Your Office

Microsoft Access 2010

COMPREHENSIVE

Amy Kinser

HAMMERLE | KINSER | LENDING

MORIARITY | NIGHTINGALE

PEARSON

Boston   Columbus   Indianapolis   New York   San Francisco   Upper Saddle River
Amsterdam   Cape Town   Dubai   London   Madrid   Milan   Munich   Paris   Montreal   Toronto
Delhi   Mexico City   Sao Paulo   Sydney   Hong Kong   Seoul   Singapore   Taipei   Tokyo

Editor in Chief: Michael Payne
Acquisitions Editor: Samantha McAfee
Product Development Manager: Laura Burgess
Development Editor: Nancy Lamm
Editorial Assistant: Erin Clark
Director of Digital Development: Zara Wanlass
Executive Editor, Digital Learning & Assessment: Paul Gentile
Director, Media Development: Cathi Profitko
Senior Editorial Media Project Manager: Alana Coles
Production Media Project Manager: John Cassar
VP/Director of IT Marketing & Customer Experience: Kate Valentine
Senior Marketing Manager: Tori Olson Alves
Marketing Coordinator: Susan Osterlitz
Marketing Assistant: Darshika Vyas
Senior Managing Editor: Cynthia Zonneveld
Associate Managing Editor: Camille Trentacoste
Operations Director: Nick Sklitsis
Senior Operations Specialist: Natacha Moore
Senior Art Director: Jonathan Boylan
Interior Design: Anthony Gemmellaro
Cover Design: Anthony Gemmellaro
Composition: GEX Publishing Services
Full-Service Project Management: GEX Publishing Services

Credits and acknowledgments borrowed from other sources and reproduced, with permission, in this textbook appear on appropriate page within text.

Microsoft, Windows, Word, PowerPoint, Outlook, FrontPage, Visual Basic, MSN, The Microsoft Network, and/or other Microsoft products referenced herein are either registered trademarks or registered trademarks of the Microsoft Corporation in the U.S.A. and other countries. Screen shots and icons reprinted with permission from the Microsoft Corporation. This book is not sponsored or endorsed by or affiliated with the Microsoft Corporation.

Pearson Education Ltd., London
Pearson Education Singapore, Pte. Ltd
Pearson Education, Canada, Inc.
Pearson Education–Japan
Pearson Education Australia PTY, Limited

Pearson Education North Asia Ltd., Hong Kong
Pearson Educación de Mexico, S.A. de C.V.
Pearson Education Malaysia, Pte. Ltd.
Pearson Education, Upper Saddle River, New Jersey

Library of Congress Cataloging-in-Publication Data

Kinser, Amy.
Microsoft Access 2010 : comprehensive / Amy Kinser.
    p. cm. — (Your office)
Includes index.
ISBN-13: 978-0-13-256088-7 (0-13-256088-7)
ISBN-10: 0-13-256088-7   1. Microsoft Access. 2. Database management. 3. Relational databases. I. Title.
QA76.9.D3K5695 2012
005.75'65—dc23
                                                                2011030751
                                                        10 9 8 7 6 5 4 3 2 1
                                                        ISBN-13: 978-0-13-256088-7
                                                        ISBN-10: 0-13-256088-7

Dedications

I dedicate this series to my Kinser Boyz for their unwavering love, support, and patience; to my parents and sister for their love; to my students for inspiring me; to Sam for believing in me; and to the instructors I hope this series will inspire!

Amy Kinser

I dedicate this book to my husband, John, and my two boys, Matthew and Adam. They provide me with all the support, love, and patience I could ever ask for—thank you boys!

Patti Hammerle

For my wife and two boys, whose inspiration, love, and endless support made this book possible.

Eric Kinser

I dedicate this book to my mother, Dagmar, for inspiring my love of books. And to Art, for keeping life going while I work too much, and for making life so much fun when I'm not working.

Diane Lending

I dedicate this book to my amazing wife, April. Without her support and understanding this would not have been possible.

Brant Moriarity

To my parents, who always believed in and encouraged me. To my husband and best friend, who gave me support, patience, and love. To my brother and my hero—may you be watching from Heaven with joy in your heart.

Jennifer Nightingale

I dedicate this to my husband, Jim. He is my support and my rock.

Joyce Thompson

About the Authors

Amy S. Kinser, Esq., Series Editor

Amy holds a B.A. degree in Chemistry with a Business minor and a J.D. from the Maurer School of Law, both at Indiana University. After working as an environmental chemist, starting her own technology consulting company, and practicing intellectual property law, she has spent the past 11 years teaching technology at the Kelley School of Business in Bloomington, Indiana. Currently, she serves as the Director of Computer Skills and Senior Lecturer at the Kelley School of Business at Indiana University.

She also loves spending time with her two sons, Aidan and J. Matthew, and her husband J. Eric.

Patti Hammerle

Patti holds a bachelor's degree in Finance and a master's degree in Business from Indiana University Kelley School of Business. She is an adjunct professor at the Kelley School of Business in Indianapolis where she teaches The Computer in Business. In addition to teaching, she owns U-Can Computer Manuals, a company that writes and publishes computer manuals primarily for libraries to teach from. She has also written and edited other computer application textbooks.

When not teaching or writing, she enjoys spending time with family, reading, and running.

Eric Kinser

Eric Kinser received his B.S. degree in Biology from Indiana University and his M.S. in Counseling and Education from the Indiana University School of Education. He has worked in a medical facility and in higher education admissions as a technology and decision support specialist. He is currently a lecturer in the Operations and Decision Technology department at the Kelley School of Business at Indiana University.

When not teaching he enjoys experimenting with new technologies, traveling, and hiking with his family.

Dr. Diane Lending

Diane Lending is a Professor at James Madison University where she has taught Computer Information Systems for 11 years. She received a Ph.D. in Management Information Systems from the University of Minnesota and a B.A. degree in mathematics from the University of Virginia. Her research interests are adoption of information technology and information systems education.

She enjoys traveling, playing card and board games, and living in the country with her husband, daughter, and numerous pets.

Brant Moriarity

Brant Moriarity earned his B.A. in Religious Studies/Philosophy at the Indiana University College of Arts and Sciences and an M.S. in Information Systems at the Indiana University Kelley School of Business. He is currently teaching at the Kelley School of Business.

Dr. Jennifer Paige Nightingale

Jennifer Nightingale, assistant professor at Duquesne University, has taught Information Systems Management since 2000. Before joining Duquesne University, she spent 15 years in industry with a focus in management and training. Her research expertise is in instructional technology, using technology as a teaching tool, and the impact of instructional technologies on student learning. She has earned numerous teaching and research honors and awards, holds an Ed.D. (instructional technology) and two M.S. degrees (information systems management and education) from Duquesne University, and a B.A. from the University of Pittsburgh.

Joyce Thompson, Common Features Author

Joyce Thompson is an Associate Professor at Lehigh Carbon Community College where she has facilitated learning in Computer Literacy and Computer Applications, Cisco, and Geographic Information Systems since 2002. She has been teaching computer applications for over 20 years. She received her M.Ed. in Instructional Design and Technology.

Joyce resides in Pennsylvania with her husband and two cats.

Brief Contents

COMMON FEATURES

ACCESS

MODULE 7

APPENDIX

Contents

ACCESS APPENDIX

Acknowledgments

The *Your Office* team would like to thank the following reviewers who have invested time and energy to help shape this series from the very beginning, providing us with invaluable feedback through their comments, suggestions, and constructive criticism.

We'd like to thank our Editorial Board:

Marni Ferner
University of North Carolina, Wilmington

Jan Hime
University of Nebraska, Lincoln

Linda Kavanaugh
Robert Morris University

Mike Kelly
Community College of Rhode Island

Suhong Li
Bryant University

Sebena Masline
Florida State College of Jacksonville

Candace Ryder
Colorado State University

Cindi Smatt
Texas A&M University

Jill Weiss
Florida International University

We'd like to thank our class testers:

Melody Alexander
Ball State University

Karen Allen
Community College of Rhode Island

Charmayne Cullom
University of Northern Colorado

Christy Culver
Marion Technical College

Marni Ferner
University of North Carolina, Wilmington

Linda Fried
University of Colorado, Denver

Darren Hayes
Pace University

Jan Hime
University of Nebraska, Lincoln

Emily Holliday
Campbell University

Carla Jones
Middle Tennessee State Unversity

Mike Kelly
Community College of Rhode Island

David Largent
Ball State University

Freda Leonard
Delgado Community College

Suhong Li
Bryant Unversity

Sabina Masline
Florida State College of Jacksonville

Sandra McCormack
Monroe Community College

Sue McCrory
Missouri State Unversity

Patsy Parker
Southwest Oklahoma State Unversity

Alicia Pearlman
Baker College, Allen Park

Vickie Pickett
Midland College

Rose Pollard
Southeast Community College

Leonard Presby
William Paterson University

Amy Rutledge
Oakland University

Cindi Smatt
Texas A&M Unversity

Jill Weiss
Florida International Unversity

We'd like to thank our reviewers and focus group attendees:

Sven Aelterman
Troy University

Angel Alexander
Piedmont Technical College

Melody Alexander
Ball State University

Karen Allen
Community College of Rhode Island

Maureen Allen
Elon University

Wilma Andrews
Virginia Commonwealth University

Mazhar Anik
Owens Community College

David Antol
Harford Community College

Kirk Atkinson
Western Kentucky University

Barbara Baker
Indiana Wesleyan University

Kristi Berg
Minot State University

Kavuri Bharath
Old Dominion University

Ann Blackman
Parkland College

Jeanann Boyce
Montgomery College

Cheryl Brown
Delgado Community College West Bank Campus

Bonnie Buchanan
Central Ohio Technical College

Peggy Burrus
Red Rocks Community College

Richard Cacace
Pensacola State College

Margo Chaney
Carroll Community College

Shanan Chappell
College of the Albemarle, North Carolina

Kuan-Chou Chen
Purdue University, Calumet

David Childress
Ashland Community and Technical College

Keh-Wen Chuang
Purdue University North Central

Amy Clubb
Portland Community College

Bruce Collins
Davenport University

Charmayne Cullom
University of Northern Colorado

Juliana Cypert
Tarrant County College

Harold Davis
Southeastern Louisiana University

Jeff Davis
Jamestown Community College

Jennifer Day
Sinclair Community College

Anna Degtyareva
Mt. San Antonio College

Beth Deinert
Southeast Commuunity College

Kathleen DeNisco
Erie Community College

Donald Dershem
Mountain View College

Bambi Edwards
Craven Community College

Elaine Emanuel
Mt. San Antonio College

Diane Endres
Ancilla College

Nancy Evans
Indiana University, Purdue University, Indianapolis

Linda Fried
University of Colorado, Denver

Diana Friedman
Riverside Community College

Susan Fry
Boise State University

Virginia Fullwood
Texas A&M University, Commerce

Janos Fustos
Metropolitan State College of Denver

Saiid Ganjalizadeh
The Catholic University of America

Randolph Garvin
Tyler Junior College

Diane Glowacki
Tarrant County College

Jerome Gonnella
Northern Kentucky University

Connie Grimes
Morehead State University

Babita Gupta
California State University, Monterey Bay

Lewis Hall
Riverside City College

Jane Hammer
Valley City State University

Marie Hartlein
Montgomery County Community College

Darren Hayes
Pace Unversity

Paul Hayes
Eastern New Mexico Universtiy

Mary Hedberg
Johnson County Community College

Lynda Henrie
LDS Business College

Deedee Herrera
Dodge City Community College

Cheryl Hinds
Norfolk State University

Mary Kay Hinkson
Fox Valley Technical College

Margaret Hohly
Cerritos College

Brian Holbert
Spring Hill College

Susan Holland
Southeast Community College

Anita Hollander
University of Tennessee, Knoxville

Emily Holliday
Campbell University

Stacy Hollins
St. Louis Community College, Florissant Valley

Mike Horn
State University of New York, Geneseo

Christie Hovey
Lincoln Land Community College

Margaret Hvatum
St. Louis Community College Meramec

Jean Insinga
Middlesex Community College

Jon (Sean) Jasperson
Texas A&M University

Glen Jenewein
Kaplan University

Gina Jerry
Santa Monica College

Dana Johnson
North Dakota State University

Mary Johnson
Mt. San Antonio College

Linda Johnsonius
Murray State University

Carla Jones
Middle Tennessee State Unversity

Susan Jones
Utah State University

Nenad Jukic
Loyola University, Chicago

Sali Kaceli
Philadelphia Biblical University

Sue Kanda
Baker College of Auburn Hills

Robert Kansa
Macomb Community College

Susumu Kasai
Salt Lake Community College

Debby Keen
University of Kentucky

Melody Kiang
California State Universtiy, Long Beach

Lori Kielty
College of Central Florida

Richard Kirk
Pensacola State College

Dawn Konicek
Blackhawk Tech

John Kucharczuk
Centennial College

David Largent
Ball State University

Frank Lee
Fairmont State University

Luis Leon
The University of Tennessee at Chattanooga

Freda Leonard
Delgado Community College

Julie Lewis
Baker College, Allen Park

Renee Lightner
Florida State College

John Lombardi
South University

Rhonda Lucas
Spring Hill College

Adriana Lumpkin
Midland College

Lynne Lyon
Durham College

Nicole Lytle
California State University,
San Bernardino

Donna Madsen
Kirkwood Community College

Paul Martin
Harrisburg Area Community
College

Cheryl Martucci
Diablo Valley College

Sherry Massoni
Harford Community College

Lee McClain
Western Washington University

Sandra McCormack
Monroe Community College

Sue McCrory
Missouri State University

Barbara Miller
University of Notre Dame

Michael O. Moorman
Saint Leo University

Alysse Morton
Westminster College

Elobaid Muna
University of Maryland Eastern Shore

Jackie Myers
Sinclair Community College

Bernie Negrete
Cerritos College

Melissa Nemeth
Indiana University–Purdue University,
Indianapolis

Kathie O'Brien
North Idaho College

Patsy Parker
Southwestern Oklahoma State
University

Laurie Patterson
University of North Carolina, Wilmington

Alicia Pearlman
Baker College

Diane Perreault
Sierra College and California State University,
Sacramento

Vickie Pickett
Midland College

Marcia Polanis
Forsyth Technical Community College

Rose Pollard
Southeast Community College

Stephen Pomeroy
Norwich University

Leonard Presby
William Paterson University

Donna Reavis
Delta Career Education

Eris Reddoch
Pensacola State College

James Reddoch
Pensacola State College

Michael Redmond
La Salle University

Terri Rentfro
John A. Logan College

Vicki Robertson
Southwest Tennessee Community
College

Dianne Ross
University of Louisiana at Lafayette

Ann Rowlette
Liberty University

Amy Rutledge
Oakland University

Joann Segovia
Winona State University

Eileen Shifflett
James Madison University

Sandeep Shiva
Old Dominion University

Robert Sindt
Johnson County Community College

Edward Souza
Hawaii Pacific University

Nora Spencer
Fullerton College

Alicia Stonesifer
La Salle University

Cheryl Sypniewski
Macomb Community College

Arta Szathmary
Bucks County Community College

Nasser Tadayon
Southern Utah Unversity

Asela Thomason
California State University Long
Beach

Joyce Thompson
Lehigh Carbon Community College

Terri Tiedeman
Southeast Community College,
Nebraska

Lewis Todd
Belhaven University

Barb Tollinger
Sinclair Community College

Allen Truell
Ball State University

Erhan Uskup
Houston Community College

Michelle Vlaich-Lee
Greenville Technical College

Barry Walker
Monroe Community College

Rosalyn Warren
Enterprise State Community College

Eric Weinstein
Suffolk County Community College

Lorna Wells
Salt Lake Community College

Rosalie Westerberg
Clover Park Technical College

Clemetee Whaley
Southwest Tennessee Community
College

MaryLou Wilson
Piedmont Technical College

John Windsor
University of North Texas

Kathy Winters
University of Tennessee, Chattanooga

Nancy Woolridge
Fullerton College

Jensen Zhao
Ball State University

Martha Zimmer
University of Evansville

Molly Zimmer
University of Evansville

Matthew Zullo
Wake Technical Community College

Additionally, we'd like to thank our my**it**lab team for their tireless work:

Jerri Williams
my**it**lab content author

Ralph Moore
my**it**lab content author

LeeAnn Bates
my**it**lab content author

Jennifer Hurley
my**it**lab content author

Jessica Brandi
Associate Media Project Manager

Jaimie Howard
Media Producer

Cathi Profitko
Director, Media Development

Preface

The *Your Office* series is built upon the discovery that both instructors and students need a modern approach to teaching and learning Microsoft Office applications, an approach that weaves in a business context and focuses on using Office as a decision-making tool.

The process of developing this unique series for you, the modern student or instructor, required innovative ideas regarding the pedagogy and organization of the text. You learn best when doing—so you will be active from Page 1. Your learning goes to the next level when you are challenged to do more with less—your hand will be held at first, but progressively the cases require more from you. Since you care about how things work in the real world—in your classes, your future jobs, your personal life—these innovative features will help you progress from a basic understanding of Office to mastering each application, empowering you to perform with confidence in Access.

No matter what career you may choose to pursue in life, this series will give you the foundation to succeed. *Your Office* uses cases that will enable you to be immersed in a realistic business as you learn Office in the context of a running business scenario—the Painted Paradise Resort and Spa. You will immediately delve into the many interesting, smaller businesses in this resort (golf course, spa, restaurants, hotel, etc.) to learn how a business or organization uses Office. You will learn how to make Office work for you now as a student and in your future career.

Today, the experience of working with Office is not isolated to working in a job in a cubicle. Your physical office is wherever you are with a laptop or a mobile device. Office has changed. It's modern. It's mobile. It's personal. And when you learn these valuable skills and master Office, you are able to make Office your own. The title of this series is a promise to you, the student: Our goal is to make Microsoft Office *Your Office*.

Key Features

- **Starting and Ending Files:** Before every case, the Starting and Ending Files are identified for students. Starting Files identify exactly which Student Data Files are needed to complete each case. Ending Files are provided to show students the naming conventions they should use when saving their files.

- **Workshop Objectives List:** The learning objectives to be achieved as students work through the workshop. Page numbers are included for easy reference.

- **Active Text:** Appears throughout the workshop and is easily distinguishable from explanatory text by the shaded background. Active Text helps students quickly identify what steps they need to follow to complete the workshop Prepare Case.

- **Quick Reference Box:** A boxed feature that appears throughout the workshop where applicable, summarizing generic or alternative instructions on how to accomplish a task. This feature enables students to quickly find important skills.

- **Real World Advice Box:** A boxed feature that appears throughout the workshop where applicable, offering advice and best practices for general use of important Office skills. The goal is to instruct students as a manager might in a future job.

- **Side Note:** A brief tip or piece of information that is aligned with a step in the workshop quickly advising students completing that particular step.

- **Consider This:** In-text questions or topics for discussion set apart from the main explanatory text, that allow students to step back from the project and think about the skills and the applications of what they are learning and how they might be used in the future.

- **Troubleshooting:** A note related to a step in the active text that helps students work around common pitfalls or errors that might occur.

- **Concepts Check:** A section at the end of each workshop made up of approximately five concept-related questions that are short answer or open ended for students to review.

- **Visual Summary:** A visual representation of the important skills learned in the workshop. Call-outs and brief explanations illustrate important buttons or skills demonstrated in a screenshot of the final solution for the Workshop Prepare Case. Intended as a visual review of the objectives learned in the workshop; it is mapped to the objectives using page numbers so students can easily find the section of text to refer to for a refresher.

Instructor Resources

The Instructor's Resource Center, available at www.pearsonhighered.com includes the following:

- Annotated Solution Files with Scorecards assist with grading the Prepare, Practice, Problem Solve, and Perform Cases.

- Data and Solution Files

- Rubrics for Perform Cases in Microsoft Word format enable instructors to easily grade open-ended assignments with no definite solution.

- PowerPoint Presentations with notes for each chapter are included for out-of-class study or review.

- Lesson Plans that provide a detailed blueprint to achieve workshop learning objectives and outcomes and best use the unique structure of the modules.

- Complete Test Bank, also available in TestGen format

- Syllabus templates for 8-week, 12-week, and 16-week courses
- Additional Perform Cases for more exercises where you have to "start from scratch."
- Workshop-level Problem Solve Cases for more assessment on the objectives on an individual workshop level.
- Scripted Lectures that provide instructors with a lecture outline that mirrors the Workshop Prepare Case.
- Online Course Cartridges
- Flexible, robust, and customizable content is available for all major online course platforms that include everything instructors need in one place. Please contact your sales representative for information on accessing course cartridges for WebCT, Blackboard, or CourseCompass.

Student Resources

- Student Data CD
- Student Data Files
- Workshop Prepare Case videos walk students through a case similar to the Workshop Prepare Case, which follows the click path and individual skills students learn in the workshop. There is one video per workshop.
- Real World Interview videos introduce students to real professionals talking about how they use Microsoft Office on a daily basis in their work. These videos provide the relevance students seek while learning this material. There is one video per workshop.

Pearson's Companion Website

www.pearsonhighered.com/youroffice offers expanded IT resources and downloadable supplements. Students can find the following self-study tools for each workshop:

- Online Study Guide
- Workshop Objectives
- Glossary
- Workshop Objectives Review
- Web Resources
- Student Data Files

myitlab for Office 2010 is a solution designed by professors for professors that allows easy delivery of Office courses with defensible assessment and outcomes-based training.

myitlab for Office 2010 Features…

- **Assessment and training built to match *Your Office 2010*** instructional content so that myitlab works with Your Office to help students make Office their own.
- **Both project-based and skill-based assessment and training** allow instructors to test and train students on complete exercises or individual Office application skills.
- **Full course management functionality** which includes all instructor and student resources, a complete Gradebook, and the ability to run a variety of reports including detailed student clickstream data.
- **The most open, realistic, high-fidelity simulation** of Office 2010 makes students feel like they are learning Office, not just a simulation.
- **Grader, a live-in-the-application project-grading tool,** enables instructors to assign projects taken from the end-of-chapter material and additional projects included in the instructor resources. These are graded automatically, with detailed feedback provided to both instructors and students.

Visual Walk-Through

Common Features workshop efficiently covers skills most common among all applications, reducing repetition and allowing instructors to move faster over such topics as save, print, and bold.

Common Features of Microsoft Office 2010

WORKSHOP 1

Objectives

1. Starting and exploring Office programs and common window elements. p. 3
2. Using the Ribbon. p. 10
3. Using contextual tools. p. 17
4. Working with files. p. 20
5. Sharing files using Windows Live SkyDrive. p. 25
6. Getting help. p. 29
7. Printing a file. p. 31
8. Exiting programs. p. 31

Understanding the Common Features of Microsoft Office

PREPARE CASE
Working with the Common Features

The gift shop at the Red Bluff Golf Club has an array of items available for purchase from toiletries to clothes to presents for loved ones back home. There are numerous part-time employees including students from the local college. Frequently, the gift shop holds training luncheons for new employees. Susan Brock, the manager, is worried about the expense of providing lunch at the trainings. Your first assignment will be to start two documents for a meeting with Susan. You will begin a Word document for meeting minutes and an Excel spreadsheet to add and analyze expenses during the meeting. To complete this task, you need to understand and work with the common features from the Microsoft Office Suite.

Courtesy of www.Shutterstock.com

Student data files needed for this workshop:

New, blank Word document

New, blank Excel workbook

You will save your files as:

Lastname_Firstname_cf01_ws01_Minutes

Lastname_Firstname_cf01_ws01_Budget

1

Unique Structure Providing for Customizability for Each Course: Instructors can choose to teach with Modules to have students achieve a higher level of understanding of the skills, or they can go more basic and traditional with the Workshops alone.

Workshops: An organizational element of the text that, similar to a chapter, introduces concepts through explanatory text and hands-on projects through Active Text, but in an integrated manner so students are working along with the Workshop Prepare Case the entire time.

Modules: An organizational structure that provides for the synthesis of skills and concepts introduced over two grouped Workshops. Requires students to successfully retain and use skills they have learned over multiple Workshops in new contexts.

Module **1**   Microsoft Office Access 2010

WORKSHOP 1

Objectives

1. Understand what Access is. p. 40
2. Maneuver in the Navigation Pane. p. 4
3. Understand what a table is. p. 47
4. Manually navigate a database. p. 54
5. Understand what a query is. p. 56
6. Understand what a form is. p. 62
7. Understand what a report is. p. 65
8. Be able to back up a database. p. 68
9. Be able to compact and repair a database. p. 69

Student data files needed
a01_ws01_Putts

Module **1**   Microsoft Office Access 2010

WORKSHOP 2

Objectives

1. Understand database design. p. 78
2. Import data from other sources. p. 81
3. Enter data manually. p. 88
4. Create a table in Design view. p. 91
5. Understand input masks. p. 95
6. Understand formatting. p. 97
7. Understand and designate keys. p. 99
8. Understand basic principles of normalization. p. 103
9. Understand relationships between tables. p. 104
10. Create a one-to-many relationship. p. 106
11. Create a many-to-many relationship. p. 109
12. Understand referential integrity. p. 114

Gathering Data into a Database

PREPARE CASE
Red Bluff Golf Club Putts for Paws Charity Tournament Database

The Red Bluff Golf Club is sponsoring a charity tournament, Putts for Paws, to raise money for the local pet shelter. You are modifying a database for the tournament that tracks money being raised from the event. The scope of this database is limited to tracking monies. Thus, in this instance, you are not tracking whether a participant is a golfer, volunteer, or other role. Anyone can donate money in the form of hole sponsorship or other donation item. You will want to track monies derived from corporate sponsorship. You'll bring in data for the event from various sources including Excel worksheets and text files.

Courtesy of www.Shutterstock.com

Student data files needed for this workshop:
a01_ws02_Putts
a01_ws02_Putts_Contacts
a01_ws02_Putts_Golfers
a01_ws02_Putts_Donors
a01_ws02_Putts_Volunteer

You will save your file as:
Lastname_Firstname_a01_ws02_Putts

77

Module **1**   Access

MODULE CAPSTONE

More Practice 1

Student data files needed:
a01_mp_Recipe
a01_mp_Recipe_Preparation
a01_mp_Recipe_Ingredients

You will save your file as:
Lastname_Firstname_a01_mp_Recipe

Indigo 5 Restaurant
Robin Sanchez, the chef of the resort's restaurant, Indigo 5, wants to keep track of recipes and the ingredients that they include in an Access database. This will allow him to plan menus and get reports and queries on the ingredients that are needed. Ingredients have already been stored in Excel worksheets and can be imported from Excel into Access. The dish preparation instructions can be cut and pasted from Excel. Other data will need to be entered. Complete the following tasks:

a. Start **Access**, and then open **a01_mp_Recipe**. Save the file as Lastname_Firstname_a01_mp_Recipe, replacing Lastname_Firstname with your own name. In the Security Warning bar, click **Enable Content**.

b. Create a new table in Design view. This table will store specific recipe items.
   • Add the following fields, data types, and descriptions:

Field Name	Data Type	Description	Field Size
RecipeID	Text	The recipe ID assigned to each menu item (primary key)	6
RecipeName	Text	The recipe name	30
FoodCategory	Text	The food category	15
TimeToPrepare	Number	Preparation time in minutes	Integer
Servings	Number	The number of servings this recipe makes	Integer
Instructions	Memo	Cooking Instructions	

   • Designate **RecipeID** as the primary key. Save the new table as tblRecipes and then close the table.

c. Create a form to enter recipes. Click the **Create tab**, and then click **Form** in the Forms group. Save the form as frmRecipes_initialLastname, replacing initialLastName with your own initial and last name.

d. Enter the following data into frmRecipes_initialLastname:

RecipeID	RecipeName	FoodCategory	TimeToPrepare	Servings
REC001	Chicken Soup	Soup	45	8
REC002	Black Beans	Beans	90	6

e. Start **Excel**, and then open **a01_mp_Recipe_Preparation**. For each recipe, copy the **Cooking Instructions** from the Excel worksheet and paste the recipe instructions into the Access field **Instructions**.

Module Capstone: An organizational section of the text that appears once per Module. The Module Capstone comprises Practice, Problem Solve, and Perform Cases that require students to use learned skills over two Workshops to complete projects.

Clear Objectives with page numbers identify the learning goals to be achieved as students work through the Workshop. Page numbers are included for easy reference. Students are introduced to the Objectives at the Workshop opener. They see them again at the Visual Summary, which shows how each Objective was put into action in a final solution from the Prepare Case.

The **Visual Summary** is intended as a quick visual review of the Objectives learned in the Workshop and is mapped to the Objectives using page numbers so students can easily refer to the section of text for a refresher.

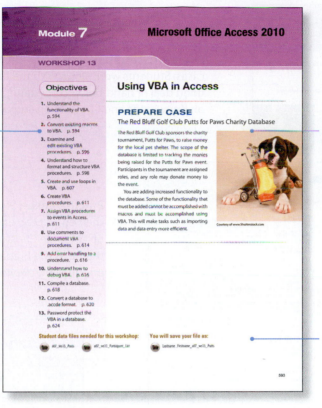

The Global Scenario is the basis of the Prepare Cases and is used to help students see the connections between businesses and how they use Microsoft Office in more than just a single case.

Starting and Ending Data Files clearly list the file names of starting data files and naming conventions for the ending data files prior to each Case.

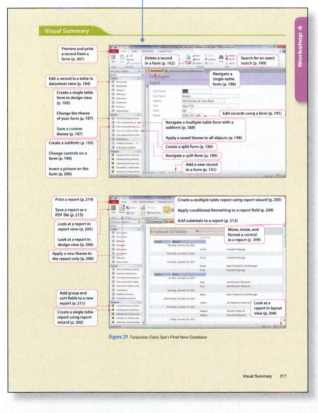

Throughout the Module we use four different kinds of cases that are characterized by the level of instruction or guidance that students receive. These cases progress with the goal of guiding students from a very introductory level all the way to mastery, so students can learn to make Office their own.

Prepare Cases: The Workshop leads students through these cases. Students work along with the instruction and receive a good deal of hand-holding or cueing. The learning emphasis is on Knowledge and Comprehension of new skills.

Practice Cases: Students complete these cases on their own at the end of a Workshop and beginning of a Module Capstone. They often continue the same theme as the Prepare Case. The learning emphasis is on Applying previously learned skills.

Problem Solve Cases: Students complete these cases independently at the end of a Module in the Module Capstone. These Cases cover skills learned over the two previous Workshops. The learning emphasis is on Analyzing and Synthesizing previously learned skills.

Perform Cases: At the end of a Module in a Module Capstone, students complete these cases entirely on their own. Most of these cases require students to work completely from scratch to solve business problems in scenarios of typical student life and future careers, and by evaluating how others have performed. The learning emphasis is on Synthesizing, Creating, and Evaluating projects using previously learned skills.

Side Note offers a very brief tip that is aligned with a step in the Workshop. This gives a quick piece of help or advice for students completing that particular step.

Troubleshooting notes relate to a step in the Active Text, helping students work around common pitfalls or errors that might occur.

Active Text boxes appear throughout the workshop and are distinguishable from explanatory text by the shaded background. These boxes help students easily identify what steps they need to follow to complete the Workshop Prepare Case and get them working hands-on from the first pages of the Workshop all the way through to the end.

Combining Operators and Multiple Criteria

The more criteria added to your query means the more difficult it will be to see if you have the correct results. With multiple criteria, it is good practice to add one criteria, run the query to make sure you are getting the correct results, and then continue adding criteria one at a time.

For this project, the spa manager would like to see all of her high-end services listed by price and then service type, and she would like to break down the criteria as follows: Beauty or Waxing services $50 or more, Facial or Microdermabrasion services over $55, Beauty or Waxing services over $45, and all Botanical Hair & Scalp Therapy services.

To Combine Operators and Multiple Criteria

a. Click the **Create tab**, click **Query Design** in the Queries group, and double-click **tblService** to add the table to the query window. Click **Close** to close the Show Table dialog box.

b. In the following order, double-click **Fee**, **Type**, and **ServiceName** to add the fields to the query design grid.

c. Click in the **Criteria** row for the Fee field, type >55, and then in the **Criteria** row for the Type field type Facial or Microdermabrasion.

d. Click the Query Tools Design tab, and then click **Run** in the Results group to run the query. The results should show six records with Facial or Microdermabrasion for the Type field, and all values in the Fee field should be greater than $55.

e. Click the Home tab, click the **View arrow** in the Views group, and then click **Design View**. In the or row for the Fee field, type >=50, and for the **or** row for the Type field type Hands & Feet or Body Massage. Click the **Design tab**, and then click **Run** in the Results group to run the query again.

The query results should show 19 records with types Facial or Microdermabrasion that have fees greater than $55, and records with types Hands & Feet or Body Massage that have fees greater than or equal to $50.

Troubleshooting

If you enter the value Hands & Feet in the Type field without quotation marks, then Access will add those quotation marks for you. In this case, Access evaluates the ampersand character (&) as separating two values, so it will put the quotation marks around the word "Hands" and around the word "Feet" so it will look like "Hands" & "Feet". This is different than having the quotations around the whole phrase, which is what you want it to look like. In this case you should put the quotation marks around the phrase in order for it to look like "Hands & Feet".

f. Click the Home tab, click the **View arrow** in the Views group, and then click **Design View**. Click in the third **Criteria** row for the Fee field, type >45, and then in the **Criteria** row the **Type** field type Beauty or Waxing. Click the **Design tab**, and then click **Run** in the Results group to run the query again.

The results should show 23 records with types Facial or Microdermabrasion that have fees greater than $55, and records with types Hands & Feet or Body Massage that have fees greater than or equal to $50, and records with types Beauty or Waxing that have fees greater than $45.

SIDE NOTE
Wider Columns
If you cannot see all the text you are entering in a column on the query design grid, you can point to the right border of the column selector bar and double-click to best fit the data. This is similar to making a column wider in Datasheet view.

Queries **163**

---

what projects. One employee might be working on several projects, and each project might have more than one employee working on it. This kind of data structure is called a many-to-many relationship. Access makes it easy to keep track of this related data by using a multi-valued lookup field. After you create the multivalued field, it appears as a check box list in Datasheet view. The selected people are stored in the multivalued field and are separated by commas when displayed.

Real World Advice | **Enforcing Referential Integrity with Multiple Values**

Access will not allow you to store multiple values if you enforce referential integrity. When Access enforces referential integrity, it is checking to see if related data exists between the primary key and foreign key. You cannot enter a value in the foreign key field of the related table that does not exist in the primary key field of the primary table. For example, a project cannot be assigned to an employee if that employee does not exist in your database. On the other hand, multiple employees may be assigned to one project. Thus, the foreign key in the Project table—EmployeeID—can have more than one EmployeeID listed and separated by a comma. The combination of the EmployeeIDs will not match any of the EmployeeIDs listed in the Employee table.

CONSIDER THIS | Multiple Values and Normalization

Does storing multiple values conform to the principles of normalization? List some examples where using this feature is useful. What are some examples where storing multiple values would be inappropriate?

Lookup Field Properties

The purpose of a Lookup field is to replace the display of a number such as an ID (or other foreign key value) with something more meaningful, such as a name. For instance, instead of displaying a product item ID number, Access can display a product name. **Lookup field properties** can be viewed in the bottom pane of the table's Design view under Field Properties. When the first property is initially configured, the list of available properties changes to reflect one's choice. Lookup field properties can be set to change the behavior of a lookup column. When the Lookup Wizard is used, many of the lookup field properties are automatically established by the wizard.

Although the wizard establishes the lookup field properties, there are some properties that may need to be modified, based on your own preferences. When the wizard creates the settings of a lookup field, many properties are not established or are configured to the Access default settings. You can set the lookup field properties to change the behavior of the lookup field.

Quick Reference | Possible Options for the Lookup Wizard Integrity Settings

- No Data Integrity: This creates a simple relationship.
- Restrict Delete: Activates referential integrity with no Cascades.
- Cascade Delete: Activates referential integrity with Cascade Delete.

Advanced Data Types **257**

Real World Advice boxes appear throughout each Workshop, offering advice and best practices for general use of important Office skills. Their goal is to instruct students as a manager might in a future career.

Consider This is an in-text question or topic for discussion, set apart from the main explanatory text. It allows students to step back from the project and think about the skills they are learning and how to apply them practically in the future.

Quick Reference boxes appear throughout the Workshop where applicable, summarizing generic or alternative instructions for accomplishing a task. The goal is to give students a place to find important skills quickly.

Concept Check is a section at the end of each Workshop with approximately five concepts-related questions. They are short answer or open-ended so students can review them quickly.

Concept Check

1. You want to report on customers and orders. You expect to create several different reports from this data. Is Access or Excel most appropriate? Why?

2. For marketing purposes, you need to create a database identifying potential customers or prospects. Suggest names for the following tables:
   Potential customers or prospects
   Salesperson who identified the prospect
   Territory that each salesperson covers

3. You work in the human resources department. Your employee table needs to contain the employee's name, date that the employee was hired, expected retirement date, and emergency contact. Suggest field names for these fields.

4. For your human resources database, you need to list all those employees who are expected to retire in 2015. How would you get this list of employees?

5. Patti Rochelle, the events coordinator at Painted Paradise, wants to share the names of the participants with the Santa Fe Animal Center. Would a report or a query be more appropriate? Why?

Key Terms

Append row 50	Form 41	Query workspace 59
Backstage view 68	Form view 62	Record 41
Backup database 68	Importing 48	Record selector 50
Compacting 69	Information 40	Recordset 58
Data 40	Layout view 62	Report 41
Database management system	Navigation bar 50	Report view 65
(DBMS) 40	Object 41	Run time 58
Datasheet view 41	Print Preview 65	Table 41
Design view 41	Query 41	Template 43
Field 42	Query design grid 59	View 41
File extension 46	Query results 58	Wizard 56

Key Terms   71

Dear Students,

If you want an edge over the competition, make it personal. Whether you love sports, travel, the stock market, or ballet, your passion is personal to you. Capitalizing on your passion leads to success. You live in a global marketplace, and your competition is global. The honors students in China exceed the total number of students in North America. Skills can help set you apart, but passion will make you stand above. *Your Office* is the tool to harness your passion's true potential.

In prior generations, personalization in a professional setting was discouraged. You had a "work" life and a "home" life. As the Series Editor, I write to you about the vision for *Your Office* from my laptop, on my couch, in the middle of the night when inspiration struck me. My classroom and living room are my office. Life has changed from generations before us.

So, let's get personal. My degrees are not in technology, but chemistry and law. I helped put myself through school by working full time in various jobs, including a successful technology consulting business that continues today. My generation did not grow up with computers, but I did. My father was a network administrator for the military. So, I was learning to program in Basic before anyone had played Nintendo's Duck Hunt or Tetris. Technology has always been one of my passions from a young age. In fact, I now tell my husband: don't buy me jewelry for my birthday, buy me the latest gadget on the market!

In my first law position, I was known as the Office guru to the extent that no one gave me a law assignment for the first two months. Once I submitted the assignment, my supervisor remarked, "Wow, you don't just know how to leverage technology, but you really know the law too." I can tell you novel-sized stories from countless prior students in countless industries who gained an edge from using Office as a tool. Bringing technology to your passion makes you well rounded and a cut above the rest, no matter the industry or position.

I am most passionate about teaching, in particular teaching technology. I come from many generations of teachers, including my mother who is a kindergarten teacher. For over 12 years, I have found my dream job passing on my passion for teaching, technology, law, science, music, and life in general at the Kelley School of Business at Indiana University. I have tried to pass on the key to engaging passion to my students. I have helped them see what differentiates them from all the other bright students vying for the same jobs.

Microsoft Office is a tool. All of your competition will have learned Microsoft Office to some degree or another. Some will have learned it to an advanced level. Knowing Microsoft Office is important, but it is also fundamental. Without it, you will not be considered for a position.

Today, you step into your first of many future roles bringing Microsoft Office to your dream job working for Painted Paradise Resort and Spa. You will delve into the business side of the resort and learn how to use *Your Office* to maximum benefit.

Don't let the context of a business fool you. If you don't think of yourself as a business person, you have no need to worry. Whether you realize it or not, everything is business. If you want to be a nurse, you are entering the health care industry. If you want to be a football player in the NFL, you are entering the business of sports as entertainment. In fact, if you want to be a stay-at-home parent, you are entering the business of a family household where *Your Office* still gives you an advantage. For example, you will be able to prepare a budget in Excel and analyze what you need to do to afford a trip to Disney World!

At Painted Paradise Resort and Spa, you will learn how to make Office yours through four learning levels designed to maximize your understanding. You will Prepare, Practice, and Problem Solve your tasks. Then, you will astound when you Perform your new talents. You will be challenged through Consider This questions and gain insight through Real World Advice.

There is something more. You want success in what you are passionate about in your life. It is personal for you. In this position at Painted Paradise Resort and Spa, you will gain your personal competitive advantage that will stay with you for the rest of your life—*Your Office*.

Sincerely,

Amy Kinser

Series Editor

Welcome to the Painted Paradise Resort and Spa Team!

Welcome to your new office at Painted Paradise Resort and Spa, where we specialize in painting perfect getaways. As the Chief Technology Officer, I am excited to have staff dedicated to the Microsoft Office integration between all the areas of the resort. Our team is passionate about our paradise, and I hope you find this to be your dream position here!

Painted Paradise is a resort and spa in New Mexico catering to business people, romantics, families, and anyone who just needs to get away. Inside our resort are many distinct areas. Many of these areas operate as businesses in their own right but must integrate with the other areas of the resort. The main areas of the resort are as follows.

- The **Hotel** is overseen by our Chief Executive Officer, William Mattingly, and is at the core of our business. The hotel offers a variety of accommodations, ranging from individual rooms to a grand villa suite. Further, the hotel offers packages including spa, golf, and special events.

  Room rates vary according to size, season, demand, and discount. The hotel has discounts for typical groups, such as AARP. The hotel also has a loyalty program where guests can earn free nights based on frequency of visits. Guests may charge anything from the resort to the room.

- **Red Bluff Golf Course** is a private world-class golf course and pro shop. The golf course has services such as golf lessons from the famous golf pro John Schilling and playing packages. Also, the golf course attracts local residents. This requires variety in pricing schemes to accommodate both local and hotel guests. The pro shop sells many retail items online.

  The golf course can also be reserved for special events and tournaments. These special events can be in conjunction with a wedding, conference, meetings, or other event covered by the event planning and catering area of the resort.

- **Turquoise Oasis Spa** is a full-service spa. Spa services include haircuts, pedicures, massages, facials, body wraps, waxing, and various other spa services—typical to exotic. Further, the spa offers private consultation, weight training (in the fitness center), a water bar, meditation areas, and steam rooms. Spa services are offered both in the spa and in the resort guest's room.

  Turquoise Oasis Spa uses top-of-the-line products and some house-brand products. The retail side offers products ranging from candles to age-defying home treatments. These products can also be purchased online. Many of the hotel guests who fall in love with the house-brand soaps, lotions, candles, and other items appreciate being able to buy more at any time.

  The spa offers a multitude of packages including special hotel room packages that include spa treatments. Local residents also use the spa. So, the spa guests are not limited to hotel guests. Thus, the packages also include pricing attractive to the local community.

- **Painted Treasures Gift Shop** has an array of items available for purchase, from toiletries to clothes, to presents for loved ones back home, including a healthy section of kids' toys for traveling business people. The gift shop sells a small sampling from the spa, golf course pro shop, and local New Mexico culture. The gift shop also has a small section of snacks and drinks. The gift shop has numerous part-time employees including students from the local college.

- The **Event Planning & Catering** area is central to attracting customers to the resort. From weddings to conferences, the resort is a popular destination. The resort has a substantial number of staff dedicated to planning, coordinating, setting up, catering, and maintaining these events. The resort has several facilities that can accommodate large groups. Packages and prices vary by size, room, and other services such as catering. Further, the Event Planning & Catering team works closely with local vendors for floral decorations, photography, and other event or wedding typical needs. However, all catering must go through the resort (no outside catering permitted). Lastly, the resort stocks several choices of decorations, table arrangements, and centerpieces. These range from professional, simple, themed, and luxurious.

- **Indigo5** and the **Silver Moon Lounge**, a world-class restaurant and lounge that is overseen by the well-known Chef Robin Sanchez. The cuisine is balanced and modern. From steaks to pasta to local southwestern meals, Indigo5 attracts local patrons in addition to resort guests. While the catering function is separate from the restaurant—though menu items may be shared—the restaurant does support all room service for the resort. The resort also has smaller food venues onsite such as the Terra Cotta Brew coffee shop in the lobby.

Currently, these areas are using Office to various degrees. In some areas, paper and pencil are still used for most business functions. Others have been lucky enough to have some technology savvy team members start Microsoft Office Solutions.

Using your skills, I am confident that you can help us integrate and use Microsoft Office on a whole new level! I hope you are excited to call Painted Paradise Resort and Spa *Your Office*.

Looking forward to working with you more closely!

Aidan Matthews

Aidan Matthews
Chief Technology Officer

Objectives

Understanding the Common Features of Microsoft Office

PREPARE CASE
Working with the Common Features

The gift shop at the Red Bluff Golf Club has an array of items available for purchase from toiletries to clothes to presents for loved ones back home. There are numerous part-time employees including students from the local college. Frequently, the gift shop holds training luncheons for new employees. Susan Brock, the manager, is worried about the expense of providing lunch at the trainings. Your first assignment will be to start two documents for a meeting with Susan. You will begin a Word document for meeting minutes and an Excel spreadsheet to add and analyze expenses during the meeting. To complete this task, you need to understand and work with the common features from the Microsoft Office Suite.

Courtesy of www.Shutterstock.com

Student data files needed for this workshop:

 New, blank Word document

 New, blank Excel workbook

You will save your files as:

 Lastname_Firstname_cf01_ws01_Minutes

 Lastname_Firstname_cf01_ws01_Budget

Working with the Office Interface and the Ribbon

When you walk into a grocery store, you usually know what you are going to find and that items will be in approximately the same location, regardless of which store you are visiting. The first items you usually see are the fruits and fresh vegetables while the frozen foods are near the end of the store. This similarity among stores creates a level of comfort for the shopper. The brands may be different, but the food types are the same. That is, canned corn is canned corn.

Microsoft Office 2010 creates that same level of comfort with its Ribbons, features, and functions. Each application has a similar appearance or user interface. Microsoft Office 2010 is a suite of productivity applications or programs. Office is available in different suites for PCs and Macs. Office Home and Student includes Word, Excel, PowerPoint, and OneNote 2010. Office Home and Business includes Word, Excel, PowerPoint, OneNote, and Outlook 2010. Office Professional includes Word, Excel, PowerPoint, OneNote, Outlook, Access, and Publisher 2010. Other suites include Office Standard, Office Professional Plus, Office Professional Academic, and Office for Mac 2011. Each of the applications in these suites can be used individually or in combination with other Office applications. Figure 1 shows the interface for Word 2010.

Figure 1 Overview of Office Word 2010 program interface

Microsoft Word is a word processing program. This application can be used to create, edit, and format **documents** such as letters, memos, reports, brochures, resumes, and flyers. Word also provides tools for creating **tables**, which organize information into rows and columns. Using Word, you can add **graphics**, which consist of pictures, clip art, SmartArt, shapes, and charts, that can enhance the look of your documents.

Microsoft Excel is a spreadsheet program. Excel is a two-dimensional database program that can be used to model quantitative data and perform accurate and rapid calculations with results ranging from simple budgets to financial and statistical analyses. Data entered into Excel can be used to generate a variety of charts such as pie charts, bar charts, line charts, or scatter charts, to name a few, to enhance spreadsheet data. The Excel files created are known as **workbooks**, which contain one or more worksheets. Excel makes it possible to analyze, manage, and share information, which can also help you make better and smarter decisions. New analysis and visualization tools help you track and highlight important data trends.

Microsoft PowerPoint is a presentation and slide program. This application can be used to create slide shows for a presentation, as part of a website, or as a stand-alone application on a computer kiosk. These presentations can also be printed as handouts.

Microsoft OneNote is a planner and note-taking program. OneNote can be used to collect information in one easy-to-find place. With OneNote, you can capture text and images, as well as video and audio. By sharing your notebooks, you can simultaneously take and edit notes with other people in other locations, or just keep everyone in sync and up to date. You can also take your OneNote notebooks with you and then view and edit your notes from virtually any computer with an Internet connection or your Windows 7 phone device.

Microsoft Outlook is an e-mail, contact, and information management program. Outlook allows you to stay connected to the world with the most up-to-date e-mail and calendar tools. You can manage and print schedules, task lists, phone directories, and other documents. Outlook's ability to manage scheduled events and contact information is why Outlook is sometimes referred to as an **information management program**.

Microsoft Access is a relational database management program. Access is a three-dimensional database program that allows you to make the most of your data. Access is known as **relational database** software (or three-dimensional database software) because it is able to connect data in separate tables to form a relationship when common fields exist—to offer reassembled information from multiple tables. For example, a business might have one table that lists all the supervisors, their shifts, and which area they supervise. Another table might accumulate data for employees and track which shift they are working. Since the common field in this example, for both database tables are shift hours, a business could use Access to query which employees are working the second shift, who the supervisor is, and produce a report with all their names. Thus, Access is used primarily for decision making by businesses that compile data from multiple records stored in tables to produce informative reports. Many businesses use Access to store data and Excel to model and analyze data by creating charts.

Microsoft Publisher is a desktop publishing program that offers professional tools and templates to help easily communicate a message in a variety of publication types, saving time and money while creating a more polished finished look. Whether you are designing brochures, newsletters, postcards, greeting cards, or e-mail newsletters, Publisher aids in delivering high-quality results without the user having graphic design experience. Publisher helps you to create, personalize, and share a wide range of professional-quality publications and marketing materials with ease.

Starting and Exploring Office Programs and Common Window Elements

There is more than one way to start Office programs. As you become familiar with the various options, you will be able to decide which method is more comfortable and efficient for your personal needs and workflow. Once you start working with these applications, also notice that it is possible to have more than one application open at a time. This is a valuable tool for users. One method for opening any Office program is from the Start menu on the taskbar.

To Start Office Programs

a. Click the **Start** button.

b. Click **All Programs**, scroll if necessary, and then click the **Microsoft Office** folder.

Office programs

Start button

Figure 2 Starting Word from the Start menu

Troubleshooting

If Microsoft Office is not listed on your menu, you can use the Search programs and files input box at the bottom of the Start menu to type keywords to help find items quickly. Type in the application name desired and a list of options will appear. Notice when "word" is the keyword typed, "Microsoft Word 2010" appears at the top of the list.

Starting Word and Opening a New Blank Document

A blank document is like a blank piece of paper. The insertion point is at the first character of the first line. This provides a clean slate for your document.

To Start Word

a. Click the **Start** button 🟢, and then click **All Programs** to display the All Programs list.

b. Click the **Microsoft Office** folder, and then point to **Microsoft Word 2010**.

c. Click **Microsoft Word 2010**. Word will start with a new blank document.

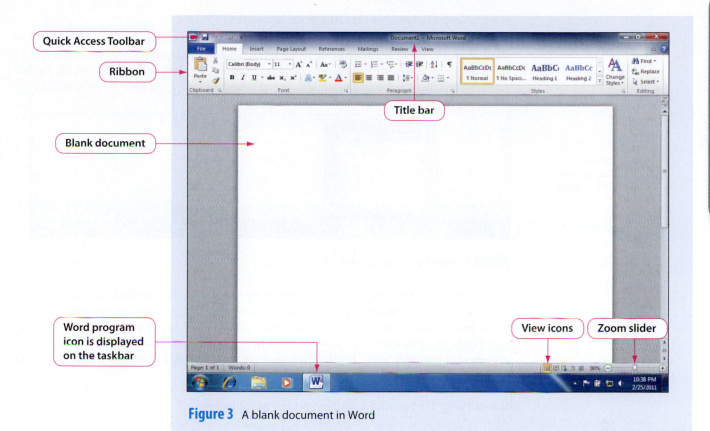

Figure 3 A blank document in Word

Starting Excel and Opening a New Blank Document

A blank spreadsheet is like a blank sheet of columnar paper. The active cell is at the first cell of the first row. This provides a clean slate for your spreadsheet.

To Start Excel

a. Click the **Start** button 🥏, and then click **All Programs** to display the All Programs list.

b. Click **Microsoft Office**, and then point to **Microsoft Excel 2010**.

c. Click **Microsoft Excel 2010**. Excel will start with a new blank workbook.

The other Office programs can be opened using the same method. As previously mentioned, more than one application can be opened at the same time. It is possible to switch between any open applications to view their contents. The taskbar contains icons for open applications, as well as any program icons that have been pinned to the taskbar to allow for quick access when starting a program.

Switching Between Open Programs and Files

When moving your mouse pointer over a taskbar icon for an open program, a **thumbnail** or small picture of the open program file is displayed, as shown in Figure 4. This is a useful feature when two or more files are open for the same application. A thumbnail of each open file for that application is displayed, and you simply click the file thumbnail you want to make active.

Figure 4 Viewing a thumbnail of Word

When two or more programs are running at the same time, you can also access them through the taskbar buttons. As you move the mouse pointer over each open application, stop and point to the Excel program button ![Excel icon]. A thumbnail will appear. If you want to switch to the Excel application file, just click the Microsoft Excel thumbnail or the button—since only one Excel document is currently open. If a different program is active, the program will switch to make Excel the active program.

Switching Between Windows Using Alt + Tab

As an alternative to using the thumbnails, you can use the keyboard shortcut to move between applications by holding down Alt and pressing Tab. A small window appears in the center of the screen with thumbnails representing each of the open programs. There is also a thumbnail for the desktop. The program name at the top of the window indicates the program that will be active when you release Alt.

To Switch Between Applications

a. On the taskbar, point to **Excel** ![Excel icon] and observe the thumbnail of the Excel file.

b. Click the **Microsoft Excel - Book1** thumbnail to make sure the Book1 Excel document is the current active program.

c. In the current active cell **A1**, type Budget, and then press Enter. In the new cell A2, type 1234, and then press Enter.

Resizing Windows and Workspaces

Office has a consistent design and layout as shown in Figure 5. This is beneficial because once you learn to use one Office program; you can use many of those skills when working with the other Office programs.

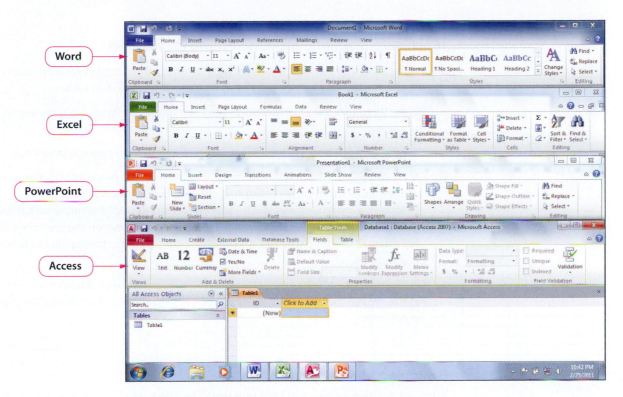

Figure 5 The Ribbons of Word, Excel, PowerPoint, and Access

One feature common among all of the applications is the three buttons that appear in the top-right corner of an application's title bar. The left button is the Minimize button. This button hides a window so it is only visible on the taskbar. The middle button is a toggle button between Restore Down and Maximize, depending on the status of the window. If the window is at its maximum size, the button will act in a Restore Down capacity by restoring the window to a previous, smaller size. Once a window is in the Restore Down mode, the button toggles to a Maximize button, which expands the window to its full size. Finally, the button on the right is the Close button, which will close a file or exit the program.

These buttons offer another layer of flexibility in the ability to size and arrange the windows to suit your purpose or to minimize a window and remove it from view. The **Maximize** button might be used most often, since it offers the largest workspace. If several applications are opened, the windows can be arranged using the **Restore Down** button so several windows can be viewed at the same time. If you are not working on an application and want to have it remain open, the **Minimize** button will hide the application on the taskbar.

Excel has two sets of buttons in the top-right corner: the set on the program title bar is for the Excel program, and the set just below that represents the workbook currently open as shown in Figure 6.

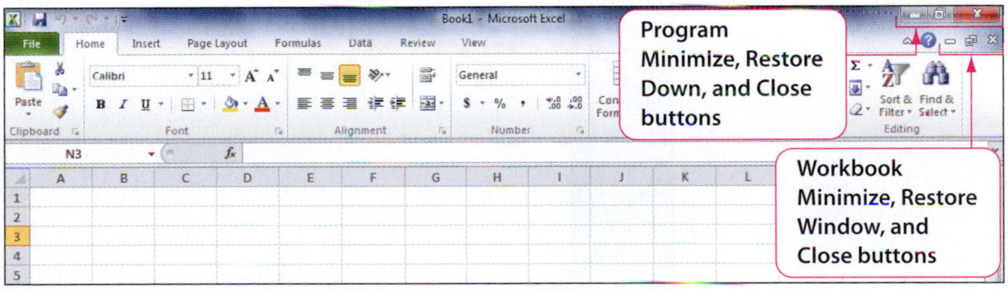

Program Minimize, Restore Down, and Close buttons

Workbook Minimize, Restore Window, and Close buttons

Figure 6 Program and workbook Minimize, Restore Window and Close buttons

To Minimize, Maximize, and Restore Down the Windows

a. On the Excel title bar, click **Minimize** to reduce the program window to an icon on the taskbar. The Word window will now be the active window in view.

b. On the Word title bar, click **Maximize** to expand the Word program window to fill the screen.

c. Click the **Restore Down** button to return Word to its previous window size.

d. Click Excel on the taskbar to make Excel the active program. On the workbook window, under the Excel set of buttons, click **Restore Window**.

   Notice the workbook window is reduced to a smaller sized window within the Excel window and the three buttons for the workbook now appear on the workbook title bar rather than under the Excel buttons, which are still located in the top-right corner of the Excel window.

e. On the workbook title bar, click **Maximize** to expand the workbook back to the original size. Notice the workbook set of buttons are again located under the Excel window set of buttons.

Switching Views

There are a variety of views in each program. The views provide different ways to display the file within the program. There are five views in Word: Print Layout, Full Screen Reading, Web Layout, Outline, and Draft. The content or file information is the same in the different views; it is merely the presentation of the document information that appears different. For example, in Word, Print Layout shows how the document appears as a printed page. Web Layout shows how the document appears as a web page. Print Layout is the most commonly used view when creating a draft of a document as shown in Figure 7.

SIDE NOTE

Switching Between Views

You can quickly switch between views using the options located on the View tab in the Document Views group, or you can use the View buttons located on the status bar at the bottom-right side of the window.

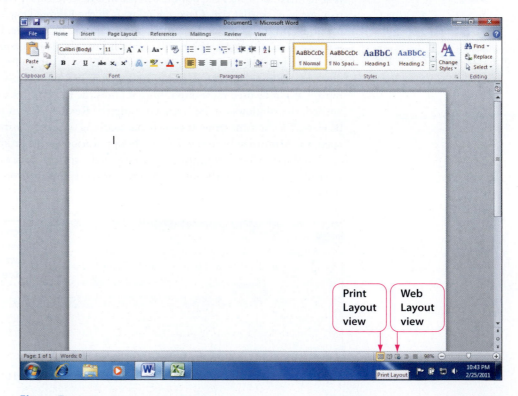

Figure 7 Print and Web Layout views

Zooming and Scrolling

To get a closer look at the content within the program, you can zoom in. Alternatively, if you would like to see more of the contents, you can zoom out. Keep in mind that the Zoom level only affects your view of the document on the monitor and does not affect the printed output of the document, similar to using a magnifying glass to see something bigger—the print on the page is still the same size. Therefore, the zoom level should not be confused with how big the text will print—it only affects your view of the document on the screen. On the right side of the status bar is a slide control that permits zooming in Word from 10% to 500%. The plus and minus propose an easy method, or you can drag the Zoom Slider. In Excel and PowerPoint, the zoom range is from 10% to 400%. When using zoom, sometimes text is shifted off the viewing screen. Depending on the program and the zoom level, you might see the vertical or horizontal scroll bars, or both scroll bars, which can be used to adjust what is displayed in the window. The scroll bars have arrows that can be clicked to shift the workspace in small increments in a specified direction and a scroll box that can be dragged to move a workspace in larger increments.

To Zoom and Scroll in Office Applications

a. On the taskbar, click **Word** . On the Word title bar, if necessary, click **Maximize** to expand the Word program window to fill the screen.

b. The insertion point should be blinking on the blank document. Type **Word**.

c. On the Word status bar, drag the **Zoom Slider** to the right until the percentage is **500%**. The document is enlarged to its largest size. This makes the text appear larger.

d. On the Word status bar, click the **Zoom level** button, currently displaying 500%. The Zoom dialog box opens. You can set a customer Zoom level or use one of the preset options.

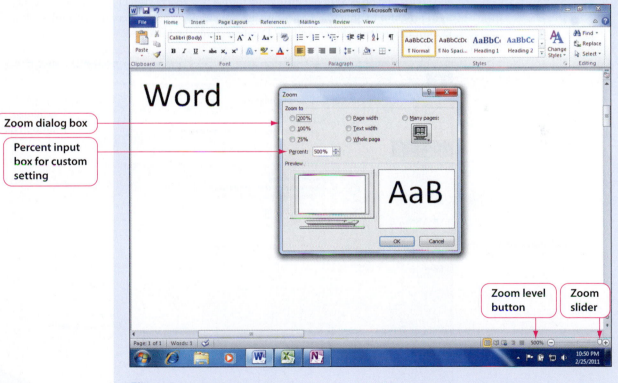

Zoom dialog box

Percent input box for custom setting

Zoom level button

Zoom slider

Figure 8 Zoom dialog box

e. Click **Page width**, and then click **OK**. The Word document is zoomed to its page width.

f. On the taskbar, click **Excel** . The Excel program should now be displayed as the active window.

g. Click cell **B1** (which is the first row cell under Column B on the worksheet).

h. Type **Firstname Lastname**, replacing Firstname Lastname with your own name.

i. Press Enter. Text has been entered in cell B1, and cell B2 is now the active cell.

j. On the status bar, notice the Zoom level and click **Zoom Out** ⊖ three times. The Zoom level magnification is now 70% (if you started at 100%).

k. On the horizontal scroll bar, click the **right scroll arrow** ▶ two times and the text is shifted to the left. Some columns may not be visible now.

l. On the horizontal scroll bar, drag the scroll box all the way to the left. The columns should be visible again.

m. Drag the **Zoom Slider** to the right to return the Zoom level to **100%**.

n. On the taskbar, click **Word** 📄. The Word program window is displayed as the active window.

Using the Ribbon

While the tabs, which contain groups of commands on the **Ribbon**, differ from program to program, each program has two tabs in common: the File tab and the Home tab. The File tab is the first tab on the Ribbon and is used for file management needs. When clicked, it opens **Backstage view**, which provides access to the file level features, such as saving a file, creating a new file, opening an existing file, printing a file, and closing a file, as well as program options, as shown in Figure 9. The Home tab is the second tab in each program Ribbon. It contains the commands for the most frequently performed activities, including copying, cutting, and pasting; changing fonts and styles; and other various editing and formatting tools. The commands on these tabs may differ from program to program. Other tabs are program specific, such as the Formulas tab in Excel, the Design tab in PowerPoint, and the Database Tools tab in Access.

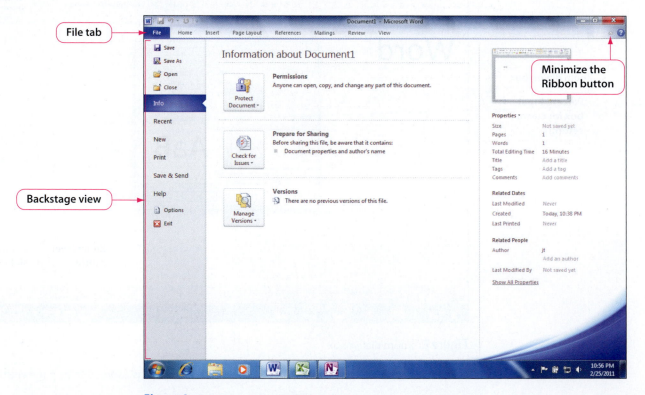

Figure 9 File tab to display Backstage view

Using the Ribbon Tabs

It is possible to enlarge your workspace by minimizing the Ribbon. The Minimize the **Ribbon button**, shown in Figure 9, is located just below the Close button in the top-right corner of the window and directly next to the Help, question mark, button. The Minimize the Ribbon button reduces the Ribbon to a single line and toggles to the Expand the Ribbon button. Click the Expand the Ribbon button to display the full Ribbon again.

To Use Ribbon Tabs

a. Word should be the active application. Click **Maximize** 🔳 to expand the Word program space so the document within the program window fills all of the screen.

b. Click **Minimize the Ribbon** ⌃, and then point to the **Page Layout tab** on the Ribbon. Notice that the Page Layout tab is highlighted but the current tab is still the active tab.

c. Click the **Page Layout tab**. The Page Layout tab Ribbon options are displayed. This tab provides easy access to the page formatting and printing options.

d. Click the **Home tab**. This displays the Home tab options on the Ribbon. If you click in the document again, notice the Ribbon options toggle out of view again. Click **Expand the Ribbon** ⌄ to toggle the Ribbon options into constant view (or alternatively, double-click any of the tab names).

SIDE NOTE
How Buttons and Groups Appear on the Ribbon

If you notice that your Ribbon appears differently from one computer to the next—the buttons and groups might seem condensed in size—there could be a few factors at play. The most common causes could be monitor size, the screen resolution, or the size of the program window. With smaller monitors, lower screen resolutions, or a reduced program window, buttons can appear as icons without labels, and a group can sometimes be condensed into a button that must be clicked to display the group options.

Clicking Buttons

Clicking a button will produce an action. For example, the Font group on the Home tab includes buttons for Bold and Italic. Clicking any of these buttons will produce an intended action. So, if you have selected text that you want to apply bold formatting to, simply click the Bold button and bold formatting is applied to the selected text.

Some buttons are toggle buttons: one click turns a feature on and a second click turns the feature off. When a feature is toggled on, the button remains highlighted. For example, in Word, on the Home tab in the Paragraph group, click the Show/Hide button ¶. Notice paragraph marks appear in your document, and the button is highlighted to show that the feature is turned on. This feature displays characters that do not print. This allows you to see items in the document that can help to troubleshoot a document's formatting, such as when Tab was pressed an arrow is displayed, or when the spacebar was pressed dots appear between words. Click the Show/Hide button again, and the feature is turned off. The button is no longer highlighted, and the paragraph characters, as well as any other nonprinting characters, in the document are no longer displayed.

Also notice that some buttons have two parts: a button that accesses the most commonly used setting or command, and an arrow that opens a gallery menu of all related commands or options for that particular task or button. For example, the Font Color button **A** on the Home tab in the Font group includes the different colors that are available for fonts. If you click the button, the last color used will be the default color applied to selected text. Notice this color is also displayed on the icon and will change when a different color is applied in the document. To access the gallery menu for other color options, click the arrow next to the Font Color button, and then click the alternate color or command option. Whenever you see an arrow next to a button, this is an indicator that more options are available.

It should also be said that the two buttons on your mouse operate in a similar fashion. The left mouse click can also be thought of as performing an action, whether it is to click a Ribbon button, menu option, or to open a document. The right-click (or right mouse button) will never perform an action, but rather it provides more options. The options that appear on the shortcut menu when you right-click change depending on the location of the mouse pointer. For example, right-click an empty area of the status bar and you will see options available for status bar features. All of these status bar options are toggles, meaning you can toggle them on or off—a check mark is displayed for the features currently on. By contrast, if you hover the mouse pointer over text in the Word document and right-click, you will see menu options that apply to text—many of the same options found in the Font group on the Home tab. When a desired option is found on a shortcut menu, simply click the option to apply it. If none of the options meets your needs, click in empty space outside the menu to cancel the shortcut menu.

CONSIDER THIS | **Changes Among Versions of Microsoft Office**

A consistent user interface helps users feel comfortable. In Office 2010, Microsoft removed the Office Button used in Office 2007 and created the File tab and Backstage view. Why do you think the company made this change? Which do you prefer? Are there any future changes you would recommend?

To Work with Buttons

a. If necessary, click **Word** W on the taskbar to make it the active window, and then click **Maximize** ▣.

b. Place the mouse pointer over the typed text **Word**, and then double-click to select the text. With the text selected, click the **Home tab**, and then click **Bold** B in the Font group. This will toggle on the Bold command. Notice that the Bold button is now highlighted and the selected text is displayed in bold format.

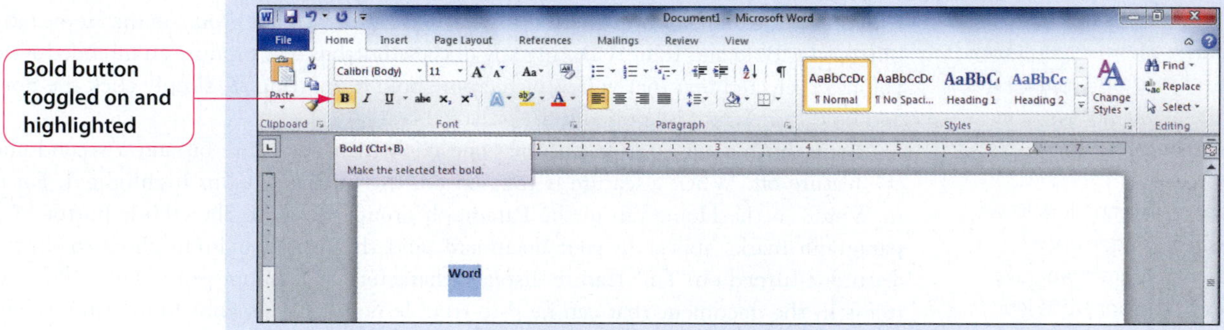

Bold button toggled on and highlighted

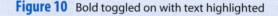

Figure 10 Bold toggled on with text highlighted

c. With the text still selected, press Backspace once to delete the text Word. Notice that the Bold button is still highlighted, which means any new text typed will be bold.

d. Type Meeting Minutes, and then press Enter. The insertion point moves to the next line of the document. If you made any typing errors, you can press Backspace to remove the typing errors and then retype the text.

e. With the insertion point on the second line, click **Bold** B again to toggle it off.

f. Position the insertion point to the left of the word **Meeting**, press and hold the left mouse button, drag the mouse until the text in the first line of text is selected, and then release the mouse button when all the text in Meeting Minutes is highlighted.

g. Click the **Home tab**, and then click the **Font Color arrow** A⏷ in the Font group. Under **Standard Colors**, point to, but do not click, **Dark Red**. Notice a Live Preview feature that shows how the selected document text will change color. As the mouse pointer hovers over a color, a ScreenTip appears to show the color name.

h. Click **Dark Red**. The selected text should now be bold and dark red.

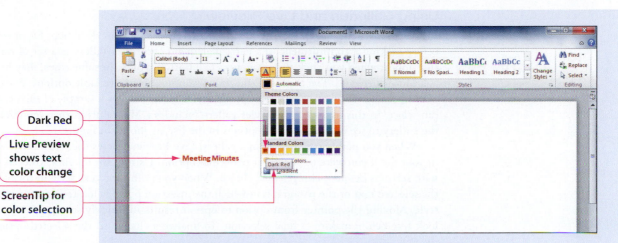

Dark Red

Live Preview shows text color change

Meeting Minutes

ScreenTip for color selection

Figure 11 Live Preview of font color

SIDE NOTE

Live Preview Feature

Live Preview, which allows you to see how formatting looks before you apply it, is available for many of the gallery libraries.

i. Click below **Meeting Minutes** to move the insertion point to the next line.

Real World Advice   Using Keyboard Shortcuts and Key Tips

Keyboard shortcuts are extremely useful because they allow you to keep your hands on the keyboard instead of reaching for the mouse to make Ribbon selections. **Key Tips** are also a form of keyboard shortcuts. Pressing [Alt] will display Key Tips (or keyboard shortcuts) for items on the Ribbon and Quick Access Toolbar. The **Quick Access Toolbar** is located at the top left of the application window and can be customized to offer commonly used buttons. After displaying the Key Tips, you can press the letter or number corresponding to the Ribbon item to request the action from the keyboard. Pressing [Alt] again will toggle the Key Tips off.

Many keyboard shortcuts are universal to all Windows programs; you will find they work not only in past versions of Office, but they also work in other Windows software. Keyboard shortcuts usually involve two or more keys, in which case you hold down the first key listed, and press the second key once. Some of the more common keyboard shortcuts are shown in Figure 12.

Keyboard Shortcut	To Do This:
Ctrl + C	Copy the selected item
Ctrl + V	Paste a copied item
Ctrl + A	Select all the items in a document or window
Ctrl + B	Bold selected text
Ctrl + Z	Undo an action
Ctrl + Home	Move to the top of the document
Ctrl + End	Move to the end of the document

Figure 12 Common keyboard shortcuts

Using Galleries and Live Preview

Live Preview lets you see the effects of menu selections on your document file or selected item before making a commitment to a particular menu choice. A gallery is a set of menu options that appear when you click the arrow next to a button which, in some cases, may be referred to as a More button ▼. The menu or grid shows samples of the available options. For example, on Word's Home tab in the Styles group, the Styles gallery shows a sample of each text style you can select. In this example, the Styles gallery includes a More button that you click to expand the gallery to see all the available options in the list, as shown in Figure 13.

When you point to an option in a gallery, Live Preview shows the results that would occur in your file if you were to click that particular option. Using Live Preview, you can experiment with settings before making a final choice. When you point to a text style in the Styles gallery, the selected text or the paragraph in which the insertion point is located appears with that text style. Moving the pointer from option to option results in quickly seeing what your text will look like before making a final selection. To finalize a change to the selected option, click on the style.

SIDE NOTE

Closing a Gallery

Esc can be used to close a gallery without making a selection, or, alternatively, you can click an empty area, such as the title bar, outside the gallery menu.

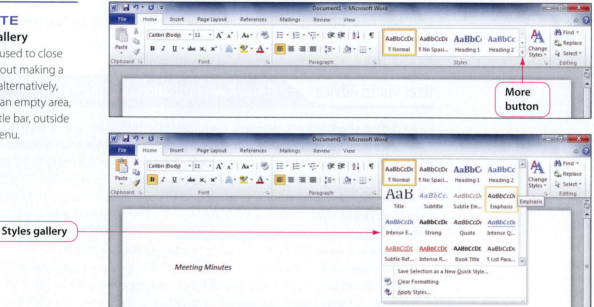

Figure 13 The More button and the Styles gallery

To Use the Numbering Library

a. Click the Home tab, and then click the **Numbering arrow** ☰▾ in the Paragraph group. The Numbering Library gallery opens.

b. Point to, but do not click, the third option in the first row, the number followed by a closing parenthesis.

c. Place the pointer over each of the remaining number styles, and then preview them in your document.

d. Click the number style with the **1)**.

The Numbering Library gallery closes, and the number 1) is added to the current line of text, which is now indented. The Numbering button remains toggled on when the insertion point is located in a paragraph line where numbering has been applied.

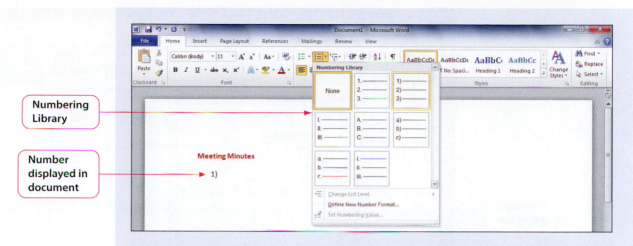

Figure 14 Numbering Library

e. With the insertion point located after the number, type Meeting was called to order at 2:15 pm.

f. Press [Enter] twice to end the numbered list.

Opening Dialog Boxes and Task Panes

Some Ribbon groups include a diagonal arrow in the bottom-right corner of the group section, called a **Dialog Box Launcher** 🗔 that opens a corresponding dialog box or task pane. Hovering the mouse pointer near the Dialog Box Launcher will display a ScreenTip to indicate more information. Click the Dialog Box Launcher to open a **dialog box**, which is a window that provides more options or settings beyond those provided on the Ribbon. It often provides access to more precise or less frequently used commands along with the commands offered on the Ribbon; thus using a dialog box offers the ability to apply many related options at the same time and located in one place. As you can see in Figure 15, many dialog boxes organize related information into tabs. In the Paragraph dialog box shown in the figure, the active Indents and Spacing tab shows options to change alignment, indentation, and spacing, with another tab that offers options and settings for Line and Page Breaks. A **task pane** is a smaller window pane that often appears to the side of the program window and offers options or helps you to navigate through completing a task or feature.

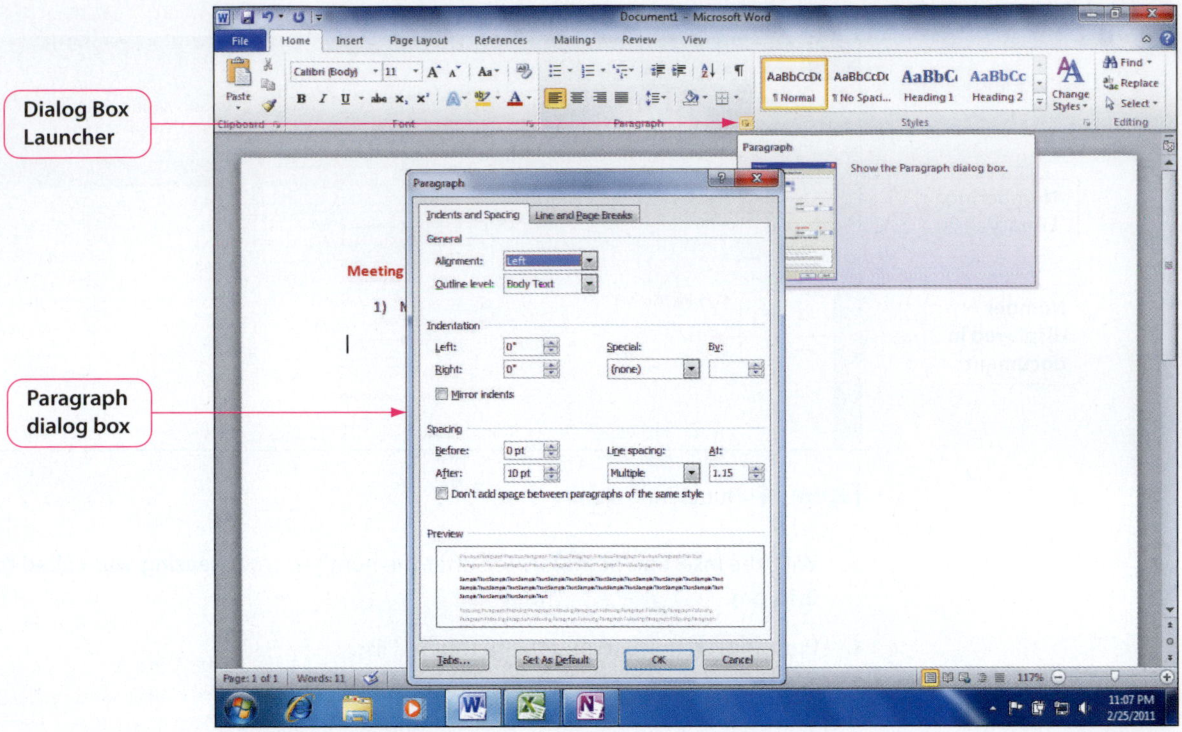

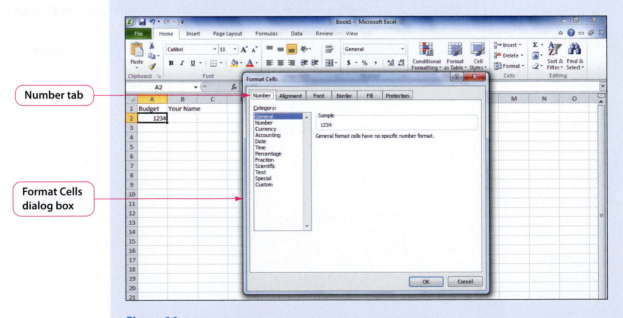

Dialog Box Launcher

Paragraph dialog box

Figure 15 Paragraph Dialog Box Launcher with dialog box overlay

To Open the Format Cells Dialog Box

a. On the taskbar, click **Excel** to make Excel the active program.

b. Click cell **A2**, the first cell in the second row.

c. Click the Home tab, if necessary. The Number group options appear on the Ribbon.

d. Click the **Dialog Box Launcher** in the Number group. The Format Cells dialog box opens with the Number tab displayed.

Number tab

Format Cells dialog box

Figure 16 Format Cells dialog box showing the Number tab

SIDE NOTE

Check Box and Radio Options

What is the difference between check box and radio options? When check box options are offered, you can check more than one check box ☑ option in a group of options, but when radio button options are offered, you can select only one radio button option in a group.

e. Under Category, click **Number**. Click the **Use 1000 Separator (,)** check box.

f. Click the **Alignment tab**. Notice, the dialog box displays options that are related to alignment of the text. If you needed to make changes, you could use the check box options or the arrows to display a list of options when appropriate to do so.

g. Click the **Fill tab**, and then click to select **Purple, Accent 4, Lighter 60%**, third row in the eighth column, which will show in the Sample box. Click **OK**. The format changes are made to the number, and the fill color is applied.

Using Contextual Tools

Whenever you see the term "contextual tools," this usually refers to tools that only appear when needed for specific tasks. Some tabs, toolbars, and menus are displayed as you work and only appear if a particular object is selected. Because these tools become available only as you need them, the workspace remains less cluttered.

A **contextual tab** is a Ribbon tab that contains commands related to selected objects so you can manipulate, edit, and format the objects. Examples of objects that can be selected to produce contextual tabs include a table, a picture, a shape, or a chart. A contextual tab appears to the right of the standard Ribbon tabs. For example, Figure 17 shows the Picture Tools Format tab that displays when a picture is selected. The contextual tabs function in the same way as a standard tab on the Ribbon. The contextual tab disappears when you click outside the target object (in the file) to deselect the object. In some instances, contextual tabs can also appear as you switch views.

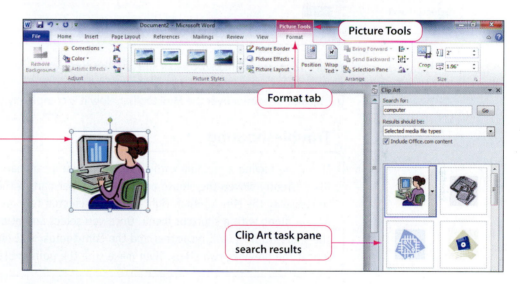

Figure 17 Contextual tab for Picture Tools in Word

Accessing the Mini Toolbar

The **Mini toolbar** appears after text is selected and contains buttons for the most commonly used formatting commands, such as font, font size, font color, center alignment, indents, bold, italic, and underline. The Mini toolbar button commands vary for each Office program. The toolbar appears transparent whenever text is selected and comes into clearer view as you move the pointer towards the toolbar. When you move the pointer over the Mini toolbar, it comes into full view, allowing you to click the formatting button or buttons. It disappears if you move the pointer away from the toolbar, press a key, or click in the workspace. All the commands on the Mini toolbar are available on the Ribbon; however, the Mini toolbar offers quicker access to common commands since you do not have to move the mouse pointer far away from selected text for these commands.

SIDE NOTE

Turning Off Mini Toolbar and Live Preview

The Mini toolbar and Live Preview can be turned off in Word, Excel, and PowerPoint. Click the File tab, click the Options command in the General options uncheck the top two appropriate check boxes in the Options dialog box, and then click the OK button.

To Access the Mini Toolbar

a. If necessary, on the taskbar, click **Excel** . Click cell **A3**, the first cell in the third row of the worksheet.

b. Type **Expenses**.

c. Press Enter . Text has been entered in cell A3, and cell A4 is selected.

d. Type **FY 2013**, and then press Enter . The year has been entered in cell A4, and cell A5 is selected.

e. Double-click cell **A3** to place the insertion point in the cell. Double-clicking a cell enables you to enter edit mode for the cell text.

f. Double-click cell **A3** again to select the text. The text appears to be opposite when selected (white text on a black background), and as you move the pointer upwards, the transparent Mini toolbar starts to appear and come into view directly above the selected text.

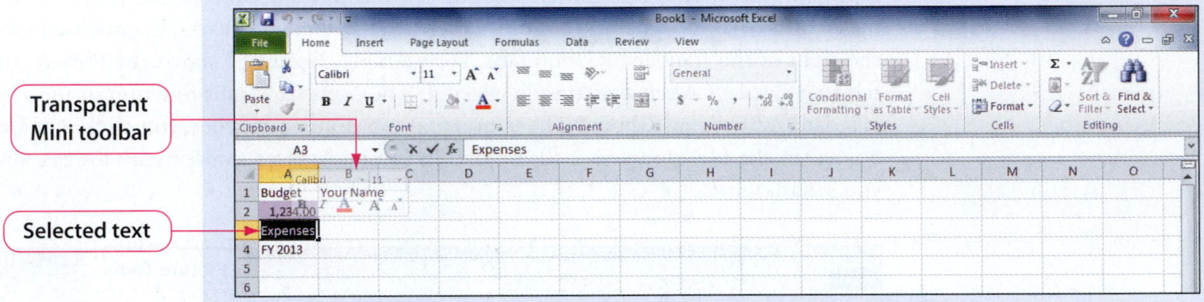

Transparent Mini toolbar

Selected text

Figure 18 Transparent Mini toolbar and selected text

g. Move the pointer over the Mini toolbar. Now it is completely visible.

Troubleshooting

If you are having a problem with the Mini toolbar disappearing, you may have inadvertently moved the mouse pointer to another part of the document. If you need to redisplay the Mini toolbar, right-click the selected text and the Mini toolbar will appear along with a shortcut menu. Once you select an option on the Mini toolbar, the shortcut menu will disappear and the Mini toolbar will remain while in use (or repeat the previous two steps, then make sure the pointer stays over the toolbar).

h. On the Mini toolbar, click **Italic** *I* .
The text in cell A3 is now italicized. The Mini toolbar remains visible allowing you to click other buttons.

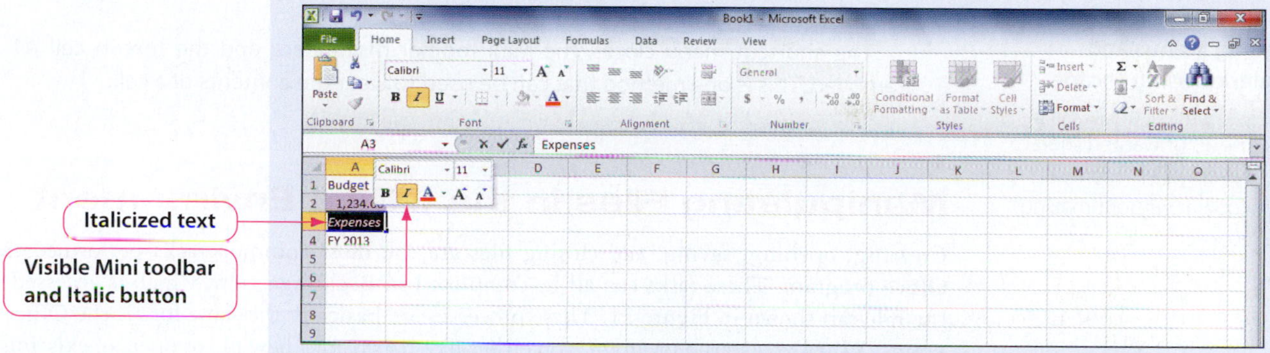

Italicized text

Visible Mini toolbar and Italic button

Figure 19 Cell A3 is now formatted with Italic from the Mini toolbar

i.   Press Enter. Cell A4 is selected, and the Mini toolbar disappears.

Opening Shortcut Menus

Shortcut menus are also context sensitive and enable you to quickly access commands that are most likely needed in the context of the task being performed. A **shortcut menu** is a list of commands related to a selection that appears when you right-click (click the right mouse button). This means you can access popular commands without using the Ribbon. Included are commands that perform actions, commands that open dialog boxes, and galleries of options that provide Live Preview. As noted previously, the Mini toolbar opens when you click the right mouse button. If you click a button on the Mini toolbar, the shortcut menu closes, and the Mini toolbar remains open allowing you to continue formatting your selection. For example, right-click selected text to open the shortcut menu *and* the Mini toolbar; the menu contains text-related commands such as Font, Paragraph, Bullets, Numbering, and Styles, as well as other program specific commands related to text.

To Use the Shortcut Menu to Delete Content

a.   Right-click cell **A1**. A shortcut menu opens with commands related to common tasks you can perform in a cell, along with the Mini toolbar.

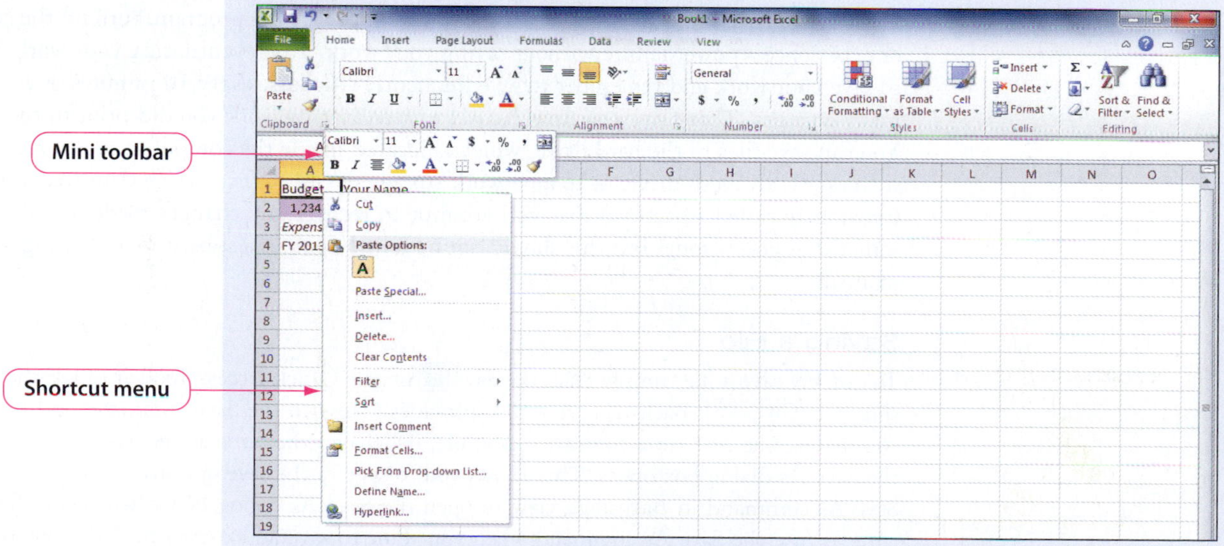

Mini toolbar

Shortcut menu

Figure 20 Shortcut menu and Mini toolbar

b. On the shortcut menu, click **Clear Contents**.

The shortcut menu closes, the Mini toolbar disappears, and the text in cell A1 is removed. This is one method that can be used to clear the contents of a cell.

Manipulating Files in the Office Environment

Creating, opening, saving, and closing files are the most common tasks performed in any Office program. These tasks can all be completed in Backstage view, which is accessed from the File tab shown in Figure 21. These processes are basically the same for all the Office programs. When you start a program, you either have to create a new file or open an existing one. When you start Word, Excel, or PowerPoint, the program opens a blank file, which is ready for you to begin working on a new document, workbook, or presentation. When you start Access, the New tab in Backstage view opens, displaying options for creating a new database or opening an existing one.

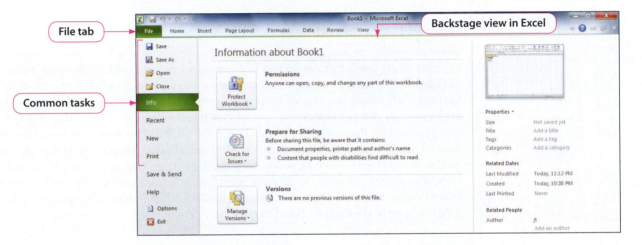

Figure 21 Backstage view in Excel

Working with Files

While working on an Office file, whether creating a new file or modifying an existing file, your work is stored in the temporary memory on your computer, not on the hard drive or your USB Flash drive. Any work done will be lost if you were to exit the program, turn off the computer, or experience a power failure without saving your work. To prevent losing your work, you need to save your work and remember to save frequently—at least every 10 minutes or after adding many changes. That saves you from having to recreate any work you did prior to the last save. You can save files to the hard drive, which is located inside the computer; to an external drive, such as a USB Flash drive; or to a network storage device. Office has an AutoRecovery feature (previously called AutoSave) that will attempt to recover any changes made to a document if something goes wrong, but this should not be relied upon as a substitute for saving your work manually.

Saving a File

To quickly save a file, simply click the Save 🔲 on the Quick Access Toolbar or use the keyboard shortcut Ctrl + S. Backstage view also provides access to the Save command and the Save As command. The first time you save a new file, it behaves the same as the Save As command and the Save As dialog box opens. This allows you to specify the save options. You can also click the Save As command in Backstage view to open the Save As dialog box when saving for the first time, or use the Save As command when you want to save an existing file as a copy or separate version—possibly with a different name. In the Save As dialog box, you name the file and specify the location in which to save it, similar to the first time you save a file. Once you save a file, the simple shortcut methods to save any changes to the file work fine to update the existing file.

No dialog box will open to save after the first time—as long as you do not need to change the file name or location as with the Save As command.

The first time a file is saved, it needs to be named. The file name includes the name you specify and a file extension assigned by the Office program to indicate the file type. The file extension may or may not be visible depending on your computer settings. By default, most computers do not display the file extension (only the file name). Use a descriptive name that accurately reflects the content of the document, workbook, presentation, or database, such as "January 2013 Budget" or "012013 Minutes." The descriptive name can include uppercase and lowercase letters, numbers, hyphens, spaces, and some special characters (excluding ? " / | < > * :) in any combination. Each Office program adds a period and a file extension after the file name to identify the program in which that file was created. Figure 22 shows the common default file extensions for Office 2010. File names can include a maximum of 255 characters including the extension (this includes the number of characters for the file path—the folder names to get to the file location). As a reminder, depending on how your computer is set up, you may or may not see the file extensions.

Application	Extension
Microsoft Word 2010	.docx
Microsoft Excel 2010	.xlsx
Microsoft PowerPoint 2010	.pptx
Microsoft Access 2010	.accdb

Figure 22 Default file extensions for Microsoft Office 2010

Real World Advice Sharing Files Between Office Versions

Different Office versions are not always compatible. The general rule is that files created in an older version can always be opened in a newer version, but not the other way around (a 2010 Office file is not easily opened in an older version of Office). With this in mind, maybe the company you work for is using Office 2010 and another company you need to share files with is using Office 2003. The concern is, prior to Office 2007 different file extensions were used. For example, .doc was used for Word files instead of docx., .xls instead of .xlsx for Excel, and so on. It is still possible to save the Office 2010 files in a previous format version. To save in one of these formats, use the Save As command, and in the Save As dialog box, click the Save as type option near the bottom of the dialog box. From the list, click the 97-2003 format option. If the file is already in the previous format, it will open in Office 2010 and save with the same format in which it was created.

To Save a File

a. On the taskbar, click **Word** [W] to make Word the active program.

b. Click the **File tab**. Backstage view opens with command options and tabs for managing files, opening existing files, saving, printing, and exiting Word.

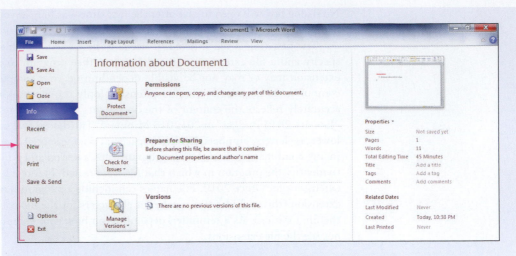

Common tasks in Word's Backstage view

Figure 23 Backstage view in Word

c. Click **Save As**.

   The Save As dialog box opens. This provides the opportunity to enter a file name and a storage location. The default storage location is the Documents folder, and the suggested file name is the first few words of the first line of the document.

d. Click the **File name** box, and if necessary, highlight the current suggested file name. Navigate to where you are storing your files, and then type Lastname_Firstname_cf01_ws01_Minutes in the File name box. This descriptive file name will help you more easily identify the file.

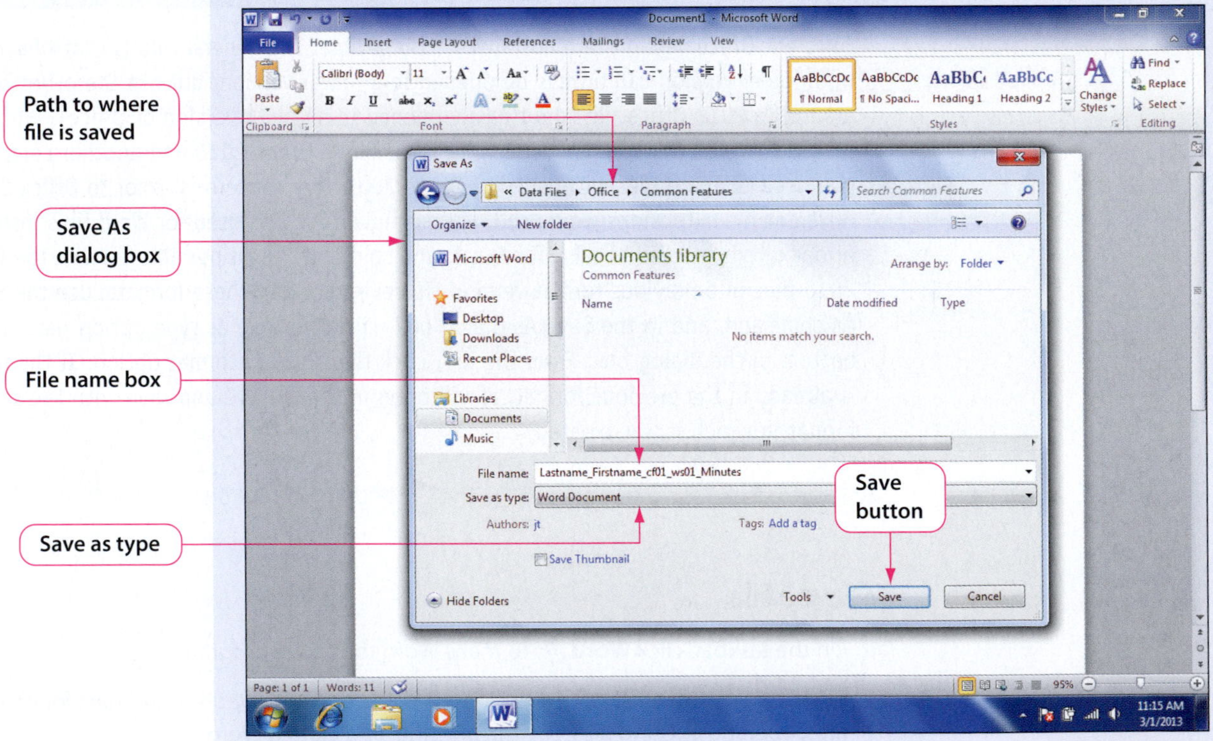

Path to where file is saved

Save As dialog box

File name box

Save as type

Save button

Figure 24 Save As dialog box

e. Click the **Save** button. The Save As dialog box closes, and the name of your file appears in the Word window title bar.

f. Click **Excel** [Excel icon] on the taskbar to make Excel the active file, repeat steps b through e and then save the file you created as **Lastname_Firstname_cf01_ws01_Budget**.

Modifying Saved Files

Saved files only contain what was in the file the last time it was saved. Any changes made after the file was saved are only stored in the computer's memory and are not saved with the file. It is important to remember to save often—after making changes—so the file is updated to reflect its current contents.

Remember, it is not necessary to use the Save As dialog box once a file has been saved unless you want a copy of the file with a different name or you want to store it in a different location.

To Modify a Saved File

a. Click **Word** [Word icon] on the taskbar to make the Word document the active window.

b. Make sure the insertion point is in the last line, below the numbered text. Type **Today's date** (the date you are doing this exercise), and then press Enter.

c. On the Quick Access Toolbar, click **Save** [icon]. The changes you made to the document have just been saved to the file stored in the location you selected earlier. Recall that no dialog boxes will open for the Save command after the first time it has been saved.

SIDE NOTE
Quick Access Toolbar
The Quick Access Toolbar provides one-click access to commonly used commands, such as saving a file and undoing recent actions.

Real World Advice   Saving Files Before Closing

It is recommended that files be saved before closing them or exiting a program. However, most programs have an added safeguard or warning dialog box to remind you to save if you attempt to close a file without saving your changes first. The warning dialog box offers three options. Click Save, and the file will be saved with any new changes. Click Don't Save if you do not want any of the changes added to the file, and the file will close without saving or adding any changes since the last Save command was applied. Click Cancel if you changed your mind about closing the program and want to get back into the file before you close the program. This warning feature helps to ensure that you have the most current version of the file saved.

Closing a File

When you are ready to close a file, you can click the Close command on the File tab in Backstage view. If the file you close is the only file open for that particular program, the program window remains open with no file in the window. You can also close a file by using the Close button [close button icon] in the top-right corner of the window. However, if that is the only file open, the file and program will close.

To Modify and Close a Document

a. With the insertion point on the line under the date, type your **course number** and **section**, replacing course number and section with the course and section you are in, on this line and press Enter. The text you typed should appear below the date.

b. Click the **File tab** to open Backstage view.

c. Click **Close**. A warning dialog box opens, asking if you want to save the changes made to the document.

d. Click **Save**.

The document closes after saving changes, but the Word program window remains open. You are able to create new files or open previously saved files. If multiple Word documents are open, the document window of the file you just closed will remain open with the other documents that are currently still open in the window.

Opening a File

You create a new file when you open a blank document, workbook, presentation, or database. If you want to work on a previously created file, you must first open it. When you open a file, it transfers a copy of the file from the file's storage location to the computer's temporary memory and displays it on the monitor's screen. There is a copy on the drive and in your computer's memory.

When opening files downloaded from the Internet, accessed from a shared network, or received as an attachment in e-mail, you may sometimes run across a file in a read-only format called Protected View, as shown in Figure 25. In **Protected View**, the file contents can be seen and read, but you are not able to edit, save, or print the contents until you enable editing. If you were to see the information bar shown in Figure 25, and you trust the source of the file, simply click the Enable Editing button on the information bar.

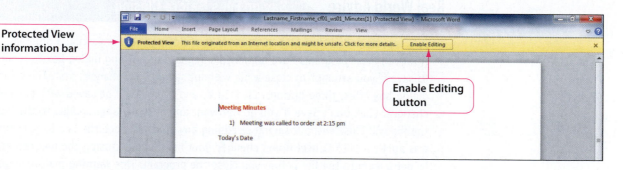

Protected View information bar

Enable Editing button

Figure 25 Open document in Protected View

To Reopen a Document

a. In Word, click the **File tab** to display Backstage view.

b. Click **Open**. The Open dialog box is displayed.

c. In the Open dialog box, click the disk drive in the left pane where your student data files are located. Navigate through the folder structure, and then click **Lastname_Firstname_cf01_ws01_Minutes**.

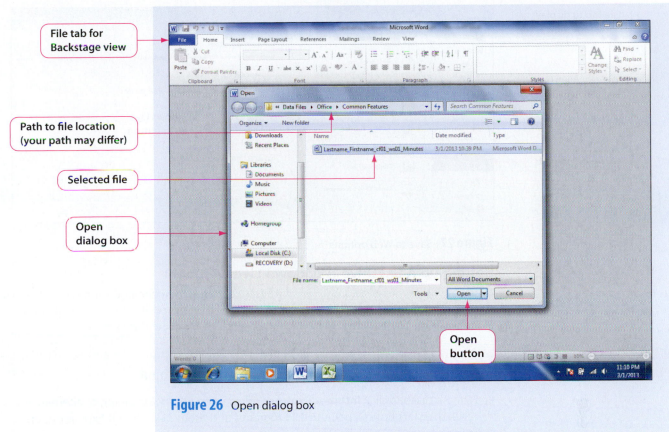

File tab for Backstage view

Path to file location (your path may differ)

Selected file

Open dialog box

Open button

Figure 26 Open dialog box

d. Click **Open**. The file opens in the Word program window.

Sharing Files Using Windows Live SkyDrive

Many times you create files in order to share them with other people. You can share files by attaching the file to an e-mail to send to someone else to read or use. Sometimes you collaborate with others by posting files on a blog. Tools for this can be found on the File tab in Backstage view, on the Save & Send tab.

When a file is sent via e-mail, a copy of the file can be attached, a link can be sent, or you can include a copy of the file in a PDF, RTF, or other file format. The file can also be saved to an online workspace where it can be made available to others for collaboration and review. The Save to Web option on the Save & Send tab in Backstage view gives you access to Windows Live **SkyDrive**, which is an online workspace provided by Microsoft. SkyDrive's online filing cabinet is a free Windows Live service. As of this writing, you are provided with 25 GB of password-protected online file storage. This makes it possible for you to store, access, and share files online from almost anywhere. This personal workspace comes with a Public folder for saving files to share, as well as a My Documents folder for saving files you want to keep private. (As of this writing, SkyDrive is not available for Access.) Figure 27 shows the Save to Web options on the Save & Send tab in Backstage view of Word.

Files saved to an online workspace can be edited by more than one person at the same time. The changes are recorded in the file with each author's name and the date of the change. A web browser is used to access and edit the files, and you can choose who can have access to the files.

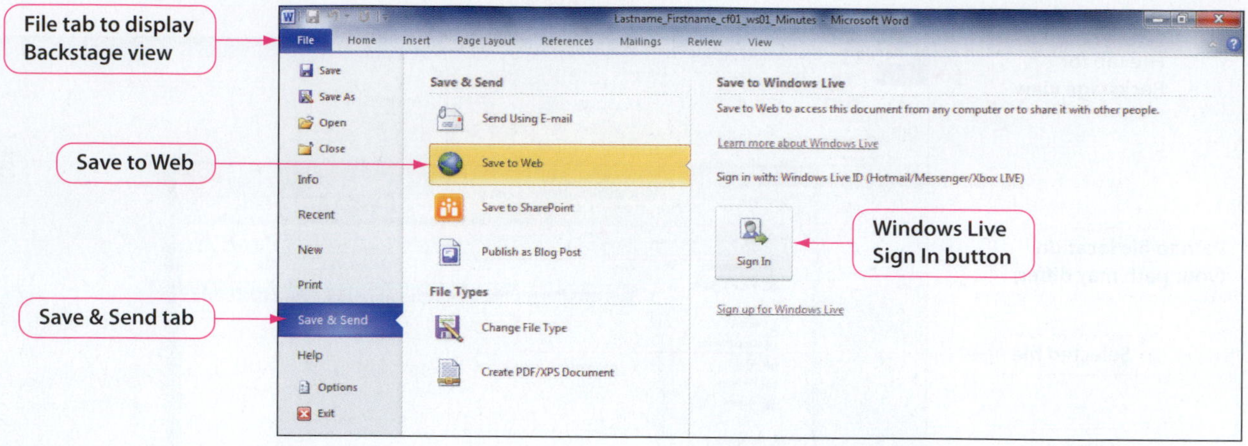

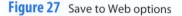

File tab to display Backstage view

Save to Web

Save & Send tab

Windows Live Sign In button

Figure 27 Save to Web options

Setting up a SkyDrive (Windows Live) Account

To use SkyDrive, you need a Windows Live ID. You can sign up for an ID at no cost. After you sign in, you can create new folders and save files into the folders. SkyDrive is a small section of Windows Live. You will need to have Internet access to complete this exercise.

To Set Up and Create a New Document in SkyDrive Account

a. On the taskbar, click **Internet Explorer** 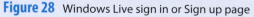 to open Internet Explorer; or alternatively, click the Start button, point to All Programs, and then click Internet Explorer to open the program.

b. In the address bar type skydrive.live.com.

c. If you already have a Windows Live account, login. If not, click the **Sign Up** button on the left side of the page. Follow the steps to set up an account.

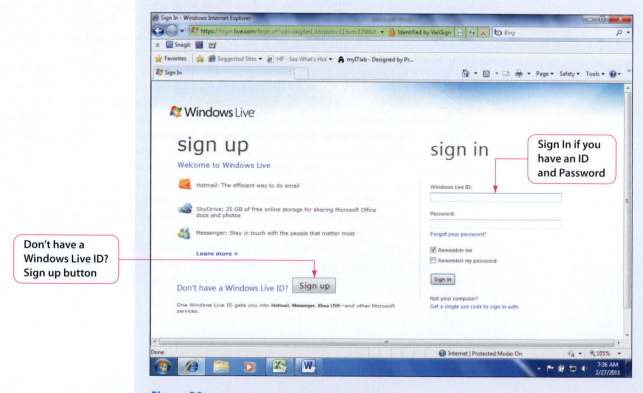

Sign In if you have an ID and Password

Don't have a Windows Live ID? Sign up button

Figure 28 Windows Live sign in or Sign up page

SIDE NOTE

Making SkyDrive the Active Screen

If SkyDrive is not the active screen, you can point to Windows Live in the upper-left corner of the window and then click SkyDrive from the menu.

d. Once your ID is created, you can log in. Once you log in you will see your SkyDrive with three areas: Documents, Favorites, and Photos.

e. To create a new document, presentation, or workbook, click the **New arrow**. Click **Word document**. Name your document Lastname_Firstname_cf01_ws01_SkyDrive. If you want to share with others, click **Change**. To add people to share with, you need to know their SkyDrive name or e-mail address.

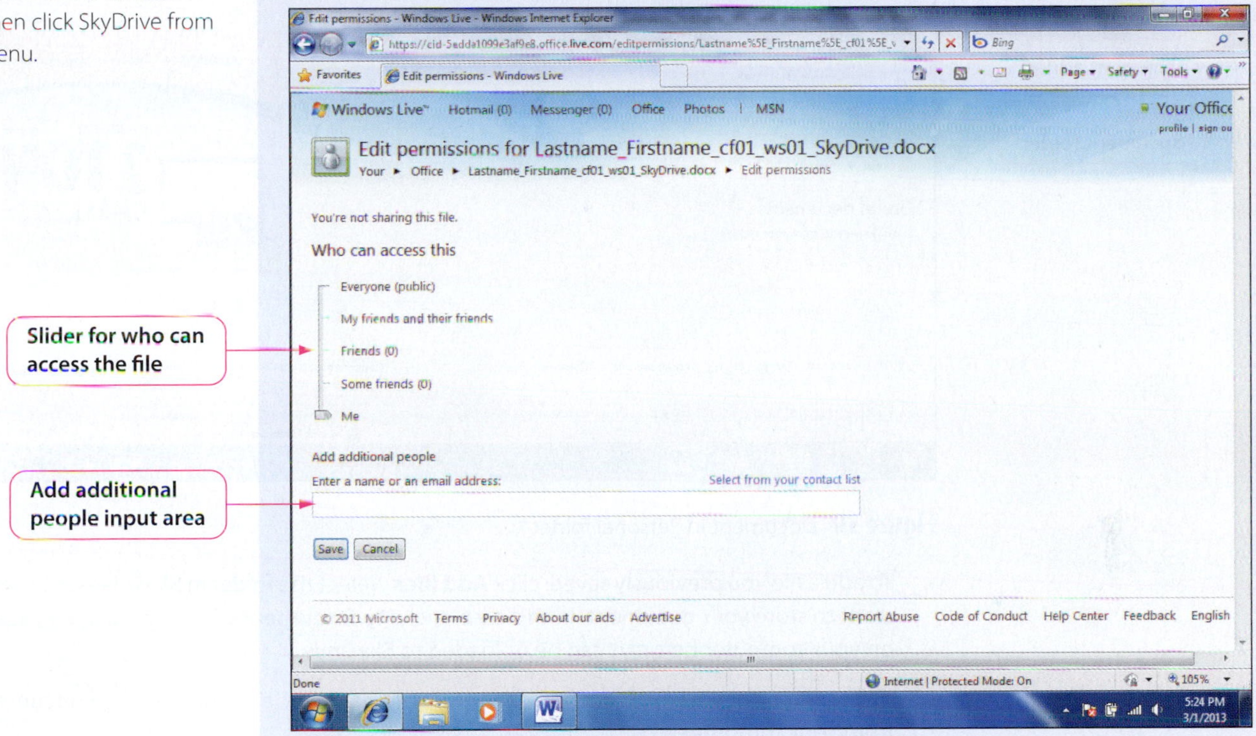

Slider for who can access the file

Add additional people input area

Figure 29 Sharing a document in SkyDrive

f. Click **Save** to save the document and to start typing the content of the file.

g. Type Firstname Lastname replacing Firstname and Lastname with your own name, click the **File tab,** and then click **Save**.

h. To return to your folders, click the Close button in the top-right corner of the document. Your document should appear in the Personal folder list because it was not shared.

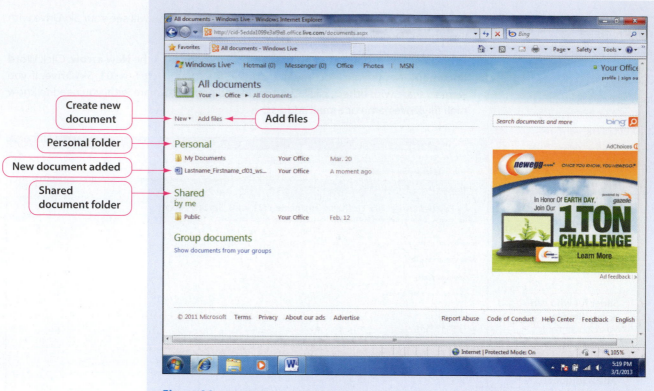

Figure 30 Document in Personal folder

i. To add a file you previously saved, click **Add files**. Select the folder in SkyDrive where you want to store your document. In this case, click **My Documents**. The file must be closed on your computer before it can be uploaded to SkyDrive.

j. Click **select documents from your computer** to navigate, and then select a document from your computer.

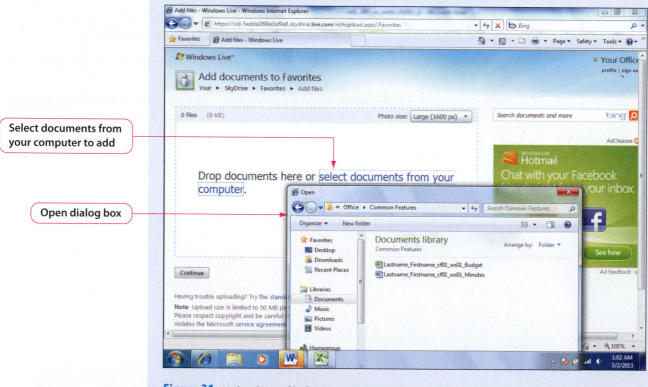

Figure 31 Uploading a file from your computer

k. Navigate to the location where your student files are stored. Select the file **Lastname_ Firstname_cf01_ws01_Minutes**, and then click **Open**. The file will upload to your SkyDrive. If necessary, click **Upload**, and then click **Continue** and you will be returned to the My Documents folder with your newly uploaded file.

l. To delete a file from the folder, hover the mouse pointer near the file name, and then click the **x** at the far right near the file name. Click **OK** to confirm that you wish to delete the file or **Cancel** if you wish to keep the file on SkyDrive. Click **sign out** to exit SkyDrive, located in the top-right corner under your sign in name.

Getting Help

If you require additional information about a feature or are not sure how to perform a task, make sure you acquaint yourself with the Office Help button and how to use it. In addition, do not overlook the ScreenTips within the program, which can also offer guidance along the way.

Viewing ScreenTips

ScreenTips are small windows that display descriptive text when you rest the mouse pointer over an object or button. You just need to point to a button or object in one of the Office applications to display its ScreenTip. In addition to the button's name, a ScreenTip might include the keyboard shortcut if one is available, a description of the command's function, and possibly more information. If you press F1 while displaying some ScreenTips it will open the Help file to the relevant topic displayed.

To Open Help

a. If necessary, on the taskbar, click **Word** [W] to make Word the active program.

b. Point to **Microsoft Word Help** [?] in the top-right corner of the window. The ScreenTip is displayed with the button's name, its keyboard shortcut, and a brief description.

c. Click the **Home tab**, and then point to the **Format Painter** button in the Clipboard group to display the ScreenTip. With the mouse pointer still over the Format Painter button and the ScreenTip showing, press the F1 key and notice that the Help window opens with information on how to use the Format Painter. Scroll down and read through the information. When you are done, click the **Close** [x] button in the top-right corner of the Word Help window.

Using the Help Window

The Help window provides detailed information on a multitude of topics, as well as access to templates, training videos installed on your computer, and content available on Office.com, the website maintained by Microsoft that provides access to the latest information and additional Help resources. To access the contents at Office.com you must have access to the Internet from the computer. If there is no Internet access, only the files installed on the computer will be displayed in the Help window.

Each program has its own Help window. From each program's Help window you can find information about the Office commands and features as well as step-by-step instructions for using them. There are two ways to locate Help topics—the search function and the topic list.

To search the Help system on a desired topic, type the topic in the search box and click Search. Once a topic is located, you can click a link to open it. Explanations and step-by-step instructions for specific procedures will be presented. There is also a Table of Contents pane, which displays a variety of topics to choose from when exploring various Help subjects and topics. It is organized similar to a book's table of contents. To access a subject or topic, click the subject links to display the subtopic links, and then click a subtopic link to display Help information for that topic.

SIDE NOTE
Help Shortcut

For those who prefer keyboard shortcuts, pressing F1 is the shortcut to access Help.

To Search Help for Information about the Ribbon in Excel

a. On the taskbar, click **Excel** to make Excel the active program.

b. Click **Microsoft Excel Help** . The Excel Help window opens.

c. If the Table of Contents is not displayed on the left side of the Help window, click the **Show Table of Contents** button on the toolbar of the Help window. Scroll down and notice the list of topics. Click the **Charts** topic and notice the subtopics displayed. Click **Charts** again to close the topic.

d. Click in the **Type words to search for** box if necessary, and then type ribbon.

e. Click the **Search arrow**. On the displayed Search menu, notice that options for both the online content—if you are connected to the Internet—and local content from your computer are available in the list.

f. If the computer has Internet access, verify there is a check mark next to **All Excel** in the Content from Office.com list. If you are not connected to the Internet, click **Excel Help** in the Content from this computer list.

g. Click the **Search** button. The Help window displays a list of the topics related to the keyword "ribbon" in the right pane.

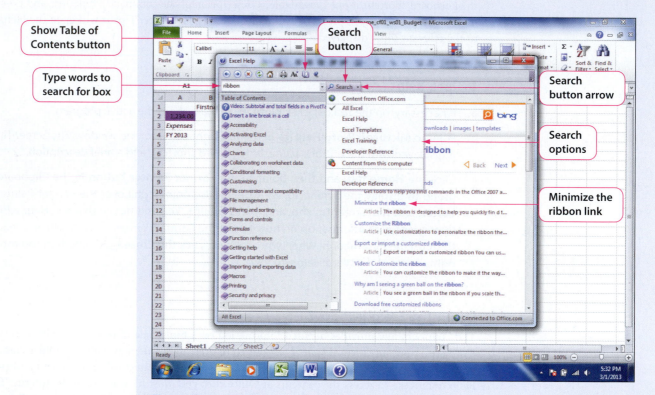

Figure 32 Excel Help

h. Scroll through the list to review the Help topics.

i. Click the **Minimize the ribbon** link from the list of results.

j. Read the information, and then click the links within this topic to explore how Help links work.

k. On the Help window title bar, click **Close** to close the window.

Printing a File

There are times you will need a paper copy, also known as a hard copy, of an Office document, spreadsheet, or presentation. Before printing, review and preview the file and adjust the print settings as needed. Many options are available to fit various printing needs, such as the number of copies to print, the printing device to use, and the portion of the file to print. The print settings vary slightly from program to program. It is advisable that you check the file's print preview to ensure the file will print as you intended. Doing a simple print preview will help to avoid having to reprint your document, workbook, or presentation, which requires additional paper, ink, and energy resources.

To Print a File

a. On the taskbar, click **Word** [W] to make Word the active program.

b. If necessary, open the **Lastname_Firstname_cf01_ws01_Minutes** file.

c. Click the **File tab** to open Backstage view.

d. Click the **Print tab**. The Print settings and Print Preview appears.

e. Verify that the Copies box displays **1**.

f. Verify that the correct printer (as directed by your instructor) appears on the Printer button (your printer choices may vary). If the correct printer is not displayed, click the Printer button arrow, and click to choose the correct or preferred printer from the list of available printers.

g. If your instructor asks you to print the document, click the Print button.

Exiting Programs

When you have completed your work with the Office program, you should exit it. You can exit the program with either a button or a command. You can use the Exit command from Backstage view or the Close button on the top-right side of the title bar. Recall that if you have not saved the final version of the file, a dialog box opens, asking whether you want to save your changes. Clicking the Save button saves the file, closes the file, and then exits the program as long as other files are not open within the same program.

Exiting programs when you are finished with them helps save system resources and keeps your Windows desktop and taskbar uncluttered, as well as prevents data from being accidentally lost.

To Exit Office Applications

a. On the Word title bar, click **Close** [x].
Both the Word document and the Word program close. Excel should be visible again.

b. Click the **File tab** to open Backstage view, and then click **Exit**. If a dialog box opens asking if you want to save the changes made to the workbook, click Don't Save since no changes need to be saved.

c. The workbook closes without saving a copy, and the Excel program closes.

Concept Check

1. Which application would you use to write a memo?

2. Explain the main purpose for using Backstage view.

3. What is the Quick Access Toolbar?

4. Which tab on the Ribbon would you use to change the font settings?

5. What are the advantages of using SkyDrive instead of a USB Flash drive?

Key Terms

Backstage view 10
Contextual tab 17
Dialog box 15
Dialog Box Launcher 15
Document 2
Graphic 2
Information management program 3
Key Tip 13
Keyboard shortcut 13

Live Preview 14
Maximize 7
Mini toolbar 17
Minimize 7
Protected View 24
Quick Access Toolbar 13
Relational database 3
Restore Down 7
Ribbon 10

Ribbon button 11
ScreenTip 29
Shortcut menu 19
SkyDrive 25
Table 2
Task pane 15
Thumbnail 6
Workbook 2

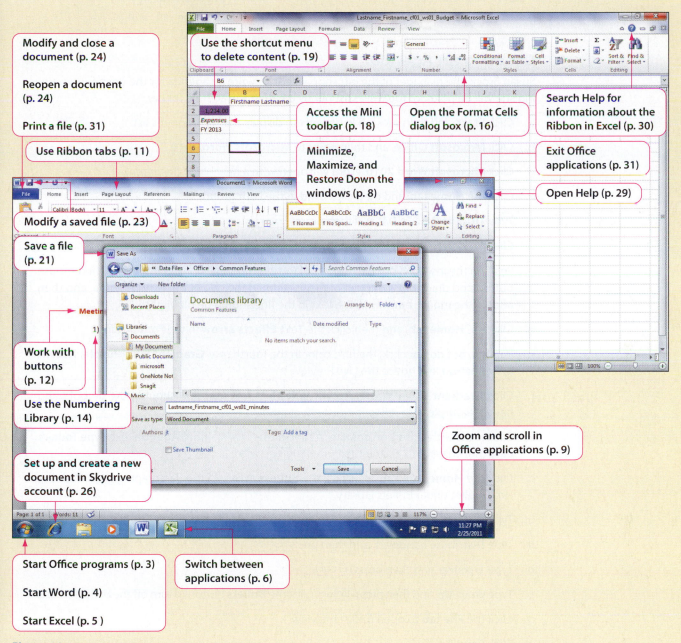

Figure 33 Working with the Common Features Final

Student data file needed:

New, blank Word document

You will save your file as:

Lastname_Firstname_cf01_ws01_Agenda

Creating an Agenda

Susan Brock, the manager of the gift shop, needs to write an agenda for the upcoming training she will be holding. You will assist her by creating the agenda for her.

a. Click **Start**, and then click **All Programs** to display the All Programs list.

b. Click **Microsoft Office**, and then point to **Microsoft Word 2010**.

c. Click **Microsoft Word 2010**. Word will open with a new blank document.

d. Click the **Home** tab, and then click **Bold** in the Font group.

e. Type TRAINING AGENDA, and then press Enter.

f. Click **Bold** to toggle the feature off.

g. Position the insertion point to the left of the word Training, press and hold the left mouse button and drag across the text of the first line to the end of the word Agenda, and then release the mouse button. All the text in the line should be highlighted.

h. Click the **Home tab**, and then click the **Text Effects arrow** in the Font group.

i. Point to, but do not click, the fifth color in the fourth row, **Gradient Fill – Purple, Accent 4, Reflection** and notice the Live Preview.

j. Click **Gradient Fill – Purple, Accent 4, Reflection**. Your text should now be bold and have the purple with reflection text effect applied.

k. Click to place the insertion point in the line under the **Training Agenda** text. Type Today's date (the current date), and then press Enter twice.

l. Click the **Home tab**, and then click the **Bullets arrow** in the Paragraph group. Click the circle bullet under Bullets Library.

m. Type Welcome trainees 2:00 pm, and then press Enter.

n. Type Distribute handouts, and then press Enter.

o. Type Training, and then press Enter.

p. Type Wrap-Up, and then press Enter. Click the **Bullets** button to turn off the bullet feature.

q. Click the **File tab** to open Backstage view.

r. Click **Save As**.

s. In the Navigation Pane, navigate to where you are saving your files. In the File name box, delete the existing file name, and then type Lastname_Firstname_cf01_ws01_Agenda.

t. Click **Save**.

u. Click **Close** in the top-right corner of the title bar to close the document and exit Word.

Practice 2

Student data file needed:
cf01_ws01_Budget

You will save your file as:
Lastname_Firstname_cf01_ws01_Budget_Update

Using the Ribbon for Event Planning

You have been asked to make some changes to the budget spreadsheet for the upcoming book publisher's conference. The publishers will be at the resort for the weekend and will be renting rooms and having a banquet dinner Saturday night. You will be working on a small portion of the banquet budget for the event planning and catering manager. You will need to apply some formatting so the document is not plain.

a.   Click **Start**, and then click **All Programs** to display the All Programs list.

b.   Click **Microsoft Office**, and then point to **Microsoft Excel 2010**.

c.   Click **Microsoft Excel 2010**. Excel starts with a new blank workbook.

d.   Click the **File tab** to open Backstage view.

e.   Click **Open**.

f.   In the Open dialog box, click the disk drive in the left pane where your student data files are located. Navigate through the folder structure, click **cf01_ws01_Budget**, and then click **Open**.

g.   If necessary, click the **Home tab**.

h.   Click cell **A1** to make it the active cell. Click **Bold** in the Font group to make the text Banquet Budget bold.

i.   Highlight column **B** by placing the mouse pointer over column letter B and clicking when the mouse pointer displays a down arrow over the B. Click the **Accounting Number Format** in the Number group.

j.   Click the **File tab**, and then click **Save As**. In the Save As dialog box, navigate to where you are saving your files, and then type Lastname_Firstname_cf01_ws01_Budget_Update in the File name box. This descriptive file name will help you more easily identify the file.

k.   Click **Save**.

l.   Click the **File tab**, and then click **Exit**.

Problem Solve 1

Student data file needed:
cf01_ps01_Agenda

You will save your file as:
Lastname_Firstname_cf01_ps01_Agenda_Updated

Adding More Formatting to a Document

Susan Brock, the manager of the gift shop, was very pleased with the training agenda you created. She decided she would like it a little more stylized. You have been asked to add some more custom formatting to the document.

a.   Start **Word**, and then open **cf_ps01_Agenda**.

b.   Click the **Page Layout tab**, and then click **Margins** in the Page Setup group.

c.   Change the Margins to **Wide**. This will provide space to take notes.

d. Position the insertion point to the left of the words **Training Agenda**, and then drag across the text of the first line to the end of the word **Agenda** to select the text. All the text in the line should be highlighted.

e. Click the **Home tab**, and then click the **Text Highlight Color arrow** in the Font group. Use Live Preview to view the available colors. Select **Turquoise**.

f. Click the **File tab**. Click **Save As** in Backstage view. Navigate to the location where your student files are stored. Save the updated file as Lastname_Firstname_cf01_ps01_Agenda_Updated.

g. Close the document. Close Word.

Perform 1: Perform in Your Career

Student data file needed:	You will save your file as:
New, blank Excel workbook	Lastname_Firstname_cf01_pf01_Training_Schedule

Creating a Training Schedule

One of the managers you worked for recommended you to Aidan Matthews, chief technology officer of the Red Bluff Golf Club. Aidan has asked you to create a training schedule in Excel for several of the trainings he is planning to schedule. The trainings include Windows 7, Word 2010, Excel 2010, and PowerPoint 2010. The trainings will be offered on Mondays, January 14, January 28, February 4, and February 11, 2013. Each training is three hours in length, with one hour between sessions. The first session starts at 9:00 am. There are two trainings per day. You will create an attractive schedule using features you worked with in this workshop.

a. Start **Excel**. Using the features of Excel, create a training spreadsheet that is attractive and easy to read. Some suggestions follow: Create column headings for the application and the date. Fill in the times in the cells where the application and date meet. Format the date (under the Number group use the drop-down list to select long date), format the column headings, format a title for the workbook, use bold, colors, etc.

b. Save the file in your folder as Lastname_Firstname_cf01_pf01_Training_Schedule. Close Excel.

Perform 2: How Others Perform

Student data file needed:

New, blank Word document

You will save your file as:

Lastname_Firstname_cf01_pf02_Critique

Improving the Look of Files

Prior to your tenure at the Red Bluff Golf Club, many different students passed through the doors as interns. You have been touted as an expert in how to format documents and spreadsheets. You have been asked to review a spreadsheet and a document and make suggestions on what to do to improve their look. Examine the following figures and answer the statements.

a. Open a new Word 2010 blank document.

b. List five items you would change in the document and why.

c. List five items you would change in the worksheet and why.

d. Save the file as Lastname_Firstname_cf01_pf02_Critique. Submit the file as directed.

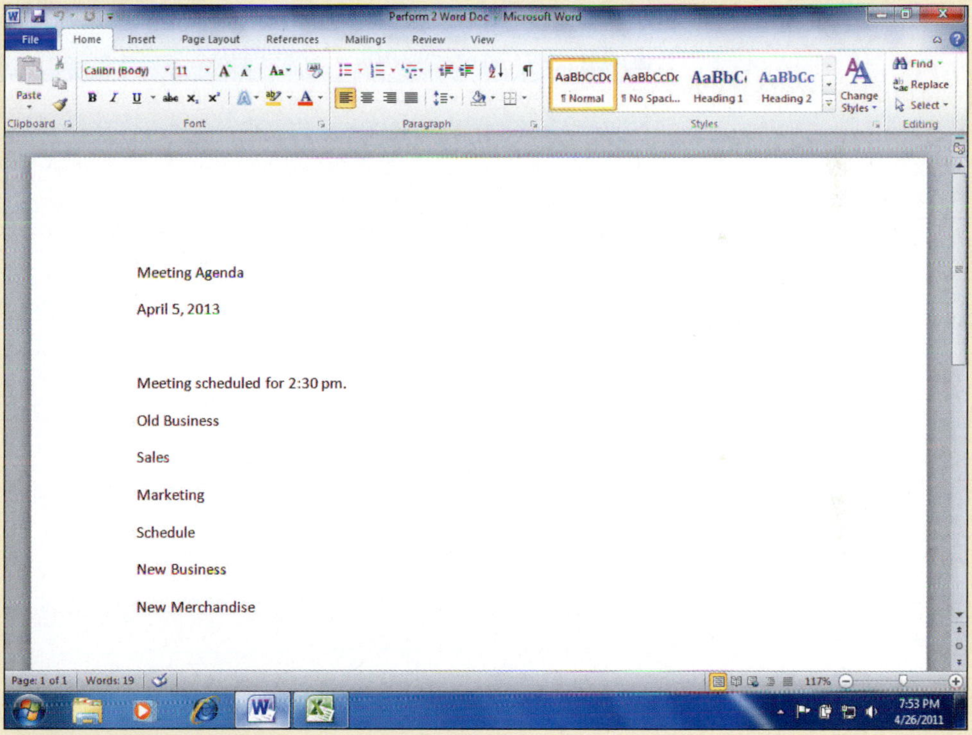

Figure 34 Word document

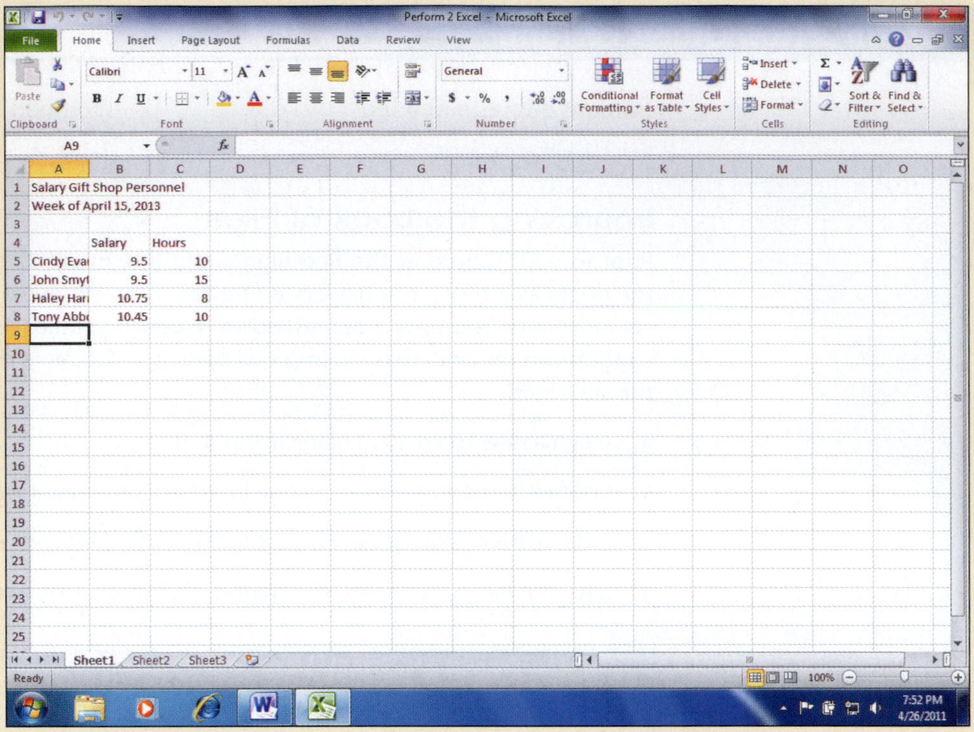

Figure 35 Excel worksheet

Understanding the Four Main Database Objects

PREPARE CASE
Red Bluff Golf Club Putts for Paws Charity Tournament

The Red Bluff Golf Club is sponsoring a charity tournament, Putts for Paws, to raise money for the Santa Fe Animal Center. An intern created a database to use to run the tournament but didn't finish it before leaving. You have been asked to finish the database to track the participants who enter the tournament, the orders they've placed, and the items they've purchased.

Courtesy of www.Shutterstock.com

Student data files needed for this workshop:

 a01_ws01_Putts

 a01_ws01_Participant

You will save your file as:

 Lastname_Firstname_a01_ws01_Putts

Understanding Database Basics and Tables

Businesses keep records about everything they do. If a business sells products, it keeps records about its products. It keeps records of its customers, the products it sells to each customer, and each sale. It keeps records about its employees, the hours they work, and their benefits. These records are collected and used for decision making, for sales and marketing, and for reporting purposes. A **database** is a collection of these records. The purpose of a database is to store, manage, and provide access to these business records.

In the past, many databases were paper-based. Paper records were stored in files in file cabinets. Each file would be labeled and put in a drawer in a file cabinet. Elaborate filing schemes were developed so that one record could be located quickly. This was highly labor-intensive and error prone. Today while most businesses use automated databases to store their records, you still see the occasional paper-based system. For example, your doctor's office may still use paper files for patient records.

Data are facts about people, events, things, or ideas, and they are an important asset to any organization as data allows companies to make better business decisions after converting it into useful information. **Information** is data that has been manipulated and processed to make it meaningful. For example, if you saw the number 2,000 out of context, the number has no meaning. If you are told that 2,000 represents the amount of an order in dollars, that piece of data becomes meaningful information. Businesses can leverage meaningful information to gain a competitive advantage, for example, by providing discounts to those who order more expensive items. An automated database management system, such as Microsoft Access, makes that possible.

Databases are used for two major purposes; for operational processing and for analytical purposes. In operational or transaction-based databases, each sale or transaction that a business makes is tracked. The information is used to keep the business running. Analytical databases are used for extracting data for decision-making. The data in these databases are summarized and classified to make information available to the decision makers in the firms.

Automated databases provide many advantages over paper databases. The information in the databases is much easier to find in automated form. The information can be manipulated and processed more rapidly. Automated databases can be used to enforce accuracy and other quality standards. In today's fast-paced world, a business needs to manipulate information quickly and accurately to make decisions. Without today's automated databases, a business cannot compete.

What Is Access?

Access is a relational **database management system (DBMS)** program created by Microsoft. It provides a tool for you to organize, store, and manipulate data, as well as to select and report on data.

Microsoft Access stores data in tables. Similar data are stored in the same table. For example, if you are storing data about participants in an event, you would include all the participants' names, addresses, and telephone numbers in one table.

The power of a database system comes with the ability to link tables together. A separate table of purchases for the tournament can be linked with the participant table. This allows users to easily combine the two tables; for example, the tournament manager would be able to print out the participants with a record of their tournament purchases.

Real World Advice   Why Use Microsoft Access?

There are many database management system software (DBMS) packages available. Why should you use Access?

- Access is an easily available DBMS. It is included with many Microsoft Office suites, which makes Access very attractive to businesses.

- Access is a relational DBMS. What you learn about Access is transferable to other relational DBMSs.

- Access allows for easy interaction with other products in the Microsoft Office suite. You can export data and reports into Word, PowerPoint, or Excel. You can also import from Excel and Word into Access.

- Access is often used as a stand-alone DBMS, meaning a DBMS used by a single user. Even if a company uses another DBMS for many users, you can easily link to that database with Access. You can use Access queries to output the data you need to interact with other MS Office applications to perform tasks such as mail merges.

What Are the Four Main Objects in a Database?

Access has four main database **objects**: tables, queries, forms, and reports. A **table** is the database object that stores data organized in an arrangement of columns and rows. A **query** object retrieves specific data from other database objects and then displays only the data that you specify. Queries allow you to ask questions about the data in your tables. You can use a **form** object to enter new records into a table, edit or delete existing records in a table, or display existing records. The **report** object summarizes the fields and records from a table or query in an easy-to-read format suitable for printing.

Access objects have several views. Each **view** gives you a different perspective on the objects. For example, the **Datasheet view** of a table shows the data contents within a table. Figure 1 shows Datasheet view of a participant table. **Design view** shows how fields are defined. Depending on the object, other views may exist. Figure 1 shows a toggle button ![toggle] you can use to switch between Datasheet view and Design view. Figure 2 shows how a participant table would appear in Design view. In Datasheet view, you see the actual participants and their related information. In Design view, you see how the information is defined and structured. Figure 1 shows the charity event participant table. Each row contains corresponding pieces of data about the participant listed in that row. Each row in Access is called a **record**. A record is all of the data pertaining to one person, place, thing, or event. There are 17 participant records in the table. The second participant is John Trujillo.

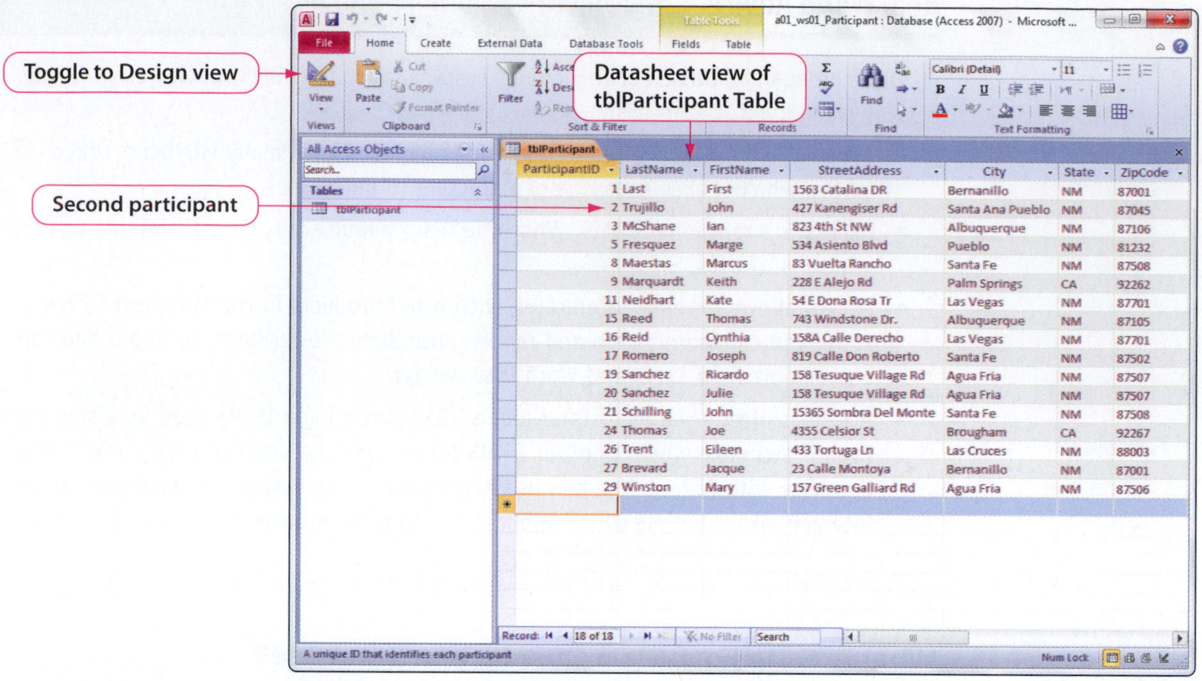

Figure 1 Datasheet view of tblParticipant table

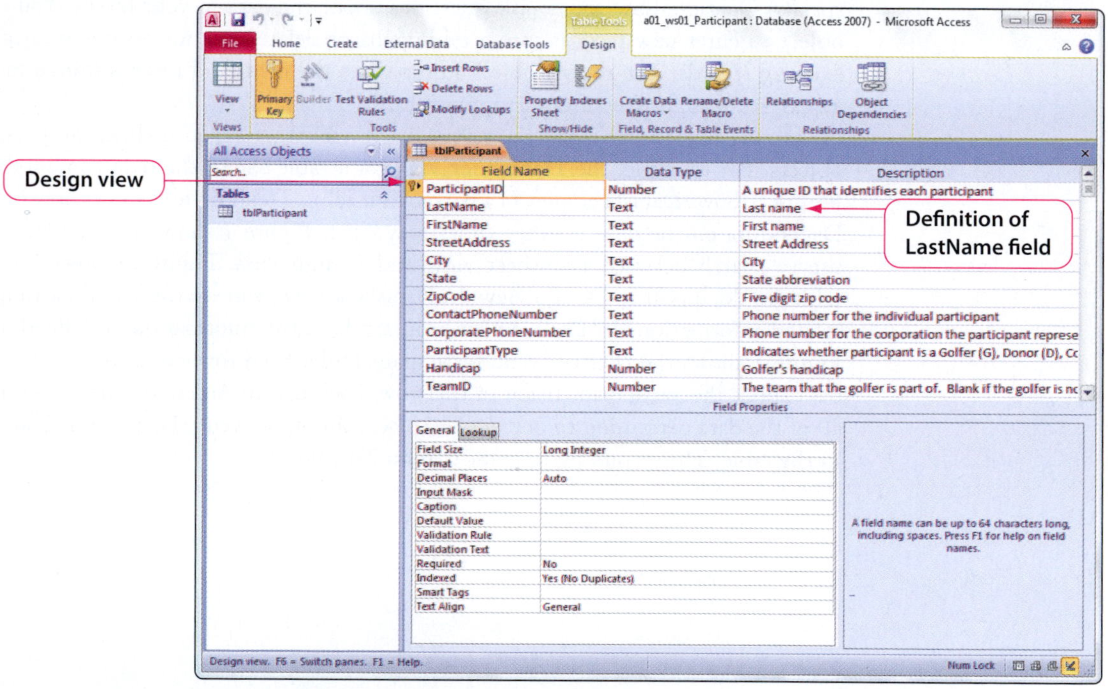

Figure 2 Design view of tblParticipant table

Each column in Access is called a **field**. A field is a specific piece of information that is stored in every record. LastName is a field that shows the participant's last name. As you go across the table rows, you will see fields that represent the participant's first name and address.

Creating a New Database and Templates

When you create a new database, you can design it yourself starting with an empty database. If you take this approach, you develop the tables, fields, and the relationships between the tables. This requires you to decide what information you want to keep in your database, how this information should be grouped into tables, what relationships you need, and what queries and reports you need.

The other option in creating a new database is to start with a prebuilt template. A **template** is a structure of a database with tables, fields, forms, queries, and reports. Templates are professionally designed databases that you can either use as is or adapt to suit your needs. You can download a wide variety of templates from Microsoft's website Office.com. Figure 3 provides a sample of database templates used for managing Assets, Contacts, Issues & Tasks, Non-profit, and Projects.

Templates are created by Microsoft employees or other users. Microsoft then allows users to rate the template so you can see what others have found useful. You can also download sample databases to experiment with. The difference between a template and a sample database is that a sample database has presupplied data, whereas a template is empty except for the structure and definitions. One of the popular databases among Access users is Microsoft's Northwind database, which has sales, customer, and employee data for a fictitious company named Northwind Traders.

For the tournament, the intern created an empty database and defined tables specifically for Putts for Paws. You will work with the database that has already been created. You need to open Access to get started.

To Start Access

a. Click the **Start button** 🎴. From the Start Menu, locate and then start **Microsoft Access 2010**.

Troubleshooting

If you don't see a folder called Microsoft Office, look for Microsoft Office Access 2010 in the list of available programs. Access may also be on the Start menu if it has been opened before. If you still don't see it, type Access in the Search programs and files box.

In Access you have the options of opening a blank database, opening an already existing database, or creating a new database from a template. If you start with a blank database, you'll need to define your tables and fields. Microsoft provides several templates with tables and fields already defined to help you create a database.

Maneuvering in the Navigation Pane

An intern started the database for the Putts for Paws charity event. You'll open it up, explore it, and make changes to it.

To Open a Database

a. Click the **File tab**, and then click **Open**.

b. In the Open dialog box, click the disk drive in the left pane where your student data files are located. Navigate through the folder structure and click **a01_ws01_Putts**, and then click **Open**. Access opens the database.

c. Click the File tab click **Save Database As**. In the Save As dialog box, navigate to the location where you are saving your files. In the File name box, type **Lastname_Firstname_ a01_ws01_Putts**, replacing Lastname_Firstname with your own name.

SIDE NOTE

Don't Confuse a DBMS with a Database

Access is a DBMS—it's software—whereas a database is a collection of data. You could use paper files to manage your Putts for Paws database, but you've chosen to use the Access DBMS software instead.

d. Click **Enable Content** in the Security Warning.

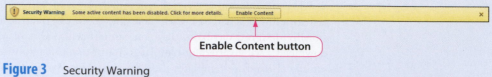

Figure 3   Security Warning

Real World Advice   **Why Does Access Give You a Security Warning About Your Database?**

Access displays a security warning asking you whether you trust the content of the database. If you download files from the Internet or get them from an unknown source, they may contain viruses. Until you tell Access that you trust this content, Access disables features that might allow the virus to infect your computer.

- Make sure you run a virus scan on any file before you say it should be trusted. You don't want to trust content that you are unsure about.

- You can trust the content for a single use. Click Enable Content to say that you trust the file.

- To trust a database permanently, you can store it in a trusted location. Depending on your computer and operating system, certain locations are predefined as trusted. Click File, and then select Trust Center Settings for the Access Trust Center where you can add other locations to the trusted locations.

Ways to View the Objects in the Navigation Pane

When you open a database, Access displays the Navigation Pane on the left side as shown in Figure 6. This pane allows you to view the objects in the database. The standard view in the Navigation Pane shows all objects in the database separated by types. You can see that the database has three tables: tblItem, tblOrder, and tblOrderLine. There is one query, one form, and one report.

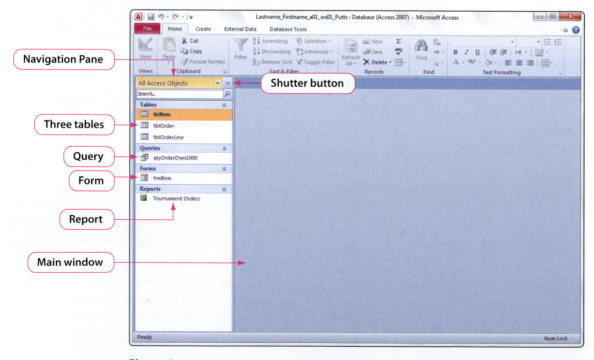

Figure 4   Opening screen for Lastname_Firstname_a01_ws01_Putts

Shutter Button

You can work with the Navigation Pane open or closed. The Shutter Bar Open/Close button at the top of the pane opens and closes the pane.

To Open and Close the Navigation Pane

a. Click the **Shutter Bar Close** button ⟪ to close the Navigation Pane. Access closes the pane, allowing for a larger working space in the database, but leaves the Navigation Pane on the side of the window for when you need it.

b. Click the **Shutter Bar Open button** ⟫ to open the pane again.

Customizing the Navigation Pane

While the default view of the Navigation Pane is all objects such as tables, queries, forms, and reports, organized by object type, you have several choices of views.

To Customize the Navigation Pane

a. Click the **Navigation Pane arrow** ⊙ to display the Navigation Pane view options. The default view is displayed, which is **Object Type** and **All Access Objects**.

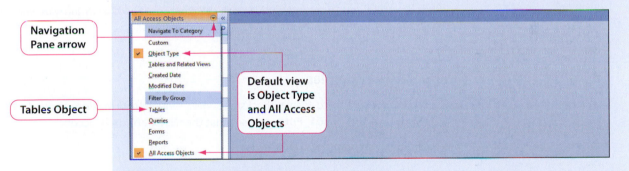

Navigation Pane arrow

Tables Object

Default view is Object Type and All Access Objects

Figure 5   Navigation Pane options (default view)

b. Click **Tables**.

Only the three tables are displayed in the Navigation Pane. When you have many objects in a database, it helps to restrict objects that are shown in the Navigation Pane.

c. Click the **Navigation Pane arrow** ⊙ again, and then click **Tables and Related Views**.

The objects are organized by tables. Any query, report, or form related to that table is listed with the table.

tblItem table has a form related to it

tblOrder table has a query and a report related to it

Figure 6   Table and related views in Navigation Pane

Using the Search Box

Currently, there are only a few objects in your database. However, as you work with a database, more objects may be added as you develop reports and queries. As a result, to help you find objects, Access provides a Search box.

To Search for an Object

a. In the Search box, type **Order**. Access searches for and displays all objects with the word Order in their name.

b. Click the **Clear Search String button** to see all objects again.

c. Click the **Navigation Pane arrow** again. Click **Object Type**, click the **Navigation Pane arrow**, and then select **All Access Objects**. This returns you to the default view, which is what will be used throughout this module.

File Extensions in Access

A **file extension** is the suffix on all file names that helps Windows understand what information is in a file and what program should open the file. However, Windows automatically hides these extensions so you often do not notice them. Access 2007 and Access 2010 both use the file extension .accdb indicating that databases created in the two versions are compatible with one another. The file name at the top of the window in Figure 11 shows that the file version is Access 2007. Be careful not to confuse DBMS with the database. The DBMS software you are using is Access 2010, but the database is in Access 2007 format.

To View a File Extension

a. Click the **File tab** to display Backstage view. Under **Information about Lastname_Firstname_a01_ws01_Putts**, you see that the file extension is .accdb.

b. Click the **Home tab**.

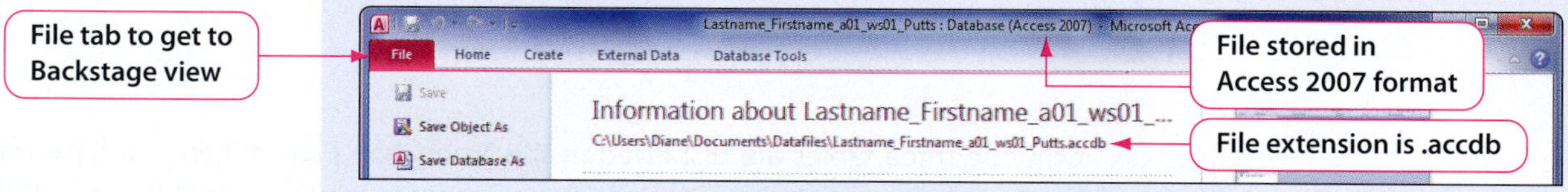

File tab to get to Backstage view

File stored in Access 2007 format

File extension is .accdb

Figure 7 Backstage view showing file extension

Quick Reference — File Extensions in Access 2003, 2007, and 2010

Extension	Description	Version of Access	Compatibility
ACCDB	Access database files.	2010 and 2007	Cannot be opened in Access 2002-2003.
ACCDE	Access database files that are in "execute only" mode. Visual Basic for Applications (VBA) source code is hidden.	2010 and 2007	Cannot be opened in Access 2002-2003.
ACCDT	Access database templates	2010 and 2007	Cannot be opened in Access 2002-2003.
MDB	Access 2002-2003 database files.	2003 and 2002	Can be opened in Access 2007 and 2010. Access 2007 and 2010 can save files in this format.
MDE	Access database files that are in "execute only" mode. Visual Basic for Applications (VBA) source code is hidden.	2003 and 2002	Can be opened in Access 2007 and 2010. Access 2007 and 2010 can save files in this format.

Introducing Tables

Tables store data organized in an arrangement of columns and rows. For illustration, think about the charity event, Putts for Paws. There are many ways participants and companies can participate in the event and help the charity. For example, a participant can play in the event, a company can pay for a foursome to play in the event, or it can sponsor various items such as a cart, hole, or flag. As a result, Painted Paradise needs to keep a record of the available options and what corporations or participants have purchased as shown in Figure 8.

ItemID	ItemDescription	QuantityAvailable	AmountToBeCharged	Notes
G1	Golfer – one	100	$200.00	
TEAM	Golfers – team of four	10	$550.00	
CTEAM	Golfers – corporate team of four	10	$850.00	Includes hole sponsorship
CART	Cart Sponsor	40	$2,000.00	Logo or brand displayed on cart
HOLE	Hole Sponsor	18	$500.00	Logo or brand displayed on hole
FLAG	Flag Sponsor	18	$500.00	Logo or brand displayed on flagstick

Figure 8 Data in the tblItem table

As mentioned previously, the power of a relational database comes when you link tables. The tblItem table shown in Figure 8 contains information about items that a participant or corporation can buy to support the charity, including the items available, a description, the quantity available to be sold, the amount that will be charged for the item, and notes about the item. However, you cannot see who has ordered these items. That additional information becomes available when you use relationships to look at other tables.

Import a Table

Recently, a colleague compiled a list of participants in an Access table in another database. You'll begin your work for Putts for Paws by importing this participant table from the Participant database into your database. **Importing** is the process of copying data from another file, such as a Word file or Excel workbook, into a separate file, such as an Access database.

To Import an Access Object

a. Click the **External Data tab**, and then click **Access** in the Import & Link group. The Get External Data – Access Database dialog box is displayed.

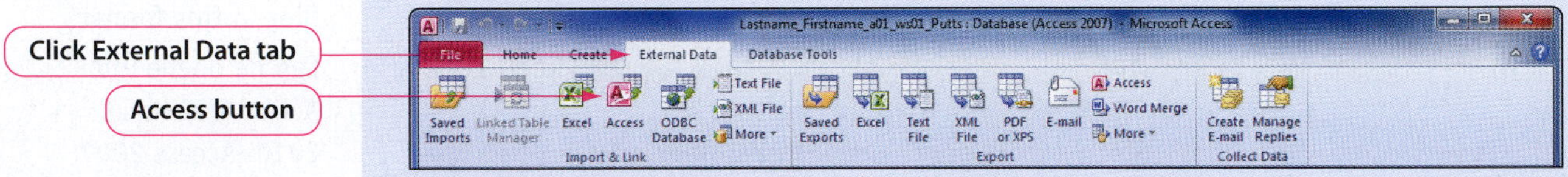

Figure 9   External Data tab

b. Click **Browse**, navigate to your student data folder, and then select the **a01_ws01_ Participant** database. Click **Open**, and then click **OK**. Access opens the Import Objects dialog box.

Troubleshooting

If your dialog box doesn't look like Figure 14, you may have chosen Access from the Export group on the Ribbon rather than from the Import & Link group.

c. If necessary, click the **Tables tab**. Click **tblParticipant**, and then click **OK**. Access displays the message: All objects were imported successfully.

d. Click **Close** at the bottom of the dialog box. Close ⊠ the tblOrder table.

e. Double-click **tblParticipant** in the Navigation Pane to open the table.
    Access opens the table. You may not see exactly the same number of columns and rows in your table because how much of the table is visible is dependent on how large your Access window is. You can change the size of the Access window by using your mouse to resize it or by clicking the Maximize button to maximize the Access window.

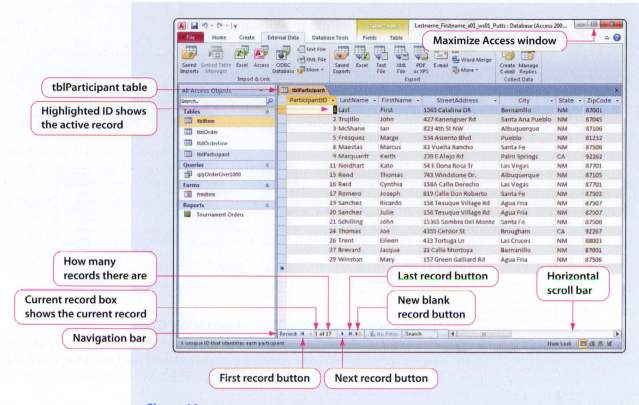

tblParticipant table

Highlighted ID shows the active record

Maximize Access window

How many records there are

Last record button

Horizontal scroll bar

Current record box shows the current record

New blank record button

Navigation bar

First record button

Next record button

Figure 10   Imported tblParticipant table

Real World Advice · What Should You Name Your Tables?

You want to use a name that is easy to understand. While Access allows you to give any name you want to a table, the name tblParticipant follows a standard naming convention:

- Use a name that starts with *tbl*. That allows you to distinguish tables from queries at a glance.

- Follow that with a name that is descriptive. You want it to be easy to remember what is in the table.

- Make the name short enough that it is easy to see in the Navigation Pane.

- You can use spaces in table names (e.g., tbl Participant), but avid Access users avoid them because it makes advanced tasks more difficult.

- You can use special characters in names. Some people use underscores where a space would otherwise be, such as tbl_Participant.

Navigate Through a Table

Carefully examine the tblParticipant table. Each row of data contains information about the participant listed in the LastName field. There are 17 participant records in the table with the second record being John Trujillo. You'll change the name in the record for the first participant to your name.

To Change the First Record to Your Name

a. If necessary, click the **First record button** ◄ to return to the first participant.

b. Press Tab to move to the LastName column.

c. Replace Last in the first record of the LastName column with your last name.

d. Press Tab to move to the next column, and then replace First with your first name in the FirstName column.

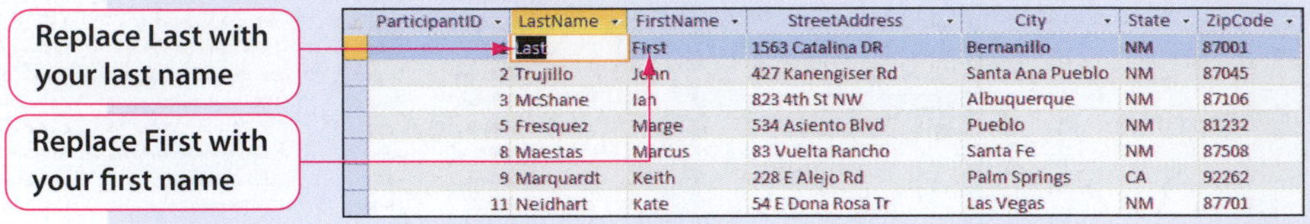

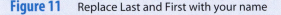

ParticipantID	LastName	FirstName	StreetAddress	City	State	ZipCode
	Last	First	1563 Catalina DR	Bernanillo	NM	87001
2	Trujillo	John	427 Kanengiser Rd	Santa Ana Pueblo	NM	87045
3	McShane	Ian	823 4th St NW	Albuquerque	NM	87106
5	Fresquez	Marge	534 Asiento Blvd	Pueblo	NM	81232
8	Maestas	Marcus	83 Vuelta Rancho	Santa Fe	NM	87508
9	Marquardt	Keith	228 E Alejo Rd	Palm Springs	CA	92262
11	Neidhart	Kate	54 E Dona Rosa Tr	Las Vegas	NM	87701

Replace Last with your last name

Replace First with your first name

Figure 11   Replace Last and First with your name

Navigate Through a Table with Navigation Bar

At the bottom of the table, Access provides a **Navigation bar** that allows you to move through the table. You can move record by record, skip to the end, or if you know a specific record, jump to that record. The highlighted ID shows the active record. When you open the table, the first record is active.

Examine the various parts of the Navigation bar as shown in Figure 16. The Current Record box shows which record is active and how many records are in the table. There are four arrow buttons in the navigation bar that you can use to move between records.

To Navigate Through the Table Using the Navigation Bar

a. Click the **Next record** button ► to move to the second record. The **Current Record** box changes to show **2 of 17**. Access highlights the first name of participant John Trujillo.

b. Click the **Next record** button ► to move to the third participant. The **Current Record** box changes to show **3 of 17**.

c. Click the **First record** button ◄ to return to the first participant.

d. Click the **New (blank) record** button ►✱ to go to the first blank row. Alternatively, you could click in the ParticipantID of the first blank row.

The first blank row at the end of the table is the **append row**. This row allows you to enter new records to the table. Notice that Access displays an asterisk in the **record selector** box (the small box at the left of the record) to indicate that it is the append row. When you type information here, you create a new participant record. Whenever you add a participant, you want to make sure you are in the append row so you are not changing the information for an existing participant. You'll add a participant to this empty row.

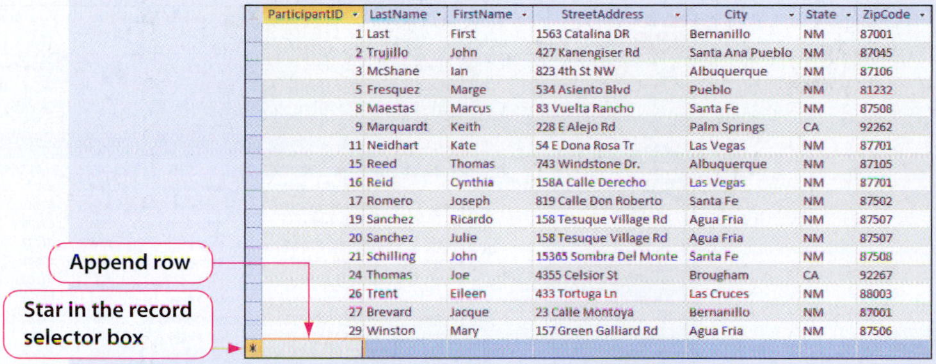

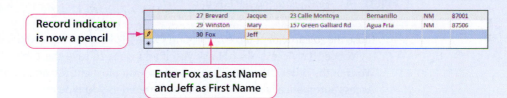

ParticipantID	LastName	FirstName	StreetAddress	City	State	ZipCode
1	Last	First	1563 Catalina DR	Bernanillo	NM	87001
2	Trujillo	John	427 Kanengiser Rd	Santa Ana Pueblo	NM	87045
3	McShane	Ian	823 4th St NW	Albuquerque	NM	87106
5	Fresquez	Marge	534 Asiento Blvd	Pueblo	NM	81232
8	Maestas	Marcus	83 Vuelta Rancho	Santa Fe	NM	87508
9	Marquardt	Keith	228 E Alejo Rd	Palm Springs	CA	92262
11	Neidhart	Kate	54 E Dona Rosa Tr	Las Vegas	NM	87701
15	Reed	Thomas	743 Windstone Dr.	Albuquerque	NM	87105
16	Reid	Cynthia	158A Calle Derecho	Las Vegas	NM	87701
17	Romero	Joseph	819 Calle Don Roberto	Santa Fe	NM	87502
19	Sanchez	Ricardo	158 Tesuque Village Rd	Agua Fria	NM	87507
20	Sanchez	Julie	158 Tesuque Village Rd	Agua Fria	NM	87507
21	Schilling	John	15365 Sombra Del Monte	Santa Fe	NM	87508
24	Thomas	Joe	4355 Celsior St	Brougham	CA	92267
26	Trent	Eileen	433 Tortuga Ln	Las Cruces	NM	88003
27	Brevard	Jacque	23 Calle Montoya	Bernanillo	NM	87001
29	Winston	Mary	157 Green Galliard Rd	Agua Fria	NM	87506

Append row

Star in the record selector box

Figure 12   Append a new record

e.   Make sure that the append row (blank row) is selected and that the record selector box contains an asterisk. In the Participant ID type **30**. Press Tab to get to the next field. In the LastName column, type **Fox**.

Alternatively, you can press Enter after typing text in a field to move to the next field. Also, notice that when you start typing, the record indicator changed from an asterisk to a pencil 🖉. The pencil means that you are in edit mode. The record after Fox now becomes the new append row.

Record indicator is now a pencil

	27	Brevard	Jacque	23 Calle Montoya	Bernanillo	NM	87001
	29	Winston	Mary	157 Green Galliard Rd	Agua Fria	NM	87506
🖉	30	Fox	Jeff				

Enter Fox as Last Name and Jeff as First Name

Figure 13   Enter participant Fox into the append row

f.   Continue entering the data for Fox using the following information:

FirstName	Jeff
Street Address	1509 Las Cruces Drive
City	Las Cruces
State	NM
Zip	88003
ContactPhoneNumber	5055558786
CorporatePhoneNumber	(leave blank)

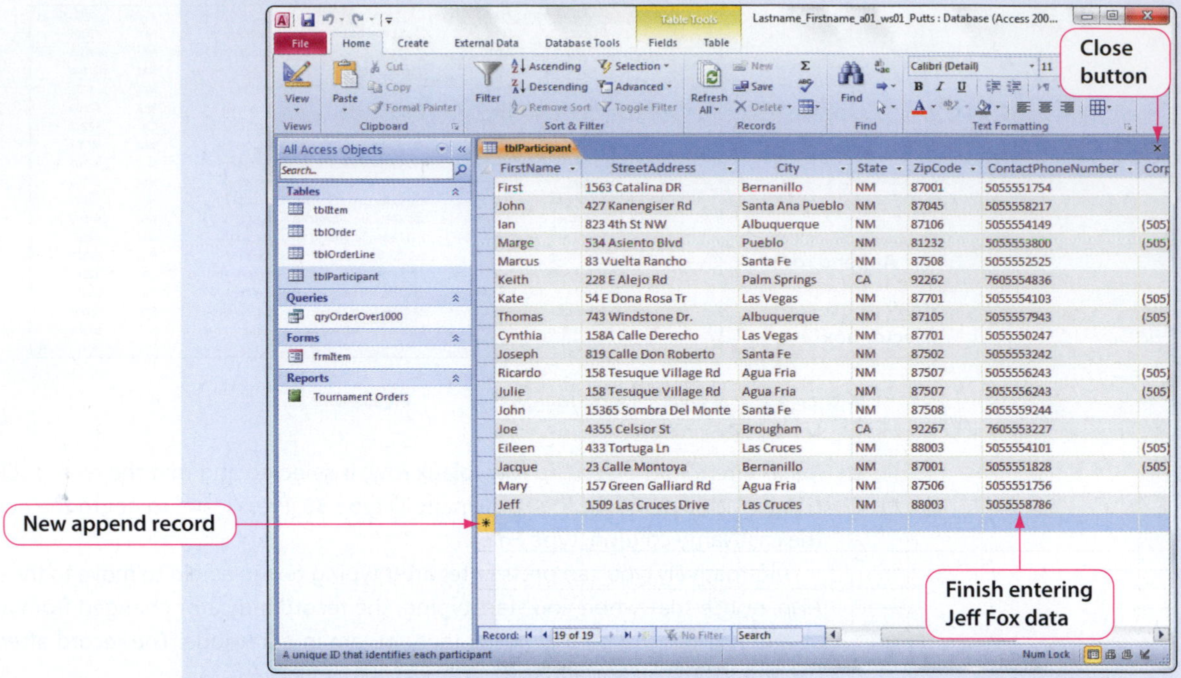

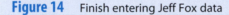

Figure 14 Finish entering Jeff Fox data

g. Close the tblParticipant table by clicking **Close** ☒. Keep Access and the database open.
Notice that Access did not ask you if you want to save the table. Access is not like
Word or the other Office applications where you must choose an option to save the file.
Access automatically saves the data you entered as you type it.

Real World Advice   Break Compound Fields into Their Parts

You might wonder why the name field and address fields are divided into multiple
fields. Wouldn't it be easier to have a single field for Name and a single field for
Address? It might be easier for data entry, but it is much more difficult for reporting.

- Break names into first name and last name fields. That means you can report on
  people alphabetically by last name, and if two people have the same last name, by
  first name.

- Break addresses into fields such as StreetAddress, City, State, and ZipCode. This
  allows reporting by state, city, or other fields.

- For other fields, consider whether you might want to report on smaller parts of the
  field. For example, for PhoneNumber in some applications, you might want to report
  on AreaCode. However, that would be rare, and so you usually use just one field.

Differences Between Access and Excel

An Access table looks similar to an Excel worksheet. Both have numbered rows of data and columns with labels. In addition, in both applications the columns are called *fields* and both allow
you to manage data, perform calculations, and report on the data. The major difference between
the two applications is that Access allows multiple tables with relationships between the tables,
thus the term *relational database*. For example, if you are keeping track of participants and the

items that they order, you create a table of participants and another table of orders. In Excel, you would have to repeat the participant information on each order.

When you look at Access, you notice that several tables are used for an order. Why use multiple tables for a single order? Figure 22 shows how an order would look in Access and in Excel. The Excel version has to repeat the participant's information on multiple lines. This leads to problems:

- Data redundancy—With repetition, you create redundant information. John Trujillo bought a cart and a team, so in Excel you have two lines. You'd have to repeat the address information on both records. It is not efficient to enter the address information twice.

- Errors—Redundant information leads to errors. If the address needs to be changed, you have to look for all records with that information to make sure it is fixed everywhere.

- Loss of data—Suppose that John Trujillo orders just one item. If you deleted the ordered item, it would mean deleting all the information about him as well as the order.

tblParticipant

ParticipantID	LastName	StreetAddress	City	State	ZipCode	ContactPhoneNumber	CorporatePhoneNumber
2	Trujillo	427 Kanengiser Rd	Santa Ana Pueblo	NM	87045	5055558217	

tblOrder

OrderID	AmountPaid	MethodOfPayment	ResortRoomNumber	ParticipantID
1	$2,550.00	CC		2

tblOrderLine

OrderID	LineNum	ItemID	Quantity
1	1	CART	1
1	2	TEAM	1

tblItem

ItemID	Itemdescription	QuantityAvailable	AmountToBeCharged
CART	Cart sponsor	40	$2,000.00
TEAM	Golfers - team of four	10	$550.00

Order in Access

Order in Excel

	A	B	C	D	E	F	G	H	I	J	K	L	M
1	Last Name	First Name	Street Address	City	State	Zip Code	Contact Phone Number	Corporate Phone Number	Order ID	Amount Paid	Method of Payment	Item ID	Quantity
2	Trujillo	John	427 Kanengiser Rd	Santa Ana Pueblo	NM	87045	5055558217		1	$2,000.00	CC	CART	1
3	Trujillo	John	427 Kanengiser Rd	Santa Ana Pueblo	NM	87045	5055558217		1	$ 550.00	CC	TEAM	1

Figure 15   John Trujillo's order in Access and in Excel

Because Access and Excel have so many common functionalities, many people use the tool that they are more confident using. If you prefer to use both, however, you can easily switch by exporting your data from Access to Excel or from Excel into Access. You can also use one tool for most uses and import your data to the other when you need to.

Generally, Access is designed to store data, and Excel is designed to analyze data and model situations. Fortunately, you can easily store data in Access and export a query to Excel for analysis.

Use Access when

- you need to store data in multiple tables.
- you have a very large amount of data (thousands of records).
- you have large amounts of nonnumeric data.
- you want to run many different queries and reports from your data.
- you have multiple users accessing your data.

Use Excel when

- your data fits well into one table.
- you want to primarily do calculations, summaries, or comparisons of your data.
- you are using a report that you create just one time or in just one format.

Discovering a Database (Manual Query)

Before you explore the database using Access queries, you will explore the database manually. This will give you an understanding of what Access can do. Patti Rochelle, the events coordinator at Painted Paradise, wants to send follow-up letters to those participants that have booked a corporate team for the Putts for Paws charity event. She asks you which participants have booked a team. First, you have to discover how a team is indicated in the database. Teams are items that participants can order, so you'll start in the tblItem table.

To Manually Navigate a Database

a. In the Navigation Pane, double-click **tblItem**.

Access opens tblItem in Datasheet view. Explore the data, and you'll notice that a corporate team is indicated as CTEAM.

Figure 16 tblItem table

b. **Close** ☒ the tblItem table.

Next you need to determine which orders include CTEAM. Orders are composed of data from tblOrderLine and tblOrder.

c. Double-click **tblOrderLine** to open the table.

Scan for orders that include CTEAM. There are two, OrderID 4 and OrderID 11.

d. **Close** ☒ the tblOrderLine table.

e. Double-click **tblOrder** to open the table and find OrderID 4 and 11.

You need to find which participants placed these orders. Access uses common fields to relate tables. tblParticipant and tblOrder have ParticipantID in common. You find that the ParticipantID for OrderID 4 is 5 and for OrderID 11 is 19.

Figure 17　tblOrder table

f. **Close** [×] tblOrder table.

g. Double-click **tblParticipant** to open the table.

Scan for the participants that match the two ParticipantIDs you identified earlier, 5 and 19. You find that OrderID 44 was placed by ParticipantID Marge Fresquez. In addition, OrderID 11 was placed by PartcipantID Ricardo Sanchez.

Figure 18　tblParticipant table

h. Close [×] the tblParticipant table.

SIDE NOTE

Knowing Your Data

It is important to know what data is in your database. While Access will do the hard part of matching tables on common fields and finding the results, you still need to tell it what fields you want and where the fields are located.

You now can tell Ms. Rochelle which participants have booked corporate teams and the address that the follow-up should be sent to. However, it may seem like a lot of work to find out who booked the corporate teams. Access queries make this task easier.

Understanding Queries, Forms, and Reports

You've explored tables, the first of the four main objects in Access. As mentioned previously, the other three objects are queries, forms, and reports. Each object provides a different way to work with data stored in tables. A query is used to ask questions about your data. A form is primarily used to enter data into your database or display data in your database. Reports are used to provide professional looking displays of your tables that are suitable for printing. In this section, you will work with queries, forms, and reports within your database.

Introducing Queries

A query is a way to ask questions about your data. For our charity golf tournament, you can use queries to get answers to questions such as "What is Ian McShane's phone number?" "What has John Trujillo ordered?" "What orders are over $1,000?"

You can also conduct more complex queries such as calculating a score given a player's strokes and their handicap.

One of the strengths of Access is the ability to ask such questions and get answers quickly. You traced who ordered corporate teams earlier in the workshop. That was difficult because you had to keep track of fields such as ParticipantID in one table and then look them up in another table. By using queries, Access will match common fields in the tables and trace the order for you.

You'll look at two different views of queries in this workshop:

- *Datasheet view* shows the results of your query.

- *Design view* shows how the query is calculated. It shows the tables, fields, and selection criterion for the query.

Creating a Query Using a Wizard

Access provides wizards to help you with tasks. A **wizard** is a step-by-step guide that walks you through tasks by asking you questions to help you decide what you want to do. Once you have some experience, you can also do the task yourself without a guide. You'd like to know which participants are from Bernanillo, New Mexico. You'll use the Query Wizard to create the query getting all participants, and then you will modify the query design to select those from Bernanillo.

To Create a Query With a Wizard

a. Click the **Create tab**, and then click **Query Wizard** in the Queries group.

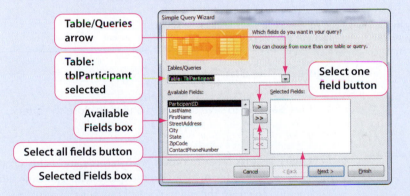

Figure 19 Create tab on the Ribbon

Access displays the New Query dialog box and asks you what kind of query you want.

Troubleshooting

If this is the first time that you've used this wizard, Access may tell you that the feature is not currently installed and ask if you want to install it. Reply Yes and wait while Access configures this wizard.

b. If necessary, click **Simple Query Wizard**. Click **OK**.

Access asks you which fields you want. You have choices of tables or queries as the source for your fields. Your database has four tables to select as a source. You will choose only one table. You could choose fields from multiple tables, but that isn't necessary in this query.

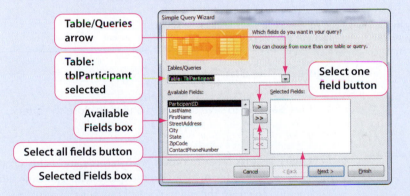

Figure 20 Select tblParticipant

c. Click the **Tables/Queries arrow** to see available field sources. Select **Table: tblParticipant** as the source of your fields.

The dialog box has two list boxes. The box on the left shows you all available fields from this table or query. The box on the right shows you all the fields that you have selected for this query. You use the buttons between the two list boxes to move fields from one box to the other. Selecting a field and clicking the One Field button **>** moves that field from the Available Fields box to the Selected Fields box. Clicking the All Fields button **>>** moves all fields.

d. Click **LastName** under Available Fields, and then click the **One Field button >**. Access moves the LastName field to the Selected Fields box.

e. Click **FirstName**, and then click the **One Field button >**.

f. Click **City**, and then click the **One Field button >**.

Your field list in the right box should be in the following order: LastName, FirstName, and City.

Troubleshooting

If you accidently add the wrong field to the Selected Fields box, use the One Field Back button < to place it back in the Available Fields box.

If you select the fields in the wrong order, Access doesn't have a way to reorder the fields. It is best to place them all back to the Available Fields window using the All Fields Back button << and then select them again in the right order.

g. Click **Next** to continue to the next page of the wizard. In the What title do you want for your query? box type **qryParticipantBernanillo**.

h. Click **Open the query to view information**, and then click **Finish**.

Access shows you the results of your query. Once you have created this query, the name is displayed under All Access objects in the Navigation Pane.

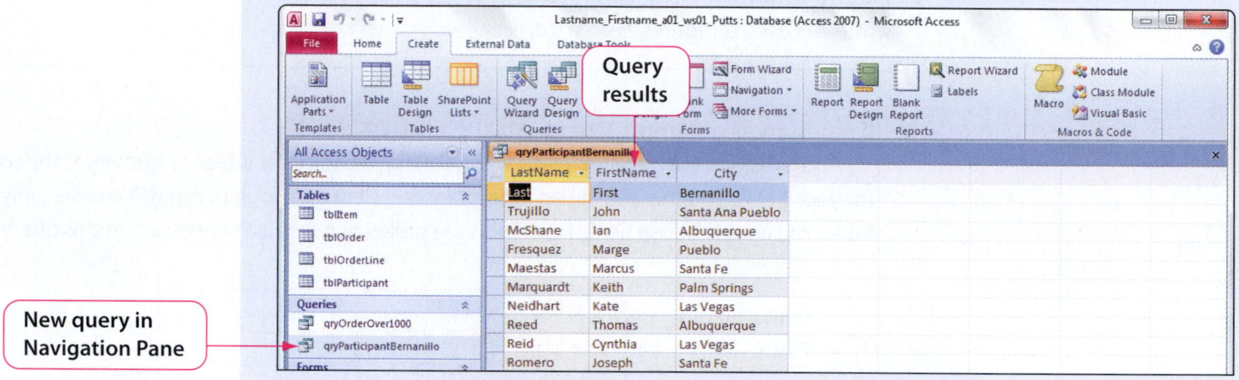

Figure 21   Results of your query

i. Click **Save** 💾 to save the query, and then close the query.

Query results are a recordset with records and fields created at **run time**, which means that it is created each time you run the query. This run time table is referred to as a **recordset**. The method to create the query is saved but not the actual results. That means that if you add a participant who meets the query criteria to the participant table, the next time you run this query, that participant will appear in the results of this query.

Real World Advice   Naming Your Queries

Access will allow you to give your query any name you want. There are two important considerations:

- You want to remember what a query does, so make the name as descriptive as possible. A query named *tblParticipant Query* will probably have no meaning for you in a few days. It will be easier to remember that *qryParticipantBernanillo* shows participants from Bernanillo.

- When you are looking at field sources, you often have a choice between tables and queries. Starting all your tables with *tbl* and all your queries with *qry* makes it easy to distinguish what you are choosing.

Real World Advice — Using Wizards in Access

Access wizards are shortcuts to building objects, such as reports and forms. They select fields, format the data, and perform calculations. After the wizard does the initial formatting, you can modify the resulting report or form to get exactly what you want.

Selecting a Value Using Design View

The Query Wizard uses a question-and-answer dialog box to create a query. The other method of creating a query is using Design view. Design view goes behind the scenes of the data and shows you the detailed structure of an Access object.

To Switch to Design View of a Query

a. Right-click **qryParticipantBernanillo** in the Navigation Pane.

b. Select **Design view** from the shortcut menu.

     Access opens the Design view of your query. The Query Tools Design tab is open on the Ribbon. The left side of the screen shows the Navigation Pane. The top half of the screen shows the **query workspace**, which is the source for data in the query. In this case, the source is the table tblParticipant. The bottom half is called the **query design grid**. It shows which fields are selected in this query: LastName, FirstName, and City.

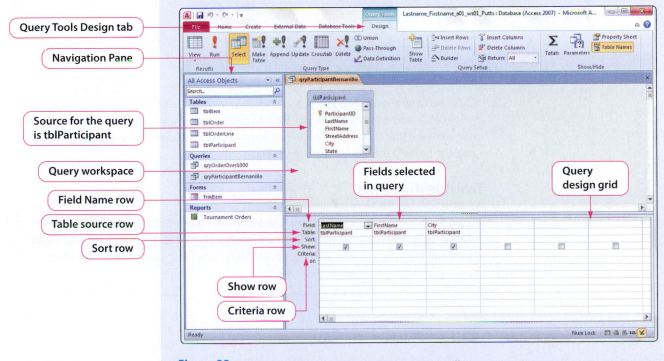

Figure 22   Design view for the qryParticipantBernanillo

Selecting Values in a Query

Each row in the design grid shows information about the field. The top row is Field name. The next row shows the table or source for this field. The Sort row allows you to specify the order of records shown in your query results by setting one or more sort fields. The Show row is a check box that specifies whether the field is shown in the table of query results. The Criteria rows allow you to select certain records by setting conditions for the field contents. You are going to change this query to see which participants are from Bernanillo. You'll do that by adding selection criteria.

To Select a Value in a Query

a. Click the **Criteria cell** in the City column.

b. Type **Bernanillo** in the cell.

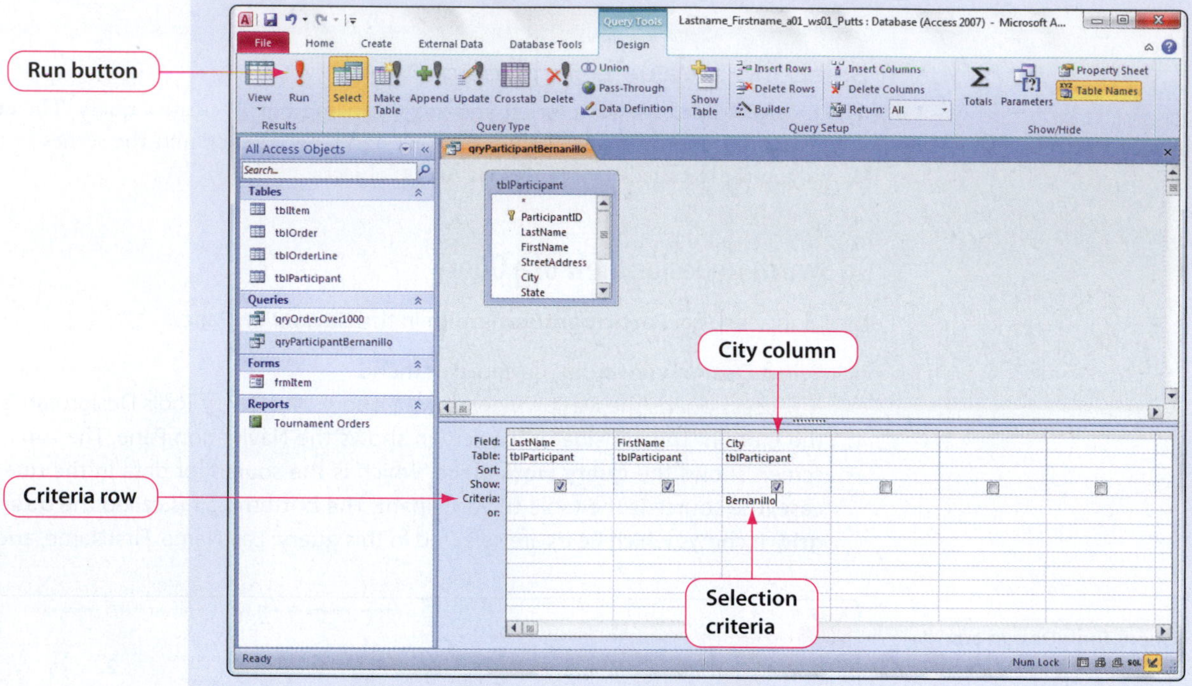

Figure 23   Enter criteria in a query selection

c. Click the Query Tools Design tab, and click **Run** in the Results group.

Access returns the query results. When you run a query, you should check the results to make sure that they make sense. You wanted the participants with a city of Bernanillo, and the participants shown are only in Bernanillo.

Troubleshooting

If your results are different than what is shown in Figure 35, you made an error in entering your selection criteria. Click View on the Home tab to switch back to Design view. Compare your criteria with Figure 34. Make sure that you spelled *Bernanillo* correctly and that it is in the City column.

Quick Reference   Selecting in a Query

When you typed *Bernanillo* in the criteria, you asked Access to select those participants that had a City equal to Bernanillo. The equal sign is implied, though you can enter it if you wish. Figure 24 shows other operators that can be entered in the selection criterion.

Operator	Meaning	Description
=	Equal to	Selects the records where the field value is equal to the value provided. If no operator is used, equal to is assumed.
<	Less than	Selects the records where the field value is less than the value provided.
>	Greater than	Selects the records where the field value is greater than the value provided.
< =	Less than or equal	Selects the records where the field value is less than or equal to the value provided.
> =	Greater than or equal	Selects the records where the field value is greater than or equal to the value provided.
< >	Not equal	Selects the records where the field value is not equal to the value provided.
Between	Between	Selects the records where the field values listed are within the two values. For example, between 1 and 7 is true for any value between 1 and 7 (includes the value of 1 and the value of 7).

Figure 24   Common selection criterion

Printing Query Results

If you want to print your query results, you can do this from the File tab. Printing tables is done the same way.

To Print a Query

a.   Click the **File tab** in the Ribbon to display Backstage view.

b.   Click **Print**, and then click **Print Preview** to see what the results would look like if printed.

c.   If your instructor asks you to print your results, on the **Print Preview tab** click **Print**. In the Print dialog box, select the correct printer, and then click **OK**.

d.   Click the **Print Preview tab**, click **Close Print Preview**.

e.   Click **Save** in the Quick Access toolbar.

f.   **Close** the qryParticipantBernanillo query.

Troubleshooting

If you accidently closed Access instead of just the query, open Access the same way you did at the beginning of the workshop. Click the File tab, and then double-click the name Lastname_Firstname_a01_ws01_Putts to open the database again.

Introducing Forms

A form provides another interface to a table beyond the table in Datasheet view. In corporate databases, end users of a database computer system often use forms to enter and change data. You can also use forms to limit the amount of data you see from a table. In a personal database, you can create forms for entering data if you wish.

Forms have three views:

- **Form view** shows the data in the form. This is the view you use to enter or change data. You cannot change the form design in this view.

- **Layout view** shows the form and the data. Some of the form design such as field lengths and fonts can be changed in this view. The data cannot be changed.

- **Design view** shows the form design but not the data. Any aspect of the report design can be changed. The data cannot be changed.

Creating a Form

You want to create a form to make it easier to enter a participant. There are different types of forms that can be created. The default form shows one participant at a time and has each field clearly labeled.

To Create a Form

a. Click **tblParticipant** in the Navigation Pane, click the **Create tab**, and then click **Form** in the Forms group.

b. Click **Save** 🖫 to save the form. In the Save As dialog box, type **frmParticipant** as the Form Name, and then click **OK**.

Access creates a form. Notice that the form displays the same Navigation bar that you had in the table. That is because a form is a data entry or display tool for the table. You can use it to navigate through your table. The form is created in Layout view, which allows you make minor changes to the design.

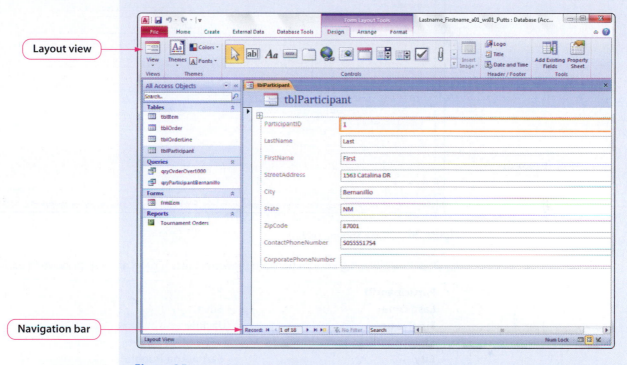

Figure 25 Form in Layout view

c. Click the title of the form **tblParticipant**, and then click again to select the title. Replace the old title with **Participant form Lastname_Firstname**, replacing LastName and FirstName with your own name.

d. Press ⎯Enter⎯, and then click **Save** 🖫 to save your form.

Entering Data via a Form

Jackie Silva has asked to register for the tournament. You'll use your newly created form to add her to the participant table. It is very important that you navigate to the append row so you enter her information into a blank form. If you see data about a participant in the form, you will be replacing that participant with Jackie Silva instead of adding a new participant.

To Enter Data Using a Form

a. Click the **View arrow** in the Views group, and then click **Form view**. This view allows you to use the form to enter data into the table.

b. Click the **New (blank) record** button on the Navigation bar. If you see a participant's name in the form, try again. This will be record 19 of 19 in the Navigation bar.

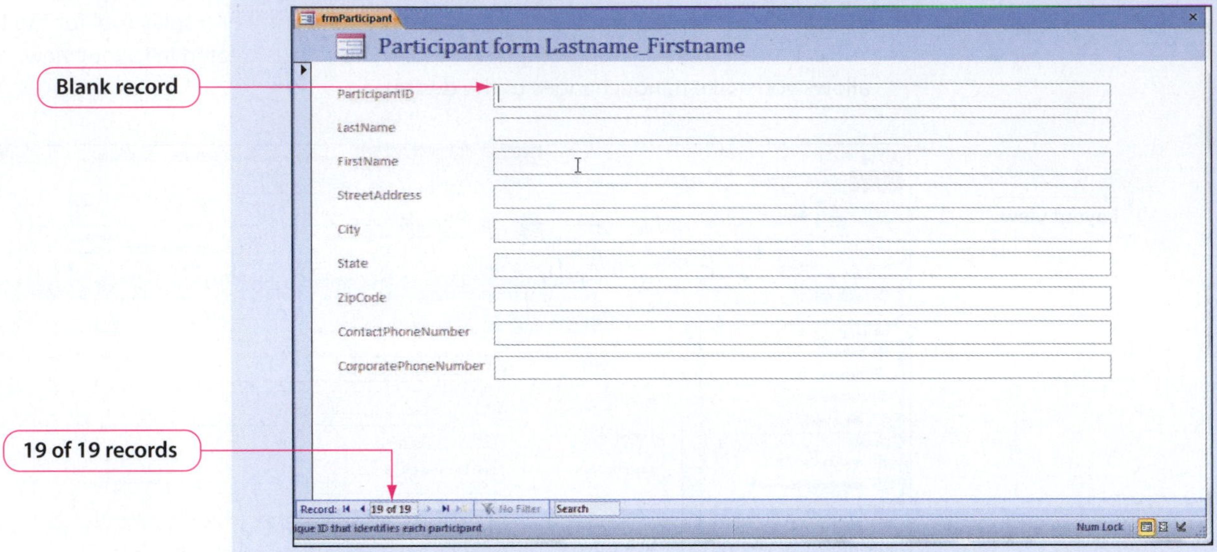

Figure 26 Blank append record

c. Type the following information into the form. Press Enter or Tab to move to each field.

ParticipantID	31
LastName	Silva
FirstName	Jackie
StreetAddress	1509 Main Street
City	Santa Ana Pueblo
State	NM
ZipCode	87044
ContactPhoneNumber	5055553355
CorporatePhoneNumber	Leave blank

d. **Close** the form. The participant data you entered in the form is saved to the table.

e. Double-click **tblParticipant** under Tables on the Navigation Pane.

f. Click the **Last Record button** on the Navigation bar. Verify that Jackie Silva has been added to your table.

g. **Close** the table.

SIDE NOTE

Saving in Access

Unlike Word and Excel, Access saves your data as it is entered. Unless you notice while you are typing, you cannot undo an inserted record once you've moved to the next record. Typing over the data in another record means that you lose the data that was there.

CONSIDER THIS | Adding Data Directly into a Table vs. Adding Data via a Form

You've added two participants to your table. Earlier, you added a row to the table and added Jeff Fox. Now, you've added Jackie Silva via a form. Which was easier for you? Why would most companies use forms to enter data?

Introducing Reports

A report provides an easy-to-read format suitable for printing. A sample report is shown in Figure 44. As you can see, the report has page headers (the column headings) and footers. You can easily provide column totals. When printing data for management presentations, you usually use a report rather than a query. The source of data for a report can be a table or query.

Reports have four views:

- **Report view** shows how the report would look like in a continuous page layout.

- **Print Preview** shows how the report will look on the printed page. This view allows you to change the page layout.

- **Layout view** shows the report and the data. Some of the report design such as field lengths and fonts can be changed in this view.

- **Design view** shows the report design but not the data. Any aspect of the report design can be changed.

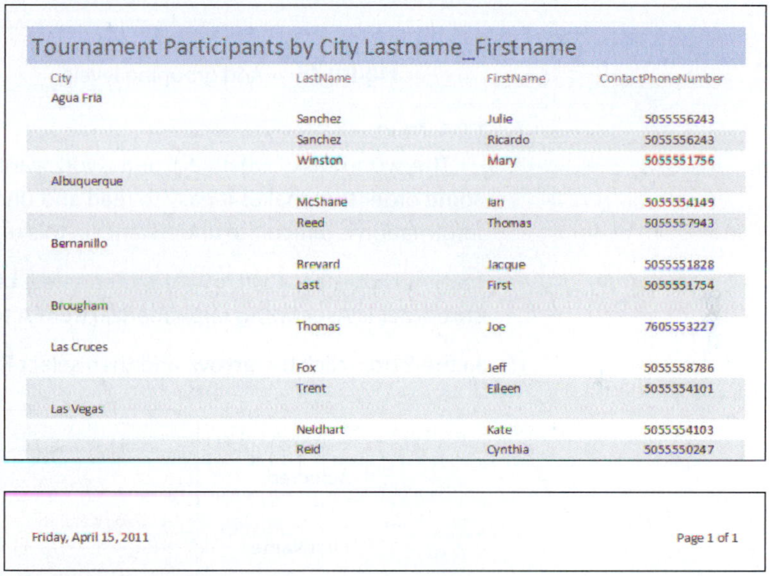

Tournament Participants by City Lastname_Firstname			
City	LastName	FirstName	ContactPhoneNumber
Agua Fria			
	Sanchez	Julie	5055556243
	Sanchez	Ricardo	5055556243
	Winston	Mary	5055551756
Albuquerque			
	McShane	Ian	5055554149
	Reed	Thomas	5055557943
Bernanillo			
	Brevard	Jacque	5055551828
	Last	First	5055551754
Brougham			
	Thomas	Joe	7605553227
Las Cruces			
	Fox	Jeff	5055558786
	Trent	Eileen	5055554101
Las Vegas			
	Neidhart	Kate	5055554103
	Reid	Cynthia	5055550247

Friday, April 15, 2011   Page 1 of 1

Figure 27   An Access report

Creating a Report Using a Wizard

The report feature in Access allows us to easily design reports that can serve management purposes and look professional. You'll create a report listing the participants in the database. You'll use the Report Wizard to create the report.

The Report Wizard starts similarly to the Query Wizard in selecting fields for the report. After that the wizard asks questions about report formatting that were not part of the Query Wizard.

You want to create a list of participants entered in the tournament with their contact phone numbers. You'll group all the participants in a single city in a single group. You'll print the participants in alphabetic order within each group.

To Create a Report Using a Wizard

a. Click the **Create tab**, and then click **Report Wizard** in the Reports group. Click the **Tables/Queries arrow**, and then click **Table: tblParticipant**.

b. Using the **One Field** button  move these the fields to the Selected Fields box: **LastName**, **FirstName**, **City**, and **ContactPhoneNumber**.

c. Click **Next**. The wizard asks if you want to add grouping levels.

d. Click to select **City**, and then click the **One Field** button > to group by City. When you make this selection the box on the right of the dialog box shows a preview of what the report grouping will look like.

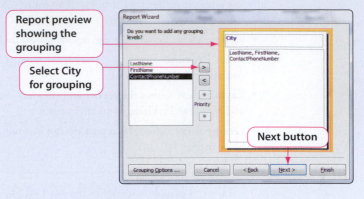

Report preview showing the grouping

Select City for grouping

Next button

Figure 28 Add grouping levels

e. Click **Next**.

The wizard asks what sort order you want. You always want to put your report in some order that makes it easy to read and understand. Otherwise a report with a lot of information is difficult to understand. In this report, you'll list participants alphabetically.

f. In the 1 box, click the **arrow**, and then select **LastName**. If necessary, make sure that the sort order is **Ascending** (alphabetical from A to Z).

g. In the 2 box, click the **arrow**, and then select **FirstName**.

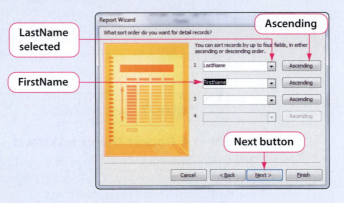

LastName selected

FirstName

Ascending

Next button

Figure 29 Add sorting

h. Click **Next**. If necessary, change the layout to **Stepped** and the orientation to **Portrait**.

i. Click **Next**. In the What title do you want for your report? box, type **Tournament Participants by City** as the title for your report.

j. Click **Finish**.

Access displays the report in Print Preview. You notice that the ContactPhoneNumber heading is not fully shown. You can fix that easily in Layout view.

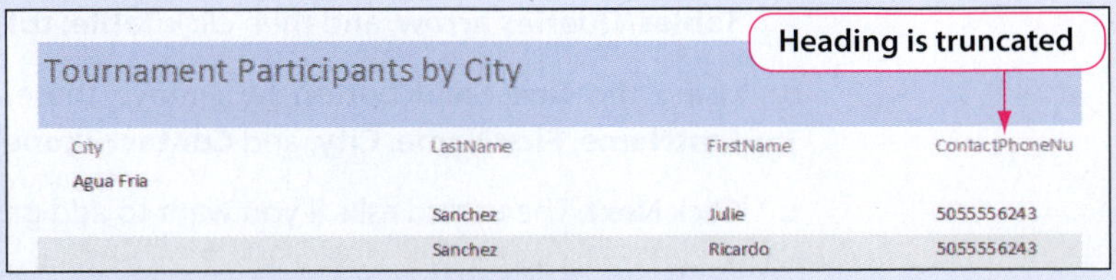

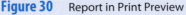

Heading is truncated

Figure 30 Report in Print Preview

k. Right-click anywhere on the report, and then click **Layout View** from the shortcut menu. Click the heading of the **ContactPhoneNumber** column.

l. Point to the **left border** of the selected heading until the Horizontal Resize pointer displays ↔.

m. Drag to the left until you can see the entire column heading.

n. Double-click the **title** of the report. At the end of the report title after **City**, add Lastname_Firstname using your own name.

o. Click **Save** 💾 to save the report.

Notice that the City data is a line above the data in the other columns. That is because the participants are grouped by city. Within city, participants are sorted alphabetically.

CONSIDER THIS | **Grouping vs. Sorting**

Grouping arranges records together by the value of a single field. Sorting puts the records within a group in a specific order based on field values. When would you choose to sort your records, and when would you group before sorting?

Printing a Report

You can print reports the same way that you printed a query earlier using the File tab. You can also take advantage of the Print Preview view to print a report. You are currently in Layout view and need to change to Print preview view. You'll use the button on the status bar to switch views.

To Print a Report

a. Click **Print preview** 🔍 to change to Print preview. Alternatively, you could change to Print preview view using the button on the Ribbon as you've done before.

b. If your instructor directs you to print the report, click **Print** in the Print group, and then click **OK**.

c. Click **Close Print Preview**. **Close** ☒ the report.

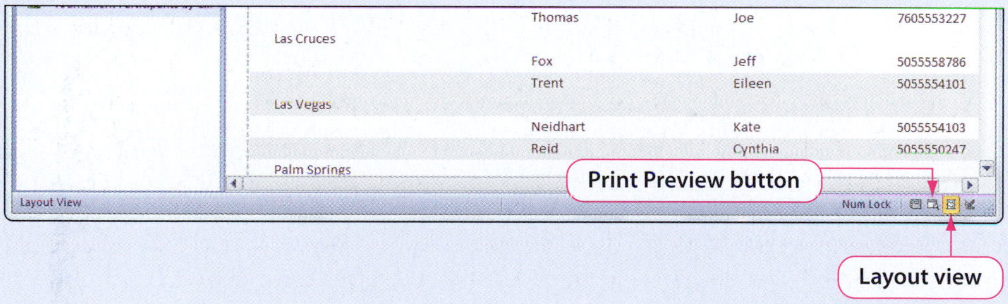

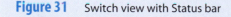

Figure 31 Switch view with Status bar

Both reports and queries can be used to report on your data. A report provides a more formal presentation of your data and is designed for printing. A query has more selection capabilities, but the formatting is not as attractive. You can combine the two capabilities by first creating the query object and then creating a report using the query as your source.

Backing Up Your Database

A **backup database** is an extra copy of your database that you can use to protect yourself from accidental loss of your database. Backups can help in cases of accidental deletion of data. You can return to the backup copy if you accidently delete the real database. It may not be as current as your real database, but it may save you from having to recreate the whole database. If you store the backup on another storage medium, it can also help in cases of hardware failure (such as a hard drive crash).

In Access, you make backups by using the Back Up Database command, which is available in the **Backstage view** on the Save & Publish tab. If you make multiple backup copies, you will want to give them different names. The backup feature appends the current date to the suggested file name. That allows you to easily distinguish various versions of the backups. You can be sure that you are getting the most recent one.

If you ever need a backup, simply return to the most recent copy that you have and start working with that file. You can copy it to the name of the file you want to work with.

To Back Up a Database

a. Click on the **File tab**, and then click **Save & Publish**. Access displays Save Database As options in the right pane.

b. Under Advanced, click **Back Up Database**, and then click **Save As**. The Save As dialog box appears with a suggested file name that has the date appended.

c. Navigate to the drive and folder where you want to store your backup. Change the file name if necessary, and click **Save**.

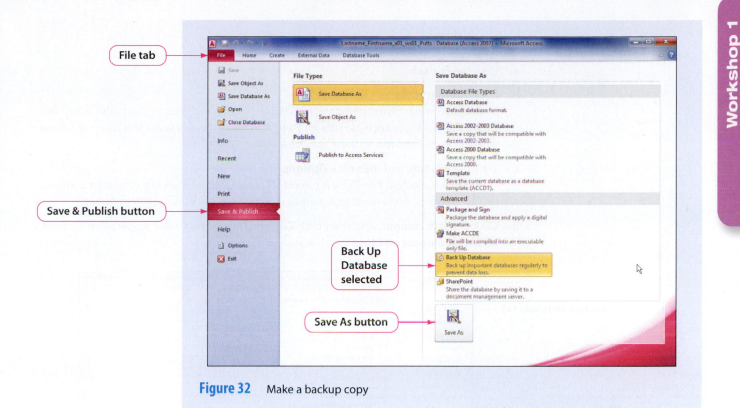

Figure 32   Make a backup copy

CONSIDER THIS | Backups

What would you lose if your PC's hard drive crashed? Do you have copies of school work, photographs, or music? You may never need one, but which would be worse: making unnecessary backups or losing all your files?

Compact and Repair

While you work on an Access database, the size of the database file increases. When you delete a record or object or if you make changes to an object, Access does not reuse the original space. Access provides a compacting feature that makes more efficient use of disk space. **Compacting** rearranges objects to use disk space more efficiently and releases the now unused space. If you don't compact your database, its size can get very large quickly. The compact option also looks for damaged data and tries to repair it.

You have two options for compacting: (1) you can perform a single Compact and Repair Database at any time, or (2) you can select Compact on Close. If you select Compact on Close, Access automatically compacts your database anytime you close it. Both options are available through Backstage view.

To Compact a Database

a. Click the **File tab**.

b. Click **Compact & Repair Database**.

Access compacts your database, fixes it if necessary, and returns you to the Home tab. On a small database such as Putts for Paws, this action is very fast. On a larger database with many changes made, there may be a noticeable delay.

c. Click the **File tab**, and then click **Options**.

By default, Compact on Close is turned off. Many professionals like to turn on Compact on Close so they don't need to remember to compact the database themselves.

d. Click the **left column**, and then click **Current Database**. Under Application Options, click the **Compact on Close** check box.

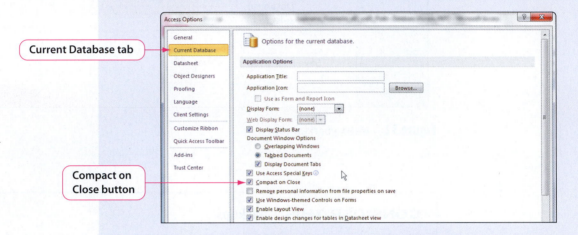

Figure 33   Select Compact on Close

e. Click **OK** to turn this option on. Access warns you that the option will not take effect until you close and reopen the database.

f. Click **OK**, and then **Close** Access.

Concept Check

1. You want to report on customers and orders. You expect to create several different reports from this data. Is Access or Excel most appropriate? Why?

2. For marketing purposes, you need to create a database identifying potential customers or prospects. Suggest names for the following tables:

   Potential customers or prospects

   Salesperson who identified the prospect

   Territory that each salesperson covers

3. You work in the human resources department. Your employee table needs to contain the employee's name, date that the employee was hired, expected retirement date, and emergency contact. Suggest field names for these fields.

4. For your human resources database, you need to list all those employees who are expected to retire in 2015. How would you get this list of employees?

5. Patti Rochelle, the events coordinator at Painted Paradise, wants to share the names of the participants with the Santa Fe Animal Center. Would a report or a query be more appropriate? Why?

Key Terms

Append row 50
Backstage view 68
Backup database 68
Compacting 69
Data 40
Database management system
   (DBMS) 40
Datasheet view 41
Design view 41
Field 42
File extension 46

Form 41
Form view 62
Importing 48
Information 40
Layout view 62
Navigation bar 50
Object 41
Print Preview 65
Query 41
Query design grid 59
Query results 58

Query workspace 59
Record 41
Record selector 50
Recordset 58
Report 41
Report view 65
Run time 58
Table 41
Template 43
View 41
Wizard 56

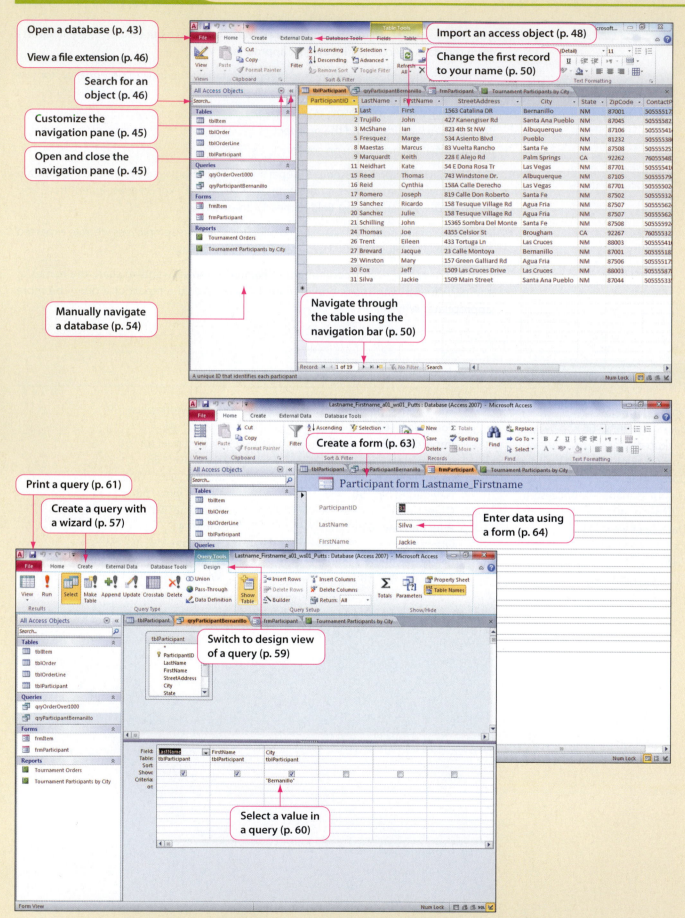

Open a database (p. 43)

View a file extension (p. 46)

Import an access object (p. 48)

Change the first record to your name (p. 50)

Search for an object (p. 46)

Customize the navigation pane (p. 45)

Open and close the navigation pane (p. 45)

Manually navigate a database (p. 54)

Navigate through the table using the navigation bar (p. 50)

Print a query (p. 61)

Create a query with a wizard (p. 57)

Create a form (p. 63)

Enter data using a form (p. 64)

Switch to design view of a query (p. 59)

Select a value in a query (p. 60)

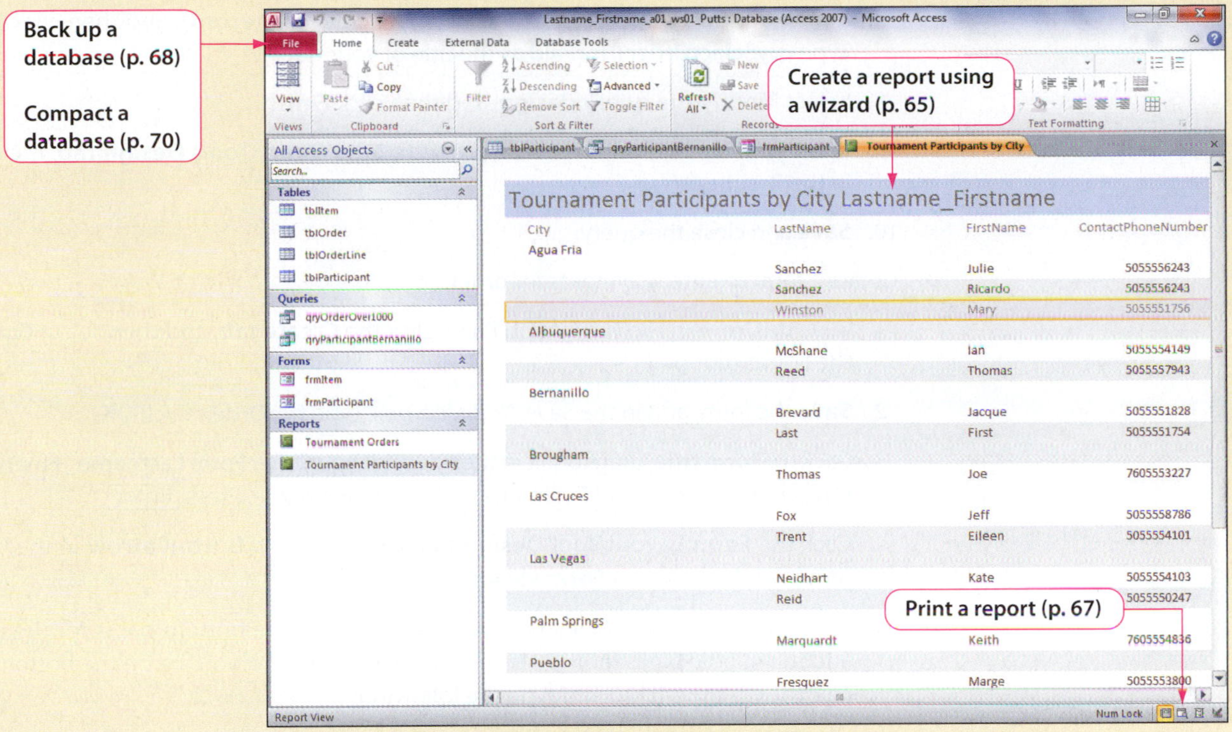

Back up a database (p. 68)

Compact a database (p. 70)

Create a report using a wizard (p. 65)

Print a report (p. 67)

Figure 34   Putts for Paws Charity Tournament Participants Final Database

Practice 1

Student data file needed:

a01_ws01_Putts2

You will save your file as:

Lastname_Firstname_a01_ws01_Putts2

Putts for Paws

You have been working with your Putts for Paws database for some time and you want to make it more complete. You've found that people often call to book a spot or to sponsor an item and pay later. You'd like a form where you can enter the information about which participants have paid.

a. Create a query to find those orders that have not been paid for.

1. Start **Access**, and then open **a01_ws01_Putts2**.

2. Click the **File tab**, and then click **Save Database As**. In the Save As dialog box, navigate to where you are saving your files and type Lastname_Firstname_a01_ws01_Putts2, replacing Lastname and Firstname with your own name. Click **Save**.

3. In the Security Warning, click **Enable Content**.

4. Click the **Create tab**, and then click **Query Wizard** in the Queries group. Select **Simple Query Wizard**, and then click **OK**.

5. Click the **Tables/Queries arrow**, and then select **Table: tblOrder** as the source of your fields.

6. In the Available Fields box, select fields **OrderID**, **AmountPaid**, **MethodOfPayment**, **ResortRoomNumber**, and **ParticipantID** and move them to the Selected Fields box. Click **Next**.

7. If necessary, click **Detail (shows every field of every record)**, and then click **Next**. Type qrySelectOrdersNotPaid as the title of your query.

8. Select **Modify the query design**, and then click **Finish**.

9. In the AmountPaid Criteria cell, type 0, Click the **Query Tools Design tab**, click **Run** in the Results group.

10. **Save** and close the query.

b. Create a form to enter payments for orders.

1. Click **tblOrder** in the Navigation Pane, click the **Create tab**, and then select **Form** in the Forms group.

2. **Save** the form, and in the Save As dialog box, type frmOrder. Click **OK**.

3. Click the **form title**, drag to select the title and type Order Form Lastname_ Firstname, replacing Lastname and Firstname with your own name. Press Enter .

4. Click the **Form Layout Tool Design tab**, click the **View button arrow** in the Views group, and then select **Form view**.

5. Notice there are two Navigation bars for this form. The bottom bar is for the order and the middle bar is for the order line. Making sure that you are on the bottom bar, navigate to OrderID 10 and type the following:

   a. **AmountPaid** $200

   b. **MethodOfPayment** ROOM

   c. **ResortRoomNumber** 204

6. **Save** and close the form.

c. Create a report on Orders.

1. Click the **Create tab**, and then select **Report Wizard** in the Reports group.

2. Click the **Tables/Queries arrow**, and then click **Table: tblOrder**.

3. Select the **OrderID**, **AmountPaid**, **MethodOfPayment**, **ResortRoomNumber**, and **ParticipantID** fields and move them to the Selected Fields box. Click **Next**.

4. Under the Do you want to add any grouping levels, double-click **MethodOfPayment**, and then click **Next**.

5. In the 1 box, click the **arrow**, and then select **ParticipantID**. In the 2 box, click the **arrow**, and then select **OrderID**. Click **Next**.

6. If necessary, change the Layout to **Stepped** and the Orientation to **Landscape**. Click **Next**.

7. Under What title do you want for your report? type Orders by Payment Method as the title for your report, and then click **Finish**.

8. Switch to Layout view, and then type Lastname_Firstname at the end of the report title, making it **Orders by Payment Method Lastname_Firstname** and replacing Lastname and Firstname with your own name.

9. **Save** and close the report, and then close Access.

Student data files needed:

a01_ws01_Painted_Treasures

a01_ws01_Products

You will save your file as:

Lastname_Firstname_a01_ws01_Painted_Treasures

Painted Treasures Gift Shop

The Painted Treasures Gift Shop sells many products for the resort patrons. These include jewelry from local artists, Painted Paradise Linens, products from the resort's restaurant, and spa products. You'll create a database that stores the gift shop's products. You'll create a form to enter products and an inventory report.

a. Create your database.

1. Start **Access**, and then open **a01_ws01_Painted_Treasures**.

2. Click the **File tab**, and then select **Save Database As**. In the Save As dialog box, navigate to where you are saving your files and then type **Lastname_Firstname_a01_ws01_Painted_Treasures**, replacing Lastname Firstname with your own name. Click **Save**.

3. In the Security Warning, click **Enable Content**.

4. Click the **External Data tab**, and then click **Access** in the Import & Link group.

5. In the Get External Data – Access Database dialog box, click **Browse**, navigate to your student data files, and then select **a01_ws01_Products**. Click **Open**, and then click **OK**.

6. In the Import Objects dialog box, select **tblProduct**, click **OK**, and then click **Close**.

b. Create a query to find the clothing products.

1. Click the **Create tab**, and then click **Query Wizard** in the Queries group. Click **Simple Query Wizard**, and then click **OK**.

2. Select **Table: tblProduct** as the source of your fields.

3. In this order, select the **ProductID**, **Category**, **ProductDescription**, **Color**, **Size**, and **Price** fields and move them to the Selected Fields box. Click **Next**, click **Detail (shows every field of every record)**, and then click **Next**.

4. Under What title do you want for your query? type **qryProductsClothingType**.

5. Click **Modify the query design**, and then click **Finish**.

6. Type **Clothing** in the Category Criteria cell, and then click **Run** in the Results group.

7. Save and close the query.

c. Create a form to enter new products.

1. Click **tblProduct** in the Navigation Pane, click the **Create tab**, and select **Form** in the Forms group.

2. Click **Save**, and then in the Save As dialog box type **frmProduct**. Click **OK**.

3. In Layout view, select the form title, and then change the title of the form to **Products Form Lastname_Firstname** using your own name. Save the form.

4. Click the **Form Layout Tools tab**, click the **View button arrow** in the Views group, and then select **Form view**. Click **New (blank) record**, and then enter the following product in the blank append record:

ProductID	42
ProductDescription	Polo Shirt
Category	Clothing
QuantityInStock	35
Price	30.00
Size	L
Color	Blue

5. Close the form.

d. Create an inventory report.

1. Click the **Create tab**, and then select **Report Wizard** in the Reports group.

2. Click the **Tables/Queries arrow**, and then click **Table: tblProduct**.

3. Select the fields in the following order: **Category**, **ProductDescription**, **Color**, **Size**, and **QuantityInStock**. Click **Next**.

4. Under Do you want to add any grouping levels? double-click **Category** and **ProductDescription**. Click **Next**.

5. In the 1 box, click the **arrow**, and then select **Color**. In the 2 box, click the **arrow**, and then select **Size**. Click **Next**.

6. Change the Layout to **Stepped** and the Orientation to **Landscape**, and then click **Next**.

7. Type Inventory Report in the title for your report, and then click **Finish**.

8. Switch to Layout view, and then at the end of the report title add Lastname_ Firstname, making it Inventory Report Lastname_Firstname using your own name.

9. **Save** and close the report, and then close the database.

Objectives

1. Understand database design.   p. 78
2. Import data from other sources.   p. 81
3. Enter data manually. p. 88
4. Create a table in Design view.   p. 91
5. Understand input masks.   p. 95
6. Understand formatting. p. 97
7. Understand and designate keys.   p. 99
8. Understand basic principles of normalization.   p. 103
9. Understand relationships between tables.   p. 104
10. Create a one-to-many relationship.   p. 106
11. Create a many-to-many relationship.   p. 109
12. Understand referential integrity.   p. 114

Gathering Data into a Database

PREPARE CASE

Red Bluff Golf Club Putts for Paws Charity Tournament Database

The Red Bluff Golf Club is sponsoring a charity tournament, Putts for Paws, to raise money for the local pet shelter. You are modifying a database for the tournament that tracks money being raised from the event. The scope of this database is limited to tracking monies. Thus, in this instance, you are not tracking whether a participant is a golfer, volunteer, or other role. Anyone can donate money in the form of hole sponsorship or other donation item. You will want to track monies derived from corporate sponsorship. You'll bring in data for the event from various sources including Excel worksheets and text files.

Courtesy of www.Shutterstock.com

Student data files needed for this workshop:

 a01_ws02_Putts

 a01_ws02_Putts_Golfers

 a01_ws02_Putts_Volunteers

 a01_ws02_Putts_Contacts

a01_ws02_Putts_Donors

You will save your file as:

 Lastname_Firstname_a01_ws02_Putts

Inserting Data into a Database

In designing a database, you will develop the tables, fields, and relationships of the tables. In order to manage the golf tournament, you will need to keep track of participants, the corporations that participate, the tee times, and the items each of the participants purchase. Each of these will be a table in your database. In this section, you will load tables from already existing databases and from Excel worksheets, in addition to creating two tables.

Database Design

Database design can be thought of as a three-step process:

1. Identify your entities—they become the tables.
2. Identify the attributes—they become the fields.
3. Specify the relationships between the tables.

An **entity** is a person, place, item, or event that you want to keep data about. You decide that you need to keep track of participants including golfers, donors, and corporate representatives. You need a participant table to track these people. A single participant is an instance of the participant entity and will become a record in the participant table.

An **attribute** is information about the entity. For example, for each participant you will want to keep information, such as name and address. These attributes will become the fields in your table.

A **relationship** is an association between tables based on common fields. The power of Access comes when you relate tables together. For example, you can relate participants to orders that the participants place.

Later in the workshop, you will look more closely at designing a database. While you explore the database tables and data, think about these general principles or steps to follow.

1. Brainstorm a list of all the types of data you will need.
2. Rearrange data items into groups that represent a single entity. These groups will become your tables.
3. If one item can have several attributes, such as a credit card number, expiration date, name on a card, and a security code, then put it into one group. In this example, it would be a group named credit card.
4. Break each attribute into the smallest attributes; they will become the fields. Give each attribute a descriptive name. For example, split addresses into street, city, state, and zip code.
5. Do not include totals, but do include all of the data needed so the calculation can be done in a query. For example, include the price of an item and the quantity ordered so the total cost can be calculated.
6. Remove any redundant data that exists in multiple groupings. For example, don't repeat customer name in both the customer grouping and the sales grouping.
7. Ensure common fields connect the groupings. For example, make sure that there is a common field between the customer grouping and the sales grouping so they can be connected. Later in this workshop, you will learn more about common fields.

You start with the participant entity, which is the tblParticipant table. You notice that it contains the fields shown in Figure 1 to track the participants in the tournament.

Field Name	Data Type	Maximum Length	Description
ParticipantID	Number—Long Integer		A unique ID that identifies each participant
LastName	Text	25	The participant's last name
FirstName	Text	20	The participant's first name
StreetAddress	Text	35	Street address
City	Text	25	City address
State	Text	2	State abbreviation
ZipCode	Text	5	Five-digit zip code
ContactPhoneNumber	Text	14	Phone number for the individual participant
CorporatePhoneNumber	Text	14	Phone number for the corporation the participant represents

Figure 1 Fields for tblParticipant

Illustrating some of the basic principles, notice that the participant's name is split into two fields and the address is split into four fields. Why should you do this? When you have fields such as name or address that are composed of several smaller fields, you should split them into their component parts. This allows for more flexibility for reporting. For example, often a report is needed in alphabetic order by last or first name. You could not do this if you had stored the first and last name combined in the same field. Further, a field named "name" is confusing, leading to inconsistent data such as nicknames and incomplete names. This also allows us to report or query on just part of the field such as which participants are from a particular state.

CONSIDER THIS | **Street Address Components**

Street addresses contain two parts, the number and street name. While some databases split these apart, this isn't necessary for most business uses. What are some businesses that benefit from separating these?

Real World Advice   First and Last Names

Painted Paradise is a U.S. company with guests who primarily use a first name followed by a last name. However, not all cultures around the world break names into first and last. For example, Korean names are designated as family name followed by given name. Designing database fields to accommodate all of the different cultures in the world is challenging. Always keep in mind the typical name for the database, but try to design it in such a way that other naming practices can fit into the database. Since businesses today are global, designing a database sensitive to all global cultures is difficult but important.

To Open a Database

a. Click the **Start button** 🔵. From the Start Menu, locate and then start **Microsoft Access 2010**.

b. Click the **File tab**, and then click **Open** to display the Open dialog box.

c. In the Open dialog box, click the disk drive in the left pane where your student data files are located. Navigate through the folder structure and click **a01_ws02_Putts**.

d. Click **Open**. Access opens the database.

e. On the File tab, click **Save Database As**. In the Save As dialog box, navigate to the location where you are saving your files. In the File name box, type Lastname_Firstname_a01_ws02_Putts, replacing Lastname_Firstname with your own name. Click **Save**.

f. Click **Enable Content** in the Security Warning.

g. Double-click the **tblParticipant table** to open it.

When you open the tblParticipant table, it opens in Datasheet view. In Datasheet view, you can see the information about the participants.

h. If necessary, click the **First record button** ◄ in the Navigation bar to return to the first participant.

i. Press Tab to move to the LastName column.

j. Replace **Last** in the first record of the LastName column with your last name and then press Tab to move to the next column. Replace **First** with your first name in the FirstName column.

Replace Last and First with your actual name

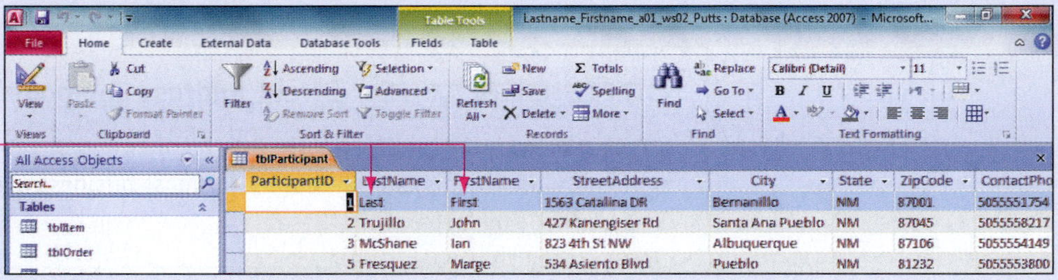

Figure 2 Datasheet view of tblParticipant table

k. Click the **Home tab**, click the **View arrow** in the Views group, and then click **Design View**.

When you switch to Design view, you see the structure of the fields and the field properties.

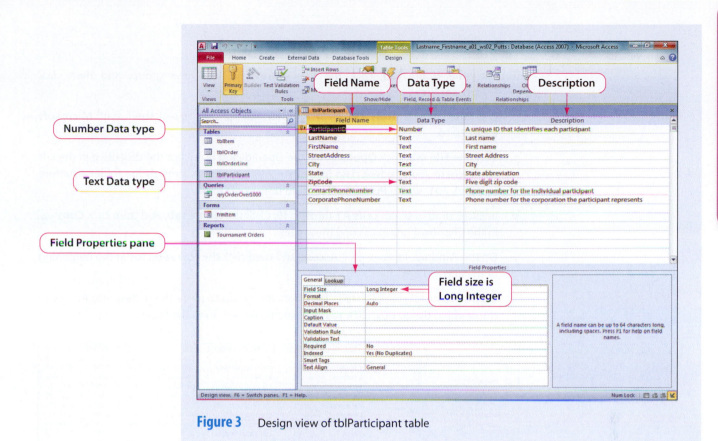

Figure 3   Design view of tblParticipant table

The upper pane of Design view has three columns: Field Name, Data Type, and Description. The Field Name is the column label in Datasheet view. **Data types** are the characteristic that defines the kind of data that can be entered into a field, such as numbers, text, or dates. The data type tells Access how to store and display the field. Number and Text are the two most common data types. In this table, you can see some fields are stored as a **Number data type**. That means that the data can only contain numeric data. The **Text data type** allows any text and numeric characters to be stored. Street Address is text data type, as a street address in this database can contain numbers, letters, and special characters. The third column, Description, helps the user discern the meaning of the field.

The Field Properties pane in Design view gives more information on how the data is stored, entered, and processed. If your insertion point is on ParticipantID, you can see that the Field Size is Long Integer.

Importing Data from Other Sources

Painted Paradise has had different employees collecting data in different ways. Luckily, the applications within the Microsoft Office suite work together. This allows you to easily move data between Excel and Access. After importing the data, you will be able to further analyze and refine the table structure for the database. Even though other employees have kept track of the roles that each participant plays, remember that the scope of this database does not include tracking the participants' roles in the event. You are only tracking corporate involvement.

Copy and Pasting

Only a few golfer participants were entered into the tblParticipant table. Some others were put in an Excel worksheet. You'll cut and paste them from Excel into your Access table.

To Copy and Paste Data from Excel

a. Click the **Home tab**, click the **View arrow** in the Views group, and then click **Datasheet View**.

b. Click the **Start button** 🌐. From the Start Menu, locate and then start **Microsoft Excel 2010**.

c. Click the **File tab**, click **Open**, and in the Open dialog box, click the disk drive in the left pane where your student data files are located. Navigate through the folder structure and click **a01_ws02_Putts_Golfers**, and then click **Open**.

d. In Excel, drag to select **cells A1** through **I9**. Click the **Home tab**, and then click **Copy** 📋 in the Clipboard group to copy these cells.

e. On the Windows taskbar, click **Access**, and then click the **row selector** at the beginning of the append row.

f. On the Home tab, click **Paste** in the Clipboard group to paste the golfers into Access. In the warning dialog box, click **Yes** to paste the records in to the table.

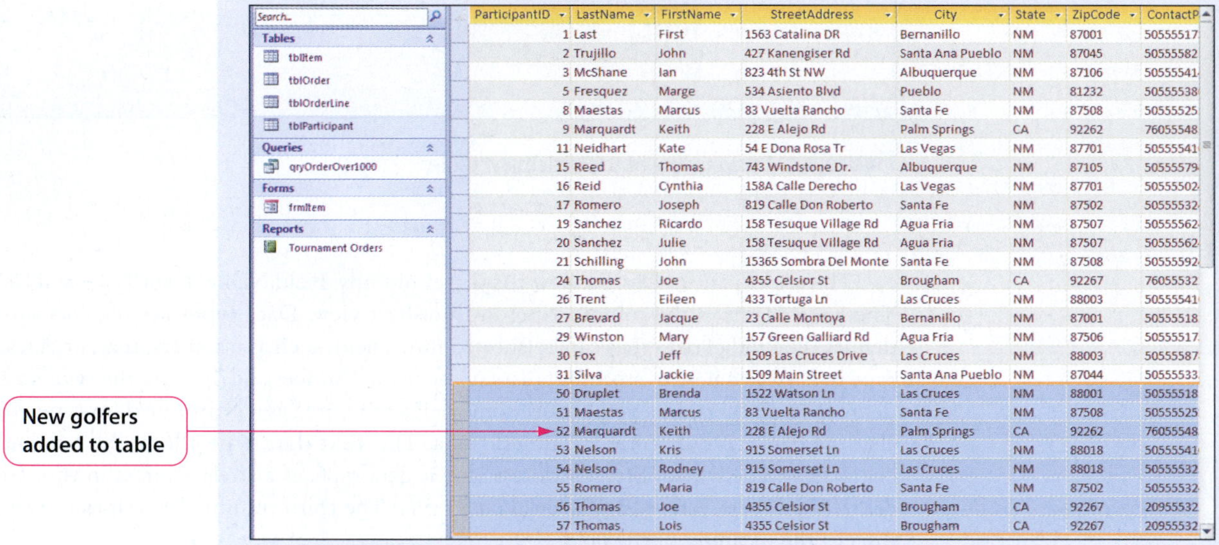

New golfers added to table

Figure 4 New golfers at the end of the tblParticipant table

Troubleshooting

If you accidently click in a single cell of the append row and try to paste there, you get the error message "The text is too long to be edited." It appears that you are trying to paste all the data into one cell and Access will not let you continue. If this happens, click OK, indicating that you do not want to put all the text into the one cell.

After that it may be difficult to exit that row and click in the row selector column. It appears you are trying to paste an invalid row and Access will not let you continue. You will get an error message saying "Index or primary key cannot contain a Null value." When you click OK and try to recover, the message will reappear. If this happens, click [Esc] indicating that you do not want to keep that record.

g. **Close** ✕ the tblParticipant table, leaving Access open.

Real World Advice — Cutting and Pasting from Excel Into Access

Cutting and pasting requires that the columns be exactly the same in Excel and Access. There cannot be missing columns or columns in different orders. You cannot paste fields that are nonnumeric into numeric fields. If you have any doubt about the files being compatible, use import to append the data to the table.

Use Cut and Paste when:

- you first export the data into Excel, make additions, and now want to put it back into Access. That way you know that the columns are the same.
- you are cutting and pasting the contents of a field from Excel into Access, such as a street address.

Importing a Worksheet

Access allows you to import an entire worksheet or a smaller portion of a worksheet into a table. This is quite useful as Excel is so frequently used in organizations. Excel column headings are frequently imported as field names.

The golf club has been keeping corporate contacts for the event in an Excel worksheet. You will import this Excel worksheet into your tblParticipant table.

To Import an Excel Worksheet

a. On the Windows taskbar, click **Excel. Close** ⊠ the Golfers worksheet.

b. Click the **File tab**, and then click **Open**. In the Open dialog box, click the disk drive in the left pane where your student data files are located. Navigate through the folder structure, click **a01_ws02_Putts_Contacts**, and then click **Open**.

Notice that the contacts data looks like the tblParticipant table in many ways. However, the corporate phone number immediately follows the participant's name rather than being at the end of the record as it is in the Access table. An import from Excel into an existing Access table is ideal for this type of import because as long as the columns have the same name, Access will match up the columns, skipping any missing column. You cannot copy and paste the way you did earlier because the columns are not arranged the same.

CorporatePhoneNumber immediately follows FirstName

	A	B	C	D	E	F	G	H	I	J
1	ParticipantID	LastName	FirstName	CorporatePhoneNumber	StreetAddress	City	State	ZipCode	ContactPhoneNumber	
2	40	Levant	Ronald	5055551200	672 N Mesquite St	Las Cruces	NM	88001	5055553878	
3	41	Dearman	Seth	5055551000	1717 Junior Hills Rd	Santa Ana Pueblo	NM	87044	5055559217	
4	42	Reed	Thomas	5055552000	743 Windstone Dr.	Albuquerque	NM	87105	5055557943	
5										
6										
7										
8										
9										

Figure 5   Contact data in Excel

c. **Close** ⊠ Excel.

d. In Access, click the **External Data tab**, and then click **Excel** in the Import & Link group.

e. In the Get External Data – Excel Spreadsheet dialog box, click **Browse**, navigate through the folder structure where your student data files are located, click **a01_ws02_Putts_Contacts**, and then click **Open**.

f. Select **Append a copy of the records to the table**. Click the **arrow**, and then select **tblParticipant**.

Access starts the Import Spreadsheet Wizard, which displays worksheets and ranges in the Excel workbook.

g. Click **OK**. Make sure **Show Worksheets** is selected and the **Corporate contacts** worksheet highlighted.

Access displays the next page of the wizard. This shows that Access found the column headings in Excel and matched them to the field names in Access.

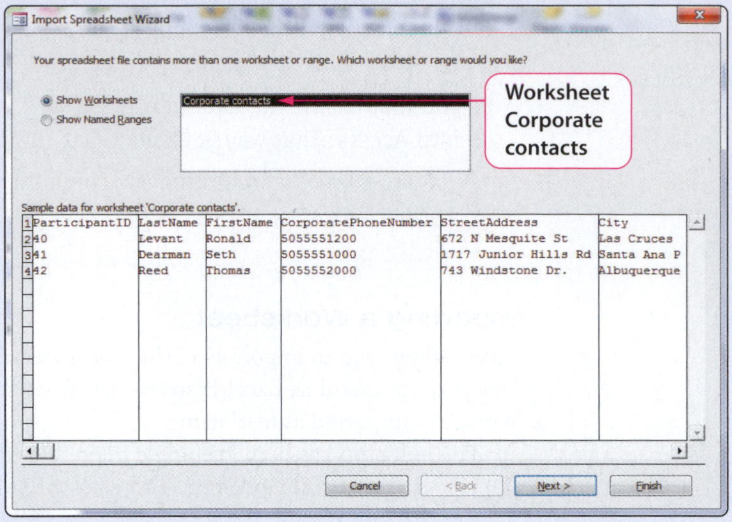

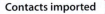

Figure 6   Worksheet to be imported

h. Click **Next**.

i. Click **Next**. Click **Finish**, and then click **Close**.

j. In the Navigation Pane, double-click **tblParticipant table** to open the table.

Your table has the three corporate contacts added. The contacts were imported and since the field names in Access matched the Excel column headings, the fields were rearranged to match the Access table order.

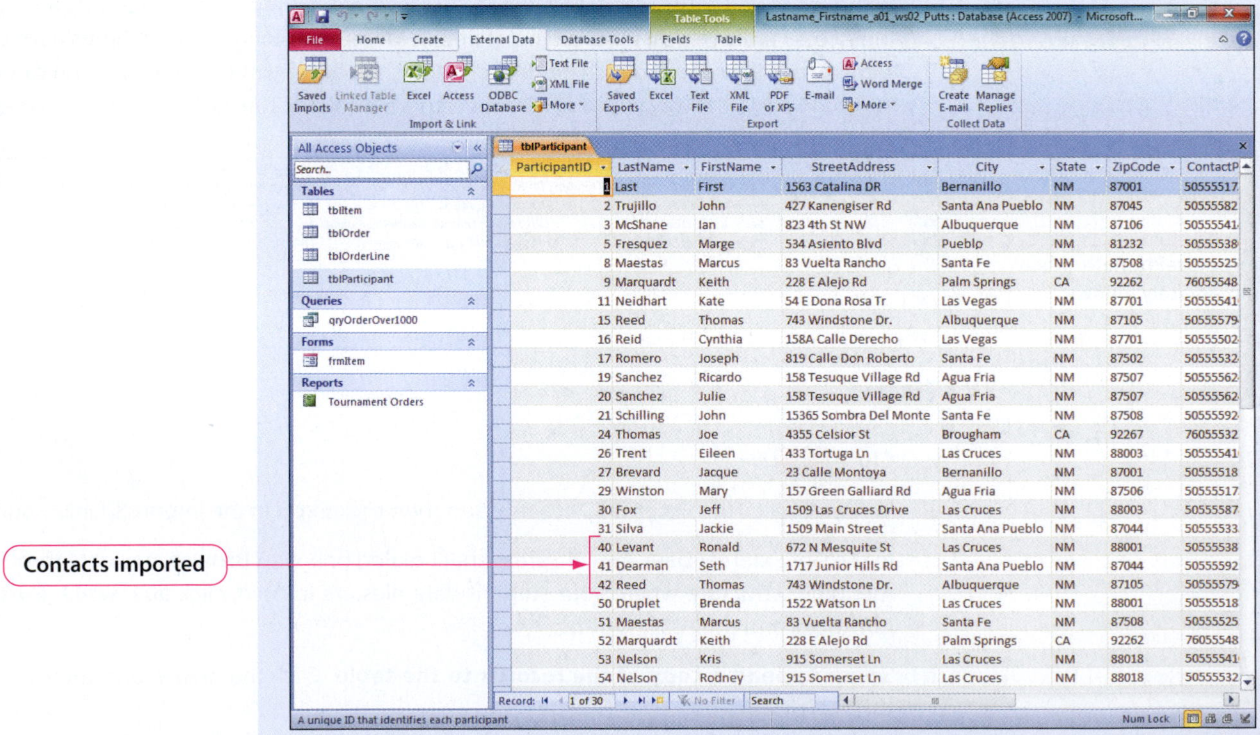

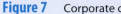

Figure 7   Corporate contacts imported into tblParticipant table

k. Close ☒ the tblParticipant table.

Importing from a Named Range

Access allows you to import a smaller portion of a worksheet known as a named range into a table. A named range is a set of cells that have been given a name that can then be used within a formula or function. This part of the worksheet can then be referenced in formulas or graphs by name rather than by cell address or range address.

The golf club has been keeping information about the volunteers for the event in an Excel worksheet. This worksheet contains other information about volunteering that you won't need. The contact information for the volunteers has been named VolunteersNamesAddress.

SIDE NOTE

Tables Are Ordered by Primary Key

When you added the contacts, Access added them in the middle of the table. That's because Access orders tables by the primary key. These records had lower keys than some records already in the table.

To Import a Named Range

a. Click the **Start button** 🟦. From the Start Menu, locate and then start **Microsoft Excel 2010**.

b. Click the **File tab**, click **Open**, and then in the Open dialog box click the disk drive in the left pane where your student data files are located. Navigate through the folder structure and click **a01_ws02_Putts_Volunteers**, and then click **Open**.

Notice the Volunteers worksheet contains the volunteer information as well as other data. The volunteer information has been given the name VolunteersNamesAddress.

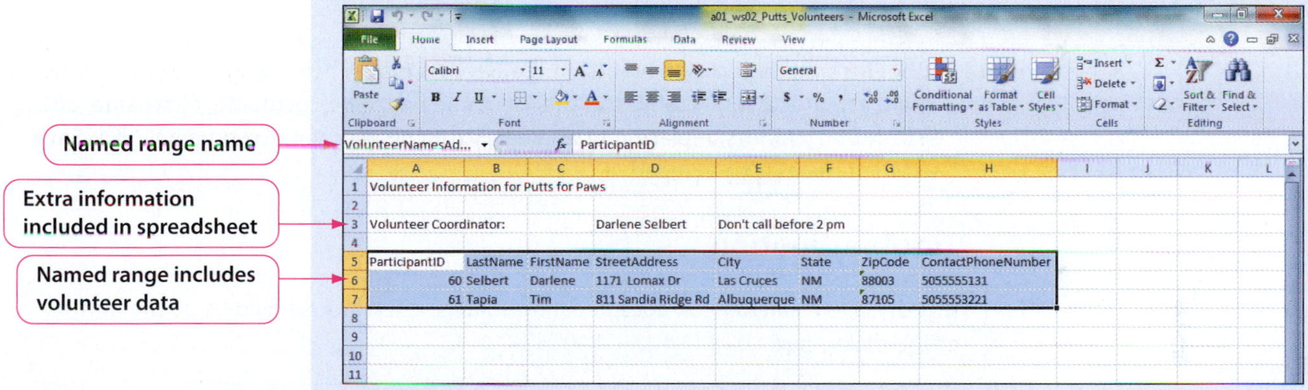

Figure 8 Volunteers file with extra information

c. Close ☒ Excel.

d. In Access, click the **External Data tab**, and then click **Excel** in the Import & Link group. Access starts the Get External Data – Excel Spreadsheet dialog box.

e. Click **Browse**, navigate through the folder structure, click **a01_ws02_Putts_Volunteers**, and then click **Open**.

f. Select **Append a copy of the records to the table**, click the **arrow**, and then select **tblParticipant**.

g. Click **OK**. Click **Show Named Ranges**.

One named range, VolunteerNamesAddress, is displayed and highlighted in the list box.

h. Click **Next**. Access tells you that it found your column headings in Excel and matched them to the field names in Access.

i. Click **Finish**, and then click **Close**.

Importing from a Text File

Access enables you to import from text and Word files. Typically these files would have been organized in tables. In Word, these tables will have actual rows and columns. In text files, the tables are implied by the separation of the columns. This separation is done by delimiter characters. A **delimiter** is a character that separates the fields. A typical delimiter is a tab or comma. The rows in the text tables will be imported as records into your Access table.

The golf course has been keeping information about the donors for the event in a text file. You want to import that data into your Access database.

To Import From a Text File

a. Click the **Start button** 🏁. From the Start Menu, locate and then start click **Notepad**. If necessary, point to **All Programs**, and then click **Accessories** to find Notepad.

b. Click **File**, click **Open**, and in the Open dialog box click the disk drive in the left pane where your student data files are located. Navigate through the folder structure and click **01_ws02_Putts_Donors**, and then click **Open**.

  Notice that there are three donors in this file. The fields are separated by (unseen) tabs.

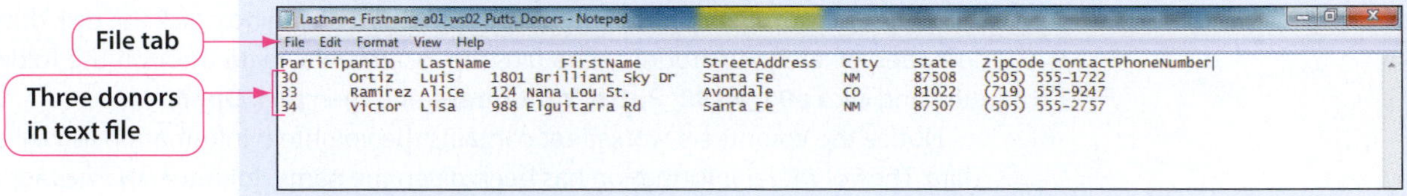

File tab

Three donors in text file

Figure 9   Donors text file in Notepad

c. Click **File**, and then click **Save As**. In the Save As dialog box, navigate to the location where you are saving your files. In the File name box, type **Lastname_Firstname_a01_ws02_Putts_Donors**, replacing Lastname_Firstname with your own name. Click **Save**, and then **close** ❌ Notepad.

Troubleshooting

> If your Save As dialog box does not show folders, click Browse Folders at the bottom of the dialog box.

d. In Access, click the **External Data tab**, and then click **Text File** in the Import & Link group. Access displays the Get External Data – Text File dialog box of the Import Text Wizard.

e. Click **Browse**, and then click the disk drive in the left pane where you are saving your student data files. Navigate through the folder structure, click **Lastname_Firstname_a01_ws02_Putts_Donors**, and then click **Open**.

f. Click **Append a copy of the records to the table**. Click the **arrow** to select **tblParticipant**, and then click **OK**. Access recognizes that this data has columns that are delimited (separated by tabs or commas.)

g. Click **Next**. Select the **Tab** delimiter, and click the **First Row Contains Field Names** check box.

h. Click **Next**, and then click **Finish**.

  Access responds with an error message. This says that Access is unable to append all the data to the table and that one record was lost because of key violations. The first field in your table is a primary key that must be unique. Apparently one of the donors has a ParticipantID that was already used in the Access table.

i. Click **Yes**, and then click **Close**.

j. Double-click **tblParticipant** to open it in Datasheet view.

k. Click the **Start button** 🙂. From the Start Menu, locate and then start **Notepad**.

l. Click **File**, click **Open**, and in the Open dialog box, click the disk drive in the left pane where your student data files are located. Navigate through the folder structure and click **Lastname_Firstname_a01_ws02_Putts_Donors**. Click **Open**. There are three donors in the file that have ParticipantIDs of 30, 33, and 34.

> Participant ID 30 used for Luis Ortiz →

```
ParticipantID  LastName     FirstName     StreetAddress     City      State   ZipCode  ContactPhoneNumber|
30      Ortiz     Luis       1801 Brilliant Sky Dr  Santa Fe   NM      87508   (505) 555-1722
33      Ramirez   Alice      124 Nana Lou St.       Avondale   CO      81022   (719) 555-9247
34      Victor    Lisa       988 Elguitarra Rd      Santa Fe   NM      87507   (505) 555-2757
```

Figure 10   Donor text file

m. Compare the donor data in the text file to the records in the tblParticipant table. Notice, ParticipantID 30 has been used twice, once for Jeff Fox and once for Luis Ortiz. You talk to the person keeping records of donors and discover she meant to type 32 for Luis Ortiz.

n. In Notepad, select the text **30** and type **32**.

> Change 30 to 32 →

```
ParticipantID  LastName     FirstName     StreetAddress     City      State   ZipCode  ContactPhoneNumber
32      Ortiz     Luis       1801 Brilliant Sky Dr  Santa Fe   NM      87508   (505) 555-1722
33      Ramirez   Alice      124 Nana Lou St.       Avondale   CO      81022   (719) 555-9247
34      Victor    Lisa       988 Elguitarra Rd      Santa Fe   NM      87507   (505) 555-2757
```

Figure 11   Change ParticipantID from 30 to 32

o. **Close** ☒ Notepad, and save the file. On the taskbar, click **Access**, and then **Close** ☒ the tblParticipant table.

p. Repeat the import Steps d–i. This time Access says that two records could not be imported. This makes sense since two donors were already imported.

q. Click **Yes**, and then click **Close** ☒. Double-click **tblParticipant** to open the table and verify that the records for Luis Ortiz, Alice Ramirez, and Lisa Victor were imported.

r. **Close** ☒ the tblParticipant table.

Real World Advice   Importing an Excel Worksheet into a New Table

In all the previous examples of importing, you imported into an already existing table. You can also import into a new table. Access creates a table using the column headings for field names. Access defines fields with standard definitions. After performing the import, open the table in Design view and adjust fields and properties as necessary. Some things that you should consider in these adjustments are the following:

- What did Access make the primary key for the table? Access defaults to creating a new field called ID for the key. Later in the workshop, you'll learn what might be better as a key.

- Access defaults the length of all text fields to be 255 characters. Adjust the field size properties to sizes that are appropriate for your fields. Check all field definitions for errors.

- Are the field names descriptive? The column headings from Excel might not be appropriate as field names in Access.

Manual Data Entry

If the data does not already exist in another form, you can type the data directly into Access. There are two methods: entering data directly into the table or entering the data in a form.

Entering Data Using Datasheet View

When you open a table in Datasheet view, you can type data directly into the table. You want to enter a new order. You'll need to enter data into tblOrder and the details of the order in tblOrderLine. The order to enter is your own; you are entering the tournament as a golfer.

To Enter Data in Datasheet View

a. In the Navigation Pane, double-click **tblOrder**, click in the **AmountPaid column** of the append row, and then enter **200**.

As you type the 200, a pencil icon ![pencil] appears in the row selector on the left. The pencil icon means that this record is actively being modified. Additionally, the OrderID was filled in with 12. This happens because the field has a data type of AutoNumber, which means that Access assigns the next highest number.

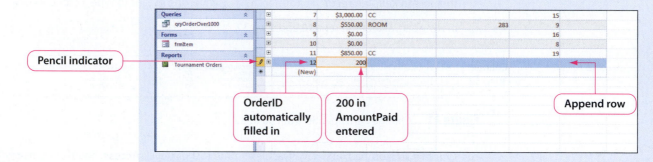

Pencil indicator

OrderID automatically filled in

200 in AmountPaid entered

Append row

Figure 12   Enter 200 in AmountPaid

b. Press ⟨Tab⟩ to continue filling in the record with a MethodOfPayment of **CC**, leave the ResortRoomNumber empty, and type **1** in ParticipantID.

c. Press ⟨Tab⟩ to go to the next record. The pencil icon disappears. Unlike Word and Excel, Access immediately saves the data change.

d. Close ⊠ the tblOrder table.

e. In the Navigation Pane, double-click **tblOrderLine**, click in **OrderID** of the append row, and then type **12**.

f. Press ⟨Tab⟩ to continue filling in the record with LineNum **1**, ItemID **G1**, and Quantity **1**.

g. Close ⊠ the tblOrderLine table.

Real World Advice | Undoing in Access

Access immediately saves the changes you make to data. There is very limited undo/redo functionality in Access. If the Undo button 🔄 is dimmed, you cannot undo the change you made.

- Typically you can undo a single typing change even if you have gone on to the next record. However, if you made several changes to different records, you cannot undo more than the changes to the last record.

- If you have made changes to several fields in a single record, you can click Undo to undo each of them.

- You can also press Escape to stop editing a record and revert to the record before you started changing the record.

- If you make an error, you can press Escape to get you out of the error.

Because of the limited undo features, do not count on undoing your changes. You will often find that you cannot undo. For example, when you delete a record or records, you cannot undo the delete.

Design changes are not saved until you save the object you changed. Thus, you can undo design changes until you save.

Removing Data

You can delete records from a table. These are permanent deletions and cannot be undone. Golfer Kate Neidhart needs to withdraw from the tournament.

To Delete Data in Datasheet View

a. In the Navigation Pane, double-click **tblParticipant** to open it in Datasheet view.

b. Click the **record selector** for record 7, Kate Neidhart, ParticipantID 11. Access selects the row.

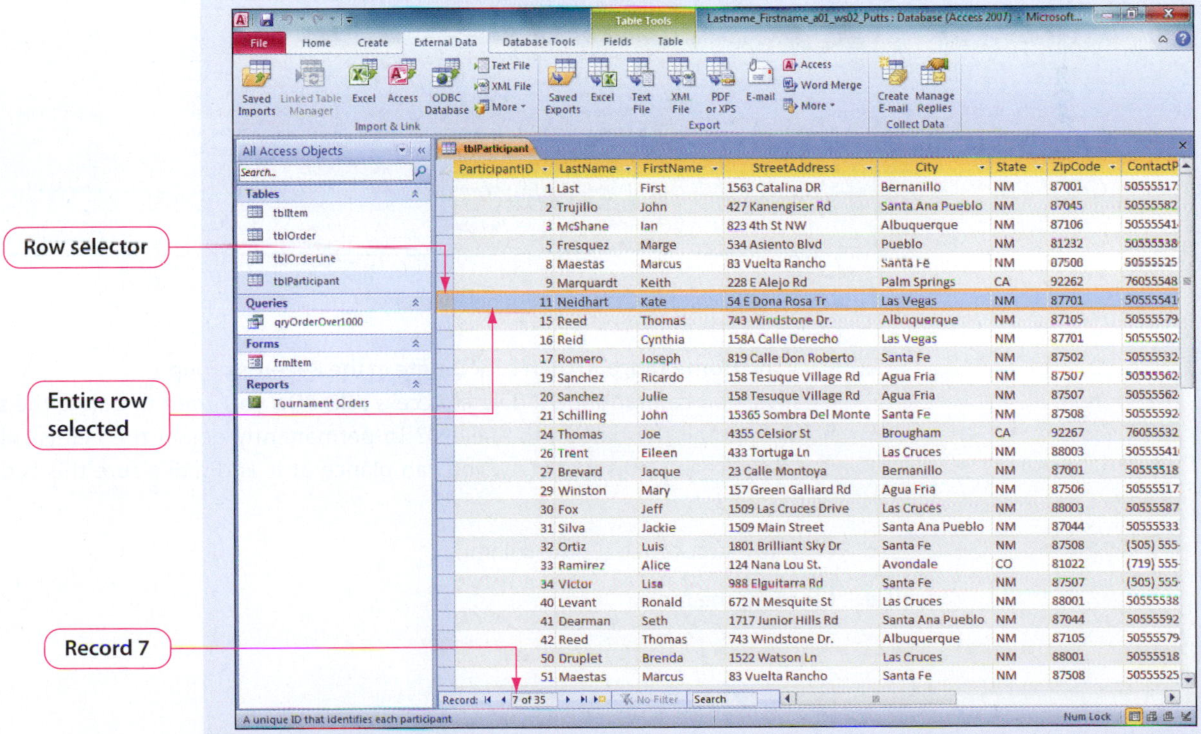

Figure 13   Delete Kate Neidhart record

c. Right-click in this row, and then select **Delete Record**. Since you cannot undo a delete, Access asks if you are sure you want to delete this record.

d. Click **Yes**. Access removes this record.

Troubleshooting

If you do not get the Access confirmation message asking if you are sure you want the deletion to occur, the confirmation message may be turned off. If you would like to turn it back on, on the File tab click Options, and then click Client Settings. Scroll down to find the Confirm section, and click the Document deletions check box.

You can also delete individual fields from a table. These are also permanent deletions and cannot be undone. You decide that you will create a table for corporations involved with the tournament, tblCorporate, and that the CorporatePhoneNumber will be a part of that table. Thus, you will not need CorporatePhoneNumber for each tblParticipant record, and you'll delete that field. You can delete a field in either Design view or Datasheet view. In Datasheet view, you can see the contents of the field that you are deleting, which gives you an extra check on whether you really want to delete the field.

To Delete a Field in Datasheet View

a. Scroll to the right to find the CorporatePhoneNumber column. Move the mouse pointer in the column heading until it changes to a black down arrow and click so the entire column is highlighted. Make sure that you selected CorporatePhoneNumber and not ContactPhoneNumber.

Figure 14   Select the CorporatePhoneNumber column

b. Click the **Home tab**, and then click **Delete** in the Records group.

Since you cannot undo a delete, Access asks, "Do you want to delete the selected field(s) and all the data in the field(s)? To permanently delete the field(s), click Yes." Since you're in Datasheet view, you can glance at it and make sure this is data you want to delete.

c. Click **Yes**. Access deletes the column.

d. **Close** ⊠ the table.

Troubleshooting

If when you clicked in the column heading you accidently double-clicked and then clicked Delete, Access blanked out the field name rather than deleting the column. This put you in edit mode, ready to rename the field. Press [Esc] to cancel edit mode and try again.

Understanding Tables and Keys

Now that you have imported data into the tblParticipant table, you need to further examine and evaluate how the tables have been set up. Tables represent entities or people, places, things, or events that you want to track. Each row represents a single person, place, and so on. To identify that entity, you use a primary key field. A **primary key** field is a field that uniquely identifies the record; it can be any data type, but it should be a field that will not change. For example, a person's name is not a good primary key for two reasons. First of all, it is not unique—several people may have the same name—and second, a person's name could change. If you define a primary key for a table, the field cannot be blank.

In this section you will create a table from scratch, minimize file size, facilitate quick data entry, minimize errors, and encourage data consistency as shown in Figure 15.

Goal	Example
Minimize file size	If a field is an integer that is always less than 32,767, use Integer rather than Long Integer to define the field.
Facilitate quick data entry, including removing redundant data	Store a state abbreviation rather than the state name spelled out.
Minimize errors	Use the Date/Time data type for dates and not a text data type. Access will then only accept valid dates (and not 2/31/2013, which is invalid).
Encourage data consistency	Use a Yes/No check box rather than having the word Yes or No typed into a text field where misspellings could occur.

Figure 15 Table design goals

Creating a Table in Design View

You want to keep track of corporations who are involved with the tournament. You don't have a source so you will need to design and create the table. You'll use Design view to enter fields, data types, and descriptions.

Data Types

Data types are the characteristic that defines the kind of data that can be entered into a field, such as numbers, text, or dates. The data type tells Access how to store and display the field.

Quick Reference | Data Types

Data Type	Description	Examples
Text	Used to store textual or character information. Any character or number can be entered into this type of field. You should store any data that will never be used in calculations, such as a Social Security number, as text, not a number. There is an upper limit of 255 characters that can be stored in a Text field.	Names, addresses
Memo	Used to capture free text. Can store up to 1 gigabyte of characters, of which you can display 65,535 characters in a control on a form or report. This is a good data type to use if you need more than 255 characters in one field.	Comments
Number	Used for numeric data.	Quantity
Date/Time	Used to store a date and/or time.	Start time
AutoNumber	Used for keys. Access generates the value by automatically incrementing the value for each new record to produce unique keys. For example, it would set the value as 1 for the first record, 2 for the next, and 3 for the third.	ProductID
Currency	A numeric value that is used for units of currency. It follows the regional settings preset in Windows to determine what the default currency should be. In the United States, the data is displayed with a dollar sign and two decimal places.	Salary
Yes/No	A checked box where an empty box is no, and a checked box is yes.	EntryPaid
Hyperlink	Text or combinations of text and numbers stored as text and used as a hyperlink address.	CompanyWebsite
Calculated Field	A field calculated from other fields in the table. A calculated field is read-only as it performs a calculation on other data that is entered.	GrossPay (calculated based upon HoursWorked and HourlySalary)
Lookup	Displays either a list of values that is retrieved from a table or query, or a set of values that you specified when you created the field.	ProductType (giving a list of valid types)
Attachment	Attached images, worksheet files, documents, charts, and other types of supported files to the records in your database, similar to attaching files to e-mail messages.	EmployeePhoto
OLE Object	Use to attach an OLE Object, such as a Microsoft Office Excel worksheet, to a record. An OLE object means that when you open the object, you open it in its original application such as Excel. It allows cross-application editing.	SalarySpreadsheet

Real World Advice Number or Text?

Any character can be used in a text field. However, if you are expecting the field to have only numbers, you should only store it in a text field if the numbers will never be used in a calculation. If you store numbers as text, you cannot use them in calculations. Conversely, if you improperly store numeric text as a number, Access will remove any leading zeros. For example, you would not add zip codes together, so a zip code should be stored as text. A person living in Boston might have a zip code of 02108. If you stored the zip code as a number, Access would convert this to 2108.

Field Size

Field size indicates the maximum length of a data field. Whenever you use a text data type, you should determine the maximum number of text characters that can exist. That number would then be the field size. For example, a state abbreviation can only be two characters long, so the size for this field should be two. If you allow more than two, you are likely to get a mix of abbreviations and spelled-out state names. Limiting the size will limit errors in the data. There is an upper limit of 255 characters for a text field. If you need more than 255 characters, use the Memo data type.

For numeric fields, the type defines the maximum length or value. You should use the number size that best suits your needs. For example, if a value in a field is never going to be above 20,000 then Integer is the best data type. If the number is currency, you should use the Currency data type instead of Number.

Quick Reference Number Field Sizes

Field Size	Description
Integer	For integers that range from -32,768 to +32,767. Must be whole numbers. Integers cannot have decimal places.
Long Integer	For integers that range from -2,147,483,648 to +2,147,483,647. Long Integers cannot have decimal places. (AutoNumber is a long integer.)
Decimal	For numeric values that contain decimal places. Numbers can be negative or positive. For numeric values that range from $-9.999... \times 10^{27}$ to $9.999... \times 10^{27}$.
Single	For very large numbers with up to seven significant digits. Can contain decimal places. Numbers can be negative or positive. For numeric floating point values that range from -3.4×10^{38} to $+3.4 \times 10^{38}$.
Double	For very large numbers with up to 15 significant digits. Can contain decimal places. Numbers can be negative or positive. For numeric floating point values that range from -1.797×10^{308} to $+1.797 \times 10^{308}$.
Byte	For integers that range from 0 to 255. These numbers can be stored in a single byte.

You determine that your corporation table, tblCorporate, should contain the company name, address, and phone number.

To Create a Table Design

a. Click the **Create tab**, and then select **Table Design**.

Access opens your blank table in Design view. You'll enter each field in the appropriate row.

b. Type CompanyName for the Field Name. Press Tab to move to the Data Type column.

Notice that Text is the default data type, so you do not need to make a selection to keep Text for this field. For other data types, click the arrow and select the data type. Alternatively, you can type the first letter of the data type, and it will appear, such as "N" for Number.

c. Press Tab to move to the Description column, and then type Company name.

d. In the Field Properties pane, type 50 in the Field Size box.

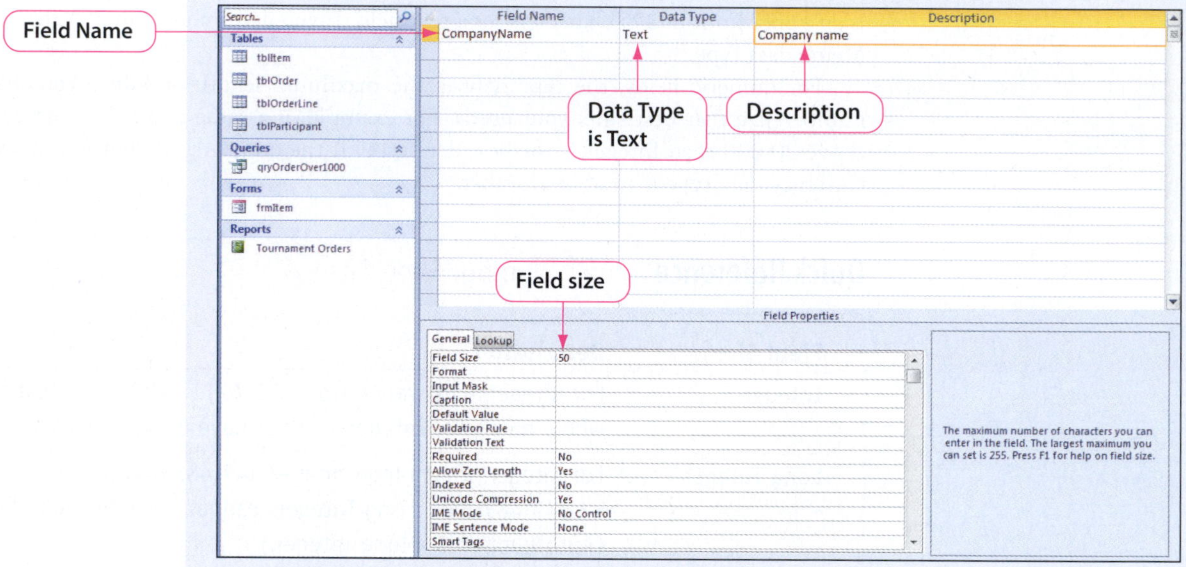

Figure 16 First field in the tblCorporate table

e. Continue defining the table with the following information, being sure to enter maximum length in field size.

Field Name	Data Type	Description	Maximum Length
CompanyName	Text	Company name	50
StreetAddress	Text	Company's street address	40
City	Text	Company's city	40
State	Text	State abbreviation	2
ZipCode	Text	Zip code either 5- or 9-character format	10
PhoneNumber	Text	Phone number with area code	14

Figure 17 Table fields

f. **Save** 💾 the table, naming it tblCorporate, and then click **OK**. In the warning message that asks if you want to create a primary key, click **No**. You'll define a key later.

Input Masks

Access provides a way to consistently enter data called **input masks**. For example, phone numbers can be typed (555) 555-5555, 555-5555, or 555-555-5555. An input mask defines a consistent template and provides the punctuation. Access also has a wizard that creates automatic masks for Social Security numbers, zip codes, passwords, extensions, dates, and times. You can also create your own custom masks. Input masks can affect how data is stored.

The characters used in masks are shown in the Quick Reference table.

Quick Reference — Characters Used in Masks

Character	Interpretation
0	Must enter a number
9	Can enter a number
#	Can enter a number, space, or plus or minus sign; if not entered, Access enters a blank space
L	Must enter a letter
?	Can enter a letter
A	Must enter a letter or number
A	Can enter a letter or number
&	Must enter a character or a space
C	Can enter characters or spaces
.	Decimal point
,	Comma separating thousands in numbers
:	Colon as time or other separator
-	Dash as date or other separator
/	Slash as date or other separator
>	All characters following are converted to uppercase
<	All characters following are converted to lowercase
!	Characters are filled from left to right
\	The character immediately following will be entered in the field. This is used when a standard character is to be automatically inserted.
" "	One or more characters enclosed in double quotation marks will be entered in the field. This is used when standard characters need to be inserted.

To Create an Input Mask

a. With the PhoneNumber field selected, in the Field Properties pane, click in the **Input Mask** box.

b. Click the **Build button** [...] to start the Input Mask Wizard. If necessary, select **Phone Number**.

c. Click **Next** to start the phone number input mask wizard.

Access suggests the format !(999) 000-0000. This means that area code is optional and will be enclosed in parentheses. The rest of the phone number is required and will have a dash between the two parts.

d. Click **Next** to accept the format.

e. Access asks if you want to store the symbols with the data. Select **With the symbols in the mask, like this**.

f. Click **Next**, and then click **Finish**.

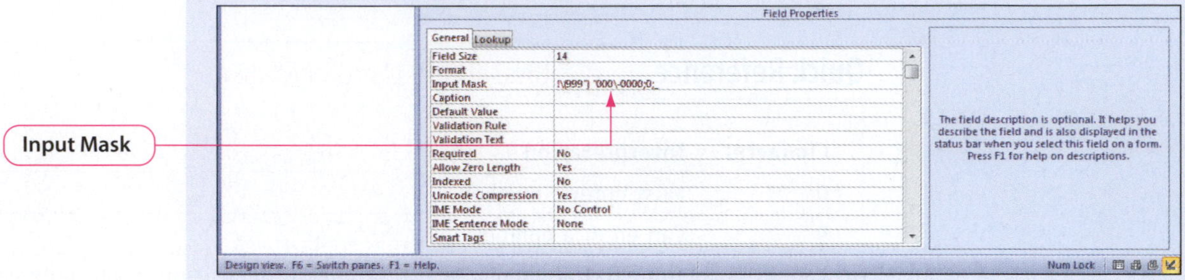

Field Properties

General | Lookup

Field Size	14
Format	
Input Mask	!\(999") "000\-0000;0;_
Caption	
Default Value	
Validation Rule	
Validation Text	
Required	No
Allow Zero Length	Yes
Indexed	No
Unicode Compression	Yes
IME Mode	No Control
IME Sentence Mode	None
Smart Tags	

Input Mask

The field description is optional. It helps you describe the field and is also displayed in the status bar when you select this field on a form. Press F1 for help on descriptions.

Design view. F6 = Switch panes. F1 = Help.   Num Lock

Figure 18   Finished input mask

g. **Save** 🖫 the table design. Click the **Home tab**, click the **View arrow** in the Views group, and then click **Datasheet View**.

h. Notice that the columns are not wide enough for the entire heading text to show. Move your mouse pointer to the border between **CompanyName** and **StreetAddress** until it becomes the Horizontal resize ⟺ symbol. Double-click the **border** to widen the column.

i. Double-click the **border** after the StreetAddress and PhoneNumber headings to widen the columns.

j. Click in the **append row for CompanyName**, and then type Tesuque Mirage Market. Press ⟦Tab⟧ to move to StreetAddress.

k. Continue entering the records as follows. Notice that the phone number mask that you entered means that you don't need to type the parentheses and dashes in PhoneNumber.

CompanyName	StreetAddress	City	State	ZipCode	PhoneNumber
Tesuque Mirage Market	8 Tesuque Mirage Rd	Santa Fe	NM	87506	5055551111
Hotel Playa Real	125 Madison Avenue	Santa Fe	NM	87508	5055551800
Bouzouki Museum	716 Camino Cercano	Santa Fe	NM	87505	5055551200
McDoakes Restaurant	2017 High St	Santa Fe	NM	87501	5055551000
Benson & Diaz	1953A Piazza Pl, Suite 101	Santo Domingo	NM	87052	5055552000

l. **Close** ✕ the table, and reply **Yes** to save the layout.

You recall that the phone number in the tblParticipant table had no format so you want to add a mask to that phone number too.

m. Right-click **tblParticipant** in the Navigation Pane, and then select **Design View**.

n. Click the **ContactPhoneNumber** field.

o. In the Field Properties pane, click in the **Input Mask** box, and then click the **Build button** 🔳 to start the Input Mask Wizard.

p. If necessary, select **Phone Number**, and then click **Next**.

q. Accept the format **!(999) 000-0000** by clicking **Next**.

r. Access asks if you want to store the symbols with the data. Select **With the symbols in the mask, like this**, click **Next**, and then click **Finish**.

s. **Close** ☒ the table, replying **Yes** to save the layout.

Formatting

In a table design, you can define a Format field property that customizes how data is displayed and printed in tables, queries, reports, and forms. **Format** tells Access how data is to be displayed. It does not affect the way that the data is stored. For example, you can specify that currency fields are displayed in dollars (e.g., $1,234.56) in American databases or in Euros (e.g., €1.234,56) in European databases. Formats are available for Date/Time, Number, Currency, and Yes/No data types. You can also define your own custom formats for Text and Memo fields.

Quick Reference | Format Field Property

Data Type	Format	Example
Date/Time	General Date	11/9/2011 10:10:10 PM
	Long Date	Wednesday, November 9, 2011
	Medium Date	9-Nov-11
	Short Date	11/9/2011
	Long Time	10:10:10 PM
	Medium Time	10:10 PM
	Short Time	22:10
Number and Currency	General Number	Display the number as entered
	Currency	Follows the regional settings preset in Windows. In the United States: $1,234.56. In much of Europe, €1.234,56.
	Euro	Uses the euro symbol regardless of the Windows setting.
	Fixed	Displays at least one digit after the decimal point. In Decimal, you choose how many fixed digits to show after the decimal point.
	Standard	Use the regional settings preset in Windows for thousands divider. 1,234 in the United States; 1.234 in much of Europe.
	Percent	Multiply the value by 100 and follow with %.
	Scientific	Use standard scientific notation, for example, $4.5 * 10^{13}$.
Yes/No	Check Box	A check box.
	Yes/No	Yes or No display options.
	True/False	True or False display options.
	On/Off	On or Off display options.

To Define a Date Field

a. In the Navigation Pane, right-click on **tblOrder**, and select **Design View**.

b. In the first blank row, in the Field Name column, type OrderDate and then enter a Data Type of Date/Time and Description of Date order was placed.

c. Click in the **Format** box in the Field Properties pane.

d. Click the **Format arrow**, and then select **Short Date**.

Notice that the Property Update Options button 🗟 appears. Clicking it would display an option to change the format of OrderDate wherever else it appears. Since it doesn't appear anywhere else yet, you don't need to click the button.

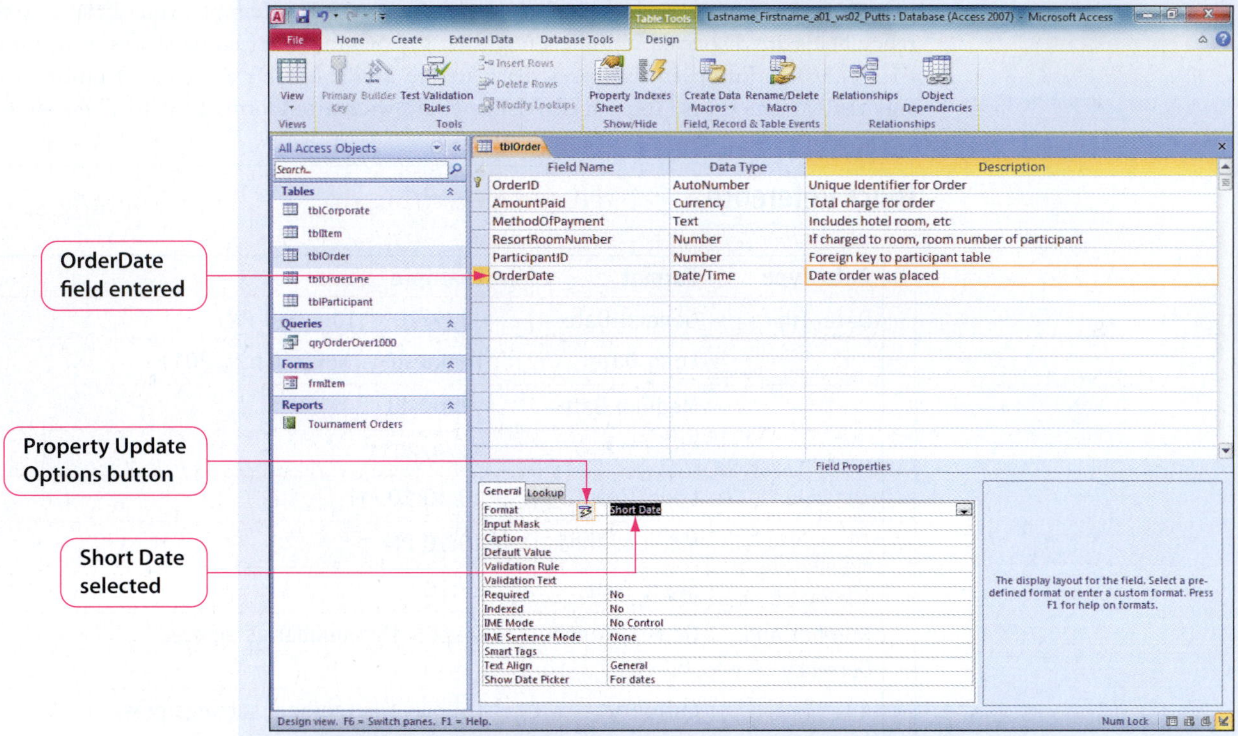

Figure 19   Adding a Short Date field

e. **Save** 🖫 the table design. Click the **Home tab**, and then click the **View** button in the Views group to switch to Datasheet view.

The orders were placed on May 4, 2012, but no date was entered.

f. For the first order, in the OrderDate field type May 4, 2012. Press ↓ to move to the next record. Notice that Access changes the display to 5/4/2012, the short date display.

g. For the second order, type 05/04/2012. Press ↓ to move to the next record. Again Access changes the display.

h. For the next order, type May 4 12. Press ↓ to move to the next record. Once again Access changes the display to 5/4/2012.

i. Continue typing May 4 12 for all the orders.

j. **Close** ⊠ the table.

It is important to keep in mind that this only affects the display of the field. The stored format is the same for any date field. This allows multiple people to enter dates in many formats, but each date is displayed in the format that was selected for the field. (Access actually stores dates in a floating-point number format that indicates how many days before or after December 30, 1899, the date is. December 29, 1899, is -1; December 30, 1899, is 0; December 31, 1899, is +1; November 6, 2000, is 36836.)

CONSIDER THIS | **Database Design Principles**

Some principles for database design are shown in Figure 15. How do field sizes, formatting, and input masks facilitate these principles? When do you use a format? When do you use an input mask?

Understanding and Designating Keys

Each table should have a field that uniquely identifies each of the records in the table. This field is called the primary key. If you know the primary key, you know exactly what record you want. Another type of key is a **foreign key**. A foreign key is the primary key of one table stored in a second table. The primary and foreign keys form the common field between tables that allow you to form a relationship between the two tables.

Primary Keys

Each row of a table represents a single person or item. The primary key field is the field that says which person or item it is. It uniquely identifies the record. Remember that a primary key field should be a field that has values that will not change. When you define a primary key for a table, the field cannot be blank. A common way of defining a primary key is to use a field specifically designed to identify the entity. This is an arbitrary **numeric key** that is assigned to represent an individual item, such as CustomerID or ProductID. A numeric key is often assigned an AutoNumber data type that Access will fill as the data is entered. Instead of using a numeric key, you can also use an already existing field that uniquely identifies the person or item such as Social Security number.

CONSIDER THIS | **Social Security Number as a Primary Key**

While Social Security number seems like the perfect primary key, it is seldom used. What privacy concerns might arise in using Social Security numbers? Are there other issues that might arise with using Social Security numbers?

Real World Advice   **Do You Need a Primary Key?**

While Access does not require a primary key for every table, you almost always want to give the table a primary key. What are the advantages of having a primary key?

- It helps organize your data. Each record is uniquely identified.
- Primary keys speed up access to your data. Primary keys provide an index to a record. In a large table, that makes it much faster to find a record.
- Primary keys are used to form relationships between tables.

Foreign Keys

A foreign key is a column in a table that stores a value that is the primary key in another table. It is called foreign because it does not identify a record in this table—it identifies a record in another (foreign) table. For example, you have two tables, tblParticipant and tblOrder, in your database. You want to know which participants have placed certain orders. The primary key for your Participant table is ParticipantID. You can add a field called ParticipantID to the Order table that indicates which participant placed the order. ParticipantID is foreign key in the tblOrder table; it identifies the participant in the tblParticipant table. Figure 20 illustrates this relationship. Foreign keys do not need to be unique in the table. Participants can place several orders.

You'll use the ParticipantID to form a relationship between the two tables later in this workshop.

ParticipantID is primary key in the tblParticipant table

John Trujillo is ParticipantID 2

tblParticipant

ParticipantID	LastName	FirstName	StreetAddress	City	State	ZipCode	ContactPhoneNumber	Click to Add
1	Last	First	1563 Catalina DR	Bernanillo	NM	87001	(505) 555-1754	
2	Trujillo	John	427 Kanengiser Rd	Santa Ana Pueblo	NM	87045	(505) 555-8217	
3	McShane	Ian	823 4th St NW	Albuquerque	NM	87106	(505) 555-4149	
5	Fresquez	Marge	534 Asiento Blvd	Pueblo	NM	81232	(505) 555-3800	
8	Maestas	Marcus	83 Vuelta Rancho	Santa Fe	NM	87508	(505) 555-2525	
9	Marquardt	Keith	228 E Alejo Rd	Palm Springs	CA	92262	(760) 555-4836	
15	Reed	Thomas	743 Windstone Dr.	Albuquerque	NM	87105	(505) 555-7943	
16	Reid	Cynthia	158A Calle Derecho	Las Vegas	NM	87701	(505) 555-0247	
17	Romero	Joseph	819 Calle Don Roberto	Santa Fe	NM	87502	(505) 555-3242	
19	Sanchez	Ricardo	158 Tesuque Village Rd	Agua Fria	NM	87507	(505) 555-6243	
20	Sanchez	Julie	158 Tesuque Village Rd	Agua Fria	NM	87507	(505) 555-6243	
21	Schilling	John	15365 Sombra Del Monte	Santa Fe	NM	87508	(505) 555-9244	
24	Thomas	Joe	4355 Celsior St	Brougham	CA	92267	(760) 555-3227	
26	Trent	Eileen	433 Tortuga Ln	Las Cruces	NM	88003	(505) 555-4101	
27	Brevard	Jacque	23 Calle Montoya	Bernanillo	NM	87001	(505) 555-1828	
29	Winston	Mary	157 Green Galliard Rd	Agua Fria	NM	87506	(505) 555-1756	
30	Fox	Jeff	1509 Las Cruces Drive	Las Cruces	NM	88003	(505) 555-8786	
31	Silva	Jackie	1509 Main Street	Santa Ana Pueblo	NM	87044	(505) 555-3355	
32	Ortiz	Luis	1801 Brilliant Sky Dr	Santa Fe	NM	87508	(505) 555-1732	
33	Ramirez	Alice	124 Nana Lou St.					
34	Victor	Lisa	988 Elguitarra Rd					
40	Levant	Ronald	672 N Mesquite					
41	Dearman	Seth	1717 Junior Hills					
42	Reed	Thomas	743 Windstone Dr					

ParticipantID is foreign key in the tblOrder table

Order 1 was placed by ParticipantID 2

tblOrder

OrderID	AmountPaid	MethodOfPayment	ResortRoomNumber	ParticipantID	OrderDate	Click to Add
1	$2,550.00	CC		2	5/4/2012	
2	$2,000.00	CC		3	5/4/2012	
3	$1,000.00	CC		17	5/4/2012	
4	$2,850.00	CC		5	5/4/2012	
5	$400.00	ROOM	217	24	5/4/2012	
6	$200.00	CC		29	5/4/2012	
7	$3,000.00	CC		15	5/4/2012	
8	$550.00	ROOM	283	9	5/4/2012	
9	$0.00			16	5/4/2012	
10	$0.00			8	5/4/2012	
11	$850.00	CC		19	5/4/2012	
12	$200.00	CC		1	5/4/2012	

Figure 20 Relationship between tblParticipant and tblOrder tables

Composite Keys

Sometimes, two fields are needed to uniquely identify a record. In that case, both fields are used to create the key and are called a **composite key**. For example, a university might identify a class by subject area and course number. The university could have classes Math 101, Math 102, and MIS 101. It takes both subject and course number to identify a single course. The combination of the two fields is called a composite key.

A typical use of a composite key is on an order form. Figure 21 shows a paper form that the golf tournament organizers used before they used Access. To store the items that have been ordered, a composite key can be made combining the order number with the line number of the order form. You notice that this composite key is used for orders in the golf tournament database.

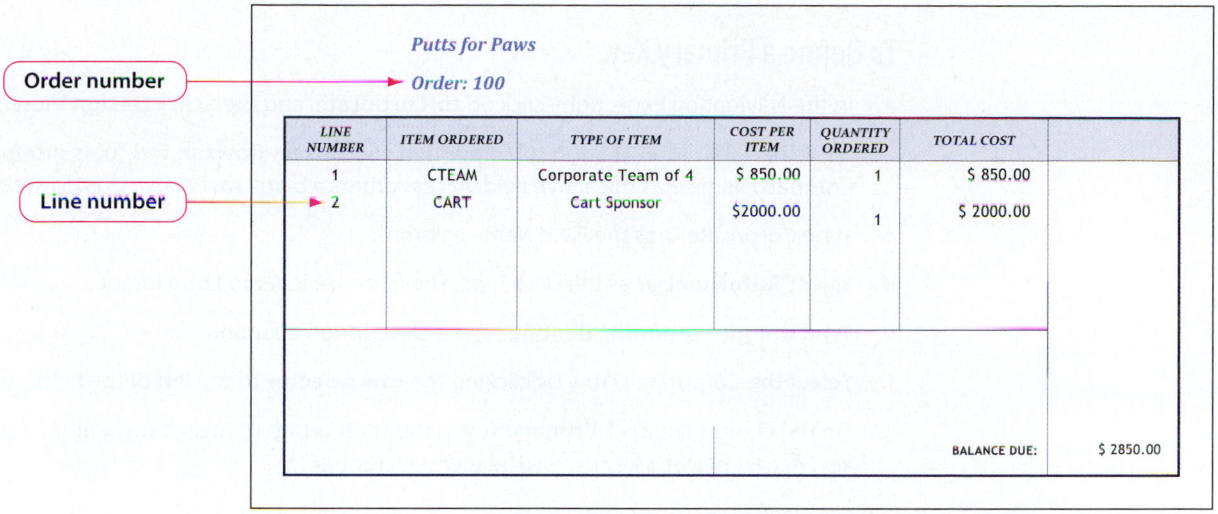

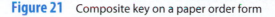

Order number → *Putts for Paws*
Order: 100

LINE NUMBER	ITEM ORDERED	TYPE OF ITEM	COST PER ITEM	QUANTITY ORDERED	TOTAL COST
1	CTEAM	Corporate Team of 4	$ 850.00	1	$ 850.00
2	CART	Cart Sponsor	$2000.00	1	$ 2000.00

Line number → 2

| | | | | BALANCE DUE: | $ 2850.00 |

Figure 21 Composite key on a paper order form

To Find a Composite Key

a. In the Navigation Pane, right-click the **tblOrderLine** table, and then click **Design View**. Notice that there are two fields marked as key: OrderID and LineNum.

b. **Close** ☒ the table.

Order number

Line number

Field Name	Data Type	Description
OrderID	Number	Order identifier
LineNum	Number	Line number within order
ItemID	Text	Identifier of Item purchased
Quantity	Number	Quanity of this item purchased

Tables: tblCorporate, tblItem, tblOrder, tblOrderLine, tblParticipant

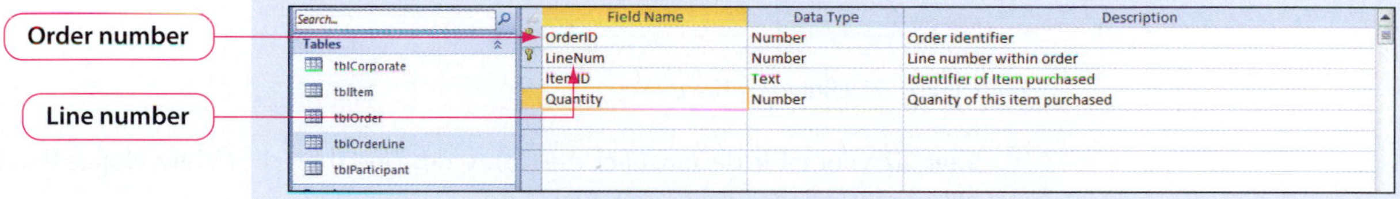

Figure 22 Composite key in the tblOrderLine table

Natural vs. Numeric Keys

Sometimes your data will have a unique identifier that is a natural part of your data. When that is true, you can use the field as a **natural primary key**. If you already identify orders by order number, that would make a good primary key.

The important point is that the natural primary key is a value that will not change. You might start by thinking that telephone number is a natural way to identify a customer. But people change their telephone numbers. When the natural key might change, it is better to use an arbitrary unique number to identify the customer. When natural keys do exist, they are favored over numeric keys.

You can use the data type AutoNumber for the primary key. In that case, Access will automatically assign a unique value for that record. You can also define a key as numeric, and fill the key values yourself.

You decide that you need to create a numeric primary key for your tblCorporate table named CorporateID. You'll let Access automatically create the key by using an number AutoNumber data type.

To Define a Primary Key

a. In the Navigation Pane, right-click on **tblCorporate**, and then click **Design View**.

b. Click the Table Tools **Design tab**, and then click **Insert Rows** in the Tools group. Since CompanyName was the active field, Access enters a blank row above CompanyName.

c. Type CorporateID as the Field Name column.

d. Select **AutoNumber** as the Data Type. The field size is set to Long Integer.

e. Type Unique corporate identifier in the Description column.

f. Select the CorporateID row by clicking the **row selector** to the left of the field.

g. On the Design tab, click **Primary Key** in the Tools group to make CorporateID a primary key. Access places a key icon in the row selector bar.

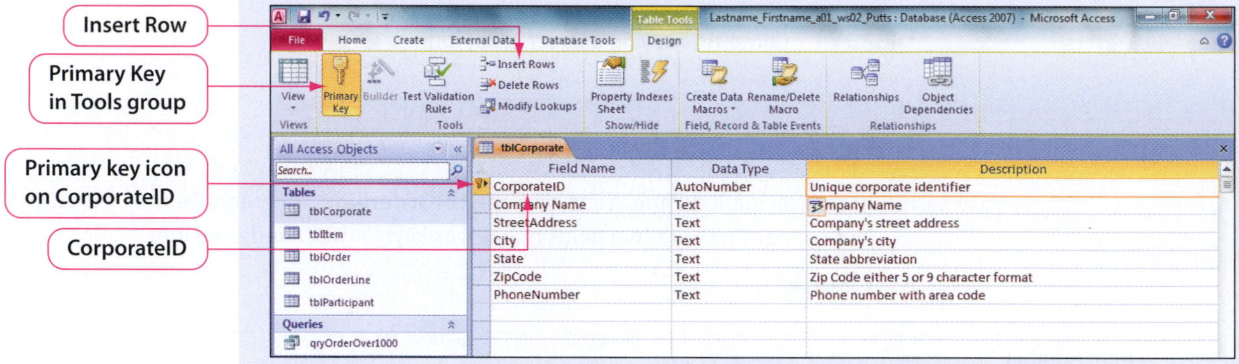

Figure 23 Defining a primary key

h. **Save** 💾 your table design. Click the **Home tab**, and then click **View**. Notice that Access has populated the CorporateID with automatic numbers.

i. **Close** ❌ tblCorporate table.

Real World Advice   Read Your Error Messages

The error message "Index or primary key cannot contain a Null value" is one example of an error message that Access gives when you make changes to an Access database that would break the rules you set up in your design. You should read the error message carefully to understand what it is telling you.

If you get the error message "Index or primary key cannot contain a Null value," that means that one of your records has no entry in the primary key field. Look for that record, and enter the primary key. Often the issue is that you accidently entered data in the append record. If you don't want that record to be created, press Escape to cancel the addition of the record.

Understanding Relational Databases

One of the benefits of Access comes when you add relationships to the tables. This allows you to work with two or more tables in the same query, report, or form. For your tournament database, when you relate tables together, you can ask such questions as "What golfers are playing for the Tesuque Mirage Market?" "Did the market agree to purchase any other items?" "Have they paid for those items yet?"

Relationships in a relational database are created by joining the tables together. A **join** is created by creating a relationship between two tables based upon a common field in the two tables, as shown in Figure 24. The tblParticipant table has a field (column) named ParticipantID. tblOrder also has a field named ParticipantID. When you create the relationship, Access will match the ParticipantIDs between the two tables to find those participants that play for a corporation. Looking at the table, you can mentally join the two tables to see that John Trujillo has placed an order for $2,550. When Access runs a query, it uses an existing join to find the results. In this section, you will form relationships between tables, create a report, and check to make sure the relationships you are creating between tables make sense.

ParticipantID in tblParticipant

ParticipantID in tblOrder

tblParticipant

ParticipantID	LastName	FirstName	StreetAddress	City	State	ZipCode	ContactPhoneNumber	Click to Add
1	Last	First	1563 Catalina DR	Bernalillo	NM	87001	(505) 555-1754	
2	Trujillo	John	427 Kanengiser Rd	Santa Ana Pueblo	NM	87045	(505) 555-8217	
3	McShane	Ian	823 4th St NW	Albuquerque	NM	87106	(505) 555-4149	
5	Fresquez	Margo	534 Asiento Blvd	Pueblo	NM	81232	(505) 555-3800	
8	Maestas	Marcus	83 Vuelta Rancho	Santa Fe	NM	87508	(505) 555-2525	
9	Marquardt	Keith	228 E Alejo Rd	Palm Springs	CA	92262	(760) 555-4836	
15	Reed	Thomas	743 Windstone Dr.	Albuquerque	NM	87105	(505) 555-7943	
16	Reid	Cynthia	158A Calle Derecho	Las Vegas	NM	87701	(505) 555-0247	
17	Romero	Joseph	819 Calle Don Roberto	Santa Fe	NM	87502	(505) 555-3242	
19	Sanchez	Ricardo	158 Tesuque Village Rd	Agua Fria	NM	87507	(505) 555-6243	
20	Sanchez	Julie	158 Tesuque Village Rd	Agua Fria	NM	87507	(505) 555-6243	
21	Schilling	John	15365 Sombra Del Monte	Santa Fe	NM	87508	(505) 555-9244	
24	Thomas	Joe	4355 Celsior St	Brougham	CA	92267	(760) 555-3227	
26	Trent	Eileen	433 Tortuga Ln	Las Cruces	NM	88003	(505) 555-4101	
27	Brevard	Jacque	23 Calle Montoya	Bernalillo	NM	87001	(505) 555-1828	

tblOrder

OrderID	AmountPaid	MethodOfPayment	ResortRoomNumber	ParticipantID	OrderDate	Click to Add
1	$2,550.00	CC		2	5/4/2012	
2	$2,000.00	CC		3	5/4/2012	
3	$1,000.00	CC		17	5/4/2012	
4	$2,850.00	CC		5	5/4/2012	
5	$400.00	ROOM	217	24	5/4/2012	

Figure 24 Tables joined between primary and foreign keys

Understanding Basic Principles of Normalization

When you work with tables in Access, you want each table to represent a single item and have data only about that entity. For example, you want a tblParticipant table to have data about participants and nothing else. You do not want to have data about the corporation they represent or the order they placed. You want the data about the participant to be in the participant table and no data about any other item in the tblParticipant table as shown in Figure 24. There is no data that is not about the participant in the tblParticipant. This is why you deleted the CorporatePhoneNumber field earlier in the exercise.

Entities, Entity Classes, and Attributes

Recall that an entity is a person, place, or item that you want to keep data about. The data you keep about an entity are called attributes. An entity is generally stored in a single table in a relational database. The attributes form the fields or columns of the table. **Normalization** is the process of minimizing the duplication of information in a relational database through effective database design. If you know the primary key of an entity in a normalized database, each of the attributes will have just one value. When you normalize a database, you will have multiple smaller tables, each representing a different thing. There will be no redundant data in the tables. A complete discussion of normalization is beyond the scope of this workshop, but the following sections will give you an idea of why you normalize your tables.

Figure 25 shows a nonnormalized view of tblParticipant. Suppose John Trujillo places two orders, Order 1 for $2,550 and Order 2 for $500. You can easily fill in his name and address. However, when you get to the order fields, you cannot fill in the attributes with just one value. You want to enter Order 1 for Order ID and Order 2 for Order ID. You want to enter $2,550 for AmountPaid and $500 for AmountPaid. But you only have one field for each.

Participant ID	Last Name	First Name	Street Address	Other address fields	Order ID	Amount Paid
2	Trujillo	John	427 Kanengiser Rd		??????	????

Figure 25   Nonnormalized tblParticipant Table

For each record's ParticipantID, you don't have a single value for OrderID and AmountPaid because each participant may make several orders. You could have a column for OrderID1 and OrderID2. But, how many columns would you make? What if this was for a grocery store where one transaction might contain hundreds of items? Any time you do not know how many columns to repeat, the table is not normalized and you need another table. Thus, this table does not fit the principles of normalization. It has two entities in the table: participants and orders.

> **CONSIDER THIS** | **Why Is a Nonnormalized Table Undesirable?**
>
> If you have a table as shown in Figure 25, you could simply enter a record for each item. So, if you had five items, you would enter five records in the table. What kind of redundancy does that create? If you used this method, is there a primary key?

Redundancy Minimization

Figure 26 shows a nonnormalized view of the tblParticipant table. In this case, when you know the ItemID, you do know the value of each field.

OrderID	Amount Paid	Method of Payment	Last Name	First Name	Address	Other Address Fields
1	$2,550.00	CC	Trujillo	John	427 Kanengiser Rd	
12	$500.00	CC	Trujillo	John	427 Kanengiser Rd	

Figure 26   Nonnormalized tblItem

However the table has redundant data. **Redundancy** is when data is repeated several times in a database. All of the data about the John Trujillo is repeated for each order he makes. That means that the data will need to be entered multiple times. Beyond that, if the data changes, it has to be changed in multiple places. If his address or phone number changes, it will need to be changed on all his order records. Forgetting to change it in one place will lead to inconsistent data and confusion. Again, this table is not normalized because it contains data about two different entities: participant and orders.

In a normalized database, redundancy is minimized. The foreign keys are redundant, but no other data about the entity is repeated.

Understanding Relationships

To make the database normalized, you need to have two tables: one for participants and one for orders. How then do you form a relationship between them? A table represents an entity—or the nouns—in the database. The relationship represents the verb that connects the two nouns. In our example, your two nouns are "participant" and "order." Is there a relationship between these two nouns? Yes. You can say that a participant places an order.

Once you determine that there is a relationship between the entities, you need to describe the relationship. You do that by asking yourself two questions starting with each entity in the relationship:

- Question 1 (starting with the Participant entity): If you have one participant, what is the maximum number of orders that one participant can place? The only two answers to consider are one or many. In this case, the participant can place many orders.

- Question 2 (starting with the Order entity): If you have one order, what is the maximum number of participants that can place that order? Again, the only answers to consider are one or many. An order is placed by just one participant.

The type of relationship where one question is answered "one" and the other is answered "many" is called a one-to-many relationship. A **one-to-many relationship** is a relationship between two tables where one record in the first table corresponds to many records in the second table. One-to-many is called the cardinality of the relationship. **Cardinality** indicates the number of instances of one entity that relates to one instance of another entity.

Using the Relationships Window

Access stores relationship information in the Relationships window as shown in Figure 27.

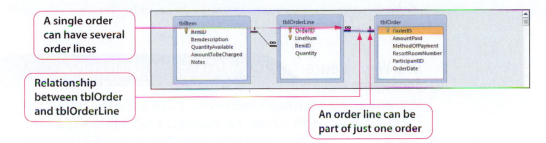

A single order can have several order lines

Relationship between tblOrder and tblOrderLine

An order line can be part of just one order

Figure 27 Relationships window

SIDE NOTE

Other Uses for the Relationships Window

The Relationships window gives you an overview of all your tables and the relationships between them. It is often helpful to return to the window when writing queries and reports.

To Open the Relationships Window

a. Click the **Database Tools tab**.

b. Click **Relationships** in the Relationships group.

The Relationships window opens. The window shows tables and the relationships between those tables. Notice the join line between tblOrder and tblOrderLine. There is an infinity symbol on the line next to tblOrderLine. The infinity symbol indicates that a single order can have several order lines. There is a "1" on the line next to tblOrder. The "1" indicates that an order line can be on just one order. Access indicates a one-to-many relationship in this way, putting a "1" on the one-side of the relationship line and an infinity symbol on the many-side.

Relationship Types

The relationship between tblParticipant and tblOrder is a one-to-many relationship. There are other types of relationships. Consider the relationship between tblOrder and tblItem. There is a relationship: an item can be on an order. What is the cardinality? You need to ask yourself the two questions to determine the cardinality:

- Question 1 (starting with the Order entity): If you have one order, what is the maximum number of items that can be part of that order? You care only about two answers: one or many. In this case, the order can contain many items. For example, a golfer could buy an entry into the tournament and a T-shirt.

- Question 2 (starting with the Item entity): If you have one item, what is the maximum number of orders that that item can be part of? Again, the only answers to consider are one or many. Obviously you want more than one person to be able to order an entry to the tournament. Therefore, you say that an item can be on many orders.

With both answers being many, this is a many-to-many relationship. A **many-to-many relationship** is a relationship between tables in which one record in one table has many matching records in a second table, and one record in the related table has many matching records in the first table. Since these two tables in the charity database do not have a common field, in

Access this kind of many-to-many relationship must have an additional table in between these two. This intermediate table is referred to by several synonymous terms: "intersection," "junction," or "link table." You'll look at this later in the workshop.

A one-to-one relationship occurs when each question is answered with a maximum of one. A **one-to-one relationship** is a relationship between tables where a record in one table has only one matching record in the second table. In a small business, a department might be managed by no more than one manager, and each manager manages no more than one department. That relationship in that business is a one-to-one relationship.

There are three types of relationships; one-to-many, many-to-many, and one-to-one. The relationship type is based upon the rules of the business. In the charity golf tournament, the relationship between the order and the item is many-to-many, but in another business it might not be. For example, consider a business that sells custom-made jewelry where each item is one of a kind. In this case, an item can appear on just one order. Thus, the relationship between order and item in that business would be one-to-many.

Real World Advice — Use of One-to-One Relationships

When you have a one-to-one relationship, you could combine the two tables into a single table. A single table is simpler than two tables with a relationship between them.

- You could keep the two tables separate when the two tables are obviously two different things like manager and department. You might want to keep private information about the manager in the manager table. Additionally this would be easier to change if business rules change and multiple managers might manage the same department.

- You should combine the two tables when there are just a few attributes on one of the tables. For example, suppose you only wanted to keep the manager's name in the manager table with no other information about the manager. Then you might consider the manager's name to be an attribute of the department.

Create a One-to-Many Relationship

Consider the relationship between tblParticipant and tblOrder. This is a one-to-many relationship. To form a relationship between two tables, you need the tables to have a column in common. The easiest way to accomplish this is to put the primary key from the one side in the table on the many side. In this case, this means that you use the ParticipantID from the one side table and add it as a field to the tblOrder table. The field that you add to the many side is called a foreign key because it is a key to another (foreign) table. ParticipantID is already a field on the many-side table, so you can use it to form the relationship.

Quick Reference — Creating a One-to-Many Relationship in Access

Creating a one-to-many relationship in Access takes three steps:

1. Make sure the two tables have a field in common. Use the primary key from the one-side, and add it as a foreign key in the many-side table.

2. Form the relationship in the Relationships window. This is done by connecting the primary key of the one-side table to the foreign key of the many-side table.

3. Populate the foreign key by adding data to the foreign key in the many-side table.

Forming the Relationship

Since the tables already have a field in common, you can form the relationship. You'll connect the primary key of the one-side table to the foreign key on the many-side table.

To Form a Relationship

a. Click **Show Table** in the Relationships group, click **tblParticipant**, and then click **Add**.

b. Click **Close** to close the Show Table dialog box. Drag the **tblParticipant** table in the Relationships window. Resize **tblParticipant** so all fields show.

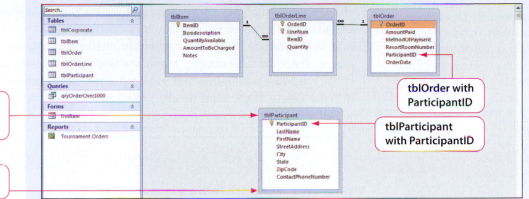

tblParticipant table moved in Relationships window

tblParticipant resized so all fields show

tblOrder with ParticipantID

tblParticipant with ParticipantID

Figure 28 Move the table in the Relationships window

SIDE NOTE

Adding Tables to the Relationships Window

You can also add tables to the Relationships window by clicking on a table in the Navigation Pane and dragging it to the Relationships window.

c. Drag the primary key, **ParticipantID**, from tblParticipant to **ParticipantID** in tblOrder. Alternatively, you could drag from ParticipantID in tblOrder to ParticipantID in tblParticipant.

Access displays the Edit Relationships dialog box. Notice that Access calls the relationship a one-to-many relationship. This is because the relationship is between a primary key and a foreign key.

d. Click **Enforce Referential Integrity** to select it, and then click **Create**. Later in the workshop you will look further at what referential integrity accomplishes.

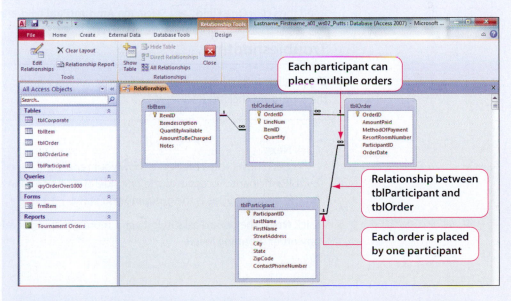

Each participant can place multiple orders

Relationship between tblParticipant and tblOrder

Each order is placed by one participant

Figure 29 tblParticipant and tblOrder relationship

e. **Close** ☒ the Relationships window, and then click **Yes** to save changes to the layout of the relationships.

Troubleshooting

If you get the error message "The database engine could not lock table 'tblParticipant' because it is already in use by another person or process," this means that the tblParticipant is still open. Close the table, and try again to form the relationship. You should get in the habit of closing tables when you are done with them.

If you get the error message "Relationship must be on the same number of fields with the same data type," this means that the data types for the primary key and the foreign key are different. For example, they must be both Numeric and Long Integer or both Text. Make sure that you're creating the relationship between the correct fields. If you are, check the table designs, and fix the field with the wrong data type.

If you add a relationship that you don't want, right-click on the relationship line and click Delete. If you want to edit a relationship, right-click the relationship line and click Edit Relationship.

Using Two Related Tables in a Report

The reason you created a relationship is to join two tables in queries, reports, and forms. You'll create a simple report showing participants and their orders.

To Create a Report From Two Tables

a. Click the **Create tab**, and then click **Report Wizard** in the Reports group.

b. In the Report Wizard dialog box, click the **Tables/Queries arrow**, and then select **Table: tblParticipant**. Select the **LastName** field, and then click **One Field** > . Select the **FirstName** field, and then click the **One Field** > .

c. Click the **Tables/Queries arrow**, and then select **Table: tblOrder**. Select the **OrderID** field, and then click **One Field** > . Select the **AmountPaid** field, and then click **One Field** > .

Troubleshooting

If you clicked Next instead of selecting the tblOrder fields, you can go back a step in the wizard by clicking Back.

d. Click **Next**.

Access shows you a preview of how your report will look if you group the participants by tblParticipant. Access uses the *one* side of a one-to-many relationship as the default for the grouping. This is the grouping you want.

e. Click **Next**. The wizard asks if you want more grouping levels; however, you don't want any other grouping levels.

f. Click **Next**.

g. Use the arrow to select **OrderID**. Ascending sort order is already selected. Click **Next**.
  The wizard asks you to choose a layout for your report. You will accept the default layout.

h. Click **Next**.

i. Title your report, **Participants and Orders_initialLastname** where initial is your first initial and Lastname is your last name.
  Access connects the team and participants in a report.

j. Click **Finish**.

k. If your instructor directs you to print the report, click **Print** in the Print group, and then click **OK**. Click **Close Print Preview**, and then close your report.

Create a Many-to-Many Relationship

Unless you are connecting a common field such as a foreign key to the same foreign key in a different table, Access cannot form a many-to-many relationship with a single relationship. Instead you need to make two one-to-many relationships to represent the many-to-many relationship. As stated before, tblOrder and tblItem have a many-to-many relationship. An order can have many items on it. Each item can be on many orders. To form this relationship, a new table, tblOrderLine needs to be added. Both tblOrder and tblItem are related to the new table. The third table is called a junction table. A **junction table** breaks down the many-to-many relationship into two one-to-many relationships.

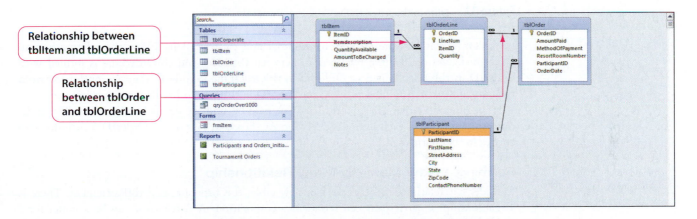

Relationship between tblItem and tblOrderLine

Relationship between tblOrder and tblOrderLine

Figure 30 Relationship between tblOrder and tblItem with tblOrderLine

Look at the relationship between tblOrder and tblOrderLine. It is a one-to-many relationship with orders having many order lines but each order line on just one order. There is also a relationship between tblOrderLine and tblItem. It also is a one-to-many relationship with each order line having just one item but an item able to be on many order lines as shown in Figure 31.

OrderID 4 has two order lines, one with an item of a corporate team, one with a cart. By traveling left to right across the three tables, you see that OrderID 4 has many items on it. OrderID 6 has one line, an entry to the tournament. By traveling from right to left across the three tables, you see that an entry to the tournament can be on many orders. Hence the junction table tblOrderLine forms a many-to-many relationship between tblOrder and tblItem.

tblOrder table:

OrderID	AmountPaid	MethodOfPayment	ResortRoomNumber	ParticipantID	OrderDate	Click to Add
1	$2,550.00	CC		2	5/4/2012	
2	$2,000.00	CC		3	5/4/2012	
3	$1,000.00	CC		17	5/4/2012	
4	$2,850.00	CC		5	5/4/2012	
5	$400.00	ROOM	217	24	5/4/2012	
6	$200.00	CC		29	5/4/2012	
7	$3,000.00	CC		15	5/4/2012	
8	$550.00	ROOM	283	9	5/4/2012	
9	$0.00			16	5/4/2012	
10	$0.00			8	5/4/2012	
11	$850.00	CC		19	5/4/2012	
12	$200.00	CC		1	5/4/2012	
(New)						

Callout: OrderID 4 in tblOrder

tblOrderLine table:

OrderID	LineNum	ItemID	Quantity	Click to Add
1	1	CART	1	
1	2	TEAM	1	
2	1	CART	1	
3	1	FLAG	1	
3	2	HOLE	1	
4	1	CTEAM	1	
4	2	CART	1	
5	1	G1	2	
6	1	G1	1	
7	1	CART	1	
7	2	HOLE	1	
7	3	FLAG	1	
8	1	TEAM	1	
9	1	G1	1	
10	1	G1	1	
11	1	CTEAM	1	

Callout: OrderID 4 in tblOrderLine
Callout: OrderID 5 includes two G1 items
Callout: OrderID 6 includes one G1 item

tblItem table:

ItemID	Itemdescription	QuantityAvailable	AmountToBeCharged	Notes	Click to Add
CART	Cart sponsor	40	$2,000.00	Logo or brand displayed on cart	
CTEAM	Golfers - corporate team of four	10	$850.00	Includes hole sponsorship	
FLAG	Flag sponsor	18	$500.00	Logo or brand displayed on flagstick	
G1	Golfer - one	100	$200.00		
HOLE	Hole sponsor	18	$500.00	Logo or brand displayed on hole	
TEAM	Golfers - team of four	10	$550.00		

Callout: G1 is a one golfer entry to the tournament

Figure 31   Data in tblOrder, tblOrderLine, and tblItem

tblOrderLine has foreign keys to tblOrder and tblItem. This allows the relationships to be formed. Notice that the relationship between tblOrder and tblOrderLine is formed with OrderID in tblOrder joined to OrderID in tblOrderLine. Similarly the relationship between tblItem and tblOrderLine is formed from ItemID in tblItem to ItemID in tblOrderLine.

The junction table, tblOrderLine, has one field beyond the key fields: Quantity. This indicates the quantity of each item on the order. As shown in Figure 31, OrderID 5 included two entries to the tournament.

Forming a New Many-to-Many Relationship

Consider the relationship between your new table, tblCorporate, and tblParticipant. There is a relationship: a participant can represent a corporation. A participant can be a golfer for a corporation, the corporate representative, or a donor. What is the cardinality? You need to ask yourself the two questions to determine the cardinality:

- Question 1 (starting with the Corporate entity): If you have one corporation, what is the maximum number of participants that can represent that corporation? You care only about two answers: one or many. In this case, the corporation could be represented by many participants. A corporate team might have four golfer participants.

- Question 2 (starting with the Participant entity): If you have one Participant, what is the maximum number of roles that Participant can represent for the corporation? Again, the only answers to consider are one or many. A Participant could be a golfer representing the corporation and also be a corporate representative.

Quick Reference — Creating a Many-to-Many Relationship in Access

Creating a many-to-many relationship in Access takes four steps:

1. Create a junction table. Create a primary key that will be a unique field for the junction table, and add two foreign keys, one to each of the many-to-many tables.

2. Determine if there are any fields that you want to add to the junction table beyond the keys.

3. Form two relationships in the Relationships window. This is done by connecting the primary key of one of the original tables to the appropriate foreign key of the junction table. Repeat for the second of the original tables. The junction table is on the *many* side of both relationships.

4. Populate the junction table.

Create a Junction Table

Since the relationship between tblCorporate and tblParticipant is many-to-many, you need a junction table. Recall that the junction table breaks down the many-to-many relationship into two one-to-many relationships. In this case the junction table will indicate the role that the participant has for the corporation. The primary key for the junction table will be ParticipantRoleID, an AutoNumber. You will have two foreign keys, the CorporateID and the ParticipantID. You'll also add a field that describes the role of the participant. Since the table represents roles, you call it tblParticipantRole.

To Create a Junction Table in Table Design

a. Click the **Create tab**, and then click **Table Design** in the Tables group.
    Access opens a blank table in Design view. You'll enter each field in the appropriate row.

b. In the Field Name, type ParticipantRoleID. Press ⌷Tab to move to the Data Type column. Click the **arrow**, and then select the data type of **AutoNumber**.
    Alternatively, you can type the "A," and "AutoNumber" will appear. Notice that Field Size in the Field Properties pane defaults to Long Integer.

c. Press ⌷Tab to move to the Description column, and then type Primary key for tblParticipantRole.

d. Click **Primary Key** in the Tool group to make the field the primary key.

e. Press ⌷Tab to move to the next field. Continue filling in the table with the following information, being sure to enter maximum length in field size.

Field Name	Data Type	Maximum Length	Description
ParticipantRoleID	AutoNumber	LongInteger	Primary key for tblParticipantRole
CorporateID	Number	Long Integer	Foreign key to tblCorporate
ParticipantID	Number	Long Integer	Foreign key to tblParticipant
Role	Text	40	Role that this participant fills for the corporation

f. **Close** ⌧ the table, replying **Yes** to saving the changes. Name the table tblParticipantRole and then click **OK**.

Create Two One-to-Many Relationships

The many-to-many relationship will turn in to two one-to-many relationships between each of the original tables and the junction table. The rule is that the junction table is on the many side of the two relationships. But you can ask yourself the two questions to determine the cardinality:

- Question 1 (starting with the Corporate entity): If you have one corporation, what is the maximum number of participant roles that can represent that corporation? You care only about two answers: one or many. In this case, the corporation could be represented by many participants. A corporate team might have four golfer participants.

- Question 2 (starting with the ParticipantRole entity): If you have one ParticipantRole, what is the maximum number of corporations that the participant can represent? Again, the only answers to consider are one or many. A ParticipantRole is for a single participant.

Thus tblCorporate to tblParticipantRole is a one-to-many relationship with Corporate on the *one* side.

You can ask the same questions between tblParticipant and tblParticipantRole.

To Form Two Relationships to the Junction Table

a. Click the **Database Tools tab**, and then click **Relationships** in the Relationships group.

b. Click the **Relationship Tools Design tab**, and then click **Show Table** in the Relationships group. Select **tblCorporate**, and then click **Add**. Select **tblParticipantRole**, and then click **Add**.

c. **Close** the Show Table dialog box. Drag the **tables** in the Relationships window so there is some space between the tables to form the relationships.

d. Drag the primary key **ParticipantID** from tblParticipant to **ParticipantID** in tblParticipantRole. Alternatively, you could drag from ParticipantID in tblOrder to ParticipantID in tblParticipant.

e. Access displays the Edit Relationships dialog box. Click **Enforce Referential Integrity** to select it, and then click **Create**.

f. Drag the primary key **CorporateID** from tblCorporate to **CorporateID** in tblParticipantRole.

g. Access displays the Edit Relationships dialog box. Click **Enforce Referential Integrity** to select it.

Relationship
Report button

Relationship between
tblCorporate and
tblParticipantRole

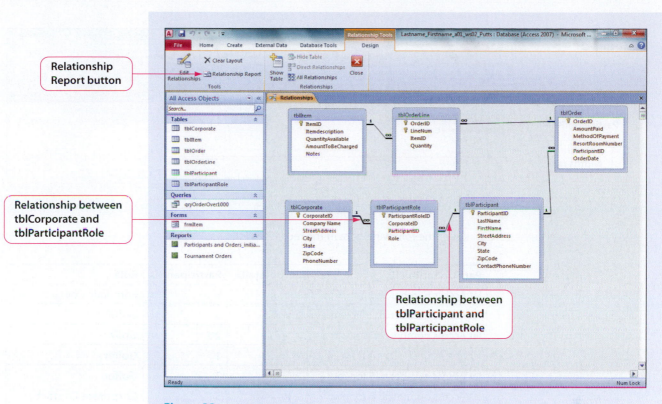

Relationship between
tblParticipant and
tblParticipantRole

Figure 32   Completed Relationship window

h. Click **Create**. Click **Relationship Report** in the Tools group to create a report on your relationship. **Save** 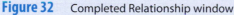 the report, accepting the name **Relationships for Lastname_ Firstname_a01_ws02_Putts**, and then click **OK**.

i. Submit your files as instructed by your instructor. **Close** ☒ the Relationship report.

j. **Close** ☒ the Relationships window, and then click **Yes** to save changes to the layout of the relationships.

Populate the Junction Table

To complete the many-to-many relationship, you need to populate the junction table.

To Format the Junction Table

a. Double-click **tblParticipantRole** to open the table in Datasheet view.

b. Click in the **CorporateID append row**. Enter a CorporateID of 1, a ParticipantID of 5 and a Role of Corporate Contact. Access automatically numbers ParticipantRoleID as 1.

c. Since the last field is not totally visible, place your pointer in the border on the right of the Role column heading. When your pointer is a double-headed arrow ⬌, double-click the **border** to resize the column. Repeat for each field.

AutoNumber in ParticipantRoleID

Column widths resized

Figure 33 tblParticiantRole columns resized

d. Enter the following data in the records as follows:

ParticipantRoleID	CorporateID	ParticipantID	Role
let Access number as 1 for you	1	5	Corporate Contact
let Access number as 2 for you	1	5	Golfer
let Access number as 3 for you	1	26	Golfer
let Access number as 4 for you	2	1	Golfer
let Access number as 5 for you	2	3	Golfer
let Access number as 6 for you	2	54	Corporate Contact
let Access number as 7 for you	2	54	Golfer

e. **Close** ☒ the table, saying **Yes** to saving the change in the table layout.

One-to-One Relationships

One-to-one relationships in Access are formed very similarly to one-to-many relationships. You can put a foreign key in either table and establish the relationship by dragging with the primary key in one table joined to the foreign key. You can also make both tables have the same primary key.

Understanding Referential Integrity

Referential integrity is a set of rules that Access uses to make sure that the relationships you are forming between records in your tables make sense. Recall that when you created the relationship between tblParticipant and tblOrder you told Access to enforce referential integrity.

Referential integrity means that Access will enforce the following rules when you define the fields in Design view:

- The field on the one side of the relationship is unique on the table. You must either use the primary key of the one side in the relationship or a field that you have set to be unique.

- You cannot add a foreign key value in the many side that does not have a matching primary key value on the one side.

- The matching fields on both sides of the relationship are defined with the same data types. For example, if the primary key is numeric and Long Integer, the foreign key must be numeric and Long Integer too. (For purposes of relationships, an AutoNumber primary key is considered Long Integer.)

If these rules are violated, when you try to form the relationship, Access will give you the following error message: "Relationship must be on the same number of fields with the same data type."

Double-check how you defined the relationship between tblParticipant and tblOrder.

To Check and Test Referential Integrity

a. Click the **Database Tools tab**, and then click **Relationships** in the Relationships group. The Relationships window is displayed. The relationship was formed between ParticipantID in tblParticipant and tblOrder.

b. **Close** the Relationships window.

c. Right-click **tblParticipant**, and then click **Design View**. Notice that ParticipantID is defined as Number and Long Integer. **Close** ⊠ tblParticipant. Right-click **tblOrder**, and then click **Design View**. Notice that ParticipantID is defined as Number and Long Integer.
   Referential integrity means that Access will also enforce rules when you work with the data in the tables. You cannot enter a value in the foreign key field on the *many* side table that is not a primary key value on the *one* side table. For example, you cannot add a participant to a team that does not exist. However, you can leave the foreign key unfilled, indicating that this participant is not part of a team.

d. Click the **Home tab**, and then click the **View** button to change to **Datasheet View** for tblOrder.

e. Scroll down to the last record in the table, and then scroll right. In ParticipantID, type **70** and then press [Enter] twice.
   Access responds with the error message "You cannot add or change a record because a related record is required in table tblParticipant." That is, you cannot add an order to participant 70 because there is no participant 70.

f. Click **OK**, and then change the ParticipantID for the last order back to **1**. Press [Enter] twice.
   ParticipantID 1 is a valid participant so you can make that change.

g. **Close** ⊠ tblOrder table.

CONSIDER THIS | **Why Enforce Referential Integrity?**

You can decline to enforce referential integrity on a relationship. What are the pros and cons of having Access enforce referential integrity? What are the pros and cons of declining to enforce referential integrity?

If you enforce referential integrity, you cannot delete a record from the *one* side table if matching records exist in the *many* side table.

To Understand Relationships Between the One and Many Side Tables

a. In the Navigation Pane, double-click **tblParticipant** to open it.

b. Click the **record selector** of the second row, John Trujillo.

c. Click the **Home tab**, and then click **Delete** in the Records group.
   Access responds that "The record cannot be deleted or changed because table 'tblOrder' includes related records." That means John Trujillo has placed an order.

d. Click **OK**.

e. **Close** ⊠ tblParticipant table.

f. **Close** ⊠ the database and Access.

You also cannot change the primary key value in the *one* side table if that record has related records.

Quick Reference | Referential Integrity

Access enforces the following rules on defining a relationship with referential integrity:

1. The primary key field on the *one* side of the relationship must be unique in the table.

2. The foreign key values on the *many* side of the relationship must exist as the primary key field for a record on the *one* side of the relationship.

3. The matching fields on both sides of the relationship are defined with the same data types.

Access enforces the following rules on data changes when referential integrity is enforced:

1. You cannot enter a value in the foreign key field on the *many* side table that is not a primary key on the *one* side table. However, you can leave the foreign key unfilled, indicating that this record is not in the relationship.

2. You cannot delete a record from the *one* side table if matching records exist in a *many* side table (unless Cascade delete has been selected for the relationship, in which case all the matching records on the many side are deleted).

3. You cannot change a primary key value in the *one* side table if that record has related records in the *many* side (unless Cascade update has been selected for the relationship, in which case all the matching records on the many side have their foreign key updated).

Cascade Update

When you ask Access to enforce referential integrity, you can also select whether you want Access to automatically cascade update or cascade delete related records. These options allow some deletions and updates that would usually be prevented by referential integrity. However, Access makes these changes and replicates (cascades) the changes through all related tables so referential integrity is preserved.

If you select Cascade Update Related Fields when you define a relationship, then when the primary key of a record in the one-side table changes, Access automatically changes the foreign keys in all related records. For example, if you change the ItemID in the tblItem table, Access automatically changes the ItemID on all order lines that include that item. Access makes these changes without displaying an error message.

If the primary key in the *one* side table was defined as AutoNumber, selecting Cascade Update Related Fields has no effect, because you cannot change the value in an AutoNumber field.

Cascade Delete

If you select Cascade Delete Related Records when you define a relationship, any time that you delete records from the *one* side table, Access automatically deletes all related records in the *many* side table. For example, if you deleted a tblParticipant record, all the orders made by that participant are automatically deleted from the tblOrder table. Before you make the deletion, Access warns you that related records may also be deleted.

CONSIDER THIS | Should You Cascade Delete Related Records?

Should you cascade delete related records? Consider a customer who has made many orders. If the customer asks to be removed from your database, do you want to remove his or her past orders? How do you think the accountants would feel?

Concept Check

1. If you wanted to create a table listing all your suppliers of products, what would be a good table name? What would be a good primary key? What data type should this key have?

2. If you have an Excel worksheet of customers, how could you move the customer data to Access? How would you decide between various ways to move the data?

3. What data types would you use for the following fields: price, phone number, street address, zip code, and directions for using a product?

4. In a university database, you have tables for students and classes. What kind of relationship is the relationship between student and class? What would you do in Access to create this relationship?

5. How many times can the number "4" appear for the ParticipantID field in the tblParticipant table? Why? How many times can the number "4" appear in the ParticipantID field in the tblOrder table? Why?

Key Terms

Attribute 78
Cardinality 105
Composite key 100
Data type 81
Delimiter 86
Entity 78
Field size 93
Foreign key 99

Format 97
Input mask 95
Join 103
Junction table 109
Many-to-many relationship 105
Natural primary key 101
Normalization 103
Number data type 81

Numeric key 99
One-to-many relationship 105
One-to-one relationship 106
Primary key 91
Redundancy 104
Relationship 78
Text data type 81

Visual Summary

Import an Excel worksheet (p. 83)

Import a named range (p. 85)

Import from a text file (p. 86)

Copy and paste data from Excel (p. 82)

Delete a field in Datasheet view (p. 90)

Delete data in Datasheet view (p. 89)

Understand relationships between the one and many side table (p. 115)

Open a database (p. 80)

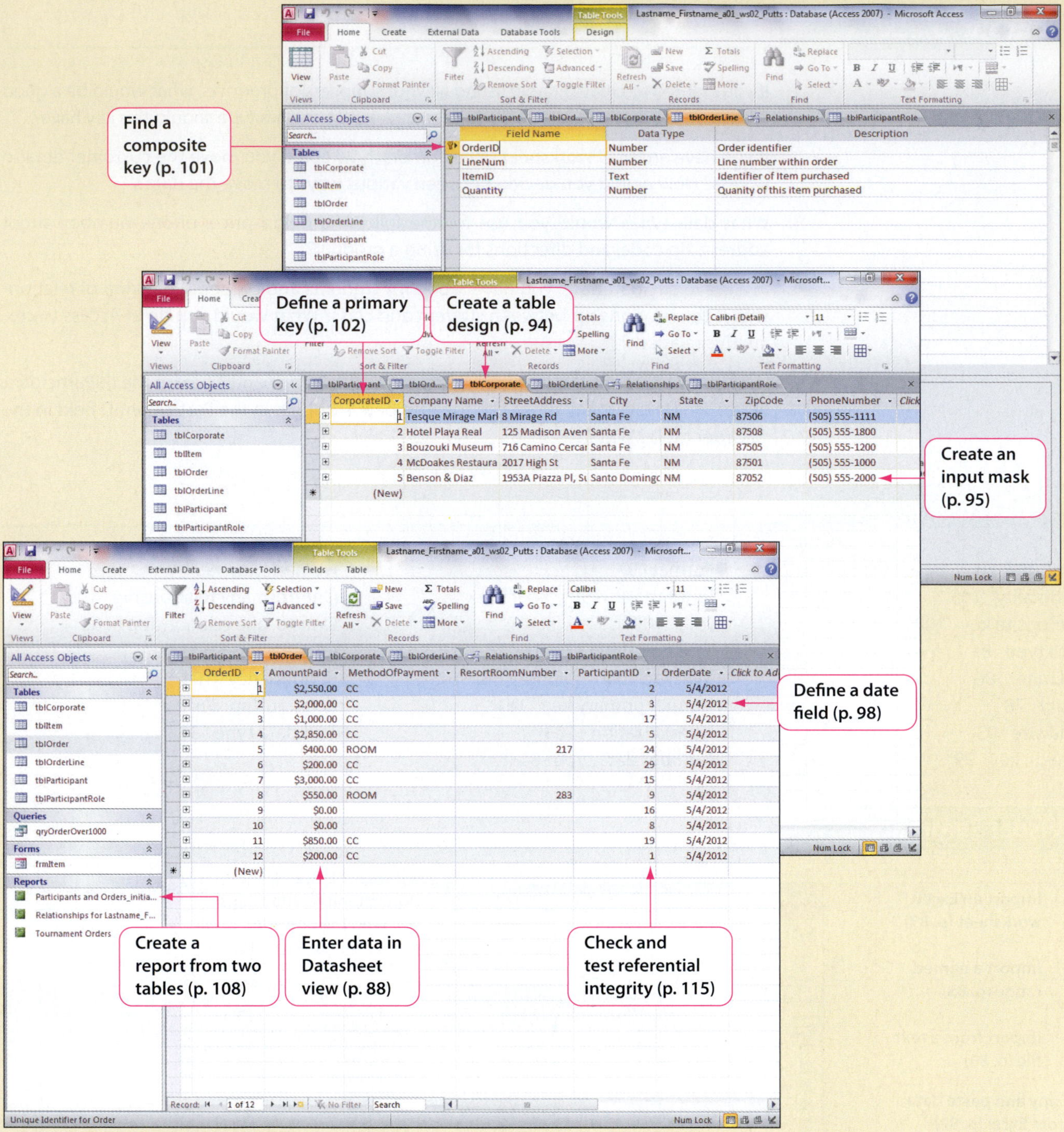

Find a composite key (p. 101)

Define a primary key (p. 102)

Create a table design (p. 94)

Create an input mask (p. 95)

Define a date field (p. 98)

Create a report from two tables (p. 108)

Enter data in Datasheet view (p. 88)

Check and test referential integrity (p. 115)

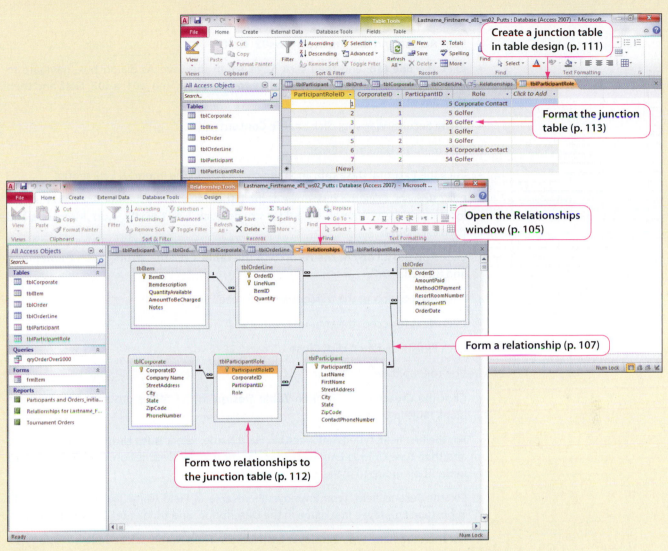

Figure 34 Putts for Paws Charity Tournament Imported Data Final Database

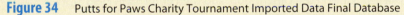

Practice 1

Student data files needed:

a01_ws02_Golf

a01_ws02_Golf_Members

You will save your files as:

Lastname_Firstname_a01_ws02_Golf

Red Bluff Golf Course

Barry Cheney, the manager of the Red Bluff Golf Course, is very pleased with your work on the Putts for Paws event. He has asked if you could create a database to keep track of members and the lessons that they sign up for. The database will have three tables: tblMember, tblMemberLessons, and tblEmployee.

The relationship between tblMember and tblEmployee that you are interested in is that a member can take a golf lesson with an employee. You ask yourself the two questions: A member can take a maximum of how many lessons with an employee? The answer is many. An employee can give how many lessons maximum to a member? Again, the answer is many. This is a many-to-many relationship that you'll create with a junction table: tblMemberLessons. A member can take many tblMemberLessons, but a MemberLesson is taken by just one member. An employee can teach many tblMemberLessons, but each MemberLesson is given by just one employee.

a. Open the Golf database.

- Start **Access**, and then open **a01_ws02_Golf**.

- Click the **File tab**, and then click **Save As**. In the Save As dialog box, navigate to where you are saving your files, type Lastname_Firstname_a01_ws02_Golf, and then click **Save**.

- In the Security Warning, click **Enable Content**.

b. Import member data from Excel.

- Click the **External Data tab**, and then click **Excel** in the Import & Link group.

- Click **Browse**. Click the disk drive in the left pane where your student data files are located, navigate through the folder structure, click **a01_ws02_Golf_Members** and then click **Open**.

- Click **Append a copy of the records to the table**. Click the **arrow**, select **tblMember**, and then click **OK**.

- Click **Next** to accept the tblMember worksheet.

- Click **Next** to accept the column headings.

- Click **Finish**, and then click **Close**.

c. Design tblEmployee.

- Click the **Create tab**, and then **Table Design** in the Tables group. Access opens a blank table in Design view.

- For the first field, type EmployeeID in Field Name, select **Auto Number** for Data Type, and then type Unique Employee Identification in the Description. Click **Primary Key** in the Tools group to make this your primary key.

- For the second field, type EmployeeFirstName in Field Name, select **Text** for Field Type, type Employee first name in the Description, and then enter 30 in Field Size.

- For the third field, type EmployeeLastName in Field Name, select **Text** for Field Type, type Employee last name in the Description, and then enter 30 in Field Size.

- For the fourth field, type EmployeeSalary in Field Name, select **Currency** for Field Type, and then type Employee annual salary in the Description.

- For the fifth field, in Field Name type EmployeeHireDate, select **Date/Time** for Field Type, and then type Date that employee was first hired in the Description. In the Field Properties pane, select **ShortDate** in Format.

- **Save** your table, naming it tblEmployee. Change to Datasheet view. Resize the columns as necessary.

- Enter the following data into the table. For the first record use your actual first and last name:

EmployeeID	EmployeeFirstName	EmployeeLastName	EmployeeSalary	EmployeeHireDate
Autonumber	YourFirstName	YourLastName	$45,000	6/1/2012
Autonumber	John	Schilling	$50,000	7/12/2007

- **Close** the table, saving the layout changes.

d. Define the foreign key.

- Open **tblMemberLessons** in Design view.

- In the first blank line after the other fields, in the Field Name, type **EmployeeID**, select **Number** as Data Type, type **Foreign Key to tblEmployee** in the Description, and then select a Field Size of **Long Integer**.

- Save your table design, and then change to Datasheet view.

- Enter the following data into the tblMemberLessons table.

MemberLessonID	MemberID	ScheduledDate	Fee	EmployeeID
1	1	4/17/2012 4:00 pm	$50.00	1
2	1	4/24/2012 4:00 pm	$50.00	1
3	2	4/17/2012 4:00 pm	$50.00	1
4	6	4/18/2012 2:00 pm	$75.00	2
5	7	4/18/2012 2:00 pm	$75.00	2

- **Save** and close the table.

e. Create relationships between tblMember, tblMemberLessons, and tblEmployee.

- Click the **Database Tools tab**.

- Click **Relationships** in the Relationships group.

- Select **tblEmployee**, **tblMemberLessons**, and **tblMember**, and then close the Show Table dialog box.

- Drag the primary key **MemberID** from tblMember to **MemberID** in tblMemberLessons.

- Click **Enforce Referential Integrity**, and then click **Create**.

- Drag the primary key **EmployeeID** from **tblEmployee** to **EmployeeID** in **tblMemberLessons**. Click **Enforce Referential Integrity**, and then click **Create**.

- Click **Relationship Report** to create a report of your relationships. Save the report, accepting the name **Relationships for Lastname_Firstname_a01_ws02_Golf**. **Close** the report.

- **Close** the Relationships window, and then click **Yes** to save your relationships.

f. Create a report that shows employees and their lessons.

- Click the **Create tab**, and then click **Report Wizard** in the Reports group.

- In the Report Wizard dialog box, click the **Tables/Queries arrow**, and then select **Table: tblEmployee**. Select the **EmployeeLastName**, and then click **One Field**. Select **EmployeeFirstName**, and then click **One Field**.

- Click the **Tables/Queries arrow**, and then select **Table: tblMemberLessons**. Select **ScheduledDate**, and then click **One Field**.

- Click the **Tables/Queries arrow** to select **Table: tblMember**. Select **FirstName**, and then click **One Field**. Select **LastName**, click **One Field**, and then click **Next**.

- Click **Next** to accept grouping by tblEmployee.

- You do not want any other grouping level so click **Next**.

- Click the **1 arrow** to sort your report by ascending **ScheduledDate**, click the **2 arrow**, and then select **LastName**. Click the **3 arrow**, select **FirstName**, and then click **Next**.

- Change the Orientation to **Landscape**, and then click **Next**.

- Title your report **Employee Lessons_initialLastname** and then click **Finish**.

- **Close** Print Preview, close the report, and then exit Access.

Student data files needed:

a01_ws02_Painted_Treasures
a01_ws02_Products
a01_ws02_Customers

You will save your file as:

Lastname_Firstname_a01_ws02_Painted_Treasures

Painted Treasures Gift Shop

The Painted Treasures Gift Shop sells many products for the resort patrons including jewelry, clothing, and spa products. You'll create a database of customers and their purchases.

The three tables that you need are customers, purchases, and products. What are the relationships between these three tables? You'll need to add a junction table between the two tables with a many-to-many relationship.

a. Import the **tblProduct** table from Excel. When you import a new table from Excel, you need to change the field definitions in Access.

- Start **Access**, and then open **a01_ws02_Painted_Treasures.**

- Click the **File tab**, and then click **Save As**. In the Save As dialog box, navigate to where you are saving your files, and then type Lastname_Firstname_a01_ws02_Painted_Treasures.

- Click **Save**.

- In the Security Warning, click **Enable Content**.

- Click the **External Data tab**, and then click **Excel** in the Import & Link group.

- **Browse** to **a01_ws02_Products**. Select the file, and then click **Open**. Make sure **Import the source data into a new table in the current database** is selected, and then click **OK**.

- In the Import Spreadsheet Wizard, note that **tblProduct** is selected, and click **Next**.

- Be sure that the **First Row Contains Column Headings** is checked. Click **Next**, and then click **Next** again.

- Select **Choose my own primary key**, click the **Primary Key arrow**, select **ProductID**, and then click **Next**.

- In the **Import to Table** box, keep the entry tblProduct, click **Finish**, and then click **Close**.

- Right-click **tblProduct**, and then open it in **Design view**.

- Change the data types as shown in the following table. Enter descriptions and change field sizes as noted.

Field Name	Data Type	Description	Field Size
ProductID	Number	Unique identifier for product	Change Field Size to **Long Integer**
ProductDescription	Text	Description of product	Change Field Size to 40
Category	Text	Product category	Change Field Size to 15
QuantityInStock	Number	Quantity of product in stock	Change Field Size to **Integer**
Price	Change to **Currency**	Price to charge customer	Change format to **Currency**
Size	Text	Size of product	Change Field Size to 10
Color	Text	Color of product	Change Field Size to 15

- **Save** the table. Access tells you that some data might be lost because you are making fields shorter in length. Accept this by clicking **Yes**. **Close** the table.

b. Create tblCustomer table in Design view.

- Click the **Create tab**, and then click **Table Design**. Access opens a blank table in Design view.

- Fill in the fields.

Field Name	Data Type	Maximum Length	Description
CustomerID	AutoNumber	Long Integer	A unique ID that identifies each customer
LastName	Text	25	The customer's last name
FirstName	Text	20	The customer's first name
StreetAddress	Text	40	Street address
City	Text	25	City address
State	Text	2	State abbreviation
ZipCode	Text	5	Five-digit zip code
ResortHotelRoom	Text	6	Leave blank if not a guest

- Highlight the **CustomerID row** by clicking the record selector to the left of the field. Click **Primary Key** to make CustomerID the primary key.

- Save your table design, naming it **tblCustomer**. Click **OK**. **Close** your table.

- Click the **External Data tab**, and then click **Excel** in the Import & Link group.

- Click **Browse**. Click the disk drive in the left pane where your student data files are located, navigate through the folder structure, click **a01_ws02_Customers**, and then click **Open**.

- Click **Append a copy of the records to the table**. If necessary, click the **arrow** to select **tblCustomer**, and then click **OK**.

- Click **Next** twice, and then in the Import Spreadsheet Wizard dialog box, keep the entry table **tblCustomer**. Click **Finish**, and then click **Close**.

- Double-click **tblCustomer** to open it in Datasheet view.

- In the first record in the table, change the LastName and FirstName to your last name and first name. **Close** tblCustomer.

c. Create relationships between your tables.

- Click the **Database Tools tab**.

- Click **Relationships** in the Relationships group, and then click **Show Table** dialog box, if necessary.

- Add all four tables in the order **tblCustomer**, **tblPurchase**, **tblPurchaseLine**, and **tblProduct** to the Relationships window, and then close the Show Table dialog box.

- Drag the primary key **CustomerID** from tblCustomer to **CustomerID** in tblPurchase.

- Click **Enforce Referential Integrity**, and then click **Create**.

- Drag the primary key **PurchaseID** from tblPurchase to **PurchaseID** in tblPurchaseLine. Click **Enforce Referential Integrity**, and then click **Create**.

- Drag the primary key **ProductID** from tblProduct to **ProductID** in tblPurchaseLine. Click **Enforce Referential Integrity**, and then click **Create**.

- Click **Relationship Report** and save it, accepting the name **Relationships for Lastname_Firstname_a01_ws02_Painted_Treasures**. Close the report.

- **Close** the Relationships window, and then click **Yes** to save the relationships.

d. Create a report of the customers, purchases, and products.

- Click the **Create tab**, and then click **Report Wizard** in the Reports group.

- In the Report Wizard dialog box, click the **Tables/Queries arrow**, and then select **Table: tblCustomer**. Select the **LastName** and **FirstName** fields.

- Click the **Tables/Queries arrow**, click **Table: tblPurchase**, and then select **PurchaseDate**.

- Click the **Tables/Queries arrow**, click **Table: tblPurchaseLine**, and then select **Quantity**.

- Click the **Tables/Queries arrow**, click **Table: tblProduct**, click **ProductDescription**, and then click **Next**.

- Accept grouping by tblCustomer and then by PurchaseDate by clicking **Next**.

- You don't want any other grouping level so click **Next**.

- Click the **arrow** to sort your report by ascending **ProductDescription**, and then click **Next**.

- Change the Orientation to **Landscape**, and then click **Next**.

- Title your report Customer and Purchases_initialLastname and then click **Finish**.

- **Close** Print Preview, close the report, and then exit Access.

MODULE CAPSTONE

Student data files needed:

a01_mp_Recipe

a01_mp_Recipe_Preparation

a01_mp_Recipe_Ingredients

You will save your file as:

Lastname_Firstname_a01_mp_Recipe

Indigo 5 Restaurant

Robin Sanchez, the chef of the resort's restaurant, Indigo 5, wants to keep track of recipes and the ingredients that they include in an Access database. This will allow him to plan menus and get reports and queries on the ingredients that are needed. Ingredients have already been stored in Excel worksheets and can be imported from Excel into Access. The dish preparation instructions can be cut and pasted from Excel. Other data will need to be entered. Complete the following tasks:

a. Start **Access**, and then open **a01_mp_Recipe**. Save the file as Lastname_Firstname_a01_mp_Recipe, replacing Lastname_Firstname with your own name. In the Security Warning bar, click **Enable Content**.

b. Create a new table in Design view. This table will store specific recipe items.

- Add the following fields, data types, and descriptions:

Field Name	Data Type	Description	Field Size
RecipeID	Text	The recipe ID assigned to each menu item (primary key)	6
RecipeName	Text	The recipe name	30
FoodCategory	Text	The food category	15
TimeToPrepare	Number	Preparation time in minutes	Integer
Servings	Number	The number of servings this recipe makes	Integer
Instructions	Memo	Cooking instructions	

- Designate **RecipeID** as the primary key. Save the new table as tblRecipes and then close the table.

c. Create a form to enter recipes. Click the **Create tab**, and then click **Form** in the Forms group. Save the form as frmRecipes_initialLastname, replacing initialLastName with your own initial and last name.

d. Enter the following data into frmRecipes_initialLastname:

RecipeID	RecipeName	FoodCategory	TimeToPrepare	Servings
REC001	Chicken Soup	Soup	45	8
REC002	Black Beans	Beans	90	6

e. Start **Excel**, and then open **a01_mp_Recipe_Preparation**. For each recipe, copy the **Cooking Instructions** from the Excel worksheet and paste the recipe instructions into the Access field **Instructions**.

f. Import **Excel a01_mp_Recipe_Ingredients**, appending it to **tblIngredients**. Use the **Ingredients** worksheet. There are headers in the first row of this worksheet. Do not save the import steps.

g. Create a new table in Design view. This table will serve as the junction table between the tblIngredients and tblRecipe tables.

- Add the following fields, data types, and descriptions (in this order):

Field Name	Data Type	Description	Field Size
RecipeIngredientID	AutoNumber	The recipe ingredient ID automatically assigned to each recipe ingredient (primary key)	
RecipeID	Text	The recipe ID from tblRecipe (foreign key)	6
IngredientID	Number	The ingredient ID from tblIngredients (foreign key)	Long Integer
Quantity	Number	The quantity of the ingredient required in the recipe	Double

- Assign **RecipeIngredientID** as the primary key.
- Save the new table as tblRecipeIngredients.

h. Close the tables and form.

i. Open the **Relationships** window.

- Create a one-to-many relationship between **RecipeID** in tblRecipes and **RecipeID** in tblRecipeIngredients. Enforce referential integrity. Do not cascade update or cascade delete.
- Create a one-to-many relationship between **IngredientID** in tblIngredients and **IngredientID** in tblRecipeIngredients. Enforce referential integrity. Do not cascade update or cascade delete.
- Save the relationships, and then close the Relationships window. If your instructor directs you to print the relationships, print your relationship report.

j. Enter the following data into tblRecipeIngredients (in this order):

RecipeIngredientID	RecipeID	IngredientID	Quantity
(Let Access assign)	REC001	7	6
	REC001	9	2
	REC001	16	2
	REC001	17	2
	REC001	6	4
	REC002	10	1
	REC002	16	1
	REC002	17	1
	REC002	21	1
	REC002	18	3
	REC002	20	1

k. Use the Query Wizard and the data in tblRecipes, tblRecipeIngredients, and tblIngredients to create a query that displays the ingredients for each dish. The query results should list **RecipeName**, **Quantity**, **Ingredient**, and **Units**. This will be a **Detail** query. Sort by **RecipeName**. Run your query. Adjust the width of the query columns as necessary. Save your query as qryRecipeIngredients_initialLastname. If your instructor directs you to print the query, print your results.

l. Create a report with the source **qryRecipeIngredients_initialLastname** using the Report Wizard. Select all fields. Group by **RecipeName**, and then sort by **Ingredient**. Name your report Recipe Ingredients Report and then modify the report title to end with your initialLastname. Fix the report columns as necessary. If your instructor directs you to print the report, print your results.

m. Close the database.

Problem Solve 1

Student data files needed:

a01_ps1_Hotel_Guests
a01_ps1_Hotel_Reservations
a01_ps1_Hotel_Rooms
a01_ps1_Hotel

You will save your file as:

Lastname_Firstname_a01_ps1_Hotel

Hotel Reservations

The main portion of the resort is the hotel. The hotel wants to store information about hotel guests, reservations, and rooms. You'll design tables, import data from Excel, and create relationships. Then you'll be able to create queries and reports from the data. Complete the following tasks:

a. Start **Access**, and then open **a01_ps1_Hotel**. Save the file as Lastname_Firstname_a01_ps1_Hotel, replacing Lastname_Firstname with your own name. In the Security Warning bar, click **Enable Content**.

b. Import tables from the Access database **a01_ps1_Hotel_Guests**, selecting the **tblGuests** table. Do not save the import steps.

c. Open **tblGuests**, and then change the name in record **25** to Your Name.

d. Create a new table in Design view. This table will store reservations.
   - Add the following fields, data types, and descriptions (in this order):

Field Name	Data Type	Description	Field Size/Format
ReservationID	AutoNumber	A unique identifier for the reservation	Long Integer
GuestID	Number	The guest ID from tblGuests (foreign key)	Long Integer
RoomNumber	Text	The room number from tblRooms (foreign key)	30
CheckInDate	Date/Time	The date the guest will check in	Short Date
NightsStay	Number	How many nights the guest will stay	Integer
NumberOfGuests	Number	The number of guests on this reservation	Integer

   - Assign **ReservationID** as the primary key.
   - Save the new table as tblReservations.

e. Import **a01_ps1_Hotel_Reservations** from Excel, using the Reservations worksheet and appending it to **tblReservations**. The Excel column headers match the Access field names so you can use them.

f. Click **Form** in the Forms group to create a form to enter reservations, and then save it as frmReservations_initialLastname, replacing initialLastname with your own initial and last name.

g. Enter the following data into the append record in frmReservations_initialLastname:

ReservationID	GuestID	RoomNumber	CheckInDate	NightsStay	NumberOfGuests
AutoNumber	25	105	4/20/2013	8	1

h. Create a new table in Design view. This table will store information about the hotel rooms.
- Add the following fields, data types, and descriptions (in this order):

Field Name	Data Type	Description	Field Size
RoomNumber	Text	The resort's room number or name (primary key)	30
RoomType	Text	The type of room this is	20

- Assign **RoomNumber** as the primary key.
- Save the new table as tblRooms.

i. Import **a01_ps1_Hotel_Rooms** from Excel, using the **Rooms** worksheet and appending it to **tblRooms**. Look to see whether there are column headings that match the Access field names.

j. Open the **Relationships** window, and then create a relationship between **GuestID** in tblGuests and **GuestID** in tblReservations. Enforce referential integrity. Do not cascade update or cascade delete.

k. Create a one-to-many relationship between **RoomNumber** in tblRooms and **RoomNumber** in tblReservations. Enforce referential integrity. Do not cascade update or cascade delete. If your instructor directs you to print the relationships, print your relationship report.

l. Use the Query Wizard to create a query. The query results should list **GuestID**, **GuestFirstName**, **GuestMiddleInitial**, **GuestLastName**, **CheckInDate**, **NightsStay** and **RoomType**. This query should show every field of every record.

m. Run your query. Save your query as qryMyReservations_initialLastname.

n. In Design view for **qryMyReservations_initialLastname**, select the guest with **GuestID = 25**. Sort by **CheckInDate**. Run the query. If your instructor directs you to print the query, print your results.

o. Create a report showing ReservationID, CheckInDate, NightsStay, and RoomType. View by tblRooms and sort by **CheckInDate** and **ReservationID**. Name your report Reservations Report and then modify the report title to end with your initialLastname. Fix the report columns as necessary. If your instructor directs you to print the report, print your results.

p. Close the database.

Student data files needed:

a01_ps2_Hotel_Staffing
a01_ps2_Hotel_Staff

You will save your file as:

Lastname_Firstname_a01_ps2_Hotel_Staffing

Hotel Staffing Database

The hotel general manager needs a human resource database to store information on employees, the areas they work in, and the hours they are scheduled to work. The database will have three new tables: tblHotelArea, tblEmployee, and tblSchedule.

a. Start **Access**, and then open **a01_ps2_Hotel_Staffing**. Save the file as Lastname_Firstname_a01_ps2_Hotel_Staffing, replacing Lastname_Firstname with your own name. In the Security Warning bar, click **Enable Content**.

b. Create a new table in Design view. This table will store employees.

- Add the following fields (in this order). Where necessary, you decide upon data types and field sizes.

Field Name	Data Type	Description	Field Size
EmployeeID	AutoNumber	A unique identifier for the employee (primary key)	
AreaID	Number	The area ID from tblHotelAreas (foreign key)	Long Integer
FirstName	Pick appropriate type	The employee's first name	30
LastName	Pick appropriate type	The employee's last name	30
StreetAddress	Pick appropriate type	Home street address	40
City	Pick appropriate type	City	30
State	Pick appropriate type	State abbreviation	Pick appropriate size
ZipCode	Pick appropriate type	Zip code (5 digit)	Pick appropriate size
Phone	Pick appropriate type	Home phone number	14
HireDate	Pick appropriate type	Date employee was hired	Short Date
JobTitle	Pick appropriate type	Employee job title	30

- Make sure you have assigned the most appropriate field to be the primary key.
- Define an input mask for the phone number. Use a mask of **(555) 555-5555** with a place holder of "-" and save with the symbols in the mask.
- Save the new table as tblEmployee.

c. Import **a01_ps2_Hotel_Staff** from Excel, using the **Employee** worksheet and appending it to **tblEmployee**. Change the name of the last employee to your name.

d. Create a new table in Design view. This table will store hotel areas.

- Add the following fields, data types, and descriptions (in this order):

Field Name	Data Type	Description	Field Size
AreaID	AutoNumber	A unique identifier for the area	Long Integer
AreaName	Text	The name of the area	30

- Make sure you have assigned the most appropriate field to be the primary key.
- Save the new table as tblHotelAreas.

e. Import **a01_ps2_Hotel_Staff** from Excel, using the **Area** worksheet and appending it to **tblHotelAreas**.

f. Create a new table in Design view. This table will store information about an employee's schedule.

- Add the following fields, data types, and descriptions (in this order):

Field Name	Data Type	Description	Field Size
ScheduleID	AutoNumber	A unique identifier for the schedule (primary key)	Long Integer
ScheduleDay	Date/Time	The day the schedule applies to	ShortDate
StartTime	Date/Time	Starting time for shift	MediumTime
HoursScheduled	Number	Number of hours on shift	Integer
EmployeeID	Number	The person being scheduled	Long Integer

- Make sure you have assigned the most appropriate primary key. Save the new table as tblSchedule.

g. Import **a01_ps2_Hotel_Staff** from Excel, using the **Schedule** worksheet, and appending it to **tblSchedule**.

h. Open the **Relationships** window, create a one-to-many relationship between **EmployeeID** in tblEmployee and **EmployeeID** in tblSchedule. Enforce referential integrity. Do not cascade update or cascade delete.

i. Create a one-to-many relationship between **AreaID** in tblHotelAreas and **AreaID** in tblEmployee. Enforce referential integrity. Do not cascade update or cascade delete. If your instructor directs you to print the relationships, print your relationship report.

j. Create a form for **tblEmployee**. Notice that Access automatically includes the related records from tblSchedule at the bottom of the form. Save the form as frmEmployeeSchedule_initialLastname.

k. Using **frmEmployeeSchedule_initialLastname**, add a new schedule for yourself to work on January 3, 2013, starting at 8 am and working for 8 hours.

l. Use data in all three tables to create a schedule query. The query results should list **AreaID**, **AreaName**, **FirstName**, **LastName**, **ScheduleDay**, **StartTime**, and **HoursScheduled**. Run your query, and then save it as qryCoffeeShopSchedule_initialLastname.

m. In Design view for qryCoffeeShopSchedule_initialLastname, select only the data from **AreaID 4**. Run the query. If your instructor directs you to print the query, print your results.

n. Create a report from qryCoffeeShopSchedule_initialLastname. Select the fields: **FirstName**, **LastName**, **ScheduleDay**, **StartTime**, and **HoursScheduled**. View by **tblSchedule**. Group by **ScheduleDay**. Access defaults to ScheduleDay by Month. Click on **Grouping Options**, and then change the **Group Intervals** to **Day**. Sort by **StartTime** and **LastName**, and then change to **Landscape** orientation.

o. Name your report CoffeeShopSchedule and then adjust the width of the report columns to make them readable. Modify the report title to end with your initialLastname.

p. If your instructor directs you to print the report, print your results. Close the database.

Student data file needed:

a01_ps3_Hotel_Event

You will save your file as:

Lastname_Firstname_a01_ps3_Hotel_Event

Group Reservations Case

Patti Rochelle, corporate event planner, wants to be able to track group reservations with the conference rooms that are booked for the event. You want to track conference rooms, groups, and events.

A group can book several events. Each event is booked by just one group.

Each event could take multiple conference rooms. Conference rooms can be booked for several events (on different days.) You'll need a junction table for this relationship.

a. Start **Access**, and then open **a01_ps3_Hotel_Event**. Browse to where you are storing your data files, and then save your database as **Lastname_Firstname_a01_ps3_Hotel_Event**, replacing Lastname_Firstname with your own name. In the Security Warning bar, click **Enable Content**.

b. Create a new table in Design view. This table will store conference rooms.

   • Add the following fields (in the following order). Where necessary, you decide upon field names, data types, and field sizes.

Field Name	Data Type	Description	Field Size
Choose the best name from the following list: Conference Room ID ConfRoomID ConferenceRoom	AutoNumber	A unique identifier for the conference room	Long Integer
RoomName	Pick an appropriate type	The name of the conference room	40
Choose the best name from the following list: Conference Room Capacity Conf Room Capacity Capacity	Pick an appropriate type	The capacity of the conference room	Integer

   • Make sure you have assigned the most appropriate field to be primary key.
   • Save the new table as **tblConfRoom**.

c. In this order, enter the following rooms into the table:

RoomName	Capacity
Musica	500
Eldorado	100
Pueblo	25

d. Create a new table in Design view. This table will store groups.

   • Add the following fields, data types, and descriptions (in the following order). Where necessary, you decide upon data types.

Field Name	Data Type	Description	Field Size
GroupID	AutoNumber	A unique identifier for the group (primary key)	Long Integer
GroupName	Pick an appropriate type	Group name	40
ContactFirstName	Pick an appropriate type	Contact person first name	30
ContactLastName	Pick an appropriate type	Contact person last name	40
ContactPhone	Pick an appropriate type	Contact phone number	14

- Define an input mask for contact phone number. Use a mask of **(555) 555-5555** with a place holder of "-" and save with the symbols in the mask.
- Make sure you have assigned the most appropriate primary key. Save the new table as tblGroup.

e. Create a new table in Design view. This table will store events.
- Add the following fields, data types, and descriptions (in the following order). Where necessary, you decide upon data types.

Field Name	Data Type	Description	Field Size
EventID	AutoNumber	A unique identifier for the event (primary key)	Long Integer
EventName	Pick an appropriate type	The name of the event	40
EventStart	Pick an appropriate type	Starting date for the event	Short Date
EventLength	Pick an appropriate type	Length of the event (in days)	Integer
GroupID	Number	The Group ID from tblGroup (foreign key)	Long Integer

- Make sure that you have assigned a primary key. Save the new table as tblEvent.

f. Create a new table in Design View. This table will serve as the junction table between tblConfRoom and tblEvent.
- Add the following fields, data types, and descriptions (in the following order). Where necessary, you decide upon data types.

Field Name	Data Type	Description	Field Size
ReservationID	AutoNumber	A unique identifier for the conference reservation (primary key)	Long Integer
EventID	Number	The Event ID from tblEvent (foreign key)	Long Integer
ConfRoomID	Number	The Conference Room ID from tblConfRooms (foreign key)	Long Integer
Choose the best name from the following list: ReservationDate Date of Reservation ShortDate	Pick an appropriate type	Reservation date	Short Date
DaysReserved	Number	Number of days reserved	Integer

- Make sure that you have assigned a primary key. Save the new table as tblConfRes.

g. Open the **Relationships** window.

- Create a one-to-many relationship between the correct field in tblGroup and the correct field in tblEvent. Enforce referential integrity. Do not cascade update or cascade delete.
- Create a one-to-many relationship between the correct field in tblEvent and the correct field in tblConfRes. Enforce referential integrity. Do not cascade update or cascade delete.
- Create a one-to-many relationship between the correct field in tblConfRoom and tblConfRes. Enforce referential integrity. Do not cascade update or cascade delete. If your instructor directs you to print the relationships, print your relationship report.

h. Enter the following data into the appropriate tables (in the following order)—you may need to determine keys along the way:

Group:	**Benson & Diaz Law Group**
	Contact: Mary Williams (505) 555-1207
Benson & Diaz's Event:	**Company Retreat**
	Start Date: 2/17/2012
	Length of Event: 2 days
Benson & Diaz's Reservation of the Pueblo Room:	
	Date: 2/17/2012
	Number of Days: 2 days

Group:	**Dental Association of Nova Scotia**
	Contact: Your Name (902) 555-8765
Dental Association's Event:	**Annual Meeting**
	Start Date: 2/17/2012
	Length of Event: 5 days
Dental Association's Reservation of the Eldorado Room:	
	Date: 2/17/2012
	Number of Days: 2 days
Dental Association's Reservation of the Pueblo Room:	
	Date: 2/20/2012
	Number of Days: 2 days

Group:	**Orchard Growers of the United States**
	Contact: Will Goodwin (212) 555-7889
Orchard Growers' Event:	**Annual Meeting**
	Start Date: 2/17/2012
	Length of Event: 2 days
Orchard Growers' Reservation of the Musica Room:	
	Date: 2/17/2012
	Number of Days: 5 days

i. Create a query using **RoomName** from tblConfRoom, and **Reservation Date** and **DaysReserved** from tblConfRes. Save your query as qryEldoradoRoom_initialLastname, replacing initialLastname with your own initial and last name. Select the room named **Eldorado**, sort by **Reservation Date**, and then run the query. Adjust the width of the query columns as necessary. If your instructor directs you to print the query, print your results.

j. Use data in four tables to create a query about the Dental Association of Nova Scotia. The query results should list **Group Name**, **EventName**, **EventStart**, **EventLength**, **RoomName**, **ReservationDate**, and **DaysReserved**. Save your query as qryDentalAssociation_initialLastname, replacing initialLastname with your own initial and last name. Select the group named **Dental Association of Nova Scotia**, sort by **ReservationDate**, and then run the query. If your instructor directs you to print the query, print your results.

k. Create a report from **qryDentalAssociation_initialLastname**. Select all fields. Accept the default grouping by GroupName and then by all tblEvent fields. Sort by **RoomName** and **ReservationDate**. Select Orientation **Landscape**. Name your report DentalAssociationBooking_initialLastname, replacing initialLastname with your own initial and last name. Adjust the width of the report columns as necessary. If your instructor directs you to print the report, print your results.

l. Close the database.

Perform 1: Perform in Your Life

You will save your file as:

Lastname_Firstname_a01_pf1_Organization

Track Events for Your Organization

Pick an organization that you belong to. You want to track the members of the organization, events, and member attendance at the events. Since a member can attend many events and an event can be attended by many members, you'll need a junction table. You'll start by creating three tables, the relationships between the tables, and reports on attendance.

Next, you'll decide on one other table that makes sense for your organization, define that table, and relate it to one of the already existing tables.

a. Start **Access**, click the **New tab**, and click **Blank database**. Browse to where you are storing your data files, and name your database Lastname_Firstname_a01_pf1_Organization, replacing Lastname_Firstname with your own name. Click the **Create** button to create the database.

b. Design a table to store members. Choose appropriate fields that would describe the members of your organization.
   - Assign a field to be primary key, and then make it **AutoNumber**. For all fields, enter appropriate data types, descriptions, field sizes, and masks. Save your table as tblMember.

c. Enter yourself and a friend into the table. Enter as many other members as you wish.

d. Design a table to store events. Use the following fields: EventID, EventName, EventDate, and Place. You may add other fields as appropriate.
   - Assign EventID to be primary key, and then make it an AutoNumber. Enter appropriate data types, descriptions, and field sizes. Save your table as tblEvent.

e. Enter two events that you attended into the table. Enter as many other events as you wish.

f. Design a junction table to relate members and attendance at events. Use the following fields: EventID and the primary key of your member table.
   - EventID is a foreign key and should be Number, Long Integer. Enter appropriate descriptions.

- Use the primary key of your member table as a foreign key in this table. Enter appropriate types and descriptions.
- Create a composite primary key using both EventID and the primary key from your member table.
- Save your table as tblAttendance.

g. Create relationships as appropriate for the tblMember, tblAttendance, and tblEvent tables.

h. Enter the following data into tblAttendance:

EventID	MemberID
Use the EventID for the first event	Your primary key in the member table
Use the EventID for the first event	Your friend's primary key in the member table
Use the EventID for the second event	Your primary key in the member table

i. Create a report on Events using **EventName**, **EventDate**, and **Place**. Sort by EventDate. Name your report Event Report and then modify the report title to end with your initialLastname. If your instructor directs you to print the report, print your results.

j. Create a query on Events including **EventName**, **EventDate**, and **Place**. Save the query as qryEventName_initalLastname and then modify the query design to select the EventName for the first event. Run the query. If your instructor directs you to print the query, print your results.

k. Create a report on event attendance. Use **EventName**, **EventDate** from tblEvent and member's name. Group the report by **Event**. Sort the report by **LastName** and **FirstName**. Name your report Event Attendance and then modify the report title to end with your initialLastname. If your instructor directs you to print the report, print your results.

l. Determine one additional table that would make sense for your organization to keep data in.

m. Design this table and the appropriate fields. Make sure to assign a primary key.

n. Enter data into the tables. Create relationships between this new table and your existing tables as appropriate. Ask yourself the two questions to determine the relationships. If your instructor directs you to print the relationships, print your relationship report.

o. Create a report showing data from your new table and data from another table that it is related to. If your instructor directs you to print the report, print your results.

p. Close the database.

Perform 2: Perform in Your Career

You will save your file as:

Lastname_Firstname_a01_pf2_PetStore

Pet Store

A pet store owner wants to create a database for the store. The database needs to include information about animals and the breeds of the animals. An animal is of one breed. The pet store can have many animals of each breed.

The pet owner will want to keep records of the purchases and the customers that bought each animal. You'll need to decide what tables you need to record purchases and customers. You'll also need to decide what relationships you want to create.

a. Start **Access**, click the **New tab**, and click **Blank database**. Browse to where you are storing your data files, and name your database Lastname_Firstname_a01_pf2_PetStore, replacing Lastname_Firstname with your own name. Click **Create** to create the database.

b. Design a table to store breeds. Use the following fields: BreedID, AnimalType, BreedName, MaximumSize (in pounds), LengthOfLife (in years).

- Assign **BreedID** to be primary key with the AutoNumber data type.
- For all fields, enter appropriate data types, descriptions, and field sizes. Save your table as tblBreed.

c. Enter the following data into the table (in this order):

BreedID	AnimalType	BreedName	MaximumSize	LengthOfLife
1	Dog	Akita	110	12
2	Dog	Papillon	9	15
3	Cat	Devon	7	18
4	Cat	Birman	10	19
5	Chinchilla	Silver Mosaic	1	15

d. After entering those five breeds, pick another breed and add it to the table.

e. Design a table to store animals. Use the following fields: AnimalID, DateOfBirth, Price, Weight, Color, Sex, and BreedID.

- Assign **AnimalID** to be primary key with the AutoNumber data type.
- BreedID is the foreign key to tblBreed.
- For all fields, enter appropriate data types, descriptions, and field sizes.
- Save your table as tblAnimal.

f. Enter the following data into tblAnimal (in this order):

AnimalID	DateOfBirth	Price	Weight	Color	Sex	BreedID
1	6/17/2011	$125.00	28	White	M	1
2	6/17/2011	$125.00	30	White	M	1
3	7/25/2011	$610.00	4	Tan	F	2
4	8/7/2011	$610.00	3	White	F	2
5	8/7/2011	$550.00	3	White	M	2
6	5/10/2011	$225.00	2	Blue	F	3
7	5/10/2011	$225.00	2	Gray	M	3
8	6/26/2011	$150.00	2	White	F	4
9	7/17/2011	$125.00	2	Gray	M	4
10	8/18/2011	$ 30.00	1	Silver	F	5

g. After adding those 10 animals, add another animal which is of the breed you entered for the prior table.

h. Open the **Relationships** window. Create a one-to-many relationship between BreedID in tblBreed and BreedID in tblAnimal. Enforce referential integrity. Do not cascade update or cascade delete.

i. Determine the tables that the store owner would need to keep store customers and their purchases.

- Design these tables and the appropriate fields. Make sure to assign primary keys.
- Create relationships between these new tables and your existing tables as appropriate. Ask yourself the two questions to determine the relationships. Add foreign keys as appropriate. If your instructor directs you to print the relationships, print your relationship report.

j. Enter the appropriate customer and purchase data to capture the following events:
- You bought the chinchilla with AnimalID = 10 yesterday.
- A friend bought the Birman cat with AnimalID = 9 and the Akita with AnimalID = 1 today.

k. Create a report showing animals by breed. Show **AnimalType**, **BreedName**, **AnimalID**, **DateOfBirth**, and **Price**. Select correct groupings and sort orders. If your instructor directs you to print the report, print your results.

l. Create a query to find out who purchased AnimalID = 10. Show **Customer name** (Firstname and Lastname), **AnimalID**, **AnimalType**, and **BreedName**. If your instructor directs you to print the query, print your results.

m. Create a report showing the animals purchased on all dates. Group and sort appropriately. If your instructor directs you to print the report, print your results.

n. Close the database.

Perform 3: Perform in Your Career

You will save your file as:

Lastname_Firstname_a01_pf3_Music

Independent Music Label

The owner of an independent music label needs to keep track of the groups, musicians, and their music. You have been asked to create a database for the label.

The label owner would like to be able to get a list of groups with all musicians, get a list of groups with albums, select an album and see all songs in the album, and select a group and see their albums with all songs in the album.

You will need to design tables, fields, relationships, queries, and reports for the label.

a. Start **Access**, click the **New tab**, and click **Blank database**. Browse to where you are storing your data files, and name your database Lastname_Firstname_a01_pf3_Music, replacing Lastname_Firstname with your own name. Click **Create** to create the database.

b. Design your tables.

c. At this point the label has three groups signed up. Enter the following data (in this order):
- Clean Green, an Enviro-Punk band. The members of the group are Jon Smith (vocalist and guitar) and Lee Smith (percussion and keyboard). The group has two albums:
  - Clean Green with the following songs:

    Esperando Verde

    Precious Drops

    Recycle Mania

    Don't Tread on Me
  - Be Kind to Animals with the following songs:

    It's Our Planet Too

    Animal Rag

    Where Will We Live?

- Spanish Moss, a Spanish Jazz band. The members of the group are Hector Caurendo (guitar), Pasquale Rodriguez (percussion), Perry Trent (vocals), and Meredith Selmer (bass). The group has one album:
  - Latin Latitude with the following songs:
    Attitude Latitude

    Flying South

    Latin Guitarra

    Cancion Cancion

- Your band. You decide on your band members, albums, and songs.

d. Create your relationships. If your instructor directs you to print the relationships, print your relationship report.

e. Create a report showing all groups with all musicians. If your instructor directs you to print the report, print your results.

f. Create a report showing all groups, the group type, and their albums. If your instructor directs you to print the report, print your results.

g. Create a query to select an album from your band and see all songs in the album. If your instructor directs you to print the query, print your results.

h. Create a query to select your band and see all your albums with all songs in the albums. If your instructor directs you to print the query, print your results.

i. Close the database.

Perform 4: How Others Perform

Student data file needed:

a01_pf4_Textbook

College Bookstore

A colleague has created a database for your college bookstore. He is having problems creating the relationships in the database and has come to you for your help. What problems do you see in his database design? He has three tables in his database: one for sections of courses, one for textbooks, and one for instructor.

a. Are there any errors in the way that fields are defined or named in the tables? List your errors by table.

b. Are there any errors in the way that tables are named or defined?

c. He wants to define these relationships. How would you want to define the relationships? What errors are there in the database that would make it difficult to define the relationships?

- An instructor can teach many sections; a section is taught by just one instructor.
- A section can have many textbooks; a textbook can be used in many sections.

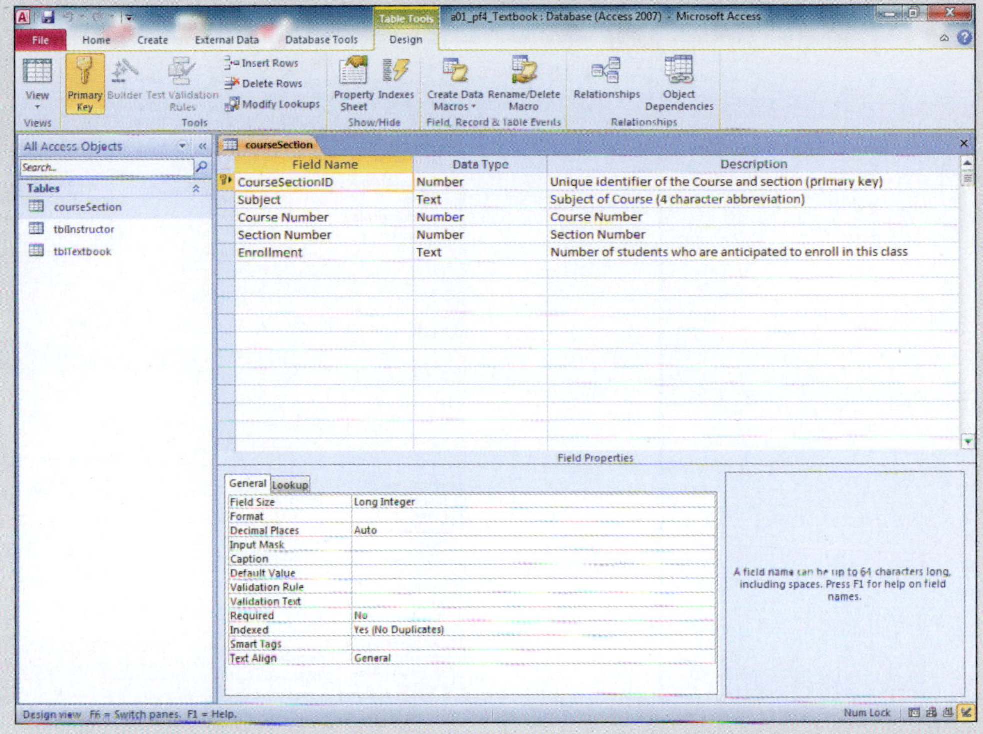

Figure 1 Table design for courseSection

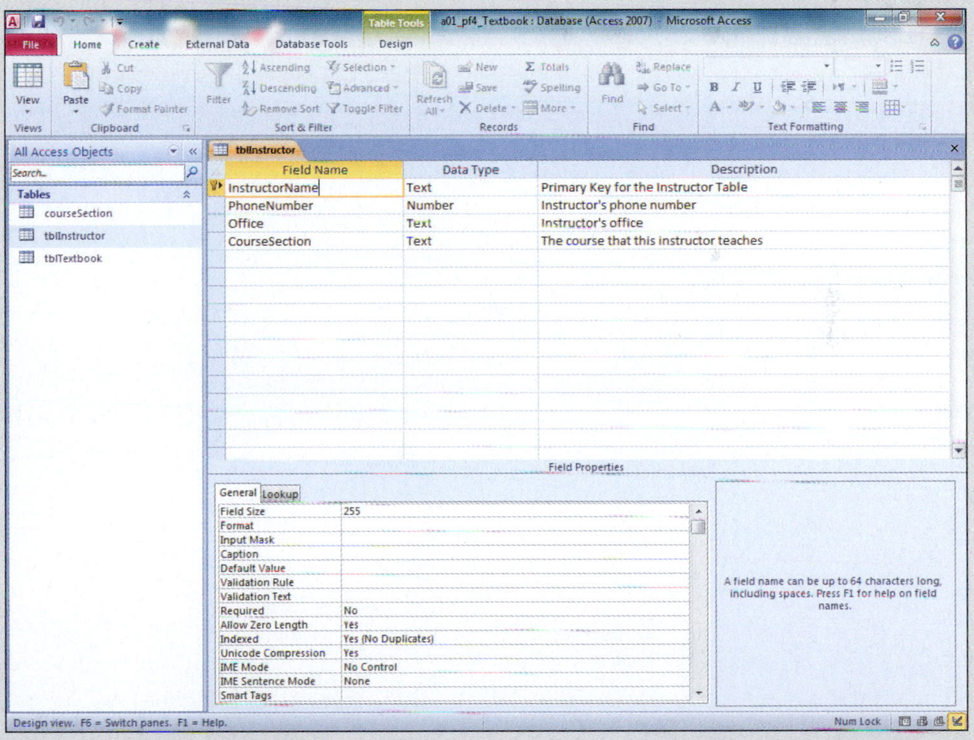

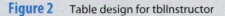

Figure 2 Table design for tblInstructor

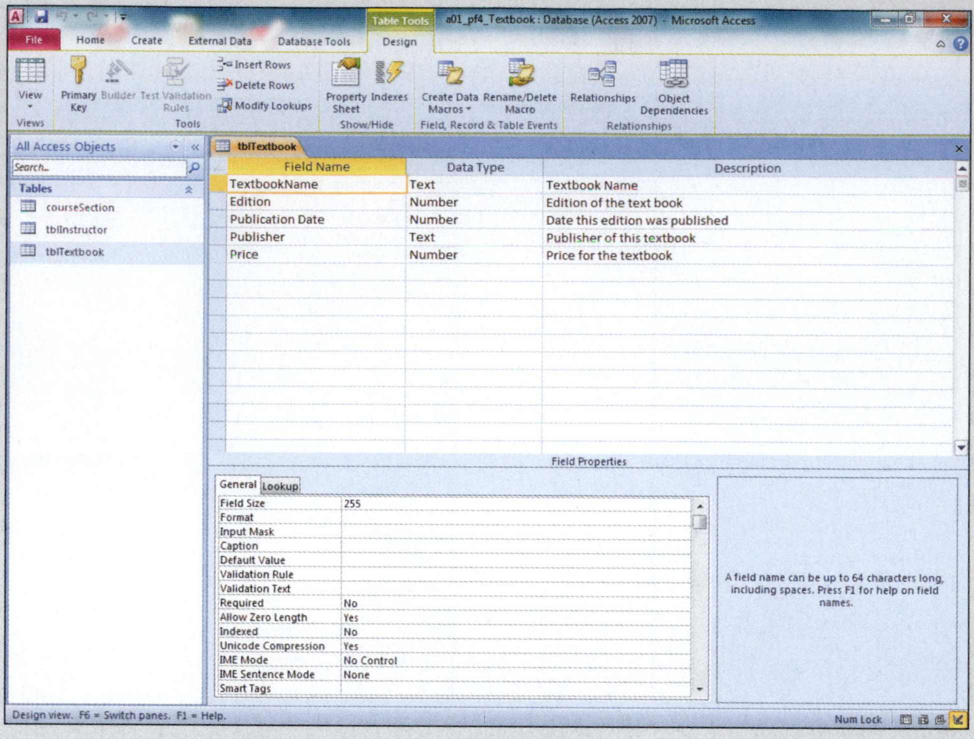

Figure 3 Table design for tblTextbook

WORKSHOP 3

Accessing Information From An Access Database

PREPARE CASE

Turquoise Oasis Spa

The Turquoise Oasis Spa has been popular with resort clients. The owners have spent several months putting spa data into an Access database so they can better manage the data. You have been asked to help show the staff how best to use the database to find information about products, services, and customers. For training purposes, not all the spa records have been added yet. Once the staff is trained, the remaining records will be entered into the database.

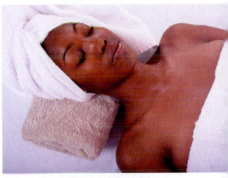

Courtesy of www.Shutterstock.com

Student data file needed for this workshop:

 a02_ws03_Spa

You will save your file as:

Lastname_Firstname_a02_ws03_Spa

Work with Datasheets

Datasheets are used to view all records in a table at one time. Each record is viewed as a row in the table. Records can be entered, edited, and deleted directly in a datasheet. When a table becomes so large that all the records and fields are no longer visible in the datasheet window without scrolling, the Find command can be used to quickly find specific values in a record. In this section, you will find records in a datasheet as well as modify the appearance of a datasheet.

Find Records in the Datasheet

The Navigation bar allows you to move to the top and bottom of a table or scroll to a specific record; however, this can be inefficient if your table is large. To manage larger tables, Access provides ways for you to quickly locate information within the datasheet. Once that information is found, it can then be easily replaced with another value using the **Replace command**.

If you do not know the exact value you are looking for because you do not know how it is spelled or how someone entered it, you can use a wildcard character. A **wildcard character** is used as a placeholder for an unknown part of a value or to match a certain pattern in a value. For example, if you know the value you are looking for contains the word "market" you can use a wildcard character at the beginning and end such as *market*.

Finding Records in a Table

In Datasheet view, you can use the **Find command** to quickly locate specific records using all or part of a field value. For this project, a staff member found a book left by one of the guests. A first name was printed on the inside of the book cover. They remember helping a gentleman named Guy who said he was from North Carolina, but they are not certain of his last name. You will show them how to use the Find command to quickly navigate through the table to search for this guest.

SIDE NOTE
Spelling Counts

Spelling counts in Access, so if you enter a search item and Access cannot find it, your search value may be spelled wrong.

To Find Records in the Datasheet

a. Click the **Start** button. From the Start Menu, locate and then start **Microsoft Access 2010**. Click the **File** tab, and then click **Open**. In the Open dialog box, click the disk drive in the left pane where your student data files are located, navigate through the folder structure, and then click **a02_ws03_Spa**. Click **Open**.

b. Click the **File tab**, and then click **Save Database As**. In the Save As dialog box, browse to where you are saving your files, change the file name to Lastname_Firstname_a02_ws03_Spa replacing Lastname and Firstname with your own name, and then click **Save**. In the Security Warning, click **Enable Content**.

c. Double-click **tblCustomer** to open the table.

d. Add a record at the end of the table with your First name, Last name, Address, City, State, Phone and E-mail Address. Press Tab until the record selector is on the next row and your record has been added to the table.

e. On the Navigation bar, click **First Record** to go to the first record in the table. Click the Home tab, and then click **Find** in the Find group to open the Find and Replace dialog box.

f. Replace the text in the Find What box with Guy. Click the **Look In arrow**, and then select **Current document**.

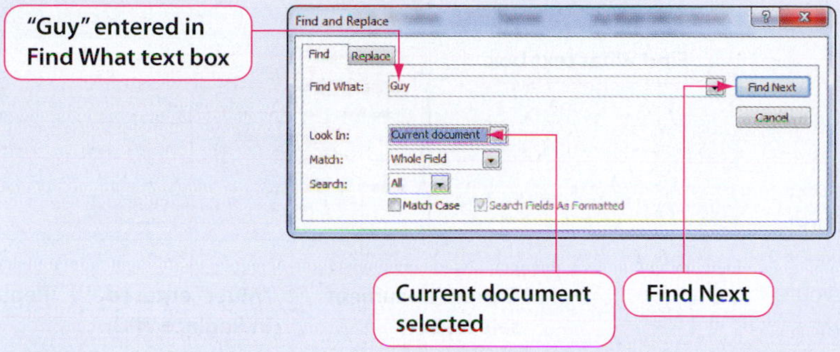

"Guy" entered in Find What text box

Current document selected

Find Next

Figure 1 Find and Replace dialog box to find all "Guy" records

g. Click **Find Next**. Access highlights the first record found for Guy Bowers from Derby, North Carolina (NC).

h. Click **Find Next** again to check for more records with Guy. When Access is done searching and cannot find any more matches, you will see the message that Microsoft Access has finished searching the records. The search item was not found. Click **OK**, and then click **Cancel** to close the Find and Replace dialog box.

i. **Close** ☒ the table.

Troubleshooting

If you did not get the results shown above, go back and carefully check the settings in the Find and Replace dialog box. In particular, check the setting for Match Case to make sure it is not checked. When Match Case is checked, the search will be case sensitive. Also check to make sure the Look In box shows Current document. If the Look In box shows Current field, Access will only look in the field selected, which may not be the field that contains the value you are looking for.

Finding and Replacing Data in a Datasheet

Not only can you find records using the Find command, but you can also replace records once you find them with the Replace command. In a large table, it is helpful to locate a record using the Find command, and then replace the data using the Replace command.

For this project, the receptionist receives a notice from Erica Rocha about her upcoming marriage. The receptionist wants to go through the database and find any records related to Erica and change her last name to her married name, Muer. You will show the receptionist how to find Erica in the database and replace her last name of Rocha with Muer.

To Find and Replace Records

a. Double-click **tblCustomer** to open it. Click the **Home tab**, and then click **Find** in the Find group to open the Find and Replace dialog box.

b. In the Find and Replace dialog box, click the **Replace tab**. In the Find What box type Rocha and then in the Replace With box, type Muer.

c. Click the **Look In arrow**, and then select **Current document**. Leave all other options as they are.

Data Is Automatically Saved

When table data is changed, Access automatically saves the changes when you close the table without prompting you to save it. This is unlike other programs that ask you to save all changes before you close a document or spreadsheet.

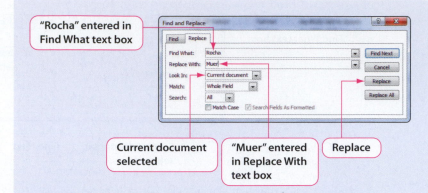

Figure 2 Find and Replace box options

d. Click **Find Next**. Notice the first record found has the last name Rocha, but the first name is Emily. Click **Find Next** again. Notice this is the record for Erica Rocha. Click **Replace**. Click **OK** when you get the message Microsoft Access has finished searching the records. The Last Name should now be Muer instead of Rocha. Click **Cancel** to close the Find and Replace dialog box.

e. **Close** ☒ the table.

Using a Wildcard Character

A wildcard character is used as a placeholder for an unknown part of a value or to match a certain pattern in a value. A wildcard character can replace a single character or multiple characters and text or numbers as shown in Figure 3.

Wildcard character	Example
*	To match any number of characters; to search for a word that starts with "ar" you would enter **ar***
#	To match any single numeric character; to search for a three digit number that starts with "75" you would enter **75#**
?	To match any single character; to search for a three letter word that starts with "t" and ends with "p" you would enter **t?p**
[ ]	To match any single character within the brackets; to search for a word that starts with "e," contains any of the letters "a" or "r," and ends with "r," you would enter **e[ar]r** and get "ear" or "err" as a result
!	To match any single character *not* within the brackets; to search for a word that starts with "e," contains any letter other than "a" or "r," and ends with "r," you would enter **e[!ar]r** to get anything except "err" or "ear"
-	To match any range of characters in ascending orders (a to z); to search for a word beginning with "a" and ending in "e" with any letter between "b" and "t" in between, you would enter **a[b-t]e**

Figure 3 Wildcard characters

For this project, the staff is looking for products with the word "butter" in the name so they can put together a weekly promotion for all these products. You will show them how to use a wildcard character to find the products.

To Use a Wildcard Character to Find a Record

a. Double-click **tblProduct** to open the table.

b. In the first record, click in the **ProductDescription** field. Click the Home tab, and then click **Find** in the Find group to open the Find and Replace dialog box. Replace the text in the Find What box with *butter*. Click the **Look In arrow**, and then click **Current field**.

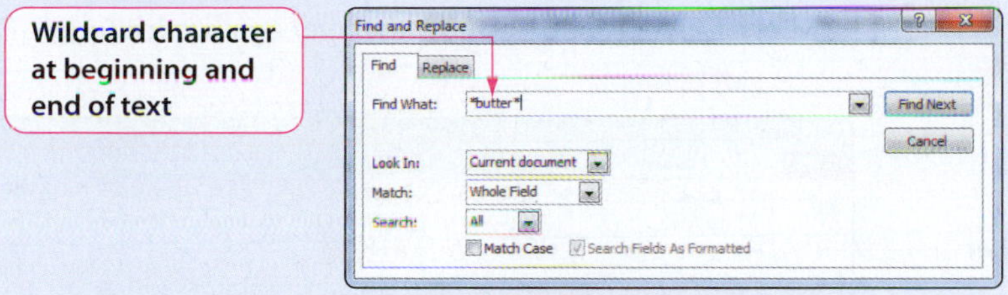

Wildcard character at beginning and end of text

Figure 4 Find records with "butter" in the ProductDescription field

c. Click **Find Next**. The first record found is for ProductID PO18 Cocoa Body Butter. Click **Find Next** again to find the record for ProductID P021 Lemon Body Butter.

d. Click **Find Next** again until Access has finished searching the records. When Access is done searching and cannot find any more matches, you will see the message Microsoft Access finished searching the records. The search item was not found. Click **OK**, and then click **Cancel** to close the Find and Replace dialog box.

e. **Close** ☒ the table.

SIDE NOTE
I Cannot See the Highlighted Record

If Access highlights a record in the table and you cannot see it, you may have to drag the Find and Replace dialog box to another area of the screen.

Apply a Filter to a Datasheet

A **filter** is a condition you apply temporarily to a table or query. All records that do not match the filter criteria are hidden until the filter is removed or the table is closed and reopened. A filter is a simple technique to quickly reduce a large amount of data to a much smaller subset of data. You can choose to save a table with the filter applied so when you open the table later the filter is still available.

You can filter a datasheet by selecting a value in a record and telling Access to filter records that contain some variation of the record you choose, or you can create a custom filter to select all or part of a field value.

Filtering by Selection

When you **filter by selection**, you select a value in a record and Access filters the records that contain only the values that match what you have selected. For this exercise, a customer came into the spa and stated that she was from Minnesota and had previously been a spa customer but was just browsing today. She left her glasses on the counter and the staff wants to return them to her. You will help the staff members find all customers from Minnesota to see if they can find the customer's name.

To Select Specific Records Using a Selection Filter

a. Double-click **tblCustomer** to open the table, locate the first record with an address in the state of Minnesota (MN), and then click in the **State** field. Click the Home tab, click **Selection** in the Sort & Filter group, and then choose the **Equals "MN"** option.

Access displays three records where all states are MN for Minnesota. Toggle Filter in the Sort & Filter group allows you to go back and forth between viewing the filtered records and all the records in the table. To remove the filter, click Toggle Filter in the Sort & Filter group. To show the filter again, click Toggle Filter in the Sort & Filter group.

Toggle Filter

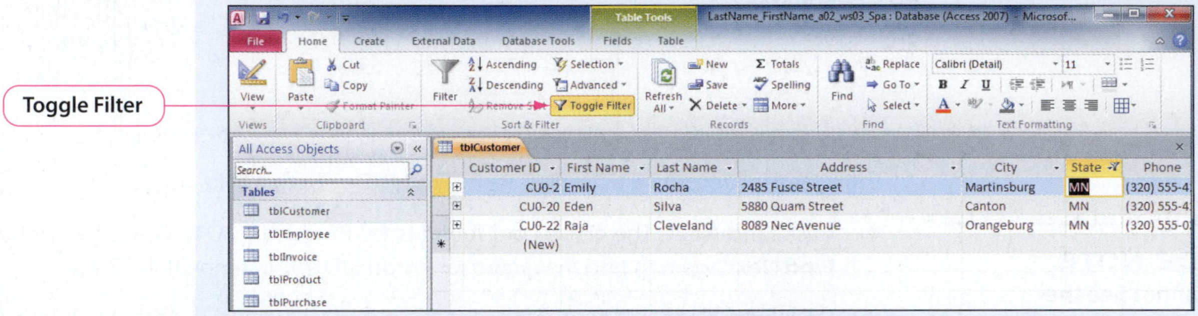

Figure 5 Filtered table for all records containing a state of MN

b. The filter is temporary unless you choose to save it with the table or query. If you do save it, the next time you open the table or query, you only have to click Toggle Filter to see the records from the state of Minnesota. To save the table with the filter, click **Save** 💾 on the Quick Access Toolbar. **Close** ✕ the table.

c. Double-click **tblCustomer** to open the table. Click the Home tab, click **Toggle Filter** in the Sort & Filter group to see the filtered records. **Close** ✕ the table.

SIDE NOTE

How to Clear a Filter

To delete a filter from the table, click Advanced in the Sort & Filter group, and select Clear all Filters.

Using a Text Filter

Text filters allow you to create a custom filter to match all or part of the text in a field that you specify. For this exercise, the staff wants to create a mailing of sample products but cannot send the products to customers with a post office box. You will help the staff find all customers who have P.O. Box as part of their address.

To Select Specific Records Using a Text Filter

a. Double-click **tblCustomer** to open the table. Select the entire **Address** column by clicking the column name. Click the **filter arrow** in the column heading, point to **Text Filters**, and then on the submenu, click **Begins With**.

b. In the Custom Filter box, type **P** and then click **OK**.

Access retrieves the nine records where the addresses contain a P.O. Box number. Notice that Toggle Filter in the Sort & Filter group is selected and the Filtered indicator in the Navigation bar is highlighted. You can toggle between the filtered table and the whole table by clicking on either Toggle Filter or the Filtered indicator.

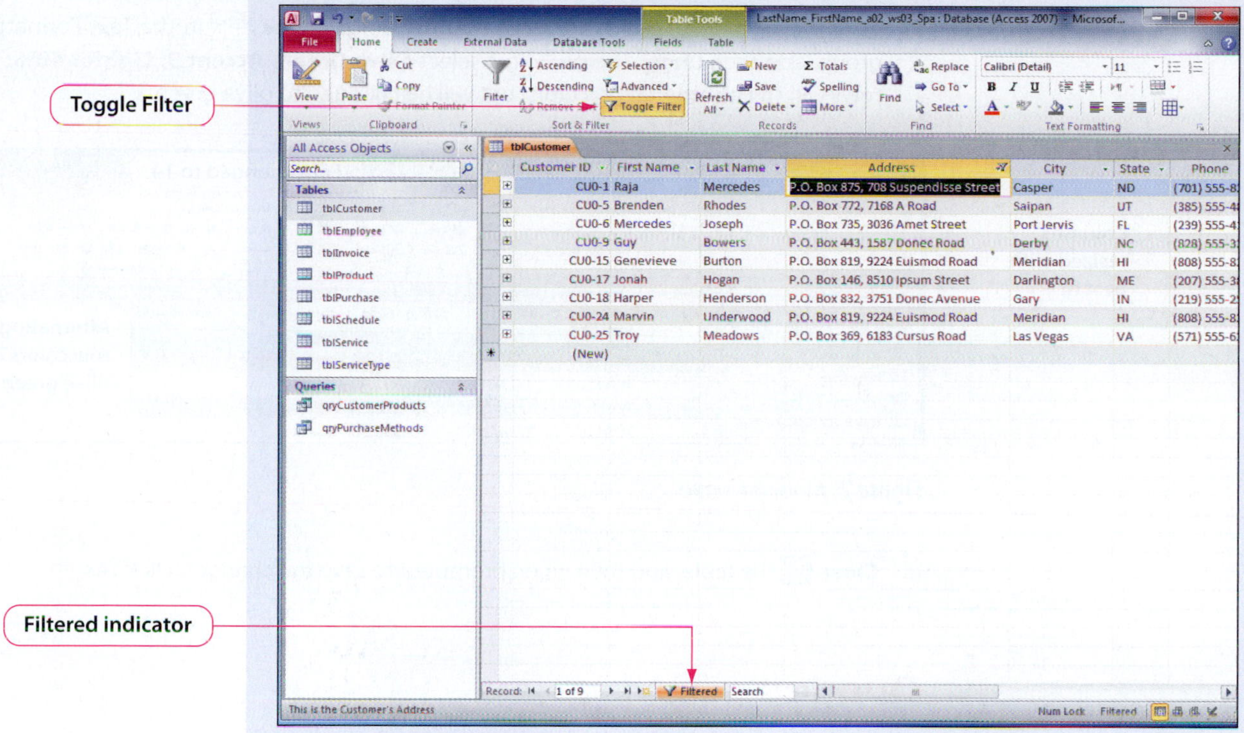

Toggle Filter

Filtered indicator

Figure 6 Results of the filter

c. Click **Save** 💾 on the Quick Access Toolbar to save the table with the new filter applied. **Close** ☒ the table.

Modify Datasheet Appearance

You can change the appearance of your datasheet by changing the font type, font size, column widths, and background colors to make it more readable. By changing the font size and column width of a table or query, you can often include more data on one page or see all the data in a particular field.

Changing the Look of a Datasheet

For this exercise, the manager is upset because the font is too small and she cannot see all the field headings in the invoice table. You will show her how to make the text larger and the column wider.

SIDE NOTE

The Invoice Table

The Invoice table tracks the balance due from a customer, not necessarily the total amount of charges incurred since some charges are billed directly to the customer's room.

SIDE NOTE

Alternate Method for Changing Column Width

You can also drag a column to make it wider.

To Change Font Size, Column Width, and Alternating Row Colors

a. Double-click **tblInvoice** to open the table.

b. Click the **Home tab**, click the **Font Size arrow** 11 ▾ in the Text Formatting group, and then click **14** to make the font size larger.

c. Point to the **right border** of the first field name and double-click. This resizes the column to best fit the data. Repeat this action for all the columns.

d. Click the Home tab, click the **Alternate Row Color arrow** ⊞ ▾ in the Text Formatting group, and then under Theme Colors select **Olive Green, Accent 3, Lighter 40%**. The rows will still be alternating colors, but will be changed to olive green.

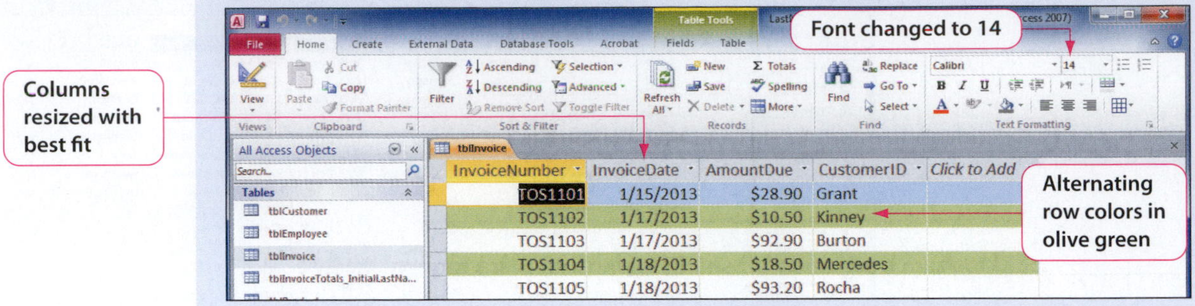

Figure 7 Modified table

e. **Close** ✕ the table, and then when prompted to save the changes, click **Yes**.

Queries

While the Find and Filter features can quickly help you find data, a query can be created for data that you may need to find again in the future. If you recall, the Simple Query Wizard is used to display fields from one or more tables or queries with the option to choose a detailed or summary query if working with more than one table. The Simple Query Wizard does not provide the opportunity to select data criteria.

Queries can also be created in Query Design view, which not only allows you to choose the tables and fields to include in the query, but also allows you to select criteria for the field values, create calculated fields, and select sorting options.

In this section, you will create and define selection criteria for queries, create aggregate functions and calculated fields as well as sort query results.

Run Other Query Wizards

Two other query wizards, Find Duplicates and Find Unmatched query wizards, allow you to find duplicate records or identify orphans by selecting criteria as part of the wizard steps. An **orphan** is a foreign key in one table that does not have a matching value in the primary key field of a related table.

Quick Reference

Cross-Tab, Find Duplicates, and Find Unmatched Queries

In addition to the Simple Query Wizard, there are three additional query wizards available to make quick, step-by-step queries.

1. **Cross-tab:** Used when you want to describe one field in terms of two or more other fields in the table. Example: summarizing information or calculating statistics on the fields in the table.

2. **Find Duplicates:** Used when you want to find records with the same specific value. Example: duplicate e-mail addresses in a customer database.

3. **Find Unmatched:** Used when you want to find the rows in one table that do not have a match in the other table. Example: identifying customers who currently have no open orders.

Creating a Find Duplicates Query

The Find Duplicates Query Wizard finds duplicate records in a table or a query. You select the fields that you think may include duplicate information, and the Wizard creates the query to find records matching your criteria.

For this exercise, the spa receptionist sends out mailings and reminders to its customers throughout the year. She wants to be able to prevent multiple mailings to the same address to help reduce costs. You will show her how she can use a Find Duplicates query to check for duplicate addresses.

To Find Duplicate Customer Information

a. Click the **Create tab**, and then click **Query Wizard** in the Queries group. Access displays the New Query dialog box and lists the different queries you can select.

b. Select **Find Duplicates Query Wizard**, and then click **OK**.

c. Select **Table:tblCustomer** as the table to search for duplicate field values, and then click **Next**.

d. Under Available fields, click **CustAddress**, and then click the **One Field** button > . Access moves the CustAddress field to the Duplicate-value fields list. This is the field you think may have duplicate data. Click **Next**.

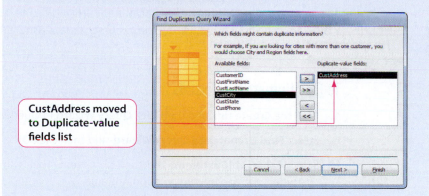

CustAddress moved to Duplicate-value fields list

Figure 8 Select the field that may have duplicate data

e. Click the **All Fields** button >> to move all available fields to the Additional query fields list in order to display all the fields in the query results. Click **Next**.

f. Under "What do you want to name your query?" type **qryDuplicateCustomers_Initial LastName**, replacing InitialLastName with your own first initial and last name, and then click **Finish**. The query should have two records with the same address.

Figure 9 Results from the Find Duplicates query

g. **Close** ✕ the query.

Creating a Find Unmatched Query

The Find Unmatched query is designed to find records in a table or query that have no related records in a second table or query. This can be very helpful if you are looking to contact inactive customers or mail a notice to past clients who are still listed in the database. The wizard uses the primary key from the first table and matches it with the foreign key in the second table in order to determine if there are unmatched records. If a one-to-many relationship exists between the two tables, then the Wizard will join the two correct fields automatically.

For this project, spa management would like to identify customers who have used the spa's services in the past but do not have a current appointment. This means a record for the customer would be listed in the customer table but not in the schedule table as shown in Figure 10.

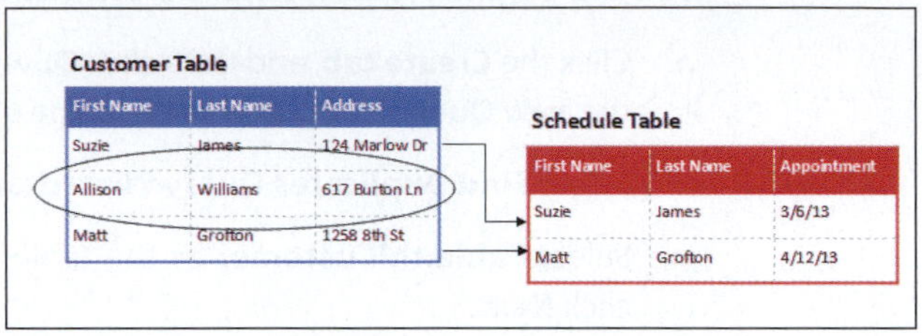

Figure 10 Tables in a Find Unmatched query

Notice Allison Williams is a past customer so she is listed in the customer table, but she does not have an appointment scheduled in the schedule table. Her record would be found in a Find Unmatched query comparing the customer and schedule table.

To Find Unmatched Records

a. Click the **Create tab**, and then click **Query Wizard** in Queries group.

b. Select **Find Unmatched Query Wizard**, and then click **OK**.

c. Select **Table: tblCustomer**, and then click **Next**. This is the table you think has past customers with no upcoming appointments.

d. Select **Table: tblSchedule**, and then click **Next**. This is the table that has customers with upcoming appointments you want to compare to the main tblCustomer table.

e. Under Fields in 'tblCustomer', verify **CustomerID** is selected and under Fields in 'tblSchedule', verify **Customer** is selected. This is the common field that the Wizard will use to compare the tables. Click **Next**.

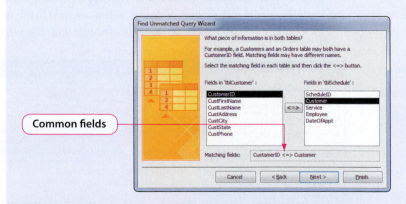

Figure 11 Compare the two tables using their common field

Troubleshooting

The wizard will try to match the primary key field and the foreign key field if there is a one-to-many relationship between the two tables. If there is not a one-to-many relationship, you can select the matching fields manually and use the ⟨=⟩ button to confirm the match. The matching fields will then appear at the bottom of the window in the Matching fields box.

f. Click the **All Fields** button ⟩⟩ to add all the fields to the query results table. Click **Next**.

g. Under "What would you like to name your query?" type **qryCustomersWithout Appointments_InitialLastName**, replacing InitialLastName with your own first initial and last name, and click **Finish**. You should see the names and e-mails of three customers who do not currently have appointments at the spa including yourself. **Close** ✕ the query.

Create Queries in Design View

The query wizards work by prompting you to answer a series of questions about the tables and fields to display and then creating the query based upon your responses. Alternatively, you can use Design view to manually create queries. The query window in Design view allows you to specify the data you want to see by building a **query by example**. A query by example provides a sample of the data you want to see in the results. Access takes that sample of data and finds records in the tables you specify that match the example. In the query window, you can include specific fields, define criteria, sort records, and perform calculations. When you use the query window, you have more control and more options available to manage the details of the query design than with the Simple Query Wizard.

When you open Design view, by default, the Show Table dialog box opens with a list of available tables and queries to add. You can either select a table name and click Add, or you can double-click the table name. Either way the table will be added to the Query window. If the Show Table dialog box is closed, you can drag a table or query from the Navigation Pane to the Query window to add it to the query.

The next step in building your query is to add the fields you want to include from the various tables selected to the query design grid. There are a number of ways to add fields to the query design grid as shown in Figure 12.

Action	Description
Drag	Once you click the field name, drag it to any empty column in the query design grid.
Double-click field name	Double-click the field name to add it to the first empty column in the query design grid.
Select from drop-down list	Click in the first row of any empty column, click the selection arrow, and select the field name from the list.
Double-click the title bar	Double-click the title bar for the table with the fields you want to add and all the fields will be selected. Drag the fields to the first empty column.
Click, Shift, Click	Click on a field name, press and hold down the Shift key, and click another name to select a range of field names. Drag the selected fields to the query design grid.

Figure 12 Methods to add fields to a query design grid

If you add a field to the wrong column in the query design grid, you can delete the column and add it again, or you can drag it to another position in the grid.

All fields that have values you want included in a query—either for the criteria or to show in the results—must be added to the query design grid. For example, you may want to find all customers from New Mexico, but not necessarily show the state field in the query results. You can use the Show check box to indicate which fields to show in the results and which fields not to show.

Real World Advice — Increasing Privacy Concerns

There are many instances where the person running the query does not have the right to see confidential information in the database. An example of this is Social Security numbers. Although companies are doing away with this practice, many existing databases still use Social Security numbers as a unique identifier. You can include a Social Security number in query criteria, but uncheck the Show box so the actual value does not show in the query results.

Creating a Single-Table Query

A single-table query is a query that is based on only one table in your database.

For this exercise, the manager of the spa needs your help to print out a price list for all the products. She only wants to see the product description, size, and price for each product, and she wants to see all the records. You will show her how to add only the fields she wants to the query.

To Create a Single-Table Query

a. Click the **Create tab**, and then click **Query Design** in the Queries group to open the query window with the Show Table dialog box.

b. In the Show Table dialog box, click **tblProduct**, and then click **Add**. Click **Close** to close the Show Table dialog box.

c. Double-click **ProductDescription** to add it to the first column of the query design grid. Repeat for **Price** and **Size**.

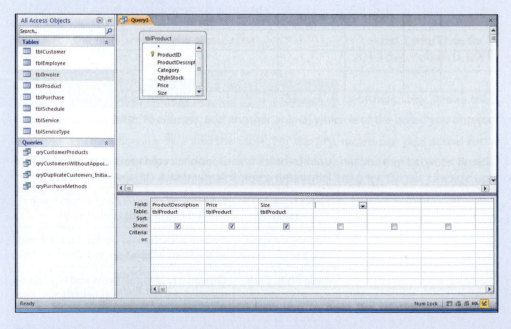

Figure 13 Fields from tblProduct added to the query design grid

Troubleshooting

If you cannot see the query design grid at the bottom of the query design window, use the pointer ⊞ to drag the top border of the grid up.

---

d. Click the Query Tools Design tab, and then click **Run** in the Results group to run the query. You should have 25 records showing the ProductDescription, Price, and Size fields.

e. Click the Home tab, click **View arrow** in the View group, and then click **Design View**. To move the Size field to the left of the Price field, click the **top border** of the Size field to highlight the column. Again pointing to the top border of the field, drag the **Size field** to the left of the ProductDescription field. Click **Run** in the Results groups to run the query again. The query will still have 25 records, but the field order will be Size, ProductDescription, and Price.

f. Click **Save** 🖫 on the Quick Access Toolbar. In the Save As box, type **qryProductPriceList_ InitialLastName**, replacing InitialLastName with your own first initial and last name, and then click **OK**. **Close** ✕ the query.

Real World Example The Importance of Knowing Your Data

Many times databases are shared by many users. Different people may enter data differently causing errors or inconsistency. Inconsistent data entry can affect the validity of query results. By misspelling a value or abbreviating a value that should be spelled out, a query may not find the record when it searches using criteria. You must know what your data looks like when you create queries. A quick scan of the records, or using Find with a wildcard for certain values, may help you find misspellings or other data entry errors before you run your query.

Having some idea of what the query results should look like will also help make sure your query has found the right record set. For example, if you query all customers from New Mexico and think there should be a dozen, but your query shows 75, you should check your table records and your query criteria to see why there might be such a big discrepancy from what you expected.

Viewing Table Relationships

A multiple-table query retrieves information from more than one table or query. For Access to perform this type of query, it must be able to "connect" tables using a common field that exists in both tables.

If two tables do not have a common field, Access will join the two tables by combining the records, regardless of whether they have a matching field. This is called the multiplier effect. For example, if one table has 100 records and another table also has 100 records, and if these two tables do not have a common field, all records in the first table will be matched with all records in the second table for a total of 10,000 records!

You can view how your tables are related in the Relationships window. The lines connecting the tables represent relationships. The field that the line is pointing to in each table represents the common field between the tables. It is helpful to understand how tables are related before you try and create a multiple table query.

To View Table Relationships

a. Click the **Database Tools tab**, and then click **Relationships** in the Relationships group. Click the **Shutter Bar Open/Close** button ⟨«⟩ to hide the Navigation Pane and display the whole Relationships window. Take a moment to study the table relationships.

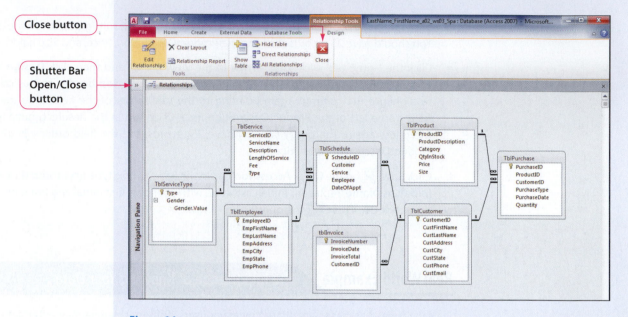

Figure 14 Spa Database table relationships

b. Click the Relationship Tools Design tab, and then click **Close** in the Relationships group to close the Relationships window. Click the **Shutter Bar Open/Close** button ⟨»⟩ to show the Navigation Pane again.

Real World Advice   Which Tables to Choose?

You should only select the tables you need when creating a query in the query window. Access treats all the tables selected as part of the query when it executes the query, which means unnecessary tables added to the query may cause performance problems. Best practice is to do the following:

- Understand the table structure and relationships before you construct your query—refer to the relationships window often.
- Only choose those tables you need data from.
- If no data from a table is needed, do not add the table. The exception to this rule is if a table is required to link the many-to-many relationship together. In other words, no table will be left unconnected and tables can be added to create that connection.

Creating a Query from Multiple Tables

All tables added to a query should be connected by relationships and have a common field. For this project, the staff would like to see one table that includes the services scheduled for each employee. tblEmployee includes the employee names, and tblSchedule lists the services scheduled for each employee. You will create a query that combines the two tables into one query.

SIDE NOTE
Adding Tables from the Navigation Pane
Remember, in addition to selecting tables from the Show Table dialog box, you can also add tables to the query by dragging them from the Navigation Pane.

SIDE NOTE
Only Add Necessary Tables
Adding a table to a query without adding fields will change the query results, although the results may not make any sense. Be sure to add only those tables that have fields you are going to use to a query.

To Create a Query from Multiple Tables

a. Click the **Create tab**, click **Query Design** in the Queries group, click **tblEmployee**, and then click **Add**. Close the Show Table dialog box.

b. Double-click **EmpFirstName** and **EmpLastName** in that order to add the fields to the query design grid.

c. Click the Query Tools Design tab, and then click **Run** in the Results group. Notice there are 14 employees' records.

d. Click the **Home tab**, click **View arrow** in the View group, and then click **Design View**. From the Navigation Pane, drag **tblSchedule** to the Query window. Click the **Query Tools Design tab**, and then click **Run** in the Results group to run the query again.

   Scroll through the table and notice there are 53 records in the query results now. Employee names have been matched up with each scheduled service, of which there are 53, but you cannot see any information about the services because no fields from that table have been added.

e. Click the **Home tab**, click **View arrow** in the Views group, and then click **Design View**. In the tblSchedule table, in the following order, double-click **Service**, **DateOfAppt**, and **Customer** to add the fields to the query design grid. Click the **Design tab**, and then click **Run** in the Results group to run the query.

   Notice there are 53 records again for each service scheduled, but now the detail for those services are included in the query because you added the fields to the query design grid.

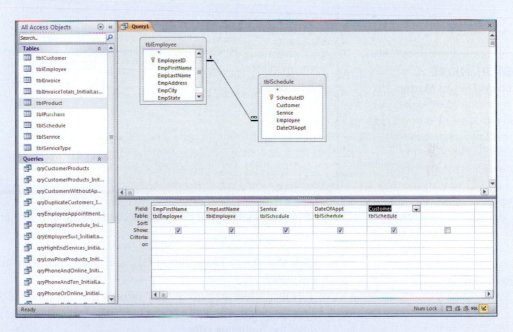

Figure 15 Query window for multiple-table query

f. Click **Save** 💾 on the Quick Access Toolbar, under Query Name type **qryEmployee Schedule_InitialLastName** replacing InitialLastname with your own first initial and last name, and then click **OK**. **Close** ✕ the query.

Correcting the Multiplier Effect

When two tables without a common field are used in a query, you will see the multiplier effect. For this exercise, someone in the spa wanted to find out all the products that were purchased by each customer, so they created a multiple table query using two tables without a common field. One table has 25 records and the other has 26, so the multiplier effect caused the query result to have 650 records! You will run their query and then fix it so the information they want can be found.

To Correct a Multiplier Effect

a. Double-click **qryCustomerProducts** to run the query. Notice there are 650 records because every customer name is matched up with every product.

b. Click the **Home tab**, click the **View arrow** in the Views group, and then click **Design View**. Notice there is no relationship between tblProduct and tblCustomer. On the Navigation Pane, drag **tblPurchase** into the query window. Now there should be relationships between all three tables.

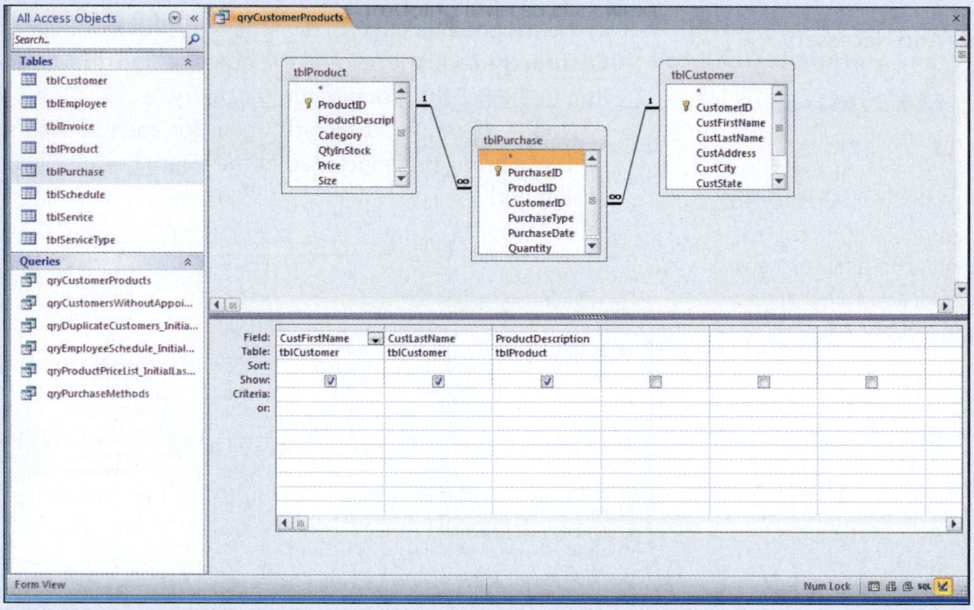

SIDE NOTE
Looks Do Not Matter

Where the tables are laid out in the query window will not affect how the tables are related or added to the query. You can even move the tables by dragging the title bar of each table to a new location. If it is hard to see how the tables are related, move the table windows until the relationship lines are untangled.

Figure 16 Three tables added to the query window, all with relationships

c. Click the Query Tools Design tab, and then click **Run** in the Results group to run the query.

   Notice there are now only 27 records that the tables all connect with relationships. Simply adding the table in the middle to establish the many-to-many relationship gets rid of the multiplier effect.

d. Click the **File tab**, click **Save Object As**, under Save qryCustomerProducts type **qryCustomerProducts_InitialLastName** replacing InitialLastname with your own first initial and last name, and then click **OK**. Click the **Home tab**, and then **close** ✕ the query.

Define Selection Criteria for Queries

Databases, including Access, provide a robust set of selection criteria that you can use to make your queries well focused. You can use the different kinds of operators described below to choose criteria for one or more fields in one or more tables.

Using a Comparison Operator

Comparison operators compare the values in a table or another query to the criteria value you set up in a query. The different comparison operators, descriptions, and examples are shown in Figure 17. Comparison operators are generally used with numbers and dates to find a range or a specific value. Equal to and Not equal to can also be used with text to find an exact match to criteria. For example, to find all states that are not NY you could enter < >"NY" for the state criteria.

Operator	Description	Example
=	Equal to	=100
< =	Less than or equal to	<=100
<	Less than	<100
>	Greater than	>100
> =	Greater than or equal to	>=100
< >	Not equal to	< >100

Figure 17 Comparison operators

For this project, the manager of the spa wants to see all products $10 and under so she can plan an upcoming special on the spa's lower-priced products. You will show her how to use a comparison operator in a query to find those products.

To Use a Comparison Operator in a Query

a. Click the **Create tab**, click **Query Design** in the Queries group, click **tblProduct**, and then click **Add**. Click **Close** to close the Show Table dialog box.

b. In the following order, double-click **ProductID**, **ProductDescription**, **Size**, **Category**, **QtyInStock**, and **Price** to add the fields to the query design grid.

c. Click in the **Criteria** row for the Price field and type <=10.

d. Click the Query Tools Design tab, and then click **Run** in the Results group to run the query. The results should show six records all with prices $10 or less.

e. Click **Save** 🖫 on the Quick Access Toolbar, under Query Name type **qryLowPrice Products_InitialLastName** replacing InitialLastName with your own first initial and last name, and then click **OK**. **Close** ✕ the query.

SIDE NOTE
Formatting Criteria

Text is identified by quotation marks around it and dates with # in front of and at the end of the date. For example, 1/1/16 would appear as #1/1/16#. Access adds the necessary quotation marks and pound signs, but it is a good idea to double check.

Hiding Fields That Are Used in a Query

For a field to be used in a query, it must be added to the query grid. If you just want to use the field to define criteria but do not want to see the results of that field in the query, it cannot be removed from the query grid, but it can be hidden from the results.

For this project, the manager is happy with the results of the Low Price Products query you created above, but she would like to post a list of the products without the prices so she can advertise the list as all under $10. You tell her that is possible by using the Show check box in the query design grid.

To Use a Field Value in a Query but Not Show the Field in the Results

a. Click the **Create tab**, click **Query Design** in the Queries group, click **tblProduct**, and then click **Add**. Click **Close** to close the Show Table dialog box.

b. Double-click **ProductID**, **ProductDescription**, **Size**, **Category**, **QtyInStock**, and **Price** in that order to add them to the query design grid.

c. Click in the **Criteria** row for the Price field, type **<=10**, and then click the **Show** check box to remove the check mark in the Price field.

d. Click the Query Tools Design tab, and then click **Run** in the Results group to run the query. The results should show the same six records you found in the previous query, but without the price field showing.

e. Click **Save** 💾 on the Quick Access Toolbar, under Query Name type **qryTenAndUnder_ InitialLastName** replacing InitialLastName with your own first initial and last name, and then click **OK**. **Close** ✕ the query.

Using the AND Logical Operator

When you create a query, you can select criteria for one field or for multiple fields. If you use multiple criteria, then you must also use **logical operators** to combine these criteria. Logical operators are operators that allow you to combine two or more criteria. For example, if you want a record selected when both criteria are met, then you would use the AND logical operator, but if you want a record selected if only one of the criteria is met, then you would use the OR logical operator. For an even more advanced query, you can combine the AND and the OR logical operators.

When you want to specify multiple criteria, and all criteria must be true for a record to be included in the results, then the AND logical operator is used, and the criteria must be in the same Criteria row in the query design grid. Access will look at the first field in the query design grid for criteria and continue moving from left to right looking for criteria. When criteria are in the same row, all criteria must match for the record to be included in the query results. For this project, you want to help the manager narrow down a sales strategy. She is trying to determine which customers place phone orders for products over $10.

To Use the AND Logical Operator

a. Click the **Create tab**, click **Query Design** in the Queries group, and then double-click **tblProduct**, **tblPurchase**, and **tblCustomer** to add the tables to the query window. Click **Close** to close the Show Table dialog box.

b. In the following order, double-click **PurchaseType** from tblPurchase, **ProductDescription** and **Price** from tblProduct, and **CustFirstName** and **CustLastName** from tblCustomer to add them to the query design grid.

c. Click in the **Criteria** row for the PurchaseType field, type **Phone**, and then for the Price field type **>10**.

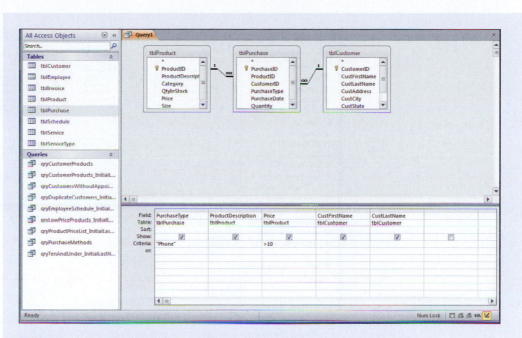

Figure 18 Criteria added for PurchaseType and Price fields

d. Click the **Query Tools Design tab**, and then click **Run** in the Results group to run the query. The results show five records, with Phone as the Purchase Type and a price greater than $10.

e. Click **Save** 🖫 on the Quick Access Toolbar, under Query Name type **qryPhoneAndTen_ InitialLastName** replacing InitialLastName with your own first initial and last name, and then click **OK. Close** ✕ the query.

Using the OR Logical Operator

When you want to specify criteria in multiple fields, and at least one of the criteria must be true for a record to be included in the results, then the OR logical operator is used, and the criteria must be in different Criteria rows in the query design grid. Access will look at the first field in the first Criteria row for criteria and continue moving from left to right, then it will start at the left again on the next criteria row which is labeled "or". For this exercise, you want to help the manager find all customers who make purchases either by phone or online.

To Use the OR Logical Operator

a. Click the **Create tab**, click **Query Design** in the Queries group, and double-click **tblProduct**, **tblPurchase**, and **tblCustomer** to add the tables to the query. Click **Close** to close the Show Table dialog box.

b. Double-click **PurchaseType** from tblPurchase, double-click **ProductDescription** from tblProduct, and then double-click **CustFirstName** and **CustLastName** from tblCustomer in that order to add them to the query design grid.

c. Click in the **Criteria** row for the PurchaseType field, type **Phone**. In the **or** row just below the Criteria line in the PurchaseType field, type **Online**.

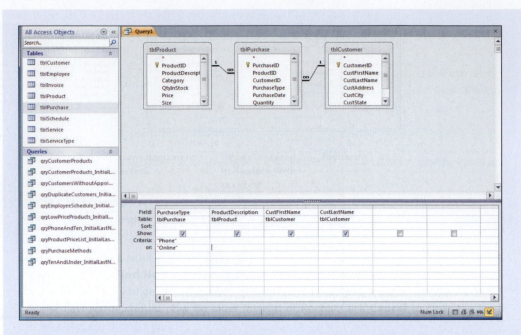

Figure 19 Two criteria added for PurchaseType

d. Click the **Design tab**, and then click **Run** in the Results group to run the query. The results should show 12 records, all with Phone or Online as the purchase type.

e. Click **Save** 🖫 on the Quick Access Toolbar, name the query **qryPhoneOrOnline_ InitialLastName** replacing InitialLastName with your own first initial and last name, and then click **OK**. **Close** ⊠ the query.

Combining the AND and OR Logical Operators

There may be times when you want to use two logical operators, AND and OR, at the same time. Depending on the desired results, you may have to use one or both Criteria rows. If you use both Criteria rows for criteria for two fields, then Access treats it like two AND logical operators and one OR logical operator. For this project, the manager wants you to find all phone purchase types for products over $10 or all online purchase types for products under $10.

To Combine the AND and the OR Logical Operator

a. Click the **Create tab**, click **Query Design** in the Queries group, and then double-click **tblProduct**, **tblPurchase**, and **tblCustomer** to add the tables to the query. Click **Close** to close the Show Table dialog box.

b. Double-click **PurchaseType** from tblPurchase, double-click **ProductDescription** and **Price** from tblProduct, and then double-click **CustFirstName** and **CustLastName** from tblCustomer in that order to add them to the query design grid.

c. Click in the **Criteria** row for the PurchaseType field, type **Phone** and then in the same **Criteria** row for the Price field, type **>10**. In the **or** row below the Criteria row, type **Online** for the PurchaseType field, and then in the same **or** row type **<10** for the Price field.

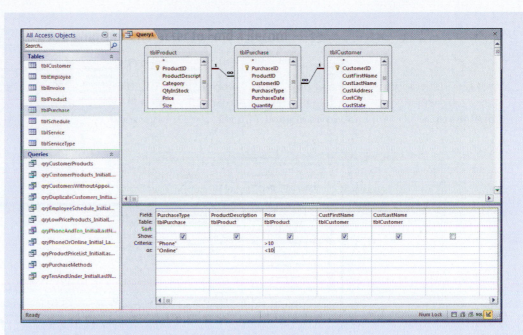

Figure 20 Two Criteria rows added for PurchaseType and Price

d. Click the **Design tab**, and then click **Run** in the Results group to run the query. The results should show seven records, all with Phone purchase types with prices greater than $10 or Online purchase types with prices less than $10.

e. Click **Save** 🖫 on the Quick Access Toolbar, name the query **qryPhoneAndOnline_InitialLastName** replacing InitialLastName with your own first initial and last name, and then click **OK. Close** ☒ the query.

Combining Multiple AND and OR Logical Operators

You cannot always use two rows for the OR criteria when you combine both logical operators. In cases like this, the word "or" can be used for two criteria used in the same field and the same Criteria row. For this project, the manager of the spa wants you to find all phone and online purchase types for products over $10. If you put the purchase type criteria on two rows and the price of >10 in one row, your results will show all records with phone purchase types over $10 *or* Online purchase types of any amount. Remember, Access moved left to right on the first criteria so it will treat "Phone" and >10 as AND criteria and then move to the next row, which it will consider OR criteria.

To Combine Multiple AND and OR Logical Operators

a. Click the **Create tab**, click **Query Design** in the Queries group, and then double-click **tblProduct**, **tblPurchase**, and **tblCustomer** to add the tables to the query. Click **Close** to close the Show Table dialog box.

b. In the following order, double-click **PurchaseType** from tblPurchase, **Product Description** and **Price** from tblProduct, and **CustFirstName** and **CustLastName** from tblCustomer to add them to the query design grid.

c. Click in the **Criteria** row for the PurchaseType field, type **Phone**, and then in the **Criteria** row for the Price field type **>10**. In the **or** row for the PurchaseType field type **Online**.

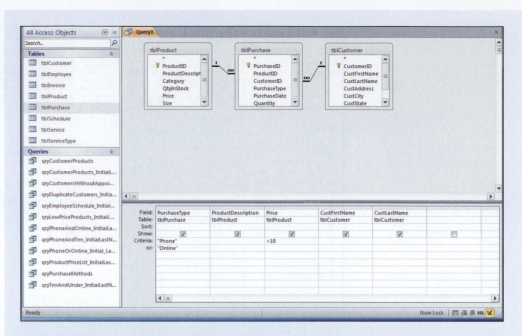

Figure 21 AND and OR criteria added to the query design grid

d. Click the Query Tools Design tab, and then click **Run** in the Results group to run the query. Notice the results are all Phone purchase types with prices over $10 or all Online purchase types, regardless of the price. The manager wants to see Phone or Online purchase types over $10, so this is not correct.

e. Click the Home tab, click the **View arrow**, and then click **Design View**. In the **or** row for PurchaseType field, delete Online. Click in the **Criteria** row for the PurchaseType field, and change the criteria to **Phone or Online**. Click the **Design tab**, and then click **Run** in the Results group to run the query again. The results should now show Phone or Online purchase types that are over $10.

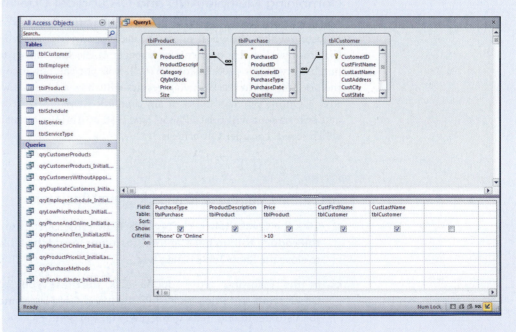

Figure 22 OR criteria in one row with AND criteria

f. Click **Save** 🖫 on the Quick Access Toolbar, under Query Name type **qryPhoneOr OnlineOverTen_InitialLastName** replacing InitialLastName with your own first initial and last name, and click **OK. Close** ☒ the query.

Combining Operators and Multiple Criteria

The more criteria added to your query means the more difficult it will be to see if you have the correct results. With multiple criteria, it is good practice to add one criteria, run the query to make sure you are getting the correct results, and then continue adding criteria one at a time.

For this project, the spa manager would like to see all of her high-end services listed by price and then service type, and she would like to break down the criteria as follows: Beauty or Waxing services $50 or more, Facial or Microdermabrasion services over $55, Beauty or Waxing services over $45, and all Botanical Hair & Scalp Therapy services.

To Combine Operators and Multiple Criteria

a. Click the **Create tab**, click **Query Design** in the Queries group, and double-click **tblService** to add the table to the query window. Click **Close** to close the Show Table dialog box.

b. In the following order, double-click **Fee**, **Type**, and **ServiceName** to add the fields to the query design grid.

c. Click in the **Criteria** row for the Fee field, type **>55**, and then in the **Criteria** row for the Type field type Facial or Microdermabrasion.

d. Click the Query Tools Design tab, and then click **Run** in the Results group to run the query. The results should show six records with Facial or Microdermabrasion for the Type field, and all values in the Fee field should be greater than $55.

e. Click the Home tab, click the **View arrow** in the Views group, and then click **Design View**. In the **or** row for the Fee field, type **>=50**, and for the **or** row for the Type field type Hands & Feet or Body Massage. Click the **Design tab**, and then click **Run** in the Results group to run the query again.

The query results should show 19 records with types Facial or Microdermabrasion that have fees greater than $55, and records with types Hands & Feet or Body Massage that have fees greater than or equal to $50.

Troubleshooting

If you enter the value Hands & Feet in the Type field without quotation marks, then Access will add those quotation marks for you. In this case, Access evaluates the ampersand character (&) as separating two values, so it will put the quotation marks around the word "Hands" and around the word "Feet" so it will look like "Hands" & "Feet". This is different than having the quotations around the whole phrase, which is what you want it to look like. In this case you should put the quotation marks around the phrase in order for it to look like "Hands & Feet".

f. Click the Home tab, click the **View arrow** in the Views group, and then click **Design View**. Click in the third **Criteria** row for the Fee field, type **>45**, and then in the **Criteria** row the **Type** field type Beauty or Waxing. Click the **Design tab**, and then click **Run** in the Results group to run the query again.

The results should show 23 records with types Facial or Microdermabrasion that have fees greater than $55, and records with types Hands & Feet or Body Massage that have fees greater than or equal to $50, and records with types Beauty or Waxing that have fees greater than $45.

SIDE NOTE

Wider Columns

If you cannot see all the text you are entering in a column on the query design grid, you can point to the right border of the column selector bar and double-click to best fit the data. This is similar to making a column wider in Datasheet view.

g. Click the Home tab, click the **View arrow** in the Views group, and then click **Design View**. Click in the **Criteria** row for the Type field and type **Botanical Hair & Scalp Therapy**, Click the **Design tab**, and then click **Run** in the Results group to run the query again.

The results should show 25 records with types Facial or Microdermabrasion that have fees greater than $55, records with types Hands & Feet or Body Massage that have fees greater than or equal to $50, records with types Beauty or Waxing that have fees greater than $45, and all Botanical Hair & Scalp Therapy types.

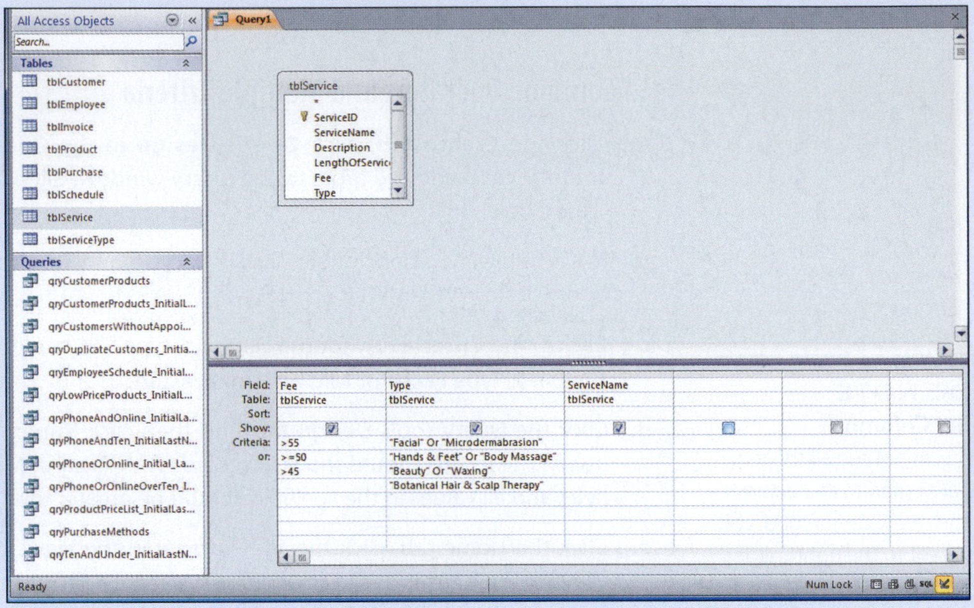

Figure 23 All criteria added to query design grid

h. Click **Save** 💾 on the Quick Access Toolbar, name the query **qryHighEndService_ InitialLastName** replacing InitialLastName with your own first initial and last name, and then click **OK. Close** ✕ the query.

Using Special Operators

Special operators are used to compare text values using wildcards (LIKE) or to determine whether values are between a range of values (BETWEEN). Commonly used special operators are shown in Figure 24.

Operator	Description
LIKE	Matches text values by using wildcards
BETWEEN	Determines if a number or date is within a range
IN	Determines if a value is found within a set of values

Figure 24 Special operators

The BETWEEN special operator will return results that include and fall between the criteria you enter. If you recall, when working with dates as criteria, a # in front of and at the end of each date is required to identify the numbers as dates and not a string of text.

For this project, the manager of the spa would like you to find all weekday services scheduled from Monday, January 14, through Friday, January 18, 2013, along with the customer who is scheduled for that service.

To Use the BETWEEN Special Operator

a. Click the **Create tab**, click **Query Design** in the Queries group, and then double-click **tblSchedule** and **tblCustomer** to add the tables to the query. Click **Close** to close the Show Table dialog box.

b. Double-click **Service**, **Employee**, and **DateOfAppt** from tblSchedule, and then double-click **CustFirstName** and **CustLastName** from tblCustomer in that order to add them to the query design grid.

c. Click in the **Criteria** row for the DateOfAppt field and type **Between 1/14/13 and 1/18/13**.

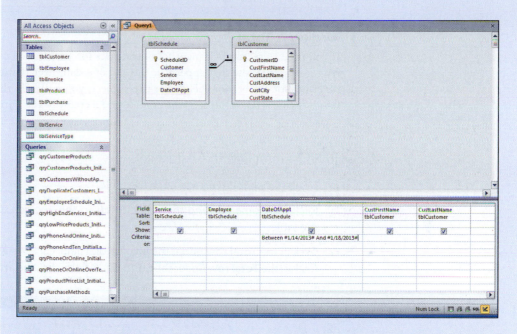

Figure 25 Criteria added for DateOfAppt

SIDE NOTE

Formatting Criteria

While it is a good habit to remember to put the pound signs around a date or the quotation marks around text, if you forget, Access will add them for you.

d. Click the Query Tools Design tab, and then click **Run** in the Results group to run the query. The results should show 31 records all with a date between January 14 and January 18, 2013.

e. Click **Save** 💾 on the Quick Access Toolbar, under Query Name type **qryWeekdayDates_InitialLastName** replacing InitialLastName with your own first initial and last name, and then click **OK. Close** ✖ the query.

Create Aggregate Functions

Aggregate functions perform arithmetic operations, such as calculating averages and totals, on records displayed in a table or query. An aggregate function can be used in Datasheet view by adding a total row to a table, or it can be used in a query on records that meet certain criteria.

Quick Reference — Commonly Used Aggregate Functions

There are a number of different aggregate functions that can be used depending on the type of calculation you want to perform.

1. **Sum:** Calculates the total value for selected records
2. **Average:** Calculates the average value for selected records
3. **Count:** Displays the number of records retrieved
4. **Minimum:** Displays the smallest value from the selected records
5. **Maximum:** Displays the largest value from the selected records

Adding a Total Row

If you need to see a quick snapshot of statistics for a table, you can use the total row. The **total row** is a special row that appears at the end of a datasheet that enables you to show aggregate functions for one or more fields. For this project, you will help the manager quickly find a total for all invoices listed in the invoices table and a count of the number of invoices in the table.

To Add a Total Row to a Datasheet

a. Double-click **tblInvoice** to open the table.

b. Click the Home tab, and then click **Totals** in the Records group to add a total row to the table.

c. Click in the **Total row** under the InvoiceTotal field, click the **arrow**, and then select **Sum**. Click in the **Total row** under the CustomerID field, click the **arrow**, and then select **Count**.

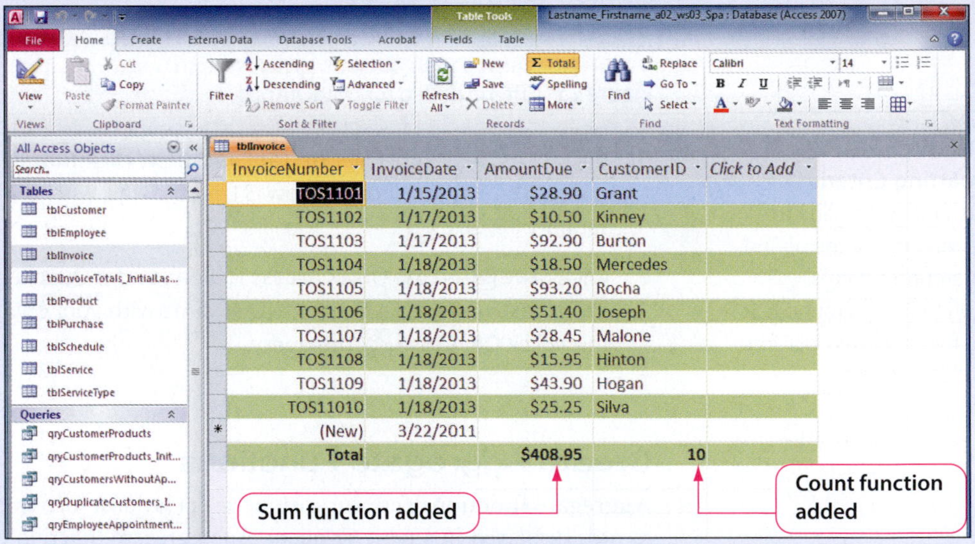

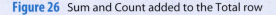

Figure 26 Sum and Count added to the Total row

d. Click the **File tab**, click **Save Object As**, in the Save 'tblInvoice' to text box type **tblInvoiceTotals_InitialLastName** replacing InitialLastName with your own first initial and last name, and then click **OK**. **Close** ☒ the table.

SIDE NOTE

Removing a Total Row

To remove the total row, on the Home tab, click Totals.

Using Aggregate Functions in a Query

Aggregate functions can be used in queries to perform calculations on selected fields and records. One advantage to using aggregate functions in queries, rather than just a total row, is that you can group criteria and then calculate the aggregate functions for a group of records. By default, the query design grid does not have a place to enter aggregate functions, so the total row must be added from the Design tab. Each column or field can calculate only one aggregate function, so to calculate multiple functions on the same field, the field must be added to the grid multiple times.

For this project, you have been asked to come up with a statistical summary of the spa's products prices. The manager would like to see how many products are offered, what the average product price is, and the minimum and maximum product prices.

To Use Aggregate Functions in a Query

a. Click the **Create tab**, click **Query Design** in the Queries group, and double-click **tblProduct** to add the table to the query. Click **Close** to close the Show Table dialog box.

b. Double-click **Price** four times to add the field four times to the query design grid.

c. Click the Query Tools Design tab, and then click **Totals** in the Show/Hide group to add a total row to the query design grid.

d. In the first Price column, click in the **Total** row, click the **arrow**, and then select **Count**. In the second Price column, in the **Total** row, click the **arrow**, and then select **Avg**. Repeat for the next two **Price** columns selecting **Min** for the third column and **Max** for the last column.

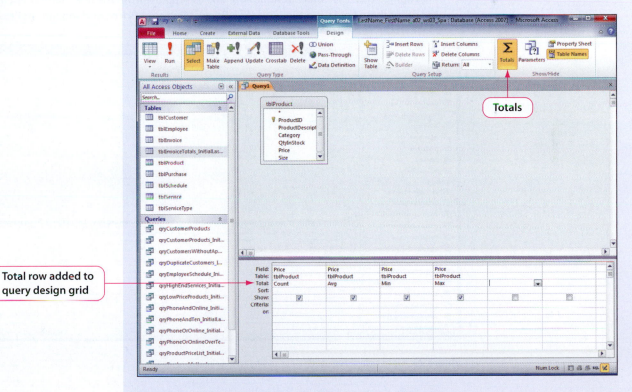

Figure 27 Aggregate functions selected for each column

e. Click the Query Tools Design tab, and then click **Run** in the Results group to run the query. Since this is an aggregate query and you are calculating one statistic per column, there will only be one record in the results.

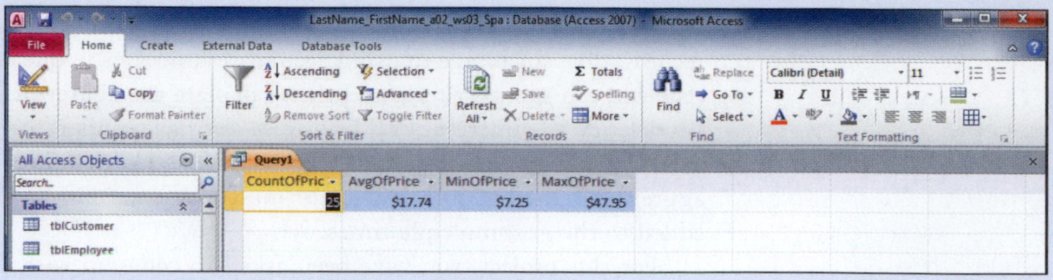

Figure 28 Aggregate query results

Changing Field Names

The field names assigned in an aggregate query can easily be changed either before or after the query is run. However, you must keep the field name in the query design grid so Access knows what field to perform the calculation on. For this project, you will change the names of the fields in the aggregate query you just created.

To Change the Field Names in an Aggregate Query

a. Click the Home tab, click the **View arrow** in the Views group, and then click **Design View**.

b. Click in the **Field** row of the first column, and then press [Home] to move the insertion point to the beginning of the field name. Type **Count of Products:**. Do not delete the field name Price. The colon identifies the title as separate from the field name. Repeat for the other three fields and type **Average Price:**, **Minimum Price:**, and **Maximum Price:**.

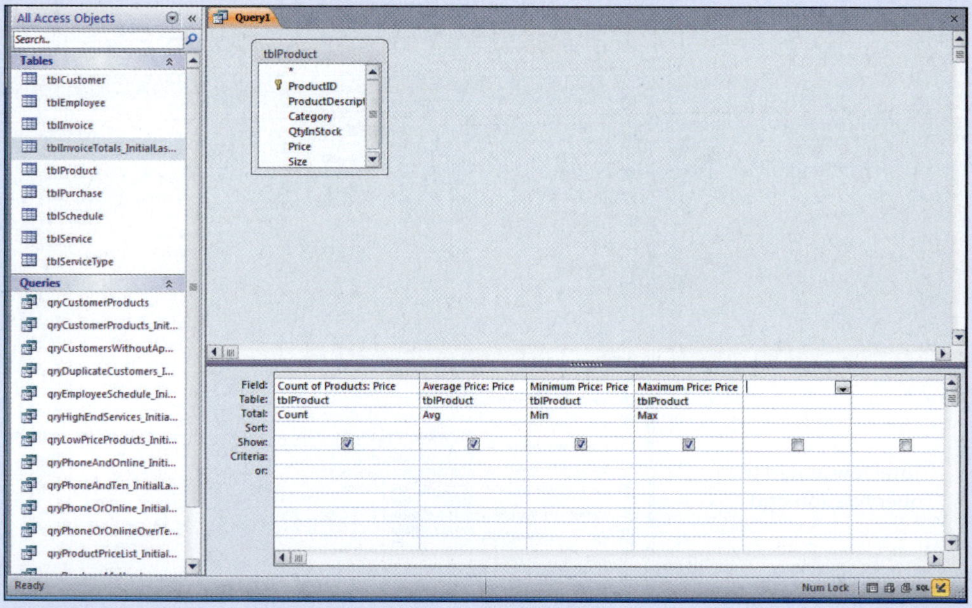

Figure 29 Field titles changed

c. Click the Query Tools Design tab, and then click **Run** in the Results group to run the query. Resize the columns to see the complete column names.

d. Click **Save** 📑 on the Quick Access Toolbar, under Query name type **qryProductStatistics_InitialLastName** replacing InitialLastName with your own first initial and last name, and then click **OK**. **Close** ✖ the query.

Creating Calculations for Groups of Records

Not only can you find statistics information on selected records using aggregate functions in a query, or for all records using the total row, you can also calculate statistics for groups of records. Creating a group to calculate statistics for works the same way as an aggregate query but must include the field to group by. The additional field will not have a statistic selected for the total row, but instead have the default Group By entered in the total row.

For this exercise, you will help the spa manager find the same product price statistics you calculated above but this time grouped by product category.

To Create a Group Calculation

a. Click the **Create tab**, click **Query Design** in the Queries group, and then double-click **tblProduct** to add the table to the query. Click **Close** to close the Show Table dialog box.

b. Double-click **Category** to add it to the query design grid, and then double-click **Price** four times to add the field four times to the query design grid.

c. Click the Query Tools Design tab, and then click **Totals** in the Show/Hide group to add a total row to the query design grid.

d. In the first Price column in the **Total** row, click the **arrow**, and then select **Count**. In the second Price column in the **Total** row, click the **arrow**, and then select **Avg**. Repeat for the next two **Price** columns selecting **Min** for the third column and **Max** for the last column. Notice that the Category Total row displays Group By so the statistics will be grouped by each category type.

e. Click the Query Tools Design tab, and then click **Run** in the Results group to run the query.

f. Click the Home tab, click the **View arrow** in the Views group, and then click **Design View**.

g. Change the titles for the Price fields to the following: **Number of Products**, **Average Price**, **Minimum Price**, and **Maximum Price**. Run the query again. Resize the columns to best fit the data.

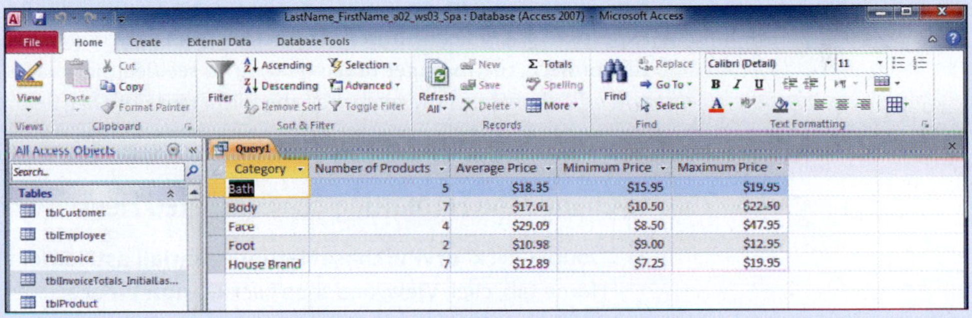

Figure 30 Query results with field titles changed

h. Click **Save** 💾 on the Quick Access Toolbar, under Query Name type **qryPriceStatisticsByCategory_InitialLastName** replacing InitialLastName with your own first initial and last name, and then click **OK**. **Close** ☒ the query.

Troubleshooting an Aggregate Query

Caution should be used when using aggregate functions. Forgetting to add a function in the total row can cause a large number of records to be retrieved from the database, or a combination of records that do not make any sense. You must carefully select which field should have the Group By operator in the total row; many times only one field will use Group By. Combining search criteria and aggregate functions in a single query can make the query complex. It also makes trouble-shooting more difficult if the query does not work. When in doubt, set all your criteria in one query and then use the aggregate functions in another query based on the query with the criteria. This way, you can first verify that your criteria worked and then concentrate on the aggregate function results.

For this exercise, the manager tried to create an aggregate query to calculate the total number of items and average number of items purchased by different methods—phone, online, and in person. The results made no sense, and she has asked you to help her figure out why.

To Troubleshoot an Aggregate Query

a. Double-click **qryPurchaseMethods** to open the query. Notice the second and third columns are exactly the same, when the intent was to have one column be a count and the other column contain a total.

b. Click the Home tab, click the **View arrow** in the Views group, and then click **Design View**. Look at the second column, Quantity, and notice the Total row shows the Group By operator instead of a function. Change this to **Sum**.

c. Rename the second and third column field titles to Total Quantity and Average Quantity.

d. Click the **Design tab**, and then click **Run** in the Results group to run the query. Resize the columns to best fit the data.

e. Click the **File tab**, click **Save Object As**, and then under Query Name type qryPurchaseMethods_InitialLastName, replacing InitialLastName with your own first initial and last name. **Close** ⊠ the query.

Formatting a Calculated Field

An aggregate query may give you the correct results but the formatting may not be what you expected. Query fields must be formatted in the query grid using the Field properties sheet. For this project, the manager does not want to see decimal places for the Average Price column, so you will show her how to change the formatting of that field.

To Change the Formatting of a Calculated Field

a. Double-click **qryPurchaseMethods_InitialLastName** to open the query. Click the Home tab, click **View**, and then click **Design View**.

b. Click the **Average Quantity: Quantity** column. Click the Query Tools Design tab, and then click **Property Sheet** in the Show/Hide group.

c. Click in the **Format** box, click the **arrow**, and then select **Fixed**. Click in the **Decimal Places** box, and then type 0.

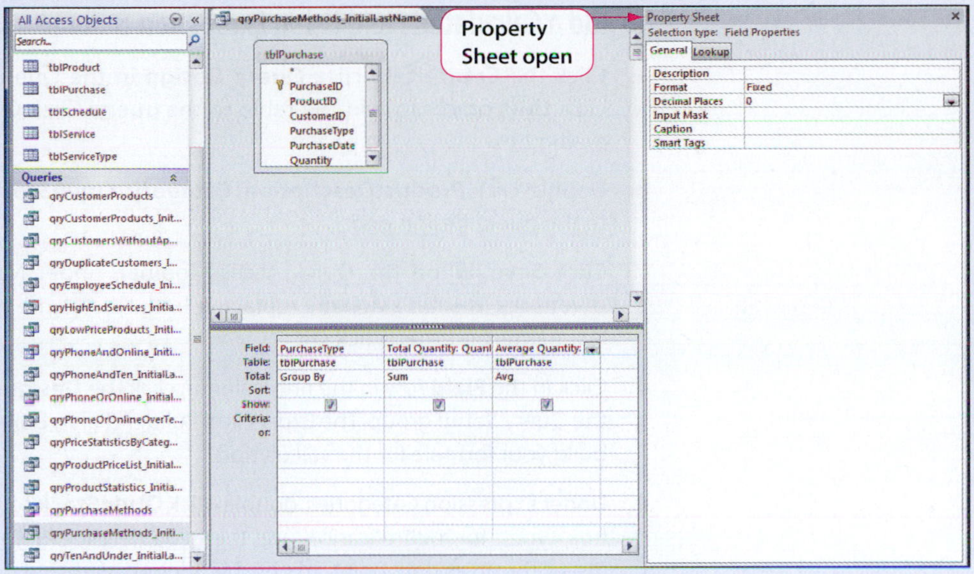

Figure 31 Property sheet open with changes

d. **Close** ✕ the property sheet, and then run the query again. The results should be formatted with no decimal places.

e. Click the **File tab**, click **Save Object As**, under Query Name type **qryPurchaseMethods NoDecimals_InitialLastName** replacing InitialLastName with your own first initial and last name, and then click **OK. Close** ✕ the query.

Create Calculated Fields

In addition to statistical calculations using aggregate functions, you can also perform an arithmetic calculation within a row of a query to create a new field. The result of the calculated field is displayed each time you run the query. However, this new field is not part of any other table.

A calculated field can be added to a query using the fields in the query or even fields in another table or query in the database. The calculation can use a combination of numbers and field values, which allows you flexibility in how you perform the calculation. For example, you can multiply a product price stored in the table by a sales tax rate that you enter into the calculation.

Building a Calculated Field Using Expression Builder

Expression Builder is a tool in Access that can help you format your calculated fields correctly. The builder provides a list of expression elements, operators, and built-in functions. The capabilities of Expression Builder range from simple to complex.

For this exercise, you will help the spa manager create a query to show what the value of her inventory is using the Quantity in Stock and Price fields for each product.

To Add a Calculated Field Using Expression Builder

a. Click the **Create tab**, click **Query Design** in the Queries group, and then double-click **tblProduct** to add the table to the query. Click **Close** to close the Show Table dialog box.

b. Double-click **ProductDescription**, **Category**, **QtyInStock**, and **Price** to add the fields to the query design grid.

c. Click **Save** 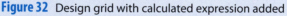 on the Quick Access Toolbar, under Name query type **qryProduct Inventory_InitialLastName** replacing InitialLastName with your own first initial and last name, and then click **OK**.

d. Click in the **Field** row in the fifth column, click the **Design tab**, and then click **Builder** in the Query Setup group. The Expression Builder dialog box opens, which is where you will build your formula for the calculation.

e. Under Expression Categories, double-click **QtyInStock** to add the field to the expression box, type ***** for multiplication, and then double-click **Price** under Expression Categories. Move the insertion point to the beginning of the expression, and then type **Total Inventory:**. Click **OK** to save the expression and add it to the query design grid.

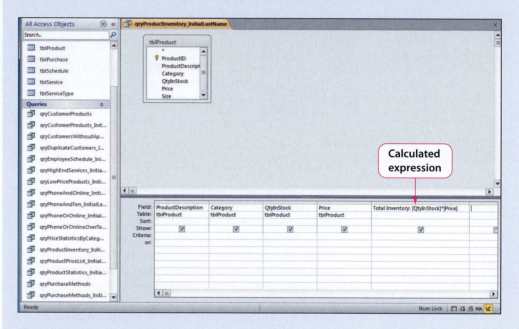

Figure 32 Design grid with calculated expression added

Troubleshooting

Where Are My Field Names?
When you click Expression Builder to create a calculated field, and you do not see your field names listed in the Expression Categories box in the middle of the dialog box, it may be that the query has not been saved yet. If the query is not saved, then the field names will not appear and you will have to type them in the Expression Builder manually instead of clicking them to select them. It is good practice to save your query first, and then open the Expression Builder to create a calculated field.

SIDE NOTE
Expression Box

When working with multiple tables, Access puts the table name in front of the field name with an exclamation mark. If you are using a single table, however, the table name is optional and will not be added by default.

f. Click the **Design tab**, and then click **Run** in the Results group to run the query. Resize the Total Inventory column to best fit the data. The results should show 25 records with a new column titled Total Inventory that multiplies the QtyInStock by the Price fields.

g. **Close** ☒ the query, and then click **Yes** when prompted to save changes.

Sort Query Results

Sorting is the process of rearranging records in a specific order. By default, records in a table or query are sorted by the primary key field. You can change the sorting of a table in a query, which will not affect how the data is stored, only how it will appear in the query results.

Sorting by One Field

To sort records, you have to select a **sort field**, or a field used to determine the order of the records. The sort field can be a Text, Number, Date/Time, Currency, AutoNumber, Yes/No, or Lookup Wizard field as shown in Figure 33. A field may be sorted either in ascending order or descending order.

Type of Data	Sorting Options
Text	Ascending (A to Z); Descending (Z to A)
Numbers (including Currency & AutoNumber)	Ascending (lowest to highest); Descending (highest to lowest)
Date/Time	Ascending (oldest to newest); Descending (newest to oldest)
Yes/No	Ascending (yes, then no values); Descending (no, then yes values)

Figure 33 Methods for sorting data

If you have numbers that are stored as text—phone number, Social Security number, zip code—then the characters 1–9 come before A to Z in the appropriate order sorted as alphanumeric text.

A table may be sorted by a single field in Datasheet view. When a table is sorted using a single field, a sort arrow will appear in the field name so you can see that it is sorted. For this project, you will show the spa manager how to sort the Product table by category.

SIDE NOTE
Alternative Method to Sorting Fields
Alternatively, you can select the field to be sorted and click Ascending or Descending on the Home tab in the Sort & Filter group.

To Sort by a Single Field

a. Double-click **tblProduct** to open the table.

b. Click the **selection arrow** in the field name next to Category, and then click **Sort A to Z**. This will sort the Category field in ascending order.

c. **Close** ☒ the table, and then click **Yes** when prompted to save the changes.

Sorting by More Than One Field

You can also sort by multiple fields in Access. The first field you choose to sort by is called the **primary sort field**. The second and subsequent fields are called **secondary sort fields**. You can sort multiple fields from the datasheet by selecting all the fields at one time and using the buttons on the Ribbon, but there are some restrictions. First, the fields must be next to each other and the sort is executed left to right; that is, the leftmost field is the primary sort field, the next field is a secondary sort field, and so on. Secondly, you can only sort in ascending or descending order for all fields, you cannot have one field sorted in ascending order and another in descending order. Because of all the restrictions, it is more efficient to create a query and sort by multiple fields using Design view.

Using Design view to sort records allows you to sequence the fields from left to right in an order that makes sense for your desired sort results and allows you to combine ascending and descending sorts. You can also sort in an order different than left to right by adding a field multiple times and clearing the Show check box. For this exercise, you will show the staff how to sort the tblScheduleschedule table by Employee, then Date, and then Service by creating a query from the table and setting up the sort options.

To Sort a Query by Multiple Fields

a. Click the **Create tab**, click **Query Design** in the Queries group, and double-click **tblSchedule** to add the table to the query. Click **Close** to close the Show Table dialog box.

b. Double-click the **tables title bar**, and then drag all the fields to the query design grid.

c. Click at the top of the **Employee** field to highlight it and then drag it to the first column of the query design grid in front of ScheduleID. Drag the **DateOfAppt** field to the second column after the **Employee** field, and then drag the **Service** field to the third column after the **DateOfAppt** field.

d. Click the **Sort** row for Employee, click the **selection arrow**, and then click **Ascending**. Click **Ascending** for both the **DateOfAppt** and **Service** fields.

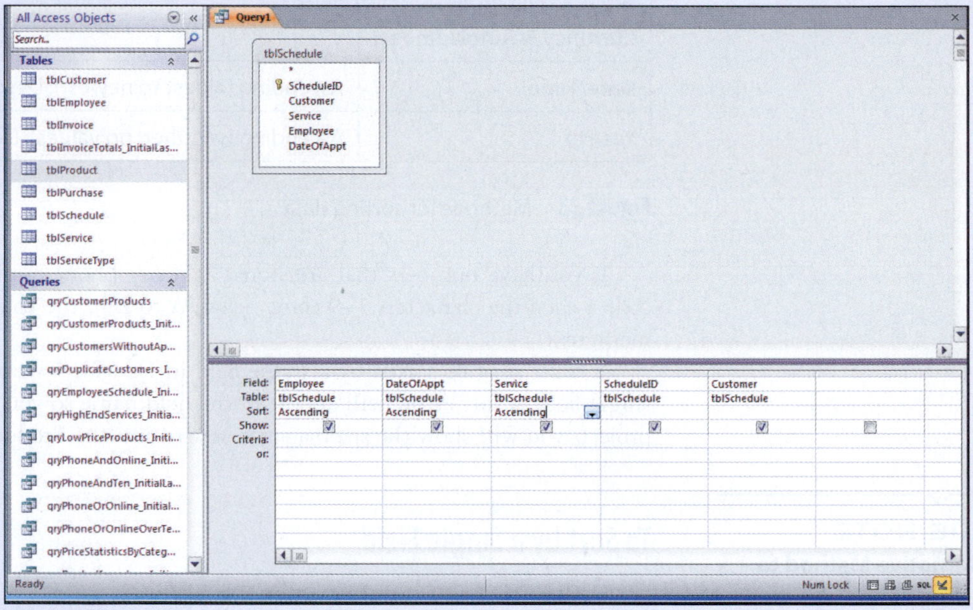

Figure 34 Sort options selected

e. Click the **Design tab**, and then click **Run** in the Results group to run the query. The table should be sorted by Employee, then Date, then Service.

f. Click **Save** 💾 on the Quick Access Toolbar, name the query **qryEmployeeAppointments_ InitialLastName** replacing InitialLastName with your own first initial and last name, and then click **OK**. **Close** ✖ the query.

SIDE NOTE

How Many Fields Is Too Many?

You may choose up to 10 fields to sort by in Design view.

Rearranging the Sort Order

For this exercise, the manager would like a query similar to the one created above, but she would like it to show employees' first and last names. She would also like it to sort by employee last name and then employee first name, but have the first name show first in the query results. You will show her how to use two tables to create this query and how to add a field multiple times to the query design grid to sort fields one way but display them another.

To Sort a Query by Multiple Fields in a Different Sort Order

a. Click the **Create tab**, click **Query Design** in the Queries group, and then double-click **tblSchedule** and **tblEmployee** to add the tables to the query. Click **Close** to close the Show Table dialog box.

b. Double-click **EmpFirstName**, **EmpLastName**, and then **EmpFirstName** again from tblEmployee to add the fields to the query design grid. Double-click **DateofAppt**, **Service**, and **Customer** in that order from tblSchedule to add the fields to the query design grid.

c. Click the **Sort** row for EmpLastName, click the **selection arrow**, and then click **Ascending**. Click the **Sort** row for the second EmpFirstName in the third column, click **Ascending**, and then then select **Ascending** for both the DateOfAppt and Service fields. Click the **Show** check box under the second EmpFirstName field in the third column to clear it.

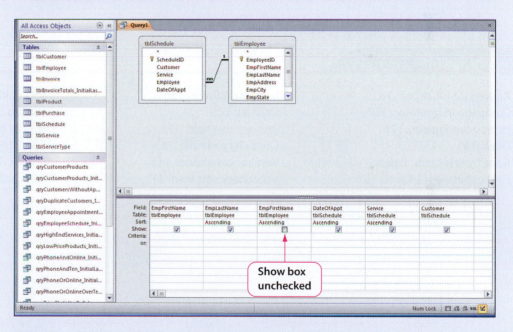

Figure 35 Sort options selected and EmpFirstName Show check box cleared

d. Click the **Design tab**, and then click **Run** in the Results group to run the query. The results should show 53 records sorted by employee last name, first name, date, and service. Notice that Alex Weaver comes before Joseph Weaver in the sort.

e. Click **Save** 💾 on the Quick Access Toolbar, name the query **qryEmployeeSort_InitialLastName** replacing InitialLastName with your own first initial and last name, and click **OK**. **Close** ✕ the query **Exit** Access.

1. You applied a filter to a table to find specific records. The next time you opened the table, Toggle Filter did not show your filtered records. What did you do wrong?

2. You used the Find command to search for someone's first name, which you are sure is in the table. The results keep coming up with nothing. What option could be preventing Access from finding the record you are looking for? What else could you do to find the record?

3. When is there an advantage to finding one record at a time and replacing a value compared to using Replace All?

4. What is the difference between the Find Duplicates Query Wizard and the Find Unmatched Query Wizard? Give an example of when you would use each.

5. Why should you only add the tables you are going to use to a query?

6. What is the multiplier effect, and how can you prevent it from happening?

7. Using logical operators allows you to create powerful queries. When do you put criteria for different fields in the same row in the query design grid? When do you put the criteria for different fields in different rows? How can you combine AND and OR criteria in the same query?

8. Why would you add the same field multiple times to the query design grid?

Key Terms

Aggregate functions 165
Comparison operator 157
Expression Builder 171
Filter 145
Filter by selection 145
Find command 142

Logical operator 158
Orphan 148
Primary sort field 173
Query by example 151
Replace command 142
Secondary sort field 173

Sort field 173
Sorting 173
Special operator 164
Text filter 146
Total row 166
Wildcard character 142

Visual Summary

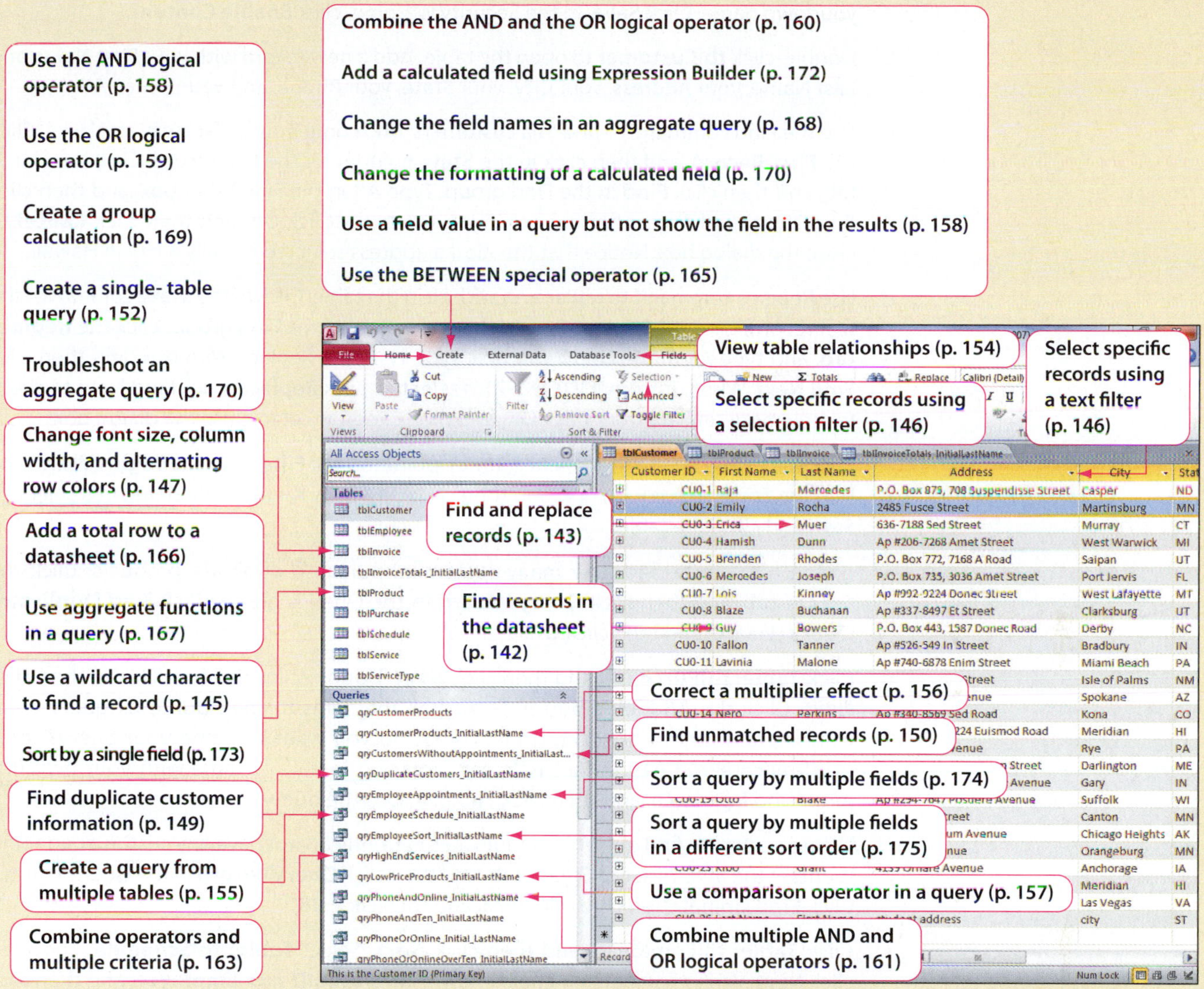

Combine the AND and the OR logical operator (p. 160)

Add a calculated field using Expression Builder (p. 172)

Change the field names in an aggregate query (p. 168)

Change the formatting of a calculated field (p. 170)

Use a field value in a query but not show the field in the results (p. 158)

Use the BETWEEN special operator (p. 165)

Use the AND logical operator (p. 158)

Use the OR logical operator (p. 159)

Create a group calculation (p. 169)

Create a single- table query (p. 152)

Troubleshoot an aggregate query (p. 170)

Change font size, column width, and alternating row colors (p. 147)

Add a total row to a datasheet (p. 166)

Use aggregate functions in a query (p. 167)

Use a wildcard character to find a record (p. 145)

Sort by a single field (p. 173)

Find duplicate customer information (p. 149)

Create a query from multiple tables (p. 155)

Combine operators and multiple criteria (p. 163)

View table relationships (p. 154)

Select specific records using a selection filter (p. 146)

Select specific records using a text filter (p. 146)

Find and replace records (p. 143)

Find records in the datasheet (p. 142)

Correct a multiplier effect (p. 156)

Find unmatched records (p. 150)

Sort a query by multiple fields (p. 174)

Sort a query by multiple fields in a different sort order (p. 175)

Use a comparison operator in a query (p. 157)

Combine multiple AND and OR logical operators (p. 161)

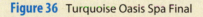

Figure 36 Turquoise Oasis Spa Final

Practice 1

Student data file needed:

a02_ws03_Spa2

You will save your file as:

Lastname_Firstname_a02_ws03_Spa2

Turquoise Oasis Spa

The Resort is considering hosting a large convention and is trying to sign a multiple-year contract with an out-of-town group. The Spa is being asked to provide information about the services, products, and packages it offers. All the information can be found in the database, but it needs to come together in a coherent fashion. You have been asked to answer a number of questions about the spa and provide information to help answer those questions. You will also look for discrepancies or mistakes in the data and correct them as necessary.

a. Start **Access**, and then open **a02_ws03_Spa2**. Click the **File tab**, and then click **Save Database As**. In the Save As dialog box, navigate to where you are storing your files, and then type Lastname_Firstname_a02_ws03_Spa2, replacing Lastname_Firstname with your own name. Click **Save**. In the Security Warning, click **Enable Content**.

b. Double-click **tblCustomer** to open the table. Add a new record with your First Name and Last Name, your Address, your City, your State, your Phone, and your E-mail Address.

c. Use the Find command to find Spa customers who come from as far away as Alaska. Click the **First Record**, and then click in the **State** column for the first record. Click the Home tab, and then click **Find** in the Find group. Type AK in the Find What box, and then click **Find Next** until Access finishes searching the table. Click **OK**, and then click **Cancel** to close the dialog box. Notice that the Alaska address selected is really a city in Hawaii.

d. Use Replace command to replace AK with HI in the table. Click in the **State** column for the first record. Click the **Home tab**, and then click **Find** in the Find group. Click the **Replace tab**, and type AK in the Find What box. Type HI in the Replace With box, and then click **Find Next**. When Customer ID CUO-21 is selected, click **Replace**. Click **Find Next** to check for any more similar errors. Click **OK**, and then click **Cancel** to close the dialog box.

e. Click the **arrow** on the **State** field column, point to **Text Filters**, select **Begins With**, type H in the State begins with box, and then click **OK**. Verify there are three records selected. Save and close the table.

f. Create a query to find how many customers purchase duplicate products. Click the **Create tab**, and then click **Query Wizard** in the Queries group. Click **Find Duplicates Query Wizard**, and then click **OK**.

g. Click **Table: tblPurchase**, and then click **Next**. Double-click **ProductID**, and then click **Next**. Click the **All Fields** button to add all the fields to the Additional query fields column, and then click **Next**. Under "What do you want to name your query?" type qryDuplicateProducts_InitialLastName replacing InitialLastName with your own first initial and last name, and then click **Finish**. Close the query.

h. Create a query to find out which employees currently do not have any customer appointments at the Spa. Click the **Create tab**, and then click **Query Wizard** in the Queries group. Click **Find Unmatched Query Wizard**, and then click **OK**.

i. Click **Table: tblEmployee**, and then click **Next**. Select **Table: tblSchedule**, and then click **Next**. Verify that Matching fields shows **EmployeeID <=> Employee**, and then click **Next**. Click the **All Fields** button to add all the fields to the Selected fields column, and then click **Next**.

j. Click **Save** on the Quick Access Toolbar, name the query qryEmployeesWitoutAppointments_InitialLastName, replacing InitialLastName with your own first initial and last name, and then click **Finish**.

k. Click the **Home tab**, click the **View arrow** in the View group, and then click **Design View**. Click the **Sort** row for the EmpLastName field, click the **sort arrow**, and then click **Ascending** to sort the query in ascending order by Last Name. Click the **Design tab**, and then click **Run** in the Results group to run the query. Close the query, and then click **Yes** when prompted to save the changes.

l. Create a query to list the Spa's services by Type, Name, Description, and Fee. Click the **Create tab**, and then click **Query Design** in the Queries group. Double-click **tblService** and **tblServiceType** to add the tables to the query window. Click **Close** to close the Show Table dialog box.

m. In the following order, from tblServiceType double-click **Type**, and from tblService double-click **ServiceName, Description**, and **Fee** to add the fields to the query design grid. Click the **Sort** row for the Type field, select **Ascending**, and then for the Fee field, select **Descending**. Click the **Design tab**, and then click **Run** in the Results group to run the query.

n. Double-click the **border** between the ServiceType and ServiceName field names to best fit the data. Repeat for all the columns. Click **Save** on the Quick Access Toolbar, name the query qryServicesAndFees_InitialLastName replacing InitialLastName with your own first initial and last name, and then close the query.

o. Create a query to find how much each customer spent on their product purchase, but only if the purchase was a quantity greater than 1, including 8% sales tax. Click the **Create tab**, click **Query Design** in the Queries group, and add **tblProduct** and **tblPurchase** to the query window. Click **Close** to close the Show Table dialog box. From tblProduct, double-click **ProductDescription** and **Price**, and from tblPurchase double-click **Quantity** and **CustomerID** in that order to add the fields to the query design grid.

p. Click in the **Criteria** row for Quantity and type **>1**. Click **Save** on the Quick Access Toolbar, name the query qryTotalPurchase_InitialLastName replacing InitialLastName with your own first initial and last name, and click **OK**.

q. In the fifth column, click in the **Field** row, click the **Design tab**, and click **Builder** in the Query Setup group. Double-click **Price** to add it to the expression, type *****, double-click **Quantity** to add it to the expression, type *****, and then type **1.08**. Click at the beginning of the expression, type Total Purchase with tax:, and then click **OK**.

r. Click the **Sort** row for the Quantity field, click the **selection arrow**, and then click **Ascending**. Click the **Design tab**, and then click **Run** in the Results group to run the query.

s. Click the Home tab, click the **View arrow**, and then click **Design View**. Click the Total Purchase with tax field, click the **Design tab**, and then click **Property Sheet** in the Show/Hide group. Click the **Format arrow**, and then select **Currency**. Click the **Decimal Places arrow**, and then select **2**. Close the property sheet, click the **Query Tools Design tab**, and then click **Run** in the Results group to run the query. The Total Purchase with tax field should be formatted with currency and two decimal places.

t. **Close** the query, and then click **Yes** when prompted to save the changes.

u. Create an aggregate query to find the average, total, minimum, and maximum fee for each type of service the spa offers. Click the **Create tab**, click **Query Design** in the Queries group, and add **tblService** to the query window. Click **Close** to close the Show Table dialog box. Double-click **Type** one time, and double-click **Fee** three times in that order to add the fields to the query design grid. Click the **Query Tools Design tab**, and then click **Totals** in the Show/Hide group to add the Total row to the query design grid.

v. Click in the **Total** row, for the first Fee column, click the **arrow**, and then click **Avg**. For the second Fee column select **Min**, and for the third Fee column select **Max**. Click in the **Sort** row in the Type field, click the **arrow**, and then select **Ascending**. Click the **Query Tools Design tab**, and then click **Run** in the Results group to run the query.

w. Click the **Home tab**, and then click **View** to return to Design view. Change the names of the three Fee columns to Fee Average, Minimum Fee, and Maximum Fee in that order. Click the **Query Tools Design tab**, and then click **Run** in the Results group to run the query.

x. Double-click the **border** between the Service Type and Fee Average field names to best fit the data. Repeat for all the columns.

y. Click **Save** on the Quick Access Toolbar, name the query qryFeeStatistics_InitialLastName replacing InitialLastName with your own first initial and last name, and click **OK**. Close the query. Close Access.

Student data file needed:

a02_ws03_Events

You will save your file as:

Lastname_Firstname_a02_ws03_Events

Event Planning

The event planning department at the resort has a database of clients, upcoming events, and decoration items. The event planning staff members would like your help in gathering information from their database to answer questions a client has. You will work with the three tables in the database and develop queries to help answer the questions. You will also help with some maintenance issues the staff members need help with.

a. Start **Access**, and then open **a02_ws03_Events**. Click the **File tab**, and click **Save Database As**. In the Save As dialog box, navigate to where you are saving your files, type Lastname_Firstname_a02_ws03_Events, and then click **Save**. In the Security Warning, click **Enable Content**.

b. Double-click **tblClients** to open the table. Add a new record to the tblClients with your First Name and Last Name, your Address, your City, your Zip, and your Phone. Click the **Home tab**, click the **Font Size arrow** in the Test Formatting group, and then click **12**. Double-click the **border** between the ID and First Name column headings to best fit the data. Repeat for all the columns.

c. Click the Home tab, click the **Alternate Row Color arrow** in the Text Formatting group, and then select **Blue, Accent 1, Lighter 60%**. Click the **File tab**, click **Save Object As**, and then name the table tblClientFormatted_InitialLastName, replacing InitialLastName with your own first initial and last name. Click **OK**, and then **close** the table.

d. Click the **Create tab**, click **Query Design** in the Queries group, and add **tblDecorations** to the query window. Click **Close** to close the Show Table dialog box. Double-click **DecorItem**, **Color**, and **Category** to add the fields to the query design grid. Click the **Color** field to highlight the column, and then drag it to the left of the DecorItem field.

e. A client wants to use red and white for their colors, but only wants the resort to provide the linens and flowers. Click in the **Criteria** row for Color and type Red or White. Click the same **Criteria** row for Category and type Linens or Flowers. Click in the **Sort** row for the Color field, click the **arrow**, and then click **Ascending**. Click the Query Tools Design tab, and then click **Run** in the Results group to run the query. Click **Save** on the Quick Access Toolbar, name the query qryRedOrWhite_InitialLastName replacing InitialLastName with your own first initial and last name, and then click **OK**. **Close** the query.

f. Another client wants to order decorations for their event, but they would like everything green or blue and want to know what the linen and centerpiece color options are. Click the **Create tab**, click **Query Design** in the Queries group, and add **tblDecorations** to the query window. Click **Close** to close the Show Table dialog box. Double-click **Color**, **DecorItem**, and **Category** to add the fields to the query design grid. In the **Criteria** row for the Color field and type Green or Blue. In the **or** row below the Category field and type Linens or Centerpieces.

g. Click in the **Sort** row for the Category field, click the **arrow**, and then click **Ascending**. Click the Design tab, and then click **Run** in the Results group to run the query. Click **Save** on the Quick Access Toolbar, name the query qryGreenOrBlue_InitialLastName replacing InitialLastName with your own first initial and last name, and then click **OK**. **Close** the query.

h. The event planning manager wants to know the total rates being charged for upcoming events and how many events that includes. Double-click **tblEvents** to open the table. Click the Home tab, and then click **Totals** in the Records group. In the Rate field, click in the **Total** row, click the **arrow** and then click **Sum**. In the **ClientID** field, click in the **Total** row, click the **arrow** and then click **Count**.

i. Click the **File tab**, click **Save Object As**, name the table **tblEventStatistics_InitialLastName** replacing InitialLastName with your own first initial and last name, and then click **OK**. **Close** the query.

j. Create a query to find out the total rates for each event that is currently planned at the resort, how many of each event is planned, and the total attendees for each kind of event. Click the **Create tab**, click **Query Design** in the Queries group, and add **tblEvents** to the query window. Click **Close** to close the Show Table dialog box. Double-click **EventName**, **TotalAttendees**, **Rate**, and **EventName** in that order to add the fields to the query design grid. Click the Query Tools Design tab, and then click **Totals** to add the Total row to the query design grid.

k. In the TotalAttendees field, click in the **Total** row, click the **arrow** and then click **Sum**. Select **Sum** for the Rate field, and select **Count** for the EventName field. Click in the **Sort** row for the TotalAttendees field, click the **arrow**, and then click **Ascending**. Click the Query Tools Design tab, and then click **Run** in the Results group to run the query.

l. Click the Home tab, and then click **View** to switch to Design view. Change the column names, starting with the **TotalAttendees** to **TotalAttendees**, **Total Rate**, **Number of Events**. Click the **top edge** of the second EventName field in the fourth column. With the field highlighted, drag it to the left of **TotalAttendees**. Click the **Design tab**, and then click **Run** in the Results group to run the query.

m. Double-click the **border** between the Event Name and Number of Events field names to best fit the data. Repeat for all the columns. Click **Save** on the Quick Access Toolbar, name the query **qryTotalEvents_InitialLastName** replacing InitialLastName with your own first initial and last name, and then click **OK**. Close the query.

n. Create a query to find all Wedding Receptions scheduled, the date, location, total attendees, and the contact information for each. Click the **Create tab**, click **Query Design** in the Queries group, and add **tblEvents** and **tblClients** to the query window. Click **Close** to close the Show Table dialog box. Double-click **EventName**, **EventDate**, **Location**, and **TotalAttendees** from tblEvents and **FirstName**, **LastName**, and **Phone** from tblClients in that order to add the fields to the query design grid.

o. Click in the **Criteria** row for the EventName field and type **Wedding Reception**. Click the **Show** box to remove the check. Click in the **Sort** row for the EventDate field, click the **arrow**, and then click **Ascending**. Click in the **Design tab**, and then click **Run** in the Results group to run the query. Click **Save** on the Quick Access Toolbar, name the query **qryWeddings_InitialLastName** replacing InitialLastName with your own first initial and last name, and click **OK**. Close the query.

p. Create a query to find all events with total attendees greater than 50 or all events scheduled for some time in the month of February. Click the **Create tab**, click **Query Design** in the Queries group, and add **tblEvents** to the query window. Click **Close** to close the Show Table dialog box. Double-click **EventName**, **EventDate**, **Location**, and **TotalAttendees** from tblEvents in that order to add the fields to the query design grid.

q. Click in the **Criteria** row for the TotalAttendees field and type **>50**. Click in the **or** row for the EventDate field and type **Between 2/1/13 and 2/28/13**. Click in the **Sort** row for the EventDate field, click the **arrow**, and then click **Ascending**. Click the Query Tools Design tab, and then click **Run** in the Results group to run the query.

r. Click **Save** on the Quick Access Toolbar, name the query **qryFebruary&Fifty_InitialLastName** replacing InitialLastName with your own first initial and last name, and then click **OK**. Close the table, and then close Access.

Objectives

1. Compare navigation and edit modes.   p. 184

2. Navigate forms.   p. 186

3. Use the Find command with a form.   p. 189

4. Update table records using forms.   p. 190

5. Create a form using the Form Wizard.   p. 193

6. Modify a form's design.   p. 196

7. Print forms.   p. 200

8. Create a report using the Report Wizard. p. 201

9. Use and customize Access themes.   p. 207

10. Modify a report's design.   p. 208

11. Printing and saving a report as a PDF file. p. 214

Maintaining and Presenting Data

PREPARE CASE

Turquoise Oasis Spa's New Database

The Turquoise Oasis Spa has a database with customer, employee, product, and service information for easier scheduling and access. An intern created the database, and the manager and staff members are struggling to use the database to its fullest capacity. You have recently been hired to work in the office of the spa and you have knowledge of Access, so the manager has asked for your help in maintaining the records and creating forms and reports to help better use the data in the database.

Courtesy of www.Shutterstock.com

Student data files needed for this workshop:

 a02_ws04_Spa3

a02_ws04_Spa_Image

You will save your files as:

 Lastname_Firstname_a02_ws04_Spa3

Lastname_Firstname_a02_ws04_Theme

 Lastname_Firstname_a02_ws04_pdfEmployeeSchedule

Maintain Records in Tables

Data may be updated directly in the table where it is stored. When updating data directly in a table, you will be in Datasheet view. Datasheet view shows all the fields and records at one time, which provides all the information you need to update your data, unlike in a form or query, where some of the fields or records may not be in view.

Compare Navigation and Edit Modes

As you may recall, you can navigate from record to record or field to field in a database using the Navigation bar, or in Navigation mode by using Tab, Enter, Home, End, ↑, ↓, ←, and →. **Navigation mode** allows you to move from record to record and field to field using keystrokes. To update data in a table, you must be in Edit mode. **Edit mode** allows you to edit, or change, the contents of a field as shown in Figure 1. To switch between Navigation mode and Edit mode, press F2.

Keystroke	Navigation Mode	Edit Mode
→ and ←	Move from field to field	Move from character to character
↑ and ↓	Move from record to record	Switch to Navigation mode and move from record to record
Home	Moves to the first field in the record	Moves to the first character in the field
End	Moves to the last field in the record	Moves to the last character in the field
Tab and Enter	Moves one field at a time	Switches to Navigation mode and moves from field to field
Ctrl+Home	Moves to the first field of the first record	Moves to the first character in the field, same as Home
Ctrl+End	Moves to the last field of the last record	Moves to the last character in the field, same as End

Figure 1 Keystrokes used in Navigation mode and Edit mode

SIDE NOTE
Look for the Blinking Insertion Point
When you can see the blinking insertion point in a field, you are in Edit mode. When the text of a field is selected and highlighted, you are in Navigation mode.

Editing a Table in Datasheet View

Datasheet view shows all the records and fields at one time, which is one advantage to using Datasheet view to update your records. Another advantage is the ability to see all the records in the table, which gives you a perspective on the data you are entering. For this exercise, the staff has received a note from a customer who has changed their phone number. You will show the spa staff how to change that customer's record in the Customer table.

To Edit a Record in a Table in Datasheet View

a. Click the **Start** button. From the Start Menu, locate and then start **Microsoft Access**. Click the **File tab**, and then click **Open**. In the Open dialog box, click the disk drive in the left pane where your student data files are located, navigate through the folder structure, click **a02_ws04_Spa3**, and then click **Open**.

b. Click the **File tab**, and then click **Save Database As**. In the Save As dialog box, navigate to where you are saving your files, and then type Lastname_Firstname_a02_ws04_Spa3 replacing Lastname_Firstname with your own name, and then click **Save**.

c. In the Security Warning, click **Enable Content**.

d. Double-click **tblCustomer** to open the table.

e. Locate the customer with the Customer ID CUO-12 and Last Name Hinton.

f. Click in the **Customer ID** field, and then press Tab. You are now in Navigation mode, and the First Name field should be highlighted.

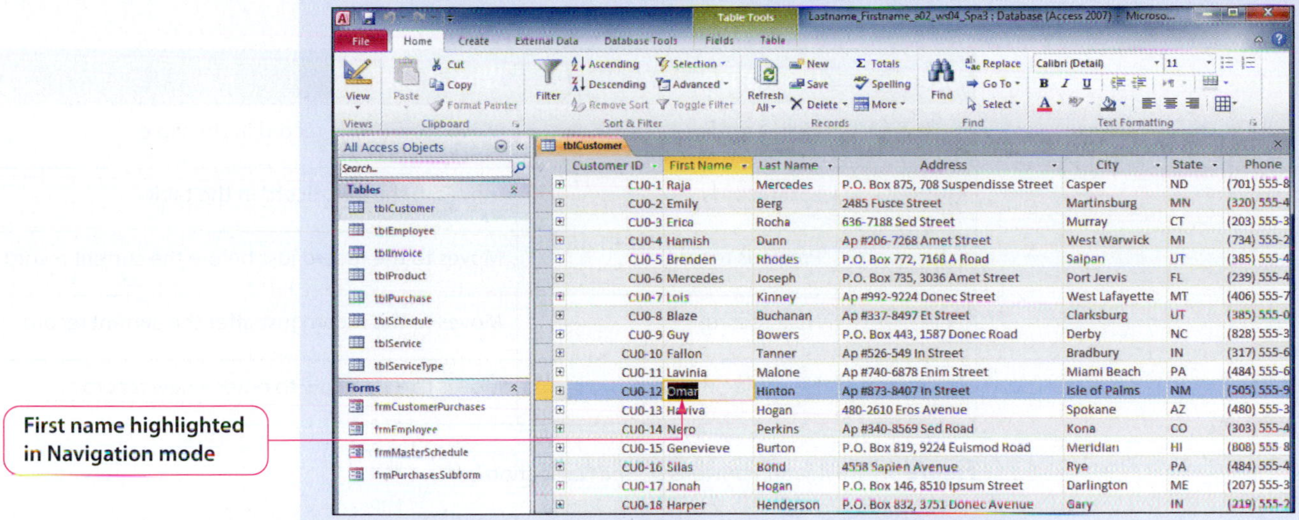

First name highlighted in Navigation mode

Figure 2 Table in navigation mode

g. Continue pressing Tab until the Phone field is highlighted. Press F2 to switch from Navigation mode to Edit mode. Notice the insertion point is at the beginning of the Phone field and the first character is highlighted. Type **5055552923** to enter the new phone number. Because the field is already formatted as a phone number, it is not necessary to enter parentheses or dashes in the phone number.

h. Press Tab to switch to Navigation mode and move to the next field.

i. **Close** × the table.

Maintain Records in Forms

If you recall, a form is an object in Access that you can use to enter, edit, or view records in a table. A simple form allows you to see records one at a time rather than as a group in Datasheet view.

When you create a form from two tables that have a one-to-many relationship, the first table selected becomes the **main form** and the second table you select becomes the **subform**. A form with a subform allows you to see one record at a time from the main form and multiple records in Datasheet view from the other related table. Since you only see one record at a time or one record and a datasheet, navigation tools become important when you are working with forms as you cannot see all the records at one time.

Real World Advice — Data Overload!

You may be asked to create a database for someone else that is not familiar with how a database works or even how the computer works. Your role is to make their job as easy as possible so they can get their work done with as few errors as possible.

Looking at a database table with hundreds or thousands of records in Datasheet view can be very intimidating to some people. Trying to keep track of the record or field you are in can be more difficult as the table grows larger and larger. Often seeing one record at a time in a form can eliminate data entry errors and allow the user to focus on the information for that particular record.

Navigate Forms

You navigate records in a form the same way you navigate a table, using the Navigation bar to move from record to record. As a reminder, the Navigation bar has a number of buttons to use for navigation as shown in Figure 3.

Button	Description	What it does
◄	First record	Moves to the first record in the table
►►	Last record	Moves to the last record in the table
◄	Previous record	Moves to the record just before the current record
►	Next record	Moves to the record just after the current record
►✱	New (blank) record	Moves to a new row to enter a new record

Figure 3 Navigation buttons on the Navigation bar

Navigating a Main Form

Within each record, you can use a combination of Tab, Home, Ctrl, End, and the arrow keys to move from field to field as shown in Figure 4.

Keystroke	What it does
Tab	Moves from field to field within a record; at the last field in a record, it moves you to the first field in the next record
Home	Moves to the first field of the current record
Ctrl + Home	Moves to the first field of the first record of the table
End	Moves to the last field of the current record
Ctrl + End	Moves to the last field of the last record of the table
Arrow keys	Move up or down a field of the current record

Figure 4 Different navigation methods for forms

For this exercise, you will show the spa staff how to navigate the form frmEmployee, which is a list of all employees one record at a time.

To Navigate a Single-Table Form

a. Double-click **frmEmployee** to open the form.

b. Click **Last record** ►► to go to the last record of the table.

c. Click **First record** ◄ to return to the first record in the table.

d. Click **Next record** ► to go to the next record in the table.

e. Click **Previous record** ◄ to go back to the previous record in the table.

f. **Close** ✕ the form.

Navigating a Form with a Subform

When navigating forms with a subform, the Navigation bar buttons at the bottom of the main window are used to navigate the records in the main form, and a second Navigation bar at the bottom of the subform datasheet is used to navigate the records in the subform.

The same navigation keystrokes listed in Figure 4 are still available; however, they work a little differently when a subform is included, as shown in Figure 5.

Keystroke	What it does
Tab	Moves from field to field within a main record. At the last field in a record, it moves to the first field in the subform. At the last record in the subform, it moves to the first field in the next record of the main form.
Home	From the main form, moves to the first field of the current record. From the subform, moves to the first field of the current record in the subform.
Ctrl + Home	From the main form, moves to the first field of the first record. From the subform, moves to the first field of the first record in the subform.
End	From the main form, moves to the last field of the current record in the subform. From the subform, moves to the last field of the current record in the subform.
Ctrl + End	From the main form, moves to the last field of the last record of the subform. From the subform, moves to the last field of the current record of the subform.
Arrow keys	Move up or down a field in the current record in either the form or subform.

Figure 5 Different navigation methods for subforms (continued)

For this exercise, you will show the spa staff members how to navigate the form frmCustomerPurchases that shows one customer at a time with all their recent product purchases.

To Navigate a Multiple-Table Form with a Subform

a. Double-click **frmCustomerPurchases** to open the form.

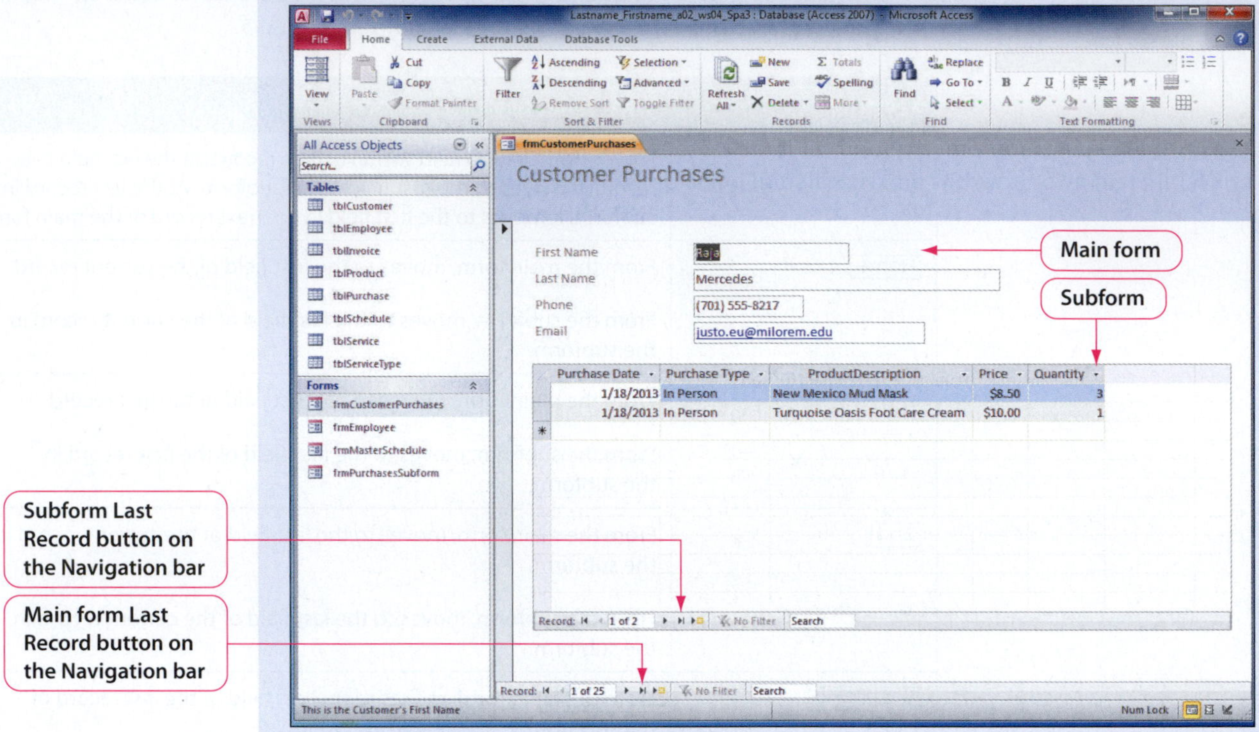

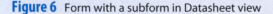

Figure 6 Form with a subform in Datasheet view

b. Click **Last record** ▶| on the subform Navigation bar to highlight the last record in the subform.

c. Click **Last record** ▶| on the main form Navigation bar to go to the last record in the table.

d. Click **Previous record** ◀ repeatedly to go to record 20 with the customer name Eden Silva.

e. Click **Next record** ▶ in the subform to go to the next record in the subform.

f. **Close** ✕ the form.

Navigating a Split Form

A **split form** is a form created from one table, but it has a Form view and a Datasheet view in the same window. You can view one record at a time at the top of the window, and see the whole table in Datasheet view at the bottom of the window. This kind of form is helpful when you want to work with one record at a time and still see the big picture in the main table. In a split form, there are buttons on the Navigation bar to move only from record to record, and each record shown at the top is the record highlighted in the datasheet at the same time. You cannot highlight a different record in the form part and the datasheet part at the same time.

For this exercise, you will show the spa staff how to navigate the form frmMasterSchedule, which shows the schedule as a form and a datasheet in the same window.

To Navigate a Split Form

a. Double-click **frmMasterSchedule** to open the form.

b. Click **Last record** ▶ on the Navigation bar to highlight the last record in both the form and the datasheet.

c. Click the record in the datasheet with Schedule ID S046. The record will be highlighted in the datasheet and also show at the top in Form view.

d. **Close** ⊠ the form.

Use the Find Command with a Form

Finding data in a form is similar to finding data in a datasheet and uses the same Find command. Since you only see one record at a time with a form, using Find can be a quick way to find a record with a specific value in a field and prevents you from having to scroll through all the records in the table one at a time in Form view.

Finding an Exact Match in a Form

When you are looking for a specific value in a field you are looking for an exact match. For this exercise, a staff member has asked you to search the employee table to find any employees who may live in Las Vegas so they can try to set up a carpool with them. You will show the staff member how to use a form to look for that information.

To Search for an Exact Match

a. Double-click **frmEmployee** to open the form. Press ⎵Tab⎴ to move to the City field in the first record.

b. Click the Home tab, and then click **Find** in the Find group to open the Find and Replace dialog box.

c. In the Find What box, type **Las Vegas**. In the Look In text box, click **Current field**, and then click **Find Next**. Move the Find and Replace dialog box to see all the fields for the current record. The first record with Las Vegas as a value in the City field will be shown.

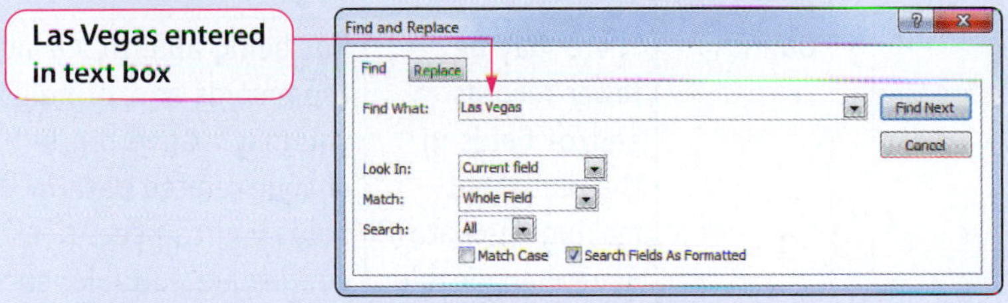

Figure 7 Find and Replace dialog box

d. Continue to click **Find Next** until Access gives you the message Microsoft Access finished searching the records. The search item was not found. Click **OK**, and then click **Cancel** to close the Find and Replace dialog box.

e. **Close** ⊠ the form.

We have become accustomed to using tabs in our browsers, and we tend to have many tabs open at one time. In fact, it makes our work more efficient so we do not have to keep opening and closing those windows. Unfortunately, Access does not work the same way. Every time you open an object in Access it opens in a new window with a tab. Those tabs, however, do not work the same way as tabs in our browser. While websites can be updated when they are open in a tab on our desktop, Access objects cannot be updated when they are open. It is therefore a good idea to close an object when you are done working with it, and then reopen it again later when you need it.

Update Table Records Using Forms

Just as you can update data in a datasheet, you can also update data in a form. Remember, a form is just another way to view the data in the table so when you see a record, you are seeing the record that is actually stored in the table. Nothing is actually stored in the form.

To make changes to data in a form, you must be viewing the form in Form view. You can also add a record to a table using the form. Using the Navigation bar you can go directly to a new record.

Quick Reference   Updating Tables

Data can be edited in tables, queries, or forms. There are advantages and disadvantages to each method. The table below will help you decide the most appropriate place to edit data.

Method	Advantages	Disadvantages	Typical Situation to Use
Tables	All the records and fields are visible in the datasheet.	The number of records and/or fields in the datasheet can be overwhelming.	A user familiar with Access needs to add a record quickly to a smaller table.
Queries	There may be fewer records and/or fields in the datasheet making the data more manageable. A form can be based on a query rather than a table.	Not being able to see all the records and/or fields, you may inadvertently change related data in the fields you can see. Not all queries are editable, such as aggregate queries.	A user familiar with Access needs to see and modify appointments booked for a particular day.
Forms	Being able to view one record at a time can make the data seem more manageable.	Not all fields may be included in a form. If fields are missing, some data may mistakenly be left out of a record. Provides view of only one record at a time.	A user unfamiliar with Access needs to add data to a large table with many records.

Adding Records

When you add a record to a form, you are actually adding the record to the table it will be stored in. The form will open in Form view, which is the view that allows you to edit the data. Just like in a datasheet, new records are added at the end of the table, which means you must go to a blank record to enter new data. For this exercise, you will use the frmEmployee form to add your name to the list of employees in the tblEmployee table.

To Add a New Record in a Form

a. Double-click **frmEmployee** to open the form. On the Navigation bar, click **New (blank) record** ▶◻.

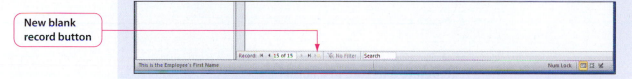

New blank record button

Record: ◄ ◄ 15 of 15 ▶ ▶ ▶◻ ☒ No Filter | Search

This is the Employee's First Name   Num Lock ◻ ◻ ◻

Figure 8 frmEmployee open

b. Type your **First Name**, **Last Name**, **Address**, **City**, **State** and **Phone** in the new record. **Close** ☒ the form.

c. Double-click **tblEmployee** to open the table and to see that your record was added. **Close** ☒ the table.

Editing Records

When you edit a record in a form, you are actually editing the record in the table it is stored in. The form will open in Form view, which is the view that allows you to edit the data. Changes to data are saved automatically but can be undone while the table or form is open by using the Undo button ↺▾ or by pressing ⎋Esc just after the change is made while still in Edit mode.

For this exercise, you are asked to update the tblEmployee table with recent changes. Mary Murphy has recently changed her phone number but it has not been changed in the table yet. You will show the staff how to find her record using a form and update her phone number.

To Edit Records Using a Form

a. Double-click **frmEmployee** to open the form. Press ⎀Tab⎀ to move to the **Last Name** field. Click the Home tab, click **Find** in the Find group, and then in the Find What box type **Murphy**. Click **Find Next**.

b. When the record for Mary Murphy is displayed, click **Cancel** to close the Find and Replace dialog box, and then press ⎀Tab⎀ to go to the Phone field. Change Mary's phone number to **5055551289**.

c. **Close** ☒ the form.

Deleting Records

Records can be deleted from a single table without additional steps if the table is not part of a relationship. If the table is part of a relationship, referential integrity has been enforced, and the cascade delete option has not been chosen, a record cannot be deleted if there are related records in another table until those records have also been deleted. For example, if you want to delete a customer from tblCustomer, and that customer has appointments in tblSchedule, then the appointments for the customer have to be deleted from the tblSchedule before the customer can be deleted from the tblCustomer. This prevents leaving a customer scheduled in one table without the corresponding customer information in another table.

For this exercise, the spa manager would like you to remove Peter Klein from tblEmployee since he has taken a new job and is leaving the spa. You explain to her that if he has any appointments scheduled in tblSchedule that those will have to be removed first. She tells you that rather than removing those records she would like to give those appointments to Alex instead. By changing the name to Alex, those appointments will no longer be linked to Peter, and Peter will be able to be deleted from tblEmployee.

> **CONSIDER THIS** | **Delete with Caution**
>
> Deleting records in a table is permanent. Once you confirm a deletion, you cannot use the Undo button. This is very different than programs like Excel or Word. Can you think of ways you could safeguard your data from accidental deletion?

To Delete a Record in a Form

a. Double-click **frmEmployee** to open the form. Click the Home tab, click **Find** in the Find group, and then in the Find What box type **Peter**. Click **Find Next**, and then click **Cancel** to close the Find and Replace dialog box.

b. Click the **Home tab**, click the **Delete arrow** in the Records group, and then click **Delete Record**. Access displays a message saying The record cannot be deleted or changed because table 'tblSchedule' included related records. Click **OK**.

c. Double-click **tblSchedule** to open the table. Press ⎄Tab to move to the Employee field. Click the **arrow** next to Peter, and then click Alex.

d. Click the Home tab, click **Find** in the Find group, and then in the Find What box type **Peter**. Click **Find Next**. Click the **arrow** next to the name, and then click **Alex**. Click **Find Next**, and then repeat for all three records that have Peter listed as the Employee. Click **Cancel** to close the Find and Replace box.

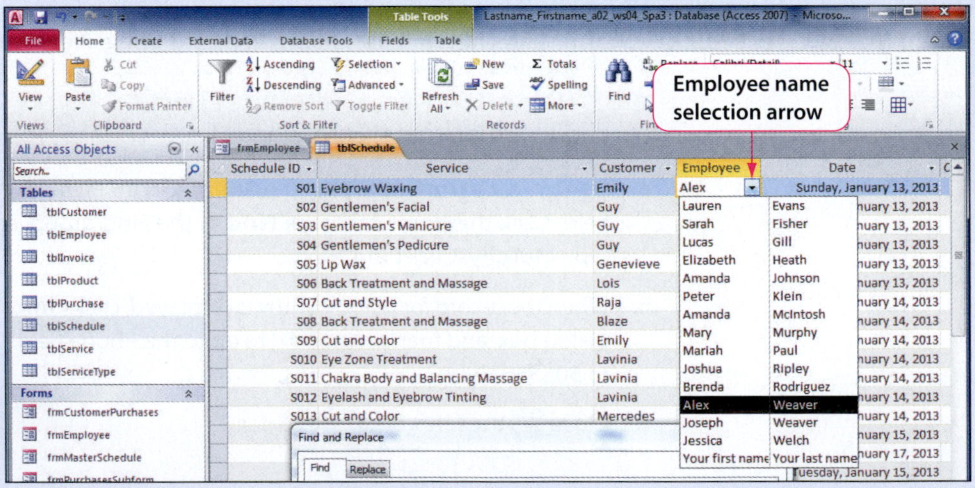

Figure 9 Replacing employee name using selection arrow

e. **Close** ⊠ the table. On the form, make sure the record showing is for Peter. Click the **Home tab**, click the **Delete arrow** in the Records group, and then select **Delete Record**. Click **Yes** to confirm the deletion.

f. **Close** ⊠ the form.

Create a Form Using the Form Wizard

Recall that the Query Wizard walks you through the steps in order to create a query, asking you questions and using your answers to build a query that you can then make changes to if necessary. The Form Wizard works in a similar fashion, walking you through step-by-step to create a form from one or more tables in your database.

Unlike creating a simple form using the Form button on the Create tab, when you create a form using the Wizard, it opens automatically in Form view ready for you to enter or edit your records. To make changes to the form, you have to switch to either Layout view or Design view.

Different Form Views

Form view is only for viewing and changing data, so to make any changes to the form you need to switch to either Layout view or Design view. Layout view allows you to make changes to the form while viewing the data at the same time. The effects of your changes can be viewed right away. Design view is a more advanced view that allows you to change the properties or structure of the form. Data is not shown while you are in Design view.

Both Layout view and Design view work with controls. A **control** is a part of a form or report that you use to enter, edit, or display data. There are three kinds of controls: bound, unbound, and calculated. A **bound control** is a control whose data source is a field in the table such as the customer name. An **unbound control** is a control that does not have a source of data such as the title of the form. A **calculated control** is a control whose data source is a calculated expression that you create. Every field from the table is made up of two controls: a label and a text box. A **label** may be the name of the field or some other text you manually enter and is an unbound control. A **text box** represents the actual value of a field and is a bound control. When you add a text box to a form, the label is automatically added as well. However, a label can be added independently from a text box.

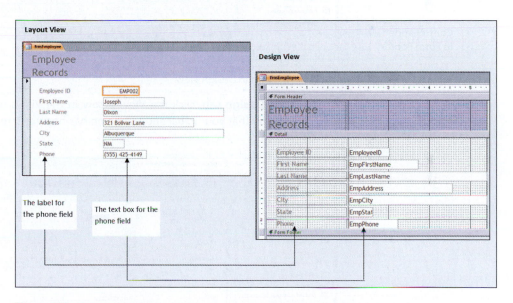

Figure 10 Text box and label controls in Layout view and Design view

For this exercise, the manager of the spa wants the staff to be able to enter and update customer information easily. She thinks it would be much easier to enter data in a form rather than in Datasheet view. You agree with her and offer to help set up the form.

To Create a Single Table Form in Design View

a. Click the **Create tab**, and then click **Form Wizard** in the Forms group. The Form Wizard dialog box opens.

b. Click the **Table/Queries arrow**, and select **Table: tblCustomer**. Click the **All Fields** button ▶▶ to add all the available fields to the Selected Fields box, and then click **Next**.

SIDE NOTE
Alternative Method to Add a Label

You can either expand the footer and then add the label, or you can add the label and the footer will automatically expand to fit what you add.

c. Verify that **Columnar** is selected as the form layout, and then click **Next**.

d. Under "What title do you want for your form?" type **frmCustomerInput_InitialLastName** replacing InitialLastName with your own name. Verify that **Open the form to view or enter information** is selected, and then click **Finish**.

The form opens in Form view so you can immediately start adding or editing records. The form name is also displayed in the Navigation Pane.

e. Click the Home tab, click the **View arrow** in the Views group, and then click **Design View**. Notice the Form Footer at the bottom of the form window. Click the Form Design Tools Design tab, and then click **Label** Aa in the Controls group. Point to the Form Footer area, and then when your mouse pointer changes to ^{+}A click and drag your pointer to draw a label control wide enough to fit your first initial and last name in the top-left corner of the Form Footer section. In the new label type your **First Initial** and **Last Name**.

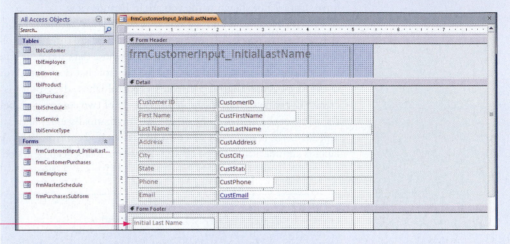

Control added in Form Footer

Figure 11 Form in Design view

f. Click the **Design tab**, click the **View arrow** in the Views group, and then click **Form View**. Verify that your initial and last name has been entered in the bottom-left corner of the form.

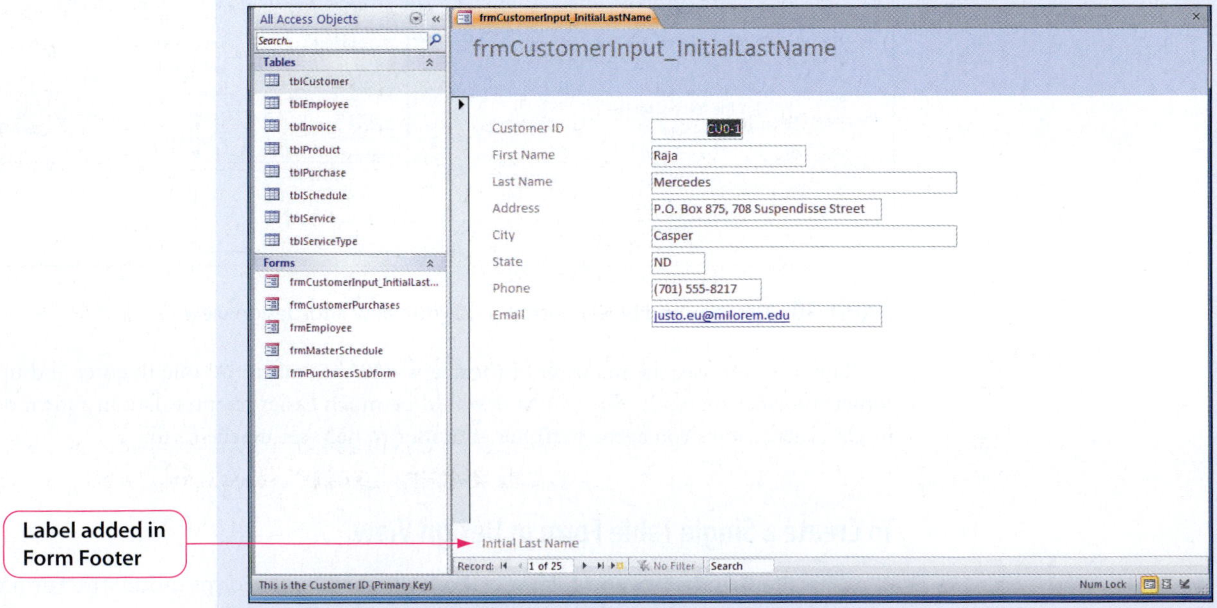

Label added in Form Footer

Figure 12 Form with first initial and last name added

g. **Close** ⊠ the form, and then click **Yes** to save the changes.

Creating Subforms (Multiple-Table Forms)

There may be times when you want to create a form using two tables. Before you can use two tables in a form, you must make sure there is a one-to-many relationship between the tables. Access will automatically use the common field between the tables to create the form.

The main form will display the first table one record at a time just like a single table form. This is the "one" record in the one-to-many relationship. The subform will be displayed as a datasheet below the main form record. This will display the "many" records in the one-to-many relationship.

For this project, you will help the staff create another form that shows each customer in the main form and the customer's scheduled appointments in the subform.

To Create a Subform

a. Click the **Create tab**, and then click **Form Wizard** in the Forms group. The Form Wizard dialog box opens.

b. Click the **Table/Queries arrow**, and then click **Table: tblCustomer**. Click the **All Fields** button ⟩⟩ to add all the available fields to the Selected Fields list.

c. Click the **Tables/Queries arrow**, and then select **Table: tblSchedule**. Click the **All Fields** button ⟩⟩ to add all the available fields to the Selected Fields list, and then click **Next**.

d. Verify that **by tblCustomer** is selected and that **Form with subform(s)** is selected, and then click **Next**.

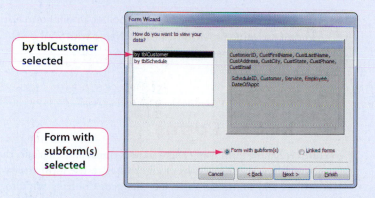

Figure 13 Form options are selected

e. Verify that **Datasheet** is selected for the subform layout, and then click **Next**.

f. Under "What titles do you want for your forms?" in the Forms field, type frmCustomer-Schedule_InitialLastName, replacing IntialLastName with your own initial and last name. In the Subform field type frmCustomerSubform_InitialLastName verify that Open the form to view or enter information is selected, and then click **Finish**.

The form opens in Form view so you can immediately start adding or editing records. The form and subform names are shown in the Navigation Pane.

g. Click the Home tab, click the **View arrow** in the Views group, and then click **Design View**. Scroll to the bottom of the form to see the Form Footer. Click the Design tab, click **Label** Aa in the Controls group, when your mouse pointer changes to ⁺A click and drag your pointer to draw a label control wide enough to fit your first initial and last name in the top-left corner of the Form Footer section. In the new label type your First Initial and Last Name.

h. Click the **Design tab**, click **View arrow** in the Views group, and then click **Form view**. Verify that your name has been entered in the bottom-left corner of the form.

i. **Close** ⊠ the form, and then click **Yes** to save the changes.

Creating a Split Form

A split form is created from one table and displays each record individually at the top of the window and then again as part of the whole table datasheet in the bottom of the window. This type of form gives you the advantage of seeing each record and the whole table in one place.

For this exercise, the manager would like to see each customer's record individually along with all the records from the customer table. You will show her how to create a split form from the customer table.

To Create a Split Form

a. Click **tblCustomer** one time in the Navigation Pane to select the table, but do not open it.

b. Click the **Create tab**, click **More Forms**, and then select **Split Form**. A window will open with the split form for the customer table.

c. Click the **Design tab**, click the **View arrow**, and then click **Design View**. Click **Label** **Aa** in the Controls group, when your mouse pointer changes to **⁺A**, click and drag your pointer to draw a label control wide enough to fit your first initial and last name in the top-left corner of the Form Footer section. In the new label type your **First Initial** and **Last Name**.

d. Click the **Design tab**, click **View arrow** in the Views group, and then click **Form View**. Verify that your name has been entered in the bottom-left corner of the form.

e. Click **Save** 🖫 on the Quick Access Toolbar, under Form Name type **frmCustomerSplit_ InitialLastName** replacing InitialLastName with your own first initial and last name, and then click **OK**. **Close** ☒ the form.

Customize Forms

While creating a form using the wizard is quick and efficient, there may be times you will want to change how the form looks or add things to the form after you have created it. Formatting, like colors and fonts, can easily be changed. Controls can also be added to a form to include additional fields or labels with text. Pictures and other objects can also be added to a form to make the form more visually appealing.

Modify a Form's Design

Oftentimes, forms are customized to match company or group color themes, or other forms and reports already created by a user. Customizing forms can make them more personal and sometimes easier to use.

Colors, font types, and font sizes are just a few of the formatting changes you can make to an existing form.

Changing the Form Theme

By default, Access uses the Office theme when you create a form using the Form Wizard. Even though there is not a step in the wizard to select a different theme, you can change it once the form has been created. A **theme** is a built-in combination of colors and fonts. By default, a theme will be applied to all objects in a database: forms, reports, tables, and queries. However, you can select to apply a theme to only the object you are working with or to all matching objects. You can also select a theme to be the default theme instead of Office.

Because the form is displayed in Form view, once it is created, the first step is to switch to Layout view to make changes to the form itself. Changing the theme will not only change the colors of the form but also the font type and size and any border colors or object colors added to the form. Once a theme is applied to the form, the colors and fonts can be changed independently of the theme, so you can combine the colors of one theme and a font of another.

For this exercise, the manager of the spa would like to make the customer input form look more like the colors in the spa. You will show her how to change the theme, the colors, and the fonts for the form. The theme will only be applied to the form and not to all the objects.

To Change the Theme of Your Form

a. Double-click **frmCustomerInput_InitialLastName** to open the form. Click the Home tab, click **View arrow**, and then click **Layout View**.

b. Click the **Design tab**, and then click **Themes** in the Themes group to open the Themes gallery. Scroll to find **Solstice** under Built-In themes, right-click the **theme**, and then click **Apply Theme to This Object Only**.

c. Click the **Design tab**, and then click **Colors** in the Themes group. Scroll down and click the color scheme **Elemental**.

d. Click the **Design tab**, and then click **Fonts** in the Themes group. Scroll down and click the Font theme **Opulent**.

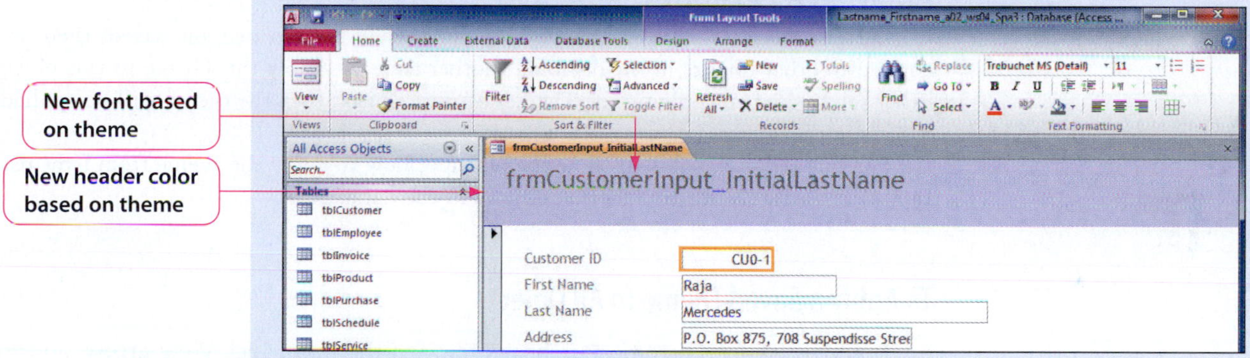

New font based on theme

New header color based on theme

Figure 14 Form with custom formatting

e. Click **Save** on the Quick Access Toolbar to save the form.

Saving a Custom Theme

If you put together a combination of fonts and colors you like, you can save that combination as a custom theme. That custom theme can then be used for other objects in Access like forms, reports, and tables.

For this exercise, you will show the manager how to save the theme from frmCustomerInput_InitialLastName as a custom theme so she can apply it to other objects.

To Save a Custom Theme

a. If necessary, double-click **frmCustomerInput_InitialLastName** to open the form. Click **View arrow**, and then select **Layout View**. Click the Design tab, and then click **Themes** in the Themes group. Click **Save Current Theme**.

b. In the Save Current Theme dialog box, navigate to where you are saving your files and type **Lastname_Firstname_a02_ws04_Theme** in the File Name box, replacing LastName_Firstname with your own last name. Click **Save**.

c. Click the **Design tab**, and then click **Themes** in the Themes group. Point to the second theme shown under the In this Database section of the gallery and notice your saved theme is listed as Solstice used by frmCustomerInput_InitialLastName.

d. **Close** the form.

Applying a Custom Theme

If a custom theme is applied to only one object when it is created and saved, then it can be applied to other objects in the database another time. If Apply the Theme to this object only is not selected when applying the Theme to a new object, then the theme will be applied to all objects in the database.

For this exercise, you will show the manager how to apply the theme from frmCustomer-Input_InitialLastName to the other objects in the database.

To Apply a Saved Theme to All Objects

a. Double-click **frmCustomerPurchases** to open the form. Click **View arrow**, and then select **Layout View**. Click the **Design tab**, click **Themes** in the Themes group, and then select **Solstice used by frmCustomerInput_InitialLastName**.

b. **Close** [×] the form. Double-click **frmEmployee** to open the form. Notice the Theme is Solstice used by frmCustomerInput_InitialLastName.

c. **Close** [×] the form.

Resizing and Changing Controls

Controls can be resized to make the form more user friendly. When you create a form using the wizard, the order that you choose the fields in the wizard step is the order the fields are added to the form. Once the form is created, you may decide the fields should be in a different order. When you click on a control in Layout view, an orange border appears around the control. When you select a subform control, an orange border appears around the control and a layout selector appears in the top-left corner. The **layout selector** allows you to move the whole table at one time. Once the control is selected you can move it or resize it. You can also change its appearance by adding borders or fill color.

For the following exercise, you will work with the spa staff to rearrange the controls on the Customer Schedule form to make it easier for data entry.

SIDE NOTE
Selecting Different Controls

There are two controls for each field—the label and the text box. The name of the field shows in the label, while the value of the field shows in the text box.

SIDE NOTE
Limited Visibility

If you cannot see the whole subform, use the scroll arrow on the right side of the window to scroll down the form.

To Change Controls on a Form

a. Double-click **frmCustomerSchedule_InitialLastName** to open it.

b. Click the Home tab, click **View**, and then click **Layout View**. Click the **Last Name** text box and an orange border appears around the control. Point to the right border of the control and drag it to the left so it lines up with the right border of the First Name text box above.

c. Click the **Address** text box, and then drag the right border to the right until it lines up with the right border of the City text box below.

d. Use the scroll bar on the Navigation bar of the subform to scroll to the right to see all the fields. Resize each column to best fit the data. Drag the right border of the subform to the right so that all fields are visible.

e. Double-click the **form title**, select the existing text, which by default is the name of the form, and type Customer Schedule. Press [Enter] when you are done typing.

f. Click the **Customer ID** label, press and hold [Shift], and then click the **Customer ID** text box to select both controls. Press [Delete] to delete both controls from the form.

g. Click the subform label **frmCustomer**, and then press [Delete] to delete it from the form.

h. Click the **Phone** label, hold down [Shift], click the **Phone** text box, the **Email** label, and the **Email** text box.

i. Point to any of the selected controls. When the mouse pointer changes to drag all four controls up and to the right until they are right next to the First Name and Last Name controls.

j. Click the **subform** datasheet to select it. Click the **Layout Selector**, and then drag it up and to the left so it is just under the State controls.

k. Click the **title** of the form to select it. Click the **Home tab**, click **Bold** in the Text Formatting group, click the **Font size arrow** in the Text Formatting group, and then select 28.

l. Click the **First Name** text box, hold down [Shift], and then click the **Last Name** text box. Click the **Home tab**, and then click **Bold** in the Text Formatting group.

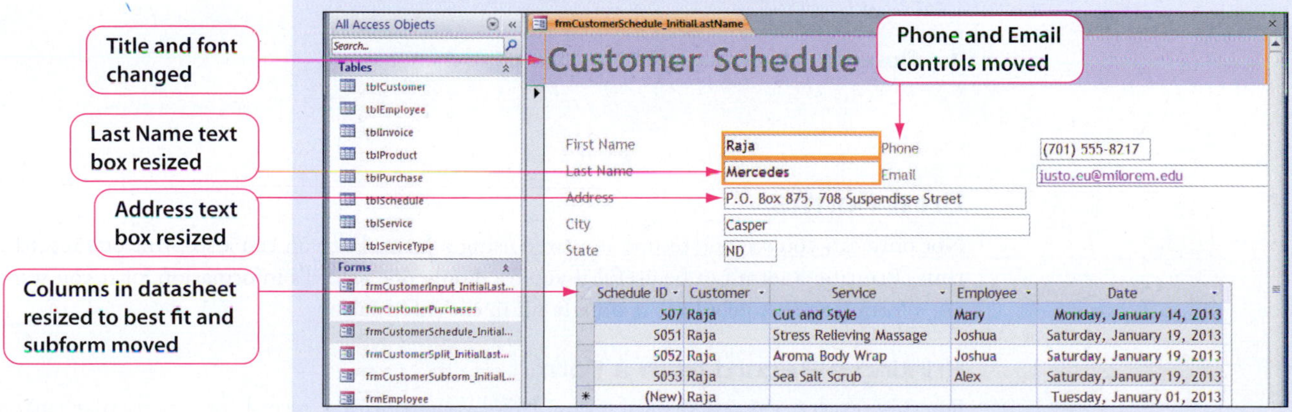

Figure 15 Formatted form and subform

m. Click **Save** on the Quick Access Toolbar to save the form.

Adding a Picture to the Form

Pictures can be added to forms to make them more appealing. When a picture is added to a form, then the same picture will appear for every record in the table. A different picture cannot be added for each record. A picture can be inserted in the header, footer, or the detail area of the form where the record values are shown. For this exercise you will insert a picture in the detail area of the form to make it more personal for the spa.

To Insert a Picture on the Form

a. Click the Home tab, click the **View arrow**, and then click **Layout View**. Click in the detail area of the form to select it. If a text box or label is selected, then the Insert Image button will not be available to use.

b. Click the **Design tab**, click **Insert Image** in the Controls group, and then click **Browse**.

c. In the Insert Picture dialog box, navigate to where your student files are located, click **a02_ws04_Spa_Image**, and click **OK**. With the image control pointer 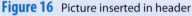, click in the form detail to insert the picture. Click the **Layout Selector** ⊞ and move the picture under the Email text box. With the top-left corner of the picture under the left border of the Email text box, point to the bottom-right corner of the picture and drag the corner until the picture fits between the Email text box and the subform.

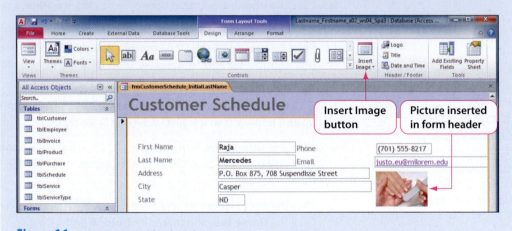

Figure 16 Picture inserted in header

d. **Close** ☒ the form and click **Yes** to save the changes.

Print Forms

Not only can you see one record at a time using a form, but you can also print one record at a time. Printing a form can be useful if you need only one record's information, or if you want to use a form for other people to manually fill in the information.

Printing a Record from a Form

For this project, the spa manager would like you to print a record for a particular customer from the customer form. You will show her how to preview the form first and then send it to the printer.

To Preview and Print a Record from a Form

a. Double-click **frmCustomerInput_InitialLastName** to open it. Click the Home tab, click the **View arrow**, and then click **Layout View**.

b. Double-click the **title**, select the **text**, and change it to Customer Record.

c. Click the **Address** text box, and then drag the right border to the right until it is lined up with the Last Name and City text boxes.

d. Click the **File tab**, click **Print**, and then click **Print Preview**. Notice all the records will print in Form view.

e. Click **Last Page** ▶ on the Navigation bar to go to the last record. Notice in the Navigation bar that the number of pages for the printed report will be seven.

f. Click the Print Preview tab, and then click **Close Print Preview** in the Close Preview group.

g. Using the Navigation bar, advance through the customer records to find the record for Jonah Hogan.

h. Click the **File tab**, select **Print**, and then click **Print**. In the Print dialog box, in the Print Range section, click **Selected Record(s)**. Click **OK** to print the record if instructed to do so.

SIDE NOTE
Selecting Records

When you view all the records in Print Preview, you cannot choose Selected Record(s) in the Print dialog box. To choose Selected Record(s) you must have one record showing in Form view when you click Print.

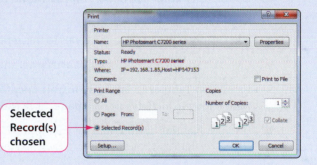

Selected Record(s) chosen

Figure 17 Print one record as a form

i. **Close** ✕ the form, and click **Yes** to save the changes.

Use the Report Wizard

While a report and a form may look similar, a form is a method for data entry and a report is a formatted printout of that data. A report can be created from either a table or query. Reports may be based on multiple tables in a one-to-many relationship using a common field to match the records. The records from the "one" table in the relationship will be shown first as the primary table (similar to a main form) with the records from the many" relationship shown as detailed records as the **subreport** (similar to a subform).

Create a Report Using the Report Wizard

The Report Wizard will walk you through step by step to build your report. You will choose the table or query to base the report on, and choose the fields to include in the report. You will have the option to group the data in your report. A **group** is a collection of records along with introductory and summary information about the records. Grouping allows you to separate related records for the purpose of creating a visual summary of the data. Groups can be created with data from individual tables or from multiple tables.

For example, a report grouped by the primary table containing customer records would show all the selected fields for a customer, and then would list that customer's individual appointments from the secondary table below the customer's record.

Within a report you can also sort using up to four fields in either ascending or descending order. Once a report is created using the wizard, it will open in Print Preview. Print Preview provides a view of the report representing how it will look when it is actually printed and provides you with printing options such as orientation, margins, and size. The current date and page numbers are added, and you can navigate the report in this view using the Navigation bar. To make any changes to the report, you can switch to Layout view using the View button.

Creating a Single Table Report

A report can be created using one table or multiple tables. A single table report is a report created from one table. Any or all of the fields can be selected, and the report can be created from a table or query. For this project, the spa manager would like to have a report to help the staff with scheduling. The report will be a list of employee names and phone numbers so the staff can contact each other if necessary.

To Create a Single Table Report Using Report Wizard

a. Click the **Create tab**, and then click **Report Wizard** in the Reports group.

b. Click the **Tables/Queries arrow**, and then select **tblEmployee**.

c. Double-click **EmpFirstName**, **EmpLastName**, and **EmpPhone** from the Available Fields list. Click **Next**.

d. You will not add any grouping levels to this report so click **Next**.

e. Click the **Sort arrow**, select **EmpLastName**, and then click **Next**.

f. Verify that **Tabular** layout and **Portrait** orientation are selected, as well as **Adjust the field width so all fields fit on a page**. Click **Next**.

g. Under "What title do you want for your report?" type rptEmployeeList_InitialLastName replacing InitialLastName with your own first initial and last name, and then click **Finish**.

h. Click the Print Preview tab, and then click **Close Print Preview** in the Close Preview group. Click the Design tab, click **Label** Aa in the Controls group, and then when your mouse pointer changes to ⁺A, click and drag your pointer to draw a label control wide enough to fit your first initial and last name in the top-left corner of the Report Footer section. In the new label type your First Initial and Last Name.

i. Click the Design tab, click the **View arrow** in the Views group, and then click **Report View**. Verify that your name has been entered in the bottom-left corner of the form.

j. **Close** ☒ the report, and then click **Yes** to save the changes.

Creating a Multiple Table Report

Similar to other objects created using more than one table, a multiple-table report must use tables that have a common field. The first table chosen for the report becomes the primary table, and the next and subsequent tables chosen become the secondary tables.

In this exercise, the manager would like a report that will show each employee name and their upcoming appointments. This way the staff members can help coordinate their services for a guest who may be seeing more than one staff member in a day.

SIDE NOTE

It is a Matter of Order

The order you add the fields in the report wizard is the order the fields will appear on the report.

To Create a Multiple Table Report Using Report Wizard

a. Click the **Create tab**, and then click **Report Wizard** in the Reports group.

b. Click the **Tables/Queries arrow**, and then select **Table: tblEmployee**. Double-click **EmpFirstName** and **EmpLastName** in the Available Fields list.

c. Click the **Tables/Queries arrow**, and then select **Table: tblSchedule**. Double-click **Service, DateOfAppt**, and **Customer** from the Available Fields list. Click **Next**.

d. Verify that **by tblEmployee** is highlighted to view the data by Employee, and then click **Next**.

e. Double-click **DateOfAppt** to group by the date. Click **Grouping Options**, and then under Grouping intervals select **Normal**. Click **OK**, and then click **Next**.

f. Click the **Sort arrow**, select **Customer**, and then click **Next**.

g. Verify that **Stepped** is selected under Layout, and then click **Landscape** under Orientation. Verify that **Adjust the field width so all fields fit on a page** is checked. Click **Next**.

h. Under "What title do you want for your report?" type rptEmployeeSchedule_InitialLastName, replacing InitialLastName with your own first initial and last name, and then click **Finish**. The report will open in Print Preview.

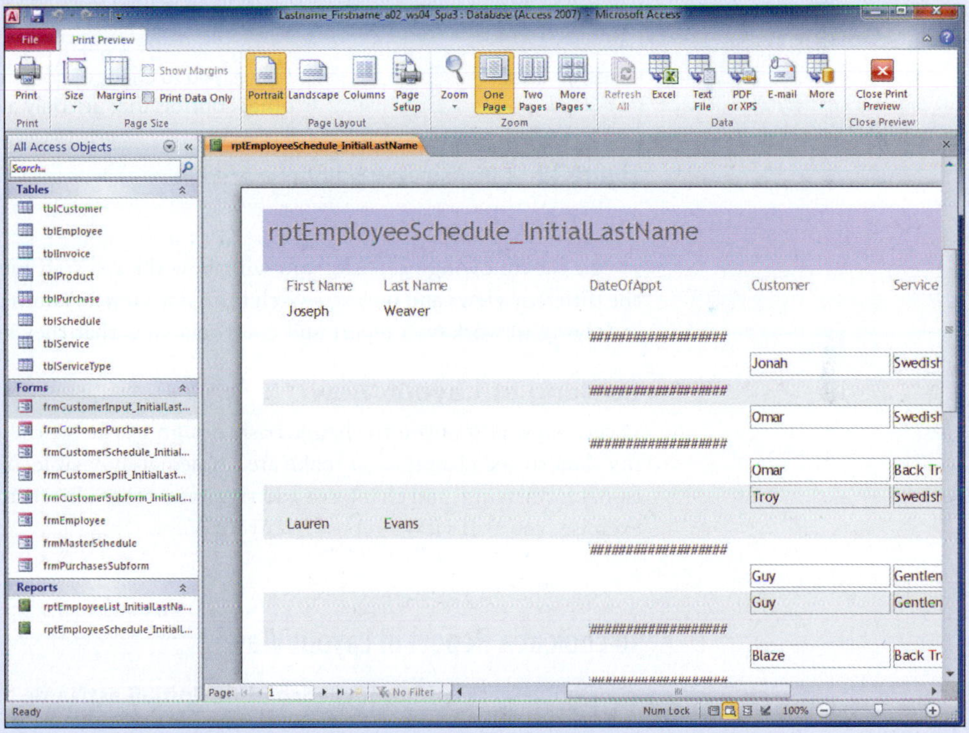

Figure 18 Report open in Print Preview

i. Click the Print Preview tab, and then click **Close Print Preview** in the Close Preview group. You should see the report in Design view.

j. Click the Design tab, click **Label** Aa in the Controls group, and then when your mouse pointer changes to $^+\!A$ click and drag your pointer to draw a label control wide enough to fit your initial and last name in the top-left corner of the Report Footer section. In the new label type your **First Initial** and **Last Name**.

k. Click the Design tab, click the **View arrow**, and then click **Report View**. Verify that your name has been entered in the bottom-left corner of the report. **Close** $\boxed{\times}$ the report, and then click **Yes** to save the changes.

Looking at Different Report Views

You have seen a report in Print Preview when the Report Wizard is done creating the report, which is the view that shows you exactly what the report will look like when it is printed. Print preview adds the current date and page numbers in the page footer at the bottom of each page. Each type of view has its own features as shown in Figure 19.

View name	What the view is used for
Print Preview	Shows what the printed report will look like
Layout view	Allows you to modify the report while seeing the data
Report view	Allows you to filter data, or copy parts of the report to the Clipboard
Design view	Allows you to change more details of the report design, or add other controls that are only available in Design view

Figure 19   Different view options for a report

In the following exercises, you will show the spa staff members what a report looks like in the different views and how to switch from one view to another. This will be helpful in case they are trying to work on a report and click on a view that they have not worked with in the past.

Looking at Layout View

Layout view allows you to change basic design feature of the report while the report is displaying data so the changes you make are immediately visible. You can resize controls, add conditional formatting, and change or add titles and other objects to the report in Layout view. In this exercise, you will view a report in Layout View.

To Look at a Report in Layout View

a. Double-click **rptEmployeeSchedule_InitialLastName** to open it.

b. Click the Home tab, click the **View arrow** in the Views group, and then click **Layout View**. Notice the orange border around the first Customer field.

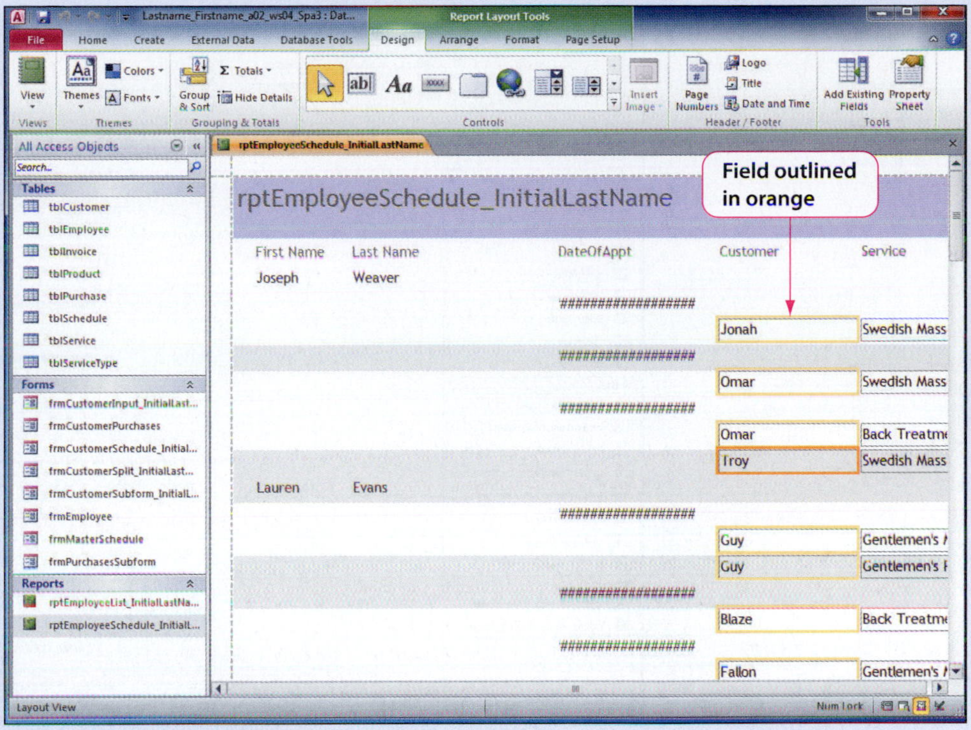

Figure 20 Report in Layout view

SIDE NOTE
Page Numbers

Notice there is the date and page number in the page footer, but the page number shows page 1 of 1. The actual number of pages will not be calculated until you switch to Print Preview.

c. Scroll to the bottom of the report.

Looking at Report View

Report view provides an interactive view of your report. In Report View you can filter records or you can copy data to the clipboard. There will be no page breaks shown in Report View so the number of pages at the bottom will show Page 1 of 1. In this exercise, you will just look at the report in Report View.

To Look at a Report in Report View

a. Click the Design tab, click the **View arrow** in the Views group, and then click **Report View**.

b. Scroll to the bottom of the report.

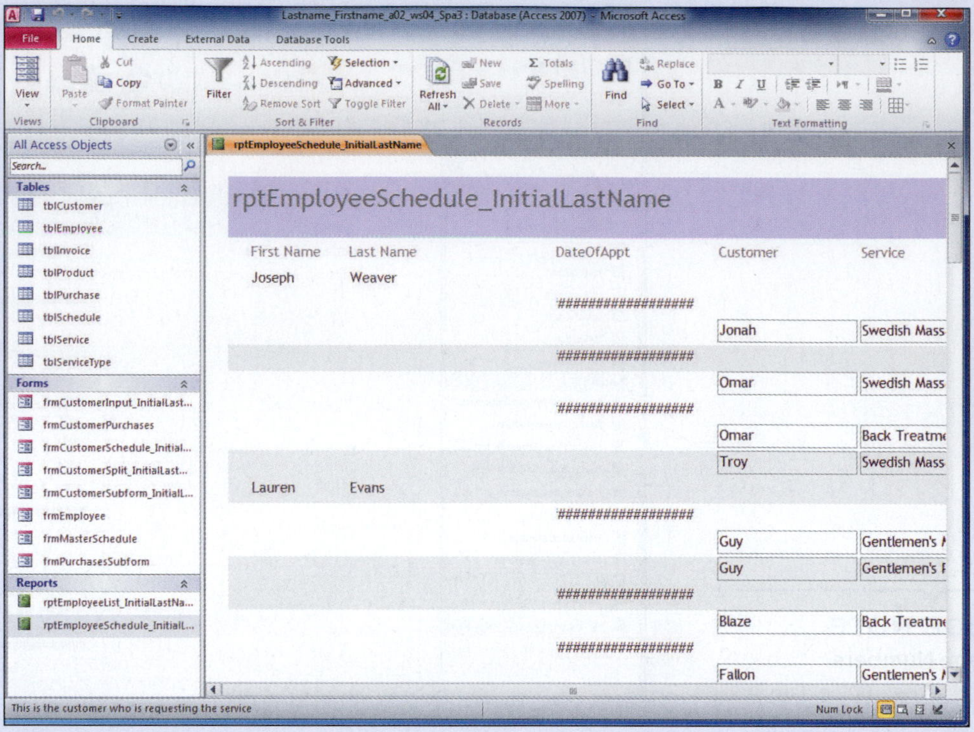

Figure 21 Report in Report view

Looking at Design View

Design view offers more options for adding and editing controls on a report, as well as options not available in any of the other views. In this exercise, you will look at a report in Design View.

To Look at a Report in Design View

a. Click the **Home tab**, click the **View arrow** in the Views group, and then click **Design View**. Data in Design view is not visible, only the controls in each section of the report are.

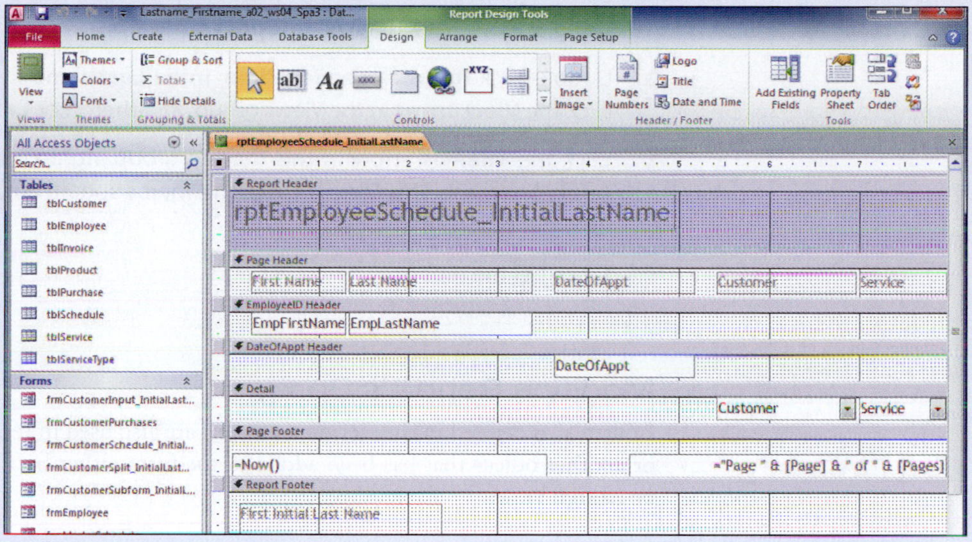

Figure 22 Report in Design view

b. **Close** ☒ the report.

Customize a Report

Reports created by the Wizard can be easily customized after they have been created and saved. Themes can be applied to just the report or the whole database to change the colors, fonts or both. Controls, bound and unbound, can be added or modified on the report to make room for more information or to rearrange the information already there.

In order to break a report into smaller sections, subtotals or groups may be added. Additional sorting options may also be applied or modified.

Conditional formatting may also be applied in order to highlight fields that meet certain criteria.

Use and Customize Access Themes

By default, Access uses the Office theme when you create a report using the Report Wizard just like when you create a form with the Form Wizard. However, even though there is not a step in the wizard to select a different theme, you can change it once the report has been created.

Applying a Theme

Changing the theme will not only change the colors of the report, but also the font type, size, and any border colors or object colors added to the report. Once a theme is applied to the report, the colors and fonts can be changed independently of the theme, so you can combine the colors of one theme and a font of another.

As you recall, by default, a theme will be applied to all objects in a database: forms, reports, tables, and queries. However, you can select to apply a theme to only the object you are working with or to all matching objects. For the following exercises, you will change the theme of the Employee schedule report to the custom theme you saved earlier.

To Apply a New Theme to the Report Only

a. Double-click **rptEmployeeSchedule_InitialLastName** to open it. Click the Home tab, click the **View arrow** in the Views group, and then click **Layout View**.

b. Click the **Themes** arrow in the Themes group, right-click **Composite**, and then click **Apply Theme to This Object Only**. The Theme should only be applied to the report and no other objects in the database.

c. **Close** ☒ the report.

Modify a Report's Design

Controls, as defined in the section on forms, are also used in reports. A control can be a text box, or another object that has been added to the form either by the wizard or manually in Layout or Design view.

Moving, Resizing, and Formatting Report Controls

Controls can be moved or resized to make the report more readable. When you create a report using the wizard, the order that you choose the fields in the wizard step is the order the fields are added to the report. Once the report is created, you may decide that the fields should be in a different order. When you click on a control in Layout view, an orange border appears around the control. Once the control is selected you can move it or resize it. You can also change its appearance by adding borders or fill color.

For this exercise, you will change the rptEmployeeSchedule schedule report to make it look more like what the manager expected. You will move the date, service, and customer name fields below the employee name, change the heading, and change the formatting.

To Move, Resize, and Format a Control in a Report

a. Double-click **rptEmployeeSchedule_InitialLastName** to open it. Click the **Home tab**, click the **View arrow** in the Views group, and then click **Layout View**.

b. Click the **DateOfAppt** text box control to select it, and then drag the field to the left so it is just slightly indented under the employee name. Drag the right border of the control to make the whole date visible.

c. Click the **First Name** label, press and hold ⟨Shift⟩, click the **Last Name** label and the **DateofAppt** label, and then press ⟨Delete⟩.

d. Click the **Customer label**, press and hold ⟨Shift⟩, and then click the **Customer** text box, the **Service label**, and the **Service** text box. Point and click on any field to drag all the controls to the left, just next to the date field.

e. Click the **Service** text box. Drag the **right border** of the text box to the right to fit all the service description. Click the **Service label**, and then press ⟨Delete⟩.

f. Click the **Service** text box, press and hold ⟨Shift⟩, and then click the **Customer** text box. Click the **Format tab**, click **Shape Outline** in the Control Formatting group, and then select **Transparent**.

g. Click the **First Name** text box, press and hold ⟨Shift⟩, and then click the **Last Name** text box. Click the Format tab, click **Shape Fill** in the Control Formatting group, and then select **Light Blue 3** under Standard colors. Click **Bold** ⟨B⟩ in the Font group.

h. Double-click the **title**, select the **text**, type Employee Schedule, and then press ⟨Enter⟩.

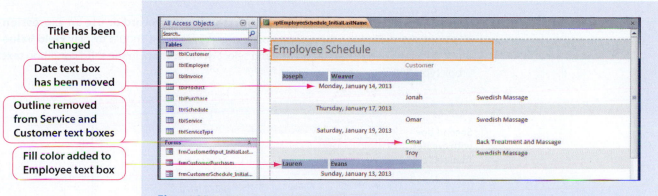

Title has been changed

Date text box has been moved

Outline removed from Service and Customer text boxes

Fill color added to Employee text box

Figure 23 Formatted report in Layout view

i. **Close** ☒ the report, and then click **Yes** to save the changes.

Enhancing a Report with Conditional Formatting

In the previous section you changed the colors and fonts of fields. You can also change the fonts and colors of fields only when certain conditions are met in the field. This is called **conditional formatting**. If a field value meets the conditions you specify, then the formatting will be applied. This is a useful tool to automatically highlight sales numbers on a report if they meet a certain threshold, or to highlight students grades when they exceed a certain limit.

To apply conditional formatting, you must select the field value in the field to which you want the formatting applied. You can select a different font color and font effects for the formatting.

For this exercise, the spa manager would like you to create a report and apply conditional formatting to all services currently scheduled that are over $100. These customers usually get some special treatments like complimentary coffee and tea, and the staff would like to be able to easily see which customers will get this service.

To Apply Conditional Formatting to a Report Field

a. Click the **Create tab**, and then click **Report Wizard** in the Reports group.

b. Click the **Tables/Queries arrow**, and then select **Table: tblSchedule**. Double-click **DateOfAppt, Customer**, and **Service** in the Available Fields list.

c. Click the **Tables/Queries arrow**, and then select **Table: tblService**. Double-click **Fee** from the Available Fields list, and then click **Next**.

d. Verify that **by tblSchedule** is highlighted, and then click **Next**. You will not add any grouping to this report, so click **Next**.

e. Click the **Sort arrow**, click **DateofAppt**, and then click **Next**. Verify that **Tabular** is selected under Layout and **Portrait** under Orientation. Verify that **Adjust the field width so all fields fit on a page** is checked. Click **Next**.

f. Under "What title do you want for your report?" type **rptHighFees_InitialLastName** replacing InitialLastName with your first initial and last name, and then click **Finish**. The report will open in Print Preview.

g. Click the Print Preview tab, and then click **Close Print Preview**. Click the **Home tab**, click the **View arrow** in the Views group, and then select **Layout View**.

h. Double-click the **title**, select the **text**, type **High Service Customers**, and press Enter.

i. Click in the **Fee** text box, click the **Format tab**, and then click **Conditional Formatting** in the Control Formatting group.

j. Click **New Rule**. Verify that **Check values in the current record or use an expression** is highlighted. Find the three condition text boxes. The first should display **Field Value Is**. Click in the second condition box and select **greater than**. In the third condition text box type **100**.

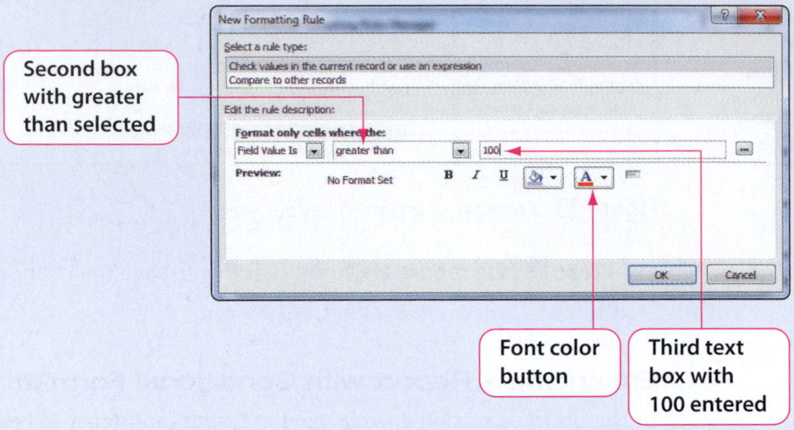

Figure 24 New Formatting Rule dialog box

k. Below the condition text boxes select the formatting. Click **Bold** B, click the **Font color arrow**, and then click **Dark Red**. Click **OK**, verify that your rule states Value >100, and then click **OK**.

All values greater than $100 in the Fee field should be highlighted in dark red and bold.

l. Click the **Home tab**, click the **View arrow** in the Views group, and then click **Design View**. Click the Design tab, click **Label** [Aa] in the Controls group, when your mouse pointer changes to [†A] click and drag your pointer to draw a label control wide enough to fit your name in the top-left corner of the Report Footer section. In the new label type your **First Initial** and **Last Name**.

m. Click the **Design tab**, click the **View arrow**, and then click **Report View**. Verify that your name has been entered in the bottom-left corner of the report.

n. Scroll through the report to make sure all your data is visible. Click the **Home tab**, click the **View arrow**, and then click **Layout View**. If necessary, click the **Date** text box, and then drag the left border to the left until the whole field is visible.

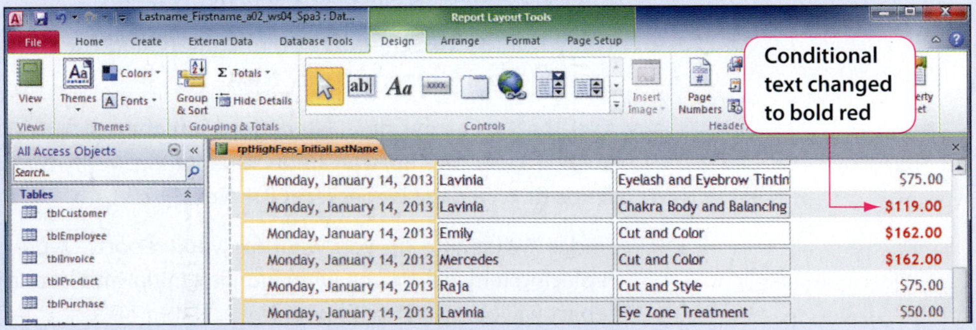

SIDE NOTE
Delete Conditional Formatting

You can delete a conditional formatting rule by clicking the Format tab in Layout view, click the field that has the conditional formatting applied, click Conditional Formatting in the Control Formatting group, and then click the rule you wish to delete and click Delete Rule.

Figure 25 Report with resized fields and conditional formatting applied

Troubleshooting

If the DateOfAppt text box shows ######## instead of the date, the field is not wide enough to display the whole date. Switch to Layout view, click the DateOfAppt text box, and drag the right border to the right to make the control wider.

o.   **Close** ☒ the report, and then click **Yes** to save the changes.

Applying Grouping and Sorting

The Report Wizard gives you the opportunity to sort and group records, but sometimes seeing the report changes your mind about what and how to group and sort. You can change the sorting and grouping options from either Layout or Design view. Groups are added to a section of the report called the **group header**. Calculations performed on a group in a report are added to a section called the **group footer**. A report may have one or more group headers, group footers, both, or neither.

In Layout view you will use the Group, Sort, and Total pane to select the sort fields and grouping fields for a report. This is done after the report has been created by the Report Wizard.

For this exercise, the spa manager would like a report that shows appointment dates and services scheduled for those dates. You will show her how to create the report, and then you will make some changes to it until she likes how the information is presented.

To Add Group and Sort Fields to a New Report

a.   Click the **Create tab**, and then click **Report Wizard** in the Reports group.

b.   Click the **Tables/Queries arrow**, and then select **Table: tblSchedule**. Double-click **DateOfAppt**, **Service**, **Customer**, and **Employee** from the Available Fields list. Click **Next**.

c.   Click the **One Field Back** button ◄ to remove the Service grouping level. Click **DateOfAppt**, and then click the **One Field** button ► to add the date as a grouping level. Click **Grouping Options**, and then under Grouping intervals select **Normal**. Click **OK**, and then click **Next**.

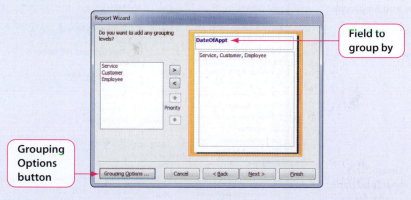

Figure 26 Report Wizard grouping step

d.   Click the **Sort arrow**, select **Service**, and then click **Next**.

e.   Select **Stepped** layout and **Portrait** orientation. Verify that **Adjust the field width so all fields fit on a page** is checked. Click **Next**.

f. Under "What title do you want for your report?" type **rptAppointments_InitialLastName** replacing InitialLastName with your own first initial and last name, and then click **Finish**. Click the Print Preview tab, and then click **Close Print Preview**.

g. Click the **Design tab**, click **Label** $\boxed{Aa}$ in the Controls group, and then when your mouse pointer changes to $\boxed{^+_A}$ click and drag your pointer to draw a label control wide enough to fit your name in the top-left corner of the Report Footer section. Click in the new label you just added, and then type your **First Initial** and **Last Name**.

h. Click the **Design tab**, click the **View arrow** in the Views group, and then click **Report View**. Verify that your name has been entered in the bottom-left corner of the report.

i. Click the Home tab, click the **View arrow** in the Views group, and then click **Layout View**. Click the **DateOfAppt** text box, click the **Format tab**, and then click **Align Text Left** $\boxed{\equiv}$ in the Font group. Drag the right border of the **DateOfAppt** text box to line up with the left border of the Service text box. All the date values should be visible.

j. Click the **Service** text field, and then drag the left border to the left to make the control wider so all the text can be displayed. Scroll down to the appointments scheduled on Friday, January 18, 2011, and then confirm that the Microdermabrasion Treatment (six sessions) is showing.

k. Double-click the **title**, select the **text**, and then type **Daily Appointments**.

l. Click the **Design tab**, click **Group & Sort** in the Grouping & Totals group, and notice the Group, Sort, and Total pane that opens at the bottom of the report.

m. Click on the line that displays **Sort by Service**, and then click **Delete** $\boxed{\times}$ on the far right of the line. This will delete the sort that was added in the Report Wizard.

n. Click **Add a group** in the Group, Sort, and Total pane, and then select **Employee**.

o. Click the **Employee** text box, and then drag it to the left until it is under the month name in the date. Click the **Employee** label, press and hold $\boxed{\text{Shift}}$, click the **DateOfAppt** label, and then press $\boxed{\text{Delete}}$.

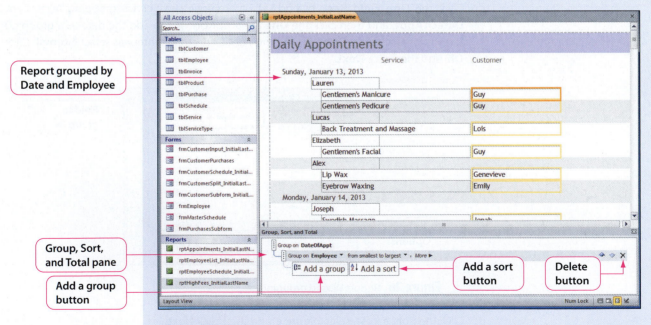

Figure 27 New grouping added to report

p. **Close** $\boxed{\boxtimes}$ the Group, Sort, and Total pane. **Close** $\boxed{\times}$ the report, and then click **Yes** to save the changes.

Adding Subtotals

Subtotals can be added to a report to calculate totals for smaller groups of records. In Layout view, the subtotal is added in the Group, Sort, and Total pane when selecting or modifying groups and sorts for the reports.

For this exercise, the spa manager would like a report that shows all invoices grouped by date and subtotaled for each date.

To Add Subtotals to a Report

a. Click the **Create tab**, and then click **Report Wizard** in the Reports group.

b. Click the **Tables/Queries arrow**, and then select **Table: tblInvoice**. Double-click **InvoiceDate, CustomerID, InvoiceNumber,** and **InvoiceTotal** from the Available fields list. Click **Next**.

c. Click the **One Field Back** button < to remove the CustomerID grouping level. Click **InvoiceDate**, and then click the **One Field** button > to add the date as a grouping level. Click **Grouping Options**, and then under Grouping intervals select **Normal**. Click **OK**, and then click **Next**.

d. Click the **Sort arrow**, select **CustomerID**, click the second **Sort arrow**, select **InvoiceNumber**, and then click **Next**.

e. Select **Stepped** layout and **Portrait** orientation. Verify that **Adjust the field width so all fields fit on a page** is checked. Click **Next**.

f. Under "What title do you want for your report?" type **rptInvoices_InitialLastName** replacing InitialLastName with your first initial and last name, and then click **Finish**.

g. Click the Print Preview tab, and then click **Close Print Preview** in the Close Preview group. Click the **Design tab**, click **Label** [Aa] in the Controls group, and then when your mouse pointer changes to [ᵗA] click and drag your pointer to draw a label control wide enough to fit your name in the top-left corner of the Report Footer section. Click in the new label you just added, and then type your First Initial and Last Name.

h. Click the **Design tab**, click the **View arrow**, and then click **Report View**. Verify that your name has been entered in the bottom-left corner of the report. Click the Home tab, click the **View arrow** in the Views group, and then click **Layout View**.

i. Click the **InvoiceTotal** text box. Click the **Design tab**, click **Totals** in the Grouping & Totals group, and then click **Sum**.

Subtotals for each InvoiceDate group will show under the InvoiceTotal details. A grand total will show at the bottom of the report.

j. Right-click one of the subtotal controls, and then click **Set Caption**. A control label will be added next to each subtotal amount that says InvoiceTotal Total. Double-click the **control**, select the **text**, and then type Invoice Subtotal. Repeat the same steps to set a caption for the grand total control, and then change the text to Invoice Total.

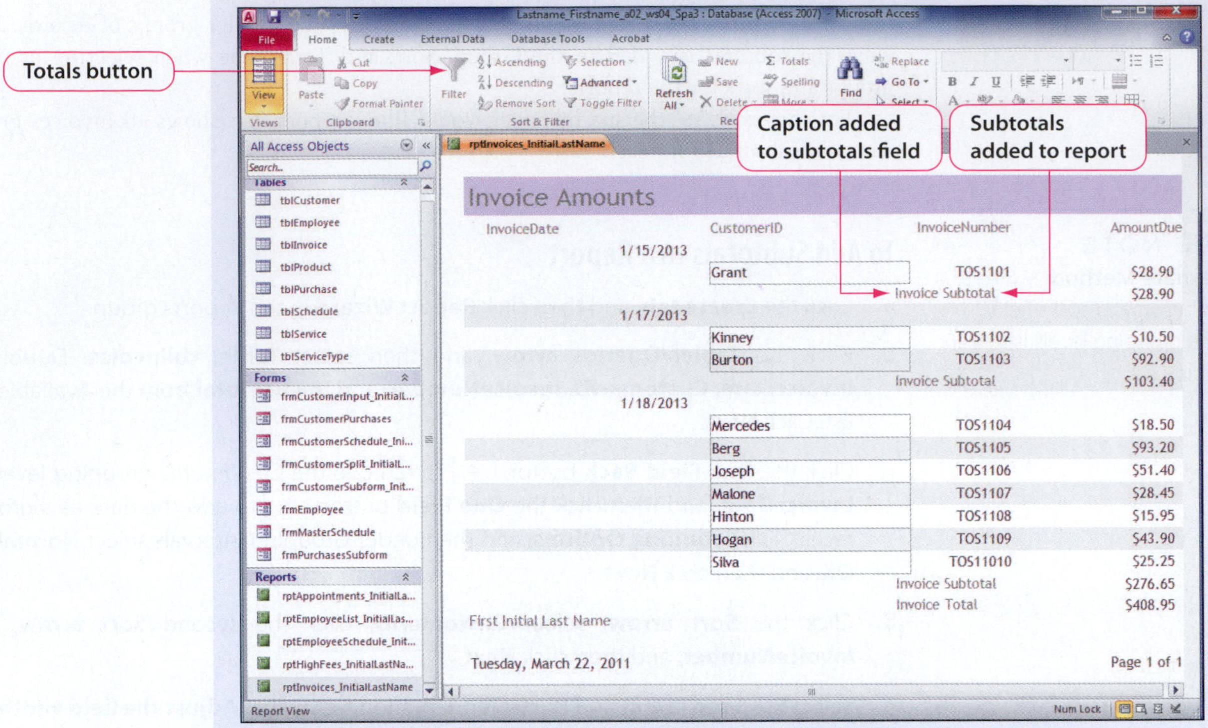

Figure 28 Report with subtotals added

k. Double-click the **title**, select the **text**, and then type **Invoice Amounts**. **Close** ☒ the report, and then click **Yes** to save the changes.

Print and Save a Report as a PDF File

Reports are formatted printable documents of your data, so the final result of a report will usually be a printout. If not printed, then the report may be shared with other people electronically. When you send a report to someone electronically, they have to have the same program in which the report was created in order to open the report. To avoid this problem, you can save a report as a PDF file, which can be read by Adobe Reader, a free program that you can download from the Internet.

Printing a Report

To print a report, you will use the Print dialog box on the File tab to select your printing options. Before you print, it is always a good idea to view the report in Print Preview to make sure it looks the way you want. Viewing the report in Layout view and Report view does not show you page breaks and other features of the report as it will look when actually printed. In Print Preview, you have many options to make design changes to your report before you send it to the printer. You can change the margins and orientation, and you can select how many pages, if not all, you want to print.

For this exercise, you will show the staff members how to print the employee schedule report so they can hang it up in the break room.

SIDE NOTE
Print Options
The Print dialog box allows you to print the whole report or a range of pages in the report.

To Print a Report

a. Double-click **rptEmployeeSchedule_InitialLastName** to open the report. Click the **File tab**, click **Print**, and then select **Print Preview**. Scroll through the pages to make sure the records fit on the pages correctly.

SIDE NOTE
Printing Part of a Report

To print a range of pages, under Print Range in the Print dialog box, select Pages and enter the first and last page of the range you want to print.

b. Click the Print Preview tab, and then click **Print** in the Print group.

c. Under Print Range, select **All**, and then click **OK**.

d. **Close** ☒ the report.

Creating a PDF File

If you need to distribute the report electronically, you also have the option to save the report as an Adobe PDF file. An **Adobe PDF file** is usually smaller than the original document, easy to send through e-mail, and preserves the original document look and feel so you know exactly what it will look like when the recipient opens it. For this exercise, you will show the staff how to create a PDF file of the employee schedule so it can easily be e-mailed to the staff each week.

SIDE NOTE
Publish a PDF

The correct terminology for saving a report as a PDF file format is to "publish" the report. When you are saving the report as a PDF you will see the option to Publish, not to Save or Print.

To Save a Report as a PDF File

a. Double-click **rptEmployeeSchedule_InitialLastName** to open the report. Click the **File tab**, and then click **Save & Publish**.

b. Click **Save Object As**. Under Database File Types, click **PDF or XPS** under Save the current database object. Click **Save As**.

c. In the Publish as PDF or XPS dialog box, locate the folder where you are saving your files, and in the File name box type **Lastname_Firstname_a02_ws04_pdfEmployeeSchedule** replacing Lastname_Firstname with your first name and last name. Click **Publish**.

d. The report will open as a PDF file in Adobe Reader. Close ☒ Adobe Acrobat to return to Access. **Close** ☒ the report, and then close ☒ Access.

SIDE NOTE
Adobe Reader

If you do not have Adobe Reader installed on your computer, the PDF file will not be able to open. To get Adobe Reader, you will need to download the free program from the Adobe Acrobat website.

1. What is the difference in editing and entering data in a form versus a table? When is it better to enter data in a form? When is it better to enter data directly in a table? What about a query? Are there times when editing data in a query can be useful?

2. What is the difference between a main form and a subform? What is a split form? When would you use each of these?

3. What view will you see when the Form Wizard is done creating the form? What are the difference between Layout view, Form view, and Design view?

4. What are controls? What is the difference between a label control and a text box control?

5. What is the difference between sorting and grouping in a report?

6. What is the difference between Report view, Print Preview, Layout Print preview, Layout view, and Design view when you are creating a report? Which view will show you the most accurate picture of what your printed report will look like?

7. What is conditional formatting, and when would you use it?

8. What is a PDF file, and why would you want to save your report as a PDF? What software do you need to read a PDF file? How can you get this software?

Key Terms

Adobe PDF file 215
Bound control 193
Calculated control 193
Conditional formatting 209
Control 193
Edit mode 184
Group 201

Group footer 211
Group header 211
Label 193
Layout selector 198
Main form 185
Navigation mode 184
Split form 188

Subform 185
Subreport 201
Subtotals 213
Text box 193
Theme 196
Unbound control 193

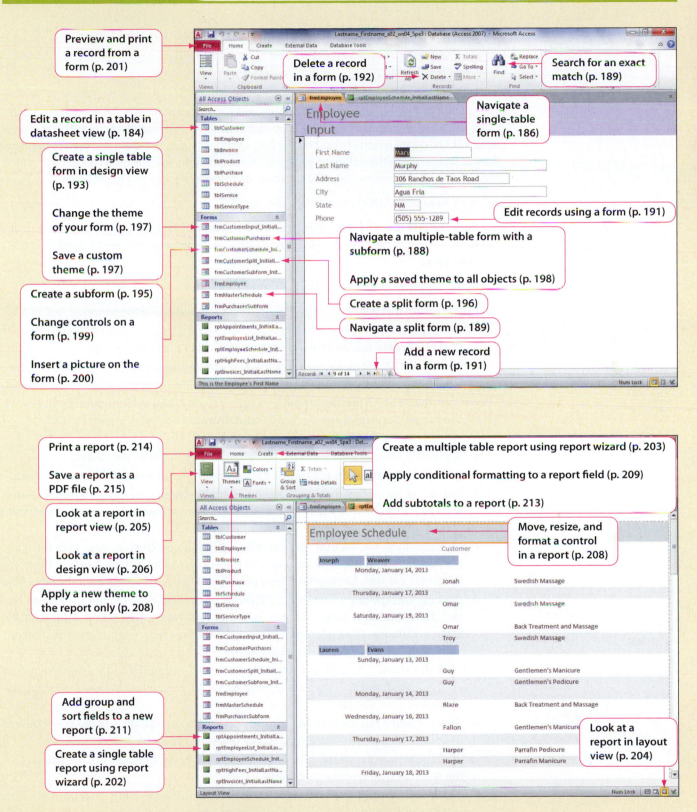

Preview and print a record from a form (p. 201)

Edit a record in a table in datasheet view (p. 184)

Create a single table form in design view (p. 193)

Change the theme of your form (p. 197)

Save a custom theme (p. 197)

Create a subform (p. 195)

Change controls on a form (p. 199)

Insert a picture on the form (p. 200)

Delete a record in a form (p. 192)

Search for an exact match (p. 189)

Navigate a single-table form (p. 186)

Edit records using a form (p. 191)

Navigate a multiple-table form with a subform (p. 188)

Apply a saved theme to all objects (p. 198)

Create a split form (p. 196)

Navigate a split form (p. 189)

Add a new record in a form (p. 191)

Print a report (p. 214)

Save a report as a PDF file (p. 215)

Look at a report in report view (p. 205)

Look at a report in design view (p. 206)

Apply a new theme to the report only (p. 208)

Add group and sort fields to a new report (p. 211)

Create a single table report using report wizard (p. 202)

Create a multiple table report using report wizard (p. 203)

Apply conditional formatting to a report field (p. 209)

Add subtotals to a report (p. 213)

Move, resize, and format a control in a report (p. 208)

Look at a report in layout view (p. 204)

Figure 29 Turquoise Oasis Spa's Final New Database

Student data file needed:

a02_ws04_Spa4

You will save your file as:

Lastname_Firstname_a02_ws04_Spa4

Turquoise Oasis Spa

The spa has just redecorated the staff lounge and has added bulletin boards and even a computer for the staff members to check their appointments and sign in and out. The manager would like to create reports to post on the bulletin boards with schedule and service information, as well as make the database as easy to use as possible. You will help create some of the reports as well as forms to make the database easy for data entry and maintenance.

a. Start **Access**, and then open **a02_ws04_Spa4**.

b. Click the **File tab**, and then select **Save Database As**. In the Save As dialog box, browse to where you are saving your files, type Lastname_Firstname_a02_ws04_Spa4, and then click **Save**.

c. In the Security Warning, click **Enable Content**.

d. Create a form that will allow employees to edit their personal information as well as their upcoming appointments:

- Click the **Create tab**, and then click **Form Wizard** in the Forms group.

- In the Form Wizard dialog box, click the **Tables/Queries arrow**, and then select **Table: tblEmployee**. Click the **All Fields** button to add all the fields to the Selected Fields list.

- Click the **Tables/Queries arrow**, and then select **Table: tblSchedule**. Double-click **Customer**, **Service**, **Employee**, and **DateOfAppt** to add all the fields to the Selected Fields list. Click **Next**.

- Verify that the data will be viewed **by tblEmployee**, and then click **Next**.

- Verify that **Datasheet** is selected as the layout for the subform, and then click **Next**.

- Name the form frmEmployeeSchedule_InitialLastName replacing InitialLastName with your first initial and last name, name the subform frmSubform_InitialLastName, and then click **Finish**.

- Click the Home tab, click the **View arrow**, and then select **Design view**. Click the Form Design Tools Design tab, click **Label**, and then draw a label in the left side of the Form Footer for the main form section. Type your First Initial and Last Name in the label box.

- Click the **Design tab**, and then click **View** to go to Form view. On the Navigation bar, click **New (blank) record**, and then add your First Name, Last Name, Address, City, State, and Phone. On the Navigation bar, click **First record** to return to the first record in the table, and then click in the **Last Name** field.

- Click the Home tab, and then click **Find** in the Find group. In the Find What text box, type Rodriguez and then click **Find Next**. When you find the record for Brenda Rodriguez, click **Cancel**.

- Click the Home tab, click the **Delete arrow** in the Records group, and then click **Delete Record**. Click **Yes** when prompted to delete the record.

- Click the Home tab, and click **View** to go to Layout view. Double-click the **title**, select the text and type Employee Schedule.

- Click the **Last Name** text box, and then drag the right border of the text box to line up with the right border of the First Name text box.

- Click the **subform** label, and then press Del to delete the control. Click the **Subform** and using the layout selector, drag it to the left so it is right below the Phone label.

- Click the **Employee** heading in the subform datasheet, and then press Del to delete the field. Click the **subform** control, and then drag the right border to the right until you can see all the fields in the subform. Click the **Date** heading in the subform data-sheet, and then drag it to the left of the Customer field. Resize all the columns to best fit the data.

- Close the form, and then click **Yes** when prompted to save the changes.

e. Create a report to show a list of customers and their purchases.

- Click the **Create tab**, and then click **Report Wizard** in the Reports group.

- In the Report Wizard dialog box, click the **Tables/Queries arrow**, and then select **Table: tblCustomer**. Double-click **CustFirstName**, **CustLastName**, **CustState**, and **CustPhone** to add the fields to the Selected Fields list.

- Click the **Tables/Queries arrow**, and then select **Table: tblProduct**. Double-click **ProductDescription** to add the field to the Selected Fields list. Click the **Tables/Queries arrow**, and then select **Table: tblPurchase**. Double-click **PurchaseType**, **PurchaseDate**, and **Quantity** to add the fields to the Selected Fields list. Click **Next**.

- Verify that the data will be viewed by **tblCustomer**, and then click **Next**.

- Double-click **ProductDescription** to add it as a grouping level, and then click **Next**.

- Click the **Sort arrow**, click **PurchaseDate**, and then click **Next**. Select a **Stepped** layout and **Portrait** orientation, and then click **Next**.

- Name the report rptCustomerPurchases_InitialLastName replacing InitialLastName with your first initial and last name, and then click **Finish**.

- Click the Print Preview tab, and then click **Close Print Preview** in the Close Preview group. Click the Design tab, click **Label**, and then draw a label in the left side of the Report Footer section. Type your First Initial and Last Name in the label box.

- Click the Design tab, click the **View arrow**, and then select **Layout View**.

- Click the **Date** text box, and then drag the left border to the left until the date is visible. Move the Date text box to the left until it lines up under the First Name field.

- Click the **ProductDescription** label, press and hold Shift, click the **PurchaseDate** label, click the **PurchaseType** label, and then press Del to delete the controls.

- Click the **Phone** text box, and then drag the right border so the whole field is visible. Click the **ProductDescription** text box, and then drag the right border to the right until the whole field is visible.

- Double-click the **title**, select the **text**, and then type Customer Purchases. Click the **Design tab**, click **Colors** in the Themes group, and then select **Elemental**. On the Design tab, click **Fonts** in the Themes group, and then select **Technic**.

- Click the **Design tab,** click **Group & Sort** in the Grouping & Totals group to open the Group, Sort, and Total pane. Click **Group on ProductDescription**, and then click **Delete** to delete the group.

- In the Group, Sort, and Total pane, click **Add a group**, and then select **PurchaseType**. Click the **PurchaseType** text box, and then drag it to just below the customer's first name and just above the date.

- In the Group, Sort, and Total pane, click **Add a sort**, and then select **ProductDescription**. Close the Group, Sort, and Total pane.

- Click the **PurchaseType** text box. Click the **Format tab**, click **Conditional Formatting** in the Control Formatting group, and then click **New Rule**. In the second box, select **equal to**, and then in the third text box type Online. Click **Font color**, and then select **Purple**. Click **OK**, and then click **OK** again.

- Click the **PurchaseType** text box. Click the **Design tab**, click **Totals** in the Grouping & Totals group, and then select **Count Records**. Select the **PurchaseType** text box, press and hold Shift, and then click the **subtotal** text box. Click the **Format tab**, click **Shape Outline**, and then select **Transparent**.

- Right-click the **Subtotal** text box, and then select **Set Caption**. Replace the text in the caption box with orders.

- Scroll to the bottom of the report. Click the **Grand Total** text box, and then move it under the product description. Right-click the **Grand Total** text box, and then select **Set Caption**. Replace the text in the caption box with Total orders.
- **Close** the report, and then click **Yes** when prompted to save the changes.

Student data files needed:

a02_ws04_Events4
a02_ws04_Events_Image

You will save your files as:

Lastname_Firstname_a02_ws04_Events4
Lastname_Firstname_a02_ws04_pdfClientEvents

Event Organizing

The event planning department at the resort has a database of past clients, upcoming events, and decoration items. The data is all there, but no one has created any forms or reports so the data is difficult to edit and report on. You have been brought in to create forms for data entry and reports that will be useful for the staff in managing the events and providing information to the clients.

a. Start **Access**, and then open **a02_ws04_Events4**.

b. Click the **File tab**, and then select **Save Database As**. In the Save As dialog box, browse to where you are saving your files, change the file name to Lastname_Firstname_a02_ws04_Events4, and then click **Save**.

c. In the Security Warning, click **Enable Content**.

d. Double-click **tblClients** to open the table. Click **New Record** in the Navigation bar to add a new record. Add your First Name, Last Name, Address, City, State, Zip Code, and Phone. Close the table.

e. Create a form to use to enter data into the clients table:
- Click the **Create tab**, and then click **Form Wizard** in the Forms group.
- In the Form Wizard dialog box, click the **Tables/Queries arrow**, and then select **Table: tblClients**. Click the **All Fields** button to add all the fields to the Selected Fields list. Click **ClientID**, and then click the **One Field Back** button to move it back to the Available Fields list. Click **Next**.
- Verify that **Columnar** is selected, and then click **Next**. Name the form frmClients_InitialLastName replacing InitialLastName with your first initial and last name, and then click **Finish**.
- Click the Home tab, and click **View** in the Views group to switch to Layout view. Double-click the **title**, and then change it to say Client Information. Click the **Phone** label, press and hold Shift, click the **Phone** text box, and then move them to the right of the First Name text box.
- Click the **Last Name** text box, and then drag the right border to the left so it lines up with the right border of the First Name text box.
- Click the **Design tab**, click the **View arrow**, and then select **Design view**. Click the **Design tab**, click **Label**, and then draw a label in the left side of the Form Footer section. Type your First Initial and Last Name in the label box.
- Click the **Design tab**, and then click **View** in the Views group to return to Form view. Click the **Last Name** field. Click the Home tab, click **Find** in the Find group, and then in the **Find What** text box, type Finch. In the **Look In** text box verify that it displays

Current field, and then click **Find Next**. Click **Cancel** to close the Find and Replace dialog box.

- Change the phone number for Adrian Finch to 8735552598. **Close** the form, and then click **Yes** to save the changes.

f. Create a split form for the clients table.

- Click **tblClients** on the Navigation pane to select the table. Click the **Create tab**, click **More Forms** in the Forms group, and then select **Split Form**.
- Double-click the **title**, select the **text**, and then change the title to Complete Client List.
- Select the **ID label**, press and hold Shift, select the **ID text box**, and then press Delete. Click the **First Name** label, press and hold Shift, click the **First Name** text box, the **Last Name** label and text box, and the **Address** label and text box. Move all the controls up to the top of the form where ID was deleted.
- Click the **Phone** label, press and hold Shift, click the **Phone** text box, and then move them to the left under the Address label and text box.
- Click the **Home tab**, click the **View arrow**, and then select **Design View**. Click the **Design tab**, click **Label**, and then draw a label in the left side of the Form Footer section. Type your First Initial and Last Name in the label box.
- Click **Save** on the Quick Access Toolbar, and then name the form frmClientSplit_InitialLastName, replacing InitialLastName with your first initial and last name. **Close** the form.

g. Create a report that shows a list of clients with their contact information along with any events they have scheduled.

- Click the **Create tab**, and then click **Report Wizard** in the Reports group.
- In the Report Wizard dialog box, click the **Tables/Queries arrow**, and then select **Table: tblClients**. Double-click **FirstName**, **LastName**, and **Phone** to add the fields to the Selected Fields list.
- Click the **Tables/Queries arrow**, and then select **Table: tblEvents**. Double-click **EventName**, **EventDate**, **Location**, and **TotalAttendees** to add the fields to the Selected Fields list. Click **Next**.
- Verify that the data will be viewed **by tblClients**, and then click **Next**.
- Do not add any grouping, and then click **Next**.
- Click the **Sort arrow**, select **EventDate**, and then click **Next**.
- Select a **Stepped** layout and **Landscape** orientation, and then click **Next**.
- Name the report rptClientEvents_InitialLastName replacing InitialLastName with your first initial and last name, and then click **Finish**.
- Click the Print Preview tab, and then click **Close Print Preview** in the Close Preview group. Click the **Design tab**, click **Label**, and then draw a label in the left side of the Report Footer section. Type your First Initial and Last Name in the label box.
- Click the **Design tab**, click the **View arrow**, and then select **Layout View**. Double-click the title, and then change it to Client Events.
- Click the **Last Name** text box, and then drag the **right border** left to fit the widest name. Click the **Phone** label, press and hold Shift, and then click the **Phone** text box. Drag the **left border** to the left so the whole phone number is visible.
- Click the **Date** text box, press and hold Shift, click the **Date** label, and then drag the **left border** to the left so the whole date is visible.
- Click the **Location** label, press and hold Shift, and then click the **Location** text box. Drag the **left border** to the left so the whole description is visible.
- Click the **Attendees** label, press and hold Shift, click the **Attendees** text box, and then press Delete.

- Click the **Design tab,** click **Colors** in the Themes group, scroll down to find **Verve**, and then click on it to apply it to only the report.
- Click the **Design tab**, click **Logo** in the Header/Footer group, navigate to your student files, and then select **a02_ws04_Events_Image**. Click **OK**. Click the **picture**, and then drag it to the right of the title.
- Click the **File tab**, click **Save & Publish**, under File Types click **Save Object As**, and then under Save the current database object select **PDF or XPS**. Click **Save As**.
- Locate the folder where you are saving your files, name the file LastName_FirstName_a02_ws04_pdfClientEvents replacing LastName_FirstName with your own first name and last name, and then click **Publish**. Close Adobe Reader.
- Close the report, and then click **Yes** when prompted to save the changes. Close Access.

MODULE CAPSTONE

More Practice

Student data files needed:

a02_mp_Recipes

a02_mp_Recipes_Logo

You will save your files as:

Lastname_Firstname_a02_mp_Recipes

Lastname_Firstname_a02_mp_pdfRecipes

Indigo5 Restaurant

Robin Sanchez, the chef of the resort's restaurant, Indigo5, has started a database to keep track of recipes and the ingredients that the restaurant includes. Right now there are no forms, queries or reports created for this database, so the information available is very limited. You will help create some queries as well as forms for data entry and reports for the daily management of the food preparation.

a. Start **Access** and open **a02_mp_Recipes**. Save the file as Lastname_Firstname_a02_mp_Recipes. In the Security Warning bar, click **Enable Content**.

b. Click the **Create tab**, click **Form Wizard**, and add all of the fields from **Table: tblRecipes**. Include **IngredientID**, **Quantity**, and **Measurement** from **Table: tblRecipeIngredients**. View the form **by tblRecipes** and show the subform as a Datasheet. Save the form as frmRecipe_InitialLastName and save the subform as frmRecipeSubform_InitialLastName. Switch to **Design View**. Click the **Design tab**, click **Label**, and then add a label to the form footer with your first initial and last name.

c. Switch to **Layout View**, change the title of the form to Recipe Input. Click the **Format tab**, change the title font to font size 28, and apply **Bold**.

d. Delete the **subform** label and move the subform to the left under the Instructions label. Delete the Subcategory.Value label and text box. Move the remaining controls and the subform up to fill in the blank space.

e. Click the **Design tab**, click in the form body, click **Insert Image**, click **Browse**, navigate to your student data files, and locate **a02_mp_Recipes_Logo**. Insert the image to the right of the Recipe information. Resize the image as necessary to fit above the Instructions text box.

f. Switch to **Form View**. Click the **Home tab**, click **Find**, and locate the record for the Recipe Name Pasta Napolitana. Change the Quantity for the IngredientID Honey to 1.

g. Click the **New (blank) Record** button on the Navigation bar and enter the following data into frmRecipe_InitialLastname:

Recipe Name	Food Category ID	Subcategory	Prep Time (minutes)	Servings	Instructions
Avocado salsa	Appetizer	Vegetarian	10	6	Peel and mash avocados. Add cayenne pepper, salt, chopped onion, and chopped tomato. Add lime juice and mix well. Refrigerate for at least 4 hours.

Enter the following data into the subform:

IngredientID	Quantity	Measurement
Avocado	2	whole
Tomato	1	cup
Cayenne pepper	.5	teaspoon
Salt	.5	teaspoon
Onions	1	cup
Lime juice	3	tablespoons

Close the form and save the changes.

h. Click the **Create tab**, click **Query Design** and then add **tblRecipes, tblRecipeIngredients**, and **tblIngredients**. Include the **RecipeName, Ingredient**, and **Quantity**, in the results. Add criteria to the **Ingredient** field so only recipes that contain cumin or paprika are selected. Sort in **Ascending** order by Quantity. Adjust the width of the query columns as necessary. Save your query as qryCuminOrPaprika_InitialLastName. Close the query.

i. Click the **Create tab**, click **Query Wizard**, and create a Find Unmatched Query to find foods in **Table: tblIngredients** that are not used in any recipes in **tblRecipeIngredients**. The **IngredientID** will be the common field between the tables. Include all the available fields. Save the query as qryUnusedIngredients_InitialLastName. Sort in Ascending order by **IngredientID**.

j. Use the Query Wizard to create a **Find Duplicates Query** to find food categories that may be duplicated in **Table: tblRecipes**. Show the **RecipeName, TimeToPrepare**, and **Servings** in the results. Sort in **Acsending** order by FoodCategoryID. Save the query as qryMultipleFoodCategories_InitialLastName.

k. Click the **Create tab**, click **Query Design**, and then add **tblRecipes** and **tblFood Categories**. Include **RecipeName, Time To Prepare**, and **FoodCategory** in the results. Add criteria to the TimetoPrepare field to find all recipes that include all recipes that take less than 30 minutes to prepare. Add criteria to the FoodCategory field to find all recipes that are listed as soup or pizza. The results should show all recipes that take less than 30 minutes to prepare or are listed with the category of soup or pizza. Sort the query in **Ascending** order by **TimeToPrepare**. Adjust the column widths as necessary. Save the query as qryTimeOrCategory_InitialLastName. Close the query.

l. Click the **Create tab**, click **Query Design** and add **tblRecipes, tblRecipeIngredients**, and **tblIngredients**. Include **RecipeName, Ingredient, Quantity, Measurement**, and **RecipeID** in the results, in that order. Sort in **Ascending** order by **RecipeID**. Adjust the column widths as necessary. Save the query as qryRecipeIngredients_InitialLastName. Close the query.

m. Click the **Create tab**, click **Report Wizard** and from tblRecipes add the fields **RecipeName, Instructions, TimeToPrepare**, and **Servings** and from qryRecipeIngredients_InitialLastName add the fields **IngredientID, Quantity**, and **Measurement** in that order. View your report **by tblRecipes**. Group by **RecipeName**. Sort in **Ascending** order by IngredientID. Accept all other default settings and name the report rptRecipes_InitialLastName.

n. Switch to **Layout View**, and move the **Ingredient** and **Quantity** text boxes to the left under the Instructions field. Delete the **Ingredient**, **Quantity**, and **Measurement** labels. Make the **Prep Time** and **Servings** labels wider so the text is visible. Move the **Servings** text box to the right under the Servings label. Change the title to Recipes.

o. Make the **RecipeName** text box wide enough to fit all the text for every record. Apply conditional formatting to the **Prep Time** field so it is **Bold** and **Red** if the Prep Time is greater than 15.

p. In Design view, click **Label** and add your first initial and last name in the **Report Footer**. Click the **File tab**, click **Save & Publish** and **Save Object As**, click **PDF or XPS**, and click **Save As**. Navigate to the folder where you are saving your files, type Lastname_Firstname_a02_mp_pdfRecipes, and click **Publish**. Close the Adobe Reader window, close the report, and then save all the changes.

q. Click the **Create tab**, click **Report Wizard**, and from tblRecipeIngredients add the fields **IngredientID**, **Quantity**, and **Measurement**; and from tblRecipes add **RecipeName** in that order. View your data **by tblRecipeIngredients** and add grouping by **RecipeName**. Accept default options and name the report rptIngredientCount_InitialLastName. Insert your first initial and last name in a label in the Report footer.

r. Switch to Layout view, click the Design tab, click **Group & Sort**, and delete the grouping by **RecipeName**. Click **Add a group** and add a grouping by **IngredientID**. Move the **IngredientID** text box to the left under the **RecipeName** label. Click the **IngredientID** text box. Click the **Format tab**, and click **Align Text Left**. Delete the **RecipeName**, **IngredientID**, **Quantity**, and **Measurement** labels.

s. Change the title to Ingredient List. Click the **IngredientID** text box, click the Format tab, click **Shape Outline**, and make the border transparent. Click **Shape Fill** and change the shape fill to **Red, Accent 2, Lighter 80%**.

t. Click the **Quantity** field. Click the **Design tab**, click **Totals**, and then click **Sum** to add subtotals. Right-click the **subtotal** text box, select **Set Caption**, and change it to Total. Click the **subtotal** text box and on the **Format tab**, click **Align Text Left** to change the alignment. Delete the grand total text box.

u. Close the Group, Sort, and Total pane. Close the report and save your changes. Close Access.

Problem Solve 1

Student data files needed:

a02_ps1_Hotel
a02_ps1_Hotel_Image

You will save your files as:

Lastname_Firstname_a02_ps1_Hotel
Lastname_Firstname_a02_ps1_pdfGuestCharges

Hotel Reservations

A database has been started to keep track of the hotel reservations with guest information, reservation information, and additional room charge information. There are no reports, forms, or queries built yet, so the staff feels like the database is not easy to use. You will create reports, forms, and queries to help the staff better manage the data in the database.

a. Start **Access** and open **a02_ps1_Hotel**. Save the database as Lastname_Firstname_a02_ps1_Hotel.

b. Open **tblGuests** and add a new record with your Last Name, First Name, Address, City, State, ZipCode, and Phone. Close the table.

c. Create a query using **tblReservations** to calculate the average rate, the minimum rate, and the maximum rate for each **DiscountType** of the rooms that are currently reserved. Rename the fields Average Rate, Minimum Rate, and Maximum Rate. **Sort** the query in **Descending** order by **DiscountType**. Resize the columns to best fit the data. Save the query as qryDiscountTypeStatistics_InitialLastName. Close the query.

d. Use the **Form Wizard** to create a form to enter guest information as well as reservation information. Add all fields from both tables EXCEPT **GuestID**. The data should be viewed by **Guest information** first, and the subform should be in **Datasheet** layout. Accept all other default options and name the form frmGuestReservations_InitialLastName and the subform frmGuestSubform_InitialLastName.

e. Change the form **title** to Guest Reservations. Change the theme to **Black Tie**. Delete the subform label. Make the title font size **28** and **bold**.

f. Delete the **subform** label. Insert **a02_ps1_Hotel_Image** into the form body to the left of the subform so that the top border of the image lines up with the top border of the subform and the image width is reduced to fit in that position.

g. Resize the column widths in the subform datasheet and resize the object so all columns are visible. Find the record for Elaine Foley. Add a new reservation from the information below.

CheckInDate	1/25/2014
Nights Stay	3
# of Guests	2
Crib	No
Handicapped	No
RoomType	Double (1 king bed)
RoomRate	$289
DiscountType	None

h. Add your first initial and last name to the form footer. Close the form and save the changes.

i. Create a query to find all guests who may not have reservations. Include the fields **GuestLastName**, **GuestFirstName**, **Address**, **City**, **State**, and **ZipCode**. Sort the query by **GuestLastName** in **Ascending** order. Name the query qryGuestsWithoutReservations_InitialLastName.

j. Change the Font size of the query to 14, change the **Alternate Row Color** to **Brown, Accent 6, Lighter 60%**, and **AutoFit** all the columns. Close the query and save the changes.

k. Create a query that will calculate the total due for each guest based on the number of nights they have stayed and the room rate for each guest. Select only guests who checked in between **December 1, 2013** and **December 31, 2013**. The results should show the **GuestFirstName**, **GuestLastName**, **NightsStay**, and **RoomRate** in that order.

l. Save the query as qryDecemberRoomCharges_InitialLastName. Name the new field TotalRoomCharge. Sort the query in Ascending order by **GuestLastName**. AutoFit the new column. Close the query and save the changes.

m. Use the Report Wizard to create a report to show all room charges incurred for each guest (not including the charge for their room). Add the **GuestFirstName**, **GuestLastName**, **ChargeCategory**, and **ChargeAmount** to the report. View the report by the **Guest**

Name. Sort by **ChargeAmount** in ascending order. Accept all other default options and name the report rptRoomCharges_InitialLastName.

n. Add a subtotal to the **Amount** field, set a caption, and type Total Charges. Left align the subtotal text box. Add conditional formatting to the subtotal text box to highlight in **Red** and **Bold** all subtotals that are over $200.

o. Resize the **Category** text box to fit on one page. Resize the **page number** control to fit on one page. Change the title to say Room Charges by Guest.

p. Add your first initial and last name to the report footer. Save and close the report.

q. Save the report as a PDF file and name it Lastname_Firstname_a02_ps1_pdfGuestCharges.

r. Create a split form from **tblReservations**. Name the form frmReservationSplit_ InitialLastName. Change the title to Reservations.

s. Close the form and close Access.

Problem Solve 2

Student data files needed:

a02_ps2_Hotel2
a02_ps2_Charges_Image

You will save your files as:

Lastname_Firstname_a02_ps2_Hotel2
Lastname_Firstname_a02_ps2_Theme

More Hotel Reservations

A database has been started to keep track of the hotel reservations with guest information, reservation information, and additional room charge information. There are no reports, forms, or queries built yet, so the staff feels like the database is not easy to use. You will create reports, forms and queries to help the staff better manage the data in the database.

a. Start **Access** and open **a02_ps2_Hotel2**. Save the database as Lastname_Firstname_ a02_ps2_Hotel2.

b. Open **tblGuests** and add a new record with your Last Name, First Name, Address, City, State, ZipCode, and Phone. Close the table.

c. Use the Form Wizard to create a form that will allow the staff to enter Room Charges for each guest during their stay. Include the **GuestLastName**, **GuestFirstName**, **City**, **State**, **ChargeCategory**, **ChargeAmount**. View the data **by tblGuests**. The subform should be in **Datasheet** layout. Accept all other default options and name the form frmGuestRoomCharges_InitialLastName and the subform frmGuestSubform_ InitialLastName.

d. **Delete** the subform label. Change the title to Guest Room Charges. Change the font size to **28** and the font to **Bold**. Resize the title as necessary.

e. Add your first initial and last name to a label in the form footer.

f. Insert **a02_ps2_Charges_Image** to the form body to the left of the subform.

g. Align the top of the image with the top of the subform and resize the image to fit between the edge of the form and the left border of the subform. Close and save the form.

h. Create a query to count the number of times a RoomType has been reserved. Include the average **RoomRate** for each RoomType. Sort the query in ascending order by **RoomRate**. Change the field names to Number of Reservations and Average Room Rate. Resize the column widths. Save the query as qryRoomStatistics_InitialLastName. Close the query.

i. Create a query to find Guests that have reservations but do not have any room charges. Include the **GuestID**, **NightsStay**, **CheckInDate**, and **RoomType** in the results. Sort the query in ascending order by **CheckInDate**. Save the query as qryGuestsWithoutRoomCharges_InitialLastName. Close the query.

j. Create a query to find guests with multiple room charges. Include **ReservationID**, **ChargeCategory**, and **ChargeAmount** in the results. Sort the query in ascending order by **ReservationID**. Save the query as qryMultipleRoomCharges_InitialLastName. Close the query.

k. Create a query to find all guests who have reservations in 2014 and who are staying more than two nights. Include **GuestFirstName**, **GuestLastName**, **CheckInDate**, **NightsStay**, and **NumberOfGuests**. Sort in ascending order by **CheckInDate**. Save the query as qry2014And2_InitialLastName. Close the query.

l. Create a query to find all guests who have reservations in 2013 with more than three guests or all guests who are staying three or more nights regardless of their check-in date. Include **GuestFirstName**, **GuestLastName**, **CheckInDate**, **NightsStay**, and **NumberOfGuests**. Sort in ascending order by **GuestLastName**. Save the query as qryGuestRelations_InitialLastName. Close the query.

m. Create a query to find all guests who are checking in sometime in April 2014 and are staying between two and four nights. Include **GuestFirstName**, **GuestLastName**, and **NightsStay** in the results. Sort in ascending order by **CheckInDate**. Save the query as qryAprilReservations_InitialLastName. Close the query.

n. Use the Form Wizard to create a form to enter new Guest information. Add all the fields except **GuestID**. Accept all other default options and name the form frmGuestInput_InitialLastName.

o. Change the title of the form to Guest Input. Apply the **Angles** theme to all the objects in the database. Change the font theme to **Concourse**. Save the custom theme to your student folder as Lastname_Firstname_a02_ps2_Theme. Add your first initial and last name to the form footer. Close the form and save the changes.

p. Use the Report Wizard to create a report for all guests with their reservation information. Include **GuestFirstName**, **GuestLastName**, **CheckInDate**, **NightsStay**, **NumberOfGuests**, **RoomType**, and **RoomRate**. View the data by tblReservation. Group the report by **CheckInDate** with normal date grouping options. Sort in ascending order by **GuestLastName**. Accept all other default options and name the report rptGuestReservations_InitialLastName.

q. Change the report title to Guest Reservations. Insert your first initial and last name in a label in the report footer. Move or resize all necessary fields so all the text is visible. Highlight any **NightsStay** that is more than two nights in **Dark Red** and **Bold**.

r. Close the report and save the changes. Close Access.

Problem Solve 3

Student data files needed:

a02_ps3_Hotel3
a02_ps3_Hotel_Image

You will save your files as:

Lastname_Firstname_a02_ps3_Hotel3
Lastname_Firstname_a02_ps3_pdfRoomTypes

Additional Hotel Reservations

A database has been started to keep track of the hotel reservations with guest information, reservation information, and additional room charge information. There are no reports, forms, or queries built yet, so the staff feels like the database is not easy to use. You will create reports, forms and queries to help the staff better manage the data in the database.

a. Start **Access** and open **a02_ps3_Hotel3**. Save the database as Lastname_Firstname_a02_ps3_Hotel3.

b. Open **tblGuests** and add a new record with your Last Name, First Name, Address, City, State, Zipcode, and Phone. Close the table.

c. Create a query to calculate the total room charges per guest. Use the **GuestID** and the **ChargeAmount** fields. Rename the field RoomCharges. Sort in Descending order by **RoomCharges**. Resize the **RoomCharges** field. Save the query as qryTotalRoomCharges_InitialLastName and close the query.

d. Create a query to calculate the total amount due for each guest who had reservations in December 2013, including room rate and room charges. Include **GuestLastName**, **GuestFirstName**, **NightsStay**, **RoomRate**, and **RoomCharges**. Save the query as qryTotalDue_InitialLastName.

e. Add a new calculated field to the query to calculate each guest's total amount due based on the room rate, the number of nights they stayed, and room charges. Name the new field TotalDue. Sort the query by **GuestLastName** in **Ascending** order. Save the changes and close the query.

f. Use the Report Wizard to create a report showing the **TotalDue** for each guest. Include all the fields. Do not add a grouping level. Sort by **TotalDue** in descending order. Accept all other default options and name the report as rptTotalDue_InitialLastName.

g. Add your first initial and last name in the Report footer. Change the title to Guest Total Charges. Highlight in **Dark Red** and **Bold** all NightsStay between three and five nights. Adjust all the label sizes to see the headings. Save and close the report.

h. Use the Report Wizard to create a report with the **RoomDescription**, **RoomRate**, **DiscountType**, **NightsStay**, and **CheckInDate**. View the data **by tblRoomTypes**, do not add a grouping level, and sort by **CheckInDate** in ascending order. Accept all other default options and name the report rptRoomTypes_InitialLastName.

i. Add your first initial and last name to the report footer. Change the title to Room Types. Remove the outline around the DiscountType text box.

j. Calculate the number of reservations for each RoomRate. Add a caption and type Number of reservations. Resize the calculated field so the caption is visible. Add the fill color **Blue, Accent 1, Lighter 60%** to the field.

k. Calculate the average night stay for each RoomDescription. Add a caption and type Average Night Stay. Add the fill color **Blue, Accent 1, Lighter 60%** to the field.

l. Add a new sort by **RoomDescription** and move it above the group on **RoomID**. Resize the width of all the labels so all text is visible. Save and close the report.

m. Publish the report as a PDF file. Save the file as Lastname_Firstname_a02_ps3_pdfRoomTypes.

n. Use the Form Wizard to create a form to enter room charges along with the charge details. Include the **RoomChargeID**, **GuestID**, **ChargeCategory**, **ChargeAmount**, and **Purchase**. View the form **by tblRoomCharges** and view the subform in a tabular layout. Accept all other default options, name the form frmRoomCharges_InitialLastName and name the subform frmRoomSubform_InitialLastName.

o. Add your first initial and last name to the form footer. Change the title to Room Charges. Insert **a02_ps3_Hotel_Image** to the right of the main form detail with the top border of the image lined up with the top border of the GuestID text box and the bottom border of the image lined up with the bottom border of the Amount text box.

p. Delete the **frmRoom** label. Change the theme for just the form to **Austin**. Save and close the form and close Access.

Perform 1: Perform in Your Life

Student data file needed:

Blank database

You will save your file as:

LastName_FirstName_a02_pf1_Schedule

Class Schedule

One way to stay organized during the semester is to keep track of your schedule. You will create a database of all your classes and grades. The database should track the class information, your personal schedule, and the location of the class. In order to use this for more than one semester, you will keep each of that data in separate tables.

Once the tables are created, you will set up forms to make data entry easier, run queries to get more information, and create reports to help you manage your schedule. You will start by adding data from your current schedule. Assume the current semester is Fall 2012 and the previous semester is Spring 2012.

a. Start **Access**. Click **Blank** database. Browse to find where you are storing your data files and save your database as Lastname_Firstname_a01_pf1_Schedule. Click the **Create** button to create the database.

b. To keep track of class information design a table that includes fields for the Class Number, Class Description, Credits Offered, and Professor name. Assign an appropriate primary key and save the table as tblClasses.

c. Add the class information for your classes from last semester, or fictitious classes if necessary. Add at least six classes to the table.

d. To keep track of your class locations, design a table that includes fields for the Building Number, building Name, and Campus the building is located on. Assign an appropriate primary key and save the table as tblBuilding.

e. Add the location of the classes you entered in step c. Include at least three different locations.

f. To keep track of your schedule, design a table that includes fields for the Class number, Semester, Meeting Days, Meeting Time, Location, Midterm Grade (as a number), and Final Grade (as a number). Resize all the column widths so all text is visible. Assign an appropriate primary key and save the table as tblSchedule.

g. Enter last semester's schedule, or a fictitious one, that includes at least six classes in at least three different locations. The classes and locations should be the ones entered in tblClasses and tblBuildings.

h. Create relationships as appropriate for tblSchedule, tblClasses, and tblBuilding.

i. You would like to be able to enter all your class and schedule information at one time. Create one form that will allow you to enter all the information. Save the form as **frmSchedule**.

j. Use the form to enter a new record for this semester. You should enter all the information except your grade. Add a new theme to the form, change the title to something more meaningful than the form name, then save and close the form.

k. You would like to see each class individually as well as all the class records at once. Create a form that will show you this view of the data. Save the form as **frmClasses**.

l. You want to find out what your average midterm grade and average final grade was each semester. Even though there are only grades entered for one semester, create a query to perform this calculation.

m. Rename the fields to something more meaningful and format the fields to show only two decimal places. Sort the query by Semester in descending order. Save the query as **qryAverageGrades**.

n. You want a schedule of last semester's classes only. Create a query that will show you last semester's classes, the instructor, and where and when it occurred. Save the query as **qrySchedule**.

o. Create a report that will show you last semester's schedule organized by each day. Sort it in order of class time.

p. Make sure all the fields print on one page of the report and that all the fields are visible. Add your **first initial** and **last name** in the report footer. Save the report as **rptSchedule**.

q. You want to know how to schedule your weekends. Create a query to see if you have classes after 9 a.m. on Friday. Save the query as **qryFridayClasses**.

r. You also want to know your average grade for your classes between midterm and final. Create a query to calculate the average grade in each class. Sort the query by an appropriate field. Save the query as **qryGrades**.

s. You want to print a report to show your parents your grades by class for the semester, including the average grade. Create a report that shows the **Class Number**, **Description**, **Credits**, **Midterm**, **Final**, and **Average Grade** for each class. Sort by an appropriate field. Resize all labels so all the text is visible. Change the title to something more appropriate. Save the report as **rptGrades**.

t. Add your **first initial** and **last name** in the report footer. Highlight all average grades over 90. Save and close the report.

u. Close Access.

Student data file needed:

a02_pf2_Fitness

You will save your file as:

Lastname_Firstname_a02_pf2_Fitness

Fitness Center

A new fitness center has opened and is developing a database for keeping track of members. So far the fitness center has two tables for Membership information and Member information. It has no queries, forms, or reports created, so the center has asked you to help answer some questions with queries, make data entry easier with forms, and print some reports for reference.

a. Start **Access** and then open **a02_pf2_Fitness**. Save the file as Lastname_Firstname_a02_pf2_Fitness.

b. Open each table and familiarize yourself with the fields. Open the relationships window and note how the tables are related.

c. The staff wants to be able to enter all new member and membership information in the database at one time. Create a form that will allow them to enter the member records and the related membership records for a new member. Insert your first initial and last name in the form footer. Save the form as frmMemberInput.

d. Using frmMemberInput, enter yourself as a member. Use your actual name and address; all other information can be fictitious. Change the title to something more meaningful.

e. The staff wants to know how old each member is (in whole numbers) as of the date they joined the club. This will help them plan age appropriate activities. Create a query to calculate the age of each member as of the date they joined the club. Hint: when you subtract one date from the other you get a total number of days, not years. Save the query as qryMemberAge.

f. The manager wants to know which membership types are creating the most revenue and are the most popular. Create a query to calculate the total number of each membership type and the total fees collected for each membership type. Format the query so the manager will understand exactly what each field represents. Save the query as qryMembershipStatistics.

g. The manager would like to know if any membership types have not been applied for. Find any membership types that are not assigned to a current member. Save the query as qryInactiveMemberships.

h. The staff likes to celebrate birthdays at the club. Assume the current year is 2012. Everyone born in 1972 will turn 40 this year and the staff would like a list of all those members along with their actual birthdays so they can quickly see who is celebrating a birthday each day. Save the query as qry1972Birthdays.

i. The staff likes to see each member's data as an individual record while still being able to view the whole table of data. Create a form that will allow the staff to view the data this way. Save the form as frmMemberRecords.

j. The staff needs a master list of members with their membership information. Create a report that will show the relevant information so the staff knows who is a current member and what kinds of membership each person has. Insert your first initial and last name in the report footer. Save the report as rptExpirationDate.

k. Modify rptExpirationDates so the records are grouped by the month of the expiration date. Highlight the expiration date field with a color so it stands out from the other fields.

l. The staff needs a list of members with the facilities their membership gives them access to. Create a report so the staff can quickly locate a member's name and determine which facilities they are allowed to access. Save the report as **rptFacilities**.

m. Change the report theme, change the report title to something other than the name of the report, save the report, and close the report.

n. Close Access.

Perform 3: Perform in Your Career

Student data file needed:

a02_pf3_Internships

You will save your files as:

Lastname_Firstname_a02_pf3_Internships
LastName_FirstName_a02_pf3_pdfCompanySchedule

Internship Coordinator

You take a job with an organization that matches students from Indiana schools to internship opportunities. The database you use keeps track of the companies that offer internships, the potential intern's information, and interview information dates for the interns.

You are often called upon to add new records to the table, find information for a company or intern, and provide reports for your staff. Currently there are no reports, forms, or queries, so you will have to build them from the existing data.

a. Start **Access** and then open **a02_pf3_Internships**. Save the file as **Lastname_Firstname_a02_pf3_Internships**. In the Security Warning bar, click **Enable Content**.

b. Open each table and familiarize yourself with the fields. Open the relationships window and note how the tables are related.

c. Create a form to enter data for new interns and their upcoming interviews. Save the form as **frmInterns** and the subform as **frmInternSubform**.

d. Add your name as a new intern with one interview date and company of your choice.

e. You are scheduling for January and March and need to know which students already have interviews scheduled for those months, as well as the interview date and company the interview is with. Save the query as **qryJanuaryOrMarch**.

f. Indiana University Purdue University Indianapolis (IUPUI) would like to know which of its students have interviews with Del Monte Foods Company or MMI Marketing and when those interviews are scheduled. Save the query as **qryIUPUI**.

g. Your boss wants to know the total number of interns in the database from each university. Create a query with descriptive field names and sorted appropriately to provide this information. Save the query as **qrySchoolCount**.

h. In the past there have been problems with interns being scheduled more than once with the same company, or scheduled for interviews on the same day. You need to find all students who have multiple interviews scheduled to check for conflicts. Save the query as **qryMultipleInterviews**.

i. Your boss has asked for a master list of all interns who have interviews scheduled. He would like to be able to look up a student in the report to see when their interview is and who the interview is with. Save the report as **rptInterviewsScheduled**.

j. You need a report that counts and highlights how many interviews are scheduled each month. The report should also show the interview and intern information. Save the report as **rptInterviewDates**.

k. When a company comes to interview, you need to quickly find who the interview is with. Create a report that will provide a master list of interviews that allows you to quickly see who is interviewing with each company. Save the report as **rptCompanySchedule**.

l. Save rptCompanySchedule as a PDF file so you can easily e-mail it to your boss and name it **Lastname_Firstname_a02_pf3_pdfCompanySchedule**.

m. You would like to stay one step ahead of your boss. Create two more queries that may be helpful in analyzing the database information. Name the queries something descriptive so your boss will know what information is provided.

n. Close Access.

Perform 4: How Others Perform

Student data file needed:

a02_pf4_Lessons

You will save your file as:

Lastname_Firstname_a02_pf4_Lessons

Music Lessons

You have just taken a new job in a music store and one of your responsibilities is to manage the music instructors and their students. A database has been created, but as you run the queries you notice they are either missing data or have wrong results. Answer the following questions about each of the objects as completely as possible:

a. Open rptListOfTeachers. Why is the image repeated after each record? How could the image have been added to the report so it would not repeat like that?

b. Open qryGuitarPianoAndBeginners. The query is supposed to show all teachers who are teaching piano or guitar and are taking new students. Why are other records in the results? Switch to Design view and explain how you would correct the query criteria to show the correct results.

c. Open qryLessonTimes. The query is supposed to show the average lesson length for each teacher. Instead, the query shows different lesson times for each teacher. What is wrong with this query and how can you fix it to show the average lesson length for each teacher?

d. Open rptLessonList. Can you tell what the report is grouped by and sorted by without looking the Group, Sort, and Total pane? Describe how you would change the grouping to group by Instrument.

e. Open qryInstrumentList. The query was supposed to find all teacher names, student names, and the instrument the student plays. Instead there are over 200 records. What happened and why did this happen? How can you fix the query so it will provide the information you really want?

f. Open frmStudents. This form was created to see only one student at a time? Why is it showing one student and the whole student table? How was this form created? How would you create the form with only one student record at a time?

Objectives

1. Control the way data is entered with data validation rules, lookup fields, and input masks.   p. 236

2. Apply advanced data type properties to fields.   p. 256

3. Create filters to view specific records.   p. 273

4. Use the Table Analyzer Wizard to ensure data integrity.   p. 277

Using Advanced Tables and Queries

PREPARE CASE

The Red Bluff Golf Club: Modifying Database Tables

The Red Bluff Golf Club generates revenue through its golfers and golfer services. The current database tracking this data has erroneous data from a lack of good table design. Barry Cheney, the Golf Club Manager, has given you a copy of the database. To keep the file small while you work with the database, he removed most of the data and left only some sample data. You have been asked to modify the tables used to track employees and members. This will make data entry easier and more consistent. Once Barry accepts your changes, he will load all of the data and roll out the new database.

Courtesy of www.Shutterstock.com

Student data files needed for this workshop:

 a03_ws05_Golf1

 a03_ws05_ginger_liu.jpg

 a03_ws05_darnell_carter.jpg

 a03_ws05_joe_condon.jpg

 a03_ws05_liu.pdf

You will save your file as:

Lastname_Firstname_a03_ws05_Golf1

Controlling the Way Data Is Entered: Advanced Field Options

By ensuring your data is consistent and accurate, you are enhancing the usability of the data. The quality of data that is entered into your database will determine the quality of data that is displayed in your query datasets. The **GIGO principle**—which stands for "Garbage In, Garbage Out"—means that inconsistent or inaccurate data leads to an inconsistent or inaccurate output. Humans are not perfect when it comes to data entry. Thus, database designers have to place constraints—rules—on the data to prevent GIGO errors. In this section, you will learn how to help control the way data is entered through the use of advanced field options such as using input masks, custom formatting, designing validation rules, and requiring data. Additionally, you will learn how to work with field captions and create indexes.

Real World Advice — Why Worry About How Data Is Entered?

The quality of the information you produce solely depends on the quality of data entered into your database. For example, you may want to query all customers who live in Pennsylvania. If you did not restrict the amount of data permitted in a State field or create an input mask to assist in data entry, users could enter the 2-character abbreviation or completely spell out the state name. Once you have multiple versions of the state name within the State field, you run the risk of not returning all the customers who reside in a given state, such as Pennsylvania, in your query dataset. This can lead to poor decision making, which is never a goal in the business world.

- Be sure to set constraints or rules on as many fields as possible. This will ensure that users are entering data the way you want it to be entered.

- Do not restrict what data can be entered into a field so much that it becomes difficult for users to enter data. You do not want to discourage users from using the database.

- Verify that all restrictions will adequately accept every variant of accurate data. You do not want valid data excluded.

- Remember that garbage in leads to garbage out.

Understanding Input Masks as Compared to Formatting

Multiple ways exist to control your data in a database. One of the most common methods includes an input mask. An **input mask** controls the way data is entered. Thus, in most cases, an input mask controls the way that data is stored. This minimizes the likelihood that people will omit information or enter the wrong data by mistake. The input mask defines a pattern for how all data will be entered in a field. Consequently, users know whether to include parentheses around an area code or not.

Illustratively, you could create an input mask that ensures all data entered into a Last Name field is an uppercase first letter while the rest remain lowercase, no matter what capitalization the user types. Thus, the data actually exists as a first capital and the rest lowercase. You could also format the last name to all uppercase, but the data would still be stored as it was entered and will appear as if it is formatted as all uppercase letters.

Defining Input Masks

You can manually create an input mask and use special characters to require part of the data to be entered, but other parts of the field are optional. For instance, you can require the data that must be entered (such as the area code for a phone number) and that other data is optional (such as the additional 4-digits of a zip code). These characters specify the type of data—such as a number or character—needed for each character in the input mask.

You can also set the Format property for the same field to define how the data is displayed. For example, your input mask can define that a date is entered in a format such as YYYY/MM/DD, but have the date be displayed as DD-MM-YYYY.

CONSIDER THIS | **What Would You Do If You Had International Data?**

Because business is global, many customers can be located all over the world. Think about what would happen if you had international data along with American data that had to be entered into your table. International postal codes are formatted differently. For example, the postal code for the city of Niagara Falls in Ontario, Canada is L2G 2A6. Or what about a phone number for a hotel near the Eiffel Tower in Paris, France? The format of a hotel's phone number would be +331 45 55 55 55. Or consider how most of the world formats a date with the day first, then the month, and then the year— 05-07-1967 would be read as July 5, 1967, in many countries outside the United States; however, it would be read as May 7, 1967, here in the United States. How could you change your input masks to allow for these variations?

Quick Reference | **Define Custom Input Masks Using the Following Characters**

Input Mask Character	Description
0	Digit (0 to 9, data entry is required, plus [+] and minus [–] signs are not permitted)
9	Digit or space (data entry is not required; plus [+] and minus [–] signs are not permitted)
#	Digit or space (data entry is not required; spaces are displayed as blanks when editing, but blanks are removed when data is saved; plus and minus signs are permitted)
L	Letter (A to Z, data entry is required)
?	Letter (A to Z, data entry is not required)
A	Letter or digit (data entry is required)
a	Letter or digit (data entry is not required)
&	Any character or a space (entry required)
\	Displays the character that follows as the literal character (for example, \A is displayed as just A)
"	Enclosed characters display as the literal character (for example, "Cat" is displayed as Cat)
C	Any character or a space (entry optional)
>	Characters that follow are displayed in uppercase
<	Characters that follow are displayed in lowercase
!	Input mask fills from right to left, instead of the default of left to right
;	Used to separate the three parts of an input mask setting

Figure 1 Custom Input Mask Characters and Descriptions

To Create a Custom Input Mask

a. Click the **Start** button, and then select **Microsoft Access 2010**.

b. Click the **File tab**, click **Open** and browse to your student data files. Locate and select **a03_ws05_Golf1**. Click **Open**.

c. Click the **File tab**, and then select **Save Database As**. In the File name box, type Lastname_Firstname_a03_ws05_Golf1, replacing Lastname_Firstname with your actual name. Click **Save**.

d. Click **Enable Content** in the Security Warning, if necessary.

e. Open **tblMember** in **Design view**.

f. Click the **State** field, and then type > in Format under Field Properties.

State field ►

Format property

Field Properties

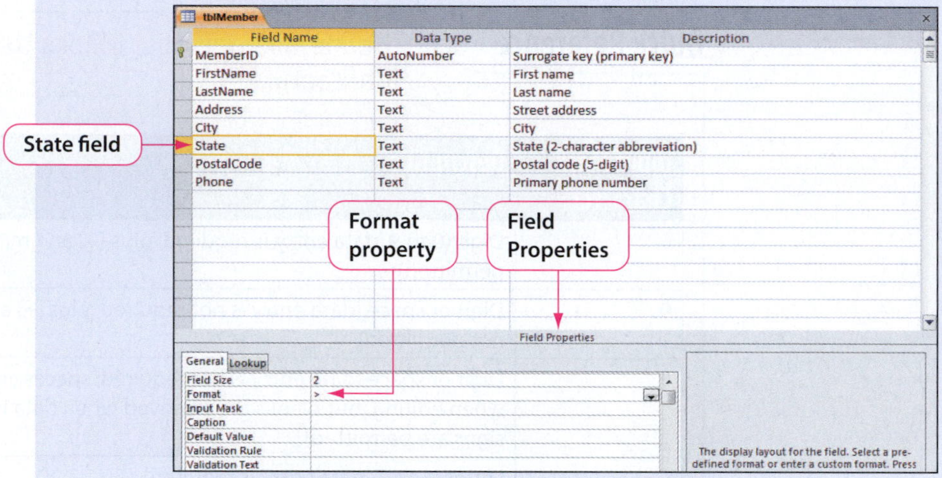

Figure 2 Design view of tblMember table

g. Click **Save** 💾 on the Quick Access Toolbar to save your changes.

h. To see how this formatting works, switch to **Datasheet view**, and then enter the following record, replacing First Name and Last Name with your own name:

FirstName	LastName	Address	City	State	ZipCode	Phone
First Name	Last Name	572 Winter Avenue	Santa Fe	nm (enter as lowercase)	87594	(505) 555-6793

Notice when you enter data as lowercase in the State field it is displayed as upper-case. However, if you click back into the data, the state you entered returns to all lower-case. Now you will reformat this field using a custom input mask.

i. Return to **Design view**.

j. Click the **State** field, click in **Input Mask** under Field Properties, and then click the **Build** button 🔳 to open the Input Mask Wizard. If Access prompts you to save your table first, click **Yes**.

k. Because there is not an input mask for the State field, you need to create a custom input mask. Begin by clicking **Edit List**.

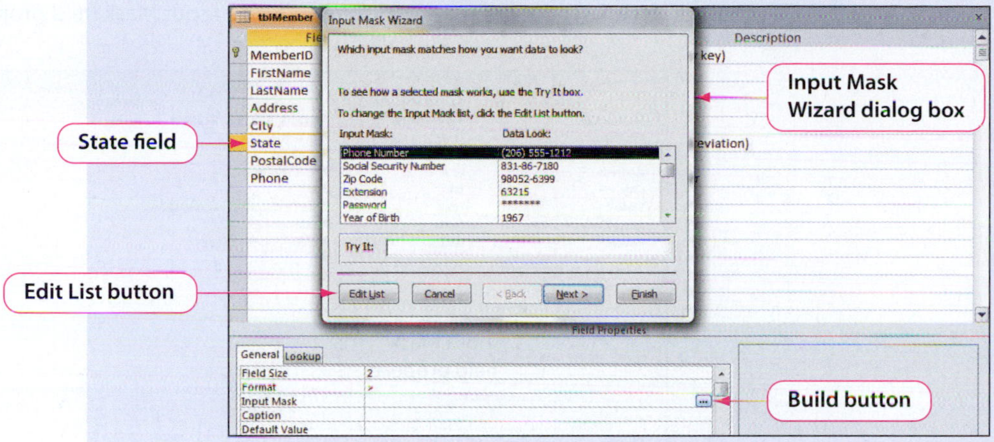

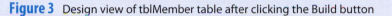

Figure 3 Design view of tblMember table after clicking the Build button

SIDE NOTE
Changing Custom Input Masks

Custom input masks can be customized by either changing a predefined mask or manually changing the Input Mask property.

l. Click the **New (blank) record** button ⯈⯈. To create a custom input mask, enter the following:

Where to enter	What to enter	Why you entered this
Description	State	This will be listed in the Input Mask Wizard.
Input Mask	>LL	The ">" is to format the field as uppercase. The "L" indicates that a letter must be entered; thus, users must enter two letters into this field.
Placeholder	_ (type an underscore)	This will make it easy to see how much data can be entered into this field.
Sample Data	NM	This is the example that will be displayed in the wizard.
Mask Type	Text/Unbound	This means that you will type the text in the field.

m. Click **Close**. Scroll down in the **Input Mask Wizard** dialog box, and then select **State**.

n. Place your insertion point in the left side of the **Try It** box, and then enter **nm** in lowercase. Notice how Access automatically displays it in uppercase and does not allow you to enter more than two letters.

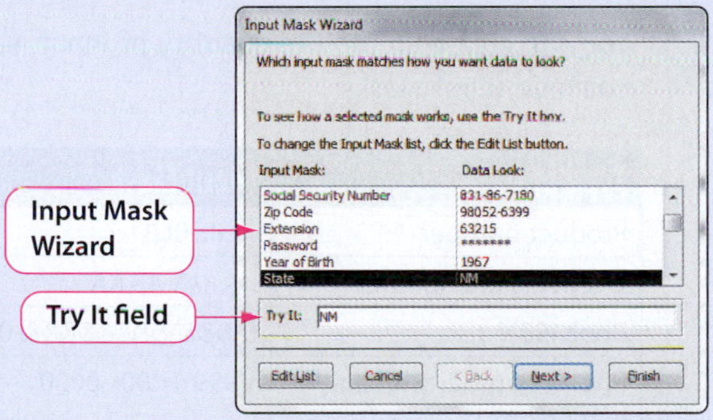

Figure 4 Input Mask Wizard dialog box

o. Click **Next** two times. Because there are no symbols in the custom input mask you created, it does not matter which option you choose on the screen that asks how you want your data to be stored. Keep the default selection, and then click **Next**.

p. Click **Finish**. Notice the mask is displayed in the Input Mask field property.

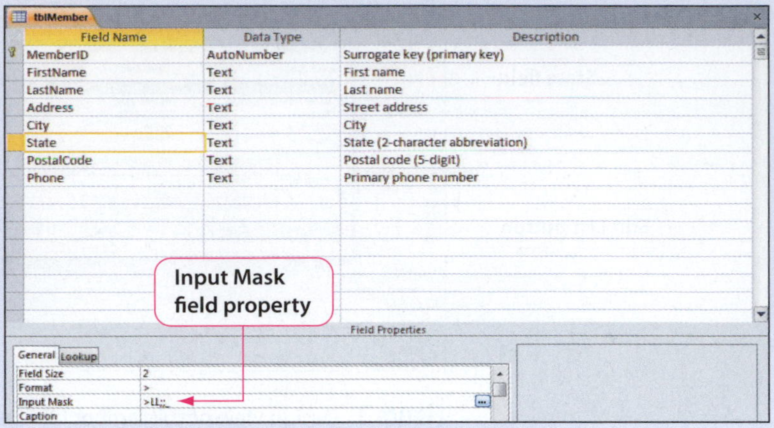

Figure 5 Design view of tblMember table with new input mask property

q. Save your changes. To see how this input mask works, switch to **Datasheet view**, and then enter the following record:

FirstName	LastName	Address	City	State	ZipCode	Phone
Stephanie	O'Neil	191 Mallard Drive	Santa Fe	nm (enter as lowercase)	87594	(505) 555-0145

r. Click the **State** field.

Notice the data used to be stored in lowercase when only the Format property was set. After you added the input mask, Access changed the storage of the state into uppercase letters.

Quick Reference   Useful Custom Input Masks

You can create an infinite quantity of input masks. Below are some of the more common input masks:

Type of Data	Input Mask	Data Results
Product number	>L0L 0L0	J7N 6C3
License plate number	>AAA\-AAAA	JPN-1234
Book ISBN-13	0-&&&-&&&&&&&&-0	9-123-12345678-0
Phone number with an extension	\(999\) 000\-0000\"x"aaaa	(412) 555-1234 x1155

Figure 6 Common Input Masks and Examples

Using the Input Mask Wizard

Microsoft Access also includes several predefined input masks for more common formats such as date, time, Social Security number, password, phone number, and zip code. To apply one of these masks, you can use the **Input Mask Wizard** in the table's Design view. Regardless of the method—manually or wizard—you want to select a mask that is most appropriate for the field. If all the field values contain data with a consistent pattern, you should define an input mask.

To Create an Input Mask Using the Input Mask Wizard

a. Switch tblMember to **Design view**.

b. Click the **Phone** field, and then click the **Build** button in the Input Mask under Field Properties to open the Input Mask Wizard.

c. Select **Phone Number**, and then click **Next**.

Notice how the Input Mask characters are already defined for you. You can enter your phone number in the Try It box to see what your users will see when they enter data into the Phone field.

d. Click **Next** two times.

e. When prompted how you want to store your data, select **With the symbols in the mask**.

f. Click **Next**, and then click **Finish**.

You will notice the mask is displayed in the Input Mask field property.

g. Save your changes.

h. To see how this input mask works, switch to **Datasheet view**, and then enter the following record:

FirstName	LastName	Address	City	State	ZipCode	Phone
Chuck	Smithfield	14 26th Street	Spring Hill	NM	87588	(505) 555-9922 (without the symbols)

Notice how the phone input mask makes it easier to enter and view data. It also saves time because Access enters the symbols for you.

i. Close tblMember.

j. Open **tblEmployee** in **Design view**.

k. Click the **HireDate** field, and then click the **Input Mask** under Field Properties. Click the **Build** button to open the Input Mask Wizard.

l. Select **Short Date**. You can enter today's date in the Try It box to see what your users will see when they enter data into the HireDate field.

m. Click **Next**, and then click **Finish**.

n. Save your changes.

o. To see how this input mask works, switch to **Datasheet view** and enter the following record:

FirstName	LastName	Salary	HireDate	Position
Mary Ann	Teeter	15500	5/26/2013	Golf Caddy

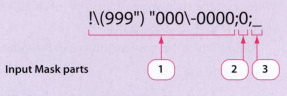
Using Custom Formatting

Another common way to control your data is through formatting. A **field format** is like makeup. Makeup may change the way a person looks, but makeup does not change a person's underlying face. The same is true with formatting. Consider an American telephone number. You place parentheses around the area code and a dash between the prefix and last four numbers. The parentheses and dash make the number easier to read, but do not change the actual number. You can also create your own type of formatting, called **custom formatting**. You can use the Format property to customize the way numbers, dates, times, and text are displayed and printed by using predefined formats or custom formats. If you set a field's Format property in Design view of a table, Microsoft Access uses that format to display data in datasheets, new form controls, and new report controls.

To Create a Custom Format Property

SIDE NOTE
Formatting Your Data
Custom formats can be customized by manually changing the Format property where you want the format applied.

a. Switch tblEmployee to **Design view**.

b. Click the **EmployeeID** field, and then click the **Format** property under Field Properties.

c. Customize the Format property of the AutoNumber field because the default AutoNumber property is only displayed as a number. Enter **"EMP"0** in the Format property. The zero will serve as a digit placeholder.

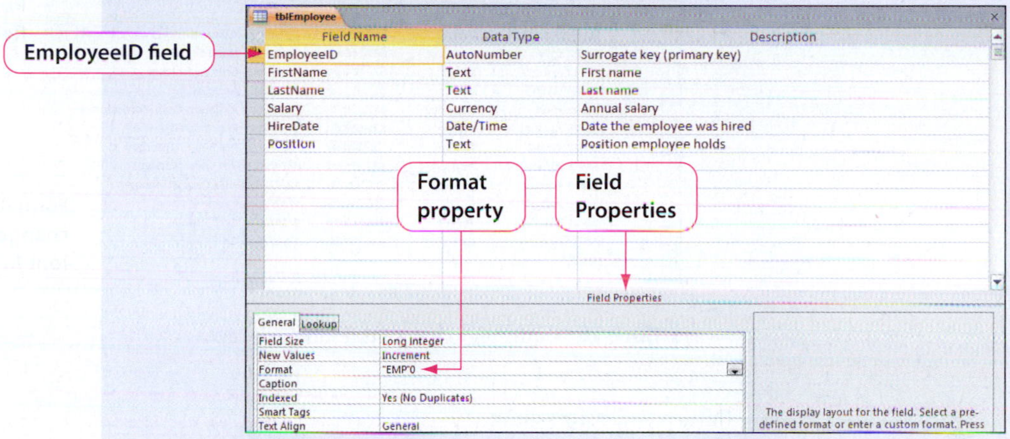

EmployeeID field

Format property

Field Properties

Figure 8 EmployeeID field with custom format property

d. Save your changes.

e. To see how this format works, switch to **Datasheet view**, and then enter the following record:

FirstName	LastName	Salary	HireDate	Position
Darnell	Carter	16750	12/1/2013	Golf Caddy

f. Click the **EmployeeID** field of the record you just entered. Notice that the format did not change the way the data is stored, just its appearance.

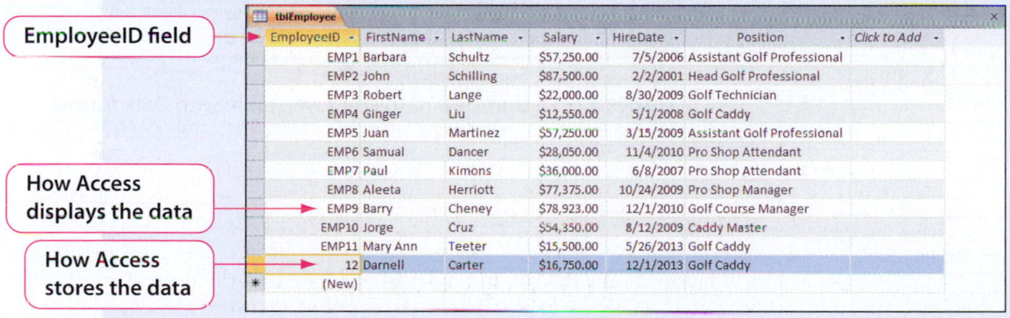

EmployeeID field

How Access displays the data

How Access stores the data

Figure 9 Datasheet view of tblEmployee table with custom formatting in EmployeeID field

g. Return to **Design view**.

h. Customize the Format property of the Position field to change the color of the text. Enter **&&[Blue]** in the Format property.

i. Save your changes.

j. To see how this format works, switch to **Datasheet view**, and then view the data in the Position field. Notice that the data is now blue.

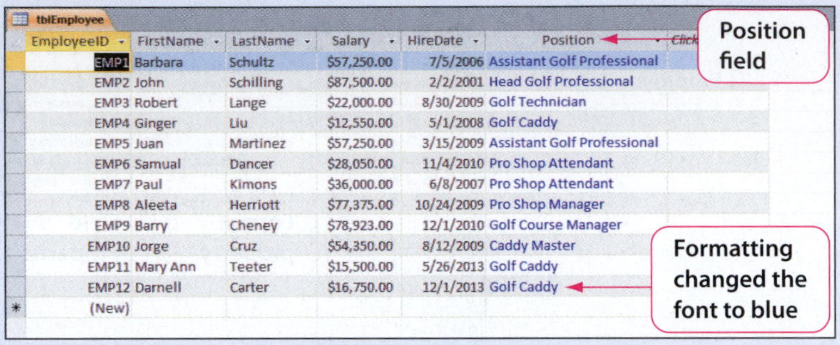

Figure 10 Datasheet view of tblEmployee table

k. Return to **Design view**.

l. Customize the Format property of the HireDate field to format the date. Select **Medium Date** in the Format property.

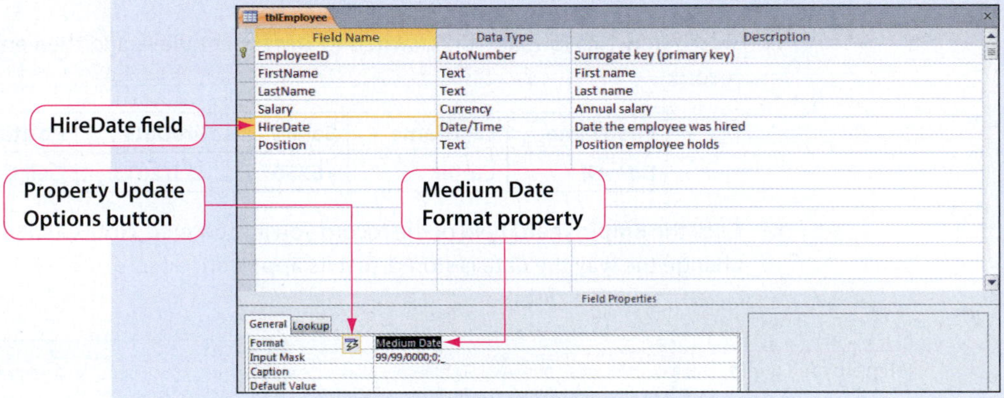

Figure 11 Design view of tblEmployee table with Date format

Troubleshooting

You may have noticed the Property Update Options button ⬚ appeared after you changed the HireDate property to Medium Date. If you click the button and choose "Update Format everywhere HireDate is used", Access will automatically update all lookup properties everywhere throughout your database where Medium Date is used, including forms, reports, and queries.

m. Save your changes.

n. To see how this format works, switch to **Datasheet view**, and then enter the following record:

FirstName	LastName	Salary	HireDate	Position
Max	Burrell	34500	12/1/2013	Pro Shop Attendant

Notice that because of the input mask you were able to enter the HireDate as a short date. However, because you formatted the field as a Medium Date, it is displayed in the Medium Date format.

o. Click the **HireDate** field.

Notice how the formatting does not change back into a short date. The data remains in the longer format because the Format property takes precedence.

Real World Advice — **Can One Property Take Precedence over Another Property?**

When you define an input mask that is different from the Format property in the same field, the Format property takes precedence when the data is displayed. Some items to note:

- If you save an input mask, the input mask is ignored when you define a format in the field's Format property.
- The data in the table does not change, regardless of how you define the Format property.
- The Format property only affects how data is displayed, not how it is stored.

Quick Reference

Define Custom Formats Using the Following Characters

You can enter different characters—placeholders, separators, literal characters, colors—in the Format property of a field to create a custom format. By combining these characters, you can make the data easier to read.

Character	Description
Space	Entering a space displays a space
"ABC"	Characters inside quotes are displayed
!	Forces left alignment in the field
*	Fills the available space with the next character
\	Displays the character that follows
[color]	A color inside square brackets changes the font color. Colors available are Black, Blue, Green, Cyan, Red, Magenta, Yellow, and White.

Figure 12 Custom Format Characters

Custom number formats can have one to four sections with semicolons separating each section. Each section also holds the format specification for a different type of number.

Section	Description
First	The format for positive numbers
Second	The format for negative numbers
Third	The format for zero values
Fourth	The format for null values

Figure 13 Custom Number Format Properties by Section

You can also create custom number formats by using the following symbols:

Symbol	Description
.	Decimal separator
,	Thousand separator
0	Display a digit or 0
#	Display a digit or blank
$	Display a dollar sign
%	Value is multiplied by 100 and a percent sign added
E– or e–	Scientific notation with a minus sign (–) next to negative exponents. This symbol must be used with other symbols such as 0.00E–00 or 0.00E00.
E+ or e+	Scientific notation with a minus sign (–) next to negative exponents and a plus sign (+) next to positive exponents. This symbol must be used with other symbols, as in 0.00E+00.

Figure 14 Custom Number Formats

For example, a custom format for a Date/Time field can contain two sections—one for the date and another for time. Both sections are then separated with a semicolon. Thus, you can combine the Short Date format—mm/dd/yyyy—and Medium Time format—hh:mm followed by AM or PM—as shown in Figure 15.

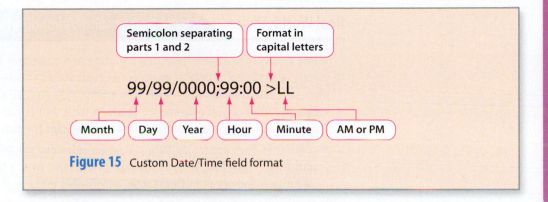

Figure 15 Custom Date/Time field format

Defining Data Validation Rules

You can validate data as it is entered to help improve its accuracy and consistency by using data validation rules. **Data validation rules** prevent bad data from being entered and consequentially stored in your database. Validation rules can be set for a specific field or an entire record. For example, a validation rule could be created to ensure that a product price is greater than zero.

When data is entered, Access checks to see whether the data meets the validation rule. If the data is not accepted, Access displays a message—known as validation text—designed to help users understand why there is a problem. The **Validation Text property** allows you to enter the error message.

You can create two basic types of validation rules: field validation rules and record validation rules. **Field validation rules** are used to verify the value that is entered in just one field. If the validation rule is violated, Access prevents the user from leaving the current field until the problem is fixed. For example, you may want to make sure that a product price entered is greater than 0. In the ProductPrice field, you would enter >0 as the Validation Rule property. If a user enters 0 in the field, Access would not permit the user to move to another field until the problem is corrected.

CONSIDER THIS | What Would You Recommend?

What if the resort wants to offer a free item in the inventory? What effect would configuring a validation rule on ProductPrice to >0 have? What would you recommend doing in this instance?

A **record validation rule** refers to other fields in the same record. In other words, you need to validate the values in one field against the values in another field in the same record. For example, suppose your business requires you to ship products within 14 days from when an order was placed. You can define a record validation rule on the ScheduledShippingDate field, ensuring that someone does not schedule a ship date that breaches the company's 14-day rule.

The only difference between establishing a field validation rule and a record validation rule is its structure. In a record validation rule, you would reference field names as opposed to simply entering an expression. If your business follows the above 14-day shipping rule, the Validation Rule property compares the date entered in the OrderDate field against the date entered in the ScheduledShippingDate field. You can enter [ScheduledShippingDate]<=[OrderDate]+14.

To Create and Test Validation Rules and Validation Text

a. Switch tblEmployee to **Design view**.

b. Click the **HireDate** field, and then click the **Validation Rule** property under Field Properties. You will notice that the Build button [...] is displayed.

c. Create a field validation rule on the HireDate field so employees cannot be entered into the system after 14 days from the hire date as it could cause problems with the payroll department. Enter [HireDate]>=Date()-14 as the Validation Rule property.

d. Enter the following validation text including the punctuation: **This employee began working more than 14 days ago. Please call the Corporate Office at (800) 555-4022.**

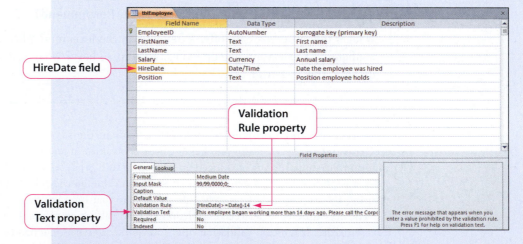

HireDate field

Validation Rule property

Validation Text property

Figure 16 Design view of tblEmployee table with validation rule and text

Troubleshooting

At times, entering data into field properties can become difficult to see. To enlarge your work area and font, right-click the property on which you are working and then click Zoom.

e. Save your changes.

f. Click **No** when Access prompts you to confirm whether you want to test the existing data against the new rules.

Troubleshooting

You will notice a warning message stating that you have made changes to the table's data integrity rules and that existing data may not meet the new rules. Access wants to confirm whether you want to test the existing data against the new rules. If you know that the data meets the new rules, you can click No. If you are not sure and you want to make certain that all records meet the requirements, click Yes.

g. To see how the validation rule and validation text work, switch to **Datasheet view**, and then enter the following record:

FirstName	LastName	Salary	HireDate	Position
Dean	Falcon	22000	Enter a date that is at least 15 days before today's date	Golf Technician

Notice that because you entered a date that was more than 14 days ago, Access keeps you from moving to the next field until you correct the mistake.

h. Click **OK**, and then change the date to today's date and finish entering the record.

i. Switch to **Design view**, click the **Salary** field, and then click the **Validation Rule** property under Field Properties.

j. Create a validation rule on Salary so all salaries entered do not exceed $200,000. Enter **<=200000** as the Validation Rule property.

k. Enter the following validation text with the punctuation: **The maximum salary an employee can earn is $200,000. Please re-enter this employee's salary.**

l. Save your changes, and then click **Yes** to make sure that all existing data meets the new validation rule.

m. To see how the validation rule and validation text work, switch to **Datasheet view**, and then enter the following record:

FirstName	LastName	Salary	HireDate	Position
Allie	Madison	310000	Today's date	Golf Professional

Notice that because you entered a salary that was more than $200,000, Access keeps you from moving on until you correct the mistake.

> ### SIDE NOTE
> **Entering Numbers into Validation Rules**
>
> When entering numbers or currency into a validation rule, do not enter symbols such as commas or a dollar sign.

Figure 17 Datasheet view of tblEmployee table with validation text displayed

n. Click **OK**, change the salary to **200000**, and then finish entering the record.

Working with Captions

When naming fields, you want to use a name that is easy to understand. Although the field name may be the best choice when designing a database, sometimes those names may not be what you want to display on other database objects—forms, reports, and queries. Or you may be working with a database that someone else created, someone who did not understand the principles of good design.

Instead of having to modify field names, which could require you to modify other objects or settings in your database (e.g., relationships), it would be easier to simply define the **Caption property**. A caption is like an alias. An alias is another name that someone may use to hide their true identity, but their legal name is still what is listed on their birth certificate. A caption does not change the actual field name, just the way users see it—like an alias. Once this property is established, every object you create will display what the caption is instead of the field name. For example, a field named HomePhone would be displayed as "Home Phone" on forms and reports by entering "Home Phone" in the Caption property.

To Create Captions for Existing Fields

a. Switch tblEmployee to **Design view**.

b. Click the **FirstName** field, and then click the **Caption** property under Field Properties. Enter First Name in the Caption property.

FirstName field

Caption field property

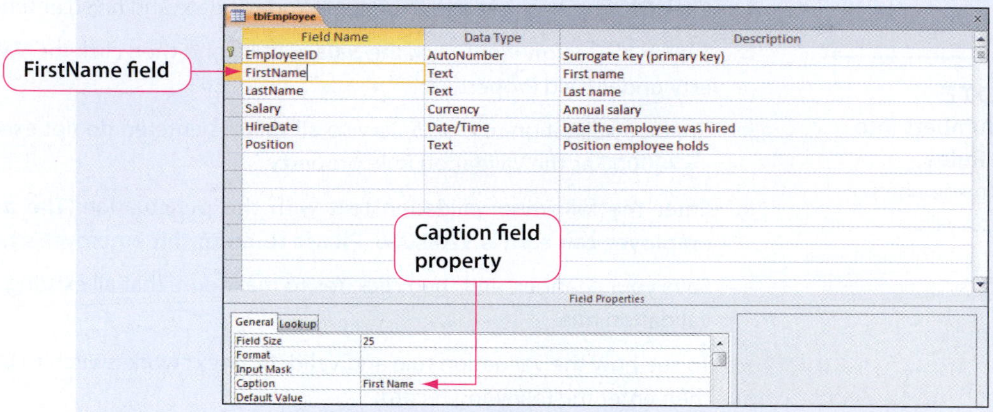

Figure 18 Design view of tblEmployee table with caption entered

c. Save your changes. To see how the Caption property works, switch to **Datasheet view**, and then look at the field heading.

FirstName field with new caption

Figure 19 Datasheet view of tblEmployee table

d. Return to **Design view**, and then enter the following captions for each field:

LastName: **Last Name**

HireDate: **Date of Hire**

Position: **Job Title**

e. Save your changes. To see how the table looks after creating your captions, switch to **Datasheet view**, and then view the field headings. Resize your fields if you cannot see the entire caption.

f. Close tblEmployee.

Real World Advice | Captions Enable You to Use Reserved Words

All relational databases have specific words and symbols that cannot be used as field names because they have a specific meaning. If you use a reserved word or symbol as a field name, Access will warn you that it is reserved and you will experience errors when working with the database. The error message you receive will not necessarily communicate that the cause of the problem stems from using a reserved word or symbol. Thus, it can be challenging to identify what needs to be revised.

Because there are hundreds if not thousands of reserved words, it is impractical to list them all. Therefore, it is important to read all warning messages thoroughly when working in Access. Remember that you can use whatever word or symbol you would like as a caption. When naming fields, create names that are compliant—Access will let you know if it is not—then create a caption for the field as you so choose.

Creating Indexes

Many databases contain a large amount of data. Indexes are created and used to increase performance. For example, if you repeatedly search or sort your data on a specific field, you could create an index to speed up the procedure. An **index** in Access is similar to an index in a book. It is a lot easier and faster to find a topic in a book's index than having to search through the book page by page. By creating an index for a field or fields in a table, Access can quickly locate all the records that contain specific values for those fields without having to read through each record in the table.

CONSIDER THIS | What Will Happen in the Future?

Right now, the resort database is small enough that you will not recognize a difference in performance after creating an index. If this database is used for three years, how large do you think this database will get? What would happen in year 3 if you did not set indexes? Would your database run slower?

Real World Advice — How Do You Decide What Fields to Index?

- You can index every field if you want to, but do not. Indexes can accelerate searches and queries, but they can slow down performance when you add or update data.
- You cannot index a field whose data type is an OLE Object, Hyperlink, Memo, or Attachment.
- Index a field when the data is generally unique and when there are more different entries than duplicate entries.
- Index a field when you plan to frequently search or sort it.
- The strategy to indexing efficiently is that an index should improve performance. Do not apply an index for any other reason.

Defining a Single-Field Index

If you create a **single-field index**, Access will not let you enter a new value in the field if that value is already entered in the same field within another record. Access automatically creates an index for primary keys, but you might also want to prevent duplicate values in other fields. For example, you may want to create an index on a field that stores a Universal Product Code (UPC) to ensure that all products have a unique UPC.

Defining Multiple-Field Indexes

You can also create an index for a combination of fields with a maximum of 10 fields. For example, if you frequently specify criteria for the Supplier and UPC fields in the same query, database performance would be improved if you create a multiple-field index on both fields.

When you create a **multiple-field index**, you specify the order of the fields. Once you sort a table by defining a multiple-field index, Access sorts the index in the order in which you enter each field into the Indexes dialog box. If there are records with duplicate values in the first field, Access then sorts by the second field defined for the index, and so on.

To Define Single- and Multiple-field Indexes

a. Open **tblMember** in **Design view**.

b. Click the **PostalCode** field, and then look at the Indexed property in Field Properties. Notice that Access automatically created an index for this field when the table was built.

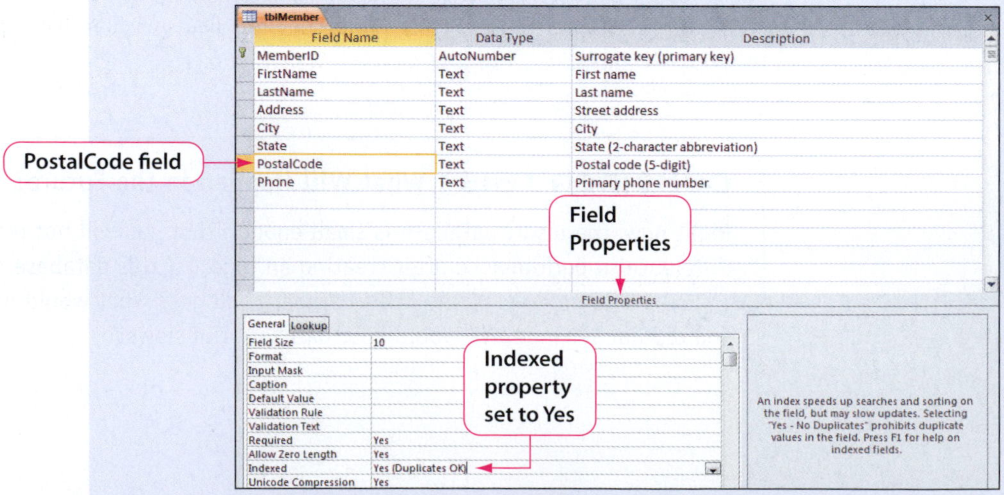

Figure 20 Design view of tblMember table with modified Indexed property

c. Click **Indexes** on the Table Tools Design tab to create a multiple-field index. The Indexes dialog box will open.

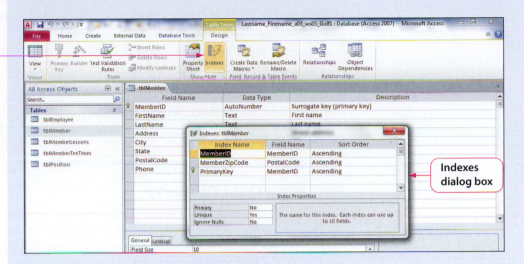

SIDE NOTE
Some Indexes Are Automatically Created

An index stores the location of your records based on the field or fields that you select. In some occasions, such as when a primary key is defined, Access automatically creates an index for you.

Figure 21 Indexes for tblMember table

d. Enter the following index properties starting at the first blank row in the Indexes dialog box:

Index Name	Field Name	Sort Order
MemberName	LastName	Ascending
	FirstName	Ascending

Index Properties for MemberName Index

Primary	No
Unique	No
Ignore Nulls	No

SIDE NOTE
Reviewing Your Indexes

By clicking Indexes on the Table Tools Design tab, you can easily view and modify all existing indexes.

SIDE NOTE
Is Something Missing?

At first glance, it appears that something is missing in the last row. This is how multiple-field indexes are created: the index name appears only once.

MemberName Custom Index

Index properties

Figure 22 Indexes dialog box

e. Save your changes, and then close the Indexes dialog box.

Requiring Data Property

Data within Access fields can be required, ensuring that necessary information cannot be omitted from the database, either accidentally or deliberately. For example, in a customer database, a first name, last name, and address might be required, while a phone number may be optional. You can use the **Required property** to specify whether a value is required in a field, ensuring that the field is not left blank, or in database terms, is not **null**. If the Required property is set to Yes, and a user attempts to leave a field blank or removes a value from a required field when trying to save the record, Access will display an error message. The user will need to enter data before moving to the next field.

The Required property applies only to new records, not existing ones. Thus, if that is all that is set, you can cause an existing last name to be blank, even if it is required. To require data in a field, you must set the Required property to Yes and either a length of zero or a validation rule of "is not null". That way, both new and existing records require that field to have data.

Real World Advice — Changing the Required Setting When a Table Contains Data

If you change the Required property to Yes for a field that already contains data, Access allows you to verify whether existing records have values entered in that field. You can require that a value be entered in this field for all new records even if there are existing records without values in the field.

To Set Properties for Required Fields

a. Click the **FirstName** field, and then click the **Required** property.

b. Change the Required property from No to **Yes**.

c. Change the Required property of the LastName, Address, City, State, and PostalCode fields from No to **Yes**.

Troubleshooting

To enforce a relationship between related tables that do not allow null values, set the Required property of the Foreign Key field in the related table to Yes.

d. Save your changes, and then click **Yes** in the Data Integrity warning dialog box.

Data about customers gives companies a way to contact the customers for marketing and customer service purposes. Some customers may not want to give out personal information. Do not restrict the database too much to allow for customers' personal preferences. For example, a customer may have an unlisted phone number. Should this be considered when determining whether data in a field is required?

Default Values

Default values are one of the easiest ways to help with data entry. A **default value** is a value automatically entered into a field when a new record is created. For example, perhaps the majority of your customers live in a specific city. In a Customers table, you can set the default value for the City field to Pittsburgh. When users add a record to the table, they can either accept this value by just tabbing to the next field or by entering the name of a different city.

To Set Additional Properties for Required Fields

a. Click the **City** field, and then click the **Default Value** property.

b. Change the Default Value to "Santa Fe".

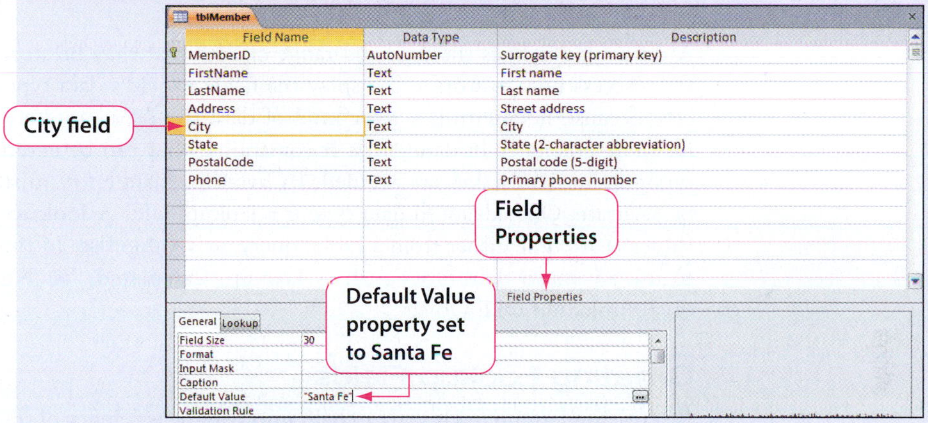

Figure 23 Design view of tblMember table with new Default value added to the City field

Troubleshooting

Quotation marks are needed around text, also known as string data, to let Access know that it is text. Different data types require specific delimiters or symbols when they become part of an expression—text needs to be enclosed in quotation marks and dates need to be enclosed in number signs. Eliminating the quotes would confuse Access because it would think you entered a number or keyword when you really entered text. Notice that Access automatically places quotes around the **string** if you forget. A string is comprised of a set of characters that can also contain spaces, symbols, and numbers. Additionally, if you type in Santa Fe, Access will automatically recognize it as a string and enter the quotes, unless the word is an operator. For example, if you have a field where the default value contains the word "like", you have to physically type the quotes because "like" is a reserved word.

SIDE NOTE

What a Default Value Cannot Do

Default values can be used in all fields except AutoNumber or OLE Object data types.

c. Click the **State** field, click the **Default Value** property, and then change the Default Value to "NM".

d. Save your changes.

e. To see how the Default Value property works, switch to **Datasheet view**, and then click the **New (blank) record** button 📑. Notice that the City and State fields are already populated for you.

f. Enter the following records:

FirstName	LastName	Address	City	State	ZipCode	Phone
Josh	Pendleton	4 Forbes Avenue	Santa Fe	NM	87594	(505) 555-9030
Gary	Way	222 Spring Hill Avenue	Snowflake	AZ	85937	(928) 555-2123

Notice that you saved time entering the first record because the City and State fields were already populated for you. You also were easily able to enter a different city and state when needed.

g. Close tblMember.

Advanced Data Types

A **data type** defines the type and range of data that may be stored in the field. The data type tells Access how to store and display the field. A field's data type is the most important property because it determines what kind of data the field can store. Advanced data types allow for more efficiency in data entry. It constrains what can be entered into a field, ensuring that typographical mistakes are avoided. By avoiding data entry mistakes, your query results will be accurate. One advanced data type is a lookup field. A **lookup field** is a table field that has values that come either from a table, query, or a value list. In this section, you will learn how to use advanced data types such as Lookup, Calculated, Yes/No, Autonumber, Attachment, Hyperlink, and OLE Object.

Creating Lookup Fields

By creating lookup fields you can help improve the efficiency of the data entry process. A lookup field can display a user-friendly list that is either linked to another field in a related table or a value list—a list of values that the database designer manually creates. For example, the lookup field can display a company name that is linked to a respective contact identification number in another table, query, or list.

When you create a lookup field that gets data from a table or query (called a source), Access uses the primary key field from the source to determine which value goes with which record. A lookup field replaces what is displayed, which would be the primary key field by default, with something more meaningful, such as an employee name. The value that is stored is called the bound value. The value that is displayed is called the display value.

Using the Lookup Wizard

Although a lookup field can be manually defined, the **Lookup Wizard** is the easiest way to create a lookup column. The wizard simplifies the process by automatically populating the appropriate field properties and creating the appropriate table relationships. The Lookup Wizard feature has been enhanced in Access 2010 by automatically creating referential integrity settings. At the end of the wizard, you can make a choice to enable referential integrity. The wizard not only creates a relationship, but makes the correct referential integrity settings.

Another feature in Access is the ability to store multiple values in a **multivalued field**. This helps you keep track of multiple related facts about a subject. For example, suppose you have a project management database that helps you manage which employees are assigned to what projects. One employee might be working on several projects, and each project might have more than one employee working on it. This kind of data structure is called a many-to-many relationship. Access makes it easy to keep track of this related data by using a multi-valued lookup field. After you create the multivalued field, it appears as a check box list in Datasheet view. The selected people are stored in the multivalued field and are separated by commas when displayed.

Real World Advice | Enforcing Referential Integrity with Multiple Values

Access will not allow you to store multiple values if you enforce referential integrity. When Access enforces referential integrity, it is checking to see if related data exists between the primary key and foreign key. You cannot enter a value in the foreign key field of the related table that does not exist in the primary key field of the primary table. For example, a project cannot be assigned to an employee if that employee does not exist in your database. On the other hand, multiple employees may be assigned to one project. Thus, the foreign key in the Project table—EmployeeID—can have more than one EmployeeID listed and separated by a comma. The combination of the EmployeeIDs will not match any of the EmployeeIDs listed in the Employee table.

CONSIDER THIS | Multiple Values and Normalization

Does storing multiple values conform to the principles of normalization? List some examples where using this feature is useful. What are some examples where storing multiple values would be inappropriate?

Lookup Field Properties

The purpose of a Lookup field is to replace the display of a number such as an ID (or other foreign key value) with something more meaningful, such as a name. For instance, instead of displaying a product item ID number, Access can display a product name. **Lookup field properties** can be viewed in the bottom pane of the table's Design view under Field Properties. When the first property is initially configured, the list of available properties changes to reflect one's choice. Lookup field properties can be set to change the behavior of a lookup column. When the Lookup Wizard is used, many of the lookup field properties are automatically established by the wizard.

Although the wizard establishes the lookup field properties, there are some properties that may need to be modified, based on your own preferences. When the wizard creates the settings of a lookup field, many properties are not established or are configured to the Access default settings. You can set the lookup field properties to change the behavior of the lookup field.

Quick Reference | Possible Options for the Lookup Wizard Integrity Settings

- No Data Integrity: This creates a simple relationship.
- Restrict Delete: Activates referential integrity with no Cascades.
- Cascade Delete: Activates referential integrity with Cascade Delete.

To Create a Lookup Field

SIDE NOTE

Lookup Fields Have Limitations

The only data types for which you can create a lookup field are Text and Number.

a. Open **tblMemberLessons** in **Datasheet view**.

Notice how only numbers exist in the MemberID and EmployeeID fields. By creating a lookup field, you will be able to display something other than a number—a key from a different table. This will make it easier to see who is scheduling lessons.

b. Switch to **Design view**, and then click the **MemberID** field.

c. Select **Lookup Wizard** from the Data Type menu. The Lookup Wizard dialog box will open.

d. Click the **I want the lookup field to get the values from another table or query** option, and then click **Next**.

Troubleshooting

If a relationship already exists on the field you want to use the Lookup Wizard for, you must open the Relationships window and delete the existing relationship before going through the Lookup Wizard. Access will re-create the relationship automatically upon completion.

e. Select **tblMember**, and then click **Next**.

f. Select the MemberID, LastName, and FirstName fields to be included in your lookup field. You can move them to the right-hand side by either double-clicking the field name or clicking once on the One Field button [>].

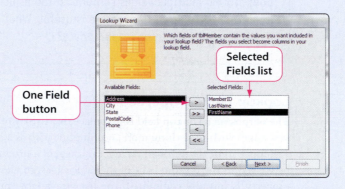

Figure 24 Lookup Wizard dialog box Screen 4

g. Click **Next**, and then sort the following fields in ascending order: LastName, FirstName.

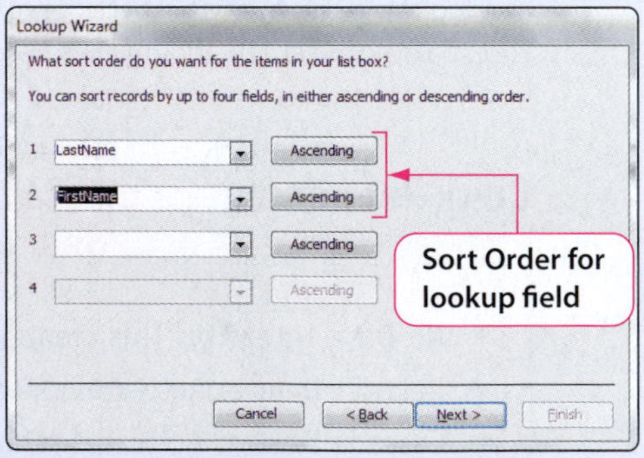

Figure 25 Lookup Wizard dialog box Screen 5

h. Click **Next**, and Access automatically selects the Hide key column check box. Clear this check box.

Figure 26 Lookup Wizard dialog box Screen 6

Notice how the key is displayed. If this box is left unchecked, the key column would be displayed in the lookup field. Because the key has no meaning other than helping you relate tables, hide it so that anyone using the lookup column sees only the values that you want them to see and not the values in the primary key field.

i. Click **Hide key column**, and then click **Next**.

j. Select **Enable Data Integrity** and **Restrict Delete**.

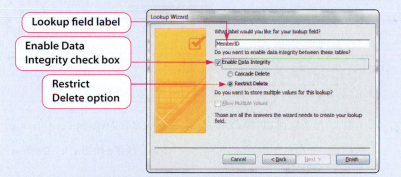

Figure 27 Lookup Wizard dialog box Screen 7

SIDE NOTE
Should You Rename the Lookup Field Label?

If your field is already named, you do not need to rename it.

k. Click **Finish**. Access will automatically create the relationship between tblMemberLessons and tblMember. Click **Yes** when prompted to save the table.

l. Switch to **Datasheet view**.
Notice how the lookup field displays the data in the MemberID field. It is much easier to determine which member has scheduled a lesson.

m. Return to **Design view**, and then click in the MemberID field. Click the **Lookup tab** under Field Properties. Notice that the Lookup Wizard configured many of the settings for you.

n. Change the Column Heads property to **Yes**, and then save your changes.

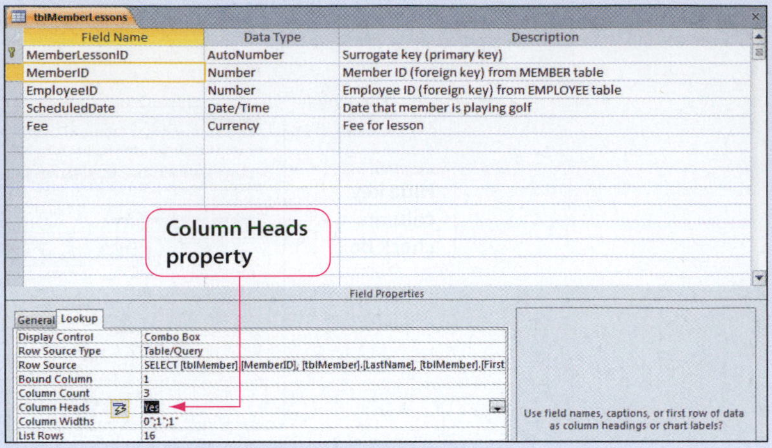

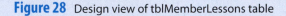

Figure 28 Design view of tblMemberLessons table

o. Switch to **Datasheet view**, click the **MemberID** field, and then click the **Selection arrow** to expand your lookup field's list. Notice that there are headings in the columns.

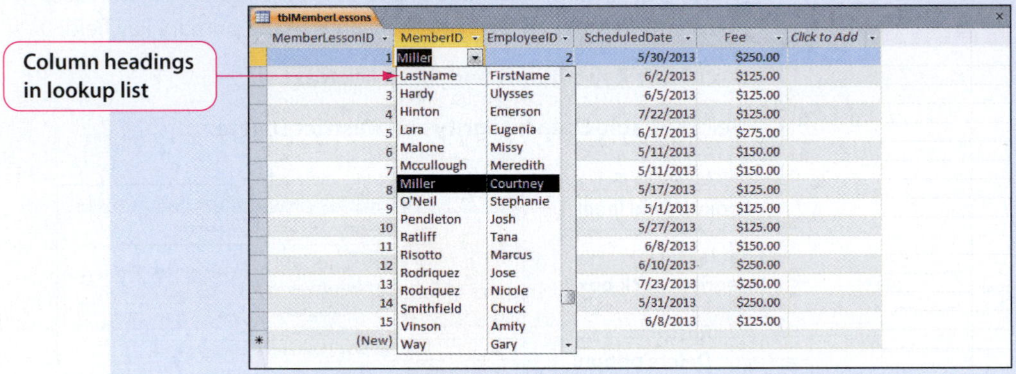

Figure 29 Datasheet view of tblMemberLessons table

p. Close tblMemberLessons. Open **tblPosition** in **Design view**, and then click in the PositionType field.

q. Select **Lookup Wizard** from the Data Type list. The Lookup Wizard dialog box will open.

r. Select **I will type in the values that I want**, and then click **Next**.

s. Enter the following options:

Row 1: **Full-time**

Row 2: **Part-time**

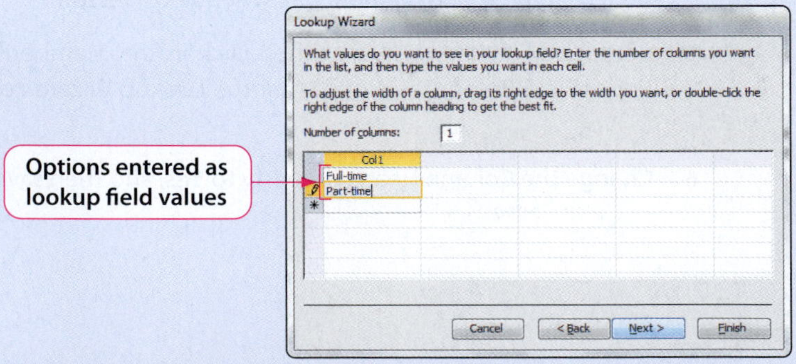

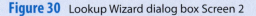

Figure 30 Lookup Wizard dialog box Screen 2

t. Click **Next**. You want to limit the user's selection to the list because there are only part-time and full-time positions at the golf resort. Click **Limit To List**.

u. You do not want to store multiple values in this field because positions entered in this table are categorized as either part-time or full-time. Leave the box next to Allow Multiple Values cleared, and then click **Finish**.

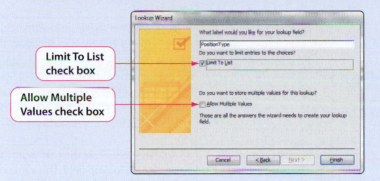

Figure 31 Lookup Wizard dialog box

v. Click **Finish**, and then save your changes.

w. Switch to **Datasheet view**, click in the **PositionType** field in the first record, and then type the word **Both**. Press **Enter**. Notice that Access displays a message explaining that you must select an item from the list or type text that is an item in the list.

x. Click **OK**, and then select **Full-time** from the list.

Troubleshooting

If you had to edit the list, you can also see the Edit List Items button ⬚ when you are in Datasheet view and entering a value (the list is showing). However, it is really hard to see and it is faint.

y. Enter the following from the list in the PositionType field:

Assistant Golf Professional: **Full-time**

Caddy Master: **Full-time**

Golf Caddy: **Part-time**

Golf Course Manager: **Full-time**

Golf Technician: **Full-time**

Head Golf Professional: **Full-time**

Part-time Golf Professional: **Part-time**

Pro Shop Attendant: **Part-time**

Pro Shop Manager: **Full-time**

Troubleshooting

As you are entering the PositionType data, you may not be able to see the EmployeePosition field. To make it easier to view the EmployeePosition field while entering the PositionType data, highlight the EmployeePosition field, right-click, and then select Freeze Fields from the menu.

z. Close tblPosition.

Quick Reference
Define Custom Lookup Field Properties

Property	Description
Display Control	You can set the control type to Check Box, Text Box, List Box, or Combo Box. Combo Box is the most common choice for a lookup field.
Row Source Type	Choose whether to fill the lookup field with values from another table or query or from a list of values that you enter.
Row Source	Specify the table, query, or list of values that provides the values for the lookup field. When the Row Source Type property is set to Table/Query or Field List, this property should be set to a table or query name. When the Row Source Type property is set to Value List, this property should contain a list of values separated by semicolons.
Bound Column	Specify the column in the row source that supplies the value stored by the lookup field. This value can range from 1 to the number of columns in the row source.
Column Count	Specify the number of columns in the row source that can be displayed in the lookup field. To select which columns to display, you provide a column width in the Column Widths property.
Column Heads	Specify whether to display column headings.
Column Widths	Enter the column width for each column. If you do not want to display a column, such as an ID column, specify 0 for the width.
List Rows	Specify the number of rows that appear when you display the lookup field.
List Width	Specify the width of the control that appears when you display the lookup field.
Limit To List	Choose whether you can enter a value that is not in the list. If you have referential integrity set to Yes, this is irrelevant.
Allow Multiple Values	Indicates whether the lookup field allows multiple values to be selected. You cannot change the value of this property from Yes to No. To remove the option, delete the relationship(s) to the field and rerun the Lookup Wizard.
Allow Value List Edits	Specify whether you can edit the items in a lookup field that is based on a value list. When this property is set to Yes and you right-click a Lookup field that is based on a single column value list, you will see the Edit List Items menu option. If the lookup field has more than one column, this property is ignored.
List Items Edit Form	Name an existing form to use to edit the list items in a lookup field that is based on a table or query.
Show Only Row Source Values	Show only values that match the current row source when Allow Multiples Values is set to Yes.

Figure 32 Lookup Field Properties

Calculated Data Type

Access has added a new data type called a **Calculated data type**. A Calculated data type allows you to display the results of a calculation in a read-only field. The calculation must refer to other fields in the same table and is created in the **Expression Builder**. The Expression Builder is a tool that helps you create formulas and functions.

This feature can be useful for many reasons. For example, in an Invoice table, you could calculate the ExtendedPrice field by multiplying the Quantity and Price fields. In an Inventory table, you could calculate CurrentQuantityOnHand by subtracting the TotalProductsSold from TotalProductsOnHand. In a Customer table, you could combine—called **concatenate**—FirstName and LastName fields for address labels.

Some database designers say that adding calculated fields in a table violates normalization rules. In some situations, they are right. However, sometimes it is acceptable to break the rules. For example, if you know that you will need the calculation in every object—query, form, or report—based on the table and you know that the expression will not change over time, then use this data type. Additionally, if having the calculation in the table makes your data easier to understand, then this is an acceptable data type to use.

> **CONSIDER THIS** | **Could the Calculated Data Type Cause Challenges?**
>
> The Calculation data type in a table is new to Access 2010. Do you think that the use of this data type will affect the speed or size of a database at all? Give examples of when using Calculated data types in a table is and is not appropriate.

Real World Advice   Using the Expression Builder

The Expression Builder is a tool you can use to help write expressions, such as calculations in forms, reports, and queries, along with field properties in tables. You can easily retrieve names of fields and controls in your database, as well as built-in functions available when writing expressions. The Expression Builder allows you to build expressions from scratch or select from many prebuilt expressions. Think of the Expression Builder as a way to retrieve and insert fields and functions you might have trouble remembering, such as identifier names (fields, tables, forms, or queries), functions, and arguments.

SIDE NOTE

The Table Name Is Listed

The Expression Elements box already displays the table you are using.

SIDE NOTE

Square Brackets Around Field Names

Access adds square brackets around field names to denote that the data will come from an existing field.

To Create a Calculated Field

a. Open **tblEmployee** in **Design view**.

b. Create a new field named **NameTag**, and then select the Calculated data type. The Expression Builder dialog box will open as soon as you change the data type to Calculated.

c. Double-click **FirstName** to add it to the Expression box.

d. Type **&** (an ampersand), which is the symbol that will help you combine data from different fields.

e. Type **"** (a quotation mark) as they indicate literal characters, press Spacebar, and then type **"** (a quotation mark).

f. Type **&** (an ampersand) again to join the FirstName field to the LastName field.

g. Double-click **LastName** to add it to the Expression box.

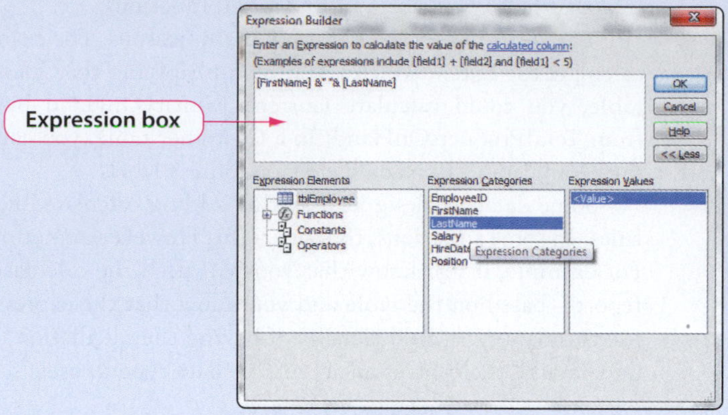

Figure 33 Expression Builder dialog box

h. Click **OK**. Notice that Access added your expression to the Expression property under Field Properties.

i. Enter **Used for printing name tags** into the Description field.

j. Save your changes.

k. To see how the Calculated field property works, switch to **Datasheet view**, and then enter the following record:

FirstName	LastName	Salary	HireDate	Position
Joe	Condon	62500	Today's date	Assistant Golf Professional

Notice that Access automatically adds the FirstName and LastName to the NameTag field.

Troubleshooting

A Calculated field is a read-only field and cannot be edited. If you made errors in entering the FirstName or LastName, make the changes you need to make in those fields. Access will automatically update the NameTag field.

Yes/No Data Type

The **Yes/No data type** allows you to set the Format property to either the Yes/No, True/False, or On/Off predefined formats or to a custom format for the Yes/No data type. Access uses a check box as the default display for the Yes/No data type. A **check box** shows whether an option is selected by using a check mark to indicate that the option is selected. Predefined and custom formats apply only to data that is displayed in a text box, and therefore they are ignored when a check box control is used.

Access's predefined formats of Yes, True, and On are comparable just as No, False, and Off are. If you select one predefined format and then enter an equivalent value, the predefined format of the equivalent value will be displayed. For example, if you enter True or On in a Text Box control where the Format property is set to the Yes/No data type, the value is automatically converted to Yes. Regardless of which format is selected, Access stores the values in this field as either a 0 (for No, False, and Off) or a -1 (Yes, True, and On). The 0 and 1 (or -1 depending on the system you are using) are a throwback to the earlier days of programming. Called **Boolean algebra**, which is still used today, a 1 and 0 are used to represent one of two values—true or false.

Custom formats can also be created with the Yes/No data type. For example, in a Customer table, you may want to have the words "Completed" or "Not Completed" in a field that tracks whether or not a customer has completed a survey sent out by the company. Additionally, you could have the words "Not Completed" displayed in red font, so it is easier to view those customers who have yet to complete the survey.

Quick Reference   The Three Parts of a Custom Yes/No Data Type

The Yes/No data type can use custom formats containing up to three sections.

1. First section: This section has no effect on the Yes/No data type. However, a semicolon is required and used as a placeholder.

2. Second section: This part contains the text to display in place of Yes, True, or On values.

3. Third section: This part contains the text to display in place of No, False, or Off values.

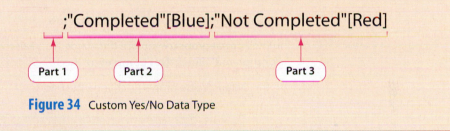

;"Completed"[Blue];"Not Completed"[Red]

Part 1   Part 2   Part 3

Figure 34 Custom Yes/No Data Type

To Create a Yes/No Field

a. Switch **tblEmployee** to **Design view**.

b. Create a new field called **Orientation**, and then select the Yes/No data type.

c. Enter Is new hire orientation complete? into the Description field.

d. Save your changes.

e. To see how the Yes/No field property works, switch to **Datasheet view**, and then check the box for **Barbara Schultz's** record, indicating that her orientation has been completed.

Salary	Date of Hire	Job Title	NameTag	Orientation
$57,250.00	05-Jul-06	Assistant Golf Professional	Barbara Schultz	☑
$87,500.00	02-Feb-01	Head Golf Professional	John Schilling	☐
$22,000.00	30-Aug-09	Golf Technician	Robert Lange	☐
$12,550.00	01-May-08	Golf Caddy	Ginger Liu	☐
$57,250.00	15-Mar-09	Assistant Golf Professional	Juan Martinez	☐
$28,050.00	04-Nov-10	Pro Shop Attendant	Samual Dancer	☐
$36,000.00	08-Jun-07	Pro Shop Attendant	Paul Kimons	☐
$77,375.00	24-Oct-09	Pro Shop Manager	Aleeta Herriott	☐
$78,923.00	01-Dec-10	Golf Course Manager	Barry Cheney	☐
$54,350.00	12-Aug-09	Caddy Master	Jorge Cruz	☐
$15,500.00	26-May-13	Golf Caddy	Mary Ann Teeter	☐
$16,750.00	01-Dec-13	Golf Caddy	Darnell Carter	☐
$34,500.00	01-Dec-13	Pro Shop Attendant	Max Burrell	☐
$22,000.00	03-Mar-13	Golf Technician	Dean Falcon	☐
$200,000.00	03-Mar-13	Golf Professional	Allie Madison	☐
$62,500.00	03-Mar-13	Assistant Golf Professional	Joe Condon	☐

Orientation field

Check box indicates orientation is complete

Figure 35 Datasheet view of tblEmployee table

f. Return to **Design view**, and then click on the Orientation field.

g. Under Field Properties, click the **Lookup tab**, and then change the Display Control from Check Box to Text Box.

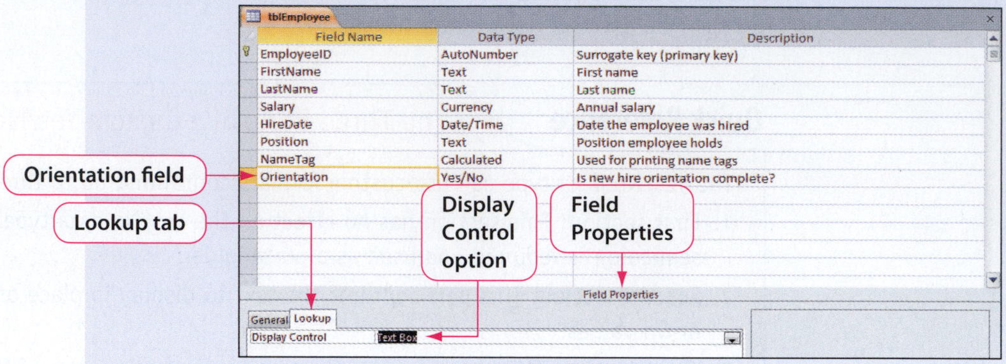

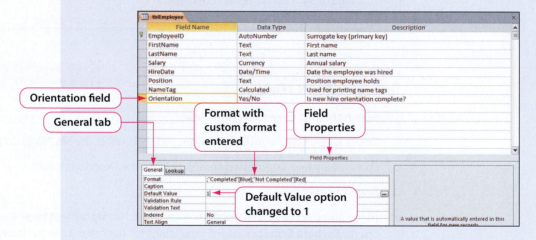

Figure 36 Design view of tblEmployee table

h. Under Field Properties, click the **General tab**.

i. In the Format property, replace the words True/False with ;"Completed"[Blue];"Not Completed"[Red].

j. In the Default Value property, change the 0 to **1**.

Figure 37 Design view of tblEmployee table

k. Save your changes, and then switch to **Datasheet view**.

SIDE NOTE

Using 1 as a Default Value

All new employees entered into the system will automatically have Orientation listed as Completed. If you click back into the field, Access changes the value to -1.

Troubleshooting

Seeing all number signs in a field indicates that a field is too narrow for the data it contains. Simply resize the field to see the data. If you do resize the field, be sure to save your changes.

l. Change the following employees' orientation status to Completed by entering a 1 in the Orientation field:

John Schilling
Robert Lange
Ginger Liu
Juan Martinez
Samuel Dancer
Paul Kimons
Aleeta Herriott
Mary Ann Teeter
Darnell Carter
Max Burrell

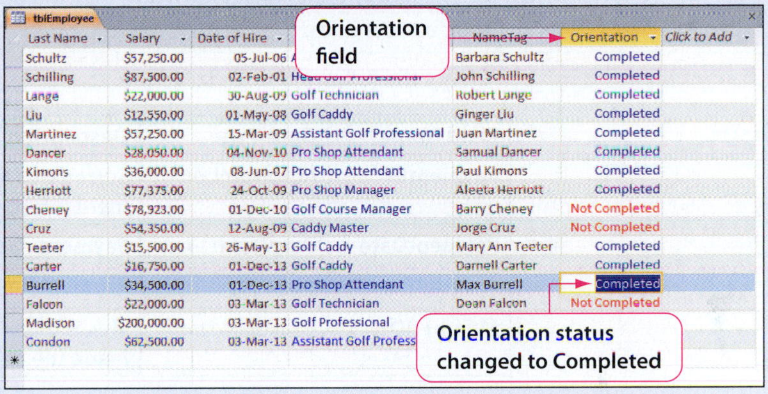

Figure 38 Datasheet view of tblEmployee table

Notice how the word "Completed" is displayed after you enter a 1 in the Orientation field.

m. Save and close tblEmployee.

SIDE NOTE

Check Box or Text Box

Certainly checking a box is easier than typing a 1. Choose a format based on your customization needs and personal preferences.

AutoNumber (and Preference for Natural Keys)

A primary key uniquely identifies the record. A **surrogate key** is an artificial column added to a table to serve as a primary key that is unique and sequential when records are created. However, these unique, sequential values are meaningless to users from a value standpoint; they are only meaningful in regard to creating relationships between tables.

An ideal surrogate key is short, numeric, and never changes. In Access, a surrogate key is known as the **AutoNumber data type**. The AutoNumber data type stores an integer that Access creates automatically as you add new records. These AutoNumbers can be categorized as increment or random. An **increment AutoNumber** is the most common and is the default setting in Access when selecting the AutoNumber data type. A **random AutoNumber** will generate a random number that is unique to each record within the table. Either type of AutoNumber will serve as a good primary key. AutoNumbers are a great method for ensuring that records are uniquely identified.

Some challenges do exist when working with AutoNumbers, but one in particular causes some stress with users. An AutoNumber of a deleted record will never be used again. For example, if you have a table with 10 records and the primary key is an AutoNumber—meaning that the records are numbered incrementally from 1 through 10—and you delete record number 7, Access will never use 7 again in the AutoNumber field. If this happens to you, do not think you did something wrong. This is simply how relational databases operate. Because of the way that Access does not reuse numbers, they are not designed to count records and they should never be used for that purpose.

To Create an AutoNumber Field

a. Create a new table in **Design view** that will help users track when members have paid their annual dues.

b. Create the following table structure:

Field Name	Data Type	Description	Field Properties
PaymentID	AutoNumber	Surrogate key for each payment (primary key)	Primary Key
PaymentDate	Date/Time	Payment date	Short Date Format
AmountPaid	Currency	Payment amount	
MemberID	Lookup Wizard	This is the member who made the payment.	

c. When the Lookup Wizard opens, click **I want the lookup field to get the values from another table or query**.

d. Click **Next**, and then select **tblMember**.

e. Click **Next**, and then select the following fields to be included in your lookup field: **MemberID**, **LastName**, and **FirstName**.

f. Click **Next**, and then select the following ascending sort order for the data in your lookup field: **LastName**, **FirstName**.

g. Click **Next** two times, and then select **Enable Data Integrity** and **Restrict Delete**.

h. Click **Finish**, and then click **Yes** when Access prompts you to save the table.

i. Save your table as **tblPayment**, and then click **OK**.

j. Add Member who made the payment to the Description field.

k. Save your changes.

Troubleshooting

Sometimes you may see a warning message that states "tblPayment has been changed since the last time you opened it, either by another user or because another instance was opened on your own machine." If you know you have not made changes outside the database, click Yes.

l. To see how the AutoNumber data type works, switch to **Datasheet view**, and then enter the following records. You may have to scroll down in the list to find the names.

PaymentDate	AmountPaid	MemberID
1/26/2013	1200	Jena Duke
2/23/2013	1500	Marcus Risotto

Notice as you enter the data, Access automatically enters the PaymentID for you.

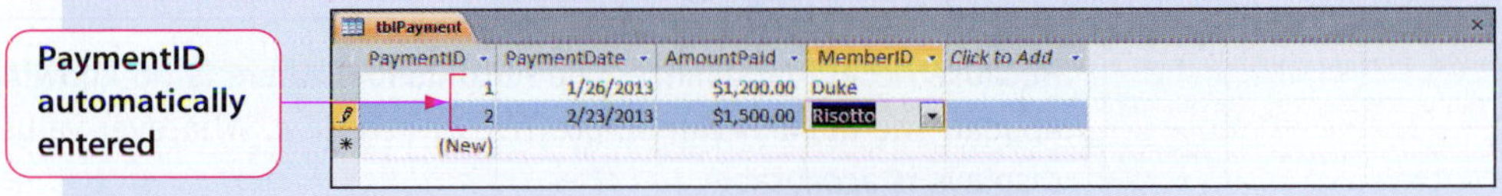

PaymentID automatically entered

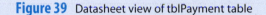

Figure 39 Datasheet view of tblPayment table

SIDE NOTE

The Lookup Fields Do Not Display All the Data

Lookup fields that have multiple fields in the menu only display the data that is in the first column.

m. Delete the record where the PaymentID is 1. Click **Yes** to confirm the deletion of this record.

n. Enter the following record to see how the AutoNumber data type behaves when a record is deleted:

PaymentDate	AmountPaid	MemberID
3/5/2013	500	Josh Pendleton

Notice as you enter the data, Access enters a PaymentID of 3.

o. To see how the random AutoNumber data type works, return to **Design view**.

p. Click the **PaymentID** field, and then under Field Properties, select the **New Values** property.

q. Change the Increment property to **Random**. As soon as you do, Access will warn you that once you change this property, you will not be able to change it back.

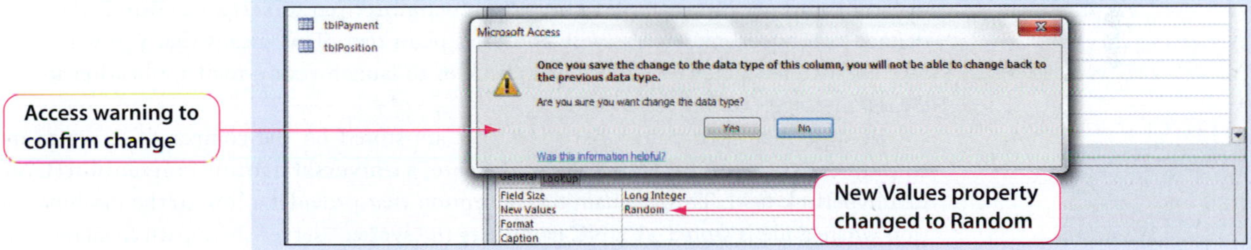

Access warning to confirm change

New Values property changed to Random

Figure 40 Design view of tblPayment table

r. Click **Yes**, and then save your changes.

s. To see how the random AutoNumber data type works, switch to **Datasheet view**, and then enter the following records:

PaymentDate	AmountPaid	MemberID
4/8/2013	800	Gary Way
5/25/2013	2250	Fiona Britt

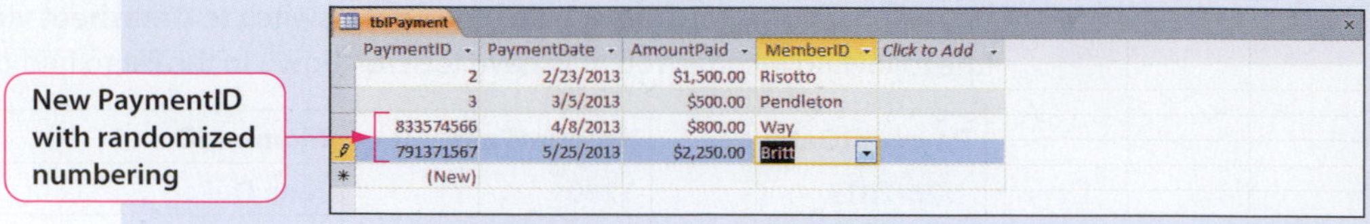

New PaymentID with randomized numbering

Figure 41 Datasheet view of tblPayment table

Troubleshooting

Because Access randomizes the AutoNumber, there is no knowing what number will appear. The number can be positive or negative. Whatever value Access enters and displays is acceptable.

t. Close tblPayment.

Attachments, Hyperlinks, and OLE Objects

You can attach images, spreadsheet files, documents, charts, and other types of supported files to the records in your database, much like you attach files to an e-mail message. Access allows you to view and edit the attached files, depending on how the database designer configures the **Attachment** field properties. Where you need to use caution is that attachments do increase the size of your database, and developers need to ensure that attachments will not use too much storage space.

You are probably familiar with how all Microsoft applications can change e-mail or website addresses to a hyperlink formatting once you finish typing it into the application. In Access, fields that contain e-mail or website addresses should be defined as the Hyperlink data type. A **hyperlink** is an address that specifies a protocol (such as HTTP or FTP) and a location of an object, document, World Wide Web page, or other destination on the Internet, an intranet, or local computer. An example is **http://www.paintedparadiseresort.com**. If the field is not defined as a hyperlink, Access will store it as plain text. This means that you will not be able to click it to navigate to a particular website or to launch your e-mail application and write an e-mail message.

Because many companies have files that are stored on the company's server so multiple employees have access to them, you can also enter a **universal naming convention (UNC)** path in a hyperlink field. This is a naming convention that provides a link to the machine and location where a file is stored. A UNC name uses the syntax \\server\share\path\filename and works the same way a Uniform Resource Locator (URL) works.

Access can also store images inside a database field by using the OLE Object data type. An **OLE Object**, which stands for Object Linking and Embedding, is a technology developed by Microsoft that creates a **bitmap** or image of the object. The OLE Object data type can be used in much the same way, but is less efficient than a bitmap as it consumes a great deal of space within the database. OLE is a legacy data type that needs to be included for existing databases, but attachments are far more functional and efficient and do not even use an OLE. A **legacy data type** is an old or outdated data type that is still used—usually because it still works for the user—even though newer technology or more efficient methods exist. An attachment is the more efficient of the two data types because they do not consume as much space.

To Create an Attachment, Hyperlink, or OLE Object Field

a. Open **tblEmployee** in **Design view**.

b. Add the following new fields:

Field Name	Data Type	Description
EmailAddress	Hyperlink	Email address
Photo	OLE Object	Golf photo
OrientationSignOff	Attachment	Form verifying orientation completion

c. Save your changes. To see how the E-mail data type works, switch to **Datasheet view**, and then enter the following data. Resize the field so you can see what you are typing.

EmployeeID	NameTag	E-mailAddress
EMP4	Ginger Liu	gliu@paintedparadiseresort.com
EMP12	Darnell Carter	dcarter@paintedparadiseresort.com
EMP16	Joe Condon	jcondon@paintedparadiseresort.com

Notice that a hyperlink is automatically created once you enter the e-mail addresses.

Troubleshooting

When entering an e-mail address into a Hyperlink field, Access automatically formats it as a link to a web page. You need to define it as an e-mail address by taking a couple of extra steps.

d. Right-click on **Joe Condon's** e-mail address, click **Hyperlink**, and then select **Edit Hyperlink**. The Edit Hyperlink dialog box opens.

e. Click **E-mail Address** in the Link to section on the left side of the dialog box. Notice that the pane changes and allows you to enter Joe Condon's e-mail address.

f. Enter Joe Condon's e-mail address into the E-mail Address text box by either typing it or copying and pasting it from the Text to Display text box, if necessary. Notice that Access adds "mailto:" at the beginning of the e-mail address.

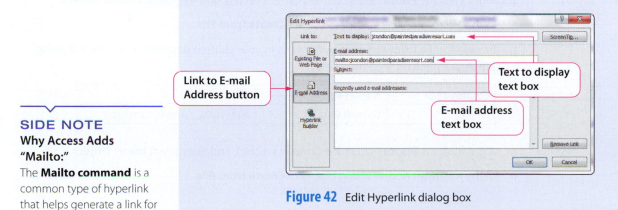

Link to E-mail Address button

Text to display text box

E-mail address text box

Figure 42 Edit Hyperlink dialog box

SIDE NOTE

Why Access Adds "Mailto:"

The **Mailto command** is a common type of hyperlink that helps generate a link for sending e-mail.

g. Click **OK**. To enter an OLE Object into the Photo field, right-click the **Photo** field in Ginger Liu's record, and then select **Insert Object**. The Microsoft Access dialog box opens.

h. Click **Create from File**.

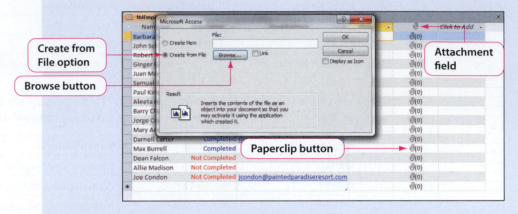

Figure 43 Microsoft Access dialog box

i. Browse for the following employee photo in your student data files. Enter the following employee photo in the Photo field:

EmployeeID	NameTag	Photo
EMP4	Ginger Liu	a03_ws05_ginger_liu.jpg

Notice that once the photo is inserted into the Photo field, the object is displayed as a Package.

Troubleshooting

Sometimes Access can be a little tricky when entering objects like photos or attachments. If you enter one and it will not let you enter any others, click in another field and check to see if Access will let you right-click into the OLE Object field. If that still does not work, close and then reopen the table.

j. Right-click the **Photo** field in Darnell Carter's record, and then select **Insert Object**.

k. In the Microsoft Access dialog box, click **Create from File**.

l. Browse for the following employee photo in your student data files. Enter the following employee photo in the Photo field:

EmployeeID	NameTag	Photo
EMP12	Darnell Carter	a03_ws05_darnell_carter.jpg

m. Right-click the **Photo** field in Joe Condon's record, and then select **Insert Object**.

n. In the Microsoft Access dialog box, click **Create from File**.

o. Browse for the following employee photo in your student data files. Enter the following employee photo in the Photo field:

EmployeeID	NameTag	Photo
EMP16	Joe Condon	a03_ws05_joe_condon.jpg

p. To enter an attachment into the OrientationSignOff field, double-click the **Paperclip** button ⬚ in Ginger Liu's record. The Attachments dialog box opens.

q. Click **Add**, and then browse for a03_ws05_liu.pdf in your student data files.

r. Click **a03_ws05_liu.pdf** once, and then click **Open**.

s. The a03_ws05_liu.pdf should now be displayed in your Attachments dialog box.

t. Click **OK**. To view the attachment, double-click Ginger Liu's **Attachment** field. The Attachments dialog box opens.

u. Click **a03_ws05_liu.pdf**, and then click **Open**. The PDF document will open in another window.

Troubleshooting

If the PDF document did not open, you probably do not have Adobe Acrobat Reader installed on your computer. You can download this free application at http://www.adobe.com.

v. Close the PDF document, and then close the Attachments dialog box by clicking **OK**.

w. Close tblEmployee. Click **Yes** to save.

SIDE NOTE

Numbers in Parentheses

In the Attachment field, the numbers in the parentheses indicate how many attachments exist in that field.

Filtering Data

Filtering is very useful where you can view and print only the desired and required information from your database. Because this is a temporary view of the data, you may want to save the filter as a query if you want to filter the records on the basis of the same criteria again and again.

Three types of filtering exist. Access provides the ability to filter records containing similar values of data for a specific field. For example, you may want to filter the records that have a "Santa Fe" value in the "City" field. The **Filter by Form** type could be used, which allows you to filter data in a form or datasheet. The Filter by Form method creates a blank table for the selected table. This blank table contains all the fields of the table with a list for each field. Each list contains all the unique values of records for each field. This method allows you to easily select the field value for which you want to filter the table records.

In some cases, the **Filter by Selection** method may not be very helpful as it may require extra steps to find your initial value. This displays only the rows in a table containing a value that matches a selected value in a row by filtering the Datasheet view. In the above scenario, you may find that the Filter by Form method is better.

Because the Filter by Form or Filter by Selection filters may not give enough options, as they are fairly basic, you might want to apply a filter that is an **advanced filter** in which you write the filter criterion yourself. For example, you may want to find products that contain dates occurring during the past seven days. After you apply an advanced filter, you can further limit the results to those that have a price of over $100. Using the advanced filters does require writing expressions. In this section, you will learn how to filter data using Filter by Form, Filter by Selection, and advanced filter options.

To Create a Filter

a. Open **tblMember** in **Datasheet view**.

b. To filter by selection, click the **City** field of Record 1. Notice there are 30 records in tblMember.

c. Click the **Selection arrow** ⏷ on the Home tab.

d. Four options are displayed. Select **Equals "Santa Fe"**. Notice that all 13 members who live in Santa Fe are displayed. Additionally, the Filter button ⫟ appears at the top of the field where the filter has been applied.

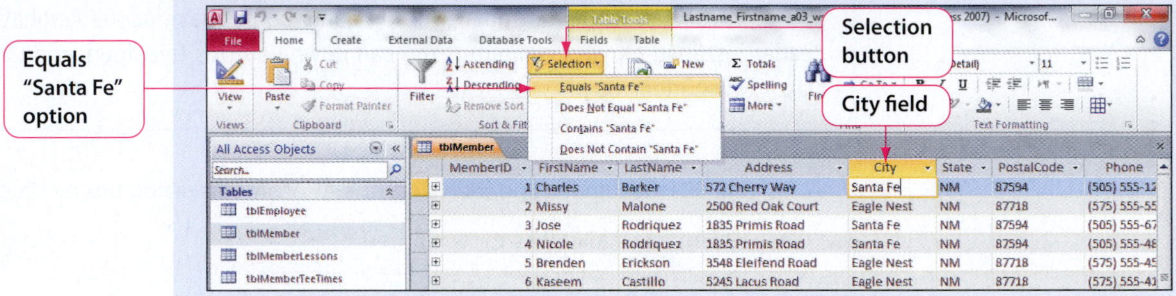

Figure 44 Datasheet view of tblMember table

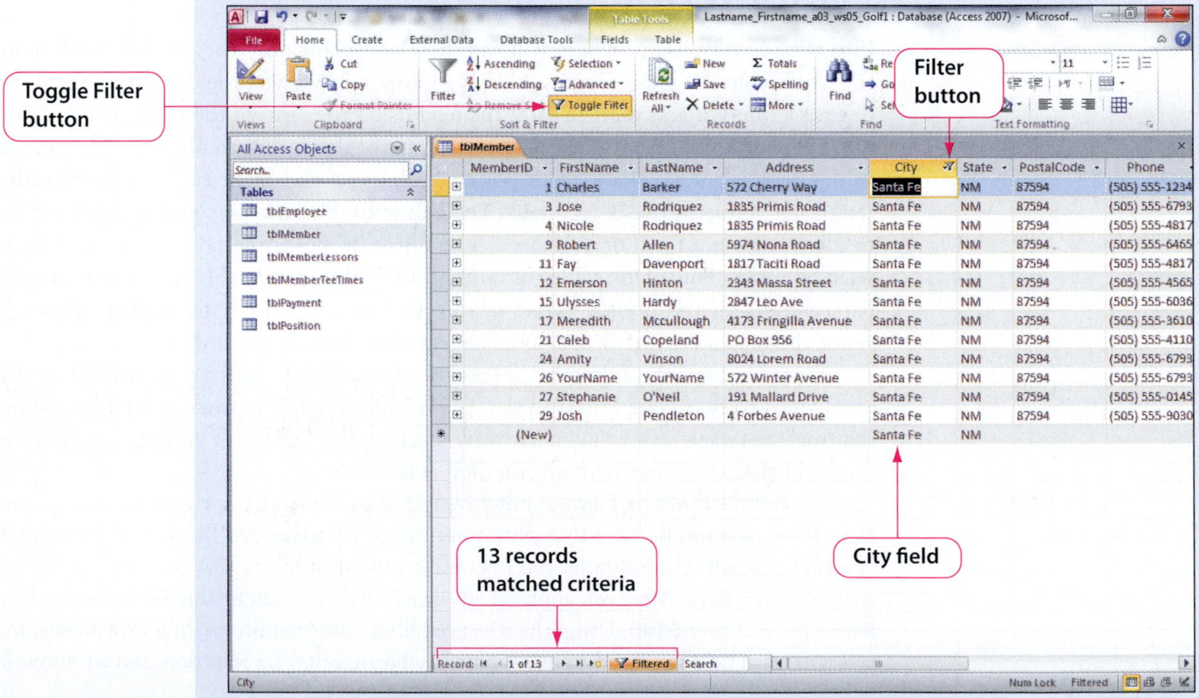

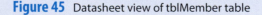

Figure 45 Datasheet view of tblMember table

e. Click **Toggle Filter** on the Home tab. Notice that the filter is now removed.

f. Click **Toggle Filter** again, and the filter is reapplied.

g. Click **Toggle Filter** again to remove it.

h. To filter by form, click **Advanced** on the Home tab, and then click **Filter By Form**.

i. Click in a few of the fields. Notice that "Santa Fe" still remains in the City field and each field has a menu and looks much like a form. An Or tab also appears at the bottom of the table.

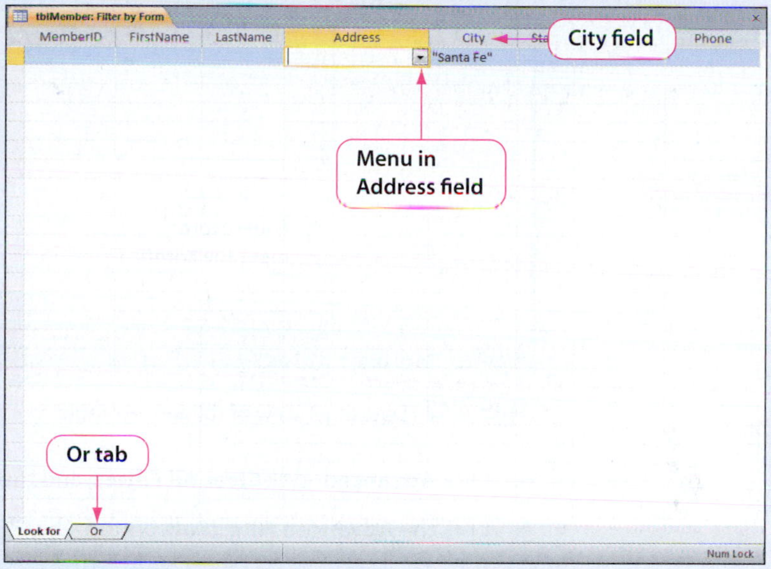

Figure 46 tblMember Filter by Form pane

j. Select **Eagle Nest** from the menu in the City field.

k. Click **Toggle Filter** on the Home tab. Three records meet the selected criteria.

l. Click **Advanced** on the Home tab, and then click **Filter By Form**.

m. Leave Eagle Nest in the City field. At the bottom of the tblMember: Filter by Form pane, click the **Or tab**.

   This will allow you to search for one criterion or another. The Or operator indicates that either of the criteria can be in a record in order to display in the filter results.

n. In the State field, select **AZ**, and then click **Toggle Filter**. Notice that four records meet the filter criteria. The Filter is displayed at the top of the City and State fields, indicating that you have applied a filter to both fields.

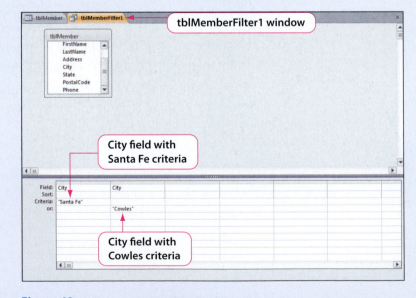

Figure 47 Datasheet view of tblMember table

o. Click **Advanced**, click **Clear All Filters**, and then click **Advanced**.

p. Click the **Advanced Filter/Sort** button. The tblMemberFilter1 pane opens.

q. Select the following fields and enter the following criteria in the tblMemberFilter1 grid:

Field	Field Name	Criteria
1	City	Santa Fe
2	City	Cowles (enter under "or" line below Criteria)

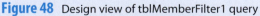

Figure 48 Design view of tblMemberFilter1 query

r. Click **Toggle Filter**. Notice the results of the Advanced Filter are now displayed in tblMember.

s. Click the **File tab** on the Ribbon.

t. Click **Save Object As**, and then select **Query**. Save your filter with the name **qrySantaFeMembers_initialLastname**.

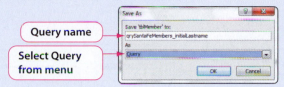

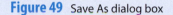

Figure 49 Save As dialog box

u. Click **OK**, and then click the **Home tab** on the Ribbon. Notice there is a new object named **qrySantaFeMembers_initialLastname**. This is the query you just created and saved.

v. Close tblMember, tblMemberFilter1, and qrySantaFeMembers_initialLastname. When Access prompts you to save the changes to **tblMember**, click **No**.

Using the Table Analyzer Wizard

Many times employees will store data in an Excel spreadsheet because they know how to use Excel, but not Access. Although Excel is a great tool for many tasks, Excel does not allow users to create sophisticated queries. Because of this, there are times that you will want to import a spreadsheet into Access and work with the data. However, Excel spreadsheets often contain repetitive information that is not normalized, making the data impossible to move directly into an efficient Access database.

By using the Access **Table Analyzer Wizard**, you can divide the table created from an imported Excel spreadsheet into several tables as well as automatically create the relationships needed between them. The Table Analyzer Wizard minimizes the need for data re-entry, saving you valuable time and resources. However, the Table Analyzer Wizard is unable to restructure all the imported data properly. In this section, you will learn how to normalize tables by using the Table Analyzer Wizard.

To Use the Table Analyzer Wizard

a. Click **tblMember**, and then click **Analyze Table** on the Database Tools tab.

b. The Table Analyzer Wizard opens to the first introduction dialog box.

c. Click **Next**. The next introduction screen is displayed.

d. Click **Next** again, and then select **tblMember**, if necessary.

e. Click **Next**, and then click **Yes, let the wizard decide**.

f. Click **Next**.

g. Access will create two new tables, noted as **Table1** and **Table2**. Double-click the current table names and rename them as follows:

Table1: **tblMemberData**
Table2: **tblCityState**

h. Click **Next**. The primary key in the new tblCityState table will be an AutoNumber, which is an ideal primary key. Access has **Generated Unique ID** as the first field in this table, which implies AutoNumber. You may have to resize the tables to see the whole table and field names.

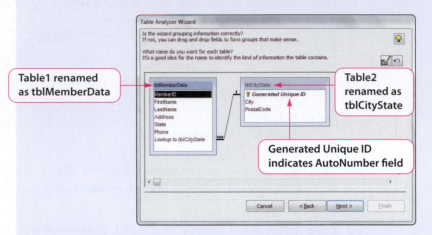

Figure 50 Table Analyzer Wizard dialog box

i. Click **Next**.

j. There are no typographical errors that need to be fixed. Click **Next**. Access will ask if you are sure you want to move on. Click **Yes**.

k. Access asks if you want to create a query that resembles your old table. Because your old table will be saved automatically, you will not need a query with the same data. Click **No, don't create the query**.

l. Click **Finish**. Both tables you just created—tblMemberData and tblCityState—will open.

Troubleshooting

Access sometimes opens the Help window to offer further assistance with analyzing the table. Just close it if it opens.

Troubleshooting

Access sometimes displays an error message that says it cannot tile the tables horizontally. Just close it if it opens.

m. Save **tblMemberData** and **tblCityState**, and then close **tblMemberData** and **tblCityState**.

n. Close the Lastname_Firstname_a03_ws05_Golf1 database.

SIDE NOTE
The Navigation Pane Minimized

After finishing the Table Analyzer Wizard, the Navigation Pane may minimize. Click the Shutter Bar Open/Close button if it does.

SIDE NOTE
tblMember Looks Like a Table

You can check to see what object type tblMember is by switching to Design view.

Real World Advice — Why Worry About Analyzing Tables?

When Access creates new tables in the Table Analyzer Wizard, it is looking for a way to minimize storage space in the analyzed table by storing data more efficiently. When a table contains repeating information in one or more fields, such as a city or state, you can use the Table Analyzer Wizard to move the data into related tables. This process is called normalization.

Quick Reference — About the Table Analyzer Wizard

Access takes you through a series of screens when you are working through the wizard:

- Looking at the Problem: This contains an explanation and examples of how duplicate data causes problems in a database.
- Solving the Problem: This contains an explanation and examples of how Access may split the table in multiple tables if there is redundant data in your tables.
- Select Table: Select the table you want to analyze.
- What Fields Go in What Tables Decision: This is where you decide whether you want Access to decide or if you want to decide what fields go in what tables.
- Review Grouping: This is where you will either review or edit what Access has created, or where you will create your new tables based on your decision in the previous step.
- Create Primary Keys: Bold fields will indicate what the new primary keys will be. You can either keep them the way they are or edit them.
- Correct Typographical Errors: The wizard gives you the opportunity to fix any errors in your data.
- Create a Query: Access can create a query that resembles your old table. This is a smart idea to have as a backup copy.

Concept Check

1. Explain why it is important to worry about the way data is entered into a database.

2. What are the similarities and differences between an input mask and formatting?

3. Describe the differences between a Filter by Form and Filter by Selection.

4. Why is the AutoNumber data type ideal to use as a primary key?

5. How can the creation of too many constraints or rules on a field or fields cause challenges for users?

Key Terms

Advanced filter 273
Attachment 270
AutoNumber data type 267
Bitmap 270
Boolean algebra 265
Calculated data type 263
Caption property 250
Check box 264
Concatenate 263
Custom formatting 242
Data type 256
Data validation rule 247
Default value 255
Expression Builder 263
Field format 242

Field validation rule 247
Filter by Form 273
Filter by Selection 273
Filtering 273
GIGO principle 236
Hyperlink 270
Increment AutoNumber 267
Index 251
Input mask 236
Input Mask Wizard 241
Legacy data type 270
Lookup field 256
Lookup field properties 257
Lookup Wizard 256
Mailto command 271

Multiple-field index 252
Multivalued field 256
Null 254
OLE Object 270
Random AutoNumber 267
Record validation rule 247
Required property 254
Single-field index 252
String 255
Surrogate key 267
Table Analyzer Wizard 277
Universal naming convention
  (UNC) 270
Validation Text property 247
Yes/No data type 264

Visual Summary

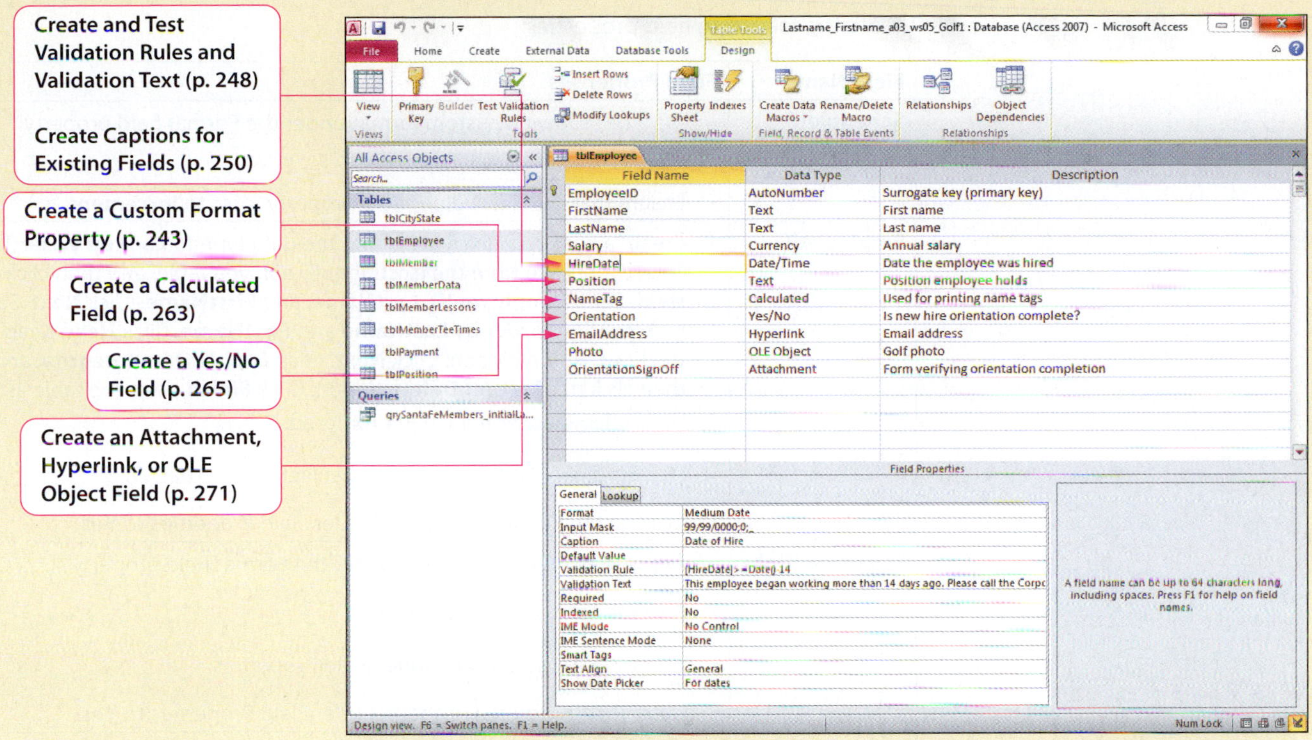

Create and Test Validation Rules and Validation Text (p. 248)

Create Captions for Existing Fields (p. 250)

Create a Custom Format Property (p. 243)

Create a Calculated Field (p. 263)

Create a Yes/No Field (p. 265)

Create an Attachment, Hyperlink, or OLE Object Field (p. 271)

Figure 51 The Red Bluff Golf Club Pro Shop final database

Practice 1

Student data file needed:

a03_ws05_Golf2

You will save your file as:

Lastname_Firstname_a03_ws05_Golf2

Scheduling Employees at the Red Bluff Golf Club

Generally, the Red Bluff Golf Club schedules one caddy for every two reservations because not everyone uses a caddy. Golfers may either carry their own bag or rent a cart. You have been asked to add a table—including advanced formatting and controls—to track the golf caddies' work schedule.

a. Open the **a03_ws05_Golf2** database. Save it as Lastname_Firstname_a03_ws05_Golf2.

b. Create a new table in **Design view** by clicking the **Table Design** button on the Create tab. This table will help track caddies' work schedules.

c. Add the following fields, data types, and descriptions:

Field Name	Data Type	Description
ScheduleID	AutoNumber	Surrogate key for each scheduled employee shift (primary key)
EmployeeID	Number	EmployeeID (foreign key) from the tblEmployee
ScheduledDate	Date/Time	Date employee is scheduled to work
StartTime	Date/Time	Time employee's shift begins
EndTime	Date/Time	Time employee's shift ends
OnTime	Yes/No	Did employee arrive on time

d. Create the following field properties:

Field Name	Field Properties
ScheduleID	• Add the following custom format under the Format field property: "SID-0"0 • Ensure that the New Values field property is set to **Increment**.
EmployeeID	• Create a Lookup field by changing the data type to **Lookup Wizard**. Select your data from the existing tblEmployee table, and then click **Next**. Select **EmployeeID**, **LastName**, and **FirstName**. Click **Next**. Sort in **Ascending order** by **LastName** and **FirstName**. Click **Next**. Keep the Key Column hidden. Click **Next**. Click **Enable Data Integrity**, and then click the **Restrict Delete** option. Click **Finish**. Save the table as tblEmployeeSchedule when prompted. • Add Employee as the caption under Field Properties. • Change the Required property under Field Properties to **Yes**.
ScheduledDate	• Apply the **Long Date** format under the Format field property. • Add the Short Date Input Mask. • Add Date as the caption under Field Properties. • Change the Required property under Field Properties to **Yes**.
StartTime	• Add the **Medium Time** format under the Format field property. • Add Medium Time as the Input Mask. • Add Shift Begins as the caption under Field Properties. • Add 8:00 AM as the Default Value under Field Properties. • Change the Required property under Field Properties to **Yes**.
EndTime	• Add the **Medium Time** format under the Format field property. • Add **Medium Time** as the Input Mask. • Add Shift Ends as the caption under Field Properties. • Add 6:00 PM as the Default Value under Field Properties. • Add the following Validation Rule: >="[StartTime]". • Add the following Validation Text: You must enter a time that ends AFTER the scheduled start time.
OnTime	• Add the following custom format under the Format field property: ;"Yes"[Blue];"No"[Red]. • Click the **Lookup tab** under Field Properties, and then change the Display Control to **Text Box**. • Add On Time? as the caption under Field Properties.

e. While still in Design view, add a Calculated field with the following properties:

Field Name	Data Type	Description
PostedSchedule	Calculated	Calculated field of employee's ScheduleDate, BeginTime, and EndTime

Field Properties
• Enter the following fields into the Expression Builder dialog box, and then separate each one with the appropriate notation as follows: [ScheduledDate]&", "&[StartTime]&"-"&[EndTime]. Click **OK**. • Add Posted Schedule as the caption under Field Properties.

f. Save your changes, and then switch to **Datasheet view**. Add the following records to test the properties in your new table—resize your fields as needed to view the data:

Employee	Date	Shift Begins	Shift Ends	On Time
Ginger Liu	7/4/2013	12:00 PM	6:00 PM	Yes
Mary Lou Lovelace	7/8/2013	8:00 AM	6:00 PM	No
Darnell Carter	7/4/2013	8:00 AM	12:00 PM	Yes
Mary Ann Teeter	7/15/2013	8:00 AM	6:00 PM	Yes

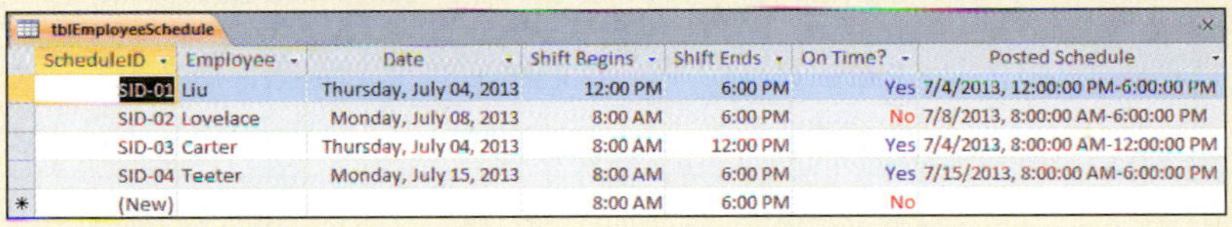

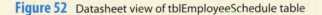

Figure 52 Datasheet view of tblEmployeeSchedule table

g. Switch to **Design view**. Click **Indexes** on the Table Tools Design tab to create a **multiple-field index**.

h. Enter the following index properties starting at the first blank row in the Indexes dialog box:

Index Name	Field Name	Sort Order
ScheduleTime	StartTime	Ascending
	EndTime	Ascending

Index Properties

Primary	No
Unique	No
Ignore Nulls	No

i. Save your changes, and then close the Indexes dialog box.

j. Close tblEmployeeSchedule.

k. Close the Lastname_Firstname_a03_ws05_Golf2 database.

Student data file needed:

a03_ws05_Events

You will save your file as:

Lastname_Firstname_a03_ws05_Events

Event Planning at the Red Bluff Golf Club

From weddings to conferences, the resort is a popular destination. The resort has several facilities that can accommodate groups from 30 to 600 people. Packages and prices vary by size, room, and other services, such as catering. The Event Planning and Catering team works closely with clients to ensure the clients have everything they need for their event. The resort stocks several choices of decorations, table arrangements, and centerpieces. These range from professional, simple, themed, and luxurious.

a. Open the **a03_ws05_Events** database. Save it as Lastname_Firstname_a03_ws05_Events.

b. Open **tblClients**, and then add your information in record 25. Replace **Your Name** in the First Name and Last Name fields with your first and last name. Close tblClients.

c. Create a new table in **Design view** by clicking **Table Design** on the Create tab. This table will help track specific items requested for an event.

d. Add the following fields, data types, and descriptions:

Field Name	Data Type	Description
EventItemID	AutoNumber	Surrogate key for each selected item (primary key)
EventID	Number	This is the scheduled event
ClientID	Number	Client ID (foreign key) from the tblClient table
DecorID	Text	What the client wants to have at the event
Theme	Text	Can be professional, simple, themed, or luxurious

e. Save the new table as tblEventItems, and then create the following field properties:

Field Name	Field Properties
EventItemID	• Add the following custom format under the Format field property: "ITEM"0 • Ensure that the New Values field property is set to **Increment**.
EventID	• Create a Lookup field by changing the data type to **Lookup Wizard**. Select your data from the existing tblEvents table, and then click **Next**. Select **EventID**, **EventName**, and **EventDate**. Click **Next**. Sort in **Descending order** by **EventDate**. Click **Next**. Hide the **Key Column**. Click **Next** two times. Click **Enable Data Integrity**, and then click **Restrict Delete**. Click **Finish**. Save the table when prompted. • Add Event as the caption under Field Properties. • Change the Required property under Field Properties to **Yes**.

Field Name	Field Properties
ClientID	• Create a Lookup field by changing the data type to **Lookup Wizard**. Select your data from the existing tblClients table, and then click **Next**. Select **ClientID**, **LastName**, and **FirstName**. Click **Next**. Sort in **Ascending order** by **LastName** and **FirstName**. Click **Next**. Keep the Key Column hidden. Click **Next**. Click **Enable Data Integrity**, and then click **Restrict Delete**. Click **Finish**. Save the table when prompted. • Add Client as the caption under Field Properties. • Change the Required property under Field Properties to **Yes**.
DecorID	• Create a Lookup field by changing the data type to **Lookup Wizard**. Select your data from the existing tblDecorations table, and then click **Next**. Select **DecorID**, **DecorItem**, and **Color**. Click **Next**. Sort in **Ascending order** by **DecorItem** and **Color**. Click **Next**. Keep the Key Column hidden. Click **Next**. Click **Enable Data Integrity**, and then click **Restrict Delete**. Click **Finish**. Save the table when prompted. • Add Item as the caption under Field Properties. • Change the Required property under Field Properties to **Yes**.
Theme	• Create a Lookup field by changing the data type to **Lookup Wizard**. Click **I will type in the values that I want**. Click **Next**. Enter the following options: Row 1: Professional Row 2: Simple Row 3: Themed Row 4: Luxurious Click **Next**, click **Limit to List**, and then click **Finish**. • Change the Field Size property under Field Properties to 12.

f. Save your changes, and then switch to **Datasheet view**. Add the following records to test the field properties in your new table:

Event	Client	Item	Theme
Wedding Reception 11/23/2013	Bennett	Tablecloth White	Luxurious
Wedding Reception 11/23/2013	Bennett	Napkins White	Luxurious
Wedding Reception 11/23/2013	Bennett	Candles with Flowers Silver	Luxurious
Wedding Reception 11/23/2013	Bennett	Fountain (large)	Luxurious

g. Close tblEventItems. Open **tblEvents** in **Datasheet view** to create a query from a filter.

h. Click the **Location** field, and then click **Filter** on the Home tab.

i. Select all events being held in the Eldorado Room. Save this filter as a query named qryEldoradoRoom_initialLastname.

j. Click the **Home tab**, and then close qryEldoradoRoom_initialLastname.

k. Click **Advanced**, click **Clear All Filters**, and then click **Advanced**.

l. Click the **Advanced Filter/Sort** button. The tblEventsFilter1 pane opens.

m. Select the following fields, and then enter the following criteria in the tblEventsFilter1 grid:

Field	Field Name	Criteria
1	EventName	
2	EventDate	
3	StartTime	
4	EndTime	>5:00 PM

n. Click **Toggle Filter**. Notice the results of the Advanced Filter are now displayed in the tblEvents table.

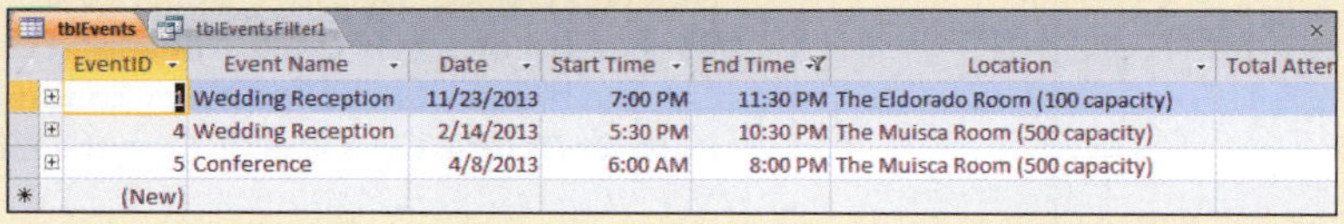

Figure 53 Filtered data from tblEvents table

o. Save this filter as a query named qryEveningEvents_initialLastname.

p. Click the **Home tab**, and then close qryEveningEvents_initialLastname.

q. Close tblEvents and tblEventsFilter1. Do not save the changes when prompted.

r. Click **Analyze Table** on the Database Tools tab. The Table Analyzer Wizard opens to the first introduction screen.

s. Click **Next** two times, and then select **tblEvents**, if necessary.

t. Click **Next**, and then click **Yes, let the wizard decide**.

u. Click **Next**. Access will create three new tables, noted as **Table1**, **Table2**, and **Table3**. Double-click the **current table names**, and rename them as follows:

Table1: tblEventData
Table2: tblEventName
Table3: tblEventLocation

v. Click **Next** two times. Access asks if you want to create a query that resembles your old table. Because your old table will be saved automatically, you will not need a query with the same data. Click **No, don't create the query**.

w. Click **Finish**. All three tables you just created will open. Close tblEventData, tblEvent-Name, and tblEventLocation. Click **Yes** if Access prompts you to save any changes.

x. Close the Lastname_Firstname_a03_ws05_Events database.

Objectives

1. Create queries that use wildcard characters in string comparisons. p. 288

2. Find records with the "most" or "least" values. p. 292

3. Create queries that use parameters to ask for input. p. 294

4. Join data in fields using the Concatenate function. p. 296

5. Create queries that use Not, In, and other advanced operators. p. 298

6. Create queries that use the IIf function. p. 300

7. Create queries using the IsNull function. p. 303

8. Create queries using different Date functions. p. 304

9. Create queries using the Round function. p. 312

Querying Databases

PREPARE CASE

The Red Bluff Golf Club: Creating Queries

The Red Bluff Golf Club needs useful information in order to run its business efficiently. Barry Cheney, the Golf Club Manager, has asked you to query the tables used to track the golfers who have scheduled tee times and private lessons. Additionally, you need to create queries for decision making, such as scheduling when golf pros give private lessons or verifying how many golf caddies are needed on a busy day. To keep the file small while you work with the database, he removed most of the data and left only some sample data. Once Barry accepts your changes, he will load all of the data and roll out the new database.

Courtesy of www.Shutterstock.com

Student data file needed for this workshop:

 a03_ws06_Golf1

You will save your file as:

 Lastname_Firstname_a03_ws06_Golf1

Advanced Criteria and Calculations

The most important functionality of a database is to create useful information. Queries enable the user to retrieve data, filter data, calculate data totals, update data, append data, and delete records in bulk. Becoming proficient at building queries will improve your ability to manage and understand your data. Building queries helps turn data into useful information and is critical in creating quality information. Knowing the features of query design allows you to perform advanced analyses quickly.

Once you have quality information and make a decision based on that information, you now have knowledge about your organization. This knowledge can help you make decisions about your business. This **knowledge** is defined as applied information once you make the decision. For example, what if you want to reward your high-value customers on their birthdays? You could create a query that shows all customers who have spent more than $500 over the past six months and limit the results to those who were born in the current month. In this section, you will create advance queries that use wildcard characters in string comparisons, find records with the "most" or "least" values, and make a query ask for input. Additionally, you will create queries that use the concatenate function, and not, in and other advanced operators.

Quick Reference / Understanding Expressions

In Access, the term "expression" is synonymous with "formula." An expression consists of several possible elements that you can use—alone or in combination—to yield a result. Those elements include:

1. Identifiers: The names of a field, a control on a form or report, or the properties of the fields or controls
2. Operators: Such as [+] or [-] signs
3. Logical operators: Includes And, Or, and Not
4. Functions: There are a large number of functions within Access including Sum, Count, and Avg—average—just to name a few.
5. Constants: These are values that do not change like strings of text or numbers that are not calculated by an expression.

You can use expressions in a number of ways such as performing calculations, retrieving values of a control—like on a form or report, supplying criteria to a query, and more.

Using Wildcard Characters in String Comparisons

Wildcard characters, such as an asterisk (*) or question mark (?), substitute for other characters when used in a query.

LIKE Function

You can use the **Like function** to find values in a field that match a specified pattern. For a value, you can specify the value within an entire field. For example, you may want to search for a customer with the last name of Smith. This would only return records where the whole last name field is equal to Smith. Thus, someone with the last name of Smithe, Smithers, or Smithfield would not be included in the dataset.

Wildcard Characters

You also can use **wildcard characters** to find a range of values. Many times these are combined with the Like operator to ensure that your query is returning all the data you need within the dataset. For example, you may want to search for all products that begin with the letters "ch"; that would return products such as cheese, chips, chocolate, and chicken. Or you may want to query a JobTitle field to search for any employees who have a manager position. By using a wildcard, the results of your dataset may include senior manager, assistant manager, manager of sales, and manager.

To Use Wildcard Characters in String Comparisons

a. Click the **Start** button, and then select **Microsoft Access 2010**.

b. Click the **File tab**, click **Open** and browse to your student data files. Locate and select **a03_ws06_Golf1**. Click **Open**.

c. Click **File** and then select **Save Database As**. In the File name box, type Lastname_Firstname_a03_ws06_Golf1, replacing Lastname_Firstname with your actual name.

d. Click **Enable Content** in the Security Warning, if necessary.

e. Click the **Create tab**, and then in the Queries group, click **Query Design**.

f. When the Show Table dialog box opens, click **tblEmployee**, and then click **Add**.

g. Close the Show Table dialog box.

h. Add the FirstName, LastName, Salary, HireDate, and Position fields to the Query design grid.

i. In the Criteria property under Position, type Like "*caddy".

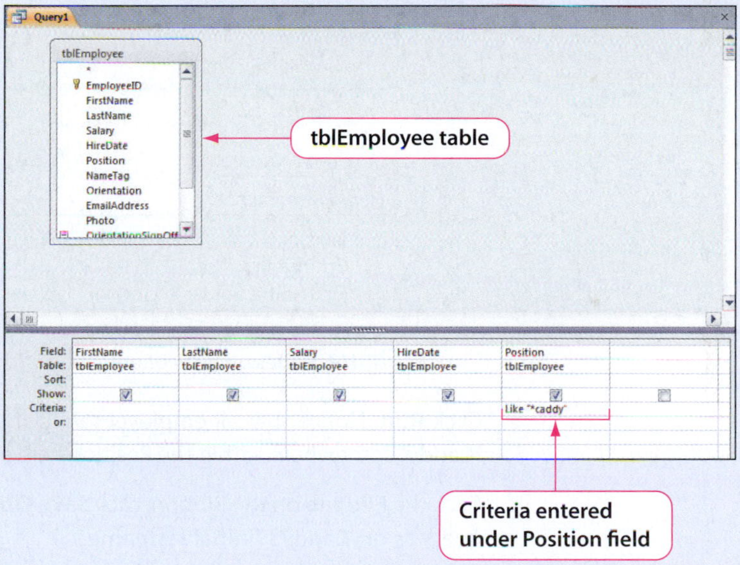

Figure 1 Design view of Query1 query

j. Click **Run** on the Query Tools Design tab of the Ribbon.

Notice that all records returned in the dataset have the word "Caddy" at the end of the field. The asterisk replaced any characters that were before the word "Caddy" in the Position field.

Figure 2 Datasheet view of Query1 query

k. Save your query as **qryCaddy1_initialLastname**, replacing initialLastname with the first initial of your first name and your full last name.

l. Return to **Design view**, and then in the Criteria property under Position, type **Like "*caddy*"**. Notice that all you need to do is add an asterisk to the existing criteria.

m. Click **Run**.

Notice that all records returned in the dataset have the word "Caddy" somewhere within the field. The asterisk replaced any characters that were before and/or after the word "Caddy" in the Position field.

n. Click the **File tab** on the Ribbon, click **Save Object As**, and then select **Query**. Save your query as **qryCaddy2_initialLastname**.

o. Click the **Home tab**, and then return to **Design view**.

p. In the Criteria property under FirstName, type **Like "Mary"**.

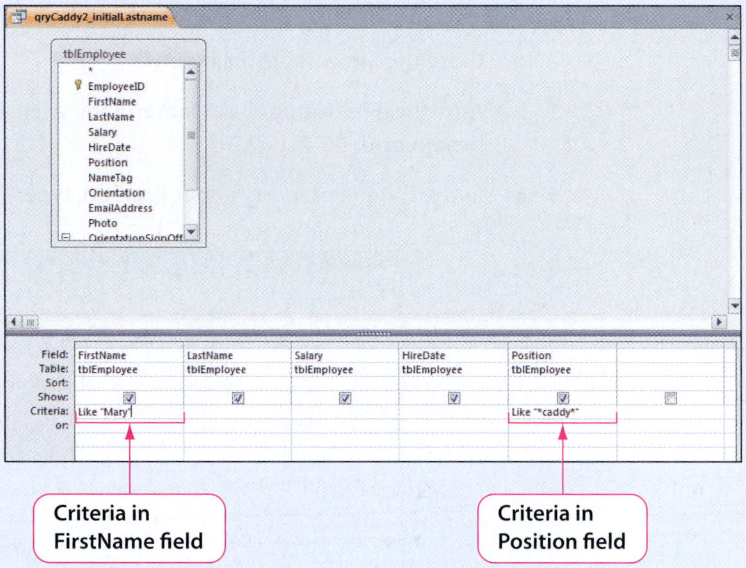

Criteria in FirstName field

Criteria in Position field

Figure 3 Design view of qryCaddy2_initialLastname

q. Click **Run**. Notice that all employees with the first name of Mary who have the word "Caddy" somewhere within the Position field are included in the dataset.

r. Click the **File tab** on the Ribbon, click **Save Object As**, and then select **Query**. Save your query as **qryCaddy3_initialLastname**.

s. Click the **Home tab**, and then close qryCaddy3_initialLastname.

t. Click the **Create tab**, and then click **Query Design** on the Ribbon.

u. When the Show Table dialog box opens, click **tblMember**, and then click **Add**. Close the Show Table dialog box.

v. Add the **FirstName**, **LastName**, **Address**, **City**, **State**, and **ZipCode** fields to the Query design grid.

w. In the Criteria property under LastName, type **Like "[A-M]*"**.

x. Sort the **LastName** field in **Ascending** order.

y. Click **Run**. Notice that all members whose last names begin with "A" through "M" are displayed in ascending order.

z. Save your query as **qryMemberAM_initialLastname**, and then close it.

Quick Reference | Using Wildcard Characters in Access

Built-in pattern matching provides a handy tool for making string comparisons in queries. Below are the wildcard characters you can use with the Like function and the number of characters they can match.

Wildcard Characters	What Wildcards Match	Example
? or _ (underscore)	Any single character	C?t in the criteria of a Notes field would return cat, cot, and cut.
* or %	Zero or more characters	ch* in the criteria of a FoodName field would return churros, chimichanga, cheese, chips, chives, chicken, or chocolate.
#	Any single digit (0–9)	4#2 in the criteria of an AreaCode field would return 402, 412, 422, 432, and so on. You could use this character for multiple digits such as 4##. This would return 400, 401, 402, 403, 404...499.
[charlist]	Any single character in charlist	[A-D]* in the criteria of a ProductName field would return any products that begin with the letters A, B, C, or D.
[!charlist]	Any single character not in charlist	[!A-D]* in the criteria of a ProductName field would return any products that begin with the letters E through Z, inclusive.
– (hyphen)	Any character within a range	b[a-o]ll in the criteria of a field would return ball, bell, and bill, but not bull.

Figure 4 Wildcard Characters

You can use a group of one or more characters (**charlist**) enclosed in brackets ([ ]) to match any single character in an expression, and charlist can include almost any characters and digits. Additionally, when you specify a range of characters, the characters must appear in ascending sort order (A–Z or 0–100). [A–Z] is a valid pattern, but [Z–A] is not. Finally, Access is not **case sensitive** in regard to the Criteria property. You can enter lowercase or uppercase letters in the Criteria property. Access will return all the applicable data, regardless how it was entered into the table.

CONSIDER THIS | **Text Matching and Input Masks**

You have a PhoneNumber field with an input mask with symbols stored. Most numbers would look like (555) 555-5555. What criteria would you use to find 7-digit phone numbers such as 555-5555?

Find Records with the "Most" or "Least" Values

An occasion may exist where you only want to view a subset—portion or part—of your query dataset by selecting either a percentage or a fixed number of records. For example, you may want to view the customers who are the bottom 10% of overall customer purchases. You could then target your marketing plan toward them, because they may not appear to be as loyal as other customers. Instead of viewing a percentage of your data, you may want to see the top three salespeople within the company. This would help you determine the best salespeople who are eligible for a promotion, raise, or bonus.

Top Values

You can use a **Top Values query** when you need to find records that contain the top or bottom values in a field. You can use a Top Values query to answer such questions as:

- Which is the most or least expensive product sold at our company?
- Which departments generated the greatest or least sales last year?
- Which products are in the top or bottom 5% of sales?

A Top Values query first sorts and then filters your data to return the top or bottom values within a field. You can use a Top Values query to search for numeric, currency, and date values.

To Create a Top Values Query

a. Click the **Create tab** on the Ribbon.

b. In the Queries group, click **Query Design**.

c. When the Show Table dialog box opens, click **tblMemberLessons**, and then click **Add**.

d. Close the Show Table dialog box.

e. Add the ScheduledDate and Fee fields to the Query design grid.

f. Click **Run** to view all records. Notice there are 8 different prices listed in the 15 records displayed.

g. Return to **Design view**.

h. Sort **Fee** in **Descending** order.

i. Click the **Return (Top Values) arrow** in the Query Setup group on the Query Tools Design tab. Select **25%** from the Return (Top Values) list.

SIDE NOTE
Sorting Fields in Top Values Queries

You must set the sort to ascending or descending on the fields containing your top or bottom values before finding the top or bottom values.

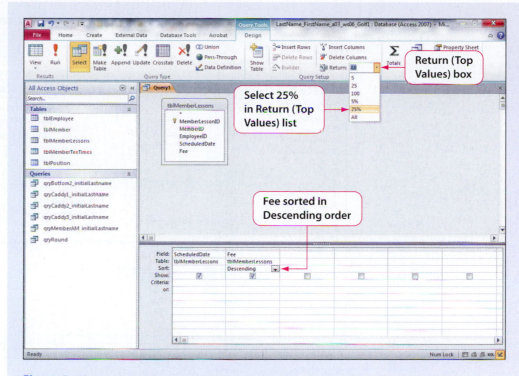

Figure 5 Design view of Query1 query

j. Click **Run**. Notice that all records displayed include the top 25% of the records in your table.

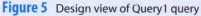

Figure 6 Datasheet view of Query1 query

k. Save your query as **qryTop25_initialLastname**, and then return to **Design view**.

l. Change the sort order in the Fee field from Descending to **Ascending**.

m. Delete the 25% in the Return (Top Values) box, and then type **2**.

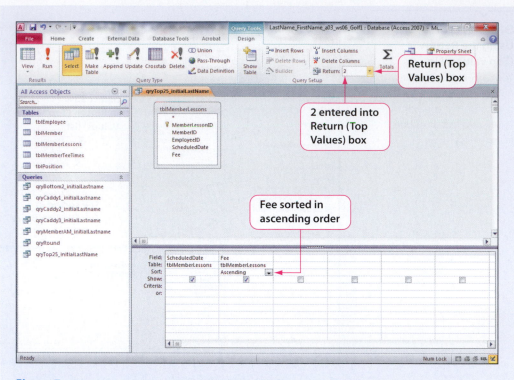

Figure 7 Design view of qryTop25_initialLastname

n. Click **Run**. Notice that by sorting the field in Ascending order, Access now displays the two bottom—or lowest—values.

o. Click the **File tab** on the Ribbon.

p. Click **Save Object As**, and then select **Query**. Save your query as **qryBottom2_initialLastname**.

q. Click the **Home tab**, and then return to **Design view**.

r. Close qryBottom2_initialLastname.

Make a Query Ask for Input

Queries can be designed to prompt users for criteria without having to make changes in Design view. These queries are known as parameter queries.

Using Parameters in a Query

Parameter queries can be designed when you may need to change the criteria for which you want to search. In this case, a variable parameter can be used. When a parameter query is run, the user is prompted to enter the value for each parameter. Using parameters in queries is exceptionally powerful and converts static queries, where the criteria are already entered into the Design view, to flexible, dynamic queries that are customized to a user's needs. The use of parameters can significantly reduce the number of queries you need to create, make queries more useful, and simplify database maintenance.

Parameters can easily be added to a query. Rather than entering the value of criteria, enter the prompt you want the user to see when the query is run, and enclose the prompt within square brackets. The value the user enters will replace the parameter and create a dataset based on what the user enters. For example, a parameter [Enter Zip Code] could be entered in the Criteria property of a Zip Code field. When the user runs the query, the user is prompted to enter a zip code, and the records matching that entered value are retrieved. This type of query can put the user in control of creating queries, even if they have never used Access.

Specify Parameter Data Types

Parameters can be used for any data type within a table, and you can specify what type of data a parameter should accept. Specifying **parameter data types** is particularly important when you have numeric, currency, or date/time data. When you specify a data type that the parameter should accept, users see a more helpful error message if they enter the wrong type of data, such as entering text when currency should be entered.

CONSIDER THIS | **Have You Used Parameter Queries Before?**

Think about the systems you have previously used. Perhaps you have called the bank to update information—maybe you have a new address or phone number—and before you can speak with a customer service representative, you have to enter your Social Security number or account number. Can you think of other systems you have used that require you to enter data in order for the system to retrieve your information?

To Create a Parameter Query

a. Click the **Create tab**, and then in the Queries group, click **Query Design**.

b. When the Show Table dialog box opens, hold down Control , click **tblEmployee**, **tblMember**, **tblMemberLessons**, and then click **Add**.

c. Close the Show Table dialog box.

d. Add the following fields to the Query design grid:

   tblEmployee: **FirstName**, **LastName**
   tblMember: **FirstName**, **LastName**
   tblMemberLessons: **ScheduledDate**, **Fee**

e. Under Criteria for the Employee's LastName field, type **[Enter the Employee's Last Name]**.

f. Click **Run**. When prompted to enter the employee's last name, type **Schilling**, and then click **OK**.

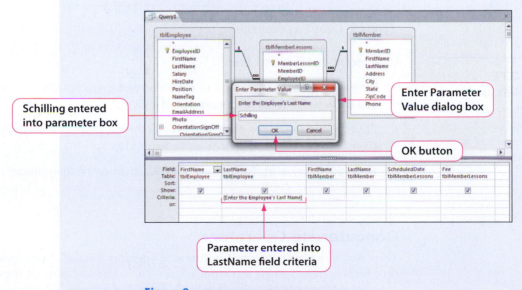

Figure 8 Design view of Query1 query

g. Click **OK**. Notice that John Schilling's four scheduled private lessons are easy to retrieve with a parameter query.

h. Save your query as **qryParameter_initialLastname**, and then close it.

i. Click the **Create tab**, and then in the Queries group, click **Query Design**.

j. When the Show Table dialog box opens, hold down Control, click **tblMember** and **tblMemberLessons**, and then click **Add**.

k. Close the Show Table dialog box.

l. Add the following fields to the Query design grid:
   tblMember: FirstName, LastName
   tblMemberLessons: ScheduledDate, Fee

m. Under Criteria for the Fee field, type [Enter the Fee].

n. Click the **Query Tools Design tab** and then click **Parameters** in the Show/Hide group. The Query Parameters dialog box opens.

o. Enter the following into the Query Parameters dialog box:

Parameter	Data Type
[Enter the Fee]	Currency

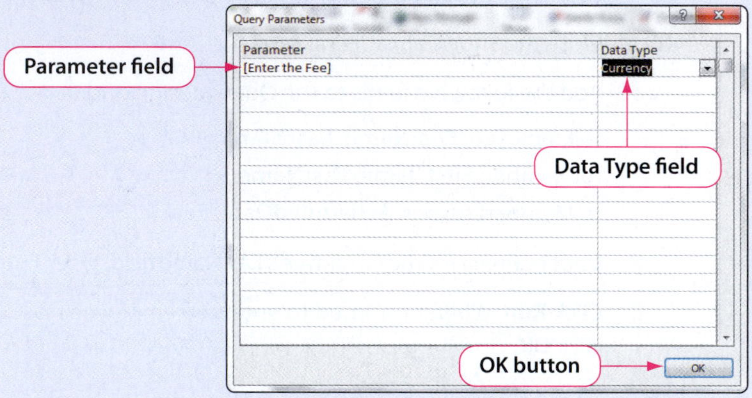

Figure 9 Query Parameters dialog box

SIDE NOTE
Parameter Prompts Must Match
Make sure that each parameter matches the prompt that you use in the Criteria row of the Query design grid.

SIDE NOTE
No Error Messages
If a parameter is configured to accept text data, any input is interpreted as text, and no error message is displayed.

p. Click **OK**, and then click **Run**.

q. When prompted to Enter the Fee, enter dog and then click **OK**. Notice that Access lets you know you entered the wrong type of data.

r. Click **OK**, and then when prompted to enter the fee, enter 125 and then click **OK**. Notice there are four scheduled lessons with a fee of $125.

s. Save your query as **qryParameter2_initialLastname**, and then close it.

Concatenate Operator

There may be a time to use the **Concatenate operator** when you want to join data from multiple fields to create a single text string of data. This is done by using an ampersand (&) to create a single field by combining data in multiple fields. For example, if you have an Employees table that contains the fields FirstName and LastName, you can use the concatenate function to create a text string that displays the values of the employee's first name and last name fields separated by a space, creating a full name field in the dataset.

To Create a Query Using the Concatenate Operator

a. Click the **Create tab**, and then click **Query Design** in the Queries group.

b. When the Show Table dialog box opens, click **tblEmployee** and **tblPosition**, and then click **Add**.

c. Close the Show Table dialog box.

d. Right-click the **first blank field** in the Query design grid, and then select **Zoom**. The Zoom dialog box opens and gives you more room to work.

e. In the Zoom dialog box, type Employee:[FirstName]&" "&[LastName]. Be sure to type a space between the quotation marks.

f. Click **OK**.

g. Right-click the **next blank field** in the Query design grid, and then select **Zoom**.

h. In the Zoom dialog box, type Job Title:[PositionType]&" "&[Position].

i. Click **OK**, and then click **Run**. Notice that Access concatenated data within multiple fields into one field—Employee and Job Title. If needed, resize your fields to view all the data.

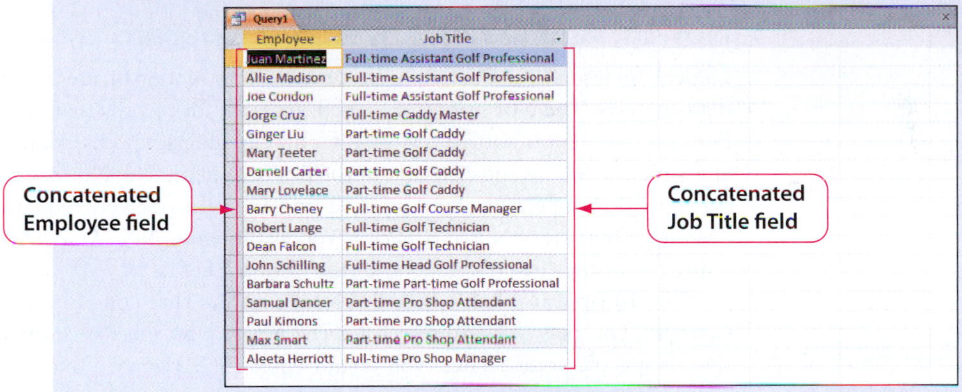

Concatenated Employee field

Concatenated Job Title field

Figure 10 Design view of Query1 query

Troubleshooting

After clicking OK from within the Zoom dialog box, you may not see the entire function you just entered. Your field on the Query design grid just needs to be resized. It can be resized just like you would resize a column in Excel or a field in an Access table.

j. Save your query as qryConcatenate_initialLastname, and then close it.

At first glance, using the ampersand to concatenate fields can appear complicated. However, if you break it into sections, it can actually be quite simple. Below are some notes to remember about the concatenate function.

1. You are creating a **virtual field**. This means that the concatenated field imitates its "real" equivalent or equivalents—such as combining FirstName and LastName fields. This concatenated field will not be saved in the table, only in your query. However, you can create this type of field in a table by using the Calculated data type.

2. When writing an expression, including the use of the concatenate function, everything to the left of the colon is the field name; everything to the right of the colon is the expression.

3. If you are using multiple tables that have the same field name in two or more tables, be sure to preface your field name with the table name, separated by an exclamation point—[tblEmployee]![FirstName].

Not, In, and Other Advanced Operators

Logical operators—or Boolean operators—such as Not or In, are used to perform more advanced data analysis. The **Not operator** is used to search for records that do not match specific criteria. For example, if you wanted to search for all customers who live outside of the USA, you would enter Not "USA" as the criterion in the Country field. The Not operator can be combined with other Boolean operators, such as And and Or. Illustratively, you may want to search for all customers outside of North America. You would enter Not "USA" And Not "Canada" And Not "Mexico" in the Criteria property of the Country field.

The **In operator** can be used to return results that contain one of the values in a list. For example, you may want to search for customers who meet certain criteria, such as those who live in specific states. Thus, you would enter In("Arizona", "Nevada", "New Mexico") as the criterion in the State field. This would return all customers who live in Arizona, Nevada, or New Mexico. Notice how the customers would only have to meet one of the stated criteria to display in the dataset.

The **Between...And operator** verifies whether the value of a field or expression falls within a stated range of numeric values. For example, you may want to view all products with a selling price between $1 and $10. Or you may want to view all customers who live between certain zip codes. By using the And operator in conjunction with the Between operator, you are testing to see if your values are greater than the lower value—such as $1—and less than the higher value—such as $10. One thing to note is that this operator finds values between the stated range of numeric values. In the above example, the results would not include $1 or $10. If you wanted to include $1 and $10, depending on your pricing structure, you could enter Between $0 And $11 or Between $.99 And $10.01.

You also can combine the Not and Between...And operators to return records that do not fall within a stated range of numeric values. For example, you may want to view all products with a selling price that are not between $5 and $10. Or you may want to view all customers who do not live between certain zip codes.

Because Access treats values entered into the Between...And operator as actual characters, wildcard characters cannot be used in this operator. For example, if you want to find all clients who were born in the 1960s or 1970s, you cannot use 196* and 197* to find all years that start with 196 and 197. You could write a more advanced expression to allow for wildcard usage, but it would be easier to write your expression as Between 1959 And 1980.

To Create a Query Using the Not, In, And, Between...And Operators

a. Click the **Create tab**, and then in the Queries group, click **Query Design**. Add **tblEmployee** to Design View, and then close the Show Table dialog box.

b. Add the FirstName, LastName, and Salary fields to the Query design grid.

c. Type Between 50000 And 75000 into the Criteria property of the Salary field.

d. Click **Run**. Notice that the employees listed have a salary that is between $50,000 and $75,000.

First Name	Last Name	Salary	
Barbara	Schultz	$57,250.00	
Juan	Martinez	$57,250.00	
Jorge	Cruz	$54,350.00	Results of salaries between $50,000 and $75,000
Joe	Condon	$62,500.00	

Figure 11 Datasheet view of Query1 query

e. Save your query as qryBetween_initialLastname.

f. Return to **Design view,** and then modify your expression in the Criteria property of the Salary field to Not Between 50000 And 75000.

g. Click **Run**. Notice that the employees listed have a salary that is not between $50,000 and $75,000.

h. Click the **File tab** on the Ribbon, click **Save Object As**, and then save your query as qryNotBetween_initialLastname.

i. Close qryNotBetween_initialLastname.

j. Click the **Create tab**, and then click **Query Design** in the Queries group. Add **tblEmployee** to Design View, and then close the Show Table dialog box.

k. Add the FirstName, LastName, Salary, and Position fields to the Query design grid.

l. Type In ("Golf Caddy","Caddy Master") into the Criteria property of the Position field.

m. Click **Run**. Notice that the employees listed hold a position as either a Golf Caddy or Caddy Master.

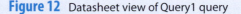

First Name	Last Name	Salary	Job Title	
Ginger	Liu	$12,550.00	Golf Caddy	
Jorge	Cruz	$54,350.00	Caddy Master	
Mary	Teeter	$15,500.00	Golf Caddy	Employees who are a Golf Caddy or Caddy Master
Darnell	Carter	$16,750.00	Golf Caddy	
Mary	Lovelace	$25,000.00	Golf Caddy	

Figure 12 Datasheet view of Query1 query

n. Save your query as qryIn_initialLastname, and then close it.

Advanced Functions in Queries

Knowing how to write queries in Access by using advanced functions, such as IIf functions, allows you to perform advanced analysis quickly without knowing any type of programming language. In this section, you will create queries that include using the IIf function, the IsNull function, date functions, and the Round function.

IIf Functions

IIf functions can be used to determine if a specific condition is true or false. The IIf function introduces decision making into a database. Depending on whether or not specified criteria are met, the IIf function returns a different result depending on the outcome of the condition.

Basic IIf Function for Individual Condition

The **IIf function** in Access, which stands for Immediate If, is similar to the IF function in Excel. The results of this function returns one value if a specified condition is true or another value if it is false. You can use the IIf function anywhere you can use expressions. For example, you may have a database that you use to manage your store's inventory. You may want to use the IIf function to assist in determining what items need to be reordered. You could write an IIf function that checks to see if your current on-hand values in the Quantity field fall below a certain level. You would enter IIf([Quantity]<=3, "Reorder", "OK"), which returns the string "Reorder" for any values in the Quantity field that are less than or equal to 3, and "OK" if the value is greater than 3, which means you do not need to reorder that specific product.

Quick Reference / IIf Function Syntax

The IIf function syntax, noted as IIf(expr, truepart, falsepart), has these arguments:

1. expr: Field or expression you want to evaluate. This argument is required.

2. truepart: Value or expression returned if expr is true. This argument is required.

3. falsepart: Value or expression returned if expr is false. This argument is required.

To Create a Query Using IIf Functions

a. Click the **Create tab**, and then click **Query Design** in the Queries group. Add **tblEmployee** to Design View, and then close the Show Table dialog box.

b. Add the FirstName, LastName, and Salary fields to the Query design grid.

c. Right-click the **first blank field** in the Query design grid, and then select **Zoom**.

d. In the Zoom dialog box, type
Raise Assessment:IIf([Salary]<=30000,"Give Raise","No Raise").

e. Click **OK**.

f. Right-click the **next blank field** in the Query design grid, and then select **Zoom**.

g. For those employees who earned a salary increase, you want to calculate what the new salary will be if employees receive a 3% raise. In the Zoom dialog box, type
New Salary:IIf([Salary]<=30000,[Salary]*1.03,[Salary]).

h. Click **OK**, and then click **Run**. Notice that the new salary is not in Currency format.

i. Return to **Design view**, and then click the **New Salary** field.

j. Click the **Query Tools Design tab** and then click **Property Sheet** in the Show/Hide group. Format the field as **Currency**.

k. Click **Run**. Notice that Access determined which employees have earned a raise and if so, the amount of the new salary.

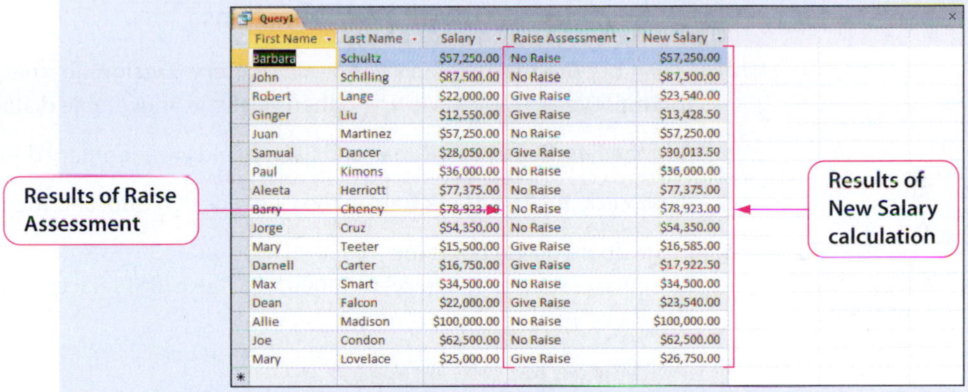

Results of Raise Assessment

First Name	Last Name	Salary	Raise Assessment	New Salary
Barbara	Schultz	$57,250.00	No Raise	$57,250.00
John	Schilling	$87,500.00	No Raise	$87,500.00
Robert	Lange	$22,000.00	Give Raise	$23,540.00
Ginger	Liu	$12,550.00	Give Raise	$13,428.50
Juan	Martinez	$57,250.00	No Raise	$57,250.00
Samual	Dancer	$28,050.00	Give Raise	$30,013.50
Paul	Kimons	$36,000.00	No Raise	$36,000.00
Aleeta	Herriott	$77,375.00	No Raise	$77,375.00
Barry	Cheney	$78,923.00	No Raise	$78,923.00
Jorge	Cruz	$54,350.00	No Raise	$54,350.00
Mary	Teeter	$15,500.00	Give Raise	$16,585.00
Darnell	Carter	$16,750.00	Give Raise	$17,922.50
Max	Smart	$34,500.00	No Raise	$34,500.00
Dean	Falcon	$22,000.00	Give Raise	$23,540.00
Allie	Madison	$100,000.00	No Raise	$100,000.00
Joe	Condon	$62,500.00	No Raise	$62,500.00
Mary	Lovelace	$25,000.00	Give Raise	$26,750.00

Results of New Salary calculation

Figure 13 Datasheet view of Query1 query

l. Save your query as **qryIIf_initialLastname**, and then close it.

Nested IIf Functions for Various Conditions

In business, there are many occasions when you need to test for multiple conditions. You saw in the previous section how a basic IIf function allows you to test for one of two conditions. You can also create a **nested IIf function**, or place one IIf function inside another, allowing you to evaluate a series of dependent expressions. A **dependent expression** is an expression that relies on the outcome of another expression.

To continue with the preceding example, you might want to test for several different inventory levels, and then display the appropriate status depending on which value exists. Perhaps you want to see which items are close to having to be reordered, as noted by "Reorder Soon" in the second or nested IIf function. To add this condition to the IIf function from our previous example, you would enter IIf([Quantity]<=3, "Reorder", IIf([Quantity]<=5, "Reorder Soon", "OK")), which returns the string "Reorder" for any values in the Quantity field that are less than or equal to 3, "Reorder Soon" for any values that are either equal to 4 or 5, and "OK" if the value is greater than 5, which means you do not need to reorder that specific product. Notice how the second IIf function becomes the falsepart of the first IIf function.

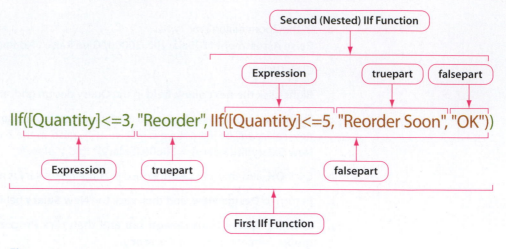

$\text{IIf([Quantity]<=3, "Reorder", IIf([Quantity]<=5, "Reorder Soon", "OK"))}$

Figure 14 Nested IIf function

To Create a Query Using Nested IIf Functions

a. Click the **Create tab**, and then click **Query Design** in the Queries group. Add **tblEmployee** to Design View, and then close the Show Table dialog box.

b. Add the FirstName, LastName, and Salary fields to the Query design grid.

c. Right-click the **first blank field** in the Query design grid, and then select **Zoom**.

d. In the Zoom dialog box, type
Raise Assessment:IIf([Salary]<=30000,"7% Raise",IIf([Salary]<=60000,"4% Raise", "No Raise")).

e. Click **OK**.

f. Right-click the **next blank field** in the Query design grid, and then select **Zoom**.

g. For those employees who received a salary increase, you want to calculate what the amount of the salary increase will be for employees depending on the percentage of the increase. If the employee will not receive a raise, a zero will be displayed. In the Zoom dialog box, type
Amount of Raise:IIf([Salary]<=30000,[Salary]*.07,IIf([Salary]<=60000, [Salary]*.04,0)).

h. Click **OK**.

i. Click the **Query Tools Design tab** and then click **Property Sheet** in the Show/Hide group. Format the field as **Currency**.

j. Click **Run**. Notice that the Raise Assessment has been determined and Amount of Raise has been calculated for you. If necessary, resize your fields to see all the data.

SIDE NOTE
Count Your Parentheses
There should always be an equal amount of opening and closing parentheses in your expression.

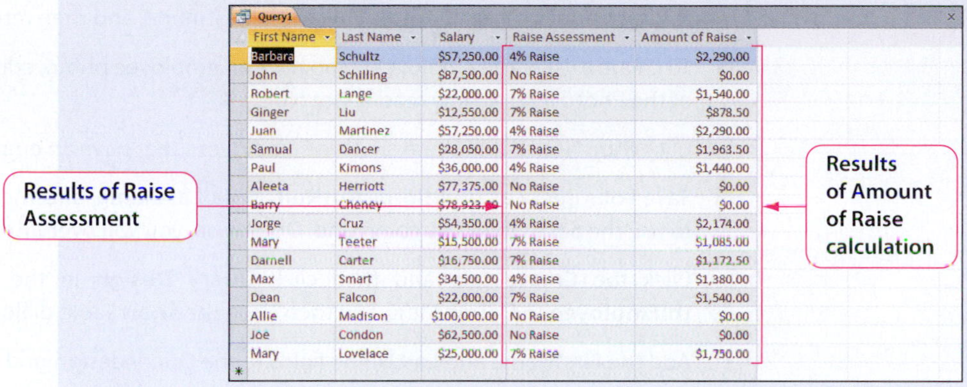

First Name	Last Name	Salary	Raise Assessment	Amount of Raise
Barbara	Schultz	$57,250.00	4% Raise	$2,290.00
John	Schilling	$87,500.00	No Raise	$0.00
Robert	Lange	$22,000.00	7% Raise	$1,540.00
Ginger	Liu	$12,550.00	7% Raise	$878.50
Juan	Martinez	$57,250.00	4% Raise	$2,290.00
Samual	Dancer	$28,050.00	7% Raise	$1,963.50
Paul	Kimons	$36,000.00	4% Raise	$1,440.00
Aleeta	Herriott	$77,375.00	No Raise	$0.00
Barry	Cheney	$78,923.[illegible]	No Raise	$0.00
Jorge	Cruz	$54,350.00	4% Raise	$2,174.00
Mary	Teeter	$15,500.00	7% Raise	$1,085.00
Darnell	Carter	$16,750.00	7% Raise	$1,172.50
Max	Smart	$34,500.00	4% Raise	$1,380.00
Dean	Falcon	$22,000.00	7% Raise	$1,540.00
Allie	Madison	$100,000.00	No Raise	$0.00
Joe	Condon	$62,500.00	No Raise	$0.00
Mary	Lovelace	$25,000.00	7% Raise	$1,750.00

Figure 15 Datasheet view of Query1 query

k. Save your query as qryNestedIIf_initialLastname, and then close it.

IsNull Function

To understand how to use the **IsNull function**, you need to understand what is meant by "null." First and foremost, null is not zero. Null is used to indicate that a value is unknown, and it is treated differently than other values because it has no value. Instances exist when querying records that contain fields with null values are necessary.

Working with Fields that Contain No Valid Data

The result of the IsNull function returns a Boolean value—True or False—that indicates whether an expression contains no valid data. For example, consider a human resources database that you would use to manage current and past employees' data. To create a list of current employees, you could build a query that searches for missing values in the Date Terminated field, showing that the value would be null for all active employees.

Because the IsNull function, written as IsNull(expression) or IsNull([field]), returns a result of either True or False, it is commonly nested or combined with other functions, such as an IIf function. Consider the previous example of using a human resources database to manage current and past employees' data. You could nest the IsNull function inside of an IIf function to return values other than True and False, such as Current Employee and Terminated Employee.

It is important to note that the IsNull function is slightly different than using Is Null and Is Not Null in your query's criteria. When you use Is Null and Is Not Null as field criteria in the Query design grid, you are checking to see if a field contains valid data. For example, if you use **Is Null** in the criteria of a Date Terminated field, the dataset would include all the employees' names and the null Date Terminated field. Using the **Is Not Null** criteria would return each employee name and the date in which each employee was terminated.

To Create Queries Using Null Criteria and the IsNull Function

a. Click the **Create tab**, and then click **Query Design** in the Queries group. Add **tblEmployee** to Design View, and then close the Show Table dialog box.

b. Add the FirstName, LastName, and Photo fields to the Query design grid.

c. To create a list of the employees who need to have their employee photo taken, type Is Null into the Criteria property of the Photo field.

d. Click **Run**. Notice that there are 14 employees who need to have their photo taken.

SIDE NOTE
You Can Hide the Photo Field
It is best to uncheck the Photo field's Show field box. However, leaving it checked when you first run the query is a good way to verify it was written correctly.

e. Save your query as **qryPhotoIsNull_initialLastname**, and then return to **Design view**.

f. To create a list of the employees who have an employee photo, edit the Criteria property of the Photo field to now read **Is Not Null**.

g. Click **Run**. Notice that there are three employees that have an employee photo.

h. Save your query as **qryPhotoIsNotNull_initialLastname**, and then close it. Remember to use the Save Object As command. Otherwise, you will overwrite the previous query.

i. Click the **Create tab**, and then click **Query Design** in the Queries group. Add **tblEmployee** to Design View, and then close the Show Table dialog box.

j. Add the **FirstName** and **LastName** fields to the Query design grid.

k. To create a list of all employees and whether or not they need to have a photo taken, type **PhotoStatus:IIf(IsNull([Photo]),"Needs Photo","Has Photo")** into the first blank field on the query grid.

l. Click **Run**. Notice that all employees are listed along with whether or not a photo needs to be taken.

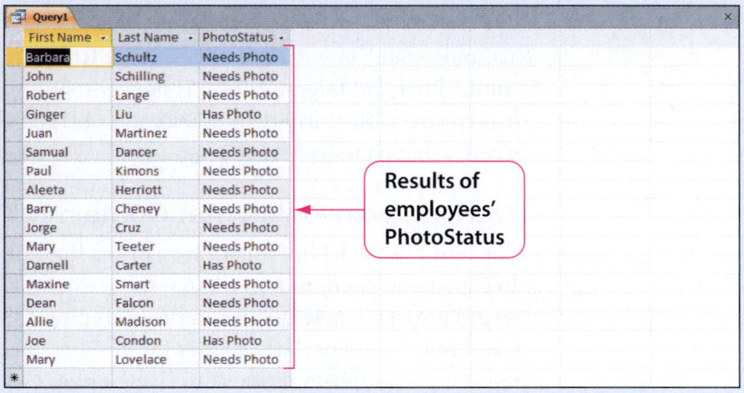

First Name	Last Name	PhotoStatus
Barbara	Schultz	Needs Photo
John	Schilling	Needs Photo
Robert	Lange	Needs Photo
Ginger	Liu	Has Photo
Juan	Martinez	Needs Photo
Samual	Dancer	Needs Photo
Paul	Kimons	Needs Photo
Aleeta	Herriott	Needs Photo
Barry	Cheney	Needs Photo
Jorge	Cruz	Needs Photo
Mary	Teeter	Needs Photo
Darnell	Carter	Has Photo
Maxine	Smart	Needs Photo
Dean	Falcon	Needs Photo
Allie	Madison	Needs Photo
Joe	Condon	Has Photo
Mary	Lovelace	Needs Photo

Results of employees' PhotoStatus

Figure 16 Datasheet view of Query1 query

m. Save your query as **qryIsNullFunction_initialLastname**, and then close it.

Using the IsNull Function and Null Criteria Can Come in Handy

It may seem a waste of time to learn how to use the IsNull function and Null criteria. In the databases you have been using, most if not all the fields have data entered into them. In business, you will find that databases can contain many null fields. Think about when you fill out an online form. Not every field is required—meaning that you can leave values empty, or null. Companies make key data required for tasks such as determining its target market. Companies also permit some fields to remain null for its customers' convenience. Some customers do not want to give all of their information, and companies do not want to deter customers from creating an account or making a purchase. If the company mandated that all the data on a form is required, they could potentially lose customers. Although a form's fields may be marked as optional, a field still has to exist in the database table to store the data when a customer does give the information. Do you always complete an online form, or are there times when you leave fields empty? Are there ever times you do not complete an online form because there are too many required fields? How do you think it affects the company's database?

Dates

Access includes a variety of techniques that enable the use of dates and date ranges in the criteria of a query. Date functions are useful when working with the complex logic in a database that contains dates.

Date Vs. Now Function

Two of the more commonly used date functions are the Date and Now functions. Both behave similarly as they can be used in expressions. Additionally, both retrieve a date and/or time according to your computer's system date and time. The **Date function** returns the current system date. This can be very helpful if you want to track the date that a record was entered into a table, where the time of day is not a concern. The **Now function** retrieves the current system date and time. For example, you may want to have a time stamp of when a document was uploaded to a system, such as a student uploading an assignment to a course management system. If an assignment is due at 1:00 PM, the Now function could log the date and time in which the upload occurred. The instructor would then know if the student met the deadline.

Real World Advice **Should You Use the Now or the Date Function?**

Avoid mixing the Now and Date functions. If you set the default value of a field to Now, Access will record the time. If you then query that field with the criteria of a date without specifying a time, you might not get the results you expect. For example, if your criteria is >12/28/2013, Access will return any records greater than >12/28/2013 at midnight. Thus, a field placed at 12/28/2013 at 8 AM would be returned in the results. The criteria of >12/28/2013 suggests that you only wanted dates starting on 12/29/2013 at midnight in the results. Generally, use the Now function only when you need time, and make sure you know the data when writing queries.

Use DateDiff to Determine a Time Interval

The **DateDiff function** is used to determine the difference between two dates. Generally one date is obtained from a field, and the second date is obtained by using the Date() function. Many instances exist in which you could use the DateDiff function. For example, suppose you have a form that you use to automatically refill customer prescriptions. In the Orders table, you have a field named Refill On that contains the earliest date that the prescription can be refilled. You can use the DateDiff function with a text box on the form to display the number of days left before the prescription can be refilled and shipped.

Quick Reference **Five Parts of a DateDiff Function**

The DateDiff function syntax, noted as DateDiff(interval, date1, date2, [firstdayofweek], [firstweekofyear]), has five arguments:

1. The first part, interval, is the interval of time—day, month, year, and so on—used to calculate the difference between date1 and date2. This argument is required.

2. The second and third parts, date1 and date2, are the dates you want to use in the calculation. These can include a field name or expression. These arguments are required.

3. The fourth part, firstdayofweek, is a constant that indicates the first day of the week. If not specified, Access assumes that you want to begin on Sunday. This argument is optional.

4. The fifth part, firstweekofyear, is a constant that indicates the first week of the year. If not specified, Access assumes the week in which January 1 occurs. This argument is optional.

To Create a Query Using the DateDiff Function

a. Click the **Create tab**, and then click **Query Design** in the Queries group. Add **tblPayments** to Design View, and then close the Show Table dialog box.

b. Add the MemberID and PaymentDate fields to the Query design grid.

c. Right-click the **first blank field** in the Query design grid, and then select **Zoom**.

d. To see how many days it has been since a member paid the club's annual dues, in the Zoom dialog box, type DaysSincePmt: DateDiff("d",Date(),[PaymentDate]).

e. Click **OK**, and then click **Run**. Notice that you are given how many days ago or in advance a member paid his or her annual dues.

f. Save your query as qryDateDiffDays_initialLastname, and then return to **Design view**.

g. Modify the DaysSincePmt expression to see how many months it has been since a member paid the club's annual dues by typing
MonthsSincePmt: DateDiff("m",Date(),[PaymentDate]).

h. Click **OK**, and then click **Run**. Notice that you are given how many months ago or in advance a member paid his or her annual dues.

i. Save your query as qryDateDiffMonths_initialLastname, and then close it.

SIDE NOTE
What Does the Minus Sign Mean?

Negative numbers in your DateDiff field means that the days have passed. Positive numbers mean that it has not happened yet.

Use DateAdd to Subtract a Time Interval

You can use the **DateAdd function** to add or subtract a specific time interval from a date. For example, you can use DateAdd to calculate a date 10 days from today or a time 30 minutes from now. Business professionals work with dates on a regular basis. A human resources manager may want to calculate when a newly hired employee is eligible for benefits, which is generally 90 days after the date of hire. Additionally, the human resources manager may want to calculate the earliest date an employee can retire.

Real World Advice — Access Uses the 1900 Date System

Access uses the 1900 date system to store dates—January 1, 1900, was day 1; January 2, 1900, was day 2; and so forth. When you enter a date into a Date/Time field, Access identifies it as a date and compares it to the calendar to make sure it is an actual date. If you try to enter a date that does not exist—such as September 31—an error message will appear. Access then stores the date as a number called the date serial. You do not need to know the date serial number to use a date field in a calculated field.

Quick Reference — Three Parts of a DateAdd Function

The DateAdd function syntax, noted as DateAdd(interval, number, date), has three arguments, all of which are required:

1. The first part, interval, contains a string expression that represents the interval of time you want to add or subtract.

2. The second part, number, refers to the numeric expression that indicates the number of intervals you want to add. It can be positive (to calculate dates in the future) or negative (to calculate dates in the past).

3. The third part, date, is the date to which the interval is added.

Quick Reference — Settings for the Date Interval

Setting	Description
yyyy	Year
q	Quarter
m	Month
y	Day of year
d	Day
w	Weekday
ww	Week
h	Hour
n	Minute
s	Second

Figure 17 Date Interval Settings

Although date intervals make it easy to calculate dates in Access, it is very important to use the date intervals carefully. For example, DateDiff for the "yyyy" in Access calculates without regard to the day. If you enter the wrong interval, you can create many problems within your data. Be certain you are selecting the appropriate one.

Many times you can test your output using simple math. For example, Date()+10 would result in the same output as using the DateAdd function to add 10 to the current date—DateAdd("d", 10, Date()). Simplify your functions as much as possible. If you can calculate the same result entering a function that is half the length, you decrease the possibility of creating errors while typing in your function.

CONSIDER THIS | Calculating Age with Date Functions

Many companies use an employee's date of birth to calculate such dates as retirement or benefits eligibility. Is the DateDiff function with a year interval appropriate for calculating age? Explain why or why not.

To Create a Query Using the DateAdd Function

a. Click the **Create tab**, and then click **Query Design** in the Queries group. Add **tblMember** and **tblPayments** to Design View.

b. Add the following fields to the Query design grid:

tblMember: FirstName, LastName

tblPayments: Amount, PaymentDate

c. Right-click the **first blank field** in the Query design grid, and then select **Zoom**.

d. To see when members' next annual membership dues will need to be paid, in the Zoom dialog box, type Next Due Date: DateAdd("y", 365, [PaymentDate]).

e. Click **OK**, and then click **Run**. Notice that all due dates have been created and look the same as the previous year—just the year has changed. However, look at Robert Allen's record. Access does calculate correctly if someone were to pay during a leap year.

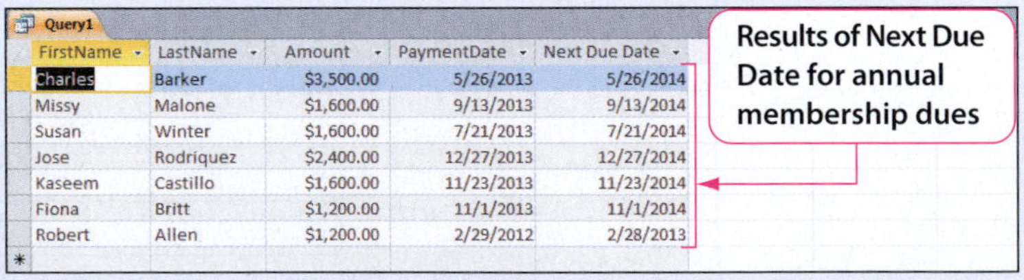

FirstName	LastName	Amount	PaymentDate	Next Due Date
Charles	Barker	$3,500.00	5/26/2013	5/26/2014
Missy	Malone	$1,600.00	9/13/2013	9/13/2014
Susan	Winter	$1,600.00	7/21/2013	7/21/2014
Jose	Rodriguez	$2,400.00	12/27/2013	12/27/2014
Kaseem	Castillo	$1,600.00	11/23/2013	11/23/2014
Fiona	Britt	$1,200.00	11/1/2013	11/1/2014
Robert	Allen	$1,200.00	2/29/2012	2/28/2013

Results of Next Due Date for annual membership dues

Figure 18 Datasheet view of Query1 query

f. Save your query as qryDateAdd1_initialLastname, and then return to **Design view**.

g. Modify the Next Due Date field to add 52 weeks onto the date that the dues were last paid by typing Next Due Date: DateAdd("ww", 52, [PaymentDate]).

h. Click **Run**. Notice that Access now calculates 52 weeks from the last payment date. Robert Allen's last payment was on Wednesday, February 29, 2012. His next payment would be exactly 52 weeks from his last payment. Accounting for leap year, the next payment would be due on Wednesday, February 27, 2013.

i. Save your query as **qryDateAdd2_initialLastname**, and then close it.

Use DateSerial to Return a Date (Year, Month, and Day)

To display specific dates, you can use the **DateSerial function**, written as DateSerial(year, month, day) to manipulate the day, month, and year of a date. DateSerial is very flexible because you can manipulate each part individually or together in any combination that meets your needs.

The best way to understand the power of this function is through an example. When the human resources manager wants to prepare paperwork for an employee's retirement, the manager can use the DateSerial function to calculate 90 days prior to the employee's 65th birthday. Naturally, you would take the birthdate and add 65 years. Then take that date and subtract 3 months. Using the DateSerial function, you can do this in one step. The Employee table includes a field representing Date of Birth called DOB. The function would be written as DateSerial(Year([DOB]) + 65, Month([DOB]) – 3, Day([DOB])). Thus, if an employee was born on July 5, 1967, the date returned would be April 5, 2032.

To Create a Query Using the DateSerial Function

a. Click the **Create tab**, and then click **Query Design** in the Queries group. Add **tblEmployee** and **tblPosition** to Design View, and then close the Show Table dialog box.

b. Add the following fields to the Query design grid:

tblEmployee: **FirstName, LastName, HireDate**
tblPosition: **PositionType**

c. In Criteria for the PositionType field, type **"Full-time"**.

d. Under the PositionType field, clear the Show check box.

e. Right-click the **first blank field** in the Query design grid, and then select **Zoom**.

f. Each full-time employee is eligible for health benefits after 90 days of employment, which means that the benefits begin on the 91st day of employment. To determine the date when eligibility begins, in the Zoom dialog box type
Benefits Begin:DateSerial(Year([HireDate]),Month([HireDate]), Day([HireDate])+91).

Troubleshooting

> The DateSerial function returns a number that represents a date from January 1, 1900 through December 31, 9999. If the date specified by the three arguments falls outside the acceptable range of dates, an error will occur.

g. Format the field as Medium Date by clicking **Property Sheet** on the Query Tools Design tab.

h. Click **Run**. Notice that Access calculated the date in which all full-time employees are eligible for benefits.

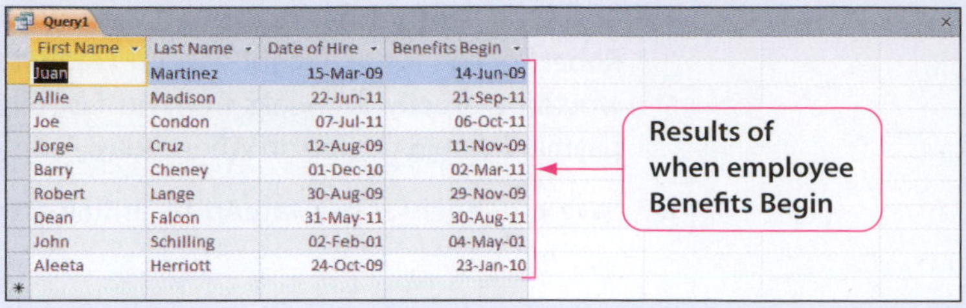

First Name	Last Name	Date of Hire	Benefits Begin
Juan	Martinez	15-Mar-09	14-Jun-09
Allie	Madison	22-Jun-11	21-Sep-11
Joe	Condon	07-Jul-11	06-Oct-11
Jorge	Cruz	12-Aug-09	11-Nov-09
Barry	Cheney	01-Dec-10	02-Mar-11
Robert	Lange	30-Aug-09	29-Nov-09
Dean	Falcon	31-May-11	30-Aug-11
John	Schilling	02-Feb-01	04-May-01
Aleeta	Herriott	24-Oct-09	23-Jan-10

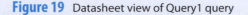

Figure 19 Datasheet view of Query1 query

Troubleshooting

Be careful where you place the numbers used to calculate. For example, in the above function, the 91 is placed after the parenthesis—Day([HireDate])+91—because the parentheses are enclosing the Day function, not the calculation.

i. Save your query as qryDateSerial_initialLastname, and then close it.

Quick Reference — Three Parts of a DateSerial Function

The DateSerial function syntax—noted as DateSerial(year, month, day)—has three arguments, all of which are required:

1. The first part, year, is a number between 1900 and 9999, inclusive, or a numeric expression. (A numeric expression is any expression that evaluates to a number. The expression can be any combination of variables, constants, functions, and operators.)
2. The second part, month, refers to either an integer or any numeric expression.
3. The third part, day, refers to either an integer or any numeric expression.

Use DatePart to Evaluate a Date

You can use the **DatePart function** to examine a date and return a specific interval of time. For example, you can use DatePart to calculate the day of the week for an order's ship date. As presented in the DateAdd function, an interval is the interval of time that is returned. For example, perhaps you want to compare the number of golfers you had this summer as compared to last summer. Each tee time contains a Scheduled Date. You can use the DatePart function to extract the year from the Scheduled Date in order to group your records in the query.

To Create a Query Using the DatePart Function

a. Click the **Create tab**, and then click **Query Design** in the Queries group. Add **tblEmployee** to Design View, and then close the Show Table dialog box.

b. Add the FirstName, LastName, and HireDate fields to the Query design grid.

c. Right-click the **first blank field** in the Query design grid, and then select **Zoom**.

d. Each employee is eligible for a bonus after 5 years of service. To determine the year when eligibility begins, in the Zoom dialog box, type
5 Year Anniversary: DatePart("yyyy", ([HireDate]))+5.

e. Click **OK,** and then click **Run**. Notice by looking at the HireDate field that the new field you created is accurate.

f. Save your query as **qryDatePart_initialLastname**, and then close it.

Quick Reference | **Four Parts of a DatePart Function**

The DatePart function syntax, noted as DatePart(interval, date, [firstdayofweek], [firstweekofyear]), has four arguments:

1. The first part, interval, contains a string expression that represents the interval of time you want to return. This argument is required.

2. The second part, date, refers to the date you want to evaluate. This argument is required.

3. The third part, firstdayofweek, is a constant that indicates the first day of the week. If not specified, Access assumes that you want to begin on Sunday. This argument is optional.

4. The fourth part, firstweekofyear, is a constant that indicates the first week of the year. If not specified, Access assumes that you want to begin with the week of January 1. This argument is optional.

Quick Reference | **The DatePart Function Argument Settings**

Setting	Description
1	Sunday (default)
2	Monday
3	Tuesday
4	Wednesday
5	Thursday
6	Friday
7	Saturday

Setting	Description
1	Start with the week in which January 1 occurs (default).
2	Start with the first week that has at least four days into the new year.
3	Start with first full week of the year.

Figure 20 *firstdayofweek* Argument Settings   **Figure 21** *firstdayofyear* Argument Settings

Round

There is a Decimal Places field property that only affects the way the data is displayed, not the way it is stored. The number will appear to be rounded, but when you sum these numbers, the total may not add up correctly. If you round the field when calculating your data, your calculation will be correct.

Rounding to a Specific Number of Decimal Places

In Access, the **Round function** returns a number rounded to a specific number of decimal places. This is different from formatting a field to a specific number of decimals. When you format a field property as Decimal and set the Decimal Places property to 1, the values displayed will automatically round to the nearest tenth in this case. The key to this formatting option is how the data is displayed; this format does not affect how the data is stored. For example, if you enter 2.64 into this field, it will be displayed as 2.6; however, the data is actually stored as 2.64. The number will appear to be rounded, but when you calculate these numbers, the total may not calculate correctly.

Distinguishing Between Rounding and Formatting

The Round function behaves differently than the Format property. For example, you may have a form where employees can enter the time they clock in and clock out of work each day, which then calculates the total hours worked each week. If the fraction portion of the number is below 0.5, then you may want to round the number down, and if the fraction portion is greater than or equal to 0.5, then the fraction should be 0.5. This is a scenario where the Round function is useful, and by using this function, your calculations will be accurate.

Quick Reference   The Precision Argument

When using the Round function, you can also determine the precision of the rounding. The **precision** argument allows you to determine how many decimal places you want to round your numbers. The syntax would be Round (expression, [precision]). The precision argument is an optional argument. Access will round to 2 decimals—hundredths—if the precision is not entered. Because currency is rounded to 2 decimals, the precision is generally not entered.

To Create a Query Using the Round Function

a. Open the **qryRound** query in **Design view**.

b. Right-click the **first blank field** in the Query design grid, and then select **Zoom**.

c. New Salary has already been calculated. However, the Golf Club wants to pay salaries in whole numbers. To round the New Salary field, in the Zoom dialog box, type
Final Salary: Round([New Salary]).

d. Click **OK**.

e. Format the Final Salary field to **Currency** by clicking **Property Sheet** on the Query Tools Design tab.

f. Click **Run**. Notice by looking at the Final Salary field that the values in the New Salary field are rounded off.

SIDE NOTE
Using Calculated Fields in Expressions
Calculated fields can be used in other expressions within your query. Just enclose the calculated field name in square brackets like you would any field name.

g. Using the Save Object As option, save your query as **qryRound_initialLastname**, and then close it.

h. Close the Lastname_Firstname_a03_ws06_Golf1 database.

CONSIDER THIS | **Databases Can Have Thousands of Records...or More!**

Remember, the database you are using was scaled down by Barry Cheney, the Golf Club Manager, and now only contains an extremely small amount of stored data. Think about running queries using advanced criteria and calculations in a database that has hundreds or thousands of records in a table. How could these types of advanced queries save you time? Improve efficiency? Help with decision making?

1. What is the most important functionality of a database? Explain why.

2. What is the difference between rounding and formatting?

3. Describe what knowledge is and why it is important to have knowledge when making decisions.

4. Explain the difference between an IIf function and a nested IIf function. Give two examples of when you would use each one.

5. In what situation would you define parameter data types within a parameter query?

Key Terms

Visual Summary

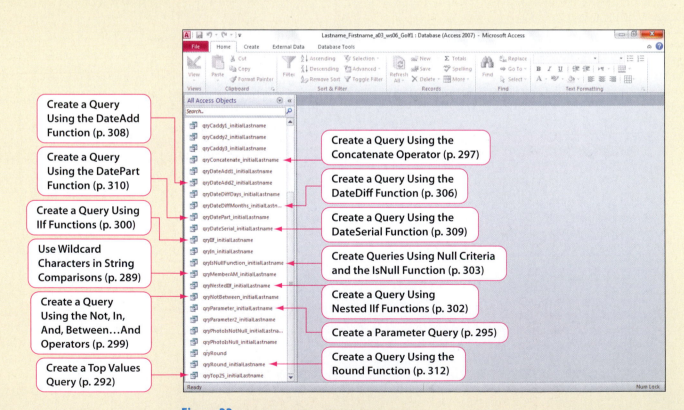

Create a Query Using the DateAdd Function (p. 308)

Create a Query Using the DatePart Function (p. 310)

Create a Query Using IIf Functions (p. 300)

Use Wildcard Characters in String Comparisons (p. 289)

Create a Query Using the Not, In, And, Between...And Operators (p. 299)

Create a Top Values Query (p. 292)

Create a Query Using the Concatenate Operator (p. 297)

Create a Query Using the DateDiff Function (p. 306)

Create a Query Using the DateSerial Function (p. 309)

Create Queries Using Null Criteria and the IsNull Function (p. 303)

Create a Query Using Nested IIf Functions (p. 302)

Create a Parameter Query (p. 295)

Create a Query Using the Round Function (p. 312)

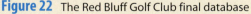

Figure 22 The Red Bluff Golf Club final database

Student data file needed:

a03_ws06_Golf2

You will save your file as:

Lastname_Firstname_a03_ws06_Golf2

Managing Payroll at the Red Bluff Golf Club Pro Shop

The Red Bluff Golf Club's Pro Shop manager has to manage all employee activities including tracking sales for commissions and hours for payroll. You have been asked to perform advanced queries that will help the Accounts Payable department generate paychecks every two weeks. The queries will mainly focus on part-time employees because their pay varies based on the hours worked. Full-time employees do not have to track their hours worked in the database. However, they still receive a paycheck every two weeks.

a. Open the **a03_ws06_Golf2** database. Save it as Lastname_Firstname_a03_ws06_Golf2.

b. Open **tblEmployee**, and then add your information in record 18. Replace YourName in the FirstName and LastName fields with your first and last name. Close tblEmployee.

c. To create a query that calculates full-time employees' payroll for the 2-week period from January 2, 2013, through January 15, 2013:

   • Click the **Create tab**, and then in the Queries group, click **Query Design**. Add **tblEmployee**, **tblPayroll**, and **tblPosition** to Design View.

   • Add the following fields to the Query design grid:

     tblEmployee: FullName, Salary
     tblPayroll: MaritalStatus, FTBenefits, BenefitsFee
     tblPosition: PositionType

   • You want to nest the Not and Like functions to be sure only full-time employees show in the dataset. In the Criteria property under PositionType, enter Not Like "Part-time".

   • Next, you need to calculate each full-time employee's paycheck before taxes. Because they get paid every two weeks and they are salaried employees, you can calculate the gross income by dividing Salary by 26—the number of pay periods in a year. This is called gross income. Gross income is the amount an employee is paid before any deductions are taken—taxes, benefits, and so forth. Click in the **first blank field** in the Query design grid, and then type GrossIncome:[Salary]/26.

   • To format GrossIncome as Currency, right-click the **GrossIncome** field, and then click **Properties** and the property sheet will open. On the General tab, select **Currency** under the Format option.

   • Run your query, save it as qryFulltimePay_initialLastname, and then return to **Design view**.

d. To modify the qryFulltimePay_initialLastname query to calculate full-time employees' estimated taxes and net pay for the 2-week period from January 2, 2013 through January 15, 2013:

   • You want to nest the IIf, Like, and Round functions to estimate the taxes that will be deducted from the gross pay. You will name this new field EstTaxes. If an employee is single, 30% of their gross income goes to taxes. If an employee is married, 25% of their gross income goes to taxes. Because this is just an estimate of how much the employee will pay in taxes, you want to use the Round function to work in whole dollars. Click the **next blank field** in the Query design grid, and then type EstTaxes:IIf([MaritalStatus] Like "Single", Round([GrossIncome]*0.3),Round([GrossIncome]*0.25)). Format this field as **Currency**.

   • To create a new calculated field named NetPay (GrossIncome minus BenefitsFee and EstTaxes), click the **next blank field** in the Query design grid, and then type NetPay: [GrossIncome]-[BenefitsFee]-[EstTaxes]. Format this field as **Currency**.

   • Run your query, save it as qryFullTimeNetPay_initialLastname using the Save Object As option, and then close it.

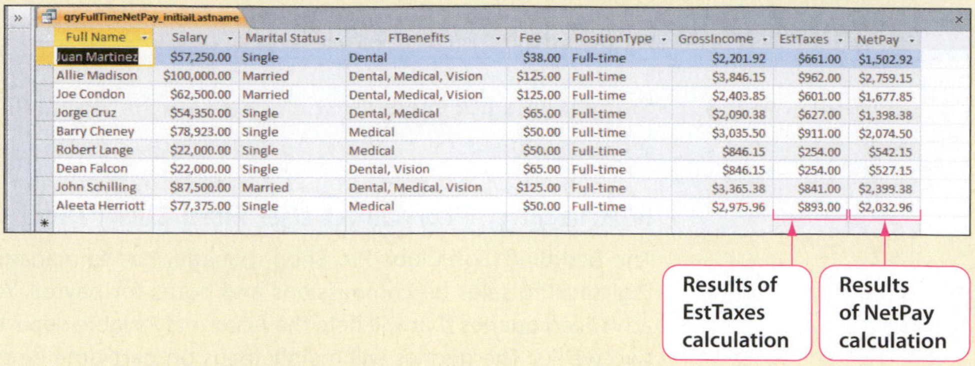

Full Name	Salary	Marital Status	FTBenefits	Fee	PositionType	GrossIncome	EstTaxes	NetPay
Juan Martinez	$57,250.00	Single	Dental	$38.00	Full-time	$2,201.92	$661.00	$1,502.92
Allie Madison	$100,000.00	Married	Dental, Medical, Vision	$125.00	Full-time	$3,846.15	$962.00	$2,759.15
Joe Condon	$62,500.00	Married	Dental, Medical, Vision	$125.00	Full-time	$2,403.85	$601.00	$1,677.85
Jorge Cruz	$54,350.00	Single	Dental, Medical	$65.00	Full-time	$2,090.38	$627.00	$1,398.38
Barry Cheney	$78,923.00	Single	Medical	$50.00	Full-time	$3,035.50	$911.00	$2,074.50
Robert Lange	$22,000.00	Single	Medical	$50.00	Full-time	$846.15	$254.00	$542.15
Dean Falcon	$22,000.00	Single	Dental, Vision	$65.00	Full-time	$846.15	$254.00	$527.15
John Schilling	$87,500.00	Married	Dental, Medical, Vision	$125.00	Full-time	$3,365.38	$841.00	$2,399.38
Aleeta Herriott	$77,375.00	Single	Medical	$50.00	Full-time	$2,975.96	$893.00	$2,032.96

Results of EstTaxes calculation

Results of NetPay calculation

Figure 23 Datasheet view of qryFullTimeNetPay_initialLastname query

e. To create a query that will help the human resources department keep track of the days off each employee has taken throughout the year:
  - Click the **Create tab**, and then in the Queries group, click **Query Design**. Add **tblTimeCard** to Design View.
  - Add the following fields to the Query design grid: EmployeeID, TotalHours, DateWorked, WorkCode.
  - You will use the Between...And function to ensure that you are only displaying records for the year 2013. In the Criteria property under DateWorked, type Between 12/31/2012 And 1/1/2014.
  - In the Criteria property under WorkCode, type In("Vacation","Sick Day","Comp Day","Training").
  - Run your query, save it as qryOtherHoursTotal_initialLastname, and then close it.

f. To create a query that shows the employees who have selected benefits but for whom the human resources department has yet to enter the fee:
  - Click the **Create tab**, and then in the Queries group, click **Query Design**. Add **tblPayroll**, **tblEmployee**, and **tblPosition** to Design View.
  - Add the Employee, MaritalStatus, PTBenefits, BenefitsFee, and PositionType fields to the Query design grid.
  - In the Criteria property under BenefitsFee, type Is Null.
  - In the Criteria property under PositionType, type Like "Part-time".
  - Run your query, save it as qryFees_initialLastname, and then close it.

g. To create a query that will determine how much part-time employees will pay for benefits:
  - Click the **Create tab**, and then in the Queries group, click **Query Design**. Add **tblEmployee**, **tblPayroll**, and **tblPosition** to Design View.
  - Add the following fields to the Query design grid:

    tblEmployee: EmployeeID, FullName

    tblPayroll: MaritalStatus, PTBenefits

    tblPosition: PositionType

  - In the Criteria property under PositionType, type Like "Part-time".
  - Because part-time employees pay different fees for their benefits, you want to nest the IIf, IsNull, and Like functions to calculate the total benefits fees for each employee. To do this you will create a new field named BenefitsFee that determines the employees' fee. Employees can only select one option and are charged accordingly. If an employee has not selected any benefit option, he or she will not need to pay a fee—thus, the fee will be $0. If an employee has selected Dental, the fee is $5. If the employee has

selected Vision the fee is $10. If the employee has selected Medical, the fee is $25. Click the **first blank field** in the Query design grid, and then type **BenefitsFee:IIf(IsNull([PTBenefits]),0,IIf([PTBenefits] Like "Dental",5,IIf([PTBenefits] Like "Vision",10,25)))**. Format this field as **Currency**.

- Run your query, save it as **qryPTBenefitsFee_initialLastname,** and then close it.

h. Close the Lastname_Firstname_a03_ws06_Golf2 database.

Practice 2

Student data file needed:

a03_ws06_Events

You will save your file as:

Lastname_Firstname_a03_ws06_Events

Managing Events at the Red Bluff Golf Club

From weddings to conferences, the resort is a popular destination. The resort has several facilities that can accommodate groups from 30 to 600 people. Packages and prices vary by size, room, and other services, such as catering. The Accounts Receivable department needs to ensure that the clients are billed appropriately and pay in full for their event. The fees include the room, decorations, table arrangements, centerpieces, and food.

a. Open the **a03_ws06_Events** database, and then save it as **Lastname_Firstname_a03_ws06_Events**.

b. Open **tblClients**, and then add your information in record 25. Replace YourName in the FirstName and LastName fields with your first and last name. Close tblClients.

c. To create a query that shows how many days are left until an event takes place:

- Click the **Create tab**, and then in the Queries group, click **Query Design**. Add **tblEvents** and **tblClients** to Design View.

- To concatenate the FirstName and LastName fields from tblClients to create a new field named ClientName, click the **first blank field** in the Query design grid, and then type **ClientName: [FirstName] & " " & [LastName]**.

- Add the following fields to the Query design grid: tblEvents: **EventName, EventDate, StartTime, EndTime**.

- You want to use the Date function and enter criteria so only events that are either occurring today or have not occurred are shown in your dataset. In the Criteria property under EventDate, enter **>=Date()**. Your results will vary from those in Figure 24 because you are using the current date.

- Next you want to create a new field named DaysOut and use the DateDiff function to calculate how many days are left until an event occurs. Click the **first blank field** in the Query design grid, and then type **DaysOut:DateDiff("d",Date(),[EventDate])**.

- You want to create a new field named FinalCountDue that will be used to let the Event Coordinator know when the client needs to give the final guest list. To do this you will use the DateAdd function to calculate the date 14 days prior to the event date. Click the **next blank field** in the Query design grid, and then type **FinalCountDue:DateAdd("d",-14,[EventDate])**.

- The next field you need to create is named OrderMenuItems and will be used to let the kitchen manager know when food for the event needs to be ordered. You will use the DateAdd function to calculate the date 7 days prior to the event date. Click the **next blank field** in the Query design grid, and then type **OrderMenuItems:DateAdd("d",-7,[EventDate])**.

- Run your query, save it as **qryDates_initialLastname**, and then close it.

ClientName	Event Name	Date	Start Time	End Time	DaysOut	FinalCountDue	OrderMenuItems
Maryam Bennett	Wedding Reception	11/23/2013	7:00 PM	11:30 PM	996	11/9/2013	11/16/2013
Malcolm Gould	Conference	1/11/2013	8:00 AM	4:00 PM	680	12/28/2012	1/4/2013
YourName YourName	Training Seminar	2/7/2013	7:30 AM	3:30 PM	707	1/24/2013	1/31/2013
Cassandra Cochran	Wedding Reception	2/14/2013	5:30 PM	10:30 PM	714	1/31/2013	2/7/2013
Graiden Kidd	Conference	4/8/2013	6:00 AM	8:00 PM	767	3/25/2013	4/1/2013
Kyra Mccall	Wedding Reception	7/4/2013	7:30 PM	12:00 AM	854	6/20/2013	6/27/2013

Results of DaysOut calculation

Results of FinalCountDue calculation

Results of OrderMenuItems calculation

Figure 24 Datasheet view of qryDates_initialLastname query

d. To create a query that shows how much a client is spending on decorations and what amount of a deposit is needed if any:

- Click the **Create tab**, and then click **Query Design** in the Queries group. Add **tblEvents**, **tblEventItems**, **tblDecorations**, and **tblClients** to Design View.
- Add the following fields to the Query design grid:

   tblClients: FirstName, LastName

   tblEvents: EventName

   tblDecorations: DecorItem, Price

   tblEventItems: Quantity

- Next you want to create a parameter that allows you to enter a client's last name when the query is run. In the Criteria property under LastName, type [Enter the client's last name].

- Because there is no charge for using the facility's chairs, you nest the Not and Like functions to make sure that Chair does not show in the DecorItem field. In the Criteria property under DecorItem, type Not Like "Chair".

- Create a field named ExtendedPrice that calculates an extended price for the chosen items by multiplying Price from tblDecorations and Quantity from tblEventItems. Click the **first blank field** in the Query design grid, and then type ExtendedPrice: [Price]*[tblEventItems]![Quantity].

- The resort obtains some items, such as the fountains, from outside vendors; these items are in high demand throughout the year. Thus, some items require a 50% deposit. The deposit will go toward the final bill. However, if the client cancels the item or event, he or she will lose the deposit. You want to create a new field named DepositAmt that shows if a deposit is required. To do this, you will write an IIf function that determines the amount of the deposit, and you will incorporate Like and Wildcard functions into your IIf function. Items that require a 50% deposit are Chocolate Fountain, Fountain (small), and Fountain (large). (Hint: Use the ExtendedPrice field to calculate the total deposit required.) If no deposit is required, a zero should be displayed in the field. Click the **next blank field** in the Query design grid, and then type DepositAmt:IIf([DecorItem] Like "*Fountain*",[ExtendedPrice]*0.5,0). Format the DepositAmt field as **Currency**.

- Run your query. Test your query using Bennett as the client's name. Save your query as qryDecor_initialLastname, and then close it.

e. To create a query that shows the decorations needed during a given time period:

- Click the **Create tab**, and then click **Query Design** in the Queries group. Add **tblEvents**, **tblEventItems**, **tblDecorations**, and **tblClients** to Design View.
- Add the following fields to the Query design grid:

   tblClients: FirstName, LastName

   tblEvents: EventName,

   tblDecorations: DecorItem, PriceEventDate

   tblEventItems: Quantity

- To create a parameter using the Between...And operators that allows you to enter a beginning and an ending date, in the Criteria property under EventDate, type **Between [Enter Start Date] And [Enter End Date]**.
- Because this is a field that has a Date data type, you need to set the parameter data types. Click **Parameters** under Show/Hide on the Query Tools Design tab. Under Parameter, type **[Enter Start Date]** in the first row. Select **Date/Time** under Data Type. In the second row, type **[Enter End Date]**, select **Date/Time** under Data Type, and then click **OK**.
- Test your query by entering **1/1/2013** as the Start Date and **5/31/2013** as the End Date. Save your query as **qryParameter_initialLastname**, and then close it.

f. To create a Top Values query to determine which decorations generate the top 10% of profit for the resort:

- Click the **Create tab**, and then in the Queries group, click **Query Design**. Add **tblDecorations** to Design View.
- Add the following fields to the Query design grid: **DecorItem**, **Color**, **Category**, **ExtendedPrice**.
- The resort makes different profits on decorations depending on the color or item. If the item is metallic in color—silver or gold—or if the item is a fountain—Fountain (small), Fountain (large), or Chocolate Fountain—the profit margin is 70%. This means that 70% of the ExtendedPrice field is profit. All other items generate 50% profit. You want to create a new field named Profit that shows how much of a profit is made on each item. To do this you use a nested IIf function to calculate the profit and incorporate Like and Wildcard functions into your IIf function. Click the **first blank field** in the Query design grid, and then type **Profit:IIf([DecorItem] Like "*Fountain*", [ExtendedPrice]*0.7,IIf([Color] Like "Silver",[ExtendedPrice]*0.7,IIf([Color] Like "Gold", [ExtendedPrice]*0.7, [ExtendedPrice]*0.5)))**. Format this field as **Currency**, and then sort the Profit field in **Descending**—highest to lowest—order.
- Click the **Return (Top Values) arrow** in the Query Setup group on the Query Tools Design tab. Select **25%** from the Top Values list.
- Run your query, save it as **qryTopValues_initialLastname**, and then close it.

g. Management wants to encourage all couples who were married at the Red Bluff Golf Club to come back and celebrate their 5-year anniversary at the resort. You have been asked to create a query so an invitation can be sent two months in advance.

- Click the **Create tab**, and then in the Queries group, click **Query Design**. Add **tblClients** and **tblEvents** to Design View.
- Add the following fields to the Query design grid:

  tblClients: **FirstName**, **LastName**, **Address**, **City**, **State**, **ZipCode**
  tblEvents: **EventDate**

- Next, you want to create a new field named MailInvite and use the DateSerial function to calculate how many days are left until an event occurs. Click the **first blank field** in the Query design grid, and then type **MailInvite: DateSerial(Year([EventDate])+4, Month([EventDate])+10,Day([EventDate]))**.
- Run your query, save it as **qryMailInvite_initialLastname**, and then close it.

h. Close the Lastname_Firstname_a03_ws06_Events database.

Student data file needed:

a03_mp_Menu

You will save your file as:

Lastname_Firstname_a03_mp_Menu

Building and Querying the Indigo5 Menu Items Database

The Painted Paradise Golf Resort and Spa is home to a world class restaurant with a top chef, Robin Sanchez. The cuisine is balanced and modern. From steaks to pasta to local southwestern meals, this restaurant attracts local patrons in addition to resort guests. You will modify tables and then query the database that is used to manage menu items.

a. Open the **a03_mp_Menu** database, and then save it as Lastname_Firstname_a03_mp_Menu.

b. To create a new table named tblMenu that will help track specific menu items, add the following fields, data types, and descriptions:

Field Name	Data Type	Description
MenuID	AutoNumber	The menu ID automatically assigned to each menu item (primary key)
RecipeID	Number	The recipe ID assigned to each recipe in tblRecipes (foreign key)
Season	Text	Season this menu item is served
Meal	Text	Time of day this is served
Special	Yes/No	Is this item one of the daily specials?
Price	Currency	The price that guests are charged
Cost	Calculated	The cost for the restaurant to prepare this item

c. For your calculated field, multiply the Price by 40%. Make the Result Type a decimal. Set the precision to **2**.

d. Create the following field properties:

Field Name	Field Properties
MenuID	Make this field the primary key. Add a custom format under the Format field property so the MenuID is displayed as MENU03. Ensure that the New Values field property is set to sequential—Increment.
RecipeID	Create a Lookup field. Select your data from the existing tblRecipes table. Select **RecipeID** and **RecipeName**. Sort in **Ascending** order by **RecipeName**. Keep the key column hidden. Enable Data Integrity and Restrict Delete. Add Recipe as the caption under Field Properties. Make data in this field required.
Season	Create a Lookup field. Enter the following values: Fall, Winter, Spring, Summer. Limit the user's selection to what is on the list. Allow multiple values.
Meal	Create a Lookup field. Enter the following values: Breakfast, Lunch, Dinner, Late Night, Anytime. Limit the user's selection to what is on the list. Allow multiple values.

e. Save your changes, and then close it.

f. Create a relationship between tblMenu and tblRecipes.

g. Enter the following data into tblMenu:

RecipeID	Season	Meal	Special	Price
Avocado Salad	Spring, Summer	Lunch	No	$18.95
Black Beans	Fall, Winter	Lunch	No	$12.95
Chicken Soup	Fall, Winter	Lunch	No	$6.95
Gambas al Ajillo (Shrimp with Garlic)	Fall, Spring, Summer, Winter	Dinner, Lunch	Yes	$26.95
Pasta Napolitana	Spring, Summer	Dinner	Yes	$18.95
Pueblo Green Chili Stew	Winter	Lunch	No	$14.95
Eggs Benedict	Fall, Spring, Summer, Winter	Breakfast	No	$11.95
Fresh Mozzarella and Basil Pizza	Fall, Spring, Summer, Winter	Dinner, Late Night, Lunch	No	$24.95
Goat Cheese Pizza	Fall, Spring, Summer, Winter	Dinner, Late Night, Lunch	No	$24.95
Reuben Panini	Fall, Spring, Summer, Winter	Dinner, Late Night, Lunch	No	$12.95
Spinach and Mushroom Frittata	Spring, Summer	Breakfast	No	$13.95

h. Create the following queries:

- Use data in tblMenu to create a query that displays the spring and summer lunch menu. Use the In operator and Like function. The query results should list RecipeID, Season, Meal, Special, and Price from tblMenu. Run your query, and then save it as qrySpSuLunch_initialLastname.

- Create a Top Values query that displays the RecipeID, Season, Meal, Special, and Price from tblMenu. Enter 3 in the Return (Top Values) box to view the three highest priced items. (Hint: Do not forget to sort your data.) Run your query, and then save it as qryTopValues_initialLastname.

- Create a parameter query that allows you to enter two parameters—one that prompts the user to Enter season and one that prompts the user to Enter meal. Use tblMenu and display RecipeID, Season, Meal, Special, Price, and Cost. Use tblRecipes and display Subcategory and TimeToPrepare. Design the query to allow users to enter a value for the Season and Meal fields. Test your query using Fall for Season and Lunch for Meal. Save your query as qryParameters_initialLastname.

- Create a query that uses the Round function. Use tblMenu and display RecipeID, Season, Meal, Special, Price, and Cost. Create a new field named Rounded Cost. Use the Round function to round the data stored in the Cost field with a precision of 1. Format the field as Currency. Run your query, and then save your query as qryRound_initialLastname.

- Create a query that displays the RecipeID, Season, Meal, Special, and Price from tblMenu. Display the RecipeName and Instructions field from tblRecipes. Use the Like function and wildcards to view all menu items whose names begin with the letters "A" through "G". Sort your data on the RecipeName field in ascending order. Run your query, and then save it as qryLike1_initialLastname.

- Create a query that displays the Ingredient field from tblIngredients. Sort Ingredients in ascending order. Use the Like function and wildcards to view all ingredients whose names begin with the letters "D" through "P". Run your query, and then save it as qryLike2_initialLastname.

Student data file needed:

a03_ps1_Hotel1

You will save your file as:

Lastname_Firstname_a03_ps1_Hotel1

Working with Tables and Queries in the Hotel Database

The main portion of the resort is the hotel. The hotel area must track all aspects of a reservation including the types of packages including Spa, Golf, and special events. If guests register for a package, the Price field must be updated to reflect the package price. You have been asked to modify the tables to ensure ease of use and functionality. Complete the following tasks:

a. Open the **a03_ps1_Hotel1** database, and then save it as Lastname_Firstname_a03_ps1_Hotel1.

b. Add your first and last name in record 25 of the tblGuests table.

c. Make the following modifications to the tblGuests table:

- State: Create an input mask to ensure that all data entered in this field is in uppercase format for two characters. Change the field size to only allow two characters. Do not specify any of the optional parts for this property.

- ZipCode: Create an input mask for the ZipCode. The ZipCode should appear in the format 54378-1234. Access should store the symbols in the mask and use the underscore as a placeholder. Change the field size to only allow 10 characters. Change the caption to Zip Code.

- Phone: Create an input mask using the Phone format. The Phone number should appear in the format (555) 555-5555. Access should store the symbols in the mask and use the underscore as a placeholder. Change the field size to only allow 14 characters.

d. Make the following modifications to the tblPackages table:

- PackageID: Change the Data Type to AutoNumber. Create a custom format that adds PKG0 at the beginning of each number. For example, record 20 should look like PKG020.

- Package: Change the field size to 40. Set the appropriate properties to make data entry in the Package field required for both new and existing records.

- Description: Set the appropriate properties to make data entry in the Description field required for both new and existing records.

- Price: Change the Data Type to Currency. Because all packages offered at the resort are at least $250, you need to ensure that no one enters a lower price. Ensure that any number entered is greater than or equal to 250. Set the appropriate property that if a user enters values less than 250, the resulting error states: Packages must be greater than or equal to $250. Include the punctuation. Create an index on the field.

e. Make the following modifications to the tblReservations table:

- NightsStay: Set the appropriate property to ensure that any number entered is greater than or equal to 1. Set the appropriate property so if users enter zero, the resulting error states NightsStay must be 1 or greater. Include the punctuation. Set the appropriate property so 1 is the default value.

- NumberOfGuests: Set the appropriate property to ensure that any number entered is greater than or equal to 1. Set the appropriate property so if users enters zero, the resulting error states NumberOfGuests must be 1 or greater. Include the punctuation. Set the appropriate property so 1 is the default value.

- Create a new field named Package. This should look up data in tblPackages. Display the following fields in your lookup field: PackageID, Package, Description, and Price. Sort the Package field in ascending order. Hide the primary key field. Enable data integrity and select Restrict Delete. Edit the lookup properties so Column Headings will show. (Hint: You do not do this in the wizard.) Enter the following as the field description: **This is the vacation package chosen (if applicable).**

f. Enter the following data in the tblPackages table:

Package	Description	Price
Golf Weekend	Enjoy a 2-day package filled with 3 rounds of golf and 1 lesson with the golf pro.	1095.00
Spa Special	Enjoy a 2-day package filled with pampering.	1295.00
Golf and Spa Special	Enjoy 3 days filled with pampering and golf.	2275.00

g. Modify the RoomRate and Package in the following records of the tblReservations table:

ReservationID	RoomRate	Package
R0001	1095.00	Golf Weekend
R0005	1295.00	Spa Special
R0006	2275.00	Golf and Spa Special
R0011	1095.00	Golf Weekend
R0016	2275.00	Golf and Spa Special

h. Create a query from the tblReservations table. Include the following fields: ReservationID, GuestID, NumberOfGuests, CheckInDate, NightsStay, RoomType, RoomRate, DiscountType, and Package. Calculate the nonpackage guests' total room rate in a new field named **TotalCharges** where NumberOfGuests is **2** and RoomType is **Double (1 king bed)**. If a guest has purchased a package, they are not eligible for a discount. Therefore, total charges are already determined and should display the RoomRate field. If the guest is paying a daily rate, multiply the room rate by the number of nights. Subtract any discount from the total. If the guest is an AARP or AAA member, they receive a 15% discount. Format the TotalCharges field as **Currency**. Run your query, and then save it as **qry2DoubleCharges_initialLastname.**

Problem Solve 2

Student data file needed:

a03_ps2_Hotel2

You will save your file as:

Lastname_Firstname_a03_ps2_Hotel2

Querying the Hotel Database

The main portion of the resort is the hotel. The hotel has rooms that range from individual rooms to a grand villa suite. The hotel area must track all aspects of a reservation including special requests for items such as a crib. The hotel also has to track room charges that guests have made.

Room rates vary according to size, season, demand, and discount. The hotel has discounts for typical groups, such as AARP. Additionally, managers need the ability to "comp" a room—give a guest a complimentary room—and charge a rate of $0 for a night or stay.

a. Open the **a03_ps2_Hotel2** database, and then save it as **Lastname_Firstname_a03_ps2_Hotel2.**

b. Add your **first name** and **last name** in record 25 of the tblGuests table.

c. Create the following queries:

- Create a parameter query that allows you to look up a reservation by entering a customer's full name. Use the tblGuests table. The parameter should display **Enter a Guest's First and Last Name with a space in between, such as John Smith** when you run the query. You will need to combine the GuestFirstName and GuestLastName fields into a calculated field named FullName from tblGuests. The first and last names are separated by a space. The query results should also list FullName, ReservationID, CheckInDate, NightsStay, and NumberOfGuests. Sort the query in ascending order by CheckInDate. Make sure that all reservations that are displayed have not occurred yet. Run the query, and then enter **Susan Wenner** to test it. Save your query as **qryFindReservation_initialLastname**.

- Create a query to list all reservations, the guest's room service and restaurant charges, and calculates a mandatory gratuity. Use the tblReservations and tblRoomCharges tables. Your query results should show ReservationID, CheckInDate, ChargeCategory, ChargeAmount, and Gratuity. Gratuity is a calculated field. The Gratuity calculated field should use the ChargeAmount field and add a gratuity of 18%. Format the Gratuity field as **Currency**. Sort your query in ascending order by CheckInDate. Run your query, and then save it as **qryCharges_initialLastname**.

- Create a query that lists the guests that have future reservations for a double room. Use the tblReservations table. Look at the data carefully. Notice that double rooms have a room type of either Double (1 king bed) or Double (2 queen beds). Ensure your query lists all the reservations for both kinds of Double room. The query results should list GuestID, CheckInDate, Crib, Handicapped, and RoomType. Sort in ascending order by CheckInDate. Run your query, and then save it as **qryDoubleRoom_initialLastname**.

- Create a query that lists the guests who reside in AK, MT, or IA. Use the tblReservations and tblGuests tables. The query results should list GuestFirstName, GuestLastName, Address, City, State, and ZipCode, CheckInDate, and RoomRate. The query should list the guests who reside in AK, MT, or IA. This list also should only contain guests who will be paying between $300 and $400 for their room. Sort in ascending order by CheckInDate. Create a new field that calculates the date that is 14 days before the CheckInDate so front desk employees can call the guest and confirm the reservation 2 weeks prior to the arrival date. The new field should be called **RSVPCallDate**. The RSVPCallDate field should use the CheckInDate field to calculate when the phone call should be made. Run your query, and then save it as **qryGuests_initialLastname**.

- Create a query that calculates the guests' check out date based on when they check in and how many nights they are staying. Use the tblReservations and tblGuests tables. The query results should list GuestFirstName, GuestLastName, ReservationID, CheckInDate, NightsStay, NumberOfGuests, and CheckOutDate. CheckOutDate is a new field that calculates the guests' check-out date. Sort in ascending order by CheckOutDate. Run your query. Save your query as **qryCheckOutDate_initialLastname**.

Problem Solve 3

Student data file needed:

a03_ps3_Hotel3

You will save your file as:

Lastname_Firstname_a03_ps3_Hotel3

Using the Hotel Database for Advanced Querying

The main portion of the resort is the hotel. Guests may charge anything from the resort to their room. Thus, the hotel area must track all of these charges, such as those from the spa, golf, gift shop, restaurants, movies, personal trainers, and sessions with golf professionals. These services are eligible for a discount.

a. Open the **a03_ps3_Hotel3** database, and then save it as **Lastname_Firstname_a03_ps3_Hotel3**.

b. Open **tblGuests**, and then add your **first name** and **last name** in record 25.

c. Create a new table named **tblPayments** that will track guest payments upon guest check-out.

d. Add the following fields, data types, and descriptions:

Field Name	Data Type	Description
PmtID	AutoNumber	The payment ID automatically assigned to each transaction (primary key)
GuestID	Number	A nine-digit alphanumeric code unique to every guest matching a guest in tblGuests (foreign key)
ReservationID	Number	A five-digit numeric code unique to every reservation and matches a reservation in tblReservations (foreign key)
PmtAmount	Currency	The amount the guest paid
PmtDate	Date/Time	The date the guest made the payment
PmtMethod	Text	How the customer paid (Cash, Check, MasterCard, Visa, American Express, Discover)
AuthNumber	Text	The authorization number if paid by credit or debit card. Authorization numbers can begin with the number zero.

e. Create the following field properties:

Field Name	Field Properties
PmtID	Change the appropriate property so that the PmtID is displayed as PMT03 but that the underlying value is still 3. New values need to be sequential—Increment.
GuestID	Create a Lookup field using the tblGuests table. Select **GuestID**, **GuestLastName**, and **GuestFirstName**. Sort in ascending order by GuestID. Keep the key column hidden. Type **Guest** as the caption. Make data in this field required both for new and existing records.
ReservationID	Create a Lookup field. Select **ReservationID**, **CheckInDate**, **GuestLastName**, and **GuestFirstName**. Unhide the key column. Enable data integrity and restrict deletions. Type **RSVP ID** as the caption. Make data in this field required for both new and existing records.
PmtAmount	Type **Amount** as the caption.
PmtDate	This field should be displayed as "Medium Date" but have an input mask of Short Date with a 4-digit year. Make certain when users enter data that an underscore is displayed in the field where users can enter digits. Type **Date** as the caption.
PmtMethod	Create a Lookup field that lists the following values: Cash, Check, MasterCard, Visa, American Express, Discover. Limit the user's selection to what is on the list. Allow multiple values. Type **Method** as the caption.
AuthNumber	Set the maximum number of characters for the field to **6**. Type **Auth #** as the caption.

f. Enter the following data in the tblPayments table:

GuestID	ReservationID	PmtAmount	PmtDate	PmtMethod	AuthNumber
Bennett	R0005	$1,229.00	02-Jan-13	American Express	22597
Cote	R0006	$168.30	01-Jan-13	Cash	
Wong	R0007	$483.23	03-Jan-13	MasterCard	877456
Bridges	R0008	$346.50	01-Jan-13	Check	
Finch	R0010	$31.19	15-Feb-13	Cash	
Sharp	R0011	$395.80	14-Feb-13	Visa	01123
Woodward	R0012	$391.31	28-Feb-13	Visa	08556
Mcmahon	R0014	$137.62	02-Apr-13	Cash, Discover	22113
Wenner	R0016	$807.49	10-Apr-13	American Express	88945
YourName	R0017	$1,682.71	06-Jul-13	Discover	612876

g. Create the following queries:

- Create a query that calculates the attendants' tip on a room service order (18%) or spa treatment (25%). Use the tblReservations and tblRoomCharges tables. Your query results should list ReservationID, CheckInDate, ChargeCategory, ChargeAmount, and Gratuity. Gratuity is a calculated field. If the ChargeCategory is not a spa treatment or room service, a zero should be displayed in the field. Format the Gratuity field as **Currency**. Sort in ascending order by CheckInDate. Run your query, and then save it as qryTips_initialLastname.

- Create a query that calculates the guest's total room charges. Use the tblReservations and tblGuests tables. Your query results should list GuestFirstName, GuestLastName, ReservationID, CheckInDate, NightsStay, RoomRate, DiscountType, and TotalRoomCharges. TotalRoomCharges is a calculated field. Be sure to subtract any discount from the total charges. In addition to the discount data in the database, AARP and AAA members receive a 10% discount. Military personnel receive a 20% discount. Guests without a discount should still have their total room charges calculated. Sort in ascending order by ReservationID. Run your query, and then save your query as qryTotalRoomCharges_initialLastname.

- Create a query that enables you to enter the guest's full name—first and last name separated by a space—to find out what services they had while staying at the resort. Use the tblGuests, tblChargeDetails, and tblRoomCharges tables. Concatenate the GuestFirstName and GuestLastName fields into a new field named **Guest**. Be sure to leave a space between the GuestFirstName and GuestLastName fields. The Parameter should ask the user to **Enter a Guest's First and Last Name**. Your query results should also list ChargeCategory, ChargeAmount, Purchase, and Guest fields. Combine the Not and Like functions to ensure that your results do not include any Gifts/Sundries in the results. Test your query using your **first name** and **last name**. Save your query as qryParameter_initialLastname.

- Create a query that finds all reservations between 6/1/2010 and 6/1/2011. Use the tblReservations and tblPayments tables. The query results should list ReservationID, CheckInDate, NightsStay, NumberOfGuests, RoomType, RoomRate, PmtAmount, PmtDate, and PmtMethod. Only show the guests who paid by credit card—MasterCard, Visa, American Express, and Discover. Sort in ascending order by PmtAmount. Run your query, and then save it as qryDates_initialLastname.

- Create a query to see what the total charges will be for each guest. Use the tblReservations and tblPayments tables and qryTotalRoomCharges_initialLastname query. Your query results should list ReservationID, CheckInDate, NightsStay, RoomRate, and TotalCharges from qryTotalRoomCharges_initialLastname. Also include PmtAmount from tblPayments and DiscountType from tblReservations. Create a new field named AmountDue that calculates whether an amount is due. (Hint: If the total charges are less than the payment amount, then the guest owes money.) Create a new field named RefundDue that calculates whether a refund is owed to a guest. Format the AmountDue and RefundDue fields as **Currency**. Run your query, and then save it as qryTotalCharges_initialLastname.

- Create a Top Values query that displays the 10 highest room rates being charged to guests who have made a reservation. Use the tblReservations and tblGuests tables. The query results should list GuestFirstName and GuestLastName from tblGuests. Also include CheckInDate, NightsStay, and RoomRate from tblReservations. Enter 11 in the Return (Top Values) box. (Hint: Do not forget to sort your data.) Run your query, and then save it as qryTopValues_initialLastname.

Perform 1: Perform in Your Life

Student data file needed:	**You will save your file as:**
a03_pf1_JobSearch	Lastname_Firstname_a03_pf1_JobSearch

Creating a Job Search Database

The Job Search database will help you track your job search process, including contacting prospective employers and following up after interviews. Even if you are not currently looking for employment, this database will help keep track of associates you may need to contact in the future. Enter data into each table. Ensure that at least one table has 20 records. If you prefer, you are welcome to make up fictitious reasonable data rather than use real data.

a. Open the **a03_pf1_JobSearch** database, and then save it as Lastname_Firstname_a03_pf1_JobSearch.

b. This database must keep track of companies, contacts within those companies, and any interactions with those contacts.

c. To ensure consistency and ease of understanding the information, modify your tables—add fields and/or change data types—to include appropriate data types, such as Lookup, Yes/No, Attachment, Hyperlink, OLE Object, and Calculated. Additionally, consider appropriate field properties such as Required, Default values, Input Masks, Formats, Captions, Sequential or Random AutoNumbers, Validation rules, and Validation text.

d. Use functions, operators, and expressions to create at least two queries about your job search efforts.

e. Create at least one parameter query.

f. Use at least two different Date functions in your queries.

g. Create appropriate indexes in each table.

h. Save and close your database.

Student data file needed:

a03_pf2_Inventory

You will save your file as:

Lastname_Firstname_a03_pf2_Inventory

Modifying an Inventory Database

As an Inventory Manager for Gibby's Great Groceries, Inc., you were asked to modify an existing database to make it more functional for completing tasks such as when to reorder items and to track inventory within your company. Consider the marketing and sales departments as you modify your database. The employees in these departments will need to know current inventory levels and when inventory will be replenished so they can better service the company's clientele.

You will deliver results of your queries to the marketing and sales departments upon completion. Enter data into each table. Ensure that at least one table has 20 records. If you prefer, you are welcome to make up fictitious reasonable data rather than use real data.

a. Open the **a03_pf2_Inventory** database, and then save it as Lastname_Firstname_a03_pf2_Inventory.

b. Add your name to the tblSuppliers table.

c. To ensure consistency and ease of understanding the information, modify your tables to include appropriate data types and field properties.

d. Create a query using the Concatenate operator.

e. Create a query using Is Null in the criteria.

f. Create a query that includes an IIf and nested IIf function.

g. Use Date functions in two of your queries.

h. Use a wildcard character in a query.

i. Create a query using either the Not, In, or Between...And operator.

j. Create a Top Values query.

k. Save and close your database.

Student data file needed:

a03_pf3_Cupcakes

You will save your file as:

Lastname_Firstname_a03_pf3_Cupcakes

Managing Employees at Jellybean's Cupcakes

You are the manager of the Human Resources department of Jellybean's Cupcakes, a bakery franchise specializing in traditional and trendy cupcakes. You need to create a database that will help you track current employees along with training efforts for all the bakeries' employees. Currently all data is kept in a notebook. It is difficult to keep track of training efforts and to track what training sessions that employees have attended.

After creating the database and running queries, you will distribute employee and training information to each bakery manager.

a. Open the **a03_pf3_Cupcakes** database, and then save it as Lastname_Firstname_a03_pf3_Cupcakes.

b. Modify the tables. Use appropriate data types and field properties as you see fit.

c. Add your information to tblEmployee as a new record.

d. Add the following fields to tblEmployee:

Field Name	Data Type	Description
Email	Hyperlink	The employee's email address.
Resume	Attachment	The employee's resume.
Photo	OLE Object	The employee's photo.

e. Create appropriate indexes in each table.

f. Create two filters using Filter by Form. Save both as queries.

g. Create two filters using Filter by Selection. Save both as queries.

h. Create one filter using an Advanced Filter. Save as a query.

i. Analyze tblEmployee using the Table Analyzer Wizard. Make appropriate changes as you see fit.

j. Save and close your database.

Perform 4: How Others Perform

Student data file needed:

a03_pf4_RealEstate

You will save your file as:

Lastname_Firstname_a03_pf4_RealEstate

Being an Entrepreneur, Rhubarb Realtors

You are the president of a small real estate agency—Rhubarb Realtors. Your intern created a database for you and your employees to use for tracking properties. At first glance, you notice that it is missing quite a few field properties within the tables that would make the database more functional and easy to use. You also noticed that there are no queries, which would help answer many questions about the properties you have listed. You need to assess the database and make some changes to make it more useful.

a. Open the a03_pf4_RealEstate database. Save it as **Lastname_Firstname_a03_pf4_ RealEstate**.

b. Open **Word**. Create a new blank document, and save it as **Lastname_Firstname_a03_ pf4_RealEstate**. This will be used to answer any questions below.

c. Evaluate the data within the tables. Are the field sizes large enough for the data stored within them? Make any changes that you deem necessary.

d. Consider each table's structure. Make any changes that you deem necessary to field properties and data types for:
   - tblAgents
   - tblProperties
   - tblSubDivision

e. Add or delete fields that will enhance the database. Consider data types such as Hyperlink, Attachment, and OLE Object. Explain how adding these fields will benefit the users.

f. Consider how the data will be used. Suggest five queries that can be created to assist with decision making.
   - Explain what question the query would answer, such as listing all properties that sold within a specific date range.
   - Explain which functions or operators you would use.
   - Denote which functions and operators would be used to create a new field in your query.
   - Write the structure of each function and operator, such as Commission: [SalePrice]*.07.

g. Save and close your files.

WORKSHOP 7

Objectives

1. Use the Group By clause in aggregated calculations.   p. 332

2. Use the Where clause in aggregated calculations.   p. 335

3. Create subqueries using business calculations.   p. 339

4. Create basic Structured Query Language (SQL) queries.   p. 345

5. Create a two-dimensional query called a crosstab query using the Crosstab Query Wizard.   p. 351

Creating Business Information Using Aggregation with Advanced Calculations

PREPARE CASE

The Turquoise Oasis Spa Database: Querying with Advanced Calculations

The Turquoise Oasis Spa generates revenue through its spa services. The spa needs useful information in order to run its business efficiently. The spa manager, Meda Rodate, has hired you as an intern and has given you a copy of the database. To keep the file small while you work with the database, he removed most of the data and left only some sample data. Meda has asked you to query the data for decision making, such as scheduling employees, booking client services, and managing services. Once Meda accepts your changes, he will load all of the data and roll out the new database.

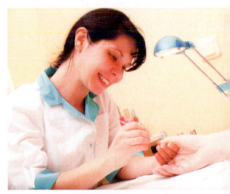

Courtesy of www.Shutterstock.com

Student data file needed for this workshop:

 a04_ws07_Spa1

You will save your file as:

Lastname_Firstname_a04_ws07_Spa1

Understanding the Group By Clause in Aggregated Calculations

Grouping data in a query can be very informative. By using the **Group By clause**, you can combine records with identical values in a specified field list into a single record. Unless the field data type is Memo or OLE Object data, a field in the Group By field list can refer to any field in a table. When you use tables to record transactions or store regularly occurring numeric data, it is useful to be able to review that data in an aggregate, such as a sum or average. In this section, you will learn how to calculate sales volume and use the Group By clause to summarize duplicate data.

Calculating Sales Volume

Many managers require summarized data in order to make decisions. For example, the spa has many different products that are sold. If a select query is created on the data, it would simply list all the products. However, the Group By clause could group the data by category, such as soap, lotion, and hair care, and calculate the total sales in each category with the Sum clause. By having summary data, you as a manager could learn which category is your best seller. You also could see which category generates the least revenue. This information could assist in making business decisions related to marketing and inventory replenishment.

Not all data within a table can be summed or averaged. Another way that the Group By clause can be used is to take a count, such as a count of products or a count of customers. For example, the spa manager may want to view how many customers each employee serviced in a given day or week. The Group By clause could group the data by employee and count the customers with the Count clause. Businesses can look at this as sales volume, or the quantity of items sold such as bottles of shampoo or massages given. **Sales volume** is the number of items sold or services rendered during normal business hours. All these figures would be taken over a specific period—week, month, year, and so on—and can be expressed in either dollars or percentages.

Real World Advice   Making Management Decisions with Grouped Data

In the world of business, specifically sales, summarized data can help managers make decisions. The data are current, relevant, and concise and depending on the nature of the organization and goals set forth by the strategic sales plan, the data can help grow their business. Some decisions that the spa manager could make include the following:

- Reorder inventory to ensure proper stocking levels are maintained.
- Advertise items that are not selling as well as others.
- Train employees on selling techniques.
- Place items on sale if the products are generating the lowest revenue.
- Determine whether sales figures are on target to meet sales goals.

To Create a Query Using the Group By Clause

a. Click the **Start** button, and then select **Access 2010**.

b. Click the **File tab**, click **Open** to browse to your student data files, locate and select **a04_ws07_Spa1**, and then click **Open**.

c. Click the **File tab**, and then click **Save Database As**. Browse to where you are storing your student files. In the File name box, type Lastname_Firstname_a04_ws07_Spa1, replacing Lastname_Firstname with your actual name. Click **Save**.

d. Click **Enable Content** in the Security Warning.

e. Click the **Create tab**, and then in the Queries group, click **Query Design**. In the Show Table dialog box, click **tblProduct**, press Ctrl and click **tblPurchase**, and then click **Add**. Close the Show Table dialog box.

f. Add the following fields to the Query design grid:

Category, **Price**, and **Quantity**

g. Click the **Query Tools Design tab** and then click **Totals**.

h. Rename the Price field by typing Revenue: in front of the field name **Price**.

i. To see how much money the spa made by category, you can modify how you want the data to be displayed by using the SUM clause. In the Total row of the Query design grid, select the following **Group By** options:

Category: Leave as **Group By**
Revenue Price: Select **Sum**
Quantity: Select **Sum**

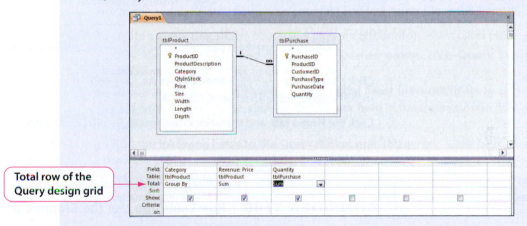

Total row of the Query design grid

Figure 1 Design view of Group By query

j. Click **Run**. Resize your fields if you cannot see all the data or column headings. Notice that you can see how many products you sold within each category and the total sales that were generated.

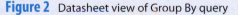

How many products sold within each category

Total sales that were generated

Figure 2 Datasheet view of Group By query

k. Save your query as qryGroupBy1_initialLastname. Click **OK**.

l. Return to **Design view**, and then delete the Quantity field.

m. Click **Run**. Because of the relationship between the two tables none of the fields from tblPurchase needed to be used. Access still includes calculations for the list of those products that were purchased. Click **OK**.

n. Click the **File tab**, then click **Save Object As**. Save your query as qryGroupBy2_initialLastname. Click **OK**.

o. Click the **Home tab**. Return to **Design view**, and then delete Revenue Price from the Query design grid.

p. Add **ProductID** from tblPurchase table to the grid.

q. To see how many times an item was purchased, you can modify how you want the data to be displayed by using the Count clause. In the Total row of the Query design grid, select the following:

   Category: Leave as **Group By**
   ProductID: Select **Count**

r. Click **Run**. Notice that your output is not the same as when you used the SUM clause to see the quantity of items purchased. The output is actually showing you how many transactions are included for each of the items.

SIDE NOTE

Sum vs. Count

Sum can only be performed on number and currency fields. Count can be done on any field data type, including text.

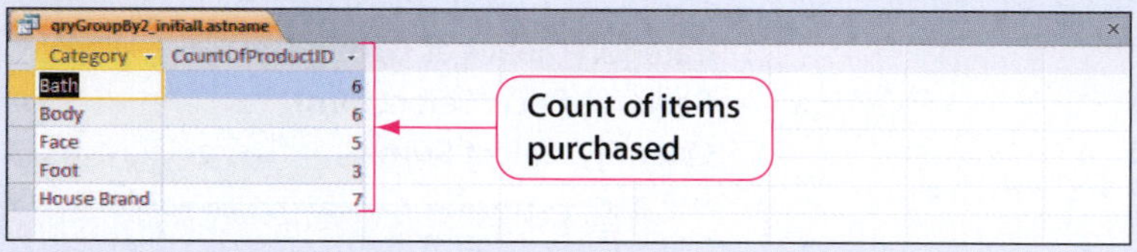

Figure 3 Datasheet view of qryGroupBy2_initialLastname query

s. Click the **File tab**, then click **Save Object As**. Save your query as qryGroupBy3_initialLastname. Click **OK**.

t. Click the **Home tab**, and then close qryGroupBy3_initialLastname.

CONSIDER THIS | How Could You Use the Grouped Data?

Now that you can see how each product category performed in regard to sales, what decisions could you make? What would you do about the low sales numbers in the Foot category? Do you think the spa's House Brand should be higher in sales? What would you do to increase sales?

CONSIDER THIS | What Would Happen If You Forgot a Step?

What would happen if you forgot to select an aggregate function in the Totals row of the Query design grid? Or what would happen if you selected the Count clause instead of the Sum clause? What would the data look like? How could it affect decision making?

Using Group By to Summarize Duplicate Data

Another way a Group By clause can be used is to summarize duplicate data. For example, what if you wanted a list of all customers (along with their mailing information) who have made a purchase during a given period of time? You can simply add a transactions table to the Query Design view and only include the customers who have made a purchase. Additionally, you could exclude people who were added to the Customers table, but never made a purchase—maybe they canceled their appointment. Initially, those who made many purchases will be listed multiple times. However, you can add the totals row to group them and therefore remove duplicates.

To Create a Query Using the Group By Clause to Summarize Duplicate Data

a. Click the **Create tab**, and then in the Queries group, click **Query Design**. Add **tblCustomer** and **tblPurchase** tables to the Design view. Close the Show Table dialog box.

b. Add the following fields to the Query design grid:

   CustFirstName, CustLastName, CustAddress, CustCity, and **CustState**

c. To view a list of customers, click **Run**. Notice that there are several duplicate names within the 27 records displaying.

d. Return to **Design view**, click the **Query Tools Design tab**, and then click **Totals**.

e. In the Total row of the Query design grid, leave all fields set to Group By, and then click **Run**. Notice that by adding the Totals row to group the records, the duplicates were grouped together and only 12 records are displayed in the dataset.

f. Save your query as **qryGroupBy4_initialLastname**, and then close the query.

SIDE NOTE

Using Group By Without Aggregate Functions

The Group By clause does not actually have to be used with Sum, Count, and so on to display aggregated data.

Understanding the Where Clause in Aggregated Calculations

The **Where clause** allows you to limit the results of your query by specifying criteria that field values must meet without using that field to group the data mathematically. When using a Where clause within your select query, you need to enter query criteria. Access selects the records that meet the condition listed in the query criteria. For example, suppose your customer service representatives need to be able to retrieve customers' e-mail addresses or phone numbers throughout the day, but the representative only knows the customer's last name. You could use a Where clause to limit the results of the query and make it easier for your employees to find the information they need. In this section, you will calculate sales revenue using the Where clause.

Real World Advice   When Do You Need to Use the Where Clause?

Determining when you need a Where clause can be difficult at first. Generally, though not in all cases, you want to use a Where clause on a field that is needed to define the criteria, but you do not want displayed in the query results. If you just clear the Show box, then Access will still use the field to group the records. You can also use a Where clause to compare values. You can use other comparison operators, such as greater than (>), less than (<), or equals (=).

Calculating Revenue

Revenue is one of the most important pieces of information that a company uses to learn more about its financial progress. **Revenue**—or gross sales—is income that a company receives from its normal business activities—the sale of goods and services to customers. Using the Where clause can assist with this calculation. For example, you may want to calculate all sales where the date falls in a specific range, such as a fiscal year. A **fiscal year** is a period businesses and other organizations use for calculating annual financial statements. This can be different from a calendar year and can vary throughout different businesses and organizations because they can choose whatever dates they want to use as the "year." Therefore, if your company uses a fiscal year, you may need to add all sales that are between July 1st of this year and June 30th of the next year. Additionally, you may want to calculate the revenue for a specific department, such as spa services, for the fiscal year.

In the business world, other criteria must be considered to accurately calculate revenue. Another valuable calculation is net revenue. **Net revenue**—or net sales—is the revenue minus sales returns, sales allowances, and sales discounts. For example, if customers return products or are given a special discount—10% off— because a product they want to purchase is damaged, it has to be accounted for and subtracted from your gross sales. By using the Where clause to limit the results, you can make it easier to find the specific data you want and calculate data accurately.

Real World Advice — Setting Up Queries Incorrectly Could Give Zero Results

In these complicated queries, you can actually get zero results if the ENTIRE totals row is not set correctly. Think about querying departments with revenue over $10,000. If you put the criteria of >=10000 under revenue, but have *not* specified the sum on the revenue, then you will get zero results (unless one item purchased equaled over $10,000).

To Create Queries That Calculate Revenue Using a Where Clause

a. Click the **Create tab**, and then in the Queries group, click **Query Design**. Add **tblSchedule** and **tblService** to the Design view. Close the Show Table dialog box.

b. Add the following fields to the Query design grid:

   Service, Fee, and **Type**

c. Click the **Query Tools Design tab** and then click **Totals**.

d. In the Total row of the Query design grid, select the following:

   Service: Leave as **Group By**
   Fee: Select **Sum**
   Type: Select **Where**

e. Type the following into the criteria portion of the Type field: **Like "*Wax*"**.

f. Click **Run**. Notice that Access totaled all waxing services performed on clients and grouped the results by each waxing service that was given.

SIDE NOTE
Why Did Access Clear the Show Check Box?
Notice that the Show check box is automatically cleared once you select Where. Access cannot display a field when it is included in an aggregate function.

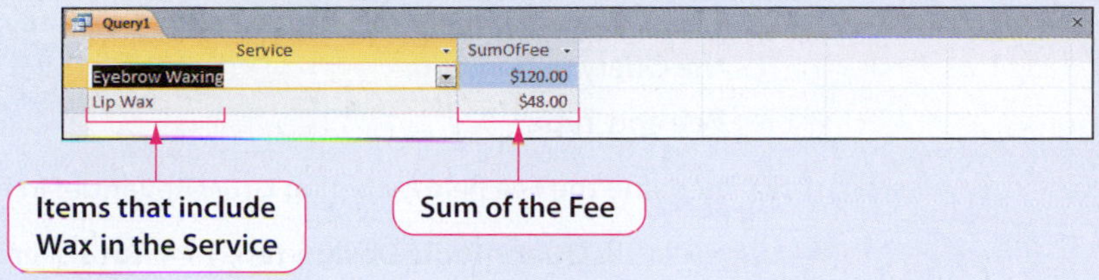

Items that include Wax in the Service

Sum of the Fee

Figure 4 Datasheet view of Where clause query

g. Save your query as **qryWhere1_initialLastname**, and then close the query.

h. Click the **Create tab**, and then in the Queries group, click **Query Design**. Add **tblSchedule** and **tblService** to the Design view. Close the Show Table dialog box and right-click the first blank field on the Query design grid, and then click **Zoom**.

i. For some of the spa services given, 38% of the gross revenue needs to be deducted due to sales returns, sales allowances, and sales discounts. Enter the following expression into the **Zoom dialog box** that will calculate the net revenue:

NetRevenue: Sum([Fee])-(Sum([Fee])*0.38)

j. Click **OK**, format the NetRevenue field as **Currency**, and then add the following fields to the Query design grid:

Fee and **Type**

k. Rename the Fee field by typing **GrossRevenue:** in front of the field name **Fee**.

l. Click the **Query Tools Design tab** and then click **Totals**.

m. In the Total row of the Query design grid, select the following:

NetRevenue: Select **Expression**
GrossRevenue: Select **Sum**
Type: Select **Where**

n. You can modify the query to view the net revenue of a specific category. In the Criteria row of the Type field, type **Like "Body Massage"**.

o. Click **Run**. Resize your fields if you cannot see all the data or column headings. Notice that you now can see the GrossRevenue—SumOfFee—and the NetRevenue for the Body Massage category.

Net revenue calculation

Total Fees calculation

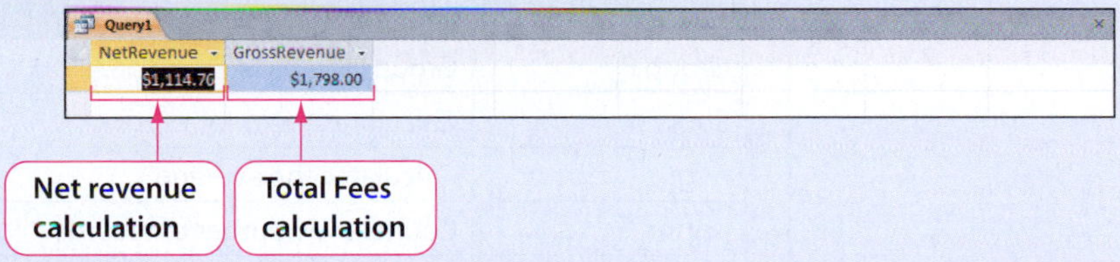

Figure 5 Datasheet view of Where clause query

p. Save your query as **qryWhere2_initialLastname**, and then close the query.

q. Click the **Create tab**, and then in the Queries group, click **Query Design**. Add **tblSchedule** and **tblService** to the Design view. Close the Show Table dialog box and right-click the first blank field on the Query design grid, and then click **Zoom**.

r. For some spa services that were given, 16% of the gross revenue needs to be deducted due to sales returns, sales allowances, and sales discounts. Enter the following expression into the Zoom dialog box, which will calculate the net revenue:
NetRevenue:[Fee]*(1-.16)

SIDE NOTE

Sales Returns, Sales Allowances, and Sales Discounts

In business, these deductions are tracked individually and totaled at the end of the year or when needed. Once totaled, they are deducted from the gross revenue.

s. Click **OK**, format the NetRevenue field as **Currency**, and then add the following fields to the Query design grid:

Fee and **Type**

t. Rename the Fee field by typing GrossRevenue: in front of the field name **Fee**.

u. Click the **Query Tools Design tab**, click **Totals**, and then in the Total row of the Query design grid, select the following:

NetRevenue: Select **Sum**
GrossRevenue: Select **Sum**
Type: Select **Group By**

v. You can modify the query to view the net revenue of a specific category. In the Criteria row of the Type field, type Like "Hands & Feet".

w. Click **Run**. Resize your fields if you cannot see all the data or column headings. Notice that you now can see the GrossRevenue and the NetRevenue for the Hands & Feet category.

x. Save your query as qryWhere3_initialLastname, and then close the query.

Real World Advice   Expressions Can Be Flexible

Did you think about the calculation you were performing when you typed Sum([Fee])-(Sum([Fee])*0.38)? Think about different calculations that are equally correct. For example, here Sum([Fee]*(1-.38)) or Sum([Fee]*.62) are also mathematically correct. Which of the expressions are more efficient for the computer to calculate? Does it really matter which calculation you use as long as the mathematical result is the same? Would the size of the database play a role in this? What if this was Amazon with billions of records?

Quick Reference   Standard Aggregate Functions in Access

Function	Use
Group By	Groups the data
Sum	Calculates the total
Avg	Calculates the average
Count	Counts the number of records
Min	Displays the minimum value
Max	Displays the maximum value
StDev	Calculates the standard deviation
First	Displays the value in the first record
Last	Displays the value in the last record
Var	Calculates the variance
Expression	Allows an expression to be entered
Where	Limits the results without grouping the data by the field

Figure 6   Functions and Uses of Aggregate Functions

Real World Advice — The Calculated Fields and Aggregate Functions

An **aggregated calculation** returns a single value calculated from multiple values in a column. Common aggregate functions include Average, Count, Maximum, Median, Minimum, Mode, and Sum. You may need to create a custom field that includes an aggregate calculation.

An aggregate function differs from a calculated field in that when you create a calculated field, you are calculating or summarizing data across a single row at a time. However, when you create an aggregated field, you are calculating or summarizing data across entire groups of rows. The word **aggregate** simply means a summative calculation, such as a total or average, or summarizing data.

When you combine calculated fields and aggregate functions, pay careful attention to the aggregate function and what data it is aggregating. If you use an aggregate function around a calculated field, Access first calculates each record and then performs the aggregation. For example, if you have a custom field AverageMarkup: average(([RetailPrice]-[WholeSaleCost])/[WholeSaleCost]), Access first calculates the markup for each product and then averages all of the markups.

Business Calculations Using Subquerying

Some managers may want to calculate the sales volume—how much has been sold of a particular item or items. Some of the salon and spa's products were sold to clients who are interested in taking their favorite products home with them. A manager would want to keep track of how many items are sold per day, week, or month. Thus, the need to first take a count of each item is critical to having an accurate calculation.

What is physical volume? **Physical volume** measures how much space is within an object. For example, clients can also phone in orders or place orders online. Thus, the manager would want to pack the products most efficiently and use the smallest shipping box possible to pack and ship the orders as it will save on shipping costs.

Because decision making is an important part of a manager's daily routine, some managers may want to calculate the percentages of physical volume, sales volume, or sales revenue to see how the business is performing or to monitor inventory. Once Access provides them with this information, they will be able to make staffing, training, marketing, and inventory decisions. In this section, you will create subqueries that calculate the percentage of sales revenue, the percentage of sales volume, physical volume, and the percentage of physical volume.

Creating a Query on a Query

Because more sophisticated queries require more advanced manipulation of data, you may need to create a subquery. A subquery simply is a select query that is nested inside of another select query. This is used when you want to create a query from previously queried data. For example, when calculating the percentage of sales volume or the percentage of physical volume, a subquery will make the calculation easier.

Calculating the Percentage of Sales Revenue

In business, the percentage of sales revenue can be a valuable piece of data and can teach a manager a lot about his or her business. The **percentage of sales revenue** can compare the portion of the gross revenue to the total gross revenue. As a manager, you may want to forecast or predict what next year's sales will be based on past sales—usually calculated based on the past three years of data. Or you may want to see how each category is performing this year as compared to last year's sales figures. For example, the spa manager may want to see how each product category's sales contributed to the overall sales of the spa. When calculating the percentage of sales revenue, you need to consider the method used to calculate percentage of sales revenue—the number of units sold—as well as the time period over which you plan on measuring the sales.

To calculate the percentage of sales revenue, you first need to calculate the total sales revenue in one query. Then you need to create a subquery that uses the total sales revenue calculation to calculate the percentage of sales revenue, where the percentage of a whole is the individual item divided by the grand total. For example, if the sales revenue for all spa services given last month was $27,325, the spa manager could create a query that divides the total sales revenue of each service given last month, such as Sea Salt Scrub, by the sales revenue for all spa services given last month. If the sales revenue for Sea Salt Scrubs was $1,768, the query results would illustrate that Sea Salt Scrubs contributed to 6.47% of the total sales revenue.

To Create a Query That Calculates the Percentage of Sales Revenue

a. Click the **Create tab**, and then in the Queries group, click **Query Design**. In the Show Table dialog box, click the **Queries tab**, add **qryGroupBy1_initialLastname** to the Design view. Close the Show Table dialog box.

b. Add the following field to the Query design grid:

   Revenue

c. First you need to calculate what the total revenue is before you can calculate the percentage of sales revenue. To do this, click the **Query Tools Design tab** and then click **Totals**.

d. In the Total row of the Query design grid, select the following:

   Revenue: Select **Sum**

e. Click **Run**. Resize your field if you cannot see all the data or column heading.

f. Save your query as qryTotalRev_initialLastname, and then close the query.

g. Click the **Create tab**, and then in the Queries group, click **Query Design**. In the Show Table dialog box, click the **Queries tab**, add **qryGroupBy1_initialLastname** and **qryTotalRev_initialLastname** to the Design view. Close the Show Table dialog box.

h. Add the following fields to the Query design grid:

   Category and **Revenue**

i. The equation needed to calculate what percentage of each category's sales contributed to the gross revenue is the category total revenue divided by the overall gross revenue. In the first blank field of the Query design grid, open the **Zoom dialog box**, and then type the following expression:

   PercentToGrossRevenue:[Revenue]/[SumOfRevenue]

j. Click **OK**.

k. Format the PercentToGrossRevenue field as **Percent**.

l. Click **Run**. Resize your fields if you cannot see all the data or column headings. Notice that you can see the percentage of sales within each category and how the category revenue that contributed to the gross revenue.

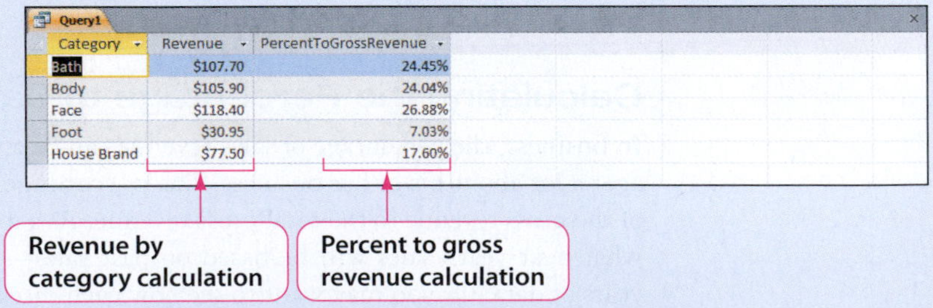

Figure 7 Datasheet view of percentage of sales volume query

m. Not only can you view the percentage of sales volume, you can also format the query output to see the grand totals of each field. Click the **Home tab** and then click **Totals**. A Total row will appear at the bottom of your datasheet.

n. Click in the **Total** row of the Revenue field, and then select **Sum** from the list.

o. Click in the **Total** row of the PercentToGrossRevenue field, and then select **Sum** from the list. Notice that you can use this as a way to communicate information better, and it can also help you double-check that your percentage calculations add up to 100%.

Query1			
Category	Revenue	PercentToGrossRevenue	
Bath	$107.70	24.45%	
Body	$105.90	24.04%	
Face	$118.40	26.88%	
Foot	$30.95	7.03%	
House Brand	$77.50	17.60%	
Total	$440.45	100.00%	← Total row

Figure 8 Datasheet view of percentage of sales volume query including Totals row

p. Save your query as **qryPctToGrossRev_initialLastname**, and then close the query.

Calculating the Percentage of Sales Volume

The **percentage of sales volume** can help compare how two or more numbers are related. As a manager, you may want to forecast or predict how many products you will sell next year based on past sales. Or you may want to see how each category is performing this year as compared to last year's sales volume. For example, the spa manager may want to track how many clients schedule services, and then find out how the total quantity of each service contributed to the overall total quantity of services given. For example, if the spa manager wants to see how many services were given last month, the spa manager could simply create a query that counts each appointment for last month.

To perform this calculation, you need to create a query that counts each service given during a specific period of time. Then you need to create a subquery that displays each service along with a calculation of the total quantity of each service contributed divided by the overall total quantity of services given. For example, if the total spa services given last month were 143, the spa manager could create a query that divides the count of each service given last month, such as Sea Salt Scrub, by the total spa services given last month. If 26 Sea Salt Scrubs were given last month, the query results would illustrate that 18.2% of all services given were Sea Salt Scrubs.

When calculating the percentage of sales volume, you need to consider the method used to calculate percentage of sales volume—the number of units sold—as well as the time period over which you plan on measuring the sales volume.

CONSIDER THIS | **How Could You Use the Percentage of Sales Volume Data?**

Once you can see how services performed relates to the total sales volume, what decisions could you make? What if a service did not sell as well as it did last year? How would that affect marketing? Would you not offer the service anymore? What if you notice that a particular service is more popular than you initially thought? How would that affect staffing?

To Create a Query That Calculates the Percentage of Sales Volume

a. Click the **Create tab**, and then in the Queries group, click **Query Design**. In the Show Table, click the **Queries tab**, add **qryGroupBy1_initialLastname** to the Design view. Close the Show Table dialog box.

b. Add the following field to the Query design grid:

   SumOfQuantity

c. You need to calculate what the total quantity of items sold is before you can calculate the percentage of sales volume. To do this, click the **Query Tools Design tab** and then click **Totals**.

d. In the Total row of the the Query design grid, select the following:

   SumOfQuantity: Select **Sum**

e. Rename the SumOfQuantity field by typing TotalQuantity: in front of the field name **SumOfQuantity**.

f. Click **Run**. Resize your field if you cannot see all the data or column heading. You will notice that there was a total of 63 items sold.

g. Save your query as qryTotalQty_initialLastname, and then close the query.

h. Click the **Create tab**, and then in the Queries group, click **Query Design**. In the Show Table, click the **Queries tab**, add **qryGroupBy1_initialLastname** and **qryTotalQty_initialLastname** to the Design view. Close the Show Table dialog box.

i. Add the following field to the Query design grid:

   Category

j. The equation needed to calculate what percentage of each category's sales contributed to the sales volume is the category total sales volume divided by the overall total sales volume. In the first blank field of the Query design grid, open the **Zoom dialog box**, and then type the following expression:

   PercentToSalesVolume: [SumOfQuantity]/[TotalQuantity]

k. Click **OK**.

l. Format the PercentToSalesVolume field as **Percent**.

m. Click **Run**. Resize your fields if you cannot see all the data or column headings. Notice that you can see the percentage of sales volume within each category and how the category sales volume contributed to the total sales volume.

n. Not only can you view the percentage of sales volume, you can also format the query output to see the grand totals of each field. Click the **Home tab** and then click **Totals**. A Total row will appear at the bottom of your datasheet.

o. Click in the **Total** row of the PercentToSalesVolume field, and then select **Sum** from the list. Notice that you can use this as a way to communicate information better, and it can also help you double-check that your percentage calculations add up to 100%.

p. Save your query as qryPctToSalesVolume_initialLastname, and then close the query.

Real World Advice   Why Are You Renaming Fields?

In the previous exercise, you renamed the SumOfQuantity field to TotalQuantity. If you had not done that, your calculation would have been [SumOfQuantity]/ [SumOfQuantity]. This would have confused Access as you would have had two fields named the same. In that case, you would have had to specify the table or query name before the field name like this [qryGroupBy1_initialLastname]![SumOfQuantity]/ [qryTotalQty_initialLastname]![SumOfQuantity]. Renaming one of the fields is easier than having to specify the table or query that the field came from.

CONSIDER THIS │ How Could You Use the Grouped Data?

Now that you can see how each product category performed in regard to gross revenue, what decisions could you make? What if a category did not sell as well as it did last year? What if you displayed the average instead of the sum at the bottom of your query results in Datasheet view? Would this change your decisions?

Calculating Physical Volume

Sometimes you might hear a question like "How much can the box hold?" You need to calculate physical volume to determine the answers to this question. For example, many companies sell products online and have to determine the best size of box to use for packing the order. The packaging volume is the difference between the volume of the shipping container and the volume of the object you are shipping. Because some shipping companies can apply surcharges for larger boxes, it is important to use the best size box to keep the overall shipping charge as low as possible. Imagine some of the largest online retailers you know and how much money using the correct box size can generate in terms of cost savings. If you know how to calculate packaging volume, you can select the appropriate size box.

Consider the Turquoise Oasis Spa. There are times when clients will either phone in an order or order products online and want them shipped to their home. If you know how much space or volume a product takes up within the box, you can determine what size box to use for the entire shipment.

To Create a Query That Calculates Physical Volume

a. Click the **Create tab**, and then in the Queries group, click **Query Design**. Add **tblProduct** to the Design view. Close the Show Table dialog box.

b. Add the following fields to the Query design grid:

ProductDescription and **Size**

c. In the criteria row of the ProductDescription field, type **Like "*soap*"**.

d. To calculate the volume that each bar of soap consumes, you need to multiply (length)* (width)*(depth). The result will be in cubic inches. In the first blank field in the Query design grid, type the following into the Zoom dialog box: **Volume:[Width]*[Length]* [Depth]**.

e. Click **OK**.

f. The smallest carton that the spa has to ship items to customers is 136 cubic inches. To calculate the packaging volume that a bar of soap consumes within the smallest box available, subtract the volume of the bar of soap from the volume of the smallest carton. The result will be in cubic inches. In the next blank field in the Query design grid, type the following into the Zoom dialog box:

RemainingPkgVolume:136-[Volume]

g. Click **OK**.

h. Calculate the total bars of soap that can fit into the spa's smallest carton. The result will be in cubic inches. In the next blank field in the Query design grid, type the following into the Zoom dialog box:

TotalPkgVolume:Int(136/[Volume])

i. Click **OK**, and then click **Run**. Resize your fields if you cannot see all the data or column headings. Notice that you can ship up to 22 bars of soap within the smallest shipping carton.

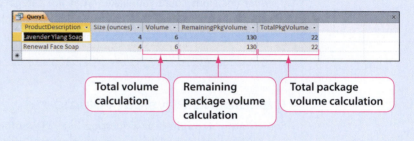

Figure 9 Datasheet view of physical volume query

j. Save your query as **qryPhysicalVolume_initialLastname**, and then close the query.

Real World Advice   Things to Note When Calculating Physical Volume

When calculating volume, consider:

- The basic formula for calculating volume is length*width*depth.

- If the item is not a perfect rectangle, take the average width and length. For example, if the object is 6 inches at its widest point and 2 inches at its narrowest point, use 4 inches for the width.

- If you are wrapping the item in bubble wrap, take your measurements after it is wrapped.

- If you take your measurements in inches, your final calculation will be in cubic inches. If you take them in centimeters, your final calculation will be in cubic centimeters, and so on.

- Finally, consider the overall dimensions of the package. A 6x3x1 bar of soap (18 cubic inches in volume) will not fit in a 3x3x3 box even if it has 50% more volume at 27 cubic inches. That would require a table that holds data regarding the types of packaging used.

Calculating the Percentage of Physical Volume

Consider a 1-gallon container of shampoo. Some of the salon and spa's products are purchased in pints, quarts, half gallons, or gallons. However, you would not use an entire bottle of shampoo on one client. Thus, the need to first convert these measurements is critical to having an accurate calculation.

If you use two 1-ounce pumps of shampoo on one client, and you purchased a 1-gallon container of shampoo, you would have to calculate how many ounces are in the 1-gallon container of shampoo. It does not make a difference if you were to convert the gallons to ounces or ounces to gallons, but it tends to be easier to go from large amounts to small amounts. The key is to be consistent.

In a second query, you can easily find the daily **percentage of physical volume** used by dividing the amount used per day by the total amount that comes in the gallon container. For example, if you use 54 pumps or ounces of shampoo per day and the container holds 1 gallon or 128 ounces, you would divide 54 by 128, then format it as percentage to find out the percent of the container being used each day. Thus, 42.2% of the can is being used each day, which means you would use 1 gallon of shampoo about every 2 days. As a manager, you could ensure that you have enough inventory for your business and know that you will not run out of product. If needed, you can change the percentage into a decimal or a fraction in order to calculate the percentage of a whole number.

To Create a Subquery That Calculates the Percentage of Physical Volume

a. Click the **Create tab**, and then in the Queries group, click **Query Design**. In the Show Table dialog box, click the **Queries tab**, add **qryPhysicalVolume_initialLastname** to the Design view. Close the Show Table dialog box.

b. Add the following fields to the Query design grid:

ProductDescription and **Size**.

c. To calculate the percentage of physical volume, you need to divide the volume of the item by the total volume the package can hold. Use the size of smallest carton that the spa has to ship items to customers—136 cubic inches. In the first blank field in the Query design grid, type the following into the Zoom dialog box: PercentOfPhysicalVolume:[Volume]/136.

d. Click **OK**, and then format the PercentOfPhysicalVolume field as **Percent**.

e. Click **Run**. Resize your fields if you cannot see all the data or column headings. Notice that each bar of soap consumes 4.41% within the smallest shipping carton.

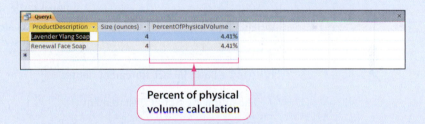

Percent of physical volume calculation

Figure 10 Datasheet view of percentage of physical volume query

f. Save your query as qryPhysicalVolumePercent_initialLastname, and then close the query.

Understanding Structured Query Language

Structured Query Language (SQL—pronounced *SEE-quel*) is an internationally recognized standard database language used by many relational databases—although many databases incorporate modified versions of the current standard SQL. The benefit of learning SQL is that once you know it, you can easily adapt to other relational database management systems. In this section, you will learn SELECT statement basics, how to view SQL statements, how to create a basic SQL query, how to use the WHERE clause, how to use the HAVING clause with AS and GROUP BY, how to create a Union query, and how to create a SQL subquery.

SELECT Statement Basics

In Access, SQL can be used to query data, just like when you create a select query in the Query design grid. As long as you know the basic structure of an SQL SELECT statement, it is fairly easy to create a SQL query. The fundamental framework for an SQL query is the SQL **SELECT statement**. The statement begins with the SELECT keyword. The basic SELECT statement has three clauses—SELECT, FROM, and WHERE, as shown in Figure 11. The SELECT clause specifies the table columns that are retrieved. The FROM clause specifies the tables accessed. The WHERE clause, which is optional in a SELECT statement, specifies which table rows are used. Finally, the SELECT statement ends with a semicolon—if you forget to add it, Access will automatically add it.

Clause	Required?	Include	Explanation	Example
SELECT	Yes	Field name(s)	Includes one or more columns from which data are retrieved	SELECT EmpFirstName, EmpLastName
FROM	Yes	Table name(s)	Name of the table(s) from which the information is retrieved	FROM tblEmployee
WHERE	No	Conditions	Specifies which table rows are used	WHERE EmpLastName Like "[A-M]*";

Figure 11   Basic SELECT statement clauses

The following SELECT statement

SELECT EmpFirstName, EmpLastName
FROM tblEmployee
WHERE EmpLastName Like "[A-M]*";

lists the results shown in Figure 12.

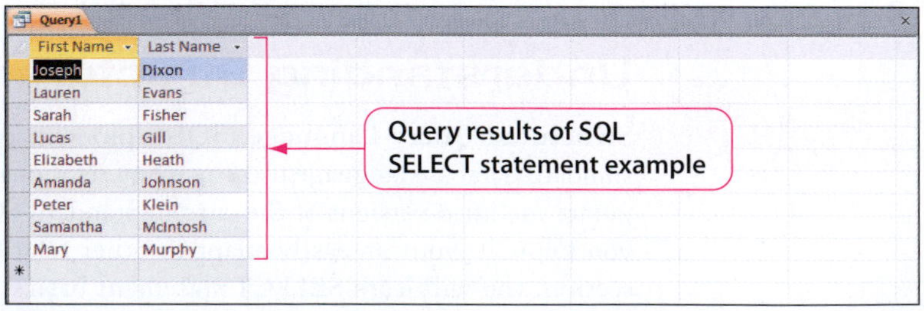

Query results of SQL SELECT statement example

Figure 12   Datasheet view of SQL query

Viewing SQL Statements

Each query that you create has an **underlying SQL statement**, which means that even when you create a query in Design view, Access automatically generates the SQL statement in the background. In Access, you can easily change between Design and SQL views of your query with the click of a mouse.

To View a Query in SQL View

a. Click the **Create tab**, and then in the Queries group, click **Query Design**. Add **tblCustomer** to the Design view. Close the Show Table dialog box.

b. Add the following fields to the Query design grid:

CustFirstName, **CustLastName**, **CustEmail**, and **CustState**

c. In the Criteria row of the CustState field, type Like "MN".

d. Click **Run**. Notice that there are three customers who live in MN.

e. Instead of returning to Design view, click the **View arrow**, and then select **SQL View**.

   Notice that Access created the SQL statement in the background as you created your query in Design view. Access prefaced each field name in the SELECT statement with the table name and added parentheses in the WHERE statement.

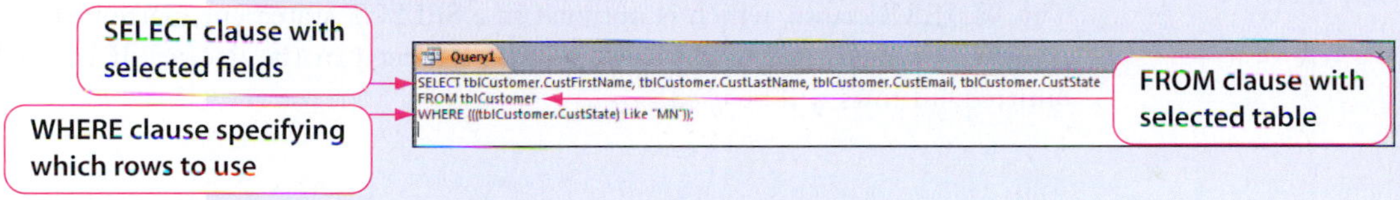

SELECT clause with selected fields

WHERE clause specifying which rows to use

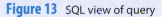

FROM clause with selected table

Figure 13 SQL view of query

f. Save your query as qrySQL1_initialLastname, and then close the query.

Creating a Basic SQL Query

SQL is used to interact with your data, and whenever a query is run Access uses SQL to filter the data and perform all the data functions of its Query Design tool. If you know SQL, you can create several types of queries in Access by typing your SQL statement in SQL view.

To Create a Basic Query in SQL View

a. Click the **Create tab**, and then in the Queries group, click **Query Design**. Close the Show Table dialog box.

b. Click the **Query Tools Design tab**, and then click the **View arrow** in the Results group. Click **SQL View**. Notice that Access has already started writing the SELECT clause.

c. Delete the **SELECT**;, and then type the following into SQL view:

SELECT InvoiceNumber, InvoiceDate, AmountDue, CustomerID
FROM tblInvoice;

d. Click **Run**. Notice that there are 10 records included in your dataset.

SIDE NOTE
Using an Asterisk in a SQL Query
The asterisk selects and returns all fields in the table when you run the query.

Troubleshooting

If any **Syntax error** dialog boxes appear, check your spelling and make sure no spaces are in the field or table names.

e. Save your query as **qrySQL2_initialLastname**, and then close the query.

f. Click the **Create tab**, and then in the Queries group, click **Query Design**. Close the Show Table dialog box.

g. Click **SQL View**, and then type the following:

SELECT *
FROM tblInvoice;

h. Click **Run**. Notice that the same 10 records were included in the qrySQL2_initialLastname dataset.

i. Save your query as **qrySQL3_initialLastname**, and then close the query.

Using the WHERE Clause

The WHERE clause, which is optional in a SELECT statement, narrows the query results by specifying which rows in the table will be returned in the dataset. If the WHERE clause is omitted, all rows will be used.

To Create a Basic Query with the WHERE Clause in SQL View

a. Click the **Create tab**, and then in the Queries group, click **Query Design**. Close the Show Table dialog box.

b. Click **SQL View**, and then type the following:

SELECT *
FROM tblInvoice
WHERE InvoiceDate BETWEEN #1/15/2013# AND #1/17/2013#;

c. Click **Run**. Notice that there are three records included in your dataset.

d. Save your query as **qrySQLwhere1_initialLastname**, and then close the query.

e. Click the **Create tab**, and then in the Queries group, click **Query Design**. Close the Show Table dialog box.

f. Click **SQL View**, and then type the following into SQL view:

SELECT ServiceName, Description, Fee
FROM tblService
WHERE Fee >= 75;

g. Click **Run**. Notice that there are 13 records included in your dataset.

h. Save your query as **qrySQLwhere2_initialLastname**, and then close the query.

i. Click the **Create tab**, and then in the Queries group, click **Query Design**. Close the Show Table dialog box.

j. Click **SQL View**, and then type the following into SQL view:

SELECT *
FROM tblCustomer
WHERE CustState In ("UT","MN","HI","PA");

k. Click **Run**. Notice that there are eight records included in your dataset.

l. Save your query as **qrySQLwhere3_initialLastname**, and then close the query.

Quick Reference   **Operators Allowed in the WHERE Clause**

Operator	Description
=	Equal
<>	Not equal
>	Greater than
<	Less than
>=	Greater than or equal
<=	Less than or equal
BETWEEN…AND	Between an inclusive range
LIKE	Search for a pattern
IN	The exact value you want to return for at least one column
AND	All conditions must be true to return a value
OR	At least one condition must be true to return a value

Figure 14   Operators Used in the WHERE Clause

Real World Advice   **Design View vs. SQL View**

Everything you have learned how to do in Design view can also be done in SQL view. If you are not sure how to write the SQL statement for a particular query, you can create it in Design view and then switch to SQL view to see how Access generated the code. Even though Access adds some extra words to the SQL statement, it is still correct and will return the proper dataset. Additionally, when you make changes to the query in SQL view, Access modifies Design view to represent the updated SQL statement.

Using the HAVING Clause with AS and GROUP BY

If a field includes an aggregate function, you need to use a **HAVING clause**, which specifies the aggregated field criteria and restricts the results based on aggregated values—sum, average, and so forth. The HAVING clause is similar to the WHERE clause. However, the WHERE clause restricts the results based on individual row values. Another way of saying this is that the WHERE clause can eliminate records from the results before the aggregates are calculated. The HAVING clause eliminates entire groups of records from the results based on the aggregated calculations. Because the HAVING clause works on aggregated rows, it always uses an aggregate function as its test. In Access, you cannot use the HAVING clause in the Query design grid; thus, you must switch to SQL.

When writing a SQL SELECT statement that includes a HAVING clause, you must also include an AS clause and a GROUP BY statement. When you do not name a field in a query, regardless whether you are working in SQL view or Design view, Access names it for you with a name such as SumOfQuantity. Thus, the **AS clause** allows you to name or rename a field, which is displayed in the dataset. The GROUP BY clause is used in conjunction with the aggregate functions to group the dataset by one or more columns.

To Create a Query Using the HAVING Clause

a. Click the **Create tab**, and then in the Queries group, click **Query Design**. Close the Show Table dialog box.

b. If you put a criteria of >5 under the Sum([Quantity]) field in the Query design grid, Access will sum any quantity that is individually greater than 5. The HAVING clause will show records where the sum of the Quantity field is greater than 5. Click **SQL View**, and then type the following:

SELECT CustomerID, PurchaseDate, ProductID, Sum(Quantity) AS Total
FROM tblPurchase
GROUP BY CustomerID, PurchaseDate, ProductID
HAVING (Sum([Quantity]))>5;

c. Click **Run**. Notice that there are three clients who have purchased a total of five or more products from the spa.

d. Save your query as **qrySQLhaving1_initialLastname**, and then close the query.

e. Click the **Create tab**, and then in the Queries group, click **Query Design**. Close the Show Table dialog box.

f. Click **SQL View**, and then type the following:

SELECT InvoiceNumber, InvoiceDate, Sum([AmountDue]) AS Total, CustomerID
FROM tblInvoice
GROUP BY InvoiceNumber, InvoiceDate, CustomerID
HAVING Sum([AmountDue])<=25;

g. Click **Run**. Notice that there are three clients who have invoices that total $25 or less.

h. Save your query as **qrySQLhaving2_initialLastname**, and then close the query.

SIDE NOTE
You Cannot Use the New Field Name

Notice that you had to use Sum(AmountDue) and cannot use the renamed field Total from the AS clause.

SIDE NOTE
Why Was the Asterisk Not Used?

Even though you're selecting all the fields from the tblInvoice table, you cannot use an asterisk in a query in which you are using the GROUP BY clause.

Creating a Union Query

A **union query** is used to query unrelated tables or queries and combine the results into a single dataset. This type of query is different from querying related tables as it combines two SQL SELECT statements. The datasets must have a similar structure—the data types must match, but field names do not need to be the same and the columns in each SELECT statement must be in the same order.

For example, you have a Client table and Employee table in which you want to create a phone directory from both sets of data. If you were restricted to using the Query design grid, you would have to create two queries, one for each table, and then combine the results. A union query can examine both tables at the same time and present the results as a single dataset.

To Create a Union Query

a. Click the **Create tab**, and then in the Queries group, click **Query Design**. Close the Show Table dialog box.

b. To create a phone directory of all employees and customers, click the **Query Tools Design tab**, click **Union**, and then type the following:

SELECT CustFirstName, CustLastName, CustPhone
FROM tblCustomer
UNION
SELECT EmpFirstName, EmpLastName, EmpPhone
FROM tblEmployee;

c. Click **Run**. Notice that there are 39 records in the dataset; however, also notice that the field headings displayed are those from the first SELECT statement.

d. Save your query as **qryUnion_initialLastname**, and then close the query.

Creating a SQL Subquery

A SQL subquery is a separate SELECT statement that is nested inside the main SELECT statement. This type of query is an alternate way of returning data from multiple tables and will be performed once for each row of the resulting dataset. A subquery is usually added in the WHERE clause of the SQL SELECT statement. Most of the time, a subquery is used when you know how to search for a value using a SELECT statement but do not know the exact value.

For example, you may want to query your StoreSalesData table to find sales data for a specific district or region. However, if you do not know all the store numbers but know the district or region where the stores are located, you can write a subquery that will retrieve the information you desire.

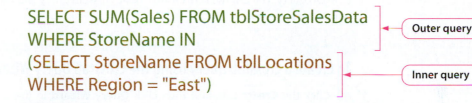

SELECT SUM(Sales) FROM tblStoreSalesData
WHERE StoreName IN — Outer query
(SELECT StoreName FROM tblLocations
WHERE Region = "East") — Inner query

Figure 15 Structure of a SQL Subquery

To Create a SQL Subquery

a. Click the **Create tab**, and then in the Queries group, click **Query Design**. Close the Show Table dialog box.

b. To create an e-mail list for all out-of-state customers, click **SQL View**, and then type the following:

SELECT CustomerID, CustFirstName, CustLastName, CustState, CustEmail
FROM tblCustomer
WHERE CustomerID NOT IN (SELECT CustomerID
FROM tblCustomer
WHERE CustState = 'MN');

c. Click **Run**. Notice that there are 22 records in the dataset.

d. Save your query as **qrySubquery_initialLastname**, and then close the query.

Creating a Crosstab Query

A **crosstab query** is different than the aggregate functions that you have been completing thus far because it groups the aggregates by the column and row headings. The added value in decision making is that crosstab queries are useful for summarizing data, calculating statistics, identifying bad data, and looking for trends. Additionally, they can be a useful way to present data in a compact and summarized format.

A crosstab query is a special type of query that can be created when you want to describe one number in terms of two other numbers. For example, suppose you wanted to know how much money was made from each service at the spa each month? This would require the construction of a crosstab query to display the information. A crosstab query uses aggregate functions and then groups the results by two sets of values—one down the side of the datasheet as rows and the other across the top as columns—and transforms rows of data to columns.

When you create a crosstab query, you specify which fields will be used as the row headings, which field's values will be used as the column headings, and which fields contain values to summarize. Only one field can be used when you specify the column heading and value to summarize. However, up to three fields can be used as row headings. Furthermore, expressions can be used to create row headings, column headings, or values to summarize. In this section, you will create and edit a crosstab query.

Crosstab Query Wizard

As with other wizards in Access, the **Crosstab Query Wizard** is the easiest way to create a crosstab query. While the wizard does help automate the creation process, there are some things that the wizard cannot do for you. Even though the wizard may not be able to create the perfect crosstab query, you can use it to create a basic crosstab query and then modify the query's design within Design view.

To Create a Crosstab Query Using the Crosstab Query Wizard

a. Click the **Create tab**, and then click **Query Wizard** in the Queries group to create a new query.

b. In the New Query dialog box, click **Crosstab Query Wizard**, and then click **OK**.

c. Click the **tblSchedule** table, which will be used to create a crosstab query, and then click **Next**.

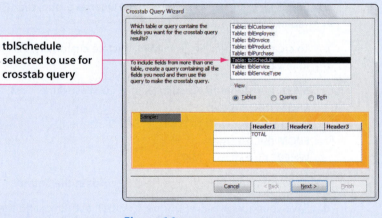

Figure 16 Crosstab Query Wizard

d. Double-click the **Employee** field, which will be used as the row heading in the crosstab query, and then click **Next**.

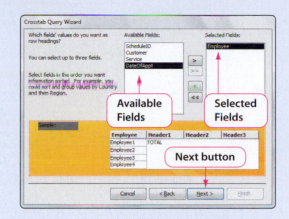

Figure 17 Crosstab Query Wizard with selected fields

e. Click the **DateOfAppt** field, which will be used as the column headings in the crosstab query, and then click **Next**.

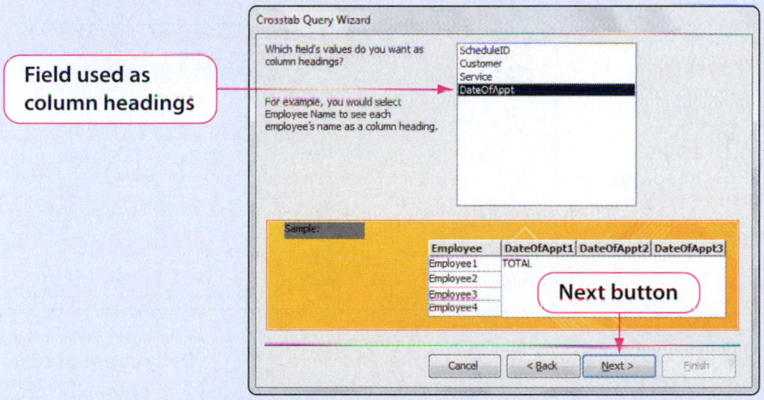

Figure 18 Crosstab Query Wizard with column heading selected

f. Click **Date** as the interval, and then click **Next**.

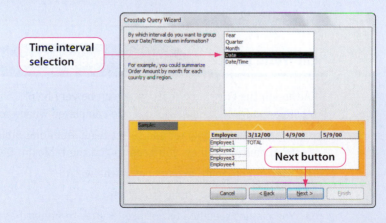

Figure 19 Crosstab Query Wizard with interval selected

g. Click **Customer** under Fields and **Count** under Functions to view how many customers each employee has on a given day, and then click **Next**.

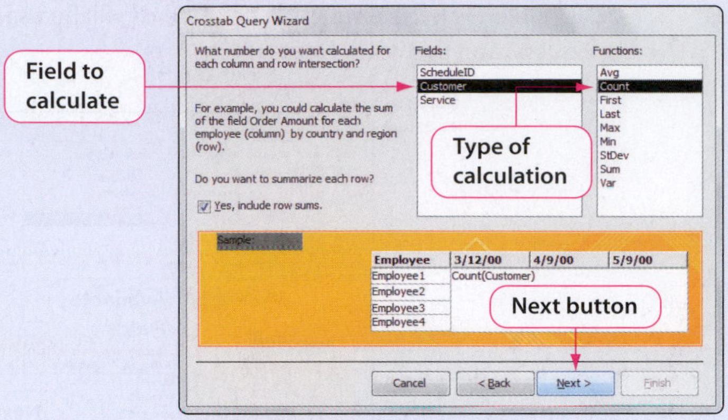

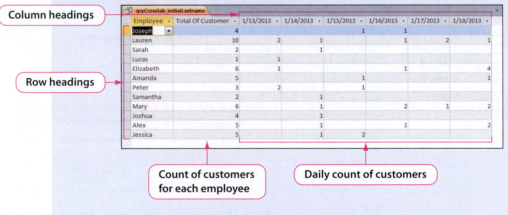

Figure 20 Crosstab Query Wizard with calculation type selected

h. Name your query **qryCrosstab_initialLastname**.

i. Click **Finish**. Resize your fields if you cannot see all the data or column headings. Notice that each employee is listed along with the total customers and a count of how many appointments each employee has per day. Empty fields indicate the employee does not have any appointments on the given day.

Employee	Total Of Customer	1/13/2013	1/14/2013	1/15/2013	1/16/2013	1/17/2013	1/18/2013
Joseph	4			1	1		
Lauren	10	2	1		1	2	1
Sarah	2		1				
Lucas	1	1					
Elizabeth	6	1			1		4
Amanda	5			1			1
Peter	3	2		1			
Samantha	2		1				
Mary	6		1		2	1	2
Joshua	4		1				
Alex	5		1		1		2
Jessica	5		1	2			

Figure 21 Datasheet view of Crosstab Query Wizard

j. Save any changes, and then close qryCrosstab_initialLastname.

Real World Advice — What the Crosstab Query Wizard Cannot Do

Although the Crosstab Query Wizard can be very helpful in creating crosstab queries, there are a few things that cannot be completed when progressing through the wizard.

1. The wizard will only let you select fields from one table. If you want to use fields from multiple tables, you need to add the tables in Design view.
2. You cannot create expressions in the wizard.
3. You cannot add a parameter prompt.
4. You cannot specify a list of fixed values to be used as column headings.

Although these tasks cannot be completed within the wizard, any of these tasks can be added to the Query design grid by simply going into Design view.

Editing a Crosstab Query

When you work in Design view, you have more control over your query design, which enables features to be added that are not available in the wizard. When you edit a crosstab query in Design view, you use the Total and Crosstab rows in the design grid to specify three criteria:

- Which field value becomes the column heading
- Which field values become row headings
- Which field's value to calculate

To Edit a Crosstab Query

a. Open the **qryCrosstab_initialLastname** query, and save it as a query named qryCrosstabEdit_initialLastname.

b. Click the Home tab if necessary and switch to **Design view**, and then resize your fields if you cannot see all the fields you selected.

c. Edit the query so the manager can enter a specific employee number and view how many appointments are scheduled for that week. In the Criteria row of the Employee field, type [Enter Employee Number].

d. On the Design tab, in the Show/Hide group, click **Parameters**.

e. In the Query Parameters dialog box, in the Parameter column, enter the same parameter that you used in the Criteria row:

[Enter Employee Number]

f. Click **Integer** in the Data Type column.

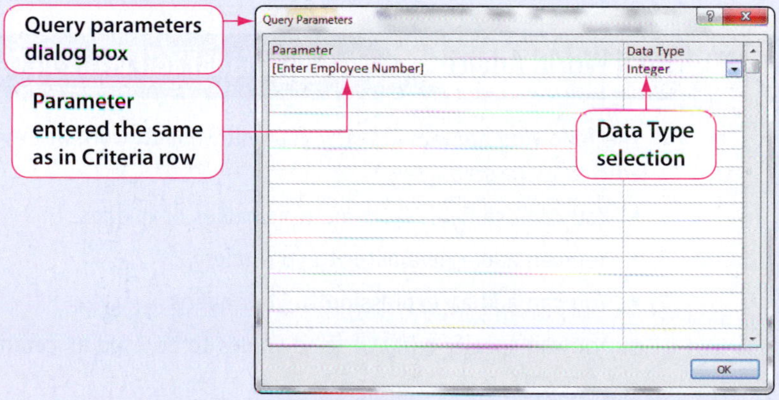

> Query parameters dialog box
>
> Parameter entered the same as in Criteria row
>
> Data Type selection

Figure 22 Query Parameters dialog box

g. Click **OK**, and then click **Run**. Test your query by entering 2 when the Parameter prompt appears.

h. Click **OK**. Notice how you can only see Joseph's appointments for the week.

Results display Joseph's appointments

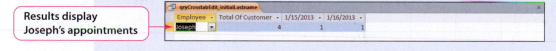

Figure 23 Datasheet view of qryCrosstabEdit_initialLastname query

i. Return to **Design view**, and then edit the query so the manager can enter a specific employee number or a specific date. In the Or area under the Format([DateOfAppt], "Short Date") field, enter [Enter Date].

j. On the Design tab, in the Show/Hide group, click **Parameters**.

k. In the Query Parameters dialog box, in the Parameters column, under the previous Parameter entry, enter the same parameter prompt that you used in the Criteria row: [Enter Date].

l. Click **Date/Time** in the Data Type column, and then click **OK**.

m. To view a specific employee's appointments or all employees' appointments, click **Run**.

n. When the [Enter Employee Number] Parameter prompt appears do not enter anything, and then click **OK**.

o. When the [Enter Date] Parameter prompt appears, type 01/18/2013, and then click **OK**. Notice how you can see all employees' appointments for 1/18/2013.

Troubleshooting

If you do not use the leading zero in the month, no data will be displayed in your dataset.

p. Save your changes, and then close qryCrosstabEdit_initialLastname. If Access prompts you to enter parameters as you are saving your changes, click **OK** twice.

SIDE NOTE
Only a Week of Appointments Appears
Remember that the spa manager only gave you a portion of the data. If you had the full database, you would see every date, which could extend over months or years.

Real World Advice   When Should You Work in Design View?

The following are reasons why you will want to work in Design view when creating or editing a crosstab query.

- You can use fields from multiple tables or queries.
- You can add a parameter to your query.
- You can add an expression to your query.
- You can specify a list of fixed values to be used as column headings.

Concept Check

1. Give two business examples outside of this workshop of when you could use the volume—either physical or sales—calculation.

2. Give two business examples outside of this workshop of when you could use the sales revenue calculation.

3. Explain how an aggregate function differs from a calculated field.

4. What is the difference between using the WHERE clause and the HAVING clause?

5. When could a crosstab query be more beneficial or helpful to use instead of a SELECT or standard aggregated query?

Key Terms

Aggregate 339
Aggregated calculation 339
AS clause 349
Crosstab query 351
Crosstab Query Wizard 352
Fiscal year 336
Group By clause 332

HAVING clause 349
Net revenue 336
Percentage of physical volume 345
Percentage of sales revenue 339
Percentage of sales volume 341
Physical volume 339
Revenue 336

Sales volume 332
SELECT statement 346
Structured Query Language (SQL) 345
Underlying SQL statement 347
Union query 350
Where clause 335

Visual Summary

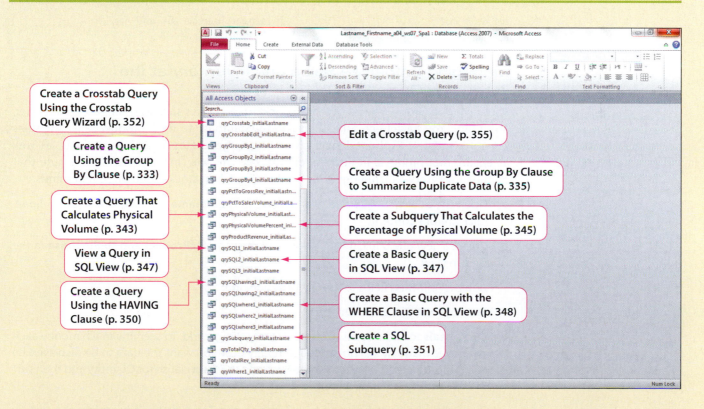

Create a Crosstab Query Using the Crosstab Query Wizard (p. 352)

Create a Query Using the Group By Clause (p. 333)

Create a Query That Calculates Physical Volume (p. 343)

View a Query in SQL View (p. 347)

Create a Query Using the HAVING Clause (p. 350)

Edit a Crosstab Query (p. 355)

Create a Query Using the Group By Clause to Summarize Duplicate Data (p. 335)

Create a Subquery That Calculates the Percentage of Physical Volume (p. 345)

Create a Basic Query in SQL View (p. 347)

Create a Basic Query with the WHERE Clause in SQL View (p. 348)

Create a SQL Subquery (p. 351)

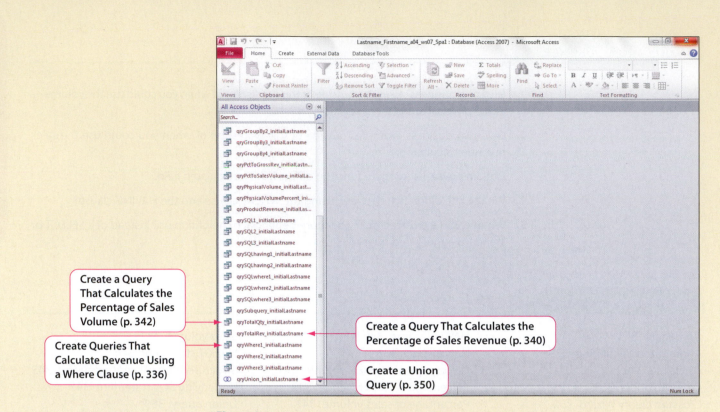

Create a Query That Calculates the Percentage of Sales Volume (p. 342)

Create Queries That Calculate Revenue Using a Where Clause (p. 336)

Create a Query That Calculates the Percentage of Sales Revenue (p. 340)

Create a Union Query (p. 350)

Figure 24   The Turquoise Oasis Spa final database

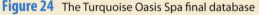

Practice 1

Student data file needed:

a04_ws07_Spa2

You will save your file as:

Lastname_Firstname_a04_ws07_Spa2

Managing Employee Sales and Inventory at the Turquoise Oasis Spa

The Turquoise Oasis Spa uses Access to track product sales such as shampoo, conditioner, and soaps. You have been asked to query the database to track product sales, the sales revenue, and sales volume that each employee generates in selling products, as well as ensure that products fit into shipping boxes. This way, management can ensure that enough inventory—including boxes for shipping—is in stock based on selling trends.

a. Open the **a04_ws07_Spa2** database. Save it as Lastname_Firstname_a04_ws07_Spa2. Click **Enable Content**.

b. Create a new query in **Query Design**, and then add **tblProduct** and **tblPurchase** to the Design view.

c. Add the following fields to the Query design grid:

   EmployeeID, **Price**, and **Quantity**

d. Click **Totals** to add a Totals row to the Query design grid. To see how much money each employee made by selling products, modify how you want the data to be displayed by using the **Expression** option for the Price and the **Sum** clause for Quantity and then sort in **Descending** order by **Price**.

e. Right-click the **Price** field and click **Zoom**. In the Zoom dialog box replace the text by typing SalesRevenue: Sum([Price]*[Quantity]) and click **OK**. Rename the Quantity field by typing SalesVolume: in front of the field name **Quantity**.

f. Click **Run**. Click **Totals** on the Home tab to sum your SalesRevenue field to ensure it totals $918.85, and then sum your SalesVolume field to ensure it totals 63.

g. Save your query as **qrySalesRevVol_initialLastname**, and then close the query.

h. Click the **Create tab**, and then click **Query Design**, in the Queries group. Add **qrySalesRevVol_ initialLastname** and **qryGrossRevenueSalesVolume** to the Design view.

i. Add the following fields to the Query design grid:

EmployeeID, **SalesRevenue**, and **SalesVolume**

j. In the first blank field in the Query design grid, create an expression that calculates how each employee's sales revenue contributed to the total gross sales revenue. Enter the following expression, and then format the PercentToGrossSalesRevenue field as **Percent**:

PercentToGrossSalesRevenue:[SalesRevenue]/[GrossSalesRevenue]

k. In the first blank field in the Query design grid, create an expression that calculates how each employee's sales volume contributed to the total gross sales volume. Enter the following expression, and then format the PercentToGrossSalesVolume field as **Percent**:

PercentToGrossSalesVolume:[SalesVolume]/[GrossSalesVolume]

l. Click **Run**. Click the **Home tab** and then click **Totals** to average your SalesRevenue and SalesVolume fields. This will determine if employees are selling at, above, or below average. Sum your PercentToGrossSalesRevenue and PercentToGrossSalesVolume fields to ensure they total 100%.

EmployeeID	SalesRevenue	SalesVolume	PercentToGrossSalesReve	PercentToGrossSalesVolume
Paul	$57.50	3	6.26%	4.76%
Dixon	$328.15	23	35.71%	36.51%
Evans	$10.00	1	1.09%	1.59%
Fisher	$50.45	5	5.49%	7.94%
Gill	$22.50	1	2.45%	1.59%
Heath	$62.40	3	6.79%	4.76%
Johnson	$8.50	1	0.93%	1.59%
Klein	$47.95	1	5.22%	1.59%
McIntosh	$66.95	7	7.29%	11.11%
Murphy	$43.50	5	4.73%	7.94%
Ripley	$109.40	5	11.91%	7.94%
Rodriguez	$67.10	4	7.30%	6.35%
Weaver	$12.95	1	1.41%	1.59%
Welch	$31.50	3	3.43%	4.76%
Total	$65.63	4.5	100.00%	100.00%

Figure 25 Datasheet view of qryRevenueAnalysis_initialLastname query

m. Save your query as **qryRevenueAnalysis_initialLastname**, and then close the query.

n. Click the **Create tab**, and then click **Query Design** in the Queries group. Add **tblProduct** to the Design view.

o. Add the following field to the Query design grid:

ProductDescription

p. Determine the physical volume by calculating length*width*depth. In the first blank field in the Query design grid, type the following into the Zoom dialog box:

PhysicalVolume:[Width]*[Length]*[Depth]

q. The medium-sized carton that the spa has to ship items to customers is 526 cubic inches and you will calculate the remaining package volume. In the next blank field in the Query design grid, type the following into the Zoom dialog box:

RemainingPkgVolume:526-[PhysicalVolume]

r. Calculate the total volume by item that can fit into the spa's medium-sized carton. In the next blank field in the Query design grid, type the following into the Zoom dialog box:

TotalPkgVolume:Int(526/[PhysicalVolume])

s. To calculate the percentage of physical volume, use the size of a medium-sized carton that the spa has to ship items to customers—526 cubic inches. In the next blank field in the Query design grid, type the following into the Zoom dialog box, and then format the PercentOfPhysicalVolume field as percent with 1 decimal place:

PercentOfPhysicalVolume:[PhysicalVolume]/526

t. Click **Run**. Save your query as qryVolumePercent_initialLastname, and then close the query.

u. Click the **Create tab**, and in the Queries group, click **Query Wizard**. Create a Crosstab query using the wizard that will use the **tblPurchase** table and click **Next**, and then double-click the **ProductID** field as the row heading and click **Next**.

v. Click the **EmployeeID** field as the column heading and click **Next**.

w. Click **Quantity** under Fields and **Sum** under Functions to view the products each employee has sold and click **Next**. Save your query as qryCrosstab_initialLastname, and then click **Finish**.

x. Switch to **Design view**. Add the **tblEmployee** table to the Design view, and then change the Field Criteria in the Column Heading for EmployeeID to **EmpFirstName**.

y. Click **Run**. Save your changes, and then close qryCrosstab_initialLastname.

z. Close Lastname_Firstname_a04_ws07_Spa2.

Practice 2

Student data file needed:

a04_ws07_Spa3

You will save your file as:

Lastname_Firstname_a04_ws07_Spa3

Managing Salon Services at the Turquoise Oasis Spa

The Turquoise Oasis Spa uses Access to track how many customers each employee services and how much revenue each employee makes for the spa. This database is also used to track the types of services that clients choose. You have been asked to query the database to track services—both revenue and client preferences. By reviewing the data, management can ensure that the spa services offered are generating enough revenue to continue being offered to clients.

a. Open the **a04_ws07_Spa3** database. Save it as Lastname_Firstname_a04_ws07_Spa3. Click **Enable Content**.

b. Create a new query that will show the client appointments for January 19, 2013. Type the following in SQL view, and then click **Run**:

SELECT *
FROM tblSchedule
WHERE DateOfAppt Like #1/19/2013#;

c. Save your query as qryJanuary19_initialLastname, and then close the query.

d. Create a new query that will show all services that are priced between $25 and $50. Type the following in SQL view, and then click **Run**:

SELECT ServiceName, Description, LengthOfService, Fee

FROM tblService

WHERE Fee BETWEEN 25 AND 50;

e. Save your query as qrySvcs2550_initialLastname, and then close the query.

f. Create a new query that will show a count of clients for each employee. Type the following in SQL view, and then click **Run**:

SELECT Employee, COUNT(DateOfAppt) AS TotalAppts

FROM tblSchedule

GROUP BY Employee;

g. Save your query as qryTotalAppts_initialLastname, and then close the query.

h. Create a new query that will show which services have only been given once. Management may want to consider discontinuing these services. Type the following in SQL view, and then click **Run**:

SELECT Service, COUNT(Service) AS Count

FROM tblSchedule

GROUP BY Service

HAVING (COUNT([Service]))=1;

i. Save your query as qryCount1_initialLastname, and then close the query.

j. Create a union query that will show all contact information for both employees and customers. Type the following in SQL view, and then click **Run**:

SELECT FirstName, LastName, Address, City, State, Phone, Email

FROM tblCustomer

UNION

SELECT FirstName, LastName, Address, City, State, Phone, Email

FROM tblEmployee;

k. Save your query as qryDirectory_initialLastname, and then close the query.

l. Create a subquery that will list all services names that are not in the category of "facial". Type the following in SQL view, and then click **Run**:

SELECT ServiceName, Fee, Type

FROM tblService

WHERE ServiceName IN (SELECT ServiceName

FROM tblService

WHERE Type <> 'Facial');

m. Save your query as qrySubquery_initialLastname, and then close the query.

n. Click the **Create tab**, click **Query Wizard** to use the wizard, click **Crosstab Query Wizard** in the New Query dialog box and click **OK**. Under View, click the **Queries** option, click **qryEmpSvcs_initialLastname** query and click **Next**, and then double-click the **ServiceName** field, which will be used as the row heading. Click **Next**.

o. Click the **FirstName** field, which will be used as the column heading. Click **Next**.

p. Click **Fee** under Fields and **Sum** under Functions to view the total revenue generated by each employee for each service. Click **Next**.

q. Name your query as **qryEmpSvcsCrosstab_initialLastname**, and then click **Finish**.

r. Switch to **Design view**.

s. Edit the query so the manager can enter a specific service and view how much revenue was generated for the service and by which employees. Add **ServiceName** to the Query design grid. Change Group By to **Where** in the Total row. In the Criteria row of the ServiceName field, type [Enter Service Name].

t. On the Query Tools Design tab, click **Parameters**. In the Query Parameters dialog box, enter the same parameter that you used in the Criteria row:

Parameters	Data Type
[Enter Service Name]	Text

u. Click **OK**, click **Run**, and then test your query by entering Back Treatment and Massage in the parameter prompt.

Results display Back Treatment and Massage data

Figure 26 Datasheet view of qryEmpSvcsCrosstab_initialLastname query

v. Close qryEmpSvcsCrosstab_initialLastname and save changes, and then close Lastname_Firstname_a04_ws07_Spa3.

WORKSHOP 8

Objectives

1. Create, test, and run make table queries. p. 364

2. Create, test, and run append queries. p. 368

3. Edit and delete data in tables. p. 370

4. Create, test and run update queries. p. 371

5. Create, test, and run delete queries. p. 376

6. Create inner joins. p. 380

7. Create outer joins. p. 381

8. Use the Find Unmatched Query Wizard. p. 383

Creating Action Queries and Advanced Relationships

PREPARE CASE

The Turquoise Oasis Spa: Understanding Action Queries

The Turquoise Oasis Spa generates revenue through its spa services and product sales. The spa needs updated information in order to run its business efficiently and make decisions about the business. The spa manager, Meda Rodate, and salon manager, Irene Kai, have asked you to automate the creation of tables and data updates through the use of action queries. This will make data management easier and more efficient for spa employees. Additionally, the managers will be able to track marketing campaigns such as viewing the customers that have redeemed coupons and discounts.

Courtesy of www.Shutterstock.com

Student data files needed for this workshop:

 a04_ws08_Spa1

 a04_ws08_Spa2

 a04_ws08_Spa3

 a04_ws08_Marketing1

 a04_ws08_Marketing2

You will save your files as:

 Lastname_Firstname_a04_ws08_Spa1

Lastname_Firstname_a04_ws08_Spa2

Lastname_Firstname_a04_ws08_Spa3

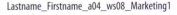 Lastname_Firstname_a04_ws08_Marketing1

Lastname_Firstname_a04_ws08_Marketing2

Understanding Action Queries

Thus far you have been creating select queries. Select queries are used to display data but not change the data. An **action query** is a query that makes changes to records or moves many records from one table to another. Action queries are used to change the data in existing tables or make new tables based on a query's dataset. Access offers four different types of action queries:

- A make table query creates a new table based on a query dataset.
- An append query is similar to a make table query, except that a query dataset is appended—added—to an existing table.
- An update query allows the values of one or more fields in a query dataset to be modified.
- A delete query deletes all the records in the underlying table of a query dataset that meet specific criteria.

One important note is that action queries permanently modify the data in tables. Because there is no undo feature for action queries, it is important to be cautious when running any action query. It is a good idea to create a backup of the database in case you need to restore any of the changed data. In this section, you will create and run new table queries, delete queries, and append queries.

Real World Advice — Turning Off the Action Query Warning

When you run an action query, Access will always warn you that you are about to make a change to your data as well as ask you to confirm the change. You can turn the Access warnings off. However, there are dangers to doing so because you will not know for sure if the action query executed. For example, if you are running an update query to update employee salaries by $500, every time you run the query, you will add $500 on to each employee's salary. If you turn off the warning, before you know it, you can increase each employee's salary by $2,500. Of course, employees would not complain, but this can cause tremendous problems for the payroll department and the company's budget. To avoid being prompted when you run such queries, do the following:

- Click the File tab.
- Click Options.
- In the Access Options dialog box, click Client Settings.
- Under Editing, under Confirm, clear the Action queries check box.

Creating a New Table

When you create a database, you store your data in tables—objects that contain records and fields. For example, you can create a customer table to store a list of customers' first and last names, addresses, and telephone numbers, or an inventory table to store information about the products your company sells. Because other database objects—queries, forms, reports—depend on tables, you should design your database by creating all of its tables first. You have learned that the manual process of creating tables can take some time if you want to create a database that is constructed properly and functions well.

There are times, however, that you will decide to store and track different data than what the database was initially designed to do. Thus, you may use existing data to add a new table that will allow you to make better decisions about your business. The process of creating a new table can be automated through a make table query. For example, your database may have been initially built to track customers and the orders they placed. Now you may want also to track marketing efforts and the number of customers who use coupons that were mailed or e-mailed to them. You would need to create a new table to track which customers redeemed coupons and when they were redeemed.

Creating a Make Table Query

A **make table query** acquires data from one or more tables, and then automatically loads the resulting dataset into a new table once you run the query. The new table can be added to the current database that you have open to build the new table. You can create a make table query by first creating a select query and then changing it to a make table query. Your initial select query can include calculated fields and expressions to return the desired data along with verifying your results before running the query.

You can also create the make table query in one database and then have Access build the table in another database. This allows you to use data in one database—the one in which the make table query resides—and copy that data into a new table within another database. For example, you may decide at some point, perhaps once you have a few years' worth of data, that you want to archive some of the older data into another database.

Archiving data is an important task in business. Managers do not want to delete historical data because it can be used to help manage and develop their business. A major use of historical data is for **forecasting**—to predict or estimate future sales trends, budget, and so forth. Archiving data from the company's **operational database**—the database used to carry out regular operations, such as payroll and inventory management, of an organization—or **transactional database**—the database used to record daily transactions—into another database, one that is used for storing older data, is a concept known as **data warehousing**. A **data warehouse** contains a large amount of different types of data that present a clear picture of your business environment at a specific point in time.

Data warehousing is a technology used to establish business intelligence. **Business intelligence (BI)** helps an organization attain their goals and objectives by giving them a better understanding of past performance as well as information on how the organization is progressing toward its goals. **Business intelligence tools** are a classification of software applications that aide in collecting, storing, analyzing, and providing access to data that helps managers make improved business decisions.

One way BI tools are used is for **data mining**, which helps expose trends, patterns, and relationships within the data that might have otherwise remained undetected. For example, the queries that you have been creating in Access are searching for data that you know exists. You have created queries to find customers who live in specific cities and states as well as queries that help calculate employee raises, just to name a few. With data mining, you are searching, or mining the data within the data warehouse, for unknown trends. The salon manager could mine archived data in the data warehouse to see what two products are most likely to sell together or what two services are most likely to be given to one customer.

Think about how this can help a manager make decisions. What about forecasting? The spa manager could learn a lot about the business and use this information to help increase sales. If the manager knows that two items are most likely to sell together in one transaction, he could ensure he has equal amounts of inventory in stock. He can also train his employees to use a **suggestive sell**—a sales technique used to add more revenue to a sale by suggesting another product to the customer's purchase.

Running a Make Table Query

Once your make table query is ready, the table is created once you click the Run button on the Query Tools Design tab as shown in Figure 1. The challenge with clicking Run is that you cannot see what Access is going to do nor can you verify that the data will be displayed how you want it to look. For example, you may be creating a make table query that includes calculated fields and expressions. You probably would want to view the query dataset before actually creating a table. The way around this is to switch from Design view to Datasheet view. This enables you to preview the data that will be added to the new table before actually creating it.

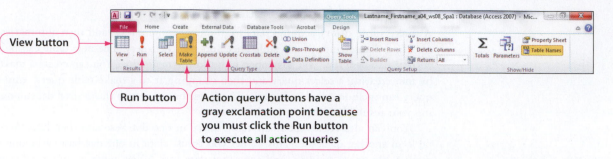

Figure 1 The different action query buttons

Real World Advice — Archiving Data

There are times when you need to copy or archive data, and you will want to make a table from data within your database. For example, you may have a table of past sales data that is used in reports. The sales figures will not change because the transactions have occurred in the past. Continually running a query to retrieve the data can take time, especially if you run a complex query against a large amount of data. Loading the historical data into a separate table and using that table as a data source can reduce time and provide a convenient data archive. Remember, however, that the data in your new table is just a snapshot—an image—of the data at a specific time. It has no relationship or link to other tables in the database.

To Create and Run a Make Table Query

a. Click the **Start** button, and then select **Access 2010**.

b. Click the **File tab**, click **Open**, locate and select **a04_ws08_Spa1**, and then click **Open**.

c. Click the **File tab**, and then click **Save Database As**. Browse to where you are storing your student files. In the File name box, type **Lastname_Firstname_a04_ws08_Spa1**, replacing Lastname_Firstname with your actual name and click **Save**. This will be the database in which you make a new table.

d. Click **Enable Content** in the Security Warning.

e. Click the **File tab**, click **Close Database**.

f. Click the **File tab** if necessary, click **Open**, locate and select **a04_ws08_Marketing1**, and then click **Open**.

g. Click the **File tab**, and then click **Save Database As**. Navigate to where you are storing your student files. In the File name box, type **Lastname_Firstname_a04_ws08_Marketing1**, replacing Lastname_Firstname with your actual name.

h. Click **Enable Content** in the Security Warning.

i. You need to create a query that will create a new table in the Lastname_Firstname_a04_ws08_Spa1 database. Create a new query in **Query Design view**, and then add **tblCampaign** and **tblMailing** to Design view.

j. Add the following fields to the Query design grid:

MailingID, **CustomerID**, and **Redeemed** from the tblMailing table, and then add **CampaignName**, **CampaignType**, **StartDate**, **EndDate**, **DiscountCode**, **Department**, and **Details** from the tblCampaign table.

k. In the Criteria property of the Department field, type Like "Turquoise Oasis Spa", and then clear the Show check box.

l. Click **Datasheet view**. Notice that you can see the nine fields and 52 records that will be added to your new table. Return to **Design view**.

m. Click the **Query Tools Design tab**, and then click **Make Table** to change the query type to make table query.

n. When the Make Table dialog box opens, type **tblCampaign** in the Table Name box to name your new table, click **Another Database**, click **Browse**, and then browse to select the **Lastname_Firstname_a04_ws08_Spa1** database and click **OK** two times.

Figure 2 Make Table dialog box

o. Return to **Design view**, and then click **Run**. Click **Yes** when Access asks you to confirm that you want to paste 52 rows into a new table.

p. Save your query as **qryMakeTable_initialLastname**, and then close the query.

q. Open the **Lastname_Firstname_a04_ws08_Spa1** database, and then open the **tblCampaign** table. Notice how all 52 records were exported from the Lastname_Firstname_a04_ws08_Marketing1 database, but all the formatting—such as a check box for the Redeemed field—was not copied.

r. Switch to **Design view**, and then make the following changes to the Field Properties and Descriptions:

Field	Field Properties	Description
MailingID	Change this field to the primary key Change the format to "MID"0	The Mailing ID (primary key)
CustomerID	Change the caption to Customer	The Customer ID (foreign key)
Redeemed	Change the lookup control to a check box	Was the coupon redeemed?
CampaignName	Change the caption to Campaign Name	The campaign name
CampaignType	Change the caption to Campaign Type	The campaign type
StartDate	Change the caption to Start Date	The campaign start date
EndDate	Change the caption to End Date	The campaign end date
DiscountCode	Change the caption to Discount Code	The POS discount code
Details		The details of the campaign

Figure 3

SIDE NOTE
Verifying That the Action Query Worked Correctly
The only way to verify that an action query worked correctly is to look in the table to see that the proper action occurred. In this case, the table was created with the correct data.

CONSIDER THIS | **Why Not Just Create the New Table from Scratch?**

You did have to do some editing after running your make table query, and this is normal. However, you did not have to create the fields, select the field types, and enter the data. Some minor editing took a few minutes. Additionally, you still would have had to create the relationship, whether you built the table from scratch or created it from a make table query. How long would it have taken you if you created it from scratch? What if the table had two or three times as many fields? Could you have created it faster from scratch?

Adding Data to a Table

You can use an append query when you need to add new records to an existing table by using data from other sources such as an Excel workbook, a Word document, a text file, or another database. An **append query** selects records from one or more data sources and copies the selected records to an existing table.

Creating an Append Query

Suppose that you have access to another database that contains a table of potential customers. However, you already have a table in your existing database that stores this type of data. Thus, you decide to import it from the other database. To avoid having to import it into a new table and then manually enter the data into your existing table, you can use an append query to copy the records into your existing table. For example, the Painted Paradise Resort and Spa's marketing department regularly updates their database with new marketing campaigns, customers, and redemption status of discounts. If the spa manager wants to ensure he has current data for decision making, he needs to regularly add new records to the table that is storing the marketing data in the spa database. An append query could help the spa's manager easily and regularly add new records to the existing table.

Real World Advice — Benefits of Using an Append Query

1. You can append—add—multiple records to a table at one time. If you copy data manually, you usually have to do it multiple times. By using an append query, you eliminate the copy-and-paste process, which can ensure that no mistakes are made and all records are appended.

2. You can review the data that will be appended before you run the query. You can view your selection in Datasheet view and modify the data as needed before you append any data. This can be helpful if your query includes criteria or expressions.

3. You can use criteria to refine your selection. For example, you might want to only append customers who live within a certain state.

4. You can append records when some of the data source fields do not exist in the destination table. For example, suppose that your existing customer table has 11 fields, and the external prospective customers table only has 10 of the 11 fields. You can still use an append query to copy and add the data from the 10 fields that match.

Running an Append Query

The data is not appended to your table until you click the Run button on the Query Tools Design tab. Before you append the records, you can switch to Datasheet view for a preview of the records. If you need to modify your dataset, you can switch back to Design view and make the needed changes. This can be done as many times as needed before running the query. It is important to emphasize that you cannot undo an append query. If you make a mistake, you must either restore your database from a backup or correct your error, either manually or by using a delete query. Therefore, you should back up your database or the destination table before running an append query.

To Create and Run an Append Query

a. Click the **File tab**, click **Open** to browse to your student data files, locate and select **a04_ws08_Marketing2**, and then click **Open**.

b. Click the **File tab**, and then click **Save Database As**. Navigate to your student files and in the File name box, type **Lastname_Firstname_a04_ws08_Marketing2**, replacing Lastname_Firstname with your actual name.

c. Click **Enable Content** in the Security Warning.

d. The marketing department has added the spring promotions for the Turquoise Oasis Spa, and you need to append the new data to the tblCampaign table in the Lastname_Firstname_a04_ws08_Spa1 database. Create a new query in **Query Design view**, and then add **tblCampaign** and **tblMailing** to Design view.

e. Add the following fields to the Query design grid:

   MailingID, **CustomerID**, and **Redeemed** from the tblMailing table, and then add **CampaignName**, **CampaignType**, **StartDate**, **EndDate**, **DiscountCode**, **Department**, and **Details** from the tblCampaign table.

f. In the Criteria property of the Department field, type **Like "Turquoise Oasis Spa"**, and then clear the Show check box.

g. In the Criteria property of the StartDate field, type **Like #4/1/2013#**.

SIDE NOTE
To Use or Not Use "Like"
Sometimes Access allows users to enter criteria multiple ways. If you do not include "Like", the query will still return the correct dataset.

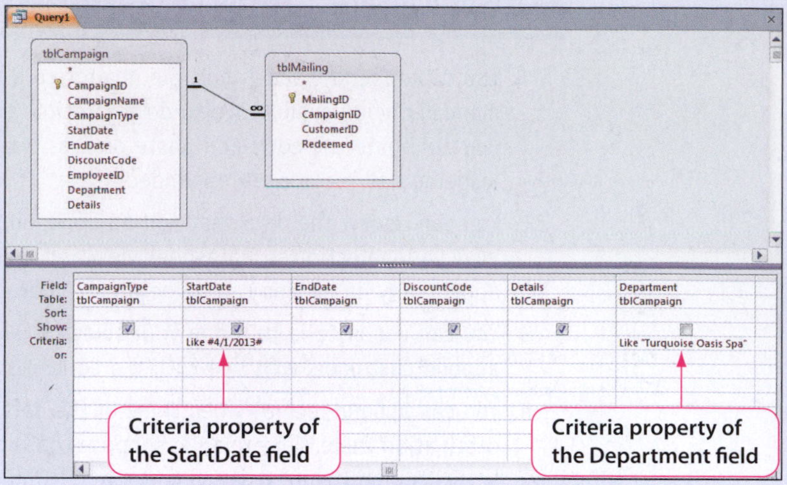

Figure 4 Design view of append query

h. Click **Append** on the Query Tools Design tab to change the query type to an append query.

i. When the Append dialog box opens, append the data to the **tblCampaign** table, click **Another Database**, and then browse and select the **Lastname_Firstname_a04_ws08_Spa1** database. Click **OK** two times.

j. Switch to **Datasheet view** to preview the data that will be included in your table. You should have 78 records that will be appended automatically into your table.

k. Return to **Design view**, and then click **Run**. Click **Yes** when Access asks you to confirm that you want to append 78 rows.

l. Save your query as **qryAppendData_initialLastname**, and then close your query.

m. Open the **Lastname_Firstname_a04_ws08_Spa1** database, and then open the **tblCampaign** table. Notice how all 78 records were exported from the Lastname_Firstname_a04_ws08_Marketing2 database, along with the formatting, and you now have 130 records in your tblCampaign table.

n. Close the tblCampaign table, and then close the Lastname_Firstname_a04_ws08_Marketing2 database.

Editing and Deleting Data

Because many databases contain a tremendous amount of data, it would be extremely time consuming to manually update data record by record. For example, many new area codes have been created in the United States over the past few years. It would take too much time to have an employee look through each customer's data and modify the area code as needed. This is when an update query can be helpful. An **update query** can be used to add, change, or delete data in one or more existing records. Update queries are similar to the Find and Replace dialog box, but much more powerful.

You also have the option of using a delete query depending on the type of deletion you need to perform. A **delete query** is used to remove entire records from a table at one time. Delete queries remove all the data in each field, including the primary key. When you need to delete old records from your database, you could search through the table and delete each individual record, which could take some time, or you could use a delete query to delete them all at once. A delete query cannot be used to delete an actual table from the database, but it can be used to delete all of the data from within a table.

Running update and delete queries are different than using the Cascade Update and Cascade Delete Related Records property in the Relationships window. When you set the Cascade Update Related Records property, Access updates the primary key in all related tables if it changes on the one side of the relationship. When you set the Cascade Delete Related Records property, Access deletes the related records in all related tables if the key field is deleted on the one side of the relationship. If you want to delete data from several related tables, you must enable the Enforce Referential Integrity and Cascade Delete Related Records properties for each relationship. This allows your query to delete data from the tables on the one *and* many sides of the relationship.

Be careful that you fully understand what Cascade Update and Cascade Delete do before using them. A vast amount of data can be updated or deleted at once and unintentionally if you are not careful. For example, if you delete an employee by accident—because you should not *ever* do this—then it would wipe out every transaction the employee was associated with. This is why it is extremely important to create a backup of your database before making any major changes in the data.

Creating, Testing, and Running Update Queries

You can use an update query when you have to update or change existing data in multiple records. As a best practice, there are two steps that you must follow to create and run an update query. First, create a select query that identifies the records to update, and then change the query to an update query that upon running will update the records.

Simple Update Queries

A **simple update query** involves updating data in one table, allowing you to specify two values—the value you want to replace and the value to use as a replacement. To create and run an update query, first begin with a select query that identifies the records to be updated. Then change the query to an update query and click Run. The key thing to remember is that although the data types for each table field do not have to match, they must be compatible.

A simple update query can be an easy way to update large amounts of data. For example, perhaps an employee no longer works at the salon and there are dozens of future appointments that need to be changed to a different employee's name. If the same employee—perhaps the person you hired to fill that employee's position—is now going to handle these appointments, you could create an update query that changes the name of the employee for all future appointments from the employee who left to the new employee.

To Create and Run a Simple Update Query

a. The marketing department has extended the date for all in-house promotions that currently expire on 3/31/2013, and you need to update the data in the tblCampaign table in the Lastname_Firstname_a04_ws08_Spa1 database. Create a new query in **Query Design view**, and then add **tblCampaign** in Design view.

b. Add the following fields to the Query design grid:

MailingID, **CampaignType**, and **EndDate**

c. In the Criteria property of the CampaignType field, type **Like "In-house Promotion"**.

d. In the Criteria property of the EndDate field, type **Like #3/31/2013#**.

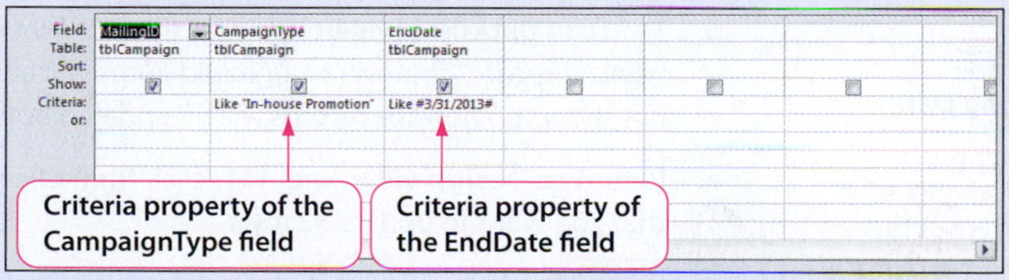

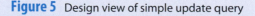

Figure 5   Design view of simple update query

e. Click the **Query Tools Design tab**, and then click **Update** to change the query type to an update query.

f. In the Update To property of the EndDate field, type **#6/30/2013#**.

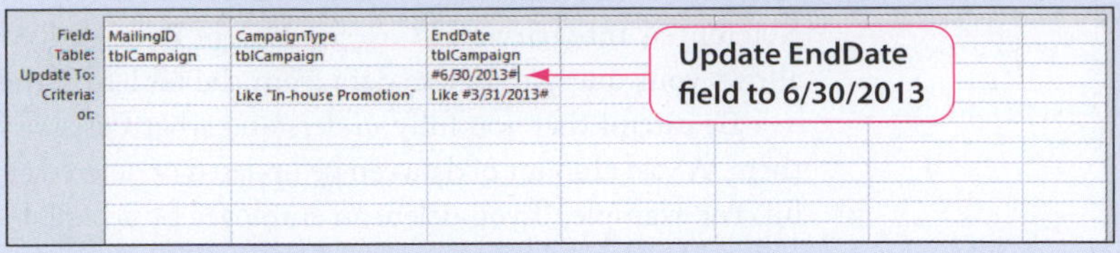

Field:	MailingID	CampaignType	EndDate
Table:	tblCampaign	tblCampaign	tblCampaign
Update To:			#6/30/2013#
Criteria:		Like "In-house Promotion"	Like #3/31/2013#
or:			

Update EndDate field to 6/30/2013

Figure 6 Design view of simple update query

SIDE NOTE

What Is Access Showing in Datasheet View?

When you preview the data, notice that Access does not show you how the data will look after the update, but shows you which records will be updated.

g. Switch to **Datasheet view** to preview the data that will be included in your update. You should have 52 records that will be updated automatically in your table.

h. Return to **Design view**, and then click **Run**. Click **Yes** when Access asks you to confirm that you want to update 52 rows.

i. Save your query as **qryUpdateData_initialLastname**, and then close your query.

j. Open the **tblCampaign** table. Notice that all In-house Promotions now have an EndDate of 6/30/2013. Close the tblCampaign table.

k. The marketing department has changed the details for all in-house promotions, and you need to update the data in the tblCampaign table. Create a new query in **Query Design view**, and add **tblCampaign** to Design view.

l. Add the following fields to the Query design grid:

CampaignType and **Details**

m. In the Criteria property of the CampaignType field, type **Like "In-house Promotion"**.

n. Click the **Query Tools Design tab**, and then click **Update** to change the query type to an update query.

o. The marketing department has informed you that in order for clients to receive this promotion, they have to spend a minimum of $50. To keep the text that is already in the Details field and add the additional information, you can concatenate the existing data with the marketing department's update. In the Update To property of the Details field, type **[Details] & " " & "Minimum purchase of $50 is required"**.

Field:	CampaignType	Details
Table:	tblCampaign	tblCampaign
Update To:		[Details] & " " & "Minimum purchase of $50 is required."
Criteria:	Like "In-house Promotion"	
or:		

Update field to concatenated value

Figure 7 Design view of simple update query

SIDE NOTE

Concatenating Data Saves Time

Access did not delete what was in the field prior to the update and simply concatenated what was already in the field with the new data.

p. Switch to **Datasheet view** to preview the data that will be included in your table. You should have 52 records that will be updated automatically in your table. Notice that Access does not show you how the records will be updated but rather just that 52 records will change.

q. Return to **Design view**, and then click **Run**. Click **Yes** when Access asks you to confirm that you want to update 52 rows.

r. Save your query as **qryUpdateDetails_initialLastname**, and then close your query.

s. Open the **tblCampaign** table. Notice that all In-house Promotions have been adjusted in the Details, for example, some entries listed as: Receive 10% off. Minimum purchase of $50 is required.

t. Close the tblCampaign table, and then close the Lastname_Firstname_a04_ws08_Spa1 database.

Complex Update Queries

There are times when you will need to update data from one table to another through the use of a **complex update query**. When doing so, the data types for both the source and destination fields must either match or be compatible. Additionally, when you update data from one table to another and use compatible data types instead of matching data types, Access converts the data types of the fields in the destination table. As a result, some of the data in the destination fields may be **truncated**—shortened or trimmed.

To Create and Run a Complex Update Query

a. Click the **File tab**, click **Open**, locate and select **a04_ws08_Spa2**, and then click **Open**.

b. Click the **File tab**, and then click **Save Database As**. Navigate to your student files and in the File name box, type Lastname_Firstname_a04_ws08_Spa2, replacing Lastname_Firstname with your actual name.

c. Click **Enable Content** in the Security Warning.

d. The marketing department has updated some of their customer data, and you need to update the tblCustomer table in the Lastname_Firstname_a04_ws08_Spa2 database with the new data from the marketing department's database. The table from the marketing department's database has already been imported into your database. Open **tblMktgImport** and **tblCustomer**. Changes in data between the two tables are the addition of data in the Zip Code field and the update of area codes, as well as a few changes to customer cities and states.

e. Close tblMktgImport and tblCustomer.

f. Create a new query in **Query Design view**, and then add **tblCustomer** and **tblMktgImport** to Design view.

g. Create an inner join between the CustomerID fields in each table, and then add the following fields to the Query design grid:

   CustomerID, CustCity, CustState, CustZipCode, and **CustPhone** from tblCustomer

h. Click the **Query Tools Design tab**, and then click **Update** to change the query type to an update query.

i. To update data from one table to another and match the fields between the two tables, type the following into the Update To property:

Field	Update To
CustCity	[tblMktgImport]![CustCity]
CustState	[tblMktgImport]![CustState]
CustZipCode	[tblMktgImport]![CustZipCode]
CustPhone	[tblMktgImport]![CustPhone]

Figure 8

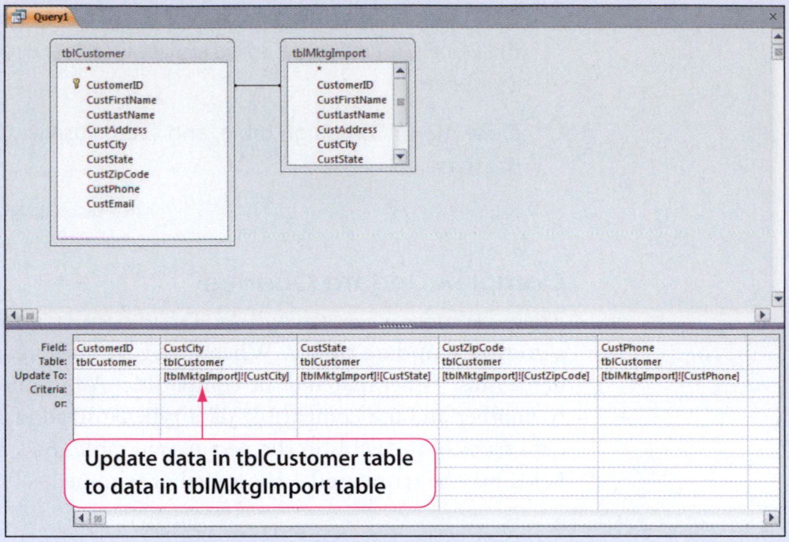

Figure 9 Design view of complex update query

j. Switch to **Datasheet view** to preview the data that will be included in your update. You should have 25 records that will be updated automatically in your table.

k. Return to **Design view**, and then click **Run**. Click **Yes** when Access asks you to confirm that you want to update 25 rows.

l. Save your query as **qryComplexUpdate_initialLastname**, and then close your query.

m. Open the **tblCustomer** table. Notice that all applicable data—such as area codes and zip codes—have been updated.

n. Close tblCustomer.

Quick Reference — Restrictions on Data Type Conversions

The following table outlines the restrictions on how to convert data types and briefly describes any data loss that might occur during conversion.

Convert to	Convert from	Changes or restrictions
Text	Memo	Deletes all except the first 255 characters
	Yes/No	The value –1 converts to Yes The value 0 converts to No
	Hyperlink	Truncates links longer than 255 characters
Memo	Yes/No	The value –1 converts to Yes The value 0 converts to No
Number	Text	Must consist of numbers, valid currency, and decimal separators. The number of characters in the Text field must fall within the size set for the Number field.
	Memo	Must contain only text and valid currency and decimal separators. The number of characters in the Memo field must fall within the size set for the Number field.
	Number with a different field size or precision	Must not be larger or smaller than what the new field size can store. Changing precision might cause Access to round some values.
	Date/Time	Dates depend on the size of the Number field. To accommodate all possible dates, set the Field Size property of your Number field to Long Integer or greater.
	Currency	Values must not exceed (or fall below) the size limit set for the field
	AutoNumber	Values must fall within the size limit set for the field
	Yes/No	Yes values convert to –1 No values convert to 0
Date/Time	Text	Must be a recognizable date or date/time combination
	Memo	Must be a recognizable date or date/time combination
	Number	Value must fall between –657,434 and 2,958,465.99998843
	Currency	Value must fall between –$657,434 and $2,958,465.9999
	AutoNumber	Value must exceed –657,434 and be less than 2,958,466
	Yes/No	The value –1 (Yes) converts to December 29, 1899 The value 0 (No) converts to midnight (12:00 AM)
Currency	Text	Must consist of numbers and valid separators
	Memo	Must consist of numbers and valid separators
	Yes/No	The value –1 (Yes) converts to $1 The value 0 (No) converts to $0
AutoNumber	Text	Not allowed if AutoNumber field serves as primary key
	Memo	
	Number	
	Date/Time	

(continued)

Convert to	Convert from	Changes or restrictions
	Currency	
	Yes/No	
Yes/No	Text	Must consist only of Yes, No, True, False, On, or Off
	Memo	Must consist only of Yes, No, True, False, On, or Off
	Number	Zero or Null converts to No All other values convert to Yes
	Date/Time	Null or 12:00:00 AM converts to No All other values convert to Yes
	Currency	Zero or Null converts to No All other values convert to Yes
	AutoNumber	All values convert to Yes
Hyperlink	Text	Converts a valid hyperlink in text format to a hyperlink
	Memo	Converts a valid hyperlink in text format to a hyperlink
	Number	Not allowed when a Number field is part of a relationship. If the original value is in the form of a valid Internet Protocol (IP) address (four number triplets separated by a period: nnn.nnn.nnn.nnn) and the numbers happen to coincide with a Web address, the conversion results in a valid link. Otherwise, Access appends http:// to the beginning of each value, and the resulting links are not valid.
	Date/Time	Access appends http:// to the beginning of each address, but the resulting links will almost never work.
	Currency	Access appends http:// to the beginning of each value, but like dates, the resulting links will almost never work.
	AutoNumber	Not allowed when the AutoNumber field is part of a relationship. Access appends http:// to the beginning of each value, but the resulting links will almost never work.
	Yes/No	Access converts all Yes values to −1 and all No values to 0, and appends http:// to the beginning of each value. The resulting links do not work.

Figure 10 Restrictions on Data Type Conversions (continued)

Creating, Testing, and Running Delete Queries

You can use an update query to delete data in one or more fields in a database. However, to delete entire records, including the primary key value that makes the record unique, you can use a delete query.

Simple Delete Queries

A **simple delete query** is used to remove one or more records from a table or another query. The number of rows deleted is dependent upon the criteria within the Where clause of the delete query. Typically, you use delete queries when you need to remove large amounts of data quickly. If you want to remove a very small number of records, you may want to simply delete them by hand. Undoubtedly, by running a delete query you reduce and/or eliminate the chance of not deleting—missing—a record if the process is done manually.

To Create and Run a Simple Delete Query

a. The spa manager has decided to discontinue selling soaps because they are not generating enough revenue for the spa. Create a new query in **Query Design view**, and add **tblProduct** to the Design view.

b. Add this field to the Query design grid:

ProductDescription

c. In the Criteria property of the ProductDescription field, type Like "*soap*".

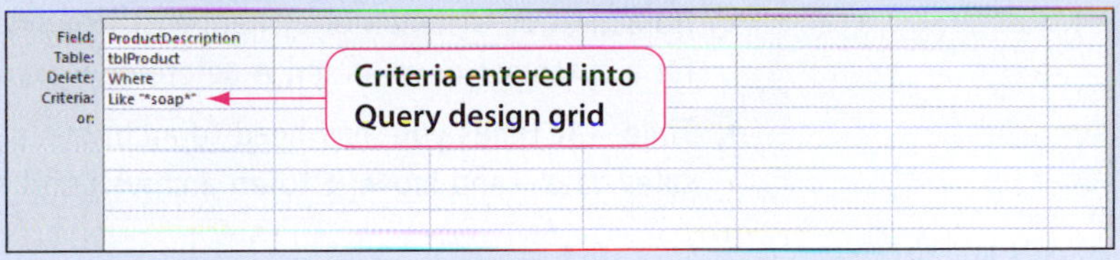

> **Field:** ProductDescription
> **Table:** tblProduct
> **Delete:** Where
> **Criteria:** Like "*soap*"
> **or:**
>
> Criteria entered into Query design grid

Figure 11 Design view of delete query

d. Click the **Query Tools Design tab**, and then click **Delete** to change the query type to a delete query.

e. Switch to **Datasheet view** to preview the data that will be deleted. You should have two records that will be deleted automatically in your table.

f. Return to **Design view**, and then click **Run**. Click **Yes** when Access asks you to confirm that you want to delete two rows.

Troubleshooting

> If you had your table open when you ran your delete query, #Deleted is displayed in the fields or records that were affected by the delete query. The message is displayed until you close and then reopen the table.

g. Save your query as qrySimpleDelete_initialLastname, and then close your query.

h. Open the **tblProduct** table. Notice that all applicable records—Lavender Ylang Soap and Renewal Face Soap—has been deleted.

i. Close tblProduct.

CONSIDER THIS | **What If You Try to Delete Records That Have Related Records?**

What do you think would happen if you tried to run a delete query and the records had related records in another table? Would you still be able to delete the records? Would it change anything if you set your Relationships property to Cascade Delete Related Records?

Real World Advice — Why Use a Delete Query?

It is important to ensure that the data within your database is current. Removing unneeded data is a good organizational strategy that all database users should practice. Cleansing outdated or incorrect data creates a database that is easy to use and maintain. Of course, before performing a delete query, you should always back up your database just in case you either make a mistake or decide to use the data at a later point in time. Data can become unneeded for several reasons:

- Real-world changes—You may need to delete discontinued products or employees who no longer work at your company.
- Human error—Human error happens. Users could accidently enter duplicate data for a customer or an order. A delete query can make it easier to fix errors.
- Time—At times you may need to archive older data—past employees or last year's sales data—and move it to an archive database or data warehouse.

Complex Delete Queries

There are times when you will need to delete data in multiple tables. This is a more **complex delete query**. For example, the salon manager may want to remove all coupons that were not redeemed and have now expired. This will keep the database cleansed. **Data cleansing** is a process where the delete query will remove data that is not useful or needed anymore.

To Create and Run a Complex Delete Query

a. The marketing department has been notified that two customers want to be removed from the Painted Paradise Resort and Spa's mailing list as they are moving out of the country and will not be customers anymore. You need to delete the records from your database to ensure that the data you have is current and cleansed. Open the **Relationships** window.

b. Right-click the joining line between the tblCampaign and tblCustomer and click **Edit Relationship**. Click **Cascade Delete Related Records** to modify the relationship between tblCustomer and tblCampaign and click **OK**.

c. Click **OK** to close the Edit Relationships dialog box, and then close the Relationships window.

d. Create a new query in **Query Design view**, and then add **tblCustomer** to Design view.

e. Add the following fields to the Query design grid:

   CustomerID, **CustFirstName**, and **CustLastName**

f. Click the **Query Tools Design tab**, if necessary, and then click **Delete** to change the query type to a delete query.

g. To delete the two customers, type "Dunn" into the Criteria property of the CustLastName field and type "Cleveland" into the Or property of the CustLastName field.

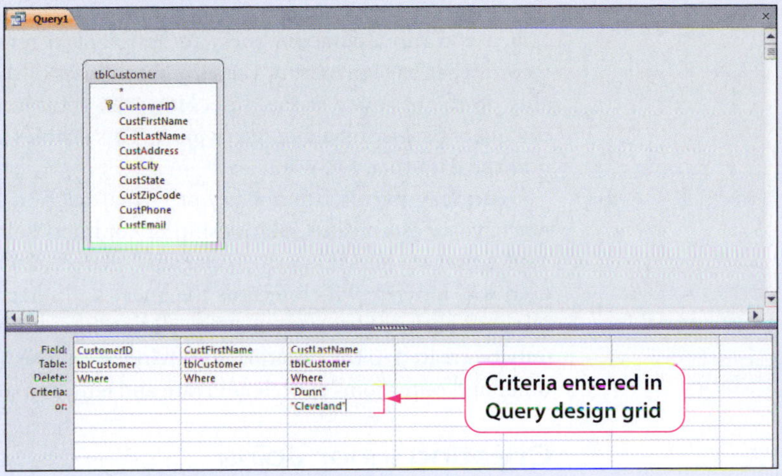

Figure 12 Design view of complex delete query

SIDE NOTE
Deleting Records on the One Side of a Relationship

To delete records on the one side of the relationship and related records on the many side, enable Referential Integrity and Cascade Delete Related Records.

SIDE NOTE
Deleting Records on the Many Side of a Relationship

If you need to remove data only on the many side of the relationship, you can create and run your delete query without having to change the relationship.

h. Switch to **Datasheet view** to preview the data that will be deleted. You should have two records that will be deleted automatically in your table once you run the query.

i. Return to **Design view**, and then click **Run**. Click **Yes** when Access asks you to confirm that you want to delete two rows.

j. Save your query as **qryComplexDelete_initialLastname**, and then close your query.

k. Open the **tblCustomer** table. Notice that all applicable data—customers with the last names of Dunn and Cleveland—have been deleted.

l. Open the **tblCampaign** table. Notice that all applicable data—customers with the CustomerID of 4 and 22—have been deleted.

m. Close tblCustomer and tblCampaign.

n. Close the Lastname_Firstname_a04_ws08_Spa2 database.

Quick Reference   Tips When Using a Delete Query

The reason you deleted records from the tblCustomer table and not the tblCampaign table is because tblCustomer resides on the one side of the relationship. Additionally, you did not have to change any of the other relationships because there were not any related records. In the future, you may need to edit all relationships and ensure the Cascade Delete Related Records property is selected. You first need to decide which records exist on the one side of the relationship and which exist on the many side.

- To delete records on the one side of the relationship and the related records on the many side, enable the Referential Integrity and Cascade Delete Related Records properties.

- To delete records only on the one side of the relationship, first delete the relationship, and then delete the data.

- To remove data only on the many side of the relationship, create and run the delete query without changing the relationship.

Advanced Relationships Using Multiple Tables

When you run a database query to find data in related tables, Access automatically looks for records that have matching values on both sides of the relationship. This is what you will probably do the majority of the time. However, you can control which records will be displayed in the query dataset by using query joins. This enables you to enhance your dataset even further to find the data that you want.

A **query join** is a temporary or virtual relationship between two tables in a query that do not have an established relationship or common field with the same field name and data type. Tables that are joined in a query are only related in that query and nowhere else. The type of join used will indicate which records the query will select or perform an action on. Creating a query join will not establish a permanent relationship between the tables. Permanent relationships can only be created in the Relationships window. In this section, you will create queries that include inner and outer joins as well as create and edit unmatched data queries.

Creating Inner Joins

An **inner join**, the default join type in Access, is a join that selects only those records from both database tables that have matching values. One or more fields can serve as the join fields. Records with values in the joined field that do not appear in both of the database tables will be excluded from the query dataset. For example, consider the spa and how the managers track sales of products to customers. By creating an inner join—a union or marriage of the data—the resulting dataset could include a customer and the products that customer has purchased. However, all products or all customers may not be included in the dataset because all products may not be included on an invoice (maybe the spa just started selling a new product and no one has purchased it yet), or all customers may not have purchased any products because they visit the spa or salon to receive services but not to purchase products.

To Create and Run Inner Join Queries

a. Click the **File tab**, click **Open**, locate and select **a04_ws08_Spa3**, and then click **Open**.

b. Click the **File tab**, and then click **Save Database As**. Navigate to your student files and in the File name box, type Lastname_Firstname_a04_ws08_Spa3, replacing Lastname_Firstname with your actual name. Click **Save**.

c. Click **Enable Content** in the Security Warning.

d. Create a new query in **Query Design view**, and then add **tblPurchase** and **tblCustomer** to Design view.

e. Double-click on the relationship between **tblPurchase** and **tblCustomer** to open the Join Properties dialog box. Notice that the default selection is set to only include rows where the joined fields from both tables are equal. This is an inner join. Close the Join Properties dialog box.

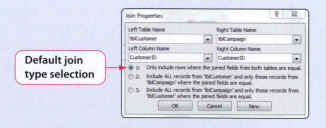

Figure 13 Join Properties dialog box

f. Add the following fields to the Query design grid:

CustomerID, **CustFirstName**, and **CustLastName**, **ProductID**, **PurchaseDate**, and **Quantity**

g. Click **Run**. Notice that there are 23 customers who have purchased products from the spa. However, if you open tblCustomer there are 46 records. Thus, the query only included the records from both tables that matched.

h. Save your query as qryInnerJoin1_initialLastname, and then close your query.

i. Create a new query in **Query Design view**, and add **qryInnerJoin1_initialLastname** and **tblCampaign** to Design view.

j. Create a relationship on the CustomerID field between the **qryInnerJoin1_initialLastname** query and the **tblCampaign** table, and then double-click the relationship to open the Join Properties dialog box. Notice that the default selection is set to only include rows where the joined fields from both tables are equal. Close the Join Properties dialog box.

k. Add the following fields to the Query design grid:

CustomerID, **CustFirstName**, **CustLastName**, **ProductID**, **PurchaseDate**, **Quantity**, **CampaignName**, and **Redeemed**

l. Click **Run**. Notice that there are 143 records in the dataset. However, look at each record. Because the join property is set to inner join, Access is listing each purchase multiple times to coincide with each coupon the customers received. Thus, an inner join may not always be the best option for you to view data.

m. Save your query as qryInnerJoin2_initialLastname, and then close your query.

Creating Outer Joins

An **outer join** selects *all* of the records from one database table and only those records in the second table that have matching values in the joined field. One or more fields can serve as a join field. For example, consider again the spa and how the managers track sales of products to customers. An outer join query that includes these two tables could include all customers and only the products that have been purchased. Therefore, you could find out what products are the most popular.

To Create and Run Outer Join Queries

a. Create a new query in **Query Design view**, and then add **tblProduct** and **tblPurchase** to Design view.

b. Double-click on the relationship between **tblProduct** and **tblPurchase** to open the Join Properties dialog box. Notice that the default selection is set to only include rows where the joined fields from both tables are equal—an inner join. To change this to an outer join, select the option that includes all records from tblProduct and only those records from tblPurchase where the joined fields are equal, and then click **OK**.

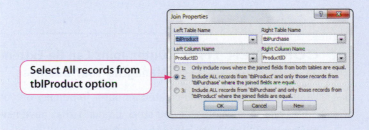

Select All records from tblProduct option

Figure 14 Join Properties dialog box

c. Add the following fields to the Query design grid:

ProductDescription and **CustomerID**

d. Click **Run**. Notice that all records from tblProduct appear—even those products in which no customers have purchased. However, the customers who have not purchased any products, such as Buchanan, do not appear. Additionally, products purchased by more than one customer appear multiple times.

e. Save your query as qryOuterJoin1_initialLastname, and then close your query.

f. Create a new query in **Query Design view**, and then add **tblProduct** and **tblPurchase** to Design view.

g. Double-click on the relationship between **tblProduct** and **tblPurchase** to open the Join Properties dialog box. To change this to an outer join, select the option that includes all records from tblProduct and only those records from tblPurchase where the joined fields are equal, and then click **OK**.

h. Add the following fields to the Query design grid:

ProductDescription and **CustomerID**

i. Click **Totals** on the Query Tools Design tab, and then in the Total property of the CustomerID field, click **Count**.

j. Rename the CustomerID field by typing TotalSold: in front of **Customer ID**.

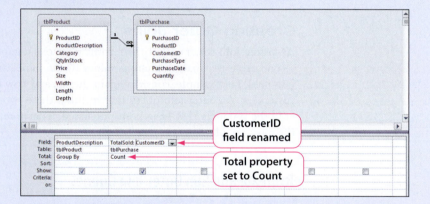

Figure 15 Design view of query

k. Click **Run**. Notice how you can now see a count of each item sold. Access automatically places a zero in the fields where there is no record of a customer purchasing an item or items.

l. Save your query as qryOuterJoin2_initialLastname, and then close your query.

CONSIDER THIS | **Outer Joins Can Be Extremely Helpful in Managing Your Business**

What would you do if you created an outer join query on your Product and Invoice tables and discovered that you stock products that have never been purchased by a customer? Should you place the products on sale? Develop a better advertising or marketing plan? Discontinue the products?

Use the Find Unmatched Query Wizard

By creating a query using the Find Unmatched Query Wizard, you will be able to edit, analyze, and cleanse data. The **Find Unmatched Query Wizard** finds records in one table that do not have related records in another table. After the wizard constructs your query, you can modify the query's design to add or remove fields or to add a join between the two tables. You can also create your own query to find unmatched records without using the wizard, but at times it is easier to at least begin building such a query by using the wizard.

This type of query can be very helpful in business. What if the spa or salon had a walk-in client—a client who wants to have a service, but did not schedule an appointment. The receptionist could find all employees who do not have an appointment scheduled for a specific time to determine who would be able to assist the walk-in client.

Additionally, you can use the Find Unmatched Query Wizard to cleanse data in a table. For example, perhaps the spa manager decided to discontinue a product or stop offering a specific service and probably will not need to use any of the transactional data in the future. The manager could find unmatched records between the Products and Purchases tables to ultimately delete the transactions in which the discontinued items reside. Thus, finding unmatched records may be the first of several steps that you want to take—you may want to then create a delete query to help you delete records that are no longer needed.

To Create Queries Using the Find Unmatched Query Wizard

a. Click the **Create tab**, and then click **Query Wizard** in the Queries group to create a new query that will find which employees do not have any scheduled appointments.

b. Click **Find Unmatched Query Wizard**, and then click **OK**.

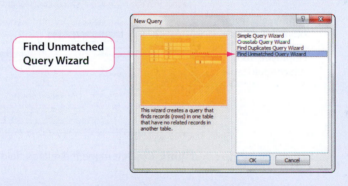

Find Unmatched Query Wizard

Figure 16 New Query Wizard

c. Access prompts you to select the table that contains the records you want in your query results. Select **Table: tblEmployee**, and then click **Next**.

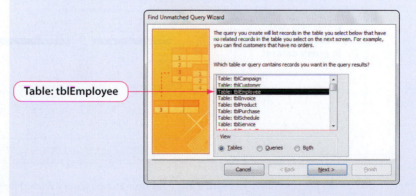

Table: tblEmployee

Figure 17 Find Unmatched Query Wizard table selection one

d. Access prompts you to select the table that contains the related records. Select **Table: tblSchedule**, and then click **Next**.

Table: tblSchedule

Figure 18 Find Unmatched Query Wizard table selection two

e. Access prompts you to select the piece of information that is in both tables, and it should have already selected EmployeeID from tblEmployee and Employee from tblSchedule. Click **Next**.

EmployeeID from tblEmployee table

Employee from tblSchedule table

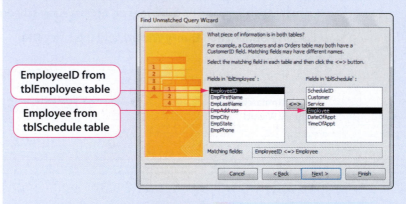

Figure 19 Determine the related field between the selected tables

f. Double-click **EmpFirstName** and **EmpLastName** as the fields you want to see in your query results, and then click **Next**.

Fields selected to be displayed in query dataset

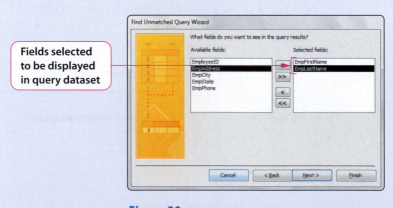

Figure 20 Find Unmatched Query Wizard field selection

g. Save your query as qryUnmatched1_initialLastname, and then click **Finish**. Notice that there are two employees listed in your dataset.

h. Close the qryUnmatched1_initialLastname query.

i. Click the **Create tab**, click **Query Wizard** in the Queries group to create a new query that will find which services have not been given to any clients.

j. Select **Find Unmatched Query Wizard**, and then click **OK**.

k. Access prompts you to select the table that contains the records you want in your query results. Select **Table: tblService**, and then click **Next**.

l. Access prompts you to select the table that contains the related records. Select **Table: tblSchedule**, and then click **Next**.

m. Access prompts you to select the piece of information that is in both tables, and it should have already selected ServiceID from tblService and Service from tblSchedule. Click **Next**.

n. Double-click **ServiceName** and **Description** as the fields you want to see in your query results, and then click **Next**.

o. Save your query as qryUnmatched2_initialLastname, and then click **Finish**. Notice that there are six services listed in your dataset.

p. Switch to **Design view**. Notice that Access created an outer join to allow you to view the results you were interested in seeing.

q. Change Is Null in the Criteria property of the Service field to Is Not Null, and then add the **Fee** field to the Query design grid.

r. Click the **Query Tools Design tab**, click **Totals**, click **Sum** in the Fee field, and then rename the Fee field by typing GrossRevenue: in front of Fee.

s. Click **Run**, and then add totals at the bottom of your dataset. Click **Sum** in the GrossRevenue field. Notice that the spa will generate gross revenue of $5339 if all scheduled appointments are kept.

t. Save your changes, and then close the qryUnmatched2_initialLastname query.

u. Close the Lastname_Firstname_a04_ws08_Spa3 database.

CONSIDER THIS | **Unmatched Records Can Help You Manage Your Business**

Now that you know there are five services that clients never requested, should you offer some sort of discount or promotion? Develop a better advertising or marketing plan? Discontinue the services?

Concept Check

1. Explain the difference between an inner join and outer join. Why is it important to understand joins when trying to retrieve data for decision making?

2. Explain the four types of action queries.

3. Give a business example of how you could use each of the four action queries.

4. How can using the Find Unmatched Query Wizard help you manage your data?

5. What is the difference between a simple action query and a complex action query?

Key Terms

Action query 364
Append query 368
Business intelligence (BI) 365
Business intelligence tools 365
Complex delete query 378
Complex update query 373
Data cleansing 378
Data mining 365

Data warehouse 365
Data warehousing 365
Delete query 370
Find Unmatched Query Wizard 383
Forecasting 365
Inner join 380
Make table query 365
Operational database 365

Outer join 381
Query join 380
Simple delete query 376
Simple update query 371
Suggestive sell 365
Transactional database 365
Truncated 373
Update query 370

Visual Summary

Create and Run a Simple Update Query (p. 371)

Create and Run a Make Table Query (p. 366)

Create and Run an Append Query (p. 369)

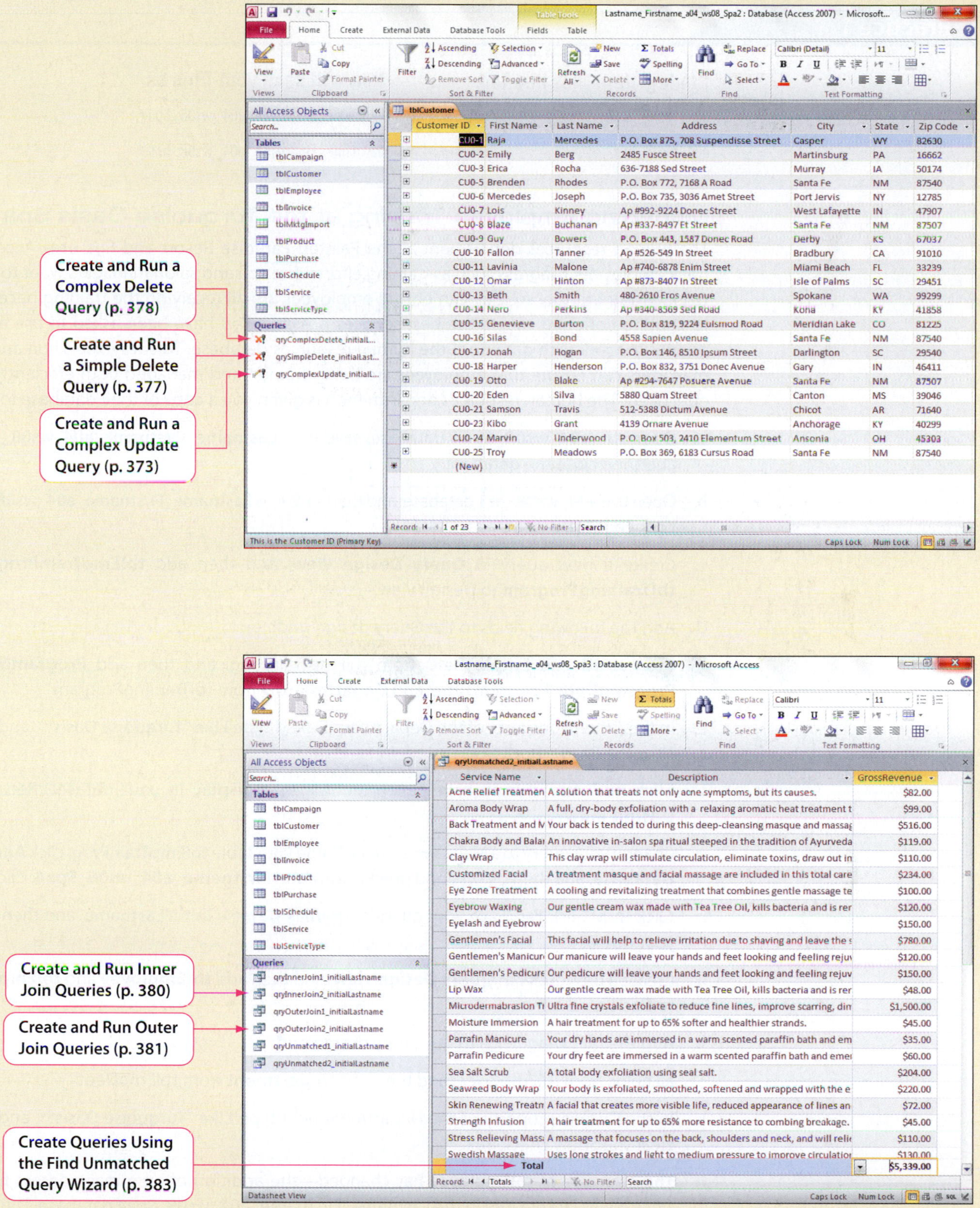

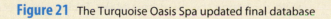

Create and Run a Complex Delete Query (p. 378)

Create and Run a Simple Delete Query (p. 377)

Create and Run a Complex Update Query (p. 373)

Create and Run Inner Join Queries (p. 380)

Create and Run Outer Join Queries (p. 381)

Create Queries Using the Find Unmatched Query Wizard (p. 383)

Figure 21 The Turquoise Oasis Spa updated final database

Student data files needed:

a04_ws08_Spa4

a04_ws08_hr1

You will save your files as:

Lastname_Firstname_a04_ws08_Spa4

Lastname_Firstname_a04_ws08_hr1

Managing Employee Training at the Turquoise Oasis Spa

The human resources department at the Painted Paradise Resort and Spa uses Access to track employees' progress such as training efforts. The spa and salon managers want to keep track of training too, so they can ensure employees are all receiving the training necessary to continue offering clients the best services possible. You have been asked to use action queries to work with data from the human resources database. This way, the salon and spa managers can ensure that employees are being trained and managed both efficiently and effectively. The human resources department has given you a copy of their database to use.

a. Open the **a04_ws08_Spa4** database, save it as Lastname_Firstname_a04_ws08_Spa4, and then close the database.

b. Open the **a04_ws08_hr1** database, and then save it as Lastname_Firstname_a04_ws08_hr1. Click **Enable Content**.

c. Create a new query in **Query Design view**, and then add **tblEmpTrainProg** and **tblTrainingProgram** to Design view.

d. Add the following fields to the Query design grid:

ProgramID and **EmployeeID** from tblEmpTrainProg, and then add **ProgramName**, **ProgramDate**, **ProgramTime**, and **DepartmentID** from tblTrainingProgram

e. In the Criteria property of the DepartmentID field type Like "Turquoise Oasis*", and then clear the Show check box.

f. Click **Run**. You should have seven records that display in your dataset. Return to **Design view**.

g. Change your query to a Make Table query. Name your table tblEmpTrainProg, click **Another Database**, and then browse and open **Lastname_Firstname_a04_ws08_Spa4**. Click **OK**.

h. Click **Run**. Click **Yes**. Save your query as qryMakeTable1_initialLastname, and then close your query.

i. Create a new query in **Query Design view**, and then add **tblEmployee** and **tblEmpDept** to Design view.

j. Add the following fields to the Query design grid:

all fields from tblEmployee, and then add **Department** from tblEmpDept

k. In the Criteria property of the Department field type Like "Turquoise Oasis*", and then clear the Show check box.

l. The structure of tblEmployee has changed—the addition of an e-mail address field—since it was last created in the Lastname_Firstname_a04_ws08_Spa4 database. Thus, you need to change the query to a **Make Table** query, recreate the tblEmployee as **Table Name** to **Another Database** Lastname_Firstname_a04_ws08_Spa4 database. Access will delete the existing tblEmployee table once you run this query. Switch to **Datasheet view**. You should have 22 records that displayed in your dataset. Return to **Design view**.

m. Click **Run**, and then click **Yes** when Access prompts you to confirm the deletion of the existing tblEmployee in Lastname_Firstname_a04_ws08_Spa4. Click **Yes** again to add 22 rows. Save your query as qryMakeTable2_initialLastname, and then close your query.

n. Close the Lastname_Firstname_a04_ws08_hr1 database, and then open the **Lastname_ Firstname_a04_ws08_Spa4** database.

o. Open **tblEmployee** in **Design view**, and then make and save the following changes to the Field Properties and Descriptions:

Field	Field Properties	Description
EmployeeID	Change this field to the primary key Change the format to "EMP"0	The Employee ID (primary key)
FirstName	Change the caption to First Name	The employee first name
LastName	Change the caption to Last Name	The employee last name
Address		The employee address
City	Change the default value to Santa Fe	The employee city
State	Format as all uppercase letters Change the default value to NM	The employee state
Phone	Change the input mask to the Phone Number format	The employee phone number
EmailAddy	Format as all lowercase letters Change the caption to E-mail Address	The employee e-mail address
JobTitle	Change the caption to Job Title	The employee job title

p. Open **tblEmpTrainProg** in **Design view**, and then make and save the following changes to the Field Properties and Descriptions:

Field	Field Properties	Description
Create a new AutoNumber field named **EmpTrainProgID**	Change this field to the primary key Change the format to "ETP"0	The Employee Training Program ID (primary key)
ProgramID	Change the caption to Program ID	The program ID (foreign key)
EmployeeID	Change the caption to Employee Change the data type to lookup the employee ID in tblEmployee. Be sure to enforce referential integrity and restrict delete.	The employee ID (foreign key)
ProgramName	Change the caption to Program Name	The program name
ProgramDate	Change the caption to Date	The program date
ProgramTime	Change the caption to Time	The program time

q. You need to recreate a relationship between tblEmployee and tblSchedule using EmployeeID and **Enforce Referential Integrity**. Open the **Relationships window**, and then create a relationship between the two tables using the EmployeeID (tblEmployee), Employee (tblSchedule) fields, and **Enforce Referential Integrity**.

r. Create a new query in **Query Design view**, add **tblEmployee** to the Query design grid, and then add the following field to the Query design grid:
EmailAddy

s. Change your query to an update query. Because EmailAddy is a new field, you need to update the table to enter all employee e-mail addresses to the EmailAddy field. The format of employee e-mail addresses is initialLastname@paintedparadise.com. In the Update To property type Left([FirstName],1) &""&[LastName]&"@paintedparadise.com".

t. Click **Run**. Click **Yes** to update 2 rows. Save your query as **qryUpdateEmail_initialLastname**, and then close your query.

u. Open **tblEmployee**. Notice that all e-mail addresses have been added to the EmailAddy field. Close tblEmployee.

EmployeeID	First Name	Last Name	Address	City	State	Phone	Email Address	Jo
EMP1	Mariah	Paul	567 N 53rd Street	Santa Ana	NM	(505) 555-8217	mpaul@paintedparadise.com	Assist
EMP2	Joseph	Dixon	321 Bolivar Lane	Albuquerque	NM	(505) 555-4149	jdixon@paintedparadise.com	Assist
EMP3	Lauren	Evans	783 W Point Drive	Pueblo	NM	(505) 555-3800	levans@paintedparadise.com	Assist
EMP4	Sarah	Fisher	9982 N Red Oak Road	Santa Fe	NM	(505) 555-2525	sfisher@paintedparadise.com	Assist
EMP5	Lucas	Gill	492 NW Lake Park Avenue	Santa Fe	NM	(505) 555-4836	lgill@paintedparadise.com	Assist
EMP6	Elizabeth	Heath	901 Mesa Boulevard	Rio Rancho	NM	(505) 555-4103	eheath@paintedparadise.com	Assist
EMP7	Amanda	Johnson	8441 Lomas Avenue	Santa Fe	NM	(505) 555-7943	ajohnson@paintedparadise.com	Assist
EMP8	Peter	Klein	672 Los Ranchos Drive	Santa Fe	NM	(505) 555-0247	pklein@paintedparadise.com	Stylist
EMP9	Samantha	McIntosh	2245 Cedar Grove Lane	Santa Fe	NM	(505) 555-3242	smcintosh@paintedparadise.com	Stylist
EMP10	Mary	Murphy	306 Ranchos de Taos Road	Agua Fria	NM	(505) 555-6201	mmurphy@paintedparadise.com	Stylist
EMP11	Joshua	Ripley	1837 El Dorado Avenue	Agua Fria	NM	(505) 555-6243	jripley@paintedparadise.com	Stylist
EMP12	Brenda	Rodriguez	245 E Bend Avenue	Santa Fe	NM	(505) 555-9244	brodriguez@paintedparadise.com	Stylist
EMP13	Alex	Weaver	268 NW 42nd Street	Rio Rancho	NM	(505) 555-3227	aweaver@paintedparadise.com	Stylist
EMP14	Jessica	Welch	7056 17th Street	Carlsbad	NM	(505) 555-4101	jwelch@paintedparadise.com	Stylist
EMP63	Irene	Kai	399 Velit Road	Santa Fe	NM	(505) 555-8196	ikai@paintedparadise.com	Salon
EMP64	Meda	Rodate	3164 Tellus Road	Santa Fe	NM	(505) 555-3986	mrodate@paintedparadise.com	Spa M
EMP65	Kelly	Masters	8474 Deedy Road	Santa Fe	NM	(505) 555-0806	kmasters@paintedparadise.com	Recep
EMP66	Christy	Istas	8035 Ante Avenue	Santa Fe	NM	(505) 555-0527	cistas@paintedparadise.com	Massa
EMP67	Kendra	Mault	495 Duel Avenue	Santa Fe	NM	(505) 555-7154	kmault@paintedparadise.com	Massa
EMP68	Jason	Niese	74 Massa Street	Santa Fe	NM	(505) 555-4928	jniese@paintedparadise.com	Massa
EMP69	Leslie	Dixon	62 Nulla Road	Santa Fe	NM	(505) 555-0704	ldixon@paintedparadise.com	Nail T
EMP70	Susan	Hemmerly	106 Ace Road	Santa Fe	NM	(505) 555-4618	shemmerly@paintedparadise.com	Nail T
(New)				Santa Fe	NM			

Figure 22 Datasheet view of tblEmployee table with added e-mail address

v. Create a new query in **Query Design view**, and then add **tblEmployee** and **tblEmpTrainProg** to Design view.

w. To change the relationship to an outer join, right-click the join line and click **Join Properties**, select the option that includes all records from tblEmployee and only those records from tblEmpTrainProg where the joined fields are equal, click **OK**. Add **FirstName** and **LastName** from tblEmployee to the Query design grid, and then add **ProgramName**, **ProgramDate**, and **ProgramTime** from tblEmpTrainProg to the Query design grid.

x. Click **Run**. Save your query as qryOuterJoin_initialLastname, and then close your query.

y. Close the Lastname_Firstname_a04_ws08_Spa4 database.

Practice 2

Student data files needed:

a04_ws08_Spa5

a04_ws08_hr2

You will save your files as:

Lastname_Firstname_a04_ws08_Spa5

Lastname_Firstname_a04_ws08_hr2

Managing Annual Evaluations Data at the Turquoise Oasis Spa

The spa and salon managers have been keeping track of training not only to ensure that employees stay up to date on current techniques but also to use as a component during the annual review process. You have been asked to use action queries to work with data from the human resources database. This way, the salon and spa managers can ensure that employees are being evaluated fairly. Additionally, the managers can view who is participating in training and working on developing their skills—and who isn't!

a. Open the **a04_ws08_Spa5** database, save it as Lastname_Firstname_a04_ws08_Spa5, and then close the database.

b. Open the **a04_ws08_hr2** database, and then save it as Lastname_Firstname_a04_ws08_hr2. Click **Enable Content**.

c. You need to create a query that will append the new employees hired into the spa's database. Create a new query in **Query Design view**, add **tblEmployee** to the Query design grid, and then add **FirstName**, **LastName**, **Address**, **City**, **State**, **Phone**, **EmailAddy**, **JobTitle**, and **HireDate** to the Query design grid.

d. In the Criteria property of the HireDate field type > #1/1/2013#, and then clear the Show check box.

e. Change your query to an append query, and then select **tblEmployee** in the database Lastname_Firstname_a04_ws08_Spa5 database.

f. Click **Run**. You should have six records that will be appended to tblEmployee. Click **Yes**. Save your query as **qryAppend_initialLastname**, and then close your query.

g. Close the Lastname_Firstname_a04_ws08_hr2 database, and then open the **Lastname_ Firstname_a04_ws08_Spa5** database and click **Enable Content**.

h. You need to create a query that will append data into tblEmpTrainProg. Create a new query in **Query Design view**, add **tblEmployee** to Design view, and then add **EmployeeID** from tblEmployee to the Query design grid.

i. Because you only want to work with the newly hired employees, in the Criteria property of the EmployeeID field type > =71.

j. Change your query to an append query, append the data to the **tblEmpTrainProg** table, and then click **Current Database**.

k. Click **Run**. You should have six records that will be appended to tblEmpTrainProg. Click **Yes**. Save your query as **qryAppend_initialLastname**, and then close your query.

l. You need to create a query that will update the training session that the new employees attended. Create a new query in **Query Design view**, add **tblEmpTrainProg** to Design view, and then add **ProgramID** to the Query design grid.

m. Because you only need to update the Null fields, in the Criteria property of the ProgramID field type Is Null.

n. Change your query to an update query, and then in the Update To property of the ProgramID field type 45.

o. Click **Run**. You should have six records that will be updated. Click **Yes**. Save your query as qryUpdate_initialLastname, and then close your query.

p. Because you will not need the training records for the year 2010 anymore, you can create a delete query to cleanse these records from your database. First, modify the relationship between tblEmpTrainProg and tblTrainingProgram to allow **Cascade Delete Related Records**.

q. Create a new query in **Query Design view**, add **tblTrainingProgram** to Design view, and then add **ProgramDate** to the Query design grid.

r. Because you only need to delete the training that was offered in 2010, in the Criteria property of the ProgramDate field type Between #1/1/2010# And #12/31/2010#. Change your query to a **Delete** query.

s. Click **Run**. You should have eight records that will be deleted. Click **Yes**. Save your query as qryDelete_initialLastname, and then close your query.

t. You want to view a list of employees along with the training sessions they have attended. Create a new query in **Query Design view**, add **tblEmployee** and **tblEmpTrainProg** to the Design view, and then leave the join as an inner join.

u. Add the following fields to the Query design grid:

   FirstName and **LastName** from tblEmployee, and then add **ProgramID** from tblEmpTrainProg

v. Click **Run**. You should have 38 records in your dataset. Save your query as qryInnerJoin_initialLastname, and then close your query.

w. Use the Find Unmatched Query Wizard to create a query to view which employees have not attended any training sessions.

x. Click **tblEmployee** as the table that contains the records you want in your query results, select **tblEmpTrainProg** as the table that contains the related records, and then select **EmployeeID** as the matching fields in both tables.

y. Double-click **FirstName**, **LastName**, and **JobTitle** as the selected fields you want to see in your query results, save your query as qryUnmatched_initialLastname, and then click **Finish**.

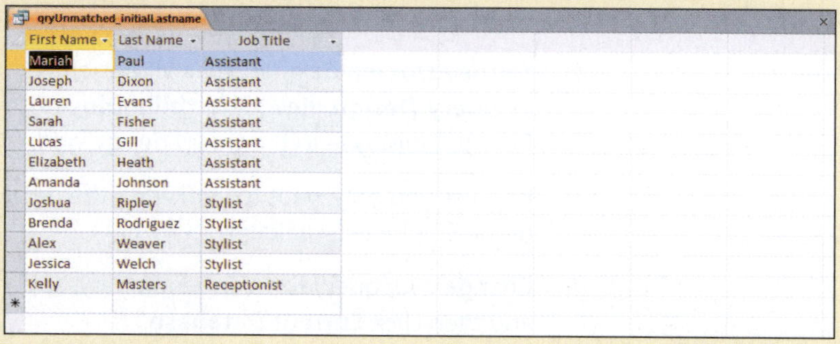
qryUnmatched_initialLastname

First Name	Last Name	Job Title
Mariah	Paul	Assistant
Joseph	Dixon	Assistant
Lauren	Evans	Assistant
Sarah	Fisher	Assistant
Lucas	Gill	Assistant
Elizabeth	Heath	Assistant
Amanda	Johnson	Assistant
Joshua	Ripley	Stylist
Brenda	Rodriguez	Stylist
Alex	Weaver	Stylist
Jessica	Welch	Stylist
Kelly	Masters	Receptionist

Figure 23 Datasheet view of qryUnmatched_initialLastname query

z. Close the qryUnmatched_initialLastname query, and then close the Lastname_Firstname_a04_ws08_Spa5 database.

MODULE CAPSTONE

Student data files needed:

a04_mp_Menu

a04_mp_ArchiveMenu

You will save your files as:

Lastname_Firstname_a04_mp_Menu

Lastname_Firstname_a04_mp_ArchiveMenu

Updating the Indigo5 Menu Items Database

The Painted Paradise Golf Resort and Spa is home to a world class restaurant with a top chef, Robin Sanchez. Robin is regularly updating data in his database to make certain he has all the ingredients and recipes needed to offer the high quality food for which the restaurant is known. You have been asked to manage and cleanse the data in the Indigo5 menu items database.

a. Open the a04_mp_Menu database, and then save it as **Lastname_Firstname_a04_ mp_Menu**. Open the a04_mp_ArchiveMenu database, and then save it as **Lastname_ Firstname_a04_mp_ArchiveMenu**.

b. Create the following queries in Lastname_Firstname_a04_mp_Menu:
- Create an outer join query that lists all records from tblFoodCategories and only those records from tblRecipes where the joined fields are equal. The query should include FoodCategory and RecipeName. Run your query, and then save your query as **qryRecipeCats_inititalLastname**.
- Create an inner join query that includes the tables tblIngredients, tblRecipeIngredients and tblRecipes that lists all records from tblIngredients and tblRecipes where joined fields are equal. The query should include RecipeName from tblRecipes and Ingredient from tblIngredients. Run your query, and then save your query as **qryRecipeIngredients_inititalLastname**.
- Create a Find Unmatched query that lists Ingredient from tblIngredients. The query should find all ingredients that are not listed in tblRecipeIngredients. Use IngredientID as the matching field. Run your query, and then save your query as **qryUnusedIngredients_inititalLastname**.

c. Create the following action queries:
- Create an update query that will update each menu item's price and cost. The query should include Price from tblMenu. Because the cost of ingredients has increased, the Price field needs to be updated to the current price plus $3. Enter an expression that adds $3 to the current menu price. Run your query, and then save your query as **qryPriceCostUpdate_initialLastname**.
- Create an append query that enables you to add data to tblRecipes from the tbl-RecipesOld table in Lastname_Firstname_a04_mp_ArchiveMenu. Select **RecipeName**, **FoodCategoryID**, **TimeToPrepare**, and **Instructions**. Append the data to the tbl-Recipes table in Lastname_Firstname_a04_mp_Menu. Run your query. Hint: Be sure to close the Lastname_Firstname_a04_mp_Menu database before running your query. Save your query as **qryRecipes_initialLastname**. Close the Lastname_Firstname_a04_mp_Menu database.
- Create a make table query in Lastname_Firstname_a04_mp_ArchiveMenu that copies all records and fields from tblReviews in the Lastname_Firstname_a04_mp_ ArchiveMenu database into the Lastname_Firstname_a04_mp_Menu database.

Name the new table **tblReviews**. Run your query, and then save your query as **qryReviewsTable_initialLastname**.

- Create a delete query that deletes all pizza recipes from tblRecipes. Hint: Be sure to delete all items from related tables. Run your query, and then save your query as **qryPizza_initialLastname**.

d. Close the Lastname_Firstname_a04_mp_ArchiveMenu database.

Problem Solve 1

Student data file needed:	You will save your file as:
a04_ps1_Hotel1	Lastname_Firstname_a04_ps1_Hotel1

Querying and Maintaining the Hotel Database

The hotel area uses an Access database to track all aspects of a reservation including the types of packages, room rates, discounts, and charges to each room. The database is used to analyze revenue and reservations. Additionally, there are times that the database needs to be updated and cleansed to ensure that all data stored within is current and accurate. You have been asked to create useful information through the use of queries and update information through the use of Action queries.

Complete the following tasks:

a. Open the a04_ps1_Hotel1 database, and then save it as **Lastname_Firstname_a04_ps1_Hotel1**.

b. Open tblGuests, and add your **first name** and **last name** in the appropriate field for record 25. Close tblGuests.

c. Create the following queries:

- Create a query that lists all discount types from tblReservations and counts how many times each discount type has been redeemed. The query should include DiscountType and CountOfDiscountType. Hint: CountOfDiscountType is an aggregated field. Name your CountOfDiscountType field **Total Discount**. Run your query, and then save your query as **qryTotalDiscount_initialLastname**.

- Create a query that calculates the gross revenue before room charges are added or discounts are subtracted. The query should include a calculated field named **GrossRevenue** that multiplies the RoomRate and NightsStay. Be sure not to include any reservations for a package as these rates are not for each night's stay. Do not show the Package field in your query results. Run your query, and then save your query as **qryRoomRevenue_initialLastname**.

- Create a query that calculates the revenue for each customer before room charges are added or discounts are subtracted. The query should include a calculated field named **Revenue** that multiplies the RoomRate and NightsStay. Be sure not to include any reservations for a package as these rates are not for each night's stay. Do not show the Package field in your query results. Run your query, and then save your query as **qryGuestRevenue_initialLastname**.

- Create a subquery that calculates how each customer contributed to the hotel's gross revenue. Include GuestID and Revenue from qryGuestRevenue_initialLastname. Type the following expression and then format the PercentToRevenue field as percentage with 1 decimal point: **PercentToRevenue:[Revenue]/[GrossRevenue]**

  Hint: Do not forget to add qryRoomRevenue_initialLastname to your Design grid so you can use the GrossRevenue field in your expression. Run your query. Sum your Revenue and PercentToRevenue fields in Datasheet view. Save your query as **qryGuestRevenueAnalysis_initialLastname**.

d. Create the following action queries:

- Create an update query that updates tblRoomCharges for customers who have checked out and paid their bill. This query will update the ChargeAmount field to 0 for customers with the last name of Wenner and Woodward. Hint: You will need the GuestID for each guest. Run your query, and then save your query as **qryUpdateAmountCharged_initialLastname**.

- Create an update query that updates prices in tblPackages. This query will update the Price field and increase each package price by $150. Run your query, and then save your query as **qryUpdatePrices_initialLastname**.

- Create a delete query that will delete all reservations for the year 2012 in tblReservations. Hint: You will also need to delete related records. Run your query, and then save your query as **qryDelete2012_initialLastname**.

e. Create a crosstab query that uses the RoomType field from tblReservations as the row heading and the CheckInDate field as the column heading. Use Month as the interval and total the NumberOfGuests field. Add totals at the bottom of your crosstab query, and then sum all fields in your dataset. In Design view, rename the Total Of NumberOfGuests field to **Total Guests**. Run your query, and then save your query as **qryTotalGuestsByMonth_initialLastname**.

f. Create an outer join query that lists all records from tblReservations and only those records from tblPackages where the joined fields are equal. Your query should include ReservationID, RoomType, and RoomRate from tblReservations and Package from tblPackages. Run your query, and then save your query as **qryRoomRatesPkgs_initialLastname**.

g. Close the Lastname_Firstname_a04_ps1_Hotel1 database.

Problem Solve 2

Student data file needed:

a04_ps2_Hotel2

You will save your file as:

Lastname_Firstname_a04_ps2_Hotel2

Using SQL to Query the Hotel Database

The main portion of the resort is the hotel. The hotel supports individual rooms to a grand villa suite. The Hotel area must track all aspects of a reservation including special requests for items such as a crib. The Hotel also has to track room charges that guests have made.

a. Open the a04_ps2_Hotel2 database, and then save it as **Lastname_Firstname_a04_ps2_Hotel2**.

b. Open tblGuests, and then add **your name** in record 25. Close tblGuests.

c. Create the following queries in SQL view:

- Create a query that lists all discount types from tblReservations and counts how many times each discount type has been redeemed. The query should include DiscountType and CountOfDiscountType. Hint: CountOfDiscountType is an aggregated field. Name your CountOfDiscountType field **Total Discounts**. Run your query, and then save your query as **qrySQLTotalDiscount_initialLastname**.

- Create a query that calculates the gross revenue before discounts are subtracted on all double rooms. The query should include a calculated field named **GrossRevenue** that multiplies the RoomRate and NightsStay. Be sure not to include any reservations for a package as these rates are not for each night's stay. Do not show the Package field in your query results. Run your query, and then save your query as **qrySQLRoom-Revenue_initialLastname**.

- Create a query that calculates the revenue for each customer before room charges are added. The query should include GuestID from tblReservations and a calculated field named **Revenue** that multiplies the RoomRate and NightsStay. Be sure not to include any reservations for a package as these rates are not for each night's stay. Do not show the Package field in your query results. Run your query, and then save your query as **qrySQLGuestRevenue_initialLastname**.

- Create a union query that lists the guests' and employees' name, address, city, state, and phone number. Sort in ascending order by GuestLastName, GuestFirstName. Rename GuestLastName to **LastName** and rename GuestFirstName to **FirstName**. Run your query, and then save your query as **qrySQLContactInfo_initialLastname**.

- Create a query that lists GuestID and Revenue from **qrySQLGuestRevenue_initialLastname**. Use the Between[el]And operator to view the guests who will be paying between $1500 and $3000. Run your query, and then save your query as **qrySQLRevenueBetween_initialLastname**.

- Create a subquery that lists all reservations where the guests need a crib. The query should include GuestID, CheckInDate, NightsStay, RoomRate, and Crib from tblReservations. Run your query, and then save your query as **qrySQLSubquery_initialLastname**.

d. Close the Lastname_Firstname_a04_ps2_Hotel2 database.

Problem Solve 3

Student data file needed:

a04_ps3_Hotel3

You will save your file as:

Lastname_Firstname_a04_ps3_Hotel3

Calculating Revenue and Maintaining the Hotel Database

The main portion of the resort is the hotel. Guests may charge anything from the resort to their room. Thus, the Hotel area must track all of these charges, such as those from the spa, golf, gift shop, restaurants, movies, personal trainers, and sessions with golf professionals. These services are eligible for a discount.

a. Open the a04_ps3_Hotel3 database, and then save it as **Lastname_Firstname_a04_ps3_Hotel3**.

b. Open tblGuests, and add your **first name** and **last name** in record 25. Close tblGuests.

c. Create the following queries:

- Create a query that calculates sales revenue and sales volume for all reservations. Your query should include an expression that totals a calculated field named **SalesRevenue** that multiplies the RoomRate and NightsStay fields. Your query should include a field named **SalesVolume** that counts the number of reservations. Group the results by RoomType. Run your query, and then save your query as **qrySalesRevVol_initialLastname**.

- Create a query that calculates gross sales revenue and gross sales volume. Rename your fields appropriately. Run your query, and then save your query as **qryGrossRevVol_initialLastname**.

- Create a subquery that shows sales revenue and sales volume and calculates percentage of sales revenue and percentage of sales volume for each room type. The sales calculations will list how much money a specific type of room has generated through reservations and the percent that each room's sales revenue contributes to the gross revenue. The sales volume calculations will list how many times a specific type of room has been reserved and the percent that each room's sales volume contributes to the total sales volume. Your query should include the RoomType.Value field from the tblReservations. Group your data by RoomType.Value. Hint: You will need to add the qrySalesRevVol_initialLastname and qryGrossRevVol_initialLastname queries to the query design. Rename and format your fields appropriately. Run your query. Add totals to sum the sales revenue, sales volume, percentage of sales revenue, and percentage of sales volume fields. Save your query as qryRevenueAnalysis_initialLastname.

d. Create the following action queries:

- Create an append query that appends updated data from the accounting department, which has been imported into the database and stored in tblNewRoomCharges. Your query should append all records from the tblNewRoomCharges table to the tblRoomCharges table. Run your query, and then save your query as qryAppendRoomCharges_initialLastname.

- Create a delete query that deletes all the records in the tblNewRoomCharges table. Run your query, and then save your query as qryDeleteRecords_initialLastname.

- Create a make table query to store data about older reservations, which will eventually be exported to a data warehouse. The new table should include the ReservationID, GuestID, CheckInDate, NightsStay, NumberOfGuests, RoomRate, DiscountType, and EmployeeID fields from the tblReservations table with check-in dates on or before 12/31/2012. Name your new table tblArchivedReservations. Run your query, and then save your query as qryArchivedReservations_initialLastname.

- Create an update query that adds a $5 delivery charge onto all room service orders in the tblRoomCharges table. Run your query, and then save your query as qryUpdateRecords_initialLastname.

e. Close the Lastname_Firstname_a04_ps3_Hotel3 database.

Perform 1: Perform in Your Life

Student data file needed:
a04_pf1_StudentOrg

You will save your file as:
Lastname_Firstname_a04_pf1_StudentOrg

Managing a Student Organization Database

The Student Organization database will help you track your organization's membership, including companies who attend events. You need to manage the data as it has not been used in the most efficient way possible. You also need to calculate the revenue generated through membership dues.

a. Open the a04_pf1_StudentOrg database, and then save it as Lastname_Firstname_a04_pf1_StudentOrg.

b. Add your first name and last name into record 2 of the tblMembers table. Close tblMembers.

c. To normalize the tblMeetings table, use a make table query to create a table that holds the company names and contacts. Name your table tblCompanies. Modify your table to include appropriate data types and field properties. Delete the appropriate fields in tblMeetings after creating your new table. Create appropriate relationships to tblCompanies.

d. Create a union query that lists all members, companies, and the first employer representative.

e. Create a query that calculates the gross revenue from member dues.

f. Create at least one delete query that will help you delete members after they have graduated.

g. Create a subquery that calculates the percentage of revenue for each semester. Add totals to your dataset in Datasheet view.

h. Create a query with an outer join that lists all members and the total amount of dues they have paid since they joined the organization. Add data aggregates to the dataset in Datasheet view.

i. Create two queries that use the WHERE function.

j. Create a GROUP BY query that performs an aggregated calculation.

k. Create two queries that use an inner join.

l. Create two queries that perform aggregated calculations.

m. Save all your changes. Close the Lastname_Firstname_a04_pf1_StudentOrg database.

Perform 2: Perform in Your Career

Student data file needed:

a04_pf2_Charity

You will save your file as:

Lastname_Firstname_a04_pf2_Charity

Querying and Modifying a Charity Database

As a manager for a local non-profit organization that helps raise money for worthy causes, you were asked to query an existing database to track such things as gross revenue for each campaign. Additionally, you will need to manage the data through the use of an Action query. This will ensure that your data is current and cleansed.

a. Open the a04_pf2_Charity database, and then save it as Lastname_Firstname_a04_pf2_Charity.

b. Add your first name and last name in record 1 of the tblContributors table. Close tblContributors.

c. Create a query that calculates gross revenue and percent to gross revenue for all donations based on the campaign. Add data aggregates to the dataset when in Datasheet view.

d. Create a query that calculates sales volume and percent of sales volume for all donations based on the campaign. Add data aggregates to the dataset when in Datasheet view.

e. Create a crosstab query that uses the ContributorID and CampaignID fields from tbl-Events as the row heading and the EventID field as the column heading. Use Sum as the interval, and then total the Amount field. Modify the column heading to display the event name as the heading. Change the field name of the Total Of Amount field to Total. Add totals to sum all fields in Datasheet view.

f. Create a query that calculates the net revenue after administration fees of 15%.

g. Create an outer join query that lists all campaigns and the contributors and donation amount where the joined fields are equal.

h. Create a find unmatched query that lists all contributors who did not donate to any campaign.

i. Use an action query to remove those contributors who have not donated to any campaign from the mailing list.

j. Save all your changes, and then close the Lastname_Firstname_a04_pf2_Charity database.

Perform 3: Perform in Your Career

Student data file needed:

a04_pf3_Roadhouse

You will save your file as:

Lastname_Firstname_a04_pf3_ Roadhouse

Querying the Beverage Database at The Roadhouse Bar and Grill

You are the bar manager at The Roadhouse Bar and Grill, a local restaurant that specializes in home-cooked meals for breakfast, lunch, and dinner. The general manager has given you a scaled-down version of the database with one days' worth of transactions. You need to manage the inventory of beverage items to ensure you have enough beverages for each day you are open for business.

a. Open the a04_pf3_Roadhouse database, and then save it as Lastname_Firstname_a04_pf3_Roadhousea04.

b. Add your full name In record 1 of the tblSuppliers table, and then close tblSuppliers.

c. Create a query that calculates the percentage of physical volume for milk and orange juice that is used based on the beverage container size.

d. Create a query that calculates the number of servings per container. Format the physical volume calculation as an integer.

e. Create an inner join query that lists all suppliers and beverages they supply.

f. Create a query that calculates the sales volume of how much inventory is used in a typical day. Group your data by the sales date and beverage name. Add data aggregates to sum the sales volume calculation in Datasheet view.

g. Create a query that calculates gross revenue by sales date.

h. Create a subquery that determines how much inventory you would need to order each week. Format the containers needed calculation as an integer.

i. Create the following queries in SQL view:
   - Create a query that calculates the net revenue for each beverage. The Roadhouse Bar and Grill makes 66% on each beverage sold. Display beverages that have net revenue of at least $1.25.
   - Create a subquery that calculates the net revenue for each beverage sold.
   - Create a union query that lists all suppliers and beverage names. Rename your displaying field as Name.
   - Create a query that lists the beverage name and total beverages sold where the totals are between 10 and 20. Rename your total beverages sold field as TotalSold.

j. Save all changes, and then close the Lastname_Firstname_a04_pf3_Roadhouse database.

Perform 4: How Others Perform

Student data file needed:

a04_pf4_CarRental

You will save your files as:

Lastname_Firstname_a04_pf4_CarRental

Lastname_Firstname_a04_pf4_CarRental.docx

Being an Entrepreneur—Cappy's Car Rental

You are the owner of a small rental car company—Cappy's Car Rental. Your intern created a database for you and your employees to use for tracking rentals and assessing monthly performance. At first glance, you notice that it has very few queries, which would help answer many questions about the cars you've rented. You need to evaluate the database, create useful queries, evaluate the existing queries, and cleanse the data as the intern left a fair amount of older data in the tables.

a. Open the a04_pf4_CarRental database, and then save it as **Lastname_Firstname_a04_pf4_CarRental**.

b. Open Word, create a new blank document, and then save it as **Lastname_Firstname_a04_pf4_CarRental**. This will be used to answer any questions below.

c. Add your first name and last name in record 1 of the tblCustomers table. Close tblCustomers.

d. Consider how the data will be used. Create five queries that can be used to assist you and your employees with decision making. In your Word document, explain what question the query would answer, such as calculating sales revenue within a specific date range.

e. Create three action queries. In your Word document, explain what the query would do if you clicked Run, such as updating prices or deleting older data. If you would need to make changes to relationships for the query to run properly, please note that as well.

f. Evaluate and modify the two existing queries to make them easier to read and use.

g. Save all changes to your Word document and database. Close the Lastname_Firstname_a04_pf4_CarRental database and Lastname_Firstname_a04_pf4_CarRental document.

WORKSHOP 9

Working with Advanced Forms and Reports

PREPARE CASE

The Red Bluff Golf Club: Providing Form Interfaces

The Red Bluff Golf Club generates revenues through golfers signing up for tee times and taking golf lessons. You have provided a database to Barry Cheney, the golf manager, where he can track employees and members. He would like to have an interface to the database where any of the golf club workers could easily sign up members for lessons. You have been asked to set up forms that the workers can use.

Courtesy of www.Shutterstock.com

Student data files needed for this workshop:

 a05_ws09_Golf

a05_ws09_Golf_Logo

You will save your file as:

Lastname_Firstname_a05_ws09_Golf

Advanced Form Settings

Recall that a **form** is an object used to enter new records into a table, edit or delete existing records in a table, or display existing records. A form can present a single record at a time rather than displaying all records the way that a table does. This presentation makes it easier for a person using the database to focus on a single record and thus helps prevent data entry errors.

Forms have three views:

- Form view shows the data in the form. This is the view you use to enter or change data. You cannot change the form design in this view. This is the view that the golf course employees would use when they are performing their jobs.

- Layout view shows the form and the data. Some of the form design such as field lengths and fonts can be changed in this view. The data cannot be changed. This view gives you an easy way to resize fields and check form appearance while you are creating the form.

- Design view shows the form design but not the data. Any aspect of the report design can be changed. The data cannot be changed. This view is used for creation of the form.

Barry Cheney would like to have a form that can be used to add a member. You decide to create it using the standard form format.

To Create a Member Form

a. Click the **Start** button, and then select **Microsoft Access 2010**.

b. Click the **File tab**, click **Open**, and then browse to your student data files. Locate and select **a05_ws09_Golf**, and then click **Open**.

c. Click the **File tab**, and then click **Save Database As**. In the File name box, type Lastname_Firstname_a05_ws09_Golf replacing Lastname_Firstname with your actual name.

d. Click **Enable Content** in the Security Warning.

e. Click **tblMember** in the Navigation Pane. Click the **Create tab**, and then click **Form Wizard**.

f. Click **Select all fields** >> to select all fields from tblMember.

g. Click **Next**, make sure that **Columnar** is selected, and then click **Next**.

h. Name your form frmAddMember, and then click **Finish**. Save 🖫 your form.

i. On this first member, tab from field to field. Note that you can tab to every field.

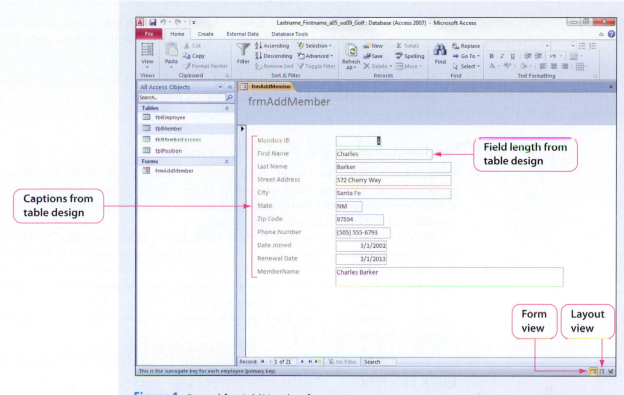

Captions from
table design

Field length from
table design

Form
view

Layout
view

Figure 1 Bound frmAddMember form

The form you created is a **bound form**. That means that it is directly connected to a data source such as a table or query and can be used to enter, edit, or display data from that data source. When you create a form from a table using the wizard, the form is bound to the table you used to run the wizard. The field labels are the captions defined for the fields in the table design. The formatting for the fields is based upon the field definitions in the table design. The field lengths are based upon the field lengths in the table design. All of these can be changed after the form is created. An **unbound form** is not linked directly to a data source. Unbound forms can be used for operating your database by allowing you to specify parameters, create buttons to print reports, and other operations.

Remember that in your member form, you could tab to each field. In a form created using the Form Wizard, a user can move to and make changes to any fields. This may be appropriate for a form used for adding a member but might lead to errors when an employee is changing a phone number or address and inadvertently changes the date the member first joined. You and Barry decided that this form will be used solely for adding a member. You will need to change the title of this form to indicate this.

Field sizes in a form are based upon field length. However, the MemberName field is a calculated field composed of FirstName and LastName, and so Access set its length longer than needed. You will start by resizing the MemberName field so that it is smaller.

Recall that Layout view allows a database developer to see a form with data in the fields and make changes to the form layout. Because you can see the data in the fields, it is an ideal view for resizing fields in a form. In this section, you will change the view of your form to Layout view.

To Change Format in Layout View

a. On the status bar, click **Layout View** 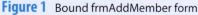.

b. Click **Charles Barker** in MemberName. Access highlights the field.

c. Move your pointer to the right border of the field until it becomes a double-headed arrow ↔. Move the border to the left until it lines up with the address and city fields above it.

d. Move your pointer to the lower border of the field until it becomes a double-headed arrow ↕. Move the border up until the field is a single line.

Understanding the Property Sheet

Every field on a form has certain characteristics or properties about the field stored in the **property sheet**. There are also characteristics of the form and sections within the forms stored in their respective property sheets. Making changes to these properties will change the formatting that was determined from the table design.

Property sheets have five tabs: Format, Data, Event, Other, and All. The Format tab is where properties that change the display of a field or form part are listed. The Data tab contains the properties including the field source and the properties that affect the values that can be entered into a field. On the Event tab, you can set procedures to determine what happens when a user performs an action such as clicking on a field. The Other tab contains all other properties that are not on one of the other tabs, such as name or datasheet caption. Finally, the All tab repeats all the properties.

Quick Reference   Property Sheet Tabs

Property Sheet Tab	Properties Included	Examples
Format tab	Properties related to the formatting and design of a field or form	For a field • Decimal places • Width • Font For a form or form part • Background color • Special effects
Data tab	Properties related to the source of a field and how the field data is entered	For a field • Source for the field • Input masks • Validation rules
Event tab	Macro procedures that should be used when a user performs an action	Actions to be taken upon • A click • An update • On double-click
Other tab	Any properties not included elsewhere	For a field • Field name • Caption For a form • Printing information
All tab	All properties	Repeats all properties from the other tabs

Figure 2

Understanding the Data Tab of the Property Sheet

The Data tab of the Property Sheet pane for Phone is shown in Figure 3. Remember that this shows properties including the field source and the properties that affect the values that can be entered into the State field. Phone is a **control**, which is an object on a form or report that displays data, performs actions, and lets you view and work with information. The properties on the Data tab are similar to the properties you use when defining the fields in a table.

To Show the Property Sheet for a Control

a. Click **(505) 555-6793**, the value for Phone Number.

b. Click **Property Sheet** on the Design tab of the Ribbon. If necessary, click the **Data tab**. Alternatively, you could right-click the **value**, and then select **Properties** from the shortcut menu.

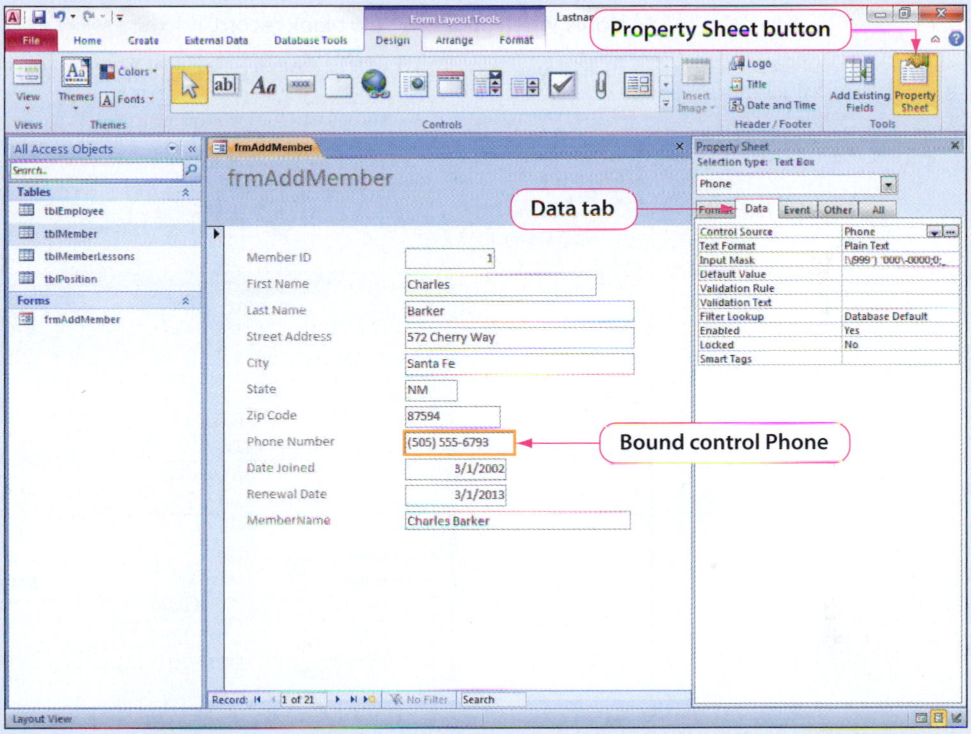

Figure 3 Property sheet for Phone Number

The first property on the Data tab is the Control Source. The control, Phone, is a **bound control**, that is, it is a field that retrieves its data from an underlying table. In this case, the Control Source tells you that the source for the data is the field Phone. You could change the source to another field or use the Expression Builder to calculate the source.

The next property is the Text Format. This is the format that the entered text will have in the form. The normal text format is Plain Text, but fields with a data type of Memo could have a Rich Text format.

The Input Mask is the next property. This mask is the same mask that is used to define input rules for a field in a table. Phone Number has a mask that was created when the table was defined.

The **Default Value** allows you to define a value that will show up in a new blank record. If a field has a typical value, you can define it here and speed up data entry.

The **Validation Rule** and **Validation Text** are respectively an expression that defines the range of data that will be accepted in a field and the error message that shows when a user enters data that violates the validation rule.

The **Locked** property determines whether data can be entered into the field using this form. A value of No means that data can be entered; a value of Yes means that the field is locked and data cannot be entered. The **Enabled** property is stronger than a lock. If the enabled property is No, the data cannot be entered or copied. The default is that bound controls are unlocked and enabled.

Barry tells you that most members are from Santa Fe, New Mexico. You will enter those values as default values for the City and State. The user will be able to change these values but will not need to enter them for members with this address.

To Change Default Values in the Property Sheet

a. Click **Santa Fe**, the value for City. The Property Sheet pane now shows the properties of the City control.

b. Click **Default Value**. Type **Santa Fe**, and then press $\boxed{\text{Tab}}$. Access puts quotation marks around the value.

This does not mean that Access changes the city to be Santa Fe. The default is used only when adding a new blank record.

c. Click **NM**, the value for State. Click **Default Value**, type **NM**, and then press $\boxed{\text{Tab}}$.

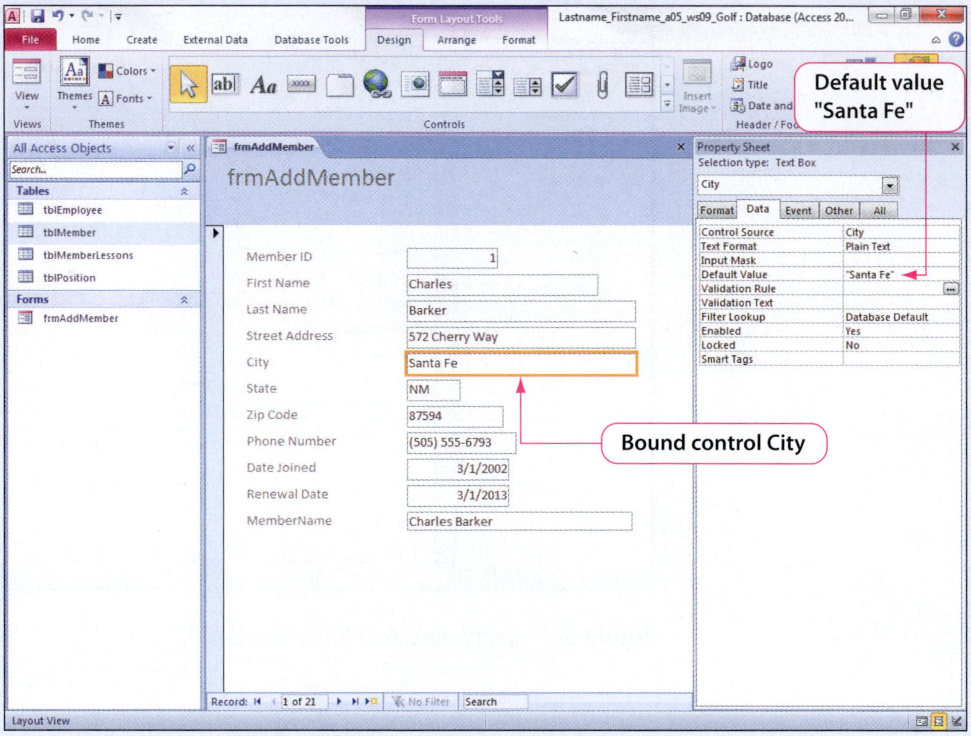

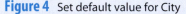

Figure 4 Set default value for City

You can also use Date functions and calculations in the default value. There are two date fields in the form; the first is Date Joined, which refers to the original date that the member joined the golf club. Date Joined is the caption for the field; in the database, the field is named DateJoined. You will set the default value for Date Joined to today's date. To do that, you will use Access's function Current Date.

The second date on the form is Renewal Date, which refers to the date that the membership expires. Renewal Date is the caption for the field; in the database, the field is named DateRenewal. You will want to set the Renewal Date default value to be one year after Date Joined. Access uses the DateAdd function to add an interval to a date. The advantage of using this function is that it always returns a valid date. The DateAdd function has the following format: DateAdd(interval,number,date). Interval can be day, month, year, or more as shown in the Quick Reference box. Number is how many of the intervals you want to add to the Date shown. You want to add one year to DateJoined. Your interval will be "yyyy", and your number will be 1. You use year rather than 365 days so that Access will automatically take account of the possibility of a leap year.

Quick Reference — Using the DateAdd Function

The DateAdd Function has the following format: DateAdd(interval,number,date).

Argument	Function Wanted	How Indicated
Interval		
	Year	yyyy
	Quarter	q
	Month	m
	Day	d
	Weekday	w
	Day of year	y
	Week	ww
	Hour	h
	Minute	n
	Second	s
Number		
	Add	Positive value
	Subtract	Negative value

Figure 5

To Use Dates in Default Values in the Property Sheet

a. Click **3/1/2002**, the value for Date Joined. In the property sheet, click **Default Value**, and then click the **Build** button ⊡.

b. In the Expression Elements pane, click **Common Expressions**.

c. Double-click **Current Date** in the Expression Categories pane, and then click **OK**.

d. Click **3/1/2013**, the value for Renewal Date. In the property sheet, click **Default Value**, and then click the **Build** button ⊡. In the Expression Builder, type =DateAdd("yyyy", 1,[DateJoined]).

e. Click **OK**, and then save your form.

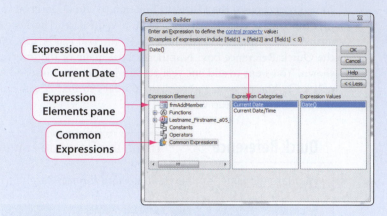

Figure 6 Expression Builder for current date

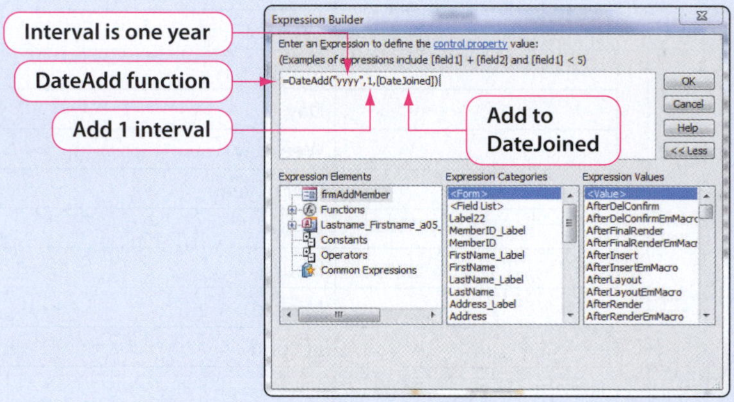

Figure 7 Expression Builder for calculated date

Notice that changing the default values did not change the renewal date for Charles Barker. The default is used only when entering new data.

f. In the Navigation bar, click the **New (blank) record**  navigation button. Notice that the new blank record has default values of Santa Fe, NM, today's date, and one year from now.

CONSIDER THIS | **Default vs. Calculated Date**

You defaulted to today's date but allowed the date to be changed. You could also have not allowed changes. When would you want to use a default that can be changed, and when would you want to force the value to be a default that cannot be changed?

To See Data Tab for Unbound Controls

a. Click the **First Name** label.

Notice that the Data tab is changed to have only a Smart Tags property. That is because a label is an **unbound control**. An unbound control does not have a data source. A label is used for form display and so needs no properties related to how the control is stored in the database. The properties shown in a tab are context sensitive and show only properties that apply to the control.

Understanding the Format Tab of the Property Sheet

The Format tab is where properties that change the display of a field or form part are listed. The properties in the Format tab are related to how the control is displayed on a form. The box for each value can be resized or moved (Width, Height, Top, Left). The Border can be changed. The font can be changed. A scroll bar can be added. None of these properties change how the field is stored in the database. They can make it easier for a user to use the form. You can also change how the form is displayed. You will first use the Format tab to change the background of the form.

To Change the Background Color of the Form

a. In the property sheet, click the **Format tab**.

b. Click the background of the Detail section. Access highlights that area by outlining it.
   Alternatively, you could have changed to the detail by clicking the Selection arrow ▾ of the Selection type at the top of the property sheet and then selecting Detail.

c. Click the **Back Color** property, and then click the **Build** button ⋯.

d. Select the light green color in the second row, **Olive Green, Accent 3, Lighter 80%**.

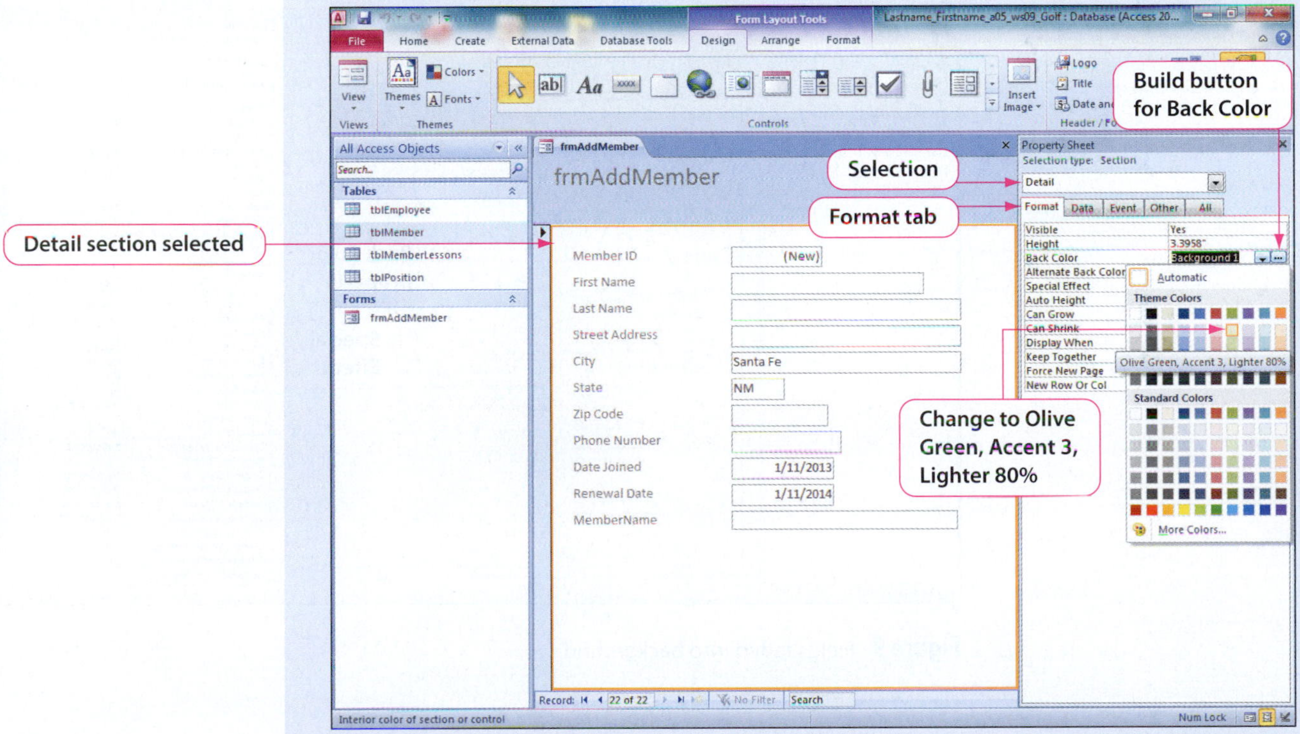

Figure 8 Change color of the background

Next you will change the display for individual fields.

To Explore the Format Tab

a. Click the **First Name** label.

Unlike the Data tab, there are many properties for an unbound control on the Format tab. That is because labels are displayed on the form, and so the properties related to the field display are relevant.

You decide that you would like to make the fields that are filled by Access a different format than the ones that the user enters. MemberID is AutoNumber, and MemberName is Calculated. You will change them to be faded in the background.

b. Click the **value** for MemberID. Click the **Special Effect** property, click the **Selection arrow** , and then change the effect to **Sunken**.

c. Click the **Back Color** property, and then click the **Build** button. Select the light green color in the second row, **Olive Green, Accent 3, Lighter 80%**.

d. Click the **value** for MemberName. In the Special Effect property, click the **Selection arrow**, and then change the effect to **Sunken**.

e. Click the **Back Color** property, and then click the **Build** button. Select the light green color in the second row, **Olive Green, Accent 3, Lighter 80%**.

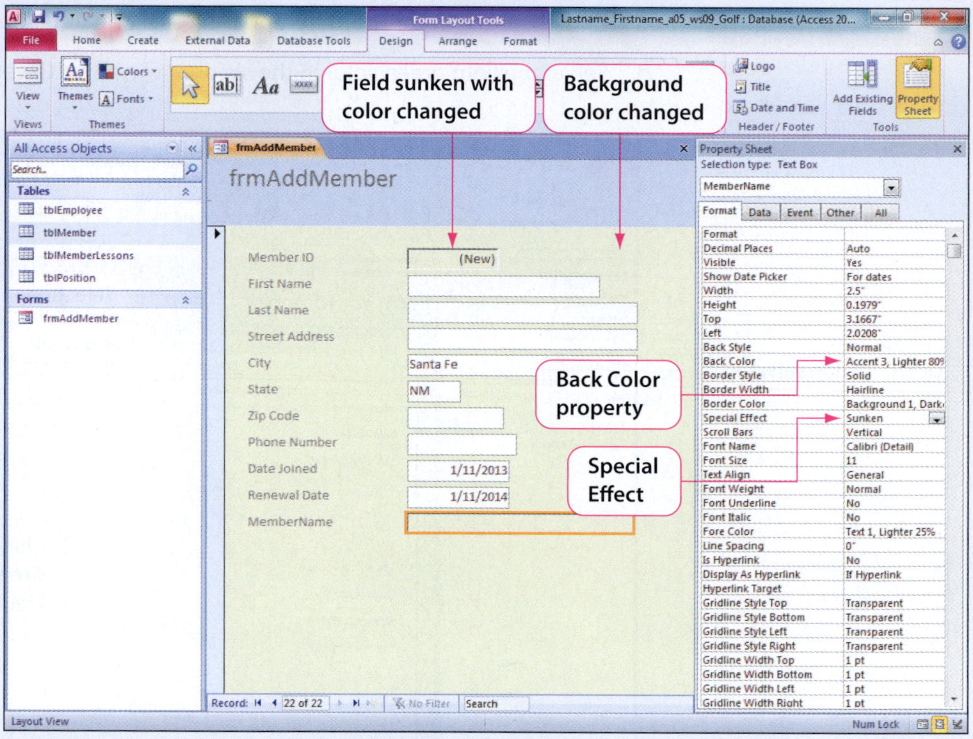

Figure 9 Fields faded into background

Real World Advice   Use Formatting Sparingly and with Purpose

It is possible to change the formatting for each label and field control. You could make one label green, with the data typed in that field blue. You could make the fonts vary for each field. However, this type of formatting is distracting and makes a form harder to use. Instead use varied formatting only if you have a reason for that variation. Two examples of when you might make this choice:

- You could use a bright color to highlight a single important control. Red is often used to catch the user's eye.
- You could use one color for fields that are protected and cannot be changed on the form and another color for fields that can be changed.

Barry asks whether you can make it easier to enter dates. Usually the Date Joined will be the current date, but occasionally it will be a day or two before or after the current date. You will add the Date Picker to make it easier for the user. The **Date Picker** is a pop-up calendar that allows users to enter dates by clicking a date in the calendar.

To Change the Date Format in the Property Sheet

a. On the status bar, click **Form View** 🔳.

b. Click the **value** for Date Joined. Notice that the date changes to have blanks after the month and day. The Date Picker is not activated.

c. On the status bar, click **Layout View** 🔳.

   In the property sheet, notice that Show Date Picker has a value of For dates. Ordinarily this would mean that a Calendar automatically pops up when you click the Date field. However, if the field has an input mask, that overrides the Date Picker. You will need to remove the mask.

d. In the property sheet, click the **Data tab**.

e. Select the **value** in the Input Mask. Press ⌦Delete to delete the mask.

f. On the form, click the **value** for Renewal Date. In the property sheet, on the Data tab, delete the input mask.

g. On the status bar, click **Form View** 🔳. Click the **value** for Date Joined. The Date Picker is activated. Click **Date Picker** 🔳 and a calendar pops up. Click the form background to deactivate the Date Picker.

h. Save 💾 your form.

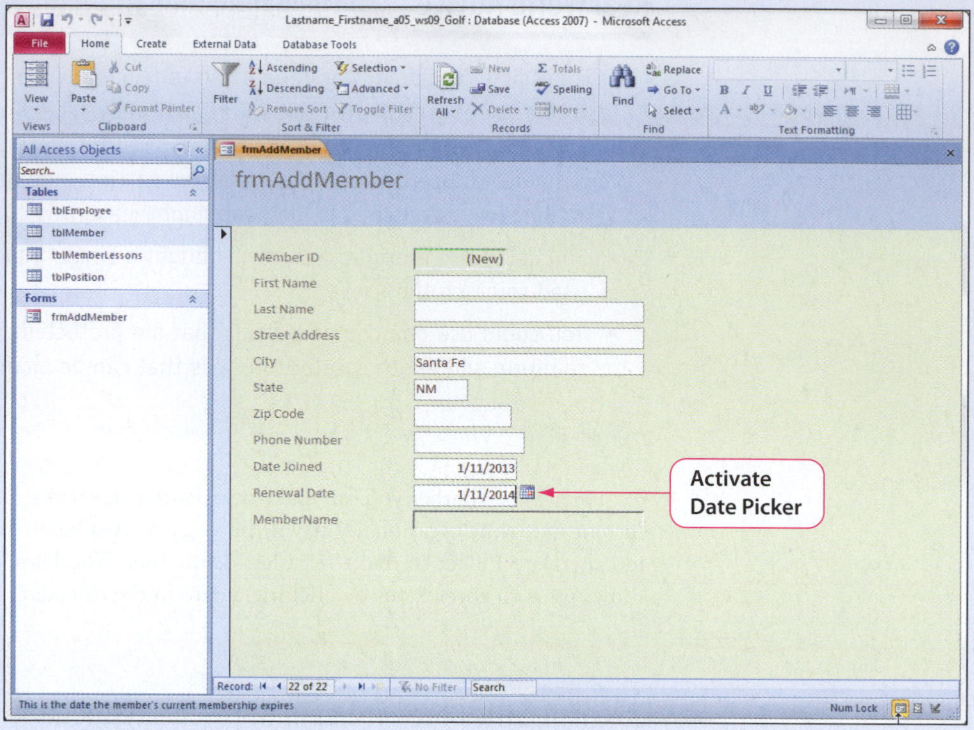

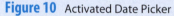

Figure 10 Activated Date Picker

Protecting Fields in a Form

The form currently allows a user to get to all fields. While MemberID and MemberName are deemphasized, a user could still try to change them. You will lock the fields. You will also change the form so the fields are skipped when a user tabs from field to field.

SIDE NOTE
Changing Tab Order in a Form

You can also rearrange the order that fields are tabbed to in your form. In Design view, the Tab Order button allows you to drag and drop fields into the desired tabbed order.

To Protect a Field from Being Updated

a. On the status bar, click **Layout View** 🔲.

b. Click the **Member ID** value. If necessary, click the **Data tab**.

c. Click the **Locked** property, and then click **Yes**.

d. Click the **Other tab**.

e. Click **Tab Stop**, and then click **No**.

f. Click the **MemberName** value. Repeat the skills you just learned in steps b through e to protect the MemberName field.

g. On the status bar, click **Form View** 🔲.

h. Tab through the fields. Notice that MemberID and MemberName are skipped.

Real World Advice **Protect Fields That Should Not Be Changed**

The reason we use forms to enter data is to make it easier for users to use the database. Anything you can do to make the form simpler will make it less likely that the user makes a mistake. If you do not want a user to change a field, lock the fields and do not allow the user to tab to it. If the fields are easily accessible, users may try to change them. Removing the ability to change the fields makes the form easier to use.

Adding a Title, Logo, Date, and Time to a Form

The detail section of your form is complete. The form also has a header section. You will make changes to the header including changing the color. You will change the title to make the form more descriptive. You will add a picture and a date and time to the form. The title of a form should be as descriptive as possible. If there are several member forms, you want it to be easy for the user to distinguish which form this is. A title of "Add a new member" will make it clear what this form is to be used for.

To Add a Title and a Logo to a Form Header

a. On the status bar, click **Layout View** 🗐.

b. Click the **header** to the right of the frmAddMember title.

c. Click the **Format tab** of the property sheet, click the **Back Color** property, and then click the **Build** button ⋯. Select the green color in the fourth row, **Olive Green, Accent 3, Lighter 40%**.

d. Close ⊠ the property sheet.

e. Click the title **frmAddMember**. Drag over the current title, and then type Add a new member. Click the **header background**.

Troubleshooting

If your title is displayed on two lines, you can resize the title by moving your pointer on the right side of the title until it is a double-headed arrow ↔. Drag the right border to the right until the title is on one line.

f. You want to have room on the left side of your title for a tournament logo. Point to the **title** until your pointer becomes a four-pointed arrow ⊞. Use your pointer to drag the **title** and move it to the right about an inch.

g. On the Ribbon, in the Header/Footer group, click **Logo**. Navigate to your student data files, and then select **a05_ws09_Golf_Logo**. Click **OK** to insert the picture.

h. Point to the lower-right corner of the logo until your pointer becomes a diagonal arrow ⬉. Resize the picture so that its height is as big as the header area.

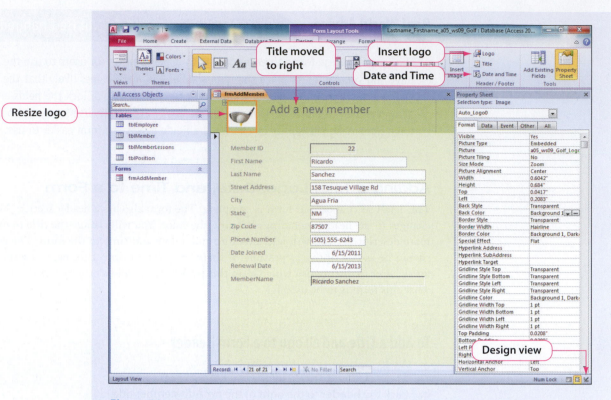

Figure 11 Insert logo

To Add the Date and Time to a Form Header

a. On the Ribbon, in the Header/Footer group, click **Date and Time**.

b. In the Date and Time dialog box, accept the defaults **Include Date**, the first format for the date, and **Include Time**, and the first format for the time.

c. Click **OK**.

Adding a Footer to a Form

You would like to add a footer to the form with a note to show the form was created by you. When a form is created, it is created with a header and a detail section. However, there is no footer created unless you insert one. This cannot be done in Layout view. You will need to switch to Design view and add the form footer.

SIDE NOTE
How Do You Know What Cannot Be Done in Layout View?

The easiest way is to try to do it in Layout view. If you cannot, switch to Design view.

To Add a Form Footer

a. On the status bar, click **Design View**.

Figure 12 shows Design view. There is a Form Header section and a Detail section. The picture and text you added to the header are in the Form Header section. Fields are shown in the Detail section. At the bottom of the form is a Form Footer section, but it is not visible. You need to display it before you can add fields to it.

b. Use your pointer to pull down the bottom edge of the bar that says **Form Footer**. Pull it down 1". You notice that the footer is white. You want to change the color to match the detail. Click the background of the form footer.

c. Click **Property Sheet**, click the **Format tab**, click the **Back Color** property, and then click the **Build** button. Select the light green in the second row, **Olive Green, Accent 3, Lighter 80%**.

d. Close ✕ the property sheet.

e. On the Ribbon, in the Controls group, click the **Label** control Aa.

f. Move your pointer to the **footer** and it becomes a Label pointer. Click and a small window appears. Type Created by FirstName LastName using your actual name. The window will get larger as you type.

g. On the status bar, click **Form View**.

h. Save your form.

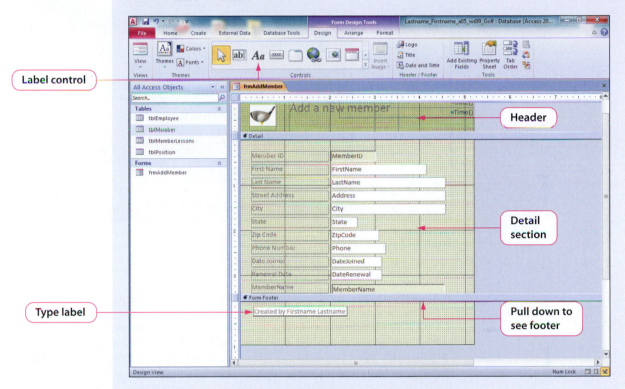

Figure 12   Design view with footer added

Your form is ready to be used. You will test it by adding yourself as a member.

To Add a Member Using a Form

a. You use the Navigation bar at the bottom of the form to navigate in a form. Click **New (blank) record** to get to a blank record.

b. Make sure you are on the New (Blank) Record, Record 22 of 22. Tab to FirstName, and then type your first name. Tab to LastName, and then type your last name.

c. Tab to Street Address, and then enter 1200 Reservoir Street.

d. Tab to City. You will accept the default of "Santa Fe" by tabbing to State.

e. Accept the default of "NM" by tabbing to Zip Code, and then enter 87593.

f. Tab to Phone Number, and then enter (505) 555-4882.

g. Tab to Date Joined, click **Date Picker**, navigate to April 11, 2011, and then click that **date**.

h. Tab to Renewal Date, and then change the date to **4/11/2013**.

i. Save and close ☒ the form.

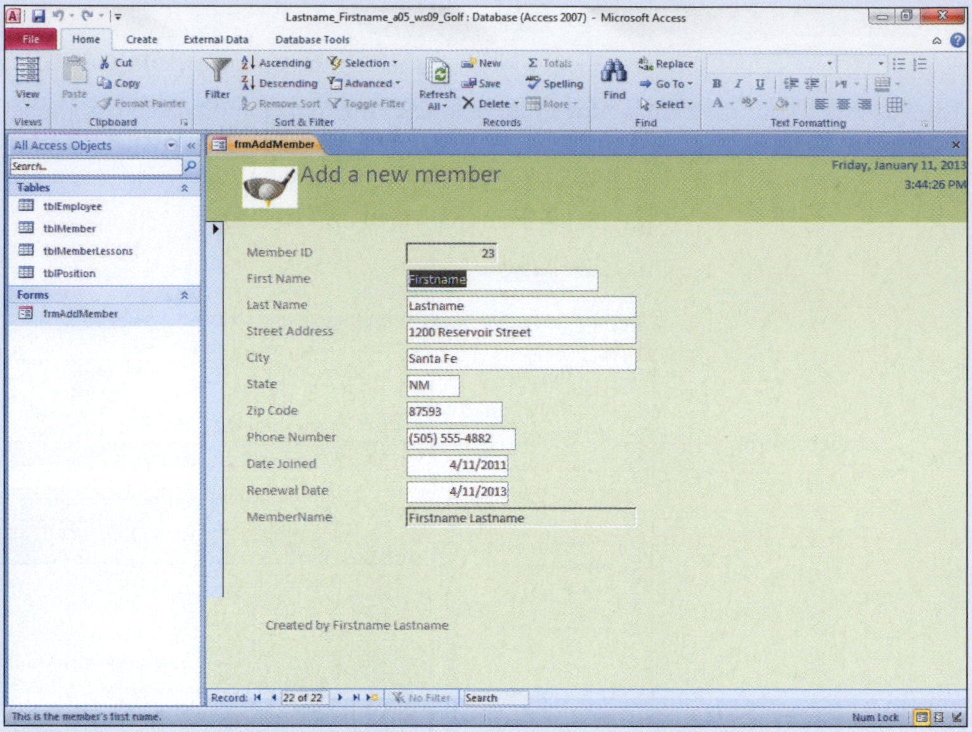

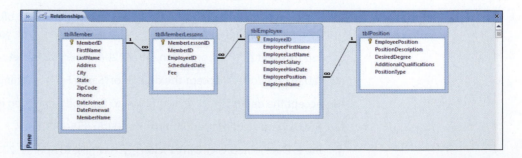

Figure 13 Completed form

Modifying a Form in Design View

Barry Cheney would like to have a form that can be used to sign a member up for a lesson. The golf club employee should be able to see the member's address and make changes if necessary. To create this form, you want to see data from two tables: tblMember and tblMemberLessons. The type of form that is ideal for two types of tables is a form with a subform. A **subform** is a form embedded in a form. The member will appear in the form. In this section, you will be able to see the lessons embedded in the form of the member.

Creating a Form with a Subform

When you create a form, it is useful to remind yourself of your database design. Figure 14 shows the relationships for this database. The relationship between tblMember and tblMemberLessons is a one-to-many relationship. A member can have many lessons; each lesson is taken by a single member. There is also a one-to-many relationship between tblMemberLessons and tblEmployee with each employee being able to give many lessons and each lesson given by a single employee.

Figure 14 Golf database relationships

You and Barry sketch the desired form and come up with the design shown in Figure 15. The header will include a way to find a member based on their name. The form will include the member's name and address. In the subform, all the lessons will be shown.

Add Lesson			
Look up Member based on name			
Member			
First name			
Last name			
Address			
City			
State			
Zip Code			
Lesson 1	Instructor name	Lesson Date	Fee
Lesson 2	Instructor name	Lesson Date	Fee
Lesson 3	Instructor name	Lesson Date	Fee

Figure 15 Sketch for Adding a Lesson form

As you compare the sketch to the database, you notice that the member lesson has EmployeeID and not the employee name. Recall that you can use a lookup field in the table design to show the name instead of the ID. If you do that, the name will also show in the form. You need to check the table design to see if tblMemberLessons was already set up that way.

Real World Advice   Think About Your Design in Advance

As you create forms and reports, a little forethought will make your task much easier. Take a minute to review your database relationships. Sketch your desired output. See which tables contain the needed data. You will often find that doing a query prior to creating the report or form will be necessary. Determining that in the beginning will save you time in the long run.

To Check the Design of tblMemberLessons

a. Right-click **tblMemberLessons**, and then click **Design View**.

b. Select the row **EmployeeID**. In Field Properties, click the **Lookup tab**. You find that the row source for the EmployeeID is a query that gets the name from the tblEmployee table. No changes are necessary.

c. Close ⊠ the table.

Now that you are sure the tblMemberLessons will appear the way you sketched them in Figure 15, you can create your form. If you create a default form without the Form Wizard, Access will select all the fields from both tables. Because you want just a selection of the fields, you will use the Form Wizard and select the fields that you and Barry agreed upon.

To Create a Form with a Subform

a. Click **tblMember**.

b. Click the **Create tab**, and then click **Form Wizard**.

c. From tblMember, select **FirstName**, **LastName**, **Address**, **City**, **State**, and **ZipCode**.

d. From tblMemberLessons, select **EmployeeID**, **ScheduledDate**, and **Fee**. Click **Next**.

e. Accept the **view by tblMember** and **Form with subform(s)**, and then click **Next**.

f. Accept **Datasheet** layout, and then click **Next**.

g. Name your form **frmAddLessons**.

h. Name your subform **frmAddLessonsSubform**.

i. Click **Finish**.

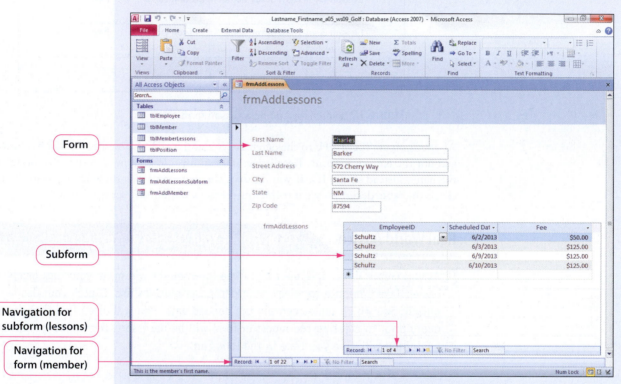

Figure 16 Form with subform

The form looks like your sketch, but it needs some formatting. You need to add the look up of members in the header which you will do with a combo box. You would like to clean up the titles of both the form and subform. The columns for the subform should be resized, and the Employee ID column should be renamed. You should check the formatting for each of your fields.

The form has two Navigation bars. The middle Navigation bar navigates through the lessons of a member. The bottom Navigation bar navigates through the members. This is difficult for users so you will add a combo box to find members and add some buttons to the form to replace the Navigation bars.

j. Tab through the fields of the member. The fields all appear formatted correctly.

k. Click the **Employee ID** for the blank (append) row in the subform. A drop-down selection box appears so that column is formatted correctly. Do not select any instructor.

Employee names are duplicated. That is because the source for the name is each lesson, and employees can teach many lessons. You need to correct that by changing the source to tblEmployee.

l. Click the **Scheduled Date** column for the blank (append) row. The Date Picker does not appear. You need to fix that by removing the input mask.

m. Click the **Fee** column for the blank (append) row. This column appears formatted correctly.

You will fix the column widths first. That is easiest to do in Layout view. While you are in Layout view, you will format the date to display the Date Picker. You will also fix the titles, add the logo, and change the background color.

To Modify the Form and Subform in Layout View

a. On the status bar, click **Layout View** 📺.

b. In the subform, click the **EmployeeID** column header. This selects the entire column. Put your pointer in the right border so it becomes a double-headed arrow ↔. Double-click to resize the column to fit the contents.

c. Resize the **Scheduled Date** and **Fee** columns the same way.

d. Use your pointer to resize the right side of the subform to fit the new column sizes.

e. Click the first **value** for EmployeeID. Click to view the property sheet, and then click the **Data tab**.

f. Click the **Row Source arrow**, and then select **tblEmployee** as your source.

g. Click the first **value** for Scheduled Date. On the property sheet, on the **Data tab**, remove the input mask.

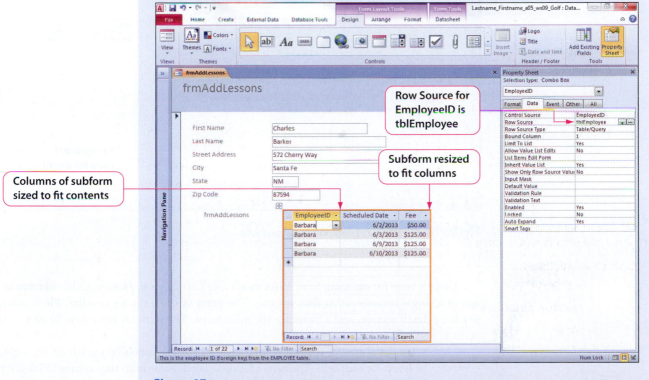

Figure 17 Resize columns in subform

h. Click the **form header**, and then on the property sheet, click the **Format tab**, and change the background color of the form header to be **Olive Green, Accent 3, Lighter 40%**.

i. Double-click **frmAddLessons** in the title of the form. Change the text to Add a lesson, and then move the revised title to the right about 1", leaving room for the logo.

j. On the Ribbon, in the Header/Footer group, click **Logo**. Navigate to your student data files, select **a05_ws09_Golf_Logo**, and then click **OK**.

k. Point to the lower-right corner of the logo until your pointer becomes a diagonal arrow. Resize the picture so that its height is as big as the header area.

l. On the Ribbon, in the Header/Footer group, click **Date and Time**. In the Date and Time dialog box, accept the defaults **Include Date**, the first format for the date, and **Include Time**, and the first format for the time. Click **OK**.

m. Click the subform label, **frmAddLessons**, in the middle of the form. Replace the text with Lessons.

n. Change the Back Color property of the form detail to **Olive Green, Accent 3, Lighter 80%**. You will not change the background color of the subform because there is no background to this part of the form.

o. Save your form.

p. Switch to Design view.

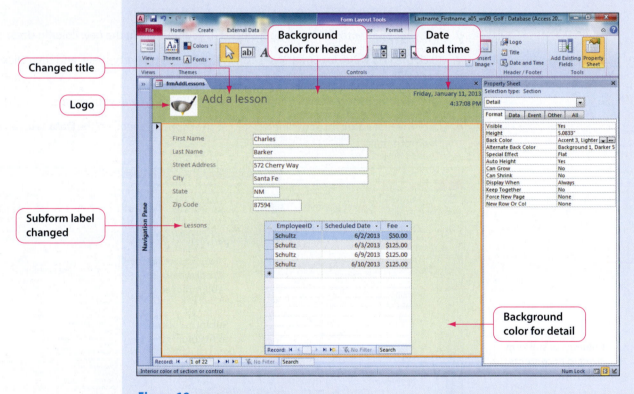

Figure 18 Fix form and subform in Layout view

Design view for the main form looks much like Layout view. However, the subform is laid out in a single column rather than in rows. The parts of the form are familiar. There is a form header, a detail section, and a footer for the main form. The subform has a form header, a detail section, and a form footer as well.

Look at the detail area for the main form. Recall that the controls on the left are the unbound controls, the labels for each field. The names for these labels come from the captions defined for the fields in the table. The controls on the right are the bound controls. In Design view, the contents are the name of the field from the database. That indicates what field this control is bound to.

In the subform, the same pattern of unbound and bound controls is shown.

To Modify a Form in Design View

a. Drag the bottom edge of the form footer down 1" (not the subform). Change the Back Color property to **Olive Green, Accent 3, Lighter 80%**.

b. Click the **Label control** $\boxed{Aa}$ in the Controls group on the Ribbon.

c. Point to the footer to display a **Label pointer** $\boxed{^{+}A}$. Click the **footer**, and then type Created by Firstname Lastname using your actual name.

d. In the subform, click the **EmployeeID** label. Change the text to read Instructor.

e. Close $\boxed{\times}$ the property sheet.

f. Save $\boxed{\blacksquare}$ your form.

Adding Fields to a Form

You show the form to Barry, and he asks that the phone number also appear on the form so a member can be contacted and the phone number could be changed on this form. You will use the Add Existing Fields button to add the field.

To Add a Member Phone Number to a Form

a. Click anywhere in the background of the main form. On the Ribbon, click the **Design tab**, and then click **Add Existing Fields** in the Tools group.

Access displays a list of fields available. The fields in the member table are shown. If you wanted, you could expand the list and see fields in other tables.

b. Click **Phone** in the Field List pane, and then drag it to the main form detail section.

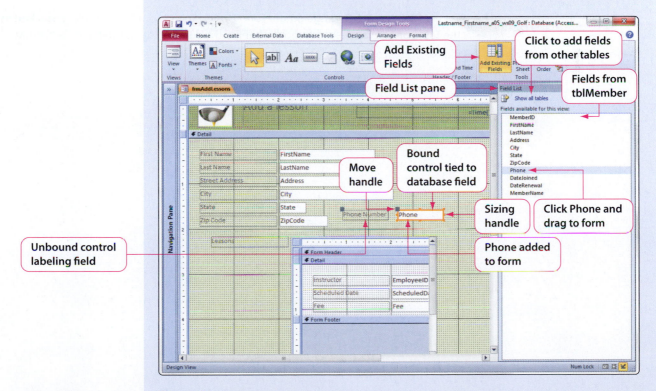

Figure 19 Add existing field to form

When you add an existing field, Access adds two controls. One is the bound control (a text box) tied to a database field. The second is an unbound control that labels the text box. The two controls are attached to each other. They can be moved as a pair or separately. When a control is selected, Access outlines the control in orange. There are eight boxes or handles on the outline. The large grey handle in the top-left corner is called the **move handle**. It is used to move the controls in the form. The smaller orange handles are **sizing handles**. Sizing handles are used to resize the control.

If you use your pointer to move the control now, without clicking on the move handle, you will move both controls at the same time. If you click the move handle, you will move just one control. You can use your mouse to move the control a large distance. You can also use the arrow keys on the keyboard to nudge the control a short distance.

c. Move your mouse to somewhere in the orange border but not on one of the handles. When the pointer becomes a four-headed arrow ⊞, move the control slightly.

d. Release the mouse and you will see that both controls moved at once.

Troubleshooting

If you accidently touched the move handle and moved one of the controls without the other, use Undo ↺▾ to undo your change.

You can also use the Arrange tab to arrange a group of controls on a form. With this feature, you do not have to worry about whether you have exactly lined up the controls. Access will take care of it for you. You decide to use this feature.

e. Place your pointer in the form background just above the First Name label. Drag diagonally to the right, selecting all of the member controls. Release your mouse when you have encircled all the controls. Access indicates that all the controls are selected by outlining them in orange.

f. On the Ribbon, click **Arrange** on the Form Design Tools tab, and then select **Stacked** in the Table group. The fields are moved behind the subform so you will need to fix that.

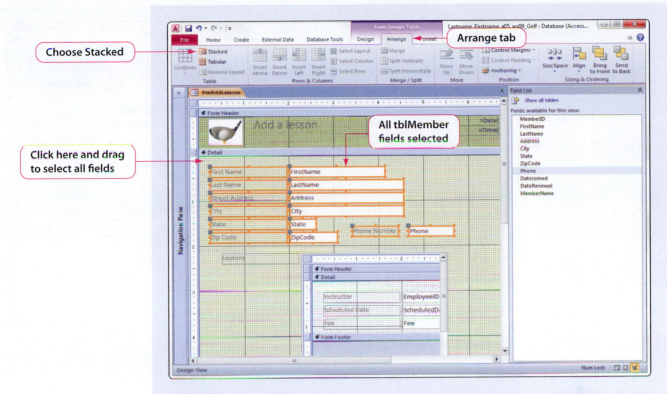

Choose Stacked

Arrange tab

All tblMember fields selected

Click here and drag to select all fields

Figure 20 Arrange fields

Access arranges all the member controls in a stacked layout. The stacked layout can be thought of as an invisible table with the matching bound and unbound controls for each field in a row. All the unbound controls are in one column; all the bound controls are in the second column. Depending on where you dropped Phone number in the form, Phone number might not be at the bottom of the layout. If Phone number is not at the bottom of the layout, you can use the Arrange tab to move it down.

g. If Phone number is not at the bottom of your layout, click in the blank space to the right of the controls to deselect the fields. Click the **Phone Number** label. On the Arrange tab, click **Select Row** in the Rows & Columns group to select both the unbound and bound controls for Phone Number. On the Arrange tab, click **Move Down** in the Move group until Phone Number is the last field.

h. On the Arrange tab, click **Select Layout** in the Rows & Columns group to select all the Member Controls. Click **Control Padding** in the Position group, and then select **Narrow**.

i. Close ☒ the Field List pane.

j. Save your form.

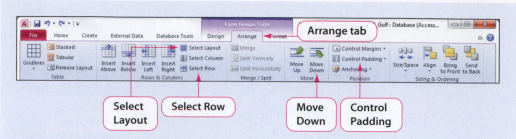

Figure 21 Arrange tab

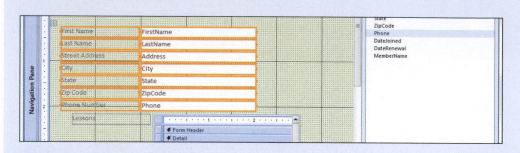

Figure 22 Narrow control padding

Adding Calculated Fields to a Form

Barry asks for a count of lessons for each member and how much they have been charged. You will create that by creating a **calculated control**, a control whose source of data is an expression rather than a field. You will use the Expression Builder to build the calculations. The functions you will use are Count (to count the number of lessons) and Sum (to sum the fees).

This is a two-step process. You will count the lessons and sum the fees in the subform. It is easier to work with a subform if you open it in another window. Then you will add new text box controls to calculate the totals in these controls. The second step involves adding the totals to the detail in the main form.

To Add Calculated Fields to the Subform

a. Click the **subform** so it is outlined in orange. With your pointer on the border, right-click, and then click **Subform in New Window**.

b. Use your pointer to pull down the bottom edge of the bar that says **Form Footer**. Make the footer 1" high. Use the ruler on the side of the form to help you judge the 1".

c. Click **Text Box** ⓐⓑ in the Controls group. Move your pointer to the footer. Your pointer will change to ⓐⓑ. Click in the middle of the footer.

Troubleshooting

If you put your controls too near the left edge of the footer, the controls will overlap. You can use Undo ↶▾ and try again. Or, you can use the two Move handles to move each field separately.

Access will add two controls—a label and an unbound control. You will want to make the unbound control a calculated control. You will do this via the property sheet.

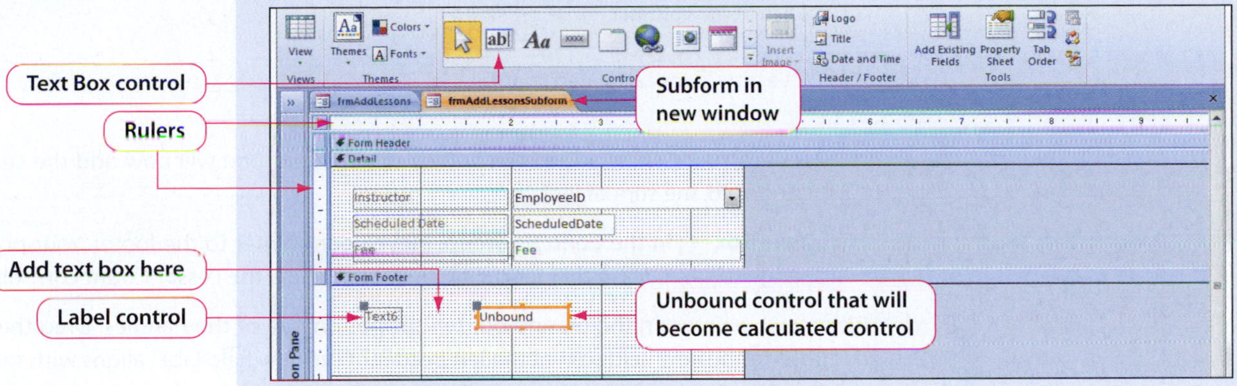

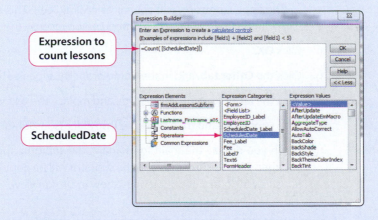

Text Box control

Rulers

Subform in new window

Add text box here

Label control

Unbound control that will become calculated control

Figure 23 Unbound control

d. If necessary, click the **text box** on the form, and then click **Property Sheet** to open the property sheet for the control.

e. Click the **Data tab**, and then in the **Control Source** property, click the **Build** button 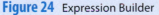.

f. In the Expression Builder , type **=Count( )**.

g. Place your pointer between the parentheses, and then double-click **ScheduledDate** in the Expression Categories pane.

   The final expression will appear as =Count([ScheduledDate]). This expression means that Access will count all the tblMemberLesson records. Alternatively, you could have typed the entire formula yourself.

Expression to count lessons

ScheduledDate

Figure 24 Expression Builder

h. Click **OK**.

i. On the property sheet, click the **Other tab**, and then in the Name property, type **LessonCount**.

j. Click the **label control** on the form, and then replace the text with **Lesson Count**.

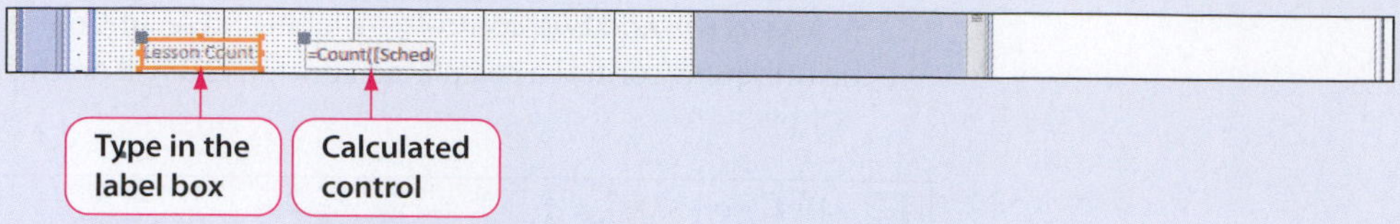

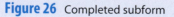

Type in the label box   Calculated control

Figure 25 LessonCount calculated control

You have successfully added the first calculated field. You will now add the second calculated field, the sum of fees.

k. Click **Text Box** 🔲 in the Controls group. Move your pointer to the footer. Your pointer will change to 🔲. Click in the middle of the footer below the LessonCount controls.

l. Place your pointer on the orange border but not on one of the handles. Drag the two controls for the new field so that the left border of the new field label aligns with the left border of the Lesson Count label.

Troubleshooting

If you accidently clicked the move handle and moved one of the controls without the other, use Undo 🔄▾ to undo your change. You can also move each control separately using their respective move handles.

m. If necessary, click the **text box**, click the **Data tab** on the property sheet, and then in the Control Source property, click the **Build** button 🔲.

n. In the Expression Builder box, type **=Sum( )**.

o. Place your pointer between the parentheses, and then double-click **Fee** in the Expression Categories pane.

The final expression will appear as =Sum([Fee]). This expression means that Access will sum the fees in all the tblMemberLesson records.

p. Click **OK**.

q. Click the **Other tab**, and in the Name property, type **FeeTotal**.

r. Click the **label control** on the form, and replace the text with **Fee Total**.

s. Save your form, and then close the frmAddLessonsSubform.

t. When you display the main form again, the subform appears blank. Click **Form View**, and then click **Design View** and the subform will be populated. The subform footer does not show in Form view, but it does show in Design view.

Figure 26 Completed subform

You have calculated the count and sum fields but you need to show them on the main form since the footer of the subform does not show in Form view. You will create text boxes and use the fields from the subform.

To Add Fields from the Subform to the Main Form

a. Click **Text Box** ⬚ in the Controls group. Place your pointer in the detail section of the form to the left of the subform. Your pointer will change to ⬚. Click to place the text box. If necessary to adjust the placement of your controls, place your pointer on the **orange border** but not on one of the handles. Drag the two controls together.

b. If necessary, click the **text box**. Click the **Data tab** in the property sheet, and then in the Control Source property, click the **Build** button ⬚.

c. In the Expression Elements pane, expand **frmAddLessons**, and then click **frmAddLessonsSubform**. This changes the fields in the Expressions Categories pane to fields from the subform.

d. In the Expression Categories pane, double-click **LessonCount**. This will build the expression [frmAddLessonsSubform].Form![LessonCount].

e. Click **OK**.

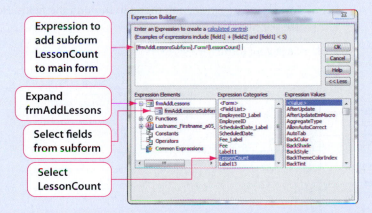

Expression to add subform LessonCount to main form

Expand frmAddLessons

Select fields from subform

Select LessonCount

Figure 27 Build LessonCount

f. Click the **Other tab**, and then in the Name property, type **LessonCount**.

g. Click the **label control**, and then replace the text with **Lesson Count**.

h. Click **Text Box** ⬚ in the Controls group. Place your pointer on the detail section of the form below Lesson Count. Your pointer will change to ⬚. Click to place the text box. If necessary to adjust the placement of your controls, place your pointer on the **orange border** but not on one of the handles. Drag the two controls together.

i. If necessary, click the **text box**. Click the **Data tab** in the property sheet, and then in the Control Source property, click the **Build** button ⬚.

j. In the Expression Elements pane, expand **frmAddLessons**. Click **frmAddLessonsSubform**.

k. In the Expression Categories pane, double-click **FeeTotal**. This will build the expression [frmAddLessonsSubform].Form![FeeTotal].

l. Click **OK**.

m. Click the **Other tab**, and then in the Name property, type **TotalFees**.

n. Click the **Format tab**, and then in the Format property, select **Currency**.

o. Click the **label control** on the form, and then replace the text with Total Fees.

p. Switch to Form view and see the calculations.

q. Click the **Lesson Count field**, and then try to change the count to 6.

You cannot type but you can click there. You want to protect these fields so the user cannot change these fields. Remember that to protect fields, you lock the property and prevent the field from being tabbed to.

To Protect a Field from Being Updated

a. Switch to Design view.

b. Click the **LessonCount** value. Click the **Data tab**, click the **Locked** property, and then select **Yes**.

c. Click the **Other tab**, click **Tab Stop**, and then select **No**.

d. Repeat steps b and c for **Total Fees**.

e. Switch to Form view, and then tab through the fields. Notice that the calculated fields are skipped.

f. Save your form.

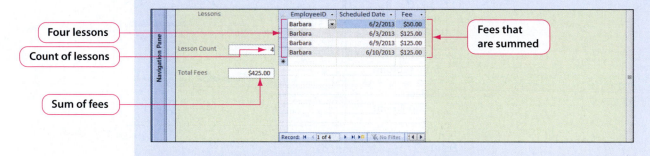

Figure 28 Calculated fields on form

Finding a Record Using a Combo Box

Your form is professional looking, but it is still not as easy to use as Barry wanted. To find a member, the user needs to use the Navigation bar and tab through all the members. They also need to decide which of the two Navigation bars to use. Barry wants a user to be able to select the member by name. You will add a combo box to select members to the form header.

To Use a Combo Box to Find a Record

a. Switch to Design view. Place your pointer on the **top border** of the Detail section bar. Drag down so that the Form Header section is 1" high.

b. Click the **More Button** in the Controls group to see all available controls.

c. Click **Combo Box** in the Controls group. Move your pointer to the header. When it changes to , click in the **form header** below the title. Access starts the Combo Box Wizard.

d. Click **Find a record on my form based on the value I selected in my combo box**, and then click **Next**.

e. Click **LastName** and **FirstName** in that order, and then click **Next**.

f. Accept the default to **Hide key column**, and then click **Next**.

g. Enter Member Name as your Label, and then click **Finish**.

h. If necessary, drag the new combo box so it fits well in the header.

i. **Save** the form. Switch to Form view.

You will use your new form to add a lesson for yourself.

To Add a Record in a Subform

a. In **Member Name** in the header, select your own name. You have no lessons.

Troubleshooting

When you try to select a member name, if you see members' names many times, close your database and reopen it. Open frmMemberLessons and try again.

b. Tab down to the Instructor. Select **John Schilling** as your instructor.

c. Use the Date Picker to schedule your lesson for **March 10, 2013**.

d. Enter 150 as your fee.

e. Tab to the next record. Notice that your lesson count and calculated fee fields were updated.

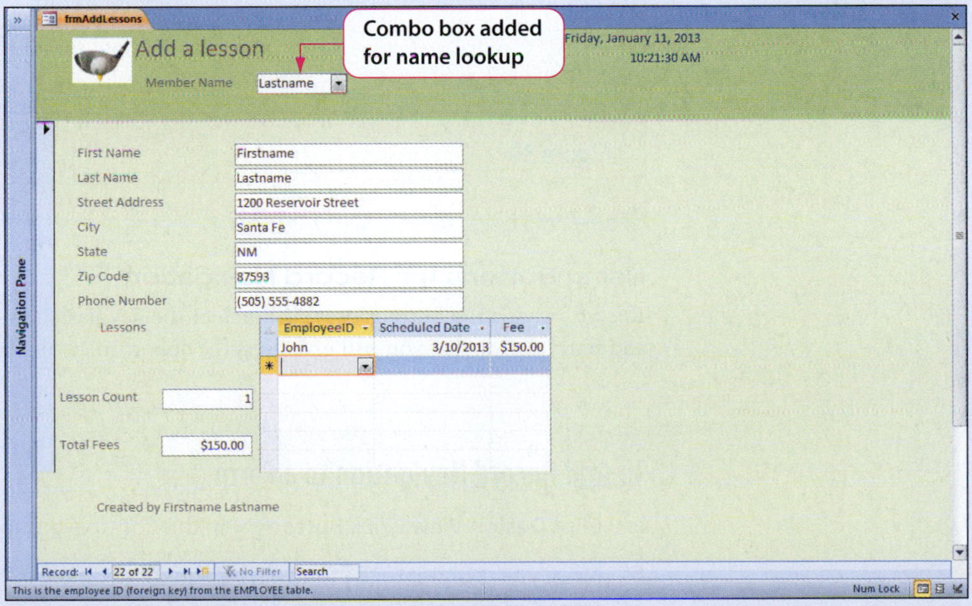

Figure 29 Form with combo box

Adding Command Buttons to a Form

The form is very easy to use. But it is still navigated with the Navigation bars. Users will not find those easy to use. You will add some buttons for navigation and turn off the Navigation bar. A button control is one of the controls available to be added to a form.

Buttons are available in several categories. Record Navigation buttons replicate most of the navigation tools available on the Navigation bar. You can create buttons to go to the first, next, last and previous records. Record Operations buttons allow the user to add, delete, and undo a record. Form Operations buttons open, close, and print forms.

Quick Reference Form Command Buttons Available

Category	Actions
Record Navigation	Find Next
	Find Record
	Go to First Record
	Go to Last Record
	Go to Next Record
	Go to Previous Record
Record Operations	Add New Record
	Delete Record
	Duplicate Record
	Print Record
	Save Record
	Undo Record
Form Operations	Apply Form Filter
	Close Form
	Open Form
	Print a Form
	Print Current Form
	Refresh Form Data

Figure 30

Using Buttons for Record Navigation

Record Navigation buttons provide much of the navigation available on the Navigation bar. You and Barry decide that you will give users the opportunity to go to the next and previous members.

To Add Record Navigation to a Form

a.   Click **Design View**. Click **Button** ▭ in the Controls group.

b.   Move your pointer to the form to the right of the member fields. Place the button on the form. Access starts the Command Button Wizard.

c.   Click **Record Navigation** and **Go To Next Record**, and then click **Next**.

d. Click **Text**, type Next Member, and then click **Next**.

e. Name the button cmdNextMember. Click **Finish**.

f. Click **Button** [⬚] in the Controls group.

g. Place your pointer below the Next Member button, and then click on the form. Access starts the Command Button Wizard.

h. Click **Record Navigation** and **Go To Previous Record**, and then click **Next**.

i. Click **Text**, type Previous Member, and then click **Next**.

j. Name the button cmdPreviousMember, and then click **Finish**.

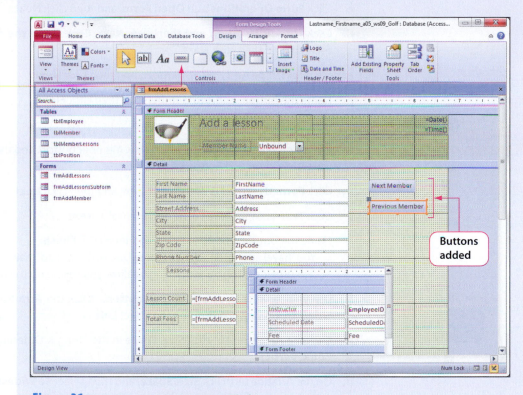

Figure 31 Previous Member button added

Real World Advice   Record vs. Member

Access suggests text for command buttons that include the word "Record". In this case, the word "Record" is a technical database term. You know that a record is a row in a table, and that it contains data about a person, place, or thing. However, a user without database training will not know what "record" means. To make your form user friendly, replace the word "Record" with the name of the person, place, or thing. For example, a record in a member table should be called "Member"; a record in an employee table should be called "Employee".

Using Buttons for Form Operations

Barry thinks that two other buttons would be useful on this form. The first would be a link to the Add Member form. That would allow the user to switch to that form. The other would close this form. Both of these are Form Operations buttons.

To Use a Button for Form Operations

a. Click **Button** 🔲 in the Controls group.

b. Place your pointer below the Previous Member button, and then click on the form. Access starts the Command Button Wizard.

c. Click **Form Operations** and **Open Form**, and then click **Next**.

d. Click **frmAddMember**, and then click **Next**. Click **Open the form and show all the records**, and then click **Next**.

e. Click **Text**, type Add a New Member, and then click **Next**.

f. Name the button cmdAddMember, and then click **Finish**.

g. Click **Button** 🔲 in the Controls group.

h. Place your pointer below the Add a New Member button, and then click the form. Access starts the Command Button Wizard.

i. Click **Form Operations** and **Close Form**, and then click **Next**.

j. Click **Text**, accept **Close Form**, and then click **Next**.

k. Name the button cmdCloseForm, and then click **Finish**.

   You have added all four buttons, but you want to make them look professional. Access provides sizing and spacing to allow you to line up the buttons.

l. Use your pointer to select **all four buttons**. Click the **Arrange tab**, click **Align** in the Sizing & Ordering group, and then select **Left**.

m. Click the **Arrange tab**, click **Size/Space** in the Sizing & Ordering group, and then select **Equal Vertical**.

n. On the Arrange tab, click **Size/Space**, and then select **To Widest**.

Once you have buttons you can hide the Navigation bars that are the normal part of the forms. You need to turn them off for both the main form and the subform. You will also turn off the Record Selector on the far left side of the form.

To Turn Off the Navigation Bar

a. Click the **Form Selector**, the small space in the top-left corner of the form. This changes the property sheet to show the properties of the entire form; verify that the property sheet Selection type is **Form**.

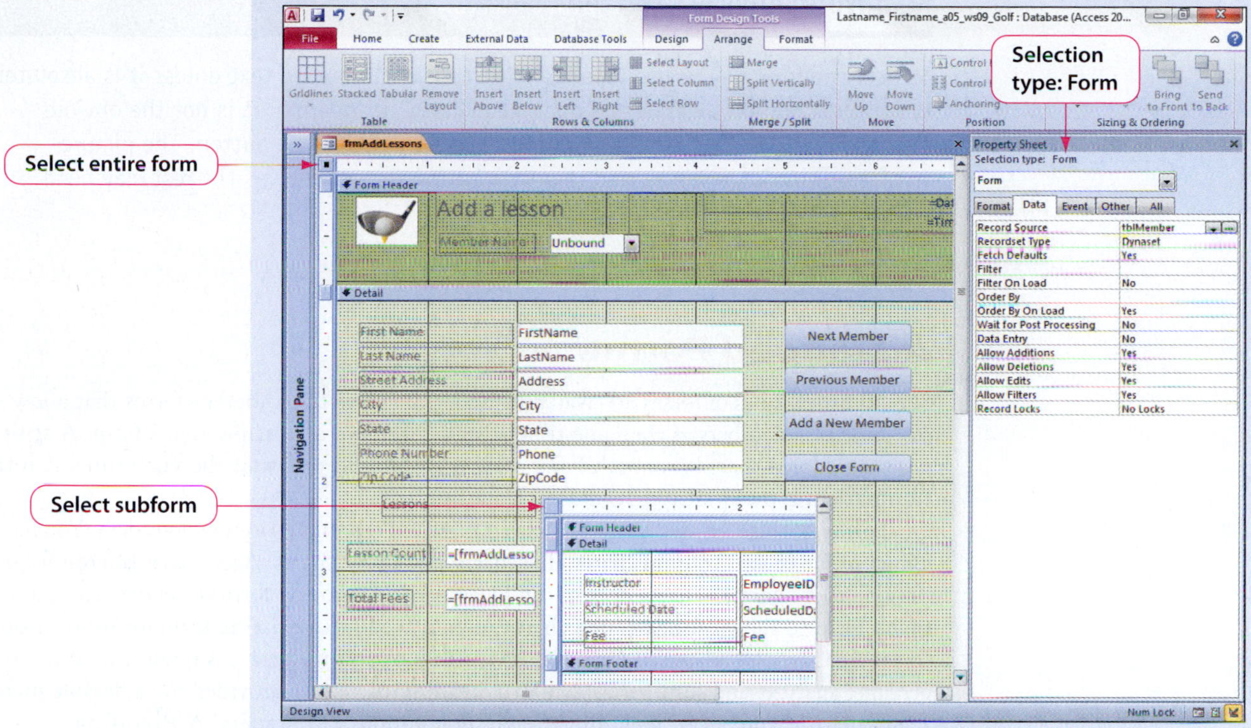

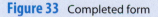

Figure 32 Select forms

b. Click the **Format tab**, and then change the Navigation Buttons to **No**.

c. Change Record Selectors to **No**.

d. Click the **Form Selector** for the subform, the small space in the top-left corner of the subform. This changes the property sheet to show the properties of the subform. Notice that the caption makes it clear that this is the subform.

e. Click the **Format tab**, and then change the Navigation Buttons to **No**.

f. Close the property sheet.

g. Save your form. Switch to Form view, and then test your buttons. Finish by clicking **Close Form** to close the form.

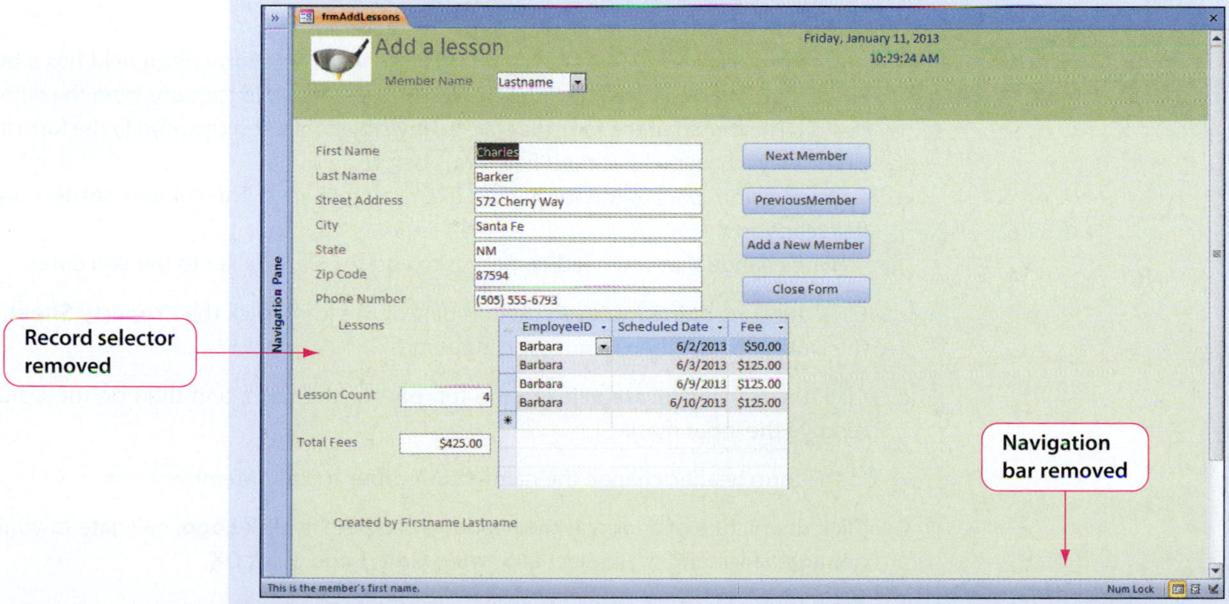

Figure 33 Completed form

Advanced Forms

Several other types of forms are available. You will create two different forms that allow you to see multiple members at the same time: a split form and a multiple items form. A **split form** is a single form that shows both Form view and Datasheet view at the same time. A **multiple items form** shows multiple records in Datasheet view.

Forms can also be used to display charts or visual representations of your data. You have your choice of pie charts, column charts, line charts, and other charts. Access uses Microsoft Graph to provide these charts. Chart controls can be embedded into any form or report. You can create a blank form to show the chart, or a chart can be placed in an existing form for illustration.

A final type of advanced form is a PivotTable. A **PivotTable** is an object used to organize, arrange, analyze, and summarize data in a meaningful way. It provides you a flexible method of manipulating your data, including swapping columns and headers. A **PivotChart** provides a graphical representation of a PivotTable.

In this section, you will create each of these types of advanced forms.

Creating a Split Form

A split form is a single form that shows both Form view and Datasheet view at the same time. You can scroll through the records at the bottom of the screen and find the record you want. That record is then displayed at the top of the screen in Form view. You can change the data in either view.

To Create a Member Split Form

a. Click **tblMember** in the Navigation Pane, click the **Create tab**, and then select **More Forms**.

b. Select **Split Form**.

   The top part of the form is a standard Form view type form. Each field has a bound and an unbound control. The unbound control uses the field captions from the database design. The format of the form is a stacked invisible table. You can modify the form in any of the ways that you have modified forms before.

   The bottom part of the form looks like the table view. The column headers are the field captions.

   One change that you need to make is to add the Date Picker to the two dates.

c. Click the **Date Joined** value in the top part of the form, click the **Property Sheet**, click the **Data tab**, and then remove the input mask.

d. Click the **Renewal Date** value in the top part of the form, and then on the Data tab, remove the input mask.

e. In the form header, change the name **tblMember** to Split Member Form.

f. Click the picture of a form in the header and delete it, click **Logo**, navigate to your student data files, and then select **a05_w09_Golf_Logo**. Click **OK**.

g. Save the form as frmSplitMember.

h. Switch to Form view. Tab to Date Joined. Notice that you are tabbing in both the top and bottom half of the form. The Date Picker is shown to the right of the field.

Troubleshooting

Does the top half of your form have just one column of fields? The number of columns depends on the size of your Access window and the size of your screen. Access will make two columns if there is room for them. If you just have one column, it means that your screen window is a little narrower than the one used to create the figure. This is fine.

i. Click in **Date Joined** in Datasheet view in the bottom half of the form. The Date Picker has also been activated for this part of the form.

j. Close the form.

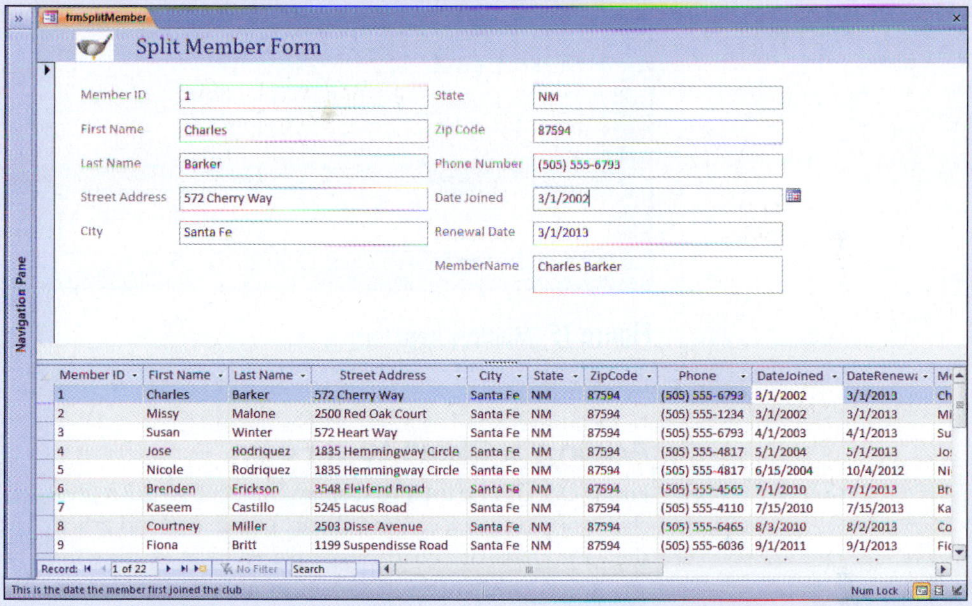

Figure 34 Split form

Creating a Multiple-Items Form

A multiple-items form shows multiple records in Datasheet view.

To Create a Member Multiple-Item Form

a. Click **tblMember** in the Navigation pane, click **Create**, and then click **More Forms**.

b. Select **Multiple Items**.

This form looks like the Datasheet view but with more space for rows and columns. The column headers are the field captions. You will make the same changes you made to the split form.

c. Scroll right to find **Date Joined**, and then click the first date field. On the property sheet, click the **Data tab**, and then remove the input mask.

d. Scroll right to find **Renewal Date**, click the **Data tab**, and then remove the input mask.

e. Scroll left. In the form header, change the name **tblMember** to Multiple Members Form.

f. Click the picture of a form in the header, and then delete it. Click **Logo**, navigate to your student data files, select **a05_w09_Golf_Logo**, and then click **OK**.

g. Save the form with the name frmMultipleMember. Close your form.

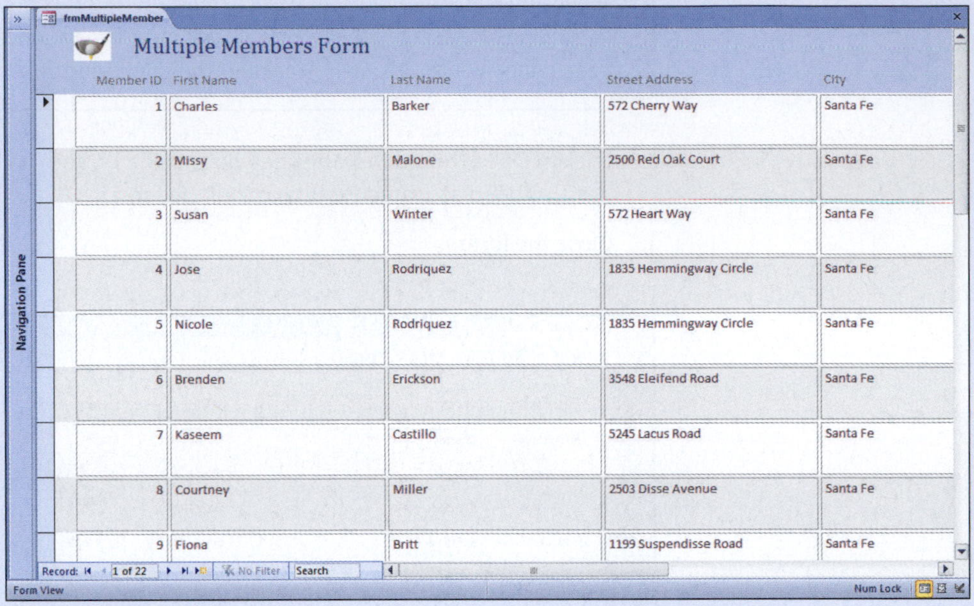

Figure 35 Multiple-item form

Adding a Chart to a Form

Forms can also be used to display charts or visual representations of your data. You have your choice of pie charts, column charts, line charts, and other charts. You can create a blank form to show the chart, or a chart can be placed in an existing form for illustration.

Access uses Microsoft Graph to provide these charts. When you start a chart, an Access wizard walks you through creating the chart. Once the chart is created, you use Microsoft Graph commands to revise the chart.

You should plan your charts before starting the Chart Wizard. Start by thinking about what data you need. You often need to create a query to bring all your data together for the wizard.

Barry would like to understand where members of the golf club who take lessons live. He asks if you could present data showing the amount of lesson fees by city of residence. You look at the data and realize that the city each member is from is in the tblMember table and fees are in the tblMemberLessons table. You need to create a query showing the combined data.

To Create a Query

a. Click the **Create tab**, and then click **Query Wizard**.

b. Click **Simple Query Wizard**, and then click **OK**.

c. From tblMember, click **FirstName**, **LastName**, **City**, and **State**.

d. From tblMemberLessons, click **ScheduledDate** and **Fee**, and then click **Next**.

e. Click **Detail**, and then click **Next**.

f. Name your query qryMemberCityFee, and then click **Finish**. Close the query.

You will use this query to create a chart. You will start with a form design and then embed the chart.

To Create a Pie Chart

a. Click the **Create tab**, and then click **Form Design**. If necessary, close ☒ the property sheet.

b. Click the **More** button ⊽ in the Controls group to see all available controls. Select **Chart** 📊 in the Controls group.

c. Move your pointer to the **detail**, and then click on the form. Access starts the Chart Wizard.

d. Click **Queries** and **qryMemberCityFee**, and then click **Next**.

e. Select **City** and **Fee**, and then click **Next**.

f. Click the **Pie Chart** in the first column of the last row, and then click **Next**.

g. Accept the default layout, and then click **Next**.

h. Name your chart Fees By City, and then click **Finish**.

i. When you first see your chart in Design view, it does not contain your data. Change your view to Layout view to view the chart data. Switch back to Design view to modify the chart.

j. Save your form with the name chartFeesByCity.

Editing of the chart is done in Microsoft Graph. You can change the formatting of the data and format the chart by adding titles and legends or by changing display options. To do that, you double-click the chart.

To Edit a Pie Chart in Microsoft Graph

a. Double-click your pie chart. Microsoft Graph opens. Examine this interface.

The chart is shown in a format similar to the form design. Below the chart is a datasheet of the values included in the chart. You could make changes to the data in the datasheet if you wanted to. You could also format the data.

The Microsoft Graph interface is very similar to interfaces from earlier versions of Excel or Access before the introduction of the Ribbon. It uses a menu system. You can click any of the choices from the menu bar such as File or Edit to bring a menu of choices. You can also click the Standard toolbar on the left, the Chart Options bar in the middle, or the Formatting toolbar on the right.

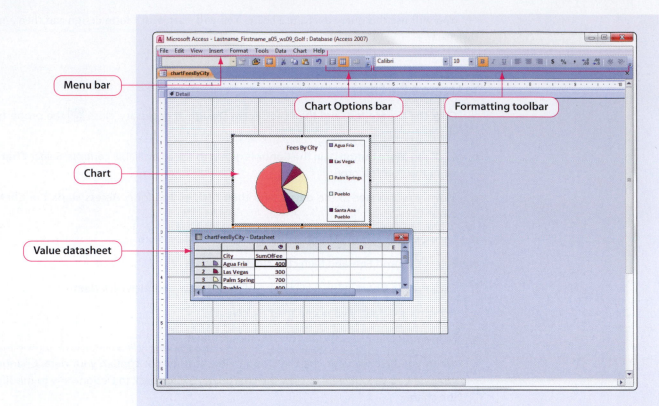

Figure 36 Microsoft Graph interface

b. On the menu bar, click **Chart**, and then select **Chart Options** from the menu.

In Chart Options, there are three tabs: Titles, Legend, and Data Labels. On the Titles tab, you can change the titles and the axes. Only Chart Title is available to be changed for a pie chart. On the Legend tab, you can decide whether or not to display a legend and where you want the legend placed. On the Data Labels tab, you can add information to the labels on the chart.

c. Click the **Data Labels tab**, click **Percentage**.

This adds Percent labels to your data. By checking this option, you are also given the option to include leader lines, which are lines between the percentage and the slice of the pie. You want those so leave it checked.

d. Click **OK**. That is all the formatting you will do in Microsoft Graph, so you will return to Access. On the menu bar, click **File**, and then click **Save**.

You are back in Access. The changes you made reduced the size of your chart. You still want to resize the chart and add a header and a footer to your chart. You do that in Access the same way that you have edited other forms. You will put the header and footer on the chart first because they also change the size of the chart.

To Edit a Form with an Embedded Chart

a. Click **Title** in the Header/Footer group. Doing this adds a header and a footer to your chart. Change the title of your form to **Lesson Fees by City of Residence**.

b. Click **Date and Time** in the Header/Footer group to put a date in the header. In the Date and Time dialog box, accept the defaults **Include Date**, the first format for the date, and **Include Time**, and the first format for the time.

c. Click **OK**.

d. Click once on your pie chart. Use the move handle to move the top-left corner of your chart to the spot 1" from the left and 1" from the top of your form. Use the bottom-right sizing handle and drag it diagonally down to the spot 5" from the left and 4" from the top of your form.

e. Drag the bottom of the form footer to make it .5" high.

f. Click **Label** [Aa] in the Controls group. Click in the form footer, and type **Created by Firstname Lastname**.

g. Save your form, and then switch to Form view.

You've given Barry a visual tool that he can use to see that the majority of golf lessons are given to members from Santa Fe. You put a date and time in the header so if the form is printed, people can see when this data was collected.

h. Close your chart.

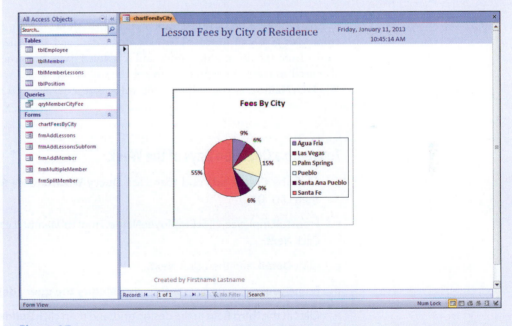

Figure 37 Completed pie chart

Real World Advice | Charting in Access vs. Charting in Excel

Both Access and Excel allow you to create charts. Which application should you use? The answer is largely a question of personal preference. You can easily export your data from Access to Excel or import from Excel into Access, so either choice is available to you. Here are some points to consider in your choice:

- Where is your data? If your data is in Access, you may want to create your charts in Access to avoid the steps of exporting the data to Excel.

- How are you going to use your charts? If you plan to embed the chart in an Access form or report, you may want to create the chart in Access. You can embed an Excel chart, but it takes extra steps.

- Which application do you find easier to use? If you are more comfortable charting in one of the two applications, you can use that application for most charts.

- Are your charts very sophisticated? Do they use advanced statistical techniques? If so, Excel is probably the better choice. Excel has a better statistical and analytical engine than Access does. If you need the multiple tables with relationships between them that Access provides, you can create a query in Access and then export the results to Excel for the statistical analysis.

- Do you want to provide a friendly user interface to your charts, particularly for many users? With forms and command buttons, Access provides that friendlier interface.

Barry asks if you could create a chart that shows which days of the week the different employees give golf lessons. You look at the data and recognize that you will need employee names from the tblEmployee table and scheduled dates from the tblMemberLessons table. You also need to create an expression to get the day of the week. Access provides a function called WeekdayName that you will use. You will create a query to get this data.

To Create a Query on Days of the Week

a. Click the **Create tab**, and then click **Query Wizard**. Click **Simple Query Wizard**, and then click **OK**.

b. From tblEmployee, click **EmployeeName**. From tblMemberLessons, click **ScheduledDate**. Click **Next**.

c. Click **Detail**, and then click **Next**.

d. Name your query **qryLessonDay**, click **Modify the query design**, and then click **Finish**.

e. Click in the **third field** in the design grid, and then click **Builder**. In the Expression Builder dialog box, type **=WeekdayName(Weekday([ScheduledDate]))**, and then click **OK**.

f. Replace Expr1 with **LessonDay**.

g. Run your query, save your query, and then close your query.

You decide to create a column chart with two sets of data on the x-axis: employee and days of the week and with count of lessons on the y-axis.

To Create a Column Chart

a. Click the **Create tab**, and then click **Form Design**.

b. Click the **More** button ▾ in the Controls group to see all available controls. Select **Chart** 📊 in the **Controls** group. Move your pointer to the 1" x 1" mark in the Detail section, and then click the form. Access starts the Chart Wizard.

c. Click **Queries** and **qryLessonDay**, and then click **Next**.

d. Click **EmployeeName** and **LessonDay**, and click **Next**.

e. Click the **Column Chart** in the first column of the first row, and then click **Next**.

f. Accept the default layout, and then click **Next**.

g. Name your chart Lessons by Day, and then click **Finish**.

h. When you first see your chart in Design view, it does not contain your data. Change your view to Layout view to view the chart. Switch back to Design view to modify the chart. Save your form with the name chartLessonsDay.

i. Click **Title** in the Header/Footer group, and then change the title of your form to Employee Lessons by Day.

j. Click **Date and Time** in the Header/Footer group to put a date in the header. In the Date and Time dialog box, accept the defaults **Include Date**, the first format for the date, and **Include Time**, and the first format for the time.

k. Click **OK**.

l. Click once on your **column chart**. Use the move handle to move the top-left corner of your chart to the spot 1" from the left and 1" from the top of your form. Use the bottom-right sizing handle and drag it diagonally down to the spot 5" from the left and 4" from the top of your form.

m. Drag the bottom of the form footer to make it .5" high.

n. Click **Label** 🄰🄰 in the Controls group, click in the form footer, and type Created by Firstname Lastname.

o. Double-click your **column chart** to open Microsoft Graph. You are happy with the chart except that the y-axis is scaled by .5 instead of 1 lesson. You will fix that. The y-axis is the line on the left of the chart that is numbered from 0 to 3.5.

p. Right-click the y-axis, and then click **Format Axis**.

q. Click the **Scale tab**, change Major unit from .5 to 1, and then click **OK**.

r. Click **File**, and then click **Save** to return to Access.

s. Save your form, and then look at your chart in Form view. Close your chart.

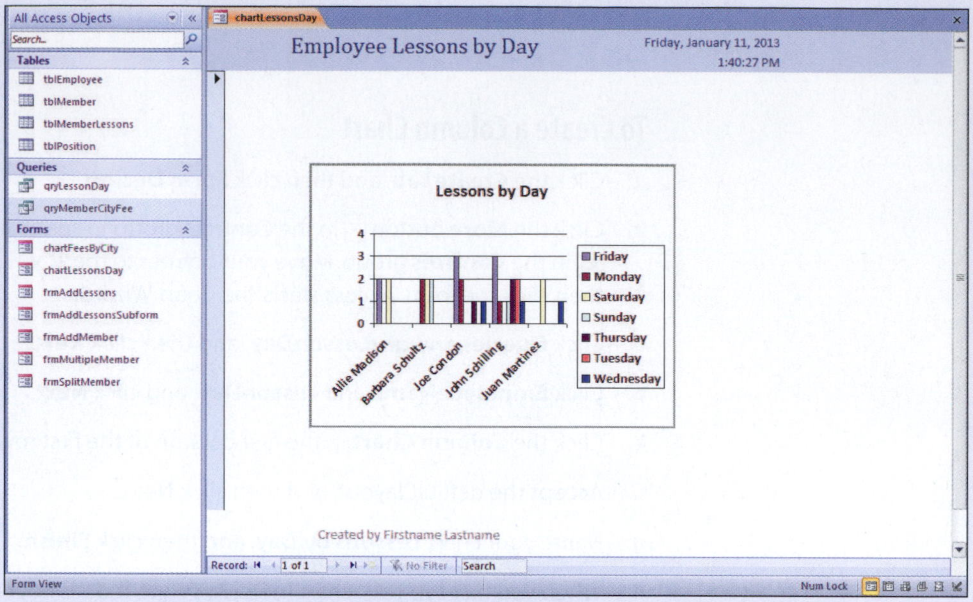

Figure 38 Finished column chart

Creating a PivotTable Form

A PivotTable is an advanced type of form. It provides you an interactive method of manipulating your data including swapping columns and headers.

You will create a new query with weekdays and fees.

To Create a New Days of the Week Query

a. Click the **Create tab**, and then click **Query Wizard**. Click **Simple Query Wizard**, and then click **OK**.

b. From tblEmployee, click **EmployeeName**. From tblMemberLessons, click **Fee** and **ScheduledDate**. From tblMember, click **MemberName**, and then click **Next**.

c. Click **Detail**, and then click **Next**.

d. Name your query **qryLessonDayMember**, click **Modify the query design**, and then click **Finish**.

e. Highlight the **MemberName** column in the design grid. Click **Insert Columns** in the Query Setup group. This inserts a blank column in the design grid as the third column. Click in the **first row** of that column, and then click **Builder**. In the Expression Builder dialog box, type **=WeekdayName(Weekday([ScheduledDate]))**, and then click **OK**.

f. Replace Expr1 with **LessonDay**.

g. Run your query, save your query, and then close your query.

To Create a PivotTable Form

a. Click **qryLessonDayMember** in the Navigation Pane, and then click **Create**, **More Forms**, and **PivotTable**.

b. Switch to Design view, and then back to PivotTable view. This will allow you to see the Field List with the fields available for this table.

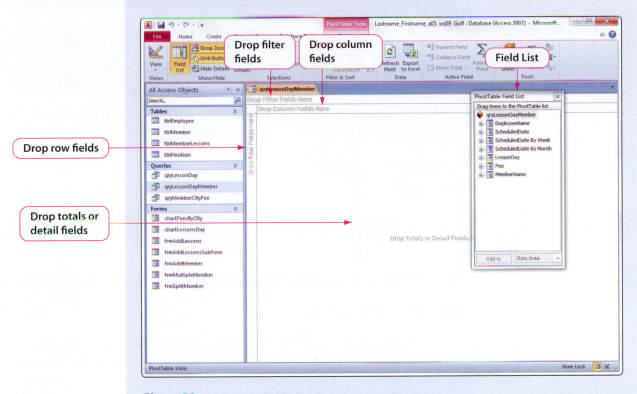

Figure 39 Empty PivotTable layout

The PivotTable has four areas: a place to drop row fields, a place to drop column fields, a place to drop filter fields, and a place to drop totals or detail fields. You can pick up fields from the Field List and drop them in each of these four areas.

c. Click **EmployeeName** in the Field List, and then drag it to the Drop Row Fields Here area. When the area is active (outlined in blue), release your mouse to drop the field.

d. Click **LessonDay** in the Field List, and then drag it to the Drop Column Fields Here area.

Troubleshooting

If the Field List disappears, click Design View on the status bar. The Field List will reappear.

e. Click **Fee** in the Field List, and then drag it to the Drop Totals or Detail Fields Here area.

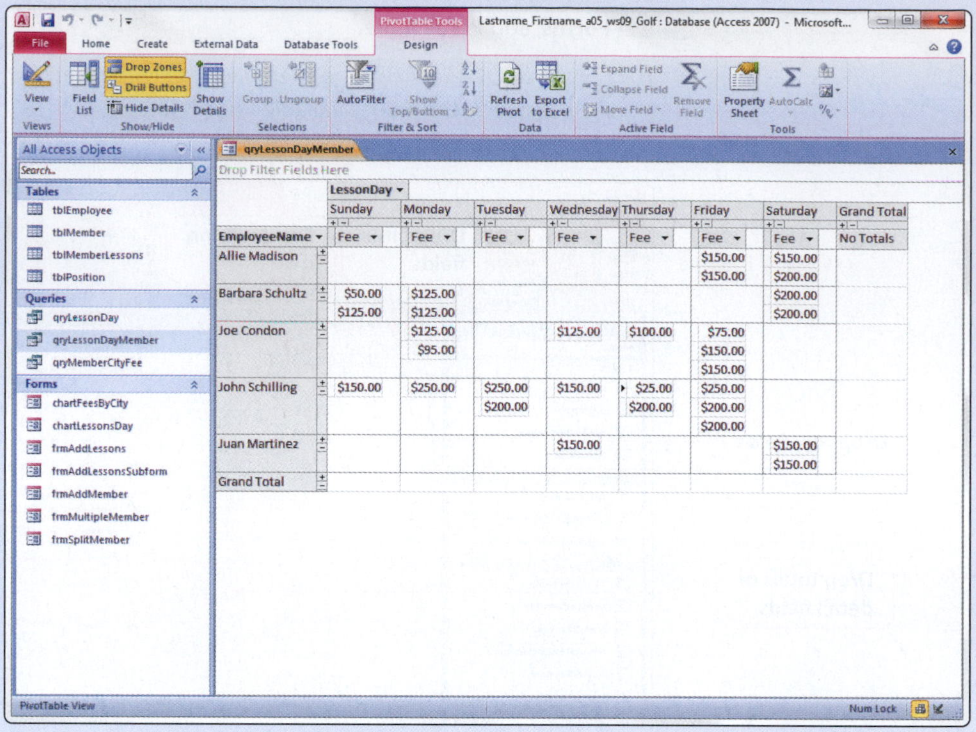

Figure 40 PivotTable with data

The purpose of a PivotTable is to allow a decision maker to analyze data. You can turn totals on and off, add filters, add additional fields, and hide detail. At this point, you can see which day different employees give lessons and how much they charge for the lesson. You would like to see totals.

f. Click the **$150** fee for Allie Madison's first lesson. Click **AutoCalc** in the Tools group, and then click **Sum**.

Now you can see totals. Next you will add a filter to show lessons by different quarters.

g. In the Field List, click the **plus sign** before **ScheduledDate by Month** to expand the field. Click **Months**, and then drag it to the Drop Filter Fields Here area.

h. In the filter area, click the **ScheduledDate by Month** arrow. Click the plus sign before 2013 to expand it. Remove the check mark before Qtr 1, and then remove the check mark before Qtr 3. Click **OK**. Now you see only lessons for Qtr 2.

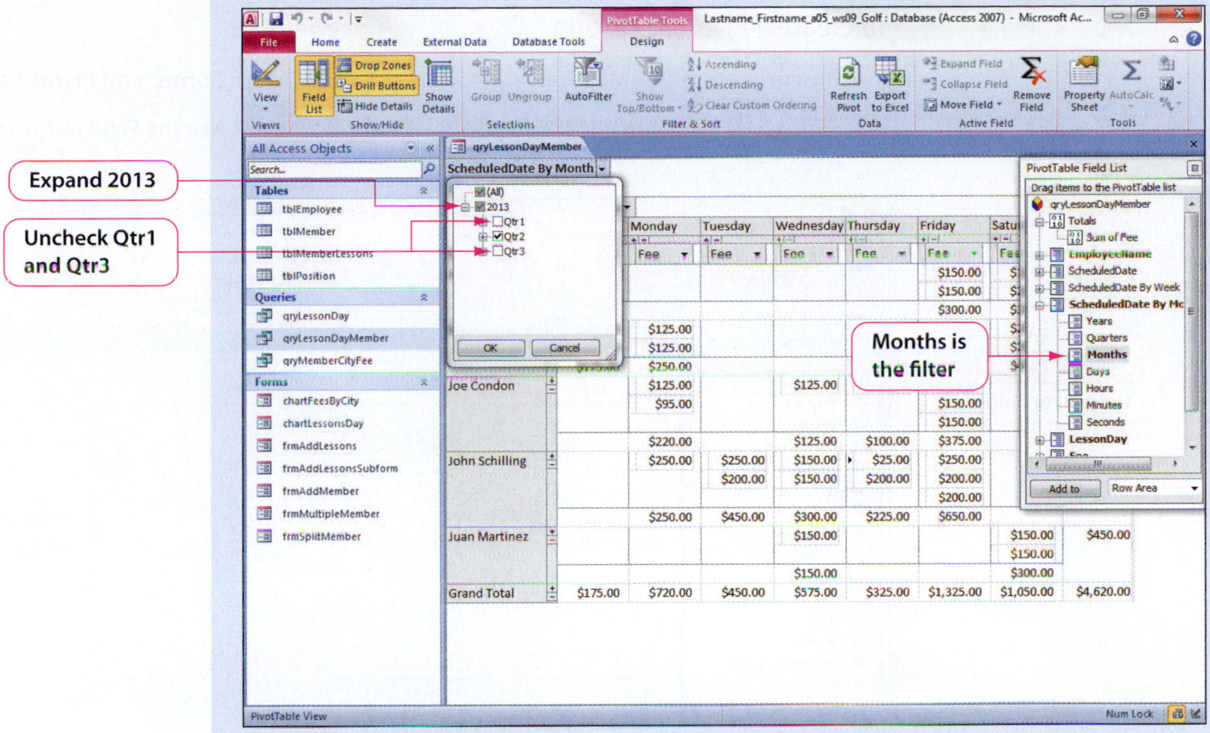

Figure 41 Filter to see just Qtr 2 of 2013

i. Click **MemberName** in the Field List, and then drag it to the right of EmployeeName. Now you can see lessons for different employees and different members.

j. Save your form as **frmPivotTableFees**, and then close ☒ your form.

Troubleshooting

If you have no Qtr 1 entries for 2013, you made a mistake when you added a lesson for yourself. Open tblMemberLessons, and then change the date on the last record (MemberLessonID 32) to 3/10/2013.

Creating a PivotChart Form

A PivotChart is similar to a PivotTable except with a graphical view of the data. You will use the same query you used for your PivotTable to see the differences between it and the PivotChart. In the column chart, you could see that John Schilling and Joe Condon have more lessons on Friday than any other day. You would like to see if Friday is the most popular day for all lessons. Swapping rows and columns is not easy in a column chart, but it is simple in a PivotChart.

To Create a PivotChart Form

a. Click **qryLessonDayMember**, and then click **Create**, **More Forms**, and **PivotChart**.

b. Switch to Design view, and then back to PivotChart view to see the Field List.

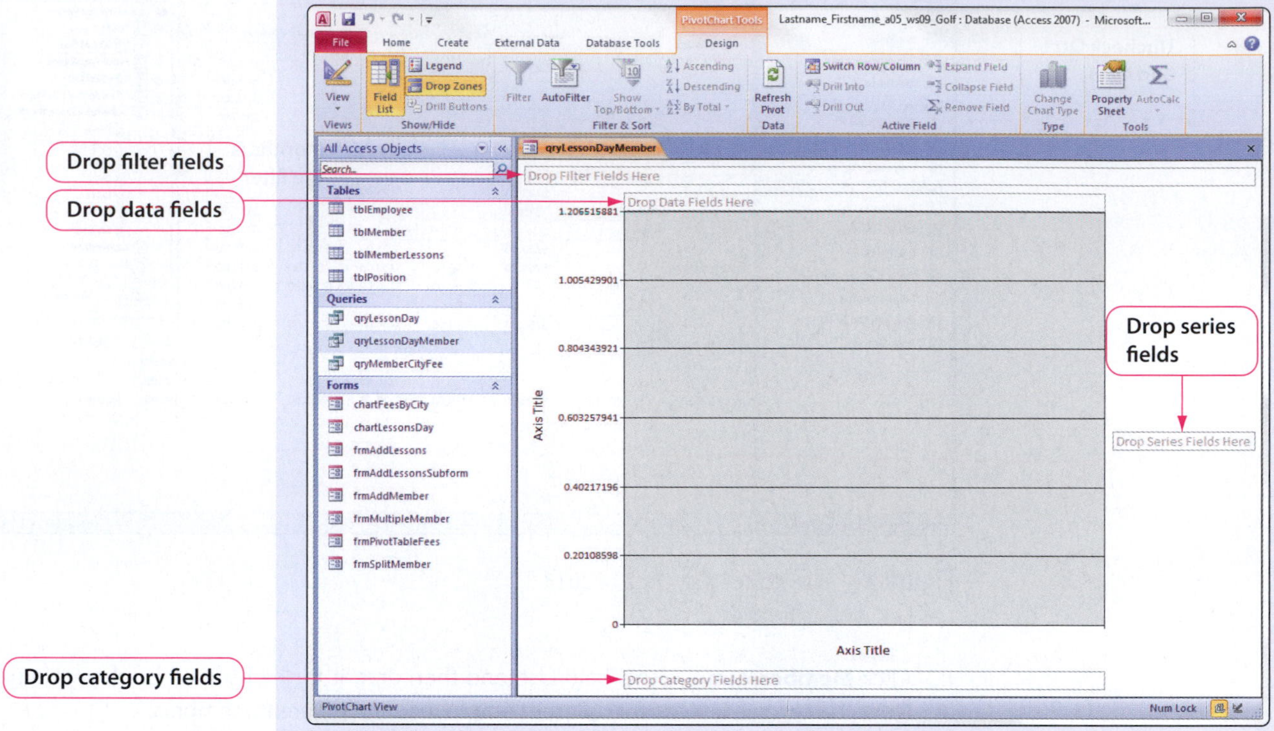

Figure 42 Blank PivotChart form

The PivotChart has four areas: a place to drop category fields, a place to drop series fields, a place to drop filter fields, and a place to drop data fields. You can pick up fields from the Field List and drop them in each of these four areas.

c. Click **EmployeeName** in the Field List, and then drag it to the Drop Category Fields Here area.

d. Click **LessonDay** in the Field List, and then drag it to the Drop Series Fields Here area.

e. Click **Fee** in the Field List, and then drag it to the Drop Data Fields Here area.

f. Click the **Design tab**, and then click **Legend** in the Show/Hide group.

This looks very similar to the column chart you created earlier. However, with a PivotChart, you can make changes and see how the chart changes.

g. Click the **Design tab**, and then click **Switch Row/Column** in the Active Field group.

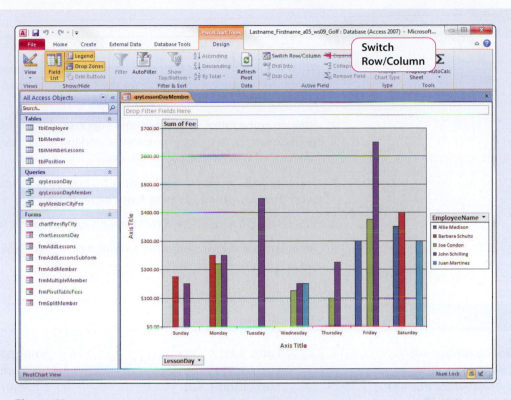

Figure 43 PivotChart with reversed rows and columns

h. In the Field List, click the plus sign before **ScheduledDate by Month** to expand the field. Click **Months**, and then drag it to the Drop Filter Fields Here area.

i. In the filter area, click the **ScheduledDate by Month arrow**. Click the plus sign before 2013 to expand it. Remove the check marks before Qtr 1 and Qtr 3. Click **OK**. Now you see only lessons for Qtr 2.

j. Save your form as **frmPivotChartFees**, and then close Access.

1. What is the difference between a bound and an unbound control? Suppose you have a form for entering customers into the table. What would be an example of a bound control on this form? An unbound control?

2. Why do some forms have subforms? Suppose you have an employee database where departments have multiple employees working in each department. What would be the main form? What would be the subform?

3. Forms provide an easy to use interface for nontechnical users. What are some features of forms that you can use to make forms easier to use?

4. What is the difference between a form with subform, a split form, and a multiple item form?

5. What is the difference between a PivotChart, a PivotTable, and a column chart? When would you use each of them?

Key Terms

Bound control 405	Form 402	Sizing handle 422
Bound form 403	Locked 406	Split form 434
Calculated control 424	Move handle 422	Subform 416
Control 405	Multiple items form 434	Unbound control 409
Date Picker 411	PivotChart 434	Unbound form 403
Default value 405	PivotTable 434	Validation rule 405
Enabled 406	Property sheet 404	Validation text 405

Visual Summary

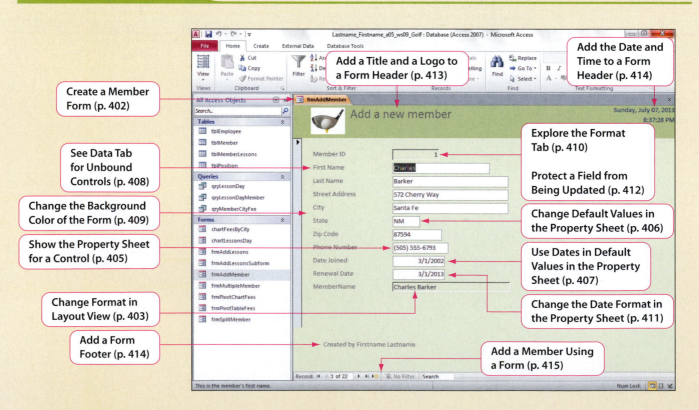

Add a Title and a Logo to a Form Header (p. 413)

Add the Date and Time to a Form Header (p. 414)

Create a Member Form (p. 402)

See Data Tab for Unbound Controls (p. 408)

Change the Background Color of the Form (p. 409)

Show the Property Sheet for a Control (p. 405)

Change Format in Layout View (p. 403)

Add a Form Footer (p. 414)

Explore the Format Tab (p. 410)

Protect a Field from Being Updated (p. 412)

Change Default Values in the Property Sheet (p. 406)

Use Dates in Default Values in the Property Sheet (p. 407)

Change the Date Format in the Property Sheet (p. 411)

Add a Member Using a Form (p. 415)

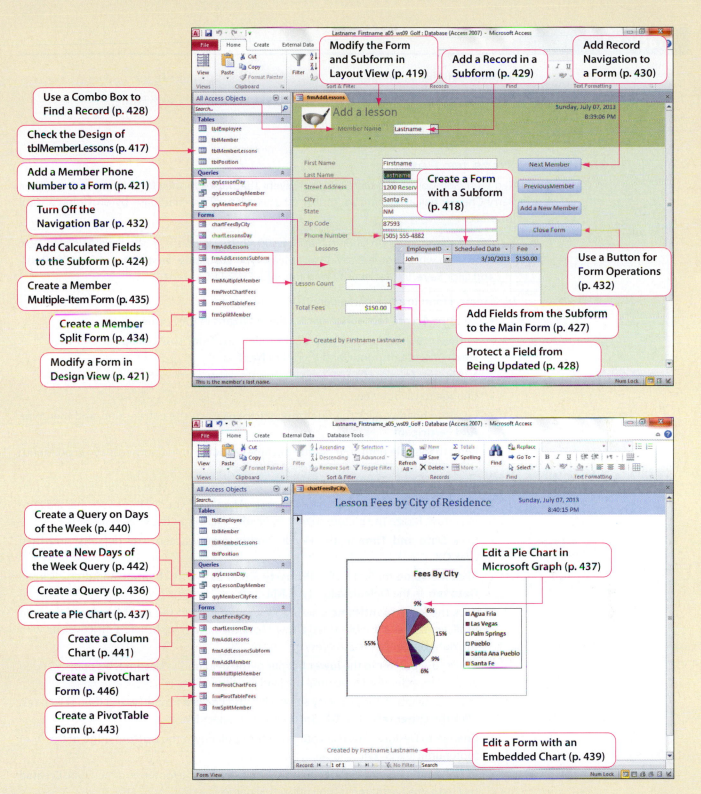

Figure 44 The Red Bluff Golf Club database with form interfaces

Student data files needed:

a05_ws09_Putts
a05_ws09_Putts_Logo

You will save your file as:

Lastname_Firstname_a05_ws09_Putts

Putts for Paws

Red Bluff Golf Course runs a charity golf event that raises money for a local animal shelter. Barry Cheney has asked you to improve the usability of the database by providing a form interface.

a. Start **Access**, and then open the **a05_ws09_Putts** database. In the Save As dialog box, browse to where you are saving your files, type Lastname_Firstname_a05_ws09_Putts, and click **Save**. In the Security Warning, click **Enable Content**.

b. Create a form to add a participant to the tournament:

- Click the **Create tab**, and then click **Form Wizard** in the Forms group.

- In the Form Wizard dialog box, select all fields from **tblParticipant** and then click **Next**. Accept **Columnar**, and then click **Next**.

- Name your form frmParticipant.

- Change to Layout view.

- Click the **header**, click the title **frmParticipant**, clear the current title, and then type Add Participant.

- Point to the **title** until your pointer becomes a four-pointed arrow. Use your pointer to drag the title and move it over to the right by 1".

- Click **Logo** in the Header/Footer group. Navigate to your student data files, and then select **a05_ws09_Putts_Logo**. Point to the **logo** until your pointer becomes a diagonal arrow. Resize the picture so that its height is as big as the header area.

- Click **Date and Time** in the Header/Footer group, accept the defaults, and then click **OK**.

- Click the **value** for State, click **Property Sheet** in the Tools group, and then click the **Data tab**. In the Default Value, type NM.

- Click the **ParticipantName** value. Move your pointer to the **right border** of the field until it becomes a double-sided arrow. Move the border to the left until it lines up with the right border of the StreetAddress field.

- Move your pointer to the **lower border** of the field until it becomes a double-headed arrow. Move the border up until the field is a single line.

- In the Data tab of the property sheet, click the **Locked** property, and then select **Yes**. Click the **Other tab**, click **Tab Stop**, and then select **No**.

- Change to Design view. Use your pointer to pull down the **bottom edge** of the form footer until it is .5" tall.

- Click the **Label** control in the Controls group, click in the footer, and then type Created by Firstname Lastname using your actual name.

- Change to Form view, change the LastName and FirstName of the first participant to your name.

- Save and close your form.

c. Create a form to see a participant's orders:

- Click the **Create tab**, and then click **Form Wizard** in the Forms group.

- In the Form Wizard dialog box, select **LastName**, **FirstName**, and **ContactPhoneNumber** from **tblParticipant**. Select **OrderDate** and **MethodOfPayment** from **tblOrder**. Select **LineNum**, **ItemID**, and **Quantity** from **tblOrderLine**. Click **Next**.

- Accept the default view, and then click **Next**. Accept **Datasheet** for the subform layouts, and then click **Next**.
- Name your form frmParticipantOrder, the first subform frmParticipantOrderSubform, and the second subform frmParticipantOrderLineSubform. Click **Finish**.
- Change to Layout view.
- Click the **header**, and then click the title **frmParticipantOrder**. Clear the current title, and then type View Tournament Orders. Point to the **title** until your pointer becomes a four-pointed arrow. Use your pointer to drag the **title** and move it over to the right by 1".
- Click **Logo** in the Header/Footer group, navigate to your student data files, and then select **a05_ws09_Putts_Logo**. Point to the logo until your pointer becomes a diagonal arrow. Resize the picture so that its height is as big as the header area.
- Click **Date and Time** in the Header/Footer group, accept the defaults, and then click **OK**.
- In the first subform, click the **OrderDate** column header. Put your pointer in the **right border** so it becomes a double-headed arrow. Double-click to resize the column to fit the contents. Resize the **MethodOfPayment** column the same way. Use your pointer to resize the **right side** of the subform to fit the new column sizes. You may need to close the Property Sheet to see right side of the subform.
- Repeat resizing of columns and forms for the second subform.
- Save your form.
- Change to Design view. Use your pointer to pull down the **bottom edge** of the form footer until it is .5" tall.
- Click the **Label** control in the Controls group, click in the footer, and then type Created by Firstname Lastname using your actual name.
- Click **Combo Box** in the Controls group. Move your pointer to the **header**. Place the combo box in the form header to the right of the title.
- In the Combo Box Wizard dialog box, click **Find a record on my form based on the value I selected in my combo box**, and then click **Next**.
- Click **LastName** and **FirstName** in that order, and then click **Next**.
- Accept **Hide key column**, and then click **Next**.
- Enter Participant Name as your Label, and then click **Finish**.
- If necessary, drag the new combo box so it fits well in the header.

Figure 45 frmParticipantOrder

d. Add buttons to the detail area of frmParticipantOrder:

- Click **Button** in the Controls group, move your pointer to the form to the right of the member fields, and then place the button on the form.
- In the Command Button Wizard, click **Record Navigation** and **Go To Next Record**, and then click **Next**. Click **Text**, type Next Participant, and then click **Next**. Name the button cmdNextParticipant, and then click **Finish**.
- Click **Button** in the Controls group. Place your pointer below the Next Participant button, and then click on the form. Click **Record Navigation** and **Go To Previous Record**, and then click **Next**. Click **Text**, type Previous Participant, and then click **Next**. Name the button cmdPreviousParticipant, and then click **Finish**.
- Click **Button** in the Controls group. Place your pointer below the Previous Participant button, and then click on the form. Click **Form Operations** and **Open Form**, and then click **Next**. Click **frmParticipant**, and then click **Next**. Click **Open the form and show all the records**, and then click **Next**. Click **Text**, type Add a New Participant, and then click **Next**. Name the button cmdAddParticipant, and then click **Finish**.
- Click **Button** in the Controls group. Place your pointer below the Add a New Participant button, and then click the form. Click **Form Operations** and **Close Form**, and then click **Next**. Click **Text**, and then accept **Close Form**. Click **Next**. Name the button cmdCloseForm, and then click **Finish**.
- Use your pointer to select all **four buttons**. Click the **Arrange tab**, click **Align** in the Sizing & Ordering group, and then select **Left**.
- Click **Size/Space** in the Sizing & Ordering group, and then select **Equal Vertical**.
- Click **Size/Space**, and then select **To Widest**.
- Save and close your form.

e. Create a split form for participants:

- Click **tblParticipant**, and then click **Create**, **More Forms**, and **Split Form**.
- Save your form, naming it frmSplitParticipant.
- Click the **header**. Click the title **tblParticipant**. Clear the current title, and then type Split Participant Form.
- Delete the current logo in the header. Click **Logo** in the Header/Footer group, navigate to your student data files, and then select **a05_ws09_Putts_Logo**.
- Click **Date and Time** in the Header/Footer group, accept the defaults, and then click **OK**.
- Change to Design view. Use your pointer to pull down the **bottom edge** of the form footer until it is .5" tall.
- Click the **Label** control in the Controls group, click in the footer, and then type Created by Firstname Lastname using your actual name.
- Save and close your form.

f. Create a query with the number of items that have been ordered for the tournament:

- Click the **Create tab**, and then click **Query Wizard**. Click **Simple Query Wizard**, and then click **OK**.
- From tblOrderLine, select **Quantity**. From tblItem, select **ItemDescription**. Click **Next**.
- Click **Detail**, and then click **Next**.
- Name your query qryItemsOrdered, and then click **Finish**. Close your query.

g. Create a column chart from qryItemsOrdered:

- Click the **Create tab**, and then click **Form Design**.
- Click the **More Button** in the Controls group to see all available controls. Select **Chart** in the **Controls** group. Move your pointer to the 1" x 1" mark in the Detail section, and then click on the form.

- In the Chart Wizard dialog box, click **Queries** and **qryItemsOrdered**, and then click **Next**.
- Select all fields, and then click **Next**.
- Click the **column chart** in the first column of the first row, and then click **Next**.
- Accept the default layout, and then click **Next**.
- Name your chart Items Ordered, and then select **No, don't display a Legend**. Click **Finish**.
- Change to Layout view to view the chart, switch back to Design view to modify the chart, and then save your form with the name chartItemsOrdered.
- Click **Title** in the Header/Footer group, and then change the title of your form to Items Ordered Summary.
- Click **Date and Time** in the Header/Footer group to put a date in the header. In the Date and Time dialog box, accept the defaults, and then click **OK**.
- Use your pointer to pull down the **bottom edge** of the form footer until it is .5" tall. Click the **Label** control in the Controls group, click in the footer, and then type Created by Firstname Lastname using your actual name.
- Click once on your **column chart**. Click the **bottom-right sizing handle**, and then drag the column chart diagonally down to the spot 5" from the left and 4" from the top of your form.
- Double-click your **column chart** to open Microsoft Graph.
- Right-click the **x-axis** (the line on the bottom of the chart that shows **Cart sponsor**), and then click **Format Axis**.
- Click the **Scale tab**, change the Number of categories between tick-mark labels to 1, and then click **OK**.
- Click **File**, and then click **Save** to return to Access.
- Save your form, and then look at your chart in Form view.

h. Close your database.

Practice 2

Student data file needed:	You will save your file as:
a05_ws09_Painted_Treasures	Lastname_Firstname_a05_ws09_Painted_Treasures

Painted Treasures

Susan Brock, the manager of the Painted Treasures gift shop, has asked you to add some forms to the Painted Treasures database. She is interested in doing some further analysis of the purchases and wants you to create charts and PivotTables to help her.

a. Start **Access**, and then open the **a05_ws09_Painted_Treasures** database. In the Save As dialog box, browse to where you are saving your files, type Latname_Firstname_ a05_ws09_Painted_Treasures, and then click **Save**. In the Security Warning, click **Enable Content**.

b. Create a form to add a customer:
- Click the **Create tab**, and then click **Form Wizard** in the Forms group.
- In the Form Wizard dialog box, select all fields from **tblCustomer**, and then click **Next**. Accept **Columnar**, and then click **Next**.
- Name your form frmCustomer.
- Change to Layout view.

- Click the **header**, click the title **frmCustomer**, clear the current title, and then type Add Customer.
- Click **Date and Time** in the Header/Footer group, accept the defaults, and then click **OK**.
- Change to Design view. Use your pointer to pull down the **bottom edge** of the form footer until it is .5" tall.
- Click the **Label** control in the Controls group, click in the footer, and then type Created by Firstname Lastname using your actual name.
- Change to Form view, and then change the **LastName** and **FirstName** of the last customer to your name.
- Save and close your form.

c. Create a query to choose clothing purchases:
- Click the **Create tab**, and then click **Query Wizard**.
- Click **Simple Query Wizard**, and then click **OK**.
- From tblPurchaseLine select **Quantity**.
- From tblProduct, select **Category**, **Size**, **Color**, and **ProductDescription** and then click **Next**.
- Click **Detail**, and then click **Next**.
- Name your query qryClothingPurchases, select **Modify the query design**, and then click **Finish**.
- In the Criteria row for Category, type Clothing.
- Run, save, and close your query.

d. From qryClothingPurchases, create a pie chart showing the percentages of clothing purchases by product description:
- Click the **Create tab**, and then click **Form Design**.
- Click the **More** button in the Controls group, and then click **Chart** in the Controls group.
- Move your pointer to the Detail section, and then click on the form at the 1" x 1" mark. In the Chart Wizard dialog box, select **Queries** and **qryClothingPurhases**, and then click **Next**.
- Select **Quantity** and **ProductDescription**, and then click **Next**.
- Click the **pie chart** in the first column of the last row, and then click **Next**.
- Accept the default layout, and then click **Next**.
- Name your chart Clothing Purchases, and then click **Finish**.
- Change to Layout view to view the chart data, and then change back to Design view.
- Save your form with the name chartClothingPurchases.
- Click **Title** in the Header/Footer group, and then change the title of your form to Clothing Purchases Summary.
- Click **Date and Time** in the Header/Footer group to put a date in the header. In the Date and Time dialog box, accept the defaults, and then click **OK**.
- Use your pointer to pull down the **bottom edge** of the form footer until it is .5" tall. Click the **Label** control in the Controls group, click in the footer, and then type Created by Firstname Lastname using your actual name.
- Click once on your **pie chart**. Using the bottom-right sizing handle, drag the chart diagonally down to the spot 5" from the left and 4" from the top of your form.
- Double-click your **pie chart**.
- On the menu bar, click **Chart**, and then select **Chart Options**.
- Click the **Data Labels tab**, click **Percentage**, and then click **OK**.
- On the menu bar, click **File**, and then click **Save**.
- Close your form.

e. From qryClothingPurchases, create a column chart showing the number of clothing purchases by size and color:

- Click the **Create tab**, and then click **Form Design**.
- Click the **More** button in the Controls group, and then click **Chart** in the Controls group.
- Move your pointer to the Details section, and then click on the form at the 1" x 1" mark. In the Chart Wizard dialog box, select **Queries** and **qryClothingPurhases**, and then click **Next**.
- Select **Quantity**, **Size**, and **Color**, and then click **Next**.
- Click the **column chart** in the first column of the first row, and then click **Next**.
- Accept the default layout, and then click **Next**.
- Name your chart Clothing Purchases, and then click **Finish**.
- Change to Layout view to view the chart data, and then change back to Design view.
- Save your form with the name chartBarChartClothingPurchases.
- Click **Title** in the Header/Footer group, and then change the title of your form to Clothing Purchases Summary.
- Click **Date and Time** in the Header/Footer group to put a date in the header. In the Date and Time dialog box, accept the defaults, and click **OK**.
- Use your pointer to pull down the **bottom edge** of the form footer until it is .5" tall. Click the **Label** control in the Controls group, and then click in the footer. Type Created by Firstname Lastname using your actual name.
- Click once on your **column chart**. Use the lower-right sizing handle and drag it diagonally down to the spot 5 inches from the left and 4 inches from the top of your form.
- Save and close your form.

f. Create a query showing the purchases of clothing on days of the week.

- Click the **Create tab** and then click **Query Wizard**. Click **Simple Query Wizard** and then click **OK**.
- From tblPurchase, select **PurchaseDate**. From tblPurchaseLine, select **Quantity**. From tblProduct, select **Category** and **ProductDescription**. Click **Next**.
- Click **Detail** and then click **Next**.
- Name your query qryPurchasesAndDates, click **Modify the query design**, and then click **Finish**.
- Click in the first row of the first empty column and then click **Builder**. In the Expression Builder dialog box, type =WeekdayName(Weekday([PurchaseDate])) and then click **OK**.
- Replace Expr1 with PurchaseDay.
- Run your query. **Save** and **close** the query.

g. Use qryPurchasesAndDates to create a PivotTable.

- Click **qryPurchasesAndDates** in the Navigation Pane and then click **Create**, **More Forms**, and **PivotTable**.
- Switch to Design View and then back to PivotTable View. This will allow you to see the Field List with the fields available for this table.
- Click **Category** in the Field List, and then drag it to the Drop Row Fields Here area. When the area is active (outlined in blue), release your mouse to drop the field.
- Click **PurchaseDay** in the Field List and then drag it to the Drop Column Fields Here area.
- Click **Quantity** in the Field List and then drag it to the Drop Totals or Detail Fields Here area.
- Right-click the **first quantity**, click **AutoCalc** and then click **Sum**.
- Click **Category** in the PivotTable and then click **HideDetails** in the Show/Hide group.
- Save your PivotTable naming it chartPivotPurchasesAndDates.

- Answer the following questions using your PivotTable:
    1. What days of the week does the gift shop have the most sales?
    2. What types of purchases are made on various days?
- Close your PivotTable.

h. Use qryPurchasesAndDates to create a PivotChart:
- Click **qryPurchasesAndDates**, and then click **Create**, **More Forms**, and **PivotChart**.
- Switch to Design view and back to PivotChart view to see the Field List.
- Click **ProductDescription** in the Field List, and then drag it to the Drop Category Fields Here area.
- Click **PurchaseDay** in the Field List, and then drag it to the Drop Series Fields Here area.
- Click **Quantity** in the Field List, and then drag it to the Drop Data Fields Here area.
- Click **Category**, and then drag it to the Drop Filter Fields Here area.
- Click the **Design tab**, and then click **Legend** in the Show/Hide group.
- In the filter area, click the **Category arrow**. Remove the check marks before **Childrens**, **Clothing**, and **Indigo 5**. Click **OK**. The PivotChart filters out all products except Spa.
- Save your PivotTable with the name chartFilterPurchasesAndDates, and then close your PivotTable.

i. Close your database.

Objectives

1. Build a report with subtotals and totals. p. 459

2. Hide duplicate values. p. 464

3. Add and remove fields from a report. p. 464

4. Add totals to a report. p. 465

5. Hide detail on a summary report. p. 467

6. Decide when totals are inappropriate. p. 468

7. Create a report with a query as a source. p. 471

8. Add conditional formatting. p. 472

9. Create a report from a parameter query. p. 474

10. Create a report based on parameters in a form. p. 476

11. Add report buttons to a form. p. 482

12. Create mailing labels. p. 484

Creating Customized Reports

PREPARE CASE

The Red Bluff Golf Club Reports

The Red Bluff Golf Club generates revenues through golfers signing up for tee times and taking golf lessons. You have provided a database to Barry Cheney, the golf club manager, that he can use to track employees and members. He would like you to create some customized reports that he can use to manage the club.

Courtesy of www.Shutterstock.com

Student data file needed for this workshop:

 a05_ws10_Golf

You will save your file as:

 Lastname_Firstname_a05_ws10_Golf

Design View

An Access **report** provides data in an easy-to-read format suitable for printing. Reports are used for providing professional-looking printed output from a database. A report is designed to fit well on the printed page, with breaks built in for each page. Column headers repeat on each page, and there are page numbers. Reports provide ways to report on data by groups, such as by each customer or product. Totals can be calculated for each grouping, and grand totals can be shown. The source of data for a report can be a table or query.

Reports can be created with the same controls that are available in forms. You can create a report with an embedded chart or image. You can also create mailing label reports or other types of labels.

Reports have four views:

- **Report view**: Shows how the report will look in a continuous page layout. If a report has multiple pages, this view shows the report as one continuous layout without individual page headers or footers. Reports cannot be changed in this view.

- **Print Preview**: Shows how the report will look on the printed page. In this view, you see the page breaks and how they will appear on paper. This view allows you to change the page layout such as from landscape to portrait view, or to change margins.

- **Layout view**: Shows the report and the data. Some of the report design, such as column widths and fonts, can be changed in this view. You can add controls in this view. Layout view is ideal for making changes where seeing the data as you make the change would be useful.

- **Design view**: Shows the report design but not the data. Any aspect of the report design can be changed in this view.

Reports can be created in four different ways: with the Report tool, with the Report Design tool, with the Blank Report tool, and with the Report Wizard. The **Report tool** creates a report with one mouse click. The report displays all of the fields from the record source that you select. The **Report Design tool** creates a blank report in Design view. You add fields or other controls to the design. The **Blank Report tool** creates a blank report in Layout view. You can insert fields or other controls while you see the data. Finally, the **Report Wizard** guides you through creating a report by asking you questions. The report is created based upon your answers to the questions.

In this section, you will learn how to work with totals and subtotals in reports and how to add or remove fields from reports.

Real World Advice | Query, Form, or Report?

There are three ways to display data from a database: a query, a form, and a report. When do you use each?

- Queries are the most versatile of the three for finding data in your database. They allow complex data selection and data calculation. But the output from a query is tabular and not always suitable for presentation to a client or manager. If you want to share the results of a query in printed form, you often create a report from the query.

- Forms are usually used for data input, but they can also be used for interactive displays such as pivot tables, multiple item forms, or charts. They are best suited for output on the screen. In fact many types of forms are very difficult to print as they can run for many pages with formatting unsuitable for the printed page, such as no page breaks or page numbers. If you want to create a bar chart or other chart for printing, you usually embed it in a report rather than in a form.

- Reports are designed for printing. You can use them to provide an easy-to-understand output for a client or manager. You can create mailing labels and other specialized printable formats.

Build a Report with Subtotals and Totals

One of the features of Access reports is the ability to summarize your data. When you have numeric data such as a sales quantity, you often want to get a grand total of that quantity. When you are creating a report with a wizard, sums, averages, minimums, and maximums are available as standard summations available. In Design view, you can build more complex formulas.

Information can be more easily understood when it is grouped. Reports have a grouping feature allowing records to be presented in sets. One common use of grouping is to use one-to-many relationships in your database and use a record from the one side to group records from the many side. For example, suppose your database has a one-to-many relationship between customers and orders: a customer can place many orders, and an order is placed by one customer. You might report on orders by first showing the customer and then grouping all of the customer's orders together. In the Report Wizard the one-to-many grouping is the first grouping suggested to you. You can also group on other fields. You could choose to group orders by date placed or by state of shipment.

Barry asks if you can create a report showing which golf course employees give lessons to which members. He would like you to group members by the employee who gave the lesson. The first step is to review the database relationships. Figure 1 shows the relationships in the golf database. Employees can give many lessons. Each lesson is given by a single employee. A lesson is taken by one member; a member can take many lessons.

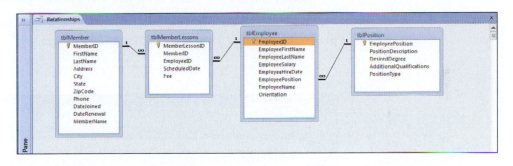

Figure 1 Golf database relationships

To Create a Report with Totals Using a Wizard

a. Click **Start** 🏁, and then select **Access 2010**.

b. Click the **File tab**, click **Open**, and then browse to your student data files. Locate and select **a05_ws10_Golf**, and then click **Open**.

c. Click the **File tab**, and then select **Save Database As**. In the File name box, type **Lastname_Firstname_a05_ws10_Golf** replacing Lastname_Firstname with your actual name.

d. Click **Enable Content** in the Security Warning.

e. Open **tblMember**, and then navigate to record 22, the last record. Change **First** and **Last** to be your actual first name and last name, and then close ⊠ tblMember.

f. Click the **Create tab**, and then click **Report Wizard** in the Reports group.

g. From tblEmployee, select **EmployeeLastName** and **EmployeeFirstName**. From tblMemberLessons, select **ScheduledDate**. From tblMember select **LastName**, **FirstName**. From tblMemberLessons, select **Fee**. Click **Next**.

h. Accept the grouping by tblEmployee, and then click **Next**. Do not add any other grouping. Click **Next**, and then sort by ScheduledDate, LastName, and FirstName accepting ascending order.

i. Click **Summary Options**. Because Fee is the only numeric value in the data, Access gives you the option to calculate summary values for Fee. Select **Sum**, and then click **OK**.

j. Click **Next**, accept **Stepped** Layout and **Portrait** Orientation, and then click **Next**.

k. Name your report **rptEmployeeLessons**, and then click **Finish**.

l. The report appears in Print Preview view. Move your pointer on the report and it changes to the zoom out indicator . **Click** to see the entire page. The Fee is shown as ## because the column is not wide enough. You will fix that.

m. Change to Layout view. Scroll right and click the first ## in the Fee column. The entire column is highlighted. Point to the left edge of the field and when the pointer changes to the horizontal resize pointer ↔, drag to the left to widen the field.

n. The subtotals and total fields also need to be widened. Scroll down to the first visible # in the Fee column. This is the subtotal for the Employee group. Click the ## in the subtotal. Point to the left edge of the field and when the pointer changes to the horizontal resize pointer ↔, drag to the left to widen the field.

o. Scroll down to the end of the report, find the grand total for Fee (the last #), and then click it. Point to the left edge of the field and when the pointer changes to the horizontal resize pointer ↔, drag to the left to widen the field.

p. On the status bar, change back to Print Preview 🔍.

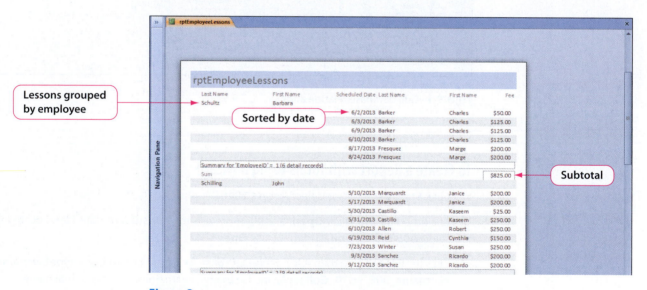

Figure 2 Employee Lessons report in Print Preview

The report shows lessons grouped by employee. Each employee's name is shown. Lessons are sorted by date and then by member's name. If an employee gives multiple lessons to a member, the member's name is repeated. Access repeated member name because tblMemberLessons is the many side of a one-to-many relationship with tblMember. A single member can take many lessons. At the end of the employee group, there is a subtotal showing the fees that the employee earned with his or her lessons. There is also a summary line showing how many detail records were in the group. If you look at the second page of the report, you see the grand total for fees. You will now switch to Design view and see how these things are designed.

To Explore Design View

a. Change to Design view.

b. Double-click **rptEmployeeLessons**, and then replace the existing text with Employee Lessons.

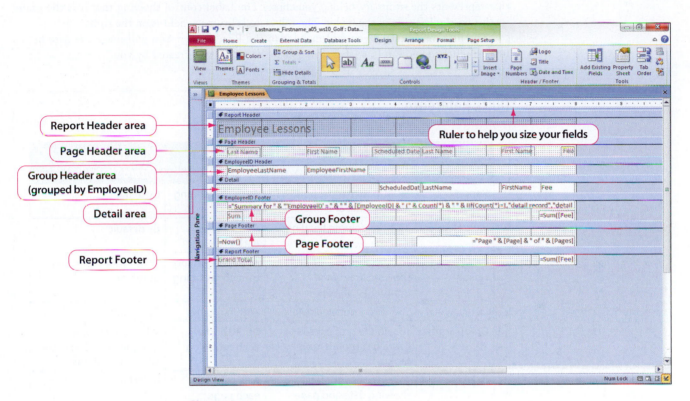

Figure 3 Employee Lessons report in Design view

A report with subtotals and totals has seven areas in Design view. The **Report Header** contains the information printed once at the beginning of a report. The default title is the name of the report. If you add a logo or date and time, they also appear in the report header. In your report, the title is now "Employee Lessons."

The **Page Header** contains the information printed at the top of every page of a report. The default information contained here is the column headers, which are taken from the captions from the table design. If no captions were defined, the values are field names. These are label controls. A **Label control** is a control that contains descriptive information, typically a field name. The Employee Lessons report has the column headers for both the grouping fields and the detail fields.

The **Group Header** contains the information printed at the beginning of every group of records. In Design view, the Group Header bar is labeled with the primary key of the record that the report was grouped by, in this case, the EmployeeID from tblEmployee. Recall when the wizard grouped by tblEmployee, the EmployeeLastName and EmployeeFirstName were the two fields in the grouping header. You see the bound controls for these two fields in the Group Header. The field labels are shown in the Page Header.

The **Detail area** shows the fields from the underlying record source. These are the bound controls showing values. The field labels are shown in the Page Header.

The **Group Footer** contains the information printed at the end of every group of records on a report. It is shown if you chose summary options in the Report Wizard. The Group Footer is labeled with the primary key of the record that the report was grouped by, in this case, the EmployeeID from tblEmployee. The fields shown include a calculated control that shows a count of detailed records, and a calculated control that represents the summary field(s) you chose. The label showing which summary option you picked is on the left side of the footer. The calculated summary field is on the right.

The **Page Footer** shows the information printed at the end of every page of a report. By default, two controls are shown: the current date using the Now function, and a calculated control representing the page number for this page.

The **Report Footer** shows the information printed once at the end of a report. It is shown if you chose summary options in the Report Wizard. The fields shown are the calculated control(s) that represents the summary field(s) you chose. The Label control showing that it is the grand total is on the left side of the footer. The calculated summary field is on the right.

The first modification you will make is to the Page Footer. You will make the date field a little smaller so you can fit a label saying that the report was created by you.

Quick Reference — Design View Areas

Area	Purpose	Where Displayed	When the Report Wizard Shows It
Report Header	To introduce the report; includes title and often logo	At the beginning of report	By default
Page Header	Includes column headings	At the top of each page	By default
Group Header	To introduce the group; shows values of the grouping variables	At the beginning of each grouping	When your report has grouping
Detail	Shows the detailed fields	Within groups	By default
Group Footer	To end the group; used to contain subtotals for the group	At the end of each grouping	When your report has grouping and you chose summary options
Page Footer	To end a page; defaults to showing date and page number	At the end of each page	By default
Report Footer	To end the report; can contain grand totals	At the end of report	When you chose summary options

Figure 4

To Add Your Name to the Page Footer

a. In the Page Footer, click the calculated Date control **=Now( )**. Point to the right edge of the field and when the pointer changes to the horizontal resize pointer ↔, drag to the left to narrow the field until it lines up with the 2.5" point on the horizontal ruler.

b. Click the **Design tab**, and then click **Label** *Aa* in the Controls group.

c. Move your pointer to the **Page Footer** and it becomes a Label pointer ⁺A. Click in the footer lining up with the 2.5" point on the horizontal ruler and a small window is displayed. Type **Created by Firstname Lastname** using your actual name. The window will get larger as you type.

d. Change to Print Preview.

Modify Group Footer

The Group Footer is named "EmployeeID Footer." Notice that the group footer contains a count of how many records are included in the group. The text is "Summary for 'EmployeeID' = 1 (6 detail records)." If you want to show the count, you would change it to be a more understandable language for a nondatabase specialist, for example "Count of Lessons = 6." However, Barry does not want to see that detail so you will remove it.

To Remove the Details Line

a.   Change to **Design View**.

b.   In the EmployeeID Footer (the Group footer) click the calculated control that begins ="**Summary for**. When it is highlighted, press ⌈Delete⌋ to delete the control.

Move and Resize Total Fields

In the next line of the Group Footer, you will move the label closer to the calculated control. You will also change the label caption to "Subtotal Fees." You will also fix the Report Footer the same way. When a control is selected, the control in outlined in orange. There are eight boxes called handles on the outline. The large gray handle in the top-left corner is called the **move handle**. It is used to move the control. The smaller orange handles are **sizing handles**. Sizing handles are used to resize the control.

To Fix Total Labels in Footers

a.   In the EmployeeID Footer, click the label **Sum**. Click the **move handle** to change your pointer to a four-headed arrow . Move the control to the right so that the left edge lines up with the 5" mark on the horizontal ruler.

b.   Click the **Sum** control so that the text is active. Enter Subtotal Fees.

c.   In the Report Footer, click the label **Grand Total**. Click the **move handle** to change your pointer to a four-headed arrow. Move the control to the right so that the left edge lines up with the 5" mark on the horizontal ruler.

d.   Click the **Grand Total** label so that the text is active. Type Total Fees.

e.   Change to Print Preview and see how the totals look.

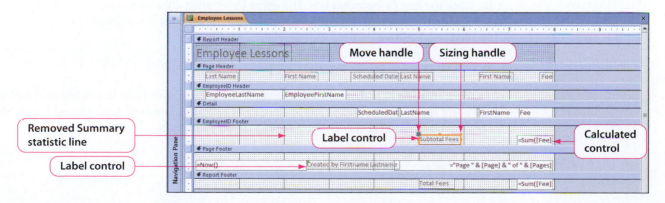

Figure 5 Design changes

Hide Duplicate Values

Lessons are sorted by date and then by member's name. As noted before, if an employee gives multiple lessons to a member, the member's name is repeated. You want to hide these duplicated values for Last Name and First Name.

Like fields on a form, every field on a report has certain characteristics or properties about the field stored in a **property sheet**. There are also characteristics of the report and sections within the report stored in their respective property sheets. The duplicate values can be hidden using the property sheet.

To Hide Duplicate Values

a. Change to Layout view, and then under the second Last Name column, click the first **Barker**.

b. Click the **Design tab**, and then click **Property Sheet** in the Tools group.

c. In the property sheet, click the **Format tab**, scroll down to find Hide Duplicates, and then select **Yes**.

d. In Layout view, under First Name, click the first **Charles**.

e. In the Property Sheet, click the **Format tab**, change Hide Duplicates to **Yes**.

f. Close ☒ the property sheet, and then save and close your report.

Add and Remove Fields from a Report

The Report Wizard selects the fields you want and formats the report with headers and footers for grouping. However, you often want to change the fields on existing reports or add grouping. Access makes this possible. You can add and delete fields in either Layout view or Design view. In the next exercise, you will make these changes in Layout view where you can see how the report will look with the changes.

Barry has a report named rptEmployeesByPosition that he has asked you to modify. He wants you to remove the Orientation field and add a Salary field to the report. The report is grouped by position and shows each employee by their hire date.

To remove a field, you must remove both the bound control and the Label control.

To Remove a Field

a. In the Navigation Pane, right-click **rptEmployeesByPosition**, and then open it in Layout view.

b. Click the first **Orientation** box. The entire Orientation column is selected. Press [Shift], and then click the **Orientation** label in the header so that is also highlighted. Right-click and select **Delete**.

Now that you have removed the orientation field, Barry would like you to add the employee's salary to the report. To add a field, you add a field from the Field List. This adds both the bound control and a Label control containing the field's caption.

To Add a Field

a. Click the **Design tab**, and then click **Add Existing Fields** in the Tools group.

b. Click **EmployeeSalary** in the Field List, and then drag it to the report. Release your mouse. The field is put on the left side of the report overlaying Employee Position.

c. Click the **layout selector** ⊞ above the highlighted controls. Your pointer becomes a four-headed arrow ⬍. Use your pointer to drag the controls to the right of **First Name** and release. If you need to drag the controls more, repeat.

d. Close ✕ the Field List pane.

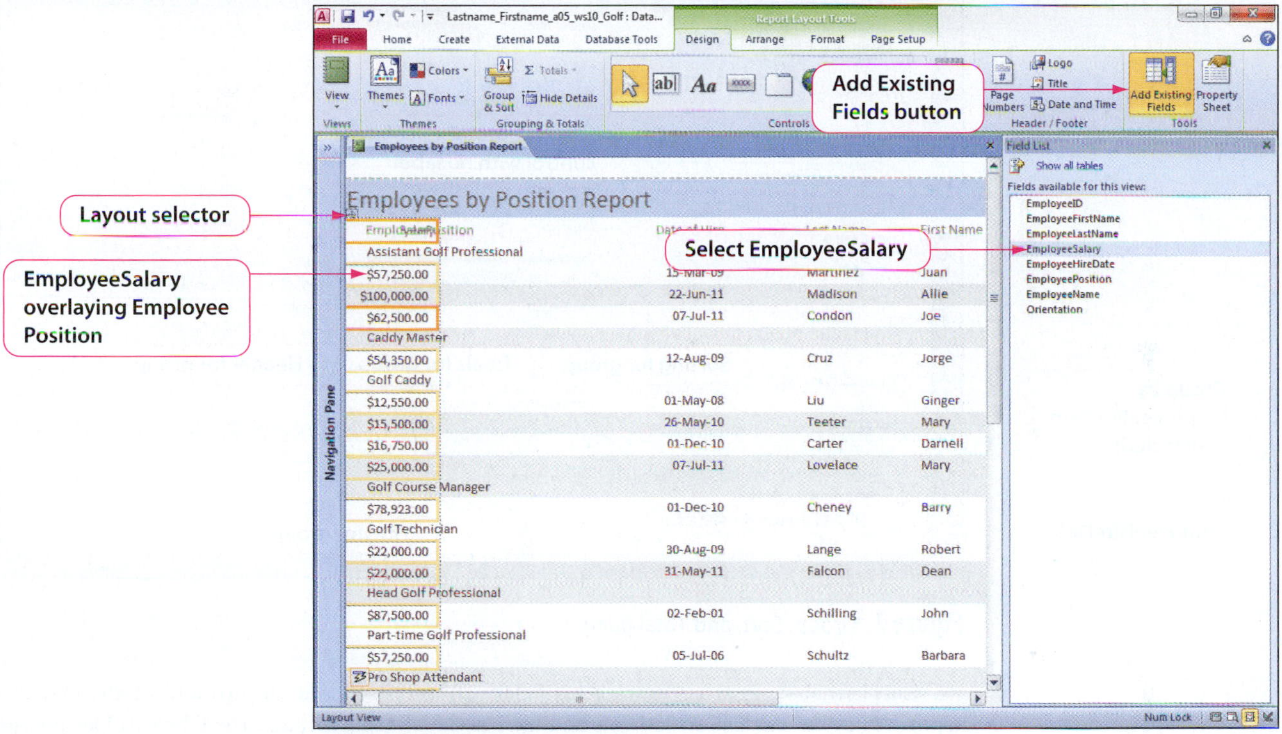

Figure 6 Add a field to the report

Add Totals to a Report

Now that the report has a numeric field, totals can be calculated. To use subtotals, you need grouping. The Employees by Position Report is grouped by employee position so it makes sense to summarize by that grouping.

Access has a Group & Sort feature that simplifies the addition of groups and totals. It can be used in either Layout or Design view. The **Group, Sort, and Total pane** lets you control how information is sorted and grouped in a report.

To Group and Sort

a. Click the **Design tab**, and then click **Group & Sort** in the Grouping & Totals group.

The Group, Sort, and Total pane is displayed at the bottom of the screen. The top line says that the data are grouped on EmployeePosition and sorted from A to Z. The second line says that the data are sorted by EmployeeHireDate. You want to add subtotals to the grouping.

b. Click **More** on the first grouping, EmployeePosition. Notice that you have many choices to add totals, titles, headers, and footers.

c. Click **with no totals**, select **EmployeeSalary** in the Total On box, select **Sum** in the Type box, and then click **Show Grand Total**. The sum is shown immediately so you need to reopen the grouping.

d. Click **More** on the first grouping. Select **with EmployeeSalary totaled**, select **Employee Salary** in the Total On box, and then select **Show subtotal in group footer**.

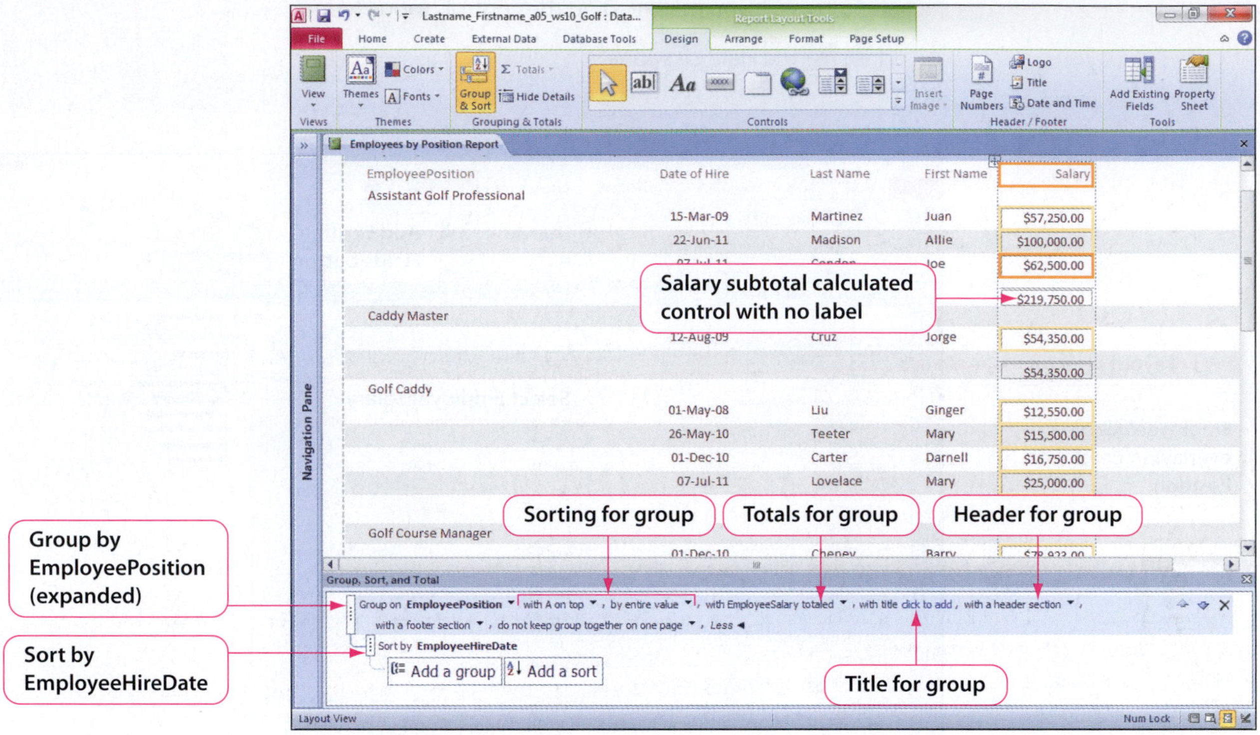

Figure 7 Group, Sort, and Total pane

Check that Access has now added Salary subtotals for the groups and at the end of the report. They are calculated controls and have no label. You will add the labels in Design view.

To Add a Horizontal Line to a Report

a. Note that the Close button for the Group, Sort, and Total pane is on the Group, Sort, and Total bar. **Close** ⊠ the Group, Sort, and Total pane. Change to Design view. In Design view, the footers are present with the calculated controls. You will add the unbound Label control.

b. Click **Label** Aa in the Controls group, move your pointer to the **EmployeePosition Footer**, and then click the 5" mark on the horizontal ruler. In the small box, type Position subtotal.

c. Click the **Label** control Aa. Move your pointer to the **Report Footer**, and then click the 5" mark on the horizontal ruler. In the small box, type Grand total.

d. Switch to Report view. The grand total does not stand out so you will add a line to distinguish it. Switch back to Design view.

e. Click the **Line** control ◻ in the Controls group, and then click to place the line in the **Report Footer**. Use your mouse to drag the line from the left side of the footer to the 8.5" mark on the horizontal ruler, holding down Shift to keep the line horizontal. Switch to Layout view.

Troubleshooting

If you have trouble keeping the Line control horizontal, you may be trying to drag it before placing the line. First, click to place the Line control in the footer. Once the line appears, you can easily drag it horizontally by holding down [Shift].

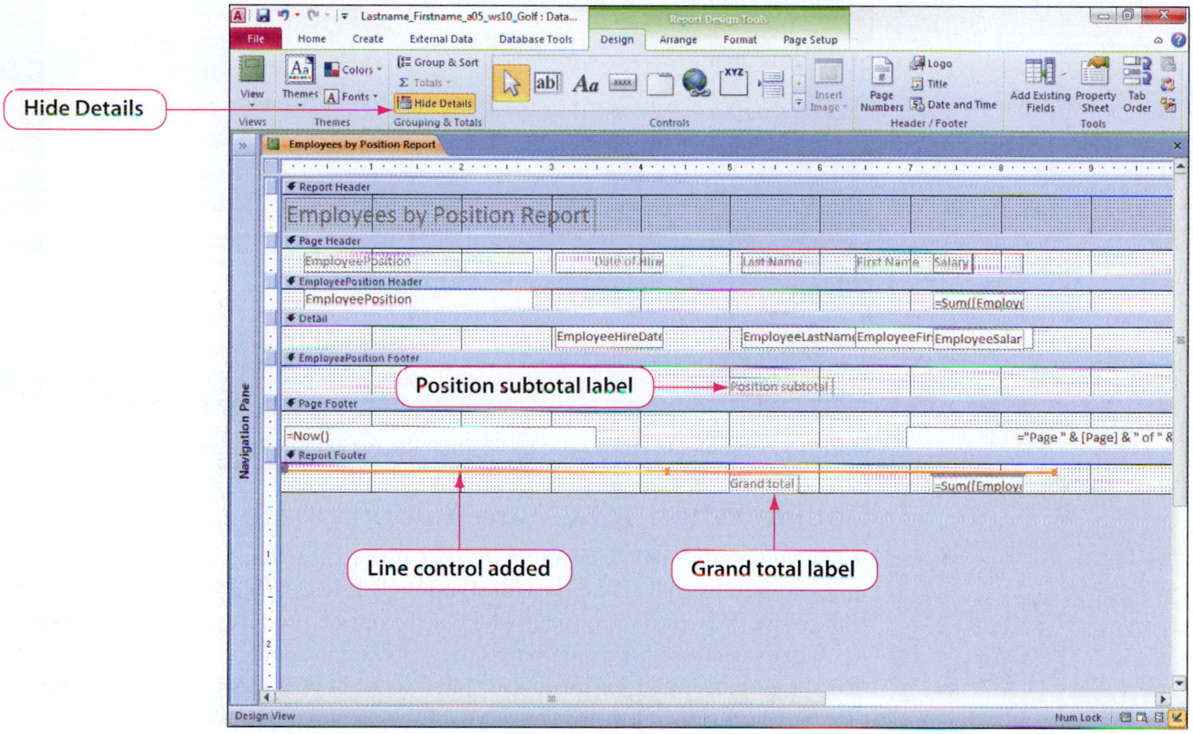

Hide Details

Figure 8 Add horizontal line in Design view

Hide Detail on a Summary Report

By default a summary report also includes a detail area showing unsummarized fields at the record level. This level can be hidden in either Layout or Design view.

To Hide Detail Lines

a. Click **Hide Details** in the Grouping & Totals group. Now the individual people are not shown.

b. Switch back to Design view. Notice that the Detail area is still shown in Design view even though it is hidden in Report view.

c. In the Page Footer, click the calculated Date control, **=Now( )**. Point to the right edge of the field and when the pointer changes to the horizontal resize pointer ↔, drag to the left to narrow the field. Move the right edge to where it lines up with the 3" point.

d. Click **Label** Aa in the Controls group.

e. Move your pointer to the Page Footer and it becomes a Label pointer ⁺A. Click the 3.5" mark on the horizontal ruler and a small window appears. Type **Created by Firstname Lastname** using your actual name.

f. Switch to Print Preview to check your report format. It should look like Figure 9.

g. Save and close your report.

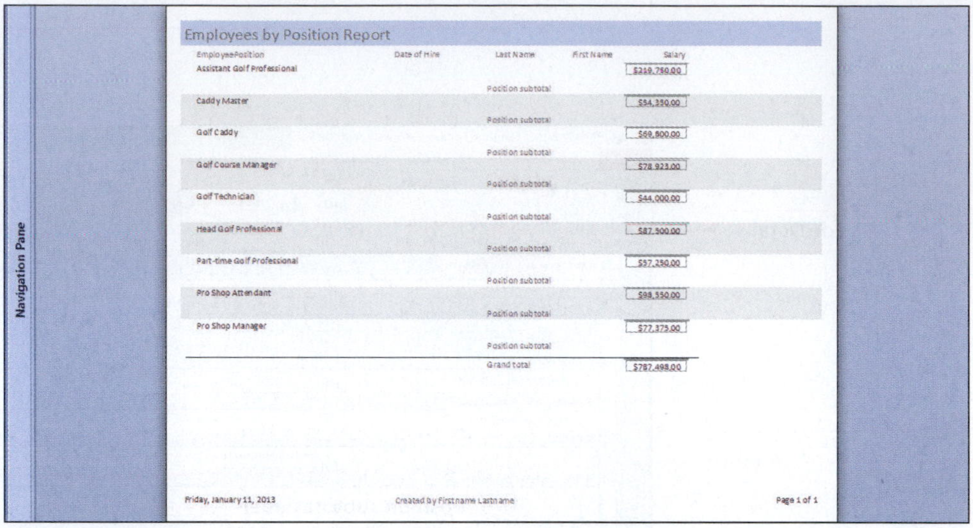

Figure 9 Completed Employees by Position Report in Print Preview

Decide When Totals Are Inappropriate

When you create a report using the Report Wizard, you have summary options for sums, averages, minimums, and maximums for all numeric fields. That does not mean that this will always make sense. You need to consider whether the option produces sensible numbers.

Barry's database has a summary query, qryLessonCount. It shows employee names, the fee that the employee gets for the lesson, and a count of how many lessons the employee gave with that fee. Barry asks if you can create a summary report from this query.

To Create a Report from a Query

a. Double-click **qryLessonCount** to open it. It shows the EmployeeName, Fee, and LessonCount. Close the query.

b. Click the **Create tab**, and then click **Report Wizard**.

c. From qryLessonCount, select all fields. Click **Next**.

d. Add grouping by EmployeeName. Click **Next**, and then sort by Fee.

e. Click **Summary Options**. Because Fee and LessonCount are numeric, you have the option to calculate summary values for both. Select **Sum** for both, click **OK**, and then click **Next**.

f. Accept Stepped Layout and Portrait Orientation, and then click **Next**.

g. Name your report rptSummaryLessonFees, and click **Finish**.

Figure 10 rptSummaryLessonFees

Look at the data for Allie Madison. She taught 3 lessons for a fee of $150.00 each. She taught 1 lesson with a fee of $200. The group summary shows a total of $350 in fees and 4 lessons. That $350 does not make sense because it simply is the addition of the two fees without taking into account that she taught 3 lessons for $150 each. You need to multiply the count by the fee and sum the product to get the correct value. You will fix that in Design view.

To Add a Calculation to a Report

a. Close Print Preview to switch to Design view. In the EmployeeName Footer, click in the first of the two calculated controls **=Sum([Fee])**, and then change it to **=Sum([Fee]*[LessonCount])**. This will multiply the values of the two fields before they are summed. Click in the background of the report design to unselect the control.

b. In the Report Footer, click in the first of the two calculated controls **=Sum([Fee])**, and then change it to **=Sum([Fee]*[LessonCount])**. Click in the background of the report design to unselect the control.

c. Switch to Layout view to verify the total is calculated correctly. Allie Madison's fees should total $650. Switch back to Design view.

Troubleshooting

If you see a prompt that asks you to enter a parameter value, you mistyped the expression for the calculation. Click Cancel and correct the expression.

d. In the EmployeeName footer, click the control that begins ="**Summary for**", and then press Delete.

e. Click **Sum** on the left side of the EmployeeName footer, point to the move handle, and then drag the field so the left side lines up with 1.5" on the horizontal ruler.

f. Click in the **control**, and then highlight **Sum**. Replace the text with **Employee Summary**.

g. Double-click **rptSummaryLessonFees** in the Report Header, and then replace the text with Summary of Lesson Fees.

h. In the Page Footer, click the calculated Date control, **=Now( )**. Point to the right edge of the field and when the pointer changes to the horizontal resize pointer ↔, drag to the left to narrow the field. Move the right edge to where it lines up with the 2" point.

i. Click **Label** Aa in the Controls group.

j. Move your pointer to the Page Footer, and then when it becomes a Label pointer ⁺A, click 2.5" mark on the horizontal ruler and a small window appears. Type Created by Firstname Lastname using your actual name.

k. Switch to Layout view. Scroll down and notice that you need to fix the size of the summary fee in the subtotals and grand total. Click John Schilling's fee summary, and then drag the left side of the box to the left so the dollar sign shows fully.

l. Click the Grand Total fees, and then repeat resizing of the field.

m. Switch to Print Preview and check that your report looks like Figure 11. Save and close your report.

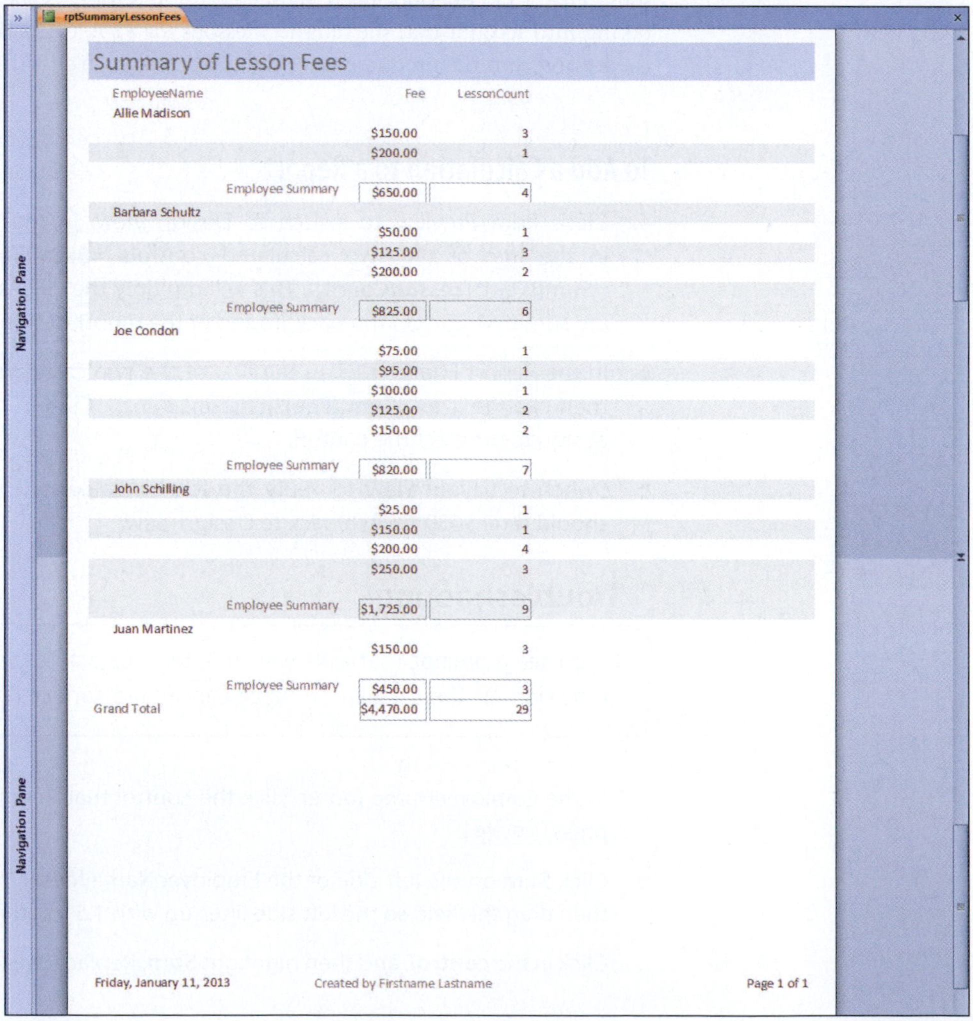

Figure 11 Completed Summary of Lesson Fees report

Parameter Report

Recall that parameter queries were used when you did not know the criteria you wanted to search for. When a **parameter query** is run, the query prompts you for criteria before running the query. A **parameter** is a value that can be changed each time you run the query. These flexible queries are customized to a user's needs. Reports can be created from parameter queries to have that same flexibility.

When reports are built from parameter queries, running the report yields different results depending on the parameter value entered. Because reports are designed to be printed, that means that after time it might not be easy to recall what parameter value was used to run that report. You will add the parameter to the report header so that it can be identified.

In this section, you will create a parameter query and a report from that query. You will add conditional formatting to the report to highlight values that meet certain criteria. You will also create a form for entering the parameters.

Create a Report with a Query as a Source

Barry asks you to create reports that show when golf club memberships are going to expire. He would like the flexibility to see expiration dates based on any date he enters. He would also like you to highlight any members whose membership has already lapsed. This is a perfect choice for a parameter query and subsequent report.

When you create a new report, you want to check where the fields are located. Barry wants to see the member's name, address, phone number, and renewal date. The relationships window provides an easy summary of all the fields. All the fields that Barry wants to see are in tblMember. You will start with a query from tblMember.

To Build a Query

a. Click **tblMember** in the Navigation Pane, and then click **Create** and **Query Wizard**.

b. Select **Simple Query Wizard**, and then click **OK**.

c. Select **FirstName**, **LastName**, **Address**, **City**, **State**, **ZipCode**, **Phone**, and **DateRenewal**. Click **Next**.

d. Title your query qryMembershipRenewals, and then click **Finish**.

e. Close your query.

Now that you have created the query, you can use it as the source for your report.

To Create a Renewal Report

a. Click the **Create tab**, and then click **Report Wizard**.

b. From qryMembershipRenewals, select all fields. Click **Next**.

c. Do not add any grouping levels. Click **Next**, sort by **DateRenewal**, and then click **Next**.

d. Accept Tabular layout, change to Landscape orientation, and then click **Next**.

e. Name your report rptMembershipRenewals, and then click **Finish**.

f. Click your report to see the entire page layout. You see that neither the Phone Number column heading nor the Phone Number data shows fully. You will fix these problems in Layout view.

g. Change to Layout view.

h. Scroll to the right, and then click the **Phone Number** column heading. Press and hold Shift, and then click the first phone number. Use the horizontal resize pointer ↔ to drag the left edge to the left so that both the column header and phone numbers show fully inside the dotted grey line.

i. Double-click the report title **rptMembershipRenewals**, and then replace the text with Membership Renewals.

j. Save your report.

Add Conditional Formatting

Barry wants to see at a glance which memberships have already expired. You will use conditional formatting to highlight those memberships. **Conditional formatting** formats a control based on one or more comparisons to a set rule. These comparisons can be based on the value of the control or on a calculation that includes other values; for example, to highlight values that are zero or negative. You can also compare the value to the value in other records; for example, you could highlight the value that is highest or lowest.

The Conditional Formatting Rules Manager dialog box is used to set the conditions. You can access the dialog box in Layout or Design view.

To Add Conditional Formatting

a. Click the first Renewal Date value, **8/4/2011**. This selects all the dates.

b. Click the **Format tab**, and then click **Conditional Formatting** in the Control Formatting group to start the Conditional Formatting Rules Manager dialog box.

c. Click **New Rule**.

d. Accept the selection Check values in the current record or use an expression.

e. In the rule description, accept Field Value Is. Change the Condition operator to **less than or equal to**. Click the **Build** button ⬚.

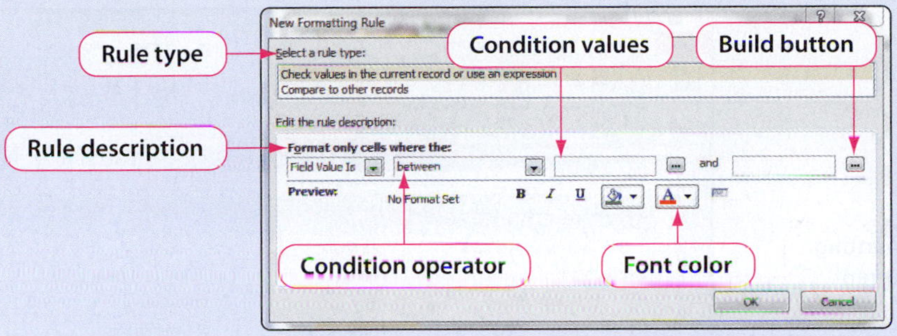

Figure 12 New Formatting Rule

f. In the Expression Elements pane, click **Common Expressions**.

g. In the Expression Categories pane, double-click **Current Date**, and then click **OK**.

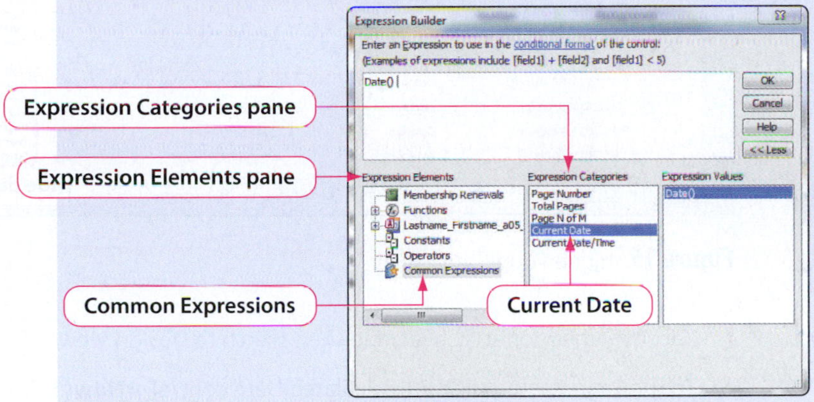

Figure 13 Expression Builder

h. Click the **Font color button** [A ▾] to select red. The preview text is now red. Click **OK**.

i. You could add more formatting rules, but that is the only one that Barry wants. Click **OK**. Depending on the date that you are working the exercise, the first few dates will turn red.

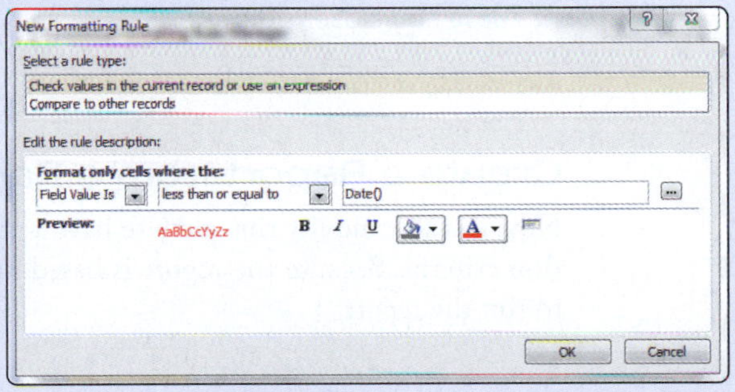

Figure 14 Completed formatting rule

If two or more members have the same renewal date, the renewal date repeats. You will hide those duplicate values the way you did before, using the property sheet.

j. Click the **Design tab**, and then click **Property Sheet** in the Tools group.

k. Click the **Format tab**, scroll down to find **Hide Duplicates**, and then select **Yes**.

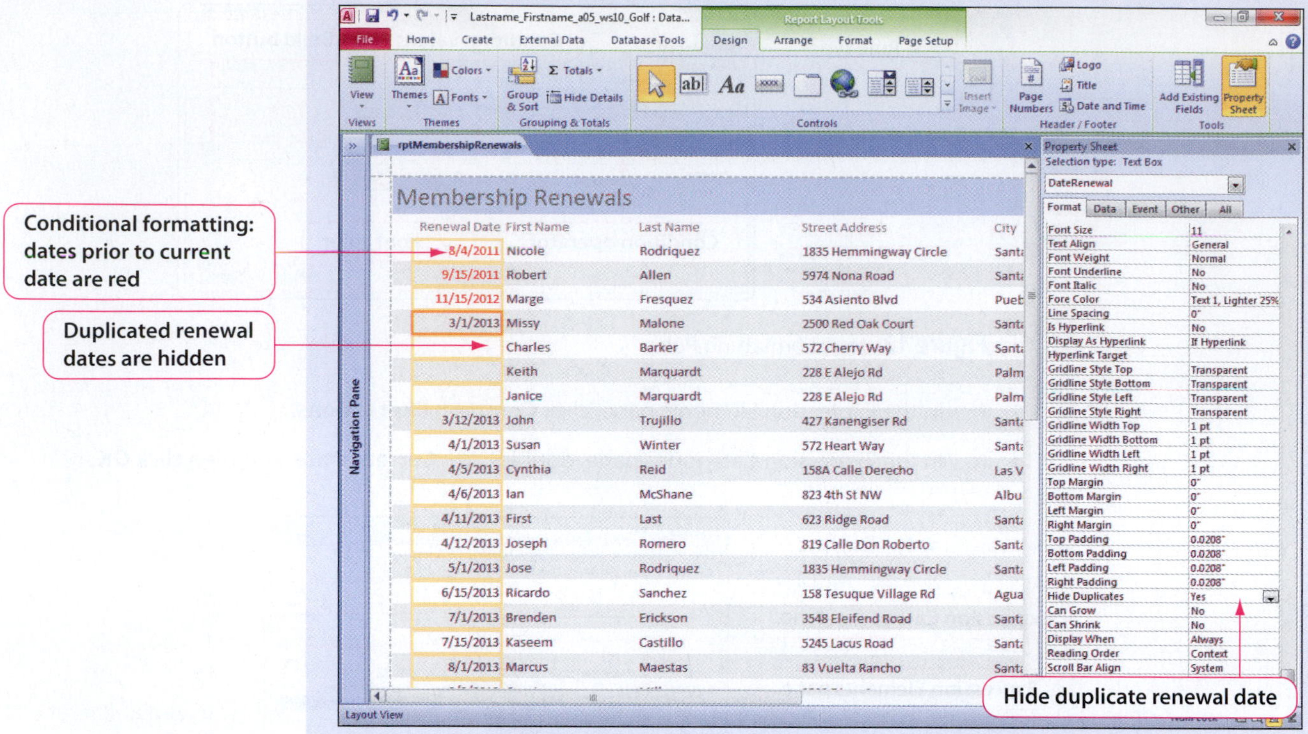

Conditional formatting: dates prior to current date are red

Duplicated renewal dates are hidden

Hide duplicate renewal date

Figure 15 Hidden duplicate values

l. Close ⊠ the property sheet, and then switch to Design view.

m. In the Page Footer, click the calculated Date control, **=Now( )**. Point to the right edge of the field and when the pointer changes to the horizontal resize pointer ↔, drag to the left to narrow the field. Move the right edge to where it lines up with the 3" mark on the horizontal ruler.

n. Click **Label** [Aa] in the Controls group.

o. Move your pointer to the Page Footer and it becomes a Label pointer ⁺A. Click the 3.5" mark on the horizontal ruler, and then type **Created by Firstname Lastname** using your actual name.

p. Save and close your report.

Create a Report from a Parameter Query

Now you will modify the query to have a parameter for entering a date range. You will use selection criteria. Because the report is based upon the query, you will need to enter the parameter to run the report.

To Add a Parameter to a Query

a. Right-click **qryMembershipRenewals**, and then select **Design View**.

b. Scroll to the right, in the Criteria row for DateRenewal, type **Between [Start Date] And [End Date]**.

c. Save and close your query.

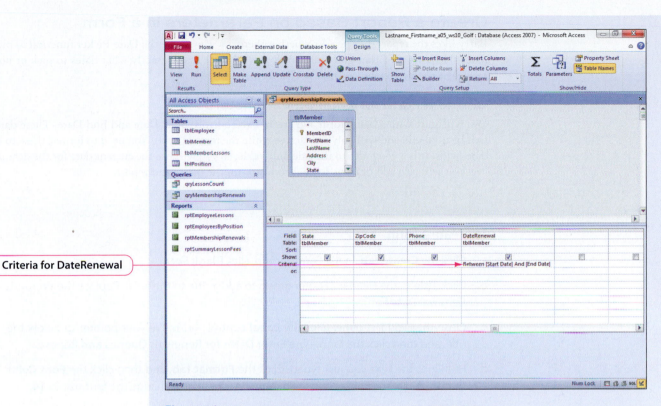

Criteria for DateRenewal

Figure 16 Enter parameters in query

d. Double-click the report **rptMembershipRenewals**.

e. In the Enter Parameter Value dialog box for Start Date, enter **1/1/2011**, and then click **OK**.

f. In the Enter Parameter Value dialog box for End Date, enter **5/1/2013**, and then click **OK**. The report contains all members that have a renewal date between these two dates.

g. Close your report.

Membership Renewals

Renewal Date	First Name	Last Name	Street Address	City
8/4/2011	Nicole	Rodriquez	1835 Hemmingway Circle	Santa Fe
9/15/2011	Robert	Allen	5974 Nona Road	Santa Fe
11/15/2012	Marge	Fresquez	534 Asiento Blvd	Pueblo
3/1/2013	Keith	Marquardt	228 E Alejo Rd	Palm Springs
	Janice	Marquardt	228 E Alejo Rd	Palm Springs
	Missy	Malone	2500 Red Oak Court	Santa Fe
	Charles	Barker	572 Cherry Way	Santa Fe
3/12/2013	John	Trujillo	427 Kanengiser Rd	Santa Ana Pueblo
4/1/2013	Susan	Winter	572 Heart Way	Santa Fe
4/5/2013	Cynthia	Reid	158A Calle Derecho	Las Vegas
4/6/2013	Ian	McShane	823 4th St NW	Albuquerque
4/11/2013	Firstname	Lastname	623 Ridge Road	Santa Fe
4/12/2013	Joseph	Romero	819 Calle Don Roberto	Santa Fe
5/1/2013	Jose	Rodriquez	1835 Hemmingway Circle	Santa Fe

Friday, January 11, 2013   Created by Firstname Lastname

Figure 17 Report selected via parameters

Create a Report Based on Parameters in a Form

Barry likes the report, but he asks whether there is a way to use the Date Picker function to pick dates. He is worried that golf club employees will not know exactly what dates to pick or how to format them. You will do that with a form.

Create a Form for Entering Parameters

You will start with a blank form and create two controls: Start Date and End Date. These dates will be unbound and will only stay active while the form is open. You need to format these to be date fields. It is a good idea to use a default value, so you will use the current date for the default. You will also add buttons to your form to run the query and report.

To Create a Form

a. Click the **Create tab**. In the Forms group, click **Blank Form**.

b. Click **Title** in the Header / Footer group to add a title to the form. Replace the title with **Renewal Date Form**.

c. Close the Field List pane. Click the **Label** control Aa, move your pointer to below the title, and then click the form. Type **Enter Dates for Renewals Queries and Reports**.

d. Highlight the **text** you just typed. Click the **Format tab**, and then click the **Font Color** button $\boxed{A \cdot}$ in the Font group to change the font to red. Change the font size to **14**.

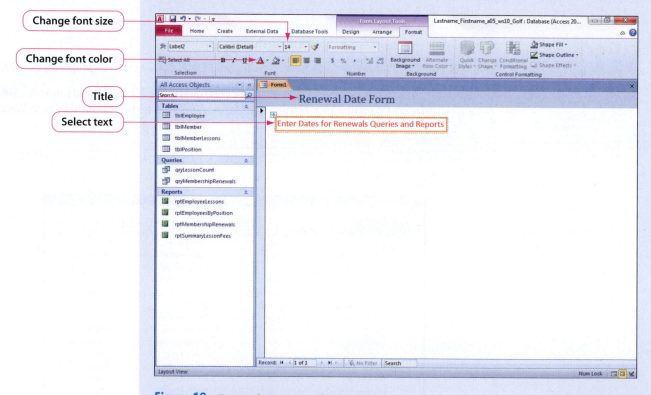

Figure 18 Change formatting of field

e. Click the **Design tab**, and then click the **Text Box** control $\boxed{abl}$. Click the form to insert a text box below the **Enter Dates for Renewal Queries and Reports** label.

f. The control on the left is the Label control. Type **Start Date** in the label.

g. The control on the right is the text box. Click in the **text box**. On the Design tab, click **Property Sheet** in the Tools group. In the property sheet, click the **Format tab**, change Format to Short Date. Click the **Data tab**, and then in Default Value, enter =Date(). Click the **Other tab**, and then in Name, enter Start Date.

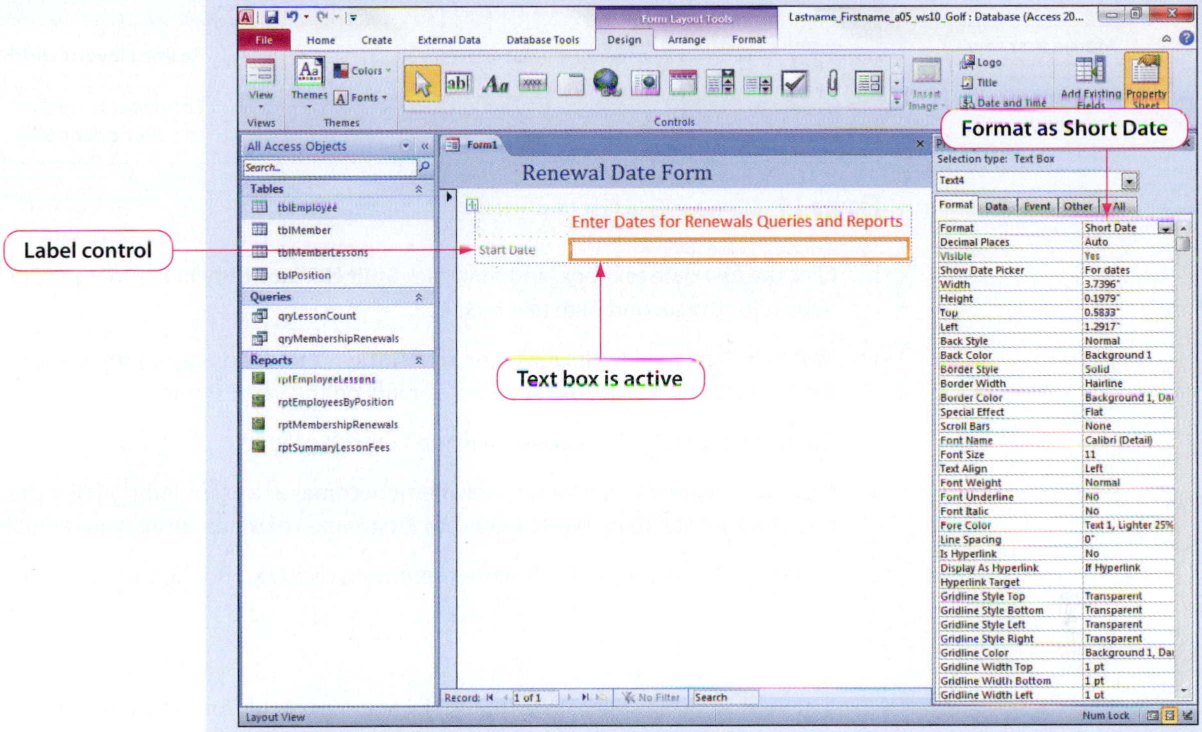

Figure 19 Enter Start Date controls

h. Click the **Design tab**, and then click the **Text Box** control [ab]. Click the form to insert a text box immediately below **Start Date**. Type End Date in the label.

i. Click in the **text box**. In the property sheet, click the **Format tab**. Change Format to Short Date. Click the **Data tab**, and then in Default Value, enter =Date(). Click the **Other tab**, and then in Name, enter End Date.

j. Close the property sheet.

Remember that Access arranges your controls in a layout that is like an invisible table. You want to fix the first row so that it is a wider single cell and make the other rows have narrower cells.

k. Click the **Arrange tab**, click the blank space above **Start Date**, and then click **Select Row** in the Rows & Columns group. Click **Merge** in the Merge / Split group, and then use your pointer to resize the entire layout to be as wide as your first row.

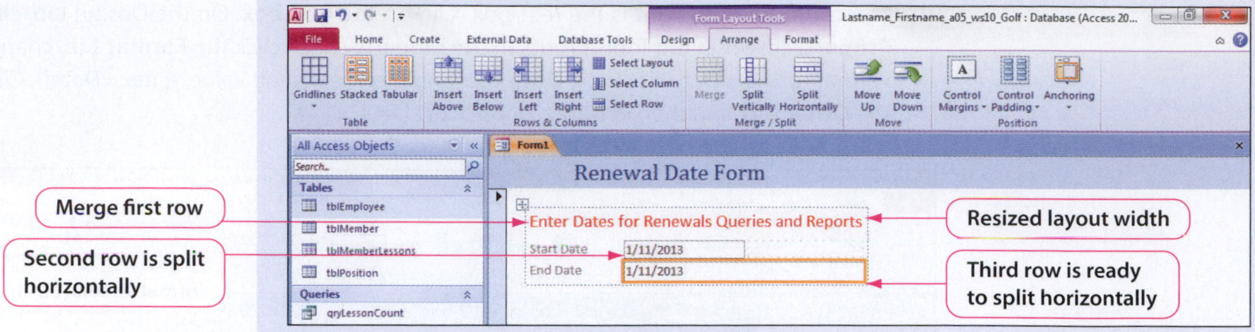

Figure 20 Merge cells in first row

l. Click the first date text box, and then click **Split Horizontally** in the Merge / Split group. Repeat for the second date text box.

m. Switch to Design view. Increase the size of the footer by dragging the bottom edge of the bar that says **Form Footer** to the .5" mark on the vertical ruler.

n. On the Design tab, click **Label** [Aa] in the Controls group.

o. Move your pointer to the footer and when it becomes a Label pointer [ᵗA] click the .5" mark on the horizontal ruler. Type **Created by Firstname Lastname** using your actual name.

p. Save your form naming it **frmMemberRenewals**, click **OK**, and then leave your form open.

You need to change your query to use the new form fields for the parameters.

To Change Query Criteria to Use Fields from Forms

a. In the Navigation Pane, right-click **qryMembershipRenewals** in the Queries group, and then open it in Design view.

b. Scroll to the right, delete the **Criteria** under **DateRenewal**, and then leave your pointer in the Criteria. If necessary, click the **Design tab**, and then click **Builder** in the Query Setup group. Type **Between** in the Expression pane.

c. In the Expression Elements pane, click the **Expand** button before **Lastname_Firstname_ a05_ws10_Golf** to expand it. Click the **Expand** button before **Forms** to expand it. Click the **Expand** button before **Loaded Forms** to expand it, and then click **frmMemberRenewals**.

d. In the Expression Categories pane, double-click **Start Date**, and then type **and** in the expression.

e. In the Expression Categories pane, double-click **End Date**. Your expression will read "Between Forms![frmMemberRenewals]![Start Date] and Forms![frmMemberRenewals]! [End Date]".

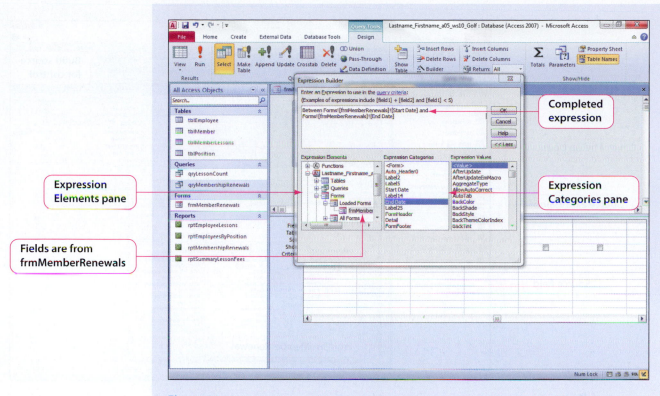

Expression Elements pane

Fields are from frmMemberRenewals

Completed expression

Expression Categories pane

Figure 21 Change query criteria to use form fields

f. Click **OK**, run the query, and then save and close your query. Leave the Renewal Date Form open.

You have successfully changed your query to use the parameters from the form. Since the report is created from the query, it will also use the parameters. You will now change the report header to show which dates are included in the report.

To Add Dates from Forms to the Report Title

a. In the Navigation Pane, right-click **rptMembershipRenewals** in the Reports group, and then open it in Design view. Use your pointer to drag the bottom edge of the **Report Header** to the 1" mark on the vertical ruler.

b. Click the **Design tab**, click **Text Box** ![abl] in the Controls group, and then click the **Report Header** below the title to insert a text box. If necessary, drag the **control** with the move handle so that the Label control lines up with the .5" mark on the horizontal ruler.

c. Click in the Label control, highlight the text, and then replace it with Start Date.

d. Click the **text box**, and then click **Property Sheet** in the Tools group. Click the **Format tab** of the property sheet, and then change Format to **Short Date**. Click the **Data tab** of the property sheet. In Control Source, click the **Build** button ![...]. In the Expression Elements pane, expand Lastname_Firstname_a05_ws10_Golf, expand Forms, expand Loaded Forms, and then click **frmMemberRenewals**.

e. In the Expression Categories pane, double-click **Start Date**, and then click **OK**.

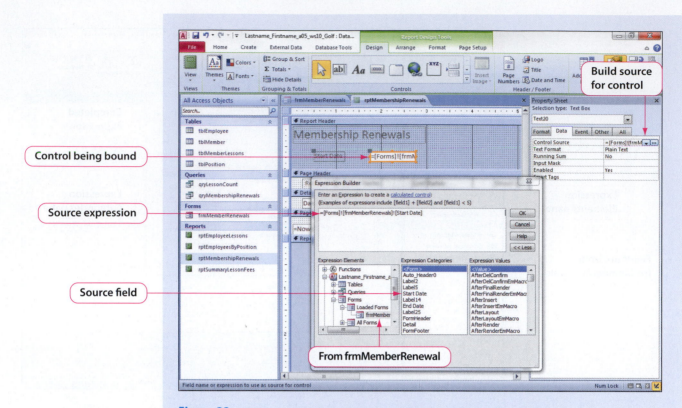

Labels pointing to the figure:
- Control being bound
- Source expression
- Source field
- Build source for control
- From frmMemberRenewal

Figure 22 Bind control in report header to form field

f. Click the **Design tab**, click **Text Box** abl in the Controls group, and then click the **Report Header** to insert a text box to the right of the first. If necessary, drag the **control** with the move handle so that the left-side of the Label control lines up with the 3" mark on the horizontal ruler.

g. Click the **Label control**, highlight the **text**, and then replace it with End Date.

h. Click the **text box**, click the **Format tab** of the property sheet, and then change Format to **Short Date**. Click the **Data tab** of the property sheet, and then in Control Source, click the **Build** button ⬚. In the Expression Elements pane, expand Lastname_Firstname_ a05_ws10_Golf, expand Forms, expand Loaded Forms, and click **frmMemberRenewals**.

i. In the Expression Categories pane, double-click **End Date**, click **OK**, and then close ⊠ the property sheet.

j. Save 🖫 and close ⊠ your report.

Whenever you create a form that calls a query or report, you need to test the form. Testing checks that your form behaves the way you expect it to.

To Test Your Form and Parameters

a. Change frmMemberRenewals to Form view.

b. In Start Date, enter 1/1/2011. In End Date, enter 5/1/2013. Notice that Date Picker is active for your dates. Press Tab. Do not close the form.

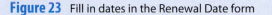

Enter dates

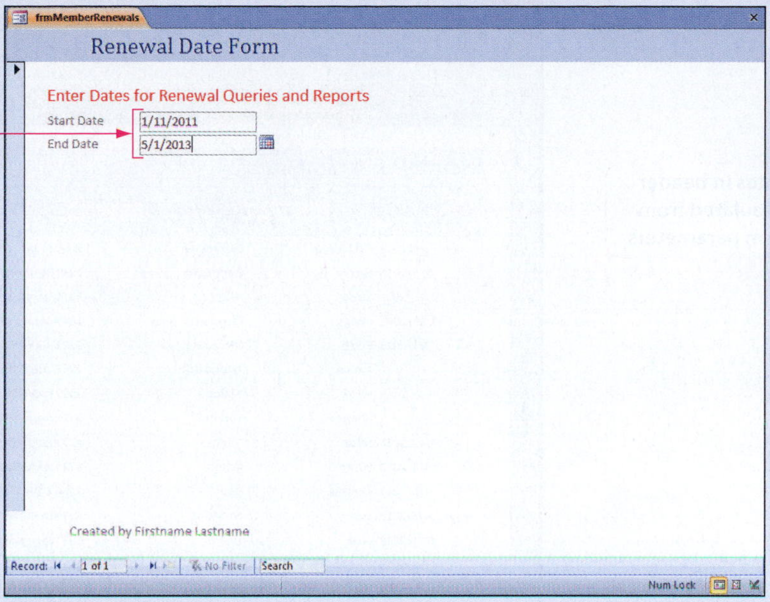

frmMemberRenewals

Renewal Date Form

Enter Dates for Renewal Queries and Reports

Start Date | 1/11/2011
End Date | 5/1/2013

Created by Firstname Lastname

Record: 1 of 1   No Filter   Search

Num Lock

Figure 23 Fill in dates in the Renewal Date form

c. In the Navigation Pane, double-click **qryMembershipRenewals** in the Queries group. The query opens showing the members who have renewals between the two dates. Close the query.

Troubleshooting

When you ran the query or report, did it ask you for parameters? Make sure that the form is open. If you close the form, Access does not know what dates you want and has to ask.

If your query is empty, close the query and press Tab. This makes sure that Access has accepted the dates. You will add buttons to the form so this will not be a problem for the golf club employees.

d. In the Navigation Pane, double-click **rptMembershipRenewals** in the Reports group. The report opens showing the members who have renewals between the two dates. The dates are filled in in the header. Close the report.

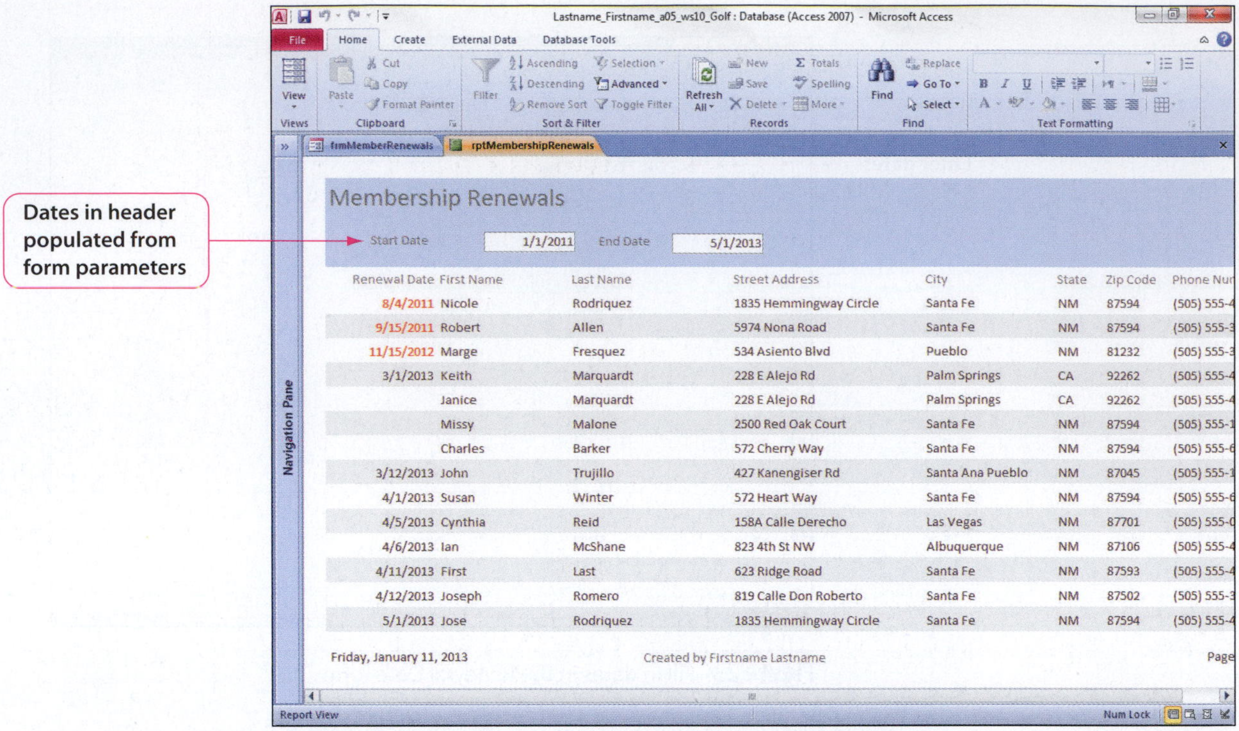

Dates in header populated from form parameters

Figure 24 Membership Renewals Report created from parameters

Real World Advice — **Show Parameter Values on the Report**

Whenever you create a report with parameters, you should add the parameter values to the report. Suppose you find this report on your desk a week from now, would you remember what dates you entered?

Add Report Buttons to a Form

To make the form more usable for the golf club employees, you will add buttons to run the query and report.

To Add Report Buttons to a Form

a. Change your form to Design view. Use your pointer to expand the Detail section of the form to the 2.5" mark on the vertical ruler.

b. Click the **Design tab**, and then click **Button** in the Controls group.

c. Move your pointer to below the dates, and click the **form**. The Command Button Wizard opens.

d. Select **Miscellaneous** and **Run Query**, and then click **Next**.

e. Select **qryMembershipRenewals**, and then click **Next**. Select **Text**, type **Run Renewals Query**, and then click **Next**.

f. Name the button **cmdQryRenewals**, and then click **Finish**.

g. Click the **Design tab**, and then click **Button** ▭ in the Controls group.

h. Move your pointer to the right of the other button, and click the **form**. The Command Button Wizard starts.

i. Select **Report Operations** and **Open Report**, and then click **Next**.

j. Select **rptMembershipRenewals**, and then click **Next**. Select **Text**, type **Run Renewals Report**, and then click **Next**.

k. Name the button **cmdRenewalsReport**, and then click **Finish**.

l. Save your form. Switch to Form view. In Start Date, enter **1/1/2011**. In End Date, enter **5/1/2013**.

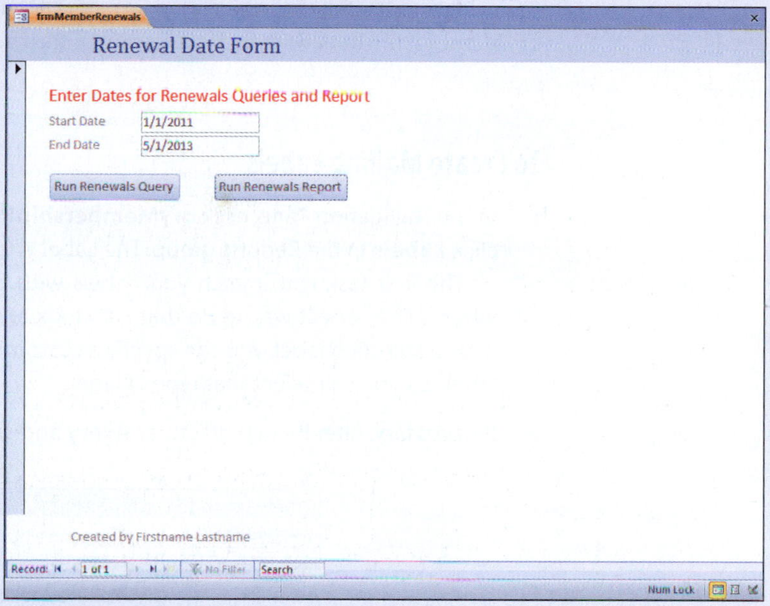

Figure 25 Form with buttons

m. Click the **Run Renewals Query** button. The query opens showing the members who have renewals between the two dates. Close ⊠ the query, but leave the form open.

n. Click the **Run Renewals Report** button. The report opens showing the members who have renewals between the two dates. The dates are filled in in the header. Close ⊠ the report, but leave the form open.

Real World Advice — Give Your Controls Meaningful Names

When you use controls in a report or form, give them meaningful names. That will allow you to easily refer to them again. Using "cmd" as a prefix for a button allows you to easily identify them as buttons.

Mailing Labels

Access has a specialized report that can be used for mailing labels, name tags, or other types of labels. Because Access is often used to keep track of customers, employees, or other types of people, this is a common need. You also could export the names and addresses to Word and then create the mailing labels in Word, but this saves a step. You can create labels based on data in tables or queries.

Access has built-in label formats for many of the leading label makers. The wizard allows you to pick the correct format.

In this section, you will create mailing labels from a query. You will add buttons to your form to request a preview view of the labels and to print the labels.

Create Mailing Labels

Barry would like to create mailing labels for members whose membership is expiring soon. The golf club can then mail a renewal letter to these members. You will use the qryMembershipRenewals query as a source for these labels.

To Create Mailing Labels

a. In the Navigation Pane, click **qryMembershipRenewals**, click the **Create tab**, and then click **Labels** in the Reports group. The Label Wizard starts.

The first task is to match your labels with the standard labels that are part of the wizard. The easiest way to do that is to look at the box or sheet of labels. If you do not have a standard label, you can specify a customized size. The golf club uses Avery C2160 labels so you will select that type of label.

b. If necessary, filter by manufacturer **Avery** and select Product Number **C2160**.

Filter by manufacturer

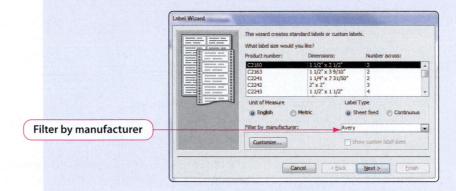

Figure 26 Choose manufacturer and label type

c. Click **Next**, change the font to **Times New Roman** and the font size to **11**, and then click **Next**.

The field selection looks like field selection in other wizard dialog boxes, but there are important differences. First, you must format your labels yourself. You will need to type spaces, commas, and line breaks. Second, there is no field back button. If you put the fields in the wrong order, it is sometimes easiest to go back a step in the wizard dialog box and try again.

d. Select **FirstName**, and then click **One Field** `>` to move it to the prototype label.

e. Press `Spacebar`, select **LastName**, and then click **One Field** `>`. Press `Enter`.

Troubleshooting

> If you omitted the space, move your pointer between the two fields and press the
> [Spacebar].

f. Select **Address**, click **One Field** [>], and then press [Enter].

g. Select **City**, click **One Field** [>], and then type **,** (a comma).

h. Press [Spacebar], select **State**, and then click **One Field** [>]. Press [Spacebar], select **ZipCode**, and then click **One Field** [>].

i. Click **Next**.

j. Sort by ZipCode, and then click **Next**.

k. Name your report **rptLabelsRenewal**, and then click **Finish**.

l. Save your report.

Troubleshooting

> When you clicked Finish did the Mailing labels report ask you for parameters? Make
> sure that the membership renewal form is open. If you close the form, Access doesn't
> know what dates you want.

Mailing labels are reports. That means that they have the four typical views: Print Preview, Report, Layout, and Design. Because of the mailing label formats, the views look different than ones you have seen before. In Print Preview, the labels look the way they will look when you print them. This particular label prints three across, and that is what is visible in this view.

To Switch Label Views

a. Switch to Report view.

In Report view, the labels are shown as a continuous report without page breaks. The labels appear as a single column.

b. Switch to Layout view.

In this view, the labels are also shown as a continuous report. You can make changes in this view. You can also check the label boundaries to make sure there is room for the addresses.

c. Click the right side of the report. The boundaries for each label appear.

d. Switch to Design view.

The format for a single label is shown. You can modify the fields here. The labels use the Trim function. This function removes all extra spaces except single spaces between words.

e. Close your report.

To make the mailing labels easier to use, you will add buttons to preview and print the labels to your renewal form.

To Add Mailing Label Buttons to a Form

a. Switch to Design view for your form.

b. Click the **Design tab**, and then click **Button** ⬚ in the Controls group.

c. Move your pointer to below the Run Renewals Query, and then click the form. The Command Button Wizard starts.

d. Select **Report Operations** and **Preview Report**, and then click **Next**.

e. Select **rptLabelsRenewal**, and then click **Next**. Select **Text**, type Preview Mailing Labels, and then click **Next**.

f. Name the button cmdPreviewLabels, and then click **Finish**.

g. Click the **Design tab**, and then click **Button** ⬚ in the Controls group.

h. Move your pointer to the right of the Preview Mailing Labels button, and then click the form. The Command Button Wizard starts.

i. Select **Report Operations** and **Print Report**, and then click **Next**.

j. Select **rptLabelsRenewal**, and then click **Next**. Select **Text**, type Print Mailing Labels, and then click **Next**.

k. Name the button cmdPrintLabels, and then click **Finish**.

l. Click the **Design tab**, and then click **Button** ⬚ in the Controls group.

m. Move your pointer below the Preview Mailing Labels button, and then click the form. The Command Button Wizard starts.

n. Select **Form Operations** and **Close Form**, and then click **Next**.

o. Select **Text**, accept Close Form, and then click **Next**.

p. Name the button cmdCloseForm, and then click **Finish**.

q. Click the **Arrange tab**. Click the top left of the **Run Renewals Query** button. Using your pointer drag to select the three buttons on the left. Click **Align** in the Sizing & Ordering group, and then select **Left**. Click **Size/Space** in the Sizing & Ordering group, and then select **Equal Vertical**. Click **Size/Space**, and then select **To Widest**.

r. Use your pointer to select the top two buttons. Click **Align** in the Sizing & Ordering group, and then select **Top**.

s. Use your pointer to select the next two buttons. Click **Align** in the Sizing & Ordering group, and then select **Top**.

t. Use your pointer to select the two buttons on the right. Click **Align** in the Sizing & Ordering group, and then select **Left**. Click **Size/Space**, and then select **To Widest**.

u. Save your form, and then switch to Form view. In Start Date, enter 1/1/2011. In End Date, enter 5/1/2013.

v. Click the **Preview Mailing Labels** button. The labels report opens showing the members who have renewals between the two dates. Close the report.

w. Click the **Close Form** button, and then close Access.

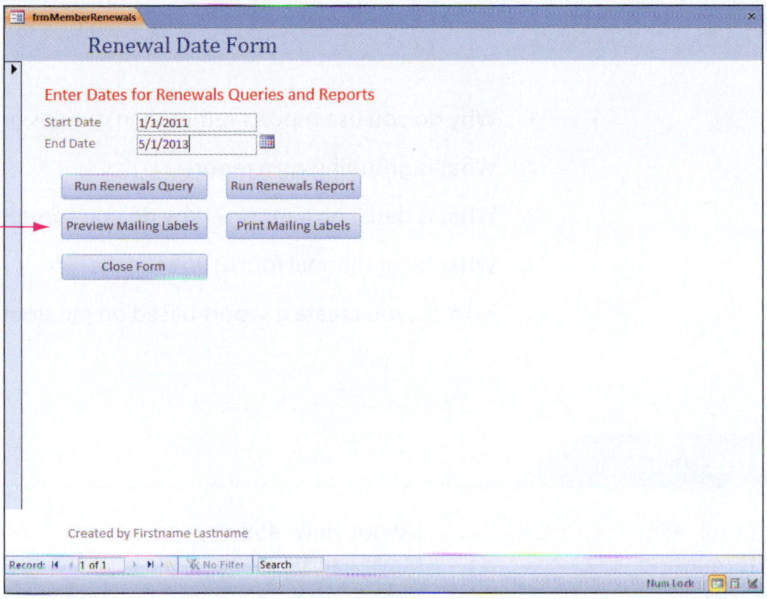

Figure 27 Completed Renewal Date Form

Real World Advice   Preview Before You Print

When you create a report, it is a good idea to preview it before you print it or send it in PDF form to someone else. Sometimes your formatting changes make the report go to two pages when you did not intend it. On mailing labels, it is common for the address to not quite fit into the label or for you to have omitted a space between fields.

1. Why do you use reports rather than queries or forms?

2. What is grouping on a report?

3. What is detail on a report? Why do you sometimes hide detail?

4. What is conditional formatting?

5. How do you create a report based on parameters?

Key Terms

Blank Report tool 458
Conditional formatting 472
Design view 458
Detail area 461
Group Footer 461
Group Header 461
Group, Sort, and Total pane 465
Label control 461

Layout view 458
Move handle 463
Page Footer 462
Page Header 461
Parameter 471
Parameter query 471
Print Preview 458
Property sheet 464

Report 458
Report Design tool 458
Report Footer 462
Report Header 461
Report tool 458
Report view 458
Report Wizard 458
Sizing handle 463

Visual Workshop

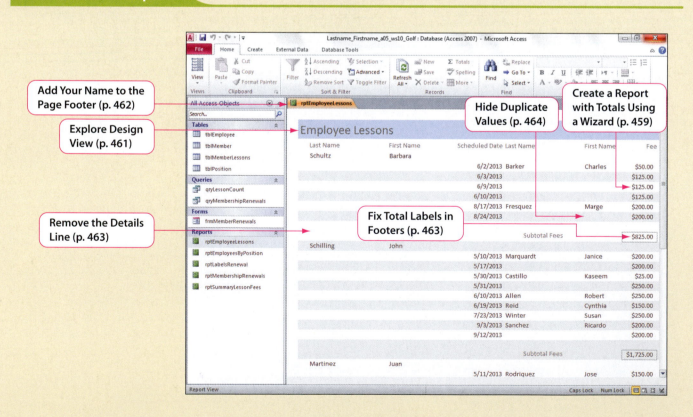

Add Your Name to the Page Footer (p. 462)

Explore Design View (p. 461)

Remove the Details Line (p. 463)

Hide Duplicate Values (p. 464)

Create a Report with Totals Using a Wizard (p. 459)

Fix Total Labels in Footers (p. 463)

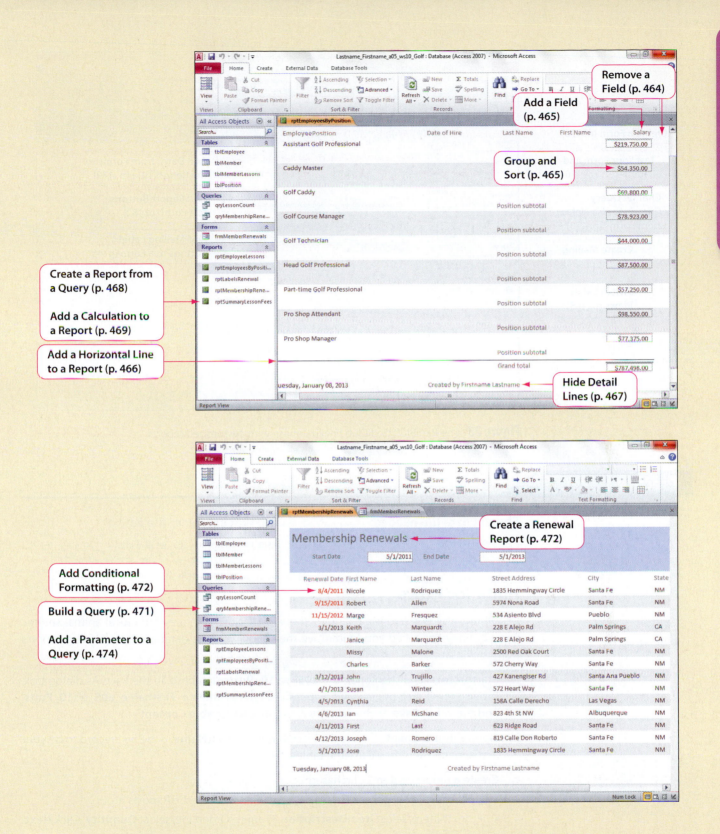

Create a Report from a Query (p. 468)

Add a Calculation to a Report (p. 469)

Add a Horizontal Line to a Report (p. 466)

Remove a Field (p. 464)

Add a Field (p. 465)

Group and Sort (p. 465)

Hide Detail Lines (p. 467)

Add Conditional Formatting (p. 472)

Build a Query (p. 471)

Add a Parameter to a Query (p. 474)

Create a Renewal Report (p. 472)

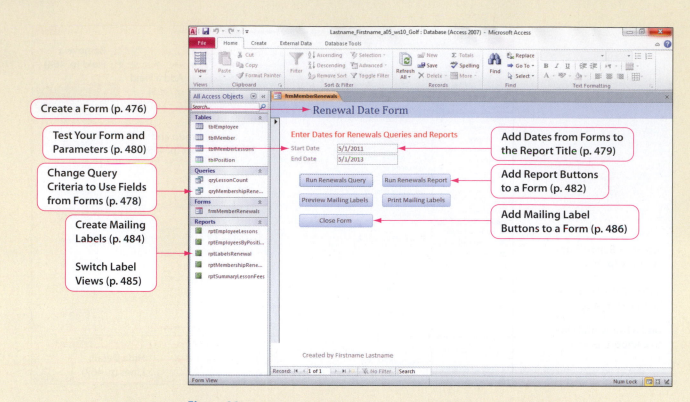

Callout labels (left side):
- Create a Form (p. 476)
- Test Your Form and Parameters (p. 480)
- Change Query Criteria to Use Fields from Forms (p. 478)
- Create Mailing Labels (p. 484)
- Switch Label Views (p. 485)

Callout labels (right side):
- Add Dates from Forms to the Report Title (p. 479)
- Add Report Buttons to a Form (p. 482)
- Add Mailing Label Buttons to a Form (p. 486)

Figure 28 The Red Bluff Golf Club final database with customized reports

Practice 1

Student data file needed:	**You will save your file as:**
a05_ws10_Putts	Lastname_Firstname_a05_ws10_Putts

Putts for Paws

Red Bluff Golf Course runs a charity golf event that raises money for a local animal shelter. Barry Cheney has asked you to improve the usability of the database by providing reports from the database.

a. Start **Access**, and then open the **a05_ws10_Putts** database. In the Save As dialog box, browse to where you are saving your files, type Lastname_Firstname_a05_ws10_Putts, and then click **Save**. In the Security Warning, click **Enable Content**.

b. Open **tblParticipant**, change the **FirstName** and **LastName** in the first record to be your actual name, and then close the table.

c. Create a report on items purchased:
- Click the **Create tab**, and then click **Report Wizard** in the Reports group.
- From tblItem, select **ItemDescription**. From tblOrderLine, select **Quantity**. Click **Next**.
- Group by tblItem, and then click **Next**. Sort by Quantity, and then click **Summary Options**. Select **Sum**, and then click **OK**. Click **Next**. Accept **Stepped** and **Portrait** layout, and then click **Next**.
- Name your report rptItemsPurchased, and then click **Finish**.
- Change to Layout view, click **rptItemsPurchased** in the header, and then change the title to Items Purchased.
- Click the line that begins **"Summary for 'ItemID'"**, and then press Delete.

- Click the **Design tab**, and then click **Hide Details** in the Grouping & Totals group.
- Change to Design view. In the Page Footer, click the calculated Date control, **=Now( )**. Use your pointer to drag the right edge left to the 2.5" mark on the horizontal ruler.
- Click **Label** in the Controls group, move your pointer and click the 2.5" mark on the Page Footer, and then type Created by Firstname Lastname using your actual name.
- Change to Report view to check your report formatting.
- Save and close your report.

d. Create a query showing participants and their purchases and a calculated total price:

- Click the **Create tab**, and then click **Query Wizard**. Click **Simple Query Wizard**, and then click **OK**.
- From tblParticipant, select **ParticipantName**. From tblOrder, select **OrderDate**. From tblOrderLine, select **Quantity**. From tblItem, select **AmountToBeCharged**, **ItemID**, and **ItemDescription**. Click **Next**.
- Click **Detail**, and then click **Next**.
- Name your query qryOrdersCalcPrice, click **Modify the query design**, and then click **Finish**.
- Click in the **Field Name** row of the first empty column, and then click **Builder** in the Query Setup group. In the Expression Builder dialog box, type [Quantity] * [AmountToBeCharged], and then click **OK**.
- Replace **Expr1** with Price.
- Run your query, and then save and close the query.

e. Create a report from qryOrdersCalcPrice:

- Click the **Create tab**, and then click **Report Wizard**. From qryOrdersCalcPrice, select all fields except ItemID. Click **Next**.
- Add grouping by ParticipantName, click **Next**, and then sort by OrderDate and ItemDescription.
- Click **Summary Options**, select **Sum** for **Quantity** and **Price**, and then click **OK**.
- Click **Next**, accept Stepped layout, change to Landscape orientation, and then click **Next**.
- Name your report rptParticipantsPurchases, and then click **Finish**.
- Change to Layout view, click **rptParticipantsPurchases** in the header, and then change the title to Participants Purchases.
- Click the line that begins **"Summary for 'ParticipantName'"**, and then press ⌑Delete⌑.
- Click the **Amount Charged** column header, press ⌑Shift⌑, and then click the first **Amount Charged** value. Click the **right edge**, and then drag it to the left to resize the column and leave room for the Price field. Click the **Amount Charged** column header, and then drag the left edge so the Amount Charged label is completely shown.
- Click the first **Price** value. Use your pointer to drag the **left edge** of the value to the left to resize the field to show values. Repeat for group totals and the grand total. Make the totals a little wider than you need because you will add a dollar sign and comma later.
- Click the **group total** for Price, and then click **Property Sheet**. Click the **Format tab**, and then change Format to Currency. Repeat for the grand total Price. Double-check that your columns are wide enough to show the full value, and then close the property sheet.
- Change to Design view, and then click **Sum** in the ParticipantName Footer. Use your pointer to drag Sum to have its left edge on the 5" mark on the horizontal ruler. Change the label from **Sum** to Participant Total.
- In the Report Footer, click **Grand Total**, and then use your pointer to drag Grand Total to have its left edge on the 5" mark on the horizontal ruler.

- Click **Label** in the Controls group. Move your pointer and then click in the **Page Footer** at the 4" mark in the horizontal ruler. Type Created by Firstname Lastname using your actual name.
- Change to Report view to check your report formatting. Save and close your report.

f. Create a form to request items:
- Click the **Create tab**, and then in the Forms group, click **Blank Form**.
- Click **Title** in the Header/Footer group, and then replace the title with Report on Item.
- Close the Field List. Click the **Label** control, move your pointer to below the title, and then place the label. Type Enter Item for Queries and Reports.
- Click the **Combo Box** control, and then click the form below the label. Select **I want the combo box to get the values from another table or query**, and then click **Next**. Select **Table: tblItem**, and then click **Next**. Select **ItemDescription**, and then click **Next**. Sort by **ItemDescription**, and then click **Next**. Adjust the width of the column to fit, and then click **Next**. Accept the name **ItemDescription** and click **Finish**.
- Click **Property Sheet** in the Tools group. Click to select the **combo box** without its label. Click the **Other tab** of the property sheet, and then change the Name to be ItemDescription.
- Place your pointer on the right edge of the label for the combo box, and double-click to adjust the width.
- Click the first row in the layout, click the **Arrange tab**, and then click **Select Row** in the Rows & Columns group. Click **Merge** in the Merge/Split group.
- Save your form naming it frmRequestItem.
- Close the property sheet.
- Change to Form view, and then select an ItemDescription of **Cart sponsor**. Do not close your form.

g. Modify **qryOrdersCalcPrice** to use the item description from the form:
- In the Navigation Pane, right-click **qryOrdersCalcPrice**, and then select **Design View**.
- Click in the **Criteria** row under ItemID, and then click **Builder** in the Query Setup group. In the Expression Elements pane, expand Lastname_Firstname_a05_ws10_ Putts, expand Forms, expand Loaded Forms, and click frmRequestItem.
- In the Expression Categories pane, double-click **ItemDescription**, and then click **OK**.
- Run, save, and close your query. Do not close your form.

h. Modify your report **rptParticipantsPurchases** to put the item description from the form in the header:
- In the Navigation Pane, right-click **rptParticipantsPurchases** in the Reports group, and then open it in Design view.
- Click **Text Box** in the Controls group, and then click to the right of the report title in the Report Header to insert a text box. If necessary, move the control so it does not overlap the title.
- Click in the **Label** control. Click the **Design tab**, and then click **Property Sheet** in the Tools group. Click the **Format tab** of the property sheet, and then change the caption to be Item Selected.
- In the Report Header, resize the Label control with the sizing handles as needed to show the full caption.
- Click the **text box**, and then click the **Data tab** of the property sheet. In Control Source, click the **Build** button. In the Expression Elements pane, expand Lastname_ Firstname_a05_ws10_Putts, expand Forms, expand Loaded Forms, and click frmRequestItem.
- In the Expression Categories pane, double-click ItemDescription, and then click **OK**.
- Change to Report view to check your work, and then save and close your report. Do not close your form.

Figure 29 frmRequestItem

i. Add buttons to your form to request the query and report:

  • Change **frmRequestItem** to Design view. Drag to change the height of the Detail area to the 2.5" mark on the vertical ruler. Close the property sheet.

  • Click **Button** in the Controls group.

  • Move your pointer to below the combo box label, and then click the form. The Command Button Wizard starts.

  • Select **Miscellaneous** and **Run Query**, and then click **Next**.

  • Select **qryOrdersCalcPrice**, and then click **Next**. Select **Text**, and then type Run Calculate Price Query. Click **Next**.

  • Name the button cmdQryCalcPrice, and then click **Finish**.

  • Click **Button** in the Controls group, move your pointer below the other button, and then click the form.

  • Select **Report Operations** and **Open Report**, and then click **Next**.

  • Select **rptParticipantsPurchases**, and then click **Next**. Select **Text**, type Run Participants Purchases Report, and then click **Next**.

  • Name the button cmdParticipantsPurchases, and then click **Finish**.

  • Use your pointer to select both buttons. Click the **Arrange tab**, click **Align** in the Sizing & Ordering group, and then select **Left**.

  • Click **Size/Space**, and then select **To Widest**.

  • Click the **Design tab**, drag the **form footer** down until it is on the .5" mark on the vertical ruler.

  • Click **Label** in the Controls group. Move your pointer to the footer, and then click the .5" mark on the horizontal ruler. Type Created by Firstname Lastname using your name.

  • Change to Form View. Test your form by selecting **ItemDescription** = **Cart Sponsor**. Run **Calculate Price** query, and then run the **Participants Purchases** report. Close the query and report.

  • Save and close your form.

j. Create mailing labels for all participants:

- In the Navigation Pane, click **tblParticipant**. Click the **Create tab**, and then click **Labels** in the Reports group.
- If necessary, filter by manufacturer Avery, select Product Number **C2160**, and then click **Next**.
- Change the font to Times New Roman, and then change the font size to 11. Click **Next**.
- Add First Name, press [Spacebar], add Last Name, and then press [Enter].
- Add StreetAddress, and then press [Enter].
- Add City, type **,** (a comma), press [Spacebar], add State, press [Spacebar], and then add ZipCode.
- Click **Next**.
- Sort by LastName and then FirstName. Click **Next**.
- Name your report rptLabelsParticipants, and then click **Finish**.
- Save and close your report.

k. Close your database.

Practice 2

Student data file needed:	You will save your file as:
a05_ws10_Painted_Treasures	Lastname_Firstname_a05_ws10_Painted_Treasures

Painted Treasures

Susan Brock, the manager of the Painted Treasures gift shop, has asked you to add some reports to the Painted Treasures database. She is interested in doing some further analysis of the purchases and wants you to create reports based on sales of items and item types.

a. Start **Access**, and then open **a05_ws10_Painted_Treasures**. In the Save As dialog box, browse to where you are saving your files, type Lastname_Firstname_a05_ws10_Painted_Treasures, and then click **Save**. In the Security Warning, click **Enable Content**.

b. Open **tblCustomer**. Change the Last Name and First Name in the last record to be your actual name, and then close the table.

c. Create a query with customer purchases:

- Click the **Create tab**, and then click **Query Wizard**. Select **Simple Query Wizard**, and then click **OK**.
- From tblCustomer, select **CustomerName**. From tblPurchase, select **PurchaseDate**. From tblPurchaseLine, select **Quantity**. From tblProduct, select **Price** and **ProductDescription**. Click **Next**, select **Detail**, and then click **Next**.
- Name your query qryPurchaseCalcPrice, select **Modify the query design**, and then click **Finish**.
- In the first empty column, click in the **Field Name** row, and then click **Builder** in the Query Setup group. In the Expression Builder dialog box, type [Quantity] * [Price], and then click **OK**.
- Replace **Expr1** with ExtendedPrice.
- Run your query, and then save and close the query.

d. Create a report grouping the query by customer:

- Click the **Create tab**, and then click **Report Wizard**. From qryPurchaseCalcPrice, select all fields. Click **Next**.
- Add grouping by CustomerName, click **Next**, and then sort by PurchaseDate and ProductDescription.
- Click **Summary Options**, select **Sum** for ExtendedPrice, and then click **OK**.
- Click **Next**, accept Stepped layout, change to Landscape orientation, and then click **Next**.
- Name your report rptPurchasesByCustomer, and then click **Finish**.
- Change to Layout view.
- Click **rptPurchasesByCustomer** in the header, and then change the title to Purchases by Customer.
- Click the line that begins **Summary for 'CustomerName'**, and then press [Delete].
- Click the **Extended Price** column header, and then use your pointer to resize that header to be very narrow. That way you can see the Price column header.
- Click the **Price** column header, press [Shift], and then click the first **Price** value. Click the **right edge**, and then drag the column to the left to leave room for the Extended Price field. Click the **Price** column header, and then with your pointer drag the header so it is above the Price values.
- Click the **ExtendedPrice** column header, and then drag the **left edge** so you can see the entire header.
- Click the first **ExtendedPrice** value. Use your pointer to drag the left edge of the value to the left to show complete values. Repeat for group totals and the grand total. Make the totals a little wider than you need because you will add a dollar sign and comma later.
- Click the **group total** for ExtendedPrice, and then click **Property Sheet**. Click the **Format tab**, and then change Format to Currency. Repeat for the grand total ExtendedPrice. Double-check that your columns are wide enough to show the full value. Close the property sheet.
- Change to Design view, and then click **Sum** in the CustomerName Footer. Use your pointer to move it to have its left edge on the 7.5" mark of the horizontal ruler. Change the label from **Sum** to Customer Total.
- In the Report Footer, click **Grand Total**. Use your pointer to move it to have its left edge on the 7.5" mark of the horizontal ruler.
- Click **Label** in the Controls group, move your pointer, and then click the 4" mark on the Page Footer. Type Created by Firstname Lastname using your actual name.
- Change to Report view to check your report formatting.
- Save and close your report.

e. Create another report grouping the query by customer and then by product. This report has two groups so many of the grouping changes will need to be made twice.

- Click the **Create tab**, and then click **Report Wizard**. From qryPurchaseCalcPrice, select all fields, and then click **Next**.
- Add grouping by CustomerName and ProductDescription. Click **Next**.
- Sort by PurchaseDate, click **Summary Options**, select **Sum** for Quantity and ExtendedPrice, and then click **OK**.
- Click **Next**, accept Stepped layout, change to Landscape orientation, and then click **Next**.
- Name your report rptPurchasesByCustomerProduct, and then click **Finish**.
- Change to Layout view.
- Click **rptPurchasesByCustomerProduct** in the header, and then change the title to Purchases by Customer and Product.

- Click the line that begins **Summary for 'CustomerName'**, and then press Delete. Click the line that begins **Summary for 'ProductDescription'**, and then press Delete.
- Click the **Extended Price** column header, and then use your pointer to resize that header to be very narrow. That way you can see the Price column header.
- Click the **Price** column header, press Shift, and then click the first **Price** value. Click the **right edge**, and then drag the column to the left to leave room for the ExtendedPrice field. Click the **Price** column header, and then with your pointer adjust the left edge so the header is shown completely.
- Click the **ExtendedPrice** column header, and drag the **left edge** so you can see the entire header.
- Click the first **ExtendedPrice** value, and then use your pointer to drag the left edge of the value to the left to show complete values. Repeat for group totals and the grand total. Make the totals a little wider than you need because you will add a dollar sign and comma later.
- Click the first **group total** for ExtendedPrice, and then click **Property Sheet**. Click the **Format tab**, and then change Format to Currency. Repeat for the other group total and the grand total ExtendedPrice. Double-check that your columns are wide enough to show the full value.
- Click the first **Price** value, click the **Format tab** on the property sheet, and then change Hide Duplicates to Yes.
- Close the property sheet.
- Change to Design view, and then click **Sum** in the ProductDescription Footer. Use your pointer to drag it to have its left edge on the 4" mark on the horizontal ruler. Change the label from **Sum** to Product Summary.
- Repeat for CustomerName Footer, changing the label from **Sum** to Customer Summary.
- In the Report Footer, click **Grand Total**. Use your pointer to drag it to have its left edge on the 4" mark on the horizontal ruler.
- Click **Label** in the Controls group. Move your pointer, and then click in the **Page Footer** at the 4" mark on horizontal ruler. Type Created by Firstname Lastname using your actual name.
- Change to Report view to check your report formatting.
- Save and close your report.

f. Create a query on products sold:

- Click the **Create tab**, and then click **Query Wizard**. Select **Simple Query Wizard**, and then click **OK**.
- From tblProduct, select **Category**, **ProductDescription**, and **Price**. From tblPurchase-Line, select **Quantity**. Click **Next**, select **Detail**, and then click **Next**.
- Name your query qryProductsSold, select **Modify the query design**, and then click **Finish**.
- In the first empty column, click in the **Field Name** row, and then click **Builder** in the Query Setup group. In the Expression Builder dialog box, type [Quantity] * [Price], and then click **OK**.
- Replace **Expr1** with ExtendedPrice.
- Run your query, and then save and close the query.

g. Create a report on products sold:

- Click the **Create tab**, and then click **Report Wizard**. From qryProductsSold, select all fields except Price. Click **Next**.
- Add grouping by Category and ProductDescription. Click **Next**.
- Click **Summary Options**, select **Sum** for Quantity and ExtendedPrice, select **Show Summary Only**, and then click **OK**.

- Click **Next**, accept Stepped layout and Portrait orientation, and then click **Next**.
- Name your report rptProductsSold, and then click **Finish**.
- Change to Layout view.
- Click **rptProductsSold** in the header, and then change the title to Products Sold.
- Click the line that begins **Summary for 'ProductDescription'**, and then press [Delete]. Click the line that begins **Summary for 'Category'**, and then press [Delete].
- Click the first **group total** for ExtendedPrice, and then click **Property Sheet**. Click the **Format tab**, and then change Format to Currency. Repeat for the second group total and grand total ExtendedPrice. Double-check that your columns are wide enough to show the full value. Close the property sheet.
- Change to Design view, and then click Sum in the ProductDescription Footer. Press [Delete].
- Click **Sum** in the Category Footer. Use your pointer to move it to have its left edge on the 4" mark of the horizontal ruler. Change the label from **Sum** to Category Summary.
- In the Report Footer, click **Grand Total**. Use your pointer to move the Layout control to have its left edge on the 4" mark of the horizontal ruler.
- In the Page Footer, click the calculated Date control, =**Now( )**. Move your pointer to the right side of the control, and then resize the right edge to where it lines up with the 2.5" mark on the horizontal ruler.
- Click **Label** in the Controls group, move your pointer, and then click the 2.5" mark on the Page Footer. Type Created by Firstname Lastname using your actual name.
- Change to Report view to check your report formatting.
- Save and close your report.

h. Create a form to specify clothing products:

- Click the **Create tab**, and then click **Blank Form** in the Forms group. Close the Field List pane.
- Click **Title** in the Header/Footer group, and then replace the title with Report on Clothing Sold.
- Click the **Combo Box** control, and then place it on the form. Select **I want the combo box to get the values from another table or query**, and then click **Next**. Select **Table: tblClothingDescription**, and click **Next**. Select **ClothingDescription**, and then click **Next**. Sort by Clothing Description, and then click **Next**. Adjust the width of the column to fit, and then click **Next**. Name your combo box Clothing Description, and then click **Finish**.
- Click **Property Sheet** in the Tools group, click the **field** on the right side of the combo box, click the **Other tab** of the property sheet, and then change the Name to be ClothingDescription.
- Click the **Combo Box** control, and then place it below Clothing Description. Select **I want the combo box to get the values from another table or query**, and then click **Next**. Select **Table: tblClothingSize**, and then click **Next**. Select **Size**, and then click **Next**. Sort by Size, and then click **Next**. Adjust the width of the column to fit, and then click **Next**. Name your combo box Size, and then click **Finish**.
- Click the **field** on the right side of the combo box, click the **Other tab** of the property sheet, and then change the Name to be Size.
- Save your form naming it frmRequestClothing.
- Close the property sheet.
- Change to Form view. Select a Clothing Description of **LS Sweatshirts**. Do not close your form.

i. Create a query of products with the selected description:

- Click the **Create tab**, and then click **Query Wizard**. Select **Simple Query Wizard**, and then click **OK**.
- From tblProduct, select **Category**, **ProductDescription**, **Price**, **Size**, and **Color**. From tblPurchaseLine, select **Quantity**. Click **Next**, select **Detail**, and then click **Next**.
- Name your query qryClothingDescriptionSold, select **Modify the query design**, and then click **Finish**.
- Click in the **Criteria** row for ProductDescription, and then click **Builder** in the Query Setup group. In the Expression Elements pane, expand Lastname_Firstname_ a05_ws10_Painted_Treasures, expand Forms, expand Loaded Forms, and then click **frmRequestClothing**. In the Expression Categories pane, double-click **ClothingDescription**, and then click **OK**.
- In the first empty column, click in the **Field Name** row, and then click **Builder** in the Query Setup group. In the Expression Builder dialog box, type [Quantity] * [Price], and then click **OK**.
- Replace **Expr1** with ExtendedPrice.
- Run your query, and then save and close the query.

j. Create a report of products with the selected description:

- Click the **Create tab**, and then click **Report Wizard**. From qryClothingDescriptionSold select **Size**, **Color**, **Quantity**, and **ExtendedPrice**. Click **Next**.
- Add grouping by Size and Color. Click **Next**.
- Click **Summary Options**, select **Sum** for Quantity and ExtendedPrice, and then click **OK**.
- Click **Next**, accept Stepped layout and Portrait orientation, and then click **Next**.
- Name your report rptClothingSoldByProductDescription, and then click **Finish**.
- Change to Layout view.
- Click **rptClothingSoldByProductDescription** in the header, and then change it to Clothing Sold by Product Description.
- Click the line that begins **Summary for 'Color'**, and then press Delete. Click the line that begins **Summary for 'Size'**, and then press Delete.
- Click the first group total for ExtendedPrice, and then click **Property Sheet**. Click the **Format tab**, and then change Format to Currency. Repeat for the other group total and the grand total ExtendedPrice.
- Close the property sheet.
- Change to Design view, and then click **Sum** in the Color footer. Use your pointer to drag the Layout control to have its left edge on the 4" mark on the horizontal ruler. Change the label from **Sum** to Color Summary.
- Repeat for the Size footer, changing the label from **Sum** to Size Summary.
- In the Report Footer, click **Grand Total**. Use your pointer to drag it to have its left edge on the 4" mark.
- In the Page Footer, click the calculated Date control, **=Now( )**. Click the right side of the control, and then resize the right edge to where it lines up with the 2.5" mark on the horizontal ruler.
- Click **Label** in the Controls group. Move your pointer, and then click in the Page Footer at the 2.5" mark on the horizontal ruler. Type Created by Firstname Lastname using your actual name.
- Click **Text Box** in the Controls group, and then click to the right of the report title in the Report Header to insert a text box. If necessary, move the control so it does not overlap the title.
- Click the **Label** control. On the Design tab, click **Property Sheet** in the Tools group, click the **Format tab** of the property sheet, and then change **Caption** to be Product Selected.

- In the Report Header, resize the Label control with the sizing handles as needed to show the full caption.
- Click the **text box**, and then click the **Data tab** of the property sheet. In Control Source, click the **Build** button. In the Expression Elements pane, expand Lastname_Firstname_a05_ws10_Painted_Treasures, expand Forms, expand Loaded Forms, and click **frmRequestClothing**.
- In the Expression Categories pane, double-click **ClothingDescription**, and then click **OK**.
- Close the property sheet. Change to Report view to check your work, and then save and close your report.

k. Create a query of products with the selected size:

- In the form, select Size of **L**.
- Click the **Create tab**, and then click **Query Wizard**. Select **Simple Query Wizard**, and then click **OK**.
- From tblProduct, select **Category**, **ProductDescription**, **Price**, **Size**, and **Color**. From tblPurchaseLine, select **Quantity**. Click **Next**, select **Detail**, and then click **Next**.
- Name your query qryClothingSizeSold, select **Modify the query design**, and then click **Finish**.
- Click in the **Criteria** row for Size, and then click **Builder** in the Query Setup group. In the Expression Elements pane, expand Lastname_Firstname_a05_ws10_Painted_Treasures, expand Forms, expand Loaded Forms, and click **frmRequestClothing**. In the Expression Categories pane, double-click **Size**, and then click **OK**.
- In the first empty column, click in the **Field Name** row, and then click **Builder** in the Query Setup group. In the Expression Builder dialog box, type [Quantity] * [Price], and then click **OK**.
- Replace **Expr1** with ExtendedPrice.
- Run your query, and then save and close the query.

l. Create report of products with the selected size:

- Click the **Create tab**, and then click **Report Wizard**. From qryClothingSizeSold, select **ProductDescription**, **Color**, **Quantity**, and **ExtendedPrice**. Click **Next**.
- Add grouping by ProductDescription and Color. Click **Next**.
- Click **Summary Options**, select **Sum** for Quantity and ExtendedPrice, and then click **OK**.
- Click **Next**, accept Stepped layout and Portrait orientation, and then click **Next**.
- Name your report rptClothingSoldBySize, and then click **Finish**.
- Change to Layout view.
- Click **rptClothingSoldBySize** in the header, and then change the title to Clothing Sold by Size.
- Click the line that begins **Summary for 'Color'**, and then press Delete. Click the line that begins **Summary for 'ProductDescription'**, and then press Delete.
- Click the first group total for ExtendedPrice, and then click **Property Sheet**. Click the **Format tab**, and then change Format to Currency. Repeat for the other group total and the grand total ExtendedPrice.
- Close the property sheet.
- Change to Design view, and then click **Sum** in the Color footer. Use your pointer to drag the **Layout** control to have its left edge on the 4" mark of the horizontal ruler. Change the label from **Sum** to Color Summary.
- Repeat for the ProductDescription footer, changing the label from **Sum** to Product Summary.
- In the Report Footer, click **Grand Total**. Use your pointer to drag the **Layout** control to have its left edge on the 4" mark of the horizontal ruler.

- In the Page Footer, click the calculated Date control, **=Now( )**. Move your pointer to the right side of the control, and then resize the right edge to where it lines up with the 2.5" mark on the horizontal ruler.
- Click **Label** in the Controls group. Move your pointer, click in the Page Footer at the 2.5" mark of the horizontal ruler, and then type Created by Firstname Lastname using your actual name.
- Click **Text Box** in the Controls group, and then click to the right of the report title in the Report Header to insert a text box. If necessary, move the control so it does not overlap the title.
- Click in the **label**. On the Design tab, click **Property Sheet** in the Tools group. Click the **Format tab** of the property sheet, and then change **Caption** to be Size Selected.
- In the Report Header, resize the Label control with the sizing handles as needed to show the full caption.
- Click the **text box**, and then click the **Data tab** of the property sheet. In Control Source, click the **Build** button. In the Expression Elements pane, expand Lastname_Firstname_a05_ws10_Painted_Treasures, expand Forms, expand Loaded Forms, and click **frmRequestClothing**.
- In the Expression Categories pane, double-click **Size**, and then click **OK**.
- Change to Report view to check your work, and then save and close your report.

m. Add buttons to your form to request the two reports:

- Change **frmRequestClothing** to Design view. Use your pointer to stretch the Detail area to be 2.5" tall on the vertical ruler. Close the property sheet.
- Click **Button** in the Controls group.
- Move your pointer to the right of the selection criteria, and then click the form.
- Select **Report Operations** and **Open Report**, and then click **Next**.
- Select **rptClothingSoldByProductDescription**, and click **Next**. Select **Text**, type Run Clothing by Description Report, and then click **Next**.
- Name the button cmdClothingDescription, and then click **Finish**.
- Click **Button** in the Controls group.
- Move your pointer to below the other button, and then click the form.
- Select **Report Operations** and **Open Report**, and then click **Next**.
- Select **rptClothingSoldBySize**, and then click **Next**. Select **Text**, type Run Clothing by Size Report, and then click **Next**.
- Name the button cmdClothingSize, and then click **Finish**.
- Click **Button** in the Controls group. Move your pointer below the other buttons, and then click the form.
- Select **Form Operations** and **Close Form**, and then click **Next**.
- Select **Text**, accept **Close Form**, and then click **Next**.
- Name the button cmdCloseForm, and then click **Finish**.
- Use your pointer to select all three buttons, click the **Arrange tab**, click **Align** in the Sizing & Ordering group, and then select **Left**.
- Click **Size/Space** in the Sizing & Ordering group, and then select **Equal Vertical**.
- Click **Size/Space**, and then select **To Widest**.
- Click the **Design tab**, use your pointer to drag the **form footer** until it is aligned with .5" on the vertical ruler. Click **Label** in the Controls group.
- Move your pointer to the footer, and then click the .5" mark on the left. Type Created by Firstname Lastname using your actual name, and then save your form.

- Change to Form view. Test your form by selecting **Clothing Description = Tshirts and Size = XL**. Click the **Run Clothing by Description Report**. Close the report. Click the **Run Clothing by Size Report**. Close the report. Click **Close Form**.

Figure 30 frmRequestClothing

n. Close your database.

MODULE CAPSTONE

Student data file needed:

a05_mp_Menu

You will save your file as:

Lastname_Firstname_a05_mp_Menu

Indigo5 Restaurant

Robin Sanchez, the chef of the resort's restaurant, Indigo5, has a database of recipes and ingredients. He uses this to plan menus and create shopping lists. He has asked you to provide forms and reports to make this database easier to use. First you will create a form listing recipes by food category.

Next, you will help him find all recipes that include an ingredient that he has in stock. You will create a query to find those recipes and a report from the query that lists the recipes. You know you will want a form to do the lookup for these recipes so you will start with the form.

He would also like a report on recipes by category that shows the minimum and maximum preparation time for each category.

a. Start **Access**, and then open the **a05_mp_Menu** database. Save the file as Lastname_Firstname_a05_mp_Menu. In the Security Warning, click **Enable Content**.

b. Create a form for finding a recipe by food category. This will be a form with a subform. The main form shows categories; the subform shows recipes. You will add a combo box to find a specific category. You will also remove the navigation bars and replace them with buttons:

- Use the Form Wizard to create the form. From tblFoodCategories, select **FoodCategory**. From tblRecipes, select **RecipeName**, **TimeToPrepare**, and **Servings**. Accept the default view and default layout. Name your form frmFindRecipe and the subform frmFindRecipeSubform.

- In Layout view, change the title of the form to Find a Recipe by Category. Fix the title so it displays on one line.

- Add Date and Time to the header, accepting the default formats.

- In the subform, resize each of the column widths to fit the contents. Resize the right side of the subform to fit the new column sizes.

- Click the **Format tab** on the property sheet, and then using the Build button, change the Back Color of the form detail to **Orange, Accent 6, Lighter 80%**. Change the Back Color of the form header to **Orange, Accent 6, Lighter 40%**.

- Change the subform label frmFindRecipe to Recipes.

- Pull down the bottom edge of the form footer until it is .5" tall. Using the **Label control** put a label in the footer that reads Created by Firstname Lastname. Change the Back Color of the form footer to **Orange, Accent 6, Lighter 80%**.

- Click the value for **FoodCategory**. Click the **Data tab** of the property sheet, change Locked to **Yes**. Click the **Other tab**, change Tab Stop to **No**. Repeat for **RecipeName**, **TimeToPrepare**, and **Servings**.

- Place a **combo box** in the form header to the right of the title. In the Combo Box Wizard dialog box, click **Find a record on my form based on the value I selected in my combo box**, click **FoodCategory**, accept the default to **Hide key column**, and then label the combo box Food Category. If necessary, drag the new combo box so it fits well in the header.

- Place a Button control in the form detail to the right of the subform fields. Select **Record Navigation** and **Go To Next Record**. Select **Text**, type Next Category, and then name the button cmdNextCategory. Place a second Button control on the form below the first. Select **Record Navigation** and **Go To Previous Record**. Select **Text**, type Previous Category, and then name the button cmdPreviousCategory.

- Place a Button control below the other buttons. Select **Form Operations** and **Close Form**. Select **Text**, and then accept **Close Form**. Name the button cmdCloseForm.

- Arrange the buttons using the Arrange tab. Use Align to align the buttons Left. Use Size/Space to Size to Widest. Use Size/Space to have Spacing of Equal Vertical.

- Click the **Form Selector** for the main form, and then click the **Format tab** on the property sheet to change the Navigation Buttons to **No**. Change Record Selectors to **No**. Click the **Form Selector** for the subform, and then repeat the navigation changes.

- View, save, and close the form.

Figure 1 frmFindRecipe

c. Create a form to request recipes by ingredient:

- Create a blank form. Add a **Title** of Request Recipes.

- Add a combo box in the detail area of the form, click **I want the combo box to get the values from another table or query**, click **Table: tblIngredients**, click **Ingredient**, and then sort by **Ingredient**. Adjust the width of the column to fit, and then label your combo box Ingredient.

- Change the name of the combo box to Ingredient using Name on the Other tab of the property sheet. Pull down the bottom edge of the form footer until it is .5" tall. Using the Label control put a label in the footer saying Created by Firstname Lastname.

- Name your form frmRequestRecipe.

- Save the form, switch to Form view, and then request Garlic.

- Leave the form open.

d. You will create a query to find those recipes that include an ingredient:

- Using the Query Wizard, select Simple Query Wizard. From tblRecipes, select **RecipeName**, **TimeToPrepare**, **Servings**, and **Instructions**. From tblIngredients, select **IngredientID** and **Ingredient**. Select **Detail** and name your query qryRecipeIngredient.

- Add a criteria to IngredientID that selects Ingredient from frmRequestRecipe.
- Run your query to test it, and then save and close the query.

e. Create a recipes report from that query:
- Using the Report Wizard, from qryRecipeIngredient select **RecipeName**, **TimeToPrepare**, **Servings**, and **Instructions**. Do not add any grouping. Sort by RecipeName. Accept Tabular, and then change the orientation to Landscape. Name your report rptRecipePreparation.
- In Layout view, move the **Servings** column to the left. Change the title of your report to Recipe Preparation.
- In Design view, use the Label control to put a label in the page footer that reads Created by Firstname Lastname.
- Add a text box to the report header. Change the label caption to Ingredient Selected, and then resize as needed. For the text box, using the Data tab of the property sheet, select a Control Source of **Ingredient**.
- Run your report to test it. Save and close the report and form.

f. Create a report of recipes by category with minimum and maximum preparation times:
- Using the Report Wizard, from tblFoodCategories select **FoodCategory**. From tblRecipes, select **RecipeName**, **TimeToPrepare**, and **Servings**.
- Group by FoodCategory, sort by RecipeName, and in Summary Options, select **Min** and **Max** TimeToPrepare. Accept the default layout, and then name your report rptRecipeTimes.
- Change the title of your report to Recipe Times to Prepare. Delete the line that starts **Summary for 'Food**.
- Move the **Min** label so that its left edge is on the 3.5" point. Change it to read Minimum Preparation Time. Repeat for the **Max** label, changing it to Maximum Preparation Time.
- Use the Label control to put a label on the 2.5" point in the page footer that reads Created by Firstname Lastname.
- Switch to Print Preview to check your report, and then save and close the report.

g. Close your database.

Problem Solve 1

Student data file needed:

a05_ps1_Hotel_Event

You will save your file as:

Lastname_Firstname_a05_ps1_Hotel_Event

Working with Forms and Reports for Event Reservations

Patti Rochelle, corporate event planner, has a database that she uses to track group reservations with the conference rooms that are booked for the event. You will create forms and reports to help her manage events.

First you will create a form to add a group. You will also create a form and subform to add an event for an already existing group. You will create a form to see rooms reserved for an event.

You will create two reports for her: a report on room reservations and a report that shows group, events, and rooms with charge totals.

You will create a PivotChart showing room charges.

a. Start **Access**, and then open the **a05_ps1_Hotel_Event** database. Save the file as Lastname_Firstname_a05_ps1_Hotel_Event. In the Security Warning, click **Enable Content**.

b. Create a form to add groups:

- Use the FormWizard to create a form containing all fields from tblGroup. Use a columnar layout. Name your form frmAddGroup.
- Change the title of the form to Add a Group. Add Date and Time with default settings.
- Change the form detail Back Color to **Red, Accent 2, Lighter 80%**. Change the header Back Color to **Red, Accent 2, Lighter 40%**.
- Lock GroupID. Change Tab Stop for GroupID to **No**.
- Add Created by Firstname Lastname to the form footer. Change the footer background to **Red, Accent 2, Lighter 80%**.
- Use your form to add a new group named Santa Fe Art Group. The contact person is you. Make your phone number (505) 555-9292.
- Save and close your form.

c. Create a form for adding an event for an existing group. This will be a form with a subform. The main form shows the group; the subform shows events. You will add a combo box to find a specific group. You will also remove the navigation bars and replace them with buttons:

- Use the Form Wizard to create the form. From tblGroup, select **GroupName**, **ContactFirstName**, **ContactLastName**, and **ContactPhone**. From tblEvent, select **EventName**, **EventStart**, and **EventLength**. Accept the default view and default layout. Name your form frmAddEvent and the subform frmAddEventSubform.
- Change the title of the form to Add an Event. Add Date and Time with default settings to the header.
- In the subform, resize each of the column widths to fit. Resize the right side of the subform to fit the new column sizes.
- Change the form detail Back Color to **Red, Accent 2, Lighter 80%**. Change the header Back Color to **Red, Accent 2, Lighter 40%**.
- Protect all the Group fields in the main form so that they are locked and cannot be tabbed to.
- Activate Date Picker for EventStartDate by removing the input mask.
- Add Created by Firstname Lastname to the form footer. Change the footer background to **Red, Accent 2, Lighter 80%**.
- Change the subform label frmAddEvent to Events.
- Place a combo box in the header to the right of the title. The combo box should find a record on your form based upon the value you select in your combo box, using the GroupName field from tblGroup. Label the combo box, Find Group. Adjust the placement of the combo box, and then make the combo box 2" wide.
- Put the following buttons on your form to the right of the group fields:

Button Function	Text Label	Button Name
Go to Next Record	Next Group	cmdNextGroup
Go to Previous Record	Previous Group	cmdPreviousGroup
Open Form, which opens frmAddGroup and shows all records	Add Group	cmdAddGroup
Close Form	Close Form	cmdCloseForm

- Align your buttons left, size them to the widest button, space them with equal vertical spacing.

- For the main form, change Record Selectors to **No**, and then use the Format tab of the property sheet to change the Navigation Buttons to **No**. Repeat for the subform.
- Use your form to add an event for the Santa Fe Art Group. The Event Name is Art Exhibition, the Event Start Date is 3/15/2013, and the Event Length is 3 days.
- Save and close the form.

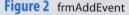

Figure 2 frmAddEvent

d. Open **tblConfRes**, and then enter a record with values ReservationID 6 (automatically assigned), EventID 5, ConfRoomID 1, ReservationDate 3/15/2013, DaysReserved 3, and Room Charge $6,000.

e. Create a query to show groups, events, and reserved rooms:
- Use the Query Wizard to create a simple detail query, using **GroupName**, **ContactFirstName**, **ContactLastName** from tblGroup, **EventName**, **EventStart** from tblEvent, **ReservationDate**, **DaysReserved**, **RoomCharge** from tblConfRes, and **RoomName** from tblConfRooms. Name your query qryReservedRooms.
- Add a field to your query called TotalCharge, which is calculated as RoomCharge * DaysReserved.
- Run, save, and close your query.

f. Create a room reservations report from the query:
- Use the Report Wizard to select **RoomName**, **ReservationDate**, **DaysReserved**, **RoomCharge**, and **TotalCharge** from qryReservedRooms. Group by RoomName, and then sort by ReservationDate. Sum TotalCharge. Accept the default layouts, and then name your report rptRoomCharges.
- Change the title of the report to Room Charges.
- Remove the **Summary for 'RoomName'** line.
- Fix any columns that overlap or do not show completely, and then adjust any numbers that require it.
- Move **Sum** in the group footer so its left edge is on the 5" mark. Change Sum to Room Summary.
- Move **Grand Total** to have its left edge on the 5" mark.
- Add Created by Firstname Lastname to the page footer.

g. Create a report on group charges from the query:

- Use the Report Wizard to select **GroupName**, **ContactFirstName**, **ContactLastName**, **EventName**, **EventStart**, and **TotalCharge** from qryReservedRooms. Accept the grouping by GroupName and then EventName. Sum TotalCharge, and then sort by TotalCharge. Use a layout of Stepped and Landscape. Name your report rptGroupEventCharges.

- Change the title of your report to Group Event Charges.

- Remove the two **Summary for** lines.

- Fix any columns that overlap or do not show completely, and then adjust any numbers that require it. Warning: The detail line charges are very easy to miss.

- Change the EventName Footer Sum to Event Summary, and then put its left edge on the 6.5" mark.

- Change the GroupName Footer Sum to Group Summary, and then put its left edge on the 6.5" mark.

- Move the Grand Total header to the 6.5" mark.

- Add Created by Firstname Lastname to the page footer.

h. Create a PivotTable from the query:

- Create a PivotTable form using qryReservedRooms.

- Drop **RoomName** on the Row Fields.

- Drop **TotalCharge** on Totals or Detail Fields.

- Drop **EventName** on the Column Fields.

- Use **ReservationDate by Month** as the Filter field. Expand the Filters until you show just February 2013.

- Use AutoCalc to see Sum of TotalCharge.

- Save your PivotTable as frmRoomChargePivotTable, and then close your form.

i. Close your database.

Problem Solve 2

Student data file needed:	You will save your file as:
a05_ps2_Hotel	Lastname_Firstname_a05_ps2_Hotel

Working with Forms in the Hotel

The main portion of the resort is the hotel. The hotel offers accommodations ranging from individual rooms to a grand villa suite. The hotel area must track all aspects of a reservation including special requests for items such as a crib. The hotel also has to track room charges that guests have made. Room rates vary according to size, season, demand, and discount. The hotel has discounts for organizations, such as AARP.

The database that is used to track charges needs some forms to make it easier to use. You will create a form to show guests and reservations. You will create a form to show charges on a reservation. You will create a split form for reservations.

You will also create a PivotTable, a PivotChart, a pie chart, and a column chart.

a. Start **Access**, and then open the **a05_ps2_Hotel** database. Save the file as Lastname_Firstname_a05_ps2_Hotel. In the Security Warning, click **Enable Content**.

b. Create a form to add guests:

- Use the Form Wizard to create a form containing all fields from tblGuests, use a columnar layout, and then name your form frmAddGuest.

- Change the title of the form to Add a Guest, and then add Date and Time with default settings to the header.
- Change the form detail Back Color to **Red, Accent 2, Lighter 80%**. Change the header Back Color to **Red, Accent 2, Lighter 40%**.
- Protect GuestID so it cannot be tabbed to or typed in.
- Add an input mask to Phone. Use the standard phone number mask, and then store the data with the symbols in the mask.
- Add Created by Firstname Lastname to the form footer. Change the footer background to **Red, Accent 2, Lighter 80%**.
- Use your form to change the 25th record to have your name and gender. Accept the address that is there. Enter the phone number (301) 555-8181.

c. Create a form for adding a reservation for an existing guest. This will be a form with a subform. The main form shows guest; the subform shows reservation. You will add a combo box to find a specific group. You will also remove the navigation buttons and replace them with buttons on the form.

- Create a form using **GuestLastName**, **GuestFirstName**, **GuestMI**, and **Phone** from tblGuests and **CheckInDate**, **NightsStay**, **NumberOfGuests**, **Crib**, **Handicapped**, **RoomRate**, **DiscountType**, and **Room Type** from tblReservations. Accept the default view and default layout. Name your form frmAddReservation and the subform frmAddReservationSubform.
- Protect the three Guest Name fields in the main form so that they are locked and cannot be tabbed to.
- Add an input mask to Phone. Use the standard phone number mask, and then store the data with the symbols in the mask.
- Add a default value of 1 to Nights Stay.
- Add a default value of 1 to # of Guests.
- Add a default value of One King to Type.
- Resize your subform as shown in Figure 3 removing the subform name.
- Create your header and footer as shown in Figure 3.
- Use colors as shown in Figure 3: **Red, Accent 2, Lighter 80%** and **Red, Accent 2, Lighter 40%**.
- Add the following buttons as shown in Figure 3:

Button Function	Text Label	Button Name
Go to Next Record	Next Guest	cmdNextGuest
Go to Previous Record	Previous Guest	cmdPreviousGuest
Open Form, which opens frmAddGuest and shows all records	Add a Guest	cmdAddGuest
Close Form	Close Form	cmdCloseForm

- Remove the Record Selectors and Navigation Buttons from the main form and subform.
- Place a Combo Box in the header to the right of the title. The combo box should find a record on your form based upon the value you select in your combo box, using the **LastName**, **FirstName**, **MiddleInitial** fields. Label the combo box, Find Guest.
- Test your form.

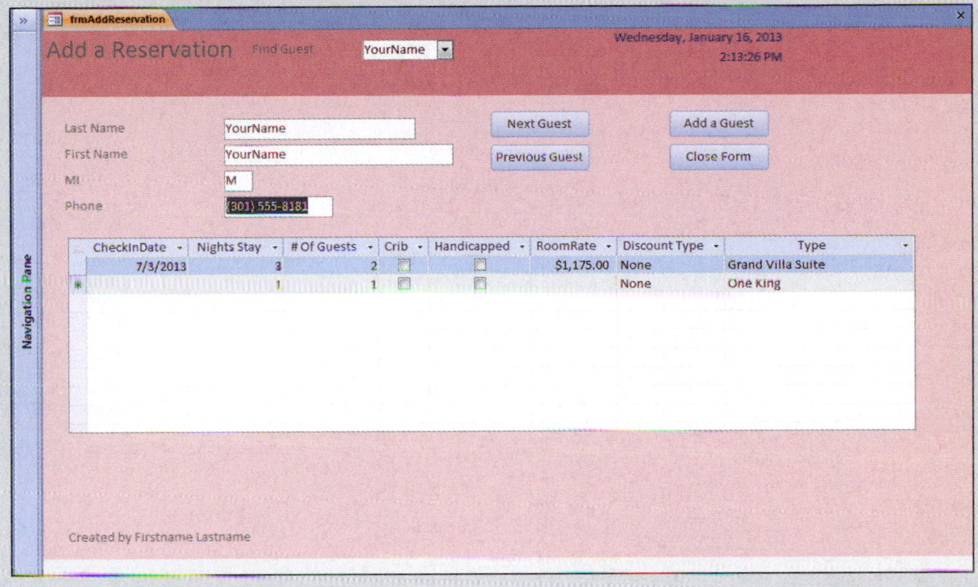

Figure 3 Add a Reservation form

d. Create a split form for payments.

- Create a split form from the table tblPayments, and then title it **frmSplitPayments**.
- Change the form title to be **Split Form Payments**, and then add Date and Time to the header.
- Fix Date so that Date Picker is activated.
- Change the form header to **Red, Accent 2, Lighter 40%** and the detail area to **Red, Accent 2, Lighter 80%**.
- Add **Created by Firstname Lastname** to the form footer, and then change the background to **Red, Accent 2, Lighter 80%**.
- Check your form.

e. Create a PivotTable form:

- Create a PivotTable from tblReservations as shown in Figure 4.
- In the row area, put **Room Type**. In the column area, put **DiscountType**. In the filter, put **CheckInDate by Month**. In the data area, put **RoomRate**. Compare by quarters.
- Save your form as **frmPivotTableReservations**.

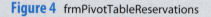

Room Type	AAA RoomRate	AARP RoomRate	Military RoomRate	None RoomRate	Grand Total Sum of RoomRate
Deluxe Suite			$492.00	$349.00	$841.00
				$492.00	
				$349.00	
Grand Villa Suite				$1,175.00	$2,350.00
				$1,175.00	
				$2,350.00	
One King	$289.00	$289.00		$289.00	$2,601.00
		$289.00		$289.00	
				$289.00	
				$289.00	
				$289.00	
				$289.00	
	$289.00	$578.00		$1,734.00	
Two Queens	$269.00			$376.00	$1,263.00
				$269.00	
				$349.00	
	$269.00			$994.00	
Grand Total	$558.00	$578.00	$492.00	$5,427.00	$7,055.00

Figure 4 frmPivotTableReservations

f. Create a pie chart of nights stay and discount type:

- Create a pie chart from tblReservations selecting **NightsStay** and **DiscountType**. Accept the default lay out, title the chart Nights Stay by Discount Type, and then name the chart frmPieChartDiscounts.
- Size the chart so the left corner is at the 1" x 1" mark and the bottom-right -corner is 5" from the left and 4" from the top.
- Show Data Labels with Percentages.
- Add a title Room Discounts, and then add Created by Firstname Lastname to the footer.

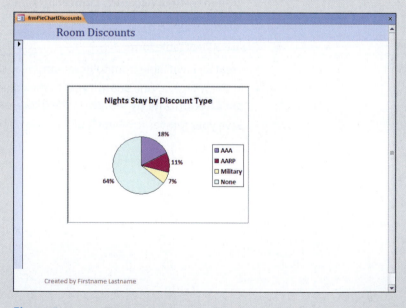

Figure 5 frmPieChartDiscounts

g. Create a PivotChart column chart showing room rates by discount type and room type:
  - Create a PivotChart from tblReservations.
  - Drop **DiscountType** into the Series Fields.
  - Drop **RoomType** into the Category Fields.
  - Drop **RoomRate** into the Data Fields.
  - Drop **CheckInDate By Month** into the Filter Fields.
  - Show the Legend.
  - Change the axis titles using Caption on the Format tab of the property sheet.
  - Save your chart as **frmPivotChartReservations**.

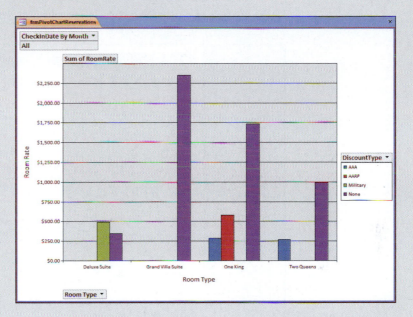

Figure 6 frmPivotChartReservations

h. Close your database.

Problem Solve 3

Student data file needed:

a05_ps3_Hotel

You will save your file as:

Lastname_Firstname_a05_ps3_Hotel

Working with Reports in the Hotel

The main portion of the resort is the hotel.

The database that is used to track charges needs some reports to make it easier to use. You will create various reports on charges.

a. Start **Access**, and then open the **a05_ps3_Hotel** database. Save the file as Lastname_Firstname_a05_ps3_Hotel. In the Security Warning, click **Enable Content**.

b. Open **tblGuests**, change the name in the last record to be your name, and then change the gender to be your gender.

c. Guest room charges are charges for items such as the spa or room service that are charged to the room. Create a report grouping these charges by customer and reservation:

- Create a report selecting **GuestLastName** and **GuestFirstName** from tblGuests, **CheckInDate** from tblReservations, and **ChargeCategory** and **ChargeAmount** from tblRoomCharges. Accept the default grouping, and then sort by ChargeCategory. Sum ChargeAmount, and then lay out your report using the Stepped and Landscape options.
- Name your report rptGuestCharges.
- Change the title of your report to Guest Charges.
- Change the report formatting to match Figure 7. The Summary labels all line up with the 6" mark.
- Be sure to check the last page to make sure your columns are wide enough.

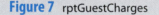

Figure 7 rptGuestCharges

d. Create a report of guest room charges that has no grouping:

- Create a report selecting **CheckInDate** from tblReservations, **GuestLastName** and **GuestFirstName** from tblGuests, and **ChargeCategory** and **ChargeAmount** from tblRoomCharges.
- View by tblRoomCharges. Add no grouping.
- Sort by CheckInDate, GuestLastName, GuestFirstName, and ChargeCategory.
- Use a Tabular layout with Landscape orientation.
- Name your report rptRoomChargesByDate.
- Change the title of your report to Room Charges by Date.
- Use Group & Sort to add to the Sort by CheckInDate a Grand Total Sum of Amount.
- Hide duplicates for CheckInDate, LastName, and FirstName.
- Add Date and Time to the Header.
- Add Created by Firstname Lastname to the footer.

e. Create a report grouping reservations by discount type and room type:

- Create a query selecting **NightsStay**, **DiscountType**, **RoomType**, and **RoomRate** from tblReservations. Add the field RoomCharge calculated as RoomRate * NightsStay. Name your query qryReservationsType.
- Create a report from qryReservationsType selecting **NightsStay**, **DiscountType**, **RoomType**, and **RoomCharge**. Group by DiscountType and then by RoomType. Sort by NightsStay. Sum NightsStay and RoomCharge. Show Summary Only.

- Accept the default layouts.
- Name your report **rptReservationsByType**.
- Change the title of your report to **Reservations by Type**.
- Change the report formatting to match Figure 8. The Summary labels all line up with the 3" mark.

Figure 8 rptReservationsByType

f. Create reports showing all charges for a selected guest. Request this report via a form. Start by creating the form:

- Create a blank form with a title of **Get Bill**.
- Add a combo box to the detail area, selecting the fields **GuestLastName** and **GuestFirstName** from tblGuests. Sort by GuestLastName and GuestFirstName. Adjust the width of the columns to fit. Name your combo box **Guest**.
- Change the name of the combo box to **GuestID** using Name on the Other tab of the property sheet.
- Put **Created by Firstname Lastname** in the footer of your form.
- Name your form **frmGetBill**.
- Request your own name.
- Leave the form open.

g. You will create a query to find charges for the guest:

- Create a query selecting **GuestID**, **GuestLastName**, and **GuestFirstName** from tblGuests, **NightsStay** and **RoomRate** from tblReservations, and **ChargeCategory** and **ChargeAmount** from tblRoomCharges. Name your query qryFindGuestCharges.
- Add the field Room Charge calculated as [NightsStay] * [RoomRate] to the query.
- Use Builder to add a Criteria to GuestID of GuestID from **frmGetBill**.
- Run your query, and then close it.

h. Create a charges report from qryFindGuestCharges:

- Select **GuestLastName**, **GuestFirstName**, **NightsStay**, **RoomRate**, **RoomCharge**, **ChargeCategory**, and **ChargeAmount** from qryFindGuestCharges. Accept the default grouping. Sort by ChargeCategory, and then Sum ChargeAmount. Use a layout of Outline and Portrait. Name your report rptGuestBill.
- Change the title of your report to Guest Bill.
- Using Group, Sort, and Total, change Group on NightsStay to be without a footer section.
- In the Data tab of the property sheet, change the Grand Total to be =Sum ([ChargeAmount]) + [Room Charge].
- Reformat the report to look like Figure 9.

Figure 9 rptGuestBill

i. Add buttons to the form frmGetBill to preview and print the guest bill.

Button Function	Text Label	Button Name
Preview Report	Preview Guest Bill	cmdPreviewGuestBill
Print Report	Print Guest Bill	cmdPrintGuestBill
Close Form	Close Form	cmdCloseForm

j. Change your form to look like Figure 10.

Figure 10 frmGetBill

k. Close your database.

Perform 1: Perform in Your Life

Student data file needed:

a05_pf1_Organization

You will save your file as:

Lastname_Firstname_a05_pf1_Organization

Make Your Organization's Database User Friendly

You have developed a database for an organization that you belong to. You use it to track the members of the organization, events, and member attendance at the events. Make the database user friendly by providing forms and reports.

a. Populate the database with at least three events and 10 members. Sign up members for the various events. If you wish, create the forms in steps b and c and use them to populate the database. One of the members should have your name.

b. Create a form to add data to one of the tables. Make the form attractive and user friendly by making sure the fields are evenly spaced.

c. Create a form with a subform. Make the form attractive and user friendly by making sure the fields are evenly spaced and buttons are available to navigate and close the form.

d. Calculate totals based upon the subform. Add those calculated totals to your form in part c.

e. Create a report with subtotals and totals. You can create a query first if it makes sense. Make the report attractive.

f. Create a chart of any kind from your choice of queries or tables.

g. Create a selection query. Create a report from that query. Create a blank form to make that selection. Add appropriate buttons to the form. Make the form attractive and user friendly by making sure the fields are evenly spaced and buttons are available to navigate and close the form.

h. Close your database.

Student data file needed:

a05_pf2_PetStore

You will save your file as:

Lastname_Firstname_a05_pf2_PetStore

Make a Pet Store Database Friendly

A pet store owner has a database to keep records of animals, breeds, purchases, and the customers that bought each animal. The pet store owner asked you to make the database easier to use. You will provide forms for data entry and for viewing data. You will also create some reports.

a. Populate the database so that there are at least 20 animals, five breeds, and five customers. Create data to track customers purchasing the animals. You may want to create your forms prior to populating the data. One of the customers should have your name.

b. Create a form to add data to one table. Make your form attractive and user friendly.

c. Create a form with a subform. Use the subform to add data. Make your form attractive and user friendly by making sure the fields are evenly spaced and buttons are available to navigate and close the form.

d. Create a split form. Make your form attractive and user friendly.

e. Create another form with a subform. Add a calculated field and protect it. Make your form attractive and user friendly.

f. Create a report with subtotals and totals.

g. Create a summary report without showing details.

h. Close your database.

Student data file needed:

a05_pf3_Inventory

You will save your file as:

Lastname_Firstname_a05_pf3_Inventory

Creating Reports, Forms, and Charts for Gibby's Great Groceries

As an inventory manager for Gibby's Great Groceries, Inc., you were asked to modify an existing database to make it more functional for completing tasks such as reordering items and tracking inventory within your company.

You have decided to create forms, reports, and charts to make the database easier to use.

a. Populate the database so that you have at least 20 transactions and five suppliers. Create at least 10 items ordered from different suppliers. You may use real or fictitious data.

b. Create a form with a subform for viewing data. Add a combo box to the form to find a record within the form. Make your form attractive and user friendly by ensuring the fields are evenly spaced and buttons are available to navigate and close the form.

c. Create another form with a subform. Use the subform to calculate totals and show them on the form. Make your form attractive and user friendly by ensuring the fields are evenly spaced and buttons are available to navigate and close the form.

d. Create a report with subtotals and totals. You can create a query and use it as your source if you wish.

e. Create a PivotTable. Add a filter to select some of the data based upon criteria. You can create a query and use it as your source if you wish.

f. Create a chart. You can create a query and use it as your source if you wish.

g. Create a query that selects data based upon dates. Create a report from that query. Create a blank form to make the selection. Add appropriate buttons to the form. Make your form attractive and user friendly by ensuring the fields are evenly spaced and buttons are available to navigate and close the form.

h. Close your database.

Perform 4: How Others Perform

Student data file needed:

a05_pf4_Appstore

You will save your file as:

Lastname_Firstname_a05_pf4_Appstore

Phil's Phone App Store Database

An intern has created a database that Phil's Phone App Store can use to sell apps for smartphones. The database is not working well, and Phil has asked you for help.

Authors can write many apps. Each app is sold to many customers. Customers can buy many apps.

a. In tblAuthor, change the third author to have your name.

b. frmAuthorSalesApp was used to show authors and the apps they have written with the charges and royalties. It is not working well. What changes would you recommend? You do not have to fix it; just describe the problems and what you would do to fix them.

c. rptSalesByAuthor shows sales by author. It is based on qryFindApps. Fix it for Phil.
- Fix the report to have subtotals and grand totals.
- Fix the report to be more attractive.
- Add a footer to the report that says Modified by Firstname Lastname.

d. Phil wants to be able to select sales by apps. The intern created a form frmFindAppSales to enter the app name and then run qryFindApps. It is not working well.
- Fix either the form or the query or both to make it work.
- Fix the form to make it attractive.
- Add a footer to the form that says Modified by Firstname Lastname.

e. The report of royalties on app sales, rptAppRoyaltiesByAuthor, looks odd to Phil. What is the matter with it? You do not need to fix it; just say what the problems are and what could be done to fix it.

f. chartSalesCount summarizes sales by app. Phil likes the idea but cannot use the chart because it has no labels.
- Fix the chart so Phil can tell what is being counted and get an idea of percentages for each app.
- Add a title.
- Add a footer that says Modified by Firstname Lastname.

g. Close your database.

Objectives

1. View a Navigation form.   p. 520
2. Create a Navigation form.   p. 522
3. Modify a Navigation form.   p. 523
4. Create a main menu.   p. 528
5. Add command buttons to the Navigation form.   p. 531
6. Set startup display options.   p. 534
7. Test the application.   p. 537

Developing Navigation Forms and User Interface

PREPARE CASE
Turquoise Oasis Spa Database

The Turquoise Oasis Spa has a well-built database with queries, forms, and reports. However, there are a lot of objects, and navigating those objects with the Navigation Pane has become tedious and sometimes confusing. The spa manager has asked you to develop a navigational system and user interface to make the whole database more user-friendly and easier to navigate, especially for someone new to Access. There are already three Navigation forms created,

Courtesy of www.Shutterstock.com

but they have to be accessed from the Navigation Pane. You will create a new Navigation form for the customer forms and reports, create a Navigation form that accesses all the Navigation forms already created, and develop an application from the database.

Student data file needed for this workshop:

 a06_ws11_Spa

You will save your file as:

 Lastname_Firstname_a06_ws11_Spa

Navigation Forms

A well-designed database includes well-thought-out tables, forms, and reports, but equally important is how the user will navigate and access the database. Whether the user is a novice or experienced user in Access, a well-planned navigation system and **user interface** provides a more streamlined experience. A user interface is what you see when you open Access. A well-designed user interface acts like a menu system, or home page, for users so they do not have to search for objects in the Navigation Pane.

Ideally, a database user should have access to the data through forms and reports. By restricting access to the tables in Datasheet view, the integrity of the data and structure of the data is not at risk. Users should be allowed to enter, edit, and delete data, but not to modify the structure or design of the database. In this section, you will create a navigation system built into a well-designed user interface to allow the user to move seamlessly from object to object to complete the task at hand.

Real World Advice   Where Did the Switchboard Go?

Many Access users are familiar with the Switchboard, a form used for database navigation. The new Navigation form has replaced the Switchboard with a new, up-to-date, weblike feel and appearance that can be built directly from the Ribbon.

For those who still want to use the Switchboard, it is available in Access 2010; however, it is not built into the Ribbon as it has been in past versions. The Switchboard Manager can be launched by adding a command to the Quick Access Toolbar, by adding a command to the Ribbon, or by running it automatically in the Immediate Window using a VBA command.

View a Navigation Form

The **Navigation form** provides a familiar weblike interface that allows you to access multiple objects in the database from one central location. Similar to websites, the Navigation form allows for top-level navigation commands across the top of the page or vertical navigation along the side of the page as well as subnavigation directly below or along the side of the page. Commands are highlighted when selected, providing users with visual cues as they navigate the form.

Open and Use a Navigation Form

In this exercise, you will look at three different Navigation forms that have already been developed in the database. Each Navigation form represents a different area of the spa: employees, products, and services. By viewing each Navigation form, you will get an idea of what the format should be for the remaining Navigation forms that you will create.

To Open and Use a Navigation Form

a. Click the **Start** button, and then select **Access**.

b. Click the **File tab**, click **Open** and browse to your student data files. Locate and open **a06_ws11_Spa**.

c. Click the **File tab**, click **Save Database As**, browse to where you are storing your files, name your database Lastname_Firstname_a06_ws11_Spa replacing Lastname_Firstname with your actual name and then click **Save**. Click **Enable Content** in the Security Warning.

d. Notice the long list of objects in the Navigation Pane. Double-click **frmEmployeeNavigation** to open the form.

Notice this is a Navigation form that provides access to all the forms and reports related to the Employees listed in the database. The blue navigation buttons on the left side represent forms, and the green navigation buttons represent reports.

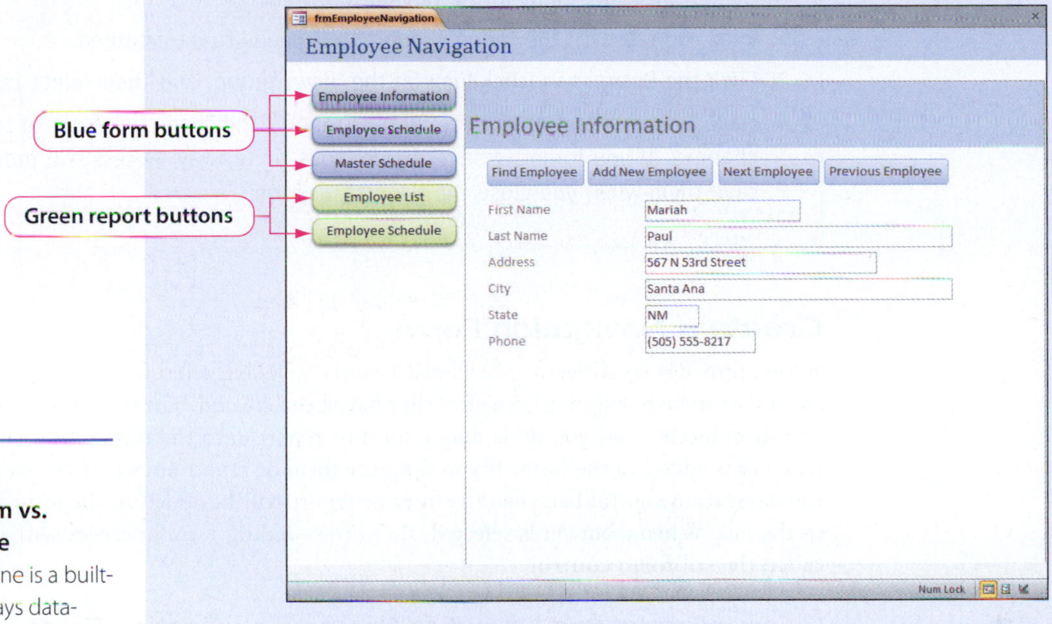

Figure 1 Employee Navigation form

SIDE NOTE

Navigation Form vs. Navigation Pane

The Navigation Pane is a built-in pane that displays database objects. A Navigation form is a type of form you create from a command on the Ribbon. A Navigation form will appear in the Navigation Pane as a form.

SIDE NOTE

Scroll Bars

Scroll bars may not appear on your screen, but may on another user's screen depending on the screen resolution and size. Best practice is to try and develop forms without scroll bars whenever possible to make the viewing less distracting.

e. Click the blue **Master Schedule** button on the left side of the Navigation form to open the Master Schedule form. Click the green **Employee Schedule** button on the left side to open the Employee Schedule report. Notice how the color and outline change slightly when a button is selected.

f. Close ☒ the Employee Navigation form.

g. Double-click **frmProductNavigation** in the Navigation Pane to open the Product Navigation form. Notice the forms and reports on the left side related to the products offered by the spa. Click each one to see the related form or report.

h. Double-click **frmServicesNavigation** in the Navigation Pane to open the Services Navigation form. Notice the forms and reports on the left side related to the services offered by the spa. Click each one to see the related form or report.

i. Close ☒ frmServicesNavigation and frmProductNavigation.

Real World Advice   Color-Coding

Color-coding can be effectively used to distinguish between different tasks or objects on a Navigation form. In the previous example, different colors were used to distinguish reports from forms. Colors can also be used to group related tasks or groups of tasks. For example, all tasks related to customers, regardless of which Navigation form they are found on, could be one color, while all tasks related to employees could be a different color. This gives you an option to group tasks on one Navigation form or on many but still keep them easy to find.

Quick Reference / Edit the Navigation Form

As you are developing your Navigation form, if there are modifications you need to make in the form or report you are adding to the Navigation form, you can make those modifications right in the Navigation form.

1. Click the tab with the form or report that needs to be modified.
2. Click the Design tab, click View in the Views group, and then select Layout View.
3. Make the modifications to the form or report, and then click Save to save the changes. If you forget to save the changes right away, Access will prompt you to save them when you close the Navigation form.

Create a Navigation Form

Access provides six different predefined layouts for Navigation forms that are customizable—and they can be redesigned even after they have been created. The predefined layouts use a drag-and-drop method; all you do is drag a form or report onto the **navigation control bar** and a new tab is added to the form. If you drop the form or report anywhere on the form other than the navigation control bar, then the form or report will be added to the form itself rather than to the tab. When a button is selected, the corresponding form or report will appear in what is called the **subform control**.

Using a Predefined Layout to Create a Navigation Form

Of the six different predefined layouts to choose from, three provide one level of navigation, either horizontal or vertical, and three provide two levels of navigation, either horizontal, vertical, or a combination of both. In this exercise, you will develop a Navigation form for customer navigation that is a vertical Navigation form similar to the ones you just viewed in the previous exercise.

To Create a New Navigation Form

a. Click the **Create tab**, click **Navigation** in the Forms group, and then click **Vertical Tabs, Left**. A new Navigation form will open.

Troubleshooting

You may see the Field list open on the right side of your window. You can close this by clicking the Design tab and then clicking Add Existing Fields in the Tools group, or by clicking the Close button.

b. Drag **frmCustomer** from the Navigation Pane to the [Add New] tab on the Navigation form.

c. Drag **frmCustomerInvoices** from the Navigation Pane to the [Add New] tab on the Navigation form.

d. Continue adding **frmCustomerSchedule**, **frmCustomerPurchases**, **rptCustomerList**, and **rptScheduleByCustomer** to the [Add New] tab on the Navigation form.

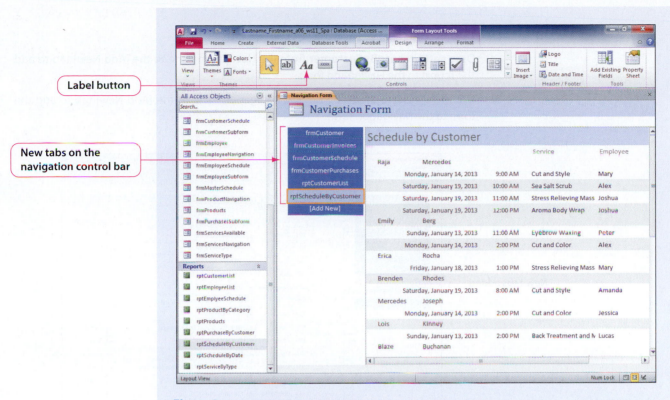

Label button

New tabs on the navigation control bar

Figure 2 Customer Navigation form with six tabs on the left side

e. Click the **Design tab**, click **View** in the Views group, and then click **Design View**. Click the **Design tab**, click **Label** Aa in the Controls group, click to add a label in the right side of the Form Header, and then type your **first initial** and **last name** in the label. Resize the labels as needed in the Form Header so text appears on one line.

f. Click the **Design tab**, click **View** in the Views group, and then click **Layout View**. Save the form as **frmCustomerNavigation_initialLastname**, replacing initialLastname with your first initial and last name.

Troubleshooting

When you save forms that are part of other forms, you may see a warning message from Access telling you that the form is being edited by another user. Go ahead and click OK to save the form. Sometimes Access thinks that if the form is opened by you, that you are another user!

Modify a Navigation Form

Once a Navigation form has been created, additional forms and reports can be added to the form, deleted from the form, or rearranged on the form.

Once tabs are added to the Navigation form, the captions, or text, can be changed or they can be replaced with icons instead of the tab caption to further customize the form. Many of the new shapes available in Access 2010 were specifically designed to use with navigation controls like Next, Previous, and Exit.

Add a Form Tab

Forms and reports can be easily added to the form by dragging the object from the Navigation Pane to the form tab; therefore, it is important to be able to see your Navigation Pane as you work on the Navigation form. In this exercise, you will add additional forms and reports to the Navigation form.

To Add New Tabs to the Form

a. Drag **rptPurchaseByCustomer** from the Navigation Pane to the [Add New] tab to add the report to the Navigation form.

b. Drag **frmMasterSchedule** from the Navigation Pane to the [Add New] tab to add the form to the Navigation form.

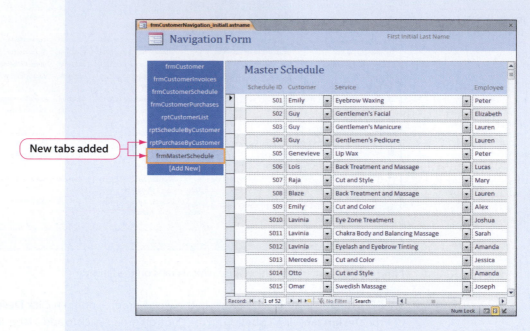

New tabs added

Figure 3 New tabs added

c. Save  the Navigation form.

Delete a Form Tab

If necessary, forms and reports may be deleted from a Navigation form. When a tab with a form or report is deleted, only the tab is deleted, not the actual form or report. In this exercise, you will delete a tab from the Navigation form.

To Delete Tabs from the Form

a. Click the **frmMasterSchedule** tab on the Navigation form.

b. Press [Delete] to delete the form from the tab.

Troubleshooting

When you delete a tab, make sure the tab is selected with an orange border around it. If you are in edit mode with the cursor blinking in the text instead of the tab selected with the orange border, you will delete the text rather than the tab.

c. Save the Navigation form.

SIDE NOTE
Alternate Method to Delete

An alternate method to delete the tab is to select the tab, right-click, and then select Delete from the menu.

Move a Form Tab

Existing tabs can easily be rearranged on their level, or they can be moved from one level of the form to another. In this exercise, you will rearrange the order of the tabs.

To Move Tabs on the Form

a. Click the **rptScheduleByCustomer** tab on the Navigation form.

b. Drag the **tab** above the rptCustomerList tab. When the yellow line is above the rptCustomerList tab, release the mouse button to move the tab.

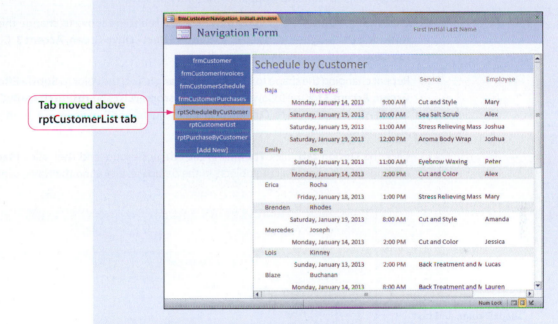

Tab moved above rptCustomerList tab

Figure 4 Tab moved to new position

c. Save 💾 the Navigation form.

Modify the Appearance of a Form Tab

Tabs can be modified in order to customize the form. The tab shape and color can be changed. A theme can be added to either the Navigation form or to the whole database, including the Navigation form. In this exercise, you will add a theme to the database, as well as change the shape and color of the tabs.

To Customize Tabs on the Form

a. Double-click the **Navigation Form** title text, select the text, change it to Customer Navigation and then press [Enter]. Select the **icon** to the left of the title, and then press [Delete].

b. Click the **frmCustomer tab**, click the **Format tab**, click **Change Shape** in the Control Formatting group, and then click **Rounded Rectangle**.

c. Click the **Format tab**, click **Quick Styles** in the Control Formatting group, and then click **Subtle Effect - Blue, Accent 1** (the option in the fourth row of the second column).

SIDE NOTE
**Alternate Method
to Rename**

An alternate method to rename the tab is to select the tab, double-click, and then type the new name.

d. Right-click the **frmCustomer** tab, and then select **Properties**. In the open Property Sheet pane on the right side of the window, select **frmCustomer** in the Caption row, and then type Customers. Close ☒ the Property Sheet pane. This should change the text on the tab to Customers.

e. Click the **frmCustomerInvoices tab**. Repeat the steps above to change the shape to **Rounded Rectangle** and the color to **Subtle Effect - Blue, Accent 1**. Change the tab caption to Invoices.

f. Repeat changing the shape to **Rounded Rectangle** and the color to **Subtle Effect - Blue, Accent 1** for the following tabs: **frmCustomerSchedule** and **frmCustomerPurchases**. Change the tab names to Appointments and Purchases.

g. Click the tab **rptScheduleByCustomer**. Repeat the steps above to change the shape to **Rounded Rectangle** and the color to **Subtle Effect - Olive Green, Accent 3**. Change the tab caption to Appointment Report.

h. Repeat changing the shape to **Rounded Rectangle** and the color to **Subtle Effect - Olive Green, Accent 3** for the following tabs: **rptCustomerList** and **rptPurchaseByCustomer**. Change the tab names to Customer List and Customer Purchases. Close the Property Sheet pane.

i. Click the **Design tab**, click **Themes** in the Themes group, and then click **Median**. This changes the theme for all the objects in the database, including the Navigation form.

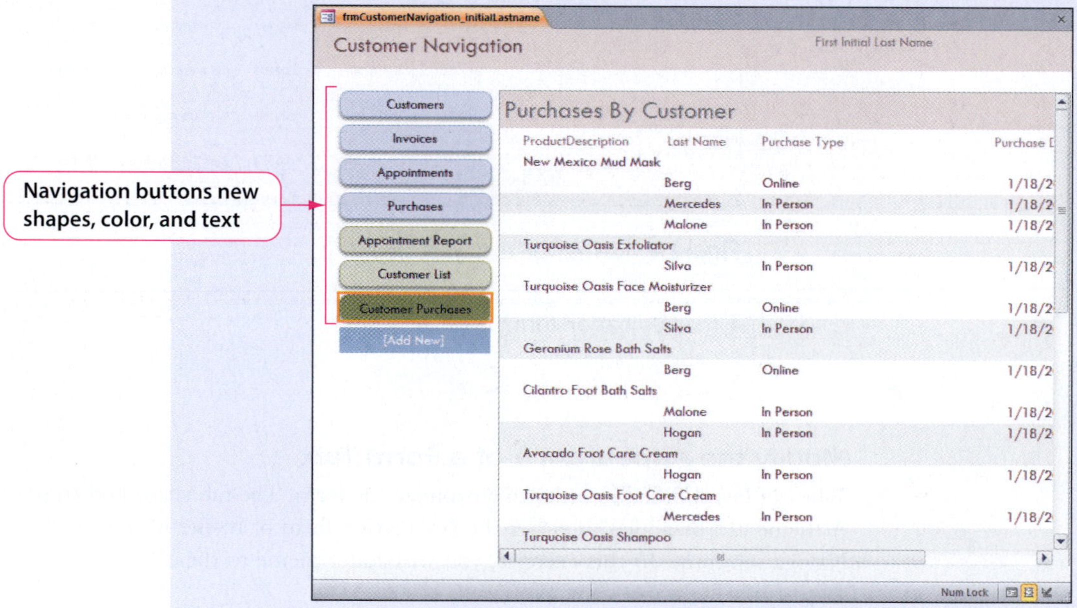

Navigation buttons new shapes, color, and text

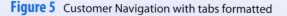

Figure 5 Customer Navigation with tabs formatted

j. Close ☒ the Navigation form, and then click **Yes** to save the changes.

Real World Advice

Navigation Forms and Tab Controls—When to Use Each?

Although tab controls and Navigation forms look similar, that is where the similarities end. The difference is that in a tab control, the tabbed windows are hidden behind each other and are all open at the same time, but you only see one at a time. You can picture the layout as pieces of paper laid on top of each other with a tab at the top of each page. As you click a tab, the piece of paper with the selected tab is moved to the top of the pile. In a Navigation form, the tabs open a new form or report in the same subform control each time so only one object is open at a time.

A Navigation form is useful when you want to provide a hierarchy of options—navigation tabs and subnavigation options. A Navigation form may also provide for better database performance because it loads only one object at a time, whereas a tab control loads all the objects for all the tabs at one time. Finally, a Navigation form is useful to provide the most up-to-date data from the database. Because the form or report loads fresh each time you click a navigation command, the data is updated as the object loads.

Refining the User Interface

Navigation forms do not display data from a table, therefore they are an unbound object. Because the user does not have to move from record to record or page to page, some of the form navigation properties can be removed. The navigation buttons and record selectors can be removed because they are not needed. The ability to access a shortcut menu can be disabled, as well as the option to copy data and close the object. Any operations that would distract the user from the purpose of the Navigation form should be disabled or removed.

If you find your Navigation form cluttered with too many objects, you can create multiple Navigation forms and have one form open another. The key to making multiple Navigation forms is to have them arranged in a way that makes intuitive sense. A Navigation form with only reports and another with only forms may not simplify the navigation process through your database. It is in effect replicating the Navigation Pane. Instead, you should consider grouping forms and reports by topic or by function.

By grouping the different business functions, you create an intuitive and well-defined user interface. A user should be able to complete all related tasks under a single tab rather than have to move from tab to tab to find different tasks. Think of how a good website works: on the Home page there are links to go to other pages. On each page of the website you are then able to view related information about one topic. To go to a new topic, you go to a new page. You can create a similar experience using multiple Navigation forms that are all linked together. In our Spa example, you might want to have different pages to navigate service, product, employee, and customer tasks.

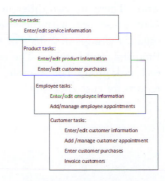

Figure 6 Different task lists

To accomplish this, you can create a main Navigation form that has four commands: Services, Products, Employees, and Customers. Clicking one of the commands opens another Navigation form with additional commands related to the area you clicked.

A well-refined user interface will make sense to any user, even one with no Access experience. The user should be able to look at the Navigation form and locate the form or report that he or she needs. In this section, you will create a user interface for the user that includes a Navigation forms, custom form buttons, and modified start-up options for the database.

CONSIDER THIS | **Websites Compared to Access**

Because so many users today are accustomed to how a website works, an Access user interface can be set up to look and work just like a webpage. Think about websites you enjoy visiting. Other than the content, what makes a web page attractive? Is it how easy things are to find? Is it the consistent color theme throughout? When you are designing your user interface, think about what makes an interface interesting and easy to use, and try to replicate that in your user interface.

Real World Advice   Planning Is Everything

How do you decide, as the designer, what a good user interface will look like? What makes sense to you may not make sense to the final user, so it is important to understand your end user and the job they have to do in order to make the best decisions for the application.

You may consider spending some time with the user, interviewing them about the task they will have to complete with the application, what they would like to make it easier, and what they do not like about it. You could even spend a day watching what they do and take notes to refer back to when you are designing the application.

Every business and every user will be different, so the more information you can get directly from the user, the better your application will be for them to use.

Create a Main Menu

A main menu is essentially a Navigation form that provides access to additional Navigation forms. In addition to Navigation forms, a main menu can also have a command to close the Access application so everything the user needs is in one place. An **application** is a collection of tools used to perform a task or multiple tasks.

When considering how the main menu will work, you have to look at how the tabs will work. There are two different ways to create a main menu form. You can create a two-level Navigation form with top-level tabs and second-level tabs. The top-level tabs can be named to organize groups of tasks. For example, the top-level tabs may be called Customer, Employee, Products, and Services. The second-level tabs could be the forms and reports associated with each task group. For example, the second-level tabs could be forms for customer data entry and reports for customer lists.

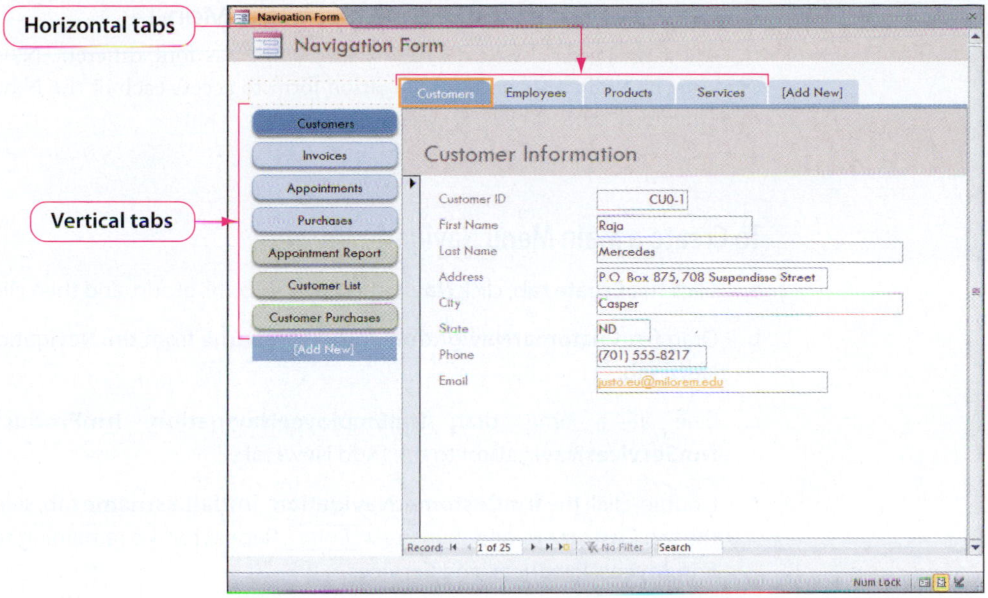

Figure 7 Navigation form created using first- and second-level tabs

Another option is to create Navigation forms for each group of tasks with only top-level tabs. Each top level points to the related forms and reports. Then, the main menu Navigation form has only top-level tabs that point to the individual Navigation forms for each task group. For example, you can create a customer Navigation form, an employee Navigation form, and so on. Each top-level tab in the main menu Navigation form can point to one of the individual Navigation forms. The effect is the same as the method described above, but the look is different.

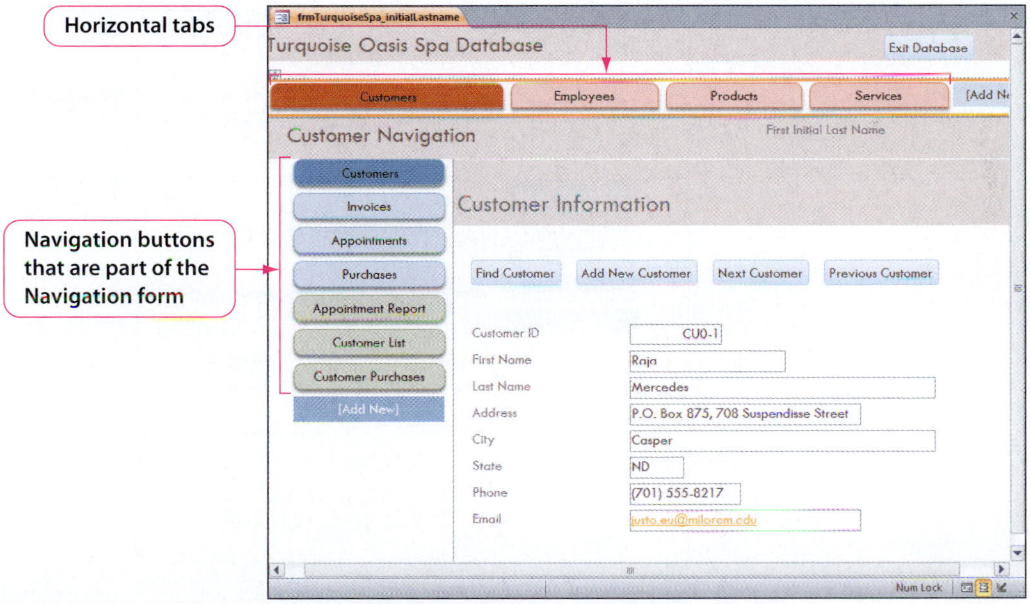

Figure 8 Navigation form created using other Navigation forms with only top-level tabs

Create a Navigation Form for a Main Menu

Because the Spa database you are working with has four different Navigation forms, in this exercise you will create a new Navigation form to access each of the Navigation forms and add a command button to close the database.

To Create a Main Menu Navigation Form

a. Click the **Create tab**, click **Navigation** in the Forms group, and then click **Horizontal Tabs**.

b. Drag **frmCustomerNavigation_initialLastname** from the Navigation Pane to the [Add New] tab.

c. One at a time, drag **frmEmployeeNavigation**, **frmProductNavigation**, and **frmServicesNavigation** to the [Add New] tab.

d. Double-click the **frmCustomerNavigation_initialLastname** tab, select the text, rename the tab Customers, and then press Enter. Repeat for the remaining tabs and name them Employees, Products, and Services.

e. Click the **Customers tab** on the Navigation form. Press and hold Shift, and then click the **Services tab**. Click the **Format tab**, click **Change Shape** in the Control Formatting group, and then click **Round Same Side Corner Rectangle**. Click the **Format tab**, click **Quick Styles** in the Control Formatting group, and then click **Subtle Effect - Orange, Accent 2** (option in fourth row, third column).

f. Double-click the **Navigation form** title, select the text, and change it to Turquoise Oasis Spa Database. Click the **icon** to the left of the title, and then press Delete.

g. Save 💾 the form as frmTurquoiseSpa_initialLastname replacing initialLastname with your first initial and last name.

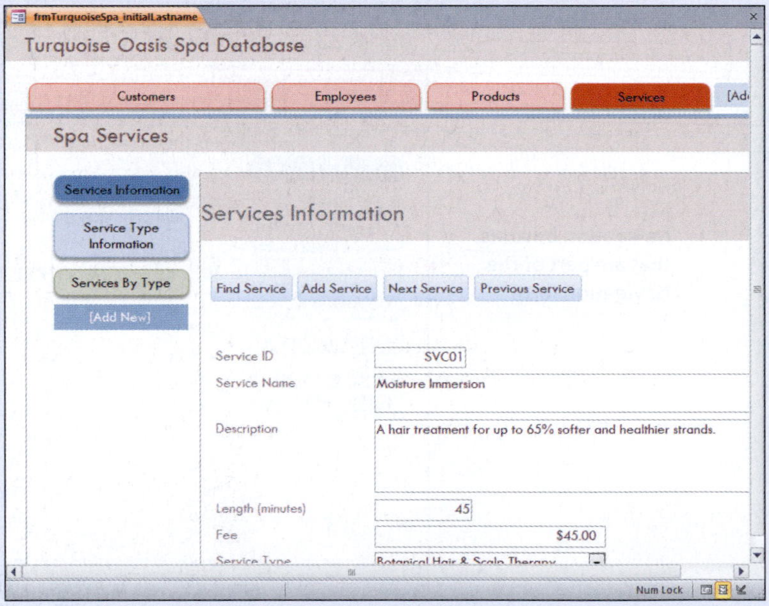

Figure 9 Turquoise Oasis Spa Navigation form

h. Close ⊠ the form.

Add Command Buttons to the Navigation Form

Command buttons can be added to the Navigation form, but they can also be added to forms and reports that are accessed through the Navigation form. Instead of requiring the user to use the selection arrows and navigation buttons on a form, you can insert buttons with navigation and selection commands for them to use. For users unfamiliar with Access, buttons are more intuitive than the navigational arrows at the bottom of a form.

Real World Advice · Images vs. Text

Sometimes people prefer to use images on a button instead of text. Images can be helpful and even more appealing on a button, but only if the meaning on the button is clear. An image on a button that invokes a question from the user about what the button does should probably be replaced with text. Remember, your user may not know that a pencil means edit or that an arrow means next record. A door may indicate open instead of exit.

Create Navigation Buttons on a Form

If you open the Employee Navigation form, Product Navigation form, or Service Navigation form, you will notice that there are buttons on the various subforms for the user to click to find a record, add a record, or go to the previous and next records. In this exercise, you will add similar buttons to the Customer form as well as an Exit Database button on the main menu Navigation form.

To Add Navigation Buttons to a Form

a. Double-click **frmCustomer** on the Navigation Pane to open the form.

b. Click the **Home tab**, click **View** in the Views group, and then click **Design View**.

c. Click the **Customer ID** text box, press and hold Shift, and then click on all the text boxes and labels in the form Detail. Move them all down about 1".

d. Click the **Design tab**, click **Button** [⬚] in the Controls group, and then click in the top-left corner of the form Detail to add the button.

e. In the Command Button Wizard, in the Categories list, verify that **Record Navigation** is selected, in the Actions list click to select **Find Record**, and then click **Next**.

f. Click **Text**, select the text, change it by typing **Find Customer**, and then click **Next**.

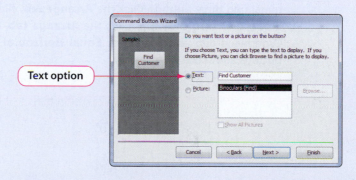

Figure 10 Text selected and changed in Command Button Wizard

g. Name the button **cmdFindCustomer**, and then click **Finish**.

h. Click the **Design tab**, click **Button** in the Controls group, and then click to the right of the first button.

i. In the Categories list click to select **Record Operations**, in the Actions list click to select **Add New Record**, and then click **Next**.

j. Click **Text**, select the text, change it by typing Add New Customer, and then click **Next**. Name the button **cmdAddNewCustomer**, and then click **Finish**.

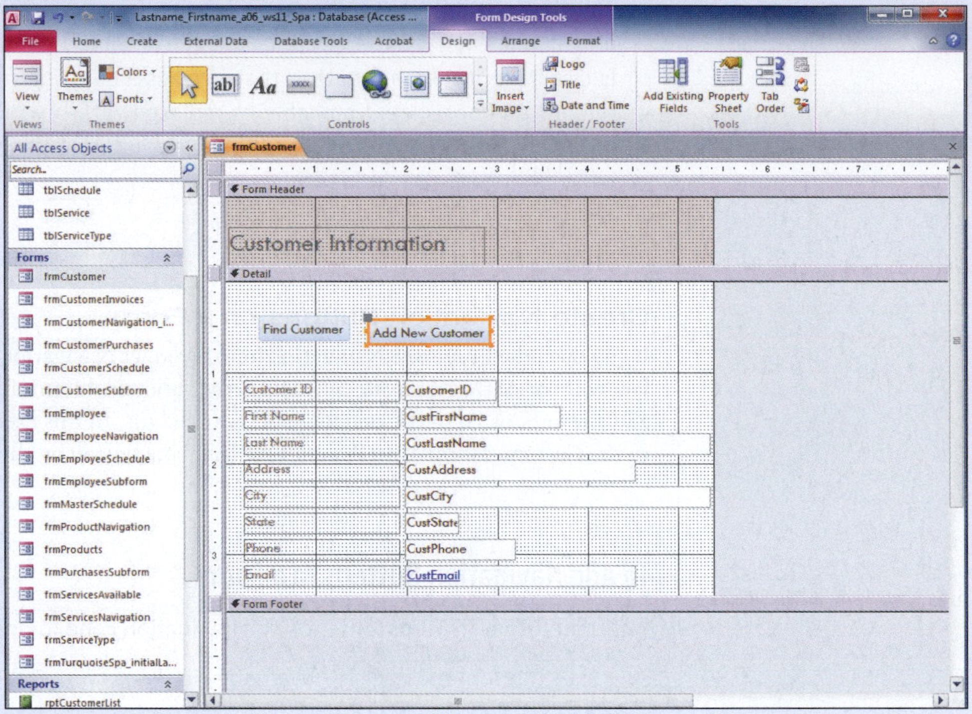

Figure 11 Two buttons added to the form

k. Repeat to add two more buttons: **Next Customer** (click the **Record Navigation** category and **Go To Next Record** action; the text should say Next Customer and the button named **cmdNextCustomer**) and **Previous Customer** (click the **Record Navigation** category and **Go To Previous Record** action; the text should say Previous Customer and the button named **cmdPreviousCustomer**).

l. Click the first button to select it. Press and hold ⇧Shift, and then click to select the remaining three buttons. Click the **Arrange tab**, click **Align** in the Sizing & Ordering group, and then click **Top**. Click the **Arrange tab**, click **Size/Space** in the Sizing & Ordering group, and then click **Equal Horizontal**. This will align the tops of the buttons and space them evenly.

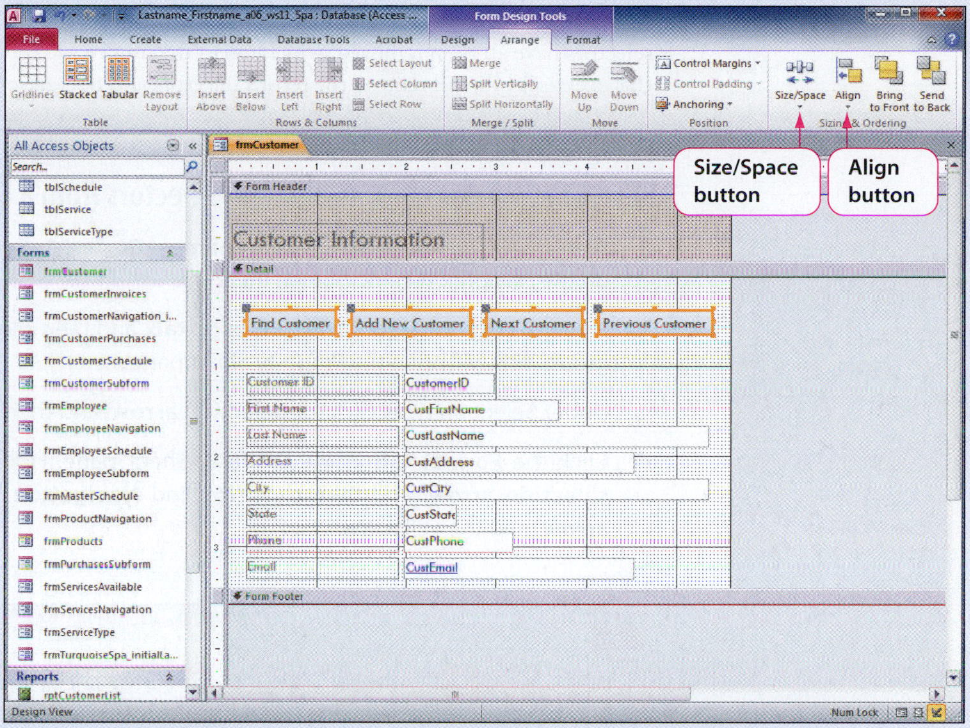

Figure 12 Align and Size/Space buttons in Design view

m. Close ☒ the form and then click **Yes** to save the changes.

n. Double-click **frmTurquoiseSpa_initialLastname** on the Navigation Pane to open the form.

o. Switch to **Design view**, click the **Design tab**, click **Button** 🔲 in the Controls group, and then click on the far right of the **Form Header**. In the Categories list, click **Application**, and then in the Actions list verify that **Quit Application** is selected. Click **Next**. Click **Text**, select the text, type **Exit Database**, and then click **Next**. Name the button **cmdExitDatabase**, and then click **Finish**. Switch to **Form view**.

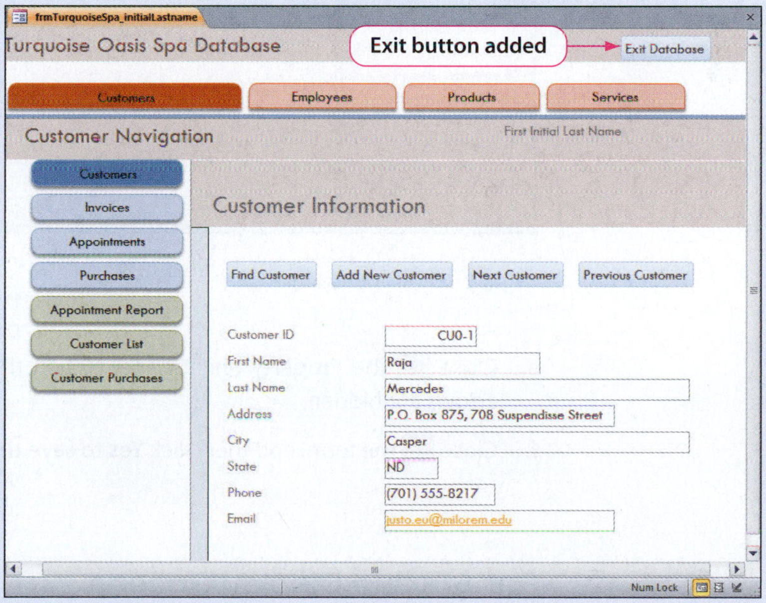

Figure 13 Exit button added to Navigation form

p. Click **Exit Database** to check your button. Click **Yes** to save the changes. Access should close.

Remove Navigation Arrows and Selectors on a Form

If you look at any of the forms with command buttons added, the navigation arrows and record selectors have all been removed, which forces the user to use the buttons to manage the records. In this exercise, you will remove the record selectors and navigation arrows from the Customer form.

To Remove Navigation Buttons and Selectors from a Form

a. **Start** Access. Open **Lastname_Firstname_a06_ws11_Spa**. Double-click **frmCustomer** on the Navigation Pane to open the form.

b. Switch to **Layout view**, click the **Design tab**, and then click **Property Sheet** in the Tools group. This will open the Property Sheet pane.

c. Under Selection type, click the **selection arrow**, and then click **Form**.

d. Click the **Format tab** in the Property Sheet pane. Find **Record Selectors**, click the **selection arrow**, and then click **No**. Find **Navigation Buttons**, click the **selection arrow**, and then click **No**.

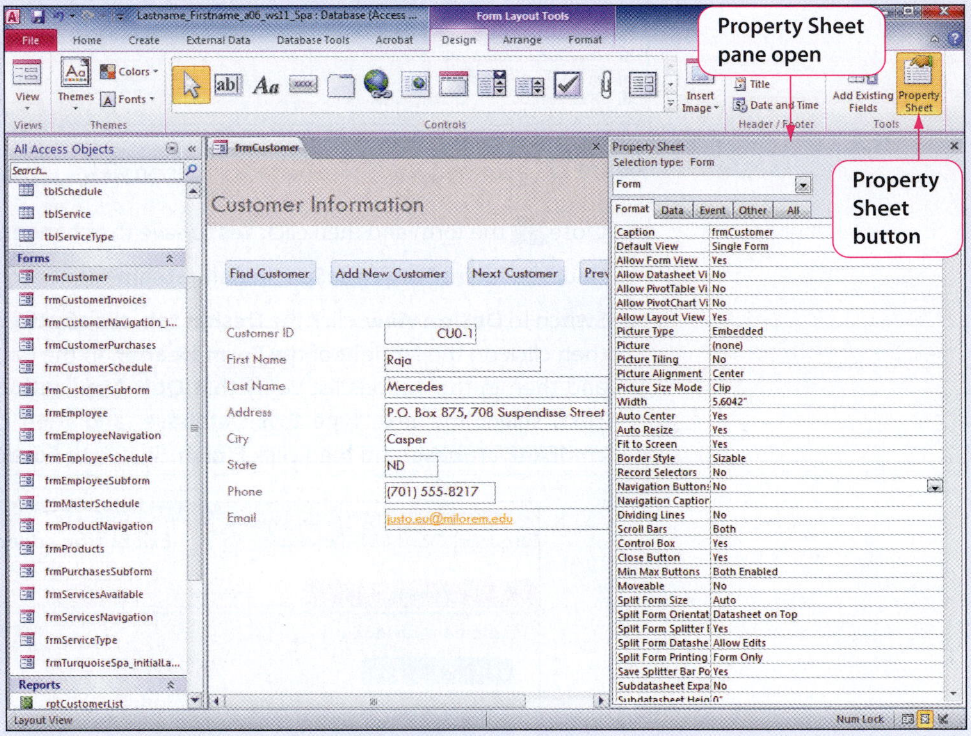

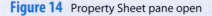

Figure 14 Property Sheet pane open

e. Close ☒ the Property Sheet pane. Notice that the record selectors and navigation arrows are hidden.

f. Close ☒ the form, and then click **Yes** to save the changes.

Set Startup Display Options

Once your database is designed, forms and reports created, and a navigation system and user interface in place, you have an application for others to use. To make the application as user friendly as possible, you can name the application and then remove options available to database designers. By doing this, you reduce the chance of changes being made to the data or the database structure either intentionally or accidentally by an end user. These options may include removing access to certain application options—the Navigation Pane, the Ribbon, and various toolbar options.

You also will want to show a **startup form** when your database opens. The startup form is the form that opens automatically when you open the database. This is generally your Navigation form, or the Navigation form that will act as your main menu.

Optional commands, such as the command to compact and repair the database when it is closed, may also be set to run automatically so the user does not have to worry about maintenance tasks.

Making Changes to the Startup Options

Changing the application title helps to better identify the application and give it an identity separate from the actual database. Selecting a startup form will determine which form opens when the application is started. Restricting access to the Navigation Pane requires the user to use the user interface you have developed. For this exercise you will change the application title to Turquoise Oasis Spa and designate your main menu Navigation form as the startup form.

CONSIDER THIS | **Creating a Pleasant Experience**

As the designer of the database, it is easy to take for granted what all the Ribbon and toolbar options do and why they are visible. To a new user in Access, these options may become overwhelming or even confusing. Because your goal is to limit the confusion of working with the application, what other options could you think of limiting? Should you password protect your application? How would this be more or less confusing? Should you only allow certain changes to be made to the data, like allowing editing but not deleting? How would these options affect the usability of your application?

To Change Startup Options

a. Click the **File tab**, click **Options**, and then click **Current Database**. In the Application Options section, click in the **Application Title** text box, and then type Turquoise Oasis Spa.

b. Click the **Display Form arrow**, and then click **frmTurquoiseSpa_initialLastname**. This will be the form that opens when the application is opened.

Troubleshooting

If None is selected in the Display Form text box, then when your application opens, no form will open.

c. Click the **Compact on Close** check box. This automatically compacts and repairs the database every time it is closed.

A database grows dynamically as data is added or manipulated; however, it does not shrink automatically when data is deleted or the manipulation is complete. Databases may also become fragmented as data is added and deleted. To maintain performance of the database, you should compact and repair the database each time it is closed.

d. In the Navigation section, clear the **Display Navigation Pane** check box. This hides the Navigation Pane.

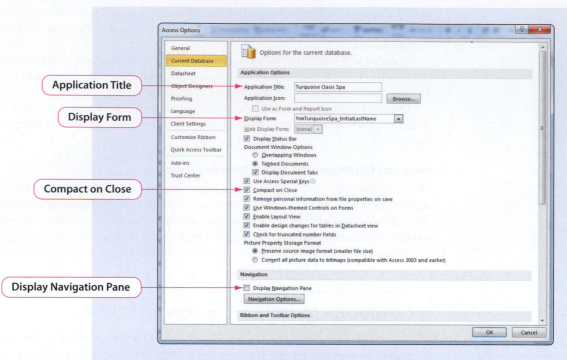

Figure 15 Access Options window

SIDE NOTE

Show Navigation Pane

If the Navigation Pane is hidden, you can press F11 to unhide it as long as the option to disable special keys was not selected in the database options.

e. Click **OK** to close the Access Options window.

f. Click **OK** at the message **You must close and reopen the current database for the specified option to take effect**.

g. Close ⊠ the database. Start **Access**, and then open **Lastname_Firstname_a06_ws11_Spa**. When the database reopens, the only form to open should be frmTurquoiseSpa_ initialLastname. Also notice the name of the application, not the database, on the title bar.

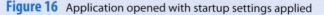

Figure 16 Application opened with startup settings applied

h. To access the complete database and not just the application, click the **File tab**, click **Options**, and then select **Current Database**. Click the **Display Navigation Pane** check box to restore the Navigation Pane. Click **OK** twice. Close, and then restart the database.

Real World Advice Even More Options

To create an even more fluid user experience, you can also hide many more options in the startup form. Actually, what you can eventually do is create two different objects—the application for the user and the database for the designer. The application could have limited options on the Ribbon, hidden tabs, status bars, and shortcut menus. The purpose of the application would be to limit the user to only commands and buttons you provide in order to limit the accessibility of the data to what you want the user to have and nothing more. By "locking down" the application, you are protecting the data and database structure from accidental or intentional modifications. Many of the options will be presented in Workshop 14.

Test the Application

A good application will be easy to use for all levels of Access users, not just the designer. Before you have a user go live with your application, it is a good practice to test it on all levels of users, especially those who will actually be using the database and those who have no experience with Access. This is called **usability testing**.

The goal of usability testing is to observe people using the application to discover what errors they may make with it and to identify areas that require modification. The four areas of usability testing include performance (how much time and how many steps are required to complete a task), accuracy (how many mistakes did users make), recall (how much did the user remember after a period of nonuse), and emotional response (how did the user feel about the tasks completed).

Usability testing requires observing a user under controlled circumstances to determine how he or she will use the application for its intended purpose. It has nothing to do with the user's opinion of the application, only how he or she interacts with it.

For successful usability testing, a realistic scenario should be set up where the user is given a list of tasks to perform in the application. In the Spa example, this could include entering a new customer, changing an existing appointment, and printing a report. While the user is performing these tasks, an observer is watching and taking notes, but not interacting with the user. The user should be allowed to make mistakes that are then noted by the observer. These mistakes will allow the designer to see what modifications may need to be made to the application.

CONSIDER THIS | Finding a Tester

All applications should be tested before they are given to the final user. If you are the only person available, you should at least run through the application as if you were a user. Unfortunately, you understand how it should work and may not be able to be objective. What are some options for you to find a tester of your application? Could you ask a co-worker, family member, or a roommate? If the application is well designed, the tester can be anyone, even if they are unfamiliar with what the database is supposed to do.

View the User Interface as a User

If you cannot test the user interface with an actual person, then you can at least view the user interface as a user rather than the developer. This will give you a better idea of what the user will see and whether modifications are required. For this exercise, you will follow a portion of a previously developed plan to test the user interface as a user rather than the developer.

To Test the User Interface as a User of the Database

a. Your Navigation form should be open in Form view.

b. Using the chart below, begin to test the application as a user. As you complete a task, fill in the Action taken section and the Comments section. This is what the developer will use to make any modifications to the application if necessary.

Task	Action taken	Comments
Enter a new customer		
Enter a new customer invoice		
Enter a new product		
Print the product list report		
Exit the database		

Figure 17

c. In addition to the above steps, click each **tab** to launch the form or report. Only one form or report should open, and it should be the one labeled on the tab.

d. Close ☒ the database, and then exit Access.

Concept Check

1. What elements should a database user have access to and why not the whole database?

2. What is a Navigation form? How is it different from the Navigation Pane?

3. What is the difference between Navigation forms and tab controls? When would you use each?

4. What is the difference between an application and a database?

5. What is usability testing, and why is it important?

Key Terms

Application 528
Navigation control bar 522
Navigation form 520

Startup form 535
Subform control 522
Usability testing 537

User interface 520

Visual Summary

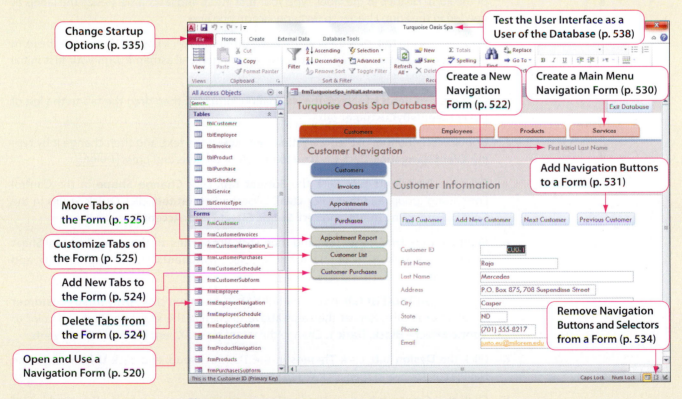

Figure 18 Turquoise Oasis Spa final database

Student data file needed:

a06_ws11_Events

You will save your file as:

Lastname_Firstname_a06_ws11_Events

Event Planning

You have been asked to create an application for the Event Planning database. The application needs to include a Navigation form built from individual Navigation forms, as well as command buttons on various forms and startup options to open the application to the Navigation form.

a. Start **Access**. Click the **File tab**, click **Open**, browse to your student data files, and then locate and open **a06_ws11_Events**. Click the **File tab**, click **Save Database As**, browse to where you are storing your files, name your database Lastname_Firstname_a06_ws11_Events replacing Lastname_Firstname with your actual name, and click **Save**. Click **Enable Content** in the Security Warning.

b. Click the **Create tab**, click **Navigation** in the Forms group, and then click **Horizontal Tabs**. Drag **frmClients** from the Navigation Pane to the [Add New] tab on the Navigation form. Continue by adding **rptEventsByClient** and **rptClientList** to the [Add New] tab on the Navigation form.

c. Click the **Design tab**, click **View** in the Views group, and click **Design View**. Click the **Design tab**, click **Label** in the Controls group, and click to add a label in the right side of the Form Header. In the label, type your first initial and last name. Resize the labels as needed in the Form Header so text appears on one line.

d. Click the **Design tab**, click **View** in the Views group, and click **Layout View**. Save the form as frmClientNavigation_initialLastname, replacing initialLastname with your first initial and last name.

e. Click the **rptClientList** tab on the Navigation form, and then drag the tab to the left of the **rptEventsByCustomer** tab.

f. Double-click the **title** of the Navigation form, select the text, and then change it by typing Client Navigation. Click the **icon** to the left of the title, and press ⎡Delete⎤.

g. Click the **frmClients tab**. Click the **Format tab**, click **Change Shape** in the Control Formatting group, and then click **Oval**. Click the **Format tab**, click **Quick Styles** in the Control Formatting group, and click **Subtle Effect - Red, Accent 2**.

h. Right-click the **frmClients tab**, and then click **Properties**. In the open Property Sheet pane on the right side of the window, select **frmClients** in the Caption row and type Clients.

i. Click the **rptClientList tab**, press and hold ⎡Shift⎤, and then click **rptEventsByCustomer** to select both tabs. Repeat the steps above to change the shape to **Oval** and color to **Subtle Effect – Black, Dark 1**. Change the tab names to Client List and Client Events.

j. Click the **Design tab**, click **Themes** in the Themes group, and click **Urban**. Close the Navigation form, and then click **Yes** to save the changes.

k. Click the **Create tab**, click **Navigation** in the Forms group, and click **Horizontal Tabs**. Drag **frmClientNavigation_initialLastname** to the [Add New] tab. Drag **frmEventNavigation** to the [Add New] tab.

l. Double-click the **frmClientNavigation_initialLastname tab**, select the text, and then rename the tab Clients. Repeat for **frmEventNavigation**, and then name it Events.

m. Click the **Clients** tab on the Navigation form. Click the **Format tab**, click **Change Shape** in the Control Formatting group, and click **Snip Single Corner Rectangle**. Click the **Format tab**, click **Quick Styles** in the Control Formatting group, and then click **Intense Effect - Indigo, Accent 1**. Repeat for the **Events tab**.

n. Double-click the **Navigation Form** title, select the text, and then change it by typing Events Database. Click the **icon** to the left of the title, and then press [Delete]. Save the form as frmEventsDatabase_initialLastname. Close the form.

o. In the Navigation Pane, double-click **frmClients** to open the form. Click the **Home tab**, click **View** in the Views group, and click **Design View**. Click the **ID** text box, press and hold [Shift], and then click all the text boxes and labels in the form Detail. Move them all down about 1". Click the **Design tab**, click **Button** in the Controls group, and click in the top-left corner of the form Detail to add the button.

p. In the Categories list verify **Record Navigation** is selected, in the Actions list click **Find Record**, and then click **Next**. Click **Text**, select the text, change it by typing Find Client, and then click **Next**. Name the button cmdFindClient, and then click **Finish**.

q. Click the **Design tab**, click **Button** in the Controls group, and click next to the first button. In the Categories list click **Record Operations**, in the Actions list click **Add New Record**, and then click **Next**. Click **Text**, select the text, change it by typing Add New Client, and click **Next**. Name the button cmdAddNewClient, and then click **Finish**.

r. Repeat to add two more buttons: **Next Client** (click the **Record Navigation** category and **Go To Next Record** action; the text should say Next Client and the button named cmdNextClient) and **Previous Client** (click the **Record Navigation** category and **Go To Previous Record** action; the text should say Previous Client and the button named cmdPreviousClient).

s. Click the first button to select it. Press and hold [Shift], and then click to select the remaining three buttons. Click the **Arrange tab**, click **Align** in the Sizing & Ordering group, and click **Top**. Click the **Arrange tab**, click **Size/Space** in the Sizing & Ordering group, and click **Equal Horizontal**. **Close** the form, and then click **Yes** to save the changes.

t. In the Navigation Pane, double-click **frmEventsDatabase_initialLastname** to open the form. Switch to **Design view**. Click the **Design tab**, click **Button** in the Controls group, and click on the far right of the **Form Header**. In the Categories list, click **Application** and in the Actions list, click **Quit Application**. Click **Next**, click **Text**, select the text and type Exit Database, and then click **Next**. Name the button cmdExitDatabase, and then click **Finish**. Switch to **Form view**.

u. Click **Exit Database** to check your button. Click **Yes** to save the changes. Open **Lastname_Firstname_a06_ws11_Events**. In the Navigation Pane, double-click **frmClients** to open the form. Switch to **Layout view** and then click **Property Sheet** in the Tools group. Under **Selection** type, click the **selection arrow**, and then click **Form**.

v. Click the **Format tab** in the Property Sheet window. Find **Record Selectors**, click the **selection arrow**, and click **No**. Find **Navigation Buttons**, click the **selection arrow**, and click **No**. Close the Property Sheet window, close the form, and then click **Yes** to save the changes.

w. Click the **File tab**, click **Options**, and then click **Current Database**. In the Application Options section, click the **Application Title** text box, and then type Events Database.

x. Click the **Display Form selection arrow**, click **frmEventsDatabase_initialLastname**. Click the **Compact on Close** check box. In the Navigation section, click **Display Navigation Pane** to deselect the option. Click **OK** to close the Access Options window. Click **OK** again. **Exit** Access.

Student data file needed:

a06_ws11_Painted_Treasures

You will save your file as:

Lastname_Firstname_a06_ws11_Painted_Treasures

Gift Shop

You have been asked to create an application for the Painted Treasures gift shop database. The application needs to include a Navigation form, as well as command buttons on various forms and startup options to open the application to the Navigation form. You will build a Navigation form with horizontal and vertical tabs.

a. Start **Access**. Click the **File tab**, click **Open**, browse to your student data files, and then locate and open **a06_ws11_Painted_Treasures**. Click the **File tab**, click **Save Database As**, browse to where you are storing your files, name your database Lastname_Firstname_ a06_ws11_Painted_Treasures replacing Lastname_Firstname with your actual name and click **Save**. Click **Enable Content** in the Security Warning.

b. Click the **Create tab**, click **Navigation** in the Forms group, and then click **Horizontal Tabs and Vertical Tabs, Left**. Double-click the horizontal [Add New] tab, type Customers, and then press Enter. Double-click the next horizontal [Add New] tab, type Products, and then press Enter.

c. Click the **Design tab**, click **View** in the Views group, and then select **Design View**. Click the **Design tab**, click **Label** in the Controls group, and then click to add a label in the right side of the Form Header. In the label, type your first initial and last name. Resize the labels as needed in the Form Header so text appears on one line. Switch to **Layout view**.

d. Select the title text in the Navigation Form, and change it to Painted Treasures Navigation. Click the **icon** to the left of the title, and press Delete.

e. Click the **Customers horizontal tab** to select it. Click **frmCustomer** on the Navigation Pane, and then drag it to the [Add New] vertical tab. Click **frmCustomerPurchases** on the Navigation Pane, and drag it to the next [Add New] vertical tab.

f. Continue by adding **rptCustomerListByID**, **rptCustomerListByLastname**, and **rptCustomerPurchases** to each of the next [Add New] vertical tabs.

g. Click the **frmCustomer vertical tab**, press and hold Shift, and then click **frmCustomerPurcases**. Click the **Format tab**, click **Change Shape** in the Control Formatting group, and click **Snip Single Corner Rectangle**. Click the **Format tab**, click **Quick Styles** in the Control Formatting group, and click **Colored Fill - Purple, Accent 4**.

h. Double-click the **frmCustomer** tab, select the text, and rename the tab Customer. Double-click the **frmCustomerPurchases tab**, and rename the tab Customer Purchases.

i. Click **rptCustomerListByID**, press and hold Shift, and then click **rptCustomerPurchases**. Click the **Format tab**, click **Change Shape** in the Control Formatting group, and click **Snip Single Corner Rectangle**. Click the **Format tab**, click **Quick Styles** in the Control Formatting group, and click **Colored Fill - Olive Green, Accent 3**. Change the tab names to Customer ID, Customer List, and Customer Purchases.

j. Click the **Design tab**, click **Themes** in the Themes group, and then click **Couture**. Save the Navigation form as frmPaintedTreasuresNavigation_initialLastname replacing initialLastname with your first initial and last name.

k. Click the **Products horizontal tab** to select it. Click **frmProduct** on the Navigation Pane, and then drag it to the [Add New] vertical tab. Continue by adding **rptProductInventory**, **rptPurchasesByCategory**, and **rptPurchasesByDate** to each of the next [Add New] vertical tabs.

l. Click the **frmProduct vertical tab**. Press and hold Shift, and then click **rptPurchasesByDate**. Click the **Format tab**, click **Change Shape** in the Control Formatting group, and click **Snip Single Corner Rectangle**. Click **frmProduct**, click the **Format tab**, click **Quick Styles** in the Control Formatting group, and then click **Colored Fill - Gray 25%, Accent 4**. Click **rptProductInventory**, press and hold Shift, and click **rptPurchasesByDate**. Click the **Format tab**, click **Quick Styles** in the Control Formatting group, and click **Colored Fill - Brown, Accent 3**.

m. Double-click the **frmProduct tab**, select the text, and rename the tab Products. Change the remaining tab names to Product Inventory, Purchases By Category, and Purchases By Date.

n. Click the **Customers horizontal tab**, and then click the **Customer vertical tab**. Click the **Design tab**, click **View** in the Views group, and select **Design View**. Click the **Design tab**, click **Button** in the Controls group, and then click in the top-left corner of the form Detail to add the button.

o. In the Categories list verify **Record Navigation** is selected, in the Actions list click to select **Find Record**, and then click **Next**. Click **Text**, select the text, change it by typing Find Customer, and click **Next**. Name the button cmdFindCustomer, and then click **Finish**.

p. Click the **Design tab**, click **Button** in the Controls group, and click next to and to the right of the first button. In the Categories list click **Record Operations**, in the Actions list click **Add New Record**, and then click **Next**. Click **Text**, select the text, change it by typing Add New Customer, and click **Next**. Name the button cmdAddNewCustomer, and then click **Finish**.

q. Repeat to add two more buttons: **Next Customer** (click the **Record Navigation** category and **Go To Next Record** action; the text should say Next Customer and the button named cmdNextCustomer) and **Previous Customer** (click the **Record Navigation** category and **Go To Previous Record** action; the text should say Previous Customer and the button named cmdPreviousCustomer).

r. Click the first button to select it. Press and hold Shift, and then click to select the remaining three buttons. Click the **Arrange tab**, click **Align** in the Sizing & Ordering group, and click **Top**. Click the **Arrange tab**, click **Size/Space** in the Sizing & Ordering group, and click **Equal Horizontal**.

s. Click the **Design tab**, click **Button** in the Controls group, and click to the right of the First Initial Lastname text label in the **Form Header**. In the Categories list, click **Application**, and then in the Actions list, click **Quit Application**. Click **Next**, click **Text**, select the text and type Exit Database, and then click **Next**. Name the button cmdExitDatabase, and then click **Finish**. Switch to **Form view**.

t. Click **Exit Database** to check your button. Click **Yes** to save the changes. Start **Access**, and then open **Lastname_Firstname_a06_ws11_Painted_Treasures**. In the Navigation Pane, double-click **frmCustomer** to open the form. Switch to **Layout view**. Click the **Design tab**, and then click **Property Sheet** in the Tools group. Under Selection type, click the **selection arrow**, and click **Form**.

u. Click the **Format tab** in the Property Sheet window. Find **Record Selectors**, click the **selection arrow**, and click **No**. Find **Navigation Buttons**, click the **selection arrow**, and click **No**. **Close** the Property Sheet window, close the form, and then click **Yes** to save the changes.

v. Click the **File tab**, click **Options**, and then click **Current Database**. In the Application Options section, click in the **Application Title** text box, and then type Painted Treasures Database.

w. Click the **Display Form selection arrow**, click **frmPaintedTreasuresNavigation_initial Lastname**. Click the **Compact on Close** check box. In the Navigation section, clear the **Display Navigation Pane** check box. Click **OK** to close the Access Options window. Click **OK** again, and then exit Access.

Objectives

1. Modify database settings for protection from macro viruses.   p. 546

2. Understand the Macro Designer.   p. 548

3. Understand how to test and troubleshoot macros.   p. 553

4. Improve database design and function by automating manual processes.   p. 557

5. Reduce processing time by combining routine tasks.   p. 559

6. Create macro groups.   p. 562

7. Create macros that run when the database opens.   p. 566

8. Increase functionality of forms and reports. p. 569

9. Implement complex business rules with data macros.   p. 573

Creating a Refined User Experience

PREPARE CASE

The Turquoise Oasis Spa Database Automates Tasks and Increases Functionality

Employees of the Turquoise Oasis Spa use the company database to store employee and customer information, record transactions, track inventory, schedule spa services, produce reports, and so on. The spa continues to experience growth, offering new products, services, and catering to more and more clients. It has become apparent that the current database no longer meets the needs of the business. You have been asked to automate some routine tasks to increase the efficiency of the database and create additional functionality to improve the overall usability of the database.

Courtesy of www.Shutterstock.com

Student data files needed for this workshop:

 a06_ws12_Spa

 a06_ws12_Spa_Products

You will save your files as:

 Lastname_Firstname_a06_ws12_Spa

 Lastname_Firstname_rptLowInventory

 Lastname_Firstname_rptScheduleByCustomer

Understanding the Purpose of Macros

A well-designed database application takes, among other things, efficiency and usability into consideration. Macros can help increase both the efficiency and the usability of a database. **Macros** are database objects that provide a method of automating routine database tasks. They can add functionality to reports and forms, as well as the controls that forms and reports contain.

There are three different kinds of macros in Microsoft Access: stand-alone, embedded, and data macros. **Stand-alone macros** are separate database objects that are displayed in the Navigation Pane. Stand-alone macros can be executed directly from the Navigation Pane by double-clicking the macro object, clicking Run in Design view, or by attaching the macro to a database object, like a button or text field. **Embedded macros** are stored as part of a database object such as a form or report or any control like a button. Embedded macros are not displayed in the Navigation Pane and are only executed when the objects they are embedded in trigger events. **Data macros** are stored in Access tables and are triggered by table events. Data macros are typically used to implement business logic into tables and automatically set values in fields. In this section you will learn the purpose of macros as well as how to build, edit, and troubleshoot them.

Modify Database Settings for Protection from Macro Viruses

Turquoise Oasis Spa collects and stores personal information about its clients in the database, such as addresses, phone numbers, and credit card information. Ensuring that this personal information is kept safe and secure is very important to the company. Before explaining how to create macros in the database, it is important to discuss some of the security risks associated with macros and what steps can be taken to mitigate those risks.

A macro is a sequence of commands that run automatically, and as mentioned above they can increase efficiency and usability of a database. However, the sequence of commands can also be harmful when executed. Harmful macros have been known to add, edit, or remove data from a database and often spread to other databases or even to the user's computer.

Creating a Trusted Location

To protect the data in the database from a macro virus, you have been asked to create a Trusted Location to store the Turquoise Oasis Spa database files while mitigating the risk of attack. A **Trusted Location** is typically a folder on your hard disk or a network share. Any file that you put in a trusted location can be opened without being checked by the Trust Center security feature.

To Add a Trusted Location

a. Click the **Start** button, and then click **Access 2010**.

b. Click the **File tab**, and then click **Options**.

c. Click **Trust Center** on the left, and then click **Trust Center Settings**.

d. Click **Trusted Locations** on the left side of the Trust Center dialog box, and then click **Add new location**.

e. Click **Browse** to navigate to the directory containing your files and click **OK**.

f. Click the **Subfolders of this location are also trusted** check box to ensure that all databases in the directory are trusted.

g. Click **OK** to close the Trusted Locations dialog box.

h. Click **OK** to close the Trust Center menu, and then click **OK** to close the Options menu.

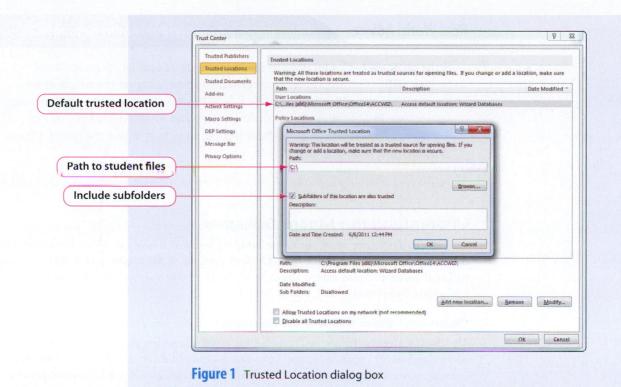

Default trusted location

Path to student files

Include subfolders

Figure 1 Trusted Location dialog box

Quick Reference — Macro Settings

Macro Settings are part of the Trust Center Settings and can be modified based on the needs of the organization. Below are the setting options and their descriptions.

Setting	Description
Disable all macros without notification	All macros and security alerts about macros are disabled.
Disable all macros with notification	This is the default setting. Disables all macros and provides security alerts if there are macros present.
Disable all macros except digitally signed macros	This setting is the same as the Disable all macros with notification option, except that the macro is digitally signed by a trusted publisher.
Enable all macros	Allows all macros to run, this setting makes your computer vulnerable to potentially malicious code and is not recommended.

Figure 2 Macro settings and descriptions

If the database is in a location defined as a Trusted Location, the macros will be ignored by the Trust Center security system. Depending on the nature of the organization, the policy may be to disable all macros. However, the most common settings are Disable all macros with notification and Disable all macros except digitally signed macros. Both of these settings help to mitigate the risk of a macro virus and still allow useful macros to run.

Understand the Macro Designer

The **Macro Designer** is an editor for building macros. In Access 2010, the macro interface has been completely revamped from previous versions of Microsoft Access. The new interface makes it easier to build robust database applications, increase productivity of business users, and reduce code errors.

Open and View the Macro Designer

The management of Turquoise Oasis Spa has asked you to improve the usability and efficiency of the database by creating macros. To create macros you must use the Macro Designer. In this exercise, you will familiarize yourself with the Macro Designer and all of its components.

To View the Macro Designer

a. Click the **File tab**, click **Open**, and browse to your student data files. Locate and select **a06_ws12_Spa**, and then click **Open**.

Troubleshooting

Be sure you have added your class files folder and subfolders as a Trusted Location as previously discussed before moving forward. If using a computer lab, changes to the Trust Center may not be allowed due to security settings.

b. Click the **File tab**, click **Save Database As**, browse to where you are storing your files, name your database Lastname_Firstname_a06_ws12_Spa replacing Lastname_Firstname with your actual name, and then click **Save**.

c. Right-click **mcrSampleMacro**, and then click **Design View** ⬚.

This mcrSampleMacro is a simple macro consisting of two actions. When executed, the macro will perform the OpenReport action, opening the rptEmployeeList report, and then it will send the report to the printer using the RunMenuCommand action.

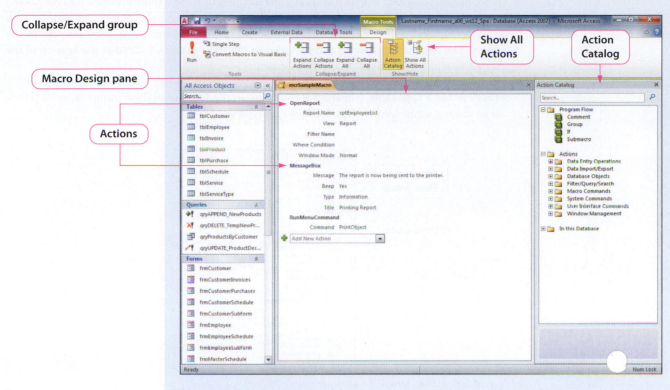

Figure 3 Macro Designer

As shown in Figure 3 the Macro Design pane consists of all the actions and logic that make up the macro. An **Action** is a self-contained instruction that can be combined with others to automate tasks and is considered to be the basic building block of macros. Actions can be added to the macro by simply selecting one from the Add New Action list or by searching the Action Catalog shown on the right side of Figure 3. The **Action Catalog** is a searchable set of macro actions that can retrieve actions based on keywords. The Action Catalog consists of three different groups: Program Flow, Actions, and In this Database.

The Program Flow group contains a list of blocks that can control the order that actions are executed or help structure the macro.

Block Name	Purpose
Comment	A form of internal documentation that can help explain the purpose of the macro.
Group	Allows for actions and program flow to be part of a named group to better organize the view of the macro in the Macro Designer. The group can be collapsed, expanded, and moved together.
If	Implements logic into a macro that will execute actions based on whether or not a condition is true. If program flow can be used to incorporate complex business rules into the database.
Submacro	Allows for a named collection of actions to be grouped together. Submacros can be incorporated into other macros by using the RunMacro or OnError actions but cannot be executed directly from the Navigation Pane.

Figure 4 A list of Program Flow blocks

The Actions group contains several different categories of actions grouped together based on purpose and function that can be used to build a macro. As the mouse hovers over each action group and action, Access displays a ScreenTip that explains the general purpose of the object. The same information is also provided in the Help window located at the bottom of the Action Catalog when an action or action group is selected.

The In this Database group contains all macros in the database. Macros can be reused inside other macros if applicable. The macros contained in the In this Database group includes stand-alone macros, embedded macros, but not data macros.

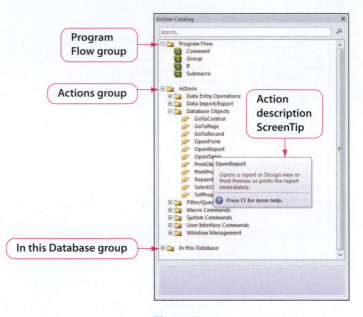

Figure 5 Action Catalog

Editing a Macro

Even a simple macro like mcrSampleMacro can be improved to create a better user experience. In this exercise, you will improve the macro by adding a comment that explains the purpose of the macro and an additional action that displays a message box informing the user that the report is being sent to the printer.

To Edit the Macro

a. Drag **Comment** from the Program Flow group in the Action Catalog to the top of the Macro Design pane, above the OpenReport macro action.

b. Type the following text in the comment field: **Edited by Firstname Lastname. This macro opens the Employee List Report and sends it to the printer.** Replace Firstname and Lastname with your first and last name.

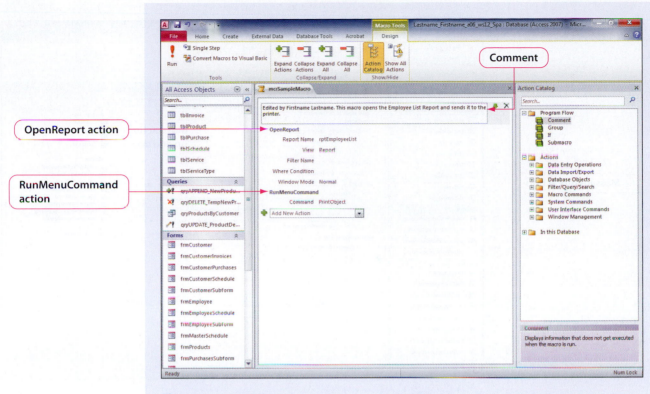

OpenReport action

RunMenuCommand action

Comment

Figure 6 mcrSampleMacro macro

c. Click **Add New Action arrow** just below the RunMenuCommand action, and then select **MessageBox** from the list of actions.

Troubleshooting

If the Action Catalog is not visible on the right, you can toggle between showing or hiding it by clicking the Action Catalog button in the Show/Hide group located on the right of the Design tab.

d. Type The report is now being sent to the printer. in the Message field.

e. Select **Yes** for Beep and **Information** for Type.

f. Type Printing Report as the Title of the message box.

g. Click the **Move up arrow** located at the far right of the MessageBox to move the action above theRunMenuCommand action. This will cause the message box to be displayed before the report is sent to the printer.

SIDE NOTE

Adding Actions to a Macro

Alternatively, you could search for the MessageBox macro in the Action Catalog and either double-click the action or drag it to the macro.

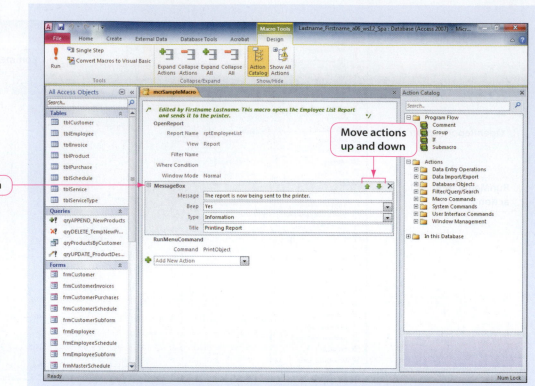

Figure 7 mcrSampleMacro edited

SIDE NOTE

Moving Actions in a Macro

Actions can also be moved around by dragging them to the desired location.

h. Save 🖫 the changes made to mcrSampleMacro.

i. To test the changes made to the macro, click **Run** to execute the macro, and then **close** ☒ the employee list report when finished.

Printing a Macro

Management at Turquoise Oasis Spa likes to document any changes made to the databases in case of an audit. You have been asked to print out the mcrSampleMacro that was just modified. Printing macros can also be helpful in analyzing the logic when troubleshooting by allowing the user to examine the printout for errors or inefficiencies.

To Print a Macro

a. With the mcrSampleMacro opened in Design view, click the **File tab**, and then click **Print**.

b. Click **Print** 🖨, click to check all **check boxes** in the Print Macro Definition dialog box, and then click **OK**.

SIDE NOTE

Alternate Method of Printing Macros

Alternatively, macros can be printed by clicking the Database Tools tab on the Ribbon, clicking Database Documenter in the Analyze group, clicking the Macros tab, and then clicking the macros check box to be printed.

Figure 8 Print Macro Definition dialog box

c. Close ☒ the macro.

In addition to the actions and arguments that make up mcrSampleMacro, the printout also includes the database name, directory path, date, and some additional information.

Real World Advice — Sharing and Backing up Macros

Both the number and complexity of macros can grow over time as the business grows and needs change. A new feature in Access 2010 allows a macro to be copied from the Macro Designer and pasted into a text editor as XML to save as a backup or to share with others. The XML then can be copied easily from the text editor and pasted directly into the Macro Designer. To copy the macro quickly, with the macro opened in Design view, on the Design tab, click Expand All in the Collapse/Expand group, press Ctrl+a to Select All, press Ctrl+c to Copy. The macro can then be pasted into any text editor for storing or sharing.

Understand How to Test and Troubleshoot Macros

Macros can get to be very complex with multiple steps and logic built in. Figuring out which actions are causing the macro to result in an error can be a tedious task. The **Single Step** feature is located next to the Run button on the Design tab in the Tools group; it allows you to observe the flow of a macro and the results of each action, isolating any action that causes an error or produces unwanted results.

When the Single Step feature is turned on, the macro executes one action at a time and pauses between actions. After each action the Macro Single Step dialog box appears that shows the name of the macro, the value of any conditions, the name of the action about to be executed, and the arguments for the action. In addition to this information, the dialog box also provides three choices on what to do next:

- Step executes the action shown in the dialog box.
- Stop All Macros stops all actions in the macro and closes the dialog box.
- Continue resumes normal operation of the macro and exits the single step process.

Single Stepping Through a Macro

An employee of Turquoise Oasis Spa had attempted to create a macro that would open the frmCustomer form, create a new record, and place the pointer in the first name field. However, the macro is not working properly, and you have been asked to troubleshoot and fix the macro. You will be using the Single Step feature to assist you in the process.

To Single Step a Macro

a. Right-click the **mcrTroubleShootingExample** macro, and then click **Design View** ☑.

b. Click the **Design tab**, click the **Single Step** button in the Tools group, and then click **Run**.
Notice the Macro Single Step dialog box and all of the information displayed. The macro name is at the top along with the action name toward the bottom. Just below the action name are the arguments for the action. This is a MessageBox action that displays a message to the user. To the right is an Error Number of 0. This means there is no error detected with this action.

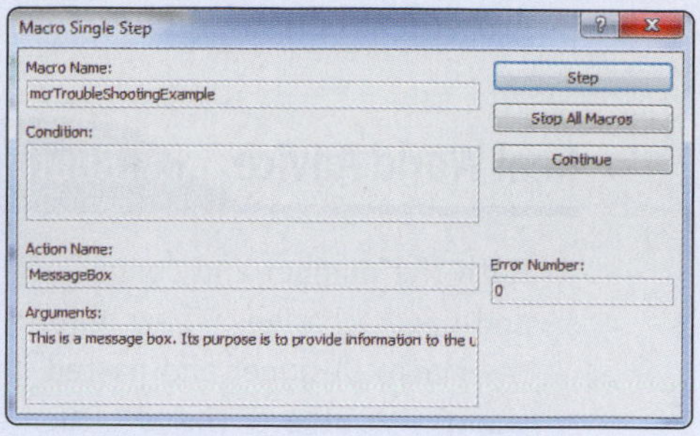

Figure 9 Macro Single Step MessageBox action

SIDE NOTE

Macro Paused with MessageBox Action

When the MessageBox action is executed the macro is paused so the message can be displayed. You need to click **OK** in order for the macro to continue.

c. Click **Step** to execute the MessageBox action, and then click **OK** to close the message box.

d. The next action is the GoToRecord action with an Error Number: 1 that indicates there is an error. Click **Step** to execute this action to get additional information.

e. An information dialog box is displayed with information about the GoToRecord action. The second statement provides some useful information. "The type of object the action applies to isn't currently selected or isn't in the active view."

Figure 10 Error message for GoToControl action

f. Click **OK**. The Macro Single Step now provides only the option to Stop All Macros so that the GoToRecord action error can be addressed. Click **Stop All Macros**.

   Notice the order of the actions in the macro. This macro has been designed to go to a specific record and then a specific field in that record before the form is even opened. The error message that was displayed indicates that this is the root cause of macro failure.

g. Click the **Move up arrow** twice in the OpenForm action to move it so it is above the GoToRecord action and below the MessageBox action.

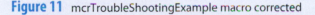

OpenForm action correct location

Figure 11 mcrTroubleShootingExample macro corrected

h. Save 🖫 the change and go through the Single Step process again to ensure there are no additional errors with the macro.

i. Click the **Single Step** button to turn off the Single Step feature, and then close ☒ the macro.

j. Double-click the **mcrTroubleShootingExample** macro in the Navigation Pane to run it and ensure the macro runs as expected.

Troubleshooting

If the Single Step feature is on when the macro ends, then it remains on. If you run another macro, it will automatically display the Macro Single Step dialog box again. To turn single stepping off, click Continue in the dialog box or on the Design tab, in the Tools group, click the Single Step button so it is not highlighted.

Real World Advice   Single Stepping Macros

If part of your macro is functioning correctly then you can begin single stepping at a specific point in the macro by adding the SingleStep macro action at the point where you wish to begin single stepping.

Real World Advice — Error Codes in Macros

Error codes provided in the single step feature and informational dialog boxes do not always provide enough information to resolve the error. If you receive an error, rest assured that many other people have experienced the same error themselves. There are many forums online that can be used to find solutions to common database errors, such as **http://answers.microsoft.com/en-us/office/forum/office_2010-access**.

Increase Efficiency and Usability of a Database by Automating Tasks

As mentioned above, macros can be used to increase the efficiency of a database by combining and automating tasks. Macros are composed of actions that often contain logic to determine when and how to perform the action. By combining various macro actions with program flow logic, routine tasks can be performed with a simple click of the mouse. In this section you will build macros that will improve the user experience and reduce processing time by automating processes and combining tasks.

Quick Reference — Common Macro Actions

Action Name	Description
ApplyFilter	Applies a filter to a table, form, or report to restrict or sort the records in the object
AutoExec	An AutoExec macro is a macro that is named AutoExec. It is automatically executed when the database is opened.
Beep	Produces a beep tone through the computer's speakers
CloseWindow	Closes the specified window, or the active window if none is specified
DisplayHourglassPointer	Provides a visual indication that the macro is running
ExportWithFormatting	Outputs the data in the specified database object to several output formats
FindRecord	Finds the first record, or the next record if the action is used again, that meets a specified criteria
GoToControl	Moves the focus to a specified field or control on the active datasheet or form
MessageBox	Displays a message box containing a warning or informational message
OpenForm	Opens a form in a specified view—Design, Form, Layout
OpenReport	Opens a report in a specified view—Design, Print Preview, Report
QuitAccess	Exits Microsoft Access
RunMacro	Runs a macro
SelectObject	Selects a specified object so you can run an action that applies to the object

Figure 12 Common macro actions and descriptions

Improve Database Design and Function by Automating Manual Processes

The management at the Turquoise Oasis Spa frequently requests copies of a report that lists the customers who have scheduled services for a particular date. The current process consists of looking through the report and copying the information for the date requested into a word processor before sending it to management.

This process takes too much time and is prone to errors because the information is being copied manually from one location to another. A macro can automate the process and reduce the risk of errors.

Exporting Database Objects Using Macros

In this exercise, you will create a macro that opens the desired report, applies a filter to only show the information for services on a particular date, and exports the report as a PDF-formatted file.

To Create a Macro

a. Click the **Create tab**, and then click **Macro** in the Macros & Code group.

b. Add a comment to the macro by double-clicking **Comment** in the Program Flow group of the Action Catalog.

c. Type the following text for the comment: Created by Firstname Lastname. Macro applies a filter to the customer schedule report and exports the report as a PDF. Replace Firstname and Lastname with your first and last name.

Troubleshooting

By default the Action Catalog and Add New Action combo box only show actions that execute in nontrusted databases. To see all actions, click **Show All Actions** in the **Show/Hide** group on the Design tab.

d. Click the **Add New Action arrow**, and then select **OpenReport** from the list of actions to add the action to the macro.

e. Select **rptScheduleByCustomer** for the report name, and then select **Report** for the View argument.

f. In the **Where Condition** argument, type the following expression: [DateOfAppt]=[Enter a date of service, Example (5/2/2013)]. This expression uses the field that stores the appointment date and prompts the user for a date to use as criteria for the filter. The message "Enter a date of service, Example (5/2/2013)" will be displayed in a parameter box when the macro is executed.

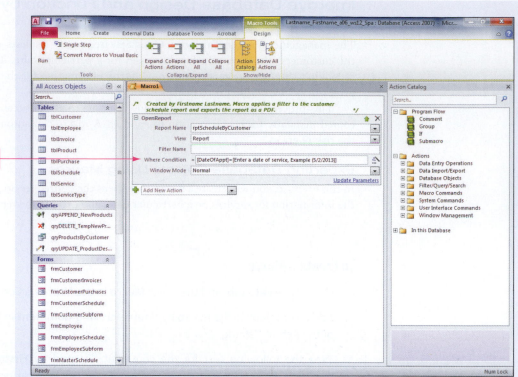

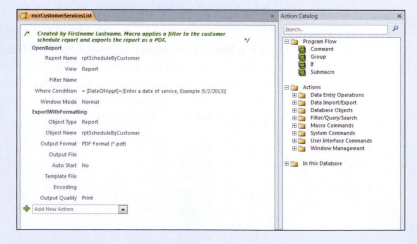

Figure 13 mcrCustomerServicesList macro in progress

SIDE NOTE
Where Condition and Filters

Alternatively, a parameter query could be created, prompting the user for a service date. The query name then could be entered into the Filter Name field.

SIDE NOTE
Output File

A file path and name can be entered in the Output File argument, such as C:\Reports\ CustomerSchedule.pdf, if a specific location has been determined to export reports.

g. Click the **Add New Action arrow**, and then select **ExportWithFormatting** from the list of actions to add the action to the macro.

h. Select **Report** for the Object Type, and then select **rptScheduleByCustomer** for the Object Name.

i. Select **PDF Format (*.pdf)** as the Output Format.

j. Leave the Output File argument blank, and keep all other arguments the same.

k. Save 🖫 the macro as **mcrCustomerServicesList**.

Figure 14 mcrCustomerServicesList macro completed

l. To test the macro, click **Run**, type **1/19/2013** in the Enter Parameter Value dialog box, and then click **OK**.

m. Save 💾 the report to your student files as **Lastname_Firstname_rptScheduleByCustomer**, replacing Lastname_Firstname with your actual name. Open the report to view the results.

n. Close the report, and then close the macro.

CONSIDER THIS | **Exporting with an Appropriate File Type**

There are several different output file types to consider when exporting database objects using macros. Some of the most commonly used output types are

- XLSX
- PDF
- HTML
- XML

What are some of the things you should take into consideration when deciding which file type to export?

Real World Advice

Comments Make Macros Easier to Understand and Maintain

Comments that describe the purpose of a macro or complex program flows are considered best practice but are many times neglected by database programmers. Appropriate comments that provide useful information about the macro and its purpose can be extremely valuable to the organization. They also can save time if a new employee is required to take over the database design and programming.

Reduce Processing Time by Combining Routine Tasks

Turquoise Oasis Spa routinely adds new products to meet the demands of their clients. When new products are acquired the information is sent in a spreadsheet with the product name and other information. This data needs to be entered into the database and is currently done manually by copying and pasting.

Automating an Import-and-Update Process

In this exercise, you will develop a macro that will automate the process of importing new products into the database by executing a query that will convert the product name to proper case and then append the modified records to the products table.

You will be adding several actions to this macro that will import the data from a spreadsheet into a temporary table, and then the data will need to be cleaned by executing an update query. The cleaned data then will be added to the products table by executing an append query. Finally, the data will be removed from the temporary table by executing a delete query.

Macros can be used to automate complex sets of actions. It is important to carefully think through all the actions that a macro will be executing to complete the tasks before beginning work on creating the macro. Taking the time to create a process flow that describes the actions and reasons for those actions can save time and reduce the chance of errors.

Step	Purpose	Specifics
Import new records to a temporary table	To update the list of products	The new product list needs to be modified before importing it into the tblProduct table.
Set warning messages off	To suppress common data-base warnings	Before action queries are executed Access issues warnings and prompts that require a user response.
Run the qryUPDATE_ ProductDescription query	To clean the data imported	Converts all product names to proper case.
Run qryAPPEND_ NewProducts	To append new products to the tblProduct table	Appends newly modified data into the tblProduct table.
Run qryDELETE_ TempNewProducts	To delete the contents of the temp table	Prevents excess data from being stored in a temporary table.

Figure 15 Process flow table example

To Automate Processes with a Macro

a. Click the **Create tab**, and then click **Macro** in the Macros & Code group.

b. Drag the **Comment** from the Program Flow group in the Action Catalog to the macro. Type the following text in the comment field: Created by Firstname Lastname. This macro automates the process of importing new products into the products table. Replace Firstname and Lastname with your first and last name.

c. Click the **Add New Action arrow**, and then select **ImportExportSpreadsheet** from the list of actions to add the action to the macro. Select **Import** as the Transfer Type and **Excel Workbook** as the Spreadsheet Type.

Troubleshooting

If the ImportExportSpreadsheet action is not available be sure to click Show All Actions in the Show/Hide group on the Design tab. Each time Access is closed the action list is restored to only showing macros that are allowed in databases that have not been trusted regardless of changes made to the Trust Center settings.

d. For the Table Name argument, type tblTempNewProducts.

e. The File Name field must include the complete path to the file being imported. Navigate to the student files using Windows Explorer, click in the address bar of the Windows Explorer, and with the path selected press Ctrl+C to copy and Ctrl+V to paste the path. After you paste the path in the File Name field, click at the end of the path and type to add the following: \a06_ws12_Spa_Products.xlsx, into the File Name argument.

f. In the **Has Field Names** argument, select **Yes**.

g. Click the **Add New Action arrow**, select **SetWarnings** from the list of actions to the macro, click the **Warnings On** argument, and if necessary, select **No**.

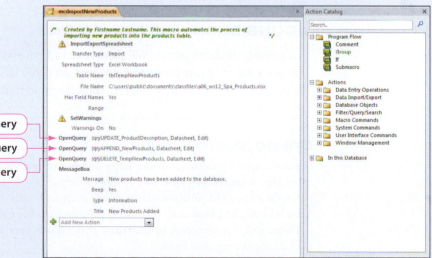

Complete path to and name of file being imported (yours may differ)

Set warning notifications to No

Figure 16 mcrImportNewProducts macro in progress

h. Select **OpenQuery** from the Add New Action list. You will be selecting to run an action query that will update the new product's names from all capital letters to all proper case so the product names are formatted consistently throughout the table.

i. Select **qryUPDATE_ProductDescription** for the Query Name argument. Select **Datasheet** for the View argument, and then select **Edit** for the Data Mode argument.

j. Add another **OpenQuery** action to this macro. Select **qryAPPEND_NewProducts** for the Query Name, select **Datasheet** for View, and then select **Edit** for Data Mode. This action will execute the append query that will add the modified products to the product table.

k. Add another **OpenQuery** action to this macro. Select **qryDELETE_TempNewProducts** for the Query Name, select **Datasheet** for View, and then select **Edit** for Data Mode. This action will execute the delete query that will remove the products from the temp table.

l. Add the **MessageBox** action to this macro. Type **New products have been added to the database.** as the Message, and then select **Yes** for the Beep argument to have the computer produce a sound from its speakers.

m. Select **Information** for the Message Box Type, and then type **New Products Added** as the Title.

n. Save 💾 this macro as **mcrImportNewProducts**.

Run Update query

Run Append query

Run Delete query

Figure 17 mcrImportNewProducts macro completed

o. Close ☒ the macro.

p. Open the **tblProduct** table to view the current list of products. Close ☒ the tblProduct table.

q. To test the macro, double-click **mcrImportNewProducts** in the Navigation Pane.

r. Click **OK** when prompted by the message box, open the products table, and then view the added records. Close ☒ the products table.

Troubleshooting

Upon running this macro, if you get an error message stating "The Microsoft Access database engine could not find the object" then you most likely entered the file path incorrectly in the File Name field in the first action. Verify the path and file name are correct.

Real World Advice | **SetWarnings Action**

The SetWarnings action is used often to suppress modal warning messages when performing various tasks like running update queries and delete queries. A **modal message** is a window or dialog box that requires the user to take some action before the focus can switch to another form or dialog box. This action must be used with caution as some warnings do provide helpful information, and the option to not perform a particular action could cause irreversible damage to the data.

The SetWarnings action does not prevent an error message from displaying if the error forces the macro to stop running. For example, if a file with sales data was incorrectly named and placed in the same directory the macro would fail with the first action.

CONSIDER THIS | **Preventing Errors**

A properly designed process will prevent users from making errors. What would happen if you tried to import the same file more than once? What role would the primary or composite key play in that process? What if warnings are turned off?

Create Macro Groups

Creating macro groups can make large number of macros in a database easier to manage and maintain. A **macro group** is two or more submacros that are similar in function, placed inside the same macro file. When a macro group is created, only the name appears in the Navigation Pane regardless of how many submacros it contains. For example a macro group could contain a submacro for every report in a database that exports and or prints each report and only appear once in the Navigation Pane.

Although Access does not require the submacros in a macro group to be similar, it is best practice to create logical groups based on function and purpose when creating them. When a macro group is executed directly from the Navigation Pane or by clicking Run in Design view, only the first submacro is executed. The most common way to run a submacro is to assign it to an event on a form or report.

You can also run submacros by creating an AutoKeys macro. An **AutoKeys macro** is a macro group that assigns keys on the keyboard to execute each submacro. The macro must be named AutoKeys, and each submacro must be named with the key or key combinations on the keyboard that will be used to execute the macros. To name a key-assignment macro, use ^ to indicate Ctrl, + for Shift, and { } around key names that are more than one letter long. You are restricted to numbers, letters, Insert, Delete, and the function keys, used in conjunction with Shift and Ctrl. If the key assignment is a combination that normally does something else, then the submacro key assignment will override the normal function; for example, Ctrl+F, which normally calls the Find and Replace dialog box, would no longer work if you created a new macro with the same key combination.

Quick Reference — Key-Assignments

Key	Macro Syntax
F5	{F5}
Ctrl+r	^r
Shift+F3	+{F3}
Insert	{INS}
Ctrl+F2	^{F2}
Delete	{DEL}

Figure 18 Keys and syntax for use in AutoKeys macro

Creating a Macro Group

The Turquoise Oasis Spa database contains several reports that provide information related to employee schedules, inventory, and client services. These reports are often printed and shared with members of management. You have been asked to create a macro group that will automate the steps of opening each report, sending it to the printer, and then closing the report.

To Create a Macro Group

a. Click the **Create tab**, and then click **Macro** in the Macros & Code group.

b. Add a Comment to the macro from the Program Flow group in the Action Catalog.

c. Type the following text in the comment: **Created by Firstname Lastname. The following macro group will open specific reports, send them to printer, and then close the reports.** Replace Firstname and Lastname with your first and last name.

d. Double-click **Submacro** from the Program Flow group in the Action Catalog to add it to the macro, and then type **PrintEmployeeSchedule** in the first argument labeled **Submacro:** to give it a name.

e. Add the **OpenReport** action to the PrintEmployeeSchedule submacro, select **rptEmployeeSchedule** for the Report Name, select **Report** for the View argument, and then select **Normal** for Window Mode.

f. Add the **RunMenuCommand** action to the PrintEmployeeSchedule submacro, and then select **PrintObject** for the Command argument.

g. Add the **CloseWindow** action to the PrintEmployeeSchedule submacro, select **Report** as Object Type, select **rptEmployeeSchedule** for Object Name, and select **No** for the Save argument. Because you are not editing the report, there are no changes that need to be saved.

SIDE NOTE
Submacro Names

Each submacro in a macro group must have a unique name.

SIDE NOTE
PrintObject

Alternatively, if you search for and add PrintObject to the macro it will automatically insert the RunMenuCommand action and select PrintObject as the Command.

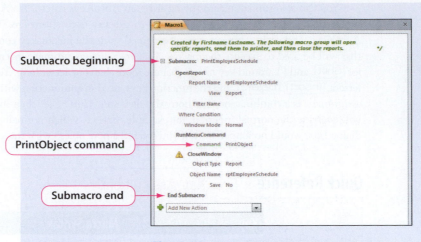

Submacro beginning

PrintObject command

Submacro end

Figure 19 macro mcrPrintReports in progress

h. Repeat steps e–g to create two more submacros for two additional reports. Create one submacro named **PrintProductInventory** that opens, prints, and closes the rptProducts report. Create another submacro named **PrintCustomerSchedule** that opens, prints, and closes the rptScheduleByCustomer report.

i. Save 💾 the macro as **mcrPrintReports**, and then close ✕ the macro.

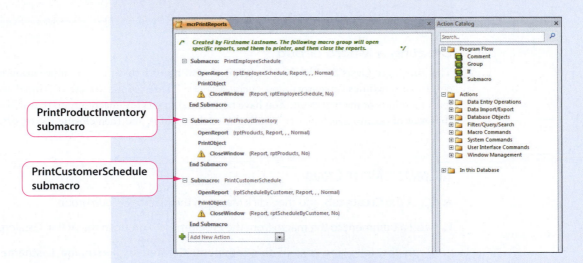

PrintProductInventory submacro

PrintCustomerSchedule submacro

Figure 20 mcrPrintReports macro completed

Real World Advice — Cutting Paper Waste

Today's businesses rely more and more on information contained in reports to make decisions. However, many businesses are cutting waste by exporting reports and having them sent in an e-mail instead of having them printed directly from a database.

Creating a Key-Assignment Macro

Because submacros cannot be executed from the Navigation Pane, you have now been asked to make the process easier by assigning keys to each submacro so that the reports can be printed simply by pressing keys on the keyboard.

To Create a Key-Assignment Macro

a. Right-click the **mcrPrintReports** macro group in the Navigation Pane, select **Copy**, right-click anywhere in Navigation Pane, and then select **Paste** to create a copy of the macro group.

b. Name the copy of the macro group AutoKeys, and then click **OK**. Now that the macro group is saved as AutoKeys, key combinations can be assigned to each submacro so that they can be executed from the keyboard.

c. Open the AutoKeys macro in Design view, and then edit the comment with the following text at the end: **Each submacro will be assigned a set of keys used to execute.**

d. Rename each of the submacros to be the key-combinations that will be used to execute them. Change the submacro name PrintEmployeeSchedule to ^e, PrintProductInventory to ^i, and PrintCustomerSchedule to ^{F1}.

e. Save the changes to the macro group, and then close the macro.

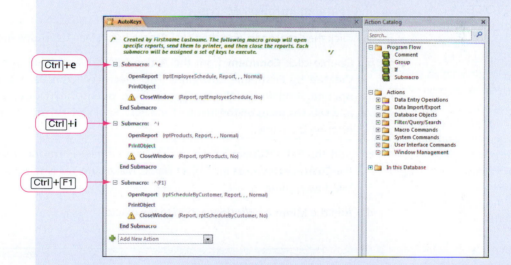

Figure 21 Completed AutoKeys macro

f. Test out the new key-assigned macro group. Press and hold Ctrl and then press **e**, **i**, or F1 to print the employee schedule, inventory, or the customer schedule report.

Troubleshooting

For the AutoKeys macro to run the database, the database may have to be closed and reopened.

Create Macros That Run When the Database Opens

If you want a set of actions to run every time a database is opened, then you can create an AutoExec macro. An **AutoExec macro** is a macro that is named AutoExec. It is automatically executed when the database is opened.

Creating an AutoExec Macro

Every morning, invoice information is entered into the database for any spa service with a remaining balance that has been charged to the customer's hotel room. You have been asked to create an AutoExec macro that will automatically minimize the Navigation Pane for optimal viewing, open the invoice form, go to a new record, and insert the pointer in the InvoiceDate field.

SIDE NOTE

Minimize the Navigation Pane

By selecting Yes for the In Database Window argument of the SelectObject action you are selecting the object in the Navigation Pane and making the Navigation Pane the active window. The MinimizeWindow action minimizes the active window, which in this case is now the Navigation Pane.

To Create an AutoExec Macro

a. Click the **Create tab**, and then click **Macro** in the Macros & Code group.

b. Double-click **Comment** from the Action Catalog, and then type the following text: **Created by Firstname Lastname. This macro will run each time the database is opened. It minimizes the Navigation Pane, opens the Invoice form in a new record, and sets the focus on the Invoice Date field.** Replace Firstname and Lastname with your first and last name.

c. Add the **SelectObject** action to the macro, select **Form** for Object Type, and select **frmCustomerInvoices** for Object Name. Make sure **Yes** is selected for the In Database Window argument.

d. Add the **MinimizeWindow** action to the macro.

Navigation Pane

Minimize Navigation Pane

Figure 22 AutoExec macro in progress

e. Add the **OpenForm** action to the macro, and then select **frmCustomerInvoices** in the Form Name argument.

f. Select **Form** for the View argument, select **Edit** for the Data Mode argument so that data can be entered and/or modified, and then select **Normal** for Window Mode.

g. Add the **GoToRecord** action to the macro. Select **Form** as Object Type, select **frmCustomerInvoices** as Object Name, and select **New** for the Record argument in order to go to a new record in the form.

h. Add the **GoToControl** action to the macro. Type InvoiceDate as the Control Name.

i. Save the macro as AutoExec, click **OK**, and then close the macro.

j. To test the AutoExec macro, close and reopen the database. Notice the Navigation Pane is minimized, the frmCustomerInvoices form is opened, and the pointer is in the InvoiceDate field.

SIDE NOTE

Bypassing AutoExec Macro

Now that this database contains a macro named AutoExec, it will automatically execute the macro every time the database is opened. An AutoExec macro can be bypassed by holding down Shift when opening the database.

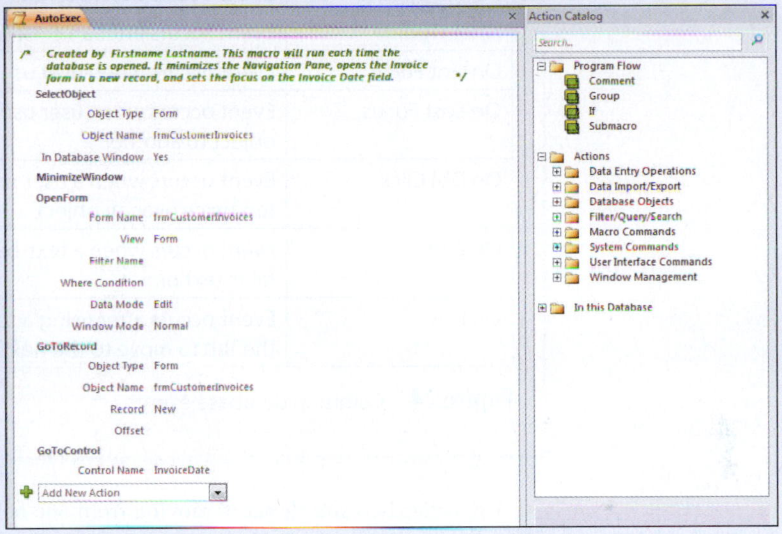

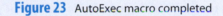

Figure 23 AutoExec macro completed

k. Close the customer invoice form.

The Benefits of Embedded Macros

The macros created so far have all been stand-alone macros that can either be executed directly from the Navigation Pane, by opening the macro in Design view and clicking Run, by assigning keys, or by having the macro execute when the database opens. Embedded macros can be used to create a better user experience and increase the functionality of a database.

Embedded macros are triggered by database events. A **database event** occurs when an action is completed on any given object. The action could be, for example, a simple click of the mouse or entering information into a specific field. When the specific event occurs the macro executes the actions.

Common Events and Descriptions

There are many different events that occur in a database. Below is a table of the most common events used to increase the effectiveness of macros and their descriptions.

Event Name	Description
On Click	Event occurs when a user presses and releases the left mouse button over an object
On Open	Event occurs when a form or report is opened
Before Update	Event occurs before an existing record has been modified
After Update	Event occurs after an existing record has been modified
On Got Focus	Event occurs when user uses the Tab to focus on an object
On Lost Focus	Event occurs when user uses the Tab to move the focus from one object to another
On Dbl Click	Event occurs when a user presses and releases the left mouse button twice over an object
On Enter	Event occurs when a text-based control is clicked whether it contains text or not
On Exit	Event occurs after using a text-based control and the user presses the Tab to move to the next control

Figure 24 Common database events

Importantly, a simple act of moving from one field in a form to another field triggers several different database events. Knowing the order the events take place is critical in determining which event to associate a macro with. For example, if you have two macros that are to be run in a certain order, you want to make sure that the events they are associated with occur in that order.

Order of Common Events for Controls

Events occur in form controls when you move the focus to another control or update and change data in a control.

A control is selected.
1. Enter
2. Got Focus

A control is exited.
1. Exit
2. Lost Focus

Data in a text box control is changed.
1. Key Down
2. Key Press
3. Dirty
4. Change
5. Key Up

Data in a control is updated and exited.
1. Before Update
2. After Update
3. Exit
4. Lost Focus

Figure 25 Order of control events

In addition to events associated with controls, such as text boxes and command buttons, there are many events associated with mouse activity. In this section you will build macros that are event driven to create a more interactive user experience with a database.

Quick Reference   Order of Common Mouse Events

Events occur when a mouse button is pressed while the mouse pointer is on a control on a form.

Click on a control.
1. Mouse Down
2. Mouse Up
3. Click

A control has focus, and the mouse selects another control.
1. Exit
2. Lost Focus
3. Enter
4. Got Focus
5. Mouse Down
6. Mouse Up
7. Click

Double-click a control.
1. Mouse Down
2. Mouse Up
3. Click
4. Double-click
5. Mouse Up

Move the mouse pointer over a control.
1. Mouse Move (This event is separate from other mouse events.)

Figure 26 Order of common mouse events

Increase Functionality of Forms and Reports

Forms can also be enhanced by embedding macros into the form or form controls to increase the functionality and improve the user experience. By embedding the macro it becomes portable, and if you export the form into another database any macros embedded will remain with the object.

Embedding a Macro to Improve User Experience

Users of the Turquoise Oasis Spa database currently enter sales information in the frmCustomerPurchases form. If the patron is a returning customer, there is no easy way to locate the customer's record before adding the transaction information. In this exercise, you will first create a Datasheet form from the tblCustomer table, which is ideal for searching. You will then embed a macro into the Datasheet form that will open the frmCustomerPurchases form for the record selected.

To Improve Form Navigation with a Macro

a. Select the **tblCustomer** table in the Navigation Pane.

b. Click the **Create tab**, in the Forms group click **More Forms**, and click **Datasheet** in the list. Notice the new Datasheet form is arranged just like a table.

c. Save 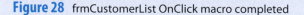 the datasheet form as **frmCustomerList**.

d. Click the column heading **Customer ID** to select the Customer ID column.

e. Click the **Datasheet tab**, and then click **Property Sheet**.

f. Click the **Event tab** in the property sheet, locate the **On Click** event, and then click the **Expression Builder** ⋯.

Figure 27 frmCustomerList Property Sheet

g. Select **Macro Builder**, and then click **OK**.

h. Add a Comment to the macro, and then type the following text: **Created by Firstname Lastname. This embedded macro will open the frmCustomerPurchases form for the Customer ID selected in frmCustomerList**. Replace Firstname and Lastname with your first and last name.

i. Add the **OpenForm** action to the macro, select **frmCustomerPurchases** for Form Name, and then select **Form** for the View argument.

j. Type the following expression in the Where Condition argument:
[CustomerID]=[Forms]![frmCustomerList]![CustomerID]

k. Select **Edit** for Data Mode, and then select **Dialog** for Window Mode.

l. Save 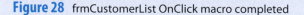 and close ✕ the Macro Builder.

Figure 28 frmCustomerList OnClick macro completed

m. The frmCustomerList form is still open in Datasheet view. Close ☒ the Property Sheet. To test this macro, click Customer ID **CU0-5** in the Customer ID field, and then observe the frmCustomerPurchases form open to the same customer record.

n. Close ☒ both the frmCustomerPurchases form and the frmCustomerList form. Click **Yes** if prompted to save changes.

Embedding a Macro to Increase Functionality

The rptProducts report contains a list of all the product details including the quantity in stock. Management is often asking for the products that are running low so that more can be ordered. Although reports can be filtered by using the Filter feature on the Home tab, it is not a very simple process. In this exercise, you will embed a macro that will apply a filter to the rptProducts report that will prompt the user for a number. The report will then only show the products that have fewer than that number in stock. The report will then be attached to an e-mail that can be sent to the appropriate person(s).

To Increase Functionality with a Macro

a. Open the **rptProducts** report in Design view.

b. Click the **Design tab**, and then click the **Button** control in the Controls group.

c. Click to create a button to the right of the Product List report title in the Report Header. Position the button in between the 5" and 6" markings on the horizontal ruler at the top.

d. Right-click the **Command Button**, and then click **Properties**. Click the **Format tab** on the Property Sheet and change the Caption property to **Low Inventory**.

Figure 29 rptProducts report with Low Inventory Command Button

e. Click the **Event tab**, click in the **On Click** event, and then click the **Expression Builder** ⋯.

f. Select **Macro Builder**, and then click **OK**.

g. Add a Comment to the macro, and then type the following text: Created by Firstname Lastname. This macro will apply a filter to the report, prompting the user for a number. The report will display products with fewer items in stock than the number provided and attach the filtered report to an e-mail. Replace Firstname and Lastname with your first and last name.

h. Add the **SetFilter** action to the macro, and then enter the following expression in the Where Condition argument: [QtyInStock]<[Enter the Maximum Number].

i. Add the **EMailDatabaseObject** action to the macro, select **Report** for Object Type, and then select **rptProducts** for Object Name.

j. Select **Excel 97 - Excel 2003 Workbook (*.xls)** for the output format argument.

k. Leave the To, Cc, and Bcc arguments blank. You may want to enter your own e-mail address in the To argument for testing purposes.

l. Type Low Inventory Report as the Subject.

m. Leave the Message Text argument blank.

n. Select **Yes** for the Edit Message argument. This allows the user to review and/or edit the e-mail before sending.

SIDE NOTE
Message Text Character Limit

The Message Text argument has a 255 character limit, just as a Text data type in tables.

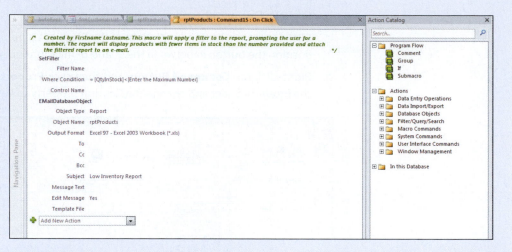

Figure 30 rptProducts Command Button macro completed

o. Save  and close ☒ the macro.

p. To test the macro, view the report in **Report view**, and then click the **Low Inventory** button. Type 25 when prompted for the number and click **OK**.

q. Once your e-mail client is opened, right-click on the attached report and click **Save As**. Browse to where you are storing your files and name the report Lastname_Firstname_ rptLowInventory. Replace Lastname_Firstname with your actual name and click **Save**. Close your e-mail window, close ☒ the report, and click **Yes** to save changes.

Troubleshooting

The EMailDatabaseObject action uses the default e-mail client on the user's computer. This is typically Outlook, Outlook Express, or Thunderbird. The database object being attached to the e-mail is stored in a temporary table that the user must have permissions to access or the object will fail to attach to the e-mail.

Implement Complex Business Rules with Data Macros

Access 2010 offers a new type of macro that can be used to enforce complex business rules in the database. This new type of macro is called a data macro. Data macros are database objects stored in Access tables and are triggered by table events. Data macros are typically used to implement business logic into tables and automatically set values in fields. Since these macros are stored in tables, the logic associated with the macros is automatically applied to any forms or queries that use the tables. This new feature allows for much more complex data validation than before so that complex business rules can be implemented.

There are five different table events that macros can be associated with: Before Change, Before Delete, After Insert, After Update, and After Delete. The table events can be divided into two categories—"Before" events and "After" events. **Before events** occur before any changes are made to the table data, and **After events** occur after the changes have been successfully made. Before events are very simple and only support a few of the data macro actions, whereas the After events are more robust and support the full range of data macro actions.

Importantly, data macros are limited in what they can do as they only have a limited number of data actions available for use. **Data actions** are a specific, limited set of macro actions that can be used in a data macro. Certain data actions are available for certain table events. For example, data macros associated with Before events cannot prevent a record from being updated or deleted. They can only set a local variable or raise an error if conditions warrant.

Quick Reference — Table-Level Events

Event	Description
After Insert	After a new record has been added to this table
After Update	After any field in a record in this table has been updated
After Delete	After a record in this table has been deleted
Before Delete	When a record in this table is about to be deleted
Before Change	When a record in this table is about to be updated

Figure 31 Table events and descriptions

Quick Reference — Common Data Actions

Action	Description
CancelRecordChange	Cancels the changes made to a record before the changes are committed
DeleteRecord	Deletes a record
ExitForEachRecord	Immediately exits a For EachRecord data block
OnError	Can specify what should happen if an error occurs in a macro
RunDataMacro	Runs a named data macros
SendEmail	Sends an e-mail message from a default e-mail client
SetField	Assigns a value to a field; has to be used inside a CreateRecord or EditRecord data block
StopMacro	Stops the currently running macro; typically used when a condition makes it necessary to stop the macro

Figure 32 Common data actions and descriptions

Data macros can incorporate the use of data blocks. **Data blocks** contain an area to add one or more data actions, and it executes all the actions contained as part of its operation. Data blocks are only able to be used with the After events with the exception of the LookupRecord data block, which can also be used with Before events.

Quick Reference — Data Blocks

Data Block	Description
CreateRecord	Actions within this block are used to create a record.
EditRecord	Actions within this block are used to edit a record.
ForEachRecord	Actions within this block will run on each record returned by the query argument.
LookupRecord	Actions within this block will run with the record selected by the query argument.

Figure 33 Different data blocks and descriptions

Creating a Data Macro

Currently when a customer makes a purchase at the spa the employee must manually adjust the inventory levels to indicate the change in the quantity in stock. You have been asked to automate this process to eliminate errors and increase the accuracy of the product inventory. You will be creating a data macro that will be triggered after a record is created in the tblPurchase table and that will deduct the Quantity ordered from the QtyInStock field in the tblProduct table.

SIDE NOTE
Alternate Method to Creating a Data Macro
Alternatively, the table you want to assign a data macro to can be opened in Design view. On the Design tab in the Field, Record & Table Events group, click Create Data Macros, and a list will appear of all the table events.

SIDE NOTE
The Query Argument
SQL Select statements can be entered into this field as well in order to select specific fields from a table, such as *SELECT tblProducts.[ProductID], tblProducts.[QtyInStock] FROM tblProducts;*

To Create a Data Macro

a. Open the **tblPurchase** table in Datasheet view.

b. Click the **Table tab**, and then click the **After Insert** table event in the After Events group.

c. Add a comment to the macro from the Program Flow group in the Action Catalog.

d. Type the following text in the comment: **Data macro created by Firstname Lastname. This macro will update the product inventory when a new record is created in the Purchase table**. Replace Firstname and Lastname with your first and last name.

e. Double-click the **LookupRecord** Data Blocks from the Action Catalog to add it to the macro.

f. Select the **tblProduct** table from the list in the **Look Up A Record In** argument.

g. Type **[tblProduct].[ProductID]=[tblPurchase].[ProductID]** into the Where Condition argument. This statement ensures that the record that will be edited is the record that has the same ProductID as the record being created in the tblPurchase table.

h. Select the **EditRecord** data block from the Add New Action list inside the LookupRecord data block.

i. Add the **SetField** action to the EditRecord data block.

j. Type **tblProduct.QtyInStock** in the Name argument for the field you want to edit.

k. Type the following statement in the Value argument: **[tblProduct].[QtyInStock]-[tblPurchase].[Quantity]**. This will subtract the number of items being purchased from that item's inventory.

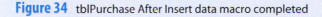

LookupRecord data block

EditRecord data block inside LookupRecord

SetField action inside EditRecord data block

Data Blocks

Data Actions

Figure 34 tblPurchase After Insert data macro completed

SIDE NOTE
Data Actions
Data macros only allow a few data actions and do not include the entire action list that is available in other macros. All Data Actions are displayed in the Action Catalog; however, the actions available for use will depend on whether you are using a Before event or an After event.

SIDE NOTE
The SetField Action
The SetField action can only be used inside of an EditRecord or CreateRecord data block.

l. Save 💾 the macro, close ✕ the Macro Builder, and then close ✕ the tblPurchase table.

m. Open the **tblProduct** table, take note of the quantity in stock for the New Mexico Mud Mask item, and then close ✕ the tblProduct table.

n. Open the **tblPurchase** table, and then enter a new record to record a new purchase of 5 New Mexico Mud Masks. Close ✕ the tblPurchase table, and then open the **tblProduct** table to verify that there are now five fewer New Mexico Mud Mask items in stock. Close ✕ the tblProduct table. Close Access.

CONSIDER THIS | **Product Returns and Cancelled Orders**

Products are often returned and online orders cancelled for various reasons. How could data macros be modified to automate the process of updating the inventory amount if a product is returned?

Concept Check

1. Explain security concerns with macros and what can be done to minimize the risk.

2. Discuss how macros can enhance the overall user experience.

3. What are the benefits of creating macro groups?

4. Discuss the purpose of an AutoKeys macro.

5. What is the purpose of a data macro, and how is it different from other macros?

Key Terms

Action   549
Action Catalog   549
After events   573
AutoKeys macro   563
AutoExec macro   566
Before events   573

Data actions   573
Data blocks   574
Data macro   546
Database event   567
Embedded macro   546
Macro Designer   548

Macro group   562
Macros   546
Modal message   562
Single Step   553
Stand-alone macro   546
Trusted Location   546

Visual Summary

Add a Trusted Location (p. 546)

Create a Data Macro (p. 574)

Improve Form Navigation with a Macro (p. 569)

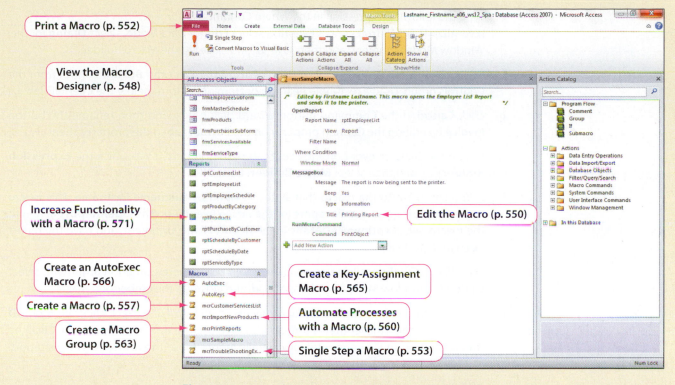

Print a Macro (p. 552)

View the Macro Designer (p. 548)

Increase Functionality with a Macro (p. 571)

Edit the Macro (p. 550)

Create an AutoExec Macro (p. 566)

Create a Key-Assignment Macro (p. 565)

Create a Macro (p. 557)

Automate Processes with a Macro (p. 560)

Create a Macro Group (p. 563)

Single Step a Macro (p. 553)

Figure 35 The Turquoise Oasis Spa database with macros

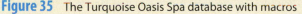

Practice 1

Student data file needed:	You will save your file as:
a06_ws12_Events	Lastname_Firstname_a06_ws12_Events

Event Planning

The event planning department at the resort has a database containing information about past and upcoming events. The current process of adding event information to the database requires the user to enter information into separate forms, and there is no easy way to calculate and view the estimated costs associated with the event. Additionally, there is a report that contains event information for all the events. Management frequently requests the event information from a specific range of dates. The current process of abstracting that information is manual and tedious.

You have been asked to improve the functionality of the Events form and report in the database by embedding macros.

a. Start **Access 2010**, click the **File tab**, click **Open**, and then browse to your student data files. Locate and open **a06_ws12_Events**.

b. Click the **File tab**, click **Save Database As**, navigate to where you are storing your files, and then name your database Lastname_Firstname_a06_ws12_Events replacing Lastname_Firstname with your actual name.

c. Open the **frmEvents** form in Design view 🖉, and then view the property sheet of the EventID field. Locate the On Click event on the **Event tab**, click the **Expression Builder** 🔲, and then click **Macro Builder**. Click **OK**.

d. Add a Comment to the macro that states: Created by Firstname Lastname. This macro will open the event items form for the active event. Add the **OpenForm** action to the macro, select **frmEventItems** for Form Name, and then for the View argument select **Form**.

e. Type the following expression in the Where Condition argument: [EventID]=[Forms]![frmEvents]![EventID], select **Edit** for Data Mode, select **Dialog** for the Window Mode argument, and then save 🖫 and close 🗵 the Macro Builder.

f. While still in Design view 🖾 of the frmEvents form, select the **Button** control from the Controls group. Drag a rectangle near the bottom of the form below the Client ID label.

g. Click **Cancel** in the Command Button Wizard dialog box, and then rename the button Invoice by editing the Caption property on the **Format tab** in the property sheet.

h. Locate the On Click event on the Event tab of the property sheet, click the **Expression Builder** 🔲, and then select **Macro Builder**. Click **OK**.

i. Add a comment to the macro that states: Created by Firstname Lastname. This macro will open the invoice details report for the active event. Add the **OpenReport** action to the macro, select **rptInvoiceDetails** in the Report Name argument, and have the report open in Report view.

j. Type [EventID]=[Forms]![frmEvents]![EventID] in the Where Condition argument, select **Dialog** for Window Mode, and then save 🖫 and close 🗵 the embedded macro.

k. To test each of these two embedded macros, switch to Form view, click the **EventID** field to view the frmEventItems form, and then close the frmEventItems form. Click the **Invoice** button to view the rptInvoiceDetails report. Close the rptInvoiceDetails report. Save 🖫 and close 🗵 the frmEvents form.

l. Click the **Create tab**, and then click **Macro** in the Macros & Code group.

m. Add a Comment to the macro and type the following text: Created by Firstname Lastname. This macro will open a report and filter the contents based on a user-provided date range and then send the report to the printer. Replace Firstname and Lastname with your first and last name.

n. Add the **OpenReport** action to the macro, select **rptEventsByDate** for the Report Name argument, and then select **Report** for the View argument.

o. Type the following expression in the Where Condition argument to create a parameter clause: [EventDate] Between [Enter first date (mm/dd/yy)] And [Enter second date (mm/dd/yy)]. Select **Normal** for the Window Mode.

p. Add the **PrintObject** action to the macro.

q. Add the **CloseWindow** action to the macro, select **Report** as Object Type, select **rptEventsByDate** for Object Name, and select **No** for the Save argument.

r. Save 🖫 the macro as mcrPrintEventsByDateRange, and then close 🗵 the macro.

s. Open **rptEventsByDate** in Design view 🖾, and then select the **Button** control from the Controls group. Create a button to the right of the Report title in the Report Header. Align the left side of the button with the 3" mark on the horizontal ruler at the top.

t. Change the name of the Button control to Events by Date Range, and then resize the button so that all text is visible.

u. Click the **Event tab**, and then click the **On Click** event arrow on the property sheet for the Command Button. Select **mcrPrintEventsByDateRange** from the list.

v. Save 🖫 the changes to the report. Switch to Report view, click the **Events by Date Range** button, and type 01/01/13 for the first date and 03/31/13 for the second date. Cancel or print as directed by your instructor. Close 🗵 the report. Exit Access.

Student data file needed:

a06_ws12_Painted_Treasures

You will save your file as:

Lastname_Firstname_a06_ws12_Painted_Treasures

Gift Shop

Employees of the Painted Treasures Gift Shop have to manually update the inventory count of each product whenever a sale is made. This process occasionally leads to errors and inaccuracies in inventory. Employees are often asked to e-mail copies of various reports throughout the week to members of management. The current process requires the user to export the report and then attach that report to an e-mail before it can be sent. Employees currently do not have any easy method of viewing the customer's information to verify identity from the Purchase form.

You have been asked to add some additional functionality to the database to allow the employees to do their jobs better, faster, and with more accuracy. You will create a data macro to automatically update the inventory table when a product is sold. You will also create a macro that will automatically e-mail each report and then embed the macro into a command button on each of the reports. Additionally, you will embed a macro into the Purchase form that will open the Customer form so that identity can be verified and/or changes can be made if necessary. Finally you will create an AutoExec macro that will open a form to a new record with the pointer in a specific field.

a. Open **Access 2010**, click the **File tab**, click **Open**, and then browse to your student data files. Locate and open **a06_ws12_Painted_Treasures**. Click the **File tab**, click **Save Database As**, navigate to where you are storing your files, and name your database **Lastname_Firstname_a06_ws12_Painted_Treasures** replacing Lastname_Firstname with your actual name.

b. Open the **tblPurchaseLine** table, click the **Table tab**, and click the **After Insert** data macro. Add a Comment to the macro that states: **Created by Firstname and Lastname. This macro will automatically decrease the number of items in stock from the product table based on the quantity of that item being purchased**. Replace Firstname and Lastname with your first and last name.

c. Double-click the **LookupRecord** in the Data Blocks in the Action Catalog, select **tblProduct** for the Look Up A Record In argument, and then type the following expression for the Where Condition argument: **[tblPurchaseLine].[ProductID]=[tblProduct].[ProductID]**. Select the **EditRecord** data block from the Add New Action list inside the LookupRecord data block, and then add the **SetField** macro to the EditRecord program flow.

d. Type **tblProduct.QuantityInStock** in the Name argument. The quantity in stock field is the field you want to edit. Type the following expression into the Value argument **[tblProduct].[QuantityInStock]-[tblPurchaseLine].[Quantity]**. Save 🖫 and close ⊠ the macro.

e. Open the **tblProduct** table, take note of the quantity in stock for Product ID 3, Jr golf clubs, and then close ⊠ the tblProduct table. Open the **tblPurchaseLine** table, and then insert a new record with the following information:

PurchaseID	PurchaseLine	ProductID	Quantity
18	4	Jr golf clubs	2

Close ⊠ the tblPurchaseLine table, open the **tblProduct** table, and then verify that there are now two fewer of Product ID 3, Jr golf clubs in stock. Close ⊠ the tblProduct table.

f. Open the **frmCustomerPurchases** form in Design view ⬚, and then open the Property Sheet for the LastName field. Locate the On Dbl Click event on the Event tab, click the **Expression Builder** ⬚, and then click **Macro Builder**. Click **OK**.

g. Add a comment to the macro that states: Created by Firstname Lastname. This macro will open the customer form when the last name field is double-clicked and filter only customers that have that last name. Replace Firstname and Lastname with your first and last name.

h. Add the **OpenForm** action to the macro. Select **frmCustomer** for the Form Name, and then select **Form** for the View argument. Type the following expression for the Where Condition argument [CustomerID]=[Forms]![frmCustomerPurchases]![CustomerID]. Select **Edit** for Data Mode, and then select **Dialog** for Window Mode. Save ⬚ and close ⬚ the macro.

i. Switch to Form view, and then double-click the last name field to test this macro. Close the frmCustomer form.

j. To create a new macro, click the **Create tab**, and then click the **Macro** button. Insert a Comment and type the following text: Created by Firstname Lastname. This macro group will call the EMailDatabaseObject action for several reports. Replace Firstname and Lastname with your first and last name.

k. Add the **Submacro** Program Flow to the macro, and then name it EmailInventory. Add the **EMailDatabaseObject** action, select **Report** for Object Type, and then select **rptProductInventory** for Object Name. Select **PDF Format (*.pdf)** as the Output Format. Leave the To, Cc, Bcc arguments blank.

l. Type Product Inventory Report for the Subject argument, and then select **Yes** for the Edit Message argument. This will allow you to edit the e-mail message before the e-mail is sent.

m. Repeat steps k–l for the next two submacros. Refer to the following table for specific setting changes for the two Submacro names and the EMailDatabaseObject action.

First Submacro

Argument	Setting
Submacro name	EmailPurchaseByCategory
Object Type	Report
Object Name	rptPurchaseByCategory
Output Format	PDF Format (*.pdf)
Subject	Purchases by Category Report
Edit Message	Yes

Second Submacro

Argument	Setting
Submacro name	EmailCustomerPurchases
Object Type	Report
Object Name	rptCustomerPurchases
Output Format	PDF Format (*.pdf)
Subject	Customer Purchases Report
Edit Message	Yes

Save ⬚ the macro group as mcrEmailReports, and then close ⬚ the Macro Designer.

n. Open the **rptProductInventory** report in Design view ⬚. Create a Command Button in the Report Header. Position the button so that the left edge of the button begins at the 5" ruler mark. Click the Property Sheet, type **E-mail Report** for the Caption, and then resize the button as needed to make sure all of the Caption is visible on the button. Locate the **On Click** event on the Event tab.

o. From the list, select the **mcrEmailReports.EmailInventory** submacro. Save 🖬 and close ☒ the report.

p. Repeat steps n–o for the **rptPurchasesByCategory** report and the **rptCustomerPurchases** report. Be sure to select the appropriate submacro for each report, Save 🖬 changes, and then close ☒ reports.

q. To test each macro, open each report, and then click the **E-mail Report** button. Close ☒ all email windows and reports.

r. Create a new macro by clicking the **Macro** button on the Create tab. Add a Comment and type: **Created by Firstname Lastname. This macro will run when the database opens and will minimize the Navigation Pane, open the customer purchase form, and place the pointer inside the first name field of a new record**. Replace Firstname and Lastname with your first and last name.

s. Add the **SelectObject** action to macro, select **Form** for Object Type, select **frmCustomerPurchases** for Object Name, and then select **Yes** for In Database Window to make the Navigation Pane the active window.

t. Add the **MinimizeWindow** action to cause the Navigation Pane to be minimized when the macro is executed.

u. Add the **OpenForm** action to the macro, select **frmCustomerPurchases** as Form Name, select **Form** for the View argument, select **Edit** for Data Mode, and then select **Normal** for Window Mode.

v. Add the **GoToRecord** action to the macro. Select **Form** for Object Type, select **frmCustomerPurchases** for Object Name, and then select **New** for the Record argument to have the form open in a new record.

w. Add the **GoToControl** action, and then type **FirstName** as the Control Name.

x. Save 🖬 the macro as **AutoExec**, close ☒ the macro, and then exit the database.

y. To test the AutoExec macro, open the database. See that the AutoExec macro runs correctly, close the database, and then exit Access.

MODULE CAPSTONE

Student data file needed:

a06_mp_Menu

You will save your file as:

Lastname_Firstname_a06_mp_Menu

Improving Navigation of the Indigo5 Restaurant Database

Indigo5 is a five-star restaurant that caters to local patrons in addition to clients of the resort and spa. The Menu database is used to store information regarding ingredients, recipes, and specials. The database consists of several forms used for entering new information as well as a few reports. You will create a navigation system that will give the employees access to the essential forms and reports. You will also implement business logic using a data macro to automatically set the cost of each menu item.

a. Open **Access 2010**. Click the **File tab**, click **Open**, navigate to where you are storing your files, and then browse to your student files. Locate and open the **a06_mp_Menu** database.

b. Click the **File tab**, click **Save Database As**, navigate to where you are storing your files and then save the database with the name Lastname_Firstname_a06_mp_Menu replacing Lastname_Firstname with your actual name.

c. Right-click the **frmFoodCategories** form, and then click **Design View**. Drag a rectangle around all fields and labels in the Details section to select them and move them down approximately 1".

d. Create a Command Button, and then place it in the top-left corner of the Detail section. In the Command Button Wizard, click **Record Navigation** in the Categories list, click **Go To Previous Record** in the Actions list, and then click **Next**. Click **Text**, and then type Previous Category as the button text. Click **Next**. Type cmdPrevCategory as the button name, and then click **Finish**.

e. Add two additional command buttons each to the right of the previous. Refer to the table below for the specific values for the Command Button Wizard.

Category	Action	Button Text	Button Name
Record Navigation	Go To Next Record	Next Category	cmdNextCategory
Record Operations	Add New Record	Add Category	cmdAddCategory

f. Select all three Command Buttons, and then click the **Arrange tab**. Click **Align** in the **Sizing & Ordering** group, and then click **Top** from the list of options. Click **Space/Size**, and then click **Equal Horizontal** to have all the buttons equally spaced apart.

g. With the buttons still selected, click the **Format tab**. Click **Quick Styles** in the Control Formatting group, and then click **Moderate Effect - Blue, Accent 1** from the list.

h. Click the **Design tab**, and then switch to **Layout View**. Click **Property Sheet** in the Tools group. Under Selection type in the Property Sheet, click the **selection arrow**, and then click **Form**. Click the **Format tab** in the Property Sheet pane, find **Record Selectors**, click the **selection arrow**, and then click **No**. Find **Navigation Buttons**, click the **selection arrow**, and then click **No**.

i. Referencing the table below make similar modifications to the **frmIngredients, frmRecipes**, and **frmMenu** forms. Place the command buttons in a similar position as described above, apply the same Quick Styles format to the navigation buttons, and then set the record selectors and navigation buttons properties to **No**.

Form Name	Button Text	Button Name
frmIngredients	Previous Ingredient, Next Ingredient, Add Ingredient	cmdPrevIngredient, cmdNextIngredient, cmdAddIngredient
frmRecipes	Previous Recipe, Next Recipe, Add Recipe	cmdPrevRecipe, cmdNextRecipe, cmdAddRecipe
frmMenu	Previous Item, Next Item, Add Item	cmdPrevItem, cmdNextItem, cmdAddItem

j. Save 🖫 and close ✕ all opened forms.

k. Click the **Create tab**, click **Navigation** in the Forms group, and then click **Vertical Tabs, Left**. Click the **File tab**, and then click **Save**. Save the Navigation Form as frmMenuNavigation_initialLastname.

l. Click the **frmMenu** form in the Navigation Pane, and then drag it to the first [Add New] vertical tab. Click the **frmRecipes** form, and then drag it to the second [Add New] vertical tab.

m. Continue adding the **frmFoodCategories** and **frmIngredient** forms and the **rptMenuItems** and **rptRecipeDetails** reports to each of the next [Add New] vertical tabs in the Navigation control.

n. Double-click the **frmMenu** tab, select the text, and then rename the tab Menu. Double-click the **frmRecipes** tab, select the text, and then rename the tab Recipes. Double-click each of the remaining tabs, select the text, and then rename the tabs Food Categories, Ingredients, Menu Items, and Recipe Details.

o. Click the first vertical tab **Menu**, press and hold ⇧ Shift, and then click the **Ingredients** tab. Click the **Format tab**, click **Change Shape** in the Control Formatting group, and click **Rounded Rectangle**. Click **Quick Styles**, and then click **Subtle Effect – Blue, Accent 1**.

p. Click the **Menu Items** vertical tab, press and hold ⇧ Shift, and then click the **Recipe Details** vertical tab. Click the **Format tab**, click **Change Shape** in the Control Formatting group, and click **Round Single Corner Rectangle**. Click **Quick Styles**, and then click **Light 1 Outline, Colored Fill – Blue, Accent 1**.

q. Delete the image in the form header, and then change the title to: Menu Navigation. Save 🖫 and close ✕ the frmMenuNavigation_initialLastname form.

r. Open the **tblMenu** table in the Navigation Pane. Click the **Table tab**, and then click the **Before Change** button in the Before Events group.

s. Add the following Comment to the data macro: Created by Firstname Lastname. This data macro will automatically set the Cost field to be 40% of the amount in the Price field.

t. Add the **SetField** action to the macro. Type Cost in the Name argument, and then type [Price]*0.4 for the Value argument. This will automatically set the cost of the menu item to be 40% of whatever price is entered. Save 🖫 and close ✕ the data macro.

u. Test the data macro by creating a new record in the tblMenu table using the information below.

MenuID	Recipe ID	Season	Meal	Special	Price	Cost
	Spinach and Mushroom Frittata	Spring, Summer	Breakfast		$8.84	

Notice that once you tab out of the Cost field is automatically set to $3.54. Changing an existing price will also cause the data macro to update the cost value.

v. Click the **File tab**, click **Options**, and then click **Current Database**. In the Application Options section, type to change the **Application Title** to Indigo5 Database.

w. Click the **Display Form arrow**, and then click **frmMenuNavigation_initialLastname**. This will be the form that opens when the application is opened.

x. Click the **Compact on Close** check box. This will automatically compact and repair the database when it is closed every time.

y. In the Navigation section, clear the **Display Navigation Pane** check box to hide the Navigation Pane, and then click **OK** to close the Access Options dialog box.

z. Click **OK** at the message **You must close and reopen the current database for the specified option to take effect**.

aa. Close ☒ the database. Start **Access**, and then open **Lastname_Firstname_a06_mp_ Menu**. When the database reopens, the only form to open should be frmMenuNavigation_initialLastname. Also notice that the name of the application, not the database, is on the title bar.

Problem Solve 1

Student data files needed:

a06_ps1_Hotel1
a06_ps1_New_Reservations

You will save your file as:

Lastname_Firstname_a06_ps1_Hotel1

Automating Tasks in the Hotel Database

The hotel provides a variety of room types and amenities to accommodate the needs of its guests. The hotel reservation database is currently used to keep track of hotel reservations including information about guests, reservations and additional purchases charged to the room from the gift shop, spa, lounge, room service, and so on.

Online and phone reservations are handled by a third party who sends a spreadsheet containing the information that is then entered into this database. You will automate this process using macros. You will also increase the functionality and usability of the database by creating a variety of macros.

a. Open **a06_ps1_Hotel1** located in your student files, and then save the database as Lastname_Firstname_a06_ps1_Hotel1. Replace Lastname_Firstname with your actual name.

b. Create a Before Change data macro for the tblReservations table:

- Add the following Comment to the data macro: Created by Firstname Lastname. This data macro will automatically set the CheckOutDate field based on the CheckInDate and the NightsStay fields. Replace Firstname and Lastname with your first and last name.

- Add the appropriate action to the macro, and then complete the required arguments to implement the business logic described in the above comment.

- Save, close, and test the macro.

- Create a new macro, and then add the following Comment: Created by Firstname Lastname. This macro will automate the process of importing guests and reservation info received by a third party. Replace Firstname and Lastname with your first and last name.

- You will need to add the ImportExportSpreadsheet action to the macro.

- You will first be importing new guest information into the tblGuests table. The guest information to be imported is part of a named range entitled Guests in the a06_ps1_New_Reservations.xlsx workbook included in your student files. The named range does include field names.
- Add a message box that displays an informational message stating: **New guests have been added to the database.** Add a beep sound and **New Guests Added** as the title.
- Add another ImportExportSpreadsheet action. You will now be importing the data from the named range Reservations in the same workbook into the tblReservations table. This range also includes field names.
- Add a message box that displays an informational message stating: **New reservations have been added to the database.** Add a beep and **New Reservations Added** as a title.
- Save the macro as **mcrImportReservationInfo_initialLastname** test, and then close it.

c. Create an embedded macro in the On Load event of the rptRoomChargesBy Reservation report.
- Add the following Comment to the macro: **Created by Firstname Lastname. This macro will prompt the user for a Reservation ID before displaying the associated charges.** Replace Firstname and Lastname with your first and last name.
- Add the SetFilter action to the macro. The filter should prompt the user to: **Please enter a Reservation ID for a list of charges.**
- Save, close, and then test the macro.

d. Create a datasheet form based on all the fields in the tblReservations table. Save it as **frmReservationsList_initialLastname**.

e. Create an embedded macro in the On Click event of the ReservationID.
- Add the following Comment: **Created by Firstname Lastname. This macro will display the frmReservationDetails form of the ReservationID clicked.** Replace Firstname and Lastname with your first and last name.
- Add the appropriate action to open the frmReservationDetails form for the same ReservationID that is clicked in this form. Have the form open in Edit mode as a dialog box.

f. Create an embedded macro in the After Insert event of the frmGuests form.
- Add the following Comment: **Created by Firstname Lastname. This macro will open the frmReservationDetails form after a new guest is entered.** Replace Firstname and Lastname with your first and last name.
- Add the appropriate action to open the frmReservationDetails form where the GuestID fields match. Have the form open in Edit mode as a dialog box.
- Save, close, and test the macro.

g. Exit Access.

Problem Solve 2

Student data file needed:
a06_ps2_Hotel2

You will save your file as:
Lastname_Firstname_a06_ps2_Hotel2

Creating a Main Menu Navigation System for the Hotel Database

The hotel database currently consists of several forms, queries, and reports that are all accessed from the Navigation Pane. You will create a comprehensive navigation system that will include a main menu that will include two Navigation forms with information pertaining to Guests and Reservations.

a. Open **a06_ps2_Hotel2**, located in your student files. Save the database as Lastname_Firstname_a06_ps2_Hotel2.

b. Apply a Hardcover theme to the database.

c. Remove the navigation buttons and record selectors from the frmGuests, frmEmployees, frmRoomCharges, and frmReservations forms.

d. Create a Navigation form with vertical tabs on the left and make the following changes:
   - Add the following objects to the navigation control:
     - frmGuests
     - rptGuestsByLastName
     - rptGuestsByState
     - rptReservationsByGuest
   - Rename the tabs to Guests, Guests by Last Name, Guests by State, and Reservations By Guest.
   - Remove the icon in the form header, and then edit the title to be Guest Navigation.
   - Change the shapes of the tabs to rounded rectangles.
   - Save the Navigation form as frmGuestNavigation_initialLastname.

e. Create a horizontal tabs Navigation form with two levels, and then make the following changes:
   - On the top level name one tab Forms and another tab Reports.
   - On the Forms tab make the following changes:
     - Add the following forms to the navigation control:
       - frmReservations
       - frmRoomCharges
       - frmEmployees
     - Rename the tabs Reservations, Room Charges, and Employees.
   - On the Reports tab make the following changes:
     - Add the following reports to the Navigation control:
       - rptReservationsCountByMonth
       - rptCountOfGuestsByMonth
       - rptTotalRoomCountByType
       - rptTotalRoomChargesByCategory
     - Rename the tabs Reservations Count By Month, Count of Guests By Month, Total Room Count By Type, and Total Room Charges By Category.
   - Change the font color of the second-tier tabs for both Forms and Reports to white.
   - Remove the icon in the form header, and then edit the text to be Reservations Navigation.
   - Save the Navigation form as frmReservationsNavigation_initialLastname.

f. Create a Navigation form with horizontal tabs to become the main menu and make the following changes:
   - Add frmGuestNavigation_initialLastname and frmReservationsNavigation_initialLastname to the Navigation control.
   - Rename the tabs Guest Navigation and Reservations Navigation.
   - Remove the icon in the form header, and then edit the text to be Main Menu.
   - Add a control button to the form header to the right of the title that will close the database when clicked. Type Exit Database as the caption and type cmdExitDatabase as the name.
   - Save the Navigation form as frmMainMenu_initialLastname.

g. Make the following modifications to the database settings:
- Change the Application title to **Hotel Database**.
- Make the database display the frmMainMenuNavigation_initialLastname form when opened.
- Make the database compact on close.
- Hide the Navigation Pane.
- Make sure users do not have access to the full menu.

h. Exit Access.

Problem Solve 3

Student data file needed:

a06_ps3_Hotel3

You will save your file as:

Lastname_Firstname_a06_ps3_Hotel3

Combining a User Interface with an AutoKeys Macro

The hotel database consists of several forms and reports that employees and management use on a daily basis to enter information in and retrieve information from. You have been asked to create a user-friendly navigation system to access all the forms required to enter a reservation. You will also create macros that will print and e-mail reports using key combinations on the keyboard.

a. Open **a06_ps3_Hotel3**, and then save the database as **Lastname_Firstname_a06_ps3_Hotel3**.

b. Apply the Elemental theme to the Navigation form.

c. Remove navigation buttons and record selectors form the frmEmployees, frmGuests, frmReservations, and frmRoomCharges forms.

d. Create a horizontal Navigation form, and then add frmReservations, frmRoomCharges, frmGuests, and frmEmployees in that order.
- Rename the tabs to be: **Reservations, Room Charges, Guests**, and **Employees**.
- Remove the icon in the form header, and then edit the text to be **Hotel Navigation**.
- Save the form as **frmHotelNavigation_initialLastname**.

e. Create an AutoKeys macro that consists of several submacro groups. Each group will open a specific report, queue the report to the printer, and close the report without prompting to save:
- Add a Comment to the macro stating **Created by Firstname Lastname**.
- See the table below for specifics.

Report Name	Key Combination
rptTotalRoomChargesByCategory	{F2}
rptTotalRoomCountByType	{F3}
rptRoomChargesByReservation	{F4}

- Create an expression in the Where Condition argument for rptRoomChargesBy Reservation that will prompt the user to enter a reservation number and only show results for that reservation number in the report. Type **Enter a Reservation number for a list of room charges** as the message prompt.

f. Modify the appropriate database settings to hide the Navigation Pane, and then have the Navigation form be displayed when the database is opened.

g. Test all macros.

h. Exit Access.

Student data file needed:

Blank database

You will save your file as:

Lastname_Firstname_ a06_pf1_Music

Music Collection Database

As a response to the rise in popularity of digital music libraries, vinyl record sales have begun to regain some lost ground and are increasing in popularity. A music collection database can help you keep track of your growing collection of vinyl records. Create a database that will keep track of artists, albums, and where and when the records were purchased or acquired.

Once the tables are created, you will create some forms to make data entry easier and create various reports. You will then create a Navigation form to provide easy access to these forms and reports.

a. Start **Access**. Click **Blank database**. Browse to find where you are storing your data files, and then save your database as **Lastname_Firstname_a06_pf1_Music**. Click **Create** to create the database.

b. The tables you create should allow you to track at a minimum:

- The names of the musicians/artists
- The album names, artist, genre, and the location and date purchased
- The location name and contact information: e-mail address, website, address, and phone number.

c. Create two reports for this database:

- Create one report that lists the albums purchased for each location. Save the report as **rptAlbumsByLocation_initialLastname**.
- Create one report that lists the albums purchased each month. Save the report as **rptAlbumsByMonth_initialLastname**.

d. Create forms for the tables so that information can be entered easily into the tables. You may want to use subforms to combine data entry into multiple tables:

- Add navigation buttons to each form that will allow users to Find, Go To Previous Records, Go To Next Record, and Add New Record.
- Apply a style and shape of your choosing to the navigation buttons.

e. Create a Navigation form with vertical tabs on the left, and then add the forms and reports.

- Rename the tabs appropriately.
- Apply a style and shape of your choosing to the tabs.
- Be sure to remove any unnecessary record selectors and/or navigation buttons from any of the forms.
- Edit the Navigation form header to: **Firstname Lastname's Music Collection**. Replace Firstname Lastname's with your name.
- Save the Navigation form as **frmMusicNavigation_initialLastname**.

f. Create an AutoKeys macro that will export each of the reports created as a PDF file to your student files directory.

- Assign the rptAlbumsByLocation_initialLastname report a key combination of Ctrl +a.
- Assign the rptAlbumsByMonth_initialLastname report a key combination of Ctrl +b.
- Test your auto keys macros.

g. Have frmMusicNavigation_initialLastname be displayed when the database opens, hide the Navigation Pane, and give the application a title of **Music Collection**.

h. Save and exit Access.

Student data file needed:

Blank database

You will save your file as:

Lastname_Firstname_a06_pf2_Independent_Films

Independent Films

Independent Films is a company that arranges screenings of independent films created by local filmmakers. Independent Films needs a database that can keep track of employees, local filmmakers, venues, scheduled screenings, available films, and a contact list of fans who want to receive e-mail updates on upcoming events.

You will create a database with the tables and forms required to track the appropriate information. You will then create several macros to increase the functionality of the database and enhance the user's experience.

a. Start **Access**. Click **Blank database**. Browse to find where you are storing your data files, and then save your database as **Lastname_Firstname_a06_pf2_Independent_Films**. Click **Create** to create the database.

b. The tables you create should allow you to track at a minimum:

- Name, address, phone, and e-mail of employees, local filmmakers, fans, and venues that host screenings
- Title, filmmaker, and genre of the films available
- Each screening should include the date, time, venue, film title, and cost of admission

c. Create two reports:

- One report should list the film titles available for each filmmaker. Save this report as **rptFilmsByFilmmakers_initialLastname**.
- One report should list the screenings occurring each month. Save this report as **rptScreeningsByMonth_initialLastname**.

d. Create forms for each of the tables so that information can be entered easily into each table:

- Add navigation buttons to each form that will allow users to Find Record, Go To Previous Record, Go To Next Record, and Add New Record.
- Apply a style and shape of your choosing to the navigation buttons.

e. Create an AutoExec macro that will minimize the Navigation Pane and display the Screenings form when the database opens and have the pointer placed in the venue field of a new record.

f. At each screening event a kiosk is available for guests to sign up for the Independent Films mailing list:

- The information stored in the kiosks is e-mailed as a spreadsheet. Create a macro that will automatically import the information into a temporary table.
- You want to be careful not to automatically import user-generated information into your database as it could create duplicate data.
- You may want to create a sample spreadsheet containing the appropriate information in order to test your macro.
- The macro should display a message box informing the user that the data has successfully been imported into the temporary table.
- Save this macro as **mcrImportFans_initialLastname**.

g. Embed a macro into the On Load event of the rptFilmsByFilmmakers_initialLastname report that will prompt the user for a filmmaker's last name and then display the films for that filmmaker.

h. Embed a macro into the On Click event of a command button on the rptScreeningsBy-Month_initialLastname report that will export the report as a PDF to your student file directory.

i. Test your macros and exit Access.

Student data file needed:

a06_pf3_SunShine_Arena

You will save your file as:

Lastname_Firstname_a06_pf3_SunShine_Arena

SunShine Event Arena

You have just taken a new internship at the SunShine Event Arena (SEA). SEA is an arena that hosts such local events as banquets, concerts, and sporting events. The database contains tables that track events, ticket sales, employees, and patrons of the arena.

You will be enhancing the database by creating a Navigation form that will allow management easy access to all necessary forms and reports for both ticket sale and event information. You will also be increasing the functionality of the database by creating some macros that can be executed using key combinations on the keyboard.

a. Open **a06_pf3_SunShine_Arena**, and then save the database as
    Lastname_Firstname_a06_pf3_SunShine_Arena.

b. Create one report that lists total revenue generated by each employee. Save the report as
    rptRevenueByEmployee_initialLastname.

c. Create one report that lists the total revenue generated from each event. Save the report
    as rptRevenueByEvent_initial_Lastname.

d. Create an After insert data macro for the tblPurchase table that will automatically deduct
    the quantity of tickets sold from the number of tickets available for each event. Add a
    Comment to the macro that states: Created by Firstname and Lastname and include a
    brief description of purpose of the macro.

e. Create an AutoKeys macro consisting of a submacro for each report in the database that
    will export the report as a PDF in a directory location of your choosing. Assign each sub-
    macro a unique key combination consisting of Ctrl and a letter of your choosing.

f. Customer orders are often processed off site, and the details of the orders are sent to
    SunShine Arena to add to their master database. Create a macro that will automate the
    process of importing a file with new patrons into the tblPatrons table as well as new
    ticket purchases into the tblPurchase table.
    - You will need to create a sample file consisting of new patrons as well as ticket pur-
      chase information in order to test your macro.
    - Be sure to add a Comment to this macro that includes Created by Firstname Lastname
      and a brief description of what the macro does.
    - Name this macro mcrImportPurchases_initialLastname.

g. Create forms for each of the tables in the database:
    - Set the navigation buttons and record selectors properties to No.
    - Create your own navigation buttons for each of the forms:
        - Each form should have a Find Record, Go To Previous Record, Go to Next Record,
          and Add New Record.
        - Apply a color style and shape of your choosing to each of the buttons for all forms.

- When saving each form append _initialLastname to the end of each form name.
- Create an additional command button on the form based on the tblPurchase table. This command button should run the mcrImportPurchases_initialLastname macro when clicked.

h. Create a horizontal Navigation form with vertical tabs on the left:

- Name the three horizontal tabs Ticket Sales, Events, and Employees.
- Add the forms created from the tblPatrons and tblPurchase table to the vertical navigation control of the Ticket Sales tab.
- Add the form based on the tblEvents table and the rptRevenueByEvent_initialLastname report you created with the event revenue to the vertical navigation control of the Events tab.
- Add the form based on the tblEmployees table and the rptRevenueByEmployee_initialLastname report you created containing revenue per employee to the Employees tab.
- Rename all tabs to provide more appropriate labels.
- Apply quick styles and shapes of your choosing to each of the tabs.
- Add a button control to the Navigation form header that lets the user exit the database when clicked.
- Edit the title text to read SunShine Arena Ticket Sales.

i. Set the appropriate database settings so that:

- SunShine Arena Database is the application title.
- The Navigation form is displayed when the database is opened.
- The Navigation Pane is not displayed.
- Access to the full menu is removed.
- The database compacts when closed.

j. Exit Access.

Perform 4: How Others Perform

Student data file needed:

a06_pf4_HipHop_Fundraising

You will save your file as:

Lastname_Firstname_a06_pf4_HipHop_Fundraising

Lastname_Firstname_a06_pf4_HipHop_fundraising.docx

HipHop Fundraising

You have just taken a new job at a local fundraising organization called HipHop Fundraising. HipHop Fundraising seeks out local hip hop talent to perform concerts in order to raise funds for various charities. A database has been created to track the various aspects of the organization. As you navigate through the database you will notice some design flaws in the Navigation forms as well as error messages when attempting to run some of the macros. You will need to make some changes to this database to increase the usability and answer some questions below.

a. Open the **a06_pf4_HipHop_Fundraising** database, and then save it as Lastname_Firstname_a06_pf4_HipHop_Fundraising.

b. Open **Word**. Create a new blank document, and then save it as Lastname_Firstname_a06_pf4_HipHop_Fundraising. This will be used to answer any questions below.

c. When the database is opened an error message is displayed. Explain what is causing the error, what can be done to correct it, and then make the appropriate change.

d. There is a data macro associated with the donations table that is not working. Explain why it is not working properly, and then make the appropriate changes so that it does.

e. mcrOpenContributors is causing error messages to be display when executed. Use the single step process to determine where the macro is failing, and then make appropriate corrections. Explain why the macro was failing and what you did to correct it.

f. The frmHipHopNavigation form needs some work to make it user friendly. List the things you feel are missing from the Navigation form in terms of both content and design. Once you have made your list, implement those changes to improve the design and function of the frmHipHopNavigation Navigation form.

g. Save and close your files.

WORKSHOP 13

Using VBA in Access

Courtesy of www.Shutterstock.com

PREPARE CASE

The Red Bluff Golf Club Putts for Paws Charity Database

The Red Bluff Golf Club sponsors the charity tournament, Putts for Paws, to raise money for the local pet shelter. The scope of the database is limited to tracking the monies being raised for the Putts for Paws event. Participants in the tournament are assigned roles, and any role may donate money to the event.

You are adding increased functionality to the database. Some of the functionality that must be added cannot be accomplished with macros and must be accomplished using VBA. This will make tasks such as importing data and data entry more efficient.

Student data files needed for this workshop:

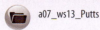 a07_ws13_Putts

 a07_ws13_Participant_List

You will save your file as:

Lastname_Firstname_a07_ws13_Putts

VBA Basics

Microsoft Office contains a powerful programming language called **Visual Basic for Applications** or more commonly known as VBA. The tools for using this language are installed by default in most instances. Many people incorrectly perceive that you need to be a "programmer" in order to use any of it. VBA can allow for a wide variety of enhancements to any Microsoft Office application. In this section, you will use VBA to enhance the functionality of databases.

Understanding the Functionality of VBA in Access

VBA is particularly valuable in automating repetitive tasks similar to macros, but it provides you with additional tools. These tools create more robust and dynamic tasks such as automatically populating a form field or prompting a user to select a file for importing. The code that you will write in this workshop is called a procedure in VBA. Each **procedure** contains a series of statements or instructions that are executed as a unit.

VBA is a form of object-oriented programming. **Object-oriented programming** uses objects—such as a form in Access—to design applications. **Objects** are combinations of data and code that are treated as a single unit. The application can respond to events that occur in relation to the object. **Event-driven programming** uses an event—moving to the next record of a form—to trigger the execution of code.

In Microsoft Access, this hierarchy has been replicated in the structure of the application. Access contains a top-level Application object that then contains objects such as forms or buttons. These objects then have changeable properties such as background colors or the value of a text box. Objects also have **methods** that are actions—such as SaveAs—that control the object's behavior.

VBA in one Microsoft Office application can also be used to interact with other Office applications. Illustratively, VBA can be used to export tables from Access to an Excel spreadsheet, or to populate an e-mail message in Outlook with data from an Access form. These are just a couple of the tasks that can be completed with VBA.

Convert an Existing Macro to VBA

Sometimes the best way to learn what VBA can do is to see how Office itself uses VBA. Consider the Putts for Paws charitable event. The event organizers must track participants and the donations made by these participants. The golf course has recently added a web service that allows participants to register for the event online. This system produces an Excel file on a daily basis that lists any new participants that have registered for the event. Given the recent success of the event, the number of participants has increased dramatically, and new participants sign up on a regular basis. You have been asked by Barry Cheney to modify the Putts for Paws database such that it can easily import these new Excel lists.

Real World Advice   Why Not Use a Saved Import?

Saved Imports in Access 2010 are extremely useful for automating the repetitive task of importing a file into Access. However, this process only works when the filename and location are always the same. Users on the go or working with filenames that change on a regular basis can be frustrated with Saved Imports. Any change in the file structure renders the Saved Import useless. VBA can accommodate for changes.

A macro already exists in the database that would import a spreadsheet from the correct folder on the user's PC. The mcrImportParticipants macro imports a list of participants from the file a07_ws13_Participant_List.xlsx into the table tblParticipant. This macro will result in an error if the file is not named exactly as listed previously or if it is in a different location. Currently, the macro is set up to import the a07_ws13_Participant_List.xlsx file from the C:\Temp folder of the user's computer. The macro is embedded in a button on the Imports tab of the frmPuttsMenu Navigational form in the Putts database.

Because the Macro Builder in Access does not allow for file selection to occur when importing files with the ImportExportSpreadsheet macro action, this process is limited in its functionality. Your task is to convert this macro into VBA and edit the macro to allow the user to select the file to import. Additionally, Barry Cheney wants users to be able to select multiple files for import. He has stated that some participants are still being tracked manually in a different Excel spreadsheet.

To Open the Database and Convert the Macro into VBA

a. Start **Access 2010**. Click the **File tab**, and then click **Open**. Navigate to where your student files are stored, and then double-click **a07_ws13_Putts**.

b. Click the **File tab**, click **Save Database As**. In the Save As dialog box, navigate to where you are saving your files, and then type **Lastname_Firstname_ a07_w13_ Putts** replacing Lastname_Firstname with your actual name. Click **Save**.

c. Click **Enable Content** in the Security Warning.

Troubleshooting

Depending on the configuration of your PC, you may not always be prompted to enable content when you first open a database in Access. Entering the Trust Center and setting the Macro Settings to Disable all macros with notification will display the Security Warning anytime you open a database that contains macros or Visual Basic. Conversely, by establishing a Trusted Location you have the option of enabling all content in databases that are stored in the specified location.

d. In the Navigation Pane, right-click the **mcrImportParticipants** macro, and then click **Design View**.

e. Click the **Design tab**, then click **Convert Macros to Visual Basic** in the Tools group.

Clear this option →

Figure 1 Convert macro message box

f. Deselect the option to **Add error handling**, and then leave the option for **Include macro comments** selected. Click **Convert**. Error handling and commenting will be discussed later in this workshop, but the conversion process will give a demonstration of this process.

SIDE NOTE

Opening the Visual Basic Editor

While converting a macro opens the Visual Basic Editor automatically, you can also access it on the Ribbon via the Database Tools tab in the Macro group or with the keyboard shortcut Alt + F11.

g. Click **OK** in the Conversion Finished message box that appears.

The Visual Basic Editor window will now open. Click 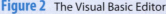 to maximize the Visual Basic Editor.

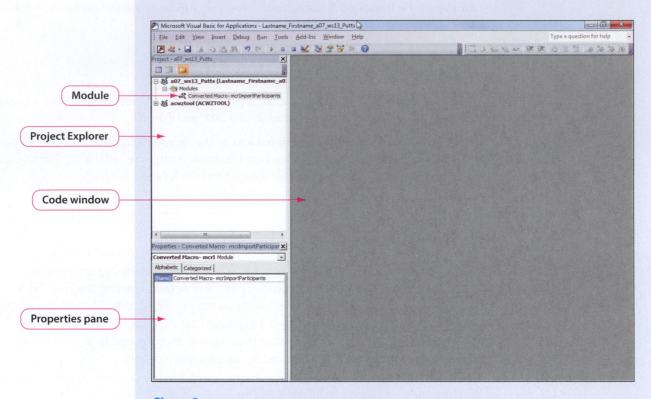

Figure 2 The Visual Basic Editor

Examine the VBA

The **Visual Basic Editor** is the tool built into Microsoft Office that is used for creating and editing VBA. At the top of the screen is the title of the database that is currently open and being edited. Directly under the application title are the File menu and Standard toolbar that are visible by default. On the left side of the Visual Basic Editor is the Project Explorer. The **Project Explorer** contains a list of the currently open Access Database objects that contain VBA procedures and a list of modules within the current database. VBA in an Access database can be contained either in a specific Access object—such as a form or a button—or within a module. **Modules** are used to store VBA procedures that can be referenced or called by other procedures in the database. This is helpful especially when a single procedure might be used in several different instances in a database. For example, a message box with a common statement could be created as a procedure and then used in other procedures throughout the database.

The larger window on the right of the Visual Basic Editor is the **Code window.** This is where you can edit the text of any procedure.

Real World Advice   Macros vs. VBA

Anything that can be done with a macro can be accomplished in VBA. In fact, most macros are created with VBA. So why use VBA if you can use a macro? VBA provides additional functionality that macros do not provide. Once you have experience with VBA it is often faster and more efficient to create a few lines of code than to create macros. In fact, best practice is to try not to switch back and forth between VBA and macros.

To Open the Converted Macro in the Code Window

a. In the Project Explorer window, double-click **Converted Macro–mcrImportParticipants** to open the module.

b. Examine the text of the module displayed currently in the Code window.

At the top of the window is the Object box. The **Object box** displays the name of the object that contains the procedure such as a form or command button. If the procedure exists within a module, the Object box will display (General). Notice that next to the Object box is the Procedure box. The **Procedure box** is a list that allows you to navigate quickly between the Declarations section and the individual procedures in the open module.

c. Examine the Code window. The Code window contains the module declarations and individual procedures.

The **Declarations section** contains declarations that apply to all procedures within the module. **Declarations** define user-defined data types, variables, arrays, and constants. By default all Access modules contain the Option Compare statement in the Declarations section. The **Option Compare** statement sets the string comparison method for the module. In a new database, the default statement is Option Compare Database. This sets the string comparison to the database default. The two settings for the Option Compare statement are Text and Binary. The **Option Compare Text** setting results in case-insensitive comparisons. The **Option Compare Binary** setting compares the ASCII values for the characters contained in a string and is therefore case sensitive.

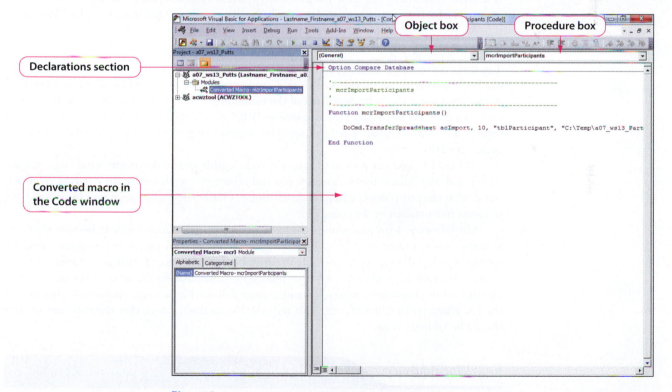

Figure 3 Converted macro in the Visual Basic Editor

Real World Advice | The Option Compare Default Setting

The default Option Compare setting can be changed in the Access Options section of Backstage view. Click the File tab, and then click Options. In the General section, the New Database Sort Order list offers options to change this feature. The default setting results in an Option Compare Binary equivalent.

After the Declarations section is the first procedure of the module. Modules can contain multiple procedures. The procedure in this module is the macro that was converted to VBA in the prior step. In this instance, the procedure is a function. A **function** executes instructions and returns a value to another procedure. Functions are called by other procedures whereas a **Sub procedure** runs on its own or can be called by another procedure. Sub procedures perform a set of instructions but do not return values to other procedures. Each function you create starts with statement "Function" followed by the name you give the function. In this case, the name is mcrImportParticipants. The function can contain multiple tasks but must end with the statement "End Function".

Formatting and Structuring VBA code

The first section in the created procedure is a comment. Comments are strings of text that will not be processed as part of the procedure. Comments will be discussed later in this workshop. Before examining the individual lines of the procedure, look over the format of the text in the Code window. An important aspect of writing VBA is to keep the code legible so that you and others can interpret what is happening. This means using indentation, comments, and line breaks liberally.

You need to take extra steps to keep the code legible and to document what steps you are taking and why. This makes it easier for you and others who work within the database to understand what the procedure is doing while editing it. One of these extra steps will be using Tab to create indentations in the code.

Also be aware, VBA procedures lack word wrapping in the Code window. Because the Code window does not word wrap like Microsoft Word or other word-processing programs, lengthy strings of code will extend continuously to the right. This creates code that is extremely difficult to read. To break a line of code across two lines, a line continuation character can be used. A **line continuation character** consists of a single space followed by a single underscore character as the last character in a line of code. This tells the Visual Basic Editor that the two lines of code should be treated as one.

Real World Advice | Lines of Code in VBA

The Visual Basic Editor interprets statements of code on a line-by-line basis. In other words, typing part of a statement on a line of the Visual Basic Editor and pressing Enter before the end of the statement will invoke an error. If you need to break a lengthy line of text across two lines of the Code window, type a line continuation character at the end of a line and continue your statements on the next line of the Code window.

The DoCmd Object

The **DoCmd object** allows Access actions to be performed from within VBA. This can include opening a report, telling Access not to show warning messages, or closing an object. Typing DoCmd into the Code window or using the Object Browser will show a list of all methods associated with the DoCmd object. The Object Browser can be opened by clicking on the Standard toolbar in the Visual Basic Editor. The **Object Browser** lists all VBA objects along with the associated methods and properties for each object. Now, you will examine the DoCmd object in more detail.

SIDE NOTE
Classes
The Object Browser refers to objects as classes. These terms are sometimes used interchangeably in help documentation and in the Visual Basic Editor environment.

To Examine the DoCmd and Break the Statement

a. Examine the line of code that begins with the DoCmd object.
   Notice that this line of code is indented. Indentations will indicate that you are taking action within the procedure. Liberal use of white space combined with line indentation creates a more legible procedure.

b. Examine the statement that follows DoCmd.
   The TransferSpreadsheet method is used to import an Excel spreadsheet into the database. The properties associated with a method will allow for further control of how the method behaves. In this example, the TransferSpreadsheet method uses several properties to control actions—such as which folder to open by default and whether to import, export, or link to the spreadsheet file.

c. Click after the portion of the TransferSpreadsheet method that reads **10,**. Press Spacebar, type _, and then press Enter. Using a line continuation character will allow you to break a single statement across two lines of code without invoking a syntax error.

Notice that the remaining portion of the mcrImportParticipants procedure contains statements used in handling potential errors that could occur in the procedure. Error handling and debugging will be discussed in further detail later in the workshop.

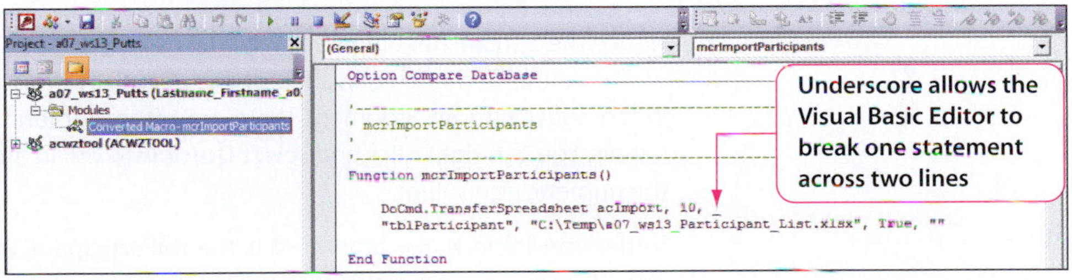

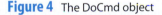

Figure 4 The DoCmd object

The TransferSpreadsheet Method

For importing, exporting, and linking tasks VBA uses the Transfer methods. The particular method used is specific to the object that is the focus of the task. The **TransferSpreadsheet method** allows for Access to import, export, or link to spreadsheet files specifically. This object has six arguments. An **argument** is a constant, variable, or expression that is passed to a procedure. Figure 5 lists the arguments for the TransferSpreadsheet method.

Argument Name	Description	Example
Transfer Type	This argument refers to the type of action that is to take place with the object.	acImport, acExport, acLink
Spreadsheet Type	This argument refers to the type of spreadsheet that will be imported by the database.	acSpreadsheet-TypeExcel12
Table Name	This is the name of the Access table that will be used during the process in the Transfer Type argument. This can also be a Select query in which the data from the query can be exported. When importing, Access will append records to an existing table. If no table exists, Access will import the records into a new table.	"tblName"
File Name	The name of the spreadsheet file to be used during the process selected in the Transfer Type argument	"C:\Temp\FileName.xlsx" When a specific file is used, the path and filename must be given in quotation marks.
Has Field Names	This argument specifies whether the spreadsheet contains field names in the first row of the spreadsheet. If the spreadsheet does contain field names this argument should be set to Yes. If the spreadsheet does not contain field names this argument should be set to No. The default is No.	Yes/No and True/False can be used interchangeably here.
Range	This optional argument can be used to define a specific range of cells from the spreadsheet to import. If this argument is left blank Access will import or link the entire worksheet.	"Data" or "" for blank

Figure 5 TransferSpreadsheet method arguments

To Examine the DoCmd and Break the Statement Across Two Lines

a. Notice in this TransferSpreadsheet method the Transfer Type is set to acImport. This tells Access to import the file.

b. Notice the Spreadsheet type is set to 10.
    This is the numeric equivalent of the default for this argument, Excel Spreadsheet. When specifying an argument there are often numeric equivalents for the property names. You can right-click and select **Quick Info** on an argument after typing it to view the numeric equivalent.

c. Notice the Table Name argument is the tblParticipant table and the table name is in quotation marks. This argument requires the name of the table to be a text string.

d. Notice the next File Name argument contains "C:\Temp\a07_ws13_Participant_List.xlsx". This is the path and name of the spreadsheet that will be imported. Here, this value is a fixed path and filename just as it was in the original macro. Using VBA, you will need to change it to make this procedure more robust.

e. Notice the Has Field Names argument is set to True. This tells Access the spreadsheet does have the appropriate column headers.

Troubleshooting

A Has Field Names argument set to True requires an exact match. If the column headings in the target Excel spreadsheet do not match the Access field names, an error message will be displayed and the data will not be imported.

f. Notice the Range argument displays "", the equivalent of a blank to indicate the default value. This directs Access to import the entire worksheet.

g. Notice the End Function statement ends the function. When the procedure comes to this statement it will not process any of the remaining code.

Editing the Routine

For this macro to work as required by Barry Cheney, it must allow the user to select the correct file or files from a dynamic location on the user's computer. VBA can be used to add this functionality and control how the user interacts with the resulting processes.

The FileDialog Object

In order to allow users to select file(s) for importing, some new code must be inserted prior to the DoCmd object. The **FileDialog object** can be used to allow the user to select the file(s) needed for the import process. The FileDialog object has the following four properties.

Property	Description	Property Name in VBA
open	This option allows the user to select one or more files that can be opened in the host application.	msoFileDialogOpen
SaveAs	This option allows the user to select a single file that can then be used to save the current file as.	msoFileDialogSaveAs
File Picker	This option allows the user to select one or more files. The file paths are stored in the SelectedItems method of the FileDialog object.	msoFileDialogFilePicker
Folder Picker	This option allows the user to select a path (folder). The file path text is stored in the SelectedItems method of the FileDialog object.	msoFileDialogFolderPicker

Figure 6 FileDialog object properties

The FileDialog object also has several methods that can be used to customize the behavior of the File Dialog window. In this example, the methods AllowMultiSelect, Title, and SelectedItems will be used. The AllowMultiSelect method lets users select multiple files for import. The Title method allows you to set a customized title to the File Dialog window. The SelectedItems method stores the names of the files that are selected for import.

Real World Advice The AutoComplete Feature

VBA uses an AutoComplete feature similar to that found in other Microsoft Office applications such as writing field names in query criteria. For example, typing "FileDialog." in the Visual Basic Editor —as seen in Figure 7— will open a list of objects and methods that are found within the FileDialog object. These can be selected with the pointer or by typing enough of the desired item to prompt Access to highlight the item, which you then can complete by pressing Tab.

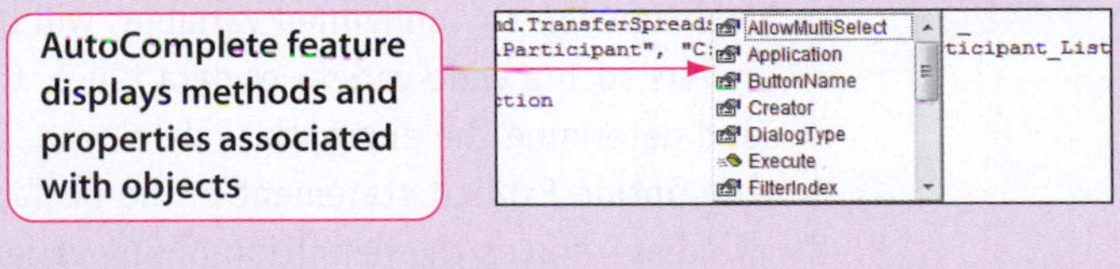

AutoComplete feature displays methods and properties associated with objects

Figure 7 The FileDialog object showing the AutoComplete feature

The first step in creating the File Dialog process is to declare a variable as a FileDialog object. Creating and declaring variables will make the procedure more efficient and easier to follow as more statements are added. **Variables** are placeholders that can be set to a hard-coded value or to an object within VBA and then later modified during the execution of the procedure. The different variable data types are listed in Figure 8. Because you can customize the names of variables in VBA, you can create variables that are easy to remember and identify. The **Dim statement** begins the process of declaring a variable. This is followed by the name the user wants to define as a variable. This can be any string that does not begin with a numeral or is not a reserved word in VBA. Following the name of the variable is the As Type portion of the statement. There are several data types in VBA to use, as shown in Figure 8.

Name	Description	Example
Byte	An integer from 0 to 255	125
Boolean	Used in true or false variables	True or False
Integer	Numeric data type for whole numbers	125
Long	Numeric data type for large integer numbers	9,000,000,000
Currency	Numeric data type that allows for four digits to the right of the decimal and 15 to the left	1234.67
Single	Numeric data type used for numbers that can contain fractions	125.25
Double	Numeric data type used for large numbers that can contain fractions	9,000,000,000.25
Date	Stores date and time data	7/1/2013 8:35:56 AM
String	A variable length of text characters	"Your import is complete"
Object	Used to create a variable that stores a VBA object	FileDialog
Variant	The default data type if none is specified; can store numeric, string, date/time, empty, or null data	125 or "One hundred and twenty-five"

Figure 8 Variable types

User-defined types can also be created in VBA modules and assigned to a variable with the Dim statement. In this instance, a variable will be created and set to be equal to the FileDialog object. This allows for easy use of the FileDialog object later in the procedure. Variables do not have to be defined using the Dim statement. Not formally defining variables often leads to errors in your VBA as the result of misspellings of variable names. This is only required if the Option Explicit statement is used in the Declarations section of the module. The **Option Explicit statement** will force any variables in a procedure to be defined using the Dim statement.

CONSIDER THIS | **Using Option Explicit**

VBA can interpret variable names without the use of the Dim statement. By default, defining a variable is not a required action. You could simply type MyVariable = 10 and the procedure would use the value "10" wherever you used the variable "MyVariable". This can lead to problems such as an unnoticed misspelling of a variable name. Additionally, any undefined variables will be of the Variant data type. Because Variant covers such a wide variety of data types, the application must evaluate the data and determine the appropriate data type. This increases the processing time. Using the Option Explicit statement in the Declarations section—the first line of the Code window—forces the definition of any variable names, preventing this type of situation from occurring. What advantages are there to using Option Explicit?

Real World Advice — What Is the Best Way to Identify the Properties of an Object?

The properties associated with an object can be referred to by name but also can sometimes be referred to by a defined constant. For example, with the FileDialog object you can choose to use the File Open dialog box by typing msoFileDialogOpen or, more simply, by typing the number 1. Using the defined constant will accomplish the same desired outcome as typing msoFileDialogOpen. The difference is that using the defined constant may be faster to type, but it may not be as intuitive to decipher when reviewing the procedure later on.

To Add the FileDialog Object to the Procedure

a. Place your pointer on the blank line above the DoCmd.TransferSpreadsheet action in the Code window.

b. Press Enter, and then press Tab to indent the code.

c. Type **Dim ParticipantDialog as Object**, and then press Enter.

This creates a variable called ParticipantDialog. This variable can be reused throughout the procedure and will be more efficient when setting the object properties later on.

d. Type **Set ParticipantDialog = Application.FileDialog(msoFileDialogOpen)**, and press Enter twice. Before completing this line of code a Microsoft Visual Basic for Applications message box may appear. If it does, click **Yes** and see the Troubleshooting tip for further explanation of this message box.

e. Examine the Set statement. The Set statement tells the application that the variable, ParticipantDialog, will be used as a FileDialog object.

Troubleshooting

Objects in VBA exist in library files. Objects become available in the Code window when these library files are referenced in the Visual Basic Editor. The FileDialog object is not included in the default libraries that are referenced in Access 2010. However, Access automatically installs a reference for the correct object library when you enter the FileDialog object into the Code window. The message box in Figure 9 is displayed when Access adds the appropriate library for the FileDialog object. Plug-in applications and legacy objects may need to be added manually to the Code window. This can be accomplished by clicking the Tools menu on the menu bar and selecting References. If the proper library file did not load, add the Microsoft Office 14.0 Object Library to the list of references.

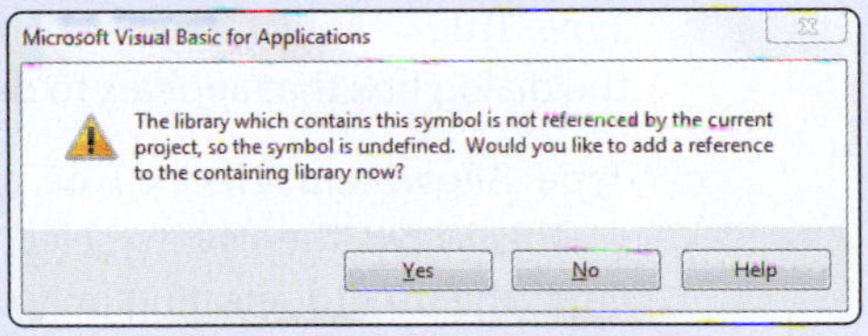

Figure 9 Add a library reference

```
Option Compare Database

'--------------------------------------------------------------
' mcrImportParticipants
'
'--------------------------------------------------------------
Function mcrImportParticipants()

    Dim ParticipantDialog As Object
    Set ParticipantDialog = Application.FileDialog(msoFileDialogOpen)


    DoCmd.TransferSpreadsheet acImport, 10, _
    "tblParticipant", "C:\Temp\a07_ws13_Participant_List.xlsx", True, ""

End Function
```

Figure 10 The FileDialog object added to the procedure

CONSIDER THIS | **Using the Filters Method**

The Filters property of the FileDialog object can prove useful for customizing the File Open dialog box. Using this method, the VBA procedure can reset the filter on the dialog box so that only spreadsheet files are initially viewed. This prevents a user from accidently selecting the incorrect file type. To accomplish this, use the .Filters method. To be safe, start by clearing out any existing filters (.Filters.Clear). Then add the filters you want the user to see. For example, .Filters.Add "Excel Spreadsheet", "*.xlsx" will allow users to select any .xlsx file in the browser. Filters.Add "All Files", "*.*" adds an all files option that displays any file in the current folder. Why might it be useful to restrict which files a user can select in a dialog box?

The With Statement

Once a variable has been assigned to serve as a placeholder for the FileDialog object there are several properties that can be set. The **With statement** allows for an efficient way of using several methods or setting multiple properties on a single object. Without it, the developer would be required to type the object's full name for each method used or property set. With statements are simple to use and provide for enormous time savings in coding. To use a With statement type "With ObjectName", where "ObjectName" is the object you want to modify. Inside of a With statement each method used or property to edit is preceded only by a single period. Each With statement must then end with the statement "End With". While With statements can be nested in order to apply settings to multiple properties within an object, they can only act upon one object at a time.

To Create a With Statement and Set the FileDialog Properties

a. Ensure that your pointer is on the line above the DoCmd statement. Type **With ParticipantDialog**, press [Enter], and then press [Tab].
   This inserts an indentation to create a more legible code structure.

b. Type **.Title = "Select New Participant List(s)"**, and then press [Enter]. This sets the title of the dialog box that appears to display "Select New Participant List(s)".

c. Type **.AllowMultiSelect = True**, and then press [Enter].
   This allows the user to select multiple files to import. Setting this method to False limits the user to selecting only one file at a time.

d. Press [Backspace] to align your pointer with the With statement.

e. Press [Enter] twice.

For the FileDialog object to function properly, the procedure must determine if the user selected any files. Alternatively, the user could end the operation by clicking the Cancel button in the File Dialog window. If this happens, the procedure should end after the Cancel button is clicked. An If statement can be implemented within the With statement to determine the outcome of the user's actions.

Real World Advice — Capitalization

While VBA is by default case sensitive, when typing the name of a variable, method, or property the Visual Basic Editor will automatically capitalize the text for you. For example, in the FileDialog property, .AllowMultiSelect, typing .allowmultiselect will be automatically corrected to the appropriate case.

If Statements in VBA

If statements in VBA work similarly to those found in Access and Excel though the syntax is slightly different. Each If statement must follow the basic syntax:

```
If [Condition] Then
[Statement]
Else
[Statement]
End If
```

Real World Advice — When to Nest If Statements in VBA

You can nest If statements to take into account multiple logical tests. In VBA, this can be accomplished in two ways. You can nest an If statement within another If statement or you can use the ElseIf statement. ElseIf can be invoked after the Else statement in order to continue to consider additional conditions being meet. The use of the ElseIf statement would look like this:

```
IF [Condition1] Then
[Statement]
ElseIf [Condition2] Then
[Statement]
Else
[Statement]
End If
```

The .Show method of the FileDialog object displays the selected type of dialog box to the user and returns to the procedure a True value if one or more files were selected. If no files were selected .Show returns a False value. For the process being created in the Putts for Paws database, if .Show returns a value of True, the procedure should import the files to the appropriate table. If .Show returns a value of False, a message should be displayed stating that the operation was cancelled and the procedure should be exited.

To Create the Import Process

a. Press Tab to indent the current line.

b. Type **If .show = True then**, and then press Enter.

c. Press Tab to create an indentation.

d. Type **Dim ImportFileName as Variant** to define a variable that will hold the names of the files selected by the user. Using the Variant type is required here and will be discussed later.

e. Click before the text **DoCmd.TransferSpreadsheet acImport, 10, _ "tblParticipant", "C:\temp\a07_ws13_Participant_List.xlsx", True, ""**, and highlight the two lines of this code. Press Tab twice to align this statement with the prior Dim statement.

This allows the import to run if the .Show property is true. Because the procedure will need to account for multiple files, additional code will be required. This will be revisited in the next step.

f. Click after the last argument of the DoCmd statement, press Enter, and then press Backspace. This aligns the pointer into the same column as the If portion of the statement.

g. Type **Else**, and then press Enter. This begins the False portion of the If statement.

h. Press Tab, and then type **Msgbox "You cancelled the import"** to create a new message box. This message box will tell the user that the import process has been stopped by clicking Cancel in the File Dialog box.

i. Press Enter, and then press Backspace.

j. Type **End If**, and then press Enter.

k. Press Backspace. This aligns the pointer with the same column as the With Statement.

l. Type **End With**, and then press Enter.

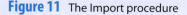

```
(General)                                          ▼   mcrImportParticipants                          ▼

   Option Compare Database

   '----------------------------------------------------------
   ' mcrImportParticipants
   '
   '----------------------------------------------------------
   Function mcrImportParticipants()

       Dim ParticipantDialog As Object
       Set ParticipantDialog = Application.FileDialog(msoFileDialogOpen)

       With ParticipantDialog
           .Title = "Select New Participant List(s)"
           .AllowMultiSelect = True

           If .Show = True Then
               Dim ImportFileName As Variant

               DoCmd.TransferSpreadsheet acImport, 10, _
               "tblParticipant", "C:\Temp\a07_ws13_Participant_List.xlsx", True, ""
           Else
               MsgBox "You cancelled the import"
           End If
       End With


   End Function
```

Figure 11 The Import procedure

Real World Advice   Message Boxes in VBA

The Msgbox function is an extremely useful function. In VBA, a message box can display customized text and buttons in addition to the standard OK, Cancel, and Yes/No buttons familiar in Microsoft applications. Similar to the process of commenting code, message boxes provide a convenient method of keeping your users informed about the status of the application that they are using.

The procedure that has been created and edited to this point will function as follows: When the procedure is executed, first it declares the variable ParticipantDialog as an Access object. The procedure then defines the variable as a FileDialog object with a File Open parameter. Next, using a With statement, the title of the File Open dialog box is set, and the object is enabled to accept multiple file selections from the user. Alternatively, Access will display a message box stating that the user cancelled the import if the Cancel button in the dialog box is clicked. To complete the procedure, a loop will be added to the True portion of the If statement to account for situations where the user selects multiple files for importing.

Looping in VBA

When the user selects a file to import, the procedure stores the name of the file in the SelectedItems property of the FileDialog object. It then imports that file into the appropriate table. If the user were to select multiple files, each filename is stored in the same property and imported. The process for importing the appropriate files listed in the .SelectedItems FileDialog property happens on a file-by-file basis. In other words, each file selected will force the procedure to access a new filename and import the file as an individualized action.

This type of repetitive action is often one of the main reasons macros or VBA are used to automate a process in Access. **Loops** are used to execute a series of statements multiple times. Loops are similar to If statements in that they evaluate a condition and act depending on the status of the condition. Loops offer a distinct difference in that they allow the statements contained within the loop to be executed multiple times depending on the constraints of the loop. Figure 12 demonstrates a programmatic loop. The number of times the loop runs can be determined two ways. Loops can run until a condition is determined to be true or false. Loops can also be set to run until they have executed a specific number of times. This can be determined by counting the number of repetitions that have run or by counting the number of items the loop should act upon.

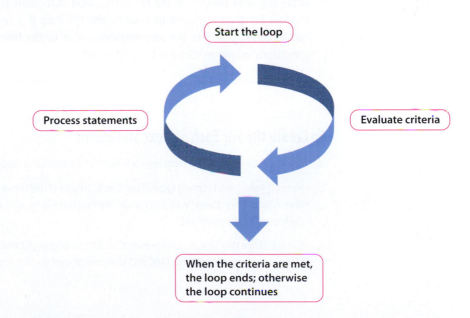

Start the loop

Process statements

Evaluate criteria

When the criteria are met, the loop ends; otherwise the loop continues

Figure 12 A loop

Loops can be conceptually difficult to understand but have a simple structure in the actual procedure. In the example of the FileDialog object, the procedure should store a filename for each file selected by the user. The problem with this specific situation is that the number of files may differ from day to day. Monday there might be three files to import while on Tuesday there may only be one. Fortunately, VBA has a statement that handles this very situation.

Quick Reference Types of Loops in VBA

1. For Loops
   a. For To...Next
   b. For Each...Next
2. Do Loops
   a. Do Loop
   b. Do Until
   c. Do While

The For Each...Next statement executes the nested statements for each item in a defined set of objects. In this example, the For Each...Next statement selects the name of each file selected by the user. When there are no more filenames to record, the loop exits. The syntax for a For Each...Next statement contains three parts and looks like the following:

For Each [element as datatype] In [group]
[Statements]
Next

The element is a variable that refers to the item that requires an action, such as a filename. The group is the object that contains the collection of items over which the statements will be repeated. The statements section contains any actions to be carried out. Once the For Each... Next statement has carried out the required actions on all of the available items, the procedure continues with the statement in the procedure after the Next statement.

CONSIDER THIS | **Exit For**

While the Next portion of the For Each...Next statement is the final piece of syntax, the Exit For statement can be used to end the loop if a certain condition is met. This can be inserted within the loop anywhere prior to the Next statement. What type of conditions might an Exit For be used with?

To Create the For Each...Next Statement

a. Click at the end of the Dim ImportFileName as Variant statement, and then press Enter.

b. Press Tab, and then type **For Each ImportFileName In .SelectedItems** to begin the loop. The loop will continue until there are no additional file names in the .SelectedItems method.

c. Click before the DoCmd statement, and then highlight the two lines of the DoCmd. Press Tab twice to indent the DoCmd statement within the For Each statement.

d. Select **"C:\Temp\a07_ws13_Participant_List.xlsx"**, and then press **Delete** to remove it. Type **ImportFileName** with no quotation marks.

This replaces the text in the FileName property of the TransferSpreadsheet statement with the variable you created to hold a file name selected by the user. Because a variable name is used in place of a text string, no quotation marks are needed.

e. Press `End`, and then press `Enter`.

Remember the TransferSpreadsheet method imports the file to the appropriate Access table. In the loop, each time a file is imported the loop starts over again with the next file name that was stored in the .SelectedItems property.

f. Press `Backspace`, and then type **Next** to complete the loop.

This aligns the pointer with the same column as the For Each statement. The Next portion of the statement exits the loop once all files have been imported.

g. Click [x] to close the Visual Basic Editor.

Click [X] to close the mcrImportParticipants macro. This completes the For...Next statement and the procedure as a whole. Now, regardless of how many files are selected by the user for import, each file will be processed separately by Access.

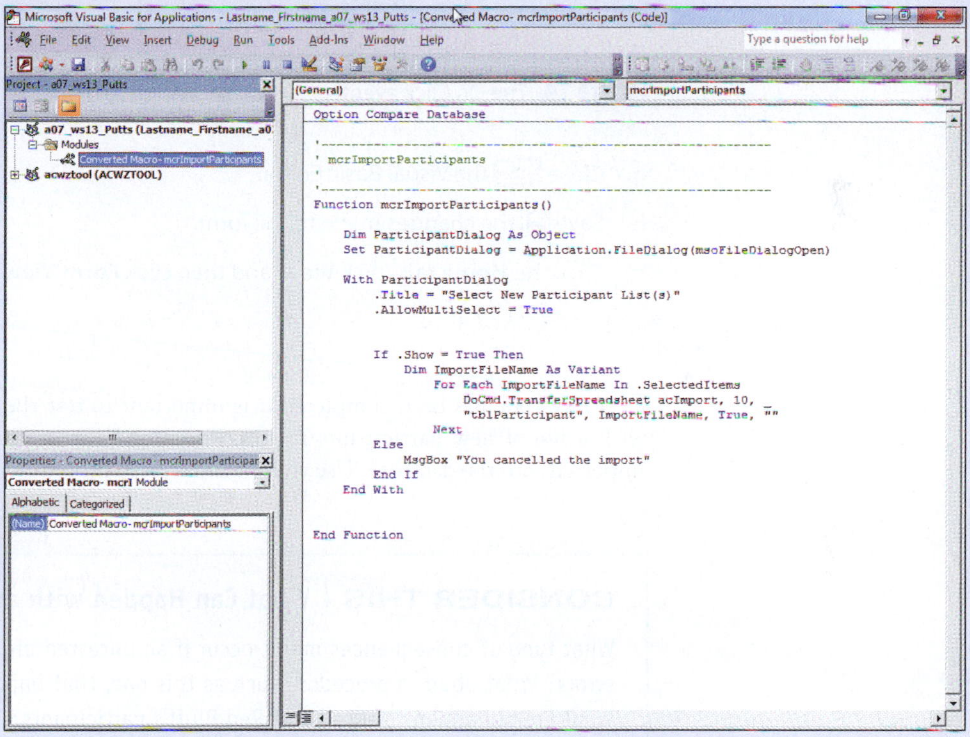

Figure 13 The finished procedure

The last step before testing the procedure is to change the assignment of the button on the Imports tab. Because the button was originally set up to run a macro when clicked, you need to change this setting to run the new procedure. To accomplish this you need to call the function that was created by converting the import macro. The **Call statement** will run another sub procedure or function from within a procedure by transferring to the called routine. Here you will call the mcrImportParticipants procedure when the Import New Participants button is clicked.

To Assign the Procedure to the Button

a. From the Navigation Pane right-click **frmPuttsMenu**, and then click **Design View**.

b. If the Property Sheet is not visible, click **Property Sheet** in the Tools group.

c. In the Design window, click the **Imports tab**, and then click **Import New Participants**.

d. In the property sheet, click the **Event tab**. The On Click event lists the macro mcrImport-Participants as the action to take when the button is clicked.

e. Click the **On Click arrow**, and then select **[Event Procedure]**.

f. Click **Builder** [...]. This will open the Visual Basic Editor. The Code window will display a new Private Sub statement. This Sub will be run when the command button is clicked. On the blank line of the Sub, press [Tab]. Type **Call mcrImportParticipants** to call the newly created VBA procedure.

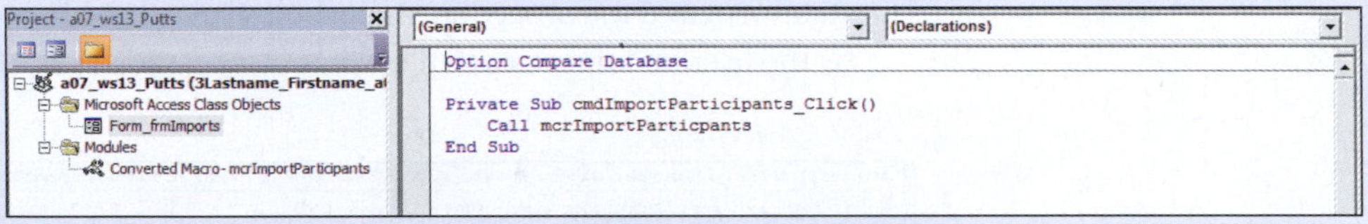

Figure 14 The On Click event

g. Close [✕] the Visual Basic Editor.

h. Save [💾] the changes made to the form.

i. Click the **Home tab**, click **View**, and then click **Form View**.

Once code has been completed it is important to test the process. You have been provided with a file of new participants for the Putts for Paws events. These participants need to be imported into the database. Use your newly created procedure to import these new participants.

CONSIDER THIS | **What Can Happen with an Untested Procedure?**

What type of consequences might occur if an untested procedure runs and contains errors? What about a procedure such as this one, that imports data into a database? What could happen to the list of Red Bluff's participants?

To Close the Procedure and Test

a. In the **Putts for Paws Database** Navigational form, click the **Imports tab**.

b. Click the **Import New Participants** button.

You will be presented with a File Open dialog box. Notice that the title of the dialog box is the same as you specified in your procedure.

c. Navigate to the folder where your student data files are stored, click **a07_ws13_Participant_List.xlsx**, and then click **Open**.

d. To verify that the import was successful, click the **Participants tab**, and then click ▶ to view the last record in the tblParticipant table. The last record should now be ParticipantID number 1009.

e. Click the **Imports tab** and click the **Import New Participants** button again.

f. Click **Cancel** to stop the import process. You will be presented with a message box stating that you cancelled the import.

g. Click **OK**. Importantly, you must test every action a user might take when developing VBA.

Figure 15 The cancellation message box

Creating VBA Procedures

You have been asked by Barry Cheney to modify the frmParticipant form of the Putts for Paws database. The database has been set up such that each entity that donates can specify a separate billing address from their designated mailing address. This works well when the two addresses are different, but when the addresses are the same the result is a duplicate data entry. To increase the efficiency of the data entry process, you have been asked to provide a method of automation to the form. Barry has requested a button that will copy the billing address fields into the mailing address fields.

Real World Advice   Creating VBA Procedures from Scratch

There will not always be a macro to begin with, and often what you will be trying to accomplish with VBA will be more involved than what a macro can be set up to do in Access. Unlike other Microsoft applications, in Access, it is not always the best practice to begin with a recorded macro.

Create an On Click Event

To add the requested functionality, a button must be added to the form that will allow a user to copy the billing address data into the mailing address data with a simple button click.

To Add a Button to the Form

a. Open the **frmPuttsMenu** form from the Navigation Pane if it is not currently open.

b. In the Views group click **View**, and then click the **Participants tab**.

c. On the Design tab click ▭ in the Controls group.

d. Move the pointer between the BillingZipCode label and the MailingStreetAddress label, and then click to place the Button control.

e. Click **Cancel** in the Command Button Wizard.

The Command Button Wizard cannot be used to associate a VBA procedure to the button. This will be accomplished in the property sheet.

f. Select the newly created **button**. Press [Ctrl], and then click the **empty cell** in the table to the right of the button. Right-click, click **Merge/Split** on the shortcut menu, and then click **Merge**.

The button should act as a separator between the mailing and billing addresses. Merging the button across the table will create a clear break between the two addresses and allow enough room for the button to have a descriptive caption.

g. Select the newly created **button**. If the Property Sheet is not visible, click **Property Sheet** on the Design tab.

h. Click the **All tab** in the property sheet. In the Name field of the property sheet, replace the default name of the button with **cmdCopyBillingAddress**.

i. In the Caption field, replace the default caption with **Mailing and billing addresses are the same**.

j. Save 🖫 the changes to the form.

Troubleshooting

To edit the VBA code of an Access object, the object (such as a form) must be opened in Design view. Opening the object in Layout view, which is often used to create and edit forms, will result in a Microsoft Access error.

Real World Advice   Renaming Command Buttons

When a new button is created on a form, Access assigns the button a name such as Command65. When using the wizard to assign functions to a button, this naming convention may not be an obstacle because you will be able to change the caption on the button as part of the wizard. When creating a button in order to assign Visual Basic code, this can present problems because the name of the button is too vague. Instead, it is helpful to rename the button to describe the event that will take place. This way when you search through your code later, you can quickly find and identify an event button that needs to be modified.

The process needed in this example is to copy the data from the billing address fields to the mailing address fields when the button cmdCopyBillingAddress is clicked. Access provides some shortcuts to assign VBA procedures to controls on objects such as forms that you can take advantage of.

To Assign a VBA Procedure to the cmdCopyBillingAddress Button

a. Click the **Home tab**, in the Views group click the **View button arrow**, and then click **Design View**.

b. Click the **Participants tab**, and then click the **Mailing and billing addresses are the same** button on the Participants form.

SIDE NOTE

Accessing the VBA Code for an Object

Often the most efficient way to access the VBA code related to an event or object is through its property sheet in Design view.

c. Click the **Event tab** in the property sheet, and then in the list of events, click **Build** [...] in the field for On Click.

d. In the Choose Builder dialog box, click **Code Builder**, and then click **OK**.

This opens the Visual Basic Editor. The basic syntax of the procedure in the Code window has been automatically completed. The Option Compare Database statement is in the Declaration section of the Code window. In the Project Explorer, a new Microsoft Access Class object has been created for the form that is being edited. The object Form_frmParticipant will contain any VBA procedures created to run in response to events occurring on this form.

e. Examine the first line of the procedure.

A Sub statement was automatically created when you chose the Code Builder option. The name of the Sub procedure, cmdCopyBillingAddress_Click(), indicates that the procedure will be run when a user clicks the cmdCopyBillingAddress_Click() button. In this procedure, the value property of the individual fields can be used to set one field value equal to that of another field value. In this example, you will use the Me keyword to identify the fields to copy. The **Me keyword** functions like a declared variable that refers to the current object.

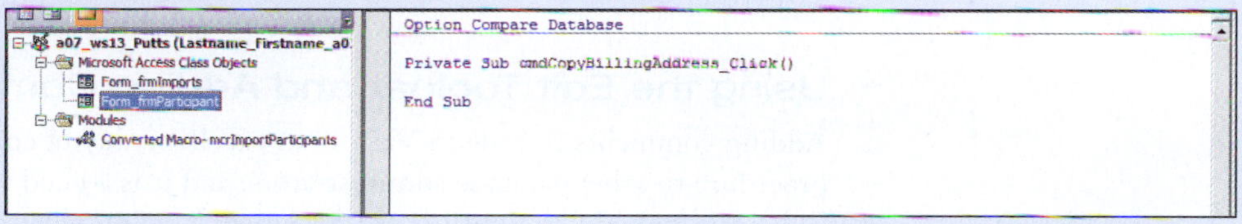

Figure 16 The Address On Click event

SIDE NOTE

Private Sub

A Private Sub is a type of Sub procedure that is only accessible by other procedures in the module in which it is located. In this example, the cmdCopyBillingAddress_Click() procedure cannot be used on another form.

f. Click the blank line in the Code window under the Private Sub statement, and then press Enter.

g. Press Tab.

This will create an indentation for your next statement. The Visual Basic Editor will use this indentation point as a reference for subsequent statements. Pressing Enter after typing a statement will align the pointer with the column in which the previous statement begins.

h. Type Me.MailingStreetAddress.Value = Me.BillingStreetAddress.Value, and then press Enter.

This uses the Me keyword as the Form object in place of typing Form![frmParticipant] to access the Form objects. The statement in its entirety sets the field value of MailStreetAddress to that of the BillingStreetAddress value.

i. Type Me.MailingCity.Value = Me.BillingCity.Value, and then press Enter.

j. Type Me.MailingState.Value = Me.BillingState.Value, and then press Enter.

k. Type Me.MailingZipCode.Value = Me.BillingZipCode.Value, and then press Enter.

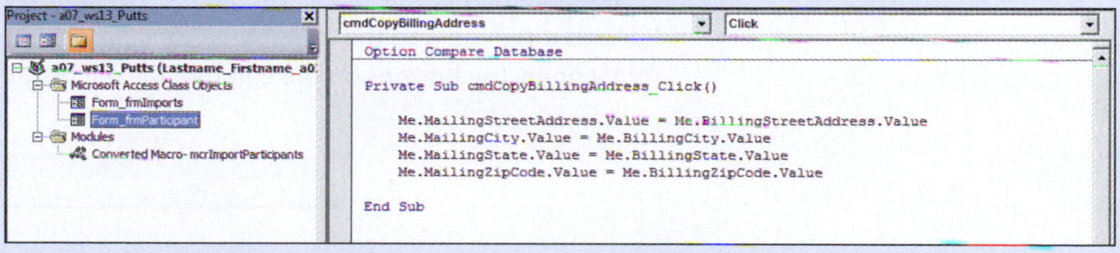

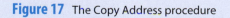

Figure 17 The Copy Address procedure

l. Close ![close button] the Visual Basic Editor, and then save ![save button] the changes to the form.

m. On the Home tab, in the Views group click the down arrow and then click **Form View**.

n. To test the new procedure on ParticipantID number 1, click the **Participants tab** and then click the **Mailing and billing address are the same** button, and then verify that the information in the Billing Address fields was copied to the Mailing Address fields.

Real World Advice   The Procedure Box and Object Box Shortcuts

Both the Procedure box and Object box can be used to create event procedures from within the Visual Basic Editor. With the Object box you can select the desired object that the event should be attached to and the corresponding Private Sub structure will appear in the Code window. Once you are editing a specific object, you can use the Procedure box to select the action that you want a procedure to run in response to an event.

Using the Edit Toolbar and Adding Comments

Adding comments to code in VBA is an excellent way of communicating the intentions of a procedure to other database administrators, and it is a good way of keeping track of your own code. You can add straightforward documentation on what the procedure is doing and what steps to take next. If you are developing more complicated procedures, you might want to leave yourself notes about what still needs to be completed or what statements are not working as expected.

Adding comments in the Code window is as simple as typing an apostrophe. The apostrophe character tells the Visual Basic Editor to ignore any text following the apostrophe on a line of the Code window. Comments can take an entire line of the Code window or begin after another statement in the Code window. The Visual Basic Editor also changes the font color of any commented text to green. Commenting only works on a line-by-line basis though. Other programming languages have block commenting methods that use special characters. In this method all text between the symbols would be omitted as part of the code. For example, in HTML any text between the characters <!-- and --> are ignored by the web browser. While Visual Basic lacks this style of commenting, the Visual Basic Editor provides commenting functionality and more on the Edit toolbar.

To Enable the Editing Toolbar

a. If you are not already in the Visual Basic Editor, press [Alt]+[F11] to open it.

b. Click **View** on the Standard menu bar, click **Toolbars**, and then click **Edit**.
    The Edit toolbar will appear as a floating toolbar. It can be docked by clicking the title bar and dragging it to the top of the Visual Basic Editor window. If no modules are currently open, the buttons on the Edit toolbar will be greyed out.

Figure 18 The Edit toolbar

The Edit toolbar has many useful features built into it. The comment block feature can be used to identify large or small strings of text in a procedure as a comment. It also includes buttons for increasing and decreasing indentations and listing the properties and methods of a statement in the Code window.

To Add a Comment

a. In the Project Explorer window, open the **Form_frmParticipant** object if is it not already displayed.

b. Click under **Private Sub** in the Code window.

c. Type This procedure will copy the Billing Address information to the Mailing Address fields. Pressing Enter at this point would result in a Visual Basic Compile error because the text above does not contain any VBA statements.

d. Click Comment Block on the Edit toolbar.

   Notice that an apostrophe now appears in the first character space of the line. The Visual Basic Editor will now ignore this entire line of text when executing the procedure.

e. Press Enter, and then type This procedure was written by Firstname Lastname replacing Firstname and Lastname with your actual name. Click **Comment Block** on the Edit toolbar, and then press Enter.

Comments in the code window display in green font

Figure 19 Comments in a procedure

Larger blocks of text can be identified as comments using this technique. Consider the macro that was converted in the "Convert an Existing Macro to VBA" section of this workshop. Several lines of comments were inserted into the procedure when Access converted the macro. This can be accomplished by using the pointer to select each line of text that you want to designate as a comment and clicking Comment Block. Likewise, if you want to remove the apostrophe from a comment, clicking Uncomment Block will remove the apostrophe from each line that is currently selected.

CONSIDER THIS | Commenting in VBA Code

Comments are an often overlooked but important aspect of coding. If you have ever examined a database someone else has created, it can be very difficult to discern a complex series of queries or decipher the relationship of poorly named objects in a database. Likewise, attempting to understand the rationale for an action in a database might be nearly impossible without comments to explain the original developer's intent. Sometimes, years later even *you* do not remember your own rationale for the action. Much of the same is true with VBA. What benefits are there to commenting your code? Can you imagine a situation where commenting is unnecessary?

Error Handling and Debugging

Creating a procedure that runs perfectly on the first run or in all situations is virtually impossible. No matter how experienced you might be at writing VBA, a simple typo or misplaced statement can invoke a Visual Basic error. These Visual Basic errors can be confusing to your users and will generally open the Visual Basic Editor in Debugging mode if not handled correctly. While as a developer this might be acceptable, the standard user will be confused by the event and should not be given access to the raw VBA code.

Debugging is the process of identifying and reducing the number of errors that can occur within your code. **Error handling** is the process of anticipating and controlling for errors. You want your application to inform the user of a problem, and your application or procedure should exit cleanly. VBA has some error-handling features installed such that when an error is encountered the procedure will be halted and you will receive an error message. You can also add customized error handling to a VBA procedure using a few key statements.

The On Error statement provides a wide array of ways to handle errors that might arise throughout the course of a procedure. It is important to note that not all errors that occur are negative. For example, when searching for the name of a person in a table the message you receive that the name cannot be found is the result of an error. The message is simply a controlled response to the error.

In the event of an error, using the On Error GoTo statement will redirect the procedure to a local error-handling routine. The GoTo portion of the statement can redirect the procedure to a line label or a specific line number. **Line labels** can be used like bookmarks in a procedure. The combination of On Error statements and line labels provide basic error handling to be built into any VBA procedure. Consider the VBA procedure created to import additional participants into the Putts database. If the Excel file being imported does not contain the appropriate column headings, Access will encounter an error and stop the import process. Because the process originates in a VBA procedure, the error will result in the termination of the process, and by default it will open the Visual Basic Editor in Debug mode. To prevent this from occurring, some simple error handling can be added to the procedure to control the outcome of any errors.

CONSIDER THIS | **Referring to Specific Lines of Code**

The Visual Basic Editor allows for two ways of referring to a line of code. Line labels are one method. On the Standard toolbar, the Code window tracks the line number and column number of the placement of your pointer. You can use a line number in much the same way you can use a line label to reference a specific place in a procedure. Would there be any differences in referencing with line labels versus line numbers?

To Add Comments and Error Handling to the mcrImportParticipants Procedure

a. In the Project Explorer, double-click the **Converted Macro–mcrImportParticipants** module to view it in the Code window. You do not need to close other modules if they are open.

b. Click the line of code below the Function statement, and then insert a new line if necessary. Type **'This procedure imports new participants into the Putts database**, and then press [Enter].

c. Type **'This procedure was written by Firstname Lastname**, and then press [Enter].

d. Type **On Error GoTo ImportParticipants_Err**, and press [Enter].

Later in this process you will create a line label named ImportParticipants_Err. If an error occurs during the execution of this procedure, Access will immediately move to the portion of the code that starts on the line that contains the identified line label.

e. Click the line of code above the End Function statement and insert a new blank line if necessary.

f. Type **ImportParticipants_Exit:**, and then press Enter.

This line label will serve as a bookmark. If no errors occur, the procedure will end on the next line.

g. Press Tab, type **Exit Function**, and then press Enter.

The **Exit Function statement** works similarly to the End Function statement in that both terminate the function. Exit Function is different as additional code can be added after this function is used whereas using End Function will not allow additional code to be added to the procedure. The Exit Function statement here serves as a stopping point for the procedure. If no error has occurred, the procedure will not execute any statements after the Exit Function statement.

h. Press Enter, and then press Backspace.

i. Type **ImportParticipants_Err:**, and then press Enter.

This is a line label and will serve as a bookmark. If an error occurs, the code will move to this line and continue running the procedure.

j. Press Tab to indent the line.

k. Type **Msgbox Error$**, and then press Enter.

The Msgbox object will display a message box to the user. The contents of the message box can be a fixed text string or a variable that can be defined elsewhere in the procedure. Here, "Error$" will display the error that Access encountered during the import process in the message box.

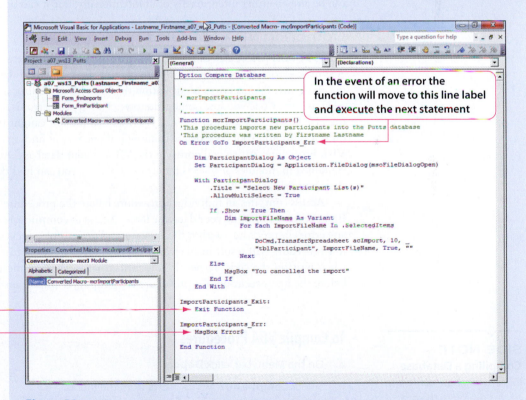

Figure 20 Error handling and comments in the mcrImportParticipants procedure

Quick Reference | Printing VBA Code

1. Open the module you want to print.
2. On the File menu, click Print.
3. To select a printer, click Setup.
4. Click OK to print to the selected printer.

Compiling and Securing Your VBA

Before implementing a database that contains VBA, all modules should be checked for potential errors. This will prevent users from encountering unnecessary and confusing errors while using the database. Importantly, you may want to secure your VBA so that it is not altered. Unsecured VBA can be altered either intentionally or unintentionally, but it can be easily secured to prevent this.

Compiling VBA Modules

Errors in VBA procedures can occur while the code is being written or when the code is executed. A **syntax error** occurs when a completed line of code is entered that the Visual Basic Editor does not recognize. Syntax errors occur within the Visual Basic Editor once the pointer leaves a line of code that the Code window cannot interpret. This type of error is identified immediately and can then be corrected. How can you detect errors that are not caught until the execution of a procedure? Compiling your code before running it is one way of finding errors before the execution of a VBA procedure. When you **compile** the VBA in your database, Access examines all of the VBA contained in modules or objects for errors. This way you can find the errors in a procedure before users stumble across them.

Access compiles an individual procedure before the procedure is executed. Using the Visual Basic Editor to compile your database forces Access to compile all existing modules. This catches any errors in procedure within those modules. For example, declaring a variable more than once in a procedure will result in an error when the procedure is executed. This error is not identified when writing the code; rather, it is identified when the module is compiled. Compiling code before the first execution of a procedure is a simple yet important process.

To Compile VBA Procedures

a. On the Menu bar, click **Debug**.

b. Select **Compile a07_ws13_Putts** from the menu.

   If there are no syntax errors with your VBA procedures, then Access returns you to the Visual Basic Editor. If an error exists, a compile error will occur and Access indicates what the error is and opens the relevant module to the incorrect line of code. To demonstrate this, you will first create a typical syntax error that the Visual Basic Editor will immediately identify. Then you will create an error that will not be identified until the code is compiled.

To Visualize Syntax Errors in VBA Procedures

a. In the Visual Basic Editor, click **Insert Module** 🧩 to create a new module. This will create a new module entitled Module1. Notice that the Option Compare Database statement is in the Declarations section by default.

b. Type **Sub TestErrorHandling**, and then press ⎣Enter⎦ twice. When you press ⎣Enter⎦, the End Sub statement is inserted by default by the Visual Basic Editor on the last line of the procedure.

c. Type **dim**, and then press ⎣Enter⎦. This will invoke a Visual Basic compile error. This happens because the Dim statement cannot exist without a variable name.

Statement causing the compile error

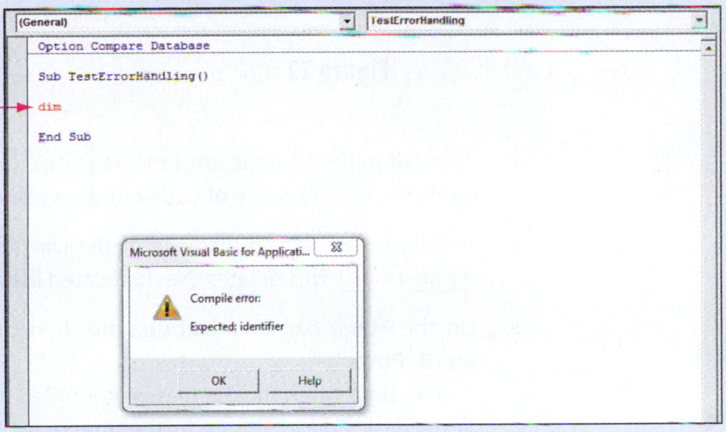

Figure 21 Compile error

Troubleshooting

If a VBA error occurs while Access is running a procedure, you are offered the choice of ending the procedure or entering debugging mode. Choosing to end the procedure halts the execution of any code and returns you to the database. Choosing to enter debugging mode opens the Visual Basic Editor with the incorrect line of code highlighted in yellow. Once you fix the code you need to click 🔳 to return the application to a state where it can again run procedures.

d. Click **OK** in the error message box.

   Notice that the Visual Basic Editor has changed the font color of the incorrect line of code to red to indicate the location of the error. Additionally, your pointer is now located in the place where the error was detected.

e. Your pointer should be located after the Dim keyword. Press the Spacebar, type **test as string** and then press ⎣Enter⎦.

f. Type **Dim test as String** once more, and then press ⎣Enter⎦.

   This time no syntax error occurs. The error here, duplicated variable names, will not be detected until the procedure is compiled.

g. On the Menu bar, click **Debug**, and then click **Compile Lastname_Firstname_a07_ws13_Putts**.

h. The duplicate variable names invokes a compile error as seen in Figure 22.

SIDE NOTE

Variant Data Types

Typing Dim Test and pressing ⎣Enter⎦ does not invoke a compile error. Why? Because if no data type is specified in the procedure the application will assign the Variant data type to the variable as a default.

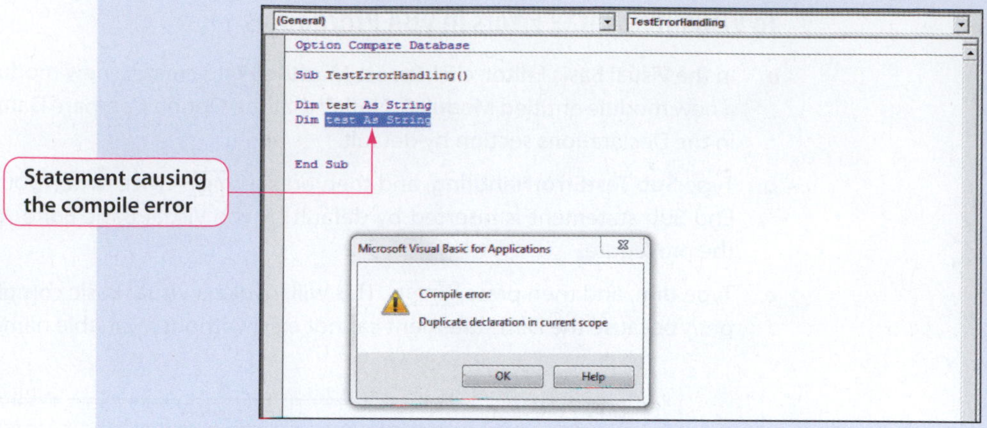

Statement causing
the compile error

Figure 22 Compile error

i. Click **OK** in the compile error message box. In this instance, the Visual Basic Editor highlights the incorrect line of code but does not change the font color.

j. Highlight the second instance of the Dim test as String line of code, and then press Backspace. This deletes the duplicated instance of the Test variable declaration.

k. On the Menu bar, click **Debug**, and then click **Compile Lastname_Firstname_a07_ws13_Putts**.

This time when the database is compiled no errors occur, and you are returned to the Visual Basic Editor without further messages. Your code has successfully compiled!

l. Close the Visual Basic Editor.

Working with ACCDE Files

Once the VBA in an Access database has been compiled it is ready to be used within the database environment. Before deploying the database you may want to consider securing the macros and Visual Basic procedures in a database. This is important so that the VBA in a database is not edited by accident, resulting in errors or incorrect execution of VBA procedures.

The default file format in Access 2010 is the .accdb extension. This format, without additional security measures, allows for full editing of the database by the user. Access provides the .accde format as a method of securing some aspects of the database. In an **.accde file**, VBA procedures will not be viewable to the user, and any errors that might occur during the execution of a VBA procedure will not result in the Visual Basic Editor being displayed. Additionally, forms and reports can be opened but not edited in .accde versions of a database. Saving a database in .accde format creates a new copy of the database that can then be given to the user.

To Create an .accde File

a. Click the **File tab**, and then click **Save & Publish**.

b. Under File Types, click **Save Database As** if it is not selected by default.

c. Under Advanced, click **Make ACCDE**.

d. Click the **Save As** button.

e. Navigate to the folder where you are saving your files, and then click **Save**.

Troubleshooting

You should have already compiled the database and tested your VBA procedures to make sure there are no errors before creating an .accde file. If Access cannot compile your code, the .accde file will not be created.

The database will now reopen in its original .accdb format. It is important to remember that converting a database into the .accde is only one aspect of securing a database for use. In an .accde database, users can still create and modify tables, queries, and macros. If your intention is to implement a fully "locked down" version of the database, there are several more steps to take. These steps are covered in the next workshop.

To Open and Test the .accde File

a. To close the Lastname_Firstname_a07_ws13_Putts.accdb database click the **File tab**, and then click **Close Database**.

b. Click **Open** to display the Open dialog box.

c. Navigate to the folder where you saved the file, and then open **Lastname_Firstname_a07_ws13_Putts.accde**.

Troubleshooting

When .accde databases are created the only difference in the filename may be the last letter of the file extension. Depending on your system settings you may or may not be able to see the extensions of files on your computer. An alternative way to identify .accde files is to look at the icon for the file. Access databases with the .accdb extension have the ![icon] icon, while .accde databases have a padlock visible on the icon ![icon].

d. If the file is not in a trusted location you will see the warning message in Figure 23. This message is to alert the user that there are macros and/or VBA code present within the database that could potentially be malicious.

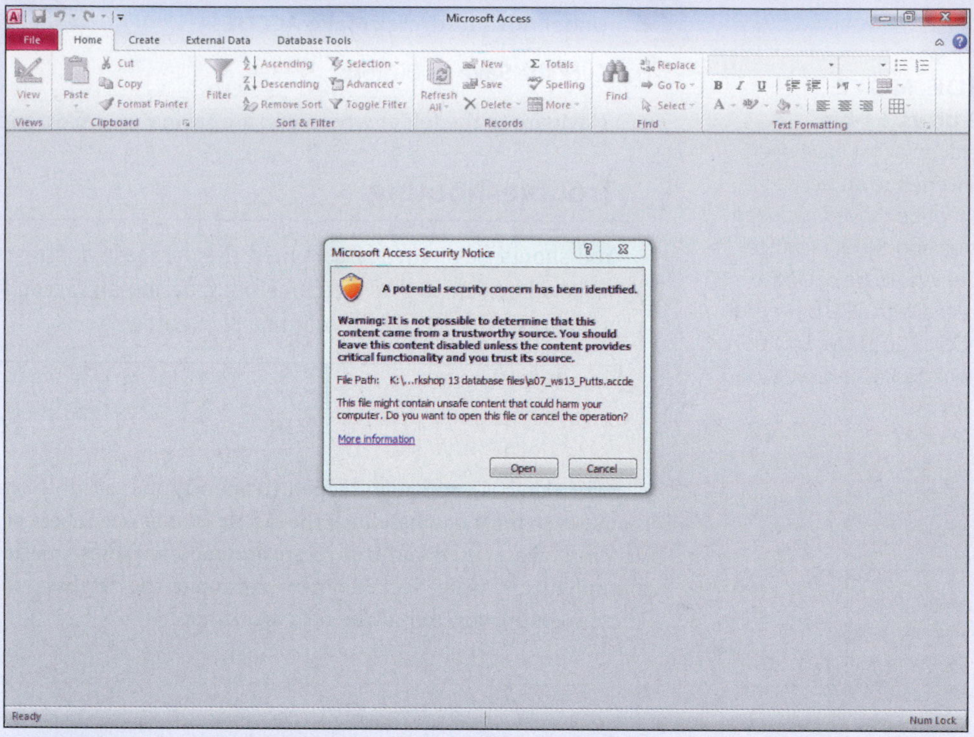

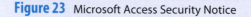

Figure 23 Microsoft Access Security Notice

If you encounter this message, click **Open**.

e. Right-click on the module **Converted Macro - mcrImportParticipants** in the Navigation Pane. Notice that Design view is greyed out and cannot be selected.

f. Press [Alt]+[F11] to open the Visual Basic Editor, and then click the ⊞ next to the **Lastname_Firstname_a07_ws13_Putts** object to expand the view.

g. Click ⊞ next to the Modules objects to expand the view.

h. Double-click the **Converted Macro–mcrImportParticipants** module. You will receive a message stating that the project is not viewable.

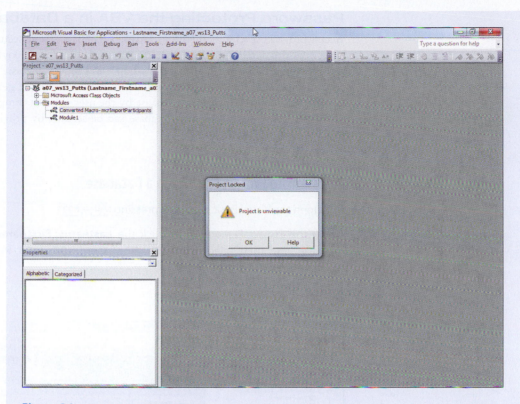

Figure 24 Project Locked dialog box

i. Click **OK**, and then close the Visual Basic Editor.

j. To close the Lastname_Firstname_a07_ws13_Putts.accde database, click the **File tab**, and then **Close Database**.

k. Click **Open** to display the Open dialog box.

l. Browse and navigate to the folder where you saved the file, and then select **Lastname_Firstname_a07_ws13_Putts.accdb**.

m. Click **Open**.

Real World Advice ACCDB and ACCDE Files

Once a database is saved as an .accde file it cannot be converted back to the .accdb file format. Therefore, no changes can be made to macros or VBA modules within the database. Instead, any changes would have to be made in the original .accdb file that would then need to be converted. This is critical because any changes that have been made to the database would be lost (or must be made again in the original file). This includes data entered into tables or new Access objects such as tables or queries that have been added to the database.

Password Protecting the VBA in a Database

Access provides several methods of securing a database. These security measures can affect many aspects of the database and are extremely useful tools for deploying databases to users. These security features are explored in Workshop 14. The Visual Basic Editor provides a method of securing the VBA in a database without implementing more general security measures. This can allow for full editing of the database by the user without compromising the integrity of the VBA code. Any VBA code in a database can be secured by providing a separate password via the Visual Basic Editor.

To Password Protect the VBA in a Database

a. Open the Visual Basic Editor by pressing Alt + F11.

b. In the Project Explorer, right-click the **Lastname_Firstname_a07_ws13_Putts** database, and then select **Lastname_Firstname_a07_ws13_Putts Properties** from the shortcut menu that appears.

c. Click the **Protection tab**.

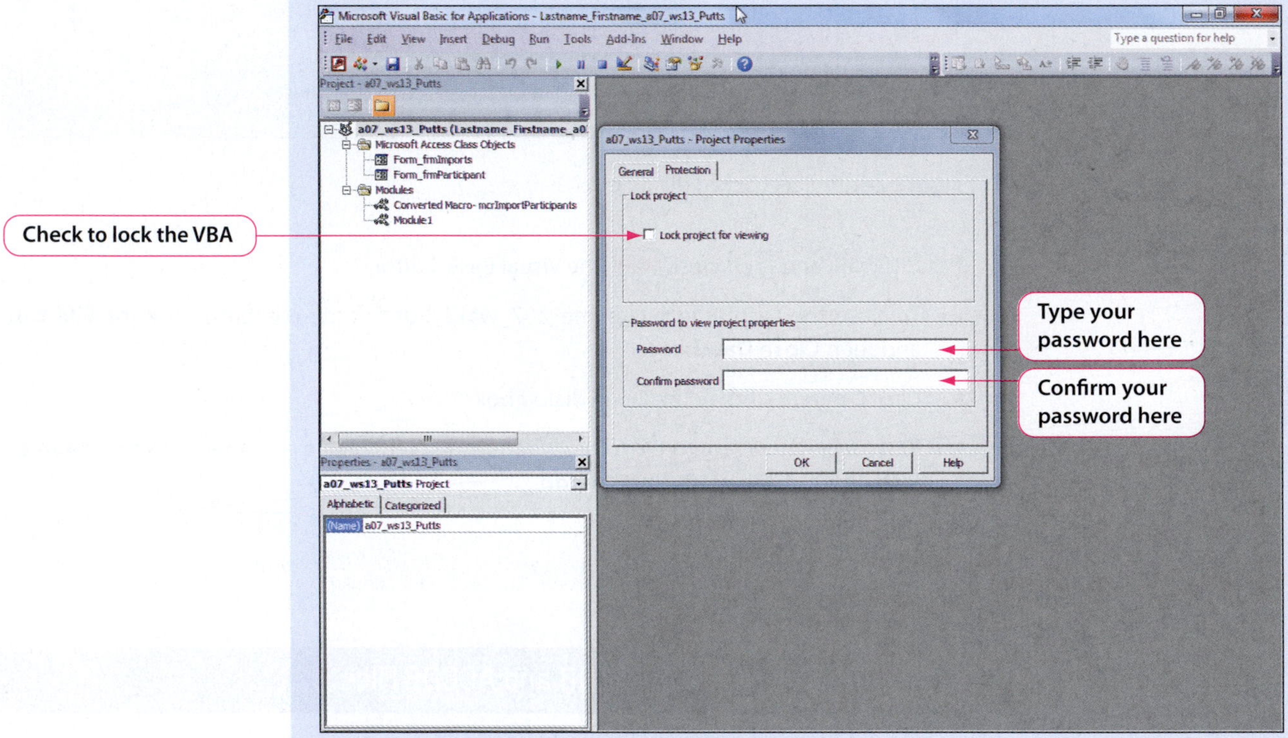

Check to lock the VBA

Type your password here

Confirm your password here

Figure 25 Password protecting your VBA

d. Check the **Lock project for viewing check box**.

e. In the Password to view project properties area, click the Password box, and then type **Zpe!82bv**, which is the password supplied by Barry Cheney.

f. Check the **Confirm password** box, retype your password, and then click **OK**.

g. Close the Visual Basic Editor and then Close Access.

Access will return you to the Visual Basic Editor without a confirmation message that the password was set. The Visual Basic Editor can still be opened by any database user. When a module or object is opened, before any code is displayed, the Visual Basic Editor will prompt you for the VBA password.

Concept Check

1. Discuss the relationship between object-oriented programming and event-driven programming.

2. Explain the difference between a function and a Sub procedure.

3. What are the benefits of debugging and error handling?

4. Macros and VBA can accomplish many of the same goals. When is it advantageous to use VBA? When would it be advantageous to use macros?

5. What are the differences between ACCDB and ACCDE files?

Key Terms

.accde file 620
Argument 599
Call statement 609
Code window 596
Compile 618
Debugging 616
Declarations 597
Declarations section 597
Dim statement 602
DoCmd object 599
Error handling 616
Event-driven programming 594
Exit Function statement 617

FileDialog object 601
Function 598
Line continuation character 598
Line labels 616
Loops 607
Me keyword 613
Method 594
Modules 596
Object 594
Object box 597
Object Browser 599
Object-oriented programming 594
Option Compare 597

Option Compare Binary 597
Option Compare Text 597
Option Explicit Statement 602
Procedure 594
Procedure box 597
Project Explorer 596
Sub procedure 598
Syntax error 618
TransferSpreadsheet method 599
Variables 602
Visual Basic Editor 596
Visual Basic for Applications 594
With statement 604

Visual Summary

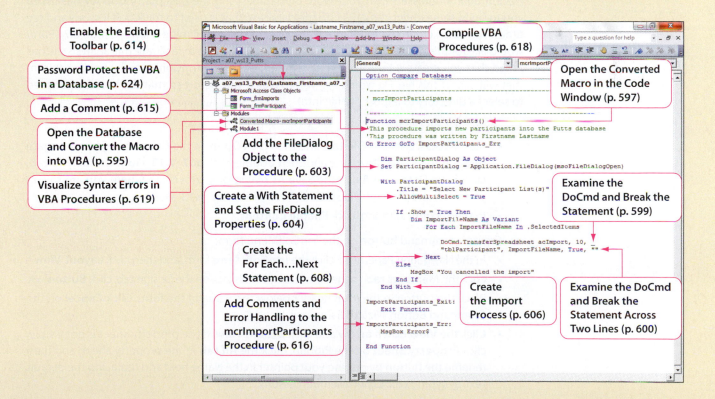

- Enable the Editing Toolbar (p. 614)
- Password Protect the VBA in a Database (p. 624)
- Add a Comment (p. 615)
- Open the Database and Convert the Macro into VBA (p. 595)
- Visualize Syntax Errors in VBA Procedures (p. 619)
- Add the FileDialog Object to the Procedure (p. 603)
- Create a With Statement and Set the FileDialog Properties (p. 604)
- Create the For Each...Next Statement (p. 608)
- Add Comments and Error Handling to the mcrImportParticpants Procedure (p. 616)
- Compile VBA Procedures (p. 618)
- Open the Converted Macro in the Code Window (p. 597)
- Examine the DoCmd and Break the Statement (p. 599)
- Create the Import Process (p. 606)
- Examine the DoCmd and Break the Statement Across Two Lines (p. 600)

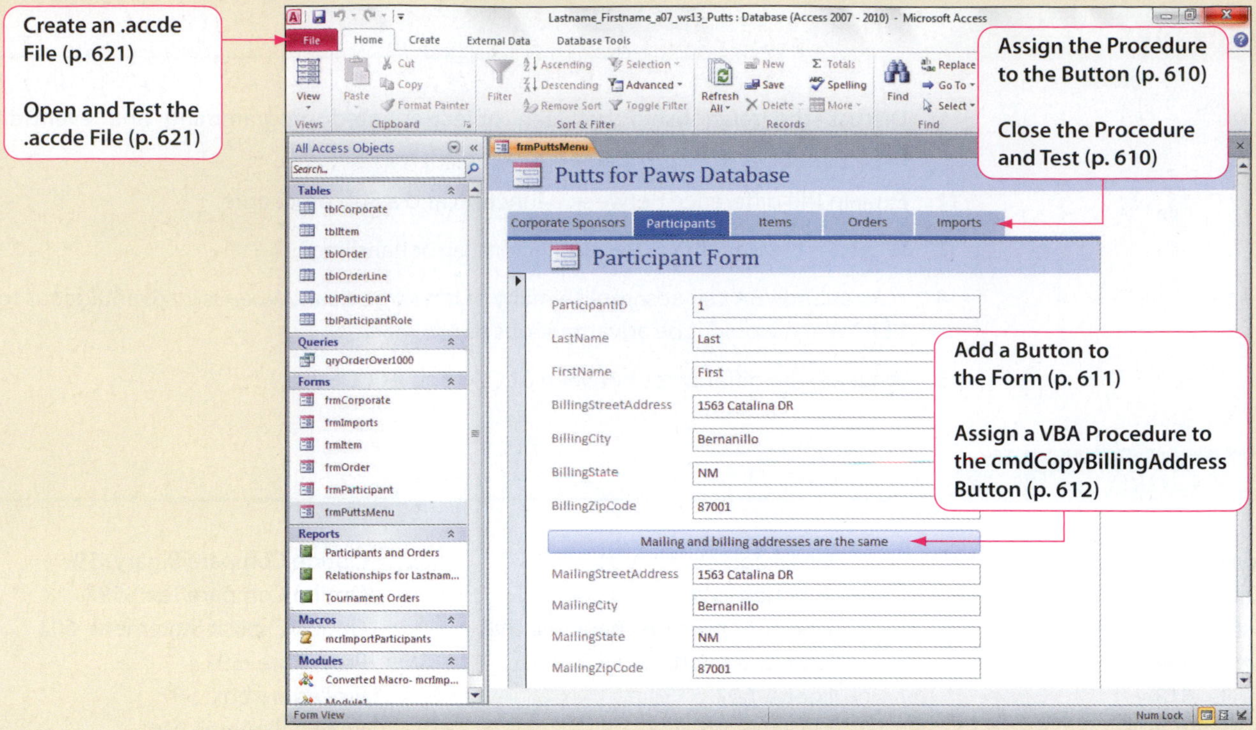
Create an .accde File (p. 621)
Open and Test the .accde File (p. 621)
Assign the Procedure to the Button (p. 610)
Close the Procedure and Test (p. 610)
Add a Button to the Form (p. 611)
Assign a VBA Procedure to the cmdCopyBillingAddress Button (p. 612)
Putts for Paws Database
Participant Form
Mailing and billing addresses are the same

Figure 26 The Red Bluff Golf Club Putts for Paws Charity final database

Practice 1

Student data file needed:

a07_ws13_Golf.accdb

You will save your file as:

Lastname_Firstname_a07_ws13_Golf

Red Bluff Golf Course

Having been impressed with your work on databases in the past, Barry Cheney has asked you to build some enhancements into the database that is used to track golf lessons and tee times. The data kept in the tblMemberLessons table will need to be analyzed regularly. Barry would like for this data to be in a Microsoft Excel spreadsheet to facilitate this analysis. He has asked that you create a button on the Members tab of the frmGolfMenu navigational form that will export this file. He would like you to create the export so that the user is prompted to select a directory to export the file into.

a. Open the Golf Database:

- Start **Access**, click the **File tab**, and then click **Open**. In the Open dialog box, navigate through the folder structure, and then double-click **a07_w13_Golf**. On the **File tab**, click **Save Database As**. In the Save As dialog box, browse to where you are saving your files, and then type Lastname_Firstname_ a07_w13_Golf.
- In the Security Warning, click **Enable Content**.

b. Create a command button on the frmGolfMenu form:

- In the Navigation Pane, right-click the **frmGolfMenu** form, and then click **Layout View**.
- Click the **Members tab**. In the Form Design Tools tab, on the Design tab, click **Button** .
- Place the button in the form header below the name of the form. Click **Cancel** on the Command Button Wizard dialog box.
- Click the **View down arrow** and click **Design View**. If the property sheet is not visible, click **Property Sheet** on the Ribbon. Click the **All tab** in the property sheet, and then rename the button by placing your pointer in the Name field and replacing the default text by typing cmdExportMemberLessons.

- Replace the default text of the button caption with **Export Member Lessons**.
- Adjust the button's shape to fit the caption text.

c. Create a new procedure for the On Click event:
  - Click the **cmdExportMemberLessons** button, and then in the property sheet, click the **Event tab**.
  - In the box for the On Click event, click **Builder** [...], in the Choose Builder dialog box select **Code Builder**, and then click **OK**. This opens the Visual Basic Editor with a newly created Private Sub statement.

d. Define the FileDialog Object:
  - On the line under the Private Sub statement, enter the comment **'Export procedure created by FirstName LastName**, replacing FirstName and LastName with your actual first and last name. Press [Enter].
  - Type **'This procedure exports tblMemberLessons**, and then press [Enter].
  - Press [Enter], and then press [Tab].
  - To declare a variable that will act as an alias for the Save As dialog box, type **Dim ExportTable as Object**, and then press [Enter].
  - Set the Export variable to be a Save As dialog box. Type **Set ExportTable = Application. FileDialog(msoFileDialogSaveAs)**, and then press [Enter] twice.
  - Begin a With statement to set the properties of the FileDialog object. Type **With ExportTable**, and then press [Enter].
  - Press [Tab], to set the title of the dialog box type **.Title = "Save tblMemberLessons as "**, and then press [Enter].

e. Create an If statement and a loop that will determine the filename and folder selected by the user or exit the procedure if no items are selected.
  - Type **If .Show = True Then** to test the condition that the user selected a filename and folder for exporting, and then press [Enter].
  - Press [Tab], and then type **Dim Filename As Variant** to declare a variable to store the filename selected by the user. Press [Enter].
  - Type **For Each Filename in .SelectedItems** to begin the loop.
  - Press [Enter], and then press [Tab].
  - Type **DoCmd.TransferSpreadsheet acExport, acSpreadsheetTypeExcel12, "tblMember", Filename, True, ""**, and then press [Enter].
  - Press [Backspace] to align your pointer with the For Each statement, type **Next** to complete the loop, and then press [Enter] and [Backspace] to align your pointer with the If statement.
  - Type **Else**, and then press [Enter].
  - Press [Tab], and then type **Msgbox "You cancelled the export."** to create a message box telling the user that the export was cancelled.
  - Press [Enter], and then press [Backspace].
  - Type **End If** to end the If statement.
  - Press [Enter], and then press [Backspace].
  - Type **End With**, and then press [Enter].

f. Add comments and error handling to the export procedure:
  - Place your pointer in the blank line under the two comment lines.
  - Type **On Error GoTo ExportMemberLessons_Err** to begin the error-handling process, and then press [Enter].
  - Place your pointer above the End Sub statement. Type **Exit Sub** to create an exit point for situations where the procedure executes as expected, and then press [Enter] twice.
  - Type **ExportMemberLessons_Err:** to add a line label that corresponds with the On Error statement added previously.

- Press Enter, and then press Tab.
- Type **Msgbox Error$** to return any error message received to a message box.

g. Compile and close the Visual Basic Editor:
- On the Menu bar, click **Debug**, and then click **Compile a07_ws13_Golf**.

  If there are no errors in the procedure you created you will be returned to the Visual Basic Editor. If there are errors, resolve them and compile the database again to confirm that all errors were corrected.
- Save the newly created Private Sub statement 🖫.

h. Password protect the VBA in the database, and then test the new export:
- In the Project Explorer, right-click the **Lastname_Firstname_a07_ws13_Golf** database.
- Click **Red Bluff Golf Club Properties** from the shortcut menu that appears, and then click the **Protection tab**.
- Check the **Lock project for viewing** check box.
- In the Password to view project properties area, click the **Password** box, and then type **423abg70**, which is the password supplied by Barry Cheney.
- Click the **Confirm password** box, retype your password, and then click **OK**.
- Close the Visual Basic Editor 🗙.
- In the Views group, click the **Views arrow**, and then click **Form View**.
- Click **Export Member Lessons** to test the export. In the Save As dialog box, browse to where you are saving your files, and then type **Lastname_Firstname_ a07_w13_ tblMemberLessons** to save the exported table.
- Click **Export Member Lessons** again to text the result of cancelling the export. In the Save As dialog box click **Cancel**, and then click **OK** on the message box that appears.

i. Click the **File tab**, and then click **Close Database**. Exit Access.

Practice 2

Student data file needed:

a07_ws13_Painted_Treaures

You will save your file as:

Lastname_Firstname_a07_ws13_ Painted_Treasures

The Painted Treasures Gift Shop

The Painted Treasures gift shop has asked for your help in modifying their database. Their current database has a report that assists in tracking inventory. They would like to be alerted when inventory is low by changing the background color and font color of the Quantity In Stock field. The default background color is Background 1 and the default font color is Text 1. If the quantities fall below a specific value, the background color should become Accent 2 and the font color should change to Background 1. The background and font colors of the text box should change when one of three events happens.
- When the form is opened
- When the quantity in stock is updated
- When the record selection changes

The specific parameters for when the changes should occur are detailed in Figure 27.

Category	Change when
Childrens or Clothing	30 or less
Indigo5 or Spa	80 or less

Figure 27 Inventory parameters

a. Open the Painted Treasures database:

- Start **Access**, click the **File tab**, and then click **Open**. In the Open dialog box, navigate through the folder structure, and then double-click **a07_w13_Painted_Treasures**. On the File tab, click **Save Database As**. In the Save As dialog box, browse to where you are saving your files, and then type Lastname_Firstname_ a07_w13_Painted_Treasures.
- In the Security Warning, click **Enable Content**.

b. Create a new procedure for the On Load event for the frmProduct form:

- In the Navigation Pane, right-click the **frmProduct** form, and then click **Design View**.
- In the property sheet, click the **Event tab**.
- In the box for the On Load event, click the **Builder** 🔲.

  The Sub procedure you will create will be contained on the frmProduct object. You can use the Builder to begin the process even though you will only call the procedure from the On Load event.

- In the Choose Builder dialog box, click **Code Builder**, and then click **OK**.

  This will open the Visual Basic Editor with a newly created Private Sub. You will not use this Sub until later.

c. Create a Private Sub that can be called by multiple events on the form. Use an If statement to evaluate the category and inventory levels:

- Click after the End Sub statement of the On Load Sub procedure.
- Create a new procedure by typing **Private Sub InventoryWarning()**, and then press ⌈Enter⌉.
- On the line of code under the Private Sub statement, enter the comment **'Inventory Warning procedure created by FirstName LastName** replacing FirstName and LastName with your actual first and last name.
- Press ⌈Enter⌉ twice, and then press ⌈Tab⌉.
- Begin an If statement that will evaluate the category of the current product. Type **If Me.Category = "Childrens" Or Me.Category = "Clothing" Then**, and then press ⌈Enter⌉.
- Press ⌈Tab⌉. A nested If statement is needed to evaluate the current inventory level. Type **If Me.QuantityInStock <= 30 Then**, and then press ⌈Enter⌉.
- Press ⌈Tab⌉. To change the font and fore colors of the text box, you need to edit multiple properties of the QuantityInStock object. Using a With statement will make this process easier. Type **With Me.QuantityInStock**, and then press ⌈Enter⌉.
- Press ⌈Tab⌉, set the background color to **Accent 2**, type **.BackThemeColorIndex = 5**, and then press ⌈Enter⌉. The BackThemeColorIndex property will set the background of the field to match one of the color themes within Access.
- To lighten the tint on the field by 40%, type **.BackTint = 60**, and then press ⌈Enter⌉.
- To set the font color to Background 1, type **.ForeThemeColorIndex = 1**, and then press ⌈Enter⌉. The ForeThemeColorIndex property will set the text of the field to match one of the color themes within Access. Press ⌈Backspace⌉.
- Type **End With**, and then press ⌈Enter⌉.
- Press ⌈Backspace⌉. Type **Else**, and then press ⌈Enter⌉.
- Press ⌈Tab⌉.

d. Reset the font color to the form defaults if the quantity of current inventory is acceptable:

- This section of the If statement will reset the font and background colors to the defaults if the low inventory criteria are not met. Type **With Me.QuantityInStock**, press ⌈Enter⌉, and then press ⌈Tab⌉.
- To set the background to Background 1, type **.BackThemeColorIndex = 1**, and then press ⌈Enter⌉.
- To remove the background tint, type **.BackTint = 100**, and then press ⌈Enter⌉.

- To set the font color to Text 1, type **.ForeThemeColorIndex = 0**, press Enter, and then press Backspace.
- Type **End With**, press Enter, and then press Backspace.
- Type **End If** to complete the If statement.

e. Create an ElseIf portion of the original If statement to handle the Indigo5 and Spa categories:
   - Press Enter, and then press Backspace.
   - Type **ElseIf Me.Category = "Indigo5" or Me.Category = "Spa" Then**, press Enter, and then press Tab.
   - A nested If statement is needed to evaluate the current inventory level. Type **If Me.QuantityInStock <= 80 Then**, press Enter, and then press Tab.
   - To change the font and fore colors of the text box, you will need to edit multiple properties of the QuantityInStock object. Using a With statement will make this process easier. Type **With Me.QuantityInStock**, press Enter, and then press Tab.
   - To set the background color to Accent 2, type **.BackThemeColorIndex = 5**, and then press Enter.
   - To lighten the tint on the field by 40%, type **.BackTint = 60**, and then press Enter.
   - To set the font color to Background 1, type **.ForeThemeColorIndex = 1**, press Enter, and then press Backspace.
   - Type **End With**, press Enter, and then press Backspace.
   - Type **Else**, and then press Enter.

f. Reset the font color to the form defaults if the quantity of current inventory is acceptable:
   - Press Tab. This section of the If statement will reset the font and background colors to the defaults if the low inventory criteria are not met. Type **With Me.QuantityInStock**, press Enter, and then press Tab.
   - To set the background to Background 1, type **.BackThemeColorIndex = 1**, and then press Enter.
   - To remove the background tint, type **.BackTint = 100**, and then press Enter.
   - To set the font color to Text 1, type **.ForeThemeColorIndex = 0**, press Enter, and then press Backspace.
   - Type **End With**, press Enter, and then press Backspace.
   - Type **End If** to end the nested If statement. Press Enter, and then press Backspace.
   - Type **End If** to end the original If statement.

g. Apply the new Private Sub to multiple events on the form:
   - Click the blank line of the Code window under **Private Sub Form_Load()**, and then type **Call InventoryWarning** to call the InventoryWarning procedure when the form is loaded.
   - Click the **Procedure arrow**, and then select **AfterUpdate**. This creates a new Private Sub that will run whenever the form data are updated.
   - Type **Call InventoryWarning**, click the **Procedure arrow**, and then select **Current**. This creates a new Private Sub that will run whenever the record selection of the form changes.
   - Type **Call InventoryWarning**.

h. Compile and close the Visual Basic Editor:
   - From the Menu toolbar, click **Debug**, and then click **Compile Lastname_Firstname_a07_ws13_Painted_Treasures**.

     If there are no errors in the procedure you created you will be returned to the Visual Basic Editor. If there are errors, resolve them and compile the database again to confirm that all errors were corrected.
   - Save ⊟ the newly created Private Sub.
   - Close ✖ the Visual Basic Editor.

i. Test the procedure and save as an .accde file.

- In the Views group on the Ribbon, click the **Views arrow**, and then click **Form View**.
- Examine record 4. The background of the Quantity In Stock field should be the theme Accent 2 and lightened by 40%. The font should be the theme Background 1.
- Examine record 8. The background of the Quantity In Stock field should be the theme Accent 2 and lightened by 40%. The font should be the theme Background 1.
- Examine record 32. The background of the Quantity In Stock field should be the theme Accent 2 and lightened by 40%. The font should be the theme Background 1.
- Examine record 38. The background of the Quantity In Stock field should be the theme Accent 2 and lightened by 40%. The font should be the theme Background 1.
- Examine record 41. The background of the Quantity In Stock field should be the theme Background 1 with no tint and the font should be the theme Text 1.
- Click the **File tab**, and then click **Save & Publish**.
- Under File Types, click **Save Database As** if it is not selected by default.
- Under Advanced, click **Make ACCDE**.
- Click the **Save As** button, navigate to the folder where you are saving your files, and then click **Save**.

j. Click the **File tab**, click **Close Database**, and then exit Access.

Objectives

1. Understand the concepts related to implementing a database.   p. 634

2. Understand Shared and Exclusive access to a database.   p. 634

3. Analyze the performance of a database.   p. 635

4. Save an Access database as a previous version.   p. 639

5. Create and refresh linked tables.   p. 641

6. Refresh linked tables with the Linked Table Manager.   p. 642

7. Split a database into front-end and back-end components.   p. 643

8. Encrypt a database with a password.   p. 645

9. Describe and disable special keys.   p. 646

10. Set startup options in Access.   p. 647

11. Describe different strategies for implementation.   p. 651

Implementing Your Database

PREPARE CASE

The Red Bluff Golf Club Putts for Paws Charity Database

The Red Bluff Golf Club sponsors the charity tournament, Putts for Paws, to raise money for the local pet shelter. The scope of the database is limited to tracking the monies being raised for the Putts for Paws event. Participants in the tournament are assigned roles, and any role may donate money to the event.

Now that a fully functioning database has been constructed, you have been asked to implement the database.

Courtesy of www.Shutterstock.com

Student data file needed for this workshop:

 a07_ws14_Putts

You will save your files as:

 Lastname_Firstname_a07_ws14_Putts

 Lastname_Firstname_a07_ws14_Putts_be

Lastname_Firstname_a07_ws14_Putts_2003

Implementing Databases

How do you prepare your database for multiple users? What are the best practices for implementing a database? These are very broad questions with many important ideas to consider. For this workshop the design of the database as well as how data are entered into the database is completed. Now you will consider how the database itself is accessed. Before this can happen, a few questions must be answered: How many people will be using the database? Should the tables for the database be stored in a centralized location? If so, how will the users access those tables? Are there macros or VBA that need to be locked? This workshop will address these concerns and more regarding the implementation of databases.

When securing a database the developer must be careful to ensure that the database is protected adequately. Any database objects that the user will not need access to should be hidden from view or otherwise protected. This way they cannot be deleted or modified—either by accident or maliciously. Often these objects include tables, macros, and Visual Basic code within the database. Securing a database is a detailed process and must be completed carefully. There might be several ways of opening or editing an object in Access. All of these methods must be accounted for when securing a database.

Once the database is secure, it can be implemented or distributed to users. Several implementation methods exist. The appropriate method can vary depending on the number of users and how data are accessed by the database. Some users may have older versions of Access. These users require a copy of the database that is compatible with these previous versions. If a large number of users will be accessing the database, Access provides a helpful utility called the Database Splitter to provide greater access to the database. In this section, you will prepare a database for implementation.

Shared and Exclusive Modes

When a database is opened in Access, by default it is opened in Shared Access mode. A database is opened with **Shared Access** when multiple users are allowed access to the database at the same time. A database opened in **Exclusive Access** allows only one user at a time the ability to open and edit the database. When establishing security in a database for implementation, Access routinely requires opening the file in Exclusive Access mode. Exclusive Access mode also ensures that no other users will be able to open the database while changes are being made. Importantly, some of the changes in this workshop will only take effect once the database or database object has been closed and reopened.

Real World Advice   Setting the Default Open Mode

You can set the default open mode to either Shared or Exclusive. However, Access only allows for this option as a setting on individual computers. It cannot be set for individual databases. If the default open mode is set to Exclusive, all databases will be opened exclusively. This setting is located in the Access Options under Client Settings and Default Open Mode.

To Open a Database with Exclusive Access

a. Open **Access**, click the **File tab**, and then click **Open**. Navigate through the folder structure, and then double-click **a07_ws14_Putts**.

b. Click the **File tab**, and then click **Save Database As**. In the Save As dialog box, navigate to where you are saving your files, and then type **Lastname_Firstname_a07_ws14_Putts** replacing Lastname_Firstname with your actual name. Click Save.

c. If you are presented with a Security Warning, click **Enable Content**.

d. Click the **File tab**, and then click **Close Database**.

e. Click **Open** to display the Open dialog box.

f. Navigate to the folder where you are saving your files, and then click **Lastname_Firstname_a07_ws14_Putts**.

g. Click the **Open arrow**, and then select **Open Exclusive**.

h. If you are presented with a Security Warning, click **Enable Content**.

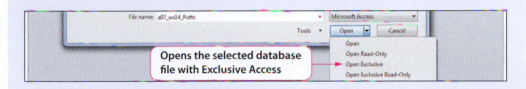

Opens the selected database file with Exclusive Access

Figure 1 Open Exclusive to provide greater access to the database

SIDE NOTE
Shared and Exclusive Access

Even if the database was originally opened with Exclusive Access, saving a database with a different filename leaves the file in Shared Access mode. To open the database with Exclusive Access, it must be opened from within Access.

Preparing the Database for a Single User

Prior workshops in this text have discussed the importance of carefully choosing the data type for a field in a table, establishing table relationships, and best practices for building queries. These practices are important in database design in part because they can improve database performance. In this section you will prepare a database for a single user.

Performance Analyzer

The **Performance Analyzer** is a tool in Access that analyzes and suggests ways to optimize the performance of a database. The Performance Analyzer can review individual Access objects or the entire database at one time.

After you run the Performance Analyzer, it provides three types of analysis results. **Suggestions** and **recommendations** can be performed by Access for you. Suggestions are actions that Access believes will improve your database performance but may have consequences that should be considered first. The Performance Analyzer provides a description of these consequences when you select a specific suggestion. **Ideas** are similar to suggestions, but the user must perform these actions. If you decide to pursue an idea from the Performance Analyzer, instructions will be provided by Access to complete the task. Recommendations can be carried out by Access directly.

To Run the Performance Analyzer

a. Click the **Database Tools tab**. In the Analyze Group, click **Analyze Performance**.

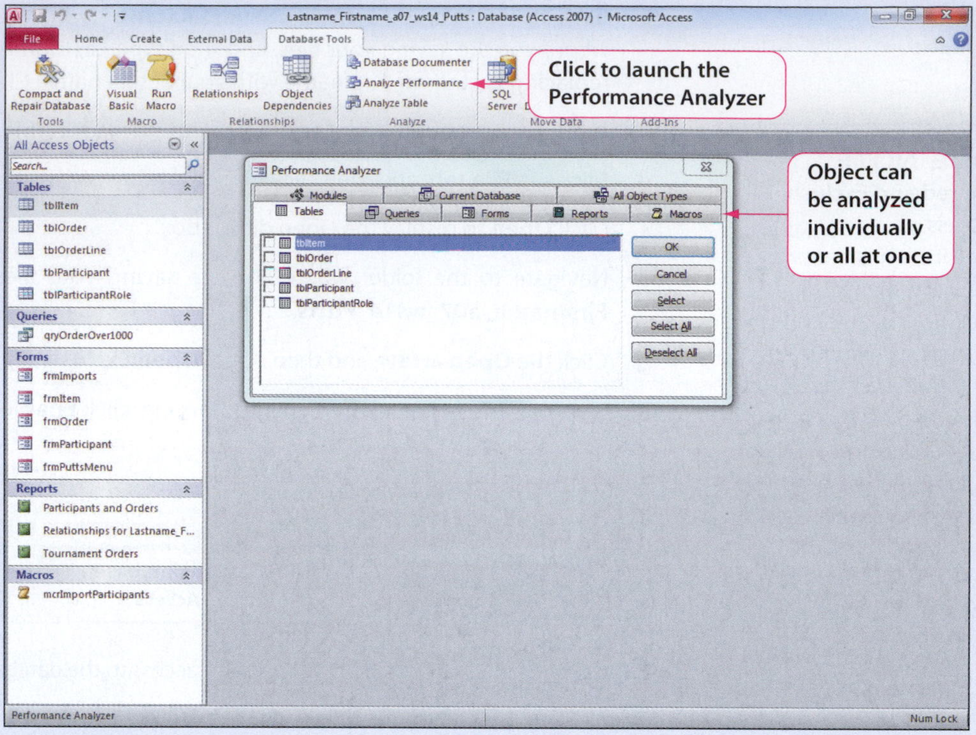

Figure 2 The Performance Analyzer

b. Click the **All Object Types tab**, and then click the **Select All** button.

This will check all items, including macros and VBA modules, within the database to be analyzed.

c. Click **OK**.

Any recommendations, suggestions, or ideas will be displayed in the Analysis Results window. A description of the results is provided in the Analysis Notes section of the window. As mentioned previously, some of the optimizations that the Performance Analyzer will make may have consequences that should be carefully considered.

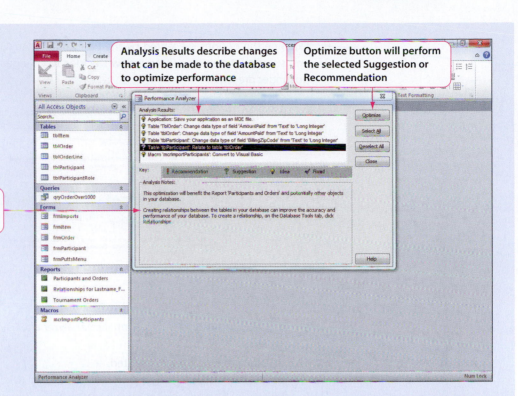

Analysis Results describe changes that can be made to the database to optimize performance

Optimize button will perform the selected Suggestion or Recommendation

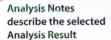

Analysis Notes describe the selected Analysis Result

Figure 3 The results of the Performance Analyzer

d. Examine the first idea presented by the Performance Analyzer. The idea is to save your database in MDE format. This concept will be revisited later in this workshop.

e. Examine the fourth idea presented by the Performance Analyzer. The idea states that the BillingZipCode field has a data type currently of Text and that this should be changed to a Long Integer data type. Access has analyzed the data in the table and determined that all of the data in this field are numeric. This is a correct conclusion as zip codes are numeric in nature. However, if a number will never be used in mathematical calculations—such as zip codes—then the correct data type is Text. Zip codes must be stored as text as some zip codes start with a zero. Changing the BillingZipCode field to a number would remove the zero at the front of any existing zip codes and any subsequent data entered into the table. Therefore, you should not take action on this suggestion.

f. Examine the second idea presented by the Performance Analyzer. This idea is to change the tblOrder field AmountPaid from Text to Long Integer. This idea complies with the best practice of a database that storing currency data in a text field can lead to problems with data management. Because this is an idea, you will need to make this change manually.

g. Click **Close** on the Performance Analyzer.

h. In the Navigation Pane, double-click the **tblOrder** table to open it in Datasheet view.

i. Select the **AmountPaid** field, click the **Table Tools Fields tab**.

j. In the Formatting group, open the **Data Type** list, and then select **Currency**.

k. Click **Yes** in the warning message that appears.

l. Save 💾 your changes, and then close the table. Because the Performance Analyzer listed several possible optimizations to the database, you should review these before proceeding.

m. Click the **Database Tools tab**. In the Analyze Group, click **Analyze Performance**, click the **All Object Types tab**, and then click **Select All**. Click **OK**.

n. Examine the options presented by the Performance Analyzer. Some of the same ideas and suggestions appear, though now the idea to change the AmountPaid data type is no longer present.

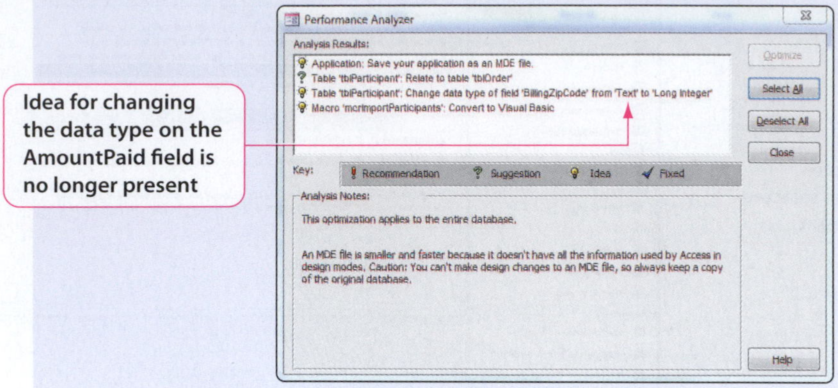

Idea for changing the data type on the AmountPaid field is no longer present

Figure 4 The Performance Analyzer after correcting the AmountPaid field

o. Examine the second option presented.

This is a suggestion by the Performance Analyzer to create a relationship between the tblParticipant table and the tblOrder table. This suggestion complies with the best practices of database design that the tblOrder table contains listings of each order participants have made. Because this is a suggestion, the Performance Analyzer can begin this process for you.

p. In the Analysis Results, click the suggestion that reads **Table 'tblParticipant': Relate to table 'tblOrder'**.

q. Click **Optimize**.

Access made the change to the database for you. Now you should review the change to ensure that it complies with your database design.

r. Click **Close**.

s. Click the **Database Tools tab** on the Ribbon, and then click **Relationships**.

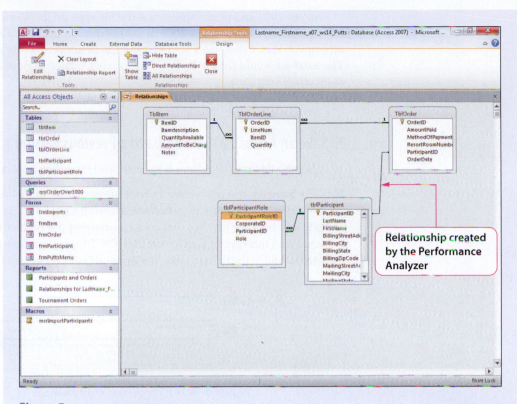

Figure 5 The Relationships window

t. Examine the relationship created by the Performance Analyzer. Notice that the relationship does not enforce referential integrity.

u. Right-click the relationship between tblParticipant and tblOrder, and then select **Edit Relationship**.

v. Click the **Enforce Referential Integrity** check box, and then click **OK**. This will create a one-to-many relationship from the tblParticipant table to the tblOrder table.

w. Click the **Relationship Tools Design tab**, and then click **Close**.

Saving Access as a Previous Version

Barry Cheney has stated that while all new computers in the office are using Access 2010, there are several computers in the Red Bluff Golf Club pro shop still using Access 2003. Thus, a copy of the database should be created in Access 2003 format.

As with most types of software, each new version of Access has features that previous versions did not. Common features of Access 2010 that are not compatible with Access 2003 are:

- Calculated fields in tables
- Data macros
- Multivalued lookup fields
- Fields with the Attachment data type
- Memo fields that have the append only property set to Yes

To convert an .accdb file to the 2003 format, these features must first be removed. The .accdb file type was first implemented in Access 2007, but there are even features new to 2010 that will not open or are limited in 2007. Some of these features include data macros and calculated fields in tables.

Access 2003 and prior versions use the file type .mdb. While 2010 can convert directly to Access versions 2002-2003 or 2000, it cannot directly convert to Access 97 or prior versions. To accomplish this, a database would first need to be converted into a 2002-2003 or 2000 version. The database would then be opened in an earlier version of Access and from there converted to an Access 97 database.

To Save an Access 2010 Database to a Previous Version

a. Click the **File tab**, click **Save & Publish**, and then click **Access 2002-2003 Database**.

b. Click **Save As**. You will receive an error message stating that you cannot save the current database in an earlier version because a feature is not backward-compatible. The message box lists possible features that could be causing the problem but does not identify the issue with this specific conversion. Click **OK**. The incompatible feature in this database is a Memo field in the tblItem table. The Append Only property of this Memo field is set to Yes.

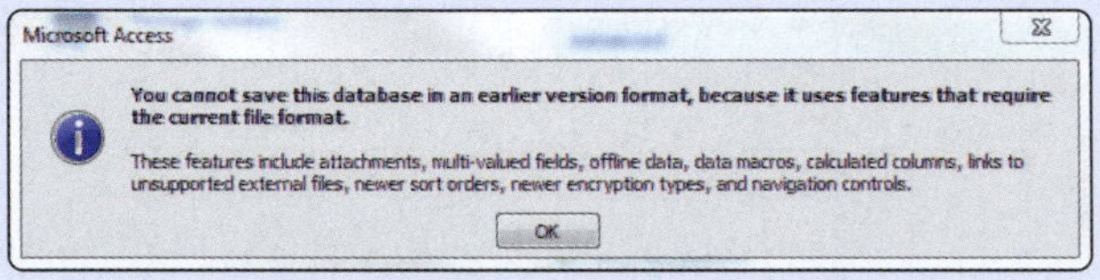

Figure 6 Access conversion error message

SIDE NOTE
Rich Text Memo Fields
Versions of Access before 2007 will not recognize Rich Text Memo fields. Instead they will display the text in the field with corresponding HTML tags.

c. Click the **Home tab**. In the Navigation Pane, right-click the table **tblItem**, and then click **Design View**.

d. Select the **Notes** field. In the Field Properties window, click the **General tab**. Scroll down to the Append Only property, click the **arrow** in the property field, and then select **No**.

e. Save the changes to the table. Click **Yes** in the error message stating that all history in the Notes column will be lost, and then close the table.

f. Click the **File tab**, click **Save & Publish**, and then click **Access 2002-2003 Database**.

g. Click **Save As**. Navigate to the folder where you are saving your files, and then save the file as Lastname_Firstname_a07_ws14_Putts_2003, and then click **Save**.

h. The database will be converted to an Access 2003 .mdb file type and remain open. Notice that the Navigation Pane view has changed. It now displays only the tables. Click the **Navigation Pane arrow**, and then click **All Access Objects**. All database objects are now visible.

i. Click the **File tab**, and then click **Close Database**.

Real World Advice   Multiple Versions of Access

It is not uncommon in large corporations or in companies that are composed of several smaller units for there to be multiple IT systems in place. In some cases, you might find multiple versions of Microsoft Office running in a company. In situations like this, backward compatibility is always a concern. When designing databases carefully consider which versions of Access are in use and which features are not backward compatible.

Preparing the Database for Multiple Users

There are times where you will need to access data that is not contained in the database currently open in Access. While importing can bring this data into the local table structure, this is not always the best option. When data are shared among many databases and is stored in a central location on a computer network, Access provides the ability to link to the data. In this section, you will prepare a database for multiple users.

Linking and Refreshing Tables

A **linked table** provides a link to data stored in another database or application. The data contained in the application becomes available to Access as a table.

Access can link to a table in another Access database, an Excel spreadsheet, or to tables in SQL and Oracle databases. Linking to data is a best practice when the core data are shared among other users or applications or when Access is used as a means of viewing and querying SQL and Oracle database systems. This can reduce data redundancy and provide an efficient way of interacting with the data.

Data for the Putts for Paws corporate partners is currently being stored in the Excel spreadsheet a07_ws14_Corporate.xlsx. This data needs to be linked to the Putts for Paws database such that it can be used later in the planning of the event.

To Reopen the Putts for Paws Database and Link to the Corporate Data Worksheet

a. Click the **File tab**, and then click **Open**.

b. Navigate to where you are saving your files, select the **Lastname_Firstname_ a07_ws14_Putts** database, and then click **Open**.

c. Click the **External Data tab**, and then in the Import & Link group, click the **Excel** button.

d. In the **Get External Data** window, click the **Browse** button, navigate to the place where your student data files are stored, select **a07_ws14_Corporate.xlsx**, and then click **Open**.

e. Click **Link to the data source by creating a linked table**, and then click **OK**.

f. The Link Spreadsheet Wizard is now visible. The wizard will display a list of worksheets and named ranges present in the file you selected. Select the **Corporate** worksheet if it is not already highlighted, and then click **Next**.

g. The wizard will now ask if you want to use the spreadsheet column headings as field names in your table. The column headings in the spreadsheet are appropriate field names in Access. Click the **First Row Contains Column Headings** check box, and then click **Next**.

h. The wizard has now finished linking the spreadsheet and needs a name for the new table. Access will suggest "Corporate" as the table name. Select this **text**, and then press Delete. Type tblCorporate, and then click **Finish**.

i. Click **OK** in the message box that appears telling you that the spreadsheet is now linked. The tblCorporate table now appears in the Navigation Pane. Notice the blue arrow in front of the Microsoft Excel symbol. This indicates that the table is linked. Data can be added, changed, or deleted from a linked table; however, the structure of the table cannot be changed.

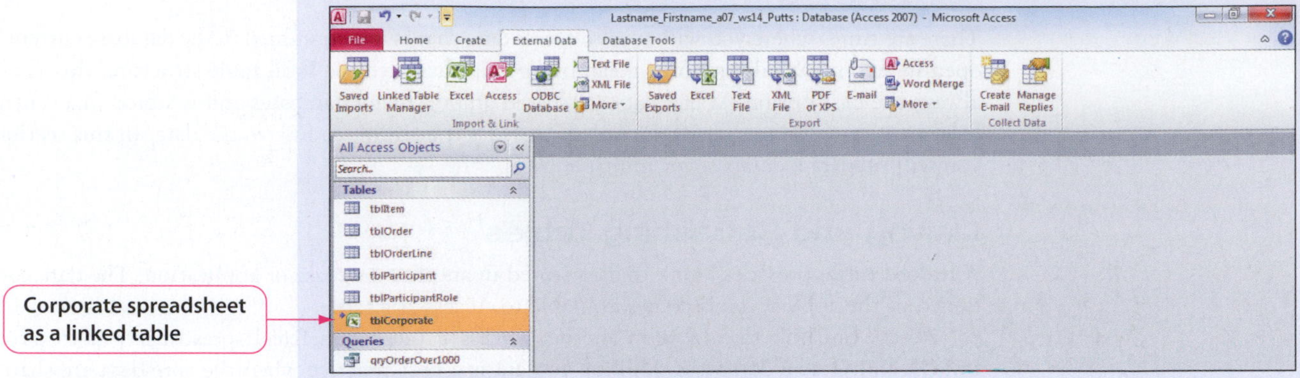

Corporate spreadsheet as a linked table

Figure 7 The linked spreadsheet in the Navigation Pane

j. Click the **Start** button, and then open Microsoft Excel 2010.

k. Click the **File tab**, and then click **Open**.

l. Navigate to the folder where your student data files are stored, select **a07_ws14_ Corporate.xlsx**, and then click **Open**.

m. In cell A7 of the Corporate worksheet, type 6. In cell B7, type your first name and last name.

n. Save your document, and then close Excel.

o. In the Putts for Paws database, in the Navigation Pane, double-click **tblCorporate**. Your name should be displayed as the sixth record in the table.

p. Close the table.

Real World Advice   Linking to Access SharePoint

Access data can be published outside of the database in many ways. They can be exported in formats such as PDF and Microsoft Excel spreadsheets. Access objects can also be published to Microsoft SharePoint sites. SharePoint is an online collaboration tool that allows teams to organize and update information online. Access can synchronize forms and reports between the online client and the offline database. You can also make changes to your Access database and update the data online.

The Linked Table Manager

When a linked table is opened, Access refreshes the data contained in the linked object. Access cannot update the data if the linked object has been moved. Linked tables are dependent on the location of the object, not the database that contains the link. This means that databases containing a linked table can be moved at will with no ill effects. However, the file containing the linked object must remain in the same location in order for the link to function properly.

If a linked object is moved, the Linked Table Manager can be used to refresh the link. The **Linked Table Manager** lists the file location of all linked tables in a database. If the location of a linked object changes, the Linked Table Manager can be used to refresh those links.

Real World Advice Linked Data in Earlier Versions of Access

If you have an Access 2010 database with links to external data that are not compatible with prior versions of Access, there is a solution. Try importing the data and then deleting the external links. This will provide the database with the ability to convert to a previous version of Access.

The Database Splitter

When implementing a database system for multiple users it can be helpful to divide the database objects into two separate database files. This splitting of the database creates a front-end and back-end system. The **front-end database** is deployed directly to users and contains nondata objects such as queries, reports, forms, macros, and VBA modules. Front-end databases can be deployed locally to user's computers. This allows the user, if given proper permissions, to modify the file to include objects for their individualized use. Front-end databases allow for the creation of temporary objects, such as temporary tables.

Back-end databases contain the tables from the original database. The front-end database accesses these tables by linking to them. This is beneficial as the back-end database can be stored in a central location where a company's technical support can ensure the data are protected and backed up regularly. Importantly, the back-end database cannot be on a shared drive with limited file permissions. That is to say, the back-end database must allow the front-end database the ability to add and delete data to its tables.

For database developers, splitting databases is beneficial as changes can be made to the front-end database without having to take the entire database offline. A new form or query can be developed and moved into the front-end system without having to shut down the back-end system.

To Split the Database

a. Open the Putts for Paws database if necessary.

b. Click on the **Database Tools tab**. In the Move Data group, click **Access Database**. This launches the Database Splitter Wizard.

c. Click **Split Database**. This will open a Create Back-end Database dialog box. The Database Splitter Wizard will first create the back-end database.

d. Navigate to the location where you store your data files, and then click **Split**.
Notice that the name of the file being created is Lastname_Firstname_a07_ws14_Putts_be. The "be" appended to the end of the file name stands for "back-end".

e. Click **OK** in the message stating that the database has been successfully split.

f. Examine the Navigation Pane.
Notice that all of the tables are now linked. This is indicated with the blue arrow next to the table icon. This front-end database can now be deployed to multiple users.

SIDE NOTE
Linked Tables in Split Databases

The links in the front-end database are based on the location of the back-end database. If the back-end database is moved, the links will not work and must be updated using the Linked Table Manager.

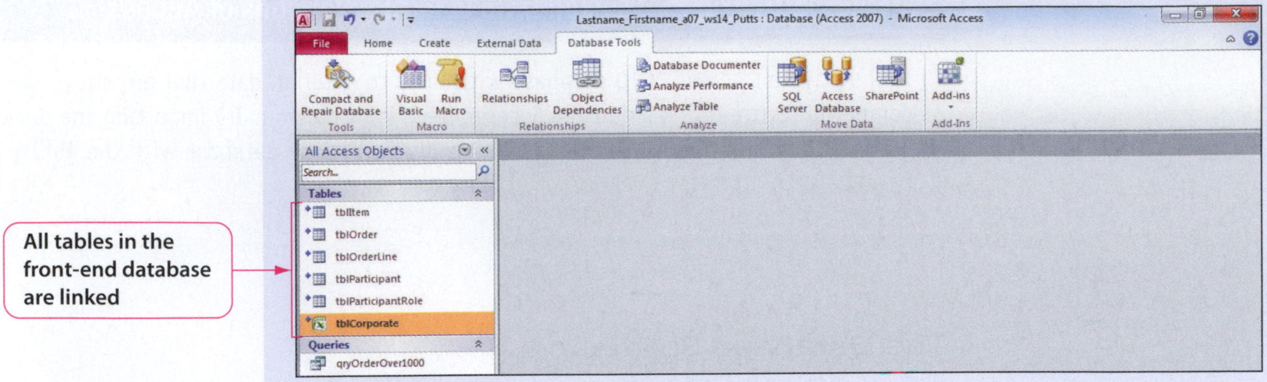

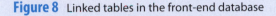

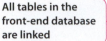

All tables in the front-end database are linked

Figure 8 Linked tables in the front-end database

g. Create a subfolder called **Putts_be** in the same folder as your student data files. Move the **Lastname_Firstname_a07_ws14_Putts_be** database into the Putts_be subfolder.

h. In Access, double-click the **tblItem** table to open it. You will receive an error listing the former file path of the back-end database. Because the file is no longer there, Access cannot open the linked table. You can use the Linked Table Manager to update the back-end database's location. Click **OK**.

i. Click the **External Data tab**, and then in the Import & Link group, click **Linked Table Manager**.

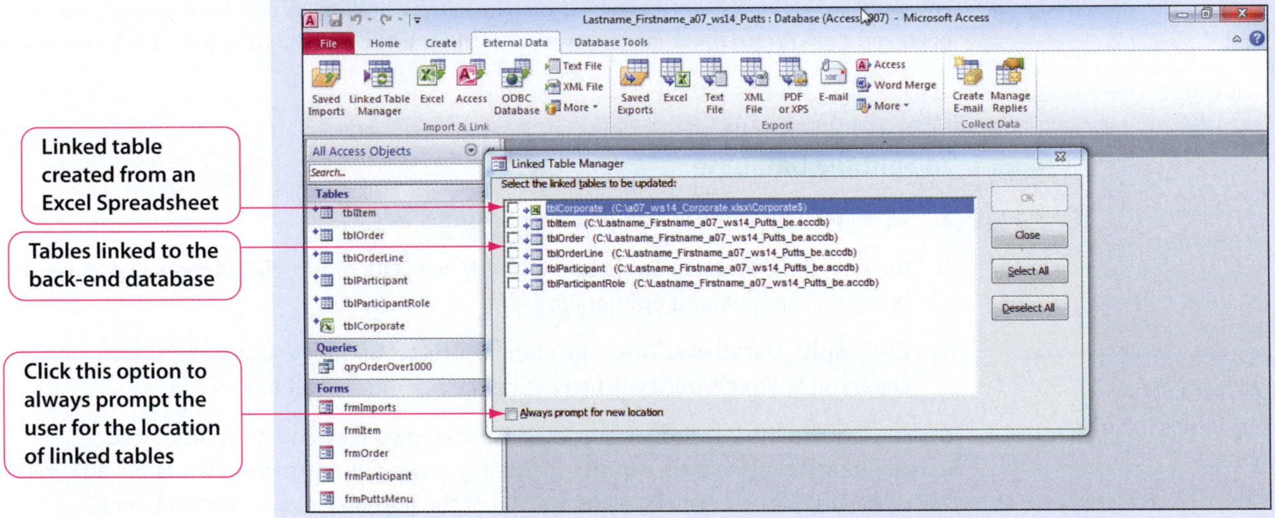

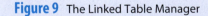

Linked table created from an Excel Spreadsheet

Tables linked to the back-end database

Click this option to always prompt the user for the location of linked tables

Figure 9 The Linked Table Manager

SIDE NOTE
The File Path of the Linked Tables

The file path of the linked tables in Figure 9 might be different from the file path of your database. This is dependent upon the configuration of your computer.

j. Click the **tblItem**, **tblOrder**, **tblOrderLine**, **tblParticipant**, and **tblParticipantRole** check boxes, and then click **OK**.

k. Navigate to the Putts_be folder, and then double-click to open it. Select the **Lastname_Firstname_a07_ws14_Putts_be** database, and then click **Open**.

l. Click **OK** in the Linked Table Manager message stating that all selected linked tables have been successfully refreshed.

m. Click **Close** to close the Linked Table Manager.

n. Click the **File tab**, and then click **Close Database**.

Encryption and Passwords

Ultimately to protect a database and its information, passwords and encryption can be implemented. **Encryption** is the process of changing text-based information into a state in which a key is required in order to read the information. An algorithm or cipher is used to process the data from text into an unreadable state. The process of **decryption** will make the encrypted information readable again. The information is decrypted using a key. In Access, the key will be a password. In other applications, the key can be a separate file.

Barry Cheney has asked that the front-end database file you created be encrypted for added security to the data.

CONSIDER THIS | **What Makes a Strong Password?**

Passwords should be created carefully. Common words and phrases in any language should be avoided. The longer and more complex a password, the more secure it will be. How do you build a strong password? What features should a strong password contain?

To Encrypt and Set a Database Password

a. Open the Putts for Paws database with Exclusive Access.

Troubleshooting

To encrypt the database it must be open in Exclusive Access mode. When Access closes and reopens a database—as it does during the split database operation—the front-end database will be opened in Shared Access mode. To encrypt a database, it must be opened in Exclusive Access mode.

b. Click the **File tab**, and then click **Info**.

c. Click **Encrypt with Password**. In the **Password** box, type 917abf70, retype your password in the **Verify** box, and then click **OK**.

d. You will receive a Microsoft Access warning stating the row level locking will be ignored. Click **OK**. Test to ensure that the next time the database is opened the user will be prompted for a password.

Troubleshooting

Row-level locking is used to ensure that, when two users are editing a table, they cannot edit the same row—record—of data. This is not compatible in an encrypted database. Access will disable this feature and provide the warning message shown in Figure 10 to this extent.

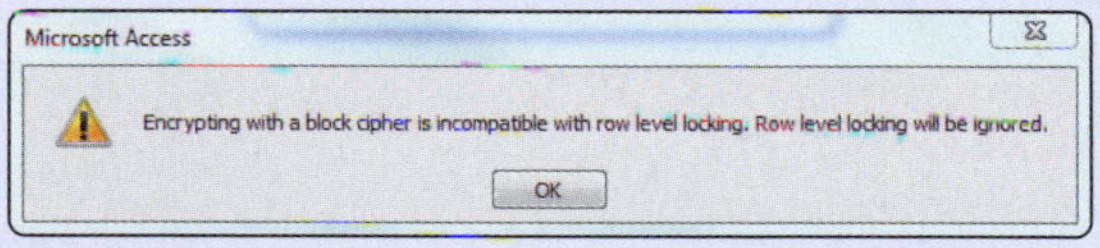

Figure 10 Row-level locking warning message

SIDE NOTE

Encrypt with Password

Encrypting an Access 2010 or 2007 database using the Encrypt with Password feature will prevent a database from being converted to a .mdb file. Removing the password will allow you to convert the database.

e. Click the **File tab**, and then click **Close Database**.

f. Click the **File tab**, and then click **Open**.

g. Navigate to where you are saving your files, select the **Lastname_Firstname_a07_ws14_Putts** database, and then click **Open**.

h. Type **917abf70** when you are prompted for the database password, and then click OK.

Setting the User's Experience

Access 2010 features several options to assist a database developer in controlling the user's experience in a database. To begin securing a database, there are several key features in Access that should be disabled or modified. This includes controlling the way users navigate to the database, preventing users from editing certain Access objects, controlling what tabs the user will see on the Ribbon, and setting a password on the database. To set a password, the database must first be opened with Exclusive Access. In this section, you will control the user interface of an Access database.

Controlling Navigation Options

To ensure the integrity of the database, access to several features must be eliminated. Barry Cheney has asked that users not be able to create new objects in the database or be able to import or export data using the Ribbon. When any of these functions are required, they will be built into the database forms as buttons or other controls. Likewise, any information stored in the database that users will need to access will be included on the navigation form that is displayed when the database is opened.

Preventing a table from being opened directly requires hiding the Navigation Pane. To prevent the creation of new database objects, the Create tab on the Ribbon must be hidden. Importing and exporting data can be prevented by hiding the External Data and Database Tools tabs. Hiding the Database Tools tab will also take one step towards securing any VBA or Macros in the database.

Often in Access there are several ways of accomplishing any single task. For example, the Visual Basic Editor can be opened using a button on the Ribbon or by pressing the keyboard shortcut Alt + F11. To properly secure a database, each of these options must be considered to adequately prevent an object from being accessed. Ultimately, any direct access to the VBA code must be locked down. The Alt + F11 keyboard shortcut is one of the special keys in Access.

Special Keys

Special keys are a subset of four keyboard shortcuts that can be disabled when securing a database. A list of special keys is provided in Figure 11. To properly secure a database, special keys should be disabled, because special keys allow users access to the Navigation Pane and the Visual Basic Editor even if these items are hidden from view initially in the database. To begin securing the Putts for Paws database, you will first hide tabs on the Ribbon, hide the Navigation Pane, and disable special keys.

Key or Key Combination	Description	Why Should This Be Disabled?
F11	Shows or hides the Navigation Pane	Prevents users from accessing tables or other objects to protect the integrity of the database
Ctrl + G	Shows the Immediate Window in the Visual Basic Editor; launches the Visual Basic Editor if it is not already open	Prevents users from accessing or creating Visual Basic code in the database
Ctrl + Break	Stops Access from retrieving records from a server	This applies when Access is designed to work as the front-end application to a SQL server
Alt + F11	Opens the Visual Basic Editor	Prevents users from accessing or creating Visual Basic code in the database

Figure 11 Table of special keys

Setting Startup Preferences

The first step in securing the database as requested by Barry Cheney is to examine the current database options. Several of the most basic steps to securing a database can be taken in the Access Options. These options will affect only the database that is currently open.

To Set the Startup Preferences on the Putts for Paws Database

a. Click the **File tab**, and then click **Options**.

b. From the navigation options on the left side of the Access Options window, click **Current Database**.

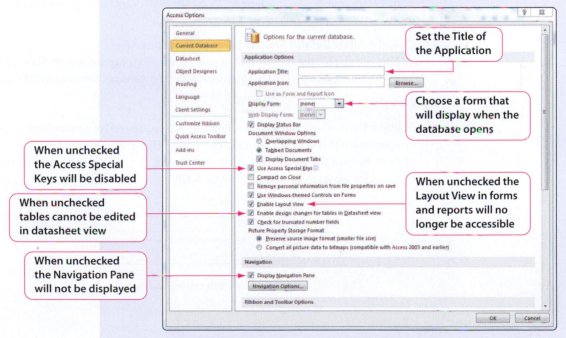

Figure 12 Access Options for the Putts for Paws database

c. In the **Application Title** box, type Putts for Paws Database. This will replace the file name on the title bar in the Access Window.

d. Click the **Display Form arrow**, and then select **frmPuttsMenu**. This will automatically open the frmPuttsMenu navigation form when the database is opened.

e. Clear the **Use Access Special Keys** check box. This step disables the four special keys described previously.

f. Clear the **Enable Layout View** check box. This will prevent users from being able to edit forms and other Access objects by removing the Layout view option from the Views group on the Ribbon.

Troubleshooting

Changes to the options in an Access database might require that a specific Access object that is open when the changes are made be closed and reopened. For example, disabling the Layout view feature will not take effect on an open form. Before the changes take effect, the form must be closed and reopened.

g. Clear the **Enable design changes for tables in Datasheet view** check box. This will prevent users from being able to edit the design of a table while viewing the table in datasheet mode.

h. Clear the **Display Navigation Pane** check box.

This will hide the Navigation Pane preventing users from opening any of the objects found there. Combined with disabling special keys, this will lock users out of accessing any objects in the Navigation Pane. Users could still access the Navigation Pane if the special keys option is checked.

i. Clear the **Allow Full Menus** check box.

This will leave only the File and Home tabs visible on the Ribbon. This restricts users from being able to use the Ribbon to create new objects in the database, import or export data, or create macros or VBA.

j. Clear the **Allow Default Shortcut Menus** check box.

This will disable the menus that appear when a user right-clicks an Access object. On forms for example, the shortcut menu provides a means of changing to Layout view.

k. Click **OK**.

l. Examine the warning message displayed by Access. Several of the settings you have just enacted will not take effect until the database is closed and reopened. This includes the options to hide the Navigation Pane, Full Menus, Shortcut Menus, and Enable design changes for tables in Datasheet view. Click **OK**.

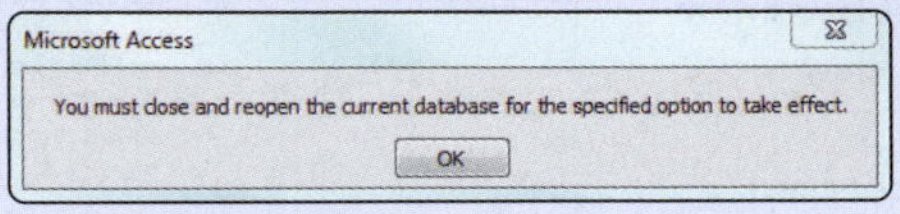

Figure 13 Startup setting warning

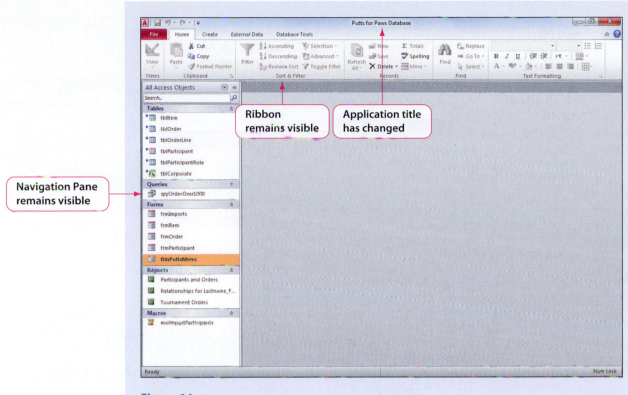

Figure 14 Access Options before closing database

m. Click the **File tab**, and then click **Close Database**.

Importantly, you should test any changes made to the user interface of a database. This provides you with a chance to verify that all options are correctly set. It also provides you with a chance to experience the database as other users will.

To Test the Startup Preferences on the Putts for Paws Database

a. To test the changes that have been made to the database click the **File tab**, and then click **Open**.

b. Navigate to where you are saving your files, and then open the **Lastname_Firstname_a07_ws14_Putts** database. Enter the password to open the file when prompted.

   Notice that only the File and Home tabs on the Ribbon are available. Likewise, the frmPuttsMenu navigation form opened with the database, but the Navigation Pane is not visible.

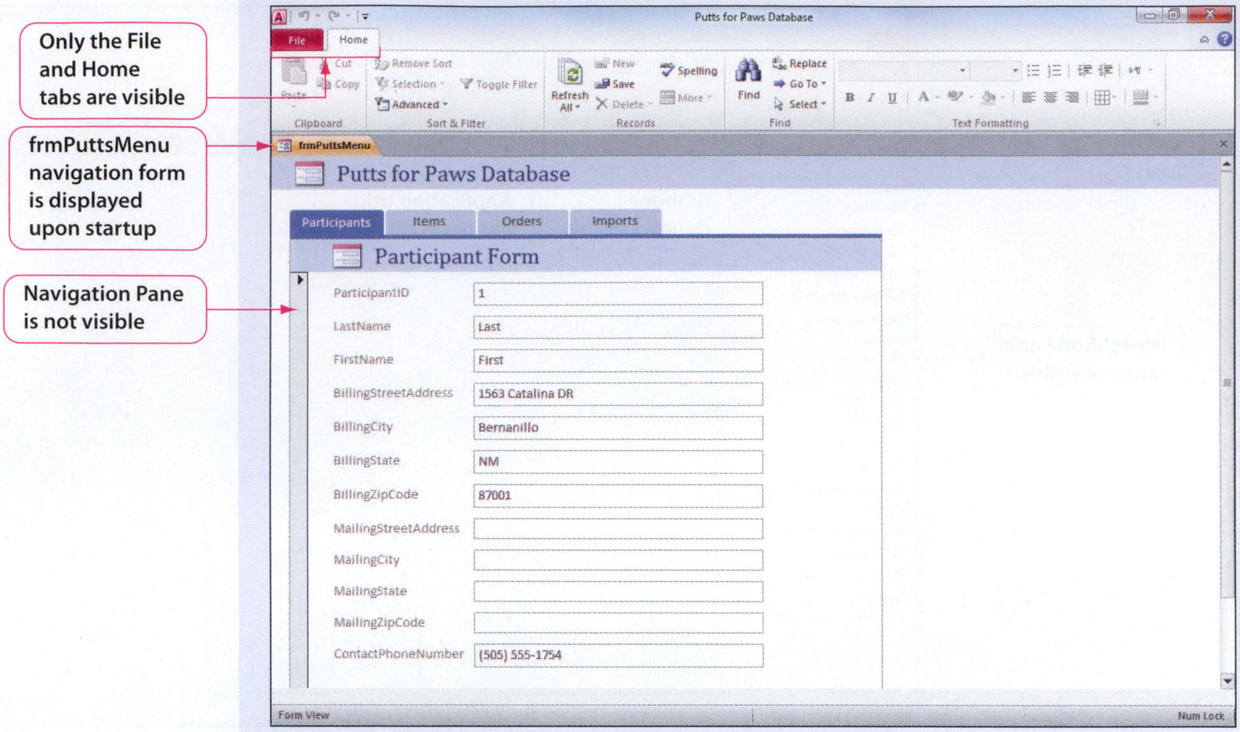

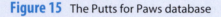

Only the File and Home tabs are visible

frmPuttsMenu navigation form is displayed upon startup

Navigation Pane is not visible

Figure 15 The Putts for Paws database

c. Press ⎡Alt⎤+⎡F11⎤.

Normally this will open the Visual Basic Editor. However, because special keys are disabled, nothing will happen as a result of this key combination.

d. Click the **File tab** to examine Backstage view.

The available options are now limited. Users are allowed to print objects and exit the database. The Privacy Options button will open the Access Options window. Importantly, users can reset the Current Database options from this menu.

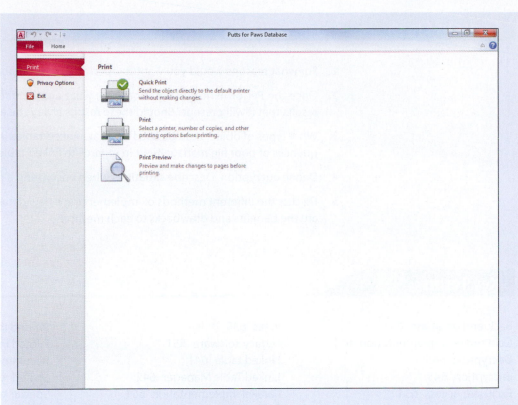

Figure 16 Putts for Paws database in Backstage view

Methods of Implementation

Selecting a method of implementing your database—or any information technology solution—is a critical decision. There are several approaches to choose from and many important factors to consider. Cost, time, and the functionality of the new system are three of the most important factors to consider. Importantly, you must choose an approach that fits your business, employees, and technical environment. Your new database will be replacing a legacy system. This might be a paper-based system or a software-based system. **Legacy software** is the old technology that is out of date but still in use. Legacy software exists because the basic needs of the business are still met by the software. Often users prefer legacy systems. They are familiar with the system, and any flaws in the system have usually been eliminated. It can be intimidating to learn a new system or business process, and thus implementations can be fraught with the anxiety of the unknown.

You might choose to implement your database all at once. This **cold turkey implementation** approach involves implementing your database in its entirety and replacing the legacy system all at once. This method leaves little room for error. Once the new system is in place, the legacy system is no longer in use. If errors are found with the new system, they must be corrected in the absence of an alternate process. Alternatively, this approach gets users into the new system quickly and limits the need for maintaining more than one active solution.

Other methods involve a more gradual approach. In **piloted implementations**, small groups of a company start using the new database. Gradually, more groups come on board as the system is perfected until the entire organization is using the new system. In **parallel implementations**, the legacy system and new system are used concurrently. In **phased implementations**, a portion of the new system is put into place and perfected before additional pieces of the system are moved into use.

These three strategies offer a robust way to test a system and correct errors before a new system is put into full use. This provides a backup if the new system needs to be taken out of use and limits the loss of productivity if such an event happens. Conversely, these implementation approaches can take more time to complete and lead to increased costs as two systems must be maintained until the new system completely replaces the legacy system.

1. For what reasons would you want to open an Access database with exclusive rights?

2. Once the Performance Analyzer has run, what are the differences in the three types of results that it will present? Should these results always be acted upon?

3. What types of objects can be used to create linked tables in Access? What are the consequences of poor file management in regards to linked tables?

4. Define encryption. Describe situations when encrypting a database would be beneficial.

5. Discuss the different methods of implementing a new database in an organization. What are the benefits and drawbacks to each method?

Key Terms

Back-end database 643
Cold turkey implementation 651
Decryption 645
Encryption 645
Exclusive Access 634
Front-end database 643

Ideas 635
Legacy software 651
Linked table 641
Linked Table Manager 642
Parallel implementation 651
Performance Analyzer 635

Phased implementation 651
Piloted implementation 651
Recommendations 635
Shared Access 634
Special keys 646
Suggestions 635

Visual Summary

Open a Database with Exclusive Access (p. 635)

Save an Access 2010 Database to a Previous Version (p. 640)

Encrypt and Set a Database Password (p. 645)

Set the Startup Preferences on the Putts for Paws Database (p. 647)

Test the Startup Preferences on the Putts for Paws Database (p. 649)

Reopen the Putts for Paws Database and Link to the Corporate Data Worksheet (p. 641)

Run the Performance Analyzer (p. 636)

Split the Database (p. 643)

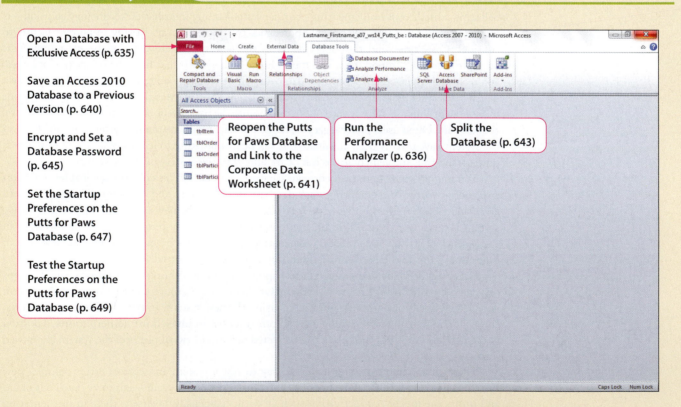

Figure 17   The Red Bluff Golf Club Putts for Paws Charity final database

Practice 1

Student data files needed:

a07_ws14_Events

a07_ws14_Hotel

You will save your files as:

Lastname_Firstname_a07_ws14_Events

Lastname_Firstname_a07_ws14_Hotel

The Events Database

Patti Rochelle has requested some changes to the database used by the resort hotel. First, she would like for you to create a link to the table in the Hotel database that contains a listing of all hotel employees. These employees will be assigned to specific events in the future, and the Events database needs easy access to an active list of all employees.

Patti has also requested that you analyze the performance of the database and ensure that any improvements that can be made to speed up the database performance are made.

a. Open the Hotel database:

- Start **Access**, click the **File tab**, and then click **Open**. In the Open dialog box, navigate through the folder structure, and then double-click **a07_ws14_Hotel**.
- Click the **File tab**, and then click **Save Database As**. In the Save As dialog box, navigate to where you are saving your files, and then type Lastname_Firstname_a07_ws14_Hotel.accdb replacing Lastname_Firstname with your actual name. Click **Save**.
- In the Navigation Pane, double-click the **tblEmployee** table to open it.
- On the New record line, type **6** in the AreaID field. Type your first name in the FirstName field, and then type your last name in the LastName field.
- Close ⌧ the table, click the **File tab**, and then then click **Close Database**.

b. Open the Events database:

- Click the **File tab**, and then then click **Open**. In the Open dialog box, navigate through the folder structure, and double-click **a07_ws14_Events.accdb**.
- Click the **File tab**, and then click **Save Database As**. In the Save As dialog box, navigate to where you are saving your files, and then type Lastname_Firstname_a07_ws14_Events.accdb replacing Lastname_Firstname with your actual last and first name. Click **Save**.
- In the Security Warning, click **Enable Content** if it appears.

c. Link to the Hotel Employee's table:

- Click the **External Data tab**, and then in the Import & Link group, click **Access**.
- In the Get External Data window, click **Browse**.
- Navigate to where your student data files are kept, select **a07_ws14_Hotel**, and then click **Open**.
- Click **Link to the data source by creating a linked table**, and then click **OK**.
- In the Link Tables window, select **tblEmployee**, and then click **OK**.

d. Analyze the performance of the database:

- Click the **Database Tools tab**. In the Analyze group, click **Analyze Performance**.
- In the Performance Analyzer window, click **All Object Types**.
- Click **Select All**, and then click **OK** to run the Performance Analyzer.
- Select the suggestion **Table 'tblEvents': Relate to table tblEventItems'**, and then click **Optimize**. This will improve the performance of the qryEventList query.
- Examine the idea **Table 'tblMenuChoice': Change data type of field 'CostPerPerson' from 'Text' to 'Double'**. The CostPerPerson field is the price each person would be charged for a meal and should be converted to Currency.
- Click **Close** in the Performance Analyzer window.

- In the Navigation Pane, double-click the **tblMenuChoice** table to open it.
- Select the **CostPerPerson** field, click the **Table Tools Fields tab**.
- In the Formatting group, click the **Data Type arrow**, and then select **Currency**. Because currency fields are smaller than text fields, Access will warn you that the potential exists for losing data. This will not be an issue in this problem. Click **Yes**.
- Save 🖫 your changes, and close ⊠ the table.

e. To encrypt the database with a password it must be open with Exclusive Access:
- Click the **File tab**, and then click **Close Database**.
- Click **Open**, navigate to the folder where you are saving your files, and then select **Lastname_Firstname_a07_ws14_Events.accdb**.
- Click the **Open arrow**, and then select **Open Exclusive**.
- Click the **File tab**, click **Info** if necessary, and then click **Encrypt with Password**.
- In the Password field, type **321efd68**, and then type **321efd68** in the Verify field. Click **OK**.
- Click **OK** in the message that Access will ignore row-level locking.
- Click the **File tab**, click **Close Database**, and then exit Access.

Practice 2

Student data file needed:

a07_ws14_Painted_Treasures

You will save your files as:

Lastname_Firstname_a07_ws14_Painted_Treasures

Lastname_Firstname_a07_ws14_Painted_Treasures_be

Painted Treasures

With their line of products encompassing many of the resort's functional areas, the number of users viewing and updating data in the Painted Treasures Gift Shop database is rapidly growing. Susan Brock would like you to secure the main database with a few key goals in mind. First, Susan would like the basic users of the database to have a more controlled experience. She does not want the average user to be able to create new Access objects or edit existing ones. She would also like to implement a password in the database to protect any data stored within the database.

a. Open the Painted Treasures database:
- Start **Access**, click the **File tab**, and then click **Open**. In the Open dialog box, navigate through the folder structure, and then double-click **a07_ws14_Painted_Treasures**.
- Click the **File tab**, and then click **Save Database As**. In the Save As dialog box, navigate to where you are saving your files, and then type Lastname_Firstname_a07_ws14_Painted_Treasures replacing Lastname_Firstname with your actual name. Click **Save**.
- In the Security Warning, click **Enable Content**.

b. Split the database into front-end and back-end components.
- Click the **Database Tools tab**, and then click **Access Database**.
- Click **Split Database**.
- Navigate to where you are saving your files, save the back-end file as **Lastname_Firstname_a07_ws14_Painted_Treasures_be**, and then click **Split**.
- Click **OK**.
- Click the **File tab**, and then click **Close Database**.

c. Open the front-end database in Exclusive Access:

- Click the **File tab**, and then click **Open**.
- Navigate to where you are saving your files, and then click the **Lastname_Firstname_ a07_ws14_Painted_Treasures** database.
- Click the **Open arrow**, and then select **Open Exclusive**. To further secure the database, you will need Exclusive Access to it.

d. Change the navigational options for the front-end database:

- Click the **File tab**, and then click **Options**.
- In the Navigation Pane, click **Current Database**.
- In the Application Options group:
  - In the text box for Application Title, type Painted Treasures Database.
  - Click the **Display Form arrow**, and then select **frmPaintedTreasuresMenu**.
  - Clear **Use Access Special Keys**. This disables the use of special keys in the database.
  - Clear **Enable Layout View**. This prevents forms and reports from being opened in Layout view in the database.
  - Uncheck the **Enable design changes for tables in Datasheet view** option.
- Under Navigation, clear **Display Navigation Pane**. This prevents the Navigation Pane from being displayed when the database is opened.
- Under Ribbon and Toolbar Options, clear **Allow Full Menus**. This hides all tabs on the Ribbon except for the File and Home tabs. If any Add-ins are installed for Access, the Add-Ins tab is also shown.
- Under Ribbon and Toolbar Options, clear **Allow Default Shortcut Menus**. This prevents the shortcut menu from appearing when a user right-clicks on a form or report.
- Click **OK** at the bottom of the Access Options dialog box. You will be prompted by Access with a message stating that you must close the database before certain options will take effect. Click **OK**.

e. Verify that the settings were correct by closing and reopening the Painted Treasures database:

- Click the **File tab**, and then click **Close Database**.
- Click **Open**. In the Open dialog box, navigate through the folder structure, and then double-click **Lastname_Firstname_a07_ws14_Painted_Treasures**.
- Examine the Ribbon. Only the File and Home tabs should be displayed. If you have an Add-in software installed, the Add-Ins tab will be displayed.
- Examine the frmPaintedTreasuresMenu form. The frmPaintedTreasuresMenu form will now open as the default object for the database. Any task in the database can be accessed from this navigational form.
- Click the **Customers tab** in the frmPaintedTreasuresMenu form, and then add a new record ▶⁎ to the database.
- In the **CustomerID** field, type 16.
- In the **LastName** field, type your last name.
- In the **FirstName** field, type your first name.
- In the **StreetAddress** field, type 3356 Hemmingway Circle.
- In the **City** field, type Santa Fe, and then in the **State** field, type NM.
- In the **ZipCode** field, type 87594.
- In the **ResortHotelRoom** field, type 123.
- Click the **File tab**, and then exit Access.

MODULE CAPSTONE

Student data files needed:

a07_mp_Menu

a07_mp_ Menu_Supplier1.xlsx

a07_mp_ Menu_Supplier2.xlsx

You will save your files as:

Lastname_Firstname_a07_mp_Menu

Lastname_Firstname_a07_mp_Menu_be

Lastname_Firstname_a07_mp_Menu.accde

Indigo5 Menu Database

Painted Paradise is home to the world-class restaurant Indigo5. The manager of Indigo5, Alberto Dimas, is looking for ways to leverage technology to make the restaurant more efficient. His discussions with Chef Robin Sanchez have led to the further development of the database that is used to maintain the menus and ingredients used at Indigo5.

Currently the database includes a list of all menus in use and the ingredients used in each recipe. Recent functionality was added to assist Indigo5 in maintaining an inventory of ingredients as well. A macro was added that will update the inventory of ingredients based on the data in a temporary table. After the inventory is updated the temporary table is deleted. You will convert the macro to VBA and create an import procedure that will allow Robin Sanchez to select multiple files from local food distributors to import into the database. After the import takes place, the original macro should then run. After the entire process is finished, a message box should alert the database user that the process has completed.

When this process is complete, Alberto has requested that the database be modified to allow multiple users and prevent the creation of new database objects.

a. Start **Access**, open **a07_mp_Menu**, and then save the file as Lastname_Firstname_a07_mp_Menu.

b. Convert the mcrUpdateIngredients macro to VBA. Include error handling and macro comments when converting the macro:

- In the Visual Basic Editor, open the converted macro in the code window.

- Insert a comment between the **Function** statement and the **On Error** statement. Type 'This procedure updates the ingredients in the database., and then press Enter.

- Insert another comment under the first one. Type 'This procedure was created by Firstname Lastname. Replace Firstname Lastname with your actual name.

c. Add an import process to the procedure. The process should allow for multiple Excel 2010 spreadsheets to be imported into the tblTempIngredients table:

- To create a new line of code after the **On Error** statement, press Enter and then press Tab.

- Type Dim IngredientDialog As Object, and then press Enter. This declares a variable that will serve as the FileDialog object.

- Set the variable as the FileDialog object, type Set IngredientDialog = Application. FileDialog(msoFileDialogOpen), and then press Enter.

- To use a With statement to more efficiently handle the IngredientDialog object, press Enter, type With IngredientDialog, and then press Enter.

- Press Tab. For the title of the file dialog window, type .Title = "Import ingredients into the database", and then press Enter.

- To allow multiple spreadsheets to be imported at the same time, type .AllowMultiSelect = True, and then press Enter.

d. Use an If statement to determine if any files were selected for import. Use a For Each Next statement to loop through the process of importing each spreadsheet selected by the user. The user should be notified with a message box if no spreadsheets were selected:

- Press [Enter], and then type **If .Show = True Then**.
- Press [Enter], and then press [Tab].
- To declare a variable that will hold the names of the files to be imported, type **Dim ImportFile As Variant**, and then press [Enter].
- Press [Tab], type **For Each ImportFile In .SelectedItems**, press [Enter], and then press [Tab].
- Type **DoCmd.TransferSpreadsheet acImport, acSpreadsheetTypeExcel12, _**, and then press [Enter]. The line continuation character will allow the Visual Basic Editor to break the statement across two lines of the code window.
- Type **"tblTempIngredients", ImportFile, True, ""**, press [Enter], and then press [Backspace].
- Type **Next**, to end the For Each Next statement after it has looped through all of the selected files.
- Press [Enter] and then press [Backspace] twice.
- Type **Else**, and then press [Enter].
- Press [Tab]. To create a message box that will inform users that they have cancelled the import procedure, type **MsgBox "You have cancelled the import process."**, and then press [Enter].
- Press [Backspace], type **End If**, and then press [Enter].
- Press [Backspace], type **End With**, and then press [Enter].

e. After the four DoCmd statements that were created by the macro conversion, create a message box that alerts users that the process is complete.

- Click in the first blank line of code after the second DoCmd.SetWarnings statement, and then press [Enter].
- Press [Tab] and then type **MsgBox "Finished importing new ingredients."**

f. Compile the code to check for any possible errors in the procedure.

- Click **Debug** on the menu bar, and then click **Compile Lastname_Firstname_a07_mp_Menu**.
- If no message appears, your code compiled successfully. If a message appears indicating a problem with your code, fix the problem and compile the VBA again.
- Close the Visual Basic Editor, and then close the mcrUpdateIngredients macro.

g. Assign the new procedure to a button on the frmIngredients form:

- Right-click the **frmIngredients form**, and then click **Design View**.
- Select all of the form labels, fields, and the subform in the Detail portion of the form, and then move them down to the .5" marker.
- On the Form Design Tools tab, click **Design**, and then click Button in the Controls group.
- Insert the new command button above the IngredientID label and text box.
- Click **Cancel** in the Command Button Wizard.
- On the Form Design Tools tab, click **Design**, and then click **Property Sheet** in the Tools group.
- Click the **All tab** in the Property Sheet, click in the **Name** field, highlight the default name of the command button, and then type **cmdImportNewIngredients**.
- Click in the **Caption** field, highlight the default caption text, and then type **Import New Ingredients**.

- Click the **Event tab** in the Property Sheet, click **Build** 🔲 in the On Click field, click **Code Builder**, and then click **OK**.
- The Visual Basic Editor will open to a new Private Sub procedure in the Form_frmIngredients object. Click on the blank line of code after the **Private Sub** statement.
- Type Call mcrUpdateIngredients.
- Close 🔲 the Visual Basic Editor.
- Adjust the width of the new command button to include the full caption text.
- Save 🔲 the frmIngredients form. Click **Yes** to save changes to the frmIngredients form and the Converted Macro- mcrUpdateIngredients module.
- Close ⊠ the frmIngredients form.

h. Split the database to accommodate more users.
- Click the **Database Tools tab**, and then click **Access Database** in the Move Data group.
- Click **Split Database**, navigate to where you are saving your files, save the back-end file as Lastname_Firstname_a07_mp_Menu_be. Click **Split**.
- Click **OK** in the confirmation message that Access split the database.

i. Alberto has also requested that the front-end database only display the File and Home tabs on the Ribbon. The database should have a title, and he would like to prevent users from editing forms by right-clicking them.
- Click the **File tab**, click **Options**, and then click **Current Database** in the left navigation pane.
- In the Application Title box, type Indigo5 Menu Database.
- Under Ribbon and Toolbar Options, clear the **Allow Full Menus** check box so that only the Home and File tabs are displayed. If any Add-in applications are installed for Access, the Add-Ins tab will appear.
- Under Ribbon and Toolbar Options, clear the **Allow Default Shortcut Menus** check box. This prevents the shortcut menus from appearing when a user right-clicks a form or report.
- Click **OK**. Click **OK** in the message window informing you that the changes you have made will not be enabled until the database is closed and reopened.

j. To further secure the database, save a copy of the front-end file as an ACCDE file. This will prevent users from being able to access any VBA or macros in the database.
- Click the **File tab**, and then click **Save & Publish**. In the Advanced list, click **Make ACCDE**, and then click **Save As**. Navigate to where you are saving your files, and then save the ACCDE file as Lastname_Firstname_a07_mp_Menu.
- Click the **File tab**, and then exit Access.

k. Test the finished ACCDE file by importing two files of ingredients into the database.
- Start Access. Click the **File tab**, and then click **Open**. Navigate to where your student data files are located, and then open the **Lastname_Firstname_a07_mp_Menu.accde** database.
- In the Navigation Pane, double-click the **frmIngredients** form to open it.
- Click **Import New Ingredients** to begin the import process. Navigate to where you are saving your student data files, press and hold [Ctrl], and then click **a07_mp_Menu_Supplier1.xlsx** and **a07_mp_Menu_Supplier2.xlsx**. Click **Open**.
- Click **OK** in the message box stating that your import has finished.
- Close 🔲 Access.

Student data file needed:

a07_ps1_Hotel

You will save your files as:

Lastname_Firstname_a07_ps1_Hotel
Lastname_Firstname_a07_ps1_Hotel_be
Lastname_Firstname_a07_ps1_Hotel.accde

Preparing the Hotel Database for Multiple Users

The Hotel at Painted Paradise needs to implement the database it uses for reservations for multiple users. There are two tasks to complete before the final project can be implemented. First, create a VBA script that will prompt the receptionist to offer any customer with five or more stays a 10% discount to the spa. This event should take place whenever the focus of the form moves from one record to another.

The entire database cannot be rolled out to different users as the reservations being made in the database must be stored in one location. Additionally, the interface that the receptionists will be using must be secured such that they cannot create new database objects or edit existing ones. Secure the database to make sure this cannot happen.

a. Start Access, open the **a07_ps1_Hotel** database, and then save the database as Lastname_Firstname_a07_ps1_Hotel.

b. Create a new function on the frmGuestSummary form that will display a message box if the number of guest stays is five or more:

- Open the **frmGuestSummary** form, enter Design view for the form, and then display the property sheet.

- Use the **Code Builder** to create an event procedure that will run when the focus of the form moves from one record to another.

- In the Visual Basic Editor, create a message box that reads Offer Guest a 10% discount at the Spa. The message box should appear if the value of the NumberOfStays field is 5 or greater.

c. Split the database into a front-end and back-end system to better accommodate multiple users.

- Name the back-end database Lastname_Firstname_a07_ps1_Hotel_be.

d. Secure the front-end database. Customize the availability of options in the database to decrease the likelihood that a user might change the database in an unwanted fashion:

- The database should have the title Hotel Reservations.

- The form **frmHotelMenu** must show when the database is opened.

- The hotel does not want the forms in the front-end database to be edited by any of the users. Ensure that users cannot open a database object in Layout or Design view.

- The Navigation Pane must not be visible when the database opens.

- Only the File and Home tabs on the Ribbon must be visible when the database opens.

- Users should not be able to use special keys.

- Save the front-end database in the ACCDE file format. Save the database as **Lastname_Firstname_a07_ps1_Hotel.accde.**

e. Close the database, and then exit Access.

Student data file needed:

a07_ps2_Hotel

You will save your file as:

Lastname_Firstname_a07_ps2_Hotel

Membership Status of Hotel Guests

The hotel at Painted Paradise wants to establish a membership system. As a pilot program for this process, they would like to identify potential guests in the Guest Summary form of the database. On the Guest Summary form, the hotel would like for the GuestID field to change format if a guest met a predetermined criteria.

Once this task is completed the VBA in the database should be password protected and locked for viewing. To further secure the database, it should be encrypted with a password.

a. Start **Access**, and then open the **a07_ps2_Hotel** database in Exclusive Access mode. Save the database as Lastname_Firstname_a07_ps2_Hotel.

b. Open the **frmGuestSummary** form, create a new VBA function, and name it GuestStatus:

- The function should change the format of the GuestID field if the guest meets specific criteria on either of two fields on the form. The criteria have been outlined as a guest that has four or more stays at the hotel or a guest that has spent at least $1,000.

- If either of these criteria is met, the BackThemeColorIndex property of the GuestID field should be Accent 3—a value of 6 in VBA. The BackTint property should be lighter by 25%—a value of 75 in VBA. The ForeThemeColorIndex property should be Background 1—a value of 1 in VBA.

- If the criterion has not been met, the BackThemeColorIndex property should be Background 1—a value of 1 in VBA. The BackTint property should be 0—a value of 100 in VBA. The ForeThemeColorIndex property should be Text 1—a value of 0 in VBA. The ForeTint property should be lighter by 25%—a value of 75 in VBA.

- Insert a comment that describes what this procedure will do.

- Add another comment that includes your first and last name as the author of the procedure.

c. The GuestStatus function must run when the frmGuestSummary form is loaded and when the focus of the form moves from one record to another:

- Call the GuestStatus function from the On Load and Current events of the frmGuest-Summary form.

d. Protect the VBA of the database with a password:

- In the VBA properties of the database, lock the project for viewing.

- Assign a password to the database to keep the VBA from being viewed and edited. Use 959acg71 as the password.

e. Secure the user interface of the database:

- The Application Title should be Hotel Reservations Database.

- The form frmHotelMenu should be displayed when the database opens.

- Only the File and Home tabs on the Ribbon should be visible.

- The Navigation Pane should not be displayed when the database is opened.

- Users should not be able to edit forms or reports in Layout view or by right-clicking a database object.

- Users should not be able to edit tables in Datasheet view.

- Users should not be able to use special keys in the database.

f. Encrypt the database to protect it from unauthorized access:

- Use 476cha65 as the password.

g. Close the database, and then exit Access.

Problem Solve 3

Student data files needed:

a07_ps3_Hotel
a07_ps3_Spa_Ads
a07_ps3_RedBluff_Ads

You will save your files as:

Lastname_Firstname_a07_ps3_Hotel
Lastname_Firstname_a07_ps3_Hotel_2003

Advertisements in the Hotel

The hotel at Painted Paradise has several large screen televisions that run promotional slide shows from other units of the organization, such as the Indigo5 restaurant and the Terra Cotta Brew coffee shop. Along the bottom of each display is a ticker line. The ticker line displays advertisements and announcements from the different areas of Painted Paradise. Each area will send their information to the hotel in an Excel spreadsheet with fixed column headings. Several files might be received in any given time period.

Create a flexible import system in the database that will allow multiple Microsoft Excel spreadsheets to be imported at one time. Analyze the performance of the database and optimize any reasonable suggestions. Then save the database in Access 2003 format.

a. Start **Access**, open the **a07_ps3_Hotel** database, and then save the database as Lastname_Firstname_a07_ps3_Hotel.

b. Create a button on the frmImports form that will initiate the import process:
   - Place a button at the top of the frmImports form. Name the button cmdImportNewAds. The caption of the button must read Import New Advertisements.
   - Assign an event procedure to the On Click event of the button.

c. The import procedure must allow for multiple Excel spreadsheets to be imported into the tblAdvertisements table:
   - Insert a comment that describes what this procedure will do. Add another comment that includes your first and last name as the author of the procedure.
   - As part of the procedure include error trapping. If an error occurs, display the error to the user, then exit the procedure.
   - In the procedure, construct a process where a user can import multiple Excel spreadsheets into the tblAdvertisements table. A template of the Excel files that the other resort areas are using has been provided for you. The files include column headings that match the Advertisements table in the a07_ps3_Hotel database.
   - The file dialog box must have the title Import Advertisement List(s).
   - If the import is cancelled, a message should be displayed. The message must display the text You cancelled the import.
   - Compile the database before exiting the Visual Basic Editor. If an error occurs during the compile process, fix the error and compile that database again.
   - Test the import process by importing the a07_ps3_Spa_Ads and a07_ps3_RedBluff_Ads Excel files.

d. Run the Performance Analyzer on the database:
   - The Performance Analyzer will recommend using the Option Explicit statement in your VBA procedure. Complete this process.

e. The computer that hosts the hotel advertising system is still running Access 2003. Save the database in Access 2003 format:
   - Save the database as Lastname_Firstname_a07_ps3_Hotel_2003.

f. Close the database.

Student data file needed:

a07_pf1_Family_Tree_PersonalDataTemplate

You will save your file as:

Lastname_Firstname_a07_pf1_Family_Tree

My Family Tree

In this project, you will create a family tree within an Access database. The database should be constructed with you as the central focus of the project. In other words, when you enter a family member into the database their relationship status will be relative to you.

A database of this nature will include intensive data entry. Build the database with this in mind. Organize the forms in a logical and efficient fashion. You will use VBA to assist you in automating tasks when possible. Family tree information may also be private information. You will take steps to secure your database not only to prevent unintentional editing of database objects but to protect any sensitive information in the database.

a. Start **Access**, and then create a new database. Save the database as Lastname_Firstname_ a07_pf1_Family_Tree.

b. Create a table that will list the different relationship possibilities. At a minimum this should include items such as mother, father, brother, sister and so on.

c. Create a table that will hold the personal information for your family members. Create an attachment field that can contain a picture.

d. Create a navigational form that contains two tabbed forms. The first should be a form to enter data into the personal information table. The second should be a form that is not based on a table that can hold command buttons.

e. On the blank form create a command button. This command button will have an import script that will run on the On Click event. Name the command button cmdImportFamilyData.

f. As part of this project you could export the personal information table as an Excel spreadsheet. This spreadsheet can serve as a data entry template that you can e-mail to family members. They could complete the form and send it back to you.
   • Create an import process that would allow you to select these files and import them into the personal information table. Assume you may be selecting more than one file at a time.
   • Compile the code in the database before exiting the Visual Basic Editor.
   • In the Visual Basic Editor, lock the project for viewing and provide a password to the VBA properties. Use 853ahe90 for the password.

g. Analyze the performance of your database. Optimize your database where appropriate.

h. This database will contain private information. Full names and dates of birth are common aspects of a family tree. Encrypt the database with a password. Use 853ahe90 for the password.

i. Close the database, and then exit Access.

Perform 2: Perform in Your Career

Student data files needed:

a07_pf2_Inventory

a07_pf2_Supplier1.xlsx

a07_pf2_Supplier2.xlsx

You will save your files as:

Lastname_Firstname_a07_pf2_Inventory

Lastname_Firstname_a07_pf2_Inventory_be

Inventory Management

As the inventory manager at a midsize office supply company, it is your duty to keep track of all items in your warehouse and reorder them when necessary. The basic database has been provided for you. Enhance the database with VBA procedures where necessary to improve efficiency. Split the database so that multiple users can access forms and reports in the database while the tables can be centralized.

a. Start **Access**, open **a07_pf2_Inventory**, and then save the database as Lastname_Firstname_a07_pf2_Inventory.

b. Split the database into a front-end and a back-end system. Name the back-end database Lastname_Firstname_a07_pf2_Inventory_be.

c. In the front-end database, on the frmInventorySummary form is a command button that imports a worksheet into the tblInventory table of the database:

- Convert this macro to a VBA procedure that allows for multiple imports.
- Include a comment in the VBA procedure that lists your first name and last name as the author of the procedure.
- Include a comment in the VBA procedure that explains the purpose of the procedure.
- Include error handling in the procedure.
- Provide the title Select Supply spreadsheet(s) to Import for the dialog box that will open for the user.
- Compile the procedure before closing the Visual Basic Editor.

d. The format of the InStock field of the frmInventorySummary form should change when the stock is below the reorder amount:

- Create a function on the form that will change the field properties of the InStock field when the quantity is equal to or below the ReorderAmount field. If this criteria is met, the BackThemeColorIndex property should change to Accent 2—a value of 5 in VBA. The ForeThemeColorIndex property should change to Background 1—a value of 1 in VBA.
- If the criteria is not met the BackThemeColorIndex property should be Background 1—a value of 1 in VBA, and the ForeThemeColorIndex property should be Text 1—a value of 0 in VBA.
- Name the function ReorderAlert.
- The function should run in response to three different events. When the form is loaded, when the record focus changes, and when the Quantity field is updated.

e. For the front-end database, secure the navigation of the database:

- The application title should be Inventory Database.
- The form frmInventorySummary should be displayed when the database opens.
- Only the File and Home tabs on the Ribbon should be visible.
- The Navigation Pane should not be displayed when the database is opened.
- Users should not be able to edit forms or reports in Layout view or by right-clicking a database object.
- Users should not be able to edit tables in Datasheet view.
- Users should not be able to use special keys in the database.
- Import the files a07_pf2_Supplier1 and a07_pf2_Supplier2 files into the database.

f. Close the database, and then exit Access.

Student data files needed:

a07_pf3_Scheduling

a07_pf3_Scheduling.xlsx

You will save your files as:

Lastname_Firstname_a07_pf3_Scheduling

Lastname_Firstname_a07_pf3_Scheduling_be

Scheduling at a Medical Facility

You have been hired as the manager of a call center at a regional medical facility. The facility houses a wide range of medical services including general physicians, x-ray services, and a lab service. You have been asked to deploy a database to a small portion of the facility before the database is expanded to additional units.

There are several requirements for the database. The performance of the database must be improved. The database must be prepared for multiple users. All computers running the database will be using Access 2010. However, users should not be able to create new objects in the database or modify existing objects in the database. The information in the database will be private data and must be protected with a password.

a. Start **Access**, **open a07_pf3_Scheduling**, and then save the database as Lastname_Firstname_a07_pf3_Scheduling.

b. Create an import process that will allow a user to import a clinician's availability as a Microsoft Excel spreadsheet:

- The command button cmdImportAppointments has been created on the frmSchedulingMenu form. Assign a function to this button that will run in response to the On Click event.
- For the import process, assume that multiple spreadsheets could be imported at the same time.
- The procedure should import Excel spreadsheets to the tblAppointments table. The clinic physicians will have an Excel template to fill out so that the fields in the spreadsheet match that of the database.
- Add comments to the procedure to explain what the procedure is doing.
- Add a comment to the procedure listing your first name and last name as the author of the procedure.
- Add error handling to the procedure. The error handling should show the user the error encountered and then exit the function.
- Provide a title to the dialog box that will be presented to the user.
- If the import is cancelled, a message box should alert the user that they have cancelled the import.
- Compile the database before closing the Visual Basic Editor.

c. Split the database into a front-end and a back-end system. Name the back-end database Lastname_Firstname_a07_pf3_Scheduling_be.

d. Secure the front-end database by encrypting it with a password:
- Close the database and open it with exclusive access.
- Use the password 727ebc67.

e. Secure the user interface of the front-end system:
- The application title should be Scheduling Database.
- The frmSchedulingMenu form menu should be displayed when the database is opened.
- Prevent users from using special keys.
- Secure the Ribbon so that only the File and Home tabs are displayed by default.
- Prevent users from editing tables in Datasheet view.

- Prevent users from editing forms and reports in Layout view or by right-clicking a database object.
- The Navigation Pane should not be visible when the database is opened.

f. Test the import process. Use the cmdImportAppointments button to import the **a07_pf3_Scheduling** Excel file.

g. Close the database, and then exit Access.

Perform 4: How Others Perform

Student data file needed:

a07_pf4_Projects

You will save your file as:

Lastname_Firstname_a07_pf4_Projects

Project Management Database

You are the project manager at a midsize technology company. As your company has grown the task of tracking projects has become overwhelming with the current paper-based process. The company decided to build an Access database that will better track projects.

You have been asked to review the database and fix any errors or improve any inefficiency that can be found. Additionally, some users will be using Access 2003 to view the database. Create a copy of the database in 2003 format.

a. Start **Access**, open **a07_pf4_Projects**, and then save the database as Lastname_ Firstname_a07_pf4_Projects.

b. Open the **frmProjectSummary** form. Examine the Project Start Date field. The BackThemeColorIndex property of this field is supposed to change under two conditions. First, when the number of days from the project start date to the date last updated is greater than 30 and the project status is "development". Second, when the number of days from the project start date to the date last updated is greater than 60 days and the project status is implementation. If neither of these conditions are met or if the project status is completed, the BackThemeColorIndex property of the Project Start date field should be Background 1—a value of 1 in VBA.

- Examine Project ID number 1:
  - **i.** The correct format presents when the form is first opened. Change from Project ID 1 to 2, then back to 1. Why does the format stay the same when records are changed? There are two reasons for why this problem is occurring. You will need to correct both before proceeding.
  - **ii.** Update the status of Project ID 3 to complete by clicking **Completed** from the Project Status list. Save 🖫 the form. This should remove the formatting from the Project Start Date field. Why did the format remain?
- Examine Project ID 1. Could a better choice of themes be used to highlight the data?
- Add comments to the procedure that explain the process.

c. Analyze the performance of the database. Make any changes categorized as suggestions or ideas.

d. Save the database in Access 2003 format. This will fail initially. Examine the tables and resolve any issues that might prevent this from happening. Save the database in Access 2003 format as Lastname_Firstname_a07_pf4_Projects_2003.

e. Close the database, and then exit Access.

APPENDIX

Objectives

1. Identify insertion, deletion, and update anomalies in data. p. 668

2. Modify a table to satisfy the first normal form. p. 670

3. Modify a table to satisfy the second normal form. p. 672

4. Modify a table to satisfy the third normal form. p. 676

5. Join tables together in relationships with referential integrity enforced. p. 678

6. Understand entity relationship diagrams. p. 679

Normalizing a Database for Effective Design

PREPARE CASE

The Terra Cotta Brew Coffee Shop Designing a Normalized Database

Aidan Matthews, the chief technology officer, wants all of the resort to be electronic. The Terra Cotta Brew coffee shop was one of the last areas of the resort still not tracking data electronically. The prior intern for the resort started an Excel spreadsheet to track the sales. When the employees started to use it, they found it to be cumbersome. Further, it requires too much time to enter data. Aidan gave you a copy of the Excel spreadsheet with four transactions in it. He asked you to analyze the data, import it into a database, and fix it.

Courtesy of www.Shutterstock.com

Student data files needed for this appendix:

 a00_Appendix_Terra_Cotta

a00_Appendix_Terra_Cotta.xlsx

a00_Appendix_Terra_Cotta_Import.xlsx

You will save your file as:

 Lastname_Firstname_a00_Appendix_Terra_Cotta

Normalizing a Database

Designing the table structure for a database is not an easy task. Some of the best relational database designers start a design and then after working with it for a while, throw it in the trash and start over. A poor relational database designer tends to structure a database like an Excel spreadsheet, which results in redundancy, inefficiencies, and anomalies. Similar to a well-written paper, one set of business requirements can lead to several different yet equally good database designs. **Normalization** is the process of minimizing the duplication of information in a relational database through effective database design. In addition to minimizing duplication, normalization also prevents anomalies, avoids the need for redesigning as the database is expanded, and provides a better structure for querying. The goal of normalization is that every field in a relation—a table—is directly dependent on every part of the key for the relation. While normalization is not the only component to a well-designed database, it is an important start.

In this workshop, you will learn how to implement the normalization process. Before starting this workshop, you should understand the basics of a database including the following terms: attribute, cardinality, composite key, entity, foreign key, join, junction table, many-to-many relationship, natural primary key, numeric key, one-to-many relationship, one-to-one relationship, primary key, record, and table. These concepts can be found in earlier workshops and the glossary.

The process of normalization holds each table to a progressive series of criteria known as **normal forms (NF)**. There are several levels of normal forms. Each level represents the table's vulnerability to redundancy, anomalies, and inaccuracies. The **highest normal form (HNF)** is the level that a table satisfies along with all levels below. Thus, if a table has an HNF of 2NF, then the table complies with the first and second normal form. If a table reaches the 3NF level, then the table is considered normalized. If a database is stated to be 3NF, this means that all tables in the database meet the criteria for the first three normal forms. Higher levels than 3NF do exist; however, discussion of the higher levels is beyond the scope of this workshop.

Identifying Anomalies

One goal of normalization is to minimize anomalies, in particular three anomalies—insert, delete, and update. An **insertion anomaly** forces you to enter data about two different entities when you may have data on only one entity. A **deletion anomaly** forces you to delete two different pieces of data when you only wanted to delete one piece of data resulting in information loss. An **update anomaly** forces you to change data in multiple records, such as when you need to change the name of a product and you must change multiple rows to make the update. Update anomalies can be difficult to detect.

To Get Started and Identify Anomalies

a. Start **Excel**.

b. Click the **File tab**, click **Open**, browse to your student data files, and then open **a00_Appendix_Terra_Cotta.xlsx**.

c. Examine the data in cells A2:N9 representing four different items ordered:

Field Name	Description
ID	An automatically generated number to represent each order
Date	Date the order was placed
EmployID	Employee ID who took the order
EmpFirst	Employee first name who took the order
EmpLast	Employee last name who took the order
Address	Employee address who took the order
City	Employee city who took the order

(continued)

Field Name	Description
State	Employee state who took the order
Zip	Employee zip code who took the order
ProductName	This is the name of the product ordered. Notice that additional products are dropped down to the next row in Excel.
RetailPrice	This is the normal price of the product.
PricePaid	This is the RetailPrice of the product. This may be different than the typical retail price if the product was at a discounted rate.
Qty	This is the quantity ordered.
Subtotal	This is the RetailPrice multiplied by the Qty.

Figure 1 Data in the spreadsheet tracking orders (continued)

d. Examine the ProductName data in column J2:J9.

Terra Cotta brew just added a new product, a breakfast soufflé. This new product cannot be added until it is sold for the first time. This is an insertion anomaly.

e. Examine the data in cells J7:L7.

This purchase of orange juice sold by Suzanne Kay was erroneous and needs to be deleted. Notice that this is the only entry for orange juice. Thus, if this order is deleted, the information that orange juice is $2.00 will be lost. This is a deletion anomaly.

f. Examine the data in cells E2:E9.

James Kilroy just got married to Jessica McAfee. He decided to change his name to a hyphenated McAfee-Kilroy. Because James has sold more than one order, his information would need to be updated in multiple places—once for every order placed. This is an update anomaly.

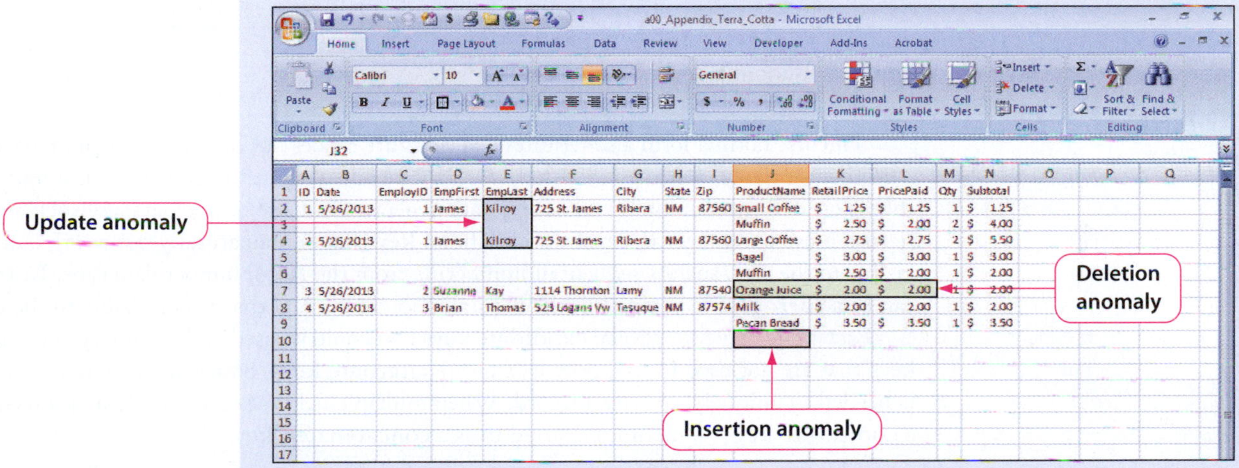

SIDE NOTE

Preventing Update Anomalies

You may think a field is highly unlikely to change. However, if it is remotely possible, you must account for that in the database design to avoid an update anomaly.

Figure 2 Insertion, deletion, and update anomalies

g. Examine the data and identify other insertion, deletion, and update anomalies.

What if this dataset had 2000 orders? It would be difficult to query, prone to typos causing inconsistent data, and inefficient at storing data.

h. Notice that many of the Excel rows are blank and that each order could span several rows.

This format is not conducive to converting into Access tables and breaks the first normal form. Aidan Matthews—the chief technology officer—knew this and already converted the data into a better starting point in another file.

i. Click **Close** ✖

Satisfying the First Normal Form

The **first normal form (1NF)** dictates that the table must not have repeating groups of values in a single column—atomicity—and that it must have a key. Also, in 1NF each nonkey field needs some sort of dependency on the key. A record is considered **atomic** when none of the values are repeating or concatenated for a single column. In Figure 3, each order has a repeating group for ProductName, PricePaid, Qty, and ItemTotal. In other words, each order may have several different products that were purchased. Thus, each row in the spreadsheet is not atomic. Rather, each database record equivalent—also known as a tuple—may be in more than one row due to this repeating group. Thus, the field of ProductName—also known as an attribute—can have multiple values. If the values are repeated in the rows that are currently blank, each row will become atomic and each row will represent one database record or tuple. This may seem like you are adding in redundancy rather than decreasing it. This redundancy will be taken care of as you progress through the normal forms.

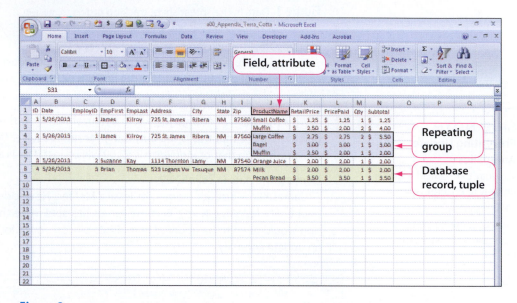

Figure 3 Unnormalized relation—table

The first normal form also requires a key. Figure 3 does not have a key. A **primary key** is a field that uniquely identifies a record. A key can be one of three kinds. It may be a **natural key** that is created from naturally occurring data generated outside of this database such as driver's license number. A key can also be an **artificial key** that is nonnaturally occurring data that is visible to the user, such as sequential numbering from the AutoNumber data type. Lastly, a key can be a **surrogate key,** which is nonnaturally occurring data that is not visible to the user.

Each table may have several **candidate keys** that could be used as the primary key. Candidate keys that are not used for the primary key are **alternate keys.** Sometimes, more than one field is needed to uniquely identify a record. When multiple fields are used to identify a record, it is a **composite key**—sometimes referred to as a **concatenated key.**

Real World Advice   Why Would You Use a Surrogate Key?

Using a surrogate key has its pros and cons. If the key never has a foreign key, you do not need a surrogate key. The advantage with a surrogate is that it can help prevent some cascading changes from primary to foreign key errors. However, a surrogate key can increase the file size and require more joins. Many database designers debate the need for surrogate keys. However, if you have a primary key with a foreign key that may need to be changed frequently or more than normal, a surrogate key should be considered.

In Figure 4, what are the potential candidate keys? Each row had the values copied down to create an atomic table. However, it still does not have a key specified. Each row represents a product purchased in an order. The ID field represents an order. So, by itself, it cannot be a key. There is also a ProductName field. Each product name is unique, but it may be purchased on multiple occasions. However, when considered together, the product name and order ID fields in combination are unique. Thus, in this example, the key is a composite key with ID—representing the order—and ProductName—representing the product ordered. Once this data is imported into Access and the composite key is designated, it will satisfy 1NF. However, it is still subject to the insertion, deletion, and update anomalies. Because further modification as you progress through the normal forms is required, in the next exercise you will import the data into an Access table, but you will not actually designate the key.

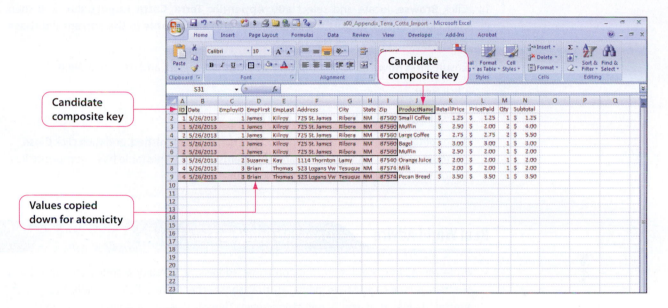

Figure 4 1NF relation—table—with a composite key

CONSIDER THIS | Appropriate Keys

In this example, product name is unique to each product. However, is it the best key to use? Could two products ever have the same product name? What if you separated the size from the product name—with small and coffee in different fields? Would a synthetic key be better?

To Satisfy Atomicity for the First Normal Form

a. Start **Excel**.

b. Click the **File tab**, click **Open**, browse to your student data files, and then open **a00_Appendix_Terra_Cotta_Import.xlsx**.

Notice the changes to this file. Aidan Matthews copied down the Date, EmpFirst, EmpLast, Address, City, State, and Zip fields, temporarily creating more redundancy. Each order is really represented in several rows—for example, the first order is in rows 2–3. Even though this is two rows in the spreadsheet, in the database it represents one database record. Further, each column represents a database field. By copying the values to each row, each row becomes atomic and a separate database record.

c. Click **Close** ![x].

d. Start **Access**.

e. Click the **File tab**, click **Open**, browse to your student data files, and then open **a00_Appendix_Terra_Cotta**.

f. Click the **File tab**, click **Save Database As**, navigate to where you are storing your files and name your database Lastname_Firstname_a00_Appendix_Terra_Cotta replacing Lastname_Firstname with your actual name. Click **Save**. Click **Enable Content** in the Security Warning bar.

g. Click the **External Data tab**, and click the **Excel button** in the Import & Link group.

h. Click **Browse**, locate and select **a00_Appendix_Terra_Cotta_Import.xlsx**, and then click **Open**. Ensure **Import the source data into a new table in the current database** is selected, and then click **OK**.

i. Ensure **First Row Contains Column Headings** is selected, and then click **Next**.

j. Click **Next**.

k. Select **No primary key**, and then click **Next**.

l. Type tblItemsOrdered for the Import to Table name. Click **Finished**, and then click **Close**.

　　You now have a table in 1NF named tblItemsOrdered. This table has a composite key, which you will specify later in this workshop.

Real World Advice　　　Does the Address Field Violate Atomicity?

While the address field represents only one address, it is really a concatenated value of street number and street name. In that sense, the address field actually has multiple values in it and is not atomic even though it is not a repeating group—because it is just a single address. You could have separate fields for street number and street name to satisfy 1NF. For many businesses, a single field for address is sufficient. You want to look at the business requirements when creating your tables and keep the future in mind. If you would never want to query how many employees live on the same street, separating the values is not necessary. However, if you were building a database for the postal office, you would want to separate the values into two fields.

Satisfying the Second Normal Form

The **second normal form (2NF)** requires that the table has no fields with partial dependencies on a composite or concatenated key and satisfies 1NF. A **dependency** is when a field relates to a key. For example, the order date is dependent on the order ID. While several orders can be placed on the same day, one order cannot be placed on more than one date. Thus, order date is dependent on the key of order ID. Further, a **determinant** is a field that determines the value of another field. For example, the order ID determines the order date. An order can be placed on one specific date. Thus, if you know the key order ID, you should be able to determine the order date. A **partial dependency** is when the field only depends on one part of a composite or concatenated key. In other words, the field is determined by only one piece of a multifield key. A **transitive dependency** is when a field depends on another field in the table, which then depends on a candidate key. A→B and B→C, thus A implies C. If C is a candidate key and B is not a candidate key, this is a transitive dependency. For 2NF, transitive dependency is acceptable, but partial dependency is not.

　　Ask yourself whether each field could still be there if one part of the key was removed. For example, can employee first name remain if the product name was not part of the composite key? The answer is yes. If you answer yes for even one field, the table is not in 2NF. Thus, employee first name is not dependent on the product that was purchased—ProductName—is a partial dependency. To get a table to satisfy 2NF, you break the table up into several tables. Dependencies are frequently shown in a **functional dependency diagram** as shown in Figure 5.

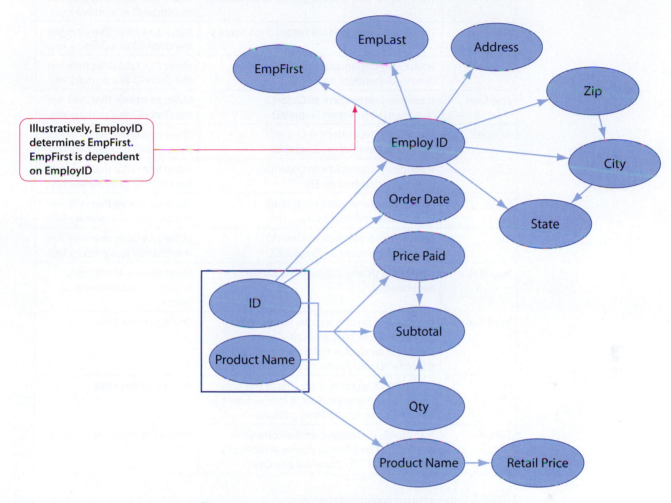

Illustratively, EmployID determines EmpFirst. EmpFirst is dependent on EmployID

Figure 5 Functional dependency diagram of tblItemsOrdered

To Remove Partial Dependencies to Satisfy the Second Normal Form

a. Open the table **tblItemsOrdered** in Design view.

b. Change the field **ID** to **OrderID** to be more easily identified.

c. Click **Save** 🖫, and then click **View** to change to Datasheet view.

d. Examine each nonkey field for partial dependencies:

Field Name	Dependent to Which Key Field: OrderID, ProductName, or Concatenated OrderID and ProductName?	Action Needed to Conform to 2NL
Date	The OrderID only and is a partial dependency	Move to a table that only has the OrderID as a primary key.
EmployID	The OrderID only and is a partial dependency	Move to a table that only has the OrderID as a primary key.
EmpFirst	Transitively dependent to OrderID. Directly dependent on EmployID.	Move to a table that only has the OrderID as a primary key.
EmpLast	Transitively dependent to OrderID. Directly dependent on EmployID.	Move to a table that only has the OrderID as a primary key.
Address	Transitively dependent to OrderID. Directly dependent on EmployID.	Move to a table that only has the OrderID as a primary key.
City	Transitively dependent to OrderID. Directly dependent on Zip.	Move to a table that only has the OrderID as a primary key.
State	Transitively dependent to OrderID. Directly dependent on City.	Move to a table that only has the OrderID as a primary key.
Zip	Transitively dependent to OrderID. Directly dependent on EmployID.	Move to a table that only has the OrderID as a primary key.
RetailPrice	The ProductName only and is a partial dependency.	Move to a table that only has the ProductName as a primary key.
PricePaid	Because this price is specific to this order—may be a discounted amount—and this particular product, it is dependent on both the order ID and ProductName.	Remain in this table
Qty	Because this quantity is specific to this order and this particular product, it is dependent on both the order ID and ProductName.	Remain in this table
Subtotal	Transitively dependent on the composite key OrderID and ProductName. It is directly dependent on the PricePaid and Qty.	Remain in this table, for now

Figure 6 Table evaluating partial dependency

e. Click the **File tab**, and then click **Save Object As**. Type **tblInventory** in the first input box for the name, and then press ⌷Enter⌷.

Troubleshooting

> If Access responds with an error message stating that there is no primary key defined, click No. You will add a key later.

f. Click the **Home tab**, and then click **View** and click **Design View** for tblInventory.

g. Delete all fields except ProductName and RetailPrice. For each field you need to delete, right-click the field's name, and then select **Delete Rows**. If prompted, click **Yes** to confirm that you want to delete the field.

Access responds with an error message when you delete some of the fields. This says that deleting a field requires Microsoft Access to delete one or more indexes. This deletion is fine. Click **Yes** when prompted with this error.

h. Click **Save** 💾. Click the **Design tab**, click **View** and click **Datasheet View** for tblInventory. To delete the record for the second occurrence of the product named **Muffin**, click the **record selector** for the row, and then press ⌨️Delete. Click **Yes** to confirm deletion.

i. Click the **Home tab**, and then click **View** and click **Design View**. Click the **ProductName** field, click the **Design tab**, and then click **Primary Key** in the Tools group to designate ProductName as a natural primary key.

You have separated the ProductName portion of the original concatenated or composite key into its own table.

Troubleshooting

If you get an error that prevents you from adding the primary key, check carefully that you deleted the second occurrence of the product named "Muffin".

j. Save 💾 and close ❌ tblInventory.

k. Open **tblItemsOrdered** in Datasheet view. Click the **File tab**, and then click **Save Object As**. Type **tblOrders** for the name, and then press ⌨️Enter.

Troubleshooting

If Access responds with an error message stating that there is no primary key defined, click No. You will add a key later.

l. Click the **Home tab**, and then click **View**, and click **Design View** for tblOrders.

m. Delete RetailPrice because that field is now in the tblInventory table. If prompted, click **Yes** to confirm the deletion.

n. Delete **ProductName**, **PricePaid**, **Qty**, and **Subtotal**. These fields will remain in the original tblItemsOrdered table. If prompted, click **Yes** to confirm deletion, and then click **Yes** again for the index message.

Access responds with an error message. This says that deleting a fi⬚ requires Microsoft Access to delete one or more indexes. This deletion is fine.

o. Click **Save** 💾. Click the **Design tab**, click **View**, and click **Datasheet View**.

p. Delete the record for the second occurrence of the OrderIDs 1 and 4. Delete the record for the second and third occurrence of the OrderID **2**.

q. Click the **Home tab**, and then click **View**, and click **Design View**. Click the **OrderID** field, and then click **Primary Key** on the Design tab to designate OrderID as an artificial primary key.

r. Save 💾 and close ❌ tblOrders.

s. Open **tblItemsOrdered** in Design view.

t. Delete all fields except: OrderID, ProductName, PricePaid, Qty, and Subtotal. If prompted, click **Yes** to confirm deletion, and then click **Yes** again if necessary for index error messages.

u. Select both **OrderID** and **ProductName**. Click **Primary Key** on the Design tab to designate OrderID and ProductName as the concatenated or composite key.

You have separated the ProductName portion of the original concatenated or composite key into its own table named tblInventory. You also have moved the field—RetailPrice—that was dependent on only that portion of the ProductName into the new table tblInventory.

All tblItemsOrdered and tblInventory tables now satisfy at least 2NF in a practical sense. In the strictest sense, tblOrders is not even 1NL as address is a multivalued field—street number and street name. Also, tblOrders and tblItemsOrdered still suffer from insertion, deletion, and update anomalies.

v. Save 💾 and close ✖ tblItemsOrdered.

Satisfying the Third Normal Form

The **third normal form (3NF)** requires that the table has to be free of transitive dependencies and that the table satisfies both 1NF and 2NF. Remember, a transitive dependency is when a field depends on another field in the table which then that field depends on a candidate key. A→B and B→C, thus A implies C. If C is a candidate key and B is not a candidate key, this is a transitive dependency. When multiple overlapping candidate keys exist, you also should satisfy an additional criterion. Known as the **Boyce–Codd normal form (BCNF, 3.5NF)**, this additional criteria requires that all determinants are candidate keys and that the table satisfies 1NF and 2NF and 3NF. By normalizing to BCNF, you are eliminating all functional dependencies.

Ask yourself, if I update this field, does another field in the table also need to be updated? If the answer is yes, then you have a transitive dependency. For example, think about a zip code. If you needed to change the zip code, then you may also have to change the city and state. In its strictest sense, 3NF would have a table of cities and zip codes, a table of cities and states, and the original table would only require you to enter the zip code. However, this level of normalization will create more joins, increase complexity, and potentially decrease the speed of the database system. Thus, the business requirements must be taken into consideration.

Other times, you clearly want to normalize to 3NF. Think about the employee last name in the orders table. The employee's last name is a nonkey field. Is the OrderID a determinant for the employee's last name? No. Instead, EmployID determines the employee's last name. Therefore, employee's last name is dependent on something other than the OrderID and needs to be moved into its own table.

To Satisfy the Third Normal Form

a. Open the table **tblOrders** in Datasheet view.

b. Examine each nonkey field for transitive dependencies:

Field Name	What Field Is This Field Dependent On and Is It a Candidate Key?	Action Needed to Conform to 3NL
Date	The OrderID—a candidate key	Remain in this table
EmployID	The OrderID—a candidate key	Remain in this table
EmpFirst	The EmployID—a noncandidate key	Move to a table with EmployID as the primary key.
EmpLast	The EmployID—a noncandidate key	Move to a table with EmployID as the primary key.
Address	The EmployID—a noncandidate key	Move to a table with EmployID as the primary key.
City	The State—a noncandidate key	Move to a table with EmployID as the primary key.
State	The City—a noncandidate key	Move to a table with EmployID as the primary key.
Zip	The EmployID—a noncandidate key	Move to a table with EmployID as the primary key.

Figure 7 Table evaluating 3NL for tblOrders

c. Click the **File tab**, and then click **Save Object As**. Type **tblEmployees** for the name, and then press Enter.

d. Click the **Home tab**, click **View**, and click **Design View**.

e. Delete the OrderID and Date fields. If prompted, click **Yes** to confirm deletion. Click **Yes** again as needed. Access responds with an error message. This says that deleting the field requires Access to delete the primary key. Click **Yes** to confirm. You will reset the primary key later.

f. Click **Save** 💾.

g. Click the **Home tab**, click **View**, and click **Datasheet View**. Delete the record for the second occurrence of the EmployID 1 and click **Yes** to confirm deletion.

h. Add a record to the tblEmployees with the following values:
- EmployID—**4**
- EmpFirst—**Your First Name**
- EmpLast—**Your Last Name**
- Address—**123 Elm Street**
- City—**Lamy**
- State—**NM**
- Zip—**87540**

i. Click **View** on the Home tab, and click **Design View**. Click the **EmployID** field, and then click **Primary Key** on the Design tab to designate EmployID as an artificial primary key.

j. Save 💾 and close ☒ tblEmployees.

k. Open **tblOrders** in Design view.

l. Delete all the fields except OrderID, Date, and EmployID. If prompted, click **Yes** to confirm deletion.

m. Save 💾 and close ☒ tblOrders.

n. Open **tblItemsOrdered** in Datasheet view.

o. Examine each nonkey field for transitive dependencies.

Field Name	What Field Is This Field Dependent On and Is It a Candidate Key?	Action Needed to Conform to 3NL
PricePaid	The Order ID and ProductName, a candidate key	Remain in this table
Qty	The Order ID and ProductName, a candidate key	Remain in this table
Subtotal	PricePaid and Qty, both noncandidate keys. Further, subtotal is value that can easily be calculated in queries.	Delete this field.

Figure 8 Table evaluating 3NL for nonkey fields in tblItemsOrdered

p. Click **View** on the Home tab to switch to Design view. Delete the Subtotal field. If prompted, click **Yes** to confirm deletion.

q. Save 💾 and close ☒ tblItemsOrdered.

The tables tblItemsOrdered, tblInventory, and tblOrders all are in 3NF. The table tblEmployee is not even 1NF because the transitive dependencies of State and City and the multivalued column of Address. For a database to be considered normalized, all tables need to be in 3NF. However, most expert database designers consider leaving the state and city in the Employees table and placing the Street Number and Name in the same column as an acceptable variation from normalization.

Quick Reference — Normal Forms

Normal Form Level	Description
First normal form (1NF)	The table must not have repeating groups of values in a single column—atomicity—and that it must have a key.
Second normal form (2NF)	The table has no fields with partial dependencies on a composite or concatenated key and satisfies 1NF.
Third normal form (3NF)	The table has to be free of transitive dependencies and satisfy all lower levels of NF.
Boyce–Codd normal form (BCNF, 3.5NF)	All determinants are candidate keys and satisfy all lower levels of NF.

Figure 9 Table of normal forms

Joining Tables with Relationships

Once the tables are set, the database needs relationships to join the data from various tables. A **one-to-many relationship (1:M or 1:N)** is a relationship between two tables where one record in the first table corresponds to many records in the second table. One-to-many is called the cardinality of the relationship. **Cardinality** indicates the number of instances of one entity that relates to one instance of another entity. For example, each employee can only be in the employees table exactly one time. However, an employee can be in the orders table many times—once for each sale. These two tables are related by a one-to-many relationship using the order ID key.

A **many-to-many relationship (M:N)** is a relationship between tables in which one record in one table has many matching records in a second table, and one record in the related table has many matching records in the first table. For example, a product can be in many different orders. Also, each order can have many products in inventory. Because these two tables do not have a common field, in Access this kind of many-to-many relationship must have an additional table in between these two. This intermediate table is referred to by several synonymous terms: "intersection," "junction," or "link table."

A **one-to-one relationship (1:1)** is a relationship between tables where a record in one table has only one matching record in the second table. In a small business, a department might be managed by no more than one manager, and each manager manages no more than one department. That relationship in the business is a one-to-one relationship.

Access allows you to add some **integrity constraints**—or rules—to your database to help ensure data's validity. The entity integrity constraint requires all primary keys have a value—not be null. **Referential integrity** in relationships requires that only values that have a corresponding value in the primary table can be entered for a foreign key. **Cascade update** will update a foreign key automatically when the primary key changes. For example, if you change an employee's ID, cascade update will change every instance in the orders table. **Cascade delete** will delete every record with the foreign key if the value is deleted from the primary table. For example, if you deleted an employee—which is not good practice—it would delete every order that the employee processed. Lastly, **domain integrity constraints** are rules that are specific for each field. For example, setting the data type of currency for price will require that the data entered is numeric. Setting all the constraints for this database is beyond the scope of this workshop but an important next step in database creation.

SIDE NOTE
Adding tables
You can also use the `Ctrl` key to select multiple tables at once (that are not in contiguous order) to add to the relationships window.

SIDE NOTE
Order of tables
Remember, the order or arrangement of the tables in the relationship view does not matter. The lines—relationships—between the fields are the important part!

SIDE NOTE
Creating relationships
Alternatively, you could drag from EmployID in tblOrders to EmployID in tblEmployees.

To Join Tables with Relationships with Referential Integrity

a. Click the **Database Tools tab**, and then click **Relationships** in the Relationships group.

b. In the Show Table dialog box, tblEmployees should already be selected. Press and hold the `Shift` key, and then click **tblOrder** to select all four tables in the list and then click **Add**.

c. Close the Show Table dialog box. Drag the **tables** in the Relationships window so there is some space between the tables to form the relationships and the tblEmployees is moved to the end, after tblOrders.

d. Drag the primary key **EmployID** from tblEmployees to **EmployID** in tblOrders.

e. Access displays the Edit Relationships dialog box. Click **Enforce Referential Integrity** to select it, and then click **Create**.

Troubleshooting

If you get this error "Microsoft Access cannot create this relationship and enforce referential integrity," double-check that your data is all correct and that you did not delete a record by accident.

f. Drag the primary key **OrderID** from tblOrders to **OrderID** in tblItemsOrdered.

g. Access displays the Edit Relationships dialog box. Click **Enforce Referential Integrity** to select it, and then click **Create**.

h. Drag the primary key **ProductName** from tblItemsOrdered to **ProductName** in tblInventory.

i. Access displays the Edit Relationships dialog box. Click **Enforce Referential Integrity** to select it, and then click **Create**. Save and close the Relationships window. Close Access.

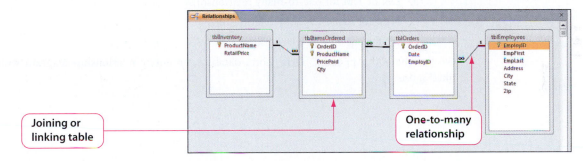

Figure 10 Final Relationships Window

Understanding an Entity Relationship Diagram

Many ways of visually expressing the database structure exist. Best practice is to use one of these methods both when designing the database and documenting the database. An **entity relationship diagram (ERD)** is a common way to visually express the tables and relationships in your database. An ERD does not tell you anything about data flow and is a fixed view of the database structure.

There are variations in how designers represent ERDs. For example, some designers may prefer the Crow's Feet approach. The Crow's Feet approach will list the table name at the top of a rectangle, draw a line, list the attributes, and underline the key.

Alternatively, under the entity relationship model these basic shapes are used to create an ERD—rectangle, diamond, and oval. Some common variations in the shapes are included below. However, all variations are beyond the scope of this workshop.

1. Identify your entities. Remember, entities are people, places, or items that you want to keep data about. Entities in ERDs are usually nouns and are drawn in rectangles. Depending on the type of entity, several variations exist:

   a. Strong entities have a primary key. These are drawn in a normal rectangle.

   b. Weak entities do not have a primary key. Rather, they have a primary key from another table—or foreign key—and a discriminator value in the table that forms the key. These are drawn in a double rectangle.

   c. Bridge entities are tables that form a join or linking table for a many-to-many relationship. Bridge entities use a composite key. A composite key consists of two foreign keys that together combine for a unique value. These are drawn in a diamond with a rectangle around it.

2. Identify the relationships. Remember, relationships are associations between tables based on common fields. Relationships in ERDs are usually verbs and are drawn in diamonds.

3. Identify the attributes. Remember, attributes are information about the entity, or the data. Consider the business requirements of the system. Ask yourself, what fields are needed in queries? What common fields and keys are needed for the relationships? You may find a new entity and need to revise your ERD in this step. Attributes in ERDs are generally drawn inside an oval. Depending on the type of attribute, several variations exist.

   a. Key attributes are underlined.

   b. A second inside circle is used for multivalued attributes, like an address that contains both street number and street name.

   c. Derived values are represented with a dashed oval line. For example, city is derived from zip which is not a candidate key.

4. Determine the cardinality of the relationships. May require you to add a join or linking table. Cardinality in ERDs are listed depending on the type of relationship.

   a. 1:N or 1:M for one-to-many relationships

   b. N:M for many-to-many relationships

   c. 1:1 for one-to-one relationships

For the a00_Appendix_Terra_Cotta database, an entity relationship diagram would look like Figure 11.

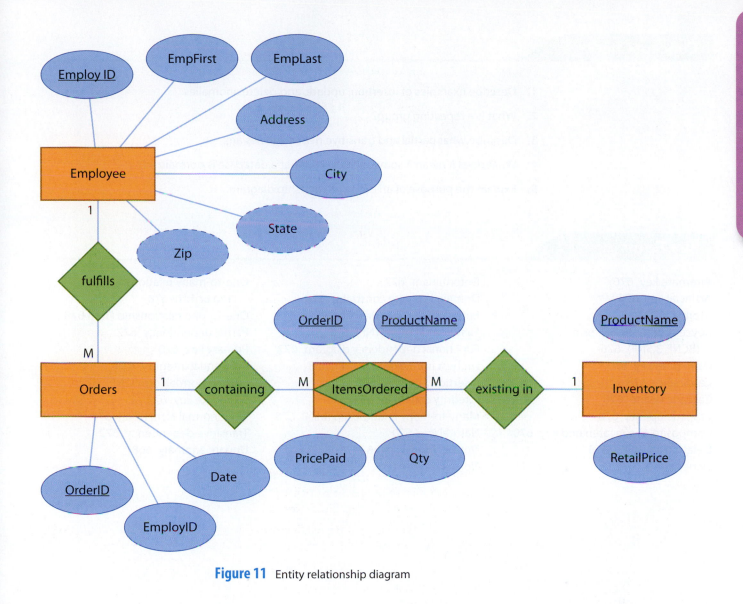

Figure 11 Entity relationship diagram

Concept Check

1. Describe examples of insertion, update, and delete anomalies.

2. What is a repeating group?

3. Describe what partial and transitive dependencies are.

4. What does it mean if someone tells you that a database is normalized?

5. Explain the purpose of an entity relationship diagram.

Key Terms

Alternate key 670
Artificial key 670
Atomic 670
Boyce–Codd normal form
  (BCNF, 3.5NF) 676
Candidate key 670
Cardinality 678
Cascade delete 678
Cascade update 678
Composite or concatenated key 670
Deletion anomaly 668
Dependency 672

Determinant 672
Domain integrity constraint 678
Entity relationship diagram (ERD) 679
First normal form (1NF) 670
Functional dependency diagram 672
Highest normal form (HNF) 668
Insertion anomaly 668
Integrity constraint 678
Many-to-many relationship (M:N) 678
Natural key 670
Normal form (NF) 668
Normalization 668

One-to-many relationship
  (1:M or 1:N) 678
One-to-one relationship (1:1) 678
Partial dependency 672
Primary key 670
Referential integrity 678
Second normal form (2NF) 672
Surrogate key 670
Third normal form (3NF) 676
Transitive dependency 672
Update anomaly 668

Visual Summary

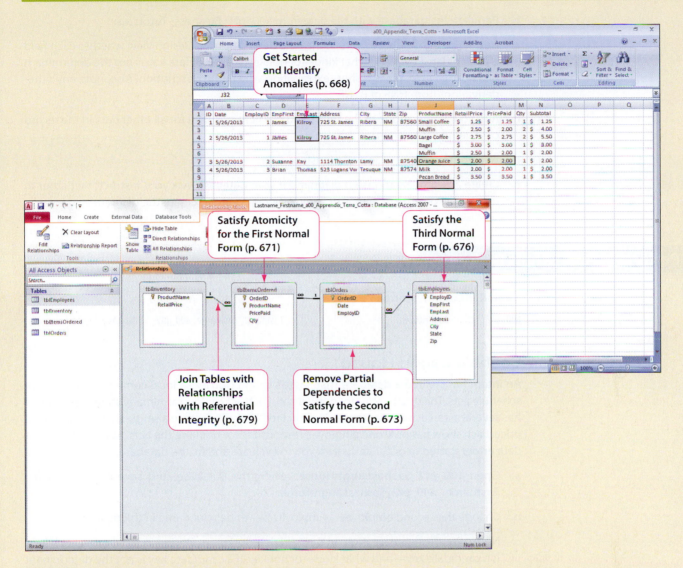

Figure 12 Terra Cotta Brew Coffee Shop Normalized Database

Perform 1: Perform in Your Career

Student data file needed:

a00_pf1_Business_Tutors.xlsx

You will save your file as:

Lastname_Firstname_a00_pf1_Business_Tutors

Normalizing Appointments for Business Tutors

A local company runs a tutoring service for local business students. Each tutor has only one topic that he or she tutors. Each tutor may have several appointments. Each appointment may have one or more students at the appointment. Only one tutor may be assigned to an appointment. The price per hour varies based on topic and number of students at the appointment. However, the price per student is the same for all students in the same appointment. Currently, the appointments are tracked in Excel. At the urging of the Access tutor, your manager has asked you to convert this spreadsheet into a normalized database.

a. Start **Access**, and then create a new blank database. Save the database as Lastname_ Firstname_ a00_pf1_Business_Tutors.

b. Populate the database with the data from a00_pf1_Business_Tutors.xlsx.

c. Normalize the database. Note in the field descriptions in Design view whether each field is a candidate key—and what kind—or nonkey. If a candidate key is not the determinant of a nonkey field, place a short explanation why in the description. Also, note any other derivations from HNF of BCNF.

d. Add your name as one of the tutors and use fictitious data for all other data in the record containing your name.

e. Add appropriate keys and relationships.

f. Create an entity relationship diagram for your database. Ask your instructor whether to use Word, PowerPoint, paper, or some other program to create the diagram.

Perform 2: How Others Perform

Student data file needed:

a00_pf2_SashasLaughHouse

You will save your file as:

Lastname_Firstname_a00_pf2_SashasLaughHouse

Sasha's Laugh House

An intern has created a database that Sasha's Laugh House—a local comedy club—uses to schedule acts. The database is not normalized. Each act can perform many shows. Each show has several acts. Each act charges a single act fee, and all tickets to a single show are the same price. Each show has only one employee responsible for booking the acts. Sasha noticed that data errors started to occur and asked you to evaluate and fix the database.

a. Open **a00_pf2_SashasLaughHouse**, review the database, and save it as Lastname_ Firstname_ a00_pf2_SashasLaughHouse.

b. Change the second employee—EmployID 2— to be your name in tblEmployee.

c. Normalize the database. Note in the field descriptions in Design view whether each field is a candidate key—and what kind—or nonkey. If a candidate key is not the determinant of a nonkey field, place a short explanation why in the description. Also, note any other derivations from HNF of BCNF.

d. Add at least two additional fields you think Sasha might find helpful. Add a description in Design view explaining why you added the field. Leave the data for the field blank.

e. Ensure you have specified all keys and added relationships.

f. In the Navigation Pane, **right-click** each table, and then select **Table Properties**. In the Description for each table, specify the HNF for the table before changes and after your changes.

Glossary

A

.accde file Allows procedures to not be viewable to the user and any errors that might occur during the execution of a VBA procedure will not result in the Visual Basic Editor being displayed.

Action A self-contained instruction that can be combined with others to automate tasks and is considered to be the basic building block of macros.

Action Catalog A searchable set of macro actions that can retrieve actions based on keywords.

Action query A query that makes changes to records or moves many records from one table to another. Action queries are used to change the data in existing tables or make new tables based on a query's dataset.

Adobe PDF file A file format that is easy to send through e-mail and preserves the original document look and feel so it opens the same way every time for the recipient.

Advanced filter This allows you to write the filter criterion yourself.

After events These occur after the changes have been successfully made to the table data.

Aggregate A summative calculation, such as a total or average, or summarizing data.

Aggregate function Calculations that perform arithmetic operations, such as averages and totals, on records displayed in a table or query.

Aggregated calculation A calculation that returns a single value, calculated from multiple values in a column. Common aggregate functions include Average, Count, Maximum, Median, Minimum, Mode, and Sum.

Alternate key A candidate key that is not used for the primary key.

Append query A query that selects records from one or more data sources and copies the selected records to an existing table.

Append row The first blank row at the end of the table.

Application A collection of tools used to perform a task or multiple tasks.

Argument A constant, variable, or expression that is passed to a procedure.

Artificial key A key comprising nonnaturally occurring data that is also visible to the user, such as sequential numbering from the AutoNumber data type.

AS clause When used in a SQL SELECT statement, the AS clause allows you to name or rename a field, which will be displayed in the dataset.

Atomic A record where none of the values are repeating or concatenated for a single column.

Attachment A data type that allows you to attach images, spreadsheet files, documents, charts, and other types of supported files to the records in your database, much like you attach files to an e-mail message.

Attribute Information about the entity.

AutoExec macro A macro that has been given the name of AutoExec. When a database is opened, Access will check for a macro with that name and run that macro before any others.

AutoFit A method to change the column width of a field to match the widest data entered in that field.

AutoKeys macro A macro group that assigns keys on the keyboard to execute each submacro. The macro must be named AutoKeys, and each submacro must be named with the key or key combinations on the keyboard that will be used to execute the macros.

AutoNumber data type The AutoNumber data type stores an integer that Access creates automatically as you add new records.

B

Back-end database Contains the tables that front-end databases link to.

Backstage view Provides access to the file-level features, such as saving a file, creating a new file, opening an existing file, printing a file, and closing a file, as well as program options.

Backup database An extra copy of a database created in case the database is lost. Access appends the current date to the file name.

Before events These occur before any changes are made to the table data.

Between…And operator This operator verifies whether the value of a field or expression falls within a stated range of numeric values and is combined with the And or Or operators. For example, to find data that falls between two dates, you type Between 2/3/2013 And 8/6/2013.

Bitmap A bitmap is an image of an object.

Blank Report tool An Access tool used to create a blank report in Layout view.

Boolean algebra Still used today, a 0 and 1 are used to represent one of two values—true or false. The 0 and 1—or -1 depending on the system you are using—are a throwback to the earlier days of programming.

Bound control A control that retrieves its data from an underlying table or query; a text box control is an example of a bound control.

Bound form A form that is directly connected to a data source such as a table or query, and can be used to enter, edit, or display data from that data source.

Boyce–Codd normal form (BCNF, 3.5NF) Additional criteria that are useful when multiple overlapping candidate keys exist. Requires that all determinants are candidate keys and that the table satisfies 1NF, 2NF, and 3NF. By normalizing to BCNF, you are eliminating all functional dependencies.

Business intelligence (BI) Helps an organization attain their goals and objectives by giving them a better understanding of past performance as well as information on how the organization is progressing toward its goals.

Business intelligence tools A classification of software applications that aid in collecting, storing, analyzing, and providing access to data that helps managers make improved business decisions.

C

Calculated control A control on a report or form whose data source is a calculated expression.

Calculated data type A Calculated data type allows you to display the results of a calculation in a read-only field.

Call statement Runs another Sub procedure or function from within a procedure by transferring to the called routine.

Candidate key Fields that could be used as the primary key.

Caption property A caption is like an alias. A caption does not change the actual field name, just the way users see it, like an alias.

Cardinality The number of instances of one entity that relates to one instance of another entity. Cardinality is expressed as one-to-many, many-to-many, or one-to-one.

Cascade delete Deletes every record with the foreign key if the value is deleted from the primary table.

Cascade update Updates a foreign key automatically when the primary key changes.

Case sensitive Access is not a case-sensitive program. Query results will return all matching data, regardless of how the data is stored, whether a user enters lowercase or uppercase letters in the criteria property.

Charlist This is a group of one or more characters.

Check box A control that shows whether an option is selected by using a check mark to indicate when the option is selected.

Code window The larger window on the right of the Visual Basic Editor where code is entered.

Cold turkey implementation The process of replacing a legacy system and implementing a new system in its entirety with no overlap between the two.

Compacting An Access function that rearranges objects in your database to use space more efficiently.

Comparison operator An operator used in a query to compare the value in a database to the criteria value entered in the query.

Compile The process of examining VBA for errors before the code is executed.

Complex delete query A query used to delete data between multiple tables.

Complex update query A query used to update data between multiple tables.

Composite key A primary key composed of two fields.

Composite or concatenated key A key where multiple fields are used to identify a record.

Concatenate A method used to combine data in multiple fields. In a Customer table, you could combine FirstName and LastName fields for address labels.

Concatenate operator A function that helps join data from multiple fields to create a single text string of data. This is done by using an ampersand (&) to create a single field by combining data in multiple fields. For example, to concatenate FirstName and LastName fields, you type FullName:[FirstName]&" " &[LastName], where FullName would become the name of the concatenated field.

Conditional formatting A way to apply formatting to specific controls based on a comparison to a rule set.

Contextual tab A Ribbon tab that contains commands related to selected objects so you can manipulate, edit, and format the objects.

Control A part of a form or report that is used to enter, edit, or display data.

Crosstab query This is a special type of query that can be created when you want to describe one number in terms of two other numbers.

Crosstab Query Wizard This wizard helps create a basic crosstab query. For a more advanced query, changes would need to be made in the query's Design view after finishing the wizard.

Custom formatting You can create your own type of formatting to customize the way numbers, dates, times, and text are displayed and printed.

D

Data Facts about people, events, things, or ideas.

Data actions A specific, limited set of macro actions that can be used in a data macro.

Data blocks These contain an area to add one or more data actions. The data block executes all the actions contained as part of its operation.

Data cleansing A process of removing data that is not useful or needed anymore.

Data macro Database objects stored in Access tables and are triggered by table events. Data macros are typically used to implement business logic into tables and automatically set values in fields.

Data mining The act of using BI tools is called data mining, which helps expose trends, patterns, and relationships within the data that might have otherwise remained undetected.

Data type The characteristic that defines the kind of data that can be entered into a field, such as numbers, text, or dates. The data type tells Access how to store and display the field.

Data validation rule A rule that prevents bad data from being entered and consequentially stored in your database. Validation rules can be set for a specific field or an entire table.

Data warehouse Data warehouses contain large amounts and different types of data that present a clear picture of business environments at specific points in time.

Data warehousing When older data is exported from transactional and operational databases into a "storage" database, called a data warehouse.

Database event This occurs when an action is completed on any given object. The action could be, for example, a simple click of the mouse or entering into a specific field.

Database management system (DBMS) Database management software that can be used to organize, store, manipulate, and report on your data.

Datasheet view A view of an Access object that shows the data.

Date function The function Date ( ) returns the current system date.

Date Picker A pop-up calendar that allows users to enter dates by clicking a date in the calendar.

DateAdd function This function can be used to add or subtract a specific time interval from a date. For example, Date()+10 results in the same output as using the DateAdd function to add 10 to the current date—DateAdd("d", 10, Date()).

DateDiff function This function is used to determine the difference between two dates. For example, to see how many days it has been since a member paid the club's annual dues, type DaysSincePmt: DateDiff("d",Date(),[PaymentDate]).

DatePart function This function can be used to examine a date and return a specific interval of time. For example, if each employee is eligible for a bonus after 5 years of service, you can determine the year when eligibility begins by typing 5 Year Anniversary: DatePart("yyyy", ([HireDate]))+5.

DateSerial function This function, written as DateSerial(year, month, day), can be used to manipulate the day, month, and year of a date. For example, if each full-time employee is eligible for health benefits after 90 days of employment, which means that the benefits begin on the 91st day of employment, you could determine the date when eligibility begins by typing Benefits Begin:DateSerial(Year([HireDate]),Month([HireDate]), Day([HireDate])+91).

Debugging The process of identifying and correcting errors that can occur within programming code.

Declarations Define user-defined data types, variables, arrays, and constants.

Declarations section Declarations that apply to all procedures within the module.

Decryption The process of making encrypted information readable again.

Default value A value displayed for new blank records.

Delete query A query that is used to remove entire records from a table at one time. Delete queries remove all the data in each field, including the primary key.

Deletion anomaly Forces you to delete two different facts such as product name and price of the product resulting in information loss.

Delimiter A character used in a text file to separate the fields; it can be a paragraph mark, a tab, a comma, or another character.

Dependency When a field relates to a key.

Dependent expression An expression that relies on the outcome of another expression.

Design view A view of an Access object that shows the detailed structure of a table, query, form, or report.

Detail area The section of a report that displays the records from the underlying table or query.

Determinant A field that determines the value of another field.

Dialog box A window that provides more options or settings beyond those provided on the Ribbon.

Dialog Box Launcher Opens a corresponding dialog box or task pane.

Dim statement The beginning of the process of declaring a variable.

DoCmd object Allows Access or Excel actions to be performed from within VBA.

Document Depending on the application a document can be a letter, memo, report, brochure, resume, or flyer.

Domain integrity constraint A rule for the database to conform to that is specific to a field.

E

Edit mode Allows you to edit or change the contents of a field.

Embedded macro These are stored as part of a database object like a form or report or any control like a button or textbox. They are triggered by database events.

Enabled A property that allows or prohibits data from being entered or copied from a control. Yes enables the field; No disables the field.

Encryption The process of changing text-based information into an unreadable state, that requires a key to unlock.

Entity Person, place, item, or event that you want to keep data about.

Entity relationship diagram (ERD) A common way to visually express the tables and relationships in your database. An ERD does not tell you anything about data flow; it is a fixed view of the database structure.

Error handling The process of anticipating and controlling errors.

Event-driven programming A technique in which the programming is created to respond to various events.

Exclusive Access Allows for only one user to open and edit a database at a time.

Exit Function statement Terminates the function.

Expression Builder A tool that helps you format your calculated fields correctly by providing a list of expressive elements, operators, and built-in functions.

F

Field A specific piece of information that is stored in every record and formatted as a column in a database table.

Field format A common way to control your data is through formatting. You can use field formats to customize the way numbers, dates, times, and text are displayed and printed by using predefined formats or custom formats.

Field size The maximum length of a data field.

Field validation rule This is used to verify the value that is entered in just one field. If the validation rule is violated, Access prevents the user from leaving the current field until the problem is fixed.

File extension A suffix that helps Windows understand what kind of information is in a file and what program should open it.

FileDialog object Can be used to allow the user to select the file(s) needed for the import process.

Filter A condition applied temporarily to a table or query to show a subset of the records.

Filter by Form This allows you to filter data in a form or spreadsheet by creating a blank table for the selected table.

Filter by Selection Selecting a value in a record and filtering the records that contain only the values that match what has been selected.

Filtering This is how you can view and print only the desired and required information from your database.

Find command A command used to find records in a database with a specific value.

Find Unmatched Query Wizard Finds records in one table that do not have related records in another table.

First normal form (1NF) Dictates that the table must not have repeating groups of values in a single column—atomicity—and that it must have a key. Also, in 1NF each nonkey field needs some sort of dependency on the key.

Fiscal year A period businesses and other organizations use for calculating annual financial statements. This can be different from a calendar year and can vary throughout different businesses and organizations because they can choose whatever dates they want to use as the "year."

Forecasting When historical data is used to predict or estimate future sales trends, to develop budgets, and so forth.

Foreign key The field that is included in the related table so the field can be joined with the primary key in another table for the purpose of creating a relationship.

Form Object that allows you to enter or view your data.

Form view Data view of a form.

Format How Access displays data.

Front-end database A database that contains nondata objects such as queries, forms, macros, and VBA modules.

Function In programming it executes instructions and returns a value to another procedure.

Functional dependency diagram A visual representation of dependencies in a table.

G

GIGO principle Stands for "Garbage In, Garbage Out" and means that inconsistent or inaccurate data leads to an inconsistent or inaccurate output.

Graphic Pictures, clip art, SmartArt, shapes, and charts that can enhance the look of your documents.

Group A collection of records along with some introductory and summary information about the records.

Group By clause A function that can help combine records with identical values in a specified field list into a single record.

Group Footer Information printed at the end of every group of records; used to display summary information for the group.

Group Header Information printed at the beginning of every new group of records, such as the group name.

Group, Sort, and Total pane A pane that is displayed at the bottom of the screen in which you can control how information is sorted and grouped in a report.

H

HAVING clause If a field includes an aggregate function, a HAVING clause specifies the aggregated field criteria and restricts the results based on aggregated values.

Highest normal form (HNF) The level of normal form that a table satisfies along with all levels below.

Hyperlink A hyperlink is an address that specifies a protocol (such as HTTP or FTP) and a location of an object, document, World Wide Web page, or other destination on the Internet, an intranet, or local computer. An example is http://www.paintedparadiseresort.com.

I

Ideas Are potential changes to the database that a Performance Analyzer presents as ways to optimize a database. Ideas cannot be completed by the Performance Analyzer.

IIf function The IIf function, which stands for Immediate If, is similar to the IF function in Excel. The results of this function returns one value if a specified condition is true or another value if it is false. For example, for employees who received a salary increase, you can calculate what the new salary will be if employees receive a 3% raise by typing New Salary:IIf([Salary]<=30000,[Salary]*1.03, [Salary]).

Importing The process of copying data from another file, such as a Word file or Excel workbook, into a separate file, such as an Access database.

In operator This operator can be used to return results that contain one of the values in a list of values. For example, you may want to search for customers who meet certain criteria, such as those who live in specific states. Thus, you would type In("Arizona", "Nevada", "New Mexico") as the criterion in the State field.

Increment AutoNumber The most common and default setting in Access when selecting the AutoNumber data type.

Index By creating an index for a field or fields in a table, Access can quickly locate all the records that contain specific values for those fields without having to read through each record in the table.

Information Data that has been manipulated and processed to make it meaningful.

Information management program Gives you the ability to keep track and print schedules, task lists, phone directories, and other documents.

Inner join The default join type in Access, an inner join selects only those records from both database tables that have matching values.

Input mask A way to control how data is entered by creating a typing guide. In most cases, an input mask controls the way that data is stored.

Input Mask Wizard The Input Mask Wizard provides input masks for most common formatting needs and helps automate the process of establishing an input mask.

Insertion anomaly Forces you to enter data about two different entities when you may have only data on one entity.

Integrity constraint A rule your database conforms to in order to help ensure the data's validity.

Is Not Null Entering this into a field's criteria in the Design view of a query, the results will include records that contain valid data. For example, to create a list of the employees who have not had an employee photo taken, type Is Not Null in the Criteria property of the Photo field.

Is Null Entering this into a field's criteria in the Design view of a query, the results will include records that do not contain valid data.

IsNull function This function is used to indicate that a value is unknown and it is treated differently than other values because it has no value. For example, to create a list of the employees who have had an employee photo taken, you could type Is Null in the Criteria property of the Photo field.

J

Join Create a relationship between two tables based upon a common field.

Junction table A table that breaks down the many-to-many relationship into two one-to-many relationships.

K

Key tip A form of keyboard shortcuts. Pressing Alt will display Key Tips (or keyboard shortcuts) for items on the Ribbon and Quick Access Toolbar.

Keyboard shortcut Keyboard equivalents for software commands that allow you to keep your hands on the keyboard instead of reaching for the mouse to make Ribbon selections.

Knowledge This is applied information once you make the decision.

L

Label An unbound control. It may be the name of a field or other text you manually enter.

Label control A control on a form or report that contains descriptive information, typically a field name.

Layout selector A tool that allows you to move a whole table at one time.

Layout view Shows data and allows limited changes to a form or report design.

Legacy data type An old or outdated data type that is still used, usually because it still works for the user, even though newer technology or more efficient methods exist.

Legacy software Out-of-date technology that is still in use.

Like function This function helps find values in a field that match a specified pattern. For example, you could find all employees who have the job title of caddy by typing Like "caddy" in the Criteria property under Position.

Line continuation character The combination of a space character and an underscore that allows a VBA statement to span multiple lines in the Code window.

Line labels Function like bookmarks in VBA procedures.

Linked table A link within Access that creates a table from data stored in another database or application.

Linked Table Manager Lists the location of all linked tables in an Access database and provides a means of updating those links.

Live preview Lets you see the effects of menu selections on your document file or selected item before making a commitment to a particular menu choice.

Locked A property that allows or prohibits data from being entered into a control. Yes unlocks the field; No locks out data entry.

Logical operator An operator used in a query to combine two or more criteria.

Lookup field A table field that has values that come either from a table, query, or a value list.

Lookup field properties Can be set to change the behavior of a lookup column.

Lookup Wizard The wizard simplifies the process by automatically populating the appropriate field properties and creating the appropriate table relationships. The Lookup Wizard feature has been enhanced in Access 2010 by automatically creating referential integrity settings.

Loops Programming code used to execute a series of statements multiple times.

M

Macro Designer An editor for creating macros that makes it easier to build robust database applications, increase productivity of business users, and reduce code errors.

Macro group Two or more submacros that are usually similar in function, placed inside the same macro file.

Macros Database objects that provide a method of automating routine database tasks and that can add functionality to reports and forms, as well as the controls that forms and reports contain.

Mailto command A common type of hyperlink that helps generate a link for sending e-mail.

Main form The primary, or first table, selected when creating a form.

Make table query A query that acquires data from one or more tables, and then automatically loads the resulting dataset into a new table once you run the query.

Many-to-many relationship (M:N) A relationship between tables in which one record in one table has many matching records in a second table, and one record in the related table has many matching records in the first table.

Maximize The button is located in the top-right corner of the title bar; it offers the largest workspace.

Me keyword Functions in a similar fashion as a declared variable. Me can be used in place of the current object name or when passing information about the currently executing instance of an object to a procedure in another module.

Method Actions—for example SaveAs—that control the objects behavior.

Mini toolbar Appears after text is selected and contains buttons for the most commonly used formatting commands, such as font, font size, font color, center alignment, indents, bold, italic, and underline.

Minimize Hides the application on the taskbar.

Modal message A window or dialog box that requires the user to take some action before the focus can switch to another form or dialog box.

Modules Store VBA procedures that can be referenced or called by other procedures in the database.

Move handle A handle on a control that is used to move a single control.

Multiple-field index Once you sort a table by defining a multiple-field index, Access sorts the index in the order in which you enter each field into the Indexes dialog box. If there are records with duplicate values in the first field, Access then sorts by the second field defined for the index, and so on.

Multiple-items form A form that allows you to display multiple records at the same time in Datasheet view.

Multivalued field This is a field that helps keep track of multiple related facts about a subject.

N

Natural key A key that is created from naturally occurring data generated outside of the database, such as driver's license number.

Natural primary key A primary key that is a natural part of your data.

Navigation bar Provides a way to move through records in table, query, report, and form objects.

Navigation control bar The area of the Navigation form where you drag a form or report to create a tab.

Navigation form Provides a familiar weblike interface that allows you to access multiple objects in the database from one central location.

Navigation mode Allows you to move from record to record or field to field using keystrokes and the Navigation bar.

Nested IIf function This function nests IIf functions, or places one inside another, allowing a series of dependent expressions to be evaluated. For example, if you wanted to determine how much of a raise each employee received, you type Raise Assessment: IIf([Salary]<=30000,"7% Raise",IIf([Salary]<=60000,"4% Raise","No Raise")).

Net revenue The revenue minus sales returns, sales allowances, and sales discounts. Also known as net sales.

Normal form (NF) A set of criteria that each table is evaluated by during the normalization process that represents the level of the table's vulnerability to redundancy, anomalies, and inaccuracies. These are a progressive series where the lower the level, the more vulnerable the table.

Normalization The process of minimizing the duplication of information in a relational database through effective database design.

Not operator This function is used to search for records that do not match specific criteria, and it can be combined with other operators. For example, you may want to search for all customers outside of North America. You would enter Not "USA" And Not "Canada" And Not "Mexico" in the Criteria property of the Country field.

Now function The Now() function retrieves the current system date and time.

Null A term used to indicate that a field is blank.

Number data type A data type that can store only numerical data. The data field will be used in calculations.

Numeric key A primary key with a number data type. AutoNumber is often used for numeric keys.

O

Object A table, form, query, or report. Combinations of data and code that are treated as a single unit in programming.

Object box Displays the name of the object that contains the procedure such as a form or command button.

Object Browser Lists all VBA objects along with the associated methods and properties for each object.

Object-oriented programming A method of programming that uses objects to design applications.

OLE Object An OLE Object, which stands for Object Linking and Embedding, is a technology developed by Microsoft that creates a bitmap or image of an object. It is a way to store images inside a database field.

One-to-many relationship (1:M or 1:N) A relationship between two tables where one record in the first table corresponds to many records in the second table—the most common type of relationship in Access.

One-to-one relationship (1:1) A relationship between tables where a record in one table has only one matching record in the second table.

Operational database The database used to carry out regular operations, such as payroll and inventory management, of an organization.

Option Compare Sets the string comparison method for the module.

Option Compare Binary Setting for the Option Compare that compares the ASCII values for the characters contained in a string and is therefore case sensitive.

Option Compare Text Setting for the Option Compare that results in case-insensitive comparisons.

Option Explicit Statement Set in the declarations and requires that all variable names be defined using a Dim statement.

Orphan An orphan is a foreign key in one table that does not have a matching value in the primary key field of a related table.

Outer join A join that selects *all* of the records from one database table and only those records in the second table that have matching values in the joined field. One or more fields can serve as a join field.

P

Page Footer Information printed at the end of every page in a report; often used to display page numbers.

Page Header Information printed at the top of every page of a report.

Parallel Implementation An implementation where the legacy system and the new system are used simultaneously until the new system is fully tested.

Parameter A value that can be changed each time you run the query.

Parameter data types When a data type that the parameter should accept is defined, users see a more helpful error message if they enter the wrong type of data, such as entering text when currency should be entered.

Parameter query This type of query can be designed when search criteria is unknown. When a parameter query is run, the user is prompted to enter the value for each parameter.

Partial dependency When a field only depends on one part of a composite or concatenated key. In other words, the field is determined by only one piece of a multifield key.

Percentage of physical volume This calculation can compare how much an object holds as compared to how much space is being used.

Percentage of sales revenue This calculation can compare a portion of the gross revenue to the total gross revenue.

Percentage of sales volume Compares how two numbers are related, such as this year's sales over last year's sales. Consider the method used to calculate sales volume as well as the time period over which you plan on measuring the sales volume.

Performance Analyzer A tool within Access that analyzes a database and makes suggestions on how to optimize the performance of a database.

Phased implementation An implementation where individual portions of the new system are used and perfected before new portions of the system are deployed.

Physical volume Measures how much space an object can hold.

Piloted implementation An implementation that starts with small groups of users and gradually incorporates more users over time.

PivotChart A graphical representation of a PivotTable.

PivotTable An object used to organize, arrange, analyze, and summarize data in a meaningful way.

Precision This allows you to determine how many decimal places you want to round your numbers when using the Round function.

Primary key The field that uniquely identifies a record in a table.

Primary sort field The first field chosen in a multiple field sort.

Print Preview A view of a report or other object that shows how it will appear if printed.

Procedure A series of statements or instructions that are executed as a unit.

Procedure box A list that allows you to navigate quickly between the Declarations section and the individual procedures in the open module.

Project Explorer A list of the currently open Access Database objects that contain VBA procedures and a list of modules within the current database.

Property sheet A list of properties for fields on a form in which you can make precise changes to each property associated with the field.

Protected view The file contents can be seen and read, but you are not able to edit, save, or print the contents until you enable editing.

Q

Query Object that retrieves specific data from one or more database objects—either tables or other queries—and then, in a single datasheet, displays only the data you specify.

Query by example A type of query where a sample of the data is set up as criteria.

Query design grid Selected fields in a query. Shown at the bottom of a query's Design view.

Query join A temporary or virtual relationship between two tables in a query that do not have an established relationship or common field with the same field name and data type.

Query results A recordset that provides an answer to a question posed in a query.

Query workspace Source for data in the query. Shown at the top of a query's Design view.

Quick Access Toolbar Located at the top left of the Office window, it can be customized to offer commonly used buttons.

R

Random AutoNumber This will generate a random number that is unique to each record within the table.

Recommendations Are potential changes to the database that the Performance Analyzer can make as ways to optimize a database.

Record All of the categories of data pertaining to one person, place, thing, event, or idea, and that is formatted as a row in a database table.

Record selector The small box at the left of a record in Datasheet view that is used to select an entire record.

Record validation rule This refers to validating data in other fields within the same record. In other words, you need to validate the values in one field against the values in another field in the same record.

Recordset A run time table.

Redundancy Data that is repeated in a manner that indicates poor database design.

Referential integrity Requires that only values that have a corresponding value in the primary table can be entered for a foreign key.

Relational database A database where data is stored in tables with relationships between the tables.

Relationship An association that you establish between two tables based on common fields.

Replace command A command used to automatically replace values in a table or query.

Report Object that summarizes the fields and records from a table or query in an easy-to-read format suitable for printing.

Report Design tool An Access tool used to create a blank report in Design view.

Report Footer Information printed once at the end of a report; used to print report totals or other summary information for the entire report.

Report Header Information printed once at the beginning of a report; used for logos, titles, and dates.

Report tool Access tool that creates a report with one mouse click, which displays all of the fields from the record source that you select.

Report view A view that allows you to see what the printed report will look like in a continuous page layout.

Report Wizard Access feature that guides you through creating a report by asking you questions.

Required property The Required property can be used to specify whether a value is required in a field, ensuring that the field is not left blank.

Restore Down Allows the user to arrange and view several windows at a time when multiple applications are open.

Revenue Income that a company receives from its normal business activities, from the sale of goods and services to customers. Also known as gross sales.

Ribbon Where you will find most of the commands for the application. The Ribbon differs from program to program, but each program has two tabs in common: the File tab and the Home tab.

Ribbon button Located just below the Minimize and Close buttons in the top-right corner of the window (and directly next to the Help button, which looks like a question mark), it can hide or show the Ribbon.

Round function This function returns a number rounded to a specific number of decimal places.

Run time An object that is created at the time of request.

S

Sales volume The number of items sold or services rendered during normal business hours. These figures would be taken over a specific period of time and can be expressed in either dollars or percent.

ScreenTip Small windows that display descriptive text when you rest the mouse pointer over an object or button.

Second normal form (2NF) Requires that the table has no fields with partial dependencies on a composite or concatenated key and satisfies 1NF.

Secondary sort field The second and subsequent fields chosen in a multiple field sort.

SELECT statement The fundamental framework for SQL query is the SQL SELECT statement.

Shared Access Allows for multiple users to access a database at the same time.

Shortcut menu A list of commands related to a selection that appears when you right-click (click the right mouse button).

Simple delete query A query that is used to remove one or more records from a table or another query. The number of rows deleted is dependent upon the criteria within the Where clause of the delete query.

Simple update query A query that involves updating data in one table, allowing you to specify two values—the value you want to replace and the value to use as a replacement.

Single-field index This is an index set on an individual field, such as a primary key.

Single Step A feature that allows you to observe the flow of a macro and the results of each action, and isolate any action that causes an error or produces unwanted results.

Sizing handle A handle on a control that is used to resize the control.

SkyDrive An online workspace provided by Microsoft. SkyDrive's online filing cabinet is a free Windows Live Service.

Sort field A field used to determine the order of the records in a table.

Sorting The process of rearranging records into a specific order.

Special keys A set of four keyboard shortcuts in Access that can be disabled in a secured database.

Special operator An operator used to compare text values in a query.

Split form A form that displays data in two views: Form view and Datasheet view.

Stand-alone macro Separate database objects that Access displays in the Navigation Pane. Stand-alone macros can be executed directly from the Navigation Pane by double-clicking the macro object, clicking Run in Design view, or embedding the macro inside a database object, like a button or text field.

Startup form A form that opens automatically when you open a database.

String A string is comprised of a set of characters that can also contain spaces, symbols, and numbers.

Structured Query Language An internationally recognized standard database language that is used by every relational database—although many databases incorporate modified versions of the current standard SQL.

Sub procedure A set of programming instructions that can run on its own or can be called by another procedure. However, it cannot return values to other procedures.

Subform A form that is embedded within another form.

Subform control The area of the Navigation form that shows the form or report associated with a tab.

Subreport The report section created for the secondary table records when creating a report from two or more tables.

Subset This is a portion or part of your query dataset.

Subtotals Controls added to a report to perform calculations on a group of records.

Suggestions Are potential changes to the database that the Performance Analyzer can make to optimize a database. Suggestions may have consequences that should be considered before they are made.

Suggestive sell A sales technique used to add more revenue to a sale by suggesting another product to the customer's purchase.

Surrogate key An artificial column added to a table to serve as a primary key that is unique and sequential when records are created. In Access, a surrogate key is known as the AutoNumber data type.

Syntax error Occurs when a line of code is entered that the Visual Basic Editor does not recognize.

T

Table The database object that stores data organized in an arrangement of columns and rows, and that is the foundation of an Access database.

Table Analyzer Wizard This tool can divide the table created from an imported Excel spreadsheet into several tables as well as automatically create the relationships needed between them.

Task pane A smaller window pane that often appears to the side of the program window and offers options or helps you to navigate through completing a task or feature.

Template A database shell providing tables, forms, queries, and reports.

Text box A bound control that represents the actual value of a field.

Text data type A data type that can store either text or numerical characters.

Text filter Filters that allow you to create a custom filter to match all or part of the text in a field that you specify.

Theme Built-in combination of colors and fonts.

Third normal form (3NF) Requires that the table has to be free of transitive dependencies and that the table satisfies both 1NF and 2NF.

Thumbnail A small picture of the open program file displayed.

Top Values query This query is used to find records that contain the top or bottom values in a field.

Total row A temporary row that can be added to the end of a datasheet that displays the results of statistical calculations of field values.

Transactional database The database used to record daily transactions.

TransferSpreadsheet method Allows for Access to import, export, or link to spreadsheet files specifically.

Transitive dependency When a field depends on another field in the table which then depends on a candidate key, A→B and B→C, thus A implies C. If C is a candidate key and B is not a candidate key, this is a transitive dependency.

Truncated When data is shortened or trimmed due to a change in the database, such as reducing the Field Size property.

Trusted Location A folder on your hard disk or a network share. Any file that you put in a trusted location can be opened without being checked by the Trust Center security feature.

U

Unbound control A control that does not have a source of data, such as a label in a form or report.

Unbound form A form that is not linked directly to a data source and can be used for operating your database.

Underlying SQL statement Even when you create a query in the QBE grid, Access automatically generates the SQL statement in the background.

Union query Used to query unrelated tables or queries and combine the results into a single dataset.

Universal naming convention (UNC) This is a naming convention for files that provides a link to the machine and location where the file is stored. A UNC name uses the syntax \\server\share\path\filename and works the same way in which a Uniform Resource Locator (URL) works.

Update anomaly Forces you to change data in multiple records.

Update query Can be used to add, change, or delete data in one or more existing records. Update queries are similar to the Find and Replace dialog box, but much more powerful.

Usability testing Testing an application on a user before the application goes live.

User interface Acts like a menu system, or home page, for an application.

V

Validation rule An expression that precisely defines the range of data that will be accepted in a field.

Validation text The error message that is displayed when a user enters a value prohibited by the validation rule.

Validation Text property When data is entered, Access checks to see whether the data meets the validation rule. If the data is not accepted, Access displays a message, known as validation text, designed to help users understand why there is a problem. The Validation Text property allows you to enter the error message.

Variables Placeholders that can be set to a hard-coded value or to an object within VBA.

View One of several perspectives of an object.

Virtual field This means that the concatenated field initiates its "real" equivalent or equivalents—such as combining FirstName and LastName fields.

Visual Basic Editor The tool built into Microsoft Office that is used for creating and editing VBA.

Visual Basic for Applications A powerful programming language run inside of Microsoft Office Applications. Also known as VBA.

W

Where clause Allows you to limit the results of your query by specifying criteria that field values must meet without using that field to group the data.

Wildcard character Characters, such as an asterisk [*] or question mark [?], substitute for other characters when used in a query.

With statement A statement that allows for an efficient way of using several methods or setting multiple properties on a single object.

Wizard Step-by-step guide to complete a task.

Workbook Contains one or more worksheets.

Y

Yes/No data type The Yes/No data type allows you to set the Format property to either the Yes/No, True/False, or On/Off predefined formats or to a custom format for the Yes/No data type.

Index

refreshing tables, 641–664
relational databases, **3**
   normalization, 103–104
   overview of, 102–103
   relationships in, 103
   SQL. *See* Structured Query Language (SQL)
relationships, **78**
   See also specific type
   advanced, using multiple
      tables, 380–385
   Cascade Update, Cascade Delete, 116
   and database design, 78–79
   joining tables with, 678–679
   between the one, and many side
      tables, 115–116
   referential integrity, checking, 114–116
   in relational databases, 104–114
   types, 105–106
   understanding, 104–105
   viewing table, 153–154
Relationships property, 377
Relationships window, 105, 107, 153
removing
   See also deleting
   data from tables, 89–90
   partial dependencies, 673–676
   total row, 166
renaming
   command buttons, 612
   fields, 343
reopening documents, 24–25
repairing databases, 69–70
Replace command, **142**
Report Design tool, **458**
Report Footer, **462**
Report Header, **461**
Report tool, **458**
Report view, **65**, 205–206, **458**
Report Wizard
   described, **458**
   using, 201–204, 459–460, 472
reports, **41**, **458**
   Access, 3
   adding, removing fields from, 464–465
   adding calculations to, 469–470
   adding dates to titles, 479–480
   building with subtotals, totals, 459–470
   changing design, 208–209
   conditional formatting, applying,
      472–474
   creating from parameter queries,
      474–482
   creating from queries, 468–469, 471–472
   creating in Design view, 458–462
   creating using wizard, 65–67, 201–204
   customizing, 207–209
   designing, 417
   embedded macros, using, 569–572
   enhancing with conditional formatting,
      209–211
   vs. forms or queries, 458
   grouping, applying, 211–212
   hiding detail on summary, 467–468
   introduction to, 65
   lines, adding horizontal, 466–467
   looking at different views, 204–207

printing, 67, 214–215, 487
   saving as PDF files, 214–215
   subtotals, adding, 213–214
   themes, 207–208
   using two related tables in, 108
Required property, **254**
reserved words, captions and, 251
resizing
   charts, 438
   controls in reports, 208–209
   forms, 198–199
   total fields in reports, 463
   windows, 6–8
Restore Down button, **7**
revenue
   calculating, 336–337
   described, **336**
Ribbon
   described, 5, **10**
   tabs, using, 10–11
Ribbon button, **11**
rich text memo fields, 640
right-clicking, 11
Round function
   described, **312**
   queries using, 312–313
rows, alternating colors in
     tables, 147–148
run time, **58**
RunMacro, 566

S

sales revenue, calculating percentage,
   339–340
sales volume, **332**
   calculating, 332
   calculating percentage of, 341–342
Save As command, 20
Save As dialog box, 21–23
Save command, 20
Saved Imports, 594
saving
   custom themes, 197–198
   data in Access, 64
   database design changes, 58
   datasheet data, 144
   files, 20–23
   filters, 274
   Office files in previous format
      version, 21
   as previous Access versions, 639–640
   reports as PDF files, 214–215
ScreenTips, 15
   theme names, 197
   viewing, 29
scrolling, in applications, 9–10
Search box, 46
searching
   See also finding
   creating indexes for, 251–254
   Help topics, 29–30
   for objects, 46
second normal form (2NF), **672**
   described, **672**
   satisfying, 672–676
secondary sort fields, **173**

security, Access warning about
   database, 44, 595
SELECT statement, **346**
selecting
   different controls, 199
   in queries, 61
   records for printing, 201
   specific records using selection
      filters, 146
   values in queries, 59
sequential AutoNumber, **267**
SetWarnings action, 561, 562
Shared Access, **634**
SharePoint, linking to Access, 642
sharing
   databases, and query results, 153
   files using SkyDrive, 25–29
shortcut menus, 19–20
Show check box, 336
Show Table dialog box, 151
simple delete queries, **376**
Simple Query Wizard, 148, 436
simple update queries, **371**
Single Step feature
   described, **553**
   using, 553–555
single-field indexes, **252**
single-table queries, 152–153
sizing handles, **422**, **463**
SkyDrive, **25**
   setting up account, 26
   setting up, creating document
      in, 26–29
   sharing files using, 25–29
social security numbers, as primary
   keys, 99
sort fields, **173**
sorting, **173**
   fields in Top Values queries, 292
   vs. grouping, 67
   query results, 173–175
   rearranging order, 175
   in reports, 211–212
special keys, **646–647**
special operators
   described, **164**
   using in queries, 164–165
spelling, 142
split forms
   creating, 196, 434–435
   described, **188**, **434**
splitting databases, 643–644
spreadsheets, 2
SQL view, creating basic queries
   in, 347–348
square brackets ([]) and calculated field
   names, 263
stand-alone macros, **546**
starting
   Access, 43
   Excel, 5
   Office programs, 3–4
   Word, 3–5
startup forms, **535**
startup preferences,
   setting, 647–651